Frequently Used Notations
Foundations of Finance, Fifth Edition

ACF_t = the annual after-tax cash flow in time period t

APR = annual percentage rate

APY = annual percentage yield

$ß$ = beta

DFN_t = discretionary financing needs for period t

$EBIT$ = earnings before interest and taxes

FV_i = the future value of $1 at the end of year i

$FVIFA_{i,n}$ = the future value interest factor of a $1 annuity at i percent for n years

$FVIF_{i,n}$ = the future value interest factor of $1 at i percent in n years

IO = the initial outlay

IRR = internal rate of return

k = rate of return or cost of capital

n = the number of years until payment will be received or during which compounding occurs

NPV = net present value

$OIROI$ = operating income return on investment

P = current selling price of a security

PI = profitability index

PMT = the annuity payment deposited or received at the end of each year

PV = the present value of a future sum of money

$PVIF_{i,n}$ = the present value interest factor of $1 received in year n at i percent

$PVIFA_{i,n}$ = the present value interest factor of a $1 annuity at i percent for n years

ROA = return on assets

ROE = return on common equity

σ = standard deviation

FIFTH EDITION

Foundations of Finance

THE LOGIC AND PRACTICE OF FINANCIAL MANAGEMENT

FIFTH EDITION

Foundations of Finance

THE LOGIC AND PRACTICE OF FINANCIAL MANAGEMENT

ARTHUR J. KEOWN

Virginia Polytechnic Institute and State University
R. B. Pamplin Professor of Finance

JOHN D. MARTIN

Baylor University
Professor of Finance
Carr P. Collins Chair in Finance

J. WILLIAM PETTY

Baylor University
Professor of Finance
W. W. Caruth Chair in Entrepreneurship

DAVID F. SCOTT, JR.

University of Central Florida
Executive Director, Dr. Phillips Institute
for the Study of American Business Activity
and Professor of Finance

PEARSON
Prentice
Hall

Upper Saddle River, New Jersey 07458

Library of Congress Cataloging-in-Publication Data

Foundations of finance : the logic and practice of financial management / Arthur J. Keown
... [et al.].—5th ed.
    p. cm.
  Includes bibliographical references and indexes.
  ISBN 0-13-185605-7
   1. Corporations—Finance.   I. Keown, Arthur J.

HG4026 .F67 2006
658.15--dc22   2005045934

AVP/Executive Editor: David Alexander
VP/Editorial Director: Jeff Shelstad
Assistant Editor: Francesca Calogero
Editorial Assistant: Michael Dittamo
Senior Media Project Manager: Nancy Welcher
Executive Marketing Manager: Sharon Koch
Marketing Assistant: Tina Panagiotou
Senior Managing Editor (Production): Cynthia Regan
Production Editor: Denise Culhane
Permissions Coordinator: Charles Morris
Manufacturing Buyer: Arnold Vila
Design Manager: Maria Lange
Art Director: K&M Design
Interior Design: Liz Harasymczuk
Cover Design: Liz Harasymczuk

Cover Illustration/Photo: Harriet Burger/Taxi/ Getty Images
Illustrator (Interior): Prepare, Inc.
Director, Image Resource Center: Melinda Reo
Manager, Rights and Permissions: Zina Arabia
Manager, Visual Research: Beth Brenzel
Manager, Cover Visual Research & Permissions: Karen Sanatar
Image Permission Coordinator: Nancy Seise
Photo Researcher: Kathy Ringrose
Print Production Manager: Christy Mahon
Composition/Full-Service Project Management: Prepare, Inc.
Printer/Binder: Quebecor World Dubuque
Typeface: 9.75/12 Janson Text

Credits and acknowledgments borrowed from other sources and reproduced, with permission, in this textbook appear on appropriate page within text.

Photo Credits
p. 4, AP Wide World Photos; p. 30, Alex Wong/Getty Images, Inc. - Liaison; p. 72, David McNew/Getty Images, Inc. - Liaison; p. 100, Kim Kulish/CORBIS- NY; p. 136, JERRY DRIENDL/Getty Images, Inc. - Taxi; p. 172, Dan Lamont/Corbis/Bettmann; p. 204, Richard B. Levine/Frances M. Roberts; p. 230, Getty Images, Inc. - Comstock Images Royalty Free; p. 258, David Young-Wolff/PhotoEdit; p. 294, Andy Rain/Bloomberg News/ Landov LLC; p. 328, Elizabeth Holmes/Omni-Photo Communications, Inc.; p. 366, Harley-Davidson Motor Company; p. 414, AP Wide World Photos; p. 446, John Chiasson/Getty Images, Inc. - Liaison; p. 468, Thomas Simon Photography; p. 490, AP Wide World Photos; p. 526, Mark Richards/PhotoEdit; COVER, Harriet Burger/Taxi/Getty Images

Microsoft® and Windows® are registered trademarks of the Microsoft Corporation in the U.S.A. and other countries. Screen shots and icons reprinted with permission from the Microsoft Corporation. This book is not sponsored or endorsed by or affiliated with the Microsoft Corporation.

Pearson Education LTD.
Pearson Education Singapore, Pte. Ltd
Pearson Education, Canada, Ltd
Pearson Education–Japan

Pearson Education Australia PTY, Limited
Pearson Education North Asia Ltd
Pearson Educación de Mexico, S.A. de C.V.
Pearson Education Malaysia, Pte. Ltd

10 9 8 7 6 5 4 3 2 1
ISBN 0-13-185605-7

To my parents, from whom I learned the most.
Arthur J. Keown

*To my grandson Luke and his little brother
who arrives in June 2005.*
John D. Martin

*To Bobbye and LaVerne, loving and supportive wives
to my brothers and the most wonderful "sisters"
I could ever have.*
J. William Petty

*To my sister, Dianne, and her husband, Ron,
who have been both supportive family
and engaging friends over so many years.*
David F. Scott, Jr.

ARTHUR J. KEOWN is the R. B. Pamplin Professor of Finance at Virginia Polytechnic Institute and State University. He received his bachelor's degree from Ohio Wesleyan University, his M.B.A. from the University of Michigan, and his doctorate from Indiana University. An award-winning teacher, he is a member of the Academy of Teaching Excellence; has received five Certificates of Teaching Excellence at Virginia Tech, the W. E. Wine Award for Teaching Excellence, and the Alumni Teaching Excellence Award; and in 1999 received the Outstanding Faculty Award from the State of Virginia. Professor Keown is widely published in academic journals. His work has appeared in *The Journal of Finance*, the *Journal of Financial Economics*, the *Journal of Financial and Quantitative Analysis*, *The Journal of Financial Research*, the *Journal of Banking and Finance*, *Financial Management*, the *Journal of Portfolio Management*, and many others. In addition to *Foundations of Finance*, two other of his books are widely used in college finance classes all over the country—*Basic Financial Management* and *Personal Finance: Turning Money into Wealth*. Professor Keown is a Fellow of the Decision Sciences Institute, a member of the Board of Directors of the Financial Management Association, and former head of the finance department at Virginia Tech. In addition, he recently served as the co-editor of *The Journal of Financial Research* for six and a half years and as the co-editor of the Financial Management Association's *Survey and Synthesis* series for six years. He lives with his wife and two children in Blacksburg, Virginia, where he collects original art from *Mad Magazine*.

JOHN D. MARTIN is Professor of Finance and the holder of the Carr P. Collins Chair of Finance at Baylor University. Dr. Martin came to Baylor University in 1998 from the University of Texas at Austin where he taught for nineteen years and was the Margaret and Eugene McDermott Centennial Professor of Finance. He teaches corporate finance and his research interests are in corporate governance, the evaluation of firm performance, and the design of incentive compensation plans. Dr. Martin has published widely in academic journals including the *Journal of Financial Economics*, *The Journal of Finance*, *Journal of Monetary Economics*, *Journal of Financial and Quantitative Analysis*, *Journal of Corporate Finance*, *Financial Management*, and *Management Science*. His work has also appeared in a number of professional publications including *Directors and Boards*, the *Financial Analysts' Journal*, the *Journal of Portfolio Management*, and the *Journal of Applied Corporate Finance*. In addition to this book Dr. Martin is co-author of nine books including *Financial Management* (9th ed., Prentice Hall), *The Theory of Finance* (Dryden Press), *Financial Analysis* (2nd ed., McGraw Hill), and *Value Based Management* (Harvard Business School Press), and he is currently writing a book on interest rate modeling. He serves on the editorial boards of eight journals and has delivered executive education programs for a number of firms including Shell Chemical, Shell E&P, Texas Instruments, and The Associates.

J. WILLIAM PETTY is Professor of Finance and the W. W. Caruth Chairholder of Entrepreneurship at Baylor University. He holds a Ph.D. and M.B.A. from the University of Texas at Austin, and a B.S. from Abilene Christian University. He has taught at Virginia Tech University and Texas Tech University, and served as the dean of the business school at Abilene Christian University. His research interests include the creation and financing of high-potential entrepreneurial firms and shareholder value-based management. He is also the Director of the Entrepreneurship Program at Baylor University. He has served as the co-editor for the *Journal of Financial Research* and the editor of the *Journal of Entrepreneurial and Small Business Finance*. He has published in a number of finance journals and is the co-author of two leading corporate finance textbooks, *Basic Financial Management* and *Foundations of Finance*, and co-author of a widely used text, *Small Business Management*. Dr. Petty serves on the board of a publicly traded oil and gas firm. He has also served as a subject matter expert on a best-practices study by the American Productivity and Quality Center on the topic of shareholder value-based management. He recently served on a research team for the Australian Department of Industry to study the feasibility of establishing a public equity market for small and medium-sized enterprises in Australia.

DAVID F. SCOTT, JR. received his Ph.D. from the University of Florida, an M.B.A. from the University of Detroit, and a B.S.B.A. from the University of Akron. He holds the Phillips-Schenck Chair in American Private Enterprise, is Executive Director, Dr. Phillips Institute for the Study of American Business Activity, and is Professor of Finance at the University of Central Florida. From 1977 to 1982 he was Area Coordinator, then Head, Department of Finance, Insurance, and Business Law at Virginia Polytechnic Institute and State University. During 1985–1986 he was President of the Financial Management Association, an international group with 9,000 members. He was a member of the Board of Trustees of FMA from 1986 to 1993.

Dr. Scott is a member of the Board of Directors of CompBenefits Corporation, headquartered in Atlanta, Georgia. He is a past member of the local Board of Directors of BankFIRST-Goldenrod (Florida), which specializes in commercial banking services for small businesses. He served on the Investment Policy Committee of the University of Central Florida Foundation for over 10 years. Dr. Scott is also past founding co-editor of the *Journal of Financial Research*, past associate editor for the *Akron Business and Economic Review*, and past associate editor for *Financial Management*. He is past president of the Southern Finance Association. In addition to *Foundations of Finance*, Dr. Scott is co-author of *Basic Financial Management*, *Cases in Finance*, and *Guide to Financial Analysis*. He is widely published in academic journals including *Financial Management*, *Engineering Economist*, *Journal of Financial and Quantitative Analysis*, *Business Economics*, and many others.

Dr. Scott's op-ed and research pieces have appeared in several leading outlets intended for consumer and practitioner audiences. These include *USA Today*, *The Miami Herald*, *The St. Petersburg Times*, *Florida Today*, *Orlando Sentinel*, and *Florida Trend*.

BRIEF CONTENTS

CONTENTS

CHAPTER 3

Understanding Financial Statements and Cash Flows 73

PART 3: INVESTMENT IN LONG-TERM ASSETS   256

CHAPTER 9
Capital-Budgeting Techniques and Practice   259

CHAPTER 10
Cash Flows and Other Topics in Capital Budgeting   295

Chapter 13

Dividend Policy and Internal Financing 415

PART 5: WORKING-CAPITAL MANAGEMENT AND INTERNATIONAL BUSINESS FINANCE 444

Chapter 14

Short-Term Financial Planning 447

Chapter 17
International Business Finance   527

PREFACE

In finance, our goal is to create wealth. This is done by providing customers with the best product and service possible, and it is the market response that determines whether we reach our goal. We are very proud of the market reaction to *Foundations of Finance*; the market's response has been overwhelming. With its success comes an even greater responsibility to deliver the finest possible textbook and supplementary package possible. We have done this with a two-pronged approach of refinement, based on users' comments, and of remaining the innovative leaders in the field, focusing on value-added innovations.

Foundations of Finance has gained the reputation for being "intuitive"—allowing the reader "to see the forest through the trees"—and "lively and easy to read." In the fifth edition of *Foundations of Finance*, we have tried to build on these strengths, introducing the latest concepts and developments in finance in a practical and intuitive manner.

PEDAGOGY THAT WORKS

This book provides students with a conceptual understanding of the financial decision-making process, rather than just an introduction to the tools and techniques of finance. For the student, it is all too easy to lose sight of the logic that drives finance and focus instead on memorizing formulas and procedures. As a result, students have a difficult time understanding the interrelationships among the topics covered. Moreover, later in life when the problems encountered do not match the textbook presentation, students may find themselves unprepared to abstract from what they learned. To overcome this problem, the opening chapter presents 10 underlying principles of finance, which serve as a springboard for the chapters and topics that follow. In essence, the student is presented with a cohesive, interrelated perspective from which future problems can be approached.

With a focus on the big picture, we provide an introduction to financial decision making rooted in current financial theory and in the current state of world economic conditions. This focus is perhaps most apparent in the attention given to the capital markets and their influence on corporate financial decisions. What results is an introductory treatment of a discipline rather than the treatment of a series of isolated problems that face the financial manager. The goal of this text is not merely to teach the tools of a discipline or trade but also to enable students to abstract what is learned to new and yet unforeseen problems—in short, to educate the student in finance.

Objective **4** | **TEN PRINCIPLES THAT FORM THE FOUNDATIONS OF FINANCIAL MANAGEMENT**

To the first-time student of finance, the subject matter may seem like a collection of unrelated decision rules. This could not be further from the truth. In fact, our decision rules, and the logic that underlies them, spring from 10 simple principles that do not require knowledge of finance to understand. *However, although it is not necessary to understand finance in order to understand these principles, it is necessary to understand these principles in order to understand finance.* Keep in mind that although these principles may at first appear simple or even trivial, they provide the driving force behind all that follows. These principles weave together concepts and techniques presented in this text, thereby allowing us to focus on the logic underlying the practice of financial management.

PRINCIPLE **1** | *The Risk–Return Trade-Off—We Won't Take On Additional Risk Unless We Expect to Be Compensated with Additional Return*

At some point we have all saved some money. Why have we done this? The answer is simple: to expand our future consumption opportunities. We are able to invest those savings and earn a return on our dollars because some people would rather forgo future consumption opportunities to consume more now. Maybe they're borrowing money to open a new business or a company is borrowing money to build a new plant. Assuming there are a lot of different people who would like to use our savings, how do we decide where to put our money?

INNOVATIONS AND DISTINCTIVE FEATURES IN THE FOURTH EDITION

PART-OPENING INTERVIEWS WITH BUSINESS PROFESSIONALS

These give students in-the-trenches insights into the application of theory to practice in the real world and provide perspective for *anyone* who is planning a career in business.

REAL-WORLD OPENING VIGNETTES

Each chapter begins with a story about a current, real-world company faced with a financial decision related to the chapter material that follows. These vignettes have been carefully prepared to stimulate student interest in the topic to come and can be used as a lecture tool to provoke class discussion.

NEW AND IMPROVED PROBLEM SETS

The end-of-chapter study problem sets have been improved and expanded to allow for a wider range of student problems.

NEW "WEB WORKS" INTERNET PROBLEMS

Internet problems have been introduced at the end of each chapter. These problems direct the student to Internet sites that allow them to explore financial issues and solve financial problems using the Web.

ACROSS THE HALL

BANKERS HAVE TO DIVERSIFY TOO

Robert A. Bennett, a banker, says that diversifying is important for any business, including banks. He makes the point that bankers need to understand the importance of diversifying, especially in uncertain times.

In the quest to increase their earnings, many banks forgot the importance of diversification. Rushing into the moment's hottest businesses, they abandoned activities that at the time seemed lackluster. The go-go businesses of the 1990s reflected the stock market's boom: investment banking, stock brokerage, wealth management and equity investment. On the other side, banks were dumping what seemed to be slow-growth activities: mortgage banking, auto financing and credit cards.

In these uncertain times it is unclear which way to turn. It appears the best gamble is to spread your bets across a wide spectrum.

Citigroup is a case in point. The decline in the stock markets walloped the earnings of its investment banking activities, where income dropped $497 million in the first quarter. That,

indeed was a severe blow that was primarily responsible for the 7% decline in Citi's year-overs-year first-quarter earnings.

But as Sandy Weill, Citi's CEO, said in the company's earnings report: "This is precisely the kind of market that demonstrates the power of our franchise. The strength and diversity of our earnings by business, geography, and customer helped to deliver a strong bottom line in a period of market uncertainty."

Considering the plunge in investment banking income, things could have been a lot worse. Despite the drop in income from investment activities, Citi succeeded in getting a 22.5% return on equity. That's even better than its 22% return last year, and better than its average ROE of 19% for the three-year period 1998–2000.

As David S. Berry, head of research at Keefe, Bruyette & Woods, put it: "Citigroup again demonstrated the benefits of diversification and leadership across its business lines."

Source: Robert A. Bennett, "When in Doubt, Diversify," *U.S. Banker*, vol. 11, no. 5 (May 2001), p. 6.

NEW "ACROSS THE HALL" BOXES

A new box feature titled "Across the Hall" has been introduced in this edition of *Foundations of Finance*. This box draws on professionals and their experiences from marketing, management, and accounting to illustrate how the material being presented pertains to what they do.

AN ENTREPRENEUR'S PERSPECTIVE

THE ENTREPRENEUR AND FINANCE

Do you ever think about wanting to someday own your own business? Does being an entrepreneur have any appeal to you? Well, it does for a lot of people. During the past decade, starting and growing companies have been the preferred avenue many have chosen for careers. In fact, while many of the large companies are reducing the number of employees, smaller companies are creating new jobs by the thousands. A lot of individuals have thought that there was greater security in working with a big company, only to be disillusioned in the end when they were informed that "Friday is your last day."

Defining an entrepreneur is not an easy thing to do. But we can say with some clarity what *entrepreneurship* is about. Entrepreneurship has been defined as a relentless pursuit of opportunity for the purpose of creating value, without concern for the resources owned.

To be successful, the entrepreneurial process requires that the entrepreneur be able to:

- **Identify a good opportunity.** Oftentimes we may have a "good idea," but it may not be a "good opportunity." Opportunities are market driven. There must be enough customers who want to buy our product or service at a price that covers our expenses and leaves an attractive profit—no matter how much we may like the idea.

- **Gain access to the resources needed.** For any venture, there are critical resources—human, financial, and physical—that must be available. The entrepreneur usually does not have

the capital to own all the resources that are needed. So the entrepreneur must have access to resources but usually cannot afford to own them. It's what we call *bootstrapping*. The goal is to do more with less.

- **Launch the venture.** All the planning in the world is not enough. The entrepreneur must be action oriented. It requires a "can do" spirit.

- **Grow the business.** A business has to grow if it is to be successful. Frequently, the firm will not break even for several years, which means that we will be burning up cash each month. Being able to survive during the time that cash flows are negative is no easy task. If we grow too slow, we lose, but also if we grow too fast, we may lose as well. During this time, additional capital will be needed, which requires that we know how to value the firm and how to structure financing.

- **Exit the business.** If a venture has been successful, the entrepreneur will have created economic value that is locked up in the business. At some point in time, the entrepreneur will want to capture the value that has been created by the business. It will be time to *harvest*.

To be successful as an entrepreneur requires an understanding of finance. At the appropriate places in *Financial Management*, we will be presenting how finance relates to the entrepreneurial journey. It is an interesting topic that we think you will enjoy.

NEW "AN ENTREPRENEUR'S PERSPECTIVE" BOXES

A new box feature titled "An Entrepreneur's Perspective" that highlights issues faced by small and medium-sized firms has been introduced. These boxes look at finance from the point of view of someone who would like to start his or her own successful business.

EXCEL SPREADSHEETS

Excel spreadsheets are used to move money through time, deal with valuation of financial assets, and evaluate capital budgeting projects. These spreadsheet solutions are integrated throughout the text with spreadsheet problems now appearing at the end of various chapters, where appropriate.

USE OF AN INTEGRATED LEARNING SYSTEM

The text is organized around the learning objectives that appear at the beginning of each chapter to provide the instructor and student with an easy-to-use integrated learning system. Numbered icons identifying each objective appear next to the related material throughout the text and in the summary, allowing easy location of material related to each objective.

WHAT'S AHEAD

These features allow students to preview what's coming up in the chapter. They include real-world examples to help students understand the relevance of the concepts to the financial world.

> ⤞ **WHAT'S AHEAD** ⤝
>
> In this chapter, we lay a foundation for the entire book by discussing what finance is and then explaining the key goal that guides financial decision making: maximization of shareholder wealth. We discuss the legal and tax environment of financial decisions and describe the golden thread that ties everything together: the 10 basic principles of finance. Finally, we briefly look at what has led to the rise in multinational corporations.

> **PAUSE AND REFLECT**
>
> A timeline often makes it easier to understand time value of money problems. By visually plotting the flow of money, you can better determine which formula to use. Arrows placed above the line are inflows, whereas arrows below the line represent outflows. One thing is certain: Timelines reduce errors.

PAUSE AND REFLECT

In-text inserts appear throughout and focus the student's attention on "the big picture." These inserts help students identify the interrelationships and motivating factors behind core concepts.

> **EXAMPLE**
>
> If we place $1,000 in a savings account paying 5 percent interest compounded annually, how much will our account accrue to in 10 years? Substituting $PV = \$1,000$, $i = 5$ percent, and $n = 10$ years into equation (5-6), we get
>
> $$FV_n = PV(1 + i)^n$$
> $$= \$1,000(1 + .05)^{10}$$
> $$= \$1,000(1.62889)$$
> $$= \$1,628.89$$
>
> Thus, at the end of 10 years we will have $1,628.89 in our savings account.

INTEGRATED EXAMPLES

These provide students with real-world examples to help them apply the concepts presented in each chapter.

> ### ETHICS IN
> ### FINANCIAL MANAGEMENT
>
> **THE ENRON LESSONS: TRUST**
>
> The bankruptcy and failure of the Enron Corporation on December 2, 2001, shook the investment community to its very core and resulted in congressional hearings that could lead to new regulations with far-reaching implications. Enron's failure provides a sober warning to employees and investors and a valuable set of lessons for students of business. The lesson we offer here reaches far beyond corporate finance and touches on fundamental principles that have always been true but are sometimes forgotten.
>
> **Lesson: Trust and Credibility Are Essential to Business Success**
> The viability of any firm hinges critically on the firm's credibility with its customers, employees, regulators, investors, and even to some degree, competitors. This is particularly critical for a trading company such as Enron, whose primary business rests on the willingness of the firm's counterpart with whom it trades to "trust" in Enron's ability to "be there" when the time to settle up arrives. When the faith of the investment community was tested with the revelation of losses from some of Enron's largest investments and the subsequent disclosure of Enron's off-balance-sheet liabilities, Enron's trading business evaporated.
>
> We also were reminded of the fact that investors must believe that a firm's published financial reports are a fair representation of the firm's financial condition. Without this trust, outside investors would refuse to invest in the shares of publicly traded firms, and financial markets would collapse.[a]
>
> Trust between two entities is hard to sustain when one of the parties has dual and conflicting motives. We refer to the presence of multiple motives as a conflict of interest, and the potential for conflict-of-interest problems was in abundance as Enron fell to earth. Some of the following sources of conflict apply only to Enron, whereas others apply to many firms:
>
> - Enron's chief financial officer (CFO) attempted to serve two masters when he was both the CFO and the general partner for a series of limited partnerships used by Enron to finance its investments and hedge certain investment returns. There were times when he represented the interests of Enron in circumstances that were in direct conflict with the interests of the partners to the partnerships. It is still not clear how he handled these circumstances, but the source of concern to Enron's shareholders is obvious.
> - Were corporate insiders (executives) selling their stock based on their privileged knowledge of the firm's true financial condition during the months prior to the firm's failure, while outside investors were being duped into holding their shares? Allegations abound that top corporate executives at Enron were selling their shares long before other employees and outside investors knew how serious the firm's problems were. Regardless of the outcome in the Enron case, this raises a serious dilemma for investors, who cannot know as much about the financial condition of the firms in which they invest as the managers know.
> - Can auditing firms that accept consulting engagements with their audit clients be truly independent, or is that independence compromised? The Enron failure has called into question the wisdom of relying on external auditing firms that are beholden to the firms they audit, both for their continued employment as an auditor and for consulting fees that can sometimes dwarf their audit fees.
> - Finally, investors often rely on the opinions of equity analysts. Investors make the assumption that the analysts are offering unfettered, independent opinions of a company's financial prospects. However, in many cases the analysts work for investment banks that, in turn, rely on investment-banking fees from the very companies the analysts cover. The potential conflict of interest is obvious.
>
> [a] This is simply a recasting of the famous result from microeconomics stating that where informational asymmetry problems between buyers and sellers are extreme, markets will collapse [George Akerlof, "The Market for Lemons: Qualitative Uncertainty and the Market Mechanism," *Quarterly Journal of Economics*, 84 (1970), pp. 488–500].

EXTENSIVE COVERAGE OF ETHICS

Ethics is covered as a core principle and *Ethics in Financial Management* boxes appear throughout. These show students that ethical behavior is doing the right thing and that ethical dilemmas are everywhere in finance.

CONCEPT CHECKS

At the end of most major sections, concept checks highlight the key ideas just presented and allow students to test their understanding of the material.

> **CONCEPT CHECK**
> 1. What is an amortized loan?

BACK TO THE FOUNDATIONS

These in-text inserts appear throughout to allow the student to take time out and reflect on the meaning of the material just presented. The use of these inserts, coupled with the use of the 10 principles, keeps the student focused on the interrelationships and motivating factors behind the concepts.

> **BACK TO THE FOUNDATIONS**
>
> *Valuing common stock is no different from valuing preferred stock; only the pattern of the cash flows changes. Thus, the valuation of common stock relies on the same three principles developed in Chapter 1 that were used in valuing preferred stock:*
>
> **Principle 1: The Risk–Return Trade-Off—We Won't Take on Additional Risk Unless We Expect to Be Compensated with Additional Return.**
>
> **Principle 2: The Time Value of Money—A Dollar Received Today Is Worth More Than a Dollar Received in the Future.**
>
> **Principle 3: Cash—Not Profits—Is King.**
>
> *Determining the economic worth or value of an asset always relies on these three principles. Without them, we would have no basis for explaining value. With them, we can know that the amount and timing of cash, not earnings, drives value. Also, we must be rewarded for taking risk; otherwise, we will not invest.*

> ### COMPREHENSIVE PROBLEM
>
> For your job as the business reporter for a local newspaper, you are given the task of putting together a series of articles that explain the power of the time value of money to your readers. Your editor would like you to address several specific questions in addition to demonstrating for the readership the use of time value of money techniques by applying them to several problems. What would be your response to the following memorandum from your editor?
>
> To: Business Reporter
> From: Perry White, Editor, *Daily Planet*
> Re: Upcoming Series on the Importance and Power of the Time Value of Money
>
> In your upcoming series on the time value of money, I would like to make sure you cover several specific points. In addition, before you begin this assignment, I want to make sure we are all reading from the same script, as accuracy has always been the cornerstone of the *Daily Planet*. In this regard, I'd like a response to the following questions before we proceed:
>
> a. What is the relationship between discounting and compounding?
> b. What is the relationship between the $PVIF_{i,n}$ and $PVIFA_{i,n}$?
> c. 1. What will $5,000 invested for 10 years at 8 percent compounded annually grow to?
>   2. How many years will it take $400 to grow to $1,671 if it is invested at 10 percent compounded annually?
>   3. At what rate would $1,000 have to be invested to grow to $4,046 in 10 years?
> d. Calculate the future sum of $1,000, given that it will be held in the bank for 5 years and earn 10 percent compounded semiannually.
> e. What is an annuity due? How does this differ from an ordinary annuity?
> f. What is the present value of an ordinary annuity of $1,000 per year for 7 years discounted back to the present at 10 percent? What would be the present value if it were an annuity due?
> g. What is the future value of an ordinary annuity of $1,000 per year for 7 years compounded at 10 percent? What would be the future value if it were an annuity due?
> h. You have just borrowed $100,000, and you agree to pay it back over the next 25 years in 25 equal end-of-year annual payments that include the principal payments plus 10 percent compound interest on the unpaid balance. What will be the size of these payments?
> i. What is the present value of a $1,000 perpetuity discounted back to the present at 8 percent?
> j. What is the present value of a $1,000 annuity for 10 years, with the first payment occurring at the end of year 10 (that is, ten $1,000 payments occurring at the end of year 10 through year 19), given an appropriate discount rate of 10 percent?
> k. Given a 10 percent discount rate, what is the present value of a perpetuity of $1,000 per year if the first payment does not begin until the end of year 10?

COMPREHENSIVE END-OF-CHAPTER PROBLEMS

A comprehensive problem appears at the end of almost every chapter, covering all the major topics included in that chapter. This comprehensive problem can be used as a lecture or review tool by the professor. For the students, it provides an opportunity to apply all the concepts presented within the chapter in a realistic setting, thereby strengthening their understanding of the material.

KEY TERMS IDENTIFIED IN THE MARGINS

Key terms are called out in the margin and highlighted in the text. They can also be found in the glossary in the back of the book with definitions, making it easier for the students to check their understanding of key terms. At the end of each chapter, key terms are listed along with page numbers as a study checklist for students.

FINANCIAL CALCULATORS

The use of financial calculators has been integrated throughout this text, especially with respect to the presentation of the time value of money. Where appropriate, calculator solutions appear in the margin.

CONTENT UPDATING

In response to both the continued development of financial thought and reviewer comments, changes have been made in the text. Some of these changes include:

CHAPTER 1 AN INTRODUCTION TO THE FOUNDATIONS OF FINANCIAL MANAGEMENT—THE TIES THAT BIND

The material in this chapter was updated and revised to reflect changes in the personal tax code that lowered the personal tax rate on dividend income and thereby lessened the impact of the double taxation of corporate dividends. This chapter also includes an expanded discussion of S-type corporations and limited liability companies (LLC). In addition, an Entrepreneur's Perspective box dealing with difficulties that entrepreneurs face in raising capital was added.

CHAPTER 2 THE FINANCIAL MARKETS AND INTEREST RATES

Several changes, updates, and additions are spread throughout this chapter in order to make it more lively and relevant to readers. Many of the alterations are in response to reviewer suggestions. The chapter opens with a review of the past six interest rate cycles with emphasis on (1) the immediate past recession that began in March 2001, (2) the ultimate business expansion that led to the tightening of monetary policy commencing in June 2004, and (3) developments related to the corporate cost of capital through the opportunity cost of funds concept. Along this line, changes in the federal funds target rate and the commercial bank prime lending rate are chronicled from 1994 to 2004.

A new section is provided on the Public Company Accounting Reform and Investor Protection Act (Sarbanes–Oxley Act of 2002). The material on Sarbanes–Oxley is related to financial controls, ethics in finance, and corporate governance. The creation of the Public Company Accounting Oversight Board is detailed.

New boxes entitled Across the Hall are provided on both investment banking and commercial banking. These are related to the need for the student to acquire a basic understanding of business finance, regardless of that student's undergraduate major. Both of these new boxes were written by practicing corporate executives.

CHAPTER 3 UNDERSTANDING FINANCIAL STATEMENTS AND CASH FLOWS

The presentation of the financial statements has been revised to be very intuitive and easy to follow with illustrations that will keep the student interested in the material. Also, at the request of adopters, the presentation of free cash flows was simplified to help the student grasp this important concept without having to spend unproductive time in computations. The result was a more intuitive presentation of the meaning and calculation of free cash flows.

CHAPTER 4 EVALUATING A FIRM'S FINANCIAL STATEMENTS

The financial analysis in this chapter uses the traditional ratios based on accounting data but then adds market-value ratios to connect the accounting data with the firm's market value. We then explain how to interpret the market-value ratios in terms of management's performance at creating shareholder value. Finally, we use Economic Value Added™ to help the student better understand how management creates shareholder value.

CHAPTER 5 THE TIME VALUE OF MONEY

This chapter went through a major revision aimed at making it more accessible to today's math-phobic students. Without a sacrifice of rigor or content, the chapter was revised to eliminate the use of summation signs. In addition, there was a large increase in the use of calculator examples. The end-of-chapter problems were also expanded and improved, allowing for a significant increase in the number of end-of-chapter problems that are calculator based.

CHAPTER 6   THE MEANING AND MEASUREMENT OF RISK AND RETURN

To make it more relevant and interesting to students, we used a firm they would be familiar with—Barnes & Noble—to illustrate the concepts and computations regarding market risk.

CHAPTER 7   VALUATION AND CHARACTERISTICS OF BONDS

This chapter was updated and revised to reflect changes in the capital markets. Several new topics, such as convertibility, call provisions, and current yield, were also added.

CHAPTER 8   VALUATION AND CHARACTERISTICS OF STOCK

This chapter was updated and revised to reflect changes in the stock market. In addition, the presentation of shareholder valuation based on a firm's expected future free cash flows was simplified and clarified.

CHAPTER 9   CAPITAL-BUDGETING TECHNIQUES AND PRACTICE

The use of a financial calculator in calculating the different capital-budgeting decision tools was expanded along with a significant expansion of margin examples on how to use a financial calculator to calculate the different capital-budgeting criteria. In addition, the modified internal rate of return (*MIRR*) was introduced. This capital-budgeting criterion has become increasingly popular thanks in part to the efforts of the consulting firm McKinsey & Company. This section can be omitted for those who choose to do so. In addition, a new Across the Hall box was introduced highlighting the relationship between marketing and capital budgeting.

CHAPTER 10   CASH FLOWS AND OTHER TOPICS IN CAPITAL BUDGETING

The presentation of the calculation of free cash flows was simplified considerably. A new Across the Hall box was introduced examining the role of marketing in calculating a project's free cash flows. In addition, the end-of-chapter problem set was expanded.

CHAPTER 11   COST OF CAPITAL

In response to users' suggestions, we simplified the discussion of the issues encountered in using the dividend growth model to estimate the cost of equity capital. Also at the request of users, we changed notation for equations to reduce the use of mathematical symbols. For example, the discounted cash flow model used for estimating the cost of debt financing now uses a three-year bond with all the terms specified. This change is geared toward making the book more accessible to students with math phobia. In addition, two new weighted average cost of capital self-test problems were added to help students develop skill in evaluating the firm's cost of capital.

CHAPTER 12   DETERMINING THE FINANCING MIX

This chapter is now rich with actual company examples and discussions on financing decisions. For instance, financial leverage, operating leverage, and the combined leverage effect are demonstrated via examples dealing with Harley-Davidson, Inc., Procter & Gamble Company, and the Boeing Company. Furthermore, General Motors' pricing strategy is discussed within the framework of break-even analysis. And Walt Disney's use of the interest-coverage ratio is presented.

A new Web Works section deals with General Motors, Coca-Cola, and the Federal Reserve Bank of St. Louis. The latter source, the St. Louis Fed Web site, introduces the student to the popular and useful FRED II database; this database is a marvelous site for financial and economic time series data and is updated daily by the bank.

CHAPTER 13   DIVIDEND POLICY AND INTERNAL FINANCING

New material now centers on the divergent nature of dividend policy across corporations. Three highly different policies are illustrated via data from Starbucks, Coca-Cola, and Harley-Davidson. Later in the chapter an in-depth look at Harley-Davidson's cash payout policy is examined over the 1997–2003 time frame and specifically related to "Objective 4" of the chapter that details three common and alternative dividend policies.

In similar fashion the unusually large Microsoft dividend payout of $3.00 per common share (some $32 billion across all shares), which was announced in the summer of 2004, is discussed within the framework of an "extra or special dividend."

Moreover, the implications of the Jobs and Growth Tax Reconciliation Act of 2003 for corporate dividend policy are presented.

CHAPTER 14 SHORT-TERM FINANCIAL PLANNING

In addition to updating the material in this chapter, a new financial forecasting exercise was created that focuses on the projection of a firm's earning power. Also, new Internet-based problems and exercises connect the book to day-to-day activities in the financial markets.

CHAPTER 15 WORKING-CAPITAL MANAGEMENT

A new self-test problem was added aimed at helping students develop the skills necessary for analyzing the cost of bank credit under a variety of loan covenants. In addition, new Internet-based problems and exercises connect the book to day-to-day activities in the financial markets.

CHAPTER 16 CURRENT ASSET MANAGEMENT

This chapter contains several alterations aimed at making the material more relevant to decision making and more up-to-date, which, in turn, will make it of more value to students. For example, recent data from Starbucks Corporation and the Walt Disney Company are used to demonstrate the value and importance of float reduction within the context of corporate cash management.

The Check Clearing for the 21st Century Act, which went into effect on October 28, 2004, is reviewed and placed within the context of the Treasury Department's mission within the firm to properly "manage the float." The implications of this act, commonly referred to as "Check 21," for the various types of float are discussed.

Additionally, a new Takin' It to the Net section introduces the student to the U.S. Department of the Treasury's comprehensive Web site at **www.treasurydirect.gov** where individuals, corporations, and governments can explore detailed information on the array of investment products offered by the U.S. Treasury.

CHAPTER 17 INTERNATIONAL FINANCIAL MANAGEMENT

This chapter was updated to reflect the changes impacting the global financial markets. In addition, a new Across the Hall box was introduced highlighting the role of marketing in international finance.

THE SUPPORT PACKAGE

PRINT SUPPLEMENTS:

FOR THE INSTRUCTOR:

TEST ITEM FILE This Test Bank, prepared by Alan D. Eastman of Indiana University of Pennsylvania, provides more than 1,600 multiple-choice, true/false, and short-answer questions with complete and detailed answers. The print Test Bank is designed for use with the new TestGen-EQ test generating software.

INSTRUCTOR'S MANUAL WITH SOLUTIONS Prepared by the authors, the Instructor's Manual follows the textbook's organization and represents a continued effort to serve the teacher in his or her goal of being effective in the classroom. Each chapter contains a chapter orientation, an outline of each chapter (also suitable for lecture notes), answers to end-of-chapter questions, and an extensive problem set for each chapter, including a large number of alternative problems along with answers.

The Instructor's Manual is also available electronically and instructors can download this file from the Instructor's Resource Center by visiting **www.prenhall.com/keown**.

COLOR TRANSPARENCIES All figures and tables from the text are reproduced as full-page, four-color acetates.

FOR THE STUDENT:

STUDY GUIDE The Study Guide to accompany *Foundations of Finance: The Logic and Practice of Financial Management*, 5th Edition, was written by the authors with the objective of providing a student-oriented supplement to the text. Each chapter of the Study Guide contains an orientation of each chapter along with a chapter outline of key topics, problems (with detailed solutions) and self-tests, which can be used to aid in the preparation of outside assignments and in studying for exams, a tutorial on capital budgeting, a set of tables that not only gives compound sum and present value interest factors but also shows how to compute the interest using a financial calculator.

TECHNOLOGY SUPPLEMENTS:

COMPANION WEBSITE (**www.prenhall.com/keown**) The Web site contains various activities related specifically to the Fifth Edition of *Foundations of Finance: The Logic and Practice of Financial Management*.

FOR THE STUDENT:

➤ **Excel Spreadsheets.** Created by the authors, these spreadsheets correspond with the end-of-chapter problems from the text.
➤ **Internet Exercises.** These activities, prepared by James M. Forjan of York College of Pennsylvania, give students the opportunity to utilize the tools and information available on the Internet by directing them to various online sites and then providing a summary and a set of questions about the experience.
➤ **Online Study Guide.** The Online Study Guide, prepared by Philip Samuel Russel of Philadelphia University, offers students another opportunity to sharpen their problem-solving skills and to assess their understanding of the text material. The Online Study Guide is a truly comprehensive set of questions with exceptional coverage of the material in the textbook and written by the authors. The Online Study Guide grades each question submitted by the students, provides immediate feedback for correct and incorrect answers, and allows students to e-mail results to up to four e-mail addresses.

FOR THE INSTRUCTOR:

➤ **Syllabus Manager.** Allows instructors to create a syllabus that they may publish for their students to access. Instructors may add exams or assignments of their own, edit any of the student resources available on the Companion Website, post discussion topics, and more.
➤ Instructors may find *downloadable resources* from the link for the Instructor's Resource Center described here.

INSTRUCTOR'S RESOURCE CENTER This password-protected site is accessible at **www.prenhall.com/keown** and hosts all of the resources that follow. Instructors should click on the "Help Downloading Instructor Resources" link for easy-to-follow instructions on getting access or may contact their sales representative for further information.

➤ **Instructor's Manual**

➤ **Solutions** to the Internet Exercise activities that are included on the student side of the Companion Website.

➤ **The PowerPoint Lecture Presentation:** This lecture presentation tool, prepared by Samuel A. Veraldi of Duke University, provides the instructor with individual lecture outlines to accompany the text. The slides include many of the figures and tables from the text. These lecture notes can be used as is or professors can easily modify them to reflect specific presentation needs.

➤ **TestGen-EQ software:** The print Test Item File is designed for use with the TestGen-EQ test generating software. This computerized package allows instructors to custom design, save, and generate classroom tests. The test program permits instructors to edit, add, or delete questions from the test bank; edit existing graphics and create new graphics; analyze test results; and organize a database of tests and student results. This new software allows for greater flexibility and ease of use. It provides many options for organizing and displaying tests, along with a search and sort feature.

ONEKEY Available by using one of the access codes shrink-wrapped with the book, OneKey is Prentice Hall's exclusive new resource for instructors and students. OneKey gives you access to the best online teaching and learning tools—all available 24 hours a day, 7 days a week. OneKey means all your resources are in one place for maximum convenience, simplicity, and success. **Instructors** have access online, in the course management system of their choosing, to all available course supplements. Instructors can create and assign tests, quizzes, or graded homework assignments. **OneKey** saves instructors time by grading all questions and tracking results in the online course grade book. **Students** have access to interactive exercises, quizzes, useful links, and much more. The following resources are available:

➤ **Study Guide.**

➤ **Self-Study Quizzes.**

➤ **Graded Homework Assignments.**

➤ **PowerPoint Lecture Notes.**

➤ **Learning Objectives.**

➤ **Chapter Summaries.**

➤ **Research Navigator.** Your OneKey course gives you direct access to Prentice Hall's powerful online research tool, Research Navigator. Research Navigator is an online academic research service that helps students learn and master the skills needed to write effective papers and complete research assignments. Research Navigator includes three databases of credible and reliable source material.

  ➤ EBSCO's ContentSelect™ Academic Journal database gives you instant access to thousands of academic journals and periodicals. You can search these on-line journals by keyword, topic, or multiple topics. It also guides students step by step through the writing of a research paper.

  ➤ The *New York Times* Search-by-Subject™ Archive allows you to search by subject and by keyword.

  ➤ Link Library is a collection of links to Web sites, organized by academic subject and key terms. The links are monitored and updated each week.

➤ **Instructor Resource Center.**

OneKey for CourseCompass allows instructors to communicate with students, distribute course material, and access student progress online. For access to this material, see **www.prenhall.com/coursecompass**.

OneKey for WebCT provides content and enhanced features to help instructors create a complete online course. See **www.prenhall.com/webct** for more information.

Finally, *OneKey for Blackboard* allows instructors to create online courses using the Blackboard tools, which include design, communications, testing, and course management tools. See **www.prenhall.com/blackboard** for more information.

SUBSCRIPTIONS:

Analyzing current events is an important skill for economic students to develop. To sharpen this skill and further support the book's theme of exploration and application, Prentice Hall offers you and your students three news subscription offers:

The *Wall Street Journal* Print and Interactive Editions Subscription
Prentice Hall has formed a strategic alliance with the *Wall Street Journal*, the most respected and trusted daily source for information on business and economics. For a small additional charge, Prentice Hall offers your students a 10-week or 15-week subscription to the *Wall Street Journal* print edition and the *Wall Street Journal* Interactive Edition. Upon adoption of a special package containing the book and the subscription booklet, professors will receive a free one-year subscription of the print and interactive versions as well as weekly subject-specific *Wall Street Journal* educators' lesson plans.

The *Financial Times*
We are pleased to announce a special partnership with the *Financial Times*. For a small additional charge, Prentice Hall offers your students a 15-week subscription to the *Financial Times*. Upon adoption of a special package containing the book and the subscription booklet, professors will receive a free one-year subscription. Please contact your Prentice Hall representative for details and ordering information.

Economist.com
Through a special arrangement with Economist.com, Prentice Hall offers your students a 12-week subscription to Economist.com for a small additional charge. Upon adoption of a special package containing the book and the subscription booklet, professors will receive a free six-month subscription. Please contact your Prentice Hall representative for further details and ordering information.

ACKNOWLEDGMENTS

We gratefully acknowledge the assistance, support, and encouragement of those individuals who have contributed to *Foundations of Finance*. Specifically, we wish to recognize the very helpful insights provided by many of our colleagues. For their careful comments and helpful reviews of the text, we are indebted to:

Ibrahim J. Affeneh
Indiana University of Pennsylvania

Sung C. Bae
Bowling Green State University

Laurey Berk
University of Wisconsin, Green Bay

Ronald W. Best
University of South Alabama

Stephen Black
University of Central Oklahoma

Laurence E. Blose
University of North Carolina, Charlotte

Robert Boldin
Indiana University of Pennsylvania

Michael Bond
Cleveland State University

Waldo L. Born
Eastern Illinois University

Joe Brocato
Tarleton State University

Paul Bursik
St. Norbert College

Soku Byoun
University of Southern Indiana

Anthony K. Byrd
University of Central Florida

P. R. Chandy
University of North Texas

Santosh Choudhury
Norfolk State University

K. C. Chen
California State University, Fresno

Jeffrey S. Christensen
Youngstown State University

M. C. Chung
California State University, Sacramento

Susan Coleman
University of Hartford

Steven M. Dawson
University of Hawaii

Karen Denning
Western Virginia University

Yashwant S. Dhatt
University of Southern Colorado

Thomas Downs
University of Alabama

Edwin Duett
Mississippi State University

John W. Ellis
Colorado State University

Suzanne Erickson
Seattle University

Slim Feriani
George Washington University

Greg Filbeck
Miami University

Jennifer Frazier
James Madison University

Bruce Fredrikson
Syracuse University

Joseph F. Greco
California State University, Fullerton

Karen Hallows
George Mason University

Ken Halsey
Wayne State College

Mary H. Harris
Cabrini College

James D. Harriss
University of North Carolina, Wilmington

Linda C. Hittle
San Diego State University

Robert Hull
Washburn University

Joel Jankowski
University of Tampa

Gerry Jensen
Northern Illinois University

Steve Johnson
University of Texas at El Paso

Ravi Kamath
Cleveland State University

James D. Keys
Florida International University

V. Sivarama Krishnan
Cameron University

Reinhold P. Lamb
University of North Carolina Charlotte

Larry Lang
University of Wisconsin

George B. F. Lanigan
University of North Carolina, Greensboro

Stephen Larson
University of Eastern Illinois

William R. Lasher
Nichols College

David E. Letourneau
Winthrop University

Ilene Levin
University of Minnesota—Duluth

David Louton
Bryant College

Lee McClain
Western Washington University

Ginette M. McManus
St. Joseph's University

Michael McMillan
Northern Virginia Community College

James E. McNulty
Florida Atlantic University

Grant McQueen
Brigham Young University

Judy E. Maese
New Mexico State University

Abbas Mamoozadeh
Slippery Rock University

Emil Meurer
University of New Orleans

Stuart Michelson
Eastern Illinois University

Eric J. Moon
San Francisco State University

Scott Moore
John Carroll University

Diane Morrison
University of Wisconsin at LaCrosse

Rick H. Mull
Fort Lewis College

M. P. Narayanan
University of Michigan

William E. O'Connell Jr.
College of William & Mary

Thomas M. Patrick
The College of New Jersey

Samuel Penkar
University of Houston—Downtown

Jeffrey H. Peterson
St. Bonaventure University

Mario Picconi
University of San Diego

Chris Pope
University of Georgia

Pradipkumar Ramanlal
University of Central Florida

P. Raghavendra Rau
Purdue University

Dan Reeder
Oklahoma Baptist University

Stuart Rosenstein
Clemson University

Ivan C. Roten
Arizona State University

Marjorie A. Rubash
Bradley University

Atul K. Saxena
Mercer University

Hari P. Sharma
Virginia State University

Chi Sheh
University of Houston

Joseph Stanford
Bridgewater State College

David Suk
Rider University

Charlene Sullivan
Purdue University

Elizabeth Sun
San Jose State University

R. Bruce Swensen
Adelphi University

Philip R. Swensen
Utah State University

Lee Tenpao
Niagara University

Philip Thames
California State University at Long Beach

Paul A. Vanderheiden
University of Wisconsin, Eau Claire

Nikhil P. Varaiya
San Diego State University

K. G. Viswanathan
Hofstra University

Al Webster
Bradley University

Patricia Webster
Bradley University

Herbert Weinraub
University of Toledo

Sandra Williams
Moorhead State University

Tony R. Wingler
University of North Carolina, Greensboro

Bob G. Wood, Jr.
Tennessee Tech University

Jian Yang
Prairie View A & M University

Ata Yesilyaprak
Columbus State University

Wold Zernedkun
Norfolk State University

Marc Zenner
Indiana University

We also thank our friends at Prentice Hall. They are a great group of folks. To David Alexander, our executive editor, we owe an immeasurable debt of gratitude. He continued to push us to make sure that we delivered the finest textbook and supplementary package possible. His efforts go well beyond what one might expect from the best of editors. On top of this, David is just a great person—thanks, David. We would also like to thank Francesca Calogero for her administrative deftness. Not only is she bright, insightful, and attentive to detail—in short, a gifted assistant editor—but she also made the revision a fun experience. She is a true friend. With Francesca watching over us, there was no way the ball could be dropped. Our thanks also go to Sharon Koch for her marketing prowess. Sharon has an amazing understanding of the market, coupled with an intuitive understanding of what the market is looking for. We also thank Nancy Welcher, our media manager, who did a great job of making sure we are on the cutting edge in terms of Web applications and offerings. To Denise Culhane, the production editor, we express a very special thank-you for seeing the book through a very complex production process and keeping it all on schedule while maintaining extremely high quality.

As a final word, we express our sincere thanks to those using *Foundations of Finance* in the classroom. We thank you for making us a part of your team. Always feel free to give any of us a call or contact us through the Internet when you have questions or needs.

—A.J.K. / J.D.M. / J.W.P. / D.F.S.

Financial Management

> G. Bennett Stewart III is a senior partner with Stern Stewart & Co. (NY). Before cofounding Stern Stewart in 1982 with Joel Stern, he was a vice president with the financial advisory arm of the Chase Manhattan Bank. Stern Stewart & Co. is a global consulting firm that specializes in helping client companies in the measurement and creation of shareholder wealth through the application of tools based on modern financial theory. We interviewed Bennett to get his thoughts on how managers should think about finance. This is what he had to say:

To be honest, I think managers should think as little about finance as possible and as much about running their business as possible. That is, finance should really be the servant of the business and not the other way around. If there is one concept that should drive what managers do, it is this: As long as managers can raise money from investors and invest it in their business [while] providing a return on the investment that is higher than what the investors could earn from an equally risky portfolio of stocks and bonds, then value is created.

I like to think of finance with an analogy of a savings account. When I worked at Chase Manhattan Bank from 1976 until 1982, Chase Bank was offering a 5% rate of interest when Merrill Lynch came out with a money market account that paid as much as 15%. It didn't take a genius to figure out that getting 15% from Merrill Lynch was a lot better than getting 5% from Chase, so people stormed the bank and took their money down the street in search of the higher rate of return. I claim that the stock market works in exactly the same way. If the rate of return a company is earning inside its business isn't up to the return that the investors could earn elsewhere, they're going to withdraw their investment from the company, and its stock price will be depressed.

A sure sign that a firm has misallocated the money entrusted to it by the firm's investors is when the market value of the company is less than its underlying book value, which is the amount that investors have put into the business. The difference in the market value of the firm and the amount of money invested in the firm is known in finance as net present value or what we at Stern Stewart like to call the *MVA* or *market value added*. The essence of finance then is taking resources of all kinds and combining them in ways such that the value of the output is worth more than the cost of the input. It's like a chef who takes a menu of ingredients, stirs them, and cooks them to make a cake. If the value of the cake is more than the value of the ingredients, value has been created. This is the concept of *net present value*—a basic premise in finance.

I think that managers often forget these very basic ideas and begin to focus on accounting measures exclusively. Frequently, people on Wall Street become focused on reported earnings, earnings per share, earnings growth, profit margins, and such. In fact, there is kind of a bewildering array of these

financial metrics and ratios and it's very easy for managers to lose sight of the forest for the trees and get away from the very simple, common-sense propositions that should guide them.

Back in the 1960s, my partner, Joel Stern, suggested that the mom and pop running the corner grocery store often know more about value creation than many senior executives. For example, mom and pop know that the key to their success is in the cigar box that holds their cash. As long as the lid on the cigar box was rising, they were doing okay for themselves. In finance, we say that as long as the "free cash flow" from the operations is increasing, all is well. But it's no different from the cigar box.

Enron is a good example of what I am describing. In its 2000 annual report, Enron reported that management was "laser-focused on earnings per share" and indeed it appears that it was. You have to conclude that the company aimed for increased earnings per share by investing too much money in unrewarding projects. In addition, it avoided issuing stock so it could maintain high earnings per share. This required Enron to use too much debt. In fact, I contend that every company that worships at the EPS altar will be tempted to either overinvest or use too much debt.

I have concluded that earnings per share is the opium of the executive suites and the Don Giovanni of corporate finance. We need to blackball this entire earnings management game!

CHAPTER 1

An Introduction to the Foundations of Financial Management—The Ties That Bind

GOAL OF THE FIRM • LEGAL FORMS OF BUSINESS ORGANIZATION • FEDERAL INCOME TAXATION • TEN PRINCIPLES THAT FORM THE FOUNDATIONS OF FINANCIAL MANAGEMENT • FINANCE AND THE MULTINATIONAL FIRM: THE NEW ROLE

Apple Computer ignited the personal computer revolution in the 1970s with the Apple II and reinvented the personal computer in the 1980s with the Macintosh, but by 1997, it looked like it might be nearing the end for Apple. Mac users were on the decline, and the company didn't seem to be headed in any real direction. It was at that point that Steve Jobs reappeared, taking back his old job as CEO of Apple, the company he cofounded in 1976. To say the least, things began to change. In fact, between then and the beginning of 2005, the price of Apple's common stock had climbed by over eightfold!

How did Apple accomplish all this? The company did it by going back to what it does best, which is to produce products that make the optimal trade-off between ease of use, complexity, and features. Apple took its special skills and applied them to more than just computers, introducing new products such as the iPod, a digital music player; Xserve, a server; Airport, wireless networking equipment; and publishing and multimedia software. In addition, Apple improved its computer offerings with the sleek iMac and iBook for the consumer and education markets and with the more powerful Power Mac and PowerBook for high-end consumers and professionals involved in design and publishing. Although all these

products have done well, the success of the iPod has been truly amazing. Between the introduction of the iPod in October 2001 and the beginning of 2005, Apple sold more than 6 million of the devices. Then, in 2004, it came out with the iPod mini, about the length and width of a business card, which has also been a huge success, particularly among women. How successful has this new product been? By 2004, Apple was selling more iPods than its signature Macintosh desktop and notebook computers.

How do you follow up on the success of the iPod? You keep improving your products and you keep developing and introducing new products that consumers want. With this in mind, in October 2004, Apple unveiled its latest version of the popular digital music player iPod, which enables users to store and share photos. The product, named iPod Photo, has a color screen, holds up to 25,000 digital photos alongside a music library, and displays them on its stunning high-resolution color screen, allowing users to scroll through their photo library almost instantly. Then in early 2005, Apple introduced the iPod shuffle at less than one ounce and smaller than a pack of gum. This tiny version of the iPod holds up to 16 hours of music and boasts 12 hours of playback time.

⨯ WHAT'S AHEAD ⨯

In this chapter, we lay a foundation for the entire book by discussing what finance is and then explaining the key goal that guides financial decision making: maximization of shareholder wealth. We discuss the legal and tax environment of financial decisions

and describe the golden thread that ties everything together: the 10 basic principles of finance. Finally, we briefly look at what has led to the rise in multinational corporations.

How did Apple make a decision to introduce the original iPod and now the iPod Photo and the iPod shuffle? The answer is through sound financial management. Financial management deals with the maintenance and creation of economic value or wealth by focusing on decision making with an eye toward creating wealth. As such, this text deals with financial decisions such as when to introduce a new product, when to invest in new assets, when to replace existing assets, when to borrow from banks, when to sell stocks or bonds, when to extend credit to a customer, and how much cash and inventory to maintain. All of these aspects of financial management were factors in Apple's decision to introduce the iPod, iPod Photo, and iPod shuffle, and the end result is having a major financial impact on Apple.

Objective **1**

GOAL OF THE FIRM

In this text we designate the goal of the firm as *maximization of shareholder wealth*, by which we mean maximization of the price of the existing common stock. Not only does this goal directly benefit the shareholders of the company, but also it provides benefits to society as scarce resources are directed to their most productive use by businesses competing to create wealth. With this goal in place, our job as financial managers is to create wealth for the shareholders. To better understand this goal, we first discuss profit maximization as a possible goal for the firm. Then we compare it to maximization of shareholder wealth to see why, in financial management, the latter is the more appropriate goal for the firm.

PROFIT MAXIMIZATION

In microeconomics courses, profit maximization is frequently given as the goal of the firm. Profit maximization stresses the efficient use of capital resources, but it is not specific with respect to the time frame over which profits are to be measured. Do we maximize profits over the current year, or do we maximize profits over some longer period? A financial manager could easily increase current profits by eliminating research and development expenditures and cutting down on routine maintenance. In the short run, this might result in increased profits, but this clearly is not in the best long-run interests of the firm. If we are to base financial decisions on a goal, that goal must be precise, not allow for misinterpretation, and deal with all the complexities of the real world.

In microeconomics, profit maximization functions largely as a theoretical goal, with economists using it to prove how firms behave rationally to increase profit. Unfortunately, it ignores many real-world complexities that financial managers must address in their decisions. In the more applied discipline of financial management, firms must deal every day with two major factors not considered by the goal of profit maximization: uncertainty and timing.

Microeconomics courses ignore uncertainty and risk to present theory more easily. Projects and investment alternatives are compared by examining their expected values or weighted average profits. Whether one project is riskier than another does not enter into these calculations; economists do discuss risk, but only tangentially.[1] In reality, projects differ a great deal with respect to risk characteristics, and to disregard these differences in the practice of financial management can result in incorrect decisions. As we discover later in this chapter, there is a very definite relationship between risk and expected return—that is, investors demand a higher expected return for taking on added risk—and to ignore this relationship leads to improper decision making.

Another problem with the goal of profit maximization is that it ignores the timing of the project's returns. If this goal is only concerned with this year's profits, we know it inappropriately ignores profits in future years. If we interpret it to maximize the average of future profits, it is also incorrect. Inasmuch as investment opportunities are available for money in hand, we are not indifferent to the timing of the returns. Given equivalent cash flows from profits, we want those cash flows sooner rather than later. Thus, the real-world

[1]See, for example, Robert S. Pindyck and Daniel Rubenfield, *Microeconomics*, 6th ed. (Upper Saddle River, NJ: Prentice Hall, 2005).

TAKIN' IT TO THE NET

As you'll soon find out, finance has a language all its own. If you ever come across terms you aren't familiar with, try looking them up in the Investopedia financial dictionary www.investopedia.com.

TAKIN' IT TO THE NET

Given the goal of maximization of shareholder wealth, we know that if a corporation is to maximize shareholder wealth, the interests of the managers and the shareholders must be aligned. The simplest way to align these interests is to structure executive compensation packages appropriately to encourage managers to act in the best interests of shareholders. However, has executive compensation gotten out of control? Take a look at the Executive Pay Watch www.aflcio.org/corporateamerica/paywatch to see where top salaries have gone.

factors of uncertainty and timing force us to look beyond a simple goal of profit maximization as a decision criterion. We now turn to an examination of a more robust goal for the firm: maximization of shareholder wealth.

MAXIMIZATION OF SHAREHOLDER WEALTH

In formulating the goal of maximization of shareholder wealth we are doing nothing more than modifying the goal of profit maximization to deal with the complexities of the operating environment. We have chosen maximization of shareholder wealth—that is, maximization of the market value of the existing shareholders' common stock—because the effects of all financial decisions are thereby included. Investors react to poor investment or dividend decisions by causing the total value of the firm's stock to fall, and they react to good decisions by pushing up the price of the stock. In effect, under this goal, good decisions are those that create wealth for the shareholder.

Obviously, there are some serious practical problems in the direct use of this goal and in using changes in the firm's stock to evaluate financial decisions. Many things affect stock prices; to attempt to identify a reaction to a particular financial decision would simply be impossible and unnecessary. To employ this goal, we need not consider every stock price change to be a market interpretation of the worth of our decisions. Other factors, such as changes in the economy, also affect stock prices. What we do focus on is the effect that our decision *should* have on the stock price if everything else were held constant. The market price of the firm's stock reflects the value of the firm as seen by its owners and takes into account the complexities and complications of the real-world risk. As we follow this goal throughout our discussions, we must keep in mind one more question: Who exactly are the shareholders? The answer: Shareholders are the legal owners of the firm.

CONCEPT CHECK

1. What are the problems with the goal of profit maximization?
2. What is the goal of the firm?

LEGAL FORMS OF BUSINESS ORGANIZATION

Objective **2**

In the chapters ahead we focus on financial decisions for corporations because, although the corporation is not the only legal form of business available, it is the most logical choice for a firm that is large or growing. It is also the dominant business form in terms of sales in this country. In this section we explain why this is so. Focusing on corporations allows us to simplify the remainder of the text by following the corporate tax code, rather than examining different tax codes for different legal forms of businesses. Keep in mind that our primary purpose is to develop an understanding of the logic of financial decision making. Taxes become important only when they affect our decisions, and our discussion of the choice of the legal form of the business is directed at understanding why we limit our discussion of taxes to the corporate form.

Although numerous and diverse, the legal forms of business organization fall into three categories: the sole proprietorship, the partnership, and the corporation. To understand the basic differences between each form, we need to define each one and understand its advantages and disadvantages. As the firm grows, the advantages of the corporation begin to dominate. As a result, most large firms take on the corporate form.

TAKIN' IT TO THE NET

If you're interested in starting your own business, take a look at the Small Business Administration's Web site www.sba.gov. It has an online library with publications, free software, and all kinds of great information.

SOLE PROPRIETORSHIP

The **sole proprietorship** is *a business owned by an individual*. The owner maintains title to the assets and is responsible, generally without limitation, for the liabilities incurred. The proprietor is entitled to the profits from the business but must also absorb any losses. This form of business is initiated by the mere act of beginning the business operations. Typically,

sole proprietorship

TAKIN' IT TO THE NET
Another great source of information on starting a business and entrepreneurial issues comes from the Wall Street Journal's Center for Entrepreneurs at www.startupjournal.com.

no legal requirement must be met in starting the operation, particularly if the proprietor is conducting the business in his or her own name. If a special name is used, an assumed-name certificate should be filed, requiring a small registration fee. Termination occurs on the owner's death or by the owner's choice. Briefly stated, the sole proprietorship is for all practical purposes the absence of any formal *legal* business structure.

PARTNERSHIP

partnership

The primary difference between a partnership and a sole proprietorship is that the partnership has more than one owner. A **partnership** is *an association of two or more persons coming together as co-owners for the purpose of operating a business for profit*. Partnerships fall into two types: (1) general partnerships and (2) limited partnerships.

GENERAL PARTNERSHIP

general partnership

In a **general partnership** *each partner is fully responsible for the liabilities incurred by the partnership*. Thus, any partner's faulty conduct even having the appearance of relating to the firm's business renders the remaining partners liable as well. The relationship among partners is dictated entirely by the partnership agreement, which may be an oral commitment or a formal document.

LIMITED PARTNERSHIP AND LIMITED LIABILITY COMPANY

limited partnership

In addition to the general partnership, in which all partners are jointly liable without limitation, many states provide for a **limited partnership**. The state statutes permit *one or more of the partners to have limited liability, restricted to the amount of capital invested in the partnership*. Several conditions must be met to qualify as a limited partner. First, at least one general partner must have unlimited liability. Second, the names of the limited partners may not appear in the name of the firm. Third, the limited partners may not participate in the management of the business. Thus, a limited partnership provides limited liability for a partner who is purely an investor.

CORPORATION

corporation

The **corporation** has been a significant factor in the economic development of the United States. As early as 1819, Chief Justice John Marshall set forth the legal definition of a corporation as "an artificial being, invisible, intangible, and existing only in the contemplation of law."[2] This entity *legally functions separate and apart from its owners*. As such, the corporation can individually sue and be sued, and purchase, sell, or own property; its personnel are subject to criminal punishment for crimes. However, despite this legal separation, the corporation is composed of owners who dictate its direction and policies. The owners elect a board of directors, whose members in turn select individuals to serve as corporate officers, including president, vice president, secretary, and treasurer. Ownership is reflected in common stock certificates, each designating the number of shares owned by its holder. The number of shares owned relative to the total number of shares outstanding determines the stockholder's proportionate ownership in the business. Because the shares are transferable, ownership in a corporation may be changed by a shareholder simply remitting the shares to a new shareholder. The investor's liability is confined to the amount of the investment in the company, thereby preventing creditors from confiscating stockholders' personal assets in settlement of unresolved claims. This is an extremely important advantage of a corporation. After all, would you be willing to invest in USAir if you would be held liable if one of its planes crashed? Finally, the life of a corporation is not dependent on the status of the investors. The death or withdrawal of an investor does not affect the continuity of the corporation. The management continues to run the corporation when stock is sold or when it is passed on through inheritance.

TAKIN' IT TO THE NET
Interested in doing well in this class? One place to find some extra help is the Companion Web site that accompanies this text www.prenhall.com/keown. Make sure you check it out. It has a study guide, current events, and Internet exercises.

---

[2]*The Trustees of Dartmouth College* v. *Woodard*, 4 Wheaton 636 (1819).

COMPARISON OF ORGANIZATIONAL FORMS

Owners of new businesses have some important decisions to make in choosing an organizational form. Whereas each business form seems to have some advantages over the others, the advantages of the corporation begin to dominate as the firm grows and needs access to the capital markets to raise funds.

WHY LARGE AND GROWING FIRMS CHOOSE THE CORPORATE FORM: EASE IN RAISING CAPITAL

Because of the limited liability, the ease of transferring ownership through the sale of common shares, and the flexibility in dividing the shares, the corporation is the ideal business entity in terms of attracting new capital. In contrast, the unlimited liabilities of the sole proprietorship and the general partnership are deterrents to raising equity capital. Between the extremes, the limited partnership does provide limited liability for limited partners, which has a tendency to attract wealthy investors. However, the impracticality of having a large number of partners and the restricted marketability of an interest in a partnership prevent this form of organization from competing effectively with the corporation. Therefore, when developing our decision models we assume we are dealing with the corporate form. The taxes incorporated in these models deal only with the corporate tax codes. Because our goal is to develop an understanding of the management, measurement, and creation of wealth, and not to become tax experts, we only focus on those characteristics of the corporate tax code that affect our financial decisions.

ORGANIZATIONAL FORM AND TAXES: THE DOUBLE TAXATION ON DIVIDENDS

In this chapter we will focus on taxes that the corporation pays. But for a moment we will set that aside and look at the taxes that a corporation's owners pay on dividends that they receive from the corporation. Historically, one of the drawbacks of the corporate form was the double taxation of dividends. This occurs when a corporation earns a profit, then pays taxes on those profits (the first taxation of earnings), pays some of those profits back to the shareholders in the form of dividends, and then the shareholders pay personal income taxes on those dividends (the second taxation of those earnings). This double taxation of earnings does not take place with proprietorships. Needless to say, that had been a major disadvantage of corporations. However, in an attempt to stimulate the economy, the tax rate on dividends was cut with the passage of the Tax Act of 2003.

Before the 2003 tax changes, you paid your regular tax rate on dividend income, which could be as high as 35 percent. However, with the new law, qualified dividends from domestic corporations and qualified foreign corporations are now taxed at a maximum rate of 15 percent. Moreover, if you're in the 10 percent or 15 percent rate bracket, your dividends will be taxed at only 5 percent, and in 2008, this rate drops to 0 percent. Unless Congress takes further action, this tax break on dividends will end after 2008 and individuals will once again be taxed at their regular personal tax rate. However, with president Bush's reelection, it looks like these tax changes will become permanent.

S-TYPE CORPORATIONS AND LIMITED LIABILITY COMPANIES (LLC)

One of the problems that entrepreneurs and small business owners face is that they need the benefits of the corporate form to expand, but the double taxation of earnings that comes with the corporate form makes it difficult to accumulate the necessary wealth for expansion. Fortunately, the government recognizes this problem and has provided two business forms that are in effect crosses between a partnership and a corporation with the tax benefits of partnerships (no double taxation of earnings) and the limited liability benefit of corporations (your liability is limited to what you invest).

The first is the **S-type corporation**, which provides limited liability while allowing the business owners to be taxed as if they were a partnership—that is, distributions back to the owners are not taxed twice as is the case with dividends in the corporate form.

S-type corporation

AN ENTREPRENEUR'S
PERSPECTIVE

LIMITED LIABILITY AND THE ENTREPRENEUR

There's no doubt that the limited liability features of the corporate form, the S-type corporation, and the LLC are extremely important; however, for the entrepreneur just starting a business, it may be irrelevant. That's because it is almost impossible for a small business that is just starting out to get a loan without a personal guarantee from the small business owner. For example, if you begin a business and go to a bank to borrow money, the bank will demand that you guarantee the repayment of the loan in the event that the corporation cannot repay the loan.

Unfortunately, a number of restrictions accompany the S-type corporation that detract from the desirability of this business form. For example, with an S-type corporation all the owners must be people. Thus, an S-type corporation cannot be used for a joint venture between two corporations. As a result, this business form has been losing ground in recent years in favor of the limited liability company.

limited liability company (LLC)

The **limited liability company** (LLC) is also a cross between a partnership and a corporation. Just as with the S-type corporation, the LLC retains limited liability for its owners but runs and is taxed like a partnership. In general, it provides more flexibility than the S-type corporation. For example, corporations can be owners in an LLC. However, since LLCs operate under state laws, both states and the IRS have rules for what qualifies as an LLC, and different states have different rules. But the bottom line in all this is that the LLC must not look too much like a corporation or it will be taxed as one.

THE ROLE OF THE FINANCIAL MANAGER IN A CORPORATION

Although a firm can assume many different organizational structures, Figure 1-1 presents a typical presentation of how the finance area fits into a corporation. The vice president for

FIGURE 1-1   How the Finance Area Fits into a Corporation

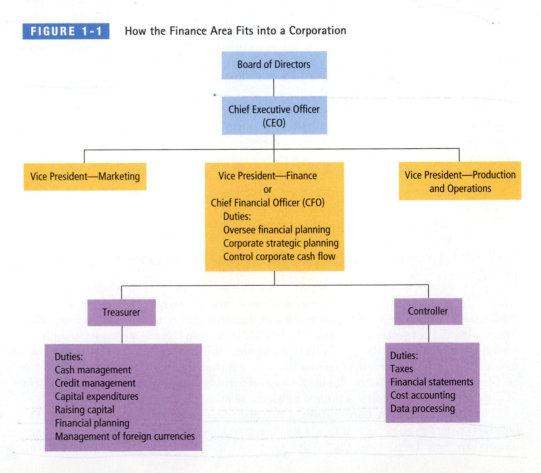

finance, also called the chief financial officer (CFO), serves under the corporation's chief executive officer (CEO) and is responsible for overseeing financial planning, corporate strategic planning, and controlling the firm's cash flow. Typically, a treasurer and controller serve under the CFO. In a smaller firm, the same person may fill both roles, with just one office handling all the duties. The treasurer generally handles the firm's financial activities, including cash and credit management, making capital expenditure decisions, raising funds, financial planning, and managing any foreign currency received by the firm. The controller is responsible for managing the firm's accounting duties, including producing financial statements, cost accounting, paying taxes, and gathering and monitoring the data necessary to oversee the firm's financial well-being. In this class, we focus on the duties generally associated with the treasurer and on how investment decisions are made.

TAKIN' IT TO THE NET

Thinking of majoring in finance? How about some information on what opportunities are out there? Try the Careers in Business Web site at www.careers-in-business.com. It covers not only finance but also marketing, accounting, and management. Also take a look at the Financial Management Association's undergrad & MBA students section page at www.fma.org.

CONCEPT CHECK

1. What are the primary differences between a sole proprietorship, a partnership, and a corporation?
2. Explain why large and growing firms tend to choose the corporate form.
3. What are the duties of the corporate treasurer? Of the corporate controller?

FEDERAL INCOME TAXATION

Objective **3**

Before presenting the 10 principles of finance that provide the conceptual underpinnings for what follow, we examine those tax features that affect our decisions. We describe the environment and set up the ground rules under which financial decisions are made. As the nation's politics change, so does the tax system. The purpose of looking at the current tax structure is not to become tax experts, but rather to gain an understanding of taxes and how they affect business decisions. There is a good chance that corporate tax rates will change significantly before you enter the workforce. However, although rates may change, taxes will continue to remain a cash outflow and, therefore, something to avoid. Thus, we pay close attention to which expenses are and are not deductible for tax purposes, and in doing so, focus on how taxes affect business decisions.

OBJECTIVES OF INCOME TAXATION

Originally, the sole objective of the federal government in taxing income was to generate financing for government expenditures. Although this purpose continues to be important, social and economic objectives have been added. For instance, a company may receive possible reductions in taxes if (1) it undertakes certain technological research, (2) it pays wages to certain economically disadvantaged groups, or (3) it locates in certain economically depressed areas. Other socially oriented stipulations in the tax laws include exemptions for dependents, old age, and blindness and a reduction in taxes on retirement income. In addition, the government uses tax legislation to stabilize the economy. In recessionary periods corporate taxes may be lowered to generate job growth. In short, three objectives may be given for the taxation of revenues: (1) the provision of revenues for government expenditures, (2) the achievement of socially desirable goals, and (3) economic stabilization.

TYPES OF TAXPAYERS

To understand the tax system, we must first ask, "Who is the taxpayer?" For the most part, there are three basic types of taxable entities: individuals, corporations, and fiduciaries. Individuals include company employees, self-employed persons owning their own businesses, and members of a partnership. Income is reported by these individuals in their personal tax returns.[3] The corporation, as a separate legal entity, reports its income and pays

---

[3]Partnerships report only the income from the partnership. The income is then reported again by each partner, who pays any taxes owed.

TAKIN' IT TO THE NET

Looking for tax information? The IRS has a great Web site at www.irs.gov with tax information for the individual and business, along with tax statistics and downloadable forms and publications. Another place to look for good information is at the TIAA-CREF Web site www.tiaa-cref.org, which annually puts out an excellent tax guide.

taxable income
gross income

any taxes related to these profits. The owners (stockholders) of the corporation need not report these earnings in their personal tax returns, except when all or a part of the profits are distributed in the form of dividends. Finally, fiduciaries, such as estates and trusts, file a tax return and pay taxes on the income generated by the estate or trust that isn't distributed to (and included in the taxable income of) a beneficiary.

Although taxation of individual and fiduciary income is an important source of income to the government, neither is especially relevant to the financial manager. Because most firms of any size are corporations, we restrict our discussion to the corporation. A caveat is necessary, however. Tax legislation can be quite complex, with numerous exceptions to most general rules. The laws can also change quickly, and certain details discussed here may no longer apply in the near future. However, the general approach should remain the same, regardless of changes.

COMPUTING TAXABLE INCOME

The **taxable income** for a corporation is based on *the gross income from all sources, except for allowable exclusions, less any tax-deductible expenses*. **Gross income** equals *the firm's dollar sales from its products or services less the cost of producing or acquiring them*. Tax-deductible expenses include any operating expenses, such as marketing expenses, depreciation, and administrative expenses. Also, *interest expense* paid on the firm's outstanding debt is a tax-deductible expense. However, dividends paid to the firm's stockholders are *not* deductible expenses, but rather distributions of income. Other taxable income includes interest income and dividend income that the corporation receives.

To demonstrate how to compute a corporation's taxable income, consider the J and S Corporation, a manufacturer of home accessories. The firm, originally established by Kelly Stites, had sales of $50 million for the year. The cost of producing the accessories totaled $23 million. Operating expenses were $10 million. The corporation has $12.5 million in debt outstanding, with an 8 percent interest rate, which resulted in $1 million interest expense ($12,500,000 × .08 = $1,000,000). Management paid $1 million in dividends to the firm's common stockholders. No other income, such as interest or dividend income, was received. The taxable income for the J and S Corporation would be $16 million, as shown in Table 1-1.

Once we know J and S Corporation's taxable income, we can next determine the amount of taxes the firm owes.

COMPUTING THE TAXES OWED

The taxes to be paid by the corporation on its taxable income are based on the corporate tax rate structure. The specific rates effective for the corporation, as of early 2005, are given in Table 1-2. Under the Revenue Reconciliation Act of 1993, a new top marginal corporate tax rate of 35 percent was added for taxable income in excess of $10 million. Also, a surtax

TABLE 1-1 J and S Corporation Taxable Income		
Sales		$50,000,000
Cost of goods sold		23,000,000
Gross profit		$27,000,000
Operating expenses		
Administrative expenses	$4,000,000	
Depreciation expenses	1,500,000	
Marketing expenses	4,500,000	
Total operating expenses		$10,000,000
Operating income		
(earnings before interest and taxes)		$17,000,000
Other income		0
Interest expense		1,000,000
Taxable income		$16,000,000

Dividends paid to common stockholders ($1,000,000) are not tax-deductible expenses.

TABLE 1-2	Corporate Tax Rates
15%	$0–$50,000
25%	$50,001–$75,000
34%	$75,001–$10,000,000
35%	over $10,000,000

Additional surtax:

- 5% on income between $100,000 and $335,000.
- 3% on income between $15,000,000 and $18,333,333.

of 3 percent was imposed on taxable income between $15 million and $18,333,333. This, in combination with the previously existing 5 percent surtax on taxable income between $100,000 and $335,000, recaptures the benefits of the lower marginal tax rates and, as a result, both the average and marginal tax rates on taxable income above $18,333,333 become 35 percent.

For example, the tax liability for J and S Corporation, which had $16 million in taxable earnings, would be $5,530,000, calculated as follows:

EARNINGS	×	MARGINAL TAX RATE	=	TAXES
$ 50,000	×	15%	=	$ 7,500
25,000	×	25%	=	6,250
9,925,000	×	34%	=	3,374,500
6,000,000	×	35%	=	2,100,000
				$5,488,250

Additional surtaxes:

- Add 5% surtax on income between $100,000 and $335,000 (5% × [$335,000 − $100,000]) 11,750
- Add 3% surtax on income between $15,000,000 and $18,333,333 (3% × [$16,000,000 − $15,000,000]) 30,000

Total tax liability $5,530,000

The tax rates shown in Table 1-2 are defined as the **marginal tax rates**, or *rates applicable to the next dollar of income*. For instance, if a firm has earnings of $60,000 and is contemplating an investment that would yield $10,000 in additional profits, the tax rate to be used in calculating the taxes on this added income is 25 percent; that is, the marginal tax rate is 25 percent. However, if the corporation already expects $20 million without the new investment, the extra $10,000 in earnings would be taxed at 35 percent, the marginal tax rate at the $20 million level of income. In the example, in which J and S Corporation has taxable income of $16 million, its marginal tax rate is 38 percent (this is because $16 million falls into the 35% tax bracket *with* a 3% surtax); that is, any additional income from new investments will be taxed at a rate of 38 percent. However, after taxable income exceeds $18,333,333, the marginal tax rate declines to 35 percent, when the 3 percent surtax no longer applies.

For financial decision making, it's the *marginal tax rate* rather than the average tax rate that we are concerned with. As becomes increasingly clear throughout the text, we always want to consider the tax consequences of any financial decision. The appropriate rate to be used in the analysis is the marginal tax rate, because it is this rate that will be applicable for any changes in earnings as a result of the decision being made. Thus, when making financial decisions involving taxes, always use the marginal tax rate in your calculations.[4]

marginal tax rates

---

[4]On taxable income between $335,000 and $10 million, both the marginal and average tax rates equal 34 percent because of the imposition of the 5 percent surtax that applies to taxable income between $100,000 and $335,000. After the company's taxable income exceeds $18,333,333, both the marginal and average tax rates equal 35 percent because the 3 percent surtax on income between $15 million and $18,333,333 eliminates the benefits of having the first $10 million of income taxed at 34 percent rather than 35 percent.

The tax rate structure used in computing J and S Corporation's taxes assumes that the income occurs in the United States. Given the globalization of the economy, it may well be that some of the income originates in a foreign country. If so, the tax rates, and the method of taxing the firm, frequently vary. As financial manager, you would minimize the firm's taxes by reporting as much income as possible in the low-tax-rate countries and as little as possible in the high-tax-rate countries. Of course, other factors, such as political risk, may discourage your efforts to minimize taxes across national borders.

OTHER TAX CONSIDERATIONS

In addition to the fundamental computation of taxes, several other aspects of the existing tax legislation have relevance for the financial manager. These are (1) the dividend-income exclusion on dividends received by corporations, (2) the effects of depreciation on the firm's taxes, and (3) the recognition of capital gains and losses. Let's look at each of these tax provisions in turn.

DIVIDEND EXCLUSION

A corporation may normally exclude 70 percent of any dividends received from another corporation. For instance, if corporation A owns common stock in corporation B and receives dividends of $1,000 in a given year, only $300 is subject to tax, and the remaining $700 (70 percent of $1,000) is tax exempt. If the corporation receiving the dividend income is in a 34 percent tax bracket, only $102 in taxes (34 percent of $300) will result.[5]

DEPRECIATION

depreciation

Depreciation is *the means by which an asset's value is expensed over its useful life for federal tax purposes.* Essentially, there are three methods for computing depreciation expenses: (1) straight-line depreciation, (2) the double-declining balance method, and (3) the modified accelerated cost recovery system. Any one of the three methods results in the same depreciation expense over the life of the asset; however, the last two approaches allow the firm to take the depreciation earlier as opposed to later, which in turn defers taxes until later. Assuming a time value of money, there is an advantage to using the accelerated techniques. (Chapter 5 fully explains the time value of money.) Also, management may use straight-line depreciation for reporting income to the shareholders while still using an accelerated method for calculating taxable income.

CAPITAL GAINS AND LOSSES

capital gain (or loss)

An important tax consideration before 1987 was the preferential tax treatment for **capital gains (or losses)**; that is, *gains (or losses) from the sale of assets not bought or sold in the ordinary course of business.* The Tax Reform Act of 1986 repealed any special treatment of capital gains and, although the Revenue Reconciliation Act of 1993 reinstituted preferential treatment in certain unique circumstances, in general, capital gains are taxed at the same rates as ordinary income. However, if a corporation has capital losses that exceed capital gains in any year, these net capital losses may not be deducted from ordinary income. The net capital losses may, however, be carried back and applied against net capital gains in each of the 3 years before the current year. If the capital loss is not completely used in the 3 prior years, any remaining capital loss may be carried forward and applied against any net capital gains in each of the next 5 years. For example, if a corporation has an $80,000 net capital loss in 2006, it may apply this loss against any net capital gains in 2003, 2004, and 2005. If any capital loss remains, it may be carried forward and applied against any capital gains through 2011.

OTHER TAX CONCERNS

As mentioned earlier, taxes are used not only to raise money but also to promote socially desirable goals and to maintain economic stability. One way in which both of these goals are met is through the creation and retention of jobs. As a result, to keep struggling firms afloat, there is a tax provision that allows a corporation with an operating loss (which is simply a loss

---

[5]If corporation A owns at least 20 percent of corporation B but less than 80 percent, 80 percent of any dividends received may be excluded from taxable income. If 80 percent or more is owned, all the dividends received may be excluded.

from operating a business) to apply this loss against income in other years. This is commonly referred to as a **net operating loss carryback and carryforward**. *This tax feature allows firms that lose money to recapture taxes they had previously paid, carrying losses back up to 2 years or forward up to 20 years to offset profits*, which hopefully allows them to deal with the problems that resulted in the loss. The bottom line is that the government wants to keep as many people employed as possible and to keep the markets as competitive as possible, and to do this it has set up a tax code that helps those in trouble stay afloat.

net operating loss carryback and carryforward

Putting It Together: An Example

To illustrate certain portions of the tax laws for a corporation, assume that the Griggs Corporation had sales during the past year of $5 million; its cost of goods sold was $3 million; and it incurred operating expenses of $1 million. In addition, it received $185,000 in interest income and $100,000 in dividend income from another corporation. In turn, it paid $40,000 in interest and $75,000 in dividends. Finally, the company sold a piece of land for $100,000 that had cost $50,000 six years ago. Given this information, the firm's taxable income is $1,225,000, as computed in the top part of Table 1-3.

Based on the tax rates from Table 1-2, Griggs's tax liability is $416,500, as shown at the bottom of Table 1-3. Note that the $75,000 Griggs paid in dividends is not tax deductible. Also, because the firm's taxable income exceeds $335,000 and the 5 percent surtax no longer applies, the marginal tax rate and the average tax rate both equal 34 percent; that is, we could have computed Griggs's tax liability as 34 percent of $1,225,000, or $416,500.

CONCEPT CHECK

1. What is the difference between the average and marginal tax rates?
2. Are the U.S. corporate tax rates progressive? Do the largest corporations get a tax break on the first dollars they earn?
3. Because all depreciation methods result in the same depreciation expense over the life of the asset, why would a firm want to use an accelerated depreciation method rather than a straight-line method?

TABLE 1-3 Griggs Corporation Tax Computations

Sales			$5,000,000
Cost of goods sold			(3,000,000)
Gross profit			$2,000,000
Operating expenses			(1,000,000)
Operating income			$1,000,000
Other taxable income and expenses:			
Interest income		$185,000	
Dividend income	$ 100,000		
Less 70% exclusion	70,000	30,000	
Interest expense		(40,000)	$ 175,000
Gain on land sale:			
Selling price		$100,000	
Cost		(50,000)	$ 50,000
Total taxable income			$1,225,000
Tax computation:			
15% × $ 50,000 =	$ 7,500		
25% × 25,000 =	6,250		
34% × 1,150,000 =	391,000		
$ 1,225,000			
Add 5% surtax for income between $100,000 and $335,000	$ 11,750		
Tax liability	$ 416,500		

TEN PRINCIPLES THAT FORM THE FOUNDATIONS OF FINANCIAL MANAGEMENT

To the first-time student of finance, the subject matter may seem like a collection of unrelated decision rules. This could not be further from the truth. In fact, our decision rules, and the logic that underlies them, spring from 10 simple principles that do not require knowledge of finance to understand. *However, although it is not necessary to understand finance in order to understand these principles, it is necessary to understand these principles in order to understand finance.* Keep in mind that although these principles may at first appear simple or even trivial, they provide the driving force behind all that follows. These principles weave together concepts and techniques presented in this text, thereby allowing us to focus on the logic underlying the practice of financial management.

PRINCIPLE

The Risk–Return Trade-Off—We Won't Take On Additional Risk Unless We Expect to Be Compensated with Additional Return

At some point we have all saved some money. Why have we done this? The answer is simple: to expand our future consumption opportunities. We are able to invest those savings and earn a return on our dollars because some people would rather forgo future consumption opportunities to consume more now. Maybe they're borrowing money to open a new business or a company is borrowing money to build a new plant. Assuming there are a lot of different people who would like to use our savings, how do we decide where to put our money?

First, investors demand a minimum return for delaying consumption that must be greater than the anticipated rate of inflation. If they didn't receive enough to compensate for anticipated inflation, investors would purchase whatever goods they desired ahead of time or invest in assets that were subject to inflation and earn the rate of inflation on those assets. There isn't much incentive to postpone consumption if your savings are going to decline in terms of purchasing power.

Investment alternatives have different amounts of risk and expected returns. Investors sometimes choose to put their money in risky investments because these investments offer higher expected returns. The more risk an investment has, the higher will be its expected return. This relationship between risk and expected return is shown in Figure 1-2.

Notice that we keep referring to *expected* return rather than *actual* return. We may have expectations of what the returns from investing will be, but we can't peer into the future and see what those returns are actually going to be. If investors could see into the future, no one would have invested money in the biotech firm Genta, whose stock dropped 50 percent on November 9, 2004, when it announced its partner Aventis had terminated its agreement to codevelop an experimental cancer treatment. Until after the fact, you are never sure what the return on an investment will be. That is why General Motors bonds pay more

FIGURE 1-2   The Risk–Return Relationship

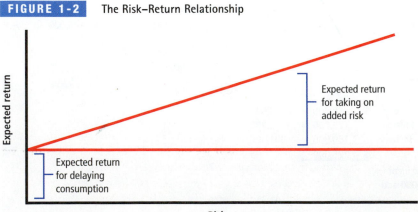

interest than U.S. Treasury bonds of the same maturity. The additional interest convinces some investors to take on the added risk of purchasing a General Motors bond.

This risk–return relationship is a key concept as we value stocks, bonds, and proposed new projects throughout this text. We also spend some time determining how to measure risk. Interestingly, much of the work for which the 1990 Nobel Prize for Economics was awarded centered on the graph in Figure 1-2 and how to measure risk. Both the graph and the risk–return relationship it depicts reappear often in this text.

PRINCIPLE 2 *The Time Value of Money—A Dollar Received Today Is Worth More Than a Dollar Received in the Future*

A fundamental concept in finance is that money has a time value associated with it: A dollar received today is worth more than a dollar received a year from now. Because we can earn interest on money received today, it is better to receive money earlier rather than later. In your economics courses, this concept of the time value of money is referred to as the opportunity cost of passing up the earning potential of a dollar today.

In this text, we focus on the creation and measurement of wealth. To measure wealth or value, we use the concept of the time value of money to bring the future benefits and costs of a project back to the present. Then, if the benefits outweigh costs, the project creates wealth and should be accepted; if the costs outweigh the benefits, the project does not create wealth and should be rejected. Without recognizing the existence of the time value of money, it is impossible to evaluate projects with future benefits and costs in a meaningful way.

To bring future benefits and costs of a project back to the present, we must assume a specific opportunity cost of money, or interest rate. Exactly what interest rate to use is determined by **Principle 1: The Risk–Return Trade-Off**, which states investors demand higher returns for taking on more risky projects. Thus, when we determine the present value of future benefits and costs, we take into account that investors demand a higher return for taking on added risk.

PRINCIPLE 3 *Cash—Not Profits—Is King*

In measuring wealth or value we use cash flows, not accounting profits, as our measurement tool. That is, we are concerned with when we have money in hand, when we can invest it and start earning interest on it, and when we can give it back to the shareholders in the form of dividends. Remember, it is cash flows, not profits, that are actually received by the firm and can be reinvested. Accounting profits, on the other hand, are shown when they are earned rather than when the money is actually in hand. As a result, a firm's cash flows and accounting profits may not occur together. For example, capital expenses, such as the purchase of new equipment or a building, are depreciated over several years, with the annual depreciation subtracted from profits. However, the cash flow associated with this expense generally occurs immediately. Therefore, cash outflows involving paying money out and cash inflows that can be reinvested correctly reflect the timing of the benefits and costs.

PRINCIPLE 4 *Incremental Cash Flows—It's Only What Changes That Counts*

In making business decisions, we are concerned with the results of those decisions: What happens if we say yes versus what happens if we say no? **Principle 3** states that we should use cash flows to measure the benefits that accrue from taking on a new project. We are now fine-tuning our evaluation process so that we only consider incremental cash flows. The **incremental cash flow** is *the difference between the cash flows if the project is taken on versus what they will be if the project is not taken on.*

incremental cash flow

When General Mills, the maker of Cheerios, Honey Nut Cheerios, Frosted Cheerios, Apple Cinnamon Cheerios, and Multi-Grain Cheerios, introduced Team Cheerios—"3 delicious O's teamed up for one sweet crunch"—it introduced a product that competed directly with General Mills' other cereals and, in particular, its Cheerios products. In fact, Team Cheerios, with its brown sugar and frosting, tastes very much like Frosted Cheerios. Certainly some of the sales dollars that ended up with Team Cheerios would have been spent on other Cheerios and General Mills products if Team Cheerios had not been available. Although General Mills was targeting younger consumers with this sweetened cereal, there is no question that Team Cheerios sales bit into—actually cannibalized—sales from Cheerios and other General Mills lines. Realistically, there's only so much cereal anyone can eat. The *difference* between revenues General Mills generated after introducing Team Cheerios versus simply maintaining its existing line of cereals is the incremental cash flow. This difference reflects the true impact of the decision.

What is important is that we *think* incrementally. Our guiding rule in deciding whether a cash flow is incremental is to look at the company with and without the new product. In fact, let's take this incremental concept beyond cash flows and look at all consequences from all decisions on an incremental basis.

PRINCIPLE 5   *The Curse of Competitive Markets—Why It's Hard to Find Exceptionally Profitable Projects*

Our job as financial managers is to create wealth. Therefore, we look closely at the mechanics of valuation and decision making. We focus on estimating cash flows, determining what an investment earns, and valuing assets and new projects. However, it is easy to get caught up in the mechanics of valuation and lose sight of the process of creating wealth. Why is it so hard to find projects and investments that are exceptionally profitable? Where do profitable projects come from? The answers to these questions tell us a lot about how competitive markets operate and where to look for profitable projects.

In reality, it is much easier evaluating profitable projects than finding them. If an industry is generating large profits, new entrants are usually attracted. The additional competition and added capacity can result in profits being driven down to the required rate of return. Conversely, if an industry is returning profits below the required rate of return, then some participants in the market drop out, reducing capacity and competition. In return, prices are driven back up. This is precisely what happened in the VCR video rental market in the mid-1980s. This market developed suddenly with the opportunity for extremely large profits. Because there were no barriers to entry, the market quickly was flooded with new entries. By 1987 the competition and price cutting produced losses for many firms in the industry, forcing them to flee the market. As the competition lessened with firms moving out of the video rental industry, profits again rose to the point at which the required rate of return could be earned on invested capital.

In competitive markets, extremely large profits simply cannot exist for very long. Given that somewhat bleak scenario, how can we find good projects—that is, projects that return more than their expected rate of return given their risk level (remember Principle 1)? Although competition makes them difficult to find, we have to invest in markets that are not perfectly competitive. The two most common ways of making markets less competitive are to differentiate the product in some key way and to achieve a cost advantage over competitors.

Product differentiation insulates a product from competition, thereby allowing a company to charge a premium price. If products are differentiated, consumer choice is no longer made by price alone. For example, many people are willing to pay a premium for Starbucks coffee. They simply want Starbucks and price is not important. In the pharmaceutical industry, patents create competitive barriers. For example, Hoffman–La Roche's Valium, a tranquilizer, is protected from direct competition by patents.

Service and quality are also used to differentiate products. For example, Levi's has long prided itself on the quality of its jeans. As a result, it has been able to maintain its market share. Similarly, much of Toyota and Honda's brand loyalty is based on quality. Service can also create product differentiation, as shown by McDonald's fast service, cleanliness, and consistency of product, which bring customers back.

Whether product differentiation occurs because of advertising, patents, service, or quality, the more the product is differentiated from competing products, the less competition it will face and the greater the possibility of large profits.

Economies of scale and the ability to produce at a cost below competition can effectively deter new entrants to the market and thereby reduce competition. Wal-Mart is one such case. For Wal-Mart, the fixed costs are largely independent of the store's size. For example, inventory costs, advertising expenses, and managerial salaries are essentially the same regardless of annual sales. Therefore, the more sales that can be built up, the lower the per-sale dollar cost of inventory, advertising, and management. Restocking from warehouses also becomes more efficient because delivery trucks can be used to full potential.

Regardless of how the cost advantage is created—by economies of scale, proprietary technology, or monopolistic control of raw materials—it deters new market entrants while allowing production at below industry cost. This cost advantage has the potential of creating large profits.

The key to locating profitable investment projects is to first understand how and where they exist in competitive markets. Then the corporate philosophy must be aimed at creating or taking advantage of some imperfection in these markets, through either product differentiation or creation of a cost advantage, rather than looking to new markets or industries that appear to provide large profits. Any perfectly competitive industry that looks too good to be true won't be for long. It is necessary to understand this to know where to look for good projects and to accurately measure the project's cash flows. We can do this better if we recognize how wealth is created and how difficult it is to create.

PRINCIPLE 6   *Efficient Capital Markets—The Markets Are Quick and the Prices Are Right*

Our goal as financial managers is the maximization of shareholder wealth. How do we measure shareholder wealth? It is the value of all the shares that the shareholders own. To understand what causes stocks to change in price, as well as how securities such as bonds and stocks are valued or priced in the financial markets, it is necessary to have an understanding of the concept of **efficient markets**. *These are markets in which the values of all assets and securities at any instant in time fully reflect all available information.*

efficient markets

Whether a market is efficient has to do with the speed with which information is impounded into security prices. An efficient market is characterized by a large number of profit-driven individuals who act independently. In addition, new information regarding securities arrives in the market in a random manner. Given this setting, investors adjust to new information immediately and buy and sell the security until they feel the market price correctly reflects the new information. Under the efficient market hypothesis, information is reflected in security prices with such speed that there are no opportunities for investors to profit from publicly available information. Investors competing for profits ensure that security prices appropriately reflect the expected earnings and risks involved and, thus, the true value of the firm.

What are the implications of efficient markets for us? First, the price is right. Stock prices reflect all publicly available information regarding the value of the company. This means we can implement our goal of maximization of shareholder wealth by focusing on the effect each decision *should* have on the stock price if everything else is held constant. That is, over time good decisions result in higher stock prices and bad ones in lower stock prices. Second, earnings manipulations through accounting changes do not result in price changes. Stock splits and other changes in accounting methods that do not affect cash flows are not reflected in prices. Market prices reflect expected cash flows available to shareholders. Thus, our preoccupation with cash flows to measure the timing of the benefits is justified.

As we will see, it is indeed reassuring that prices reflect value. It allows us to look at prices and see value reflected in them. Although it may make investing a bit less exciting, it makes corporate finance much less uncertain.

PRINCIPLE 7   *The Agency Problem—Managers Won't Work for the Owners Unless It's in Their Best Interest*

agency problem

Although the goal of the firm is the maximization of shareholder wealth, in reality the agency problem may interfere with the implementation of this goal. The **agency problem** *results from the separation of management and the ownership of the firm.* For example, a large firm may be run by professional managers who have little or no ownership in the firm. Because of this separation of the decision makers and owners, managers may make decisions that are not in line with the goal of maximization of shareholder wealth. They may approach work less energetically and attempt to benefit themselves in terms of salary and perquisites at the expense of shareholders.

To begin with, an agent is someone who is given the authority to act on behalf of another, who is referred to as the principal. In the corporate setting, the shareholders are the principals, because they are the actual owners of the firm. The board of directors, the CEO, the corporate executives, and all others with decision-making power are agents of the shareholders. Unfortunately, the board of directors, the CEO, and the other corporate executives don't always do what's in the best interest of the shareholders. Instead, they often act in their own best interest. Not only might they benefit themselves in terms of salary and perquisites, but they might also avoid any projects that have risk associated with them—even if they're great projects with huge potential returns and a small chance of failure. Why is this so? Because if the project doesn't turn out, these agents of the shareholders may lose their jobs.

The costs associated with the agency problem are difficult to measure, but occasionally we see the problem's effect in the marketplace. For example, if the market feels management of a firm is damaging shareholder wealth, we might see a positive reaction in stock price to the removal of that management. In 1989, on the day following the death of John Dorrance, Jr., chairman of Campbell's Soup, Campbell's stock price rose about 15 percent. Some investors felt that Campbell's relatively small growth in earnings might be improved with the departure of Dorrance. There was also speculation that Dorrance was the major obstacle to a possible positive reorganization.

If the management of the firm works for the owners, who are the shareholders, why doesn't the management get fired if it doesn't act in the shareholders' best interest? *In theory*, the shareholders pick the corporate board of directors and the board of directors in turn picks the management. Unfortunately, *in reality* the system frequently works the other way around. Management selects the board of director nominees and then distributes the ballots. In effect, shareholders are offered a slate of nominees selected by the management. The end result is that management effectively selects the directors, who then may have more allegiance to managers than to shareholders. This in turn sets up the potential for agency problems, with the board of directors not monitoring managers on behalf of the shareholders as they should.

We spend considerable time discussing monitoring managers and trying to align their interests with shareholders. Managers can be monitored by auditing financial statements and managers' compensation packages. The interests of managers and shareholders can be aligned by establishing management stock options, bonuses, and perquisites that are directly tied to how closely their decisions coincide with the interest of shareholders. The agency problem will persist unless an incentive structure is set up that aligns the interests of managers and shareholders. In other words, what is good for shareholders must also be good for managers. If that is not the case, managers will make decisions in their best interest rather than maximizing shareholder wealth.

TAKIN' IT TO THE NET

For information on corporate governance, try the Corporate Governance Web site www.corpgov.net, which has news links and a forum page that provides commentaries and conversations.

PRINCIPLE 8   *Taxes Bias Business Decisions*

Hardly any decision is made by the financial manager without considering the impact of taxes. When we introduced **Principle 4**, we said that only incremental cash flows should be considered in the evaluation process. More specifically, the cash flows we consider are the *after-tax incremental cash flows to the firm as a whole.*

When we evaluate new projects, we will see income taxes play a significant role. When the company is analyzing the possible acquisition of a plant or equipment, the returns from the investment should be measured on an after-tax basis. Otherwise, the company is not evaluating the true incremental cash flows generated by the project.

The government also realizes taxes can bias business decisions and uses taxes to encourage spending in certain ways. If the government wants to encourage spending on research and development projects, it might offer an *investment tax credit* for such investments. This would have the effect of reducing taxes on research and development projects, which would in turn increase the after-tax cash flows from those projects. The increased cash flow would turn some otherwise unprofitable research and development projects into profitable projects. In effect, the government can use taxes as a tool to direct business investment to research and development projects, to the inner cities, and to projects that create jobs.

PRINCIPLE **9**

All Risk Is Not Equal—Some Risk Can Be Diversified Away, and Some Cannot

Much of finance centers around **Principle 1, the Risk–Return Trade-Off**. But before we can fully use **Principle 1**, we must decide how to measure risk. As we will see, risk is difficult to measure. **Principle 9** introduces you to the process of diversification and demonstrates how it can reduce risk. We also provide you with an understanding of how diversification makes it difficult to measure a project's or an asset's risk.

You are probably already familiar with the concept of diversification. There is an old saying, "don't put all your eggs in one basket." Diversification allows good and bad events or observations to cancel each other out, thereby reducing total variability without affecting expected return.

To see how diversification complicates the measurement of risk, let's look at the difficulty Louisiana Gas has in determining the level of risk associated with a new natural gas well-drilling project. Each year Louisiana Gas might drill several hundred wells, with each well having only a 1 in 10 chance of success. If the well produces, the profits are quite large, but if it comes up dry, the investment is lost. Thus, with a 90 percent chance of losing everything, we would view the project as being extremely risky. However, if each year Louisiana Gas drills 2,000 wells, all with a 10 percent, independent chance of success, then they would typically have 200 successful wells. Moreover, a bad year may result in only 190 successful wells, whereas a good year may result in 210 successful wells. If we look at all the wells together, the extreme good and the bad results tend to cancel each other out and the well-drilling projects taken together do not appear to have much risk or variability of possible outcome.

The amount of risk in a gas well project depends on our perspective. Looking at the well standing alone, it looks like a lot; however, if we consider the risk that each well contributes to the overall firm risk, it is quite small. This occurs because much of the risk associated with each individual well is diversified away within the firm. The point is we can't look at a project in isolation. Later, we will see that some of this risk can be further diversified away within the shareholder's portfolio.

Perhaps the easiest way to understand the concept of diversification is to look at it graphically. Consider what happens when we combine two projects, as depicted in Figure 1-3. In this case, the cash flows from these projects move in opposite directions, and when they are combined, the variability of their combination is totally eliminated. Notice that the return has not changed—both the individual projects' and their combination's return averages 10 percent. In this case the extreme good and bad observations cancel each other out. The degree to which the total risk is reduced is a function of how the two sets of cash flows or returns move together.

As we will see for most projects and assets, some risk can be eliminated through diversification, while some cannot. This becomes an important distinction later in our studies. *For now, we should realize that the process of diversification can reduce risk, and as a result, measuring a project's or an asset's risk is very difficult.* A project's risk changes depending on whether you measure it standing alone or together with other projects the company may take on.

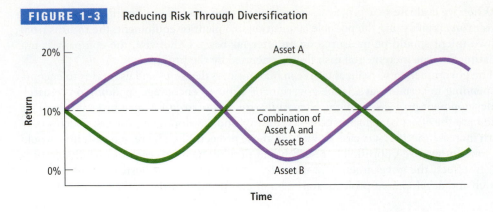

FIGURE 1-3   Reducing Risk Through Diversification

PRINCIPLE **10**   *Ethical Behavior Is Doing the Right Thing, and Ethical Dilemmas Are Everywhere in Finance*

Ethics, or rather a lack of ethics, in finance is a recurring theme in the news. During the late 1980s and early 1990s, the fall of Ivan Boesky and Drexel, Burnham, Lambert, and the near collapse of Salomon Brothers seemed to make continuous headlines. Meanwhile, the movie *Wall Street* was a hit at the box office and the book *Liar's Poker*, by Michael Lewis, chronicling unethical behavior in the bond markets, became a best-seller. As the lessons of Salomon Brothers and Drexel, Burnham, Lambert illustrate, ethical errors are not forgiven in the business world. Not only is acting in an ethical manner morally correct, but also it is congruent with our goal of maximization of shareholder wealth.

Ethical behavior means "doing the right thing." The difficulty arises, however, in attempting to define "doing the right thing." The problem is that each of us has his or her own set of values, which forms the basis for our personal judgments about what is the right thing to do. However, every society adopts a set of rules or laws that prescribe what it believes to be "doing the right thing." In a sense, we can think of laws as a set of rules that reflect the values of the society as a whole, as they have evolved. For purposes of this text, we recognize that individuals have a right to disagree about what constitutes "doing the right thing," and we seldom venture beyond the basic notion that ethical conduct involves abiding by society's rules. However, we point out some of the ethical dilemmas that have arisen in recent years with regard to the practice of financial management. So as we embark on our study of finance and encounter ethical dilemmas, we encourage you to consider the issues and form your own opinions.

Many students ask, "Is ethics really relevant?" This is a good question and deserves an answer. First, although business errors can be forgiven, ethical errors tend to end careers and terminate future opportunities. Why? Because *unethical behavior eliminates trust, and without trust businesses cannot interact.* Second, *the most damaging event a business can experience is a loss of the public's confidence in its ethical standards.* In finance we have seen several recent examples of such events. It was the ethical scandals involving insider trading at Drexel, Burnham, Lambert that brought down that firm. In 1991 the ethical scandals involving attempts by Salomon Brothers to corner the Treasury bill market led to the removal of its top executives and nearly put the company out of business.

Beyond the question of ethics is the question of social responsibility. In general, corporate social responsibility means that a corporation has responsibilities to society beyond the maximization of shareholder wealth. It asserts that a corporation answers to a broader constituency than shareholders alone. As with most debates that center on ethical and moral questions, there is no definitive answer. One opinion is that because financial managers are employees of the corporation and the corporation is owned by the shareholders, the financial managers should run the corporation in such a way that shareholder wealth is maximized and then allow the shareholders to decide if they would like to fulfill a sense of social responsibility by passing on any of the profits to deserving causes. Very few corporations consistently act in this way. For example, Bristol-Myers Squibb Co. has an ambitious

TAKIN' IT TO THE NET

Ethical problems seem to crop up all the time in finance. If you'd like more information on some of the worst, take a look at the Financial Scandals Web site www.ex.ac.uk/~RDavies/arian/scandals. It's got information on BCCI, Barings, Daiwa, Sumitomo, Credit Lyonnais, Bre-X, Lloyds, and NASDAQ.

ETHICS IN
FINANCIAL MANAGEMENT

THE ENRON LESSONS: TRUST

The bankruptcy and failure of the Enron Corporation on December 2, 2001, shook the investment community to its very core and resulted in congressional hearings that could lead to new regulations with far-reaching implications. Enron's failure provides a sober warning to employees and investors and a valuable set of lessons for students of business. The lesson we offer here reaches far beyond corporate finance and touches on fundamental principles that have always been true but are sometimes forgotten.

Lesson: Trust and Credibility Are Essential to Business Success

The viability of any firm hinges critically on the firm's credibility with its customers, employees, regulators, investors, and even to some degree, competitors. This is particularly critical for a trading company such as Enron, whose primary business rests on the willingness of the firm's counterpart with whom it trades to "trust" in Enron's ability to "be there" when the time to settle up arrives. When the faith of the investment community was tested with the revelation of losses from some of Enron's largest investments and the subsequent disclosure of Enron's off-balance-sheet liabilities, Enron's trading business evaporated.

We also were reminded of the fact that investors must believe that a firm's published financial reports are a fair representation of the firm's financial condition. Without this trust, outside investors would refuse to invest in the shares of publicly traded firms, and financial markets would collapse.[a]

Trust between two entities is hard to sustain when one of the parties has dual and conflicting motives. We refer to the presence of multiple motives as a conflict of interest, and the potential for conflict-of-interest problems was in abundance as Enron fell to earth. Some of the following sources of conflict apply only to Enron, whereas others apply to many firms:

- Enron's chief financial officer (CFO) attempted to serve two masters when he was both the CFO and the general partner for a series of limited partnerships used by Enron to finance its investments and hedge certain investment returns. There were times when he represented the interests of Enron in circumstances that were in direct conflict with the interests of the partners to the partnerships. It is still not clear how he handled these circumstances, but the source of concern to Enron's shareholders is obvious.

- Were corporate insiders (executives) selling their stock based on their privileged knowledge of the firm's true financial condition during the months prior to the firm's failure, while outside investors were being duped into holding their shares? Allegations abound that top corporate executives at Enron were selling their shares long before other employees and outside investors knew how serious the firm's problems were. Regardless of the outcome in the Enron case, this raises a serious dilemma for investors, who cannot know as much about the financial condition of the firms in which they invest as the managers know.

- Can auditing firms that accept consulting engagements with their audit clients be truly independent, or is that independence compromised? The Enron failure has called into question the wisdom of relying on external auditing firms that are beholden to the firms they audit, both for their continued employment as an auditor and for consulting fees that can sometimes dwarf their audit fees.

- Finally, investors often rely on the opinions of equity analysts. Investors make the assumption that the analysts are offering unfettered, independent opinions of a company's financial prospects. However, in many cases the analysts work for investment banks that, in turn, rely on investment-banking fees from the very companies the analysts cover. The potential conflict of interest is obvious.

[a] This is simply a recasting of the famous result from microeconomics stating that where informational asymmetry problems between buyers and sellers are extreme, markets will collapse [George Akerlof, "The Market for Lemons: Qualitative Uncertainty and the Market Mechanism," *Quarterly Journal of Economics*, 84 (1970), pp. 488–500].

program to give away heart medication to those who cannot pay for it. This program came in the wake of an American Heart Association report showing that many of the nation's working poor face severe health risks because they cannot afford such medications. Clearly, Bristol-Myers Squibb felt it had a social responsibility to provide this medicine to the poor at no cost.

How do you feel about this decision?

A FINAL NOTE ON THE 10 PRINCIPLES

Hopefully, these principles are as much statements of common sense as they are theoretical statements. These principles provide the logic behind what is to follow. We build on them and attempt to draw out their implications for decision making. As we continue, try to keep in mind that although the topics being treated may change from chapter to chapter, the logic driving our treatment of them is constant and rooted in these 10 principles.

AN ENTREPRENEUR'S PERSPECTIVE

THE ENTREPRENEUR AND FINANCE

Do you ever think about wanting to someday own your own business? Does being an entrepreneur have any appeal to you? Well, it does for a lot of people. During the past decade, starting and growing companies have been the preferred avenue many have chosen for careers. In fact, while many of the large companies are reducing the number of employees, smaller companies are creating new jobs by the thousands. A lot of individuals have thought that there was greater security in working with a big company, only to be disillusioned in the end when they were informed that "Friday is your last day."

Defining an entrepreneur is not an easy thing to do. But we can say with some clarity what *entrepreneurship* is about. Entrepreneurship has been defined as a relentless pursuit of opportunity for the purpose of creating value, without concern for the resources owned.

To be successful, the entrepreneurial process requires that the entrepreneur be able to:

- *Identify a good opportunity.* Oftentimes we may have a "good idea," but it may not be a "good opportunity." Opportunities are market driven. There must be enough customers who want to buy our product or service at a price that covers our expenses and leaves an attractive profit—no matter how much we may like the idea.
- *Gain access to the resources needed.* For any venture, there are critical resources—human, financial, and physical—that must be available. The entrepreneur usually does not have

the capital to own all the resources that are needed. So the entrepreneur must have access to resources but usually cannot afford to own them. It's what we call *bootstrapping*. The goal is to do more with less.

- *Launch the venture.* All the planning in the world is not enough. The entrepreneur must be action oriented. It requires a "can do" spirit.
- *Grow the business.* A business has to grow if it is to be successful. Frequently, the firm will not break even for several years, which means that we will be burning up cash each month. Being able to survive during the time that cash flows are negative is no easy task. If we grow too slow, we lose, but also if we grow too fast, we may lose as well. During this time, additional capital will be needed, which requires that we know how to value the firm and how to structure financing.
- *Exit the business.* If a venture has been successful, the entrepreneur will have created economic value that is locked up in the business. At some point in time, the entrepreneur will want to capture the value that has been created by the business. It will be time to *harvest*.

To be successful as an entrepreneur requires an understanding of finance. At the appropriate places in *Financial Management*, we will be presenting how finance relates to the entrepreneurial journey. It is an interesting topic that we think you will enjoy.

CONCEPT CHECK

1. According to Principle 1, how do investors decide where to invest their money?
2. Why is it so hard to find extremely profitable projects?
3. Why is ethics relevant?

Objective **5**

FINANCE AND THE MULTINATIONAL FIRM: THE NEW ROLE

In the search for profits, U.S. corporations have been forced to look beyond our country's borders. This movement has been spurred on by the collapse of communism and the acceptance of the free market system in Third World countries. All this has taken place at a time when information technology has experienced a revolution brought on by the personal computer (PC). Concurrently, the United States went through an unprecedented period of deregulation of industries. These changes resulted in the opening of new international markets, and U.S. firms experienced a period of price competition here at home that made it imperative that businesses look across borders for investment opportunities. The end result is that many U.S. companies, including General Electric, IBM, Walt Disney, American Express, and General Motors, have restructured their operations to expand internationally. However, not only do U.S. firms have a freer access to international markets, but also foreign firms have an easier job of entering U.S. markets and competing with U.S. firms on their own turf.

The bottom line is what you think of as a U.S. firm may be much more of a multinational firm than you would expect. For example, Coca-Cola earns over 80 percent of its profits from overseas sales. Moreover, Coca-Cola earns more money from its sales in Japan than it does from all its domestic sales, and this is not uncommon. In fact, Dow Chemical, Colgate-Palmolive, 3M, Compaq, Hewlett-Packard, and Gillette make over half their sales overseas and earn over half of their profits from international sales. In addition to U.S. firms venturing abroad, foreign firms have also made their mark in the United States. You need only look to the auto industry to see what changes the entrance of Toyota, Honda, Nissan, BMW, and other foreign car manufacturers have had on the auto industry. In addition, foreigners have bought and now own such companies as Brooks Brothers, RCA, Pillsbury, A&P, 20th Century Fox, Columbia Pictures, and Firestone Tire & Rubber. Consequently, even if we wanted to, we couldn't keep all our attention focused on the United States, and even more important, we wouldn't want to ignore the opportunities that are available across international borders.

CONCEPT CHECK

1. What has brought on the era of the multinational corporation?
2. Has looking beyond U.S. borders been a profitable experience for U.S. corporations?

SUMMARY

This chapter outlines the framework for the maintenance and creation of wealth. In introducing decision-making techniques aimed at creating wealth, we emphasize the logic behind those techniques. This chapter begins with an examination of the goal of the firm.

Objective **1**

The commonly accepted goal of profit maximization is contrasted with the more complete goal of maximization of shareholder wealth. Because it deals well with uncertainty and time in a real-world environment, the goal of maximization of shareholder wealth is found to be the proper goal for the firm.

The legal forms of business are examined. The sole proprietorship is a business operation owned and managed by an individual. Initiating this form of business is simple and generally does not involve any substantial organizational costs. The proprietor has complete control of the firm but must be willing to assume full responsibility for its outcomes.

Objective **2**

The general partnership, which is simply a coming together of two or more individuals, is similar to the sole proprietorship. The limited partnership is another form of partnership sanctioned by states to permit all but one of the partners to have limited liability if this is agreeable to all partners.

The corporation increases the flow of capital from public investors to the business community. Although larger organizational costs and regulations are imposed on this legal entity, the corporation is more conducive to raising large amounts of capital. Limited liability, continuity of life, and ease of transfer in ownership, which increase the marketability of the investment, have contributed greatly in attracting large numbers of investors to the corporate environment. The formal control of the corporation is vested in the parties who own the greatest number of shares. However, day-to-day operations are managed by the corporate officers, who theoretically serve on behalf of the common stockholders.

The tax environment is presented. In introducing taxes we focus on taxes that affect our business decisions. Three taxable entities exist: the individual, including partnerships; the corporation; and the fiduciary. Only information on the corporate tax environment is given here.

Objective **3**

For the most part, taxable income for the corporation is equal to the firm's operating income plus capital gains less any interest expense. The corporation is allowed an income exclusion of 70 percent of the dividends received from another corporation.

Tax consequences have a direct bearing on the decisions of the financial manager. The relationships are grounded in the taxability of investment income and the difference in tax treatment for interest expense and dividend payments. Also, shareholders' tax status may influence their preference between capital gains from stock sale and dividends, which in turn may influence corporate dividend policy.

Objective **4**   An examination of the 10 principles on which finance is built is presented. The techniques and tools introduced in this text are all motivated by these 10 principles. They are

PRINCIPLE 1   *The Risk–Return Trade-Off—We Won't Take On Additional Risk Unless We Expect to Be Compensated with Additional Return*

PRINCIPLE 2   *The Time Value of Money—A Dollar Received Today Is Worth More Than a Dollar Received in the Future*

PRINCIPLE 3   *Cash—Not Profits—Is King*

PRINCIPLE 4   *Incremental Cash Flows—It's Only What Changes That Counts*

PRINCIPLE 5   *The Curse of Competitive Markets—Why It's Hard to Find Exceptionally Profitable Projects*

PRINCIPLE 6   *Efficient Capital Markets—The Markets Are Quick and the Prices Are Right*

PRINCIPLE 7   *The Agency Problem—Managers Won't Work for the Owners Unless It's in Their Best Interest*

PRINCIPLE 8   *Taxes Bias Business Decisions*

PRINCIPLE 9   *All Risk Is Not Equal—Some Risk Can Be Diversified Away, and Some Cannot*

PRINCIPLE 10   *Ethical Behavior Is Doing the Right Thing, and Ethical Dilemmas Are Everywhere in Finance*

Objective **5**   With the collapse of communism and the acceptance of the free market system in Third World countries, U.S. firms have been spurred on to look beyond our own boundaries for new business. The end result has been that it is not uncommon for major U.S. companies to earn over half their income from sales abroad.

KEY TERMS

Agency problem, 20	Gross income, 12	Net operating loss carry-back and carryforward, 15
Capital gain (or loss), 14	Incremental cash flow, 17	
Corporation, 8	Limited liability company (LLC), 10	Partnership, 8
Depreciation, 14		Sole proprietorship, 7
Efficient markets, 19	Limited partnership, 8	S-type corporation, 9
General partnership, 8	Marginal tax rates, 13	Taxable income, 12

STUDY QUESTIONS

1-1. What are some of the problems involved in the use of profit maximization as the goal of the firm? How does the goal of maximization of shareholder wealth deal with those problems?

1-2. Compare and contrast the goals of profit maximization and maximization of shareholder wealth.

1-3. Firms often involve themselves in projects that do not result directly in profits; for example, IBM and ExxonMobil frequently support public television broadcasts. Do these projects contradict the goal of maximization of shareholder wealth? Why or why not?

1-4. What is the relationship between financial decision making and risk and return? Would all financial managers view risk–return trade-offs similarly?

1-5. Define (a) sole proprietorship, (b) partnership, and (c) corporation.

1-6. Identify the primary characteristics of each form of legal organization.

1-7. Using the following criteria, specify the legal form of business that is favored: (a) organizational requirements and costs, (b) liability of the owners, (c) continuity of business, (d) transferability of ownership, (e) management control and regulations, (f) ability to raise capital, and (g) income taxes.

1-8. Does a partnership pay taxes on its income? Explain.

1-9. When a corporation receives a dividend from another corporation, how is it taxed?

1-10. What is the purpose of the net operating loss carryback and carryforward?

SELF-TEST PROBLEM

ST-1. (*Corporate income tax*) The Dana Flatt Corporation had sales of $2 million this past year. Its cost of goods sold was $1.2 million, and its operating expenses were $400,000. Interest expenses on outstanding debts were $100,000, and the company paid $40,000 in preferred stock dividends. The corporation received $10,000 in preferred stock dividends and interest income of $12,000. The firm sold stock that had been owned for 2 years for $40,000; the original cost of the stock was $30,000. Determine the corporation's taxable income and its tax liability.

STUDY PROBLEMS

1-1. (*Corporate income tax*) The William B. Waugh Corporation is a regional Toyota dealer. The firm sells new and used trucks and is actively involved in the parts business. During the most recent year the company generated sales of $3 million. The combined cost of goods sold and the operating expenses were $2.1 million. Also, $400,000 in interest expense was paid during the year. The firm received $6,000 during the year in dividend income from 1,000 shares of common stock that had been purchased 3 years previously. However, the stock was sold toward the end of the year for $100 per share; its initial cost was $80 per share. The company also sold land that had been recently purchased and had been held for only 4 months. The selling price was $50,000; the cost was $45,000. Calculate the corporation's tax liability.

1-2. (*Corporate income tax*) Sales for L. B. Menielle, Inc., during the past year amounted to $5 million. The firm provides parts and supplies for oil field service companies. Gross profits for the year were $3 million. Operating expenses totaled $1 million. The interest and dividend income from securities owned were $20,000 and $25,000, respectively. The firm's interest expense was $100,000. The firm sold securities on two occasions during the year, receiving a gain of $40,000 on the first sale but losing $50,000 on the second. The stock sold first had been owned for 4 years; the stock sold second had been purchased 3 months before the sale. Compute the corporation's tax liability.

1-3. (*Corporate income tax*) Sandersen, Inc., sells minicomputers. During the past year the company's sales were $3 million. The cost of its merchandise sold came to $2 million, and cash operating expenses were $400,000; depreciation expense was $100,000, and the firm paid $150,000 in interest on bank loans. Also, the corporation received $50,000 in dividend income but paid $25,000 in the form of dividends to its own common stockholders. Calculate the corporation's tax liability.

1-4. (*Corporate income tax*) A. Don Drennan, Inc., had sales of $6 million during the past year. The company's cost of goods sold was 70 percent of sales; operating expenses, including depreciation, amounted to $800,000. The firm sold a capital asset (stock) for $75,000, which had been purchased 5 months earlier at a cost of $80,000. Determine the company's tax liability.

1-5. (*Corporate income tax*) The Robbins Corporation is an oil wholesaler. The company's sales last year were $1 million, with the cost of goods sold equal to $600,000. The firm paid interest of $200,000, and its cash operating expenses were $100,000. Also, the firm received $40,000 in dividend income while paying only $10,000 in dividends to its preferred stockholders. Depreciation expense was $150,000. Compute the firm's tax liability. Based on your answer, does management need to take any additional action?

1-6. (*Corporate income tax*) The Fair Corporation had sales of $5 million this past year. The cost of goods sold was $4.3 million, and operating expenses were $100,000. Dividend income totaled $5,000. The firm sold land for $150,000 that had cost $100,000 5 months ago. The firm received $150 per share from the sale of 1,000 shares of stock. The stock was purchased for $100 per share 3 years ago. Determine the firm's tax liability.

1-7. (*Corporate income tax*) Sales for J. P. Hulett, Inc., during the past year amounted to $4 million. The firm supplies statistical information to engineering companies. Gross profits totaled $1 million, and operating and depreciation expenses were $500,000 and $350,000, respectively. Dividend income for the year was $12,000. Compute the corporation's tax liability.

1-8. (*Corporate income tax*) Anderson & Dennis, Inc., sells computer software. The company's past year's sales were $5 million. The cost of its merchandise sold came to $3 million. Operating expenses were $175,000, plus depreciation expenses totaling $125,000. The firm paid $200,000 interest on loans. The firm sold stock during the year, receiving a $40,000 gain on a stock owned 6 years but losing $60,000 on stock held 4 months. Calculate the company's tax liability.

1-9. (*Corporate income tax*) G. R. Edwin, Inc., had sales of $6 million during the past year. The cost of goods sold amounted to $3 million. Operating expenses totaled $2.6 million, and interest expense was $30,000. Determine the firm's tax liability.

1-10. (*Corporate income tax*) The Analtoly Corporation is an electronics dealer and distributor. Sales for the last year were $4.5 million, and cost of goods sold and operating expenses totaled $3.2 million. Analtoly also paid $150,000 in interest expense, and depreciation expense totaled $50,000. In addition, the company sold securities for $120,000 that it had purchased 4 years earlier at a price of $40,000. Compute the tax liability for Analtoly.

1-11. (*Corporate income tax*) Utsumi, Inc., supplies wholesale industrial chemicals. Last year the company had sales of $6.5 million. Cost of goods sold and operating expenses amounted to 70 percent of sales, and depreciation and interest expenses were $75,000 and $160,000, respectively. Furthermore, the corporation sold 40,000 shares of Sumitomo Industries for $10 a share. These shares were purchased a year ago for $8 each. In addition, Utsumi received $60,000 in dividend income. Compute the corporation's tax liability.

1-12. (*Corporate income tax*) Mdyer, Inc., had taxable income of $300,000. Calculate Mdyer's federal income taxes.

1-13. (*Corporate income tax*) Fighting Dyer, Inc., had taxable income of $20 million. Calculate Fighting Dyer's federal income taxes.

1-14. Boisjoly Productions had taxable income of $19 million.

    a. Calculate Boisjoly's federal income taxes.
    b. Now calculate Boisjoly's average and marginal tax rates.
    c. What would Boisjoly's federal income taxes be if its taxable income was $29 million?
    d. Now calculate Boisjoly's average and marginal tax rates with taxable income of $29 million.

COMPREHENSIVE PROBLEM

The final stage in the interview process for an assistant financial analyst at Caledonia Products involves a test of your understanding of basic financial concepts and of the corporate tax code. You are given the following memorandum and asked to respond to the questions. Whether you are offered a position at Caledonia will depend on the accuracy of your response.

    To: Applicants for the position of Financial Analyst
    From: Mr. V. Morrison, CEO, Caledonia Products
    Re: A test of your understanding of basic financial concepts and of the corporate tax code

Please respond to the following questions:

    a. What are the differences between the goals of profit maximization and maximization of shareholder wealth? Which goal do you think is more appropriate?
    b. What does the risk–return trade-off mean?
    c. Why are we interested in cash flows rather than accounting profits in determining the value of an asset?
    d. What is an efficient market and what are the implications of efficient markets for us?
    e. What is the cause of the agency problem and how do we try to solve it?
    f. What do ethics and ethical behavior have to do with finance?

g. Define (1) sole proprietorship, (2) partnership, and (3) corporation.

h. The Carrickfergus Corporation has sales of $4 million this past year. Its cost of goods sold was $2.4 million, and its operating expenses were $600,000. Interest expenses on outstanding debts were $300,000, and the company paid $60,000 in preferred stock dividends. The corporation received $30,000 in preferred stock dividends and interest income of $22,000. The firm sold stock that had been owned for 2 years for $100,000; the original cost of the stock was $60,000. Determine the corporation's taxable income and its tax liability.

SELF-TEST SOLUTION

SS-1.

Sales		$2,000,000
Cost of goods sold		1,200,000
Gross profit		800,000
Tax-deductible expenses:		
Operating expenses	$400,000	
Interest expenses	100,000	500,000
		$ 300,000
Other income:		
Interest income		12,000
Preferred dividend income	$ 10,000	
Less 70% exclusion	7,000	3,000
Taxable ordinary income		$ 315,000
Gain on sale:		
Selling price	$ 40,000	
Cost	30,000	10,000
Taxable income		$ 325,000

Tax liability

.15 ×	$50,000 =	$	7,500
.25 ×	$25,000 =		6,250
.34 ×	$250,000 =		85,000
5% surtax			11,250
			$ 110,000

CHAPTER 2

The Financial Markets and Interest Rates

THE FINANCIAL MANAGER, INTERNAL AND EXTERNAL FUNDS, AND FLEXIBILITY • THE MIX OF CORPORATE SECURITIES SOLD IN THE CAPITAL MARKET • WHY FINANCIAL MARKETS EXIST • FINANCING OF BUSINESS: THE MOVEMENT OF FUNDS THROUGH THE ECONOMY • COMPONENTS OF THE U.S. FINANCIAL MARKET SYSTEM • THE INVESTMENT BANKER • PRIVATE PLACEMENTS • FLOTATION COSTS • REGULATION • RATES OF RETURN IN THE FINANCIAL MARKETS • INTEREST RATE LEVELS OVER RECENT PERIODS • INTEREST RATE DETERMINANTS IN A NUTSHELL • THE TERM STRUCTURE OF INTEREST RATES • FINANCE AND THE MULTINATIONAL FIRM: EFFICIENT FINANCIAL MARKETS AND INTERCOUNTRY RISK

≪ WHAT'S AHEAD ≫

This chapter focuses on the market environment in which long-term financial capital is raised. Long-term funds are raised in the capital market. By the term *capital market*, we mean all institutions and procedures that facilitate transactions in long-term financial instruments, such as common stocks and bonds.

The sums involved in tapping the capital markets can be vast. For example, new corporate securities offered to the investing marketplace for cash by U.S. corporations totaled $1.43 trillion in 2002 and $1.82 trillion in 2003. To be able to distribute and absorb security offerings of such enormous size, an economy must have a well-developed financial market system. To use that system effectively, a financial manager must possess a basic understanding of its structure. This chapter will help you gain that understanding.

Moreover, we will introduce the logic behind the determination of interest rates and required rates of return in the capital markets. We will also explore interest rate levels and risk differentials (premia) over recent time periods. This knowledge of financial market history will permit you as both a financial manager and an investor to realize that earning, say, a 40 percent annual return on a common stock investment does not occur very often.

As you work through this chapter, be on the lookout for direct applications of several of our principles that form the basics of business financial management. Specifically, your attention will be directed to: **Principle 1: The Risk–Return Trade-Off—We Won't Take On Additional Risk Unless We Expect to Be Compensated with Additional Return; Principle 6: Efficient Capital Markets— The Markets Are Quick and the Prices Are Right; and Principle 10: Ethical Behavior Is Doing the Right Thing, and Ethical Dilemmas Are Everywhere in Finance.**

From February 4, 1994, through November 10, 2004, the Federal Reserve System (Fed), the nation's central bank, voted to change the "target" federal funds rate on 37 different occasions. Eighteen of these interest rate changes were upward. Nineteen decisions, therefore, moved short-term interest rates downward, indicating a loosening of monetary policy. Eleven consecutive times, in fact, during 2001 the Federal Reserve policymakers chose to reduce the target federal funds rate. Such a pervasive stance occurs during periods of slowing aggregate economic activity, which we will shortly review. The federal funds rate is a short-term market rate of interest, influenced by the Fed, that serves as a sensitive indicator of the direction of future changes in interest rates.

We will review here six different interest rate cycles that have confronted major corporate officers. This will emphasize how alert and flexible top-level executives must be in planning their firms' cash availability and cash distributions within an always uncertain global economic environment. The discussion also stresses that interest rate changes induce changes in the cost of capital to firms, and thereby, affect their capital budgeting decisions. The funds-management process, as you will shortly see, is continual. An overview of the six distinct cycles is displayed here.

Recent Interest Rate Cycles

PHASE AND TIME PERIOD	MAIN CONCERN OR RISK	POLICY ACTION
1. Early 1994	Inflation	Raise interest rates
2. Early 1997	Inflation	Raise interest rates
3. Fall 1998	International pressures	Lower interest rates
4. Summer 1999	Tight labor markets, strong aggregate real growth, and inflation	Raise interest rates
5. Early 2001	Contracting manufacturing output, slower business capital spending, equity market sell-off, and formal recession	Lower interest rates
6. Summer 2004	Firming labor market, stronger retail sales, improving industrial production, hot housing market and home price appreciation, and high rates of increase in energy prices, all imbedded in solid real aggregate growth. In total, this suggested unacceptable future rates of inflation.	Raise interest rates

In early 1994, the central bank feared that inflationary pressures were building up in the U.S. economy; it decided to take action, via raising nominal short-term interest rates, to stem those pressures by slowing down aggregate economic growth. The Fed remained committed to a course of higher interest rates throughout 1994 and the first half of 1995; then on July 6, 1995, these monetary policymakers reversed course and began a series of three interest rate decreases. For more than a year, from January 31, 1996, to March 25, 1997, the Fed stayed on the sidelines and let the nation's financial markets direct the course of interest rates.

However, during the first quarter of 1997, the Fed again became concerned that increased inflationary pressures were building up within the U.S. economic system. For example, the national economy was growing at a faster inflation-adjusted rate in the 1997 first quarter than was experienced in the first quarter of 1987—the year of a major equity-market crash (in October 1987). As a result, the Fed chose to raise the target federal funds rate on March 25, 1997. The March interest rate increase directed by the Fed was followed by almost a year and a half of the central bank returning to the sidelines and observing the important relationship between the rate of inflation and real economic growth.

Then, during the fall of 1998, unfavorable international pressures from Brazil and Russia, among others, caused the commercial lending system to pull in the reins. This put financing strains on corporate America. Fearing a widening international economic slowdown, the Fed engineered a quick sequence of three interest rate decreases that ended on November 17, 1998, aimed at stabilizing both the credit and equity markets. By the way, this maneuvering by the central bank did, in fact, work.

Once again, commencing on June 30, 1999, the Fed became concerned about the relationship among (a) tight labor markets; (b) strong aggregate real economic growth, usually monitored by rates of change in real gross domestic product (GDP); and (c) the rate of observed inflation, as well as inflationary expectations. During this phase of the business cycle, the Fed chose to increase short-term interest rates on six different occasions over the period ended May 16, 2000.

Realize that at this stage of the business cycle the U.S. economy was in uncharted territory, as the remarkable economic expansion that began in March 1991 entered its tenth year at the close of the 2000 first quarter. Such good performance within the aggregate domestic economy stood out, as it marked the longest uninterrupted period of expansion in the U.S. economy dating back to 1854, when reliable records began to be maintained. Thus, the Fed continued its vigilant monitoring stance by putting upward pressure on short-term interest rates in hopes of meeting its twin objectives of supporting (a) maximum sustainable employment and (b) price stability. The "good times" began to be stressed during the summer of 2000. A wide-ranging series of events that included (a) a contracting manufacturing sector, (b) slower business investment in plant and equipment, (c) an equity market sell-off that made the term *dot-com* a less than desirable word, and (d) a buildup of business inventories notably suggested that the United States was poised to enter its tenth recession since the end of World War II.

On January 3, 2001, the Fed began a concerted drive that lasted all that year to stimulate the domestic economy by driving interest rates lower and reducing the cost of capital funds to businesses. In the midst of these record 11 interest rate cuts, the United States officially slipped into recession in March 2001. Thus, the record-setting U.S. commercial expansion ended at 120 months, outpacing the previous record, the 106-month expansion from February 1961 to December 1969.

The interest rate moves made by the Fed across 2001 were successful in that the tenth official recession since the end of World War II ended in November of that same year. Thus, this recession, different as all are in their complexity and internal makeup, lasted for only 8 months, just as the previous recession that began in July 1990 did. The average duration of these immediate past 10 recessions is 10.4 months. The table that follows identifies the post–World War II recessions with their respective beginning and ending dates and also includes their durations. Notice by convention in the United States, and not by legislative decree, that these dates are set by the National Bureau of Economic Research located in Cambridge, Massachusetts.

Post–World War II U.S. Business Cycle Contractions

START OF RECESSION (Peaks)	END (Troughs)	LENGTH (Months)
November 1948	October 1949	11
July 1953	May 1954	10
August 1957	April 1958	8
April 1960	February 1961	10
December 1969	November 1970	11
November 1973	March 1975	16
January 1980	July 1980	6
July 1981	November 1982	16
July 1990	March 1991	8
March 2001	November 2001	8

Source: National Bureau of Economic Research. See www.nber.org/cycles.html.

On June 30, 2004, the Fed again was alert to a plethora of stronger business conditions and extraordinary price increases in the energy sector. The latter condition was a precursor of unwelcome inflationary pressures. Predictably, the decision makers at the Fed began to increase the target federal funds rate in small increments across the rest of the year. These actions marked the beginning of the sixth interest rate cycle since early 1994. The intent here was to moderate real domestic economic growth with the ultimate aim of making such growth sustainable.

The implications for business financial officers and other corporate decision makers are important. The 37 monetary policy actions and resultant interest rate changes discussed here are displayed in the next table.

From a financial management viewpoint, the 18 overt actions by the Fed to raise rates caused the *opportunity cost of funds* to rise. This means that firms such as Harley-Davidson and the Walt Disney Company, for example, endured increases in their respective cost of capital funds. This, in turn, made it more difficult for real capital projects to be financed and to be included in those firms' capital budgets.

Changes in the Target Federal Funds Rate and Commercial Bank Prime Lending Rate, February 1994–November 2004

DATE	OLD TARGET RATE %	NEW TARGET RATE %	PRIME LENDING RATE %
1994			
February 4	3.00	3.25	6.00 (no change)
March 22	3.25	3.50	6.25
April 18	3.50	3.75	6.75
May 17	3.75	4.25	7.25
August 16	4.25	4.75	7.75
November 19	4.75	5.50	8.50

DATE	OLD TARGET RATE %	NEW TARGET RATE %	PRIME LENDING RATE %
1995			
February 1	5.50	6.00	9.00
July 6	6.00	5.75	8.75
December 19	5.75	5.50	8.50
1996			
January 31	5.50	5.25	8.25
1997			
March 25	5.25	5.50	8.50
1998			
September 29	5.50	5.25	8.25
October 15	5.25	5.00	8.00
November 17	5.00	4.75	7.75
1999			
June 30	4.75	5.00	8.00
August 24	5.00	5.25	8.25
November 16	5.25	5.50	8.50
2000			
February 2	5.50	5.75	8.75
March 21	5.75	6.00	9.00
May 16	6.00	6.50	9.50
2001			
January 3	6.50	6.00	9.00
January 31	6.00	5.50	8.50
March 20	5.50	5.00	8.00
April 18	5.00	4.50	7.50
May 15	4.50	4.00	7.00
June 27	4.00	3.75	6.75
August 21	3.75	3.50	6.50
September 17	3.50	3.00	6.00
October 2	3.00	2.50	5.50
November 6	2.50	2.00	5.00
December 11	2.00	1.75	4.75
2002			
November 6	1.75	1.25	4.25
2003			
June 25	1.25	1.00	4.00
2004			
June 30	1.00	1.25	4.25
August 10	1.25	1.50	4.50
September 21	1.50	1.75	4.75
November 10	1.75	2.00	5.00

The 19 decisions to lower the target federal funds rate had the exact opposite effect—that is, the given firm's cost of capital funds decreased. In this latter case, the company could take on more capital projects.

Note in the far right column of the table that the commercial-bank prime lending rate typically changes in the same direction and at about the same time that a shift in the federal funds rate occurs. The prime lending rate is the base rate on corporate loans set by the preponderance of the country's major commercial banks. In earlier years this was the rate charged by banks to their most creditworthy customers. Owing to intense competition across banks today, most established business firms receive pricing discounts denominated in basis points (a basis point is one hundredth of a percent) off the prime lending rate. Because the prime rate is directly linked to the federal funds target rate, the central bank's policy is transmitted quickly to the explicit cost of funds that firms face in the financial markets. The commercial banking industry helps it along. Later in this chapter in a section labeled "Across the

Hall," a practicing commercial banker will talk about the pricing of actual business loans.

As you read this chapter, you will learn (a) the importance of financial markets to a developed economy, (b) how funds are raised in the financial markets, (c) the roles played by major institutions such as the Fed and the commercial banking system in the funds-raising process, and (d) some of the fundamentals of interest rate determination. This will help you, as an emerging business executive specializing in accounting, finance, marketing, or strategy, understand the impact of federal monetary policy and actions on your firm's ability to do business and acquire financial capital in the funds marketplace.

Objective **1**

THE FINANCIAL MANAGER, INTERNAL AND EXTERNAL FUNDS, AND FLEXIBILITY

At times, internally generated funds will not be sufficient to finance all of the firm's proposed expenditures. In these situations, the corporation may find it necessary to attract large amounts of financial capital externally or otherwise forgo projects that are forecast to be profitable.[1] Business firms in the nonfinancial corporate sector of the U.S. economy rely heavily on the nation's financial market system to raise cash. Table 2-1 displays the relative internal and external sources of funds for such corporations over the 1981 to 2000 period. Notice that the percentage of external funds raised in any given year can vary substantially from that of other years. In 1982, for example, the nonfinancial business sector raised only

TABLE 2-1   Nonfinancial Corporate Business Sources of Funds, 1981 to 2000

YEAR	TOTAL SOURCES ($ BILLIONS)	PERCENT INTERNAL FUNDS	PERCENT EXTERNAL FUNDS
2000	1,166.9	68.1	31.9
1999	1,200.1	62.5	37.5
1998	899.8	79.4	20.6
1997	967.6	75.6	24.4
1996	812.0	83.4	16.6
1995	878.4	70.7	29.3
1994	733.7	77.3	22.7
1993	593.1	81.6	18.4
1992	560.5	78.2	21.8
1991	471.7	90.3	9.7
1990	535.5	76.9	23.1
1989	567.9	70.4	29.6
1988	634.2	63.7	36.3
1987	564.7	66.6	33.4
1986	538.8	62.5	37.5
1985	493.8	71.3	28.7
1984	511.4	65.8	34.2
1983	444.6	65.7	34.3
1982	331.7	74.6	25.4
1981	394.4	60.6	39.4
Mean	—	72.3	27.7

Sources: *Economic Report of the President* (February 1995), p. 384; *Federal Reserve Bulletin* (June 2000), Table 1.57; and *Flow of Funds Accounts of the U.S.*, First Quarter 2000, Table F. 102, and Third Quarter 2001, Table F. 102.

[1]By *externally generated*, we mean that the funds are obtained by means *other than* through retentions or depreciation. Funds from these latter two sources are commonly called *internally generated funds*.

25.4 percent of its funds by external means (in the financial markets). This was substantially less than the 39.4 percent raised externally only 1 year earlier, during 1981. After that, the same type of significant adjustment made by financial managers is evident. For example, during 1988 nonfinancial firms raised 36.3 percent of new funds in the external markets. By the end of 1991 this proportion dropped drastically to 9.7 percent.

Such adjustments illustrate an important point: The financial executive is perpetually on his or her toes regarding market conditions. Changes in market conditions influence the precise way corporate funds are raised. High relative interest rates, for instance, will deter the use of debt instruments by the financial manager.

The financial market system must be both organized and resilient. Periods of economic recession, for instance, test the financial markets and those firms that continually use the markets. Economic contractions are especially challenging to financial decision makers because all recessions are *unique*. This forces financing policies to become unique.

During the 1981–1982 recession, which lasted 16 months, interest rates remained high during the worst phases of the downturn. This occurred because policymakers at the Federal Reserve System decided to wring a high rate of inflation out of the economy by means of a tight monetary policy. Simultaneously, stock prices were depressed. These business conditions induced firms to forgo raising funds via external means. During 1982, we notice that 74.6 percent of corporate funds were generated internally (see Table 2-1).

The same general pattern followed after the 1990–1991 recession ended in the first quarter of 1991. During 1991 businesses paid down their short-term borrowings and relied on internally generated sources for 90.3 percent of their net financing needs.

Corporate profitability also plays a crucial role in the determination of the internal–external financing choice. In 1998, the U.S. economy began the eighth year of a vibrant economic expansion that ended during March 2001. The good economy translated into good corporate profits. Other things held equal, greater profits reduce the need for external financing. Thus, in 1998 the reliance by firms on external finance dropped to 20.6 percent of their total funds sources. Notice at the bottom of Table 2-1 that the simple (unweighted) average for external finance over the entire 1981–2000 period was a higher 27.7 percent.

The collective behavior of companies that results in firms retaining internally generated cash rather than paying it to stockholders as dividends or to creditors (bondholders) as interest is referred to by financial economists and analysts as the *internal capital market*.[2] This is because the firm allocates the cash flows to new projects. On the other hand, if the cash payments were made directly to stockholders and creditors, the funds would ultimately be allocated to new projects through the external capital markets.

As Figure 2-1 shows, the internal capital market accounted for 72.3 percent of nonfinancial corporations' sources of funds over the 1981–2000 period. Changing economic conditions cause this relationship to continually shift because executives continually adjust to the new information that encompasses the business cycle, interest rates, and stock prices.

FIGURE 2-1   Nonfinancial Corporate Business Sources of Funds, 1981 to 2000

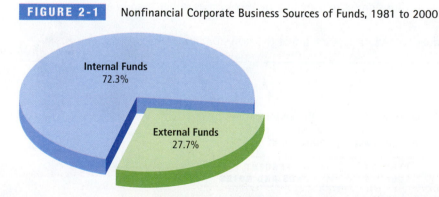

Internal Funds
72.3%

External Funds
27.7%

[2]A lengthier discussion on the relationship of the internal capital market to the external capital market is found in M. Berlin, "Jack of All Trades? Product Diversification in Nonfinancial Firms," *Business Review*, Federal Reserve Bank of Philadelphia (May–June 1999), pp. 19, 23.

CONCEPT CHECK

1. What distinguishes the internal capital market from the external capital market?
2. What important factor(s) might affect the firm's internal–external financing choice?

Objective **2**

THE MIX OF CORPORATE SECURITIES SOLD IN THE CAPITAL MARKET

When corporations decide to raise cash in the capital market, what type of financing vehicle is most favored? Many individual investors think that common stock is the answer to this question. This is understandable, given the coverage of the level of common stock prices by the popular news media. All the major television networks, for instance, quote the closing price of the Dow Jones Industrial Average on their nightly news broadcasts. Common stock, though, is not the financing method corporations most rely on; rather, they use *corporate bonds*. *The corporate debt markets clearly dominate the corporate equity markets when new funds are being raised.* This is a long-term relationship—it occurs year after year. Table 2-2 highlights this fact for the recent time period of 2001 to 2003.

In Table 2-2, we see the annual average volume (in millions of dollars) of corporate securities sold for cash over the 2001–2003 period. The percentage breakdown between equities (both common and preferred stocks) and bonds and notes (corporate debt) is also displayed. Notice that debt-type instruments represented a full 85.7 percent of the annual average dollar amount offered to investors by nonfinancial corporations over this three-year time frame. Equities, therefore, represented the other 14.3 percent. We learn from our discussions of the cost of capital and planning the firm's financing mix that the U.S. tax system inherently favors debt as a means of raising capital. Quite simply, interest expense is deductible from other income when computing the firm's federal tax liability, whereas the dividends paid on both preferred and common stock are not.

Financial executives responsible for raising corporate cash know this. When they have a choice between marketing new bonds and marketing new preferred stock, the outcome is usually in favor of bonds. The after-tax cost of capital on debt is less than that incurred on preferred stock. Likewise, if the firm has unused debt capacity and the general level of equity prices is depressed, financial executives favor the issuance of debt securities over the issuance of new common stock.

CONCEPT CHECK

1. Why might firms prefer to issue new debt securities rather than new common stock?
2. How does the U.S. tax system affect the firm's financing choices?

TABLE 2-2 Corporate Securities Offered for Cash—Nonfinancial Corporations, 3-Year Cash Weighted Average, 2001–2003

TOTAL VOLUME ($ IN MILLIONS)	PERCENT EQUITIES	PERCENT BONDS AND NOTES
$1,288,515	14.3	85.7

Source: Statistical Supplement to the *Federal Reserve Bulletin*, Table 1.46, October 2004, A29.

BACK TO THE FOUNDATIONS

Our previous discussion on the financing preferences of corporate executives provides tangible evidence of **Principle 8: Taxes Bias Business Decisions**. *The U.S. tax code allows corporations to deduct the interest expense associated with debt contracts from the income levels that are taxed. On the other hand, common and preferred stock cash dividend payments to investors are not tax deductible. Thus, the logical choice made by executives on behalf of their firms and shareholders is to finance the next dollar of externally raised capital by means of some debt contract such as bonds and notes. This decision saves the firm cash flows because the tax bill is lower. And, we remember from Chapter 1:* **Principle 3: Cash—Not Profits—Is King**. *You see how it all ties together. The firm would rather have more cash, instead of less cash, and so would its stockholders.*

WHY FINANCIAL MARKETS EXIST

Objective **3**

financial markets

Financial markets are *institutions and procedures that facilitate transactions in all types of financial claims*. The purchase of your home, the common stock you may own, and your life insurance policy all took place in some type of financial market. Why do financial markets exist? What would the economy lose if our complex system of financial markets were not developed? We will address these questions here.

Some *economic units*, such as households, firms, or governments, spend more during a given period than they earn. Other economic units spend less on current consumption than they earn. For example, business firms in the aggregate usually spend more during a specific period than they earn. Households in the aggregate spend less on current consumption than they earn. As a result, some mechanism is needed to facilitate the transfer of savings from those economic units with a surplus to those with a deficit. That is precisely the function of financial markets. Financial markets exist in order to allocate the supply of savings in the economy to the demanders of those savings. The central characteristic of a financial market is that it acts as the vehicle through which the forces of demand and supply for a specific type of financial claim (such as a corporate bond) are brought together.

Now, why would the economy suffer without a developed financial market system? The answer is that the wealth of the economy would be less without the financial markets. The rate of capital formation would not be as high if financial markets did not exist. This means that the net additions during a specific period to the stocks of (1) dwellings, (2) productive plant and equipment, (3) inventory, and (4) consumer durables would occur at lower rates. Figure 2-2 helps clarify the rationale behind this assertion. The abbreviated balance sheets in the figure refer to firms or any other type of economic units that operate in the private, as opposed to governmental, sectors of the economy. This means that such units cannot issue money to finance their own activities.

At stage 1 in Figure 2-2, only real assets exist in the hypothetical economy. **Real assets** are *tangible assets such as houses, equipment, and inventories*. They are distinguished from **financial assets**, which represent *claims for future payment on other economic units*. Common and preferred stocks, bonds, bills, and notes all are types of financial assets. If only real assets exist, then savings for a given economic unit, such as a firm, must be accumulated in the form of real assets. If the firm has a great idea for a new product, that new product can be developed, produced, and distributed only out of company savings (retained earnings). Furthermore, all investment in the new product must occur simultaneously as the savings are generated. If you have the idea, and we have the savings, there is no mechanism to transfer our savings to you. This is not a good situation.

real assets

financial assets

At stage 2, paper money (cash) comes into existence in the economy. Here, at least, you can *store* your own savings in the form of money. Thus, you can finance your great idea by drawing down your cash balances. This is an improvement over stage 1, but there is still no effective mechanism to transfer our savings to you. You see, we won't just hand you our dollar bills—we'll want a receipt.

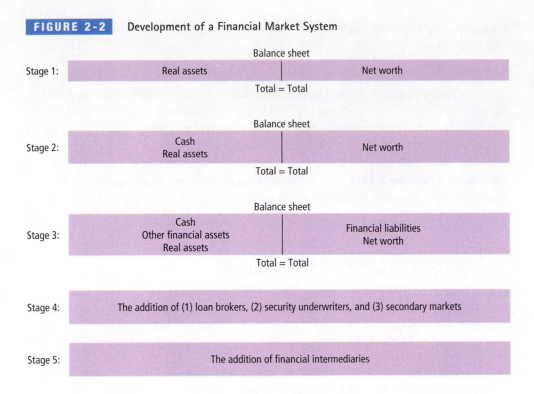

FIGURE 2-2   Development of a Financial Market System

The concept of a receipt that represents the transfer of savings from one economic unit to another is a monumental advancement. The economic unit with excess savings can lend the savings to an economic unit that needs them. To the lending unit, these receipts are identified as "other financial assets" in stage 3 of Figure 2-2. To the borrowing unit, the issuance of financial claims (receipts) shows up as "financial liabilities" on the stage 3 balance sheet. The economic unit with surplus savings earns a rate of return on those funds. The borrowing unit must pay that rate of return, but it has been able to finance its great idea.

In stage 4 the financial market system moves further toward full development. Loan brokers come into existence. These brokers help locate pockets of excess savings and channel such savings to economic units needing the funds. Some economic units actually purchase the financial claims of borrowing units and sell them at a higher price to other investors; this process is called *underwriting*. Underwriting is discussed in more detail later in this chapter. In addition, **secondary markets** develop. Secondary markets simply represent *trading in already existing financial claims*. If you buy your brother's General Motors common stock, you have made a secondary market transaction. Secondary markets reduce the risk of investing in financial claims. Should you need cash, you can liquidate your claims in the secondary market. This induces savers to invest in securities.

The progression toward a developed and complex system of financial markets ends with stage 5. Here, financial intermediaries come into existence. You can think of financial intermediaries as the major financial institutions you're used to dealing with. These include commercial banks, savings and loan associations, credit unions, life insurance companies, and mutual funds. Financial intermediaries share a common characteristic: They offer *their own financial claims*, called **indirect securities**, to economic units with excess savings. The proceeds from selling their indirect securities are then used to purchase the *financial claims of other economic units*. These latter claims can be called **direct securities**. Thus, a mutual fund might sell mutual fund shares (their indirect security) and purchase the common stocks (direct securities) of some major corporations. A life insurance company sells life insurance policies and purchases huge quantities of corporate bonds. Financial intermediaries thereby involve many small savers in the process of capital formation. This means there are more "good things" for everybody to buy.

A developed financial market system provides for a greater level of wealth in the economy. In the absence of financial markets, savings are not transferred to the economic units most in need of those funds. It is difficult, after all, for a household to build its own automobile.

secondary markets

indirect securities

direct securities

The financial market system makes it easier for the economy to build automobiles and all the other goods that economic units like to accumulate.

CONCEPT CHECK

1. What are financial markets?
2. Why will an economy suffer without a developed financial market system?
3. What distinguishes a real asset from a financial asset?
4. Distinguish between direct securities and indirect securities.

FINANCING OF BUSINESS: THE MOVEMENT OF FUNDS THROUGH THE ECONOMY

Objective **4**

The movement of financial capital (funds) throughout the economy just means the movement of savings to the ultimate user of those savings. Some sectors of the economy save more than other sectors. As a result, these savings are moved to a productive use—say, to manufacture that Corvette you want to buy.

The price of using someone else's savings is expressed in terms of interest rates. The financial market system helps to move funds to the most productive end use. Those economic units with the most promising projects should be willing to bid the highest (in terms of rates) to obtain the savings. The concepts of financing and moving savings from one economic unit to another are explored in this section.

THE FINANCING PROCESS

We now understand the crucial role that financial markets play in a capitalist economy. At this point we take a brief look at how funds flow across some selected sectors of the U.S. economy. In addition, we focus a little more closely on the process of financial intermediation that was introduced in the preceding section. Some actual data are used to sharpen our knowledge of the financing process. We will see that financial institutions play a major role in bridging the gap between savers and borrowers in the economy. Nonfinancial corporations, we already know, are significant borrowers of financial capital.

Table 2-3 shows how funds were supplied and raised by the major sectors of the U.S. economy over the 5-year period from 1995 through 1999. The dollar amounts (in billions) are annual averages over those five years. We will specifically make comments on three of the five sectors identified in the table.

Households' net increase in financial liabilities exceeded their net increase in financial assets by $50.3 billion (shown in the last column of the table). In the jargon of economics, the household sector was a *savings-deficit* sector over this period.

TABLE 2-3 Sector View of Flow of Funds in U.S. Financial Markets for 1995 to 1999 (Billions of Dollars, 5-Year Averages)

SECTOR	[1] FUNDS RAISED $	[2] FUNDS SUPPLIED $	[2] − [1] NET FUNDS SUPPLIED $
Households[a]	447.4	397.1	−50.3
Nonfinancial corporate business	447.5	383.8	−63.7
U.S. government	73.9	62.9	−11.0
State and local governments	56.4	48.4	−8.0
Foreign	320.2	561.7	241.5

[a] Includes personal trusts and nonprofit organizations.

Source: *Flow of Funds Accounts, First Quarter 2000*, Flow of Funds Section, Statistical Release Z.1 (Washington, DC; Board of Governors of the Federal Reserve System, June 9, 2000).

This financing behavior was unusual because the household sector over long periods of time is typically a major *savings-surplus* sector. This means the household sector normally is a key net supplier of funds to the financial markets. Actually, and for example, over the 6-year period of 1991 through 1996, the household sector supplied an annual average of $170 billion to the markets. Since 1991, the household sector has been a savings-surplus sector for all years except the recent three covering the period 1997 through 1999. So why were those most recent three years any different? We can see and understand the difference merely by looking at data from 1999. Due to prevailing low interest rates in the U.S. credit markets, households took on a huge $411 billion in mortgages to finance home purchases. The result made the household sector a net user of financial capital in that year, and similar financing behavior was followed in the previous two years.

Notice that over the 5 years detailed in Table 2-3 the nonfinancial business sector was likewise a savings-deficit sector, by $63.7 billion on average for each year. This means nonfinancial firms, such as General Motors, raised $63.7 billion more in the financial markets than they supplied to the markets. Although the nonfinancial business sector often is a savings-deficit sector, it can at times be a savings-surplus sector depending on aggregate economic conditions. The most important of those conditions is the level of corporate profitability.

Table 2-3 further highlights how important foreign financial investment is to the activity of the U.S. economy. On average, the foreign sector supplied a net $241.5 billion to the domestic capital markets for each year of the period. Thus, it was a crucial *savings-surplus* sector. Back in 1982, the foreign sector raised—rather than supplied—$29.9 billion in the U.S. financial markets! This illustrates the dynamic nature of financial management and why financial-management practitioners have to be in tune with current business conditions. Actual capital budgeting decisions, such as those explored in other chapters, are made in the corporate boardroom—not within the rather sterile confines of an end-of-chapter problem.

We have seen here that the financial market system must exist to facilitate the orderly and efficient flow of savings from the surplus sectors to the deficit sectors of the economy. Over long periods, the nonfinancial business sector is typically dependent on the household sector to finance its investment needs. Foreign financing also plays an important role in the U.S. economy.

MOVEMENT OF SAVINGS

Figure 2-3 provides a useful way to summarize our discussion of (1) why financial markets exist and (2) the movement of funds through the economy. It also serves as an introduction to the role of the investment banker—a subject discussed in detail later in this chapter.

We see that savings are ultimately transferred to the business firm in need of cash in three ways.

1. **The direct transfer of funds.** Here the firm seeking cash sells its securities directly to savers (investors) who are willing to purchase them in hopes of earning a reasonable rate of return. New business formation is a good example of this process at work. The new business may go directly to a saver or group of savers called venture capitalists. The venture capitalists lend funds to the firm or take an equity position in the firm if they feel the product or service the new firm hopes to market will be successful.

2. **Indirect transfer using the investment banker.** In a common arrangement under this system, the managing investment-banking house forms a syndicate of several investment bankers. The syndicate buys the entire issue of securities from the firm that is in need of financial capital. The syndicate then sells the securities at a higher price than it paid for them to the investing public (the savers). Salomon Smith Barney and Goldman Sachs are examples of investment-banking firms. They tend to be called "houses" by those who work in the financial community. Notice that under this second method of transferring savings, the securities being issued just pass through the investment-banking firm. They are not transformed into a different type of security.

FIGURE 2-3   Three Ways to Transfer Financial Capital in the Economy

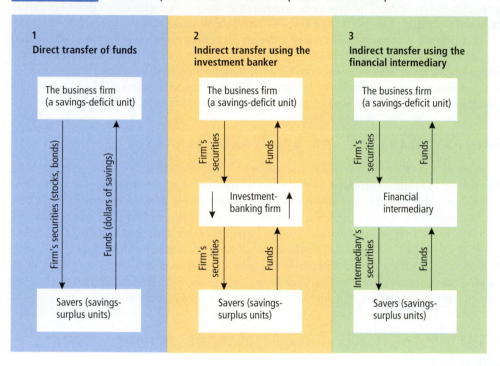

3. **Indirect transfer using the financial intermediary.** This is the type of system life insurance companies and pension funds operate within. The financial intermediary collects the savings of individuals and issues its own (indirect) securities in exchange for these savings. The intermediary then uses the funds collected from the individual savers to acquire the business firm's (direct) securities, such as stocks and bonds.

CONCEPT CHECK

1. What is the difference between a savings-surplus sector and a savings-deficit sector? Give an example of each.
2. Why can't all sectors be savings-deficit sectors?

We all benefit from the three transfer mechanisms displayed in Figure 2-3. Capital formation and economic wealth are greater than they would be in the absence of this financial market system.

COMPONENTS OF THE U.S. FINANCIAL MARKET SYSTEM

Objective **5**

Numerous approaches exist for classifying the securities markets. At times, the array can be confusing. An examination of four sets of dichotomous terms can help provide a basic understanding of the structure of the U.S. financial markets.

PUBLIC OFFERINGS AND PRIVATE PLACEMENTS

When a corporation decides to raise external capital, those funds can be obtained by making a public offering or a private placement. In a **public offering** *both individual and institutional investors have the opportunity to purchase the securities.* The securities are usually made

public offering

available to the public at large by a managing investment-banking firm and its underwriting (risk-taking) syndicate. The firm does not meet the ultimate purchasers of the securities in the public offering. The public market is an impersonal market.

private placement
direct placement

In a **private placement**, also called a **direct placement**, the securities are offered and sold to a *limited number of investors*. The firm will usually hammer out, on a face-to-face basis with the prospective buyers, the details of the offering. In this setting the investment-banking firm may act as a finder by bringing together potential lenders and borrowers. The private placement market is a more personal market than its public counterpart.

PRIMARY MARKETS AND SECONDARY MARKETS

primary markets

Primary markets are *those in which securities are offered for the first time to potential investors*. A new issue of common stock by AT&T is a primary market transaction. This type of transaction increases the total stock of financial assets outstanding in the economy.

As mentioned in our discussion of the development of the financial market system, *secondary markets* represent transactions in currently outstanding securities. If the first buyer of the AT&T stock subsequently sells it, he or she does so in the secondary market. All transactions after the initial purchase take place in the secondary market. The sales do *not* affect the total stock of financial assets that exists in the economy. Both the money market and the capital market, described next, have primary and secondary sides.

MONEY MARKET AND CAPITAL MARKET

MONEY MARKET

money market

The key distinguishing feature between the money and capital markets is the maturity period of the securities traded in them. The **money market** refers to *all institutions and procedures that provide for transactions in short-term debt instruments* generally issued by borrowers with very high credit ratings. By financial convention, *short-term* means maturity periods of 1 year or less. Notice that equity instruments, either common or preferred, are not traded in the money market. The major instruments issued and traded are U.S. Treasury bills, various federal agency securities, bankers' acceptances, negotiable certificates of deposit, and commercial paper. Keep in mind that the money market is an intangible market. You do not walk into a building on Wall Street that has the words "Money Market" etched in stone over its arches. Rather, the money market is primarily a telephone and computer market.

CAPITAL MARKET

capital market

The **capital market** refers to *all institutions and procedures that provide for transactions in long-term financial instruments*. *Long-term* here means having maturity periods that extend beyond one year. In the broad sense this encompasses term loans and financial leases, corporate equities, and bonds. The funds that comprise the firm's capital structure are raised in the capital market. Important elements of the capital market are the organized security exchanges and the over-the-counter markets.

ORGANIZED SECURITY EXCHANGES AND OVER-THE-COUNTER MARKETS

organized security exchanges

over-the-counter markets

Organized security exchanges are *tangible entities*; they physically occupy space (such as a building or a part of a building), and *financial instruments are traded on their premises*. The **over-the-counter markets** include *all security markets except the organized exchanges*. The money market, then, is an over-the-counter market. Because both markets are important to financial officers concerned with raising *long-term capital*, some additional discussion is warranted.

ORGANIZED SECURITY EXCHANGES

For practical purposes there are seven major security exchanges in the United States: (1) New York Stock Exchange, (2) American Stock Exchange, (3) Chicago Stock Exchange,

(4) Pacific Stock Exchange, (5) Philadelphia Stock Exchange, (6) Boston Stock Exchange, and (7) Cincinnati Stock Exchange. The New York Stock Exchange (NYSE) and the American Stock Exchange (AMEX) are called *national* exchanges, whereas the others are loosely described as *regionals*. All seven of these active exchanges are registered with the Securities and Exchange Commission (SEC). Firms whose securities are traded on the registered exchanges must comply with reporting requirements of both the specific exchange and the SEC.

An example of the prominent stature of the NYSE is provided by the sheer number of companies that have stocks listed on this exchange. In September 2004, the NYSE handled such listings of 2,747 firms—up from 2,570 some ten years earlier in 1994. This represented a 6.9 percent absolute increase in the number of firms listed over this period. Even though the NASDAQ, soon to be discussed, has surpassed the NYSE in trading volume, the NYSE remains the preeminent exchange in the United States. The collapse in market value of numerous high-tech and "dot-com" firms during the 2000–2001 period just reinforced the importance of the NYSE to the general credibility of the U.S. financial market system. The total market value of domestic shares listed on the NYSE in September 2004 amounted to $11.8 trillion, up from $2.7 trillion in 1990.[3] As a point of comparison, the nominal value of gross domestic product for the United States as of the 2004 third quarter was also $11.8 trillion.[4]

The business of an exchange, including securities transactions, is conducted by its *members*. Members are said to occupy "seats." There are 1,366 seats on the NYSE, a number that has remained constant since 1953. Major brokerage firms own seats on the exchanges. An officer of the firm is designated to be the member of the exchange, and this membership permits the brokerage house to use the facilities of the exchange to effect trades. During September 2004, the high price for a seat that was exchanged was $1.15 million. This amount was down from the high price in 2002 of $2.255 million.[5]

Stock Exchange Benefits

Both corporations and investors enjoy several benefits provided by the existence of organized security exchanges. These include

1. **Providing a continuous market.** This may be the most important function of an organized security exchange. A continuous market provides a series of continuous security prices. Price changes from trade to trade tend to be smaller than they would be in the absence of organized markets because there is a relatively large sales volume in each security, trading orders are executed quickly, and the range between the price asked for a security and the offered price tends to be narrow. The result is that price volatility is reduced.
2. **Establishing and publicizing fair security prices.** An organized exchange permits security prices to be set by competitive forces. They are not set by negotiations off the floor of the exchange, where one party might have a bargaining advantage. The bidding process flows from the supply and demand underlying each security. This means the specific price of a security is determined in the manner of an auction. In addition, the security prices determined at each exchange are widely publicized.
3. **Helping business raise new capital.** Because a continuous secondary market exists where prices are competitively determined, it is easier for firms to float new security offerings successfully. This continuous pricing mechanism also facilitates the determination of the offering price of a new issue. This means that comparative values are easily observed.

Listing Requirements

To receive the benefits provided by an organized exchange, the firm must seek to have its securities listed on the exchange. An application for listing must be filed and a fee paid. The requirements for listing vary from exchange to exchange; those of the NYSE are the most stringent. The general criteria for listing fall into these categories: (1) profitability, (2) size,

[3]New York Stock Exchange, *2004 Fact Book Online* (New York, December 2004), www.nysedata.com/factbook.
[4]U.S. Department of Commerce, Bureau of Economic Analysis, November 30, 2004, *Gross Domestic Product: Third Quarter 2004* (Preliminary), Table 3.
[5]New York Stock Exchange, *2004 Fact Book Online* (New York, September 2004), www.nysedata.com/factbook.

TABLE 2-4   A Sample of NYSE Listing Requirements for Domestic (U.S.) Companies

PROFITABILITY (EARNINGS)

Earnings before taxes (EBT) for the most recent year must be at least $2.5 million.
For the 2 years preceding that, EBT must be at least $2.0 million.

MARKET VALUE (GLOBAL MARKET CAPITALIZATION)

Revenues for the most recent fiscal year must be at least $100.0 million, and average (last six months) global
   market capitalization must be $1.0 billion.

PUBLIC OWNERSHIP (DISTRIBUTION CRITERIA)

There must be at least 1.1 million publicly held common shares.
There must be at least 2,000 holders of 100 shares or more.

Source: New York Stock Exchange, *2004 Fact Book Online* (New York, 2004), www.nysedata.com/factbook.

(3) market value, and (4) public ownership. To give you the flavor of an actual set of listing requirements, those set forth by the NYSE are displayed in Table 2-4.

OVER-THE-COUNTER MARKETS

Many publicly held firms do not meet the listing requirements of major stock exchanges. Others may want to avoid the reporting requirements and fees required to maintain listing. As an alternative their securities may trade in the over-the-counter markets. On the basis of sheer numbers (not dollar volume), more stocks are traded over the counter than on organized exchanges. As far as secondary trading in corporate bonds is concerned, the over-the-counter markets are where the action is. In a typical year, more than 90 percent of corporate bond business takes place over the counter.

Most over-the-counter transactions are done through a loose network of security traders who are known as broker-dealers and brokers. Brokers do not purchase securities for their own account, whereas broker-dealers do. Broker-dealers stand ready to buy and sell specific securities at selected prices. They are said to "make a market" in those securities. Their profit is the spread or difference between the price they pay for a security (bid price) and the price at which they sell the security (asked price).

PRICE QUOTES AND THE NASDAQ

The availability of prices is not as continuous in the over-the-counter market as it is on an organized exchange. Since February 8, 1971, however, when a computerized network called NASDAQ came into existence, the availability of prices in this market has improved substantially. NASDAQ stands for National Association of Security Dealers Automated Quotation system. It is a telecommunications system that provides a national information link among the brokers and dealers operating in the over-the-counter markets. Subscribing traders have a terminal that allows them to obtain representative bids and ask prices for thousands of securities traded over the counter. NASDAQ is a quotation system, not a transactions system. The final trade is still consummated by direct negotiation between traders.

The NASDAQ system has become an increasingly important element of the U.S. financial market system in recent years. It provides a nationwide communications element that was lacking in the over-the-counter side of the securities markets.

The Nasdaq Stock Market, Inc., describes itself as a "screen-based, floorless market." It has become highly popular as the trading mechanism of choice of several fast-growth sectors in the United States, including the high-technology sector. The common stock of computer chip maker Intel Corporation, for example, is traded via the NASDAQ as is that of Dell and Starbucks. About 3,300 companies are listed.[6]

NASDAQ price quotes for many stocks are published daily in *The Wall Street Journal*. This same financial newspaper also publishes prices on hundreds of other stocks traded over the counter. Local papers supply prices on stocks of regional interest.

[6]See www.nasdaq.com/investorrelations.

THE INVESTMENT BANKER

Objective **6**

We touched briefly on the investment-banking industry and the investment banker earlier in this chapter when we described various methods for transferring financial capital (see Figure 2-3). The investment banker is to be distinguished from the commercial banker in that the former's organization is not a permanent depository for funds. For the moment, it is important for you to learn about the role of the investment banker in the funding of commercial activity because of the importance of this institution within the financial market system.

Most corporations do not raise long-term capital frequently. The activities of working-capital management go on daily, but attracting long-term capital is, by comparison, episodic. The sums involved can be huge, so these situations are considered of great importance to financial managers. Because most managers are unfamiliar with the subtleties of raising long-term funds, they enlist the help of an expert. That expert is an investment banker.

DEFINITION

The **investment banker** is *a financial specialist involved as an intermediary in the merchandising of securities*. He or she acts as a "middle person" by facilitating the flow of savings from those economic units that want to invest to those units that want to raise funds. We use the term *investment banker* to refer both to a given individual and to the organization for which such a person works, variously known as an investment-banking firm or an investment-banking house. Although these firms are called investment bankers, they perform no depository or lending functions. The activities of commercial banking and investment banking as we know them today were separated by the Banking Act of 1933 (also known as the Glass-Steagall Act of 1933). Then, after considerable political debate, the Financial Modernization Act was passed by the U.S. Congress on November 12, 1999. This recent legislation is also referred to as the Gramm-Leach-Bliley Act of 1999, in honor of its congressional sponsors. The act actually repealed the depression-era Glass-Steagall Act and is aimed at increasing competitiveness among modern financial services companies. Through the creation of operating subsidiaries, the act provides for business combinations among banks, underwriters of financial securities (investment bankers), insurance firms, and securities brokers. Here we focus on investment banking and its important intermediary role. This is most easily understood in terms of the basic functions of investment banking.

investment banker

FUNCTIONS

The investment banker performs three basic functions: (1) underwriting, (2) distributing, and (3) advising.

UNDERWRITING

The term **underwriting** is borrowed from the field of insurance. It means *assuming a risk*. The investment banker assumes the risk of selling a security issue at a satisfactory price. A satisfactory price is one that generates a profit for the investment-banking house.

The procedure goes like this. The managing investment banker and its syndicate will buy the security issue from the corporation in need of funds. The **syndicate** is *a group of other investment bankers that is invited to help buy and resell the issue*. The managing house is the

underwriting

syndicate

investment-banking firm that originated the business because its corporate client decided to raise external funds. On a specific day, the firm that is raising capital is presented with a check in exchange for the securities being issued. At this point the investment-banking syndicate owns the securities. The corporation has its cash and can proceed to use it. The firm is now immune from the possibility that the security markets might turn sour. If the price of the newly issued security falls below that paid to the firm by the syndicate, the syndicate will suffer a loss. The syndicate, of course, hopes that the opposite situation will result. Its objective is to sell the new issue to the investing public at a price per security greater than its cost.

DISTRIBUTING

Once the syndicate owns the new securities, it must get them into the hands of the ultimate investors. This is the distribution or selling function of investment banking. The investment banker may have branch offices across the United States, or it may have an informal arrangement with several security dealers who regularly buy a portion of each new offering for final sale. It is not unusual to have 300 to 400 dealers involved in the selling effort. The syndicate can properly be viewed as the security wholesaler, and the dealer organization can be viewed as the security retailer.

ADVISING

The investment banker is an expert in the issuance and marketing of securities. A sound investment-banking house will be aware of prevailing market conditions and can relate those conditions to the particular type of security that should be sold at a given time. Business conditions may be pointing to a future increase in interest rates. The investment banker might advise the firm to issue its bonds in a timely fashion to avoid the higher yields that are forthcoming. The banker can analyze the firm's capital structure and make recommendations about what general source of capital should be issued. In many instances the firm will invite its investment banker to sit on the board of directors. This permits the banker to observe corporate activity and make recommendations on a regular basis.

DISTRIBUTION METHODS

Several methods are available to the corporation for placing new security offerings in the hands of final investors. The investment banker's role is different in each of these. Sometimes, in fact, it is possible to bypass the investment banker. These methods are described in this section. Private placements, because of their importance, are treated separately later in the chapter.

NEGOTIATED PURCHASE

In a negotiated underwriting, the firm that needs funds makes contact with an investment banker, and deliberations concerning the new issue begin. If all goes well, a *method* is negotiated for determining the price the investment banker and the syndicate will pay for the securities. For example, the agreement might state that the syndicate will pay $2 less than the closing price of the firm's common stock on the day before the offering date of a new stock issue. The negotiated purchase is the most prevalent method of securities distribution in the private sector. It is generally thought to be the most profitable technique as far as investment bankers are concerned.

COMPETITIVE BID PURCHASE

The method by which the underwriting group is determined distinguishes the competitive bid purchase from the negotiated purchase. In a competitive underwriting, several underwriting groups bid for the right to purchase the new issue from the corporation that is raising funds. The firm does not directly select the investment banker. The investment banker that underwrites and distributes the issue is chosen by an auction process. The syndicate willing to pay the greatest dollar amount per new security will win the competitive bid.

Most competitive bid purchases are confined to three situations, compelled by legal regulations: (1) railroad issues, (2) public utility issues, and (3) state and municipal bond issues. The argument in favor of competitive bids is that any undue influence of the investment banker over the firm is mitigated and the price received by the firm for each security should be higher. Thus, we would intuitively suspect that the cost of capital in a competitive bid situation would be less than in a negotiated purchase situation. Evidence on this question, however, is mixed. One problem with the competitive bid purchase as far as the fund-raising firm is concerned is that the benefits gained from the advisory function of the investment banker are lost. It may be necessary to use an investment banker for advisory purposes and then by law exclude the banker from the competitive bid process.

COMMISSION OR BEST-EFFORTS BASIS

Here, the investment banker acts as an agent rather than as a principal in the distribution process. The securities are *not* underwritten. The investment banker attempts to sell the issue in return for a fixed commission on each security actually sold. Unsold securities are returned to the corporation. This arrangement is typically used for more speculative issues. The issuing firm may be smaller or less established than the banker would like. Because the underwriting risk is not passed on to the investment banker, this distribution method is less costly to the issuer than a negotiated or competitive bid purchase. On the other hand, the investment banker only has to give it his or her "best effort." A successful sale is not guaranteed.

PRIVILEGED SUBSCRIPTION

Occasionally, the firm may feel that a distinct market already exists for its new securities. When a *new issue is marketed to a definite and select group of investors*, it is called a **privileged subscription**. Three target markets are typically involved: (1) current stockholders, (2) employees, or (3) customers. Of these, distributions directed at current stockholders are the most prevalent. Such offerings are called *rights offerings*. In a privileged subscription the investment banker may act only as a selling agent. It is also possible that the issuing firm and the investment banker might sign a *standby agreement*, which would obligate the investment banker to underwrite the securities that are not accepted by the privileged investors.

privileged subscription

DIRECT SALE

In a **direct sale** *the issuing firm sells the securities directly to the investing public without involving an investment banker*. Even among established corporate giants, this procedure is relatively rare. A variation of the direct sale, though, was used more frequently in the 1970s than in previous decades. This involves the private placement of a new issue by the fund-raising corporation *without* the use of an investment banker as an intermediary. Texaco, Mobil Oil, and International Harvester (now Navistar) are examples of large firms that have followed this procedure.

direct sale

INDUSTRY LEADERS

All industries have their leaders, and investment banking is no exception. We have discussed investment bankers in general at some length in this chapter. Table 2-5 gives us some idea who the major players are within the investment-banking industry. It lists the top 10 houses in 2003, based on the dollar volume of security issues that were managed.

TABLE 2-5 "Leading Managing Underwriters" or "Leading Bookrunners" of Global Stocks and Bonds

FIRM	UNDERWRITING VOLUME (BILLIONS OF DOLLARS)	PERCENT OF MARKET
1. Citigroup	$542.7	10.2%
2. Morgan Stanley	394.8	7.4
3. Merrill Lynch	380.3	7.1
4. Lehman Brothers	354.1	6.7
5. J.P. Morgan	353.9	6.6
6. Credit Suisse First Boston	338.7	6.4
7. Deutsche Bank	317.4	6.0
8. UBS	293.8	5.5
9. Goldman Sachs	293.3	5.5
10. Banc of America Securities	206.4	3.9

Source: Thomson Financial.

MANAGEMENT AND SELECTION CRITERIA FOR AN INVESTMENT BANKER

Comments and Procedure by David R. Klock, Ph.D.

Dr. David R. Klock is past CEO and currently chairman of the board of directors of CompBenefits Corporation, headquartered in Atlanta, Georgia. Dr. Klock holds a Ph.D. in finance from the University of Illinois and is a nationally known insurance economist. CompBenefits is a privately held national leader in providing a wide range of dental and vision insurance products. The firm's annual revenues are approximately $310 million. The firm continually works with venture capitalists who provide equity capital and access to debt capital in the nation's financial market system. Dr. Klock authored the following checklist that deals with selecting an investment banker within the context of seeking what are called "strategic buyers" by venture capital firms. Dr. Klock is highly familiar with the field, having spent time at the investment-banking firm of Goldman Sachs earlier in his career.

1. Competency
   - Technical skills/resources of total team
   - People skills/resources of total team
   - Knowledge of the firm
   - Knowledge of key potential buyers and their needs/ability to pay
2. Connections
   - Recent firm history of working with potential buyers
   - Individual banker's recent history of working with key potential buyers
   - Reputation of investment-banking firm with potential buyers
   - Intangibles
3. Conviction on Enterprise Value of the Firm
   - Valuation range and strength of valuation methods/matrix
   - Ability to strongly tell firm's story and to be heard/understood by key individuals at potential buyers
   - Level of commitment to this transaction within the banking firm

Notice in Table 2-5 that the U.S. investment-banking industry is a highly concentrated one. The top 10 bankers with regard to underwriting volume during 2003 accounted for a full 65.3 percent of the total market. This degree of concentration is pervasive over time. The upshot is that it is most difficult to successfully launch a new investment banking firm. The barriers to market entry are steep.

In the preceding "Across the Hall" section, a board chairman presents his checklist for selecting an investment-banking firm to work with an actual corporation. Please keep in mind that many board chairpersons and chief executive officers of business firms come from academic disciplines other than finance, for example, marketing, management, and information systems. Thus, a basic knowledge of the investment-banking industry is vital to both the employee and the employer.

CONCEPT CHECK

1. What is the main difference between an investment banker and a commercial banker?
2. What are the three major functions that an investment banker performs?
3. What are the five key methods by which securities are distributed to final investors?

Objective **7** | **PRIVATE PLACEMENTS**

Private placements are an alternative to the sale of securities to the public or to a restricted group of investors through a privileged subscription. Any type of security can be privately placed (directly placed). This market, however, is clearly dominated by debt issues. Thus, we restrict this discussion to debt securities. From year to year the volume of private placements varies greatly. However, the private placement market is always a significant portion of the U.S. capital market. In fact, according to the Federal Reserve, bonds and notes made up 35.5 percent of private securities offered for cash over the 1997–1999 period. The private placement market is not limited to fixed-income securities. There exists in the United States an extensive, organized, private equity market that is extensively participated in by venture capitalists. From the fund-raising perspective, the private placement market is especially appealing to new, small, and medium-sized companies. Such firms are the province of the venture capitalists.[7]

The major investors in private placements are still large financial institutions. Based on the volume of securities purchased, the three most important investor groups are (1) life insurance companies, (2) state and local retirement funds, and (3) private pension funds.

In arranging a private placement, the firm may (1) avoid the use of an investment banker and work directly with the investing institutions or (2) engage the services of an investment banker. If the firm does not use an investment banker, of course, it does not have to pay a fee. Conversely, investment bankers can provide valuable advice in the private placement process. They are usually in contact with several major institutional investors; thus, they will know if a firm is in a position to invest in its proposed offering, and they can help the firm evaluate the terms of the new issue.

Private placements have advantages and disadvantages compared with public offerings. The financial manager must carefully evaluate both sides of the question. The advantages associated with private placements are these:

1. **Speed.** The firm usually obtains funds more quickly through a private placement than a public offering. The major reason is that registration of the issue with the SEC is not required.
2. **Reduced flotation costs.** These savings result because the lengthy registration statement for the SEC does not have to be prepared, and the investment-banking underwriting and distribution costs do not have to be absorbed.
3. **Financing flexibility.** In a private placement the firm deals on a face-to-face basis with a small number of investors. This means that the terms of the issue can be tailored to meet the specific needs of the company. For example, all of the funds need not be taken by the firm at once. In exchange for a commitment fee, the firm can "draw down" against the established amount of credit with the investors. This provides some insurance against capital market uncertainties, and the firm does not have to borrow the funds if the need does not arise. There is also the possibility of renegotiation. The terms of the debt issue can be altered. The term to maturity, the interest rate, or any restrictive covenants can be discussed among the affected parties.

The following disadvantages of private placements must be evaluated:

1. **Interest costs.** It is generally conceded that interest costs on private placements exceed those of public issues. Whether this disadvantage is enough to offset the reduced flotation costs associated with a private placement is a determination the financial manager must make. There is some evidence that on smaller issues, say $500,000 as opposed to $30 million, the private placement alternative would be preferable.
2. **Restrictive covenants.** Dividend policy, working-capital levels, and the raising of additional debt capital may all be affected by provisions in the private-placement debt contract. This is not to say that such restrictions are always absent in public debt contracts. Rather, the financial officer must be alert to the tendency for these covenants to be especially burdensome in private contracts.
3. **The possibility of future SEC registration.** If the lender (investor) should decide to sell the issue to a public buyer before maturity, the issue must be registered with the SEC. Some lenders, then, require that the issuing firm agree to a future registration at their option.

CONCEPT CHECK

1. Within the financial markets, explain what we mean by "private placements."
2. What are the possible advantages and disadvantages of private placements?

---

[7]For a longer discussion on the private placement market and venture capital, see A. J. Keown, J. D. Martin, J. W. Petty, and D. F. Scott, Jr., *Financial Management: Principles and Applications*, 10th ed. (Upper Saddle River, N.J.: Prentice Hall, 2005), pp. 481–486.

Objective **8**

flotation costs

FLOTATION COSTS

The firm raising long-term capital incurs two types of **flotation costs**: (1) *the underwriter's spread* and (2) *issuing costs*. Of these two costs, the underwriter's spread is the larger. The *underwriter's spread* is simply the difference between the gross and net proceeds from a given security issue expressed as a percent of the gross proceeds. The *issue costs* include (1) printing and engraving, (2) legal fees, (3) accounting fees, (4) trustee fees, and (5) several other miscellaneous components. The two most significant issue costs are printing and engraving and legal fees.

Data published by the SEC have consistently revealed two relationships about flotation costs. First, the costs associated with issuing common stock are notably greater than the costs associated with preferred stock offerings. In turn, preferred stock costs exceed those of bonds. Second, flotation costs (expressed as a percentage of gross proceeds) decrease as the size of the security issue increases.

In the first instance, the stated relationship reflects the fact that issue costs are sensitive to the risks involved in successfully distributing a security issue. Common stock is riskier to own than corporate bonds. Underwriting risk is, therefore, greater with common stock than with bonds. Thus, flotation costs just mirror these risk relationships. In the second case, a portion of the issue costs is fixed. Legal fees and accounting costs are good examples. So, as the size of the security issue rises, the fixed component is spread over a larger gross proceeds base. As a consequence, average flotation costs vary inversely with the size of the issue.

CONCEPT CHECK

1. What are the two major categories of flotation costs?
2. Are flotation costs greater for a new bond issue or a new common stock issue?

REGULATION

Since late 1986, public interest has been renewed in the regulation of the country's financial markets. The key event was a massive insider trading scandal that made the name Ivan F. Boesky one of almost universal recognition—but, unfortunately, in a negative sense. This was followed by the October 19, 1987, crash of the equity markets. More recently, in early 1990, the investing community (both institutional and individual) became increasingly concerned over a weakening in the so-called junk bond market. Then several financial failures and breakdowns in corporate governance and democracy made firms such as Enron, WorldCom, Global Crossing, Adelphia, Tyco, Arthur Andersen, and HealthSouth household names in a negative context in the very recent 2001–2003 time frame. The accompanying notoriety associated with these firms and their key management personnel led Congress to pass the Sarbanes-Oxley Act of 2002. This recent act is reviewed later in this section. The upshot of all of this enhanced awareness is a new appreciation of the crucial role that regulation plays in the financial system.

Following the severe economic downturn of 1929–1932, congressional action was taken to provide for federal regulation of the securities markets. State statutes (blue sky laws) also govern the securities markets where applicable, but the federal regulations are clearly more pressing and important. The major federal regulations are reviewed here.

PRIMARY MARKET REGULATIONS

The new issues market is governed by the Securities Act of 1933. The intent of the act is important. It aims to provide potential investors with accurate, truthful disclosure about the firm and the new securities being offered to the public. This does *not* prevent firms from issuing highly speculative securities. The SEC says nothing whatsoever about the possible investment worth of a given offering. It is up to the investor to separate the junk from the jewels. The SEC does have the legal power and responsibility to enforce the 1933 act.

Full public disclosure is achieved by the requirement that the issuing firm file a registration statement with the SEC containing requisite information. The statement details particulars about the firm and the new security being issued. During a minimum 20-day waiting period, the SEC examines the submitted document. In numerous instances the 20-day wait has been extended by several weeks. The SEC can ask for additional information that was omitted in order to clarify the original document. The SEC can also order the offering to be stopped.

During the registration process, a preliminary prospectus (the red herring) may be distributed to potential investors. When the registration is approved, the final prospectus must be made available to the prospective investors. The prospectus is actually a condensed version of the full registration statement. If, at a later date, the information in the registration statement and the prospectus is found to be lacking, purchasers of the new issue who incurred a loss can sue for damages. Officers of the issuing firm and others who took part in the registration and marketing of the issue may suffer both civil and criminal penalties.

Generally, the SEC defines public issues as those that are sold to more than 25 investors. Some public issues need not be registered. These include the following:

1. Relatively small issues for which the firm sells less than $1.5 million of new securities per year. Such issues of less than $1.5 million are not entirely regulation free. They are monitored through what is usually called the *small-issues exemption*. These small issues, then, fall under the auspices of Regulation A, which is just a very short offering statement compared to the full-blown registration statement. The latter is onerous, often ending up in the 50- to 100-page range.
2. Issues that are sold entirely intrastate.
3. Issues that are basically short-term instruments. This translates into maturity periods of 270 days or less.
4. Issues that are already regulated or controlled by some other federal agency. Examples include the Federal Power Commission (public utilities) and the Interstate Commerce Commission (railroads).

SECONDARY MARKET REGULATIONS

Secondary market trading is regulated by the Securities Exchange Act of 1934. This act created the SEC to enforce federal securities laws. The Federal Trade Commission enforced the 1933 act for 1 year. The major aspects of the 1934 act can best be presented in outline form:

1. Major security exchanges must register with the SEC. This regulates the exchanges and places reporting requirements on the firms whose securities are listed on them.
2. Insider trading is regulated. Insiders can be officers, directors, employees, relatives, major investors, or anyone having information about the operation of the firm that is not public knowledge. If an investor purchases the security of the firm in which the investor is an insider, he or she must hold it for at least 6 months before disposing of it. Otherwise, profits made from trading the stock within a period of less than 6 months must be returned to the firm. Furthermore, insiders must file with the SEC a monthly statement of holdings and transactions in the stock of their corporation.[8]
3. Manipulative trading of securities by investors to affect stock prices is prohibited.
4. The SEC is given control over proxy procedures.
5. The Board of Governors of the Federal Reserve System is given responsibility for setting margin requirements. This affects the flow of credit into the securities markets. Buying securities on margin simply means using credit to acquire a portion of the subject financial instruments.

[8]On November 14, 1986, the SEC announced that Ivan F. Boesky had admitted to illegal inside trading after an intensive investigation. Boesky at the time was a very well-known Wall Street investor, speculator, and arbitrageur. Boesky was an owner or part-owner in several companies, including an arbitrage fund named Ivan F. Boesky & Co. L.P. Boesky agreed to pay the U.S. government $50 million, which represented a return of illegal profits, and another $50 million in civil penalties; to withdraw permanently from the securities industry; and to plead guilty to criminal charges. The far-reaching investigation continued into 1987 and implicated several other prominent investment figures.

BACK TO THE FOUNDATIONS

*In recent years a number of financial intermediaries, including Drexel Burnham Lambert and Salomon Brothers, have been rocked by ethical scandals. Because financial dealings demand trust, these ethical scandals closed Drexel Burnham Lambert and almost did the same to Salomon Brothers. Once again, this demonstrates the importance of **Principle 10: Ethical Behavior Is Doing the Right Thing, and Ethical Dilemmas Are Everywhere in Finance.***

THE SECURITIES ACTS AMENDMENTS OF 1975

The Securities Acts Amendments of 1975 touched on three important issues. First, Congress mandated the creation of a national market system (NMS). Only broad goals for this national exchange were identified by Congress. Implementation details were left to the SEC and, to a much lesser extent, the securities industry in general. Congress was really expressing its desire for (1) widespread application of auction-market trading principles, (2) a high degree of competition across markets, and (3) the use of modern electronic communication systems to link the fragmented markets in the country into a true NMS. The NMS is still a goal toward which the SEC and the securities industry are moving. Agreement as to its final form and an implementation date has not occurred.

A second major alteration in the habits of the securities industry also took place in 1975. This was the elimination of fixed commissions (fixed brokerage rates) on public transactions in securities. This was closely tied to the desire for an NMS in that fixed brokerage fees provided no incentive for competition among brokers. A third consideration of the 1975 amendments focused on such financial institutions as commercial banks and insurance firms. These financial institutions were prohibited from acquiring membership on stock exchanges in order to reduce or save commissions on their own trades.

SHELF REGISTRATION

shelf registration
shelf offering

On March 16, 1982, the SEC began a new procedure for registering new issues of securities. Formally it is called SEC Rule 415; informally the process is known as a **shelf registration**, or a **shelf offering**. The essence of the process is rather simple. Rather than go through the lengthy, full registration process each time the firm plans an offering of securities, it can get a blanket order approved by the SEC. *A master registration statement that covers the financing plans of the firm over the coming 2 years is filed with the SEC.* On approval, the firm can market some or all of the securities over this 2-year period. The securities are sold in a piecemeal fashion, or "off the shelf." Before each specific offering, a short statement about the issue is filed with the SEC.

Corporations raising funds approve of this procedure. The tedious, full registration process is avoided with each offering pulled off the shelf. This should result in a saving of fees paid to investment bankers. Moreover, an issue can more quickly be brought to the market. Also, if market conditions change, an issue can easily be redesigned to fit the specific conditions of the moment.

An example of a prominent firm that likes and uses the shelf registration procedure is the Walt Disney Company. In its annual report for 2001, the firm said:

> In August 2001, the company filed a new U.S. shelf registration statement, which replaced the existing U.S. shelf registration statement. As of September 30, 2001, the company had the ability to borrow under the U.S. shelf registration statement and a Euro Medium-Term Note Program, which collectively permitted the issuance of up to approximately $8.1 billion of additional debt or various other securities.[9]

---

[9]The Walt Disney Company, *Annual Report* (2001), p. 57.

As is always the case, there is another side to the story. Recall that the reason for the registration process in the first place is to give investors useful information about the firm and the securities being offered. Under the shelf registration procedure some of the information about the issuing firm becomes old as the 2-year horizon unfolds. Some investment bankers feel they do not have the proper amount of time to study the firm when a shelf offering takes place.

SARBANES-OXLEY ACT OF 2002

As mentioned previously, several disappointing lapses in corporate behavior became public information after the year 2000. Numerous unflattering instances of poor judgment occurred involving the major fundamental building blocks of Western capitalism. These included the (a) public accounting industry, (b) legal industry, (c) investment-banking industry, (d) security analysts' industry, and (e) subject firms themselves, even involving their elected boards of directors. Both individual investors and some institutional investors lost hugely significant amounts of invested capital as a result of this monumental breakdown in corporate morality.

One glaring example involved the board of directors of the energy-sector company Enron Corporation. Enron failed financially in December 2001. Prior to that formal failure (bankruptcy), the firm's board of directors overtly voted on two occasions to temporarily suspend its own code of ethics to permit its CFO to engage in risky personal financial ventures that involved the financial structure and cash flow streams of Enron. This should remind you of our **Principle 10: Ethical Behavior Is Doing the Right Thing, and Ethical Dilemmas Are Everywhere in Finance**.

In a research paper that focused on accounting practices at energy firms, Richard Bassett and Mark Storrie summarized the problems at Enron as follows:

> In brief, Enron's senior management and others engaged in a systematic attempt to use various accounting and reporting techniques to mislead investors.[10]

Under intense public scrutiny resulting from a large series of corporate indiscretions like those noted earlier, Congress passed in July 2002 the Public Company Accounting Reform and Investor Protection Act. The short name for the act became the Sarbanes-Oxley Act of 2002. The act contains 11 "titles," which are displayed in Table 2-6.[11] Those 11 titles provide the flavor of the act, which tightened significantly the latitude given corporate advisors (such as accountants, lawyers, company officers, and boards of directors) who have access to or influence company decisions.

TABLE 2-6	Sarbanes-Oxley Act of 2002, Key Elements
TITLE	**AREA OF EMPHASIS**
I	Public Company Accounting Oversight Board
II	Auditor Independence
III	Corporate Responsibility
IV	Enhanced Financial Disclosures
V	Analyst Conflicts of Interest
VI	Commission Resources and Authority
VII	Studies and Reports
VIII	Corporate and Criminal Fraud Accountability
IX	White-Collar Crime Penalty Enhancements
X	Corporate Tax Returns
XI	Corporate Fraud and Accountability

Source: U.S. Congress, H.R. 3763. Passed by the 107th Congress of the U.S. on July 25, 2002; signed by President Bush on July 30, 2002.

[10]Richard Bassett and Mark Storrie, "Accounting at Energy Firms After Enron: Is the Cure Worse Than the Disease?" *Policy Analysis: Cato Project on Corporate Governance, Audit and Tax Reform*, no. 469, February 12, 2003, p. 2.
[11]The full Sarbanes-Oxley Act can be viewed at the Library of Congress site at http://thomas.loc.gov.

In effect, such advisors are now held strictly accountable by law for any instances of misconduct. The act very simply and directly identified its purpose as being "to protect investors by improving the accuracy and reliability of corporate disclosures made pursuant to the securities laws, and for other purposes." In a speech given in March 2003, SEC Commissioner Paul S. Atkins directly recognized the relationship of the act to corporate valuations. He said:

> Fundamentally, Sarbanes-Oxley acknowledges the importance of stockholder value. Without equity investors and their confidence, our economic growth and continued technological innovations would be slowed. Sarbanes-Oxley strengthens the role of directors as representatives of stockholders and reinforces the role of management as stewards of the stockholders' interest.[12]

As evidenced by its being the initial title of the act, a critical part of this law was the creation of the Public Company Accounting Oversight Board. This board's purpose is to regulate the accounting industry relative to public companies that accounting firms audit. Table 2-7 highlights the composition of the board's membership and its duties. As recently as June 30, 2003, the oversight board itself published a set of ethics rules to police its own set of activities.[13] This ethics code was sent to the SEC for approval as was intended to "insulate itself from perceptions or accusations of conflicts of interest."

CONCEPT CHECK

1. What are the main elements of the Securities Act of 1933 and the Securities Exchange Act of 1934?
2. What is meant by "insider trading"?
3. What is a "shelf registration"?
4. What is the purpose of the Sarbanes-Oxley Act of 2002?

TABLE 2-7   Public Company Accounting Oversight Board

I. THE BOARD: ESTABLISHMENT OF AN INDEPENDENT OVERSIGHT BOARD FOR AUDITORS

The Board consists of five financially-literate members, appointed for five-year terms. Two of the members must be or have been Certified Public Accountants (CPAs), and the remaining members must not be nor have ever been CPAs. Members cannot share in the profits or receive payments from a public accounting firm (other than fixed continuing payments such as retirement benefits). Members are appointed by the SEC, after consultation with the chairman of the Federal Reserve Board and the Secretary of the Treasury. Members can be removed from the board by the SEC for good cause.

II. BOARD DUTIES:

1. Register public accounting firms.
2. Establish or adopt, by rule, auditing, quality control, ethics, independence, and other standards relating to the preparation of audit reports for issuers.
3. Conduct inspections of audit firms.
4. Conduct investigations and disciplinary proceedings, and impose appropriate sanctions.
5. Conduct such other duties or functions as necessary and appropriate.
6. Enforce compliance with the Act, the rules of the Board, professional standards, and the securities laws relating to the preparation and issuance of audit reports and the obligations and liabilities of accountants with respect thereto.
7. Set the budget and manage the operations of the Board and its staff.

Source: Sarbanes-Oxley Act of 2002.

---

[12]Paul S. Atkins, "The Sarbanes-Oxley Act of 2002: Goals, Content, and Status of Implementation," Speech by the SEC Commissioner, March 25, 2003, p. 2 of 6. See www.sec.gov/news/speech/spch032503psa.htm.
[13]See http://money.cnn.com/2003/06/30/news/companies/accounting_ethics.reut/index.htm.

RATES OF RETURN IN THE FINANCIAL MARKETS

Earlier in this chapter in discussing "the financing process" we noted that net users of funds (savings-deficit economic units) must compete with one another for the funds supplied by net savers (savings-surplus economic units). Consequently, to obtain financing for projects that will benefit the firm's stockholders, the firm must offer the supplier (savings-surplus unit) a rate of return *competitive* with the next best investment alternative available to that saver (investor). This *rate of return on the next best investment alternative to the saver* is known as the supplier's **opportunity cost of funds**. The opportunity cost concept is crucial in financial management and is referred to often.

opportunity cost of funds

Next we review the levels and variability in rates of return that have occurred over the lengthy period of 1926 to 2003. This review focuses on returns from a wide array of financial instruments. In Chapter 11 we discuss at length the concept of an *overall* cost of capital. Part of that overall cost of capital is attributed to interest rate levels at given points in time. So we follow this initial broad look at interest rate levels with a discussion of the more recent period of 1981 to 2003.

RATES OF RETURN OVER LONG PERIODS

History can tell us a great deal about the returns that investors earn in the financial markets. A primary source for an historical perspective comes from a widely used volume published by Ibbotson Associates, Inc. The volume is updated every year. In the present case it examined the realized rates of return for a wide variety of securities from 1926 through 2003.[14] The study by Ibbotson Associates calculated the average annual rates of return investors earned over the preceding 78 years, along with the average inflation rate for the same period. They also calculated the standard deviations of the returns for each type of security. The concept of standard deviation comes from our statistical colleagues, who use this measurement to indicate quantitatively how much dispersion or variability there is around the mean, or average, value of the item being measured—in this case, the rates of return in the financial markets.

The data are summarized in Figure 2-4. These returns represent the average inflation rate and the average observed rates of return for different types of securities. The average

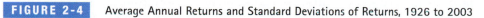

FIGURE 2-4   Average Annual Returns and Standard Deviations of Returns, 1926 to 2003

Source: Ibbotson Associates, *Stocks, Bonds, Bills, and Inflation: 2004 Yearbook* (Chicago: Ibbotson Associates, 2004), p. 33. © Ibbotson Associates. Used by permission.

---

[14]*Stocks, Bonds, Bills, and Inflation: 2004 Yearbook* (Chicago: Ibbotson Associates, 2004).

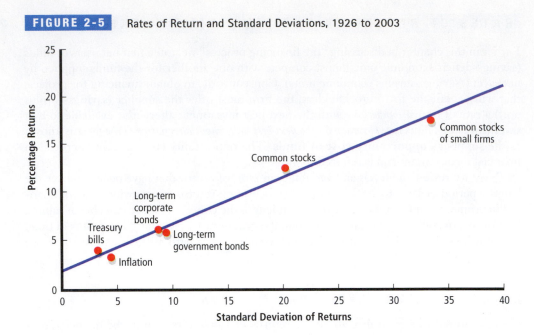

FIGURE 2-5   Rates of Return and Standard Deviations, 1926 to 2003

inflation rate was 3.1 percent for the period covered by the study. We refer to this rate as the "inflation-risk premium." The investor who earns only the rate of inflation has earned no "real return." That is, the *real return* is the return earned above the rate of increase in the general price level for goods and services in the economy, which is the inflation rate. In addition to the danger of not earning above the inflation rate, investors are concerned about the risk of the borrower defaulting, or failing to repay the loan when due. Thus, we would expect a default-risk premium for long-term corporate bonds over long-term government bonds. The premium for 1926 to 2003, as shown in Figure 2-4, was 0.4 percent, or what is called 40 basis points (6.2 percent on long-term corporate bonds minus 5.8 percent on long-term government bonds). We would also expect an even greater risk premium for common stocks vis-à-vis long-term corporate bonds, because the variability in average returns is greater for common stocks. The study verified such a risk premium, with common stocks (all firms) earning 6.2 percent more than the rate earned on long-term corporate bonds (12.4 percent for common stocks minus 6.2 percent for long-term corporate bonds).

Remember that these returns are "averages" across many securities and over an extended period of time. However, these averages reflect the conventional wisdom regarding risk premiums: The greater the risk, the greater will be the expected returns. Such a relationship is shown in Figure 2-5, where the average returns are plotted against their standard deviations; note that higher average returns have historically been associated with higher dispersion in these returns.

Objective **10**

TAKIN' IT TO THE NET

Do you need current interest rate data? Just go to www.federalreserve.gov and you will be at the Federal Reserve Board's Web site. Once you get there, click on "Research and Data." Then examine the H.15 report called "Selected Interest Rates." This provides a long-term perspective on interest rate levels in the United States for a wide variety of instruments.

INTEREST RATE LEVELS OVER RECENT PERIODS

The *nominal* interest rates on some key fixed-income securities are displayed within both Table 2-8 and Figure 2-6 for the most recent 1981–2003 time frame. The rate of inflation at the consumer level is also presented in those two exhibits. This allows us to observe quite easily several concepts that were mentioned in the previous section. Specifically, we can observe (1) the inflation-risk premium, (2) the default-risk premium across the several instruments, and (3) the approximate real return for each instrument. Looking at the mean (average) values for each security and the inflation rate at the bottom of Table 2-8 will facilitate the discussion.

Notice that the average inflation rate over this more recent period is higher than reported in the longer period covered by the Ibbotson Associates analysis. Over the period 1981 to 2003, the consumer price index (December to December change) increased by an average of 3.37 percent each year. According to the logic of the financial markets, investors

FIGURE 2-6   Interest Rate Levels and Inflation Rates, 1981 to 2003

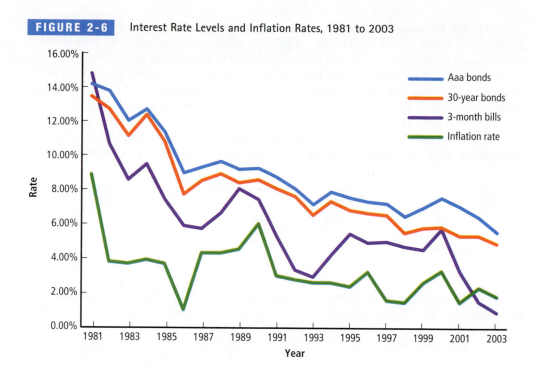

require a nominal rate of interest that exceeds the inflation rate or else their realized *real* return will be negative. Earning a negative return over long periods of time (e.g., 23 years) is not very smart.

TABLE 2-8   Interest Rate Levels and Inflation Rates, 1981 to 2003

YEAR	3-MONTH TREASURY BILLS %	30-YEAR TREASURY BONDS %	Aaa-RATED CORPORATE BONDS %	INFLATION RATE %
1981	14.08	13.44	14.17	8.9
1982	10.69	12.76	13.79	3.9
1983	8.63	11.18	12.04	3.8
1984	9.52	12.39	12.71	4.0
1985	7.49	10.79	11.37	3.8
1986	5.98	7.80	9.02	1.1
1987	5.82	8.58	9.38	4.4
1988	6.68	8.96	9.71	4.4
1989	8.12	8.45	9.26	4.6
1990	7.51	8.61	9.32	6.1
1991	5.42	8.14	8.77	3.1
1992	3.45	7.67	8.14	2.9
1993	3.02	6.59	7.22	2.7
1994	4.29	7.37	7.97	2.7
1995	5.51	6.88	7.59	2.5
1996	5.02	6.71	7.37	3.3
1997	5.07	6.61	7.26	1.7
1998	4.81	5.58	6.53	1.6
1999	4.64	5.87	7.05	2.7
2000	5.82	5.94	7.62	3.4
2001	3.40	5.43	7.08	1.6
2002	1.61	5.41	6.49	2.4
2003	1.01	4.93	5.66	1.9
Mean	5.98	8.09	8.94	3.37

Source: *Federal Reserve Bulletin*, various issues, *Federal Reserve Statistical Releases* H.15 (519), G.13 (415), various issues, and www.federalreserve.gov/releases. Analysis and presentation by the Dr. Phillips Institute for the Study of American Business Activity, College of Business Administration, University of Central Florida, Orlando, June 9, 2004.

Table 2-8 indicates that investor rationality prevailed. For example, the average return premium demanded on U.S. Treasury bills with a 3-month maturity was 2.61 percent (or 261 basis points) in excess of the inferred inflation-risk premium of 3.37 percent. That is, an average 5.98 percent yield on Treasury bills over the period *minus* the average inflation rate of 3.37 percent over the same period produces a premium of 2.61 percent. This 2.61 percent can be thought of as the real risk-free short-term interest rate that prevailed over the 1981–2003 period.

The default-risk premium is also evident in Table 2-8 and Figure 2-6. If we arrange the securities in these two exhibits from low risk to high risk, the following tabulation results:

SECURITY	AVERAGE YIELD
3-month Treasury bills	5.98
30-year Treasury bonds	8.09
Aaa corporate bonds	8.94

Again, the basic rationale of the financial markets prevailed. The default-risk premium on high-rated (Aaa) corporate bonds relative to long-term Treasury bonds of 30-year maturity was 0.85 percent, or 85 basis points.

The preceding array can also be used to identify another factor that affects interest rate levels. It is referred to as the "maturity premium." This maturity premium arises even if securities possess equal (or approximately equal) odds of default. This is the case with Treasury bills and Treasury bonds, for instance, because the full faith and credit of the U.S. government stands behind these financial contracts. They are considered risk free (i.e., possessing no chance of default).

Notice that Treasury bonds with a 30-year maturity commanded a 2.11 percent yield differential over the shorter, 3-month-to-maturity Treasury bonds. This provides an estimate of the maturity premium demanded by investors over this specific 1981–2003 period. More precisely, the **maturity premium** can be defined as *the additional return required by investors in longer-term securities (bonds in this case) to compensate them for the greater risk of price fluctuations on those securities caused by interest rate changes.*

maturity premium

When you study the basic mathematics of financial decisions and the characteristics of fixed-income securities in later chapters, you will learn how to quantify this maturity premium that is imbedded in nominal interest rates.

One other type of risk premium that helps determine interest rate levels needs to be identified and defined. It is known as the "liquidity premium." The **liquidity premium** is defined as *the additional return required by investors in securities that cannot be quickly converted into cash at a reasonably predictable price.*

liquidity premium

The secondary markets for small-bank stocks, especially community banks, provide a good example of the liquidity premium. A bank holding company that trades on the New York Stock Exchange, such as SunTrust Bank, will be more liquid to investors than, say, the common stock of Century National Bank of Orlando, Florida. Such a liquidity premium is reflected across the spectrum of financial assets, from bonds to stocks.

CONCEPT CHECK

1. What is the "opportunity cost of funds"?
2. Over long periods of time is the "real rate of return" higher on common stocks or long-term government bonds?
3. Distinguish between the concepts of the "inflation-risk premium" and the "default-risk premium."
4. Distinguish between the concepts of the "maturity premium" and the "liquidity premium."

ACROSS THE HALL

ECONOMICS—COMMERCIAL BANKING AND THE IMPORTANCE OF INTEREST RATES

Comments by Mr. Paul Garland

Mr. Paul Garland is senior vice president, commercial real estate for Franklin Bank, SSB, of Houston, Texas. The parent bank, Franklin Bank Corp., had assets exceeding $3.5 billion at the end of 2004. Most of Mr. Garland's operating responsibilities involve the state of Florida, the nation's fourth largest in terms of population and home of vibrant commercial and private real estate markets. Mr. Garland's broader oversight and activities extend across the eastern United States and cover land acquisition and builder revolving lines of credit. He has over 20 years of commercial-banking experience and holds an M.B.A. degree from Stetson University and a B.B.A. from the Walsh College of Accountancy and Business Administration. He is a graduate of the Robert Morris Associates School of Commercial Banking. Mr. Garland has also authored articles on bank-related activities for several banking publications.

Interest rates, expected inflation rates, and default risk of prospective borrowers are all important to Mr. Garland's work and decisions. His comments on these areas follow.

Many banks utilize a return on asset or equity (ROA/E) model in the underwriting process as a tool for making loan investment decisions. Inputs to a model may include the loan amount, projected balances, term, asset classification, opportunity cost of funds, applicable interest rate index with premium, allocated corporate fixed costs, and other factors.

The interest rate determinants are imbedded in the model by corporate financial analysts and considered in conjunction with the inputs discussed (i.e., the maturity premium is tied to the loan term). However, the underwriter usually determines a portion of the default-risk premium input by grading the loan for tangible internal factors and intangible external factors. The criteria utilized in building the loan grade will usually involve to some extent the "Five C's of Credit"—character, capacity, capital, collateral, and conditions.

- Character reflects the aptitude, skills, experience, and morality of the management of the entity being granted the loan and is somewhat intangible.
- Capacity reflects the liquidity and cash flow generating capability of the borrowing entity and its ability to repay debt and can be reflected through ratio and other analysis.
- Capital reflects the amount of financial support the borrowing entity exhibits and may be measured by leverage ratios.
- Collateral represents the liquidity of the asset supporting the investment and may be measured by loan-to-value or other such ratios.
- Conditions account for the state and trend of the economy, the industry, and other factors and are more subjective.

The loan grade is utilized to determine the amount of bank capital (equity and loan loss reserves) that must be allocated to support the loan and the expected losses associated with it. The model as a whole proves the loan being made is supported by an adequate interest rate as it calculates the yield to maturity inferred from the ROA/E, which can be compared to minimum standards for the loan considered.

BACK TO THE FOUNDATIONS

Our first principle, **Principle 1: The Risk–Return Trade-Off—We Won't Take On Additional Risk Unless We Expect to Be Compensated with Additional Return**, established the fundamental risk–return trade-offs that govern the financial markets. We are now trying to provide you with an understanding of the kinds of risks that are rewarded in the risk–return trade-off presented in **Principle 1**.

In the previous "Across the Hall" section, but preceding our discussion on interest rate determinants, a skilled commercial banker with over 20 years' experience puts into perspective why managers need some acquaintance with the fundamentals of interest rate levels and determinants. As you read this piece and the section that follows it, please keep in mind that many individuals in commercial-banking positions obtained their training in disciplines such as marketing, management, and economics. Such individuals who choose commercial banking as a career often spend some time in what is called "loan production." The upshot is these individuals need more than a passing familiarity with finance principles. Here the emphasis is on interest rates.

INTEREST RATE DETERMINANTS IN A NUTSHELL

nominal rate of interest

Our review of rates of return and interest rate levels in the financial markets permits us to synthesize our introduction to the different types of risk that impact interest rates. We can, thereby, generate a simple equation with the **nominal** (i.e., observed) **rate of interest** being the output variable from the equation. The nominal interest rate, also called the "quoted" rate, *is the interest rate paid on debt securities without an adjustment for any loss in purchasing power*. It is the rate that you would read about in the *Wall Street Journal* for a specific fixed-income security. That equation follows:

$$k = k^* + IRP + DRP + MP + LP \tag{2-1}$$

where: k = the nominal or observed rate of interest on a specific fixed-income security.

k^* = the real risk-free rate of interest; it is the required rate of interest on a fixed-income security that has no risk and in an economic environment of zero inflation. This can be reasonably thought of as the rate of interest demanded by investors in U.S. Treasury securities during periods of no inflation.

IRP = the inflation-risk premium.

DRP = the default-risk premium.

MP = the maturity premium.

LP = the liquidity premium.

Sometimes in analyzing interest rate relationships over time it is of use to focus on what is called the "nominal risk-free rate of interest." Again, by nominal we mean "observed." So let us designate the nominal risk-free interest rate as k_{rf}. Drawing, then, on our previous discussions and notation we can write this expression for k_{rf}

$$k_{rf} = k^* + IRP \tag{2-2}$$

TAKIN' IT TO THE NET

Timely data that enable you to estimate your own inflation-risk premium (IRP) are available at stats.bls.gov. This site from the U.S. Bureau of Labor Statistics gives you the current consumer price index report. Note that you do not enter '"www" with this site.

This equation says that the nominal risk-free rate of interest is equal to the real risk-free interest rate plus the inflation-risk premium. It also provides a quick and *approximate* way of estimating the real risk-free rate of interest, k^*, by solving directly for this rate. The basic relationship in equation (2-2) contains important information for the financial decision maker. It has also for years been the subject of fascinating and lengthy discussions among financial economists.

ESTIMATING SPECIFIC INTEREST RATES USING RISK PREMIUMS: AN EXAMPLE

By using our knowledge of various risk premia as contained in equation (2-1), the financial manager can generate useful information for the firm's financial planning process. For instance, if the firm is about to offer a new issue of corporate bonds to the investing marketplace, it is possible for the financial manager or analyst to estimate what interest rate (yield) would satisfy the market and help ensure that the bonds are actually bought by investors. It would be unwise for the firm to offer too high of a yield because it will incur unnecessary interest expense that will negatively impact earnings. On the other hand, offering too low of a yield will hinder the bonds from being attractive to investors (savers) in a competitive marketplace. The following example should help clarify and illustrate this situation.

PROBLEM SITUATION

You have been asked to provide a reasonable estimate of the nominal interest rate for a new issue of Aaa-rated bonds to be offered by Big Truck Producers, Inc. The final format that the chief financial officer (CFO) of Big Truck has requested is that of equation (2-1). Your assignment also requires that you consult the data in Table 2-8.

Some agreed-upon procedures related to generating estimates for key variables in equation (2-1) follow:

1. The financial market environment over the 1996–1998 period is considered representative of the prospective tone of the market near the time of offering the new bonds to the

investing public. This means that 3-year averages are used as benchmarks for some of the variable estimates. All estimates are rounded off to hundredths of a percent; thus, 6.288 becomes 6.29 percent.

2. The real risk-free rate of interest is the difference between the calculated average yield on 3-month Treasury bills and the average inflation rate.

3. The default-risk premium is estimated by the difference between the average yield on Aaa-rated bonds and 30-year Treasury bonds.

4. The maturity premium is estimated by the difference between the average yield on 30-year Treasury bonds and 3-month Treasury bills.

5. Big Truck's bonds will be traded on the New York Exchange for Bonds, so the liquidity premium will be slight. It will be greater than zero, however, because the secondary market for the firm's bonds is more uncertain than that of some other truck producers. It is estimated at 3 basis points. A basis point is one hundredth of 1 percent.

Now place your output into the format of equation (2-1) so that the nominal interest rate can be estimated and the size of each variable can also be inspected for reasonableness and discussion with the CFO.

SOLUTION

Let's look at the building blocks that comprise our forecast of the nominal interest rate on Big Truck's new issue of bonds. The nominal rate (k) that is forecast to satisfy the market is 7.08 percent. The following tables illustrate how we obtained this estimate. The first table generates the 3-year averages thought to be representative of the basic financial market environment. The second table is a worksheet that "builds up" the nominal interest rate. It's just equation (2-1) in worksheet form.

YEAR	(1) 3-MONTH TREASURY BILLS (%)	(2) 30-YEAR TREASURY BONDS (%)	(3) Aaa-RATED CORPORATE BONDS (%)	(4) INFLATION RATE (%)
1996	5.02	6.71	7.37	3.30
1997	5.07	6.61	7.26	1.70
1998	4.81	5.58	6.53	1.60
Mean	4.97	6.30	7.05	2.20

Thus, the real risk-free rate of interest is estimated to be 2.77 percent; it is the difference between the 3-year average yield on 3-month Treasury bills and the inflation rate (column 1 minus column 4). In similar fashion, the inflation-risk premium of 2.20 percent (*IRP*) is the 3-year average of the inflation rate (column 4). The default-risk premium (*DRP*) is the difference in the 3-year average rates that were available to investors in Aaa-rated bonds and Treasury bonds with a 30-year maturity (column 3 minus column 2). The maturity premium (*MP*) of 1.33 percent is the difference in the 3-year average rates that were earned by investors in 30-year Treasury bonds and 3-month Treasury bills (column 2 minus column 1). And the liquidity premium (*LP*) of 3 basis points was estimated for us by a sharp financial analyst like yourself.

TABLE COLUMNS (FROM PREVIOUS TABLE)	EQUATION (2-1)	
(1)–(4)	k^*	2.77
	+	+
(4)	*IRP*	2.20
	+	+
(3)–(2)	*DRP*	0.75
	+	+
(2)–(1)	*MP*	1.33
	+	+
Given	*LP*	0.03
	=	=
	k	7.08

When we put this all together as an estimate of the nominal interest rate needed to satisfy the financial markets on Big Truck's new bond issue, we have

$$k = k^* + IRP + DRP + MP + LP = \text{nominal rate on Big Truck's bonds}$$
$$k = 2.77 + 2.20 + 0.75 + 1.33 + 0.03 = 7.08\%$$

Understanding this analysis will help you deal with the comprehensive problems at the end of this chapter. We now move to an examination of the relationship between real and nominal interest rates.

THE EFFECTS OF INFLATION ON RATES OF RETURN AND THE FISHER EFFECT

real rate of interest

When a rate of interest is quoted, it is generally the nominal, or observed rate. The **real rate of interest**, on the other hand, represents *the rate of increase in actual purchasing power, after adjusting for inflation*. For example, if you have $100 today and lend it to someone for a year at a nominal rate of interest of 11.3 percent, you will get back $111.30 in 1 year. But if during the year prices of goods and services rise by 5 percent, it will take $105 at year-end to purchase the same goods and services that $100 purchased at the beginning of the year. What was your increase in purchasing power over the year? The quick and dirty answer is found by subtracting the inflation rate from the nominal rate, $11.3\% - 5\% = 6.3\%$, but this is not exactly correct. To be more precise, let the nominal rate of interest be represented by k_{rf}, the anticipated rate of inflation by IRP, and the real rate of interest by k^*. Using these notations, we can express the relationship among the nominal interest rate, the rate of inflation, and the real rate of interest as follows:

$$1 + k_{rf} = (1 + k^*)(1 + IRP) \tag{2-3}$$

or

$$k_{rf} = k^* + IRP + (k^* \cdot IRP)$$

Consequently, the nominal rate of interest (k_{rf}) is equal to the sum of the real rate of interest (k^*), the inflation rate (IRP), and the product of the real rate and the inflation rate. This relationship among nominal rates, real rates, and the rate of inflation has come to be called the *Fisher effect*.[15] It means that the observed nominal rate of interest includes both the real rate and an *inflation premium* as noted in the previous section.

Substituting into equation (2-3) using a nominal rate of 11.3 percent and an inflation rate of 5 percent, we can calculate the real rate of interest, k^*, as follows:

$$k_{rf} = k^* + IRP + (k^* \cdot IRP)$$
$$.113 = k^* + .05 + .05k^*$$
$$k^* = .06 = 6\%$$

Thus, at the new higher prices, your purchasing power will have increased by only 6 percent, although you have $11.30 more than you had at the start of the year. To see why, let's assume that at the outset of the year one unit of the market basket of goods and services costs $1, so you could purchase 100 units with your $100. At the end of the year you have $11.30 more, but each unit now costs 1.05 (remember the 5 percent rate of inflation). How many units can you buy at the end of the year? The answer is $111.30 \div \$1.05 = 106$, which represents a 6 percent increase in real purchasing power.[16]

INFLATION AND REAL RATES OF RETURN: THE FINANCIAL ANALYST'S APPROACH

Although the algebraic methodology presented in the previous section is strictly correct, few practicing analysts or executives use it. Rather, they employ some version of the

---

[15]This relationship was analyzed many years ago by Irving Fisher. For those who want to explore "Fisher's theory of interest" in more detail, a fine overview is contained in Peter N. Ireland, "Long-Term Interest Rates and Inflation: A Fisherian Approach," *Federal Reserve Bank of Richmond, Economic Quarterly* 82 (Winter 1996), pp. 22–26.

[16]In Chapter 5 we study more about the time value of money.

following relationship, an approximation method, to estimate the real rate of interest over a selected past time frame.

(nominal interest rate) − (inflation rate) = real interest rate

The concept is straightforward, but implementation requires that several judgments be made. For example, which interest rate series and maturity period should be used? Suppose we settle for using some U.S. Treasury security as a surrogate for a nominal risk-free interest rate. Then, should we use the yield on 3-month U.S. Treasury bills or, perhaps, that on 30-year Treasury bonds? There is no absolute answer to the question.

So, we can have a real risk-free short-term interest rate, as well as a real risk-free long-term interest rate, and several variations in between. In essence, it just depends on what the analyst wants to accomplish. We could also calculate the real rate of interest on some rating class of corporate bonds (like Aaa-rated bonds) and have a risky real rate of interest as opposed to a real risk-free interest rate.

Furthermore, the choice of a proper inflation index is equally challenging. Again, we have several choices. We could use the consumer price index, the producer price index for finished goods, or some price index out of the national income accounts, such as the gross domestic product chain price index. Again, there is no precise scientific answer as to which specific price index to use. Logic and consistency do narrow the boundaries of the ultimate choice.

Let's tackle a very basic (simple) example. Suppose that an analyst wants to estimate the approximate real interest rate on (1) 3-month Treasury bills, (2) 30-year Treasury bonds, and (3) Aaa-rated corporate bonds over the 1981–2003 time frame. Furthermore, the annual rate of change in the consumer price index (measured from December to December) is considered a logical measure of past inflation experience. Most of our work is already done for us in Table 2-8. Some of the data from Table 2-8 are displayed here.

SECURITY	MEAN NOMINAL YIELD (%)	MEAN INFLATION RATE (%)	INFERRED REAL RATE (%)
3 month Treasury bills	5.98	3.37	2.61
30 year Treasury bonds	8.09	3.37	4.72
Aaa-rated Corporate bonds	8.94	3.37	5.57

Notice that the mean yield over the 23 years from 1981 to 2003 on all three classes of securities has been used as a reasonable proxy for the ex-post return. Likewise, the mean inflation rate over the same time period has been used as an estimate of the inflation-risk premium (*IRP* from our earlier notation). The last column provides the approximation for the real interest rate on each class of securities.

Thus, over the 23-year examination period the real rate of interest on 3-month Treasury bills was 2.61 percent versus 4.72 percent on 30-year Treasury bonds, versus 5.57 percent on Aaa-rated corporate bonds. These three estimates (approximations) of the real interest rate provide a rough guide to the increase in real purchasing power associated with an investment position in each security. Remember that the real rate on the corporate bonds is expected to be greater than that on long-term government bonds because of the default-risk premium (*DRP*) placed on the corporate securities. We move in the next section to a discussion of the maturity premium (*MP*).

CONCEPT CHECK

1. What is the "nominal rate of interest"? Explain how it differs from the "real rate of interest."
2. Write an equation that includes the building blocks of the nominal rate of interest.

THE TERM STRUCTURE OF INTEREST RATES

Objective **11**

The relationship between a debt security's rate of return and the length of time until the debt matures is known as the **term structure of interest rates** or the **yield to maturity**. For the relationship to be meaningful to us, all the factors other than maturity, meaning factors

term structure of interest rates
yield to maturity

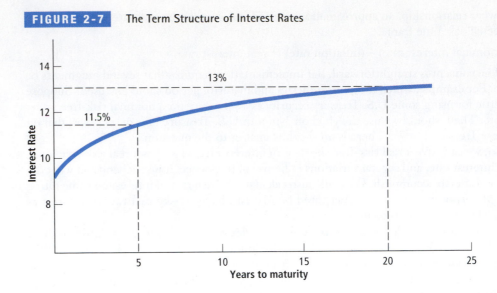

FIGURE 2-7   The Term Structure of Interest Rates

such as the chance of the bond defaulting, must be held constant. Thus, *the term structure reflects observed rates or yields on similar securities, except for the length of time until maturity, at a particular moment in time.*

Figure 2-7 shows an example of the term structure of interest rates. The curve is upward sloping, indicating that longer terms to maturity command higher returns, or yields. In this hypothetical term structure, the rate of interest on a 5-year note or bond is 11.5 percent, whereas the comparable rate on a 20-year bond is 13 percent.

OBSERVING HISTORICAL TERM STRUCTURES OF INTEREST RATES

As we might expect, the term structure of interest rates changes over time, depending on the environment. The particular term structure observed today may be quite different from the term structure a month ago and different still from the term structure 1 month from now. A perfect example of the changing term structure, or yield curve, was witnessed during the early days of the Persian Gulf Crisis in August 1990. Figure 2-8 shows the yield curves 1 day before the Iraqi invasion of Kuwait and then again just 3 weeks later. The change is noticeable, particularly for long-term interest rates. Investors quickly developed new fears about

FIGURE 2-8   Changes in the Term Structure of Interest Rates for Government Securities at the Outbreak of the Persian Gulf Crisis

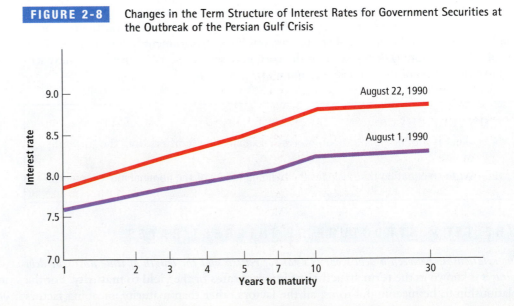

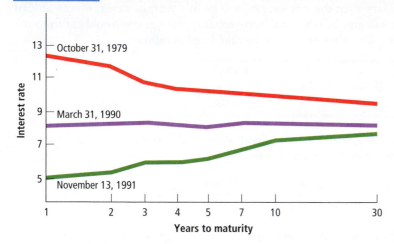

FIGURE 2-9 Historical Term Structures of Interest Rates for Government Securities

the prospect of increased inflation to be caused by the crisis and, consequently, increased their required rates of return. Although the upward-sloping term-structure curves in Figures 2-7 and 2-8 are the ones most commonly observed, yield curves can assume several shapes. Sometimes the term structure is downward sloping; at other times it rises and then falls (humpbacked); and at still other times it may be relatively flat. Figure 2-9 shows some yield curves at different points in time.

TRYING TO EXPLAIN THE SHAPE OF THE TERM STRUCTURE

A number of theories may explain the shape of the term structure of interest rates at any point. Three possible explanations are prominent: (1) the unbiased expectations theory, (2) the liquidity preference theory, and (3) the market segmentation theory.[17] Let's look at each in turn.

THE UNBIASED EXPECTATIONS THEORY

The **unbiased expectations theory** says that *the term structure is determined by an investor's expectations about future interest rates.*[18] To see how this works, consider the following investment problem faced by Mary Maxell. Mary has $10,000 that she wants to invest for 2 years, at which time she plans to use her savings to make a down payment on a new home. Wanting not to take any risk of losing her savings, she decides to invest in U.S. government securities. She has two choices. First, she can purchase a government security that matures in 2 years, which offers her an interest rate of 9 percent per year. If she does this, she will have $11,881 in 2 years, calculated as follows:[19]

unbiased expectations theory

Principal amount	$10,000
Plus: Year 1 interest (.09 × $10,000)	900
Principal plus interest at the end of year 1	$10,900
Plus: Year 2 interest (.09 × $10,900)	981
Principal plus interest at the end of year 2	$11,881

Alternatively, Mary could buy a government security maturing in 1 year that pays an 8 percent rate of interest. She would then need to purchase another 1-year security at the end of the first year. Which alternative Mary chooses obviously depends in part on the rate of

[17]See Richard Roll, *The Behavior of Interest Rates: An Application of the Efficient Market Model to U.S. Treasury Bills* (New York: Basic Books, 1970).

[18]Irving Fisher thought of this idea in 1896. The theory was later refined by J. R. Hicks in *Value and Capital* (London: Oxford University Press, 1946) and F. A. Lutz and V. C. Lutz in *The Theory of Investment in the Firm* (Princeton, NJ: Princeton University Press, 1951).

[19]We could also calculate the principal plus interest for Mary's investment using the following compound interest equation: $10,000(1 + .09)^2 = $11,881$. We study the mathematics of compound interest in Chapter 5.

interest she expects to receive on the government security she will purchase a year from now. We cannot tell Mary what the interest rate will be in a year; however, we can at least calculate the rate that will give her the same two-year total savings she would get from her first choice, or $11,881. The interest rate can be calculated as follows:

Savings needed in 2 years	$11,881
Savings at the end of year 1 [$10,000(1 + .08)]	$10,800
Interest needed in year 2	$ 1,081

For Mary to receive $1,081 in the second year, she would have to earn about 10 percent on her second-year investment, computed as follows:

$$\frac{\text{interest received in year 2}}{\text{investment made at beginning of year 2}} = \frac{\$1,081}{\$10,800} = 10\%$$

So the term structure of interest rates for our example consists of the 1-year interest rate of 8 percent and the 2-year rate of 9 percent. This exercise also gives us information about the *expected* 1-year rate for investments made 1 year hence. In a sense, the term structure contains implications about investor expectations of future interest rates; thus, this explains the unbiased expectations theory of the term structure of interest rates.

Although we can see a relationship between current interest rates with different maturities and the investor's expectations about future interest rates, is this the whole story? Are there influences other than the investor's expectations about future interest rates? Probably, so let's continue to think about Mary's dilemma.

LIQUIDITY PREFERENCE THEORY

In presenting Mary's choices, we have suggested that she would be indifferent to a choice between the 2-year government security offering a 9 percent return and two consecutive 1-year investments offering 8 and 10 percent, respectively. However, that would be so only if she is unconcerned about the risk associated with not knowing the rate of interest on the second 1-year security as of today. If Mary is risk averse (that is, she dislikes risk), she might not be satisfied with expectations of a 10 percent return on the second 1-year government security. She might require some additional expected return to be truly indifferent. Mary might in fact decide that she will expose herself to the uncertainty of future interest rates only if she can reasonably *expect* to earn an additional .5 percent in interest, or 10.5 percent, on the second 1-year investment. This *risk premium* (additional required interest rate) to compensate for the risk of changing future interest rates is nothing more than the maturity premium (*MP*) introduced earlier, and this concept underlies the liquidity preference theory of the term structure.[20] In the **liquidity preference theory**, *investors require maturity premiums to compensate them for buying securities that expose them to the risks of fluctuating interest rates.*

liquidity preference theory

MARKET SEGMENTATION THEORY

market segmentation theory

The **market segmentation theory** of the term structure of interest rates is built on the notion that legal restrictions and personal preferences limit choices for investors to certain ranges of maturities. For example, commercial banks prefer short- to medium-term maturities as a result of the short-term nature of their deposit liabilities. They prefer not to invest in long-term securities. Life insurance companies, on the other hand, have long-term liabilities, so they prefer longer maturities in investments. At the extreme, the market segmentation theory implies that *the rate of interest for a particular maturity is determined solely by demand and supply for a given maturity and that it is independent of the demand and supply for securities having different maturities.* A more moderate version of the theory allows investors strong maturity preferences, but it also allows them to modify their feelings and preferences if significant yield inducements occur.

---

[20]This theory was first presented by John R. Hicks in *Value and Capital* (London: Oxford University Press, 1946), pp. 141–145, with the risk premium referred to as the liquidity premium. For our purposes we use the term *maturity premium (MP)* to describe this risk premium, thereby keeping our terminology consistent within this chapter.

FINANCE AND THE MULTINATIONAL FIRM: EFFICIENT FINANCIAL MARKETS AND INTERCOUNTRY RISK

Objective **12**

In this chapter we have discussed and demonstrated that the United States has a highly developed, complex, and competitive system of financial markets that allows for the quick transfer of savings from those economic units with a surplus of savings to those economic units with a savings deficit. Such a system of robust and credible financial markets allows great ideas (e.g., the personal computer) to be financed and increases the overall wealth of the given economy. Real capital formation, such as a Ford Motor Company manufacturing plant in Livonia, Michigan, is enhanced by the financial market mechanism.

One major reason underdeveloped countries are indeed underdeveloped is that they lack a financial market system that has the confidence of those who must use it—such as the multinational firm. The multinational firm with cash to invest in foreign markets will weigh heavily the integrity of both the financial system and the political system of the prospective foreign country.

A lack of integrity on either the financial side or the political stability side retards direct investment in the lesser-developed nation. Consider the Walt Disney Company, headquartered in Burbank, California. Disney common stock trades on the NYSE (ticker symbol DIS), although the firm has significant overseas real investments in projects known as the Disneyland Paris Resort and Tokyo Disneyland. Disney has confidence in the French financial markets, those of western Europe, and Japan. For example, Disney executives launched three new projects in Japan during 1998—a new theme park and two new hotels.[21] However, Disney did not launch any new projects in Thailand, where the basic currency—called the "baht"—lost a full 98 percent of its value against the U.S. dollar over the short period from June 1997 to February 1998. Profits generated in Thailand and measured by the baht would have bought significantly fewer U.S. dollars after the devaluation. This type of situation is typically referred to as foreign exchange rate risk. Currencies, too, trade within financial markets, and those risks are closely studied by wise multinational firms.

SUMMARY

This chapter centers on the market environment in which corporations raise long-term funds, including the structure of the U.S. financial markets, the institution of investment banking, and the various methods for distributing securities. It also discusses the role of interest rates in allocating savings to ultimate investment.

Mix of corporate securities sold

When corporations go the capital market for cash, the most favored financing method is debt. The corporate debt markets clearly dominate the equity markets when new funds are raised. The U.S. tax system inherently favors debt capital as a fund-raising method. In an average year over the 1998–2000 period, bonds and notes made up 73.6 percent of the external cash that was raised.

Objective **1**

Objective **2**

---

[21]The Walt Disney Company, *Annual Report*, 1998, pp. 24–25, 57.

Primarily because of the transaction costs involved, corporations prefer to finance new investments out of internally generated funds before external sources of funds are tapped. Table 2-1 showed that from 62.5 percent to 90.3 percent of business sources of funds over the 1990–2000 period were generated via internal sources.

Objective **3**

Why financial markets exist
The function of financial markets is to allocate savings efficiently in the economy to the ultimate demander (user) of the savings. In a financial market the forces of supply and demand for a specific financial instrument are brought together. The wealth of an economy would not be as great as it is without a fully developed financial market system.

Objective **4**

Financing of business
Typically, households are a net supplier of funds to the financial markets. The nonfinancial business sector is usually a net borrower of funds. Both life insurance companies and private pension funds are important buyers of corporate securities. Savings are ultimately transferred to the business firm seeking cash by means of (1) the direct transfer, (2) the indirect transfer using the investment banker, or (3) the indirect transfer using the financial intermediary.

Objective **5**

Components of the U.S. financial market system
Corporations can raise funds through public offerings or private placements. The public market is impersonal in that the security issuer does not meet the ultimate investors in the financial instruments. In a private placement, the securities are sold directly to a limited number of institutional investors.

The primary market is the market for new issues. The secondary market represents transactions in currently outstanding securities. Both the money and capital markets have primary and secondary sides. The money market refers to transactions in short-term debt instruments. The capital market, on the other hand, refers to transactions in long-term financial instruments. Trading in the capital markets can occur in either the organized security exchanges or the over-the-counter market. The money market is exclusively an over-the-counter market.

Objective **6**

Investment banker
The investment banker is a financial specialist involved as an intermediary in the merchandising of securities. He or she performs the functions of (1) underwriting, (2) distributing, and (3) advising. Major methods for the public distribution of securities include (1) the negotiated purchase, (2) the competitive bid purchase, (3) the commission or best-efforts basis, (4) privileged subscriptions, and (5) direct sales. The direct sale bypasses the use of an investment banker. The negotiated purchase is the most profitable distribution method to the investment banker. It also provides the greatest amount of investment-banking services to the corporate client.

Objective **7**

Private placements
Privately placed debt provides an important market outlet for corporate bonds. Major investors in this market are (1) life insurance firms, (2) state and local retirement funds, and (3) private pension funds. Several advantages and disadvantages are associated with private placements. The financial officer must weight these attributes and decide if a private placement is preferable to a public offering.

Objective **8**

Flotation costs and regulation
Flotation costs consist of the underwriter's spread and issuing costs. The flotation costs of common stock exceed those of preferred stock, which, in turn, exceed those of debt. Moreover, flotation costs as a percent of gross proceeds are inversely related to the size of the security issue.

The new issues market is regulated at the federal level by the Securities Act of 1933. It provides for the registration of new issues with the SEC. Secondary market trading is regulated by the Securities Exchange Act of 1934. The Securities Acts Amendments of 1975 placed on the SEC the responsibility to devise a national market system. This concept is still being studied. The shelf registration procedure (SEC Rule 415) was initiated in March 1982. Under this regulation and with the proper filing of documents, firms that are selling new issues do not have to go through the old, lengthy registration process each time firms plan an offering of securities.

On July 30, 2002, President Bush signed into law the Public Company Accounting Reform and Investor Protection Act. This act is commonly known as the Sarbanes-Oxley Act of 2002. Its intended purpose as stated in the act is "to protect investors by improving the accuracy and reliability of corporate disclosures made pursuant to the securities laws, and for other purposes."

Objective **9**

The logic of rates of return and interest rate determination
The financial markets give managers an informed indication of investors' opportunity costs. The more efficient the market, the more informed the indication. This information is a useful input about the rates of return that investors require on financial claims. In turn, this becomes useful to financial managers as they estimate the overall cost of capital used as a screening rate in the capital budgeting process.

Rates of return on various securities are based on the underlying supply of loanable funds (savings) and the demand for those loanable funds. In addition to a risk-free return, investors will want to be compensated for the potential loss of purchasing power resulting from inflation. Moreover, investors require a greater return the greater the default risk, maturity premium, and liquidity premium are on the securities being analyzed.

Objective **10**

The multinational firm: efficient financial markets and intercountry risk

Objective **11**

A system of robust and credible financial markets allows great ideas to be financed and increases the overall wealth of a given economy. The multinational firm with cash to invest in foreign markets will weigh heavily the integrity of both the financial system and the political system of the prospective foreign country where the proposed investment project will be domiciled. A lack of integrity on either the financial side or the political stability side retards direct investment in a less-developed nation.

Objective **12**

KEY TERMS

Capital market, 42
Direct placement, 42
Direct sale, 47
Direct securities, 38
Financial assets, 37
Financial markets, 37
Flotation costs, 50
Indirect securities, 38
Investment banker, 45
Liquidity preference theory, 66
Liquidity premium, 58
Market segmentation theory, 66

Maturity premium, 58
Money market, 42
Nominal rate of interest, 60
Opportunity cost of funds, 55
Organized security exchanges, 42
Over-the-counter markets, 42
Primary markets, 42
Private placement, 42
Privileged subscription, 47

Public offering, 41
Real assets, 37
Real rate of interest, 62
Secondary markets, 38
Shelf offering, 52
Shelf registration, 52
Syndicate, 45
Term structure of interest rates, 63
Unbiased expectations theory, 65
Underwriting, 45
Yield to maturity, 63

STUDY QUESTIONS

2-1. What are financial markets? What function do they perform? How would an economy be worse off without them?

2-2. Define in a technical sense what we mean by *financial intermediary*. Give an example of your definition.

2-3. Distinguish between the money and capital markets.

2-4. What major benefits do corporations and investors enjoy because of the existence of organized security exchanges?

2-5. What are the general categories examined by an organized exchange in determining whether an applicant firm's securities can be listed on it? (Specific numbers are not needed here but rather areas of investigation.)

2-6. Why do you think most secondary-market trading in bonds takes place over the counter?

2-7. What is an investment banker, and what major functions does he or she perform?

2-8. What is the major difference between a negotiated purchase and a competitive bid purchase?

2-9. Why is an investment-banking syndicate formed?

2-10. Why might a large corporation want to raise long-term capital through a private placement rather than a public offering?

2-11. As a recent business school graduate, you work directly for the corporate treasurer. Your corporation is going to issue a new security and is concerned with the probable flotation costs. What tendencies about flotation costs can you relate to the treasurer?

2-12. When corporations raise funds, what type of financing vehicle (instrument or instruments) is most favored?

2-13. What is the major (most significant) savings-surplus sector in the U.S. economy?

2-14. Identify three distinct ways that savings are ultimately transferred to business firms in need of cash.

2-15. Explain the term *opportunity cost* with respect to cost of funds to the firm.

2-16. Compare and explain the historical rates of return for different types of securities.

2-17. Explain the impact of inflation on rates of return.

2-18. Define the *term structure of interest rates*.

2-19. Explain the popular theories for the rationale of the term structure of interest rates.

STUDY PROBLEMS

2-1. (*Real interest rates: financial analyst's method*) The CFO of your firm has asked you for an approximate answer to this question: What was the increase in real purchasing power associated with both 3-month Treasury bills and 30-year Treasury bonds over the 2000–2003 period? *Hints:* (1) Consult Table 2-8 in the text, and (2) simple averages on the key variables will provide a defensible response to your boss. Also, the chief financial officer wants a short explanation should the 3-month real rate of return turn out to be *less* than the 30-year real rate.

2-2. (*Real interest rates: financial analyst's method*) The CFO of your firm has asked you for an approximate answer to this question: What was the increase in real purchasing power associated with both 3-month Treasury bills and 30-year Treasury bonds over the 1991–1995 period? Hints: (1) Consult Table 2-8 in the text, and (2) simple averages on the key variables will provide a defensible response to your boss. Also, the chief financial officer wants a short explanation should the 3-month real rate turn out to be *less* than the 30-year real rate.

2-3. (*Inflation and interest rates*) What would you expect the nominal rate of interest to be if the real rate is 4 percent and the expected inflation rate is 7 percent?

2-4. (*Inflation and interest rates*) Assume the expected inflation rate to be 4 percent. If the current real rate of interest is 6 percent, what ought the nominal rate of interest be?

2-5. (*Inflation and interest rates*) Assume the expected inflation rate to be 5 percent. If the current real rate of interest is 7 percent, what would you expect the nominal rate of interest to be?

2-6. (*Term structure of interest rates*) You want to invest your savings of $20,000 in government securities for the next 2 years. Currently, you can invest either in a security that pays interest of 8 percent per year for the next 2 years or in a security that matures in 1 year but pays only 6 percent interest. If you make the latter choice, you would then reinvest your savings at the end of the first year for another year.

    a. Why might you choose to make the investment in the 1-year security that pays an interest rate of only 6 percent, as opposed to investing in the 2-year security paying 8 percent? Provide numerical support for your answer. Which theory of term structure have you supported in your answer?

    b. Assume your required rate of return on the second-year investment is 11 percent; otherwise, you will choose to go with the 2-year security. What rationale could you offer for your preference?

WEB WORKS

2-WW1. A table within the introduction to this chapter identified all of the U.S. business cycle contractions since the end of World War II. Visit the Web site of the National Bureau of Economic Research at **www.nber.org** and determine the average duration of all economic contractions over the 1854–2001 period and for all "peacetime" recessions over this same time span. Over all cycles, is this average duration much different?

2-WW2. Negative real interest rates occur when the rate of inflation exceeds the rate of interest on fixed-income financing instruments such as corporate bonds, government bonds, and U.S. Treasury bills. Negative real rates of interest generally are associated with slow periods of economic growth. During such periods, corporations usually prefer to raise external cash via new debt issues rather than equity issues. Two Web sites can give you insights into whether current real rates of interest are negative or positive. Visit **www.federalreserve.gov** to check on the H.15 Selected Interest Rates report to assess nominal interest rates. Then check on **stats.bls.gov** to assess several different inflation indices. Estimate the level of the real rate of interest on the 10-year Treasury note (and any other maturity period that excites you), using more than one inflation index. *Hint:* The consumer price index and producer price index for finished goods are two indicators commonly used by security and financial analysts.

2-WW3. Again, we will consult the central bank of the United States—the Federal Reserve. Go to **www.federalreserve.gov** and use your abilities to ascertain (1) how many times and (2) in what direction the Federal Open Market Committee (FOMC) has changed the target federal funds rate since January 2005. Additionally, what is the most recent level for this target federal funds rate? Given that knowledge, where would you place the commercial-banking prime lending rate—that is, at what percent?

COMPREHENSIVE PROBLEMS

2-1. You have been asked to provide a reasonable estimate of the nominal interest rate for a new issue of Aaa-rated bonds to be offered by Big Truck Producers, Inc. The final format that the chief financial officer of Big Truck has requested is that of equation (2-1) in the text. Your assignment also requires that you consult the data in Table 2-8.

Some agreed-upon procedures related to generating estimates for key variables in equation (2-1) follow.

a. The financial market environment over the 1993–1995 period is considered representative of the prospective tone of the market near the time of offering the new bonds to the investing public. This means that 3-year averages will be used as benchmarks for some of the variable estimates. All estimates are rounded off to hundredths of a percent; thus, 6.288 becomes 6.29 percent.

b. The real risk-free rate of interest is the difference between the calculated average yield on 3-month Treasury bills and the inflation rate.

c. The default-risk premium is estimated by the difference between the average yield on Aaa-rated bonds and 30-year Treasury bonds.

d. The maturity premium is estimated by the difference between the average yield on 30-year Treasury bonds and 3-month Treasury bills.

e. Big Truck's bonds will be traded on the New York Bond Exchange, so the liquidity premium will be slight. It will be greater than zero, however, because the secondary market for the firm's bonds is more uncertain than that of some other truck producers. It is estimated at 3 basis points. A basis point is one hundredth of 1 percent.

Now place your output into the format of equation (2-1) so that the nominal interest rate can be estimated and the size of each variable can also be inspected for reasonableness and discussion with the CFO.

2-2. You have been asked to provide a reasonable estimate of the nominal interest rate for a new issue of Aaa-rated bonds to be offered by SanBlas Jewels, Inc. The final format that the chief financial officer of SanBlas Jewels has requested is that of equation (2-1) in the text. Your assignment also requires that you consult the data in Table 2-8.

Some agreed-upon procedures related to generating estimates for key variables in equation (2-1) follow.

a. The financial market environment over the 2000–2003 period is considered representative of the prospective tone of the market near the time of offering the new bonds to the investing public. This means that 4-year averages will be used as benchmarks for some of the variable estimates. All estimates are rounded off to hundredths of a percent; thus, 3.688 becomes 3.69 percent.

b. The real risk-free rate of interest is the difference between the calculated average yield on 3-month Treasury bills and the inflation rate.

c. The default-risk premium is estimated by the difference between the average yield on Aaa-rated bonds and 30-year Treasury bonds.

d. The maturity premium is estimated by the difference between the average yield on 30-year Treasury bonds and 3-month Treasury bills.

e. SanBlas Jewels' bonds will be traded on the New York Bond Exchange, so the liquidity premium will be slight. It will be greater than zero, however, because the secondary market for the firm's bonds is more uncertain than that of some other jewel sellers. It is estimated at 4 basis points. A basis point is one hundredth of 1 percent.

Now place your output into the format of equation (2-1) so that the nominal interest rate can be estimated and the size of each variable can also be inspected for reasonableness and discussion with the CFO.

CHAPTER 3

Understanding Financial Statements and Cash Flows

INCOME STATEMENT • BALANCE SHEET • MEASURING CASH FLOWS

The announcement of its profits is a significant event for a firm. For publicly traded firms, this event occurs on a quarterly basis—much too often to suit many managers. On the other hand, investors eagerly await the announcement so they can compare the actual earnings with their expectations. There is a lot of pressure on a firm to meet investors' earnings expectations; otherwise, the company's stock price may fall significantly if the earnings are less than expected. To see what a firm might say in an earnings release, let's look at Starbucks Corporation's earnings announcement for 2004 released on November 10, 2004.

> Starbucks Corporation (NASDAQ:SBUX) today announced revenues and earnings for its fiscal fourth quarter and fiscal year ended October 3, 2004.
>
> For the 2004 fiscal year, revenues increased 30 percent to $5.3 billion from $4.1 billion for fiscal 2003. Net revenues increased 27 percent. Earnings for fiscal 2004 increased 46 percent to $392 million from $268 million for fiscal 2003.

"Fiscal 2004 has been an amazing year of outstanding performance throughout our business," stated Howard Schultz, chairman. "Our aggressive global store expansion, innovation ranging from food and beverage to music and execution of new and expanded agreements for licensing, grocery and foodservice all contributed to our results. We look forward to building on this momentum in fiscal 2005."

"We achieved remarkable financial results during fiscal 2004," stated Orin Smith, president and CEO. "In addition to posting the first year of double-digit sales increase in more than a decade—a particularly notable accomplishment … ."

Sounds like good news for Starbucks. But not according to investors. They expected more, and as a result, the firm's stock price fell about 3 percent. In the words of Dan Geiman, an investment analyst, "In the past they have tended to beat [expectations] … Some investors were hoping for a little bit more." So it matters not only what a firm earns but also how it compares to investors' expectations.

≪ WHAT'S AHEAD ≫

In Chapter 2, we looked at the workings of the financial markets. We found that these markets provide the means for bringing together investors (savers) with the users of capital (businesses that provide products and services to the consumer). There we looked at the world as the economist sees it, with an eye for understanding the marketplace where managers go to acquire capital. It is the investors in these financial markets who determine the value of a firm, and given our goal of maximizing shareholder value, no issue is more fundamental to our study. However, we now want to alter our perspective.

In this chapter, we view the world of finance more as an accountant sees it. To begin, we review the two basic financial statements that are used to understand how a firm is doing financially: the income statement, or what is sometimes called the profit and loss statement, and the balance sheet. Our goal is not to make you an accountant but instead to provide you

with the tools to understand a firm's financial situation. Without this knowledge you will be unable to understand the financial consequences of company decisions and actions—including your own.

The financial performance of a firm matters to a lot of groups—the company's management, its employees, and its investors, just to name a few. If you are an employee, the firm's performance is important to you for it determines your annual bonus, your job security, and your opportunity to advance your professional career. This is true whether you are in the marketing department, in human resources, or in the finance area. Moreover, a new or experienced employee who can see how decisions affect a firm's finances has a competitive advantage. So regardless of your position in the firm, it is in your own best interest to know the basics of financial statements—even if accounting is not your greatest love.

Let's begin our review of financial statements by looking at the format and content of the income statement.

Objective

income statement (profit and loss statement)

INCOME STATEMENT

An **income statement**, or **profit and loss statement**, indicates the amount of profits generated by a firm over a given time period, often a year. In its most basic form, the income statement may be represented as follows:

Sales – expense = profits

cost of goods sold
gross profit
operating expenses

operating income

The format for an income statement is shown in Figure 3-1. The income statement begins with sales or revenue, from which we subtract **cost of goods sold** (the cost of producing or acquiring the product or service) to yield **gross profit**. Next, **operating expenses**, consisting of marketing and selling expenses, general and administrative expenses, and depreciation expense, are deducted to determine **operating income** (also called *operating profits* or *earnings before interest and taxes* or *EBIT*).

FIGURE 3-1   The Income Statement: An Overview

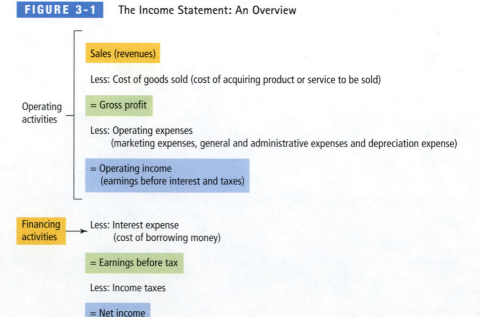

In Figure 3-1, we see that operating income is the result of management's decisions relating to the *operations* of the business. That is, *financing* expenses (interest expense resulting from the use of debt financing) have not been subtracted to this point.

Thus, the operating income of a firm reports the results of the following activities:

1. the *pricing* decisions for the products or services and the *number of units* sold (*selling price × units sold = total sales*)
2. the *cost* of producing or acquiring the goods or services that were sold (*cost of goods sold*)
3. the expenses incurred in selling and marketing the firm's products or services
4. the firm's overhead expenses (*general and administrative expenses* and *depreciation expenses*)

We then determine **earnings before taxes** by deducting the **financing costs**—the firm's interest expense on its debt—from the operating income. Next, the firm's income taxes are calculated, based on its earnings before taxes and the applicable tax rate for the amount of income reported. For instance, if a firm had earnings before taxes of $100,000 and its tax rate is 28 percent, then it would owe $28,000 in taxes (0.28 × $100,000 = $28,000).

earnings before taxes
financing costs

The resulting number is the **net income available to owners** (usually called **net income**), which represents income that may be reinvested in the firm or distributed to its owners—provided, of course, the cash is available to do so. As you will come to understand, *a positive net income on an income statement does not necessarily mean that a firm has generated positive cash flows*.

net income available to owners (net income)

INCOME STATEMENT: STARBUCKS CORPORATION

Table 3-1 contains the 2003 income statement for Starbucks Corporation. Starbucks had *sales* of $4,076 million for the 12-month period ending September 28, 2003, and *cost of goods sold* was $3,207 million. (The numbers for Starbucks are expressed in millions, so Starbucks' sales were actually about $4 billion, with cost of goods sold over $3.2 billion.) The result is a *gross profit* of $869 million. The firm then had $433 million in operating

TABLE 3-1	Starbucks Corporation Income Statement for the Year Ended September 28, 2003 ($ millions)	
Sales		$4,076
Cost of goods sold		3,207
Gross profit		$ 869
Operating expenses:		
Marketing expenses and general and administrative expenses	$227	
Depreciation expense	206	
Total operating expenses		$ 433
Operating income		$ 436
Interest expense		3
Earnings before taxes		$ 433
Income taxes		165
Net income		$ 268

At the completion of the year, a firm's net income, less any dividends paid to stockholders, is added to retained earnings in the balance sheet. For Starbucks Corporation:

Net income	$268
Less common stock dividends	(0)
Increase in retained earnings in the balance sheet	$268

STARBUCKS CORPORATION: A FIRM ON THE GO

It was 1967 and Gordon Bowker was upset about the decline in the quality of Seattle coffee. So he began buying coffee beans for himself and his friends from Vancouver, British Columbia. Then Bowker, along with two friends, Jerry Baldwin and Zev Siegl, built a store by hand. Today we know the business as the Starbucks Corporation.

Starbucks began by buying its coffee from Peet's Coffee and giving away cups of coffee to "hook customers." By 1982 Starbucks owned five stores, a small roasting facility, and a wholesale business that sold coffee primarily to local restaurants. Also in 1982, Howard Schultz was hired to manage the company's retail stores and marketing, but he left a year later to research espresso and coffee bars in Italy. He later returned to the United States and offered $4 million for the business, which the founders accepted.

Schultz's management philosophy to "hire people smarter than you are and get out of their way" certainly proved successful as Starbucks stores and ventures have grown exponentially from 11 stores in 1987 to 425 stores in 1994, and by late 2004, the firm had over 8,000 locations, employing around 74,000 employees worldwide. Starbucks also operates over 1,500 stores in 31 markets outside North America.

Not bad for such a small beginning resulting from an individual who was dissatisfied with a cup of coffee.

Source: Adapted from "Starbucks Corporation," *International Directory of Company Histories*, vol. 34. St. James Press, 2000. Reproduced in Business and Company Resource Center. Farmington Hills, MI: Gale Group, 2004 (http://galenet.galegroup.com/servlet/BCRC); "Starbucks Corp.," *Notable Corporate Chronologies*. Gale Group, 2003. Reproduced in Business and Company Resource Center. Farmington Hills, MI: Gale Group, 2004 (http://galenet.galegroup.com/servlet/BCRC).

expenses, which included marketing expenses, general and administrative expenses, and depreciation expenses. After deducting operating expenses, the firm's *operating income* (*earnings before interest and taxes*) amounted to $436 million. Recall that, to this point, we have calculated the profits resulting only from operating activities, as opposed to financing decisions, such as how much debt or equity is used to finance the company's operations.

We next deduct Starbucks' interest expense (the amount paid for using debt financing) of $3 million from operating income to arrive at the company's *earnings before taxes* of $433 million. Finally, we subtract the income taxes of $165 million to arrive at the company's *net income available to common stockholders* of $268 million.

Although not technically part of the income statement, we have added a box at the bottom of the table that shows what happened to the firm's $268 million net income. The firm paid no dividends to its common stockholders, leaving all $268 million to be retained within the company. As we will see shortly, the firm's *retained earnings* reported in the balance sheet increased by this same amount of $268 million.

What conclusions can we draw from Starbucks' income statement? Well, for one thing, we learn that for every $1 in sales, Starbucks earned:

1. 21.3 cents in gross profit ($869 million gross profit divided by $4,076 million sales)
2. 10.7 cents in operating profit ($436 million operating profit divided by $4,076 million sales)
3. 6.6 cents in net income ($268 million net income divided by $4,076 million sales)

Only by knowing if these profit-to-sales levels are high enough so that shareholder value is being created can we say if these results are good. We might also gain some insight if we could see how Starbucks' performance compares with its competition—something we will discuss in Chapter 4. For the time being, simply remember that profit-to-sales relationships, or **profit margins**, are important in assessing a firm's performance.

profit margins

CONCEPT CHECK

1. What does the income statement tell us?
2. What is the basic relationship that we see in the income statement?
3. How are gross profit, operating income, and net income different as they relate to the areas of business activity reported in the income statement?

TESTING YOUR
UNDERSTANDING

THE INCOME STATEMENT

Given the information to the right, see if you can construct an income statement. What are the firm's gross profit, operating income, and net income? Which expense is a *noncash* expense? (The solution to this problem is shown on page 79.)

Interest expense	$ 10,000	Sales	$400,000
Cost of goods sold	$160,000	Stock dividends	$ 5,000
Selling expenses	$ 70,000	Income taxes	$ 20,000
Administrative expenses	$ 50,000	Depreciation expense	$ 20,000

BALANCE SHEET

Objective **2**

A firm's income statement reports the results from operating the business for a period of time, such as a year. The **balance sheet**, on the other hand, provides a snapshot of the firm's financial position at a specific point in time, presenting its asset holdings, liabilities, and owner-supplied capital (stockholders' equity). In its simplest form, a balance sheet follows this formula:

balance sheet

Total assets = total liabilities (debt) + total shareholders' equity

Assets represent the resources owned by the firm, whereas the liabilities and shareholders' equity indicate how those resources are financed.

Figure 3-2 gives us the basic components of a balance sheet. On the left side of Figure 3-2, the firm's assets are listed according to their type; on the right side, we see a listing of the different sources of financing a company could use to finance its assets.

FIGURE 3-2   The Balance Sheet: An Overview

ASSETS	LIABILITIES (DEBT) AND EQUITY
Current assets: • Cash • Accounts receivable • Inventories • Other current assets **Total current assets**	**Current liabilities (debt):** • Accounts payable • Accrued expenses • Short-term notes **Total current debt**
+	+
Fixed assets: • Machinery and equipment • Buildings • Land **Total fixed assets**	**Long-term liabilities (debt)**
+	+
Other assets: • Goodwill • Patents **Total other assets**	**Equity:** • Preferred stock • Common stock • Retained earnings **Total stockholders' equity**
=	=
TOTAL ASSETS	**TOTAL DEBT AND EQUITY**

ACROSS THE HALL

WANT TO START A NEW BUSINESS? BETTER KNOW YOUR NUMBERS

Johnny Stites is CEO of J&S Construction, Inc. in Cookeville, Tennessee. When he graduated from college, he served in the navy for three years, and then returned home to work in the family's business. When asked if finance matters to an entrepreneur, he responds:

> When you start and run your own business, it no longer matters whether you were a marketing, management, finance, or any other specific major. As an entrepreneur, you have to know how a business operates, which requires more than having knowledge in a specific academic field.

> So whatever your major, you had best know the basics of accounting and finance. You do not need to be an accountant, but you had better be able to read and understand financial statements. Sure, you can hire an accountant, but if you do not understand what the numbers are telling you, you are in big trouble.

The construction industry is one of the riskiest industries you can enter, second only to the restaurant industry. For years, we would bid a job based on our best understanding of the costs that would be incurred. Then we would have to wait to the completion of the job to see if we made or lost money—not exactly an ideal situation to be in. Today, we have the ability to know how we are doing in terms of profits and costs on a daily basis. Not having accurate and timely accounting information would be deadly. We simply could not exist in such a competitive industry, and certainly not profitably, without understanding where we are financially.

Does accounting and finance matter to an entrepreneur? Only if you want to have a good understanding of your business.

Source: Personal interview with Johnny Stites, February 2005.

TYPES OF ASSETS

As shown in Figure 3-2, a company's assets fall into three categories: (1) current assets, (2) fixed assets, and (3) other assets.

CURRENT ASSETS

current assets

Current assets, or gross working capital as it is sometimes called, *comprise those assets that are relatively liquid, that is, those that are expected to be converted into cash within 12 months.* Current assets primarily include cash, accounts receivable, inventories, and other current assets.

➤ **Cash.** Every firm must have cash for current business operations. A reservoir of cash is needed because of the unequal flow of funds into (cash receipts) and out of (cash expenditures) the business.

accounts receivable

➤ **Accounts Receivable.** The firm's **accounts receivable** *consist of payments due from its customers who buy on credit.*

inventory

➤ **Inventories. Inventory** *consists of the raw materials, work in process, and finished goods held by a firm for eventual sale.*

➤ **Other Current Assets.** Other current assets include such items as prepaid expenses. For example, insurance premiums may be due before coverage begins, or rent may have to be paid in advance.

FIXED ASSETS

fixed assets

Fixed assets are long term in nature, such as machinery and equipment, buildings, and land. These assets will be used over a number of years. Some of these assets will depreciate in value over time, such as machinery and equipment; others will not, such as land.

OTHER ASSETS

Other assets are all assets that are not current assets or fixed assets, including for example, intangible assets such as patents, copyrights, and goodwill.

In reporting the dollar amounts of the various types of assets in the balance sheet, the conventional practice is to report the value of the assets and liabilities on a historical cost basis. Thus, the balance sheet is not intended to represent current market value of the company but rather *reports the historical transactions at their cost,* or what we call a firm's

accounting book value

accounting book value. Determining a fair value of a business is a different matter—an issue that we will give great attention to throughout future chapters.

TESTING YOUR UNDERSTANDING

THE INCOME STATEMENT: HOW DID YOU DO?

On page 77, we provided data and asked you to prepare an income statement based on the information. Your results should be as follows:

Sales	$400,000	Operating income	$100,000
Cost of goods Sold	160,000	Interest expense	10,000
Gross profit	$240,000	Earnings before tax	$ 90,000
Operating expenses:		Tax expense	20,000
Selling expenses	$70,000	Net income	$ 70,000
Administrative expenses	50,000		
Depreciation expense	20,000		
Total operating expenses	$140,000		

Notice that we did not include the $10,000 stock dividends included in the problem, which is considered a return on the stockholder's capital and deducted from retained earnings.

TYPES OF FINANCING

We now turn to the right side of the balance sheet in Figure 3-2 labeled "Liabilities (Debt) and Equity," which indicates how the firm finances its assets. **Debt** *is money that has been* **debt** *borrowed and must be repaid at some predetermined date*. **Equity**, on the other hand, *represents* **equity** *the shareholders' investment in the company*.

DEBT (LIABILITIES)

Debt capital is financing provided by a creditor. As shown in Figure 3-2, it is divided into (1) current or short-term debt and (2) long-term debt. **Current debt**, or short-term liabilities, **current debt** *includes borrowed money that must be repaid within the next 12 months*. Sources of current debt include the following.

➤ **Accounts payable** *represents credit extended by suppliers to a firm when it purchases inventories.* **accounts payable (trade credit)** The purchasing firm may have 30 or 60 days before paying for inventory that has been purchased. This form of credit extension is also called **trade credit**.

➤ **Accrued expenses** *are short-term liabilities that have been incurred in the firm's operations* **accrued expenses** *but not yet paid*. For example, employees perform work that may not be paid for until the following week or month, and these are recorded as accrued wages.

➤ **Short-term notes** *represent amounts borrowed from a bank or other lending source that are* **short-term notes** *due and payable within 12 months.*

LONG-TERM DEBT

Long-term debt *includes loans from banks or other sources that lend money for longer than 12* **long-term debt** *months*. For example, a firm might borrow money for 5 years to buy equipment or for as long as 25 to 30 years to purchase real estate, such as a warehouse or office building.

EQUITY

Equity includes the shareholders' investment—both preferred stockholders and common stockholders—in the firm.

➤ **Preferred stockholders** *receive a dividend that is fixed in amount*. In the event of the firm **preferred stockholders** failing, these stockholders are paid after the firm's creditors but before the common stockholders.

➤ **Common stockholders** *are the residual owners of a business*. They receive whatever is left **common stockholders** over in the event of bankruptcy—good or bad—after the creditors and preferred stockholders are paid. The amount of a firm's common equity as reported in the balance sheet is equal to (1) the amount the company received from selling stock to investors plus (2) the firm's retained earnings. These amounts may be offset by *any stock that has been repurchased by the company*, which is typically shown as **treasury stock**. **Retained earnings** is *the cumulative total of all the net income over the firm's life less the common stock dividends that have been paid over the years.* Thus, the common equity capital consists of the following:

Common shareholders' equity = common stock issued − common stock repurchased + cumulative net income over the firm's life − total dividends paid over the firm's life

BALANCE SHEET: STARBUCKS CORPORATION

Balance sheets for Starbucks Corporation are presented in Table 3-2 for both fiscal years ending September 28, 2002, and September 28, 2003, along with the changes in each account between years. By examining the two balance sheets, along with the income statement for 2003, we have a more complete picture of the firm's operations. We can see what Starbucks looked like at the beginning of fiscal 2003 (balance sheet on September 28, 2002), what happened during the year (income statement for 2003), and the final outcome at the end of the fiscal year (balance sheet on September 28, 2003). Our perspective of 2003 is shown graphically in Figure 3-3.

The balance sheet data for Starbucks Corporation show that the firm ended fiscal 2002 with about $2,238 million in assets, compared to $2,672 million at the end of fiscal 2003. Practically all of this growth was in long-term assets, namely, an increase of $566 million in gross fixed assets or plant and equipment. In the bottom half of the balance sheet, notice the growth in debt and equity that comes primarily from accounts payable and accruals (an increase of $70 million), additional common stock issued of $87 million, along with an increase in retained earnings (or reinvested profits) of $268 million.

To gain a better grasp of Starbucks' financial position on September 28, 2003, we graphed the major types of assets, debt, and equity in Figure 3-4. In looking at this graph, we are struck by the large proportion of the firm's assets that is invested in fixed assets—$1.75 billion in fixed

TABLE 3-2   Starbucks Corporation
Balance Sheets ($ in millions),
September 28, 2002 and 2003

	SEPTEMBER 28		
	2002	**2003**	**2003 CHANGES**
ASSETS			
Cash	$ 402	$ 350	($ 52)
Accounts receivable	98	114	16
Inventories	263	342	79
Other current assets	85	116	31
Total current assets	$ 848	$ 922	$ 74
Gross fixed assets	$2,103	$2,669	$ 566
Accumulated depreciation	(713)	(919)	(206)
Net fixed assets	$1,390	$1,750	$ 360
Total assets	$2,238	$2,672	$ 434
LIABILITIES AND EQUITY			
Accounts payable and accruals	$ 482	$ 552	$ 70
Short-term notes payable	1	1	0
Total current liabilities	$ 483	$ 553	$ 70
Long-term debt	$ 29	$ 38	9
Total liabilities	$ 512	$ 591	$ 79
Equity			
Common stock	$ 930	$1,017	$ 87
Retained earnings	796	1,064	268
Total common equity	$1,726	$2,081	$ 355
Total liabilities and equity	$2,238	$2,672	$ 434

FINANCIAL MANAGEMENT
IN PRACTICE

BEING PROFITABLE IS VITAL: JUST ASK FORD MOTOR COMPANY

Income is more than a number accountants use—it is critical to the survival of a business. Ford Motor Company's management knows firsthand that if earnings estimates are not met, something must be done. Due to the lackluster performance of Ford's luxury line of vehicles (such as Jaguar, Land Rover, Volvo, Aston Martin, and Lincoln), Ford had to make some difficult decisions in one of its Jaguar plants.

To return Jaguar to profitability, Ford cut 1,150 jobs and closed the historic Browns Lane plant in Coventry, England. An initial hit to income of $450 million caused Ford to miss its earnings estimates, but decision makers hoped that this action would enable Ford to meet its future earnings targets.

The decision to cut jobs at Browns Lane was not popular with union leaders or politicians in the British Midlands because of a 1998 pledge by Ford to continue producing luxury sedans and sports cars at the Browns Lane plant. According to Mark Fields, Ford's senior executive in Europe, if Ford "just blindly stuck to this commitment, given the changes in the business and the external factors, the survival of the business was going to be at risk."

Source: Stephen Power, "Ford Takes Hard Line at Jaguar," *The Wall Street Journal*, September 20, 2004, p. A4.

FIGURE 3-3 Starbucks Corporation: The Income Statement and Balance Sheet as One Picture

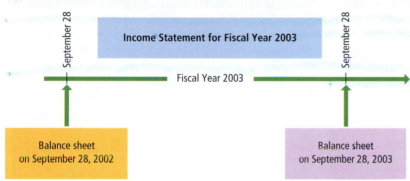

FIGURE 3-4 Starbucks Corporation Balance Sheet, September 28, 2003 ($ millions)

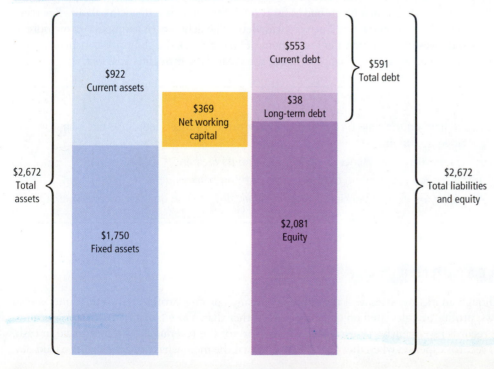

TESTING YOUR
UNDERSTANDING

THE BALANCE SHEET

Given the information to the right, construct a balance sheet. What are the firm's current assets, net fixed assets, total assets, current or short-term debt, long-term debt, total equity, and total debt and equity? (Check your solution to this problem with the answer shown on page 83.)

Gross fixed assets	$75,000	Accounts receivables	$50,000
Cash	10,000	Long-term notes	5,000
Other assets	15,000	Mortgage	20,000
Accounts payables	40,000	Common stock	100,000
Retained earnings	15,000	Inventories	70,000
Accumulated depreciation	20,000	Short-term notes	20,000

assets out of $2.67 billion in total assets. Also, there are two other relationships that can be observed in Figure 3-4: (1) the level of Starbucks' net working capital and (2) the firm's mix of debt to equity used in financing the company. Let's consider each.

net working capital

NET WORKING CAPITAL

Earlier we noted that the term *current assets* is sometimes referred to as *gross working capital*. We can now define **net working capital** as *current assets less current liabilities* (*current assets – current liabilities*). Thus, *net* working capital compares the amount of current assets (assets that should convert into cash within the next 12 months) to the current liabilities (debt that will be due within 12 months). The larger the net working capital a firm has, the more able the firm will be to pay its debt as it comes due. Thus, the amount of net working capital is important to a company's lenders who are always concerned about a company's ability to repay a loan. Also, we use the concept of net working capital at several points in our study of finance. So, don't forget: Net working capital is equal to current assets (also called *gross* working capital) less current liabilities.

For Starbucks, its net working capital as of the end of the 2003 fiscal year was $369 million ($922 million current assets – $553 million current debt).

debt ratio

DEBT RATIO

A firm's **debt ratio** is *the percentage of assets financed by debt*. Starbucks' debt ratio at the 2003 fiscal year end was about 22 percent ($591 million in total liabilities divided by $2,672 million in total assets). This means that by the end of fiscal 2003, Starbucks was financing about 78 percent of its assets with equity and only 22 percent with debt. The debt ratio is an important measure to lenders and investors, as it indicates the amount of financial risk the company is incurring—the more debt a company uses to finance its assets, the greater the firm's financial risk.

CONCEPT CHECK

1. Regarding the time frame reported, how is the balance sheet different from the income statement?
2. State the basic balance sheet formula and its meaning.
3. What is the definition of a firm's "accounting book value"?
4. What are the two principal sources of financing? Of what do these sources consist?

Objective **3**

MEASURING CASH FLOWS

Although an income statement measures a company's profits, profits are not the same as cash flows; profits are calculated on an *accrual* basis rather than a *cash* basis. Accrual-basis accounting records revenue when it is earned, whether or not the revenue has been received in cash, and records expenses when they are incurred, even if the money has not actually been paid out.

For example, sales reported in the income statement include both cash sales and credit sales. Therefore, sales for a given year do not correspond exactly to the actual cash collected from sales. Similarly, a firm must purchase inventory, but some of the purchases are financed by credit rather than by immediate cash payment so expenses are not equal to actual cash "out the door" either. Also, under the accrual system, the purchase of equipment that will last for more than a year is not shown as an expense in the income statement. Instead, the amount is recorded as an asset and then expensed as depreciation over the useful life of the equipment. An annual depreciation expense (this is not a cash flow) is recorded as a way to match the use of the asset with sales generated from its service.

We could give more examples to show why profits differ from cash flows, but the point should be clear: *Profits and cash flows are not the same thing.* In fact, a business could be profitable but have negative cash flows, even to the point of going bankrupt. So understanding a firm's cash flows is very important to managers.

There are a number of different ways to measure a firm's cash flows. For one, we could use the conventional accountant's presentation called a *statement of cash flows*, which is always included in the financial section of a firm's annual report. But for our purposes, we will instead take a finance perspective to measuring cash flows, computing what we will call *free cash flows*. This measurement will be used later in valuing a capital investment and in valuing the firm itself. So, what follows is similar to a conventional cash flow statement presented as part of a company's financial statements, but it does not follow exactly the accountant's format.

WHAT SHOULD YOU DO?

Your brother-in-law has asked you to help him finance what he considers to be a "great investment opportunity." He plans to sell a new brand of European clothing that is becoming popular in the United States. He thinks that the university located nearby, from which you both graduated, would be an ideal location. He estimates that the financing can come mostly from a bank loan and credit from suppliers. However, the two of you will need to put in $5,000, of which he would invest $3,000, leaving you to invest the remaining $2,000.

It's not that you don't trust him, but you have decided to undertake your own investigation into the opportunity. After a few hours of work, you develop what you think are realistic estimates of the potential profits for the venture. You also estimate how much money it would take to start the business.

There is a slight problem, however: Your new puppy chewed up your papers. After putting the dog in the backyard *without any supper for the time being*, you pick up the pieces and begin reconstructing your work. The remnants of your hard work—at least most of it—look as follows (numbers are in thousands):

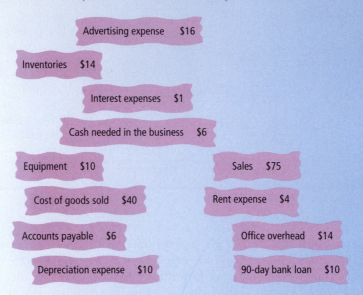

Can you reconstruct the income statement and balance sheet using the bits of information provided above? What do you conclude about your brother-in-law's great opportunity? *See page 85 for the solution to your brother-in-law problem—hopefully after you have made a good-faith effort to solve it yourself.*

FREE CASH FLOWS

We can think of a firm as a group of assets that produces cash flow. Once the firm has paid all its operating expenses and made all its investments, the remaining cash flows are *free* to be distributed to the firm's creditors and shareholders—thus, the term **free cash flows**. Being more specific, a company's *free* cash flows result from two activities:

free cash flows

1. *Cash flow from operations*, which relates to the normal operating activities of the business, including buying or producing products to be sold, selling to customers, paying wages and administrative expenses, and paying taxes.
2. *Asset investments*, which include investments in (1) a company's *net working capital* (described earlier in the chapter) and (2) its fixed assets.

Simply stated, free cash flows are equal to:

$$\begin{bmatrix} \text{After-tax cash} \\ \text{flows from operations} \end{bmatrix} less \begin{bmatrix} \text{increase or decrease in} \\ \text{net working capital} \end{bmatrix} less \begin{bmatrix} \text{increase or decrease in} \\ \text{gross fixed assets} \end{bmatrix}$$

The procedure for computing a firm's free cash flows involves three steps:

1. Compute the after-tax cash flows from operations by converting the income statement from an accrual basis to a cash basis.
2. Calculate the increase or decrease in the firm's investment in *net* working capital.
3. Compute the increase or decrease in investments made in fixed assets.

Let's look at each of the foregoing steps.

... NOW ABOUT YOUR BROTHER-IN-LAW!

With an understanding of the income statement and balance sheet, let's return to your brother-in-law's proposition to become a partner with him in the clothing business. You have constructed the income statement and the balance sheet from the fragments of your dog-chewed papers. When you do, you get the following results (in $ thousands):

PROJECTED INCOME STATEMENT			PROJECTED BALANCE SHEET	
Sales		$ 75	Cash needed in the business	$ 6
Cost of goods sold		40	Inventories	14
			Equipment	10
Gross profit		$ 35	Total assets	$ 30
Operating expenses:				
Office overhead	$14		Accounts payable	$ 6
Advertising expense	16		90-day bank loan	10
Rent expense	4		Total debt	$ 16
Depreciation expense	10		Equity:	
Total operating expenses		$ 44	Brother-in-law	$ 3
Operating income		$ (9)	Your investment	2
Interest expenses		1	Total equity	$ 5
Loss before taxes		$(10)	Total projected debt and equity	$ 21
Taxes		0	Additional financing needed	9
Net income		$(10)	Total debt and equity needed	$ 30

So, based on your estimates, the venture would expect to incur a loss of $10,000. Furthermore, the balance sheet suggests that the business will need $30,000 for investments in assets, which would come from debt financing of $16,000 (you hope); $3,000 from your brother-in-law (if he has it), and $2,000 from you, which totals $21,000, and not the $30,000 you actually need. Thus, the business will need an additional $9,000. Maybe, just maybe, this is not quite the opportunity your brother-in-law perceives it to be.

Step 1: *Determine the after-tax cash flows from operations.* For the first step, we compute the after-tax cash flows from operations as follows:

> **Operating income (earnings before interest and taxes)**
> + depreciation expense
> − income tax expense[1]
> = after-tax cash flows from operations

Thus, we compute the after-tax cash flows from operations by adding back depreciation expense to operating income, because depreciation expense is not a cash expense, and then subtracting taxes to get the cash flows on an after-tax basis.

To illustrate how to compute a firm's after-tax cash flows from operations, return to Starbucks' income statement in Table 3-1 on page 75, where we find the following information:

Operating income (EBIT)	$436
Depreciation expense	206
Income tax expense	165

[1]We should be subtracting actual taxes paid, which may frequently be different from the income tax expense shown in the income statement. But let's just keep things simple and assume they are the same for Starbucks.

FINANCIAL MANAGEMENT
IN PRACTICE

PROFITS AND CASH MATTER: THE FEDEX DILEMMA

In 2004, FedEx was facing a dilemma relating to government assistance that was recorded as income. This situation provides a prime example of the need to examine both the income and cash flow statements when analyzing the financial situation of a company.

FedEx had to take a $48 million charge to income as a result of government assistance received. This assistance was provided by the Air Transportation Safety and Stabilization Act for air carriers hurt by the September 11 attacks. Initially, FedEx recorded $119 million, the amount originally granted in income, even though it had not yet received all the payment.

The government later found that FedEx should only be entitled to $72 million and ordered the company to repay $29 million and take a charge against income of $48 million in its fiscal second quarter. FedEx plans to "vigorously contest this determination judicially and ... continue to aggressively pursue its compensation claims."

The lesson to learn is that cash flow and net income are not the same. In this case, FedEx reported the income before it received the cash. Both numbers should be examined to assess a company's economic reality.

Source: Adapted from "FedEx Ordered to Repay $29 Million to U.S.," *Journal of Commerce*. November 12, 2004, p. 1; "FedEx to Repay Government, Book Charge of $48 Million," *The Wall Street Journal Online*. November 12, 2004 (http://online.wsj.com/article/0,,SB110026862794772564,00.html).

Given this information, we compute Starbucks' after-tax cash flows from operations as follows:

Operating income (EBIT)	$ 436
Plus depreciation	206
Less income tax expense	(165)
After-tax cash flows from operations	$ 477

Step 2: *Calculate the change in the net working capital.* For the second step, the change in net working capital is equal to the:[2]

$$\begin{bmatrix} \text{change in} \\ \text{current assets} \end{bmatrix} - \begin{bmatrix} \text{change in} \\ \text{current liabilities} \end{bmatrix}$$

For Starbucks, the increase in *net working capital* is found by looking at the firm's balance sheets at the beginning and end of fiscal 2003 in Table 3-2 on page 80, where we see that:

	SEPTEMBER 28		2003
	2002	**2003**	**CHANGES**
Current assets	$848	$922	$74
Current liabilities	483	553	70
Net working capital	$365	$369	$ 4

Thus, in 2003 Starbucks invested an additional $74 million in current assets; however, current liabilities (actually accounts payables and accruals) helped finance $70 million of the increase in current assets, requiring the firm to make up the difference of $4 million ($74 million − $70 million).

Step 3: *Compute the change in fixed assets.* The final step involves computing the change in *gross* fixed assets (not *net* fixed assets). Again returning to Starbucks' balance sheets, we see that there was an increase in gross fixed assets of $566 million from $2,103 million to $2,669 million.

---

[2]To be precise, we should only be subtracting non-interest-bearing current liabilities, instead of all current liabilities, where the *non-interest-bearing current liabilities* are those liabilities incurred in the normal day-to-day operating activities of buying and selling the firm's goods, namely, accounts payable and accrued operating expenses. But, again, we will take the liberty of simplifying the computations.

Step 4: *Wrapping up.* We can now compute Starbucks' free cash flows as follows:

After-tax cash flows from operations		$477
Less 2003 investments:		
Investment in net working capital	($ 4)	
Investment in long-term assets	(566)	
Total investments		(570)
Free cash flows		$ (93)

Given these computations, we see that the firm's free cash flows are *negative* in the amount of $93 million. The firm's operations generated $477 million; however, all of this amount, plus $93 million, was consumed by the increases in net working capital ($4 million) and the investments in long-term assets ($566 million). In other words, the fast growth being experienced by Starbucks—all those new locations—was more than what the firm could finance from operations. So where did the $93 million come from to finance the shortfall? The investors, of course.

FINANCING CASH FLOWS

A firm can either receive money from or distribute money to its investors, or some of both. In general, cash flows between investors and the firm, what we will call **financing cash flows**, occur in one of four ways. The firm can:

financing cash flows

1. Pay interest to lenders.
2. Pay dividends to stockholders.
3. Increase or decrease long-term debt.
4. Issue stock to new shareholders or repurchase stock from current investors.

Let's again return to Starbucks to illustrate the process for calculating the firm's financing cash flows, which will also let us determine how the $93 million negative free cash flows that Starbucks experienced were financed.

When we speak of *investors* in this context, we include both lenders and shareholders. However, we do *not* include financing provided by current liabilities, which were recognized earlier as part of the firm's net working capital.

Let's compute the financing cash flows for Starbucks. We first determine the interest expense paid to lenders and the dividends paid to shareholders, which are provided in the firm's income statement (Table 3-1). We then refer to the balance sheet (Table 3-2) to see the changes in long-term debt and common stock. The results are as follows:

Interest paid to lenders	$ (3)	Use of cash
Common stock dividends	0	
Increase in long-term debt	9	Source of cash
Increase in common stock	87	Source of cash
Investors' cash flows	$ 93	

Thus, the firm paid $3 million in interest and nothing in dividends. The firm received $9 million from additional long-term debt and $87 million by issuing common stock. Add it all up and Starbucks received a net amount of $93 million from its long-term creditors and shareholders.

It is not a coincidence that the dollar amount of Starbucks' free cash flows exactly equals its cash flows from its investors. They will always be the same except the signs will be opposite—if one is positive (negative) the other will be negative (positive). The firm's free cash flows, if positive, will be the amount distributed to the investors; if the free cash flows are negative, it will be the amount that the investors provide to the firm to cover the shortage in free cash flows.

CONCEPT CHECK

1. Why can an income statement not provide a measure of a firm's cash flows?
2. What are *free cash flows*?
3. How do we measure free cash flows?
4. How do we compute a firm's *financing cash flows*?
5. What is the relationship between free cash flows and financing cash flows?

TESTING YOUR
UNDERSTANDING

MEASURING CASH FLOWS

Given the following information, compute the firm's free cash flows and financing cash flows. (See the solution on the next page after first working the problem.)

Change in current assets	$ 25	Change in long-term notes payables	30
Operating income	50	Dividends	5
Interest expense	10	Change in common stock	0
Increase in accounts payable	20	Increase in fixed assets	55
		Depreciation expense	7
		Income taxes	12

STARBUCKS CORPORATION: WHAT HAVE WE LEARNED?

Based on our review of Starbucks Corporation's financial statements, we can now draw some conclusions. To this point, we have learned that:

➤ For every dollar of sales, Starbucks earns 11 cents in operating income and 7 cents in net income.
➤ The firm finances its assets more with equity than with debt.
➤ Starbucks has negative free cash flows, which means that in net, the firm is relying on its lenders and shareholders to finance the firm's growth that occurred beyond the cash flows generated from operations.
➤ The company's primary investments were to expand its fixed assets, namely its store locations.
➤ The only cash flow going to investors was interest.

In Chapter 4, we continue our financial analysis of Starbucks Corporation as we use the data from this chapter to dig deeper into the relationships provided from the financial statements. Read on.

SUMMARY

Compute a company's profits, as reflected by an income statement.
A firm's profits may be viewed as follows:

Objective **1**

Gross profit = sales − cost of goods sold

Earnings before interest and tax (operating profit) = sales − cost of goods sold − operating expenses

Net profit (net income) = sales − cost of goods sold − operating expenses − interest expense −taxes

The following five activities drive a company's net income:

1. Revenue derived from selling the company's product or service
2. Cost of producing or acquiring the goods or services to be sold
3. Operating expenses related to (1) marketing and distributing the product or service to the customer and (2) administering the business
4. Financing costs of doing business—namely, the interest paid to the firm's creditors
5. Payment of taxes

Determine a firm's accounting book value, as presented in a balance sheet.
The balance sheet presents a company's assets, liabilities, and equity on a specific date. Total assets must equal debt plus equity. The assets include current assets, fixed assets, and other assets. Debt includes short-term and long-term debt. Equity includes common stock and retained earnings. All the numbers in a balance sheet are based on historical costs. As such, they are considered to equal the firm's accounting book value, as opposed to its market value.

Objective **2**

Objective **3** | Measure a company's cash flows.

In measuring a firm's cash flows we can take one of two perspectives: the cash flows produced by the firm's assets (free cash flows) or the cash flows received from or distributed to lenders and investors (financing cash flows). That is,

CASH FLOWS

Free Cash Flows	**Financing Cash Flows**
Operating income + depreciation expense – taxes – additional investments in net working capital and long-term assets	Increase (decrease) in long-term debt + increase (decrease) in common stock – interest and dividend payments

TESTING YOUR
UNDERSTANDING

MEASURING CASH FLOWS: HOW DID YOU DO?

On the previous page we asked you to calculate a firm's free cash flows and its financing cash flows. Your results should be as follows:

FREE CASH FLOWS

Operating income		$50
Depreciation expense		7
Income taxes		(12)
After-tax cash flows from operations		$45
Investments in net working capital:		
Change in current assets	$(25)	
Change in accounts payables	20	
Investments in net working capital:		$ (5)
Investment in fixed assets		(55)
Total investments		$(60)
Free cash flows		$(15)

INVESTORS' CASH FLOWS

Interest expense	($10)
Dividends	($5)
Increase in long-term notes payables	30
Change in common stock	0
Investors' cash flows	$ 15

KEY TERMS

Accounting book value, 78

Accounts payable (trade credit), 79

Accounts receivable, 78

Accrued expenses, 79

Balance sheet, 77

Common stockholders, 79

Cost of goods sold, 74

Current assets, 78

Current debt, 79

Debt, 79

Debt ratio, 82

Earnings before taxes, 75

Equity, 79

Financing cash flows, 87

Financing costs, 75

Fixed assets, 78

Free cash flows, 84

Gross profit, 74

Income statement (profit and loss statement), 74

Inventory, 78

Long-term debt, 79

Net income available to owners (net income), 75

Net working capital, 82

Operating expenses, 74

Operating income (earnings before interest and taxes), 74

Preferred stockholders, 79

Profit margins, 76

Retained earnings, 80

Short-term notes, 79

Treasury stock, 80

STUDY QUESTIONS

3-1. A company's financial statements consist of the balance sheet, income statement, and statement of cash flows.

    a. Describe the nature of the balance sheet and the income statement.

    b. Why have we not used the conventional statement of cash flows in our presentation, computing instead what we call free cash flows?

3-2. What are the differences between gross profit, operating profits, and net income?

3-3. What is the difference between dividends and interest expense?

3-4. Why is it that the preferred stockholders' equity section of the balance sheet would change only when new shares are sold or repurchased, whereas the common equity section would change from year to year regardless of whether new shares are bought or sold?

3-5. What is net working capital?

3-6. How might one firm have positive cash flows and be headed for financial trouble, whereas another firm with negative cash flows could actually be in a good financial position?

3-7. Why is the examination of only the balance sheet and income statement not adequate in evaluating a firm?

3-8. Why do a firm's free cash flows have to equal its financing cash flows?

SELF-TEST PROBLEM

ST-1. (*Measuring cash flows*) Given the following information for the M & G Corporation, compute the firm's free cash flows and its financing cash flows for 2006. What do you learn about the firm from these computations?

M & G Corporation Balance Sheet for December 31, 2005 and 2006

	2005	2006
Cash	$ 9,000	$ 500
Accounts receivable	12,500	16,000
Inventories	29,000	45,500
Total current assets	$ 50,500	$ 62,000
Land	20,000	26,000
Buildings and equipment	70,000	100,000
Less: Accumulated depreciation	(28,000)	(38,000)
Total fixed assets	$ 62,000	$ 88,000
Total assets	$112,500	$150,000
Accounts payable	$ 10,500	$ 22,000
Short-term bank notes	17,000	47,000
Total current liabilities	$ 27,500	$ 69,000
Long-term debt	28,750	22,950
Common stock	31,500	31,500
Retained earnings	24,750	26,550
Total debt and equity	$112,500	$150,000

M & G Corporation Income Statement
for the Years Ending December 31, 2005 and 2006

	2005	2006
Sales (all credit)	$125,000	$160,000
Cost of goods sold	75,000	96,000
Gross profit	$ 50,000	$ 64,000
Operating expenses		
Fixed cash operating expenses	$ 21,000	$ 21,000
Variable operating expenses	12,500	16,000
Depreciation	4,500	10,000
Total operating expenses	$ 38,000	$ 47,000
Earnings before interest and taxes	$ 12,000	$ 17,000
Interest expense	3,000	6,100
Earnings before taxes	$ 9,000	$ 10,900
Taxes	4,500	5,450
Net income	$ 4,500	$ 5,450

STUDY PROBLEMS

3-1. (*Review of financial statements*) Prepare a balance sheet and income statement for Belmond, Inc., from the following information. How much is the firm's net working capital and what is the debt ratio?

Inventory	$ 6,500
Common stock	45,000
Cash	16,550
Operating expenses	1,350
Notes payable	600
Interest expense	900
Depreciation expense	500
Net sales	12,800
Accounts receivable	9,600
Accounts payable	4,800
Long-term debt	55,000
Cost of goods sold	5,750
Buildings and equipment	122,000
Accumulated depreciation	34,000
Taxes	1,440
General and administrative expense	850
Retained earnings	?

3-2. (*Computing cash flows*) Given the following information, compute the firm's free cash flows and financing cash flows.

Increase in current assets	$50
Operating income	75
Interest expense	25
Increase in accounts payable	35
Dividends	15
Increase in common stock	20
Increase in net fixed assets	23
Depreciation expense	12
Income taxes	17

3-3. (*Review of financial statements*) Prepare a balance sheet and income statement for the Warner Company from the following scrambled list of items.

    a. What are the firm's net working capital and debt ratio?
    b. What are the profit margins?

Depreciation expense	$ 66,000
Cash	225,000
Long-term debt	334,000
Sales	573,000
Accounts payable	102,000
General and administrative expense	79,000
Buildings and equipment	895,000
Notes payable	75,000
Accounts receivable	153,000
Interest expense	4,750
Accrued expenses	7,900
Common stock	289,000
Cost of goods sold	297,000
Inventory	99,300
Taxes	50,500
Accumulated depreciation	263,000
Prepaid expenses	14,500
Taxes payable	53,000
Retained earnings	262,900

3-4. (*Free cash flow analysis*) Interpret the following information regarding Westlake Corporation's free cash flows and financing cash flows.

Westlake Corporation Free Cash Flows and Financing Cash Flows

FREE CASH FLOWS		
Operating Income (EBIT)		$1,020
Depreciation		125
Tax expense		(290)
After-tax cash flows from operations		$ 855
Increase in net working capital		
Increase in current assets	(640)	
Increase in current debt	201	
Increase in net working capital		($ 439)
(current assets – current debt)		
Increase in long-term assets:		
Purchase of fixed assets		(1,064)
Free cash flows		$ (648)

FINANCING CASH FLOWS	
Interest paid to lenders	($ 276)
Issue long-term debt	640
Issue common stock	348
Common stock dividends	(64)
Financing cash flow	$ 648

3-5. (*Computing cash flows*) Given the following information, compute the firm's free cash flows and financing cash flows.

Dividends	25
Increase in common stock	27
Increase in current assets	135
Operating income	215
Interest expense	50
Depreciation expense	20
Increase in current liabilities	48
Increase in gross fixed assets	55
Income taxes	45

3-6. (*Free cash flow analysis*) Interpret the following information regarding Maness Corporation's free cash flows and financing cash flows.

Maness Corporation Free Cash Flows and Financing Cash Flows

FREE CASH FLOWS		
Operating income (EBIT)		$ 954
Depreciation expense		60
Tax expense		(320)
After-tax cash flows from operations		$ 694
Increase in net working capital		
Increase in current assets	$ (899)	
Increase in current debt	175	
Increase in net working capital		$ (724)
Change in long-term assets:		
Sale of fixed assets		(2,161)
Free cash flows		$3,579

FINANCING CASH FLOWS	
Interest paid to lenders	($ 364)
Repayment of long-term debt	(850)
Repurchase of common stock	(1,024)
Common stock dividends	(1,341)
Financing cash flow	($3,579)

3-7. (*Measuring cash flows*) Calculate the free cash flows and financing cash flows for Pamplin, Inc., for 2006. Interpret your results.

Pamplin Inc. Balance Sheet
at 12/31/2005 and 12/31/2006

ASSETS

	2005	2006
Cash	$ 200	$ 150
Accounts receivable	450	425
Inventory	550	625
Current assets	$1,200	$1,200
Plant and equipment	$2,200	$2,600
Less: Accumulated depreciation	(1,000)	(1,200)
Net plant and equipment	$1,200	$1,400
Total assets	$2,400	$2,600

LIABILITIES AND OWNERS' EQUITY

	2005	2006
Accounts payable	$ 200	$ 150
Notes payable—current (9%)	0	150
Current liabilities	$ 200	$ 300
Bonds	$ 600	$ 600
Owners' equity		
Common stock	$ 900	$ 900
Retained earnings	700	800
Total owners' equity	$1,600	$1,700
Total liabilities and owners' equity	$2,400	$2,600

Pamplin Inc. Income Statement
for Years Ending 12/31/2005 and 12/31/2006

	2005		2006	
Sales (all credit)		$1,200		$1,450
Cost of goods sold		700		850
Gross profit		$ 500		$ 600
Operating expenses	30		40	
Depreciation	220	250	200	240
Operating income		$ 250		$ 360
Interest expense		50		64
Net income before taxes		$ 200		$ 296
Taxes (40%)		80		118
Net income		$ 120		$ 178

3-8. (*Measuring cash flows*) Calculate the free cash flows and financing cash flows for the Waterhouse Co. for the year ended December 31, 2006. Interpret your results.

Waterhouse Co. Balance Sheet for 12/31/2005 and 12/31/2006

	2005	2006
Cash	$ 75,000	$ 82,500
Receivables	102,000	90,000
Inventory	168,000	165,000
Prepaid expenses	12,000	13,500
Total current assets	$357,000	$351,000
Gross fixed assets	325,500	468,000
Accumulated depreciation	(94,500)	(129,000)
Patents	61,500	52,500
Total assets	$649,500	$742,500
Accounts payable	$124,500	$ 112,500
Short-term notes	97,500	105,000
Total current liabilities	$222,000	$217,500
Mortgage payable	150,000	0
Preferred stock	0	231,000
Common stock	225,000	225,000
Retained earnings	52,500	69,000
Total liabilities and equity	$649,500	$742,500

Additional Information

1. The only entry in the accumulated depreciation account is the depreciation expense for the period.
2. The only entries in the retained earnings account are for dividends paid in the amount of $18,000 and for the net income for the year.
3. Expenses include a $9,000 amortization of patents and $6,000 in interest expenses.   *NON cash Expense*
4. The income statement for 2006 is as follows:

Waterhouse Co. Income Statement for Year Ended 12/31/2006

Sales (all credit)	$187,500
Cost of goods sold	111,000
Gross profit	76,500
Expenses	32,000
Taxes	10,000
Net income	$ 34,500

(Cost of goods sold included depreciation expense of $34,500)

3-9. (*Measuring cash flows*) Calculate the free cash flows and financing cash flows for T. P. Jarmon Company for the year ended December 31, 2006. Interpret your results.

T. P. Jarmon Company Balance Sheet for 12/31/2005 and 12/31/2006

ASSETS

	2005	2006
Cash	$ 15,000	$ 14,000
Marketable securities	6,000	6,200
Accounts receivable	42,000	33,000
Inventory	51,000	84,000
Prepaid rent	1,200	1,100
Total current assets	$115,200	$138,300
Net plant and equipment	286,000	270,000
Total assets	$401,200	$408,300

LIABILITIES AND EQUITY

	2005	2006
Accounts payable	$ 48,000	$ 57,000
Notes payable	15,000	13,000
Accruals	6,000	5,000
Total current liabilities	$ 69,000	$ 75,000
Long-term debt	$160,000	$150,000
Common stockholders' equity	$172,200	$183,300
Total liabilities and equity	$401,200	$408,300

**T. P. Jarmon Company Income Statement
for the Year Ended 12/31/2006**

Sales (all credit)		$600,000
Less: Cost of goods sold		460,000
Gross profit		$140,000
Less: Operating and interest expenses		
General and administrative	$ 30,000	
Interest	10,000	
Depreciation	30,000	
Total		70,000
Earnings before taxes		$ 70,000
Less: Taxes		27,100
Net income available to common stockholders		$ 42,900
Less: Cash dividends		31,800
Change in retained earnings		$ 11,100

3-10. (*Measuring cash flows*) Calculate the free cash flows and financing cash flows for Abrams Manufacturing Company for the year ended December 31, 2006, both from an asset and a financing perspective. Interpret your results.

**Abrams Manufacturing Company Balance Sheet
for 12/31/2005 and 12/31/2006**

	2005	2006
Cash	$ 89,000	$100,000
Accounts receivable	64,000	70,000
Inventory	112,000	100,000
Prepaid expenses	10,000	10,000
Total current assets	275,000	280,000
Plant and equipment	238,000	311,000
Accumulated depreciation	(40,000)	(66,000)
Total assets	$473,000	$525,000
Accounts payable	$ 85,000	$ 90,000
Accrued liabilities	68,000	63,000
Total current debt	153,000	153,000
Mortgage payable	70,000	0
Preferred stock	0	120,000
Common stock	205,000	205,000
Retained earnings	45,000	47,000
Total debt and equity	$473,000	$525,000

**Abrams Manufacturing Company Income Statement
for Year Ended 12/31/2006**

	2006
Sales (all credit)	$184,000
Cost of goods sold	60,000
Gross profit	$124,000
Selling, general, and administrative expenses	44,000
Depreciation expense	26,000
Operating income	$ 54,000
Interest expense	4,000
Earnings before taxes	$ 50,000
Taxes	16,000
Preferred stock dividends	10,000
Net income	$ 24,000

Additional Information

1. The only entry in the accumulated depreciation account is for 2006 depreciation.
2. The firm paid $22,000 in common stock dividends during 2006.

WEB WORKS

3-WW1. See the annual report for Starbucks Corporation by going to **www.starbucks.com/about/ investor.asp** and then clicking on the Annual Reports options. Scan the annual report to see what is included.

3-WW2. Go to **www.homedepot.com** for the home page of the Home Depot Corporation. Select the "Company" option, then Investor Relations and finally Financial Statements. Look for keywords in the income statement that appear in this chapter, such as sales, gross profit, and net income. What do you learn about the firm from its financial statements that you find interesting?

3-WW3. Go to *The Wall Street Journal Online* **www.wsj.com**, and do a search on Barnes & Noble. Try to find the firm's earnings announcements. What did you learn about the company from the announcements?

3-WW4. In 2004, Disney was having a big stir about its CEO, Michael Eisner. Some of the Disney board members were wanting to fire him. After considerable turmoil, Eisner announced that he would retire in 2005. Conduct a web search to find out Eisner's status with Disney. Also go to the firm's Web site and look at their financial statements and see how the business is doing in terms of profits. Can you discover what parts of the business are doing well and those that are not?

COMPREHENSIVE PROBLEM

The financial statements both for PepsiCo and Coca-Cola follow.

a. How much profit is each company making per dollar of sales?

b. Calculate the free cash flows and financing cash flows for the two firms. Compare your findings.

PepsiCo, Inc. Income Statement
for Year Ended December 31, 2003 ($ millions)

Sales		$26,971
Cost of goods sold		11,359
Gross profit		$15,612
Marketing expenses and general and administrative expenses	$9,460	
Depreciation expense	1,165	
Total operating expenses		$10,625
Operating profits		$ 4,987
Interest expenses		163
Nonoperating income		168
Earnings before taxes		$ 4,992
Income taxes		1,424
Net income available to common stockholders		$ 3,568

PepsiCo, Inc. Balance Sheet
for December 31, 2002 and 2003 ($ millions)

ASSETS

	2002	2003
Cash	$ 1,845	$ 2,001
Accounts receivable	2,531	2,830
Inventories	1,342	1,412
Other current assets	695	687
Total current assets	$ 6,413	$ 6,930
Gross fixed assets	$13,395	$14,755
Accumulated depreciation	(6,005)	(7,170)
Net fixed assets	$ 7,390	$ 7,585
Investments	2,611	2,920
Intangibles, net	5,219	5,383
Other assets	1,841	2,509
Total assets	$23,474	$25,327

LIABILITIES AND EQUITY

	2002	2003
Short-term notes payable	$ 77	$ 145
Accounts payable	1,543	1,638
Taxes payable	492	611
Accrued expenses	1,690	2,245
Other current liabilities	2,250	1,776
Total current liabilities	$ 6,052	$ 6,415
Long-term debt	2,187	1,702
Deferred taxes	1,718	1,261
Other liabilities	4,226	4,075
Total liabilities	$14,183	$13,453
Equity		
Preferred stock	$ (7)	$ (22)
Capital stock	30	30
Capital surplus	–	548
Retained earnings	11,792	14,694
Treasury stock	(2,524)	(3,376)
Total common equity	$ 9,298	$11,896
Total equity	9,291	11,874
Total liabilities and equity	$23,474	$25,327

Coca-Cola Co. Income Statement
for Year Ended December 31, 2003 ($ millions)

Sales		$21,044
Cost of goods sold		7,159
Gross profit		$13,885
Marketing expenses and general and administrative expenses	$7,488	
Depreciation expense	667	
Total operating expenses		$ 8,155
Operating profits		$ 5,730
Interest expense		178
Nonoperating income		444
Extraordinary items		(501)
Earnings before taxes		$ 5,495
Income taxes		1,148
Net income available to common stockholders		$ 4,347

Coca-Cola Co. Balance Sheet
for December 31, 2002 and 2003 ($ millions)

ASSETS

	2002	2003
Cash	$ 2,345	$ 3,482
Accounts receivables	2,097	2,091
Inventories	1,294	1,252
Other current assets	1,616	1,571
Total current assets	$ 7,352	$ 8,396
Gross fixed assets	$ 9,001	$ 9,622
Accumulated depreciation	(3,090)	(3,757)
Net fixed assets	$ 5,911	$ 5,865
Investments	4,737	5,224
Intangibles, net	3,553	3,989
Other assets	2,948	3,868
Total assets	$24,501	$27,342

LIABILITIES AND EQUITY

	2002	2003
Short-term notes payable	$ 2,475	$ 2,583
Accounts payable	2,002	4,058
Taxes payable	994	922
Other current liabilities	1,870	323
Total current liabilities	$ 7,341	$ 7,886
Long-term debt	2,701	2,517
Deferred taxes	399	337
Other liabilities	2,260	2,512
Total liabilities	$12,701	$13,252
Equity		
Capital stock	$ 873	$ 874
Capital surplus	3,857	4,395
Retained earnings	21,459	24,692
Treasury stock	(14,389)	(15,871)
Total common equity	11,800	14,090
Total liabilities and equity	$24,501	$27,342

SELF-TEST SOLUTION

SS-1.

M & G Industries Free Cash Flows and Financing Cash Flows

FREE CASH FLOWS

Operating income		$ 17,000
Plus depreciation expense		10,000
Less tax expense		(5,450)
After-tax cash flows from operations		$ 21,550
Change in net working capital		
Increase in current assets	$(11,500)	
Increase in short-term debt	41,500	
Decrease in net working capital		$ 30,000
Change in fixed assets and land		
Purchase of plant and equipment	$(30,000)	
Purchase of land	(6,000)	
Change in fixed assets and land		$(36,000)
Free cash flows (asset perspective)		$ 15,550

FINANCING CASH FLOWS

Decrease in long-term notes	$ (5,800)
Dividends	(3,650)
Interest expense	(6,100)
Financing cash flows	$ 15,550

M&G Industries has positive free cash flows, which are the result of positive cash flows from operations and a significant reduction in net working capital. Some of these cash flows were then used to invest in long-term assets. The cash flows were then used to reduce long-term debt, pay interest, and pay dividends.

≼ LEARNING OBJECTIVES ≽

After reading this chapter, you should be able to:

1. Explain the purpose and importance of financial analysis.

2. Calculate and use a comprehensive set of measurements to evaluate a company's performance.

3. Describe the limitations of financial ratio analysis.

CHAPTER 4

Evaluating a Firm's Financial Performance

THE PURPOSE OF FINANCIAL ANALYSIS • MEASURING KEY FINANCIAL RELATIONSHIPS • LIMITATIONS OF FINANCIAL RATIO ANALYSIS

In this chapter, we look at financial measurements or metrics that are used to manage a business. Is using metrics to help us manage a business important? John Thompson, CEO, Symantec Corporation, a high-growth Internet security firm, thinks so:

> I don't believe you can manage what you don't measure. A firm needs metrics that serve as an indication for the team about what you're paying attention to. If employees know you're measuring market growth and customer satisfaction, they'll pay attention to those considerations and will behave based on indicators that you, as the leader, provide to the organization. Metrics help the team focus on what's important for an organization.

The best metrics are simple to understand, are simple to communicate, and make it relatively easy for everyone to get access to the data that represents the results. That makes your metrics an effective management tool. If you make your metrics difficult to gather, manage, or communicate, they won't be effective. Simplicity is key.

> My experience has proven to me the importance of picking a few metrics that are the most critical for running the business. Stick with them—and communicate them to both internal and external audiences.[1]

With this advice from an experienced CEO, we begin our study of the key financial metrics that can and must be used by companies, both large and small.

[1] David Liss, "Ask the CEO: Management by the Numbers," *Business Week Online*, New York: The McGraw-Hill Companies, Inc., at www.businessweek.com/technology/content/jul2003/tc20030721_6130.htm, July 23, 2003.

⊰ WHAT'S AHEAD ⊱

This chapter is a natural extension of Chapter 3. In this chapter, we restate financial statements in relative terms to understand how a firm is performing. Specifically, we look at key financial relationships in the form of ratios to understand three basic attributes of firm performance:

- The ability of a firm to meet current liabilities as they come due, or what financial analysts refer to as *liquidity*.
- Management's performance in generating acceptable, and hopefully even superior, profits on the capital that has been entrusted to the firm.
- Management's performance in creating or destroying shareholder value.

BACK TO THE FOUNDATIONS

*As in Chapter 3 when we talked about financial statements, a primary rationale for evaluating a company's financial performance continues to be **Principle 7: Managers Won't Work for the Owners Unless It's in Their Best Interest** to do so. Thus, the firm's common stockholders need information that can be used to monitor managers' actions. Interpreting the firm's financial statements through the use of financial ratios is a key tool in obtaining information that can be used in this monitoring. Moreover, the firm's management needs metrics to monitor firm performance so corrective actions can be taken when necessary.*

*   **Principle 5: The Curse of Competitive Markets—Why It's Hard to Find Exceptionally Profitable Markets** is also relevant in evaluating a firm's financial performance. By exceptional, we mean investments that earn rates of return that exceed the opportunity cost of the money invested. Thus, the notion of a rate of return is a primary issue in knowing whether management is creating shareholder value. Although far from perfect, certain financial ratios can help us better know if management is finding exceptional investments, or if the investments are in fact just the opposite—exceptionally bad.*

*   Finally, **Principle 1: The Risk–Return Trade-Off—We Won't Take On Additional Risk Unless We Expect to Be Compensated with Additional Return** is also at work in this chapter. As we will see, how management chooses to finance the business affects the company's risk and, as a result, the stockholders' rate of return on their investment.*

Objective **1**

THE PURPOSE OF FINANCIAL ANALYSIS

As explained in Chapter 1, the fundamental and core objective of financial management is to create shareholder value, as opposed to focusing on accounting numbers, such as earnings. In a perfect world, we would rely on market values relating to a firm's assets rather than the accounting data. However, we rarely have market values to guide decision making. Thus, we are required to fall back on accounting information.

Financial analysis entails the use of historical financial statements to measure a company's performance and to make financial projections of future performance. Whereas accounting focuses on the *preparation* of financial statements according to *generally accepted accounting principles* (GAAP), finance focuses on how to *use* the information to manage the business. The analysis is primarily based on the use of ratios that help us see critical relationships that might not otherwise be readily identifiable. Ratios are used to standardize financial information so that we can make comparisons. Otherwise, it is really difficult to compare the financial statements of two firms of different sizes and even the same firm at different times.

financial ratios

Financial ratios give us two ways of making meaningful comparisons of a firm's financial data: (1) We can examine the ratios across time (say, for the last 5 years) to compare a firm's current and past performance in order to identify trends; and (2) we can compare the firm's ratios with those of other firms. In comparing a firm with other companies, we could select a peer group of companies, or we could use industry norms published by firms such as Dun & Bradstreet, Robert Morris Associates, Standard & Poor's, and Prentice Hall. Dun & Bradstreet, for instance, annually publishes a set of 14 key ratios for each of 125 lines of business. Robert Morris Associates, the association of bank loan and credit officers, publishes a set of 16 key ratios for more than 350 lines of business. The firms are grouped according to the North American Industrial Classification System (NAICS) codes. They are also segmented by firm size to provide the basis for more meaningful comparisons.

Figure 4-1 shows the financial statement information as reported by Robert Morris Associates (RMA) for new car dealers. The report shows the information by two asset-size and sales-size categories. In the total report, other size categories are presented. The balance sheet data in the report are provided as a percentage of total assets, or what we call a

common-sized balance sheet
common-sized income statement

common-sized balance sheet. Likewise, the income statement data are reported as a percentage of sales, referred to as a **common-sized income statement**. In presenting the financial ratios in the bottom portion of the report, RMA gives three results for each ratio—the firms at the 75th, 50th, and 25th percentiles, respectively.

FIGURE 4-1   Robert Morris Associates, Industry Norms for New Car Dealers

RETAIL—NEW CAR DEALERS NAICS 4411 (SIC 5511)

CURRENT DATA SORTED BY ASSETS			CURRENT DATA SORTED BY SALES	
50-100MM %	100-250MM %	ASSETS	10-25MM %	25MM & OVER %
7.3	8.7	Cash & Equivalents	8.1	10.3
10.0	10.9	Trade Receivables (net)	7.3	8.7
48.3	45.5	Inventory	67.9	60.0
4.4	2.5	All Other Current	2.7	2.9
70.0	67.6	Total Current	85.9	81.9
16.3	20.9	Fixed Assets (net)	8.3	10.9
2.6	1.5	Intangibles (net)	1.4	1.6
11.1	10.0	All Other Non-Current	4.3	5.6
100.0	100.0	Total	100.0	100.0
		LIABILITIES		
		Notes Payable		
42.2	42.5	-Short Term	56.5	51.8
3.5	2.4	Cur. Mat. L/T/D	2.0	2.4
3.5	4.2	Trade Payables	4.3	4.4
.1	.2	Income Taxes Payable	.1	.2
9.7	12.8	All Other Current	9.5	11.2
59.0	62.2	Total Current	72.3	70.0
14.6	16.0	Long Term Debt	6.5	7.5
.6	.3	Deferred Taxes	.1	.2
3.4	2.3	All Other Non-Current	2.7	2.2
22.5	19.2	Net Worth	18.5	20.1
		Total Liabilities		
100.0	100.0	& Net Worth	100.0	100.0
		INCOME DATA		
100.0	100.0	Net Sales	100.0	100.0
15.6	15.6	Gross Profit	12.3	12.1
13.2	14.0	Operating Expenses	11.9	11.2
2.4	1.6	Operating Profit	.3	.9
		All Other		
−.3	.3	Expenses (net)	−.6	−.5
2.6	1.3	Profit Before Taxes	.9	1.4
		RATIOS		
1.3	1.2		1.3	1.3
1.2	1.1	Current	1.2	1.1
1.1	.9		1.1	1.0
.4	.4		.3	.4
.3	.3	Quick	(768) .2 (1302)	.2
.2	.2		.1	.2
5 67.2	6 61.0		3 127.5	4 102.8
10 36.1	11 33.1	Sales/Receivables	5 70.6	6 60.7
17 21.6	17 21.9		9 38.6	10 37.5

CURRENT DATA SORTED BY ASSETS			CURRENT DATA SORTED BY SALES	
50-100MM %	100-250MM %	RATIOS	10-25MM %	25MM & OVER %
52 7.1	53 6.9		60 6.1	46 8.0
67 5.4	62 5.9	Cost of Sales/Inventory	76 4.8	59 6.2
80 4.5	74 5.0		93 3.9	73 5.0
3 142.6	3 111.0		1 257.4	2 209.2
4 84.3	4 81.3	Cost of Sales/Payables	3 140.6	3 123.4
8 43.8	8 43.5		5 71.2	5 77.8
16.7	30.5		17.5	21.9
29.7	95.3	Sales/Working Capital	30.6	39.4
53.0	−98.0		88.5	134.2
8.4	12.7		6.8	11.3
(32) 4.0	(20) 4.1	EBIT/Interest	(597) 2.4	(938) 4.5
1.5	2.5		1.0	1.9
8.4		Net Profit + Depr., Dep.,	4.6	6.7
(10) 1.5		Amort./Cur. Mat. L/T/D	(64) 1.8	(174) 2.2
1.0			.6	.9
.2	.4		.2	.2
.8	1.3	Fixed Assets/Net Worth	.4	.5
1.3	4.9		1.2	1.2
2.4	3.2		3.0	2.6
3.7	5.3	Debt/Net Worth	5.8	4.8
6.6	17.0		14.0	9.8
39.3	77.4	% Profit Before	36.4	50.4
(36) 23.3	(25) 22.2	Taxes/Tangible	(692) 17.4	(1223) 28.0
10.5	13.3	Net Worth	3.0	12.2
8.6	7.7		6.1	9.2
4.4	5.0	% Profit Before Taxes/	2.3	4.8
1.5	2.9	Total Assets	.1	1.6
84.2	74.0		163.6	126.3
22.9	17.7	Sales/Net Fixed Assets	77.4	67.2
9.6	8.2		37.0	27.0
4.0	3.9		4.5	5.2
3.3	3.1	Sales/Total Assets	3.8	4.2
1.9	2.5		3.0	3.4
.3	.2		.1	.1
(37) .4	(21) .5	% Depr., Dep., Amort./Sales	(679) .3	(1214) .3
1.0	.8		.4	.4
.1			.4	.2
(17) .3		% Officers', Directors', Owners' Comp/Sales	(501) .6	(760) .4
1.1			1.1	1.0
7968935M	13431196M	Net Sales ($)	13318098M	95427461M
2604956M	3948948M	Total Assets ($)	3876849M	24306019M

M = $ thousand   MM = $ million

FINANCIAL MANAGEMENT
IN PRACTICE

ONLY WITH FINANCIAL ANALYSIS CAN WE KNOW HOW WE ARE DOING

Until recently, Greg Smith, president and CEO of the Petra Technology Group, based in Corning, New York, rarely examined how his company compared with the rest of the industry. Why would he? Sales and profits of the company, a $1.5 million systems integrator, had grown every year since the company's inception in 1993.

But in 1998 sales flattened. Petra faced losses for the first time. Though it was easy to attribute losses to the sales slump, Smith felt there was more to the story—he just couldn't pin down an answer. Was he overspending in ways he couldn't see?

Smith obtained two industry studies. One was from Robert Morris Associates and the other from a private consulting firm, which Smith found through an Internet search.

Armed with industry-wide information, Smith quickly saw a problem. Payroll and related costs for his 15-employee business exceeded 60 percent of company sales—a ratio the consulting firm generally views as a red flag for companies trying to stay in the black. "At certain points, you have to face the music to remain profitable," Smith says. Part of facing the music for

Smith meant reducing his head count by two and using contractors instead of staff employees.

Smith also checked Petra's ratio of current assets to current liabilities. It was 0.82—too low by most standards. Most of the short-term debt was the result of having to pay down a $100,000 line of credit every year. To address this issue, Smith shifted the majority of his debt from a credit line to a 7-year note.

Smith used the numbers as guides rather than as absolutes. Most research groups recommend this approach in order to take into account the vagaries of individual businesses. Also, the survey process used to collect financial data often skews information in favor of profitable companies, since they're happier to talk about their results.

Smith has also become a lot more scrupulous in other areas, paying more attention to the company's weekly break-even point and charting sales in relation to it. He's learned that a big part of financial discipline is monitoring the simple things. "Losing money for a year is a good wake-up call," he says.

Source: Adapted from Ilan Mochari, "Significant Figures," at www.inc.com, July 1, 2000.

Financial analysis is not just a tool for financial managers but also can be used effectively by investors, lenders, suppliers, employees, and customers. Within the firm, management uses financial ratios to:

➤ Identify deficiencies in a firm's performance and take corrective action.
➤ Evaluate employees' performance and determine incentive compensation.
➤ Compare the financial performance of the different divisions within a firm.
➤ Prepare financial projections, at both the firm and division levels, such as when a firm is considering the launch of a new product.
➤ Understand the financial performance of competitors.
➤ Evaluate the financial condition of a major supplier.

Outside the company financial ratios can be used by:

➤ Lenders in deciding whether or not to make a loan to a company.
➤ Credit-rating agencies in determining a firm's creditworthiness.
➤ Investors in deciding whether or not to invest in a company.
➤ Major suppliers in deciding to sell and grant credit terms to a company.

The conclusion: Financial analysis is helpful to a wide group of individuals for a variety of purposes. However, we will focus on the use of financial ratios within a firm, particularly in evaluating a firm's performance. But remember that personnel in marketing, human resources, information systems, and other groups within a firm can use financial ratios for a variety of reasons.

CONCEPT CHECK

1. What is the basic purpose of financial analysis?
2. Describe the two methods for interpreting the findings from using financial ratios.
3. Where can we find financial ratios for different companies?

MEASURING KEY FINANCIAL RELATIONSHIPS

In learning about ratios, two approaches are generally taken. The first reviews the different types or categories of ratios, whereas the second uses ratios to answer important questions about a firm's operations. We prefer the latter approach and have chosen the following five questions as a map in using financial ratios:

1. How liquid is the firm?
2. Is management generating adequate operating profits on the firm's assets?
3. How is the firm financing its assets?
4. Is management providing a good return on the capital provided by the shareholders?
5. Is the management team creating shareholder value?

Let's look at each of these five questions in turn. In doing so, we will use Starbucks Corporation to illustrate the use of financial ratios. The company's financial statements, which were originally presented in Chapter 3, are shown again in Tables 4-1 and 4-2.

TABLE 4-1	Starbucks Corporation Income Statement for Year Ending September 28, 2003 ($ millions)	
Sales		$4,076
Cost of goods sold		3,207
Gross profit		$ 869
Operating expenses:		
Marketing expenses and general and administrative expenses	$227	
Depreciation expense	206	
Total operating expenses		$ 433
Operating profit (operating income)		$ 436
Interest expense		3
Earnings before taxes		$ 433
Income taxes		165
Net income		$ 268

TABLE 4-2	Starbucks Corporation Balance Sheet ($ millions), September 28, 2003	
ASSETS		
Cash		$ 350
Accounts receivable		114
Inventories		342
Other current assets		116
Total current assets		$ 922
Gross fixed assets		$2,669
Accumulated depreciation		919
Net fixed assets		$1,750
Total assets		$2,672
LIABILITIES AND EQUITY		
Accounts payable and accruals		$ 552
Short-term notes payable		1
Total current liabilities		$ 553
Long-term debt		$ 38
Total liabilities		$ 591
Equity		
Common stock		$1,017
Retained earnings		1,064
Total common equity		$2,081
Total liabilities and equity		$2,672

To give us a basis for comparison, we also provide the average financial ratios of a peer group of similar businesses to Starbucks. In the ratio computations, we have color coded the numbers so that you can readily determine whether a particular number is coming from the income statement (red numbers) or the balance sheet (blue numbers). (Note: As in Chapter 3, an Excel spreadsheet model is available with this chapter at **www.prenhall.com/keown**. We suggest you use the model as you work through the different examples in the chapter.)

QUESTION 1: HOW LIQUID IS THE FIRM—CAN WE PAY THE BILLS?

liquidity

A liquid asset is one that can be converted quickly and routinely into cash at the current market price. So the **liquidity** of a business is a function of its ability to have cash available when needed to meet its financial obligations. Very simply, can we expect the company to be able to pay creditors on a timely basis?

This question can be answered in two complementary approaches: (1) by comparing the firm's assets that are relatively liquid (i.e., can be converted quickly and easily into cash) with the debt coming due in the near term, and (2) by examining the timeliness with which the firm's primary liquid assets—accounts receivable and inventories—are being converted into cash. Let's consider these two approaches.

MEASURING LIQUIDITY: APPROACH 1

The first approach to measuring liquidity is to compare "liquid" assets that should be converted into cash within the next 12 months against the debt (liabilities) that is coming due within 12 months. The most liquid assets shown in a balance sheet are the current assets, since these are the assets that should be converted into cash in the normal operating cycle of the business. Also, in a balance sheet, the current (short-term) liabilities represent the firm's debt that will be coming due within the next 12 months. Thus, the most commonly **current ratio** used measure of a firm's short-term solvency is the **current ratio**:

$$\text{Current ratio} = \frac{\text{current assets}}{\text{current liabilities}} \tag{4-1}$$

For Starbucks:

$$\text{Current ratio} = \frac{\$922M}{\$553M} = 1.67$$

Peer-group current ratio	2.02

Based on the current ratio, Starbucks is less liquid than the average firm in the peer group—$1.67 in current assets for every $1 in short-term debt, compared to a peer-group average current ratio of $2.02.

In using the current ratio, we assume that the firm's accounts receivable will be collected and turned into cash on a timely basis and that the inventories can be sold without any extended delay. Clearly, for most firms, inventory is less liquid than accounts receivable, since it must first be sold before any cash can be collected. So if we want to have a more stringent test of a firm's liquidity, we include only cash and accounts receivable in the **acid-test (quick) ratio** numerator of our liquidity measure. This revised ratio is called the **acid-test** (or **quick**) **ratio**, and is calculated as follows:

$$\text{Acid-test ratio} = \frac{\text{cash} + \text{accounts receivable}}{\text{current liabilities}} \tag{4-2}$$

For Starbucks:

$$\text{Acid-test ratio} = \frac{\$350M + \$114M}{\$553M} = 0.84$$

Peer-group acid-test ratio	1.44

Thus, based on the acid-test ratio, Starbucks continues to appear less liquid—$0.84 in cash and accounts receivable per $1 in current debt, compared to $1.44 for the average company in the peer group.

MEASURING LIQUIDITY: APPROACH 2

The second approach to measuring liquidity examines the firm's ability to convert accounts receivable and inventory into cash on a timely basis.

Converting Accounts Receivable to Cash

The conversion of accounts receivable into cash can be measured by computing *how long it takes to collect the firm's receivables*; that is, how many days of sales are outstanding in the form of accounts receivable? We can answer this question by computing a firm's **days of sales outstanding**, or its **average collection period**, as follows:[2]

days of sales outstanding
average collection period

$$\frac{\text{Average collection}}{\text{period}} = \frac{\text{accounts receivable}}{\text{annual credit sales}/365} = \frac{\text{accounts receivable}}{\text{daily credit sales}} \qquad (4\text{--}3)$$

To compute the average collection period, we need to know (1) a firm's accounts receivable, which represent credit sales that have not been collected, and (2) total credit sales for the year, restated on a daily basis, or credit sales per day. For Starbucks, we know that:

1. The firm's accounts receivable for year-end 2003 totaled $114 million (Table 4-2).
2. Based on information from Starbucks' 2003 annual report (not provided here), we have estimated that the firm's $4.076 billion in sales consisted of $3.465 billion in cash sales and $611 million in credit sales. Cash sales came primarily from those of us who like to have our daily cup of Starbucks and pay with cash. The credit sales of $611 million came from selling to commercial customers, such as Barnes & Noble, who buy on credit.
3. Given credit sales for 2003 of about $611 million, the firm's daily credit sales would be $1.67 million ($1.67 million = $611 million ÷ 365 days).

We can now estimate Starbucks' *average collection period*, as follows:

$$\frac{\text{Average collection}}{\text{period}} = \frac{\text{accounts receivable}}{\text{daily credit sales}}$$

For Starbucks:

$$\frac{\text{Average collection}}{\text{period}} = \frac{\$114M}{\$611M/365 \text{ days}} = \frac{\$114M}{\$1.67M/\text{day}} = 68.3 \text{ days}$$

Peer-group average collection period	93 days

So, Starbucks converts its accounts receivable into cash 25 days faster than its peer group (68 days compared to 93 days), which suggests that the firm's receivables are significantly more liquid than for competing firms.

We could have reached the same conclusion by measuring how many times accounts receivable are "rolled over" during a year, using the **accounts receivable turnover ratio**. If Starbucks collects its accounts receivable every 68 days, then it is collecting 5.34 times per year (5.34 times = 365 days ÷ 68.3 days). The accounts receivable turnover can also be calculated as follows:

accounts receivable turnover ratio

$$\frac{\text{Accounts receivable}}{\text{turnover}} = \frac{\text{annual credit sales}}{\text{accounts receivable}} \qquad (4\text{--}4)$$

[2]In computing a given ratio that uses information from both the income statement and the balance sheet, we should remember that the income statement is for a given time period (e.g., 2005), whereas balance sheet data are at a point in time (e.g., December 31, 2005). If there has been a significant change in an asset from the beginning of the period to the end of the period, it would be better to use the average balance for the year. For example, if the accounts receivable for a company have increased from $1,000 at the beginning of the year to $2,000 at the end of the year, it would be more appropriate to use the average accounts receivable of $1,500 in our computations. Nevertheless, in an effort to simplify, we will use year-end amounts from the balance sheet in our computations.

EVALUATING DISNEY'S LIQUIDITY

The following information is taken from the Walt Disney Company's financial statements:

Current assets	$8,314
Accounts receivable	4,238
Cash	1,583
Inventories	1,271
Sales (all credit)	23,373
Cost of goods sold	19,097
Total current liabilities	8,669

Evaluate Disney's liquidity based on the following norms in the broadcasting and entertainment industry, as follows:

Current ratio	1.17
Acid-test ratio	0.92
Accounts receivable turnover	10.08
Inventory turnover	18.32

Check your answer on page 110.

For Starbucks:

$$\text{Accounts receivable turnover} = \frac{\$611M}{\$114M} = 5.36\times$$

Peer-group accounts receivable turnover	3.90×

Whether we use the average collection period or the accounts receivable turnover ratio, the conclusion is the same. Starbucks Corporation is considerably faster at collecting its receivables than competing firms.

Converting Inventories to Cash

inventory turnover ratio

We now want to know how liquid Starbucks' inventories are: *How many times is the company turning over inventories during the year?* The **inventory turnover ratio** is calculated as follows:[3]

$$\text{Inventory turnover} = \frac{\text{cost of goods sold}}{\text{inventory}} \qquad \textbf{(4-5)}$$

For Starbucks:

$$\text{Inventory turnover} = \frac{\$3,207M}{\$342M} = 9.38\times$$

Peer-group inventory turnover	8.5×

Thus, Starbucks is moving (turning over) its inventory somewhat faster than the average peer-group firm—9.38 times per year at Starbucks, compared with 8.5 times for the peer group, which suggests that the firm's inventory is more liquid than the case for the peer group on average.

days of sales in inventory

We could also express the inventory turnover in terms of the number of **days of sales in inventory**. Since Starbucks turns its inventory over 9.38 times per year, then on average it is carrying its inventory for 39 days (365 days ÷ 9.38 times per year), whereas the average peer firm takes almost 43 days (365 days ÷ 8.5 times per year).

---

[3]Note that sales has been replaced by cost of goods sold in the numerator. Because the inventory (the denominator) is measured at cost, we want to use a cost-based measure of sales in the numerator. Otherwise, our answer would vary from one firm to the next solely because of differences in how each firm marks up its sales over costs. However, some of the industry norms provided by financial services are computed using sales in the numerator. In those cases, we will want to use sales in our computation of inventory turnover in order to be consistent.

To conclude, Starbucks' liquidity appears lower than the average peer-group company when we measure liquidity using the current and the acid-test ratios. However, one reason, if not the complete reason, for the lower current and acid-test ratios is Starbucks' ability to collect its receivables and turn its inventory over more quickly, which allows the firm to maintain smaller balances in these two assets. Therefore, it appears that Starbucks' liquidity is roughly on par with peer firms.

QUESTION 2: IS MANAGEMENT GENERATING ADEQUATE OPERATING PROFITS ON THE FIRM'S ASSETS?

We now switch to a different dimension of firm performance—the firm's profitability. The question here is, "Does management produce adequate profits from the firm's assets?" From the perspective of the firm's shareholders, there is no more important question to be asked. One of the most important ways that management can create shareholder value is to earn strong profits on the assets in which they have invested.

In evaluating a firm's profits on the assets, think about the process of financing a company. In its simplest form, a firm's shareholders invest in a business and over time they borrow money to use along with their own investment. The cumulative effects of this process are reflected in a firm's balance sheet. For example, Figure 4-2 indicates that Starbucks' shareholders have invested $2,081 million in the company and the company has borrowed another $591 million to finance $2,672 million of assets. These assets are then used to produce $436 million in operating profits.

At this point, we want to know the profits that have been generated on the total assets. We measure profits using *operating profit* (frequently referred to as the *operating income* or *earnings before interest and taxes*). In evaluating a firm's profits relative to its assets, we could choose between *operating profit* or *net income*. We will choose operating profit, rather than net income, because operating profit does not include the firm's cost of debt financing—the interest expense. The effect of financing will be explicitly considered in our next question, but for now we want to isolate only the operating aspects of the company's profits. In this way, we are able to compare the profitability of firms with different debt-to-equity mixes.

To examine the *level of operating profit relative to the total assets*, we use the **operating return on assets (OROA):**

operating return on assets (OROA)

$$\frac{\text{Operating return}}{\text{on assets}} = \frac{\text{operating profit}}{\text{total assets}} \qquad \textbf{(4–6)}$$

For Starbucks:

$$\frac{\text{Operating return}}{\text{on assets}} = \frac{\$436M}{\$2,672M} = 0.163 \text{ or } 16.3\%$$

Peer-group operating return on assets	14.9%

Starbucks Corporation is earning a higher return on assets relative to the average firm in the peer group. Management is generating 16.3 cents for every $1 of assets, compared to 14.9 cents on average for the peer group.

FIGURE 4-2   Starbucks Corporation Profits to Assets Relationship for Fiscal Year Ended September 28, 2003

TESTING YOUR
UNDERSTANDING

EVALUATING DISNEY'S LIQUIDITY: HOW DID YOU DO?

	DISNEY	INDUSTRY
Current ratio	0.96	1.17
Acid-test ratio	0.67	0.92
Accounts receivable turnover	5.52	10.08
Inventory turnover	15.03	18.32

Disney is not as liquid as the average firm in the industry—no matter how you measure it! It does not have the liquid assets to cover current liabilities, nor does it convert receivables and inventories to cash as quickly.

While management can be pleased that it is generating a return on the firm's assets that is higher than the competition, they will also want to know how they are achieving the superior return. The answer lies in two areas: (1) *operations management*, which includes the day-to-day buying and selling of a firm's goods or services as reflected in the income statement, and (2) *asset management*, as shown in the balance sheet. We can relate operations management and asset management through a firm's *operating return on assets* using the product of two ratios; that is,

$$\underset{\text{on assets}}{\text{Operating return}} = \underset{\substack{\text{OPERATIONS} \\ \text{MANAGEMENT}}}{\underset{\text{margin}}{\text{operating profit}}} \times \underset{\substack{\text{ASSET} \\ \text{MANAGEMENT}}}{\underset{\text{turnover}}{\text{total asset}}} \qquad \textbf{(4-7a)}$$

which is calculated as follows:

$$\underset{\text{on assets}}{\text{Operating return}} = \frac{\text{operating profits}}{\text{sales}} \times \frac{\text{sales}}{\text{total assets}} \qquad \textbf{(4-7b)}$$

[handwritten: Op. Income / Total assets]

Managing Operations

operating profit margin

The first component of the operating return on assets (OROA), the **operating profit margin**, is an indicator of a company's *effectiveness in managing its operations* (i.e., generating revenues while controlling expenses). The operating profit margin measures how well a firm is managing its cost of operations, in terms of both the cost of goods sold and operating expenses (marketing expenses and general and administrative expenses) relative to the firm's revenues. All else being equal, the objective for managing operations is to keep costs and expenses low relative to sales. Thus, we often say that the operating profit margin measures *how well the firm is managing its income statement.*

For Starbucks:

$$\underset{\text{margin}}{\text{Operating profit}} = \frac{\text{operating profits}}{\text{sales}} \qquad \textbf{(4-8)}$$

$$= \frac{\$436M}{\$4,076M} = 0.107 \text{ or } 10.7\%$$

Peer-group operating profit margin	11.8%

The foregoing results suggest that Starbucks' management is not as effective in managing its cost of goods sold and operating expenses as comparable firms. It has higher costs per sales dollar, which result in a lower operating profit margin. *Starbucks is not as good as other comparable firms at managing its income statement.*

FINANCIAL MANAGEMENT
IN PRACTICE

KEEPING YOUR EYES ON THE NUMBERS

Rick Sapio keeps a sign on the wall of his office. Its message: "Profit equals revenues less expenses." The chart is a gimmick but, nevertheless, is important to Sapio, the CEO of Dallas-based Mutuals.com.

Sapio didn't always have that sign on the wall, and he didn't believe he needed it—or anything else—as a manifesto. When he started Mutuals.com, Sapio never really thought about keeping an eye on expenses. He didn't have to. "I found it very easy to raise money," he says, and as the boom of the 1990s wore on and the marketplace was flush with investment capital, raising money got even simpler.

All that cash was not necessarily a good thing, Sapio admits now. "We were not accountable to being a profitable company at the beginning and hence our energies weren't focused on looking at expenses."

During the past few years, Sapio has made some changes. His first step was learning to keep an eye on the numbers. After reading that Cisco Systems Inc., closes its books every day, Sapio took up the practice. Now all financial transactions are entered the same day they occur to create a real-time picture of the company's revenues and expenses. It's good discipline and surprisingly easy with today's accounting software.

Today Sapio gathers his top managers in a daily huddle to go over the figures. Each person is responsible for updating at least one revenue item and one expense. "Every line item on our financial statement has a name next to it," Sapio says. "So if travel's out of whack, I'll say, 'Ernie, give us a report on how we can lower travel next week.'"

Source: Emily Barker, "Finance: Cheap Executive Officer," *Inc. Magazine*, vol. 24, no. 4 (April 2002), pp. 38–40.

Managing Assets

The second component in equation (4-7) is the **total asset turnover**. This ratio indicates how well the firm is managing its assets, or **asset efficiency**. It measures how efficiently a firm is using its assets to generate sales. To clarify, assume that Company A generates $3 in sales for every $1 in assets, whereas Company B generates the same $3 in sales but has invested $2 in assets. We may conclude that Company A is using its assets more efficiently to generate sales, which leads to a higher return on the firm's investment in assets.

total asset turnover
asset efficiency

For Starbucks:

$$\frac{\text{Total asset}}{\text{turnover}} = \frac{\text{sales}}{\text{total assets}} \qquad (4\text{-}9)$$

$$= \frac{\$4{,}076M}{\$2{,}672M} = 1.53\times$$

Peer-group total asset turnover	1.26×

Starbucks is using its assets more efficiently than its competitors as it generates about $1.53 in sales per dollar of assets, whereas the competition produces only $1.26 in sales from every dollar in assets.

We should not stop here with our analysis of Starbucks' asset utilization. We have learned that Starbucks' management is making effective use of the firm's assets, but this may not be the case for each and every type of asset. Specifically, is management efficiently managing the investment in accounts receivable, inventories, and fixed assets?

To answer the preceding question, we examine the turnover ratios for each asset category. We have already calculated these ratios for accounts receivable and inventories, where we concluded that Starbucks' managers are managing the firm's accounts receivable and inventories more efficiently than competitors. Thus, we only need to compute the turnover for fixed assets as follows:

$$\frac{\text{Fixed asset}}{\text{turnover}} = \frac{\text{sales}}{\text{net fixed assets}} \qquad (4\text{-}10)$$

TESTING YOUR UNDERSTANDING

EVALUATING DISNEY'S OPERATING RETURN ON ASSETS

Given the following financial information for the Walt Disney Company (expressed in $ millions), evaluate the firm's operating return on assets (OROA).

Accounts receivable	$ 4,238
Inventories	1,271
Sales	23,373
Operating profits	2,314
Cost of goods sold	19,097
Gross fixed assets	27,677
Accumulated depreciation	12,482
Net fixed assets	15,195
Total assets	49,988

The peer group norms are as follows:

Operating return on assets	3.84%
Operating profit margin	11.30%
Total asset turnover	0.34
Accounts receivable turnover	10.08
Inventory turnover	18.32
Fixed asset turnover	1.05

Check your answers on page 114.

For Starbucks:

$$\text{Fixed asset turnover} = \frac{\$4,076M}{\$1,750M} = 2.33\times$$

Peer-group fixed asset turnover	2.75×

Thus, Starbucks has a larger investment in fixed assets relative to the firm's sales than average for the peer group. Most likely, the significant growth in the number of new stores in recent years (some 8,000 new stores in the preceding decade) has resulted in Starbucks' larger investment in fixed assets. Also, the book value of Starbucks' fixed assets could be higher than for the peer firms since it purchased its assets in more recent times. More recent asset purchases would be at higher prices due to inflation. Also, the newer fixed assets that Starbucks owns will have less accumulated depreciation on the balance sheet.

We can now look at all the asset efficiency ratios together to summarize Starbucks' asset management:

	STARBUCKS	PEER GROUP
Total asset turnover	1.53×	1.26×
Accounts receivable turnover	5.36×	3.90×
Inventory turnover	9.38×	8.50×
Fixed asset turnover	2.33×	2.75×

Starbucks' situation with respect to asset management efficiency is now clear. Overall, Starbucks' management is utilizing the firm's assets efficiently, as based on the firm's total asset turnover. This overall asset efficiency results from better management of accounts receivable and inventories (higher turnovers of accounts receivable and inventories) and not more efficient management of fixed assets (lower **fixed asset turnover**).

Figure 4-3 provides a summary of our evaluation of Starbucks' operating and asset management performance. We began by computing the operating return on assets to determine if management is producing good returns on the assets. We then broke the operating return on assets into its two pieces, operations management (operating profit margin) and asset management (asset turnover ratios) to explain why the operating return on assets is higher or lower than the peer group.

fixed asset turnover

FINANCIAL MANAGEMENT
IN PRACTICE

MANAGING BY THE NUMBERS

Dorian S. Boyland is taking care of business as he bustles about his 29,000-square-foot Honda dealership, located in Greenfield, Wisconsin. He is preparing for a grand opening, even though the store has been open since 2001.

Boyland, 48, is excited about the festivities, but he intends to get a return on this investment. Make no mistake about it; he is meticulous about how he spends money, keeping advertising and sales salaries less than 10 percent of gross profits. No more than 10 percent of gross profits is paid in commissions to managers, and no more than 15 percent of gross profits is awarded in commissions to sales managers.

The auto dealer operates with one goal in mind: net a 3 to 3.5 percent profit on sales from all seven of his auto dealerships. "I never ask how many cars we sold," says Boyland. "I ask my sales managers how much profit did we make. I operate on the premise that if I sell a car for $20,000, I know that 3 percent (or $600) of that amount is going to go to my bottom line. Now, how I get that 3 percent is how we operate the store—from the bottom up."

Boyland's cost controls are a never-ending process. He has a system of financial analysis that is generated monthly and reviewed by all store managers. This information sharing allows every general manager and sales manager to critique one another, exchange ideas, and establish goals and guidelines.

Volume is very important to dealers because manufacturers expect them to achieve a certain level of market penetration. But as Boyland sees it, "You can be No. 1 in terms of volume, but if you are constantly losing that manufacturer money, you'll be taken out of business."

Boyland grows excited when discussing business strategies. "You have to have a passion for this business," he says. "There's a lot of money to be made and a lot of money to be lost. But whether you are selling cars or shoes, you go into business to make money. That's the bottom line."

Source: Carolyn M. Brown, "Maximum Overdrive," *Black Enterprise*, vol. 33, no. 11 (June 2003), pp. 156–162.

FIGURE 4-3   Analysis of Starbucks Corporation Operating Return on Assets (OROA)

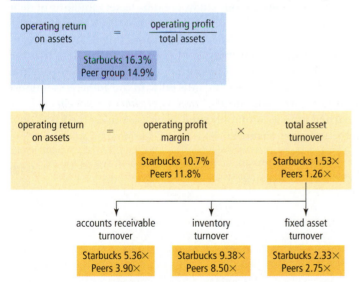

QUESTION 3: HOW IS THE FIRM FINANCING ITS ASSETS?

We now turn to the matter of how the firm is financed. (We will return to the issue of profitability shortly.) The basic issue now is how the firm finances its assets, either with debt or equity. In answering this question, we use two ratios. First, we ask *what percentage of the firm's assets is financed by debt*, including *both* short-term and long-term debt, realizing that the remaining percentage must be financed by equity. We compute the debt ratio as follows:

$$\text{Debt ratio} = \frac{\text{total debt}}{\text{total assets}}$$

(4-11)

TESTING YOUR
UNDERSTANDING

EVALUATING DISNEY'S OPERATING RETURN ON ASSETS: HOW DID YOU DO?

Disney generates a slightly higher return on its assets than the average firm in the industry, 4.63 percent compared to 3.84 percent.

Disney provided a higher operating return on assets, not by managing its operations better (as suggested by a lower operating profit margin), but by making better use of its assets (higher total asset turnover). The higher total asset turnover is due to a higher fixed asset turnover, which makes up for the less efficient management of accounts receivable and inventories (low turnovers).

	DISNEY	INDUSTRY
Operating return on assets	4.63%	3.84%
Operating profit margin	9.90%	11.30%
Total asset turnover	0.47	0.34
Accounts receivable turnover	5.52	10.08
Inventory turnover	15.03	18.32
Fixed asset turnover	1.54	1.05

For Starbucks:

$$\text{Debt ratio} = \frac{\$591M}{\$2,672M} = 0.221 = 22.1\%$$

Peer-group debt ratio	25%

Starbucks Corporation finances 22 percent of its assets with debt (taken from Starbucks' balance sheet in Table 4-2), compared with the peer-group average of 25 percent. Stated differently, Starbucks finances with 78 percent equity, whereas the average for the peer group is 75 percent equity. Thus, Starbucks used slightly less debt than the peer-group average. As we will see at several points in our study, greater (lesser) amounts of debt financing results in greater (lesser) financial risk.[4]

Our second perspective regarding the firm's financing decisions comes by looking at the income statement. When we borrow money, there is a minimum requirement that the firm pay the interest on what it has borrowed. Thus, it is informative to compare the amount of operating income that is available to pay the interest with the amount of interest that is to be paid. Stated as a ratio, we compute the *number of times we are earning our interest*. The **times interest earned** ratio is commonly used when examining the firm's debt position and is computed in the following manner:

times interest earned

$$\text{Times interest earned} = \frac{\text{operating profit}}{\text{interest expense}} \tag{4-12}$$

For Starbucks:

$$\text{Times interest earned} = \frac{\$436M}{\$3M} = 145.3\times$$

Peer-group times interest earned	46.0×

Starbucks Corporation's interest expense is only $3 million, which when compared to its operating income of $436 million indicates that its interest expense is less than 1 percent of its operating profits—hardly anything for management or investors to be worried about. Even Starbucks' peer group has a very high times interest earned ratio of 46 times. As a side note, a more "typical" times interest earned ratio for most firms is something close to 10 times earnings.[5]

---

[4]Instead of using the debt ratio, we could use the debt–equity ratio. The debt–equity ratio is simply a transformation of the debt ratio:

$$\text{Debt–equity ratio} = \frac{\text{total debt}}{\text{total equity}} = \frac{\text{debt ratio}}{1 - \text{debt ratio}} \text{ and the debt ratio} = \frac{\text{total debt}}{\text{total assets}} = \frac{\text{debt/equity}}{1 + \text{debt/equity}}$$

[5]For example, Barnes & Noble and McDonald's have times interest earned ratios of 15.0 and 7.3, respectively.

TESTING YOUR
UNDERSTANDING

EVALUATING DISNEY'S FINANCING POLICIES

Given the information to the right for the Walt Disney Company, calculate the firm's debt ratio and the times interest earned. How do Disney's practices compare to the industry? What are the implications of your findings?

Check your answers on the next page.

Total debt	$26,197
Equity	
Common stock	10,627
Retained earnings	13,164
Total liabilities and equity	49,988
Operating profits	2,314
Interest expense	793
Peer group norms:	
Debt ratio	34.21%
Times interest earned	4.50×

Why would Starbucks, and to a lesser extent the peer group, have such unusually high times interest earned ratios? There are two possible explanations. First, Starbucks and the peer group use less debt than most companies. This means less interest expense. Second, we see in Starbucks' balance sheet that almost all of its debt is accounts payable and accruals, which carry no explicit interest payments. Most of Starbucks' debt is simply liabilities incurred in the normal operating cycle of the business and not from borrowing money from banks or other financial institutions.[6]

Before concluding our discussion regarding times interest earned, we should understand that interest is not paid with income but with cash. Moreover, the firm may be required to repay some of the debt principal. Thus, the times interest earned ratio is only a crude measure of the firm's capacity to service its debt. Nevertheless, it does give us a general indication of a company's financial risk and its ability to borrow.

QUESTION 4: IS MANAGEMENT PROVIDING A GOOD RETURN ON THE CAPITAL PROVIDED BY THE SHAREHOLDERS?

We now want to look at the *accounting return on the common stockholders' investment*, or the **return on equity** (frequently shortened to *ROE*); that is, we want to know if the earnings available to the firm's owners (shareholders) are attractive when compared with the returns earned for the owners of companies in the peer group. We measure the return on equity (ROE) as follows:

return on equity

$$\frac{\text{Return on}}{\text{equity}} = \frac{\text{net income}}{\text{common equity}} = \frac{\text{net income}}{\text{common stock} + \text{retained earnings}} \quad \text{(4-13)}$$

For Starbucks:

$$\frac{\text{Return on}}{\text{equity}} = \frac{\$268M}{\$2,081M} = 0.129 \text{ or } 12.9\%$$

Peer-group return on equity	12.0%

In the preceding computation, the common equity includes all common equity in the balance sheet, both common stock and retained earnings. (Understand that profits retained within the business are as much of an investment for the common stockholders as when the shareholders bought the common stock.)

[6]Are suppliers really willing to extend credit to a firm without charging interest? In reality, suppliers imbed the cost of the credit in the price of the merchandise they sell. So there is an implicit interest cost that is not recognized in conventional financial statements prepared by accountants.

EVALUATING DISNEY'S FINANCING POLICIES: HOW DID YOU DO?

	DISNEY	INDUSTRY
Debt ratio	52.41%	34.21%
Times interest earned	2.92×	4.50×

Disney uses significantly more debt financing than the average firm in the industry. It also has lower interest coverage. The higher debt ratio implies that the firm has greater financial risk. The lower interest coverage is the result of Disney using more debt, resulting in a higher interest expense.

The return on equity for Starbucks Corporation and the peer group are 12.9 percent and 12 percent, respectively. Hence, the owners of Starbucks Corporation are receiving a somewhat higher return on their equity investment than the shareholders in peer-group firms. How are they doing it? To answer, we need to draw on what we have already learned, namely, that:

1. Starbucks Corporation is receiving a higher operating return on assets. We learned earlier that the operating return on assets was 16.3 percent for Starbucks, compared to 14.9 percent for the competition. A higher return on the firm's assets will always result in a higher return on equity.
2. On the other hand, Starbucks uses slightly less debt (more equity) financing than the average firm in the industry—22 percent debt for Starbucks and 25 percent debt for the peer group. As we will see shortly, the less debt a firm uses, the lower its return on equity will be, provided that the firm is earning a return on assets greater than the interest rate on its debt. Thus, Starbucks' peer group, on average, has increased the return for its shareholders by using slightly more debt. That's the good news. The bad news for the peer-group shareholders is that the more debt a firm uses, the greater the company's financial risk, which translates into more risk for the shareholders.

To help us understand the foregoing reason for Starbucks' higher return on equity and its implications, consider the following example.

EXAMPLE: THE EFFECT OF USING DEBT ON NET INCOME

Firms A and B are identical in size, both having $1,000 in total assets and both having an operating return on assets of 14 percent. However, they are different in one respect: Firm A uses all equity and no debt and Firm B finances 60 percent of its investments with debt and 40 percent with equity. (For the sake of simplicity, we will assume that both firms pay interest at an interest cost of 6 percent and there are no income taxes.) The financial statements for the two companies would be as follows:

	FIRM A	FIRM B
BALANCE SHEET		
Total assets	$1,000	$1,000
Debt (6% interest rate)	$ 0	$ 600
Equity	1,000	400
Total debt and equity	$1,000	$1,000
INCOME STATEMENT		
Operating income (OROA = 14%)	$ 140	$ 140
Interest expense (6%)	0	36
Net income	$ 140	$ 104

TESTING YOUR
UNDERSTANDING

EVALUATING DISNEY'S RETURN ON EQUITY

The net income and also the common equity invested by Disney's shareholders (expressed in $ millions) follow, along with the average return on equity for the industry. Evaluate the rate of return being earned on the common stockholders' equity investment. In addition to comparing Disney's return on equity to the industry, consider the implications of its operating return on assets and its debt financing practices for the firm's return on equity.

Net income	$1,300
Equity	
Common stock	10,627
Retained earnings	13,164
Industry average return on equity	2.31%

Check your answers on page 118.

Computing the return on equity for both companies, we see that Firm B has a more attractive return of 26 percent compared with Firm A's 14 percent. The calculations are as follows:

	FIRM A	**FIRM B**

$$\frac{\text{Return}}{\text{on equity}} = \frac{\text{net income}}{\text{common equity}} = \frac{\$140}{\$1,000} = 14\% \qquad \frac{\$104}{\$400} = 26\%$$

Why the difference? The answer is straightforward. Firm B is earning 14 percent on its investments, but it only has to pay 6 percent for its borrowed money. The difference between the 14 percent return on the firm's assets (operating return on assets) and the 6 percent interest rate goes to the owners, thus boosting Firm B's return on equity above that of Firm A.

This is an illustration of favorable financial leverage. What's favorable, you might ask? Well, you earn 14 percent on your investments while paying only 6 percent to the bankers, thus capturing an 8 percent spread on each dollar of debt financing. The result is an increase in the return on equity to Firm B when compared to Firm A.

What a great deal for the shareholders! So if debt enhances the owners' returns, why doesn't Starbucks borrow more?

The good outcome for Firm B shareholders is based on the assumption that the firm does in fact earn 14 percent operating return on the assets. What if the economy falls into a deep recession, business declines sharply, and Firms A and B only earn a 2 percent operating return on assets? Let's recompute the return on equity as follows:

	FIRM A	FIRM B
Operating income (OROA = 2%)	$20	$20
Less: Interest expense	(0)	(36)
Net income	$20	($16)
Return on equity:		
$\dfrac{\text{net income}}{\text{common equity}}$	$\dfrac{\$20}{\$1,000}$	$\dfrac{(\$16)}{\$400}$
Equals:	2%	−4%

Now the use of financial leverage has a negative influence on the return on equity, with Firm B earning less than Firm A for its owners. This results from Firm B earning less than the interest rate of 6 percent; consequently, the equity investors have to make up the difference. Thus, financial leverage is a two-edged sword; when times are good, financial leverage can make them very, very good, but when times are bad, financial leverage makes them very, very bad. Thus, financial leverage can enhance the returns of the equity investors, but it also increases the possibility of losses, thereby increasing the uncertainty or risk for the owners.

Figure 4-4 provides a summary of our discussion of the return on equity and helps us visualize the two fundamental drivers of a firm's return on equity:

1. There is a direct relationship between a firm's operating return on assets (OROA) and the resulting return on equity (ROE). The higher the operating return on assets (OROA), the higher will be the return on equity (ROE). More specifically, the greater the difference between the firm's operating return on assets (OROA) and the interest rate (i) being paid on the firm's debt, the higher the return on equity will be. So increasing the operating return on assets relative to the interest rate (OROA – i) increases the return on equity (ROE). But if (OROA – i) decreases, then ROE will decrease as well.

2. Increasing the amount of debt financing relative to the amount of equity (increasing the debt ratio) increases the return on equity if the operating return on assets is higher than the interest rate being paid. If the operating return on assets falls below the interest rate, more debt financing will decrease the return on equity.

In short, the return on equity is driven by (1) the spread between the operating return on assets and the interest rate (OROA – i), and (2) changes in the debt ratio.

FIGURE 4-4   Return on Equity Relationships

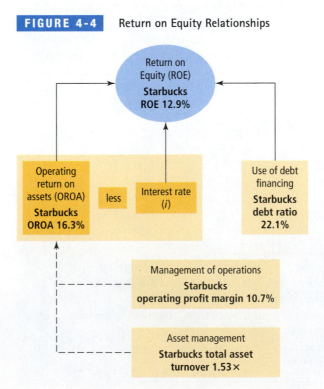

> **CONCEPT CHECK**
>
> 1. How will a firm use financial ratios? Who else might use financial ratios and why?
> 2. What questions can financial ratios answer in evaluating a firm's financial performance?
> 3. Which number in the income statement should be used in measuring profitability relative to total assets and why?
> 4. What are the two driving forces behind the operating return on assets?
> 5. What is the relationship between the use of debt and the return on equity for shareholders?

QUESTION 5: IS THE MANAGEMENT TEAM CREATING SHAREHOLDER VALUE?

To this point, we have relied exclusively on accounting data for identifying key financial relationships within a firm. We now want to look at management's performance in terms of creating or destroying shareholder value.

To answer this question, we use two approaches: (1) We examine market-value ratios, and (2) we estimate the value being created for shareholders, as measured by a popular technique called Economic Value Added (EVA™).

MARKET-VALUE RATIOS

There are two commonly used ratios that compare the firm's stock price to the firm's earnings and the accounting book value of the equity. These two ratios indicate what investors think of management's past performance and future prospects.

Price/Earnings Ratio

The **price/earnings** (P/E) **ratio** indicates how much investors are willing to pay for $1 of reported earnings. For example, for 2003, Starbucks' net income was $268 million. The firm had about 391 million common shares outstanding, so Starbucks' earnings per share was $0.69 ($0.69 = $268 million net income ÷ 391 million shares). At that time, the stock was selling for $35 per share. Thus, the price/earnings ratio was 51 times, calculated as follows:

price/earnings ratio

$$\text{Price/earnings ratio} = \frac{\text{price per share}}{\text{earnings per share}}$$

$$= \frac{\$35.00}{\$0.69} = 50.7\times \qquad \textbf{(4-14)}$$

Standard & Poor's 500 Index price/earnings ratio	24×

Starbucks' price/earnings ratio tells us that the investors are willing to pay $50.70 for every dollar of earnings per share that Starbucks produces, compared to a price/earnings ratio of 24 times for the firms making up the Standard & Poor's 500 Index (the largest 500 corporations in the United States). Clearly, investors are willing to pay a significantly higher price for Starbucks' earnings than for the average firm in the Standard & Poor's 500 Index. Why might that be? The price/earnings ratio will be higher for companies that investors think have strong growth prospects with low risk. Thus, investors are rewarding Starbucks for its growth potential and its low risk compared to the average company in the peer group.

Price/Book Ratio

A second frequently used indicator of the investors' assessment of the firm is the **price/book ratio**. This ratio compares the market value of a share of stock to the book value per share of the firm's reported equity in the balance sheet. We already know that the market price of

price/book ratio

TESTING YOUR
UNDERSTANDING

COMPUTING DISNEY'S PRICE/EARNINGS RATIO AND PRICE/BOOK RATIO

Disney's stock was selling for $24 when its net income was $1.3 billion ($1,300 million) and its common equity in the balance sheet (book equity) was $23.791 billion ($23,791 million). There were 2.031 billion shares outstanding. What was the firm's earnings per share and its book value per share? Calculate the price/earnings ratio and the price/book ratio. What do the shareholders think about the firm's performance?

Check your answer on page 121.

Starbucks' common stock was $35. To determine the equity book value per share, we divide the firm's equity book value by the number of shares of stock. From Starbucks' balance sheet (Table 4-2), we see that the equity book value is $2,081 million (including both common stock and retained earnings). Remembering that Starbucks had 391 million shares outstanding, the equity book value per share is $5.32 ($5.32 = $2,081 million book equity value ÷ 391 million shares). With this information, we determine the price/book ratio to be:

$$\text{Price/book ratio} = \frac{\text{price per share}}{\text{equity book value per share}}$$

$$= \frac{\$35.00}{\$5.32} = 6.58\times$$

(4-15)

Standard & Poor's 500 Index price/book ratio	3×

Given that the book value per share is an accounting number that reflects historical costs, we can roughly think of it as the original price investors paid for their shares. So, a ratio greater than 1 indicates that investors believe the firm is more valuable than what they originally paid for the stock. In like manner, a ratio less than 1 suggests that investors do not believe the stock is worth what they originally paid. Starbucks' investors clearly believe that the stock is worth more than their original cost, paying $6.58 for each dollar of book value. In comparison, the average firm in the Standard & Poor's 500 Index was selling for $3 for every $1 in book equity. Again, the investors are rewarding the firm for its growth prospects relative to its riskiness.

ECONOMIC VALUE ADDED (EVA™)

The price/book ratio, as just described, indicates whether the shareholders value the firm's equity above or below the amount of capital they originally invested. If the firm's market value is above the accounting book value (price/book > 1), then management has created value for shareholders, but if the firm's market value is below book value (price/book < 1), then management has destroyed shareholder value.

How is shareholder value created or destroyed? Quite simply, shareholder value is created when a firm earns a rate of return on the capital invested greater than the investors' required rate of return. If we invest in a firm and have a 12 percent required rate of return and the firm earns 15 percent on our capital, then management is creating value for investors. If instead, the firm only earns 10 percent, then equity value is being destroyed. This concept is regularly applied by firms when making accept/reject decisions on large capital investments in plant and equipment; however, it has not been applied to the analysis of a firm's day-to-day operating results. Instead, managers have traditionally focused on accounting results, such as earnings growth, profit margins, and the return on book equity.

More recently, attention has been given to determining whether a firm's management is in fact creating shareholder value on all the capital invested and linking managers' compensation, mostly through bonuses, to the amount of shareholder value created. Although several techniques have been developed for assessing whether management is creating shareholder value, the one that has captured the most attention is Economic Value Added (EVA®).

Economic Value Added, developed by the consulting firm Stern Stewart & Co., is an attempt to measure a firm's *economic* profit, rather than *accounting* profit, in a given year.

COMPUTING DISNEY'S PRICE/EARNINGS RATIO AND PRICE/BOOK RATIO: HOW DID YOU DO?

We compute Disney's price/earnings ratio and price/book ratio as follows:

$$\text{Earnings per share} = \frac{\text{net income}}{\text{number of shares}}$$

$$= \frac{\$1.3 \text{ billion}}{2.031 \text{ billion shares}} = \$0.64$$

$$\begin{array}{c}\text{Equity book} \\ \text{value per share}\end{array} = \frac{\text{common equity}}{\text{number of shares}}$$

$$= \frac{\$23.79 \text{ billion}}{2.031 \text{ billion shares}} = \$11.71$$

$$\text{Price/earnings ratio} = \frac{\text{price per share}}{\text{earnings per share}}$$

$$= \frac{\$24}{\$0.64} = 37.50$$

$$\text{Price/book ratio} = \frac{\text{price per share}}{\text{equity book value per share}}$$

$$= \frac{\$24}{\$11.71} = 2.05$$

Disney's stock is selling for 37.50 times earnings and 2.05 times book. At the same time, the average firm in the industry was selling for 36 times earnings and 2.19 times book, which is very similar to Disney. Thus, investors see Disney as similar in terms of growth prospects and/or the firm's level of risk.

Economic profits assign a cost to the equity capital (the opportunity cost of the funds provided by the shareholders) in addition to the interest cost on the firm's debt, although accountants recognize only the interest expense as a financing cost in calculating a firm's net income.

For example, assume a firm has total assets of $1,000 and is financed 40 percent with debt ($400) and 60 percent with equity ($600). If the interest rate on the debt is 5 percent, the firm's interest expense is $20 ($400 × 0.05) and would be reported in the income statement. However, there would be no cost shown for the equity financing. To compute economic profits, we recognize not only the interest cost but also the opportunity cost of the $600 equity capital invested in the firm. That is, if the shareholders could earn 15 percent on another investment of similar risk (their opportunity cost is, therefore, 15 percent), then we should count this cost just as surely as we do the interest expense. In computing economic profits, we would subtract not only the $20 in interest but also $90 ($600 equity × 0.15) as the cost of equity. Thus, economic profits exist only if our operating profits exceed $110 ($20 + $90). Stated as a percentage, the firm must earn at least an 11 percent operating return on its assets ($110 ÷ $1,000) in order to meet the investors' required rate of return.

We can calculate Economic Value Added (EVA)—the value created for the shareholders—as follows:

$$\text{EVA} = \left(\begin{array}{c}\text{operating return} \\ \text{on assets}\end{array} - \begin{array}{c}\text{cost of} \\ \text{all capital}\end{array}\right) \times \text{total assets} \qquad \textbf{(4-16)}$$

where the cost of capital is the cost of all the firm's capital, both debt *and* equity. That is, the value created by management is determined by the amount the firm earns on its invested capital relative to the cost of these funds—both debt and equity—and the amount of capital invested in the firm, which are the total assets.[7]

Continuing with our previous example, assume that our company is earning a 16 percent operating return on its assets (invested capital). Then the firm's *economic value added* is $50, calculated as follows:

$$\text{EVA} = \left(\begin{array}{c}\text{operating return} \\ \text{on assets}\end{array} - \begin{array}{c}\text{cost of} \\ \text{all capital}\end{array}\right) \times \text{total assets}$$

$$\text{EVA} = (0.16 - 0.11) \times \$1,000 = \$50$$

---

[7]In Chapter 11, we will explain how a firm's cost of capital is calculated.

ECONOMIC VALUE ADDED USED TO MEASURE A FIRM'S FINANCIAL PERFORMANCE

The California Public Employees' Retirement System (CalPERS) invests pension monies to fund retirement and health benefits for more than 2,500 employers and 1.4 million public employees, retirees, and their families. CalPERS evaluates the companies in which it invests based in part on Economic Value Added (EVA™). Using EVA, CalPERS analysts can determine if poor market performance is due to financial performance problems or other extraneous factors.

Each year CalPERS compiles a "Focus List" of companies that it feels are not performing up to their potential. For example, in 2004 the Walt Disney Company was included as one of four companies on the CalPERS's 2004 "Focus List" of firms that CalPERS considers to be underperforming for stockholders.

CalPERS would like Disney to determine long-term compensation based on performance measures such as Economic Value Added. Other earnings-based methods, such as earnings per share, can provide the wrong type of motivation for management, eventually destroying shareholder wealth. When the board of directors for Disney decides to make some changes in its governing methods, CalPERS may view the company in a more positive light.

Source: "CalPERS Releases 2004 Corporate Governance Focus List," *Business Wire*, Lexis-Nexis, June 9, 2004. Copyright 2004 Business Wire, Inc. at www.calpers.ca.gov/index.jsp?bc=/about/home.xml. Posted June 1, 2004. Accessed November 11, 2004.

The foregoing explains the EVA concept in its simplest form. However, computing EVA requires converting a firm's financial statements from an accountant's perspective (GAAP) to an economic book value. This process is much more involved than we will go into here, but the basic premise involved in its computation is the same.

Objective **3**

LIMITATIONS OF FINANCIAL RATIO ANALYSIS

We conclude this chapter by offering several caveats about using financial ratios. We have described how financial ratios may be used to understand a company's financial position, but anyone who works with these ratios needs to be aware of the limitations involved in their use. The following list includes some of the more important pitfalls that may be encountered in computing and interpreting financial ratios:

1. It is sometimes difficult to identify the industry category to which a firm belongs when the firm engages in multiple lines of business. Thus, we frequently must select our own set of peer firms and construct tailor-made norms.
2. Published peer-group or industry averages are only approximations and provide the user with general guidelines rather than scientifically determined averages of the ratios of all, or of even a representative sample, of the firms within an industry.
3. Accounting practices differ widely among firms and can lead to differences in computed ratios. For example, the use of last-in, first-out (LIFO) inventory valuation can, in a period of rising prices, lower the firm's inventory account and increase its inventory turnover ratio when compared with that of a firm that uses first-in, first-out (FIFO). In addition, firms may choose different methods of depreciating their fixed assets.
4. Financial ratios can be too high or too low. For example, a current ratio that exceeds the industry norm may signal the presence of excess liquidity, which results in a lowering of overall profits in relation to the firm's investment in assets. On the other hand, a current ratio that falls below the norm may indicate (1) the possibility that the firm has inadequate liquidity and may at some future date be unable to pay its bills on time, or (2) the firm is managing accounts receivable and inventories more efficiently than other similar firms. Given what we learned earlier about Starbucks' liquidity, Starbucks is an example of the latter situation.

TESTING YOUR
UNDERSTANDING

CALCULATING DISNEY'S EVA

Earlier in the chapter, we determined that Disney's operating return on assets (OROA) was 4.63 percent. If Disney's cost of capital (the cost of both debt and equity capital) was 9 percent at that time, what was the Economic Value Added for the firm when total assets were approximately $50 billion?[a]

Check your answer on the next page.

[a]The firm's cost of capital is an important concept in finance and will be explained in detail in Chapter 11.

5. An industry average is not necessarily a desirable target ratio or norm. There is nothing magical about an industry norm. At best, an industry average provides a guide to the financial position of the average firm in the industry. It does not mean it is the ideal or best value for the ratio. A well-managed company may be above an average, whereas another equally good firm may choose to be below the average.

6. Many firms experience seasonality in their operations. Thus, balance sheet entries and their corresponding ratios will vary with the time of year when the statements are prepared. To avoid this problem, an average account balance should be used (for several months or quarters during the year) rather than the year-end total. For example, an average of month-end inventory balances might be used to compute a firm's inventory turnover ratio when the firm is subject to a significant seasonality in its sales (and correspondingly in its investment in inventories).

In spite of their limitations, financial ratios provide us with a very useful tool for assessing a firm's financial condition. We should, however, be aware of these potential weaknesses when performing a ratio analysis. In many cases the real value derived from analyzing financial ratios is that they tell us what questions to ask.

CONCEPT CHECK

1. Why is it difficult to create industry categories, especially among larger companies?
2. What differences in accounting practices create problems in using financial ratios?
3. Why should a firm be careful when making comparisons with industry norms?

SUMMARY

Explain the purpose and importance of financial analysis.
A variety of groups find financial ratios useful. For instance, managers use them to measure and track company performance over time. The focus of their analysis is frequently related to various measures of profitability used to evaluate the performance of the firm from the perspective of the owners. Another group of users of financial ratios includes analysts external to the firm who, for one reason or another, have an interest in the firm's economic well-being. An example of this group would be a loan officer of a commercial bank who wishes to determine the creditworthiness of a loan applicant. Here the focus of the analysis is on the firm's previous use of financial leverage and its ability to pay the interest and principal associated with the loan request.

Objective **1**

Calculate and use a comprehensive set of measurements to evaluate a company's performance.
Financial ratios are the principal tool of financial analysis. Sometimes referred to simply as benchmarks, ratios standardize financial information so comparisons can be made between firms of varying sizes.

Objective **2**

TESTING YOUR
UNDERSTANDING

COMPUTING DISNEY'S ECONOMIC VALUE ADDED: HOW DID YOU DO?

Disney's Economic Value Added (EVA) is calculated as follows:

$$EVA = \left(\begin{array}{c} \text{operating return} \\ \text{on assets} \end{array} - \begin{array}{c} \text{cost of} \\ \text{all capital} \end{array} \right) \times \text{total assets}$$

$$= \left(4.63\% - 9.0\% \right) \times \$50 \text{ billion} = \left(\$2.19 \text{ billion} \right)$$

Wow! In 2003, the EVA calculation indicates that Disney destroyed $2.19 billion in shareholder value by earning a rate of return on the firm's assets that was less than the investors' required rate of return.

What we have found here is not a secret. Read the accompanying Financial Management in Practice on page 112 to see what a large institutional investor thinks about Disney from a shareholder's perspective.

Financial ratios may be used to answer at least five questions: (1) How liquid is the company? (2) Is management effective at generating profits on the firm's assets? (3) How is the firm financed? (4) Is management providing a good return on the capital provided by the shareholders? (5) Is the firm's management creating or destroying shareholder value?

Two methods may be used in analyzing financial ratios. The first involves trend analysis for the firm over time; the second involves making ratio comparisons with industry norms or a selected peer group of similar firms. In our example, a peer group was chosen for analyzing the financial position of Starbucks Corporation.

Financial ratios provide a popular way to evaluate a firm's financial performance. However, when evaluating a company's use of assets (capital) to create firm value, financial ratio analysis based entirely on the financial statements may not be enough. If we want to understand how the shareholders assess management's performance, we can use the market price of the firm's stock relative to accounting earnings and the equity book value.

Economic Value Added (EVA™) provides another approach to evaluate a firm's performance in terms of shareholder value creation. EVA is equal to the return on invested capital less the investors' opportunity cost of the funds times the total amount of capital invested.

Objective **3**

Describe the limitations of financial ratio analysis.

Some of the limitations that may be encountered in computing and interpreting financial ratios include:

1. It is sometimes difficult to identify an appropriate industry category.
2. Published industry averages are only approximations rather than scientifically determined averages.
3. Accounting practices differ widely among firms and can lead to differences in computed ratios.
4. Some financial ratios can be too high or too low, which makes the results more difficult to interpret.
5. An industry average may not provide a desirable target ratio or norm.
6. Many firms experience seasonality in their operations. Thus, ratios will vary with the time of year when the statements are prepared.

In spite of their limitations, financial ratios provide us with a very useful tool for assessing a firm's financial condition.

KEY TERMS

Accounts receivable
  turnover ratio, 107

Acid-test (quick) ratio, 106

Asset efficiency, 111

Average collection period,
  107

Common-sized balance
  sheet, 102

Common-sized income
  statement, 102

Current ratio, 106

Days of sales in inventory,
  108

Days of sales outstanding,
  107

Financial ratios, 102

Fixed asset turnover, 112

Inventory turnover ratio,
  108

Liquidity, 106

Operating profit margin,
  110

Operating return on assets
  (OROA), 109

Price/book ratio, 119

Price/earnings ratio, 119

Return on equity, 115

Times interest earned, 114

Total asset turnover, 111

STUDY QUESTIONS

4-1. Describe the "five-question approach" to using financial ratios.

4-2. Discuss briefly the two perspectives that can be taken in performing ratio analysis.

4-3. Where can we obtain industry norms?

4-4. What are the limitations of industry average ratios? Discuss briefly.

4-5. What is liquidity, and what is the rationale for its measurement?

4-6. Distinguish between operating return on assets and operating profit margin.

4-7. Why is operating return on assets a function of operating profit margin and total asset turnover?

4-8. What is the difference between gross profit margin, operating profit margin, and net profit margin?

4-9. What information do the price/earnings ratio and the price/book ratio give us about the firm and its investors?

4-10. Explain what drives a company's return on equity.

4-11. What is Economic Value Added? Why is it used?

SELF-TEST PROBLEMS

ST-1. (*Ratio analysis and short-term liquidity*) Ray's Tool and Supply Company of Austin, Texas, has been expanding its level of operation for the past 2 years. The firm's sales have grown rapidly as a result of the expansion in the Austin economy. However, Ray's is a privately held company, and the only source of available funds it has is a line of credit with the firm's bank. The company needs to expand its inventories to meet the needs of its growing customer base but also wishes to maintain a current ratio of at least 3. If Ray's current assets are $6 million, and its current ratio is now 4, how much can it expand its inventories (financing the expansion with its line of credit) before the target current ratio is violated?

ST-2. (*Ratio analysis*) The statements for M & G Industries are presented below:

M & G Industries Balance Sheet for December 31, 2005 and 2006

	2005	2006
Cash	$ 9,000	$ 500
Accounts receivable	12,500	16,000
Inventories	29,000	45,500
Total current assets	$ 50,500	$ 62,000
Land	20,000	26,000
Buildings and equipment	70,000	100,000
Less: Accumulated depreciaton	(28,000)	(38,000)
Total fixed assets	$ 62,000	$ 88,000
Total assets	$112,500	$150,000
Accounts payable	$ 10,500	$ 22,000
Short-term bank notes	17,000	47,000
Total current liabilities	$ 27,500	$ 69,000
Long-term debt	28,750	22,950
Common stock	31,500	31,500
Retained earnings	24,750	26,550
Total debt and equity	$112,500	$150,000

M & G Industries Income Statement for the Years Ended
December 31, 2005 and 2006

	2005	2006
Sales (all credit)	$125,000	$160,000
Cost of goods sold	75,000	96,000
Gross profit	$ 50,000	$ 64,000
Operating expenses		
Fixed cash operating expenses	$ 21,000	$ 21,000
Variable operating expenses	$ 12,500	16,000
Depreciation	4,500	10,000
Total operating expenses	$ 38,000	$ 47,000
Earnings before interest and taxes	$ 12,000	$ 17,000
Interest expense	3,000	6,100
Earnings before taxes	$ 9,000	$ 10,900
Taxes	4,500	5,450
Net income	$ 4,500	$ 5,450

a. Based on the preceding statements, complete the following table:

M & G Industries Ratio Analysis

	INDUSTRY AVERAGES	ACTUAL 2005	ACTUAL 2006
Current ratio	1.80		
Acid-test ratio	0.70		
Average collection period	37.00		
Inventory turnover	2.50		
Debt ratio	58%		
Times interest earned	3.80		
Operating profit margin	10%		
Total asset turnover	1.14		
Fixed asset turnover	1.40		
Operating return on assets	11.4%		
Return on common equity	9.5%		

b. Evaluate the firm's financial position at the end of 2006 in terms of liquidity, operating return on assets, financing, and return on equity.

c. If in 2006 the firm has 5,000 shares of common stock outstanding selling for $15, what is the (i) firm's earnings per share, (ii) price/earnings ratio, and (iii) price/book ratio?

STUDY PROBLEMS

4-1. (*Ratio analysis*) Brashear, Inc., currently has $2,145,000 in current assets and $858,000 in current liabilities. Management wishes to increase inventory, which will be financed by a short-term note with the bank. What level of inventories can the firm carry without its current ratio falling below 2.0?

4-2. (*Ratio analysis*) The Allen Corporation had sales in 2005 of $65 million, with total assets of $42 million and total liabilities of $20 million. The interest rate on the debt is 6 percent and the firm's tax rate is 30 percent. The operating profit margin was 12 percent. What was the 2005 operating income and net income? What was operating return on assets and return on equity? Assume that all the debt is subject to paying interest.

4-3. (*Ratio analysis*) Last year, The Davies Corporation had sales of $400,000, with a cost of goods sold of $112,000. The firm's operating expenses were $130,000 and the increase in retained earnings was $58,000. There are currently 22,000 common stock shares outstanding and the firm pays a $1.60 dividend per share.

a. Assuming a 34 percent tax rate, construct the firm's income statement.
b. Compute the firm's operating profit margin.
c. What was the times interest earned?

4-4. (*Ratio analysis*) Greene, Inc.'s, balance sheet shows the stockholders' equity value of $750,500. The firm's earnings per share was $3, resulting in a price/earnings ratio of 12.25. There are 50,000 shares of common stock outstanding. What is the price/book ratio? What does this indicate about how shareholders view Greene, Inc.?

4-5. (*Ratio analysis*) The Mitchem Marble Company has a target current ratio of 2.0 but has experienced some difficulties financing its expanding sales in the past few months. At present the firm has a current ratio of 2.5 with current assets of $2.5 million. If Mitchem expands its receivables and inventories using its short-term line of credit, how much additional short-term funding can it borrow before its current ratio standard is reached?

4-6. (*Ratio analysis*) The balance sheet and income statement for the J. P. Robard Mfg. Company are as follows:

BALANCE SHEET ($000)

Cash	$ 500
Accounts receivable	2,000
Inventories	1,000
Current assets	3,500
Net fixed assets	4,500
Total assets	$8,000
Accounts payable	$1,100
Accrued expenses	600
Short-term notes payable	300
Current liabilities	$2,000
Long-term debt	2,000
Owners' equity	4,000
Total liabilities and owners' equity	$8,000

INCOME STATEMENT ($000)

Net sales (all credit)	$8,000
Cost of goods sold	(3,300)
Gross profit	4,700
Operating expenses	
(includes $500 depreciation)	(3,000)
Operating income	1,700
Interest expense	(367)
Earnings before taxes	$1,333
Income taxes (40%)	(533)
Net income	$ 800

Calculate the following ratios:

Current ratio   Operating return on assets
Times interest earned   Debt ratio
Inventory turnover   Average collection period
Total asset turnover   Fixed asset turnover
Operating profit margin   Return on equity

4-7. (*Analyzing operating return on assets*) The R. M. Smithers Corporation earned an operating profit margin of 10 percent based on sales of $10 million and total assets of $5 million last year.

  a. What was Smithers' total asset turnover ratio?
  b. During the coming year the company president has set a goal of attaining a total asset turnover of 3.5. How much must firm sales rise, other things being the same, for the goal to be achieved? (State your answer in both dollars and percentage increase in sales.)
  c. What was Smithers' operating return on assets last year? Assuming the firm's operating profit margin remains the same, what will the operating return on assets be next year if the total asset turnover goal is achieved?

4-8. (*Using financial ratios*) The Brenmar Sales Company had a gross profit margin (gross profits ÷ sales) of 30 percent and sales of $9 million last year. Seventy-five percent of the firm's sales are on credit and the remainder are cash sales. Brenmar's current assets equal $1.5 million, its current liabilities equal $300,000, and it has $100,000 in cash plus marketable securities.

  a. If Brenmar's accounts receivable are $562,500, what is its average collection period?
  b. If Brenmar reduces its average collection period to 20 days, what will be its new level of accounts receivable?
  c. Brenmar's inventory turnover ratio is 9 times. What is the level of Brenmar's inventories?

4-9. (*Ratio analysis*) Using Pamplin, Inc.'s financial statements shown below:

a. Compute the following ratios for both 2005 and 2006.

INDUSTRY NORM	2006
Current ratio	5.00
Acid-test (quick) ratio	3.00
Inventory turnover	2.20
Average collection period	90.00
Debt ratio	0.33
Times interest earned	7.00
Total asset turnover	0.75
Fixed asset turnover	1.00
Operating profit margin	20%
Return on common equity	9%

b. How liquid is the firm?

c. Is management generating adequate operating profit on the firm's assets?

d. How is the firm financing its assets?

e. Is management generating a good return on equity?

Pamplin, Inc. Balance Sheet at 12/31/2005 and 12/31/2006

ASSETS

	2005	2006
Cash	$ 200	$ 150
Accounts receivable	450	425
Inventory	550	625
Current assets	$ 1,200	$ 1,200
Plant and equipment	$ 2,200	$ 2,600
Less: Accumulated depreciation	(1,000)	(1,200)
Net plant and equipment	$ 1,200	$ 1,400
Total assets	$ 2,400	$ 2,600

LIABILITIES AND OWNERS' EQUITY

	2005	2006
Accounts payable	$ 200	$ 150
Notes payable—current (9%)	0	150
Current liabilities	$ 200	$ 300
Bonds ($8\frac{1}{3}\%$ interest)	$ 600	$ 600
Owners' equity		
Common stock	$ 300	$ 300
Paid-in capital	600	600
Retained earnings	700	800
Total owners' equity	$1,600	$ 1,700
Total liabilities and owner's equity	$2,400	$ 2,600

Pamplin, Inc. Income Statement for Years Ending 12/31/2005 and 12/31/2006

	2005		2006	
Sales (all credit)		$1,200		$1,450
Cost of goods sold		700		850
Gross profit		$ 500		$ 600
Operating expenses	30		40	
Depreciation	220	250	200	240
Operating income		$ 250		$ 360
Interest expense		50		64
Net income before taxes		$ 200		$ 296
Taxes (40%)		80		118
Net income		$ 120		$ 178

4-10. (*Financial ratios—investment analysis*) The annual sales for Salco, Inc., were $4.5 million last year. The firm's end-of-year balance sheet appeared as follows:

Current assets	$ 500,000	Liabilities	$1,000,000
Net fixed assets	1,500,000	Owners' equity	1,000,000
	$2,000,000		$2,000,000

The firm's income statement for the year was as follows:

Sales	$ 4,500,000
Less: Cost of goods sold	(3,500,000)
Gross profit	$ 1,000,000
Less: Operating expenses	(500,000)
Operating income	$ 500,000
Less: Interest expense	(100,000)
Earnings before taxes	$ 400,000
Less: Taxes (50%)	(200,000)
Net income	$ 200,000

    a. Calculate Salco's total asset turnover, operating profit margin, and operating return on assets.

    b. Salco plans to renovate one of its plants, which will require an added investment in plant and equipment of $1 million. The firm will maintain its present debt ratio of .5 when financing the new investment and expects sales to remain constant. The operating profit margin will rise to 13 percent. What will be the new operating return on assets for Salco after the plant renovation?

    c. Given that the plant renovation in part b occurs and Salco's interest expense rises by $50,000 per year, what will be the return earned on the common stockholders' investment? Compare this rate of return with that earned before the renovation.

4-11. (*Financial Analysis*) The T. P. Jarmon Company manufactures and sells a line of exclusive sportswear. The firm's sales were $600,000 for the year just ended, and its total assets exceeded $400,000. The company was started by Mr. Jarmon just 10 years ago and has been profitable every year since its inception. The chief financial officer for the firm, Brent Vehlim, has decided to seek a line of credit from the firm's bank totaling $80,000. In the past, the company has relied on its suppliers to finance a large part of its needs for inventory. However, in recent months tight money conditions have led the firm's suppliers to offer sizable cash discounts to speed up payments for purchases. Mr. Vehlim wants to use the line of credit to supplant a large portion of the firm's payables during the summer, which is the firm's peak seasonal sales period.

The firm's two most recent balance sheets were presented to the bank in support of its loan request. In addition, the firm's income statement for the year just ended was provided. These statements are found in the following tables:

T. P. Jarmon Company, Balance Sheet for 12/31/2005 and 12/31/2006

ASSETS	2005	2006
Cash	$ 15,000	$ 14,000
Marketable securities	6,000	6,200
Accounts receivable	42,000	33,000
Inventory	51,000	84,000
Prepaid rent	1,200	1,100
Total current assets	$115,200	$138,300
Net plant and equipment	286,000	270,000
Total assets	$401,200	$408,300

LIABILITIES AND EQUITY

	2005	2006
Accounts payable	$ 48,000	$ 57,000
Notes payable	15,000	13,000
Accruals	6,000	5,000
Total current liabilities	$ 69,000	$ 75,000
Long-term debt	$160,000	$150,000
Common stockholders' equity	$172,200	$183,300
Total liabilities and equity	$401,200	$408,300

T. P. Jarmon Company, Income Statement for the Year Ended 12/31/2006

Sales (all credit)		$600,000
Less: Cost of goods sold		460,000
Gross profit		$140,000
Less: Operating and interest expenses		
General and administrative	$30,000	
Interest	10,000	
Depreciation	30,000	
Total		70,000
Earnings before taxes		$ 70,000
Less: Taxes		27,100
Net income available to common stockholders		$ 42,900
Less: Cash dividends		31,800
Change in retained earnings		$ 11,100

Jan Fama, associate credit analyst for the Merchants National Bank of Midland, Michigan, was assigned the task of analyzing Jarmon's loan request.

    a. Calculate the financial ratios for 2006 corresponding to the industry norms provided as follows:

RATIO	NORM
Current ratio	1.8
Acid-test ratio	0.9
Debt ratio	0.5
Times interest earned	10.0
Average collection period	20.0
Inventory turnover (based on cost of goods sold)	7.0
Return on common equity	12.0%
Operating return on assets	16.8%
Operating profit margin	14.0%
Total asset turnover	1.20
Fixed asset turnover	1.80

    b. Which of the ratios reported in the industry norms do you feel should be most crucial in determining whether the bank should extend the line of credit?

    c. Compute Jarmon's free cash flows for the year ended December 31, 2006. Interpret your findings.

    d. Use the information provided by the financial ratios and the cash flow statement to decide if you would support making the loan.

4-12. (*Economic Value Added*) Stegemoller, Inc.'s, management wants to evaluate its firm's prior-year performance in terms of its contribution to shareholder value. This past year, the firm earned an operating income return on investment of 12 percent, compared to an industry norm of 11 percent. It has been estimated that the firm's investors have an opportunity cost on their funds of 14 percent. The firm's total assets for the year were $100 million. Compute the amount of economic value created or destroyed by the firm. How does your finding support or fail to support what you would conclude using ratio analysis to evaluate the firm's performance?

WEB WORKS

4-WW1. Go to the Web site for IBM at **www.ibm.com/investor**. Then click on Financial Tools for a guide to reading financial statements. How does it differ from the presentation in Chapter 3 and this chapter?

4-WW2.

   a. Go to **www.investor.reuters.com**. (You will need to sign up for a free membership before being able to access all the information on the site.) Click on the Financial Statements link in the left margin of the Web page. Type in the symbol for Starbucks (SBUX) and examine Starbucks' financial statements.

   b. After becoming familiar with the financial statements for Starbucks, click on the Ratios link in the left margin to see a large number of ratios that have been calculated for the company. There are many more ratios than what we presented and some have been calculated differently than we did—a problem that occurs frequently when using different sources of ratios. Which ratios are familiar to you? How have the ratios changed for Starbucks Corporation since 2003 as presented in this chapter?

4-WW3. Being able to identify an industry to use for benchmarking your firm's results with similar companies is frequently not easy. Choose a type of business and go to **www.naics.com**. This Web site allows you to use a free search for the NAICS number for different types of businesses. Choose keywords like "athletic shoes" or "auto dealers" and others to see what industry they have been assigned.

COMPREHENSIVE PROBLEM

Return to the Chapter 3 comprehensive problem (pp. 97–98), in which we presented the financial statements for PepsiCo and Coca-Cola. These two firms are considered to be in the beverages industry (Standard Industrial Code 2080).

   a. Go to your library or online and find industry norms for the beverages industry.

   b. Are there any ratios that are not provided for the industry that prevent you from using the "five-question approach" as described in this chapter? How would you adapt your approach to compensate for any missing industry norms?

   c. Compute the financial ratios for both firms for 2003, and using your industry norms, evaluate the firms in the following areas:
   1. liquidity
   2. operating profitability
   3. financing policies
   4. return on the shareholders' investment

SELF-TEST SOLUTIONS

SS-1. Note that Ray's current ratio before the inventory expansion is as follows:

current ratio = $6,000,000/current liabilities = 4

Thus, the firm's level of current liabilities is $1.5 million. If the expansion in inventories is financed entirely with borrowed funds, then the change in inventories is equal to the change in current liabilities, and the firm's current ratio after the expansion can be defined as follows:

$$\text{current ratio} = \frac{\$6,000,000 + \text{change in inventory}}{\$1,500,000 + \text{change in inventory}} = 3$$

Note that we set the new current ratio equal to the firm's target of 3. Solving for the change in inventory in the above equation, we determine that the firm can expand its inventories by $750,000 and finance the expansion with current liabilities and still maintain its target current ratio.

SS-2.

a.
M & G Industries Ratio Analysis

	INDUSTRY AVERAGES	ACTUAL 2005	ACTUAL 2006
Current ratio	1.80	1.84	0.90
Acid-test ratio	0.70	0.78	0.24
Average collection period (based on a 365-day year and end-of-year figures)	37.00	36.50	36.50
Inventory turnover	2.50	2.59	2.11
Debt ratio	58%	50%	61.3%
Times interest earned	3.80	4.00	2.79
Operating profit margin	10%	9.6%	10.6%
Total asset turnover	1.14	1.11	1.07
Fixed asset turnover	1.40	2.02	1.82
Operating return on assets	11.4%	10.67%	11.3%
Return on common equity	9.5%	8.0%	9.4%

b. M & G's liquidity is poor, as suggested by the low current ratio and acid-test ratio in 2006; also, inventories are turning slowly compared to the industry norm. In 2006, management is doing a satisfactory job at generating profits on the firm's operating assets, as indicated by the operating return on assets. Note that the operating return on assets in 2006 is about the same as the industry average, owing to a slightly above average operating profit margin combined with a slightly below average total asset turnover. The problem with the total asset turnover ratio comes from a slow inventory turnover. M & G has increased its use of debt to the point of using slightly more debt than the average company in the industry. As a result, the firm's coverage of interest has decreased to a point well below the industry norm.

c.

(i) $$\text{earnings per share} = \frac{\text{net income}}{\text{number of outstanding shares}} = \frac{\$5,450}{5,000 \text{ shares}} = \$1.09$$

(ii) $$\text{price/earnings ratio} = \frac{\text{market price per share}}{\text{earnings per share}} = \frac{\$15}{1.09} = 13.76$$

(iii) $$\text{price/book ratio} = \frac{\text{market price per share}}{\text{book value per share}} = \frac{\$15.00}{\$11.61} = 1.29$$

$$\text{where book value per share} = \frac{\text{total book equity value}}{\text{number of outstanding shares}}$$

$$= \frac{\$31,500 + \$26,550}{5,000 \text{ shares}}$$

$$= \frac{\$58,050}{5,000 \text{ shares}} = \$11.61$$

► As a partner at Ernst & Young, a national accounting and consulting firm, Don Erickson is in charge of the business valuation practice for the firm's Southwest region. Erickson's sole job for the firm is valuing companies, or what he calls a dedicated valuation practice. He has national responsibilities for valuing certain industries. In this role, he works with managers of major companies from across the nation. Although he has valued businesses of all kinds and sizes, he primarily focuses on certain industries, such as oil and gas firms and major league sports franchises. For instance, he has valued a number of major league sports clubs, including NFL, NBA, NHL, and major league baseball teams.

Erickson explains, "Valuing a company is an interesting, even intriguing, process. It requires having an understanding of the outlook of the specific business and the nature of the industry, which allows us to predict multiple scenarios of the future. More specifically, it is crucial to understand the two key value drivers: the company's risk and expected growth. If I were to name one variable that matters the most in estimating a firm's value and is the most difficult thing to determine, it would be our estimate of the firm's *growth rate*."

Erickson continues, "In valuing a business, we use several methods, the most important being a discounted cash flow approach. I am a true believer that the value of a company is the present value of the firm's expected future free cash flows."

When asked about the discount rate used in finding the present value of a firm's cash flows, he says, "In almost all cases, we use the *effective market discount rate*. In this approach, we estimate the discount rate for companies that have recently been sold. Alternatively, we may compute an *imputed discount rate* for the industry. In both cases, we will then adjust the discount rate for company-specific risk. The greater the inherent risk, the higher the discount rate.

"Let me also say that it is essential that an operating manager be familiar with what determines firm value. Due to recent changes in accounting rules for any firm that is audited, accounting and finance are becoming increasingly interconnected. The changes will make it all the more important for a manager to understand how much value is being created, not just at the firm level, but also at the division level."

The chapters in this part of the text will provide you a basic understanding of valuation concepts and procedures—the same ones that Erickson uses in valuing a company, or almost any business asset for that matter. We will explain the role of risk, which Erickson identifies as a matter of importance, and then see how to value a company's bonds and its stock.

CHAPTER 5
THE TIME VALUE OF
MONEY

CHAPTER 6
THE MEANING AND
MEASUREMENT OF
RISK AND RETURN

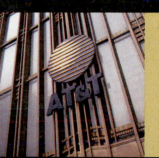

CHAPTER 7
VALUATION AND
CHARACTERISTICS OF
BONDS

CHAPTER 8
VALUATION AND
CHARACTERISTICS OF
STOCK

After reading this chapter, you should be able to:

1. Explain the mechanics of compounding, that is, how money grows over time when it is invested.

2. Be able to move money through time using time value of money tables, financial calculators, and spreadsheets.

3. Discuss the relationship between compounding and bringing money back to the present.

4. Define an ordinary annuity and calculate its compound or future value.

5. Differentiate between an ordinary annuity and an annuity due and determine the future and present value of an annuity due.

6. Explain Loan amortization.

7. Determine the future or present value of a sum when there are nonannual compounding periods.

8. Determine the present value of an uneven stream of payments.

9. Determine the present value of a perpetuity.

10. Explain how the international setting complicates the time value of money.

CHAPTER 5

The Time Value of Money

COMPOUND INTEREST AND FUTURE VALUE • TABLES, CALCULATORS, AND SPREADSHEETS—THREE ALTERNATIVES TO SOLVING TIME VALUE OF MONEY PROBLEMS • PRESENT VALUE • ANNUITIES • ANNUITIES DUE • AMORTIZED LOANS • COMPOUND INTEREST WITH NONANNUAL PERIODS • PRESENT VALUE OF AN UNEVEN STREAM • PERPETUITIES • THE MULTINATIONAL FIRM: THE TIME VALUE OF MONEY

In business, there is probably no other single concept with more power or applications than that of the time value of money. In his landmark book, *A History of Interest Rates*, Sidney Homer noted that if $1,000 were invested for 400 years at 8 percent interest, it would grow to $23 quadrillion—that would work out to approximately $5 million per person on earth. He was not giving a plan to make the world rich but effectively pointing out the power of the time value of money.

The time value of money is certainly not a new concept. Benjamin Franklin had a good understanding of how it worked when he left £1,000 each to Boston and Philadelphia. With the gift, he left instructions that the cities were to lend the money, charging the going interest rate, to worthy apprentices. Then, after the money had been invested in this way for 100 years, they were to use a portion of the investment to build something of benefit to the city and hold some back for the future. Two hundred years later, Franklin's Boston gift resulted in the construction of the Franklin Union, has helped countless medical students with loans, and still has over $3 million left in the account. Philadelphia, likewise, has reaped a significant reward from his gift with its portion of the gift growing to over $2 million. Bear in mind that all this has come from a gift of £2,000 with some serious help from the time value of money.

The power of the time value of money can also be illustrated through a story Andrew Tobias tells in his book *Money Angles*. There he tells of a peasant who wins a chess tournament put on by the king. The king then asks the peasant what he would like as the prize. The peasant answers that he would like for his village one piece of grain to be placed on the first square of his chessboard, two pieces of grain on the second square, four pieces on the third, eight on the fourth, and

⨿ WHAT'S AHEAD ⨿

In the next five chapters, we focus on determining the value of the firm and the desirability of investment proposals. A key concept that underlies this material is the *time value of money*; that is, a dollar today is worth more than a dollar received a year from now. Intuitively this idea is easy to understand. We are all familiar with the concept of interest. This concept illustrates what economists call an *opportunity cost* of passing up the earning potential of a dollar today. This opportunity cost is the time value of money.

In evaluating and comparing investment proposals, we need to examine how dollar values might accrue from accepting these proposals. To do this, all dollar values must first be comparable; because a dollar received today is worth more than a dollar received in the future, we must move all dollar flows back to the present or out to a common future date. An understanding of the time value of money is essential, therefore, to an understanding of financial management, whether basic or advanced.

so forth. The king, thinking he was getting off easy, pledged on his word of honor that it would be done. Unfortunately for the king, by the time all 64 squares on the chessboard were filled, there were 18.5 million trillion grains of wheat on the board—the kernels were compounding at a rate of 100 percent over the 64 squares of the chessboard. Needless to say, no one in the village ever went hungry, in fact, that is so much wheat that if the kernels were one-quarter inch long (quite frankly, I have no idea how long a kernel of wheat is, but

Andrew Tobias's guess is one-quarter inch), if laid end to end, they could stretch to the sun and back 391,320 times.

Understanding the techniques of compounding and moving money through time is critical to almost every business decision. It will help you to understand such varied things as how stocks and bonds are valued, how to determine the value of a new project, how much you should save for children's education, and how much your mortgage payments will be.

BACK TO THE FOUNDATIONS

*In this chapter we develop the tools to incorporate **Principle 2: The Time Value of Money—A Dollar Received Today Is Worth More Than a Dollar Received in the Future** into our calculations. In coming chapters we use this concept to measure value by bringing the benefits and costs from a project back to the present.*

Objective 1

COMPOUND INTEREST AND FUTURE VALUE

Most of us encounter the concept of compound interest at an early age. Anyone who has ever had a savings account or purchased a government savings bond has received compound interest. **Compound interest** occurs when *interest paid on the investment during the first period is added to the principal; then, during the second period, interest is earned on this new sum.*

compound interest

For example, suppose we place $100 in a savings account that pays 6 percent interest, compounded annually. How will our savings grow? At the end of the first year we have earned 6 percent, or $6 on our initial deposit of $100, giving us a total of $106 in our savings account. The mathematical formula illustrating this phenomenon is

$$FV_1 = PV(1 + i) \tag{5-1}$$

where FV_1 = the future value of the investment at the end of one year
   i = the annual interest (or discount) rate
   PV = the present value, or original amount invested at the beginning of the first year

In our example

$$
\begin{aligned}
FV_1 &= PV(1 + i) \\
&= \$100(1 + .06) \\
&= \$100(1.06) \\
&= \$106
\end{aligned}
$$

Carrying these calculations one period further, we find that we now earn the 6 percent interest on a principal of $106, which means we earn $6.36 in interest during the second year. Why do we earn more interest during the second year than we did during the first? Simply because we now earn interest on the sum of the original principal, or present value, and the interest we earned in the first year. In effect we are now earning interest on interest; this is the concept of compound interest. Examining the mathematical formula illustrating the earning of interest in the second year, we find

$$FV_2 = FV_1(1 + i) \tag{5-2}$$

which, for our example, gives

$$
\begin{aligned}
FV_2 &= \$106(1.06) \\
&= \$112.36
\end{aligned}
$$

TABLE 5-1   Illustration of Compound Interest Calculations

YEAR	BEGINNING VALUE	INTEREST EARNED	ENDING VALUE
1	$100.00	$ 6.00	$106.00
2	106.00	6.36	112.36
3	112.36	6.74	119.10
4	119.10	7.15	126.25
5	126.25	7.57	133.82
6	133.82	8.03	141.85
7	141.85	8.51	150.36
8	150.36	9.02	159.38
9	159.38	9.57	168.95
10	168.95	10.13	179.08

Looking back at equation (5-1), we can see that FV_1, or $106, is actually equal to $PV(1 + i)$, or $100(1 + .06)$. If we substitute these values into equation (5-2), we get

$$FV_2 = PV(1 + i)(1 + i)$$
$$= PV(1 + i)^2 \qquad\qquad (5\text{-}3)$$

Carrying this forward into the third year, we find that we enter the year with $112.36 and we earn 6 percent, or $6.74 in interest, giving us a total of $119.10 in our savings account. Expressing this mathematically:

$$FV_3 = FV_2(1 + i)$$
$$= \$112.36(1.06) \qquad\qquad (5\text{-}4)$$
$$= \$119.10$$

If we substitute the value in equation (5-3) for FV_2 into equation (5-4), we find

$$FV_3 = PV(1 + i)(1 + i)(1 + i)$$
$$= PV(1 + i)^3 \qquad\qquad (5\text{-}5)$$

By now a pattern is becoming apparent. We can generalize this formula to illustrate the value of our investment if it is compounded annually at a rate of i for n years to be

$$FV_n = PV(1 + i)^n \qquad\qquad (5\text{-}6)$$

where FV_n = the future value of the investment at the end of n years
n = the number of years during which the compounding occurs
i = the annual interest (or discount) rate
PV = the present value or original amount invested at the beginning of the first year

Table 5-1 illustrates how this investment of $100 would continue to grow for the first 10 years at a compound interest rate of 6 percent. Notice how the amount of interest earned annually increases each year. Again, the reason is that each year interest is received on the sum of the original investment plus any interest earned in the past.

When we examine the relationship between the number of years an initial investment is compounded for and its future value as shown graphically in Figure 5-1, we see that we can increase the future value of an investment by either increasing the number of years for which we let it compound or by compounding it at a higher interest rate. We can also see this from equation (5-6) because an increase in either i or n while PV is held constant results in an increase in FV_n.

PAUSE AND REFLECT

Keep in mind that future cash flows are assumed to occur at the end of the time period during which they accrue. For example, if a cash flow of $100 occurs in time period 5, it is assumed to occur at the end of time period 5, which is also the beginning of time period 6. In addition, cash flows that occur in time $t = 0$ occur right now; that is, they are already in present dollars.

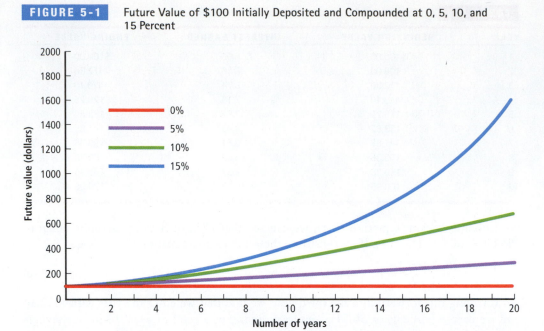

FIGURE 5-1   Future Value of $100 Initially Deposited and Compounded at 0, 5, 10, and 15 Percent

EXAMPLE

If we place $1,000 in a savings account paying 5 percent interest compounded annually, how much will our account accrue to in 10 years? Substituting $PV = \$1,000$, $i = 5$ percent, and $n = 10$ years into equation (5-6), we get

$$
\begin{aligned}
FV_n &= PV(1 + i)^n \\
&= \$1,000(1 + .05)^{10} \\
&= \$1,000(1.62889) \\
&= \$1,628.89
\end{aligned}
$$

Thus, at the end of 10 years we will have $1,628.89 in our savings account.

Objective **2**

TABLES, CALCULATORS, AND SPREADSHEETS— THREE ALTERNATIVES TO SOLVING TIME VALUE OF MONEY PROBLEMS

There are three different approaches that you can use to solve a time value of money problem. The first is to use the time value of money tables that appear in Appendix B in the back of the book. These tables do much of the math for you and solve for the present or future value of $1 for a range of values of i and n. Financial calculators are a second alternative, and there are a number of them that do a good job of solving time value of money problems. Based on many years of experience, the Texas Instruments BA II Plus calculator would be an excellent choice. Finally, spreadsheets can move money through time, and in the real world, they are without question the tool of choice. Now let's take a look at all three alternatives.

TIME VALUE OF MONEY (TVM) TABLES SOLUTION

future-value interest factor
($FVIF_{i, n}$)

Because determining future value can be quite time-consuming when an investment is held for a number of years, the **future-value interest factor** for i and n ($FVIF_{i, n}$), defined as $(1 + i)^n$, has been compiled in the back of the book for various values of i and n. An abbreviated

TABLE 5-2 $FVIF_{i,n}$, or the Compound Sum of $1

N	1%	2%	3%	4%	5%	6%	7%	8%	9%	10%
1	1.010	1.020	1.030	1.040	1.050	1.060	1.070	1.080	1.090	1.100
2	1.020	1.040	1.061	1.082	1.102	1.124	1.145	1.166	1.188	1.210
3	1.030	1.061	1.093	1.125	1.158	1.191	1.225	1.260	1.295	1.331
4	1.041	1.082	1.126	1.170	1.216	1.262	1.311	1.360	1.412	1.464
5	1.051	1.104	1.159	1.217	1.276	1.338	1.403	1.469	1.539	1.611
6	1.062	1.126	1.194	1.265	1.340	1.419	1.501	1.587	1.677	1.772
7	1.072	1.149	1.230	1.316	1.407	1.504	1.606	1.714	1.828	1.949
8	1.083	1.172	1.267	1.369	1.477	1.594	1.718	1.851	1.993	2.144
9	1.094	1.195	1.305	1.423	1.551	1.689	1.838	1.999	2.172	2.358
10	1.105	1.219	1.344	1.480	1.629	1.791	1.967	2.159	2.367	2.594
11	1.116	1.243	1.384	1.539	1.710	1.898	2.105	2.332	2.580	2.853
12	1.127	1.268	1.426	1.601	1.796	2.012	2.252	2.518	2.813	3.138
13	1.138	1.294	1.469	1.665	1.886	2.133	2.410	2.720	3.066	3.452
14	1.149	1.319	1.513	1.732	1.980	2.261	2.579	2.937	3.342	3.797
15	1.161	1.346	1.558	1.801	2.079	2.397	2.759	3.172	3.642	4.177

compound interest or future-value interest factor table appears in Table 5-2, with a more comprehensive version of this table appearing in Appendix B at the back of this book. Alternatively, the $FVIF_{i,n}$ values could easily be determined using a calculator. Note that the compounding factors given in these tables represent the value of $1 compounded at rate i at the *end* of the nth year. Thus, to calculate the future value of an initial investment, we need only to determine the $FVIF_{i,n}$ using a calculator or the tables at the end of the text and multiply this times the initial investment. In effect, we can rewrite equation (5-6) as follows:

$$FV_n = PV(FVIF_{i,n})$$ **(5-6a)**

EXAMPLE

If we invest $500 in a bank where it will earn 8 percent compounded annually, how much will it be worth at the end of 7 years? Looking at Table 5-2 in the row $n = 7$ and column $i = 8$ percent, we find that $FVIF_{8\%, 7\,yr}$ has a value of 1.714. Substituting this into equation (5-6a), we find

$$\begin{aligned} FV_n &= PV(FVIF_{8\%, 7\,yr}) \\ &= \$500(1.714) \\ &= \$857 \end{aligned}$$

Thus, we will have $857 at the end of 7 years.

In the future we will find several uses for equation (5-6a); not only can we find the future value of an investment, but we can also solve for PV, i, or n. In any case, you will be given three of the four variables and will have to solve for the fourth.

PAUSE AND REFLECT

As you read through the chapter it is a good idea to solve the problems as they are presented. If you just read the problems, the principles behind them often do not sink in. The material presented in this chapter forms the basis for the rest of the course; therefore, a good command of the concepts underlying the time value of money is extremely important.

EXAMPLE

Let's assume that the DaimlerChrysler Corporation has guaranteed that the price of a new Jeep will always be $20,000, and you'd like to buy one but currently have only $7,752. How many years will it take for your initial investment of $7,752 to grow to $20,000 if it is invested at 9 percent compounded annually? We can use equation (5-6a) to solve for this problem as well. Substituting the known values in equation (5-6a), you find

$$FV_n = PV(FVIF_{i,n})$$
$$\$20,000 = \$7,752(FVIF_{9\%,\,n\,yr})$$
$$\frac{\$20,000}{\$7,752} = \frac{\$7,752(FVIF_{9\%,\,n\,yr})}{\$7,752}$$
$$2.58 = FVIF_{9\%,\,n\,yr}$$

Thus, you are looking for a value of 2.58 in the $FVIF_{i,\,n}$ tables, and you know it must be in the 9% column. To finish solving the problem, look down the 9% column for the value closest to 2.58. You find that it occurs in the $n = 11$ row. Thus it will take 11 years for an initial investment of $7,752 to grow to $20,000 if it is invested at 9 percent compounded annually.

EXAMPLE

Now let's solve for the compound annual growth rate, and let's go back to that Jeep that always costs $20,000. In 10 years, you'd really like to have $20,000 to buy a new Jeep, but you only have $11,167. At what rate must your $11,167 be compounded annually for it to grow to $20,000 in 10 years? Substituting the known variables into equation (5-6a), you get

$$FV_n = PV(FVIF_{i,n})$$
$$\$20,000 = \$11,167(FVIF_{i,10\,yr})$$
$$\frac{\$20,000}{\$11,167} = \frac{\$11,167(FVIF_{i,10\,yr})}{\$11,167}$$
$$1.791 = FVIF_{i,10\,yr}$$

You know to look in the $n = 10$ row of the $FVIF_{i,\,n}$ tables for a value of 1.791, and you find this in the $i = 6\%$ column. Thus, if you want your initial investment of $11,167 to grow to $20,000 in 10 years, you must invest it at 6 percent.

EXAMPLE

At what rate must $100 be compounded annually for it to grow to $179.10 in 10 years? In this case we know the initial investment, $PV = \$100$; the future value of this investment at the end of n years, $FV_n = \$179.10$; and the number of years that the initial investment will compound for, $n = 10$ years. Substituting into equation (5-6), we get

$$FV_n = PV(1 + i)^n$$
$$\$179.10 = \$100(1 + i)^{10}$$
$$1.791 = (1 + i)^{10}$$

We know to look in the $n = 10$ row of the $FVIF_{i,\,n}$ table for a value of 1.791, and we find this in the $i = 6$ percent column. Thus, if we want our initial investment of $100 to accrue to $179.10 in 10 years, we must invest it at 6 percent.

Just how powerful is the time value of money? Manhattan Island was purchased by Peter Minuit from the Indians in 1626 for $24 in "knickknacks" and jewelry. If at the end of 1626 the Indians had invested their $24 at 8 percent compounded annually, it would be worth over $111 trillion today (by the end of 2005, 379 years later). That's certainly enough to buy back all of Manhattan—in fact, with $111 trillion in the bank, the $80 billion to $90 billion you'd have to pay to buy back all of Manhattan would seem like pocket change. This story illustrates the incredible power of time in compounding. There simply is no substitute for it.

FINANCIAL CALCULATOR SOLUTION

Time value of money calculations can be made simple with the aid of a *financial calculator*. In solving time value of money problems with a financial calculator, you will be given three of four variables and will have to solve for the fourth. Before presenting any solutions using a financial calculator, we introduce the calculator's five most common keys. (In most time value of money problems, only four of these keys are relevant.) These keys are

N   I/Y   PV   PMT   FV

where:

N	Stores (or calculates) the total number of payments or compounding periods.
I/Y	Stores (or calculates) the interest or discount rate.
PV	Stores (or calculates) the present value of a cash flow or series of cash flows.
FV	Stores (or calculates) the future value, that is, the dollar amount of a final cash flow or the compound value of a single flow or series of cash flows.
PMT	Stores (or calculates) the dollar amount of each annuity payment deposited or received at the end of each year.

When you use a financial calculator, remember that outflows generally have to be entered as negative numbers. In general, each problem will have two cash flows: one an outflow with a negative value, and one an inflow with a positive value. The idea is that you deposit money in the bank at some point in time (an outflow), and at some other point in time you take money out of the bank (an inflow). Also, every calculator operates a bit differently with respect to entering variables. Needless to say, it is a good idea to familiarize yourself with exactly how your calculator functions.

As previously stated, in any problem you will be given three of four variables. These four variables will always include N and I/Y; in addition, two out of the final three variables—*PV*, *FV*, and *PMT*—will also be included. To solve a time value of money problem using a financial calculator, all you need to do is enter the appropriate numbers for three of the four variables and then press the key of the final variable to calculate its value. It is also a good idea to enter zero for any of the five variables not included in the problem in order to clear that variable.

Now let's solve the previous example using a financial calculator. We were trying to find at what rate $100 must be compounded annually for it to grow to $179.10 in 10 years. The solution using a financial calculator would be as follows:

CALCULATOR SOLUTION

Data Input	Function Key
10	N
−100	PV
179.10	FV
0	PMT

Function Key	Answer
CPT	
I/Y	6.00%

Any of the problems in this chapter can easily be solved using a financial calculator, and the solutions to many examples using a Texas Instruments BA II Plus financial calculator

TAKIN' IT TO THE NET

There are a number of calculators on the Internet aimed at not only moving money through time but also solving other problems that involve the time value of money. One great site for financial calculators is Kiplinger Online Calculators www.kiplinger.com/calc/calchome.html.

TAKIN' IT TO THE NET

Another excellent site that provides financial calculators is Money Advisor www.moneyadvisor.com/calc. This site has, among other things, a loan calculator, retirement spending calculator, present value calculator, and calculators for future value of an annuity calculation.

are provided in the margins. If you are using the TI BA II Plus, make sure that you have selected both the "END MODE" and "one payment per year" ($P/Y = 1$). This sets the payment conditions to a maximum of one payment per period occurring at the end of the period. One final point, you will notice that solutions using the present-value tables versus solutions using a calculator may vary slightly—a result of rounding errors in the tables.

For further explanation of the TI BA II Plus, see Appendix A at the end of the book.

> **PAUSE AND REFLECT**
>
> The concepts of compound interest and present value follow us through the remainder of this book. Not only do they allow us to determine the future value of any investment, but also they allow us to bring the benefits and costs from new investment proposals back to the present and thereby determine the value of the investment in today's dollars.

Obviously, the choice of the interest rate plays a critical role in how much an investment grows, but do small changes in the interest rate have much of an impact on future values? To answer this question, let's look back at Peter Minuit's purchase of Manhattan. If the Indians had invested their $24 at 10 percent rather than 8 percent compounded annually at the end of 1626, they would have over $116 quadrillion by the end of 2005 (379 years later). That is 116 followed by 15 zeros, or $116,000,000,000,000,000. Actually, that is enough to buy back not only Manhattan Island but also the entire world and still have plenty left over! Now let's assume a lower interest rate—say 6 percent. In that case the $24 would have only grown to a mere $93.6 billion—less than one one-thousandth of what it grew to at 8 percent, and less than one-millionth of what it would have grown to at 10 percent. With today's real estate prices, you'd have a tough time buying Manhattan, and if you did, you probably couldn't pay your taxes! To say the least, the interest rate is extremely important in investing.

SPREADSHEET SOLUTION

Without question, in the real world most calculations involving moving money through time will be carried out with the help of a spreadsheet. Although there are several competing spreadsheets, the most popular one is Microsoft Excel. Just as with the keystroke calculations on a financial calculator, a spreadsheet can make easy work of most common financial calculations. Listed here are some of the most common functions used with Excel when moving money through time:

Calculation	Formula
Present Value	= PV(rate,number of periods,payment,future value,type)
Future Value	= FV(rate,number of periods,payment,present value,type)
Payment	= PMT(rate,number of periods,present value,future value,type)
Number of Periods	= $NPER$(rate,payment,present value,future value,type)
Interest Rate	= $RATE$(number of periods,payment,present value,future value,type, guess)

where:		
	rate	= i, the interest rate or discount rate
	number of periods	= n, the number of years or periods
	payment	= PMT, the annuity payment deposited or received at the end of each period
	future value	= FV, the future value of the investment at the end of n periods or years
	present value	= PV, the present value of the future sum of money
	type	= when the payment is made (0 if omitted)
		0 = at end of period
		1 = at beginning of period
	guess	= a starting point when calculating the interest rate; if omitted, the calculations begin with a value of 0.1 or 10%

Just like with a financial calculator, the outflows have to be entered as negative numbers. In general, each problem will have two cash flows: one positive and one negative. The idea is that you deposit money at some point in time (an outflow or negative value), and at some point later in time, you withdraw your money (an inflow or positive value). For example, let's look back on the example on page 141.

	A	B	C	D	E	F	G
1							
2		Spreadsheets and the Time Value of Money					
3							
4	If we invest $500 in a bank where it will earn 8 percent compounded						
5	annually, how much will it be worth at the end of 7 years?						
6							
7			rate (i) =	8%			
8		number of periods (n) =		7			
9		payment (PMT) =		$0			
10		present value (PV) =		$500			
11		type (0 = at end of period) =		0			
12							
13			Future value =	$856.91			
14							
15	Excel formula: =FV(rate,number of periods,payment,present value,type)						
16							
17	Entered value in cell d13: =FV(d7,d8,d9,-d10,d11)						
18	Notice that present value ($500) took on a negative value.						
19							

Entered values in cell d13:
=FV(d7,d8,d9,-d10,d11)

	A	B	C	D	E	F	G	H
1								
2			Spreadsheets: Solving for i					
3								
4		In 10 years you'd like to have $20,000 to buy a new Jeep, but you only						
5		have $11,167. At what rate must your $11,167 be compounded						
6		annually for it to grow to $20,000 in 10 years?						
7								
8		number of periods (n) =		10				
9		payment (PMT) =		$0				
10		present value (PV) =		$11,167				
11		future value (FV) =		$20,000				
12		type (0 = at end of period) =		0				
13			guess =					
14								
15			i =	6.00%				
16								
17	Excel formula: =RATE(number of periods,payment,present value,future value,type,guess)							
18								
19	Entered value in cell d15: =RATE(d8,d9,-d10,d11,d12,d13)							
20								
21	Notice that present value ($11,167) took on a negative value.							
22	Also note that if you didn't assign a value to guess, it would begin calculations							
23	with a value of 0.1 or 10%. If it could not come up with a value for i after							
24	20 iterations, you would receive the #NUM! error message. Generally a							
25	guess between 10 and 100 percent will work.							
26								

Entered values in cell d15:
=RATE(d8,d9,-d10,d11,d12,d13)

CONCEPT CHECK

1. Principle 2 states that "a dollar received today is worth more than a dollar received in the future." Explain this statement.

2. How does compound interest differ from simple interest?

3. Explain the formula $FV_n = PV(1 + i)^n$.

PRESENT VALUE

Objective **3**

Up to this point we have been moving money forward in time; that is, we know how much we have to begin with and are trying to determine how much that sum will grow in a certain number of years when compounded at a specific rate. We are now going to look at the

present value

reverse question: What is the value in today's dollars of a sum of money to be received in the future? The answer to this question will help us determine the desirability of investment projects in Chapters 9 and 10. In this case we are moving future money back to the present. We will determine the **present value** of a lump sum, which in simple terms is the *current value of a future payment.* In fact, we will be doing nothing other than inverse compounding. The differences in these techniques come about merely from the investor's point of view. In compounding, we talked about the compound interest rate and the initial investment; in determining the present value, we will talk about the discount rate and present value of future cash flows. Determination of the discount rate is the subject of Chapter 11 and can be defined as the rate of return available on an investment of equal risk to what is being discounted. Other than that, the technique and the terminology remain the same, and the mathematics are simply reversed. In equation (5-6) we were attempting to determine the future value of an initial investment. We now want to determine the initial investment or present value. By dividing both sides of equation (5-6) by $(1 + i)^n$, we get

$$PV = FV_n \left[\frac{1}{(1+i)^n} \right] \tag{5-7}$$

where FV_n = the future value of the investment at the end of n years
n = the number of years until the payment will be received
i = the annual discount (or interest) rate
PV = the present value of the future sum of money

Because the mathematical procedure for determining the present value is exactly the inverse of determining the future value, we also find that the relationships among n, i, and PV are just the opposite of those we observed in future value. The present value of a future sum of money is inversely related to both the number of years until the payment will be received and the discount rate. This relationship is shown in Figure 5-2.

> **PAUSE AND REFLECT**
>
> Although the present value equation [equation (5-7)] is used extensively in evaluating new investment proposals, it should be stressed that the present value equation is actually the same as the future value or compounding equation [equation (5-6)], where it is solved for *PV*.

FIGURE 5-2 Present Value of $100 to Be Received at a Future Date and Discounted Back to the Present at 0, 5, 10, and 15 Percent

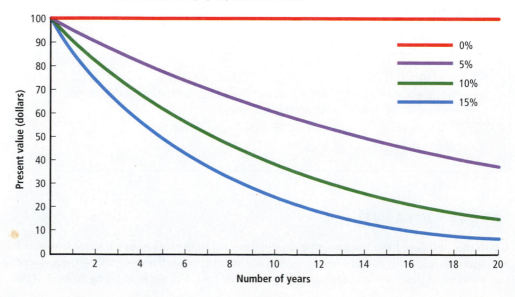

EXAMPLE

What is the present value of $500 to be received 10 years from today if our discount rate is 6 percent? Substituting $FV_{10} = \$500$, $n = 10$, and $i = 6$ percent into equation (5-7), we find

$$PV = \$500 \left[\frac{1}{(1 + .06)^{10}} \right]$$

$$= \$500 \left(\frac{1}{1.791} \right)$$

$$= \$500(.558)$$

$$= \$279$$

Thus, the present value of the $500 to be received in 10 years is $279.

CALCULATOR SOLUTION	
Data Input	**Function Key**
10	N
6	I/Y
500	FV
0	PMT
Function Key	**Answer**
CPT	
PV	−279.20

To aid in the computation of present values, the **present-value interest factor** for i and n (**$PVIF_{i, n}$**), defined as $[1/(1 + i)^n]$, has been compiled for various combinations of i and n and appears in Appendix C at the back of this book. An abbreviated version of Appendix C appears in Table 5-3. A close examination shows that the values in Table 5-3 are merely the inverse of those found in Table 5-2 and Appendix B. This, of course, is as it should be because the values in Appendix B are $(1 + i)^n$ and those in Appendix C are $[1/(1 + i)^n]$. Now, to determine the present value of a sum of money to be received at some future date, we need only determine the value of the appropriate $PVIF_{i, n}$, by either using a calculator or consulting the tables, and multiply it by the future value. In effect we can use our new notation and rewrite equation (5-7) as follows:

present-value interest factor ($PVIF_{i, n}$)

$$PV = FV_n(PVIF_{i, n}) \tag{5-7a}$$

TABLE 5-3	$PVIF_{i, n}$, or the Present Value of $1									
N	**1%**	**2%**	**3%**	**4%**	**5%**	**6%**	**7%**	**8%**	**9%**	**10%**
1	.990	.980	.971	.962	.952	.943	.935	.926	.917	.909
2	.980	.961	.943	.925	.907	.890	.873	.857	.842	.826
3	.971	.942	.915	.889	.864	.840	.816	.794	.772	.751
4	.961	.924	.888	.855	.823	.792	.763	.735	.708	.683
5	.951	.906	.863	.822	.784	.747	.713	.681	.650	.621
6	.942	.888	.837	.790	.746	.705	.666	.630	.596	.564
7	.933	.871	.813	.760	.711	.655	.623	.583	.547	.513
8	.923	.853	.789	.731	.677	.627	.582	.540	.502	.467
9	.914	.837	.766	.703	.645	.592	.544	.500	.460	.424
10	.905	.820	.744	.676	.614	.558	.508	.463	.422	.386
11	.896	.804	.722	.650	.585	.527	.475	.429	.388	.350
12	.887	.789	.701	.625	.557	.497	.444	.397	.356	.319
13	.879	.773	.681	.601	.530	.469	.415	.368	.326	.290
14	.870	.758	.661	.577	.505	.442	.388	.340	.299	.263
15	.861	.743	.642	.555	.481	.417	.362	.315	.275	.239

EXAMPLE

You're on vacation in a rather remote part of Florida and see an advertisement stating that if you take a sales tour of some condominiums "you will be given $100 just for taking the tour." However, the $100 that you get is in the form of a savings bond that will not pay you the $100 for 10 years. What is the present value of $100 to be received 10 years from today if your discount rate is 6 percent? By looking at the $n = 10$ row and

$i = 6\%$ column of Table 5-3, you find the $PVIF_{6\%, 10\ yr}$ is .558. Substituting $FV_{10} = \$100$ and $PVIF_{6\%, 10\ yr} = .558$ into equation (5-7a), you find

$$PV = \$100(PVIF_{6\%, 10\ yr})$$
$$= \$100(.558)$$
$$= \$55.80$$

Thus, the value in today's dollars of that $100 savings bond is only $55.80.

DEALING WITH MULTIPLE UNEVEN CASH FLOWS

Again, we only have one present-value–future-value equation; that is, equations (5-6) and (5-7) are identical. We have introduced them as separate equations to simplify our calculations; in one case we are determining the value in future dollars, and in the other case the value in today's dollars. In either case the reason is the same: to compare values on alternative investments and to recognize that the value of a dollar received today is not the same as that of a dollar received at some future date. We must measure the dollar values in dollars of the same time period. For example, if we looked at these projects—one that promised $1,000 in 1 year, one that promised $1,500 in 5 years, and one that promised $2,500 in 10 years— the concept of present value allows us to bring their flows back to the present and make those projects comparable. Moreover, because all present values are comparable (they are all measured in dollars of the same time period), we can add and subtract the present value of inflows and outflows to determine the present value of an investment. Let's now look at an example of an investment that has two cash flows in different time periods and determine the present value of this investment.

EXAMPLE

What is the present value of an investment that yields $500 to be received in 5 years and $1,000 to be received in 10 years if the discount rate is 4 percent? Substituting the values of $n = 5$, $i = 4$ percent, and $FV_5 = \$500$; and $n = 10$, $i = 4$ percent, and $FV_{10} = \$1,000$ into equation (5-7) and adding these values together, we find

$$PV = \$500\left[\frac{1}{(1+.04)^5}\right] + \$1,000\left[\frac{1}{(1+.04)^{10}}\right]$$
$$= \$500(PVIF_{4\%, 5\ yr}) + \$1,000(PVIF_{4\%, 10\ yr})$$
$$= \$500(.822) + \$1,000(.676)$$
$$= \$411 + \$676$$
$$= \$1,087$$

Again, present values are comparable because they are measured in the same time period's dollars.

With a financial calculator, this becomes a three-step solution. First, you'll solve for the present value of the $500 received at the end of 5 years, then you'll solve for the present value of the $1,000 received at the end of 10 years, and finally, you'll add the two present values together. Remember, once you've found the present value of those future cash flows you can add them together because they're measured in the same period's dollars.

CONCEPT CHECK

1. What is the relationship between the present-value equation (5-7) and the future-value, or compounding, equation (5-6)?
2. Why is the present value of a future sum always less than that sum's future value?

ANNUITIES

An **annuity** is a *series of equal dollar payments for a specified number of years.* When we talk about annuities, we are referring to **ordinary annuities** unless otherwise noted. With an ordinary annuity *the payments occur at the end of each period.* Because annuities occur frequently in finance—for example, as bond interest payments—we treat them specially. Although compounding and determining the present value of an annuity can be dealt with using the methods we have just described, these processes can be time-consuming, especially for larger annuities. Thus, we have modified the formulas to deal directly with annuities.

Objective **4**

annuity
ordinary annuities

(handwritten note: ★ Annuity → Beginning of the Due! look for Month. words like now)

COMPOUND ANNUITIES

A **compound annuity** involves *depositing or investing an equal sum of money at the end of each year for a certain number of years and allowing it to grow.* Perhaps we are saving money for education, a new car, or a vacation home. In any case we want to know how much our savings will have grown by some point in the future.

(margin: compound annuities)

Actually, we can find the answer by using equation (5-6), our compounding equation, and compounding each of the individual deposits to its future value. For example, if to provide for a college education we are going to deposit $500 at the end of each year for the next 5 years in a bank where it will earn 6 percent interest, how much will we have at the end of 5 years? Compounding each of these values using equation (5-6), we find that we will have $2,818.50 at the end of 5 years.

TAKIN' IT TO THE NET

USA Today also has a selection of online calculators www.usatoday.com/money/calculat/mcfront.htm aimed at helping you with all kinds of personal finance questions involving the time value of money.

$$FV_5 = \$500(1 + 0.6)^4 + \$500(1 + 0.6)^3 + \$500(1 + 0.6)^2$$
$$+ \$500(1 + 0.6) + \$500$$
$$= \$500(1.262) + \$500(1.191) + \$500(1.124)$$
$$+ \$500(1.060) + \$500$$
$$= \$631.00 + \$595.50 + \$562.00 + \$530.00 + \$500.00$$
$$= \$2,818.50$$

From examining the mathematics involved and the graph of the movement of money through time in Table 5-4, we can see that all we are really doing is adding up the future values of different cash flows that initially occurred in different time periods. Fortunately, there is also an equation that helps us calculate the future value of an annuity:

$$FV_n \text{ of an annuity} = PMT \left[\frac{FVIF_{i,\,n} - 1}{i} \right] \tag{5-8}$$

$$= PMT \left[\frac{(1 + i)^n - 1}{i} \right] \tag{5-8a}$$

where FV_n = the future value of the annuity at the end of the nth year
  PMT = the annuity payment deposited or received at the end of each year
  i = the annual interest (or discount) rate
  n = the number of years for which the annuity will last

TABLE 5-4	Illustration of a 5-Year $500 Annuity Compounded at 6 Percent					
YEAR	0	1	2	3	4	5
Dollar deposits at end of year		500	500	500	500	500
						$ 500.00
						530.00
						562.00
						595.50
						631.00
Future value of the annuity						$2,818.50

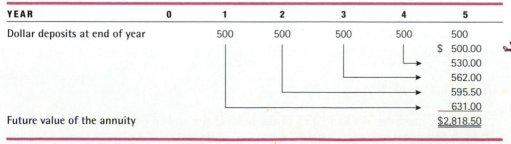

(handwritten note: ★ FV moves you to the end of the last payment. No accrued interest or compounding on the 1 cost part)

TABLE 5-5 $FVIFA_{i,n}$, or the Sum of an Annuity of $1 for n Years

N	1%	2%	3%	4%	5%	6%	7%	8%	9%	10%
1	1.000	1.000	1.000	1.000	1.000	1.000	1.000	1.000	1.000	1.000
2	2.010	2.020	2.030	2.040	2.050	2.060	2.070	2.080	2.090	2.100
3	3.030	3.060	3.091	3.122	3.152	3.184	3.215	3.246	3.278	3.310
4	4.060	4.122	4.184	4.246	4.310	4.375	4.440	4.506	4.573	4.641
5	5.101	5.204	5.309	5.416	5.526	5.637	5.751	5.867	5.985	6.105
6	6.152	6.308	6.468	6.633	6.802	6.975	7.153	7.336	7.523	7.716
7	7.214	7.434	7.662	7.898	8.142	8.394	8.654	8.923	9.200	9.487
8	8.286	8.583	8.892	9.214	9.549	9.897	10.260	10.637	11.028	11.436
9	9.368	9.755	10.159	10.583	11.027	11.491	11.978	12.488	13.021	13.579
10	10.462	10.950	11.464	12.006	12.578	13.181	13.816	14.487	15.193	15.937
11	11.567	12.169	12.808	13.486	14.207	14.972	15.784	16.645	17.560	18.531
12	12.682	13.412	14.192	15.026	15.917	16.870	17.888	18.977	20.141	21.384
13	13.809	14.680	15.618	16.627	17.713	18.882	20.141	21.495	22.953	24.523
14	14.947	15.974	17.086	18.292	19.598	21.015	22.550	24.215	26.019	27.975
15	16.097	17.293	18.599	20.023	21.578	23.276	25.129	27.152	29.361	31.772

future-value interest factor for an annuity ($FVIFA_{i,\,n}$)

To simplify our discussion, we will refer to the value in parentheses in equation (5-8a) as the **future-value interest factor for an annuity** for i and n (**$FVIFA_{i,\,n}$**), defined as $\left[\dfrac{(1+i)^n - 1}{i}\right]$, which is provided in Appendix D for various combinations of n and i; an abbreviated version is shown in Table 5-5.

Using this new notation, we can rewrite equation (5-8) as follows:

$$FV_n = PMT(FVIFA_{i,\,n}) \tag{5-8b}$$

Reexamining the previous example, in which we determined the value after 5 years of $500 deposited in the bank at 6 percent at the end of each of the next 5 years, we would look in the $i = 6$ percent column and $n = 5$ row and find the value of the $FVIFA_{6\%,\,5\text{ yr}}$ to be 5.637. Substituting this value into equation (5-8b), we get

$$FV_5 = \$500(5.637)$$
$$= \$2,818.50$$

This is the same answer we obtained earlier using equation (5-6).

Rather than ask how much we will accumulate if we deposit an equal sum in a savings account each year, a more common question is how much we must deposit each year to accumulate a certain amount of savings. This problem frequently occurs with respect to saving for large expenditures and pension funding obligations.

For example, we may know that we need $10,000 for education in 8 years; how much must we deposit in the bank at the end of each year at 6 percent interest to have the college money ready? In this case we know the values of n, i, and FV_n in equation (5-8b); what we do not know is the value of PMT. Substituting these example values in equation (5-8b), we find

$$\$10,000 = PMT(FVIFA_{6\%,\,8\text{ yr}})$$
$$\$10,000 = PMT(9.897)$$
$$\frac{\$10,000}{\$9.897} = PMT$$
$$\$1,010.41 = PMT$$

Thus, we must deposit $1,010.41 in the bank at the end of each year for 8 years at 6 percent interest to accumulate $10,000 at the end of 8 years.

CALCULATOR SOLUTION

Data Input	Function Key
5	N
6	I/Y
0	PV
500	PMT

Function Key	Answer
CPT	
FV	−2,818.55

CALCULATOR SOLUTION

Data Input	Function Key
8	N
6	I/Y
10,000	FV
0	PV

Function Key	Answer
CPT	
PMT	−1,010.36

EXAMPLE

How much must we deposit in an 8 percent savings account at the end of each year to accumulate $5,000 at the end of 10 years? Substituting the values $FV_{10} = \$5,000$, $n = 10$, and $i = 8$ percent into equation (5-8b), we find

$$\$5,000 = PMT(FVIFA_{8\%,\,10\,yr})$$

$$\$5,000 = PMT(14.487)$$

$$\frac{\$5,000}{14.487} = PMT$$

$$\$345.14 = PMT$$

Thus, we must deposit $345.14 per year for 10 years at 8 percent to accumulate $5,000.

CALCULATOR SOLUTION

Data Input	Function Key
10	N
8	I/Y
5,000	FV
0	PV

Function Key	Answer
CPT	
PMT	−345.15

PAUSE AND REFLECT

A timeline often makes it easier to understand time value of money problems. By visually plotting the flow of money, you can better determine which formula to use. Arrows placed above the line are inflows, whereas arrows below the line represent outflows. One thing is certain: Timelines reduce errors.

PRESENT VALUE OF AN ANNUITY

Pension funds, insurance obligations, and interest received from bonds all involve annuities. To compare them, we need to know the present value of each. Although we can find this by using the present-value table in Appendix C, this can be time consuming, particularly when the annuity lasts for several years. For example, if we wish to know what $500 received at the end of each of the next 5 years is worth to us given the appropriate discount rate of 6 percent, we can simply substitute the appropriate values into equation (5-7), such that

$$PV = \$500\left[\frac{1}{(1+.06)}\right] + \$500\left[\frac{1}{(1+.06)^2}\right] + \$500\left[\frac{1}{(1+.06)^3}\right]$$

$$+ \$500\left[\frac{1}{(1+.06)^4}\right] + \$500\left[\frac{1}{(1+.06)^5}\right]$$

$$= \$500(.943) + \$500(.890) + \$500(.840) + \$500(.792) + \$500(.747)$$

$$= \$2,106$$

Thus, the present value of this annuity is $2,106.00. From examining the mathematics involved and the graph of the movement of money through time in Table 5-6, we can see

[handwritten margin note: When looking at Present Value it moves you back one period]

TABLE 5-6 Illustration of a 5-Year $500 Annuity Discounted to the Present at 6 Percent

YEAR	0	1	2	3	4	5
Dollars received at end of year		500	500	500	500	500
	$ 471.50					
	445.00					
	420.00					
	396.00					
	373.50					
Present value of the annuity	$2,106.00					

[handwritten margin note: When your turn 19 its the begining of year 20 its the end of 19.]

TABLE 5-7 $PVIFA_{i,n}$, or the Present Value of an Annuity of $1

N	1%	2%	3%	4%	5%	6%	7%	8%	9%	10%
1	0.990	0.980	0.971	0.962	0.952	0.943	0.935	0.926	0.917	0.909
2	1.970	1.942	1.913	1.886	1.859	1.833	1.808	1.783	1.759	1.736
3	2.941	2.884	2.829	2.775	2.723	2.673	2.624	2.577	2.531	2.487
4	3.902	3.808	3.717	3.630	3.546	3.465	3.387	3.312	3.240	3.170
5	4.853	4.713	4.580	4.452	4.329	4.212	4.100	3.993	3.890	3.791
6	5.795	5.601	5.417	5.242	5.076	4.917	4.767	4.623	4.486	4.355
7	6.728	6.472	6.230	6.002	5.786	5.582	5.389	5.206	5.033	4.868
8	7.652	7.326	7.020	6.733	6.463	6.210	5.971	5.747	5.535	5.335
9	8.566	8.162	7.786	7.435	7.108	6.802	6.515	6.247	5.995	5.759
10	9.471	8.983	8.530	8.111	7.722	7.360	7.024	6.710	6.418	6.145
11	10.368	9.787	9.253	8.760	8.306	7.887	7.499	7.139	6.805	6.495
12	11.255	10.575	9.954	9.385	8.863	8.384	7.943	7.536	7.161	6.814
13	12.134	11.348	10.635	9.986	9.394	8.853	8.358	7.904	7.487	7.103
14	13.004	12.106	11.296	10.563	9.899	9.295	8.746	8.244	7.786	7.367
15	13.865	12.849	11.938	11.118	10.380	9.712	9.108	8.560	8.061	7.606

that all we are really doing is adding up the present values of different cash flows that initially occurred in different time periods. Fortunately, there is also an equation that helps us calculate the present value of an annuity:

$$PV \text{ of an annuity} = PMT \left[\frac{1 - PVIF_{i,\,n}}{i} \right] \tag{5-9}$$

$$= PMT \left[\frac{1 - (1+i)^{-n}}{i} \right] \tag{5-9a}$$

where PMT = the annuity payment deposited or received at the end of each year
i = the annual discount (or interest) rate
PV = the present value of the future annuity
n = the number of years for which the annuity will last

present-value interest factor for an annuity ($PVIFA_{i,n}$)

To simplify our discussion, we will refer to the value in the parentheses in equation (5-9a) as the **present-value interest factor for an annuity** for i and n ($PVIFA_{i,n}$), defined as $\left[\dfrac{1 - (1+i)^{-n}}{i} \right]$, which has been compiled for various combinations of i and n in Appendix E, with an abbreviated version provided in Table 5-7.

Using this new notation we can rewrite equation (5-9) as follows:

$$PV = PMT(PVIFA_{i,n}) \tag{5-9b}$$

Solving the previous example to find the present value of $500 received at the end of each of the next 5 years discounted back to the present at 6 percent, we look in the $i = 6$ percent column and $n = 5$ row and find the $PVIFA_{6\%,\,5\,yr}$ to be 4.212. Substituting the appropriate values into equation (5-9b), we find

$$PV = \$500(4.212)$$
$$= \$2,106$$

This, of course, is the same answer we calculated when we individually discounted each cash flow to the present. The reason is that we really only have *one* table; the Table 5-7 value for an n-year annuity for any discount rate i is merely the sum of the first n values in Table 5-3. We can see this by comparing the value in the present-value-of-an-annuity table (Table 5-7) for $i = 8$ percent and $n = 6$ years, which is 4.623, with the sum of the values in

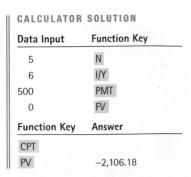

CALCULATOR SOLUTION

Data Input	Function Key
5	N
6	I/Y
500	PMT
0	FV

Function Key	Answer
CPT	
PV	−2,106.18

TABLE 5-8   Present Value of a 6-Year Annuity Discounted at 8 Percent

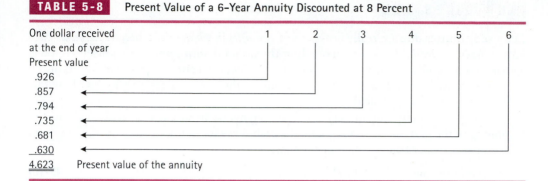

the $i = 8$ percent column and $n = 1, \ldots, 6$ rows of the present-value table (Table 5-3), which is equal to 4.623, as shown in Table 5-8.

EXAMPLE

What is the present value of a 10-year $1,000 annuity discounted back to the present at 5 percent? Substituting $n = 10$ years, $i = 5$ percent, and $PMT = \$1,000$ into equation (5-9b), we find

$$PV = \$1,000(PVIFA_{5\%,\ 10\ yr})$$

Determining the value for the $PVIFA_{5\%,\ 10\ yr}$ from Table 5-7, row $n = 10$, column $i = 5$ percent, and substituting it in, we get

$$PV = \$1,000(7.722)$$
$$= \$7,722$$

Thus, the present value of this annuity is $7,722.

CALCULATOR SOLUTION

Data Input	Function Key
10	N
5	I/Y
1,000	PMT
0	FV

Function Key	Answer
CPT	
PV	−7,721.73

As with our other compounding and present-value tables, given any three of the four unknowns in equation (5-9b), we can solve for the fourth. In the case of the present-value-of-an-annuity table, we may be interested in solving for PMT, if we know i, n, and PV. The financial interpretation of this action would be: How much can be withdrawn, perhaps as a pension or to make loan payments, from an account that earns i percent compounded annually for each of the next n years if we wish to have nothing left at the end of n years? For example, if we have $5,000 in an account earning 8 percent interest, how large an annuity can we draw out each year if we want nothing left at the end of 5 years? In this case the present value, PV, of the annuity is $5,000, $n = 5$ years, $i = 8$ percent, and PMT is unknown. Substituting this into equation (5-9b), we find

$$\$5,000 = PMT(3.993)$$
$$\$1,252.19 = PMT$$

Thus, this account will fall to zero at the end of 5 years if we withdraw $1,252.19 at the end of each year.

CONCEPT CHECK

1. Could you determine the future value of a 3-year annuity using the formula for the future value of a single cash flow? How?

2. What is the $PVIFA_{10\%,\ 3\ yr}$? Now add up the values for the $PVIF_{10\%,\ n\ yr}$ for $n = 1, 2$, and 3. What is this value? Why do these values have the relationship they do?

Objective **5**

annuities due

TAKIN' IT TO THE NET

The FinanCenter Web site www.financenter.com has a great selection of Internet calculators. In fact, many of the calculators used on the Internet actually have been developed by the FinanCenter.

ANNUITIES DUE

Because **annuities due** are really just *ordinary annuities in which all the annuity payments have been shifted forward by 1 year*, compounding them and determining their present value is actually quite simple. Remember, with an annuity due, each annuity payment occurs at the beginning of each period rather than at the end of the period. Let's first look at how this affects our compounding calculations.

Because an annuity due merely shifts the payments from the end of the year to the beginning of the year, we now compound the cash flows for one additional year. Therefore, the compound sum of an annuity due is simply

$$FV_n(\text{annuity due}) = PMT(FVIFA_{i, n})(1 + i) \tag{5-10}$$

For example, earlier we calculated the value of a 5-year ordinary annuity of $500 invested in the bank at 6 percent to be $2,818.50. If we now assume this to be a 5-year annuity due, its future value increases from $2,818.50 to $2,987.61.

$$\begin{aligned} FV_5 &= \$500(FVIFA_{6\%, \, 5 \, yr})(1 + .06) \\ &= \$500(5,637)(1.06) \\ &= \$2,987.61 \end{aligned}$$

Likewise, with the present value of an annuity due, we simply receive each cash flow 1 year earlier—that is, we receive it at the beginning of each year rather than at the end of each year. Thus, because each cash flow is received 1 year earlier, it is discounted back for one less period. To determine the present value of an annuity due, we merely need to find the present value of an ordinary annuity and multiply that by $(1 + i)$, which in effect cancels out 1 year's discounting.

$$PV(\text{annuity due}) = PMT(PVIFA_{i, n})(1 + i) \tag{5-11}$$

Reexamining the earlier example in which we calculated the present value of a 5-year ordinary annuity of $500 given an appropriate discount rate of 6 percent, we now find that if it is an annuity due rather than an ordinary annuity, the present value increases from $2,106 to $2,232.36,

$$\begin{aligned} PV &= \$500(PVIFA_{6\%, \, 5 \, yr})(1 + .06) \\ &= \$500(4.212)(1.06) \\ &= \$2,232.36 \end{aligned}$$

Present value of an annuity due:

STEP 1:

CALCULATOR SOLUTION

Data Input	Function Key
5	N
6	I/Y
500	PMT
0	FV

Function Key	Answer
CPT	
PV	−2,106.18

STEP 2:

$2,106.18
× 1.06
$2,232.55

With a financial calculator, you have two choices. First, you can reset your financial calculator to "Beginning Mode." Just as easy is to approach this as a two step-problem. First, treat it as if it were an ordinary annuity and find the present value. Then multiply the present value times $(1 + i)$, in this case times 1.06; this is shown in the margin.

The result of all this is that both the future and present values of an annuity due are larger than those of an ordinary annuity because in each case all payments are received earlier. Thus, when *compounding* an annuity due, it compounds for one additional year, whereas when *discounting* an annuity due, the cash flows are discounted for one less year. Although annuities due are used with some frequency in accounting, their usage is quite limited in finance. Therefore, in the remainder of this text, whenever the term *annuity* is used, you should assume that we are referring to an ordinary annuity.

EXAMPLE

The Virginia State Lottery runs like most other state lotteries: You must select 6 out of 44 numbers correctly in order to win the jackpot. If you come close, there are some significantly lesser prizes, which we ignore for now. For each million dollars in the lottery jackpot you receive $50,000 per year for 20 years, and your chance of winning is 1 in 7.1 million. A recent advertisement for the Virginia State Lottery went as follows: "Okay, you got two kinds of people. You've got the kind who play Lotto all the time, and the kind who play Lotto some of the time. You know, like only on a Saturday when they stop in at the store on the corner for some peanut butter cups and diet soda and the jackpot happens to be really big. I mean, my friend Ned? He's like "Hey, it's only $2 million this week." Well, hellloooo, anybody home? I mean, I don't know about you, but I wouldn't mind having a measly 2 mill coming *my* way. …"

What is the present value of these payments? The answer to this question depends on what assumption you make about the time value of money. In this case, let's assume that your required rate of return on an investment with this level of risk is 10 percent. Keeping in mind that the Lotto is an annuity due—that is, on a $2 million lottery you would get $100,000 immediately and $100,000 at the end of each of the next 19 years. Thus, the present value of this 20-year annuity due discounted back to present at 10 percent becomes

$$PV(\text{annuity due}) = PMT(PVIFA_{i\%,\, n\, \text{yr}})(1 + i)$$
$$= \$100,000(PVIFA_{10\%,\, 20\, \text{yr}})(1 + .10)$$
$$= \$100,000(8.514)(1.10)$$
$$= \$851,400(1.10)$$
$$= \$936,540$$

Just as before, you can either reset your financial calculator to "Beginning Mode" or use the two-step process. With the two-step process, in step 1, you treat it as if it were an ordinary annuity and find the present value. Then multiply the present value times $(1 + i)$, in this case times 1.10; this is shown in the margin. You'll notice this answer is a bit different from the answer you got using the tables. That's because of rounding error in the tables.

Thus, the present value of the $2 million Lotto jackpot is less than $1 million if 10 percent is the appropriate discount rate. Moreover, because the chance of winning is only 1 in 7.1 million, the expected value of each dollar "invested" in the lottery is only $(1/7.1 \text{ million}) \times (\$936,540) = 13.19¢$. That is, for every dollar you spend on the lottery you should expect to get, *on average*, about 13 cents back—not a particularly good deal. Although this ignores the minor payments for coming close, it also ignores taxes. In this case, it looks like "my friend Ned" is doing the right thing by staying clear of the lottery. Obviously, the main value of the lottery is entertainment. Unfortunately, without an understanding of the time value of money, it can sound like a good investment.

Present value of an annuity due:

STEP 1:
CALCULATOR SOLUTION

Data Input	Function Key
20	N
10	I/Y
100,000	PMT
0	FV

Function Key	Answer
CPT	
PV	−851,356

STEP 2:

$851,356
× 1.10
$936,492

CONCEPT CHECK
1. How does an annuity due differ from an ordinary annuity?
2. Why are both the future and present values greater for an annuity?

AMORTIZED LOANS

Objective 6

This procedure of solving for *PMT*, the annuity payment value when *i*, *n*, and *PV* are known, is also used to determine what payments are associated with paying off a loan in equal installments over time. <u>Loans that are paid off this way, in equal periodic payments,</u> are called **amortized loans**. Actually, the word *amortization* comes from the Latin word meaning "about to die." When you pay off a loan using regular, fixed payments, that loan is amortized. Although the payments are fixed, different amounts of each payment are applied toward the principal and the interest. With each payment you owe a bit less toward the principal. As a result, the amount that has to go toward the interest payment declines with each payment whereas the portion of each payment that goes toward the principal increases. Figure 5-3 illustrates the process of amortization.

amortized loan

FIGURE 5-3 The Amortization Process

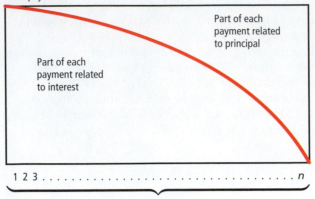

Number of payments

For example, suppose a firm wants to purchase a piece of machinery. To do this, it borrows $6,000 to be repaid in four equal payments at the end of each of the next 4 years, and the interest rate that is paid to the lender is 15 percent on the outstanding portion of the loan. To determine what the annual payments associated with the repayment of this debt will be, we simply use equation (5-9b) and solve for the value of PMT, the annual annuity. Again we know three of the four values in that equation: PV, i, and n. PV, the present value of the future annuity, is $6,000; i, the annual interest rate, is 15 percent; and n, the number of years for which the annuity will last, is 4 years. PMT, the annuity payment received (by the lender and paid by the firm) at the end of each year, is unknown. Substituting these values into equation (5-9b), we find

$$\$6,000 = PMT(PVIFA_{15\%,\,4\,yr})$$
$$\$6,000 = PMT(2.855)$$
$$\$2,101.58 = PMT$$

To repay the principal and interest on the outstanding loan in 4 years, the annual payments would be $2,101.58. The breakdown of interest and principal payments is given in the *loan amortization schedule* in Table 5-9, with very minor rounding error. As you can see, the interest portion of the payment declines each year as the loan outstanding balance declines.

CONCEPT CHECK

1. What is an amortized loan?

TABLE 5-9 Loan Amortization Schedule Involving a $6,000 Loan at 15 Percent to Be Repaid in 4 Years

YEAR	ANNUITY	INTEREST PORTION OF THE ANNUITY[a]	REPAYMENT OF THE PRINCIPAL PORTION OF THE ANNUITY[b]	OUTSTANDING LOAN BALANCE AFTER THE ANNUITY PAYMENT
0	0	0	0	$6,000
1	$2,101.58	$900.00	$1,201.58	4,798.42
2	2,101.58	719.76	1,381.82	3,416.60
3	2,101.58	512.49	1,589.09	1,827.51
4	2,101.58	274.07	1,827.51	

[a]The interest portion of the annuity is calculated by multiplying the outstanding loan balance at the beginning of the year by the interest rate of 15 percent. Thus, for year 1 it was $6,000 × .15 = $900.00, for year 2 it was $4,798.42 × .15 = $719.76, and so on.

[b]Repayment of the principal portion of the annuity was calculated by subtracting the interest portion of the annuity (column 2) from the annuity (column 1).

SPREADSHEETS: THE LOAN AMORTIZATION PROBLEM

Now let's look at a loan amortization problem in which the payment occurs monthly using a spreadsheet.

To buy a new house, you take out a 25-year mortgage for $100,000. What will your monthly interest rate payments be if the interest rate on your mortgage is 8 percent?

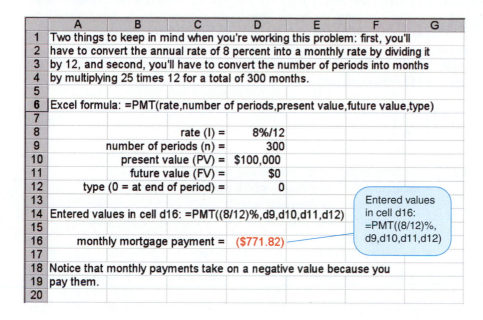

You can also use Excel to calculate the interest and principal portion of any loan amortization payment. You can do this using the following Excel functions:

Calculation	Formula
Interest portion of payment	= *IPMT*(rate,period,number of periods,present value,future value,type)
Principal portion of payment	= *PPMT*(rate,period,number of periods,present value,future value,type)

where period refers to the number of an individual periodic payment.

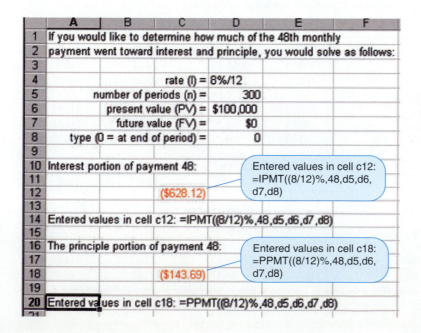

COMPOUND INTEREST WITH NONANNUAL PERIODS

Until now we have assumed that the compounding or discounting period is always annual; however, it need not be, as evidenced by savings and loan associations and commercial banks that compound on a quarterly, daily, and in some cases continuous basis. Fortunately, this adjustment of the compounding period follows the same format as that used for annual compounding. If we invest our money for 5 years at 8 percent interest compounded semi-annually, we are really investing our money for 10 six-month periods during which we receive 4 percent interest each period. If it is compounded quarterly, we receive 2 percent interest per period for 20 three-month periods. This process can easily be generalized, giving us the following formula for finding the future value of an investment for which interest is compounded in nonannual periods:

$$FV_n = PV\left(1 + \frac{i}{m}\right)^{mn}$$

(5-12)

where FV_n = the future value of the investment at the end of n years
n = the number of years during which the compounding occurs
i = annual interest (or discount) rate
PV = the present value or original amount invested at the beginning of the first year
m = the number of times compounding occurs during the year

We can see the value of intrayear compounding by examining Table 5-10. Because interest is earned on interest more frequently as the length of the compounding period declines, there is an inverse relationship between the length of the compounding period and the effective annual interest rate.

FINANCIAL CALCULATOR SOLUTION TO NONANNUAL PERIODS

With a financial calculator, the easiest way to solve a problem involving nonannual periods is to reset the "payments per year" or P/Y feature on your calculator to match the problem. While you'll want to make sure you understand how your financial calculator works, you should keep in mind that on most financial calculators N is the number of compounding

TABLE 5-10   The Value of $100 Compounded at Various Intervals

	FOR 1 YEAR AT i PERCENT			
i =	2%	5%	10%	15%
Compounded annually	$102.00	$105.00	$110.00	$115.00
Compounded semiannually	102.01	105.06	110.25	115.56
Compounded quarterly	102.02	105.09	110.38	115.87
Compounded monthly	102.02	105.12	110.47	116.08
Compounded weekly (52)	102.02	105.12	110.51	116.16
Compounded daily (365)	102.02	105.13	110.52	116.18

	FOR 10 YEARS AT i PERCENT			
i =	2%	5%	10%	15%
Compounded annually	$121.90	$162.89	$259.37	$404.56
Compounded semiannually	122.02	163.86	265.33	424.79
Compounded quarterly	122.08	164.36	268.51	436.04
Compounded monthly	122.12	164.70	270.70	444.02
Compounded weekly (52)	122.14	164.83	271.57	447.20
Compounded daily (365)	122.14	164.87	271.79	448.03

periods. Thus, for problems with annual compounding, P/Y should be set to 1, and for problems with monthly compounding, P/Y should be set to 12. If you have a TI BA II Plus calculator, to reset the P/Y feature you must first hit the 2nd button, then the I/Y button (you'll notice just above the I/Y button P/Y is listed). From there, you enter 12, then hit the ENTER button on the top row, and finally hit the CE/C, then CE/C again—hitting the CE/C button twice serves to clear the display. Once again, once you've got the "payments per year" button set, N then becomes the number of compounding periods, so if your problem involves 10 years of monthly compounding, then N equals 120, the number of months in 10 years.

EXAMPLE

First let's solve this problem without resetting the "payments per year" or P/Y feature on your calculator. If we place $100 in a savings account that yields 12 percent compounded quarterly, what will our investment grow to at the end of 5 years? Substituting $n = 5$, $m = 4$, $i = 12$ percent, and $PV = \$100$ into equation (5-12), we find

$$FV_5 = \$100\left(1 + \frac{.12}{4}\right)^{4 \cdot 5}$$
$$= \$100(1 + .03)^{20}$$
$$= \$100(1.806)$$
$$= \$180.60$$

Thus, we will have $180.60 at the end of 5 years. Notice that the calculator solution is slightly different because of rounding errors in the tables, and it also takes on a negative value. Also notice that while N becomes the number of quarters in 5 years, I/Y remains the annual interest rate.

CALCULATOR SOLUTION

First, SET P/Y = 4

Data Input	Function Key
20	N
12	I/Y
100	PV
0	PMT

Function Key	Answer
CPT	
FV	−180.61

EXAMPLE

In 2004 the average U.S. household owed $8,400 in credit card debt, and the average interest rate on credit card debt was 18.9 percent. On many credit cards the minimum monthly payment is 2 percent of the debt balance. If the average household paid off 2 percent of the initial amount owed each month, that is, made payments of $168 each month, how many months would it take to repay this credit card debt? Use a financial calculator to solve this problem.

You'll notice in the solution that appears in the margin that the value for *PMT* goes in as a negative. The answer is 99 months. Over that period you'll be paying just about as much in interest as you will in repayment of principal!

CALCULATOR SOLUTION

First, SET P/Y = 12

Data Input	Function Key
18.9	I/Y
8,400	PV
−168	PMT
0	FV

Function Key	Answer
CPT	
N	99.1

CONCEPT CHECK

1. Why does the future value of a given amount increase when interest is compounded nonannually as opposed to annually?
2. How do you adjust the present- and future-value formulas when interest is compounded monthly?

PRESENT VALUE OF AN UNEVEN STREAM

Objective **8**

Although some projects will involve a single cash flow and some annuities, many projects will involve uneven cash flows over several years. Chapter 9, which examines investments in fixed assets, presents this situation repeatedly. There we will be comparing not only the present value of cash flows between projects but also the cash inflows and outflows within a particular project, trying to determine that project's present value. However, this will not be difficult because the present value of any cash flow is measured in today's dollars and thus can be compared, through addition for inflows and subtraction for outflows, to the present value of any other cash flow also measured in today's dollars. For example, if we wished to find the present value of the following cash flows

YEAR	CASH FLOW	YEAR	CASH FLOW
1	$ 0	6	500
2	200	7	500
3	−400	8	500
4	500	9	500
5	500	10	500

given a 6 percent discount rate, we would merely discount the flows back to the present and total them by adding in the positive flows and subtracting the negative ones. However, this problem is complicated by the annuity of $500 that runs from years 4 through 10. To accommodate this, we can first discount the annuity back to the beginning of period 4 (or end of period 3) by multiplying it by the value of $PVIFA_{6\%, 7\text{ yr}}$ and get its present value at that point in time. We then multiply this value times the $PVIF_{6\%, 3\text{ yr}}$ in order to bring this single cash flow (which is the present value of the 7-year annuity) back to the present. In effect we discount twice, first back to the end of period 3, then back to the present. This is shown graphically in Table 5-11 and numerically in Table 5-12. Thus, the present value of this uneven stream of cash flows is $2,186.44.

Remember, once the cash flows from an investment have been brought back to the present, they can be combined by adding and subtracting to determine the project's total present value.

CONCEPT CHECK

1. If you wanted to calculate the present value of an investment that produced cash flows of $100 received at the end of year 1 and $700 at the end of year 2, how would you do it?

STEP 1:

Bring the $200 at the end of year 2 back to present.

CALCULATOR SOLUTION

Data Input	Function Key
2	N
6	I/Y
200	FV
0	PMT

Function Key	Answer
CPT	
PV	−178.00

STEP 2:

Bring the negative $400 at the end of year 3 back to present.

CALCULATOR SOLUTION

Data Input	Function Key
3	N
6	I/Y
−400	FV
0	PMT

Function Key	Answer
CPT	
PV	335.85

STEP 3:

Bring the 7-year, $500 annuity beginning at the end of year 4 back to the beginning of year 4, which is the same as the end of year 3.

CALCULATOR SOLUTION

Data Input	Function Key
7	N
6	I/Y
500	PMT
0	FV

Function Key	Answer
CPT	
PV	−2,791.19

STEP 4:

Bring the value we just calculated, which is the value of the 7-year annuity of $500 at the end of year 3, back to present.

CALCULATOR SOLUTION

Data Input	Function Key
3	N
6	I/Y
2,791.19	FV
0	PMT

Function Key	Answer
CPT	
PV	2,343.54

TABLE 5-11 Illustration of an Example of Present Value of an Uneven Stream Involving One Annuity Discounted to the Present at 6 Percent

YEAR	0	1	2	3	4	5	6	7	8	9	10
Dollars received at end of year	0	200	−400	500	500	500	500	500	500	500	

$ 178.00 ←
−336.00 ←
$2,791 ←
2,344.44 ←

Total present value $2,186.44

TABLE 5-12 Determination of the Present Value of an Example with Uneven Stream Involving One Annuity Discounted to the Present at 6 Percent

1. Present value of $200 received at the end of 2 years = $200(.890) = $ 178.00
2. Present value of a $400 outflow at the end of 3 years = −400(.840) =   −336.00
3. (a) Value end of year 3 of a $500 annuity, years 4–10 = $500(5.582) = $2,791.00
   (b) Present value of $2,791.00 received at the end of year 3 = $2,791(.840) =   2,344.44
4. Total present value = $2,186.44

PERPETUITIES

A **perpetuity** is *an annuity that continues forever*; that is, every year from its establishment this investment pays the same dollar amount. An example of a perpetuity is preferred stock that pays a constant dollar dividend infinitely. Determining the present value of a perpetuity is delightfully simple; we merely need to divide the constant flow by the discount rate. For example, the present value of a $100 perpetuity discounted back to the present at 5 percent is $100/.05 = $2,000. Thus, the equation representing the present value of a perpetuity is

$$PV = \frac{PP}{i} \qquad (5\text{-}13)$$

where PV = the present value of the perpetuity
$\quad\quad PP$ = the constant dollar amount provided by the perpetuity
$\quad\quad\quad i$ = the annual interest (or discount) rate

STEP 5:
Add the present value of the cash inflows and subtract the present value of the cash outflow (the $400 from the end of year 3) calculated in steps 1, 2, and 4:

$ 178.00
−335.85
+2,343.54
$2,185.69

EXAMPLE

What is the present value of a $500 perpetuity discounted back to the present at 8 percent? Substituting PP = $500 and i = .08 into equation (5-13), we find

$$PV = \frac{\$500}{.08} = \$6,250$$

Thus, the present value of this perpetuity is $6,250.

CONCEPT CHECK
1. What is a perpetuity?
2. When i, the annual interest (or discount) rate, increases, what happens to the present value of a perpetuity? Why?

THE MULTINATIONAL FIRM: THE TIME VALUE OF MONEY

From **Principle 1: The Risk–Return Trade-off—We Won't Take On Additional Risk Unless We Expect to Be Compensated with Additional Return**, we found that investors demand a return for delaying consumption, as well as an additional return for taking on added risk. The discount rate that we use to move money through time should reflect this return for delaying consumption; and as the Fisher effect showed in Chapter 2, this discount rate should reflect anticipated inflation. In the United States, anticipated inflation is quite low, although it does tend to fluctuate over time. Elsewhere in the world, however, the inflation rate is difficult to predict because it can be dramatically high and undergo huge fluctuations.

Let's look at Argentina, keeping in mind that similar examples abound in Central and South America and Eastern Europe. At the beginning of 1992, Argentina introduced the fifth currency in 22 years, the new peso. The austral, the currency that was replaced, was introduced in June 1985 and was initially equal in value to $1.25 U.S. currency. Five and a half years later, it took 100,000 australs to equal $1. Inflation had reached the point at which the stack of money needed to buy a candy bar was bigger and weighed more than the candy bar itself, and many workers received their weeks' wages in grocery bags. Needless to say, if we were to move australs through time, we would have to use an extremely high interest or discount rate. Unfortunately, in countries suffering from hyperinflation, inflation rates tend to fluctuate dramatically, and this makes estimating the expected inflation rate even more difficult. For example, in 1989 the inflation rate in Argentina was 4,924 percent; in 1990 it dropped to 1,344 percent; in 1991 it was only 84 percent; in 1992, only 18 percent; in 2000 it was close to zero and by 2003 it climbed up again to 41 percent. However, as inflation in Argentina dropped, inflation in Brazil heated up, going from 426 percent in 1991 to 1,094 percent in 1995. By 2000, the inflation rate in Brazil had dropped to 7 percent, and it has stayed at about that level since then. However, in 2000 the inflation rate in Uzbekistan, our ally in the war against terrorists based in Afghanistan, reached 1,568 percent and has since dropped to 26 percent. Finally, at the extreme, in 1993 in Serbia the inflation rate reached 360,000,000,000,000,000 percent.

The bottom line on all this is that because of the dramatic fluctuations in inflation that can take place in the international setting, choosing the appropriate discount rate of moving money through time is an extremely difficult process.

CONCEPT CHECK

1. How does the international setting complicate the choice of the appropriate interest rate to use when discounting cash flows back to the present?

SUMMARY

Objective **8**

Objective **10**

Objective **2**

To make decisions, financial managers must compare the costs and benefits of alternatives that do not occur during the same time period. Whether to make profitable investments or to take advantage of favorable interest rates, financial decision making requires an understanding of the time value of money. Managers who use the time value of money in all of their financial calculations assure themselves of more logical decisions. The time-value process first makes all dollar values comparable; because money has a time value, it moves all dollar flows either back to the present or out to a common future date. All time-value formulas presented in this chapter actually stem from the single compounding formula $FV_n = PV(1 + i)^n$. The formulas are used to deal simply with common financial situations, for example, discounting single flows, compounding annuities, and discounting annuities. Table 5-13 provides a summary of these calculations. The formulas can be solved using the time value of money tables at the book of the book, a financial calculator, or a spreadsheet.

TABLE 5-13 Summary of Time Value of Money Equations[a]

CALCULATION	EQUATION
Objective **1** — Future value of a single payment	$FV_n = PV(1 + i)^n = PV(FVIF_{i,n})$
Objective **3** — Present value of a single payment	$PV = FV_n\left[\dfrac{1}{(1+i)^n}\right] = FV_n(PVIF_{i,n})$
Objective **4** — Future value of an annuity	$FV \text{ of an annuity} = PMT\left[\dfrac{FVIF_{i,n} - 1}{i}\right] = PMT\left[\dfrac{(1+i)^n - 1}{i}\right] = PMT(FVIFA_{i,n})$
Objective **6** — Present value of an annuity	$PV \text{ of an annuity} = PMT\left[\dfrac{1 - PVIF_{i,n}}{i}\right] = PMT\left[\dfrac{1 - (1+i)^{-n}}{i}\right] = PMT(PVIFA_{i,n})$
Objective **5** — Future value of an annuity due / Present value of an annuity due	$FV_n(\text{annuity due}) = PMT(FVIFA_{i,n})(1 + i)$ / $PV(\text{annuity due}) = PMT(PVIFA_{i,n})(1 + i)$
Objective **7** — Future value of a single payment with nonannual compounding	$FV_n = PV\left(1 + \dfrac{i}{m}\right)^{mn}$
Objective **9** — Present value of a perpetuity	$PV = \dfrac{PP}{i}$

Notations: FV_n = the future value of the investment at the end of n years
n = the number of years until payment will be received or during which compounding occurs
i = the annual interest or discount rate
PV = the present value of the future sum of money
m = the number of times compounding occurs during the year
PMT = the annuity payment deposited or received at the end of each year
PP = the constant dollar amount provided by the perpetuity

[a] Related tables appear in Appendixes B through E at the end of the book.

Because of the dramatic fluctuations in inflation that can take place in the international setting, choosing the appropriate discount rate of moving money through time is an extremely difficult process.

KEY TERMS

Amortized loan, 155

Annuity, 149

Annuity due, 154

Compound annuity, 149

Compound interest, 138

Future-value interest factor ($FVIF_{i,\ n}$), 140

Future-value interest factor for an annuity ($FVIFA_{i,\ n}$), 150

Ordinary annuity, 149

Perpetuity, 161

Present value, 146

Present-value interest factor ($PVIF_{i,\ n}$), 147

Present-value interest factor for an annuity ($PVIFA_{i,\ n}$), 152

STUDY QUESTIONS

5-1. What is the time value of money? Why is it so important?

5-2. The process of discounting and compounding are related. Explain this relationship.

5-3. How would an increase in the interest rate (i) or a decrease in the holding period (n) affect the future value (FV_n) of a sum of money? Explain why.

5-4. Suppose you were considering depositing your savings in one of three banks, all of which pay 5 percent interest; bank A compounds annually, bank B compounds semiannually, and bank C compounds daily. Which bank would you choose? Why?

5-5. What is the relationship between the $PVIF_{i,n}$ (Table 5-3) and the $PVIFA_{i,n}$ (Table 5-7)? What is the $PVIFA_{10\%,\ 10\ yr}$? Add up the values of the $PVIF_{10\%,n}$ for $n = 1, \ldots, 10$. What is this value? Why do these values have the relationship they do?

5-6. What is an annuity? Give some examples of annuities. Distinguish between an annuity and a perpetuity.

SELF-TEST PROBLEMS

ST-1. You place $25,000 in a savings account paying an annual compound interest of 8 percent for 3 years and then move it into a savings account that pays 10 percent interest compounded annually. How much will your money have grown at the end of 6 years?

ST-2. You purchase a boat for $35,000 and pay $5,000 down and agree to pay the rest over the next 10 years in 10 equal annual end-of-the-year payments that include principal payments plus 13 percent compound interest on the unpaid balance. What will be the amount of each payment?

STUDY PROBLEMS

5-1. (*Compound interest*) To what amount will the following investments accumulate?

   a. $5,000 invested for 10 years at 10 percent compounded annually
   b. $8,000 invested for 7 years at 8 percent compounded annually
   c. $775 invested for 12 years at 12 percent compounded annually
   d. $21,000 invested for 5 years at 5 percent compounded annually

5-2. (*Compound value solving for n*) How many years will the following take?

   a. $500 to grow to $1,039.50 if invested at 5 percent compounded annually
   b. $35 to grow to $53.87 if invested at 9 percent compounded annually
   c. $100 to grow to $298.60 if invested at 20 percent compounded annually
   d. $53 to grow to $78.76 if invested at 2 percent compounded annually

5-3. (*Compound value solving for i*) At what annual rate would the following have to be invested?

    a. $500 to grow to $1,948.00 in 12 years
    b. $300 to grow to $422.10 in 7 years
    c. $50 to grow to $280.20 in 20 years
    d. $200 to grow to $497.60 in 5 years

5-4. (*Present value*) What is the present value of the following future amounts?

    a. $800 to be received 10 years from now discounted back to the present at 10 percent
    b. $300 to be received 5 years from now discounted back to the present at 5 percent
    c. $1,000 to be received 8 years from now discounted back to the present at 3 percent
    d. $1,000 to be received 8 years from now discounted back to the present at 20 percent

5-5. (*Compound annuity*) What is the accumulated sum of each of the following streams of payments?

    a. $500 a year for 10 years compounded annually at 5 percent
    b. $100 a year for 5 years compounded annually at 10 percent
    c. $35 a year for 7 years compounded annually at 7 percent
    d. $25 a year for 3 years compounded annually at 2 percent

5-6. (*Present value of an annuity*) What is the present value of the following annuities?

    a. $2,500 a year for 10 years discounted back to the present at 7 percent
    b. $70 a year for 3 years discounted back to the present at 3 percent
    c. $280 a year for 7 years discounted back to the present at 6 percent
    d. $500 a year for 10 years discounted back to the present at 10 percent

5-7. (*Compound value*) Stanford Simmons, who recently sold his Porsche, placed $10,000 in a savings account paying annual compound interest of 6 percent.

    a. Calculate the amount of money that will have accrued if he leaves the money in the bank for 1, 5, and 15 years.
    b. If he moves his money into an account that pays 8 percent or one that pays 10 percent, rework part (a) using these new interest rates.
    c. What conclusions can you draw about the relationship between interest rates, time, and future sums from the calculations you have completed in this problem?

5-8. (*Compound interest with nonannual periods*) Calculate the amount of money that will be in each of the following accounts at the end of the given deposit period.

ACCOUNT	AMOUNT DEPOSITED	ANNUAL INTEREST RATE	COMPOUNDING PERIOD (COMPOUNDED EVERY _ MONTHS)	DEPOSIT PERIOD (YEARS)
Theodore Logan III	$ 1,000	10%	12	10
Vernell Coles	95,000	12	1	1
Thomas Elliott	8,000	12	2	2
Wayne Robinson	120,000	8	3	2
Eugene Chung	30,000	10	6	4
Kelly Cravens	15,000	12	4	3

5-9. (*Compound interest with nonannual periods*)

    a. Calculate the future sum of $5,000, given that it will be held in the bank 5 years at an annual interest rate of 6 percent.
    b. Recalculate part (a) using compounding periods that are (1) semiannual and (2) bimonthly.
    c. Recalculate parts (a) and (b) for a 12 percent annual interest rate.
    d. Recalculate part (a) using a time horizon of 12 years (annual interest rate is still 6 percent).
    e. With respect to the effect of changes in the stated interest rate and holding periods on future sums in parts (c) and (d), what conclusions do you draw when you compare these figures with the answers found in parts (a) and (b)?

5-10. (*Solving for i with annuities*) Nicki Johnson, a sophomore mechanical engineering student, receives a call from an insurance agent, who believes that Nicki is an older woman ready to retire from teaching. He talks to her about several annuities that she could buy that would guarantee her an annual fixed income. The annuities are as follows:

ANNUITY	INITIAL PAYMENT INTO ANNUITY (AT $t = 0$)	AMOUNT OF MONEY RECEIVED PER YEAR	DURATION OF ANNUITY (YEARS)
A	$50,000	$8,500	12
B	$60,000	$7,000	25
C	$70,000	$8,000	20

13.13 %
10.74 % n = 11
9.6 %

If Nicki could earn 11 percent on her money by placing it in a savings account, should she place it instead in any of the annuities? Which ones, if any? Why?

5-11. (*Future value*) Sales of a new finance book were 15,000 copies this year and were expected to increase by 20 percent per year. What are expected sales during each of the next 3 years? Graph this sales trend and explain.

5-12. (*Future value*) Barry Bonds hit 73 home runs in 2001. If his home-run output grew at a rate of 10 percent per year, what would it have been over the following 5 years?

5-13. (*Loan amortization*) Mr. Bill S. Preston, Esq., purchased a new house for $80,000. He paid $20,000 down and agreed to pay the rest over the next 25 years in 25 equal annual end-of-year payments that include principal payments plus 9 percent compound interest on the unpaid balance. What will these equal payments be?

5-14. (*Solving for PMT of an annuity*) To pay for your child's education, you wish to have accumulated $15,000 at the end of 15 years. To do this you plan on depositing an equal amount into the bank at the end of each year. If the bank is willing to pay 6 percent compounded annually, how much must you deposit each year to obtain your goal?

5-15. (*Solving for i in compound interest*) If you were offered $1,079.50 ten years from now in return for an investment of $500 currently, what annual rate of interest would you earn if you took the offer?

5-16. (*Future value of an annuity*) In 10 years you are planning on retiring and buying a house in Oviedo, Florida. The house you are looking at currently costs $100,000 and is expected to increase in value each year at a rate of 5 percent. Assuming you can earn 10 percent annually on your investments, how much must you invest at the end of each of the next 10 years to be able to buy your dream home when you retire?

5-17. (*Compound value*) The Aggarwal Corporation needs to save $10 million to retire a $10 million mortgage that matures in 10 years. To retire this mortgage, the company plans to put a fixed amount into an account at the end of each year for 10 years, with the first payment occurring at the end of 1 year. The Aggarwal Corporation expects to earn 9 percent annually on the money in this account. What equal annual contribution must it make to this account to accumulate the $10 million in 10 years?

5-18. (*Compound interest with nonannual periods*) After examining the various personal loan rates available to you, you find that you can borrow funds from a finance company at 12 percent compounded monthly or from a bank at 13 percent compounded annually. Which alternative is more attractive?

5-19. (*Present value of an uneven stream of payments*) You are given three investment alternatives to analyze. The cash flows from these three investments are as follows:

END OF YEAR	INVESTMENT		
	A	B	C
1	$10,000		$10,000
2	10,000		
3	10,000		
4	10,000		
5	10,000	$10,000	
6		10,000	50,000
7		10,000	
8		10,000	
9		10,000	
10		10,000	10,000

Assuming a 20 percent discount rate, find the present value of each investment.

5-20. (*Present value*) The Kumar Corporation is planning on issuing bonds that pay no interest but can be converted into $1,000 at maturity, 7 years from their purchase. To price these bonds competitively with other bonds of equal risk, it is determined that they should yield 10 percent, compounded annually. At what price should the Kumar Corporation sell these bonds?

5-21. (*Perpetuities*) What is the present value of the following?

    a. A $300 perpetuity discounted back to the present at 8 percent
    b. A $1,000 perpetuity discounted back to the present at 12 percent
    c. A $100 perpetuity discounted back to the present at 9 percent
    d. A $95 perpetuity discounted back to the present at 5 percent

5-22. (*Solving for n with nonannual periods*) About how many years would it take for your investment to grow fourfold if it were invested at 16 percent compounded semiannually?

5-23. (*Complex present value*) How much do you have to deposit today so that beginning 11 years from now you can withdraw $10,000 a year for the next 5 years (periods 11 through 15) plus an *additional* amount of $20,000 in that last year (period 15)? Assume an interest rate of 6 percent.

5-24. (*Loan amortization*) On December 31, Beth Klemkosky bought a yacht for $50,000, paying $10,000 down and agreeing to pay the balance in 10 equal annual end-of-year installments that include both the principal and 10 percent interest on the declining balance. How big would the annual payments be?

5-25. (*Solving for i of an annuity*) You lend a friend $30,000, which your friend will repay in five equal annual end-of-year payments of $10,000, with the first payment to be received 1 year from now. What rate of return does your loan receive?

5-26. (*Solving for i in compound interest*) You lend a friend $10,000, for which your friend will repay you $27,027 at the end of 5 years. What interest rate are you charging your "friend"?

5-27. (*Loan amortization*) A firm borrows $25,000 from the bank at 12 percent compounded annually to purchase some new machinery. This loan is to be repaid in equal annual installments at the end of each year over the next 5 years. How much will each annual payment be?

5-28. (*Present-value comparison*) You are offered $1,000 today, $10,000 in 12 years, or $25,000 in 25 years. Assuming that you can earn 11 percent on your money, which should you choose?

5-29. (*Compound annuity*) You plan on buying some property in Florida 5 years from today. To do this you estimate that you will need $20,000 at that time for the purchase. You would like to accumulate these funds by making equal annual deposits in your savings account, which pays 12 percent annually. If you make your first deposit at the end of this year and you would like your account to reach $20,000 when the final deposit is made, what will be the amount of your deposits?

5-30. (*Complex present value*) You would like to have $50,000 in 15 years. To accumulate this amount you plan to deposit each year an equal sum in the bank, which will earn 7 percent interest compounded annually. Your first payment will be made at the end of the year.

    a. How much must you deposit annually to accumulate this amount?
    b. If you decide to make a large lump-sum deposit today instead of the annual deposits, how large should this lump-sum deposit be? (Assume you can earn 7 percent on this deposit.)
    c. At the end of 5 years you will receive $10,000 and deposit this in the bank toward your goal of $50,000 at the end of 15 years. In addition to this deposit, how much must you deposit in equal annual deposits to reach your goal? (Again assume you can earn 7 percent on this deposit.)

5-31. (*Comprehensive present value*) You are trying to plan for retirement in 10 years, and currently you have $100,000 in a savings account and $300,000 in stocks. In addition you plan on adding to your savings by depositing $10,000 per year in your savings account at the end of each of the next 5 years and then $20,000 per year at the end of each year for the final 5 years until retirement.

    a. Assuming your savings account returns 7 percent compounded annually and your investment in stocks will return 12 percent compounded annually, how much will you have at the end of 10 years? (Ignore taxes.)
    b. If you expect to live for 20 years after you retire, and at retirement you deposit all of your savings in a bank account paying 10 percent, how much can you withdraw each year after retirement (20 equal withdrawals beginning one year after you retire) to end up with a zero balance at death?

5-32. (*Loan amortization*) On December 31, Son-Nan Chen borrowed $100,000, agreeing to repay this sum in 20 equal annual end-of-year installments that include both the principal and 15 percent interest on the declining balance. How large will the annual payments be?

5-33. (*Loan amortization*) To buy a new house you must borrow $150,000. To do this you take out a $150,000, 30-year, 10 percent mortgage. Your mortgage payments, which are made at the end of each year (one payment each year), include both principal and 10 percent interest on the declining balance. How large will your annual payments be?

5-34. (*Present value*) The state lottery's million-dollar payout provides for $1 million to be paid over 19 years in 20 payments of $50,000. The first $50,000 payment is made immediately, and the 19 remaining $50,000 payments occur at the end of each of the next 19 years. If 10 percent is the appropriate discount rate, what is the present value of this stream of cash flows? If 20 percent is the appropriate discount rate, what is the present value of the cash flows?

5-35. (*Solving for i in compound interest—financial calculator needed*) In September 1963, the first issue of the comic book *X-MEN* was issued. The original price for that issue was $.12. By September 2002, 39 years later, the value of this comic book had risen to $7,500. What annual rate of interest would you have earned if you had bought the comic in 1963 and sold it in 2002?

5-36. (*Comprehensive present value*) You have just inherited a large sum of money, and you are trying to determine how much you should save for retirement and how much you can spend now. For retirement, you will deposit today (January 1, 2006) a lump sum in a bank account paying 10 percent compounded annually. You don't plan on touching this deposit until you retire in 5 years (January 1, 2011), and you plan on living for 20 additional years and then dropping dead on December 31, 2030. During your retirement you would like to receive income of $50,000 per year to be received the first day of each year, with the first payment on January 1, 2011, and the last payment on January 1, 2030. Complicating this objective is your desire to have one final 3-year fling during which time you'd like to track down all the living original cast members of *Leave It to Beaver* and *The Brady Bunch* and get their autographs. To finance this you want to receive $250,000 on January 1, 2026, and *nothing* on January 1, 2027, and January 1, 2028, as you will be on the road. In addition, after you pass on (January 1, 2031), you would like to have a total of $100,000 to leave to your children.

   a. How much must you deposit in the bank at 10 percent on January 1, 2006, to achieve your goal? (Use a timeline to answer this question.)
   b. What kinds of problems are associated with this analysis and its assumptions?

5-37. (*Spreadsheet problem*) If you invest $900 in a bank in which it will earn 8 percent compounded annually, how much will it be worth at the end of 7 years? Use a spreadsheet to do your calculations.

5-38. (*Spreadsheet problem*) In 20 years you'd like to have $250,000 to buy a vacation home, but you only have $30,000. At what rate must your $30,000 be compounded annually for it to grow to $250,000 in 20 years? Use a spreadsheet to calculate your answer.

5-39. (*Spreadsheet problem*) To buy a new house you take out a 25-year mortgage for $300,000. What will your monthly interest rate payments be if the interest rate on your mortgage is 8 percent? Use a spreadsheet to calculate your answer. Now, calculate the portion of the 48th monthly payment that goes toward interest and principal.

5-40. (*Future and present value using a calculator*) Bill Gates's Billions! Over the past few years Microsoft founder Bill Gates's net worth has fluctuated between $30 and $130 billion. In late 2004 it was about $30 billion (in late 2004 he owned just over 1.1 billion shares of Microsoft, and Microsoft's stock was trading at $27.29) after he reduced his stake in Microsoft from 21 percent to around 14 percent by moving billions into his charitable foundation. Let's see what Bill Gates can do with his money in the following problems.

   a. I'll take Manhattan? Manhattan's native tribe sold Manhattan Island to Peter Minuit for $24 in 1626. Now, 379 years later in 2005, Bill Gates wants to buy the island from the "current natives." How much would Bill have to pay for Manhattan if the "current natives" want a 6 percent annual return on the original $24 purchase price? Could he afford it?
   b. (*This part requires nonannual compounding using a calculator*) How much would Bill have to pay for Manhattan if the "current natives" want a 6% return compounded monthly on the original $24 purchase price?
   c. Microsoft Seattle? Bill Gates decides to pass on Manhattan and instead plans to buy the city of Seattle, Washington, for $60 billion in 10 years. How much would Mr. Gates have to invest today at 10 percent compounded annually in order to purchase Seattle in 10 years?
   d. Now assume Bill Gates only wants to invest half his net worth today, $15 billion, in order to buy Seattle for $60 billion in 10 years. What annual rate of return would he have to earn in order to complete his purchase in 10 years?
   e. Margaritaville? Instead of buying and running large cities, Bill Gates is considering quitting the rigors of the business world and retiring to work on his golf game. To fund his retirement, Bill Gates would invest his $30 billion fortune in safe investments with an expected annual rate of return of 7 percent. Also, Mr. Gates wants to make 40 equal annual withdrawals from this retirement fund beginning a year from today. How much can Mr. Gates's annual withdrawal be in this case?

5-41. (*Compounding using a calculator*) Bart Simpson, age 10, wants to be able to buy a really cool new car when he turns 16. His really cool car costs $15,000 today, and its cost is expected to increase 3 percent annually. Bart wants to make one deposit today (he can sell his mint-condition original *Nuclear Boy* comic book) into an account paying 7.5 percent annually in order to buy his car in 6 years. How much will Bart's car cost, and how much does Bart have to save today in order to buy this car at age 16?

5-42. (*Compounding using a calculator*) Lisa Simpson wants to have $1 million in 45 years by making equal annual end-of-the-year deposits into a tax-deferred account paying 8.75 percent annually. What must Lisa's annual deposit be?

5-43. (*Compounding using a calculator*) Springfield mogul Montgomery Burns, age 80, wants to retire at age 100 in order to steal candy from babies full time. Once Mr. Burns retires, he wants to withdraw $1 billion at the beginning of each year for 10 years from a special offshore account that will pay 20 percent annually. In order to fund his retirement, Mr. Burns will make 20 equal end-of-the-year deposits in this same special account that will pay 20 percent annually. How much money will Mr. Burns need at age 100, and how large of an annual deposit must be made to fund this retirement account?

5-44. (*Compounding using a calculator and annuities due*) Imagine Homer Simpson actually invested the $100,000 he earned providing Mr. Burns entertainment 5 years ago at 7.5 percent annual interest and starts investing an additional $1,500 a year today at the beginning of each year for 20 years at the same 7.5 percent annual rate. How much money will Homer have 20 years from today?

5-45. (*Nonannual compounding using a calculator*) Prof. Finance is thinking about trading cars. He estimates he will still have to borrow $25,000 to pay for his new car. How large will Prof. Finance's monthly car loan payment be if he can get a 5-year (60 equal monthly payments) car loan from the university's credit union at 6.2 percent?

5-46. (*Nonannual compounding using a calculator*) Bowflex's television ads say you can get a fitness machine that sells for $999 for $33 a month for 36 months. What rate of interest are you paying on this Bowflex loan?

5-47. (*Nonannual compounding using a calculator*) Ford's current incentives include 4.9 percent financing for 60 months or $1,000 cash back for a Mustang. Let's assume Suzie Student wants to buy the premium Mustang convertible, which costs $25,000, and she has no down payment other than the cash back from Ford. If she chooses the $1,000 cash back, Suzie can borrow from the VTech Credit Union at 6.9 percent for 60 months (Suzie's credit isn't as good as Prof. Finance's). What will Suzie Student's monthly payment be under each option? Which option should she choose?

5-48. (*Nonannual compounding using a calculator*) Ronnie Rental plans to invest $1,000 at the end of each quarter for 4 years into an account that pays 6.4 percent compounded quarterly. He will use this money as a down payment on a new home at the end of the 4 years. How large will his down payment be 4 years from today?

5-49. (*Nonannual compounding using a calculator*) Dennis Rodman has a $5,000 debt balance on his Visa card that charges 12.9 percent compounded monthly. Dennis's current minimum monthly payment is 3 percent of his debt balance, which is $150. How many months (round up) will it take Dennis to pay off his credit card if he pays the current minimum payment of $150 at the end of each month?

5-50. (*Nonannual compounding using a calculator*) Should we have bet the kids' college fund at the dog track? In the early 2000s investors suffered substantial declines on mutual funds used in tax-sheltered college savings plans (called 529 plans) around the country. Let's look at one specific case of a college professor (let's call him Prof. ME) with two young children who 2 years ago had deposited $160,000 hoping to have $420,000 available 12 years later when the first child starts college. However, the account's balance is now only $140,000. Let's figure out what is needed to get Prof. ME's college savings plan back on track.

    a. What was the original annual rate of return needed to reach Prof. ME's goal when he started the fund two years ago?

    b. Now with only $140,000 in the fund and 10 years remaining until his first child starts college, what annual rate of return would the fund have to earn to reach Prof. ME's $420,000 goal if he adds nothing to the account?

c. Shocked by his experience of the past two years, Prof. ME feels the college fund has invested too much in stocks and wants a low-risk fund in order to ensure he has the necessary $420,000 in 10 years. He is willing to make end-of-the-month deposits to the fund as well. He finds he can get a fund that promises to pay a guaranteed return of 6 percent compounded monthly. Prof. ME decides to transfer the $140,000 to this new fund and make the necessary monthly deposits. How large of a monthly deposit must Prof. ME make into this new fund?

d. Now Prof. ME gets sticker shock from the necessary monthly deposit he has to make into the guaranteed fund in the preceding question. He decides to invest the $140,000 today and $500 at the end of each month for the next 10 years into a fund consisting of 50 percent stock and 50 percent bonds and hope for the best. What annual rate of return would the fund have to earn in order to reach Prof. ME's $420,000 goal?

WEB WORKS

5-WW1. How fast will my money grow? Use the financial calculator provided by Financenter (**http://partners.financenter.com/financenter/calculate/us-eng/savings14.fcs**) to determine how long it will take $50,000 to grow to $90,000 if it earns 10 percent. Again using the financial calculator provided by Financenter (**http://partners.financenter.com/financenter/calculate/us-eng/savings14.fcs**), if you start with $50,000 and invest an additional $250 per month every month, how long will it take to grow to $90,000 if it earns 10 percent?

5-WW2. How much money will you need to start with if you make no additional investments? You want to have $90,000 in 6 years and your investment will grow at 10 percent. Use the financial calculator provided by Financenter (**http://partners.fmancenter.com/financenter/calculate/us-eng/savings14.fcs**) to determine how much money you will need to start with.

5-WW3. Financial Calculators. Compare some of the different financial calculators that are available on the Internet. Look at both the DinkyTown calculators (**www.dinkytown.net**) and USA Today's Internet calculators (**www.usatoday.com/money/perfi/calculators/calculator.htm**)—consumer loan, tuition, new car, mortgage, retirement, and 401(k) calculators. Also check out Kiplinger Online calculators (**www.kiplinger.com/tools/finances**), which include credit and banking, taxes, and insurance online calculators. Finally look at Interest.com calculators (**http://mortgages.interest.com/content/calculators/index.asp**). Which financial calculators do you find to be the most useful? Why?

5-WW4. Understanding annuities. Home mortgage payments are an annuity, and so are any loans where the payments remain constant. In effect, if you can understand annuities, you'll understand how mortgages and other loans are calculated. What would your monthly loan payments be if you bought a new 60-inch television for $3,400? You put $300 down and plan to finance the loan over 36 months at 12 percent interest. In addition, when you bought the new television, you received $100 for the trade-in of your old set. Use an online financial calculator (**www.calcbuilder.com/cgi-bin/calcs/AUT5.cgi/Kiplinger**) to determine your answer.

5-WW5. College Savings Planning. Try out the MSN Money Tuition Savings Calculator (**http://moneycentral.msn.com/investor/calcs/n_college/main.asp**). Assume you live in Virginia, begin with an initial balance of $1,000, there are 11 years until college, the rate of return on your college investments is 9 percent, and this is a taxable investment with a marginal tax rate of 22.35 percent. You do not pay capital gains tax when you cash out your college investments, the rate of tuition cost increase is 6 percent annually, there will be 4 years of college, 1 child, and the current annual cost of college is $10,000. How much do you need to save annually to cover the cost of college, and how much in total will be available for college?

COMPREHENSIVE PROBLEM

For your job as the business reporter for a local newspaper, you are given the task of putting together a series of articles that explain the power of the time value of money to your readers. Your editor would like you to address several specific questions in addition to demonstrating for the readership the use of time value of money techniques by applying them to several problems. What would be your response to the following memorandum from your editor?

To: Business Reporter
From: Perry White, Editor, *Daily Planet*
Re: Upcoming Series on the Importance and Power of the Time Value of Money

In your upcoming series on the time value of money, I would like to make sure you cover several specific points. In addition, before you begin this assignment, I want to make sure we are all reading from the same script, as accuracy has always been the cornerstone of the *Daily Planet*. In this regard, I'd like a response to the following questions before we proceed:

a. What is the relationship between discounting and compounding?

b. What is the relationship between the $PVIF_{i,\,n}$ and $PVIFA_{i,\,n}$?

c. 1. What will $5,000 invested for 10 years at 8 percent compounded annually grow to?
   2. How many years will it take $400 to grow to $1,671 if it is invested at 10 percent compounded annually?
   3. At what rate would $1,000 have to be invested to grow to $4,046 in 10 years?

d. Calculate the future sum of $1,000, given that it will be held in the bank for 5 years and earn 10 percent compounded semiannually.

e. What is an annuity due? How does this differ from an ordinary annuity?

f. What is the present value of an ordinary annuity of $1,000 per year for 7 years discounted back to the present at 10 percent? What would be the present value if it were an annuity due?

g. What is the future value of an ordinary annuity of $1,000 per year for 7 years compounded at 10 percent? What would be the future value if it were an annuity due?

h. You have just borrowed $100,000, and you agree to pay it back over the next 25 years in 25 equal end-of-year annual payments that include the principal payments plus 10 percent compound interest on the unpaid balance. What will be the size of these payments?

i. What is the present value of a $1,000 perpetuity discounted back to the present at 8 percent?

j. What is the present value of a $1,000 annuity for 10 years, with the first payment occurring at the end of year 10 (that is, ten $1,000 payments occurring at the end of year 10 through year 19), given an appropriate discount rate of 10 percent?

k. Given a 10 percent discount rate, what is the present value of a perpetuity of $1,000 per year if the first payment does not begin until the end of year 10?

SELF-TEST SOLUTIONS

SS-1. This is a compound interest problem in which you must first find the future value of $25,000 growing at 8 percent compounded annually for 3 years and then allow that future value to grow for an additional 3 years at 10 percent. First, the value of the $25,000 after 3 years growing at 8 percent is

$$FV_3 = PV(1 + i)^n$$
$$FV_3 = \$25,000(1 + 0.8)^3$$
$$FV_3 = \$25,000(1.260)$$
$$FV_3 = \$31,500$$

Thus, after 3 years you have $31,500. Now this amount is allowed to grow for 3 years at 10 percent. Plugging this into equation (5-6), with $PV = \$31,500$, $i = 10$ percent, and $n = 3$ years, we solve for FV_3.

$$FV_3 = \$31,500(1 + .10)^3$$
$$FV_3 = \$31,500(1.331)$$
$$FV_3 = \$41,926.50$$

Thus, after 6 years the $25,000 will have grown to $41,926.50.

SS-2. This loan amortization problem is actually just a present-value-of-an-annuity problem in which we know the values of i, n, and PV and are solving for PMT. In this case the value of i is 13 percent, n is 10 years, and PV is $30,000. Substituting these values into equation (5-9b) we find

$$\$30,000 = PMT(PVIFA_{13\%,\ 10})$$
$$\$30,000 = PMT(5.426)$$
$$\$5,528.93 = PMT$$

STEP 1:

Determine the value of $25,000 growing at 8 percent for 3 years.

CALCULATOR SOLUTION

Data Input	Function Key
3	N
8	I/Y
25,000	PV
0	PMT

Function Key	Answer
CPT	
FV	−31,492.80

STEP 2:

Determine the value of the $31,492.80, calculated in step 1, growing at 10 percent for 3 years.

CALCULATOR SOLUTION

Data Input	Function Key
3	N
10	I/Y
31,492.80	PV
0	PMT

Function Key	Answer
CPT	
FV	−41,916.92

CALCULATOR SOLUTION

Data Input	Function Key
10	N
13	I/Y
30,000	PV
0	FV

Function Key	Answer
CPT	
PMT	−5,528.69

CHAPTER 6

The Meaning and Measurement of Risk and Return

EXPECTED RETURN DEFINED AND MEASURED • RISK DEFINED AND MEASURED • RATES OF RETURN: THE INVESTOR'S EXPERIENCE • RISK AND DIVERSIFICATION • THE INVESTOR'S REQUIRED RATE OF RETURN

One of the most important concepts in all of finance deals with risk and return, and our first principle addresses this topic. As an illustration of risk and return, consider what was happening with the stock prices of the various Internet companies during 1998 through 2004.

In 1998 through early 1999, the stock prices of Internet companies, such as Amazon.com, increased in value a whopping 572 percent, compared with 36 percent for most large-company stocks. Most of us wished that we had been so "smart" as to buy a group of these Internet stocks. But then on April 19, 1999, the stock prices of Internet companies declined 17 percent on average, all within a matter of a few hours. But far more significant, from March 1999 through the end of 2001, Internet stocks on average declined an amazing 80 percent. So for every $100 you paid for an Internet stock in March 1999, it was selling for a mere $20 when you went Christmas shopping in 2001.

Internet stocks continued to fall out of favor with investors during 2002, with many of these companies failing and leaving only a remnant of survivors. By then, the perspective of investors regarding Internet and many high-tech firms had changed. Instead of trying to invest in the latest "good idea," investors began demanding that a firm demonstrate the potential for profits—if not now, then not too far in the future.

Amazingly, in the new environment, the stock values of the surviving and new Internet businesses began seeing sharp price increases. In 2003, Internet stocks as a group increased in value by 82 percent, with another increase of 25 percent in 2004. We can only speculate where things will go from here.

≼ WHAT'S AHEAD ≽

The need to recognize risk in financial decisions has already been apparent in earlier chapters. In Chapter 2, we referred to the discount rate or the interest rate as the opportunity cost of funds, but we did not look at the reasons for why that rate might be high or low. For example, we did not explain why in December 2001 you could buy bonds issued by AT&T that promised to pay a 6.5 percent rate of return, or why you could buy Lucent Corporation bonds that would give you a 9.3 percent rate of return, provided that both firms make the payments to the investors as promised.

In this chapter, we learn that risk is an integral force underlying rates of return. To begin our study, we define expected return and risk and offer suggestions about how these important concepts of return and risk can be measured quantitatively. We also compare the historical relationship between risk and rates of return. We then explain how diversifying investments can affect the expected return and riskiness of those investments. We also consider how the riskiness of an investment should affect the required rate of return on an investment.

Let's begin our study by looking at what we mean by the expected rate of return and how it can be measured.

Clearly, owning Internet stocks has not been for the faint of heart. These stocks may produce high rates of return to their owners, but they are risky investments, as demonstrated by their high volatility. As the owner of Internet stocks, you may eat well if they continue to increase in the future, but you certainly won't sleep very well some nights. Welcome to the world of high risk.

BACK TO THE FOUNDATIONS

This chapter has one primary objective, that of helping us understand **Principle 1: The Risk–Return Trade-off—We Won't Take on Additional Risk Unless We Expect to Be Compensated with Additional Return.**

Objective **1**

EXPECTED RETURN DEFINED AND MEASURED

The expected benefits or returns an investment generates come in the form of cash flows. Cash flows, not accounting profits, is the relevant variable the financial manager uses to measure returns. This principle holds true regardless of the type of security, whether it is a debt instrument, preferred stock, common stock, or any mixture of these (such as convertible bonds).

BACK TO THE FOUNDATIONS

Remember that future cash flows, not the reported earnings figure, determine the investor's rate of return. That is, **Principle 3: Cash—Not Profits—Is King.**

Accurately measuring expected future cash flows is not easy in a world of uncertainty. To illustrate, assume you are considering an investment costing $10,000, for which the future cash flows from owning the security depend on the state of the economy, as estimated in Table 6-1.

In any given year, the investment could produce any one of three possible cash flows, depending on the particular state of the economy. With this information, how should we select the cash flow estimate that means the most for measuring the investment's expected rate of return? One approach is to calculate an *expected* cash flow. The expected cash flow is simply the weighted average of the *possible* cash flow outcomes such that the weights are the probabilities of the occurrence of the various states of the economy. Let X_i designate the ith possible cash flow, n reflect the number of possible states of the economy, and $P(X_i)$ indicate the probability that the ith cash flow or state of economy will occur. The expected cash flow, $\overline{X}$, may then be calculated as follows:

$$\overline{X} = P(X_1)X_1 + P(X_2)X_2 + \cdots + P(X_n)X_n \tag{6-1}$$

For the present illustration:

$$\overline{X} = (.2)(\$1,000) + (.3)(\$1,200) + (.5)(\$1,400) = \$1,260$$

TABLE 6-1   Measuring the Expected Return

STATE OF THE ECONOMY	PROBABILITY OF THE STATES[a]	CASH FLOWS FROM THE INVESTMENT	PERCENTAGE RETURNS (CASH FLOW ÷ INVESTMENT COST)
Economic recession	20%	$1,000	10% ($1,000 ÷ $10,000)
Moderate economic growth	30%	1,200	12% ($1,200 ÷ $10,000)
Strong economic growth	50%	1,400	14% ($1,400 ÷ $10,000)

[a]The probabilities assigned to the three possible economic conditions have to be determined subjectively, which requires management to have a thorough understanding of both the investment cash flows and the general economy.

In addition to computing an expected dollar return from an investment, we can also calculate an **expected rate of return** earned on the $10,000 investment. Similar to the expected cash flow, the expected rate of return is *a weighted average of all the possible returns, weighted by the probability that each return will occur.* As the last column in Table 6-1 shows, the $1,400 cash inflow, assuming strong economic growth, represents a 14 percent return ($1,400 ÷ $10,000). Similarly, the $1,200 and $1,000 cash flows result in 12 percent and 10 percent returns, respectively. Using these percentage returns in place of the dollar amounts, the expected rate of return, $\bar{k}$, can be expressed as follows:

$$\bar{k} = P(k_1)k_1 + P(k_2)k_2 + \cdots + P(k_n)k_n \qquad \text{(6-2)}$$

In our example:

$$\bar{k} = (.2)(10\%) + (.3)(12\%) + (.5)(14\%) = 12.6\%$$

With our concept and measurement of expected returns, let's consider the other side of the investment coin: risk.

expected rate of return

CONCEPT CHECK

1. When we speak of "benefits" from investing in an asset, what do we mean?
2. Why is it difficult to measure future cash flows?
3. Define *expected rate of return.*

PROBLEM CHECK: COMPUTING EXPECTED RETURN

You are contemplating making a $5,000 investment that would have the following possible outcomes in cash flow each year. What are the expected value of the future cash flows and the expected rate of return?

PROBABILITY	CASH FLOW
0.30	$350
0.50	625
0.20	900

Check your answer on page 176.

RISK DEFINED AND MEASURED

Objective **2**

Because we live in a world where events are uncertain, the way we see risk is vitally important in almost all dimensions of our life. The Greek poet and statesman Solon, writing in the sixth century B.C., put it this way:

> There is risk in everything that one does, and no one knows where he will make his landfall when his enterprise is at its beginning. One man, trying to act effectively, fails to foresee something and falls into great and grim ruination, but to another man, one who is acting ineffectively, a god gives good fortune in everything and escape from his folly.[1]

Solon would have given more of the credit to Zeus than we would for the outcomes of our ventures. However, his insight reminds us that little is new in this world, including the need to acknowledge and compensate as best we can for the risks we encounter. In fact, the

---

[1]Translated by Arthur W. H. Adkins from the Greek text of Solon's poem "Prosperity, Justice, and the Hazards of Life," in M. L. West, ed., *Iambi et Elegi Gracci ante Alexandrum Canttati,* vol. 2 (Oxford: Clarendon Press, 1972).

significance of risk and the need for understanding what it means in our lives is noted by Peter Bernstein in the following excerpt:

> What is it that distinguishes the thousands of years of history from what we think of as modern times? The answer goes way beyond the progress of science, technology, capitalism, and democracy.
>
> The distant past was studded with brilliant scientists, mathematicians, inventors, technologists, and political philosophers. Hundreds of years before the birth of Christ, the skies had been mapped, the great library of Alexandria built, and Euclid's geometry taught. Demand for technological innovation in warfare was as insatiable then as it is today. Coal, oil, iron, and copper have been at the service of human beings for millennia, and travel and communication mark the very beginnings of recorded civilization.
>
> The revolutionary idea that defines the boundary between modern times and the past is the mastery of risk: the notion that the future is more than a whim of the gods and that men and women are not passive before nature. Until human beings discovered a way across that boundary, the future was a mirror of the past or the murky domain of oracles and soothsayers who held a monopoly over knowledge of anticipated events.[2]

In our study of risk, we want to consider these questions:

1. What is risk?
2. How do we know the amount of risk associated with a given investment; that is, how do we measure risk?
3. If we choose to diversify our investments by owning more than one asset, as most of us do, will such diversification reduce the riskiness of our combined portfolio of investments?

PROBLEM CHECK SOLUTION: EXPECTED RETURN

PROBABILITY	POSSIBLE		EXPECTED	
	CASH FLOW	RETURN	CASH FLOW	RETURN
0.30	$350	7.0%	$105.00	2.1%
0.50	625	12.5%	312.50	6.3%
0.20	900	18.0%	180.00	3.6%
Expected cash flow and rate of return			$597.50	12.0%

The possible returns are equal to the possible cash flows divided by the $5,000 investment. The expected cash flow and return are equal to the possible cash flows and possible returns multiplied by the probabilities.

WHAT IS RISK?

Without intending to be trite, risk means different things to different people, depending on the context and on how they feel about taking chances. For the student, risk is the possibility of failing an exam or the chance of not making his or her best grades. For the coal miner or the oil field worker, risk is the chance of an explosion in the mine or at the well site. For the retired person, risk means perhaps not being able to live comfortably on a fixed income. For the entrepreneur, risk is the chance that a new venture will fail.

risk

While certainly acknowledging these different kinds of risk, we limit our attention to the risk inherent in an investment. In this context, **risk** is the *potential variability in future cash flows*. The wider the range of possible events that can occur, the greater the risk. If we think about it, this is a relatively intuitive concept.

To help us grasp the fundamental meaning of risk within this context, consider two possible investments:

1. The first investment is a U.S. Treasury bill, a government security that matures in 90 days and promises to pay an annual return of 6 percent. If we purchase and hold this security for 90 days, we are virtually assured of receiving no more and no less than 6 percent on an annualized basis. For all practical purposes, the risk of loss is nonexistent.

[2]Peter Bernstein, *Against the Gods: The Remarkable Story of Risk*. John Wiley & Sons, Inc., New York, 1996, p. 1.

2. The second investment involves the purchase of the stock of a local publishing company. Looking at the past returns of the firm's stock, we have made the following estimate of the annual returns from the investment:

CHANCE OF OCCURRENCE	RATE OF RETURN ON INVESTMENT
1 chance in 10 (10%)	0%
2 chances in 10 (20%)	5%
4 chances in 10 (40%)	15%
2 chances in 10 (20%)	25%
1 chance in 10 (10%)	30%

Investing in the publishing company could conceivably provide a return as high as 30 percent if all goes well, or no return (0 percent) if everything goes against the firm. However, in future years, both good and bad, we could expect a 15 percent return on average.[3]

$$\bar{k} = (.10)(0\%) + (.20)(5\%) + (.40)(15\%) + (.20)(25\%) + (.10)(30\%) = 15\%$$

Comparing the Treasury bill investment with the publishing company investment, we see that the Treasury bill offers an expected 6 percent annualized rate of return, whereas the publishing company has an expected rate of return of 15 percent. However, our investment in the publishing firm is clearly more "risky"—that is, there is greater uncertainty about the final outcome. Stated somewhat differently, there is a greater variation or dispersion of possible returns, which in turn implies greater risk.[4] Figure 6-1 shows these differences graphically in the form of discrete probability distributions.

Although the return from investing in the publishing firm is clearly less certain than for Treasury bills, quantitative measures of risk are useful when the difference between two investments is not so evident. The standard deviation (σ) is such a measure. The **standard deviation** is simply the square root of the *weighted average squared deviation of each possible return from the expected return*; that is,

standard deviation

$$\sigma = \sqrt{\sum_{i=1}^{n}(k_i - \bar{k})^2 P(k_i)} \qquad (6\text{-}3)$$

where n = the number of possible outcomes or different rates of return on the investment
k_i = the value of the ith possible rate of return
$P(k_i)$ = the chance or probability that the ith outcome or return will occur
$\bar{k}$ = the expected value of the rates of return

FIGURE 6-1   **Probability Distribution of Returns**

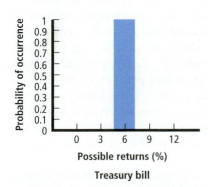

Treasury bill

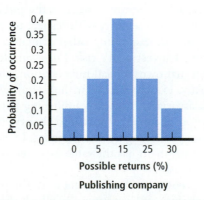

Publishing company

[3]We assume that the particular outcome or return earned in 1 year does *not* affect the return earned in the subsequent year. Technically speaking, the distribution of returns in any year is assumed to be independent of the outcome in any prior year.
[4]How can we possibly view variations above the expected return as risk? Should we even be concerned with the positive deviations above the expected return? Some would say "yes," viewing risk as only the negative variability in returns from a predetermined minimum acceptable rate of return. However, as long as the distribution of returns is symmetrical, the same conclusions will be reached.

FINANCIAL MANAGEMENT
IN PRACTICE

WANT BIG AND RISKY RETURNS: THINK SMALL

The "hottest" stocks in 2004 were those companies that were developing nanotechnology. *Nanotechnology* uses small particles to create or improve products.

John Roy, a Merrill Lynch analyst, thought that nanotechnology "could be the next great growth innovation." John Romero of Aptus Partners thought otherwise, saying, "they're way too frothy."

Some observers see similarities to the Internet bubble. In Romero's opinion, there is "far more risk than reward" in these companies whose stock prices might double or triple without

the earnings to support them. Furthermore, many companies are now simply adding "nano" to their names in hopes of attracting investor attention.

There is one difference, however, between Internet companies and nanotechnology firms—barriers to entry. Real expertise is needed to begin a nanotechnology company. But the point remains, these firms are extremely risky, and their investors will be either very wealthy or very poor!

Source: Gregory Zuckerman, "Recent Big Gainers Come from Thinking Really, Really Small," *The Wall Street Journal*, January 20, 2004, p. C1.

For the publishing company, the standard deviation would be 9.22 percent, determined as follows:

$$\sigma = \left[\begin{array}{l} (\ 0\% - 15\%)^2(.10) + (\ 5\% - 15\%)^2(.20) \\ + (15\% - 15\%)^2(.40) + (25\% - 15\%)^2(.20) \\ + (30\% - 15\%)^2(.10) \end{array} \right]^{\frac{1}{2}}$$

$$= \sqrt{85\%} = 9.22\%$$

Although the standard deviation of returns provides us with a quantitative measure of an asset's riskiness, how should we interpret the result? What does it mean? Is the 9.22 percent standard deviation for the publishing company investment good or bad? First, we should remember that statisticians tell us that two-thirds of the time, an event will fall within one standard deviation of the expected value (assuming the distribution is normally distributed; that is, it is shaped like a bell). Thus, given a 15 percent expected return and a standard deviation of 9.22 percent for the publishing company investment, we may reasonably anticipate that the actual returns will fall between 5.78 percent and 24.22 percent (15% ± 9.22%) two-thirds of the time—not much certainty with this investment.

A second way of answering the question about the meaning of the standard deviation comes by comparing the investment in the publishing firm against other investments. The attractiveness of a security with respect to its return and risk cannot be determined in isolation. Only by examining other available alternatives can we reach a conclusion about a particular investment's risk. For example, if another investment, say, an investment in a firm that owns a local radio station, has the same expected return as the publishing company, 15 percent, but with a standard deviation of 7 percent, we would consider the risk associated with the publishing firm, 9.22 percent, to be excessive. In the technical jargon of modern portfolio theory, the radio station investment is said to "dominate" the publishing firm investment. In common sense terms, this means that the radio station investment has the same expected return as the publishing company investment but is less risky.

What if we compare the investment in the publishing company with one in a quick oil-change franchise, an investment in which the expected rate of return is an attractive 24 percent but the standard deviation is estimated at 13 percent? Now what should we do? Clearly, the oil-change franchise has a higher expected rate of return, but it also has a larger standard deviation. In this example, we see that the real challenge in selecting the better investment comes when one investment has a higher expected rate of return but also exhibits greater risk. *Here the final choice is determined by our attitude toward risk, and there is no single right answer.* You might select the publishing company, whereas I might choose the oil-change investment, and neither of us would be wrong. We would simply be expressing our tastes and preferences about risk and return.

PAUSE AND REFLECT

The first Chinese symbol shown here represents danger; the second stands for opportunity. The Chinese define risk as the combination of danger and opportunity. Greater risk, according to the Chinese, means we have greater opportunity to do well but also greater danger of doing badly.

CONCEPT CHECK

1. How is risk defined?
2. How does the standard deviation help us measure the riskiness of an investment?
3. Does greater risk imply a bad investment?

PROBLEM CHECK: COMPUTING THE STANDARD DEVIATION

In the preceding problem check, we computed the expected cash flow of $597.50 and the expected return of 12 percent on a $5,000 investment. Now let's calculate the standard deviation of the returns. The probabilities of possible returns are given as follows:

PROBABILITY	RETURNS
0.30	7.0%
0.50	12.5%
0.20	18.0%

Check your answer on p. 181.

RATES OF RETURN: THE INVESTOR'S EXPERIENCE

Objective **3**

In speaking of expected rates of return and risk, we have mostly used hypothetical examples; however, it is also interesting to look at returns that investors have actually received. Such information is readily available. For example, Ibbotson and Sinquefield have provided annual rates of return as far back as 1926.[5] In their results, they summarize, among other things, the annual returns for six portfolios of securities made up of

1. Common stocks of large companies
2. Common stocks of small firms

---

[5]Roger G. Ibbotson and Rex A. Sinquefield, *Stocks, Bonds, Bills, and Inflation: 2003 Yearbook (1926–2004).* (Chicago: Dow Jones–Irwin, 2005).

3. Long-term corporate bonds
4. Long-term U.S. government bonds
5. Intermediate-term U.S. government bonds
6. U.S. Treasury bills (short-term government securities)

Before comparing these returns, we should think about what to expect. First, we would intuitively expect a Treasury bill (short-term government securities) to be the least risky of the six portfolios. Because a Treasury bill has a short-term maturity date, the price is less volatile (less risky) than the price of an intermediate- or long-term government security. In turn, because there is a chance of default on a corporate bond, which is essentially nonexistent for government securities, a long-term government bond is less risky than a long-term corporate bond. Finally, common stock of large companies is more risky than a corporate bond, with small-company stocks being more risky than the portfolio of large-firm stocks.

With this in mind, we could reasonably expect different rates of return to the holders of these varied securities. If the market rewards an investor for assuming risk, the average annual rates of return should increase as risk increases.

A comparison of the annual rates of return for the six respective portfolios for the years 1926 to 2004 is provided in Figure 6-2. Four aspects of these returns are included: (1) the nominal average annual rate of return; (2) the standard deviation of the returns, which measures the volatility or riskiness of the portfolio returns; (3) the real average annual rate of return, which is the nominal return less the inflation rate; and (4) the risk premium, which represents the additional return received beyond the risk-free rate (Treasury bill rate) for assuming risk. Also, a frequency distribution of returns is provided. Looking first at the two columns of nominal average annual returns and standard deviations, we gain a good overview of the risk–return relationships that have existed over the 79 years ending in 2004. For the most part, there has been a positive relationship between risk and return, with Treasury bills being least risky and small-company stocks being most risky.

FIGURE 6-2   Annual Rates of Return, 1926 to 2004

Securities	Nominal Average Annual Returns	Standard Deviation of Returns	Real Average Annual Returns[a]	Risk Premium[b]	Frequency of Returns Distributions
Large company stocks	12.4%	20.4%	9.3%	8.6%	
Small-company stocks	17.5%	33.3%	14.4%	13.7%	
Long-term corporate bonds	6.2%	8.6%	3.1%	2.4%	
Long-term government bonds	5.8%	8.4%	2.7%	2.0%	
Intermediate-term government bonds	5.5%	5.7%	2.4%	1.7%	
U.S. Treasury bills	3.8%	3.1%	0.7%	0%	
Inflation	3.1%	4.3%			

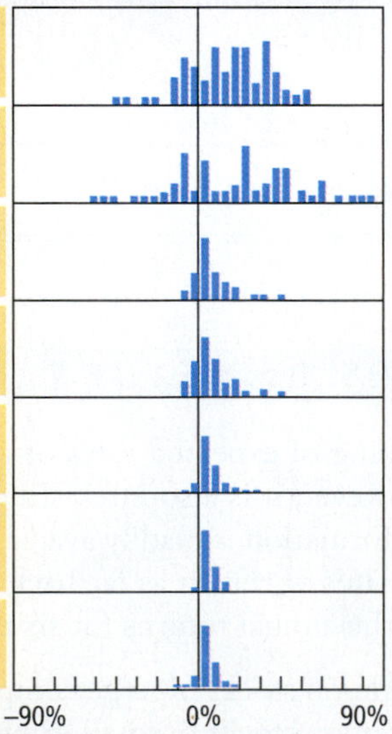

−90%   0%   90%

[a]Real return equals the nominal returns less the average inflation rate from 1926 through 2004 of 3.1 percent.
[b]Risk premium equals the nominal security return less the average risk-free rate (Treasury bills) of 3.8 percent.

PROBLEM CHECK SOLUTION: STANDARD DEVIATION

DEVIATION (POSSIBLE RETURN – 12% EXPECTED RETURN)	DEVIATION SQUARED	PROBABILITY	PROBABILITY × DEVIATION SQUARED
−5.0%	25.00%	0.30	7.500%
0.5%	0.25%	0.50	0.125%
6.0%	36.00%	0.20	7.200%
Sum of squared deviations × probability			14.825%
Standard deviation			3.850%

The return information in Figure 6-2 clearly demonstrates that only common stock has in the long run served as an inflation hedge and provided any substantial risk premium. However, it is equally apparent that the common stockholder is exposed to sizable risk, as demonstrated by a 20.4 percent standard deviation for large-company stocks and a 33.3 percent standard deviation for small-company stocks. In fact, in the 1926 to 2004 time frame, common shareholders of large firms received negative returns in 22 of the 79 years, compared with only 1 (1938) in 79 years for Treasury bills.

CONCEPT CHECK

1. What is the additional compensation for assuming greater risk called?
2. In Figure 6-2, which rate of return is the risk-free rate? Why?

RISK AND DIVERSIFICATION

Objective **4**

From the preceding discussions, we can define risk as the variability of anticipated returns, as measured by the standard deviation. However, more can be said about risk, especially about its nature, when we own more than one asset in our investment portfolio. Let's consider for the moment how risk is affected if we diversify our investment by holding a variety of securities.

As a beginning illustration, let's assume that you graduated from college in May 2004. Not only did you get the good job you had hoped for, but also you actually finished the year with a little nest egg—not enough to take that summer fling to Europe like some of your college friends but a nice surplus. Besides you suspected that they used credit cards to go anyway. So you made two stock investments based on your experience during your college studies. For the past four years, you lived on Starbucks coffee and Krispy Kreme doughnuts. They had to be great investments—they got you through those all-night study sessions. After graduating you became focused on your work, wanting to do well in your job, and seldom thought about your investments. As 2004 ended, you took a few days off to go home and just relax. On the first morning home, you picked up the local newspaper to check out how your investments were doing. You bought Starbucks at $40 per share and it was now trading at $62. Super! Then you looked at Krispy Kreme, and you were shocked. You also paid $40 per share for Krispy Kreme, and it was now trading for a meager $12 per share! How could that be? Going to the Internet, you found that the firm's sales growth was faltering combined with investigations of the firm's accounting practices. What a way to begin the day!

Clearly, what we have described about Starbucks and Krispy Kreme were events unique to these two companies, and as we would expect investors reacted accordingly; that is, the value of the stock changed in light of the new information. Although we might have wished we had owned only Starbucks stock at the time, most of us would prefer to avoid such uncertainties; that is, we are risk averse. Instead, we would like to reduce the risk associated with our investment portfolio, without having to accept a lower expected return. Good news: It is possible by diversifying our portfolio!

FIGURE 6-3   Variability of Returns Compared with Size of Portfolio

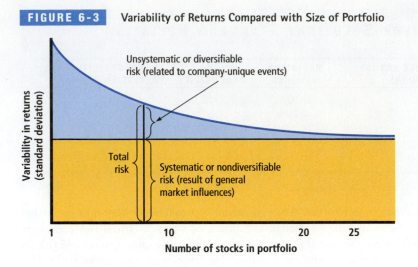

DIVERSIFYING AWAY THE RISK

If we diversify our investments across different securities rather than invest in only one stock, the variability in the returns of our portfolio should decline. The reduction in risk will occur if the stock returns within our portfolio do not move precisely together over time—that is, if they are not perfectly correlated. Figure 6-3 shows graphically what we could expect to happen to the variability of returns as we add additional stocks to the portfolio. The reduction occurs because some of the volatility in returns of a stock are unique to that security. The unique variability of a single stock tends to be countered by the uniqueness of another security. However, we should not expect to eliminate all risk from our portfolio. In practice, it would be rather difficult to cancel all the variations in returns of a portfolio, because stock prices have some tendency to move together. Thus, we can divide the total risk (total variability) of our portfolio into two types of risk: (1) **company-unique risk**, or **unsystematic risk**, and (2) **market risk**, or **systematic risk**. Company-unique risk might also be called **diversifiable risk**, in that it *can be diversified away*. Market risk is **nondiversifiable risk**; it *cannot be eliminated through random diversification*. These two types of risk are shown graphically in Figure 6-3. Total risk declines until we have approximately 20 securities, and then the decline becomes very slight.

The remaining risk, which would typically be about 40 percent of the total risk, is the portfolio's systematic or market risk. At this point, our portfolio is highly correlated with all securities in the marketplace. Events that affect our portfolio now are not so much unique events as changes in the general economy, major political events, and sociological changes. Examples include changes in interest rates in the economy, changes in tax legislation that affect all companies, or increasing public concern about the effect of business practices on the environment.

Because we can remove the company-unique or unsystematic risk, there is no reason to believe the market will reward us with additional returns for assuming risk that could be avoided by simply diversifying. Our measure of risk should, therefore, measure how responsive a stock or portfolio is to changes in a market portfolio, such as the New York Stock Exchange or the S&P 500 Index.[6]

MEASURING MARKET RISK

To help clarify the idea of systematic risk, let's examine the relationship between the common stock returns of Barnes & Noble, Inc. and the returns of the S&P 500 Index.

company-unique risk

unsystematic risk

market risk

systematic risk

diversifiable risk

nondiversifiable risk

---

[6]The New York Stock Exchange Index is an index that reflects the performance of all stocks listed on the New York Stock Exchange. The Standard & Poor's (S&P) 500 Index is similarly an index that measures the combined stock-price performance of the companies that constitute the 500 largest companies in the United States, as designated by Standard & Poor's.

TABLE 6-2 Monthly Holding–Period Returns, Barnes & Noble, Inc. and the S&P 500 Index, December 2002 to November 2004

MONTH AND YEAR	BARNES & NOBLE		S&P 500 INDEX	
	PRICE	RETURNS (%)	PRICE	RETURNS (%)
2002				
November	$23.67		$ 928.62	
December	18.07	−23.66%	876.99	−5.56%
2003				
January	17.40	−3.71%	854.72	−2.54%
February	17.63	1.32%	834.75	−2.34%
March	18.99	7.71%	864.03	3.51%
April	19.70	3.74%	917.77	6.22%
May	23.80	20.81%	953.08	3.85%
June	23.05	−3.15%	981.06	2.94%
July	23.93	3.82%	989.58	0.87%
August	26.20	9.49%	999.31	0.98%
September	25.41	−3.02%	1,002.14	0.28%
October	29.80	17.28%	1,049.29	4.70%
November	33.18	11.34%	1,055.61	0.60%
December	32.85	−0.99%	1,108.55	5.02%
2004				
January	33.85	3.04%	1,131.02	2.03%
February	34.90	3.10%	1,142.93	1.05%
March	32.60	−6.59%	1,123.93	−1.66%
April	29.87	−8.37%	1,118.54	−0.48%
May	29.94	0.23%	1,120.00	0.13%
June	33.98	13.49%	1,134.30	1.28%
July	34.38	1.18%	1,099.91	−3.03%
August	34.56	0.52%	1,102.80	0.26%
September	37.00	7.06%	1,111.39	0.78%
October	33.27	−10.08%	1,125.23	1.25%
November	27.08	−18.61%	1,180.54	4.92%
Average return		1.08%		1.04%
Standard deviation		10.26%		2.84%

The monthly returns for Barnes & Noble, Inc. and the S&P 500 Index for the 24 months ending November 2004 are presented in Table 6-2 and Figure 6-4. These *monthly returns*, or **holding-period returns**, as they are often called, are calculated as follows.[7]

holding-period returns

$$k_t = \frac{P_t}{P_{t-1}} - 1 \qquad\qquad (6\text{-}4)$$

where k_t = the holding-period return in month t for a particular firm, such as Barnes & Noble, or for a portfolio such as the S&P 500 Index

P_t = a firm's stock price, such as Barnes & Noble (or the S&P 500 Index), at the end of month t

---

[7]For simplicity's sake, we are ignoring the dividend that the investor receives from the stock as part of the total return. In other words, letting D_t equal the dividend received by the investor in month t, the holding-period return would more accurately be measured as

$$k_t = \frac{P_t + D_t}{P_{t-1}} - 1 \qquad\qquad (6\text{-}5)$$

FIGURE 6-4   Monthly Holding–Period Returns: Barnes & Noble and the S&P 500 Index, December 2002 to November 2004

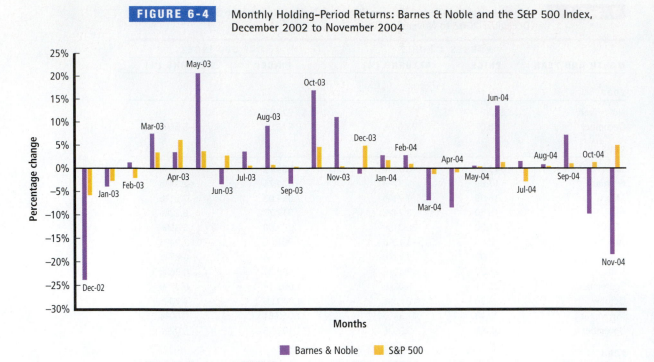

For instance, the holding-period return for Barnes & Noble and the S&P 500 Index for April 2003 is computed as follows:

$$\text{The Barnes \& Noble return} = \frac{\text{stock price end of April 2003}}{\text{stock price end of March 2003}} - 1$$

$$= \frac{\$19.70}{\$18.99} - 1 = 0.0374 = 3.74\%$$

$$\text{S\&P 500 Index return} = \frac{\text{index value at the end of April 2003}}{\text{index value at the end of March 2003}} - 1$$

$$= \frac{\$917.77}{\$864.03} - 1 = 0.0622 = 6.22\%$$

At the bottom of Table 6-2, we have also computed the averages of the returns for the 24 months, for both Barnes & Noble and the S&P 500 Index, and the standard deviation for these returns. Because we are using historical return data, we assume each observation has an equal probability of occurrence. Thus, the average return, $\bar{k}$, is found by summing the returns and dividing by the number of months; that is,

$$\text{Average return} = \bar{k} = \frac{\sum\limits_{t=1}^{n} \text{return in month } t}{\text{number of months}} = \frac{\sum\limits_{t=1}^{n} (k_t)}{n} \tag{6-6}$$

and the standard deviation σ is computed as

$$\text{Standard deviation} = \sqrt{\frac{\sum\limits_{t=1}^{n} (\text{return in month } t - \text{average return})^2}{\text{number of months} - 1}} \tag{6-7}$$

$$\sigma = \sqrt{\frac{\sum\limits_{t=1}^{n} (k_t - \bar{k})^2}{n-1}}$$

BANKERS HAVE TO DIVERSIFY TOO

Robert A. Bennett, a banker, says that diversifying is important for any business, including banks. He makes the point that bankers need to understand the importance of diversifying, especially in uncertain times.

In the quest to increase their earnings, many banks forgot the importance of diversification. Rushing into the moment's hottest businesses, they abandoned activities that at the time seemed lackluster. The go-go businesses of the 1990s reflected the stock market's boom: investment banking, stock brokerage, wealth management and equity investment. On the other side, banks were dumping what seemed to be slow-growth activities: mortgage banking, auto financing and credit cards.

In these uncertain times it is unclear which way to turn. It appears the best gamble is to spread your bets across a wide spectrum.

Citigroup is a case in point. The decline in the stock markets walloped the earnings of its investment banking activities, where income dropped $497 million in the first quarter. That,

indeed was a severe blow that was primarily responsible for the 7% decline in Citi's year-overs-year first-quarter earnings.

But as Sandy Weill, Citi's CEO, said in the company's earnings report: "This is precisely the kind of market that demonstrates the power of our franchise. The strength and diversity of our earnings by business, geography, and customer helped to deliver a strong bottom line in a period of market uncertainty."

Considering the plunge in investment banking income, things could have been a lot worse. Despite the drop in income from investment activities, Citi succeeded in getting a 22.5% return on equity. That's even better than its 22% return last year, and better than its average ROE of 19% for the three-year period 1998–2000.

As David S. Berry, head of research at Keefe, Bruyette & Woods, put it: "Citigroup again demonstrated the benefits of diversification and leadership across its business lines."

Source: Robert A. Bennett, "When in Doubt, Diversify," *U.S. Banker*, vol. 11, no. 5 (May 2001), p. 6.

In looking at Table 6-2 and Figure 6-4, we notice the following things about Barnes & Noble's holding-period returns over the 2 years ending in November 2004.

1. Barnes & Noble's stockholders have had slightly higher average monthly returns than the average stock in the S&P 500 Index, 1.08 percent compared to 1.04 percent.
2. The bad news is Barnes & Noble's greater volatility of returns—in other words, greater risk—as evidenced by Barnes & Noble's higher standard deviation. As shown at the bottom of Table 6-2, the standard deviation of the returns is 10.26 percent for Barnes & Noble versus 2.84 percent for the S&P 500 Index. Barnes & Noble's more volatile returns are also evident in Figure 6-4, where we see Barnes & Noble's returns frequently being higher and lower than the corresponding S&P 500 returns.
3. We should also notice the tendency of Barnes & Noble's stock price to increase (decrease) when the value of the S&P 500 Index increases (decreases). In 17 of the 24 months, Barnes & Noble's returns were positive (negative) when the S&P 500 Index returns were positive (negative). That is, there is a positive, although not perfect, relationship between Barnes & Noble's stock returns and the S&P 500 Index returns.

With respect to our third observation, that there is a relationship between the stock returns with Barnes & Noble and the S&P 500 Index, it is helpful to see this relationship by graphing Barnes & Noble's returns against the S&P 500 Index returns. We provide such a graph in Figure 6-5. In the figure, we have plotted Barnes & Noble's returns on the vertical axis and the returns for the S&P 500 Index on the horizontal axis. Each of the 24 dots in the figure represents the returns of Barnes & Noble and the S&P 500 Index for a particular month. For instance, the returns for January 2004 for Barnes & Noble and the S&P 500 Index were 3.04 percent and 2.03 percent, respectively, which are noted in the figure.

In addition to the dots in the graph, we have drawn a line of "best fit," which we call the **characteristic line**. *The slope of the characteristic line measures the average relationship between a stock's returns and those of the S&P 500 Index*: or stated differently, *the slope of the line indicates the average movement in a stock's price in response to a movement in the S&P 500 Index price*. For Barnes & Noble, the slope of the line is 1.43, which simply equals the rise of the line relative to the run of the line.[8] A slope of 1.43, as for Barnes & Noble, means that as the market return (S&P 500 Index returns) increases or decreases 1 percentage point, the return for Barnes & Noble on average increases or decreases 1.43 percentage points.

characteristic line

[8]Linear regression is the statistical technique used to determine the slope of the line of best fit.

FIGURE 6-5 Monthly Holding–Period Returns of Barnes & Noble and the S&P 500 Index, December 2002 to November 2004

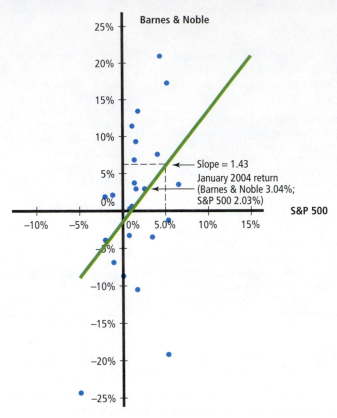

We can also think of the 1.43 slope of the characteristic line as indicating that Barnes & Noble's returns are 1.43 times as volatile on average as those of the overall market (S&P 500 Index). This slope has come to be called **beta** in investor jargon, and it *measures the average relationship between a stock's returns and the market's returns*. It is a term you will see almost any time you read an article written by a financial analyst about the riskiness of a stock.

Looking once again at Figure 6-5, we see that the dots (returns) are scattered all about the characteristic line—most of the returns do not fit neatly on the characteristic line. That is, the average relationship may be 1.43, but the variation in Barnes & Noble's returns is only partly explained by the stock's average relationship with the S&P 500 Index. There are other driving forces unique to Barnes & Noble that also affect the firm's stock returns. (Earlier, we called this company-unique risk.) If we were, however, to diversify our holdings and own, say, 20 stocks with betas of 1.43, we could essentially eliminate the variation about the characteristic line. That is, we would remove almost all the volatility in returns, except for what is caused by the general market, which is represented by the slope of the line in Figure 6-5. If we plotted the returns of our 20-stock portfolio against the S&P 500 Index, the points in our new graph would fit nicely along a straight line with a slope of 1.43, which means that the beta of the portfolio is also 1.43. The new graph would look something like the one shown in Figure 6-6. In other words, by diversifying our portfolio, we can essentially eliminate the variations about the characteristic line, leaving only the variation in returns for a company that comes from variations in the general market returns.

So beta—the slope of the characteristic line—is a measure of a firm's market risk or systematic risk, which is the risk that remains for a company even after we have diversified our portfolio. It is this risk—and only this risk—that matters for investors who have broadly diversified portfolios.

While we have said that beta is a measure of a stock's systematic risk, how should we interpret a specific beta? For instance, when is a beta considered low and when is it considered high? In general, a stock with a beta of zero has no systematic risk; a stock with a beta of 1 has systematic or market risk equal to the "typical" stock in the marketplace; and a

beta

FIGURE 6-6 Holding–Period Returns: Hypothetical Portfolio and the S&P 500 Index

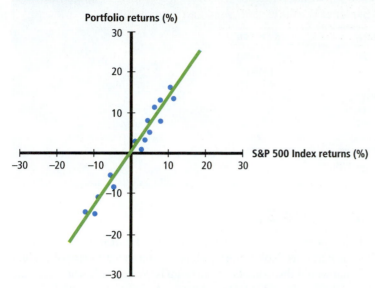

stock with a beta exceeding 1 has more market risk than the typical stock. Most stocks, however, have betas between 0.60 and 1.60.

We should also realize that calculating beta is no exact science. The final estimate of a firm's beta is heavily dependent on one's methodology. For instance, it matters whether you use 24 months in your measurement or 60 months, as most professional investment companies do. Take our computation of Barnes & Noble's beta. We said Barnes & Noble's beta is 1.43 but Value Line, a well-known investment service, has estimated Barnes & Noble's beta to be 1.13. Value Line's beta estimates for a number of firms are as follows:

	VALUE LINE
Coca-Cola	0.85
ExxonMobil	0.80
General Motors	1.10
General Electric	1.30
IBM	1.05
Merck	0.95
Nike	0.95
PepsiCo	0.70
Wal-Mart	1.15

Thus, although close in many instances, even the professionals may not agree in their measurement of a given firm's beta.

To this point, we have talked about measuring an individual stock's beta. We will now consider how to measure the beta for a portfolio of stocks.

PROBLEM CHECK: ESTIMATING BETA

On the next page we provide the end-of-month prices for Nike stock and the Standard & Poor's 500 Index for the last seven months of 2004. Given the information, compute the following both for Nike and the S&P 500: (1) the monthly holding-period returns, (2) the average monthly returns, and (3) the standard deviation of the returns. Next, graph the holding-period returns of Nike on the vertical axis against the holding-period returns of the S&P 500 on the horizontal axis. Draw a line on your graph similar to what we did in Figure 6-5 to estimate the average relationship between Nike's stock returns and the returns of the overall market as represented by the S&P 500. What is the slope of your line? What does this tell you?

(In working this problem, it would be easier if you used a computer spreadsheet. One is available for this chapter at **www.prenhall.com/keown** to help you.)

	NIKE	S&P 500
June	$75.75	$1,134.30
July	72.71	1,099.91
August	75.31	1,102.80
September	78.80	1,111.39
October	81.31	1,125.23
November	84.66	1,180.54
December	90.69	1,185.00

Check your answer on page 189.

MEASURING A PORTFOLIO'S BETA

portfolio beta

What if we were to diversify our portfolio, as we have just suggested, but instead of acquiring stocks with the same beta as Barnes & Noble (1.43), we buy 8 stocks with betas of 1.0 and 12 stocks with betas of 1.5. What would the beta of our portfolio become? As it works out, the **portfolio beta** is merely the average of the individual stock betas. Actually, the portfolio beta is a *weighted average of the individual securities' betas, with the weights being equal to the proportion of the portfolio invested in each security.* Thus, the beta (β) of a portfolio consisting of n stocks is equal to

$$\beta_{portfolio} = \sum_{j=1}^{n} [(\text{percentage invested in stock } j) \times (\beta \text{ of stock } j)] \qquad (6\text{-}8)$$

So, assuming we bought equal amounts of each stock in our new 20-stock portfolio, the beta would simply be 1.3, calculated as follows:

$$\text{Portfolio beta} = \left(\frac{8}{20} \times 1.0\right) + \left(\frac{12}{20} \times 1.50\right) = 1.3$$

Thus, whenever the general market increases or decreases 1 percent, our new portfolio's returns would change 1.3 percent on average, which says that our new portfolio has more systematic or market risk than the market has as a whole.

We can conclude that the beta of a portfolio is determined by the betas of the individual stocks. If we have a portfolio consisting of stocks with low betas, then our portfolio will have a low beta. The reverse is true as well. Figure 6-7 presents these situations graphically.

FIGURE 6-7 Holding-Period Returns: High- and Low-Beta Portfolios and the S&P 500 Index

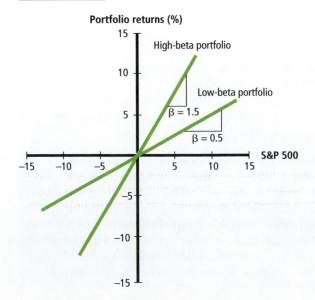

PROBLEM CHECK SOLUTION: ESTIMATING BETA

The holding-period returns, average monthly returns, and the standard deviations for Nike and the S&P 500 data are as follows:

	NIKE		S&P 500	
	PRICES	RETURNS	PRICES	RETURNS
June	$75.75		$1,134.30	
July	72.71	−4.01%	1,099.91	−3.03%
August	75.31	3.58%	1,102.80	0.26%
September	78.8	4.63%	1,111.39	0.78%
October	81.31	3.19%	1,125.23	1.25%
November	84.66	4.12%	1,180.54	4.92%
December	90.69	7.12%	1,185.00	0.38%
Average return		3.10%		0.76%
Standard deviation		3.75%		2.54%

The graph would appear as follows:

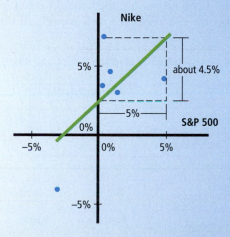

The average relationship between Nike's stock returns and the S&P 500's returns, as estimated by the slope of the characteristic line in the graph above, appears to be about 0.90, where the rise of the line is 4.5 relative to a run (horizontal axis) of 5.0 (0.90 = 4.5/5.0). If our estimates fairly represent the relationships, then Nike's stock returns are not as volatile as the market's returns. When the market rises (falls) 1 percent, Nike's stock will rise (fall) 0.9 percent. (We should, however be hesitant to draw any firm conclusions here, given the limited number of return observations.)

Before leaving the subject of risk and diversification, we want to share a study that demonstrates the effects of diversifying our investments, not just across different stocks but also across different types of securities.

RISK AND DIVERSIFICATION DEMONSTRATED[9]

Having described the effect of diversification on risk and return in a general way, let's now look at some actual numbers to demonstrate how risk and return change as you diversify your portfolio. As it was stated earlier in the chapter, our source of information is Ibbotson Associates, a firm that gathers extensive return data on a large group of investments.

[9]This presentation is taken from material developed by Ibbotson Associates, Chicago. Copyright © 1994.

To show the effect of diversification on risk and rates of return, Ibbotson compared three portfolios (A, B, and C), consisting of the following investments:

	INVESTMENT MIX IN PORTFOLIO (%)		
TYPES OF SECURITIES	**A**	**B**	**C**
Short-term government securities (Treasury bills)	0%	63%	34%
Long-term government bonds	100	12	14
Large-company stocks	<u>0</u>	<u>25</u>	<u>52</u>
	100	100	100

Figure 6-8 shows the average returns and standard deviations of the three portfolios. The results show that an investor can use diversification to improve the risk–return characteristics of a portfolio. Specifically, we can see that

1. Portfolio A, which consists entirely of long-term government bonds, had an average annual return of 5.5 percent with a standard deviation of 11.3 percent.[10]
2. In portfolio B, we diversified across all three security types, with the majority of the funds (63%) invested in Treasury bills and a lesser amount in stocks (25%) and long-term government bonds (12%). The effects are readily apparent. The average returns of the two portfolios were identical, but the risk associated with portfolio B was almost half that of

FIGURE 6-8   The Effect of Diversification on Average Return and Risk

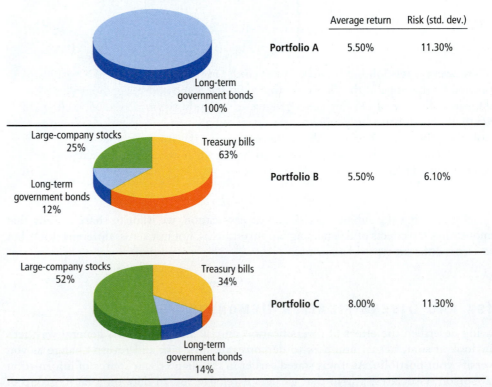

	Portfolio mix (%)		
	A	B	C
Treasury bills	0	63	34
Long-term government bonds	100	12	14
Large-company stocks	0	25	52

	Average return	Risk (std. dev.)
Portfolio A	5.50%	11.30%
Portfolio B	5.50%	6.10%
Portfolio C	8.00%	11.30%

Source: Adapted from Ibbotson Associates, Inc. Copyright © 1994, Ibbotson Assoc., Inc., Chicago.

[10]In this example, Ibbotson Associates uses 1970 to 1993 data to compute the standard deviation for the long-term government bonds; all other computations use the total 1926 to 1993 time frame.

FINANCIAL MANAGEMENT
IN PRACTICE

DO STOCKS ALWAYS GIVE HIGHER RETURNS THAN BONDS?

Investment advisers will invariably tell us to invest in stocks for the long term, largely based on the results of rates of return in American capital markets, which are summarized in Figure 6-2. For the last 79 years, stocks have outperformed bonds in almost all years. Also, analysts are quick to point out that stock returns have beat bond returns in every single 20-year period—although there are only three such periods to consider.

A recent study, presented in a book entitled *Triumph of the Optimists*, examines rates of return all the way back to 1900 for the 16 wealthiest countries in the world. The study looks at equity-risk premium, calculated as the annual return of stocks over the returns of riskless debt (government securities). Based on their findings, the authors conclude that stocks outperform government bonds in all the world's stock markets, not just the United States. However, the authors showed that in four countries—the Netherlands, Germany, Sweden, and Switzerland—

we would at times have had to hold stocks for 40 years for stocks to have outperformed government bonds.

The equity-risk premiums for the different countries are shown in the accompanying figure, with Germany having the highest premium and Denmark the lowest. The authors estimate a global average equity premium of 4.6 percentage points. (Notice that China and Russia, which were closed during Communist rule, are excluded from the study. The global premium would be even less if these countries were included.)

The true level of the equity premium is not merely an academic debate. As we will see later, overestimating the market's equity premium will cause us to overestimate the discount rate (cost of capital) used in valuing prospective capital investments. If the equity premium is overstated, managers may be rejecting profitable investments, from new factories to drug research to investments in poor countries.

SECURITY RISK PREMIUMS FOR DIFFERENT COUNTRIES

Source: Elroy Dimson, Paul Marsh, and Mike Staunton, *Triumph of the Optimists*. Copyright© 2000 by Princeton University Press. Used by permission.

portfolio A—a standard deviation of 6.1 percent for portfolio B compared with 11.3 percent for portfolio A. Notice that risk was less in portfolio B even though stocks, a far more risky security, were included in the portfolio. How could this be? Quite simply, stocks behave differently than both government bonds and Treasury bills, with the effect being a less risky (lower standard deviation) portfolio.

3. Whereas portfolio B demonstrates how an investor can reduce risk while keeping returns constant, portfolio C, with its increased investment in stocks (52%), shows how an investor can increase average returns while keeping risk constant. This portfolio had a risk level identical to that of long-term government bonds alone (portfolio A), but it achieved a higher average return of 8 percent, compared with 5.5 percent for the government bond portfolio.

The conclusion to be drawn from this example is clear. The market rewards diversification. We can indeed lower risk without sacrificing expected returns, and/or we can increase expected returns without having to assume more risk by diversifying our investments.

This example gives us real-world evidence about the merits of diversification; however, a clarification is in order. Note that the diversification in our example is across different asset types—Treasury bills versus long-term government bonds versus common stocks. *Diversifying among different kinds of assets* is called **asset allocation**, compared with diversification within the different asset classes. The benefit we receive from diversifying is far greater through effective asset allocation than from astutely selecting individual stocks to include within an asset category. For instance, Brinson, Singer, and Beebower studied quarterly data from 82 large U.S. pension funds over the period 1977 to 1987.[11] They found that the asset allocation decision accounted for over 91 percent of the differences among the returns of pension funds. Deciding what specific securities to hold accounted for only 4.6 percent of the variation in the different pension returns.[12] The point is investors in the capital markets should focus more attention on asset allocation than on selecting individual securities.

In the next section, we complete our study of risk and returns by connecting risk—market or systematic risk, that is—to the investor's *required* rate of return. After all, although risk is an important issue, it is primarily important in its effect on the investor's required rate of return.

asset allocation

CONCEPT CHECK

1. Give specific examples of systematic and unsystematic risk. How many different securities must be owned to essentially diversify away unsystematic risk?
2. What method is used to measure a firm's market risk?
3. After reviewing Figure 6-5, explain the difference between the plotted dots and the firm's characteristic line. What must be done to eliminate the variations?

Objective **5**

THE INVESTOR'S REQUIRED RATE OF RETURN

In this section, we examine the concept of the investor's required rate of return, especially as it relates to the riskiness of an asset, and then we see how the required rate of return might be measured.

THE REQUIRED RATE OF RETURN CONCEPT

An investor's **required rate of return** can be defined as the *minimum rate of return necessary to attract an investor to purchase or hold a security*. This definition considers the investor's **opportunity cost of funds** of making an investment in *the next-best investment*. This forgone return is an opportunity cost of undertaking the investment and consequently is the investor's required rate of return. In other words, we invest with the intention of achieving a rate of return sufficient to warrant making the investment. The investment will be made

required rate of return

opportunity cost of funds

---

[11]Gary P. Brinson, Ronald F. Singer, and Gilbert L. Beebower, "Determinants of Portfolio Performance," *Financial Analysts Journal* (May–June 1991) 40–47.
[12]It is also interesting to know that Brinson, Singer, and Beebower found that timing investments explained a meager 1.8 percent of the variation in pension fund returns. That is, none of the investors of these pension funds were any better than their peers at timing market movements when making investments.

only if the purchase price is low enough relative to expected future cash flows to provide a rate of return greater than or equal to our required rate of return.

To help us better understand the nature of an investor's required rate of return, we can separate the return into its basic components: the risk-free rate of return plus a risk premium. Expressed as an equation:

$$k = k_{rf} + k_{rp} \tag{6-9}$$

where k = the investor's required rate of return
k_{rf} = the risk-free rate of return
k_{rp} = the risk premium

The risk-free rate of return rewards us for deferring consumption, not for assuming risk; that is, the risk-free return reflects the basic fact that we invest today so that we can consume more later. By itself, the **risk-free rate of return** is the *required rate of return, or discount rate, for riskless investments*. Typically, our measure for the risk-free rate of return is the U.S. Treasury bill rate.

> **risk-free rate of return**

The **risk premium**, k_{rp}, is the *additional return we must expect to receive for assuming risk*. As the level of risk increases, we will demand additional expected returns. Even though we may or may not actually receive this incremental return, we must have reason to expect it; otherwise, why expose ourselves to the chance of losing all or part of our money?

> **risk premium**

EXAMPLE

Assume you are considering the purchase of a stock that you believe will provide a 14 percent return over the next year. If the expected risk-free rate of return, such as the rate of return for 90-day Treasury bills, is 5 percent, then the risk premium you are demanding to assume the additional risk is 9 percent (14% − 5%).

MEASURING THE REQUIRED RATE OF RETURN

We have seen that (1) systematic risk is the only relevant risk—the rest can be diversified away, and (2) the required rate of return, k, equals the risk-free rate, k_{rf}, plus a risk premium, k_{rp}. We will now examine how we may estimate an investors' required rates of return.

The finance profession has had difficulty in developing a practical approach to measure an investor's required rate of return; however, financial managers often use a method called the **capital asset pricing model (CAPM)**. The capital asset pricing model is *an equation that equates the expected rate of return on a stock to the risk-free rate plus a risk premium for the stock's systematic risk*. Although certainly not without its critics, the CAPM provides an intuitive approach for thinking about the return that an investor should require on an investment, given the asset's systematic or market risk.

> **capital asset pricing model (CAPM)**

Equation (6-9) on the prior page provides the natural starting point for measuring the investor's required rate of return and sets us up for using the CAPM. Rearranging this equation to solve for the risk premium (k_{rp}), we have

$$k_{rp} = k - k_{rf} \tag{6-10}$$

which simply says that the risk premium for a security, k_{rp}, equals the required return, k, less the risk-free rate existing in the market, k_{rf}. For example, if the required return is 15 percent and the risk-free rate is 5 percent, the risk premium is 10 percent. Also, if the required return for the market portfolio, k_m, is 12 percent, and the risk-free rate, k_{rf}, is 5 percent, the risk premium, k_{rp}, for the market would be 7 percent. This 7 percent risk premium would apply to any security having systematic (nondiversifiable) risk equivalent to the general market, or a beta of 1.

In this same market, a security with a beta (β) of 2 should provide a risk premium of 14 percent, or twice the 7 percent risk premium existing for the market as a whole. Hence, in general, the appropriate required rate of return for the jth security, k_j, should be determined by

$$k_j = k_{rf} + \beta_j (k_m - k_{rf}) \tag{6-11}$$

FINANCIAL MANAGEMENT
IN PRACTICE

DOES BETA ALWAYS WORK?

At the start of 1998, Apple Computer was in deep trouble. As a result, its stock price fluctuated wildly—far more than other computer firms, such as IBM. However, based on the capital asset pricing model (CAPM) and its measure of beta, the required return of Apple's investors would have been only 8 percent at the time, compared with 12 percent for IBM's stockholders. Equally interesting, when Apple's situation improved in the spring of that year and its share price became less volatile, Apple's investors, at least according to the CAPM, would have required a rate of return of 11 percent—a 3 percentage point increase from the earlier required rate of return. That is not what intuition would suggest should have happened.

So what should we think? Just when Apple's future was most in doubt and its shares most volatile, its beta was only 0.47, suggesting that Apple's stock was only half as volatile as the overall stock market. In reality, beta is meaningless here. The truth is that Apple was in such dire condition that its stock price simply decoupled itself from the stock market. So as IBM and its peer stock prices moved up and down with the rest of the market, Apple shares reacted solely to news about the company, without regard for the market's movements. Beta thus created the false impression that Apple shares were more stable than the stock market.

The lesson here is that beta may at times be misleading when used with individual companies. Instead, its use is far more reliable when applied to a portfolio of companies. A firm that was interested in acquiring Apple Computer in 1998, for instance, most likely would not have been planning to buy other computer companies in the same circumstances. If an interested acquirer used beta in computing the required rate of return for the acquisition, it would without a doubt have overvalued Apple.

So does that mean that CAPM is worthless? No, not as long as company-unique risk is not the main driving force in a company's stock price movements or if investors are able to diversify away specific company risk. Then they would bid up the price of such shares until they reflect only market risk. For example, a mutual fund that specializes in "distress stocks" might purchase a number of "Apple Computer companies," each with its own problems, but for different reasons. For such investors, beta works pretty well. Thus, the moral of the story is to exercise common sense and judgment when using beta.

---

security market line

Equation (6-11) is the CAPM. This equation designates the risk–return trade-off existing in the market, where risk is measured in terms of beta. Figure 6-9 graphs the CAPM as the **security market line**.[13] The security market line is *the graphic representation of the CAPM, where the line shows the appropriate required rate of return given a stock's systematic risk.* As presented in this figure, securities with betas equal to 0, 1, and 2 should have required rates of return as follows:

$$\text{If } \beta_j = 0: k_j = 5\% + 0(12\% - 5\%) = 5\%$$
$$\text{If } \beta_j = 1: k_j = 5\% + 1(12\% - 5\%) = 12\%$$
$$\text{If } \beta_j = 2: k_j = 5\% + 2(12\% - 5\%) = 19\%$$

where the risk-free rate, k_{rf}, is 5 percent and the required return for the market portfolio, k_m, is 12 percent.

BACK TO THE FOUNDATIONS

*The conclusion of the matter is that **Principle 1** is alive and well. It tells us, **We Won't Take On Additional Risk Unless We Expect to Be Compensated with Additional Return**. That is, there is a risk–return trade-off in the market.*

---

[13]Two key assumptions are made in using the security market line. First, we assume that the marketplace where securities are bought and sold is highly efficient. Market efficiency indicates that the price of an asset responds quickly to new information, thereby suggesting that the price of a security reflects all available information. As a result, the current price of a security is considered to represent the best estimate of its future price. Second, the model assumes that a perfect market exists. A perfect market is one in which information is readily available to all investors at a nominal cost. Also, securities are assumed to be infinitely divisible, with any transaction costs incurred in purchasing or selling a security being negligible. Furthermore, investors are assumed to be single-period wealth maximizers who agree on the meaning and significance of the available information. Finally, within the perfect market, all investors are *price takers*, which simply means that a single investor's actions cannot affect the price of a security. These assumptions are obviously not descriptive of reality. However, from the perspective of positive economics, the mark of a good theory is the accuracy of its predictions, not the validity of the simplifying assumptions that underlie its development.

FIGURE 6-9   Security Market Line

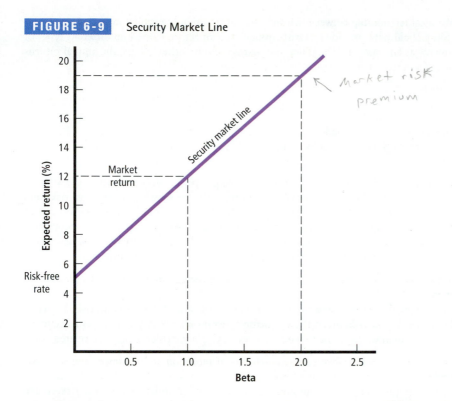

PROBLEM CHECK: COMPUTING EXPECTED RATE OF RETURN

Determine a fair expected or required rate of return for a stock that has a beta of 1.25 when the risk-free rate is 5 percent and the expected market return is 9 percent.

Check your answer on the next page.

SUMMARY

In Chapter 2, we referred to the discount rate as the interest rate or the opportunity cost of funds. At that point, we considered a number of important factors that influence interest rates, including the price of time, expected or anticipated inflation, and risk premium related to maturity (liquidity) and variability of future returns.

In this chapter, we have returned to our study of rates of return and looked ever so carefully at the relationship between risk and rates of return.

Define and measure the expected rate of return of an individual investment
In a world of uncertainty, we cannot make forecasts with certitude. Thus, we must speak in terms of *expected* events. The expected return on an investment may therefore be stated as a weighted average of all the possible returns, weighted by the probability that each return will occur.

Objective **1**

Define and measure the riskiness of an individual investment
Risk for our purposes is the variability of returns and may be measured by the standard deviation.

Objective **2**

Objective **3**

Compare the historical relationship between risk and rates of return in the capital markets

Ibbotson and Sinquefield have provided us with annual rates of return earned on different types of security investments as far back as 1926. They summarize, among other things, the annual returns for six portfolios of securities made up of

1. Common stocks of large companies
2. Common stocks of small firms
3. Long-term corporate bonds
4. Long-term U.S. government bonds
5. Intermediate-term U.S. government bonds
6. U.S. Treasury bills

A comparison of the annual rates of return for these respective portfolios for the years 1926 to 2004 shows a positive relationship between risk and return, with Treasury bills being least risky and common stocks of small firms being most risky. From the data, we are able to see the benefit of diversification in terms of improving the return–risk relationship. Also, the data clearly demonstrate that only common stock has in the long run served as an inflation hedge, and that the risk associated with common stock can be reduced if investors are patient in receiving their returns.

Objective **4**

Explain how diversifying investments affects the riskiness and expected rate of return of a portfolio or combination of assets

We made an important distinction between nondiversifiable risk and diversifiable risk. We concluded that the only relevant risk, given the opportunity to diversify our portfolio, is a security's nondiversifiable risk, which we called by two other names: systematic risk and market-related risk.

Objective **5**

Explain the relationship between an investor's required rate of return on an investment and the riskiness of the investment

The capital asset pricing model provides an intuitive framework for understanding the risk–return relationship. The CAPM suggests that investors determine an appropriate required rate of return, depending upon the amount of systematic risk inherent in a security. This minimum acceptable rate of return is equal to the risk-free rate plus a risk premium for assuming risk.

PROBLEM CHECK SOLUTION: COMPUTING EXPECTED RETURN

The appropriate rate of return would be:

$$\text{Expected return} = \text{risk-free rate} + [\text{beta} \times (\text{market return} - \text{risk-free rate})]$$
$$= 5\% + 1.25 \times (9\% - 5\%)$$

KEY TERMS

Asset allocation, 192	Expected rate of return, 175	Required rate of return, 192
Beta, 186	Holding-period returns, 183	Risk, 176
Capital asset pricing model (CAPM), 193	Market risk (see systematic risk), 182	Risk premium, 193
Characteristic line, 185	Nondiversifiable risk (see systematic risk), 182	Risk-free rate of return, 193
Company-unique risk (see unsystematic risk), 182	Opportunity cost of funds, 192	Security market line, 194
Diversifiable risk (see unsystematic risk), 182	Portfolio beta, 188	Standard deviation, 177
		Systematic risk, 182
		Unsystematic risk, 182

STUDY QUESTIONS

6-1. a. What is meant by the investor's required rate of return?

b. How do we measure the riskiness of an asset?

c. How should the proposed measurement of risk be interpreted?

6-2. What is (a) systematic risk (company-unique or diversifiable risk) and (b) systematic risk (market or nondiversifiable risk)?

6-3. What is the meaning of beta? How is it used to calculate k, the investor's required rate of return?

6-4. Define the security market line. What does it represent?

6-5. How do we measure the beta for a portfolio?

6-6. If we were to graph the returns of a stock against the returns of the S&P 500 Index, and the points did not follow a very ordered pattern, what could we say about that stock? If the stock's returns tracked the S&P 500 returns very closely, then what could we say?

6-7. Over the past six decades, we have had the opportunity to observe the rates of return and variability of these returns for different types of securities. Summarize these observations.

6-8. Describe the potential effect on returns of diversifying your portfolio.

SELF-TEST PROBLEMS

ST-1. (*Expected return and risk*) Universal Corporation is planning to invest in a security that has several possible rates of return. Given the following probability distribution of returns, what is the expected rate of return on the investment? Also compute the standard deviations of the returns. What do the resulting numbers represent?

PROBABILITY	RETURN
.10	−10%
.20	5%
.30	10%
.40	25%

ST-2. (*Capital asset pricing model*) Using the CAPM, estimate the appropriate required rate of return for the three stocks listed here, given that the risk-free rate is 5 percent and the expected return for the market is 17 percent.

STOCK	BETA
A	.75
B	.90
C	1.40

ST-3. (*Average expected return and risk*) Given the holding-period returns shown here, calculate the average returns and the standard deviations for the Kaifu Corporation and for the market.

MONTH	KAIFU CORP.	MARKET
1	4%	2%
2	6	3
3	0	1
4	2	−1

ST-4. (*Holding-period returns*) From the price data that follow, compute holding-period returns for periods 2 through 4.

PERIOD	STOCK PRICE
1	$10
2	13
3	11
4	15

ST-5. (*Security market line*)

a. Determine the expected return and beta for the following portfolio:

STOCK	PERCENTAGE OF PORTFOLIO	BETA	EXPECTED RETURN
1	40%	1.00	12%
2	25	0.75	11
3	35	1.30	15

b. Given the foregoing information, draw the security market line and show where the securities fit on the graph. Assume that the risk-free rate is 8 percent and that the expected return on the market portfolio is 12 percent. How would you interpret these findings?

STUDY PROBLEMS

6-1. (*Expected rate of return and risk*) Carter, Inc., is evaluating a security. One-year Treasury bills are currently paying 9.1 percent. Calculate the investment's expected return and its standard deviation. Should Carter invest in this security?

PROBABILITY	RETURN
.15	6%
.30	9%
.40	10%
.15	15%

6-2. (*Expected rate of return and risk*) Summerville, Inc., is considering an investment in one of two common stocks. Given the information that follows, which investment is better, based on risk (as measured by the standard deviation) and return?

COMMON STOCK A		COMMON STOCK B	
PROBABILITY	RETURN	PROBABILITY	RETURN
.30	11%	.20	−5%
.40	15%	.30	6%
.30	19%	.30	14%
		.20	22%

6-3. (*Expected rate of return and risk*) Richland Manufacturing, Inc., has prepared the following information regarding two investments under consideration. Which investment should be accepted?

COMMON STOCK A		COMMON STOCK B	
PROBABILITY	RETURN	PROBABILITY	RETURN
.20	−2%	.10	4%
.50	18%	.30	6%
.30	27%	.40	10%
		.20	15%

6-4. (*Required rate of return using CAPM*)

    a. Compute a fair rate of return for Intel common stock, which has a 1.2 beta. The risk-free rate is 6 percent, and the market portfolio (New York Stock Exchange stocks) has an expected return of 16 percent.

    b. Why is the rate you computed a fair rate?

6-5. (*Estimating beta*) From this graph relating the holding-period returns for Aram, Inc., to the S&P 500 Index, estimate the firm's beta.

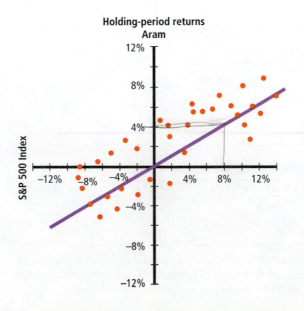

6-6. (*Capital asset pricing model*) Levine Manufacturing, Inc., is considering several investments. The rate on Treasury bills is currently 6.75 percent, and the expected return for the market is 12 percent. What should be the required rates of return for each investment (using the CAPM)?

SECURITY	BETA
A	1.50
B	.90
C	.70
D	1.15

6-7. (*Capital asset pricing model*) MFI, Inc., has a beta of .86. If the expected market return is 11.5 percent and the risk-free rate is 7.5 percent, what is the appropriate required return of MFI (using the CAPM)?

6-8. (*Capital asset pricing model*) The expected return for the general market is 12.8 percent, and the risk premium in the market is 4.3 percent. Tasaco, LBM, and Exxos have betas of .864, .693, and .575, respectively. What are the corresponding required rates of return for the three securities?

6-9. (*Computing holding-period returns*)

   a. From the price data here, compute the holding-period returns for Jazman and Solomon for periods 2 through 4.

PERIOD	JAZMAN	SOLOMON
1	$ 9	$27
2	11	28
3	10	32
4	13	29

   b. How would you interpret the meaning of a holding-period return?

6-10. (*Measuring risk and rates of return*)

   a. Given the holding-period returns shown here, compute the average returns and the standard deviations for the Zemin Corporation and for the market.

MONTH	ZEMIN CORP.	MARKET
1	6%	4%
2	3	2
3	−1	1
4	−3	−2
5	5	2
6	0	2

   b. If Zemin's beta is 1.54 and the risk-free rate is 8 percent, what would be an appropriate required return for an investor owning Zemin? (*Note:* Because the Zemin Corporation returns are based on monthly data, you will need to annualize the returns to make them compatible with the risk-free rate. For simplicity, you can convert from monthly to yearly returns by multiplying the average monthly returns by 12.)

   c. How does Zemin's historical average return compare with the return you believe to be a fair return, given the firm's systematic risk?

6-11. (*Portfolio beta and security market line*) You own a portfolio consisting of the following stocks:

STOCK	PERCENTAGE OF PORTFOLIO	BETA	EXPECTED RETURN
1	20%	1.00	16%
2	30	0.85	14
3	15	1.20	20
4	25	0.60	12
5	10	1.60	24

The risk-free rate is 7 percent. Also, the expected return on the market portfolio is 15.5 percent.

   a. Calculate the expected return of your portfolio. (*Hint:* The expected return of a portfolio equals the weighted average of the individual stocks' expected returns, where the weights are the percentage invested in each stock.)

   b. Calculate the portfolio beta.

   c. Given the foregoing information, plot the security market line on paper. Plot the stocks from your portfolio on your graph.

   d. From your plot in part c, which stocks appear to be your winners and which ones appear to be losers?

   e. Why should you consider your conclusion in part d to be less than certain?

6-12. (*Expected return, standard deviation, and capital asset pricing model*) Following you will find the end-of-month prices for both the Standard & Poor's 500 Index and Ford Motor Company common stock.

    a. Using the data here, calculate the holding-period returns for each of the months.

MONTH AND YEAR	S&P 500	FORD
2003		
November	1,055.61	13.20
December	1,108.55	16.00
2004		
January	1,131.02	14.54
February	1,142.93	13.75
March	1,123.93	13.57
April	1,118.54	15.36
May	1,120.00	14.85
June	1,134.30	15.65
July	1,099.91	14.72
August	1,102.80	14.11
September	1,111.39	14.05
October	1,125.23	13.03
November	1,180.54	14.18

    b. Calculate the average monthly return and the standard deviation of these returns for both the S&P 500 and Ford.

    c. Develop a graph that shows the relationship between the Ford stock returns and the S&P 500 Index (show the Ford returns on the vertical axis and the S&P 500 Index returns on the horizontal axis as done in Figure 6-5).

    d. From your graph, describe the nature of the relationship between Ford stock returns and the returns for the S&P 500 Index.

WEB WORKS

6-WW1. Go to **www.moneychimp.com**. Select the link to Volatility. Complete the retirement planning calculator, making the assumptions that you believe are appropriate for you. Then go to the Monte Carlo simulation calculator. Assume that you invest in large-company common stocks during your working years and then invest in long-term corporate bonds during retirement. Use the nominal average returns and standard deviations shown in Figure 6-2. What did you learn?

6-WW2. Go to **www.money.cnn.com**. Click on the option Financial Tools (in the left margin). Then choose Calculators and finally select Asset Allocator. Complete the questions to see how the calculator suggests you allocate your asset investments. Try some different options and see how the answers change. Why do you get different answers?

6-WW3. Access **http://finance.yahoo.com**. In the left margin, select the link to Education. Then choose Glossary and go to Expected Return and Expected Value. What do you learn from the definition of these terms?

6-WW4. Go to **www.investopedia.com/university/beginner**, where there is an article on "Investing 101: A Tutorial for Beginning Investors." Read the article and be able to explain what is said about risk tolerance.

COMPREHENSIVE PROBLEM

Note: Although not absolutely necessary, you are advised to use a computer spreadsheet to work the following problem. A spreadsheet (Chapter 6 comp problem) with the following data is available at **www.prenhall.com/keown**.

a. Use the price data from the table that follows for the Standard & Poor's 500 Index, Wal-Mart, and Target to calculate the holding-period returns for the 24 months from December 2002 through November 2004.

MONTH AND YEAR	S&P 500	WAL-MART	TARGET
2002			
November	$ 928.62	$ 53.90	$ 34.78
December	876.99	50.51	30.00
2003			
January	854.72	47.80	28.21
February	834.75	48.06	28.65
March	864.03	52.03	29.26
April	917.77	56.32	33.44
May	953.08	52.61	36.63
June	981.06	53.67	37.84
July	989.58	55.91	38.32
August	999.31	59.17	40.60
September	1,002.14	55.85	37.63
October	1,049.29	58.95	39.74
November	1,055.61	55.64	38.72
December	1,108.55	53.05	38.40
2004			
January	1,131.02	53.85	37.96
February	1,142.93	59.56	43.96
March	1,123.93	59.69	45.04
April	1,118.54	57.00	43.37
May	1,120.00	55.73	44.70
June	1,134.30	52.50	42.47
July	1,099.91	53.01	43.60
August	1,102.80	52.67	44.58
September	1,111.39	53.20	45.25
October	1,125.23	53.92	50.02
November	1,180.54	52.06	51.22

b. Calculate the average monthly holding-period returns and the standard deviation of these returns for the S&P 500 Index, Wal-Mart, and Target.

c. Plot (1) the holding-period returns for Wal-Mart against the Standard & Poor's 500 Index, and (2) the Target holding-period returns against the Standard & Poor's 500 Index. (Use Figure 6-5 as the format for your graph.)

d. From your graphs in part c, describe the nature of the relationship between the Wal-Mart stock returns and the returns for the S&P 500 Index. Make the same comparison for Target.

e. Assume that you have decided to invest one-half of your money in Wal-Mart and the remainder in Target. Calculate the monthly holding-period returns for your two-stock portfolio. (*Hint:* The monthly return for the portfolio is the average of the two stocks' monthly returns.)

f. Plot the returns of your two-stock portfolio against the Standard & Poor's 500 Index as you did for the individual stocks in part c. How does this graph compare to the graphs for the individual stocks? Explain the difference.

g. On the following page, you are provided the returns on an *annualized* basis that were realized from holding long-term government bonds from December 2002 through November 2004. Calculate the average *monthly* holding-period returns and the standard deviations of these returns. (*Hint:* You will need to convert the annual returns to monthly returns by dividing each return by 12 months.)

MONTH AND YEAR	ANNUALIZED RATE OF RETURN (%)
2002	
December	5.01
2003	
January	5.02
February	4.87
March	4.82
April	4.91
May	4.52
June	4.34
July	4.92
August	5.39
September	5.21
October	5.21
November	5.17
December	5.11
2004	
January	5.01
February	4.94
March	4.72
April	5.16
May	5.46
June	5.45
July	5.24
August	5.07
September	4.89
October	4.85
November	4.89

h. Now assuming that you have decided to invest equal amounts of money in Wal-Mart, Target, and long-term government securities, calculate the monthly returns for your three-asset portfolio. What are the average return and the standard deviation?

i. Make a comparison of the average returns and the standard deviations for all the individual assets and the two portfolios that we designed. What conclusions can be reached by your comparison?

j. According to Standard & Poor's, the betas for Wal-Mart and Target are 0.58 and 1.02, respectively. Compare the meaning of these betas relative to the standard deviations calculated above.

k. The Treasury bill rate at the end of November 2004 was approximately 5.5 percent. Given the betas for Wal-Mart and Target and using the above data for the S&P 500 Index as a measure for the market portfolio expected return, estimate an appropriate required rate of return given the level of systematic risk for each stock.

SELF-TEST SOLUTIONS

SS-1.

(A) PROBABILITY $P(k_i)$	(B) RETURN (k_i)	EXPECTED $\bar{k}$ $(A) \times (B)$	WEIGHTED DEVIATION $(k_i - \bar{k})^2 \, P(k_i)$
.10	−10%	−1%	52.9%
.20	5	1	12.8
.30	10	3	2.7
.40	25	10	57.6
		$\bar{k} = 13\%$	$\sigma^2 = 126.0\%$
			$\sigma = 11.22\%$

From our studies in statistics, we know that if the distribution of returns were normal, then Universal could expect a return of 13 percent, with a 67 percent possibility that this return would vary up or down by 11.22 percent between 1.78 percent (13% − 11.22%) and 24.22 percent (13% + 11.22%). However, it is apparent from the probabilities that the distribution is not normal.

SS-2.

Stock A: 5% + .75 (17% − 5%) = 14.0%
Stock B: 5% + .90 (17% − 5%) = 15.8%
Stock C: 5% + 1.40 (17% − 5%) = 21.8%

SS-3.

Kaifu

Average return: $\dfrac{4\% + 6\% + 0\% + 2\%}{4} = 3\%$

Standard deviation: $\sqrt{\dfrac{[(4\% - 3\%)^2 + (6\% - 3\%)^2 + (0\% - 3\%)^2 + (2\% - 3\%)^2]}{4 - 1}} = 2.58\%$

Market

Average return: $\dfrac{2\% + 3\% + 1\% - 1\%}{4} = 1.25\%$

Standard deviation: $\sqrt{\dfrac{[(2\% - 1.25\%)^2 + (3\% - 1.25\%)^2 + (1\% - 1.25\%)^2 + (-1\% - 1.25\%)^2]}{4 - 1}} = 1.71\%$

SS-4.

TIME	STOCK PRICE	HOLDING-PERIOD RETURN
1	$10	
2	13	($13 ÷ $10) − 1 = 30.0%
3	11	($11 ÷ $13) − 1 = −15.4%
4	15	($15 ÷ $11) − 1 = 36.4%

SS-5.

a. Portfolio expected return:

$(.4 \times 12\%) + (.25 \times 11\%) + (.35 \times 15\%) = 12.8\%$

Portfolio beta:

$(.4 \times 1) + (.25 \times .75) + (.35 \times 1.3) = 1.04$

b.

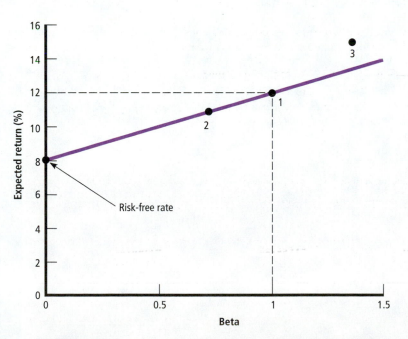

Stocks 1 and 2 seem to be right in line with the security market line, which suggests that they are earning a fair return, given their systematic risk. Stock 3, on the other hand, is earning more than a fair return (above the security market line). We might be tempted to conclude that security 3 is undervalued. However, we may be seeing an illusion; it is possible to misspecify the security market line by using bad estimates in our data.

◄ LEARNING OBJECTIVES ►

After reading this chapter, you should be able to:

1. Distinguish between different kinds of bonds.

2. Explain the more popular features of bonds.

3. Define the term *value* as used for several different purposes.

4. Explain the factors that determine value.

5. Describe the basic process for valuing assets.

6. Estimate the value of a bond.

7. Compute a bondholder's expected rate of return.

8. Explain three important relationships that exist in bond valuation.

CHAPTER 7

Valuation and Characteristics of Bonds

TYPES OF BONDS • TERMINOLOGY AND CHARACTERISTICS OF BONDS • DEFINITIONS OF VALUE • DETERMINANTS OF VALUE • VALUATION: THE BASIC PROCESS • BOND VALUATION • YIELD TO MATURITY • BOND VALUATION: THREE IMPORTANT RELATIONSHIPS

Practically all companies use debt to finance their firms, and many of those companies issue bonds, just one form of debt. Bonds provide investors a fixed income each year in the form of interest. Just as you can open a savings account at a bank and earn interest on your savings, you can buy a bond that pays interest and then repays your principal on a designated date when the bond matures. Many of these bonds are traded in the public capital markets. Three examples of companies that have issued bonds to investors are Hewlett-Packard, McDonald's, and AT&T. Each of these bonds pays $65 in interest each year on a bond that will repay the investor $1,000 when it matures. Although these bonds are similar in terms of their interest payments, investors do not value them the same.

At the end of 2004, they were selling for the following amounts:

Hewlett-Packard	$1,130
McDonald's	$1,073
AT&T	$945

Why would there be differences in the values of these bonds? Why would Hewlett-Packard's bonds be worth more than McDonald's bonds? And why would the AT&T bonds be so "cheap"? They all pay the same amount of interest. Why would investors pay $1,130 for a bond that promises $65 in interest, when they could buy AT&T bonds for only $945? Or a more general question, "What determines a bond's value?" Read on and you will find the answer to this puzzle.

⤝ WHAT'S AHEAD ⤞

Knowing the fair value or price of an asset is no easy matter. The *Maxims* of the French writer La Rouchefoucauld, written over three centuries ago, still speak to us: "The greatest of all gifts is the power to estimate things at their true worth."

Understanding how to value financial securities is essential if managers are to meet the objective of maximizing the value of the firm. If they are to maximize the investors' value, they must know what drives the value of an asset. Specifically, they need to understand how bonds and stocks are valued in the marketplace; otherwise, they cannot act in the best interest of the firm's investors.

A bond is one form of a company's long-term debt. In this chapter, we begin by identifying the different kinds of bonds. We next look at the features or characteristics of most bonds. We then examine the concepts of and procedures for valuing an asset and apply these ideas to valuing bonds.

We now begin our study by considering the different kinds of bonds.

bond

TYPES OF BONDS

Objective 1

A **bond** is a *type of debt or long-term promissory note, issued by the borrower, promising to pay its holder a predetermined and fixed amount of interest per year and the face value of the bond at maturity.* However, there is a wide variety of such creatures. Just to mention a few, we have

✓Debentures	Eurobonds
Subordinated debentures	Zero and very low coupon bonds
Mortgage bonds	Junk bonds

The following sections briefly explain each of these types of bonds.

DEBENTURES

debenture

The term **debenture** applies to *any unsecured long-term debt*. Because these bonds are unsecured, the earning ability of the issuing corporation is of great concern to the bondholder. They are also viewed as being more risky than secured bonds and as a result must provide investors with a higher yield than secured bonds provide. Often the issuing firm attempts to provide some protection to the holder of the bond by prohibiting it from issuing more secured long-term debt that would further tie up the firm's assets and leave the bondholders less protected. To the issuing firm, the major advantage of debentures is that no property has to be secured by them. This allows the firm to issue debt and still preserve some future borrowing power.

SUBORDINATED DEBENTURES

subordinated debentures

Many firms have more than one issue of debentures outstanding. In this case a hierarchy may be specified, in which some debentures are given *subordinated standing in case of insolvency*. The claims of the **subordinated debentures** are honored only after the claims of secured debt and unsubordinated debentures have been satisfied.

MORTGAGE BONDS

mortgage bond

A **mortgage bond** is a *bond secured by a lien on real property.* Typically, the value of the real property is greater than that of the mortgage bonds issued. This provides the mortgage bond-holders with a margin of safety in the event the market value of the secured property declines. In the case of foreclosure, the trustees have the power to sell the secured property and use the proceeds to pay the bondholders. In the event that the proceeds from this sale do not cover the bonds, the bondholders become general creditors, similar to debenture bondholders, for the unpaid portion of the debt.

EUROBONDS

Eurobonds

Eurobonds are not so much a different type of security. They are simply securities, in this case *bonds, issued in a country different from the one in whose currency the bond is denominated.* For example, a bond that is issued in Europe or in Asia by an American company and that pays interest and principal to the lender in U.S. dollars would be considered a Eurobond. Thus, even if the bond is not issued in Europe, it merely needs to be sold in a country different from the one in whose currency it is denominated to be considered a Eurobond.

The primary attractions of Eurobonds to borrowers, aside from favorable rates, are the relative lack of regulation (Eurobonds are not registered with the Securities and Exchange Commission [SEC]), less-rigorous disclosure requirements than those of the SEC, and the speed with which they can be issued. Interestingly, not only are Eurobonds not registered with the SEC, but they may not be offered to U.S. citizens and residents.

ZERO AND VERY LOW COUPON BONDS

Zero and very low coupon bonds allow the issuing firm to issue *bonds at a substantial discount from their $1,000 face value with a zero or very low coupon rate*. The investor receives a large part (or all with zero coupon bonds) of the return from the appreciation of the bonds. For example, in 2005, American Music, an online music provider, issued $250 million of debt maturing in 2015 with a zero coupon rate. In 2005, these bonds sold at a 60 percent discount from their par value; that is, investors paid only $400 for a bond with a $1,000 par value. Investors who purchased these bonds for $400 and hold them until they mature in 2015 will receive an effective interest rate of 9.6 percent, with all of this return coming from appreciation of the bond. Furthermore, the firm will have no cash outflows until these bonds mature; however, at that time it will have to pay back $250 million, even though it only received approximately $100 million when the bonds were issued.

zero and very low coupon bonds

As with any form of financing, there are both advantages and disadvantages of issuing zero or very low coupon bonds. As already mentioned, one disadvantage is, when the bonds mature, American Music will face an extremely large cash outflow, much greater than the cash inflow it experienced when the bonds were issued. There are several advantages of zero and low coupon bonds from the issuing firm's perspective. First, the annual cash outflows associated with interest payments do not occur with zero coupon bonds and are at a relatively low level with low coupon bonds. Second, because there is relatively strong investor demand for this type of debt, the investors will frequently accept a lower effective interest rate. For instance, American Music was able to issue zero coupon bonds at about half a percent less than it would have been if they had been traditional interest-paying bonds. Finally, the firm is able to deduct the annual amortization of the discount from taxable income, which will provide a positive annual cash flow to American Music.

JUNK BONDS (HIGH-YIELD BONDS)

Junk bonds are high-risk debt with *ratings of BB or below by Moody's and Standard & Poor's*. The lower the rating, the higher the chance of default; the lowest class is CC for Standard & Poor's and Ca for Moody's. Originally, the term "junk bonds" was used to describe bonds issued by "fallen angels," that is, firms with sound financial histories that were facing severe financial problems and suffering from poor credit ratings.

junk bonds

Junk bonds are also called **high-yield bonds** for the high interest rates they pay the investor, typically having an interest rate of between 3 and 5 percent more than AAA-grade long-term debt.

high-yield bonds

Before the mid-1970s, smaller firms simply did not have access to the capital markets because of the reluctance of investors to accept speculative-grade bonds. However, by the late 1980s, junk bonds became the way to finance hostile takeovers—buying a firm without the management's approval. For example, the purchase of RJR Nabisco for about $20 billion by the investment group KKR was largely accomplished by junk bond financing. However, the eventual bankruptcy of Drexel Burnham Lambert, the investment banker most responsible for developing a large junk bond market, the jailing of the "king of junk bonds," Michael Milken, and increasing interest rates brought an end to the extensive use of junk bonds for financing corporate takeovers. (Michael Milken, a partner at Drexel Burnham Lambert, used to have an annual conference in Beverly Hills, California, nicknamed "The Predator's Ball" to attract takeover investors and corporate raiders who needed junk bond financing to accomplish their takeovers.)

When corporate takeovers subsided from their highs, most people thought the junk bond was forever dead. By 1990, the junk bond market was virtually nonexistent. Then, in 1992, with investors looking for higher interest rates and a rebounding economy, the junk bond market was revitalized. The following year, new junk bond issues reached a record $62 billion. Also, by 1995, less than 20 percent of the proceeds from junk bonds was being used to finance mergers and acquisitions, compared with 60 percent in the 1980s. Between 1997 and 2000, corporations issued $382 billion in junk bonds, suggesting that this type of debt continues to be a significant source of capital to finance corporate growth. However, the increase came with increased risk as well, with such giants as W. R. Grace, Lucent, and Pacific Gas & Electric defaulting on their debt. Junk bonds continue to be a source of financing for a number of companies providing higher potential returns for investors—but with greater risk as well.

CONCEPT CHECK

1. What is the difference in the nature and associated risk between debentures, subordinated debentures, and mortgage bonds? How would investors respond to the varying types of risk?
2. How does an investor receive a return from a zero or very low coupon bond? Why would a company be able to deduct amortized interest over the life of the bond even though there are no cash outflows associated with interest?
3. Why do junk bonds typically have a higher interest rate than other types of bonds? Why has this market been revitalized?

Now that you have an understanding of the kinds of bonds firms might issue, let's look at some of the characteristics and terminology of bonds.

Objective **2**

TERMINOLOGY AND CHARACTERISTICS OF BONDS

Before valuing bonds, we first need to understand the terminology related to bonds. Then we will be better prepared to determine the value of a bond.

When a firm or nonprofit institution needs financing, one source is *bonds*. As already noted, this type of financing instrument is simply a long-term promissory note, issued by the borrower, promising to pay its holder a predetermined and fixed amount of interest each year. Some of the more important terms and characteristics that you might hear about bonds are as follows:

Claims on assets and income   Convertibility
Par value   Call provision
Coupon interest rate   Indenture
Maturity   Bond ratings

Let's consider each in turn.

CLAIMS ON ASSETS AND INCOME

In the case of insolvency, claims of debt, including bonds, are generally honored before those of both common stock and preferred stock. However, different types of debt may also have a hierarchy among themselves as to the order of their claim on assets.

Bonds also have a claim on income that comes ahead of common and preferred stock. In general if interest on bonds is not paid, the bond trustees can classify the firm as insolvent and force it into bankruptcy. Thus, the bondholders' claim on income is more likely to be honored than that of common stockholders, whose dividends are paid at the discretion of the firm's management.

PAR VALUE

The **par value of a bond** is its *face value, which is returned to the bondholder at maturity*. In general, corporate bonds are issued in denominations of $1,000, although there are some exceptions to this rule. Also, when bond prices are quoted, either by financial managers or in the financial press, prices are generally expressed as a percentage of the bond's par value. For example, a Time-Warner bond was recently quoted as selling for 113.68. That does not mean you can buy the bond for $113.68. It means that this bond is selling for 113.68 percent of its par value of $1,000. Hence, the market price of this bond is actually $1,136.80. At maturity in 2028 the bondholder will receive $1,000.

par value of a bond

COUPON INTEREST RATE

The **coupon interest rate** on a bond indicates the *percentage of the par value of the bond that will be paid out annually in the form of interest*. Thus, regardless of what happens to the price of a bond with an 8 percent coupon interest rate and a $1,000 par value, it will pay out $80 annually in interest until maturity (.08 × $1,000 = $80). However, as we will observe later, the interest may be paid semiannualy, like in June and December. In the foregoing example, the interest would be $40 semiannually, but the coupon rate is still calculated on the annual interest of $80.

coupon interest rate

MATURITY

The **maturity** of a bond indicates *the length of time until the bond issuer returns the par value to the bondholder and terminates or redeems the bond*.

maturity

CONVERTIBILITY

A **convertible bond** may allow the investor to exchange the bond for a predetermined number of the firm's shares of common stock. For instance, TiVo, a firm that developed the TiVo recorder for television, issued $51.8 million of 7 percent convertible debt. The bonds are convertible at any time into TiVo common stock at a conversion price of $6.73 per share. Since the par value for each bond is $1,000, a bondholder can convert one bond into 148.59 shares (148.59 shares = $1,000 ÷ $6.73 price per share). This option allows the investor to be repaid the $1,000 par value or to convert into stock if the value of the stock is greater than $1,000.

convertible bond

CALL PROVISION

If a company issues bonds and then later the prevailing interest rate declines, the firm may want to pay off the bonds early and then issue new bonds with a lower interest rate. To do so, the bond must be **callable** or **redeemable**; otherwise, the firm cannot force the bondholder to accept early payment. The issuer, however, usually must pay the bondholders a premium, such as one year's interest. Also, there frequently is a **call protection period** where the firm cannot call the bond for a prespecified time period.

callable bond (redeemable bond)

call protection period

INDENTURE

An **indenture** is the *legal agreement between the firm issuing the bonds and the trustee who represents the bondholders*. The indenture provides the specific terms of the loan agreement, including a description of the bonds, the rights of the bondholders, the rights of the issuing firm, and the responsibilities of the trustee. This legal document may run 100 pages or more in length, with the majority of it devoted to defining protective provisions for the bondholder. The bond trustee, usually a banking institution or trust company, is then assigned the task of overseeing the relationship between the bondholder and the issuing firm, protecting the bondholder, and seeing that the terms of the indenture are carried out.

Typically, the restrictive provisions included in the indenture attempt to protect the bondholders' financial position relative to that of other outstanding securities. Common provisions involve (1) prohibiting the sale of accounts receivable, (2) limiting common stock dividends, (3) restricting the purchase or sale of fixed assets, and (4) setting limits on

indenture

additional borrowing. Not allowing the sale of accounts receivable is specified because such sales would benefit the firm's short-run liquidity position at the expense of its future liquidity position. Common stock dividends may not be allowed if the firm's liquidity falls below a specified level, or the maximum dividend payout may be limited to some fraction, say, 50 percent or 60 percent of earnings under any circumstance. Fixed-asset restrictions generally require lender permission before the liquidation of any fixed asset or prohibit the use of any existing fixed asset as collateral on new loans. Constraints on additional borrowing usually involve limiting the amount and type of additional long-term debt that can be issued. All these restrictions have one thing in common: They attempt to prohibit actions that would improve the status of other securities at the expense of bonds and to protect the status of bonds from being weakened by any managerial action.

BOND RATINGS

John Moody first began to rate bonds in 1909; since that time three rating agencies—Moody's, Standard & Poor's, and Fitch Investor Services—have provided ratings on corporate bonds. These ratings involve a judgment about the future risk potential of the bond. Although they deal with expectations, several historical factors seem to play a significant role in their determination. Bond ratings are favorably affected by (1) a greater reliance on equity as opposed to debt in financing the firm, (2) profitable operations, (3) a low variability in past earnings, (4) large firm size, and (5) little use of subordinated debt. In turn, the rating a bond receives affects the interest rate demanded on the bond by the investors. The poorer the bond rating, the higher the interest rate demanded by investors. Table 7-1 provides an example and description of these ratings. Thus, bond ratings are extremely important for the financial manager. They provide an indicator of default risk that in turn affects the interest rate that must be paid on borrowed funds.

BACK TO THE FOUNDATIONS

*When we say that a lower bond rating means a higher interest rate charged by the investors (bondholders), we are observing an application of **Principle 1: The Risk–Return Trade-Off—We Won't Take On Additional Risk Unless We Expect to Be Compensated with Additional Return**.*

TABLE 7-1   Standard & Poor's Corporate Bond Ratings

AAA	This is the highest rating assigned by Standard & Poor's for debt obligation and indicates an extremely strong capacity to pay principal and interest.
AA	Bonds rated AA also qualify as high-quality debt obligations. Their capacity to pay principal and interest is very strong, and in the majority of instances, they differ from AAA issues only in small degree.
A	Bonds rated A have a strong capacity to pay principal and interest, although they are somewhat more susceptible to the adverse effects of changes in circumstances and economic conditions.
BBB	Bonds rated BBB are regarded as having an adequate capacity to pay principal and interest. Whereas they normally exhibit adequate protection parameters, adverse economic conditions or changing circumstances are more likely to lead to a weakened capacity to pay principal and interest for bonds in this category than for bonds in the A category.
BB B CCC CC	Bonds rated BB, B, CCC, and CC are regarded, on balance, as predominately speculative with respect to the issuer's capacity to pay interest and repay principal in accordance with the terms of the obligation. BB indicates the lowest degree of speculation and CC the highest. Although such bonds will likely have some quality and protective characteristics, these are outweighed by large uncertainties or major risk exposures to adverse conditions.
C	The rating C is reserved for income bonds on which no interest is being paid.
D	Bonds rated D are in default, and payment of principal and/or interest is in arrears.

Plus (+) or Minus (–): To provide more detailed indications of credit quality, the ratings from AA to BB may be modified by the addition of a plus or minus sign to show relative standing within the major rating categories.

Source: Adapted from www.standardandpoors.com, December 2004.

FINANCIAL MANAGEMENT
IN PRACTICE

CO-COS: A GOOD DEAL FOR WHOM?

When biotech company Cephalon Inc. wanted to raise money and refinance old debt, it thumbed its nose at the low rates. In fact, it didn't want to pay any interest at all on its new bonds. And thanks to an accounting loophole, it was able to fashion a 0 percent, $750 million offering of so-called contingent convertible bonds that investors snapped up.

Dubbed co-cos (short for contingent convertibles), such bonds are the latest craze in corporate finance. In 2003 more than 100 companies, including Comverse Technology and advertising agency holding company Omnicom Group, have sold them in various forms. General Motors (GM) sold the largest issue yet, placing some $4.3 billion in bonds paying 6.25 percent to bolster its underfunded pension plan. At the time, standard GM debt was yielding about 8.5 percent. As with Cephalon, GM is paying no interest after raising $600 million in June.

Raising money by selling bonds at little or no apparent cost is great for corporate bottom lines but not so great for unsuspecting shareholders. The bonds carry below-market interest rates because investors get a conversion option—the right to swap their bonds for stock—instead of interest payments. And, just as with the stock options granted to employees, companies have not had to treat the conversion options as an expense under generally accepted accounting principles (GAAP).

Even more critical for investors, companies—when counting their outstanding shares—don't have to include the shares that would be issued if the bonds were converted to stock. So shareholders can get hit with a nasty surprise. Accounting analysts at Bear Stearns & Co. say companies issuing co-cos would see their earnings per share slip by an average of 6 percent if the conversion options were included in the calculation.

For their part, the companies say they aren't hiding anything. Instead, they say they're doing the deals to get cheap capital. Robert S. "Chip" Merritt, senior director of investor relations at Cephalon, says the company has been straight with the market. "Any professional investor would understand that this conversion could occur and would have modeled for it appropriately," he says. However, Christopher Senyek, an accountant at Bear Stearns who looked at more than 100 of the contingent convertible issues, says public information on the deals is often "sketchy at best," making it hard to gauge their impact on stock prices.

So who is getting a good deal? The answer is *contingent* on what happens in the future for a given firm. Management of firms that use co-cos will help their bottom line for the present but have added a bit more risk for investors.

Source: David Henry, "The Latest Magic in Corporate Finance: How Contingent Convertible Bonds Blindside Shareholders," *Business Week*, September 8, 2003, pp. 146–147.

We are now ready to think about bond valuation. To begin, we must first clarify precisely what we mean by value. Next, we need to understand the basic concepts of valuation and the process for valuing an asset. Then we may apply these concepts to valuing a bond—and in Chapter 8 to valuing stocks.

CONCEPT CHECK

1. What are some of the important features of a bond? Which features determine the cash flows associated with a bond?
2. What restrictions are typically included in an indenture in order to protect the bondholder?
3. How does the bond rating affect an investor's required rate of return? What actions could a firm take to receive a more favorable rating?

DEFINITIONS OF VALUE

Objective **3**

The term *value* is often used in different contexts, depending on its application. Examples of different uses of this term include the following:

Book value is the *value of an asset as shown on a firm's balance sheet*. It represents the historical cost of the asset rather than its current worth. For instance, the book value of a company's common stock is the amount the investors originally paid for the stock and, therefore, the amount the firm received when the stock was issued.

book value

Liquidation value is the *dollar sum that could be realized if an asset were sold individually and not as part of a going concern*. For example, if a firm's operations were discontinued and its assets were divided up and sold, the sales price would represent the asset's liquidation value.

liquidation value

market value

A willing buyer negotiates w/ a willing seller

The **market value** of an asset is the *observed value for the asset in the marketplace*. This value is determined by supply and demand forces working together in the marketplace, where buyers and sellers negotiate a mutually acceptable price for the asset. For instance, the market price for Ford's common stock on December 14, 2004, was $15.12 per share. This price was reached by a large number of buyers and sellers working through the New York Stock Exchange. In theory, a market price exists for all assets. However, many assets have no readily observable market price because trading seldom occurs. For instance, the market price for the common stock of Vision Research Organization, a recent start-up firm in Ft. Lauderdale, Florida, would be more difficult to establish than the market value of Ford's common stock.

intrinsic or economic value
fair value

The **intrinsic or economic value** of an asset—also called the **fair value**—is the *present value of the asset's expected future cash flows*. This value is the amount an investor should be willing to pay, given the amount, timing, and riskiness of future cash flows. Once the investor has estimated the intrinsic value of a security, this value could be compared with its market value when available. If the intrinsic value is greater than the market value, then the security is undervalued in the eyes of the investor. Should the market value exceed the investor's intrinsic value, then the security is overvalued.

We hasten to add that if the securities market is working efficiently, the market value and the intrinsic value of a security will be equal. Whenever a security's intrinsic value differs from its current market price, the competition among investors seeking opportunities to make a profit will quickly drive the market price back to its intrinsic value. Thus, we may

efficient market

define an **efficient market** as *one in which the values of all securities at any instant fully reflect all available public information, which results in the market value and the intrinsic value being the same*. If the markets are efficient, it is extremely difficult for an investor to make extra profits from an ability to predict prices.

BACK TO THE FOUNDATIONS

The fact that investors have difficulty identifying stocks that are undervalued relates to **Principle 6: Efficient Capital Markets—The Markets Are Quick and the Prices Are Right**. In an efficient market, the price reflects all available public information about the security and, therefore, it is priced fairly.

The idea of market efficiency has been the backdrop for an intense battle between professional investors and university professors. The academic community has contended that someone throwing darts at the list of securities in *The Wall Street Journal* could do as well as a professional money manager. Market professionals retort that academicians are grossly mistaken in this view. The war has been intense but also one that the student of finance should find intriguing.

CONCEPT CHECK

1. Explain the different types of value.
2. Why should the market value equal the intrinsic value?

Objective **4**

DETERMINANTS OF VALUE

For our purposes, *the value of an asset is its intrinsic value or the present value of its expected future cash flows*, when these cash flows are discounted back to the present using the investor's required rate of return. This statement is true for valuing all assets, and it serves as the basis of almost all that we do in finance. Thus, value is affected by three elements:

1. The amount and timing of the asset's expected cash flows
2. The riskiness of these cash flows
3. The investor's required rate of return for undertaking the investment

The first two factors are characteristics of the asset; the third one, the required rate of return, is the minimum rate of return necessary to attract an investor to purchase or hold a security, which is determined by *the rates of return available on similar investments*, or what is called the **opportunity cost of funds**. This rate must be high enough to compensate the investor for the risk perceived in the asset's future cash flows. (The required rate of return was explained in Chapter 6.)

opportunity cost of funds

BACK TO THE FOUNDATIONS

Our discussions should remind us of three of our principles that help us understand finance:

Principle 1: The Risk–Return Trade-Off—We Won't Take On Additional Risk Unless We Expect to Be Compensated with Additional Return.

Principle 2: The Time Value of Money—A Dollar Received Today Is Worth More Than a Dollar Received in the Future.

Principle 3: Cash—Not Profits—Is King.

Determining the economic worth or value of an asset always relies on these three principles. Without them, we would have no basis for explaining value. With them, we can know that the amount and timing of cash, not earnings, drive value. Also, we must be rewarded for taking risk; otherwise, we will not invest.

Figure 7-1 depicts the basic factors involved in valuation. As the figure shows, finding the value of an asset involves the following steps:

1. Assessing the asset's characteristics, which include the amount and timing of the expected cash flows and the riskiness of these cash flows
2. Determining the investor's required rate of return, which embodies the investor's attitude about assuming risk and the investor's perception of the riskiness of the asset
3. Discounting the expected cash flows back to the present, using the investor's required rate of return as the discount rate

Thus, intrinsic value is a function of the cash flows yet to be received, the riskiness of these cash flows, and the investor's required rate of return.

CONCEPT CHECK

1. What are the three important elements of asset valuation?

FIGURE 7-1   Basic Factors Determining an Asset's Value

Asset characteristics	Investor attributes
Amount of expected cash flows	Investor's assessment of the riskiness of the asset's cash flows
Timing of expected cash flows	
Riskiness of expected cash flows	Investor's willingness to bear risk

Determine

Investor's required rate of return

Asset value = Present value of expected cash flows discounted using the investor's required rate of return

FINANCIAL MANAGEMENT
IN PRACTICE

ETHICS: KEEPING PERSPECTIVE

Ethical and moral lapses in the business and financial community, academia, politics, and religion fill the daily press. But the rash of insider trading cases on Wall Street against recent graduates of top business and law schools seems particularly disturbing because the cream of the crop, with six-figure incomes and brilliant careers ahead, is being convicted.

Most appear to have been very bright, highly motivated overachievers, driven by peer rivalries to win a game in which the score had a dollar sign in front of it. Although there have been a few big fish, most sold their futures for $20,000 to $50,000 of illicit profits. They missed the point—that life is a marathon, not a sprint.

In fact, most business school graduates become competent executives, managing people and resources for the benefit of society. The rewards—the titles and money—are merely byproducts of doing a good job.

To illustrate the point, consider the owner of a small company who had the opportunity to acquire a contract with a large Fortune 500 company to produce a product for the large firm. Verbal agreement was reached on the deal, but when the owner met with the president of the large company to sign the contract, the price of the product to be produced by the small firm was $0.25 per unit higher than originally agreed upon—in the small company owner's favor. When questioned, the president of the large firm informed the small firm owner she was to deposit the difference in a personal account and then periodically send the money to the president's personal bank account. Because the small firm owner was not directly profiting from the president's clearly unethical behavior, should she have accepted the terms? It would have increased her firm's profits significantly—but only by a legitimate amount. How about the president of the large company? Why would he be willing to act unethically for what would have meant $40,000 or $50,000 to him?

Objective 5

VALUATION: THE BASIC PROCESS

The valuation process can be described as follows: It is assigning value to an asset by calculating the present value of its expected future cash flows using the investor's required rate of return as the discount rate. The investor's required rate of return, k, is determined by the level of the risk-free rate of interest and risk premium that the investor feels is necessary to compensate for the risks assumed in owning the asset. Therefore, a basic asset valuation model can be defined mathematically as follows:

$$V = \frac{C_1}{(1+k)^1} + \frac{C_2}{(1+k)^2} + \cdots + \frac{C_n}{(1+k)^n}$$

(7-1)

where V = the intrinsic value or present value of an asset producing expected future cash flows, C_t, in years 1 through n

C_t = cash flow to be received at time t

k = the investor's required rate of return

Using equation (7-1), there are three basic steps in the valuation process:

Step 1: Estimate the C_t in equation (7-1), which is the amount and timing of the future cash flows the security is expected to provide.

Step 2: Determine k, the investor's required rate of return.

Step 3: Calculate the intrinsic value, V, as the present value of expected future cash flows discounted at the investor's required rate of return.

Equation (7-1), which measures the present value of future cash flows, is the basis of the valuation process. It is the most important equation in this chapter, because all the remaining equations in this chapter and in Chapter 8 are merely reformulations of this one equation. If we understand equation (7-1), all the valuation work we do, and a host of other topics as well, will be much clearer in our minds.

PROBLEM CHECK: COMPUTING ASSET VALUE

You purchased an asset that is expected to provide $5,000 cash flow per year for four years. If you have a 12 percent required rate of return, what is the value of the asset for you?

See below for the answer.

With the foregoing principles of valuation as our foundation, let's now look at how bonds are valued.

BOND VALUATION

Objective **6**

The value of a bond is the present value of both future interest to be received and the par or maturity value of the bond. It's that simple.

The process for valuing a bond, as depicted in Figure 7-2, requires knowing three essential elements: (1) the amount and timing of the cash flows to be received by the investor, (2) the time to maturity of the bond, and (3) the investor's required rate of return. The amount of cash flows is dictated by the periodic interest to be received and by the par value to be paid at maturity. Given these elements, we can compute the value of the bond, or the present value.

FIGURE 7-2   Data Requirements for Bond Valuation

(A) Cash flow information	Periodic interest payments For example, $65 per year
	Principal amount or par value For example, $1,000
(B) Term to maturity	For example, 12 years
(C) Investor's required rate of return	For example, 8%

PROBLEM CHECK SOLUTION: COMPUTING ASSET VALUE

The value of an asset generating $5,000 per year for four years, given a 12 percent required rate of return, would be $15,186.75 using a TI BA II plus calculator, we find the answer as follows:

CALCULATOR SOLUTION

Data Input	Function Key
12	I/Y
4	N
5,000	PMT
0	FV

Function Key	Answer
CPT PV	−15,186.75

EXAMPLE

Consider a bond issued by Toyota with a maturity date of 2008 and a stated annual coupon rate of 5.5 percent.[1] In December 2004, with 4 years left to maturity, investors owning the bonds are requiring a 3.6 percent rate of return. We can calculate the value of the bonds to these investors using the following three-step valuation procedure:

---

[1] Toyota pays interest to its bondholders on a semiannual basis on June 15 and December 15. However, for the moment, assume the interest is to be received annually. The effect of semiannual payments is examined shortly.

Step 1: Estimate the amount and timing of the expected future cash flows. Two types of cash flows are received by the bondholder:

a) Annual interest payments equal to the coupon rate of interest times the face value of the bond. In this example, the bond's coupon interest rate is 5.5 percent; thus, the annual interest payment is $55 = .055 × $1,000. Assuming that 2004 interest payments have already been made, these cash flows will be received by the bondholder in each of the 4 years before the bond matures (2005 through 2008 = 4 years).

b) The face value of $1,000 to be received in 2008.

To summarize, the cash flows received by the bondholder are as follows:

YEARS	1	2	3	4
	$55	$55	$55	$ 55
				+ $1,000
				$1,055

Step 2: Determine the investor's required rate of return by evaluating the riskiness of the bond's future cash flows. A 3.6 percent required rate of return for the bondholders is given. However, we should recall from Chapter 6 that an investor's required rate of return is equal to a rate earned on a risk-free security plus a risk premium for assuming risk.

Step 3: Calculate the intrinsic value of the bond as the present value of the expected future interest and principal payments discounted at the investor's required rate of return.

In general, the present value of a bond is found as follows:

$$\text{Bond value} = V_b = \frac{\$ \text{ interest in year 1}}{(1+\text{required rate of return})^1}$$
$$+ \frac{\$ \text{ interest in year 2}}{(1+\text{required rate of return})^2}$$
$$+ \frac{\$ \text{ interest in year 3}}{(1+\text{required rate of return})^3}$$
$$+ \vdots$$
$$+ \frac{\$ \text{ interest in year } n}{(1+\text{required rate of return})^n}$$
$$+ \frac{\$ \text{ maturity value of bond}}{(1+\text{required rate of return})^n}$$

(7-2a)

Using I_t to represent the interest payment in year t, M to represent the bond's maturity (or par) value, and k_b to equal the bondholder's required rate of return, we may express the value of a bond maturing in year n as follows:

$$V_b = \frac{\$I_1}{(1+k_b)^1} + \frac{\$I_2}{(1+k_b)^2} + \frac{\$I_3}{(1+k_b)^3} + \cdots + \frac{\$I_n}{(1+k_b)^n} + \frac{\$M}{(1+k_b)^n}$$

(7-2b)

Notice that equation (7-2b) is a restatement of equation (7-1), where now the cash flows are represented by the interest received each period and the par value of the bond when it matures. In either equation, the value of an asset is the present value of its future cash flows.

The equation for finding the value of the Toyota bonds would be as follows:

$$V_b = \frac{\$55}{(1+0.036)^1} + \frac{\$55}{(1+0.036)^2} + \frac{\$55}{(1+0.036)^3} + \frac{\$55}{(1+0.036)^4} + \frac{\$1,000}{(1+0.036)^4}$$

Finding the value of the Toyota bonds may be represented graphically as follows:

YEAR	0	1	2	3	4
Dollars received at end of year		$55	$55	$55	$55 + $1,000 $1,055
Present value	$1069.62 ←				

Using a TI BA II Plus financial calculator, we find the value of the bond to be $1,069.62, as calculated in the margin.[2] Thus, if investors consider 3.6 percent to be an appropriate required rate of return in view of the risk level associated with Toyota bonds, paying a price of $1,069.62 would satisfy their return requirement.

We can also solve for the value of Toyota's bonds using a spreadsheet. The solution using Excel appears as follows:

	A	B	C	D
1	Required rate of return	Rate	3.2%	
2	Periods left to maturity	Nper	24	
3	Annual interest payment	Pmt	37.50	
4	Future value	FV	1.000	
5	Present value	PV	($1.091.17)	
6				
7	Equation:			
8	=PV (Rate, Nper, Pmt, FV) = PV(C1,C2,C3,C4)			
9				

CONCEPT CHECK

1. What two factors determine an investor's required rate of return?
2. How does the required rate of return affect a bond's value?

SEMIANNUAL INTEREST PAYMENTS

In the preceding Toyota illustration, the interest payments were assumed to be paid annually. However, companies typically pay interest to bondholders semiannually. For example, Toyota actually pays a total of $55 per year, but disburses the interest semiannually ($27.50 each June 15 and December 15).

Several steps are involved in adapting equation (7-2b) for semiannual interest payments.[3] First, thinking in terms of *periods* instead of years, a bond with a life of n years paying interest semiannually has a life of $2n$ periods. In other words, a 5-year bond ($n = 5$) that remits its interest on a semiannual basis actually makes 10 payments. Although the number of periods has doubled, the *dollar* amount of interest being sent to the investors for each period and the bondholders' required rate of return are half of the equivalent annual figures. I_t becomes $I_t/2$ and k_b is changed to $k_b/2$; thus, for semiannual compounding, equation (7-2b) becomes

$$V_b = \frac{\$I_1/2}{\left(1+\frac{k_b}{2}\right)^1} + \frac{\$I_2/2}{\left(1+\frac{k_b}{2}\right)^2} + \frac{\$I_3/2}{\left(1+\frac{k_b}{2}\right)^3} + \cdots + \frac{\$I_{2n}/2}{\left(1+\frac{k_b}{2}\right)^{2n}} + \frac{\$M}{\left(1+\frac{k_b}{2}\right)^{2n}} \quad (7\text{-}3)$$

We can now compute the value of the Toyota bonds, recognizing that interest is being paid semiannually. We simply change the number of periods from 4 years to 8 semiannual periods and the required rate of return from 3.6 percent annually to 1.8 percent per semiannual period. The value of the bond would now be $1,070.20.

[2]As noted in Chapter 5, we are using the TI BA II Plus. You may want to return to the Chapter 5 section "Moving Money Through Time with the Aid of a Financial Calculator" or Appendix A, to see a more complete explanation of using the TI BA II Plus. For an explanation of other calculators, see the study guide that accompanies this text.
[3]The logic for calculating the value of a bond that pays interest semiannually is similar to the material presented in Chapter 5, where compound interest with nonannual periods was discussed.

This solution can be found using a calculator as shown in the margin or a spreadsheet that would look as follows:

	A	B	C	D
1	Required rate of return	Rate	9.4%	
2	Years left to maturity	Nper	15	
3	Annual interest payment	Pmt	90	
4	Future value	FV	1.000	
5	Present value	PV	($968.50)	
6				
7				
8	Equation:			
9	=PV (Rate, Nper, Pmt, FV) = PV(C1,C2,C3,C4)			
10				

CONCEPT CHECK

1. How do semiannual interest payments affect the asset valuation equation?

PROBLEM CHECK: COMPUTING BOND VALUE

La Fiesta Restaurants issued bonds that have a 6 percent coupon interest rate. Interest is paid annually. The bonds mature in 12 years. If your required rate of return is 8 percent, what is the value of a bond to you?

See page 219 for the answer.

Now that we know how to value a bond, we will next examine a bondholder's rate of return from investing in a bond, or what is called bond yields.

BOND YIELDS

There are two calculations that are used to measure the rate of return a bondholder is receiving from owning a bond: the yield to maturity and the current yield.

Objective **7**

YIELD TO MATURITY

Theoretically, each bondholder could have a different required rate of return for a particular bond. However, the financial manager is only interested in the expected rate of return that is implied by the market prices of the firm's bonds or what we call the yield to maturity.

expected rate of return

To measure the bondholder's **expected rate of return**, $\bar{k}_b$, we would find the *discount rate that equates the present value of the future cash flows (interest and maturity value) with the current market price of the bond.*[4] It is also the *rate of return the investor will earn if the bond is held to maturity*, thus the name **yield to maturity**. So, when referring to bonds, the terms *expected rate of return* and *yield to maturity* are often used interchangeably.

yield to maturity

To illustrate this concept, consider the Brister Corporation's bonds, which are selling for $1,100. The bonds carry a coupon interest rate of 9 percent and mature in 10 years. (Remember, the coupon rate determines the interest payment—coupon rate × par value.)

In determining the expected rate of return ($\bar{k}_b$), implicit in the current market price, we need to find the rate that discounts the anticipated cash flows back to a present value of $1,100, the current market price (P_0) for the bond.

The expected return for the Brister Corporation bondholders is 7.54 percent, which may be found by using the TI BA II Plus calculator as presented in the margin, or by using a computer spreadsheet, as follows:

CALCULATOR SOLUTION

Data Input	Function Key
10	N
1100	PV
90	+/– PMT
1000	+/– FV

Function Key	Answer
CPT I/Y	7.54

[4]When we speak of computing an expected rate of return, we are not describing the situation very accurately. Expected rates of return are ex ante (before the fact) and are based on "expected and unobservable future cash flows" and, therefore, can only be "estimated."

FINANCIAL MANAGEMENT
IN PRACTICE

AT&T BOND PRICES FALL THANKS TO WORLDCOM

When WorldCom announced to the public the accounting misfeasance that had occurred in the company, the firm's bond prices fell sharply—as would be expected. But the news also sent shock waves through the industry, with AT&T's bonds suffering one of their worst one-day losses in years. Investors were worried that the telephone giant would run into the same troubles as WorldCom.

AT&T's 10-year bonds fell to about 82 percent of their par value, down from about 90 percent the day before—a significant fall for an investment-grade-rated bond. A week earlier, the bonds had traded at around 96 percent of par value.

The spread, or difference in yield, between AT&T's bonds and U.S. Treasuries surged to about 4.3 percentage points, up from almost 3.8 percentage points earlier, suggesting investors are demanding more compensation for the risk of buying the bonds.

AT&T was being treated as if it had a "junk" bond rating, even though it belonged firmly in the investment-grade category. In the words of Philip Olesen, an analyst at UBS Warburg, "There was nothing but selling . . . ; it was brutal."

Source: Gregory Zuckerman, Richard A. Bravo, and Christine Richard, "AT&T's Bonds Tumble in Sell-Off as WorldCom Woes Spark Fears," *The Wall Street Journal*, May 2, 2002, p. A2.

	A	B	C	D	E
1	Years left to maturity	Nper	10		
2	Annual interest payment	Pmt	90		
3	Present value	PV	-1.100		
4	Future value	FV	1.000		
5	Required rate of return	Rate	7.5%		
6					
7		Equation:			
8		= RATE(Nper, Pmt, -PV,FV) = RATE(C1,C2,C3,C4)			
9					
10					

PROBLEM CHECK SOLUTION: COMPUTING BOND VALUE

A bond with a 6 percent coupon rate pays $60 in interest per year ($60 = 0.06 coupon rate × $1,000 par value). Thus, you would receive $60 per year for 12 years plus the $1,000 in par value in year 12. Assuming an 8 percent required rate of return, the value of the bond would be $849.28:

CALCULATOR SOLUTION

Data Input	Function Key
8	I/Y
12	N
60	PMT
1,000	FV

Function Key	Answer
CPT PV	−849.28

CURRENT YIELD

The **current yield** on a bond refers to the *ratio of the annual interest payment to the bond's current market price*. If, for example, we have a bond with an 8 percent coupon interest rate, a par value of $1,000, and a market price of $700, it would have a current yield of 11.4 percent:

current yield

$$\text{Current yield} = \frac{\text{annual interest payment}}{\text{current market price of the bond}} \tag{7-4}$$

$$= \frac{0.08 \times \$1,000}{\$700} = \frac{\$80}{\$700} = 0.114 = 11.4\%$$

We should understand that the current yield, although frequently quoted in the popular press, is an incomplete picture of the expected rate of return from holding a bond. The current yield indicates the cash income that results from holding a bond in a given year, but it fails to recognize the capital gain or loss that will occur if the bond is held to maturity. As such, it is not an accurate measure of the bondholder's expected rate of return.

PROBLEM CHECK: COMPUTING YIELD TO MATURITY AND CURRENT YIELD

The Argon Corporation bonds are selling for $925. They have a 5 percent coupon interest rate paid annually and mature in 8 years. What is the yield to maturity for the bonds if an investor buys them at the $925 market price? What is the current yield?

See page 221 for the answer.

Objective **8**

BOND VALUATION: THREE IMPORTANT RELATIONSHIPS

We have now learned to find the value of a bond (V_b), given (1) the amount of interest payments (I_t), (2) the maturity value (M), (3) the length of time to maturity (n periods), and (4) the investor's required rate of return, k_b. We also know how to compute the expected rate of return ($\bar{k}_b$), which also happens to be the current interest rate on the bond, given (1) the current market value (P_0), (2) the amount of interest payments (I_t), (3) the maturity value (M), and (4) the length of time to maturity (n periods). We now have the basics. But let's go further in our understanding of bond valuation by studying several important relationships.

FIRST RELATIONSHIP

The value of a bond is inversely related to changes in the investor's present required rate of return. In other words, as interest rates increase (decrease), the value of the bond decreases (increases).

To illustrate, assume that an investor's required rate of return for a given bond is 12 percent. The bond has a par value of $1,000 and annual interest payments of $120, indicating a 12 percent coupon interest rate ($120 \div $1,000 = 12\%$). Assuming a 5-year maturity date, the bond would be worth $1,000, computed as follows:

$$V_b = \frac{\$I_1}{(1+k_b)^1} + \cdots + \frac{\$I_n}{(1+k_b)^n} + \frac{\$M}{(1+k_b)^n} \tag{7-5}$$

$$= \frac{\$120}{(1+0.12)^1} + \frac{\$120}{(1+0.12)^2} + \frac{\$120}{(1+0.12)^3} + \frac{\$120}{(1+0.12)^4} + \frac{\$120}{(1+0.12)^5} + \frac{\$1,000}{(1+0.12)^5}$$

Using a calculator, we find the value of the bond to be $1,000.

CALCULATOR SOLUTION	
Data Input	**Function Key**
12	I/Y
5	N
120	PMT
1,000	FV

Function Key	**Answer**
CPT PV	−1,000

If, however, the investor's required rate of return increases from 12 percent to 15 percent, the value of the bond would decrease to $899.44, computed as follows:

CALCULATOR SOLUTION

Data Input	Function Key
15	I/Y
5	N
120	PMT
1,000	FV

Function Key	Answer
CPT PV	−899.44

On the other hand, if the investors' required rate of return decreases to 9 percent, the bond would increase in value to $1,116.69.

CALCULATOR SOLUTION

Data Input	Function Key
9	I/Y
5	N
120	PMT
1,000	FV

Function Key	Answer
CPT PV	−1,116.69

PROBLEM CHECK SOLUTION: COMPUTING YIELD TO MATURITY AND CURRENT YIELD

The Argon bonds pay $50 in interest per year ($50 = 0.05 coupon rate × $1,000 par value) for the duration of the bond, or for 8 years. The investor will then receive $1,000 at the bond's maturity. Given a market price of $925, the yield to maturity would be 6.2 percent:

CALCULATOR SOLUTION

Data Input	Function Key
8	N
925	PV
50	+/− PMT
1,000	+/− FV

Function Key	Answer
CPT I/Y	6.22

$$\text{Current yield} = \frac{\text{annual interest payment}}{\text{current market price of the bond}}$$

$$= \frac{\$50}{\$925} = 0.0541 = 5.41\%$$

This inverse relationship between the investor's required rate of return and the value of a bond is presented in Figure 7-3. Clearly, as an investor demands a higher rate of return, the value of the bond decreases. The higher rate of return the investor desires can be achieved only by paying less for the bond. Conversely, a lower required rate of return yields a higher market value for the bond.

Changes in bond prices represent an element of uncertainty for the bond investor. If the current interest rate (required rate of return) changes, the price of the bond also fluctuates. An increase in interest rates causes the bondholder to incur a loss in market value. Because future interest rates and the resulting bond value cannot be predicted with certainty, a bond investor is exposed to the *risk of changing values as interest rates vary*. This risk has come to be known as **interest rate risk**.

interest rate risk

FIGURE 7-3   Value and Required Rates for a 5-Year Bond at a 12 Percent Coupon Rate

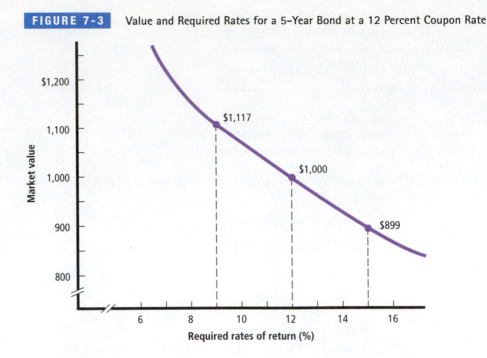

SECOND RELATIONSHIP

The market value of a bond will be less than the par value if the investor's required rate of return is above the coupon interest rate; but it will be valued above par value if the investor's required rate of return is below the coupon interest rate.

Using the previous example, we observed that

1. The bond has a *market value* of $1,000, equal to the par or maturity value, when the investor's required rate of return equals the 12 percent coupon interest rate. In other words, if

   required rate = coupon rate, then *market value = par value*
   $\quad$ 12% $\quad=\quad$ 12%, $\quad$ then $\quad$ $1,000 $\quad=\quad$ $1,000

2. When the required rate is 15 percent, which exceeds the 12 percent coupon rate, the market value falls below par value to $899.44; that is, if

   required rate > coupon rate, then *market value < par value*
   $\quad$ 15% $\quad>\quad$ 12%, $\quad$ then $\quad$ $899.44 $\quad<\quad$ $1,000

   discount bond   In this case the *bond sells at a discount below par value*; thus, it is called a **discount bond**.

3. When the required rate is 9 percent, or less than the 12 percent coupon rate, the market value, $1,116.69, exceeds the bond's par value. In this instance, if

   required rate < coupon rate, then *market value > par value*
   $\quad$ 9% $\quad<\quad$ 12%, $\quad$ then $\quad$ $1,116.69 $\quad>\quad$ $1,000

   premium bond   The *bond is now selling at a premium above par value*; thus, it is a **premium bond**.

THIRD RELATIONSHIP

Long-term bonds have greater interest rate risk than do short-term bonds.

As already noted, a change in current interest rates (required rate of return) causes an inverse change in the market value of a bond. However, the impact on value is greater for long-term bonds than it is for short-term bonds.

In Figure 7-3 we observed the effect of interest rate changes on a 5-year bond paying a 12 percent coupon interest rate. What if the bond did not mature until 10 years from today instead of 5 years? Would the changes in market value be the same? Absolutely not. The changes in value would be more significant for the 10-year bond. For example, if we vary the current interest rates (the bondholder's required rate of return) from 9 percent to 12 percent and then to 15 percent, as we did earlier with the 5-year bond, the values for both the 5-year and the 10-year bonds are shown here.

REQUIRED RATE	MARKET VALUE FOR A 12% COUPON-RATE BOND MATURING IN	
	5 YEARS	10 YEARS
9%	$1,116.69	$1,192.53
12	1,000.00	1,000.00
15	899.44	849.44

FIGURE 7-4 Market Values of a 5-Year and a 10-Year Bond at Different Required Rates of Return

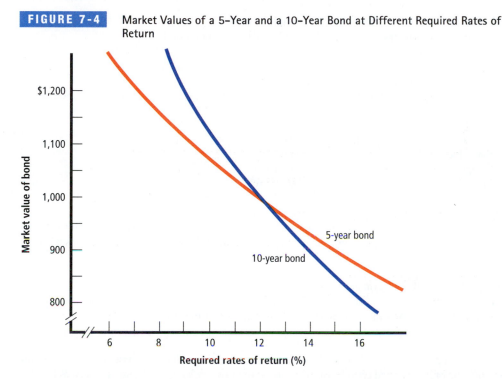

Using these values and the required rates, we can graph the changes in values for the two bonds relative to different interest rates. These comparisons are provided in Figure 7-4. The figure clearly illustrates that the price of a long-term bond (say, 10 years) is more responsive or sensitive to interest rate changes than the price of a short-term bond (say, 5 years).

The reason long-term bond prices fluctuate more than short-term bond prices in response to interest rate changes is simple. Assume an investor bought a 10-year bond yielding a 12 percent interest rate. If the current interest rate for bonds of similar risk increased to 15 percent, the investor would be locked into the lower rate for 10 years. If, on the other hand, a shorter-term bond had been purchased—say, one maturing in 2 years—the investor would have to accept the lower return for only 2 years and not the full 10 years. At the end of year 2, the investor would receive the maturity value of $1,000 and could buy a bond offering the higher 15 percent rate for the remaining 8 years. Thus, interest rate risk is determined, at least in part, by the length of time an investor is required to commit to an investment. However, the holder of a long-term bond may take some comfort from the fact that long-term interest rates are usually not as volatile as short-term rates. If the short-term rate changed 1 percentage point, for example, it would not be unusual for the long-term rate to change only .3 percentage points.

CONCEPT CHECK

1. Why does a bond sell at a discount when the coupon rate is lower than the required rate of return and vice versa?

2. As interest rates increase, why does the price of a long-term bond decrease more than a short-term bond?

SUMMARY

Valuation is an important issue if we are to manage the company effectively. An understanding of the concepts and how to compute the value of a security underlie much of what we do in finance and in making correct decisions for the firm as a whole. Only if we know what matters to our investors can we maximize the firm's value.

Objective **1**

Distinguish between different kinds of bonds
There is a variety of types of bonds, including:

Debentures	Eurobonds
Subordinated debentures	Zero and very low coupon bonds
Mortgage bonds	Junk bonds

Objective **2**

Explain the more popular features of bonds
Some of the more popular terms and characteristics that you might hear about bonds include the following:

Claims on assets and income	Indenture
Par value	Bond ratings
Coupon interest rate	Call provision
Maturity	Convertibility

Objective **3**

Define the term *value* **as used for several different purposes**
Value is defined differently depending on the context. But for us, value is the present value of future cash flows expected to be received from an investment discounted at the investor's required rate of return.

Objective **4**

Explain the factors that determine value
Three basic factors determine an asset's value: (1) the amount and timing of future cash flows, (2) the riskiness of the cash flows, and (3) the investor's attitude about the risk.

Objective **5**

Describe the basic process for valuing assets
The valuation process can be described as follows: It is assigning value to an asset by calculating the present value of its expected future cash flows using the investor's required rate of return as the discount rate. The investor's required rate of return, k, equals the risk-free rate of interest plus a risk premium to compensate the investor for assuming risk.

Objective **6**

Estimate the value of a bond
The value of a bond is the present value of both future interest to be received and the par or maturity value of the bond.

Objective **7**

Compute a bondholder's expected rate of return
To measure the bondholder's expected rate of return, we find the discount rate that equates the present value of the future cash flows (interest and maturity value) with the current market price of the bond. The expected rate of return for a bond is also the rate of return the investor will earn if the bond is held to maturity, or the yield to maturity. We may also compute the current yield as the annual interest payment divided by the bond's current market price, but this is not an accurate measure of a bondholder's expected rate of return.

Objective **8**

Explain three important relationships that exist in bond valuation
Certain key relationships exist in bond valuation, these being:

1. A decrease in interest rates (required rates of return) will cause the value of a bond to increase; an interest rate increase will cause a decrease in value. The change in value caused by changing interest rates is called interest rate risk.
2. If the bondholder's required rate of return (current interest rate):
   a. Equals the coupon interest rate, the bond will sell at par, or maturity value.
   b. Exceeds the bond's coupon rate, the bond will sell below par value, or at a discount.
   c. Is less than the bond's coupon rate, the bond will sell above par value, or at a premium.
3. A bondholder owning a long-term bond is exposed to greater interest rate risk than one owning a short-term bond.

KEY TERMS

Bond, 206

Book value, 211

Callable bond (redeemable bond), 209

Call protection period, 209

Convertible bond, 209

Coupon interest rate, 209

Current yield, 219

Debenture, 206

Discount bond, 222

Efficient market, 212

Eurobonds, 206

Expected rate of return, 218

Fair value, 212

High-yield bonds (junk bonds), 207

Indenture, 209

Interest rate risk, 221

Intrinsic or economic value, 212

Junk bonds, 207

Liquidation value, 211

Market value, 212

Maturity, 209

Mortgage bond, 206

Opportunity cost of funds, 213

Par value of a bond, 209

Premium bond, 222

Subordinated debentures, 206

Yield to maturity, 218

Zero and very low coupon bonds, 207

STUDY QUESTIONS

7-1. Distinguish between debentures and mortgage bonds.

7-2. Define (a) Eurobonds, (b) zero coupon bonds, and (c) junk bonds.

7-3. Describe the bondholder's claim on the firm's assets and income.

7-4. a. How does a bond's par value differ from its market value?

   b. Explain the difference between a bond's coupon interest rate, the current yield, and a bondholder's required rate of return.

7-5. What factors determine a bond's rating? Why is the rating important to the firm's manager?

7-6. What are the basic differences between book value, liquidation value, market value, and intrinsic value?

7-7. What is a general definition of the intrinsic value of an asset?

7-8. Explain the three factors that determine the intrinsic, or economic, value of an asset.

7-9. Explain the relationship between an investor's required rate of return and the value of a security.

7-10. Define the bondholder's expected rate of return.

SELF-TEST PROBLEMS

ST-1. (*Bond valuation*) Trico bonds have an annual coupon rate of 8 percent and a par value of $1,000, and will mature in 20 years. If you require a return of 7 percent, what price would you be willing to pay for the bond? What happens if you pay *more* for the bond? What happens if you pay *less* for the bond?

ST-2. (*Bond valuation*) Sunn Co.'s bonds, maturing in 7 years, pay 8 percent interest on a $1,000 face value. However, interest is paid semiannually. If your required rate of return is 10 percent, what is the value of the bond? How would your answer change if the interest were paid annually?

ST-3. (*Bondholder's expected rate of return*) Sharp Co. bonds are selling in the market for $1,045. These 15-year bonds pay 7 percent interest annually on a $1,000 par value. If they are purchased at the market price, what is the expected rate of return?

STUDY PROBLEMS

7-1. You own a 20-year, $1,000 par value bond paying 7 percent interest annually. The market price of the bonds is $875, and your required rate of return is 10 percent.

   a. Compute the bond's expected rate of return.
   b. Determine the value of the bond to you, given your required rate of return.
   c. Should you sell the bond or continue to own it?

7-2. (*Bond valuation*) Calculate the value of a bond that will mature in 14 years and has a $1,000 face value. The annual coupon interest rate is 7 percent, and the investor's required rate of return is 10 percent.

7-3. You recently bought a $1,000 par value corporate bond with a 6 percent annual coupon rate and a 10-year maturity date. When you bought the bond, it had an expected yield to maturity of 8 percent. Today the bond sells for $1,060.

   a. What did you pay for the bond?
   b. If you sold the bond today, what would be your one-period return on the investment?

7-4. (*Bond valuation*) Shelly, Inc. bonds have a 10 percent coupon rate. The interest is paid semiannually, and the bonds mature in 8 years. Their par value is $1,000. If your required rate of return is 8 percent, what is the value of the bond? What is the value if the interest is paid annually?

7-5. Crawford, Inc. has two bond issues outstanding, both paying the same annual interest of $85, called Series A and Series B. Series A has a maturity of 12 years, whereas Series B has a maturity of 1 year.

   a. What would be the value of each of these bonds when the going interest rate is (1) 5 percent, (2) 8 percent, and (3) 12 percent? Assume that there is only one more interest payment to be made on the Series B bonds.
   b. Why does the longer-term (12-year) bond fluctuate more when interest rates change than does the shorter-term (1-year) bond?

7-6. (*Bondholder's expected rate of return*) The market price is $900 for a 10-year bond ($1,000 par value) that pays 8 percent interest (4 percent semiannually). What is the bond's expected rate of return?

7-7. You own a bond that has a par value of $1,000 and matures in 5 years. It pays a 9 percent annual coupon rate. The bond currently sells for $1,200. What is the bond's expected rate of return?

7-8. (*Bond valuation*) ExxonMobil 20-year bonds pay 9 percent interest annually on a $1,000 par value. If bonds sell at $945, what is the bonds' expected rate of return?

7-9. (*Bondholder's expected rate of return*) Zenith Co.'s bonds mature in 12 years and pay 7 percent interest annually. If you purchase the bonds for $1,150, what is your expected rate of return?

7-10. (*Bond valuation*) National Steel 15-year, $1,000 par value bonds pay 8 percent interest annually. The market price of the bonds is $1,085, and your required rate of return is 10 percent.

   a. Compute the bond's expected rate of return.
   b. Determine the value of the bond to you, given your required rate of return.
   c. Should you purchase the bond?

7-11. (*Bond valuation*) You own a bond that pays $100 in annual interest, with a $1,000 par value. It matures in 15 years. Your required rate of return is 12 percent.

   a. Calculate the value of the bond.
   b. How does the value change if your required rate of return (1) increases to 15 percent or (2) decreases to 8 percent?
   c. Explain the implications of your answers in part b as they relate to interest rate risk, premium bonds, and discount bonds.
   d. Assume that the bond matures in 5 years instead of 15 years. Recompute your answers in part b.
   e. Explain the implications of your answers in part d as they relate to interest rate risk, premium bonds, and discount bonds.

7-12. (*Bond valuation*) New Generation Public Utilities issued a bond that pays $80 in annual interest, with a $1,000 par value. It matures in 20 years. Your required rate of return is 7 percent.

   a. Calculate the value of the bond.
   b. How does the value change if your required rate of return (1) increases to 10 percent or (2) decreases to 6 percent?
   c. Explain the implications of your answers in part b as they relate to interest rate risk, premium bonds, and discount bonds.
   d. Assume that the bond matures in 10 years instead of 20 years. Recompute your answers in part b.
   e. Explain the implications of your answers in part d as they relate to interest rate risk, premium bonds, and discount bonds.

7-13. (*Bond valuation—zero coupon*) The Logos Corporation is planning on issuing bonds that pay no interest but can be converted into $1,000 at maturity, seven years from their purchase. To price these bonds competitively with other bonds of equal risk, it is determined that they should yield 9 percent, compounded annually. At what price should the Logos Corporation sell these bonds?

7-14. (*Bond values*) You are examining three bonds with a par value of $1,000 (you receive $1,000 at maturity) and are concerned with what would happen to their market value if interest rates (or the market discount rate) changed. The three bonds are

Bond A—A bond with 3 years left to maturity that has a 10 percent annual coupon interest rate, but the interest is paid semiannually.

Bond B—A bond with 7 years left to maturity that has a 10 percent annual coupon interest rate, but the interest is paid semiannually.

Bond C—A bond with 20 years left to maturity that has a 10 percent annual coupon interest rate, but the interest is paid semiannually.

What would be the value of these bonds if the market discount rate were

a. 10 percent per year compounded semiannually?
b. 4 percent per year compounded semiannually?
c. 16 percent per year compounded semiannually?
d. What observations can you make about these results?

WEB WORKS

7-WW1. Go to http://bond.yahoo.com. Under Find Bonds by Name, type in the company name Texaco. How many bonds has Texaco issued? How are they different? Click on one of the issues. What do you learn about the issue? Choose another one and see how the two issues are different.

7-WW2. At the Web site http://bond.yahoo.com there are links under Features. Choose Calculators. Then choose the option of Which Bond Is Better. What do you learn from this calculator? Now choose How Will Rate Changes Affect My Bond's Value. Make up some examples to see what you learn from using the calculator.

7-WW3. Go to the Web site www.investinginbonds.com. What does the Web site tell us about how bond rating changes affect bond value?

7-WW4. Find the Web site www.investopedia.com/university/bonds. Scroll down the table of contents and choose the option on how to read a bond table. Describe what you find.

COMPREHENSIVE PROBLEM

Here are data on $1,000 par value bonds issued by Bell South, Dole, and Xerox, at the end of 2004. Assume you are thinking about buying these bonds as of January 2005. Answer the following questions for each of these bonds:

a. Calculate the values of the bonds if your required rates of return are as follows: Bell South, 7 percent; Dole, 7.5 percent; and Xerox, 10 percent; where

	BELL SOUTH	DOLE	XEROX
Coupon interest rate	6.375%	7.875%	7.2%
Years to maturity	27	12	11

b. At the end of 2004, the bonds were selling for the following amounts:

Bell South $ 945.00
Dole $1,002.50
Xerox $ 839.00

What were the expected rates of return for each bond?

c. How would the value of the bonds change if (1) your required rate of return (k_b) increased 2 percentage points or (2) decreased 2 percentage points?

d. Explain the implications of your answers in part b in terms of interest rate risk, premium bonds, and discount bonds.

e. Should you buy the bonds? Explain.

SELF-TEST SOLUTIONS

SS-1.

$$\text{Value}(V_b) = \frac{\$80}{(1.07)^1} + \frac{\$80}{(1.07)^2} + \cdots + \frac{\$80}{(1.07)^{20}} + \frac{\$1000}{(1.07)^{20}}$$

Using a financial calculator, we find the value of the bond to be $1,105.94:

CALCULATOR SOLUTION	
Data Input	**Function Key**
7	I/Y
20	N
80	PMT
1,000	FV
Function Key	**Answer**
CPT PV	−1,105.94

If you pay more for the bond, your required rate of return will not be satisfied. In other words, by paying an amount for the bond that exceeds $1,105.94, the expected rate of return for the bond is less than the required rate of return. If you have the opportunity to pay less for the bond, the expected rate of return exceeds the 7 percent required rate of return.

SS-2. If interest is paid semiannually:

$$\text{Value}(V_b) = \frac{\$40}{(1.05)^1} + \cdots + \frac{\$40}{(1.05)^{14}} + \frac{\$1,000}{(1.05)^{14}}$$

The value of the bond would be $901.01:

CALCULATOR SOLUTION	
Data Input	**Function Key**
5	I/Y
14	N
40	PMT
1,000	FV
Function Key	**Answer**
CPT PV	−901.01

If interest is paid annually:

$$\text{Value}(V_b) = \frac{\$80}{(1.10)^1} + \cdots + \frac{\$80}{(1.10)^7} + \frac{\$1,000}{(1.10)^7}$$

The value of the bond would be $902.63:

CALCULATOR SOLUTION	
Data Input	**Function Key**
10	I/Y
7	N
80	PMT
1,000	FV
Function Key	**Answer**
CPT PV	−902.63

SS-3. Finding the bond's yield to maturity, the expected rate of return is based on the following equation:

$$\$1,045 = \frac{\$70}{(1 + \overline{k}_b)^1} + \cdots + \frac{\$70}{(1 + \overline{k}_b)^{15}} + \frac{\$1,000}{(1 + \overline{k}_b)^{15}}$$

Using a financial calculator, we find the yield to maturity to be 6.52 percent:

CALCULATOR SOLUTION

Data Input	Function Key
15	N
70	+/– PMT
1000	+/– FV
1045	PV

Function Key	Answer
CPT I/Y	6.52

1. Identify the basic characteristics and features of preferred stock.

2. Value preferred stock.

3. Identify the basic characteristics and features of common stock.

4. Value common stock.

5. Calculate a stock's expected rate of return.

CHAPTER 8

Valuation and Characteristics of Stock

PREFERRED STOCK • COMMON STOCK • THE STOCKHOLDER'S EXPECTED RATE OF
RETURN

When you invest in a common stock, as opposed to a bond, you are not promised any fixed interest or dividends. In fact, most companies today pay less than 2 percent in dividends to their common stockholders when compared to the price of the stock. Thus, the lion's share of the return that common stockholders receive comes from the stock appreciating in value, or the *capital gains*.

As we explained in Chapter 6, a stock's performance is largely influenced by how the stock market as a whole is doing. If the overall market is increasing in value, then most stocks—but not all by any means—will increase in value as well. Predicting how the market will do brings out some interesting approaches by investors. Most investors follow the major economic indicators, such as the strength of the dollar, inflation, earnings forecasts, and the risk of a terrorist attack, just to mention a few. But some investors develop their own approach to reading the "tea leaves":

Brian Pears, a stock trader in Cleveland, pays attention to several factors, including his "Garage Indicator." He looks at how much financial television local mechanics are watching. Too much, and stocks are likely to decline in value.

Brian Belski, a market analyst in Minneapolis, tracks earnings, interest rates, and the amount of speculative froth he senses when other hockey dads sidle over to ask stock questions during his son's games.[1]

Whatever approach we might use to guide us in buying and selling stock, we know one thing for certain: Investing in common stocks is risky. There are, however, some basics that we should know about when valuing stocks, whether as an individual investor or as a manager of a company.

In this chapter, we look closely at preferred stock and common stock and what determines the intrinsic value of these investments. How else can we realize the goal as a manager of increasing shareholder value if we do not know the underlying determinants of stock valuation?

[1]E. S. Browning, "Tea Leaves: With the Stock Market Stalled, Pros Hunt for Signs of a Peak; While Most Don't Think Run Is Over, Many Feel Big Gains May Be Behind; Hints From the Hockey Dads," *The Wall Street Journal*, March 9, 2004, p. A1.

✎ WHAT'S AHEAD ✎

In Chapter 7, we developed a general concept about valuation, and economic value was defined as the present value of the expected future cash flows generated by an asset. We then applied that concept to valuing bonds.

We continue our study of valuation in this chapter, but we now give our attention to valuing stocks, both preferred stock and common stock. As already noted at the outset of our study of finance and on several occasions since, the financial manager's objective should be to maximize the value of the firm's common stock. Thus, we need to understand what determines stock value. Also, only with an understanding of valuation can we compute a firm's cost of capital, a concept essential to making effective capital investment decisions—an issue to be discussed in Chapter 12.

PREFERRED STOCK

preferred stock

Preferred stock is often referred to as a *hybrid security* because it has *many characteristics of both common stock and bonds*. Preferred stock is similar to common stock in that (1) it has no fixed maturity date, (2) failure to pay dividends does not bring on bankruptcy, and (3) dividends are not deductible for tax purposes. On the other hand, preferred stock is similar to bonds in that dividends are fixed in amount.

The amount of the preferred stock dividend is generally fixed either as a dollar amount or as a percentage of the par value. For example, Texas Utility Electric (TXU) has preferred stock outstanding that pays an annual dividend of $1.81, while AT&T has some 8.25 percent preferred stock outstanding. The AT&T preferred stock has a par value of $25; hence, each share pays 8.25 percent × $25, or $2.06 in dividends annually.

To begin, we first discuss several features associated with almost all preferred stock. Then we take a brief look at methods of retiring preferred stock. We close by learning how to value preferred stock.

Objective 1

FEATURES OF PREFERRED STOCK

Although each issue of preferred stock is unique, a number of characteristics are common to almost all issues. Some of these more frequent traits include

- ➤ Multiple series of preferred stock
- ➤ Preferred stock's claim on assets and income
- ➤ Cumulative dividends
- ➤ Protective provisions
- ➤ Convertibility
- ➤ Retirement features

All these features are presented in the discussion that follows.

MULTIPLE SERIES

If a company desires, it can issue more than one series of preferred stock, and each series can have different characteristics. In fact, it is quite common for firms that issue preferred stock to issue more than one series. These issues can be differentiated in that some are convertible into common stock and others are not, and they have varying protective provisions in the event of bankruptcy. For instance, the Xerox Corporation has a Series B and Series C preferred stock.

CLAIM ON ASSETS AND INCOME

Preferred stock has priority over common stock with regard to claims on assets in the case of bankruptcy. The preferred stock claim is honored after that of bonds and before that of common stock. Multiple issues of preferred stock may be given an order of priority. Preferred stock also has a claim on income before common stock. That is, the firm must pay its preferred stock dividends before it pays common stock dividends. Thus, in terms of risk, preferred stock is safer than common stock because it has a prior claim on assets and income. However, it is riskier than long-term debt because its claims on assets and income come after those of bonds.

CUMULATIVE DIVIDENDS

cumulative feature

Most preferred stocks carry a **cumulative feature** that *requires all past, unpaid preferred stock dividends be paid before any common stock dividends are declared*. The purpose is to provide some degree of protection for the preferred shareholder. Without a cumulative feature, there would be no reason why preferred stock dividends would not be omitted or passed when common stock dividends were passed.

PROTECTIVE PROVISIONS

protective provisions

In addition to the cumulative feature, protective provisions are common to preferred stock. These **protective provisions** generally *allow for voting rights in the event of nonpayment of* *dividends, or they restrict the payment of common stock dividends if the preferred stock sinking-fund payments are not met or if the firm is in financial difficulty.* For example, consider Tenneco Corporation and Reynolds Metals preferred stocks. The Tenneco preferred stock has a protective provision that provides preferred stockholders with voting rights whenever six quarterly dividends are in arrears. At that point the preferred shareholders are given the power to elect a majority of the board of directors. The Reynolds Metals preferred stock includes a protective provision that precludes the payment of common stock dividends during any period in which the preferred stock sinking fund is in default. Both provisions, which give protection beyond that provided by the cumulative provision and thereby reduce the preferred shareholders' risk, are desirable. Because of these protective provisions, investors do not require as high a rate of return. That is, they will accept a lower dividend payment.

CONVERTIBILITY

Much of the preferred stock that is issued today is **convertible preferred stock**; that is, *at the discretion of the holder, the stock can be converted into a predetermined number of shares of common stock.* In fact, today about one-third of all preferred stock issued has a convertibility feature. The convertibility feature is, of course, desirable to the investor and, thus, reduces the cost of the preferred stock to the issuer.

convertible preferred stock

RETIREMENT FEATURES

Although preferred stock does not have a set maturity date associated with it, issuing firms generally provide for some method of retiring the stock, usually in the form of a call provision or a thinking fund.

Callable Preferred

Most preferred stock has some type of **call provision** associated with it. A call provision *entitles a company to repurchase its preferred stock from their holders at stated prices over a given time period.* In fact, the Securities and Exchange Commission discourages firms from issuing preferred stock without some call provision. For example, on January 3, 2005, Florida Power and Light redeemed (called) its Series V preferred stock.

call provision

The call feature on preferred stock usually involves an initial premium of approximately 10 percent above the par value or issuing price of the preferred stock. Then, over time, the call premium generally falls. By setting the initial call price above the initial issue price and allowing it to decline slowly over time, the firm protects the investor from an early call that carries no premium. A call provision also allows the issuing firm to plan the retirement of its preferred stock at predetermined prices.

Sinking-Fund Provision

A **sinking-fund provision** *requires the firm periodically to set aside an amount of money for the retirement of its preferred stock.* This money is then used to purchase the preferred stock in the open market or to call the stock, whichever method is cheaper. Although preferred stock does not have a maturity date associated with it, the use of a call provision in addition to a sinking fund can effectively create a maturity date. For instance, Xerox Corporation has two preferred stock issues, one that has a 7-year sinking-fund provision and another with a 17-year sinking fund. Another firm, SCANA Corporation, a $4.5 billion energy-based holding company in South Carolina, had preferred stock outstanding that both was callable and had a sinking-fund provision. By the terms of the issue, the stock's call premium above its par value was not to exceed the amount of the annual dividend, and the firm was to retire $2.4 million of stock per year from 1996 through 2000.

sinking-fund provision

VALUING PREFERRED STOCK

Objective **2**

As already explained, the owner of preferred stock generally receives a constant dividend from the investment in each period. In addition, most preferred stocks are perpetuities (nonmaturing). In this instance, finding the value (present value) of preferred stock, V_{ps}, with a level cash-flow stream continuing indefinitely, may best be explained by an example.

FINANCIAL MANAGEMENT
IN PRACTICE

READING A STOCK QUOTE IN THE WALL STREET JOURNAL

Following is a section of *The Wall Street Journal* that gives the quotes on January 14, 2005, for some of the stocks traded on the New York Stock Exchange that day.

The stocks listed include familiar companies—such as General Electric (GE), General Mills, and General Motors—that are listed in *The Wall Street Journal* on a daily basis. To help us understand how we read the quotes, consider General Electric.

- The "YTD% Chg" indicates that the General Electric stock price has declined 3.5 percent from one year ago.
- The 52-week *high* column shows General Electric stock reached a high of 37.75 ($37.75) during the past year.
- The 52-week *low* column shows that General Electric sold at a low of 28.88 ($28.88) during the past year.

- The *stock* (GenElec) and *sym* (GE) columns give an abbreviated version of the corporation's name and the ticker symbol, respectively.
- *Div*, the dividend column, gives the amount of dividend that General Electric paid its common stockholders in the last year; $.88 per share.
- *Yld%* (2.5) is the stock's dividend yield—the amount of the dividend divided by the day's closing price ($.88 ÷ $35.23).
- *PE* (23) gives the current market price (35.23) divided by the firm's earnings per share.
- The amount of General Electric stock traded on January 14, 2005, is represented in the *Vol 100s* column, or 14,074,400 shares.
- The previous day's closing price is subtracted from the closing price (*Last*) of 35.23 for January 14, 2005, for a net change (*Net Chg*) of –0.45.

| | 52 WEEKS | | | | | | | | |
YTD% CHG	HI	LO	STOCK (SYM)	DIV	YLD%	PE	VOL 100S	LAST	NET CHG
–3.5	37.75	28.88	GenElec GE	.88	2.5	23	140,744	35.23	–0.45
–7.8	36.90	24.31	GenGrthProp GGP	1.44	4.3	27	12,249	33.33	+0.59
–2.8	50.80	17.75	GenMaritime GMR		...	8	9,928	38.85	+0.84
+1.8	51.24	43.01	GenMills GIS	1.24	2.5	18	15,112	50.59	–0.37
–6.8	54.67	36.90	GenMotor GM	2.00	5.4	5	156,141	37.32	–1.07
–6.4	31.39	15.46	Genesco GCO		...	16	1,548	29.14	+0.54

EXAMPLE

Consider Xerox's Series C preferred stock issue. In similar fashion to valuing bonds in Chapter 7, we use a three-step valuation procedure.

Step 1: Estimate the amount and timing of the receipt of the future cash flows the preferred stock is expected to provide. Xerox's preferred stock pays an annual dividend of $6.25. The shares do not have a maturity date; that is, they are a perpetuity.

Step 2: Evaluate the riskiness of the preferred stock's future dividends and determine the investor's required rate of return. The investor's required rate of return is assumed to equal 5 percent for the Xerox preferred stock.[2]

Step 3: Calculate the economic or intrinsic value of the Xerox share of preferred stock, which is the present value of the expected dividends discounted at the investor's required rate of return. The valuation model for a share of preferred stock, V_{ps}, is, therefore, defined as follows:

$$V_{ps} = \frac{\text{dividend in year 1}}{(1 + \text{required rate of return})^1}$$

$$+ \frac{\text{dividend in year 2}}{(1 + \text{required rate of return})^2}$$

(8-1)

[2]In Chapter 6, we learned about measuring an investor's required rate of return.

$$+ \cdots + \frac{\text{dividend in infinity}}{(1 + \text{required rate of return})^{\infty}}$$

$$= \frac{D_1}{(1 + k_{ps})^1} + \frac{D_2}{(1 + k_{ps})^2} + \cdots + \frac{D_{\infty}}{(1 + k_{ps})^{\infty}}$$

Notice that equation (8-1) is a restatement in a slightly different form of equation (7-1) in Chapter 7. Recall that equation (7-1) states that the value of an asset is the present value of future cash flows to be received by the investor.

Because the dividends in each period are equal for preferred stock, equation (8-1) can be reduced to the following relationship:[3]

$$V_{ps} = \frac{\text{annual dividend}}{\text{required rate of return}} = \frac{D}{k_{ps}} \qquad (8\text{-}2)$$

Equation (8-2) represents the present value of an infinite stream of cash flows, when the cash flows are the same each year. We can determine the value of the Xerox preferred stock, using equation (8-2), as follows:

$$V_{ps} = \frac{D}{k_{ps}} = \frac{\$6.25}{0.05} = \$125.00$$

In summary, the value of a preferred stock is the present value of all future dividends. But because most preferred stocks are nonmaturing—the dividends continue to infinity—we, therefore, rely on a shortcut for finding value as represented by equation (8-2).

[3]To verify this result, we begin with equation (8-1):

$$V_{ps} = \frac{D_1}{(1 + k_{ps})^1} + \frac{D_2}{(1 + k_{ps})^2} + \cdots + \frac{D_n}{(1 + k_{ps})^n} \qquad (8\text{-}1)$$

If we multiply both sides of this equation by $(1 + k_{ps})$, we have

$$V_{ps}(1 + k_{ps}) = D_1 + \frac{D_2}{(1 + k_{ps})} + \cdots + \frac{D_n}{(1 + k_{ps})^{n-1}} \qquad (8\text{-}1\text{i})$$

Subtracting (8-1) from (8-1i) yields

$$V_{ps}(1 + k_{ps} - 1) = D_1 - \frac{D_n}{(1 + k_{ps})^n} \qquad (8\text{-}1\text{ii})$$

As n approaches infinity, $D_n/(1 + k_{ps})^n$ approaches zero. Consequently,

$$V_{ps}k_{ps} = D_1 \text{ and } V_{ps} = \frac{D_1}{k_{ps}} \qquad (8\text{-}1\text{iii})$$

Because $D_1 = D_2 = \ldots = D_n$ we need not designate the year. Therefore,

$$V_{ps} = \frac{D}{k_{ps}} \qquad (8\text{-}2)$$

BACK TO THE FOUNDATIONS

Valuing preferred stock relies on three of our principles presented in Chapter 1, namely:

Principle 1: The Risk–Return Trade-Off—We Won't Take On Additional Risk Unless We Expect to Be Compensated with Additional Return.

Principle 2: The Time Value of Money—A Dollar Received Today Is Worth More Than a Dollar Received in the Future.

Principle 3: Cash—Not Profits—Is King.

Determining the economic worth or value of an asset always relies on these three principles. Without them, we would have no basis for explaining value. With them, we can know that the amount and timing of cash, not earnings, drive value. Also, we must be rewarded for taking risk; otherwise, we will not invest.

CONCEPT CHECK

1. What features of preferred stock are different from bonds?
2. What provisions are available to protect a preferred stockholder?
3. What cash flows associated with preferred stock are included in valuation model (8-1)? Why is the valuation model simplified in equation (8-2)?

PROBLEM CHECK: VALUING PREFERRED STOCK

If a preferred stock pays 4 percent on its par or stated value of $100 and your required rate of return is 7 percent, what is the stock worth to you?

Check your answer on page 237.

COMMON STOCK

common stock

Common stock is *a certificate that indicates ownership in a corporation*. In effect, bondholders and preferred stockholders can be viewed as creditors, whereas the common stockholders are the true owners of the firm. Common stock does not have a maturity date but exists as long as the firm does. Nor does common stock have an upper limit on its dividend payments. Dividend payments must be declared each period (usually quarterly) by the firm's board of directors. In the event of bankruptcy, the common stockholders, as owners of the corporation, will not receive any payment until the firm's creditors, including the bondholders and preferred shareholders, have been satisfied.

In examining common stock, we first look at several of its features or characteristics. Then we focus on valuing common stock.

Objective **3**

FEATURES OR CHARACTERISTICS OF COMMON STOCK

We now examine common stock's claim on income and assets, stockholder voting rights, preemptive rights, and the meaning and importance of its limited-liability feature.

CLAIM ON INCOME

As the owners of a corporation, the common shareholders have the right to the residual income after bondholders and preferred stockholders have been paid. This income may be paid directly to the shareholders in the form of dividends or retained within the firm and reinvested in the business. Although it is obvious the shareholder benefits immediately from the distribution of income in the form of dividends, the reinvestment of earnings also benefits the shareholder. Plowing back earnings into the firm should result in an increase in the value of the firm, in its earning power, and in its future dividends. This action, in turn, should result in an increase in the value of the stock. In effect, residual income is distributed directly to shareholders in the form of dividends or indirectly in the form of capital gains on their common stock.

The right to residual income has advantages and disadvantages for the common stockholder. The advantage is that the potential return is limitless. Once the claims of the most senior securities (bonds and preferred stock) have been satisfied, the remaining income flows to the common stockholders in the form of dividends or capital gains. The disadvantage is that if the bond and preferred stock claims on income totally absorb earnings, common shareholders receive nothing. In years when earnings fall, it is the common shareholder who suffers first.

PROBLEM CHECK SOLUTION: VALUING PREFERRED STOCK

The value of the preferred stock would be $57.14:

$$\text{Value} = \frac{\text{dividend}}{\text{required rate of return}} = \frac{0.04 \times \$100}{0.07} = \frac{\$4}{0.07} = \$57.14$$

CLAIM ON ASSETS

Just as common stock has a residual claim on income, it also has a residual claim on assets in the case of liquidation. Only after the claims of debt holders and preferred stockholders have been satisfied do the claims of common shareholders receive any consideration. Unfortunately, when bankruptcy does occur, the claims of the common shareholders generally go unsatisfied. This residual claim on assets adds to the risk of common stock. Thus, although common stock has historically provided a large return, averaging 12 percent annually since the late 1920s, it also has higher risk associated with it.

VOTING RIGHTS

The common stock shareholders are entitled to elect the board of directors and are, in general, the only security holders given a vote. With the merger boom of the 1980s, dual classes of common stock with different voting rights emerged as a defensive tactic used to prevent takeovers. However, with the increased activism of shareholders, especially large institutional shareholders during recent years, dual classes of stock have been discouraged.

Common shareholders have the right not only to elect the board of directors but also to approve any change in the corporate charter. A typical change might involve the authorization to issue new stock or to accept a merger proposal.

Voting for directors and charter changes occurs at the corporation's annual meeting. Although shareholders may vote in person, the majority generally vote by proxy. A **proxy** *gives a designated party the temporary power of attorney to vote for the signee at the corporation's annual meeting.* The firm's management generally solicits proxy votes and, if the shareholders are satisfied with the firm's performance, management has little problem securing them. However, in times of financial distress or when management takeovers are threatened, **proxy fights**—*battles between rival groups for proxy votes*—occur.

Although each share of stock carries the same number of votes, the voting procedure is not always the same from company to company. The two procedures commonly used are majority and cumulative voting. Under **majority voting**, *each share of stock allows the shareholder one vote, and each position on the board of directors is voted on separately*. Because each member of the board of directors is elected by a simple majority, a majority of shares has the power to elect the entire board of directors.

With **cumulative voting**, *each share of stock allows the stockholder a number of votes equal to the number of directors being elected*. The shareholder can then cast all of his or her votes for a single candidate or split them among the various candidates. The advantage of a cumulative voting procedure is that it gives minority shareholders the power to elect a director.

proxy

proxy fights

majority voting

cumulative voting

FINANCIAL MANAGEMENT
IN PRACTICE

WHAT DOES A STOCK LOOK LIKE?

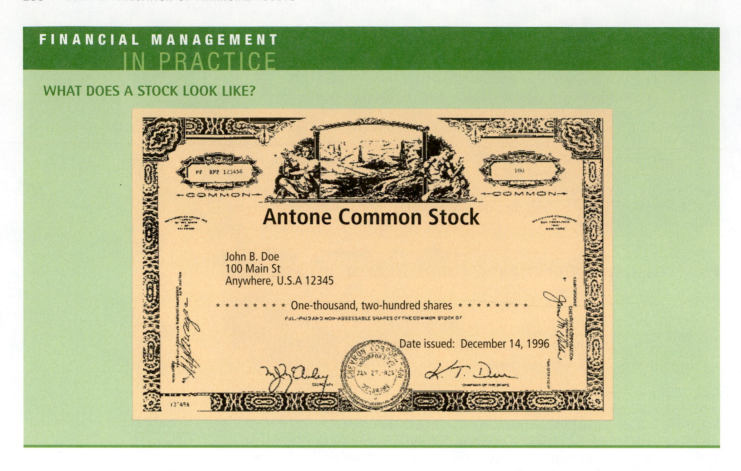

In theory, the shareholders pick the corporate board of directors, generally through proxy voting, and the board of directors, in turn, picks the management. In reality, shareholders are offered a slate of nominees selected by management from which to choose. The end result is that management effectively selects the directors, who then may have more allegiance to the managers than to the shareholders. This sets up the potential for agency problems in which a divergence of interests between managers and shareholders is allowed to exist, with the board of directors not monitoring the managers on behalf of the shareholders as they should.

PREEMPTIVE RIGHTS

preemptive right

The **preemptive right** *entitles the common shareholder to maintain a proportionate share of ownership in the firm.* When new shares are issued, common shareholders have the first right of refusal. If a shareholder owns 25 percent of the corporation's stock, then he or she is entitled to purchase 25 percent of the new shares. *Certificates issued to the shareholders giving them an option to purchase a stated number of new shares of stock at a specified price during a 2- to 10-week period* are called **rights**. These rights can be exercised (generally at a price set by management below the common stock's current market price), allowed to expire, or sold in the open market.

rights

LIMITED LIABILITY

Although the common shareholders are the actual owners of the corporation, their *liability in the case of bankruptcy is limited to the amount of their investment.* The advantage is that investors who might not otherwise invest their funds in the firm become willing to do so. This **limited liability** feature aids the firm in raising funds.

limited liability

FINANCIAL MANAGEMENT
IN PRACTICE

WHAT DO YOU TELL YOUR SHAREHOLDERS?

If you want a higher share price, what would you tell your investors? Suppose that someone asks you whether your company's share price is too high, too low, or just right. What should you say? If you think the answer depends on the circumstances, then you had best think again.

Most chief executives understand that they are, above all, salespersons, trying to convince the financial markets that their company is a good buy. But whereas ordinary salespeople are told that the customer is always right, most CEOs act as if the investors are always wrong. The CEO complains about the market's short-term focus and has little appreciation for analysts who follow the firm's stock.

Pleasing investors, however, is becoming more complicated. Besides the usual backward-looking financial measures, investors also want managers to be specific about their firm's future prospects, and they want more nonfinancial information to help them fill in the picture. Some advocates also want firms to provide more details about their "corporate governance" practices, such as boardroom procedures and ethical guidelines.

In a study by Shelley Taylor & Associates, "The Care and Feeding of Institutional Investors," the researchers examined the demands of the largest institutional investors in America, Britain, and continental Europe and compared these with what firms actually disclose. The study found that investors rate one measure above all else: *free cash flow*.

Most managers, however, have refused to believe this. Instead, they continue to rely on accrual accounting measures to make decisions, frequently destroying value in the process. This has discouraged firms from being frank with shareholders. Although the disclosure of cash flow itself is easy enough (and is required by many accounting standards), Shelley Taylor's research suggests that information that helps investors gauge future cash flows is guarded closely.

There was another interesting finding. Of the 19 kinds of corporate governance information considered, only one—executive pay—ranked among the top 20 issues investors care about. Specifically, they are concerned about the way in which pay relates to performance, not with just the amount. The rationale: An executive's incentives have a large effect on future performance.

VALUING COMMON STOCK

Objective 4

Like bonds and preferred stock, a common stock's value is equal to the present value of all future cash flows expected to be received by the stockholder. However, in contrast to bonds, common stock does not promise its owners interest income or a maturity payment at some specified time in the future. Given the uniqueness of common stock, compared with bonds and preferred stock, we will consider two approaches to valuing common stock:

1. The value of a common stock is equal to the present value of all future dividends—the same approach just used in valuing preferred stock, but with some twists and turns, as we will see.
2. The value of a common stock is equal to the total firm or enterprise value less the firm's outstanding debt, where the firm value is equal to the present value of the firm's *free cash flows*.

Each of these approaches will now be explained.

COMMON STOCK VALUE: THE PRESENT VALUE OF FUTURE DIVIDENDS

In contrast to preferred stock dividends, common stock does not provide the investor with a predetermined, constant dividend. For common stock, the dividend is based on the profitability of the firm and on management's decision to pay dividends or to retain the profits for reinvestment. As a consequence, dividend streams tend to increase with the growth in corporate earnings. Thus, the growth of future dividends is a prime distinguishing feature of common stock.

THE GROWTH FACTOR IN VALUING COMMON STOCK

What is meant by the term *growth* when used in the context of valuing common stock? A company can grow in a variety of ways. It can become larger by borrowing money to invest in new projects. Likewise, it can issue new stock for expansion. Management can also acquire another company to merge with the existing firm, which would increase the firm's assets. In all these cases, the firm is growing through the use of new financing, by issuing debt or common stock. Although management can accurately say that the firm has grown, the original stockholders may or may not participate in this growth. Growth is realized through the infusion of new capital. The firm size clearly increases, but unless the original investors increase their investment in the firm, they will own a smaller portion of the expanded business.

internal growth

Another means of growing is **internal growth**, which requires that *management retain some or all of the firm's profits for reinvestment in the firm*, resulting in the growth of future earnings and, hopefully, the value of the common stock. This process underlies the essence of potential growth for the firm's current stockholders and is the only relevant growth for our purposes in valuing a firm's common shares.[4]

EXAMPLE

To illustrate the nature of internal growth, assume that the return on equity for PepsiCo is 16 percent.[5] If PepsiCo's management decides to pay all the profits out in dividends to its stockholders, the firm will experience no growth internally. It might become larger by borrowing more money or issuing new stock, but internal growth will come only through the retention of profits. If, on the other hand, PepsiCo retained all the profits, the stockholders' investment in the firm would grow by the amount of profits retained, or by 16 percent. If, however, management kept only 50 percent of the profits for reinvestment, the common shareholders' investment would increase only by half of the 16 percent return on equity, or by 8 percent. We can express this relationship by the following equation:

$$g = ROE \times r$$

where g = the growth rate of future earnings and the growth in the common stockholders' investment in the firm

ROE = the return on equity (net income/common book value)

profit-retention rate

r = *the company's percentage of profits retained*, called the **profit-retention rate**[6]

Therefore, if only 25 percent of the profits were retained by PepsiCo, we would expect the common stockholders' investment in the firm and the value of the stock price to increase or grow by 4 percent; that is,

$$g = 16\% \times 0.25 = 4\%$$

In summary, common stockholders frequently rely on an increase in the stock price as a source of return. If the company is retaining a portion of its earnings for reinvestment, future profits and dividends should grow. This growth should be reflected in an increased market price of the common stock in future periods, provided that the return

---

[4]We are not arguing that the existing common stockholders never benefit from the use of external financing; however, such benefit is nominal if capital markets are efficient.

[5]The return on equity is the accounting rate of return on the common shareholders' investment in the company and is computed as follows:

$$\text{Return on equity} = \frac{\text{net income}}{(\text{common stock} + \text{retained earnings})}$$

dividend-payout ratio

[6]The retention rate is also equal to (1 − the percentage of profits paid out in dividends). *The percentage of profits paid out in dividends* is often called the **dividend-payout ratio**.

on the funds reinvested exceeds the investor's required rate of return. Therefore, both types of return (dividends and price appreciation) must be recognized in valuing common stock.

PROBLEM CHECK: MEASURING MICROSOFT'S GROWTH RATE

In 2003, Microsoft had a return on equity of 12 percent. The firm's earnings per share was $0.74, and the firm paid $0.32 in dividends per share. If these relationships hold in the future, what will be the firm's internal growth rate?

Check your answer below.

DIVIDEND VALUATION MODEL

The value of a common stock when defining value as the present value of future dividends relies on the same basic equation that we used with preferred stock [equation (8-1)], with the exception that we are using the required rate of return of common stockholders, k_{cs}. That is,

$$V_{cs} = \frac{D_1}{(1+k_{cs})^1} + \frac{D_2}{(1+k_{cs})^2} + \cdots + \frac{D_n}{(1+k_{cs})^n} + \cdots + \frac{D_\infty}{(1+k_{cs})^\infty} \tag{8-3}$$

> ### PAUSE AND REFLECT
>
> Turn back to Chapter 7 and compare equation (7-1) with equation (8-4). Equation (8-4) is merely a restatement in a slightly different form of equation (7-1). Recall that equation (7-1), which is the basis for our work in valuing securities, states that the value of an asset is the present value of future cash flows to be received by the investor. Equation (8-4) is simply applying equation (7-1) to valuing common stock.

PROBLEM CHECK SOLUTION: MEASURING MICROSOFT'S GROWTH RATE

Microsoft's internal growth rate would be 6.81 percent: Microsoft is paying out 43.24 percent of its earnings in dividends (43.24% = $0.32 dividends per share ÷ $0.74 earnings per share), which means that the firm is retaining 56.76 percent of its earnings (56.76% = 100% − 43.24%). Given that the firm has a 12 percent return on equity, its internal growth rate would be 8.21 percent (6.81% = 12% return on equity × 0.5676 earnings retained per dollar of earnings).

Equation (8-4) indicates that we are discounting the dividend at the end of the first year, D_1, back 1 year; the dividend in the second year, D_2, back 2 years; the dividend in the nth year back n years; and the dividend in infinity back an infinite number of years. The required rate of return is k_{cs}. In using equation (8-4), note that the value of the stock is established at the beginning of the year, say January 1, 2006. The most recent past dividend, D_0, would have been paid the previous day, December 31, 2005. Thus, if we purchased the stock on January 1, the first dividend would be received in 12 months, on December 31, 2006, which is represented by D_1.

Fortunately, equation (8-4) can be reduced to a much more manageable form if dividends grow each year at a constant rate, g. The constant-growth common-stock valuation equation may be presented as follows:[7]

$$\text{Common stock value} = \frac{\text{dividend in year 1}}{\text{required rate of return} - \text{growth rate}}$$

$$V_{cs} = \frac{D_1}{k_{cs} - g} \tag{8-4}$$

Consequently, the intrinsic value (present value) of a share of common stock whose dividends grow at a constant annual rate can be calculated using equation (8-4). Although the interpretation of this equation may not be intuitively obvious, simply remember that it solves for the present value of the future dividend stream growing at a rate, g, to infinity, assuming that k_{cs} is greater than g.

EXAMPLE

Consider the valuation of a share of common stock that paid a $2 dividend at the end of the last year and is expected to pay a cash dividend every year from now to infinity. Each year the dividends are expected to grow at a rate of 10 percent. Based on an assessment of the riskiness of the common stock, the investor's required rate of return is 15 percent. Using this information, we would compute the value of the common stock as follows:

1. Because the $2 dividend was paid last year (actually, yesterday), we must compute the next dividend to be received, that is, D_1, where

$$\begin{aligned} D_1 &= D_0(1 + g) \\ &= \$2(1 + .10) \\ &= \$2.20 \end{aligned}$$

[7]When common stock dividends grow at a constant rate of g every year, we can express the dividend in any year in terms of the dividend paid at the end of the previous year, D_0. For example, the expected dividend 1 year hence is simply $D_0(1 + g)$. Likewise, the dividend at the end of t years is $D_0(1 + g)^t$. Using this notation, the common-stock valuation equation in (8-3) can be rewritten as follows:

$$V_{cs} = \frac{D_0(1 + g)^1}{(1 + k_{cs})^1} + \frac{D_0(1 + g)^2}{(1 + k_{cs})^2} + \cdots + \frac{D_0(1 + g)^n}{(1 + k_{cs})^n} + \cdots + \frac{D_0(1 + g)^\infty}{(1 + k_{cs})^\infty} \tag{8-3i}$$

If both sides of equation (8-5) are multiplied by $(1 + k_{cs})/(1 + g)$ and then equation (8-4) is subtracted from the product, the result is

$$\frac{V_{cs}(1 + k_{cs})}{1 + g} - V_{cs} = D_0 - \frac{D_0(1 + g)^\infty}{(1 + k_{cs})^\infty} \tag{8-3ii}$$

If $k_{cs} > g$, which normally should hold, $[D_0(1 + g)^\infty/(1 + k_{cs})^\infty]$ approaches zero. As a result,

$$\frac{V_{cs}(1 + k_{cs})}{1 + g} - V_{cs} = D_0$$

$$V_{cs}\left(\frac{1 + k_{cs}}{1 + g}\right) - V_{cs}\left(\frac{1 + g}{1 + g}\right) = D_0$$

$$V_{cs}\left[\frac{(1 + k_{cs}) - (1 + g)}{1 + g}\right] = D_0 \tag{8-3iii}$$

$$V_{cs}(k_{cs} - g) = D_0(1 + g)$$

$$V_{cs} = \frac{D_1}{k_{cs} - g} \tag{8-4}$$

2. Now, using equation (8-4),

$$V_{cs} = \frac{D_1}{k_{cs} - g}$$

$$= \frac{\$2.20}{.15 - .10}$$

$$= \$44$$

BACK TO THE FOUNDATIONS

Valuing common stock is no different from valuing preferred stock; only the pattern of the cash flows changes. Thus, the valuation of common stock relies on the same three principles developed in Chapter 1 that were used in valuing preferred stock:

Principle 1: The Risk–Return Trade-Off—We Won't Take on Additional Risk Unless We Expect to Be Compensated with Additional Return.

Principle 2: The Time Value of Money—A Dollar Received Today Is Worth More Than a Dollar Received in the Future.

Principle 3: Cash—Not Profits—Is King.

Determining the economic worth or value of an asset always relies on these three principles. Without them, we would have no basis for explaining value. With them, we can know that the amount and timing of cash, not earnings, drives value. Also, we must be rewarded for taking risk; otherwise, we will not invest.

We have argued that the value of a common stock is equal to the present value of all future dividends, which is without question a fundamental premise of finance. In practice, however, managers, along with many security analysts, often talk about the relationship between stock value and earnings, rather than dividends. We would encourage you to be very cautious in using earnings to value a stock. Even though it may be a popular practice, significant evidence available suggests that investors look to the cash flows generated by the firm, not the earnings, for value. A firm's value truly is the present value of the cash flows it produces.

We now turn to our second approach for estimating the value of a common stock—the present value of free cash flows.

CONCEPT CHECK

1. What features of common stock indicate ownership in the corporation versus preferred stock or bonds?

2. What are the two ways that a shareholder benefits from ownership?

3. How does internal growth versus the infusion of new capital affect the original shareholders?

4. If a corporation decides to retain its earnings, when will the value of the market price actually decrease?

5. Describe the process for common stock valuation.

PROBLEM CHECK: CALCULATING COMMON STOCK VALUE

The Abraham Corporation paid $1.32 in dividends per share *last year*. The firm's projected growth rate is 6 percent for the foreseeable future. If an investor's required rate of return for a firm with Abraham's level of risk is 10 percent, what is the value of the stock?

Check your answer on page 244.

$$\frac{1.32\,(1.06)}{.10 - .06}$$

PROBLEM CHECK SOLUTION: CALCULATING COMMON STOCK VALUE

Abraham's stock value would be $35:

$$\text{Value} = \frac{\text{dividend year 1}}{\text{required rate of return} - \text{growth rate}}$$

$$= \frac{\$1.32 \times (1 + .06)}{0.10 - 0.06} = \frac{\$1.40}{0.04} = \$35$$

COMMON STOCK VALUE: THE PRESENT VALUE OF FREE CASH FLOWS

free cash flows

Free cash flow valuation defines the value of a firm as the present value of its expected future cash flows. More specifically, a firm's *economic* or *intrinsic* value is equal to the present value of its future **free cash flows** discounted at the company's cost of capital—the required rate of return of the firm's investors. We then compute shareholder value as the firm value less the value of outstanding interest-bearing debt, such as bonds and bank notes.

In Chapter 3 we learned to compute a firm's historical free cash flows. We specifically said that a firm's free cash flows are determined as follows:

> **Operating income**
>
> + depreciation and amortization
> − tax expense
> = after-tax cash flows from operations
> − the investment (increase) in the firm's assets, both net working capital and capital expenditures in plant and equipment
> = free cash flows

We are now interested in predicting the firm's *future*, rather than its *historical*, free cash flows and then finding the present value of these cash flows as a measure of firm value. The actual process is as follows:

competitive-advantage period

1. We decide on a **competitive-advantage period**, which represents the number of years management believes it can sustain a competitive advantage, given the present strategies.
2. We estimate the free cash flows for each year of the competitive-advantage period. For instance, if management thinks the firm has a 5-year competitive-advantage period, it will estimate the free cash flows for each year through the fifth year.
3. We next make an assumption that the free cash flows in all subsequent years (e.g., the sixth year on) will grow at a constant growth rate each year, much like we did when we were using the dividend-valuation approach described earlier. With this assumption, we can determine the free cash flow for the first year of the residual period, e.g., year 6.
4. Given the projected cash flows, we
   a. Calculate the present value of the free cash flows (FCF_t) during the competitive-advantage period expected to continue through year T, discounted at the cost of capital, k:

present value
competitive-advantage period

$$PV_{CAP^2} = \frac{FCF_1}{(1+k)^1} + \frac{FCF_2}{(1+k)^2} + \frac{FCF_3}{(1+k)^3}$$

$$+ \cdots \frac{FCF_T}{(1+k)^T}$$

(8-5)

b. Compute the firm's **residual value** as of the end of the competitive-advantage period, where the residual value is the present value of the post-competitive-advantage period cash flows.

By assuming that the firm's free cash flows will grow at a constant growth rate, we can compute the firm's residual value (RV_T) as of year T, based on free cash flows, (FCF_t), beginning one year later at $T+1$. That is,

$$\text{Residual value (year } T) = RV_T = \frac{FCF_{T+1}}{k-g} \tag{8-6}$$

c. We then calculate the present value of the residual value (RV_0)

$$\text{Present value of the residual value} = RV_0 = \frac{\text{residual value year } T}{(1+k)^T} \tag{8-7}$$

d. Firm value is then found as follows:

$$\text{Firm value} = \text{present value} \left(\begin{array}{c} \text{competitive-advantage} \\ \text{period cash flows} \end{array} \right) + \text{present value} \left(\begin{array}{c} \text{residual} \\ \text{value} \end{array} \right) \tag{8-8}$$

e. We subtract the firm's outstanding debt from the firm value to determine the shareholder or stock value:

$$\text{Shareholder value} = \text{firm value} - \text{debt} \tag{8-9}$$

f. Finally, we divide the shareholder value by the number of shares outstanding to arrive at the value per share.

ILLUSTRATING THE FREE CASH FLOW MODEL

We can best clarify the free cash flow valuation method by an illustration. Let's assume the following facts and estimates about the Fadelu Corporation:

➤ Sales for the most recent period (last year) were $1,000.
➤ Management anticipates sales to grow at 12 percent annually for 2 years, 8 percent in years 3 through 5, and 4 percent thereafter.
➤ The firm's operating profit margin (operating income ÷ sales) is expected to be 12 percent.
➤ The corporation's tax rate is 40 percent.
➤ The firm's assets as a percentage of sales are expected to be 45 percent for the foreseeable future. That is, for each increase in sales of $1, we would expect assets to increase $.45.
➤ The firm's cost of capital (the discount rate) is 12 percent.
➤ The company has $250 of debt outstanding.
➤ The firm has 100 shares of common stock outstanding.

The Excel spreadsheet used to compute the Chai Corporation's shareholder value is shown in Table 8-1. (This spreadsheet is available at **www.prenhall.com/keown**.) The calculations involve the following steps:

1. Based on the assumptions given, we compute the annual free cash flows for the competitive-advantage period (years 1 through 5) and for the first year of the post-competitive-advantage period (year 6). For instance, the free cash flow in the first year is computed below. (The numbers have been rounded to the nearest dollar, which may create rounding differences.)

Sales	$1,120	[$1,000 last year's sales × (1 + 12% growth rate)]
Operating profits	134	[$1,120 sales × 12% operating profit margin]
Taxes	54	[$134 operating profits × 40% tax rate]
After-tax profits	$ 81	[operating profits − taxes]
Increase in assets	54	[(increase in sales $1,120 − $1,000 = $120) × 45% assets-to-sales ratio]
Free cash flows	$ 27	[after-tax profits − increase in assets]

TABLE 8-1 Free Cash Flow Valuation: The Fadelu Corporation

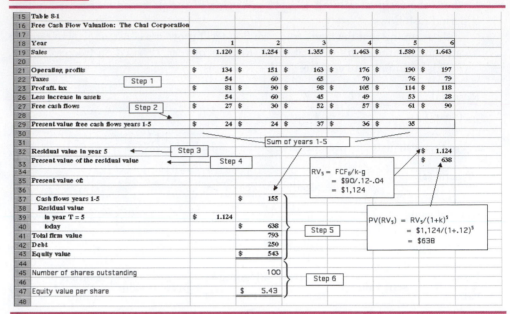

15	Table 8-1							
16	Free Cash Flow Valuation: The Chai Corporation							
17								
18	Year		1	2	3	4	5	6
19	Sales	$	1.120	$ 1.254	$ 1.355	$ 1.463	$ 1.580	$ 1.643
20								
21	Operating profits	$	134	$ 151	$ 163	$ 176	$ 190	$ 197
22	Taxes *Step 1*		54	60	65	70	76	79
23	Prof aft. tax	$	81	$ 90	$ 98	$ 105	$ 114	$ 118
26	Less Increase in assets		54	60	45	49	53	28
27	Free cash flows *Step 2*	$	27	$ 30	$ 52	$ 57	$ 61	$ 90
28								
29	Present value free cash flows years 1-5	$	24	$ 24	$ 37	$ 36	$ 35	
30								
31		Sum of years 1-5						
32	Residual value in year 5 *Step 3*							$ 1.124
33	Present value of the residual value *Step 4*							$ 638
34								
35	Present value of:							
36								
37	Cash flows years 1-5		$ 155					
38	Residual value							
39	in year T = 5	$ 1.124						
40	today		$ 638					
41	Total firm value *Step 5*		793					
42	Debt		250					
43	Equity value		$ 543					
44								
45	Number of shares outstanding		100					
46		*Step 6*						
47	Equity value per share		$ 5.43					
48								

$RV_5 = FCF_6/k-g$
   $= \$90/.12-.04$
   $= \$1,124$

$PV(RV_5) = RV_5/(1+k)^5$
   $= \$1,124/(1+.12)^5$
   $= \$638$

Note that the numbers have been rounded to the nearest dollars, which may create rounding differences.

Note that free cash flows are found by computing after-tax operating profits and subtracting the *incremental* investments, where the incremental investments are determined by computing the *change in sales for the year* multiplied by the percentage of the assets-to-sales relationship.

Also, observe that we did not add back depreciation expense, as is usually done in computing free cash flow. Instead, it is common practice in a free cash flow model to assume that the depreciation expense equals the cost of replacing fixed assets. That is, accounting depreciation is assumed to equal the economic depreciation—the actual cost of replacing depreciating assets. Therefore, we do not add back any depreciation expense, but neither do we show a cash outflow for the cost of replacing already existing fixed assets. Additions to fixed assets only include those investments resulting from firm growth, not from replacements.

2. Find the present value of the cash flows during the competitive-advantage period (years 1 to 5) by discounting each year's cash flows back to the present and summing the results:

$$\text{Present value} = \frac{\$27}{(1+0.12)^1} + \frac{\$30}{(1+0.12)^2} + \frac{\$52}{(1+0.12)^3} + \frac{\$57}{(1+0.12)^4} + \frac{\$61}{(1+0.12)^5} = \$24 + \$24 + \$37 + \$36 + \$35 = \$155$$

3. Determine the residual value (value of all future free cash flows beginning in year 6 and beyond) as of year 5 as follows:

$$\text{Residual value}_5 = \frac{FCF_6}{k-g} = \frac{\$90}{.12-.04} = \$1,124$$

4. Discount the residual value in year 5 back to the present, giving us a value of

$$\frac{\text{Present value}}{\text{of the residual value}} = \frac{\text{residual value year 5}}{(1+k)^5} = \frac{\$1,124}{(1+.12)^5} = \$638$$

5. Combine the two present values to determine a firm value of $793, and subtract the debt of $250 to find the shareholder value of $543.

6. Divide the shareholder value, $543, by the number of shares outstanding (100) to determine a value per share of $5.43.

The foregoing approach to valuing a firm and its shareholder value has become relatively popular in practice. We will see this same basic approach used in assigning value to individual fixed-asset investments when we look at capital budgeting decisions, so don't forget the process of valuing an asset or a firm based on the present value of its free cash flows.

PROBLEM CHECK: COMPUTING STOCK VALUE (A FREE CASH FLOW APPROACH)

You have been asked to determine the stock value for the Davies Corporation, a small computer supplies business. Given the following information, calculate the firm's stock value based on the free cash flow valuation approach:

1. The firm had sales last year of $2 million, and the owner expects sales to grow at 10 percent for two years and 4 percent thereafter.
2. The operating profit margin is expected to be 15 percent with a tax rate of 30 percent.
3. The firm has maintained a 40 percent asset-to-sales relationship, which should continue into the future. That is, for every $1 of sales, the firm has $0.40 in assets.
4. The company has $500,000 in outstanding debt.
5. The firm's cost of capital (discount rate for finding the present value of future cash flows) is 12 percent.
6. There are 150,000 shares outstanding.

Check your answer with the solution on page 248.

THE STOCKHOLDER'S EXPECTED RATE OF RETURN

Objective **5**

As stated in Chapter 7, the expected rate of return, or yield to maturity, on a bond is the return the bondholder expects to receive on the investment by paying the existing market price for the security. This rate of return is of interest to the financial manager because it tells the manager about the investor's expectations. The same can be said for the financial manager needing to know the expected rate of return of the firm's stockholders, which is the topic of this section.

THE PREFERRED STOCKHOLDER'S EXPECTED RATE OF RETURN

In computing the preferred stockholder's expected rate of return, we use the valuation equation for preferred stock. Earlier, equation (8-2) specified the value of a preferred stock, V_{ps}, as

$$V_{ps} = \frac{\text{annual dividend}}{\text{required rate of return}} = \frac{D}{k_{ps}} \tag{8-2}$$

Solving equation (8-2) for k_{ps}, we have

$$k_{ps} = \frac{\text{annual dividend}}{\text{preferred stock value}} = \frac{D}{V_{ps}} \tag{8-10}$$

Thus, a preferred stockholder's *required* rate of return simply equals the stock's annual dividend divided by the intrinsic value. We may also restate equation (8-8) to solve for a preferred stock's *expected* rate of return, $\bar{k}_{ps}$, as follows:[8]

$$\bar{k}_{ps} = \frac{\text{annual dividend}}{\text{preferred stock market price}} = \frac{D}{P_{ps}} \tag{8-11}$$

Note that we have merely substituted the current market price, P_{ps}, for the intrinsic value, V_{ps}. The expected rate of return, $\bar{k}_{ps}$, therefore, equals the annual dividend relative to the price the stock is currently selling for P_{ps}. Thus, the **expected rate of return**, $\bar{k}_{ps}$, is the rate of return the investor can expect to earn from the investment if bought at the current market price.

expected rate of return

---

[8] We will use $\bar{k}$ to represent a security's *expected* rate of return versus k for the investor's *required* rate of return.

For example, if the present market price of preferred stock is $50 and it pays a $3.64 annual dividend, the expected rate of return implicit in the present market price is

$$\bar{k}_{ps} = \frac{D}{P_{ps}} = \frac{\$3.64}{\$50} = 7.28\%$$

Therefore, investors (who pay $50 per share for a preferred security that is paying $3.64 in annual dividends) are expecting a 7.28 percent rate of return.

PROBLEM CHECK SOLUTION: COMPUTING STOCK VALUE (A FREE CASH FLOW APPROACH)

The solution to this problem involves the following steps:

Step 1: Compute the free cash flows for the three years of data given, where sales are growing at 10 percent for two years, followed by growth of 4 percent beginning in year 3 and continuing in perpetuity.

Step 2: Find the present value of the first two years of free cash flows.

Step 3: Using year 3 as the first year of the perpetual constant growth rate, we compute the residual value of the firm, as of year 2.

Step 4: Compute the present value of the residual value.

Step 5: Sum the present value of the cash flows, both for years 1 and 2 and for the residual value to determine the firm value, and then subtract the firm's debt to find the total equity value.

Step 6: Divide the total equity value by the number of shares outstanding to arrive at the equity value per share.

Using an Excel spreadsheet, the value per share is found to be $18.64, computed as follows (numbers rounded to the nearest dollars):

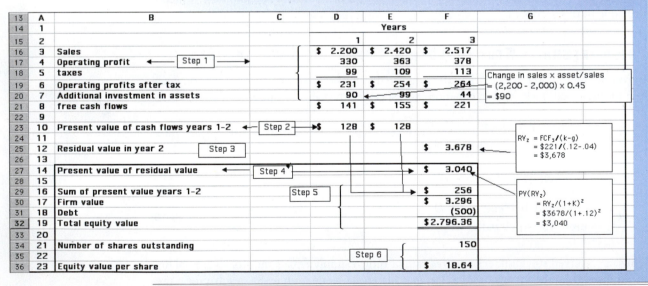

THE COMMON STOCKHOLDER'S EXPECTED RATE OF RETURN

The valuation equation for common stock was defined earlier in equation (8-4) as

$$\text{Common stock value} = \frac{\text{dividend in year 1}}{(1 + \text{required rate of return})^1} + \frac{\text{dividend in year 2}}{(1 + \text{required rate of return})^2}$$

$$+ \cdots + \frac{\text{dividend in year infinity}}{(1 + \text{required rate of return})^\infty} \qquad (8\text{-}3)$$

$$V_{cs} = \frac{D_1}{(1 + k_{cs})^1} + \frac{D_2}{(1 + k_{cs})^2} + \cdots + \frac{D_\infty}{(1 + k_{cs})^\infty}$$

Owing to the difficulty of discounting to infinity, we made the key assumption that the dividends, D_t, increase at a constant annual compound growth rate of g. If this assumption is valid, equation (8-4) was shown to be equivalent to

$$\text{Common stock value} = \frac{\text{dividend in year 1}}{\text{required rate of return} - \text{growth rate}}$$

$$V_{cs} = \frac{D_1}{k_{cs} - g}$$

(8-4)

Thus, V_{cs} represents the maximum value that an investor having a required rate of return of k_{cs} would pay for a security having an anticipated dividend in year 1 of D_1 that is expected to grow in future years at rate g. Solving equation (8-4) for k_{cs}, we can compute the common stockholder's required rate of return as follows:[9]

$$k_{cs} = \frac{D_1}{V_{cs}} + g$$

(8-12)

dividend yield | annual growth rate

From this equation, the common stockholder's required rate of return is equal to the dividend yield plus a growth factor. Although the growth rate, g, applies to the growth in the company's dividends, given our assumptions the stock's value may also be expected to increase at the same rate. For this reason, g represents the annual percentage growth in the stock value. In other words, the investor's required rate of return is satisfied by receiving dividends and capital gains, as reflected by the expected percentage growth rate in the stock price.

As was done for preferred stock earlier, we may revise equation (8-12) to measure a common stock's *expected* rate of return, $\bar{k}_{cs}$. Replacing the intrinsic value, V_{cs}, in equation (8-12) with the stock's current market price, P_{cs}, we may express the stock's expected rate of return as follows:

$$\bar{k}_{cs} = \frac{\text{dividend in year 1}}{\text{market price}} + \frac{\text{growth}}{\text{rate}} = \frac{D_1}{P_{cs}} + g$$

(8-13)

EXAMPLE

As an example of computing the expected rate of return for a common stock when dividends are anticipated to grow at a constant rate to infinity, assume that a firm's common stock has a current market price of $44. If the expected dividend at the conclusion of this year is $2.20 and dividends and earnings are growing at a 10 percent annual rate (last year's dividend was $2), the expected rate of return implicit in the $44 stock price is as follows:

$$\bar{k}_{cs} = \frac{\$2.20}{\$44} + 10\% = 15\%$$

Most of the returns on stocks come from price appreciation, or capital gains, with a smaller part of the return coming from dividends. The Standard & Poor's 500 Index, for example, returned a 12 percent annual return on average over the past 10 years. The dividend yield (dividend ÷ stock price) accounted for about 2 percent of the return, with the remaining 10 percent resulting from price appreciation.

[9]At times the expected dividend at year-end (D_1) is not given. Instead, we might only know the most recent dividend (paid yesterday), that is, D_0. If so, equation (8-7) must be restated as follows:

$$V_{cs} = \frac{D_1}{(k_{cs} - g)} = \frac{D_0(1 + g)}{(k_{cs} - g)}$$

PROBLEM CHECK: COMPUTING THE EXPECTED RATE OF RETURN

Calculate the expected rate of return for the two following stocks:

Preferred stock: The stock is selling for $80 and pays a 5 percent dividend on its $100 par or stated value.

Common stock: The stock paid a dividend of $4 last year and is expected to increase each year at a 5 percent growth rate. The stock sells for $75.

Check your answer below.

BACK TO THE FOUNDATIONS

We have just learned that on average, the expected return will be equal to the investor's required rate of return. This equilibrium condition is achieved by investors paying for an asset only the amount that will exactly satisfy their required rate of return. Thus, finding the expected rate of return based on the current market price for the security relies on two of the principles given in Chapter 1:

Principle 1: The Risk–Return Trade-Off—We Won't Take On Additional Risk Unless We Expect to Be Compensated with Additional Return.

Principle 2: The Time Value of Money—A Dollar Received Today Is Worth More Than a Dollar Received in the Future.

As a final note, we should understand that the *expected* rate of return implied by a given market price equals the *required* rate of return for investors at the margin. For these investors, the expected rate of return is just equal to their required rate of return and, therefore, they are willing to pay the current market price for the security. These investors' required rate of return is of particular significance to the financial manager because it represents the cost of new financing to the firm.

PROBLEM CHECK SOLUTION: COMPUTING THE EXPECTED RATE OF RETURN

Preferred stock:

$$\text{Expected return} = \frac{\text{dividend}}{\text{stock price}} = \frac{\$5}{\$80} = 0.0625 \text{ or } 6.25\%$$

Common stock:

$$\text{Expected return} = \frac{\text{dividend}}{\text{stock price}} + \text{growth rate}$$
$$= \frac{\$4 \times (1 + 0.05)}{\$75} + 5\% = \frac{\$4.20}{\$75} + 5\%$$
$$= 5.6\% + 5\% = 10.6\%$$

CONCEPT CHECK

1. In computing the required rate of return, why should the growth factor be added to the dividend yield?

2. How does an efficient market affect the required and expected rates of return?

SUMMARY

Valuation is an important process in financial management. An understanding of valuation, both the concepts and procedures, supports the financial officer's objective of maximizing the value of the firm.

Identify the basic characteristics and features of preferred stock

Objective **1**

Preferred stock has no fixed maturity date, and the dividends are fixed in amount. Some of the more common characteristics of preferred stock include the following:

- There are multiple classes of preferred stock.
- Preferred stock has a priority of claim on assets and income over common stock.
- Any dividends, if not paid as promised, must be paid before any common stock dividends may be paid; that is, they are cumulative.
- Protective provisions are included in the contract with the shareholder to reduce the investor's risk.
- Many preferred stocks are convertible into common stock shares.

In addition, there are provisions frequently used to retire an issue of preferred stock, such as the ability of the firm to call its preferred stock or to use a sinking-fund provision.

Value preferred stock

Objective **2**

Value is the present value of future cash flows discounted at the investor's required rate of return. Although the valuation of any security entails the same basic principles, the procedures used in each situation vary. For example, we learned in Chapter 7 that valuing a bond involves calculating the present value of future interest to be received plus the present value of the principal returned to the investor at the maturity of the bond.

For securities with cash flows that are constant in each year but when there is no specified maturity, such as preferred stock, the present value equals the dollar amount of the annual dividend divided by the investor's required rate of return; that is,

$$\frac{\text{Preferred}}{\text{stock value}} = \frac{\text{annual dividend}}{\text{required rate of return}}$$

Identify the basic characteristics and features of common stock

Objective **3**

Common stock involves ownership in the corporation. In effect, bondholders and preferred stockholders can be viewed as creditors, whereas the common stockholders are the owners of the firm. Common stock does not have a maturity date but exists as long as the firm does. Nor does common stock have an upper limit on its dividend payments. Dividend payments must be declared by the firm's board of directors before they are issued. In the event of bankruptcy, the common stockholders, as owners of the corporation, cannot exercise claims on assets until the firm's creditors, including the bondholders and preferred shareholders, have been satisfied. However, common stockholders' liability is limited to the amount of their investment.

The common stockholders are entitled to elect the board of directors and are, in general, the only security holders given a vote. Common shareholders have the right to elect the board of directors and to approve any change in the corporate charter. Although each share of stock carries the same number of votes, the voting procedure is not always the same from company to company.

The preemptive right entitles the common shareholder to maintain a proportionate share of ownership in the firm.

Value common stock

Objective **4**

For common stock when the future dividends are expected to increase at a constant growth rate, value may be given by the following equation:

$$\text{Common stock value} = \frac{\text{dividend in year 1}}{\text{required rate of return} - \text{growth rate}}$$

Growth here relates to *internal* growth only, in which management retains part of the firm's profit to be reinvested and thereby grows the firm—as opposed to growth through issuing of new stock or acquiring another firm.

Growth in and of itself does not mean that we are creating value for the stockholders. Only if we are reinvesting at a rate of return greater than the investor's required rate of return will growth result in increased value to the firm. In fact, if we are investing at rates less than the required rate of return for investors, the value of the firm will actually decline.

A second approach for calculating common stock value is based on the present value of the firm's projected free cash flows. Here we compute the expected free cash flows and find their present value. The process involves identifying the anticipated time frame for the existing competitive advantage and determining the value of the cash flows during this time period and adding the present value of the cash flows during the post-competitive-advantage period, or what we call the residual value. The basic concept suggests that the value of an asset, even a whole firm, is equal to the present value of the asset's future free cash flows.

Objective **5**

Calculate a stock's expected rate of return

The expected rate of return on a security is the required rate of return of investors who are willing to pay the present market price for the security, but no more. This rate of return is important to the financial manager because it equals the required rate of return of the firm's investors.

The expected rate of return for preferred stock is computed as follows:

$$\frac{\text{Expected return,}}{\text{preferred stock}} = \frac{\text{annual dividend}}{\text{market price}}$$

The expected rate of return for common stock is calculated as follows:

$$\frac{\text{Expected return,}}{\text{common stock}} = \frac{\text{dividend in year 1}}{\text{market price}} + \frac{\text{growth}}{\text{rate}}$$

KEY TERMS

Call provision, 233	Expected rate of return, 247	Protective provisions, 232
Common stock, 236	Free cash flows, 244	Proxy, 237
Competitive-advantage period, 244	Internal growth, 240	Proxy fight, 237
Convertible preferred stock, 233	Limited liability, 238	Residual value, 245
	Majority voting, 237	Rights, 238
Cumulative feature, 232	Preemptive right, 238	Sinking-fund provision, 233
Cumulative voting, 237	Preferred stock, 232	
Dividend-payout ratio, 240	Profit-retention rate, 240	

STUDY QUESTIONS

8-1. Why is preferred stock referred to as a hybrid security? It is often said to combine the worst features of common stock and bonds. What is meant by this statement?

8-2. Inasmuch as preferred stock dividends in arrears must be paid before common stock dividends, should they be considered a liability and appear on the right-hand side of the balance sheet?

8-3. Why would a preferred stockholder want the stock to have a cumulative dividend feature and protective provisions?

8-4. Why is preferred stock frequently convertible? Why would it be callable?

8-5. Compare valuing preferred stock and common stock.

8-6. Define the investor's expected rate of return.

8-7. State how the investor's expected rate of return is computed.

8-8. The common stockholders receive two types of return from their investment. What are they?

SELF-TEST PROBLEMS

ST-1. (*Preferred stock valuation*) What is the value of a preferred stock when the dividend rate is 16 percent on a $100 par value? The appropriate discount rate for a stock of this risk level is 12 percent.

ST-2. (*Preferred stockholder expected return*) You own 250 shares of Dalton Resources preferred stock, which currently sells for $38.50 per share and pays annual dividends of $3.25 per share.

   a. What is your expected return?

   b. If you require an 8-percent return, given the current price, should you sell or buy more stock?

ST-3. (*Preferred stock valuation*) The preferred stock of Armlo pays a $2.75 dividend. What is the value of the stock if your required return is 9 percent?

ST-4. (*Common stock valuation*) Crosby Corporation common stock paid $1.32 in dividends last year and is expected to grow indefinitely at an annual 7 percent rate. What is the value of the stock if you require an 11 percent return?

ST-5. (*Common stockholder expected return*) Blackburn & Smith common stock currently sells for $23 per share. The company's executives anticipate a constant growth rate of 10.5 percent and an end-of-year dividend of $2.50.

   a. What is your expected rate of return?

   b. If you require a 17 percent return, should you purchase the stock?

STUDY PROBLEMS

8-1. (*Preferred stock expected return*) You are planning to purchase 100 shares of preferred stock and must choose between Stock A and Stock B. Stock A pays an annual dividend of $4.50 and is currently selling for $35. Stock B pays an annual dividend of $4.25 and is selling for $36. If your required return is 12 percent, which stock should you choose?

8-2. (*Measuring growth*) The Fisayo Corporation wants to achieve a steady 7 percent growth rate. If it can achieve a 12 percent return on equity, what percentage of earnings must Fisayo retain for investment purposes?

8-3. (*Common stock valuation*) Dalton, Inc., has an 11.5 percent return on equity and retains 55 percent of its earnings for reinvestment purposes. It recently paid a dividend of $3.25 and the stock is currently selling for $40.

   a. What is the growth rate for Dalton, Inc.?

   b. What is the expected return for Dalton's stock?

   c. If you require a 13 percent return, should you invest in the firm?

8-4. (*Common stock valuation*) Bates, Inc., pays a dividend of $1 and is currently selling for $32.50. If investors require a 12 percent return on their investment from buying Bates stock, what growth rate would Bates, Inc. have to provide the investors?

8-5. (*Preferred stock valuation*) What is the value of a preferred stock when the dividend rate is 14 percent on a $100 par value? The appropriate discount rate for a stock of this risk level is 12 percent.

8-6. (*Preferred stockholder expected return*) Solitron preferred stock is selling for $42.16 per share and pays $1.95 in dividends. What is your expected rate of return if you purchase the security at the market price?

8-7. (*Preferred stockholder expected return*) You own 200 shares of Somner Resources preferred stock, which currently sells for $40 per share and pays annual dividends of $3.40 per share.

   a. What is your expected return?

   b. If you require an 8 percent return, given the current price, should you sell or buy more stock?

8-8. (*Common stock valuation*) You intend to purchase Marigo common stock at $50 per share, hold it 1 year, and sell after a dividend of $6 is paid. How much will the stock price have to appreciate for you to satisfy your required rate of return of 15 percent?

8-9. (*Common stockholder expected return*) Made-It common stock currently sells for $22.50 per share. The company's executives anticipate a constant growth rate of 10 percent and an end-of-year dividend of $2.

   a. What is your expected rate of return if you buy the stock for $22.50?

   b. If you require a 17 percent return, should you purchase the stock?

8-10. (*Common stock valuation*) Header Motor, Inc., paid a $3.50 dividend last year. At a constant growth rate of 5 percent, what is the value of the common stock if the investors require a 20 percent rate of return?

8-11. (*Measuring growth*) Given that a firm's return on equity is 18 percent and management plans to retain 40 percent of earnings for investment purposes, what will be the firm's growth rate?

8-12. (*Common stockholder expected return*) The common stock of Zaldi Co. is selling for $32.84 per share. The stock recently paid dividends of $2.94 per share and has a projected constant growth rate of 9.5 percent. If you purchase the stock at the market price, what is your expected rate of return?

8-13. (*Common stock valuation*) Honeywag common stock is expected to pay $1.85 in dividends next year, and the market price is projected to be $42.50 per share by year-end. If the investor's required rate of return is 11 percent, what is the current value of the stock?

8-14. (*Common stockholder expected return*) The market price for Hobart common stock is $43 per share. The price at the end of 1 year is expected to be $48, and dividends for next year should be $2.84. What is the expected rate of return?

8-15. (*Preferred stock valuation*) Pioneer preferred stock is selling for $33 per share in the market and pays a $3.60 annual dividend.

    a. What is the expected rate of return on the stock?
    b. If an investor's required rate of return is 10 percent, what is the value of the stock for that investor?
    c. Should the investor acquire the stock?

8-16. (*Common stock valuation*) The common stock of NCP paid $1.32 in dividends last year. Dividends are expected to grow at an 8 percent annual rate for an indefinite number of years.

    a. If NCP's current market price is $23.50 per share, what is the stock's expected rate of return?
    b. If your required rate of return is 10.5 percent, what is the value of the stock for you?
    c. Should you make the investment?

8-17. (*Preferred stock valuation*) Calculate the value of a preferred stock that pays a dividend of $6 per share if your required rate of return is 12 percent.

8-18. (*Measuring growth*) Pepperdine, Inc.'s return on equity is 16 percent, and the management plans to retain 60 percent of earnings for investment purposes. What will be the firm's growth rate?

8-19. (*Common stock valuation: free cash flows*) Given the information here, calculate the shareholder value for Hokie, Inc.

Cost of capital	10%
Most recent year's sales	$2,000
Debt	$ 250
Operating profit margin	12%
Assets/sales	40%
Tax rate	40%
Forecasted sales growth:	
1 to 2 years	14%
3 to 5 years	9%
6 to ∞	3%

WEB WORKS

8-WW1. Preferred stock is frequently used by venture capitalists when investing in a private company. Go to **www.jbv.com/lessons/lesson26.htm** and learn about the terms and conditions frequently used by venture capitalists when investing using preferred stock.

8-WW2. Find the Web site **www.bigchart.com**. Choose a publicly traded firm. At the top of the Web site, enter the firm's ticker symbol and click on Quick Chart. What information is provided about the firm and its stock? What reports has the firm filed with the Securities and Exchange Commission (SEC)? What kind of information do these reports contain?

8-WW3. Go to **http://finance.yahoo.com**. Click on the Mutual Fund icon at the top of the page. Then go to Inside Mutual Fund Education. What do you learn about investing in mutual funds?

8-WW4. Go to **http://finance.yahoo.com**. Look up Chevron Texaco (ticker symbol CVX). Then click on Key Statistics. What is the firm's dividend yield (dividend ÷ stock price)? Under the Growth Estimates, what is the firm's projected growth rate for the next five years? Assuming your required rate of return is 10 percent, what is the Chevron Texaco stock worth to you? What is the expected rate of return for the stock? Should you buy Chevron given your required rate of return?

COMPREHENSIVE PROBLEM

You are considering three investments. The first is a bond that is selling in the market at $1,100. The bond has a $1,000 par value, pays annual interest at 13 percent, and is scheduled to mature in 15 years. For bonds of this risk class, you believe that a 14 percent rate of return should be required. The second investment that you are analyzing is a preferred stock ($100 par value) that sells for $90 per share and pays an annual dividend of $13. Your required rate of return for this stock is 15 percent. The last investment is a common stock ($25 par value) that recently paid a $2 dividend. The firm's earnings per share have increased from $3 to $6 in 10 years, and this also reflects the expected growth in dividends per share for the indefinite future. The stock is selling for $20, and you think a reasonable required rate of return for the stock is 20 percent.

    a. Calculate the value of each security based on your required rate of return.

    b. Which investment(s) should you accept? Why?

    c. 1. If your required rates of return changed to 12 percent for the bond, 14 percent for the preferred stock, and 18 percent for the common stock, how would your answers to parts **a** and **b** change?

        2. Assuming again that your required rate of return for the common stock is 20 percent, but the anticipated constant growth rate changes to 12 percent, how would your answers to parts **a** and **b** change?

SELF-TEST SOLUTIONS

SS-1. Value $(V_{ps}) = \dfrac{0.16 \times \$100}{0.12}$

$\qquad\qquad = \dfrac{\$16}{0.12}$

$\qquad\qquad = \$133.33$

SS-2. **a.** Expected return $= \dfrac{\text{dividend}}{\text{market price}} = \dfrac{\$3.25}{\$38.50} = 0.0844 = 8.44\%$

    b. Given your 8 percent required rate of return, the stock is worth $40.62 to you:

$\qquad$ Value $= \dfrac{\text{dividend}}{\text{required rate of return}} = \dfrac{\$3.25}{0.08} = \$40.63$

Because the expected rate of return (8.44%) is greater than your required rate of return (8%) or because the current market price ($38.50) is less than $40.63, the stock is undervalued and you should buy.

SS-3. Value $(V_{ps}) = \dfrac{\text{dividend}}{\text{required rate of return}} = \dfrac{\$2.75}{0.08} = \$30.56$

SS-4. Value $(V_{cs}) = \dfrac{\text{last year dividend}(1 + \text{growth rate})}{\text{required rate of return} - \text{growth rate}}$

$\qquad\qquad = \dfrac{\$1.32(1.07)}{0.11 - 0.07}$

$\qquad\qquad = \$35.31$

SS-5. **a.** $\begin{array}{l}\text{Expected rate}\\ \text{of return}\end{array} (\bar{k}_{cs}) = \dfrac{\text{dividend in year 1}}{\text{market price}} + \text{growth rate}$

$\qquad\qquad \bar{k}_{cs} = \dfrac{\$2.50}{\$23.00} + 0.105 = 0.2137$

$\qquad\qquad \bar{k}_{cs} = 21.37\%$

    b. $V_{cs} = \dfrac{\$2.50}{0.17 - 0.105} = \$38.46$

The expected rate of return exceeds your required rate of return, which means that the value of the security to you is greater than the current market price. Thus, you should buy the stock.

➤ Harken Energy is an energy company located in Houston, Texas. The firm explores for oil and gas in the southwestern part of the United States and in Central and South America.

Jim Denny supervises the technical analysis for evaluating exploration prospects, acquisitions, and divestitures. In a conversation with Denny, he talked about the capital budgeting process at Harken.

In the oil and gas industry, the heart of capital budgeting requires a strong program for ranking drilling opportunities based on their potential risk and reward. The decisions made based on our capital budgeting analysis greatly affect the long-term welfare of the firm—not to mention the value for the firm's shareholders.

When we evaluate drilling prospects in oil fields where we already have experience, we use a "deterministic approach." We essentially use a decision tree to assess the likelihood of high, medium, and low oil production—and resulting cash flows. For instance, we consider such factors as drilling risk, pricing, and infrastructure. The decision tree also incorporates the chance of a dry hole or results that are economically unattractive. The probabilities assigned to the different possible events are a function of a number of technical factors, such as the structural formation, the organic matter from which the oil and gas will originate, and the ability of rock to store and flow hydrocarbons.

When we are considering drilling in geographical areas that are unfamiliar to us, we use a "probabilistic" approach. Here we build a probability distribution of outcomes. We then calculate what must happen for the drilling investment to be economically rewarding and compare these numbers against the probability distribution. Then if, for example, there is only a 20% chance of making the targeted numbers, we would reject the investment.

Once we have evaluated individual prospects, we then have to decide on a portfolio of investments, given the size of the total drilling budget. A primary concern is not running out of money before the drilling plan has been executed. To make this decision requires the assessment of a lot of intangible factors that are qualitative in nature. A decision is made and then we begin the drilling program.

CHAPTER 9
CAPITAL-BUDGETING
TECHNIQUES AND
PRACTICE

CHAPTER 10
CASH FLOWS AND
OTHER TOPICS IN
CAPITAL BUDGETING

CHAPTER 11
COST OF CAPITAL

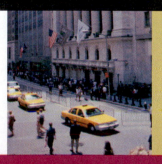

After reading this chapter, you should be able to:

1. Discuss the difficulty encountered in finding profitable projects in competitive markets and the importance of the search.

2. Determine whether a new project should be accepted or rejected using the payback period, the net present value, the profitability index, and the internal rate of return.

3. Explain how the capital-budgeting decision process changes when a dollar limit is placed on the dollar size of the capital budget.

4. Discuss the problems encountered in project ranking.

5. Explain the importance of ethical considerations in capital-budgeting decisions.

6. Discuss the trends in the use of different capital-budgeting criteria.

7. Explain how foreign markets provide opportunities for finding new capital-budgeting projects.

CHAPTER 9

Capital-Budgeting Techniques and Practice

FINDING PROFITABLE PROJECTS • CAPITAL-BUDGETING DECISION CRITERIA • CAPITAL RATIONING • PROBLEMS IN PROJECT RANKING: CAPITAL RATIONING, MUTUALLY EXCLUSIVE PROJECTS, AND PROBLEMS WITH THE IRR • ETHICS IN CAPITAL BUDGETING • A GLANCE AT ACTUAL CAPITAL-BUDGETING PRACTICES • FINANCE AND THE MULTINATIONAL FIRM: CAPITAL BUDGETING

In 1955, the Walt Disney Company changed the face of entertainment when it opened Disneyland, its first theme park in Anaheim, California, at a cost of $17.5 million. Since then Disney has opened theme parks in Orlando, Florida; Tokyo, Japan; and Paris, France. More recently, Disney broke ground in Hong Kong with the intention of launching Hong Kong Disneyland on Lantau Island, which is scheduled to open in late 2005 or early 2006. Much of the money needed for this $3.5 billion project has been provided by the Hong Kong government. Disney hopes to reach what has largely been an untapped Chinese market. Because Disney has decided not to skimp on anything, when Hong Kong Disneyland opens, it will be wildly spectacular with more than 250,000 annual flowering plants, 15,000 canopy trees, plenty of rides and attractions, and Sleeping Beauty's castle as its centerpiece complete with its trademark blue-pointed turret.

For Disney, this is an important move. Keeping its Theme Parks and Resorts Division healthy is extremely important because this division accounts for over one-quarter of the company's revenues. Certainly, there are opportunities for Disney in China. With a population of 1.26 billion people, China accounts for 20 percent of the world's total population.

To say the least, the stakes involved with an investment of this size are so large that the outcome of this decision will have a major effect on Disney's future. Only time will tell whether this was a good or a bad decision. The question we will ask in this chapter is how Disney went about making the decision to enter the Chinese market and build Hong Kong Disneyland. The answer is that Disney did it using the decision criteria we will examine in this chapter.

≪ WHAT'S AHEAD ≫

In this chapter we look first at the difficulties associated with finding profitable projects. Four capital-budgeting criteria are subsequently provided for evaluating capital investments, followed by a discussion of the problems created when the number of projects that can be accepted or the total budget is limited. We then examine capital budgeting in practice and close with a discussion of how foreign markets can provide capital-budgeting projects.

This chapter is actually the first of two chapters dealing with the process of decision making with respect to investment in fixed assets—that is, should a proposed project be accepted or rejected? We will refer to this process as capital budgeting. In this chapter we will look at methods used to evaluate new projects. In deciding whether to accept a new project, we will focus on free cash flows. Free cash flows represent the benefits generated from accepting a capital-budgeting proposal. We will assume we know what level of free cash flows is generated by a project and will work on determining whether that project should be accepted. In the following chapter, we will examine what a free cash flow is and how we measure it. In that chapter we will also look at how risk enters into this process.

Objective **1**

capital budgeting

FINDING PROFITABLE PROJECTS

Without question it is easier to *evaluate profitable projects or investment in fixed assets*, a process referred to as **capital budgeting**, than it is to find them. In competitive markets, generating ideas for profitable projects is extremely difficult. The competition is brisk for new profitable projects, and once they have been uncovered, competitors generally rush in, pushing down prices and profits. For this reason a firm must have a systematic strategy for generating capital-budgeting projects. Without this flow of new projects and ideas, the firm cannot grow or even survive for long, being forced to live off the profits from existing projects with limited lives. So where do these ideas come from for new products, or for ways to improve existing products or make them more profitable? The answer is from inside the firm—from everywhere inside the firm.

BACK TO THE FOUNDATIONS

The fact that profitable projects are difficult to find relates directly to **Principle 5: The Curse of Competitive Markets—Why It's Hard to Find Exceptionally Profitable Projects**. *When we introduced that principle, we stated that successful investments involve the reduction of competition by creating barriers to entry through either product differentiation or cost advantages. The key to locating profitable projects is to understand how and where they exist.*

TAKIN' IT TO THE NET
Capital budgeting involves coming up not only with new products but also with new ways of selling old products. A good example of this is the battle between Amazon.com (www.amazon.com) and Barnes and Noble, which introduced BarnesandNoble.com (www.barnesandnoble.com) in 1997 after giving Amazon.com a 2-year lead. Take a look at these two sites. Which one do you think will dominate in the future and why?

Typically, a firm has a research and development (R&D) department that searches for ways of improving existing products or finding new products. These ideas may come from within the R&D department or may be based on referral ideas from executives, sales personnel, anyone in the firm, or even customers. For example, at Ford Motor Company before the 1990s, ideas for product improvement had typically been generated in Ford's R&D department. Unfortunately, this strategy was not enough to keep Ford from losing much of its market share to the Japanese. In an attempt to cut costs and improve product quality, Ford moved from strict reliance on an R&D department to seeking the input of employees at all levels for new ideas. Bonuses are now provided to workers for their cost-cutting suggestions, and assembly-line personnel who can see the production process from a hands-on point of view are now brought into the hunt for new projects. The effect on Ford has been positive and significant. Although not all suggested projects prove to be profitable, many new ideas generated from within the firm turn out to be good ones.

Another way an existing product can be applied to a new market is illustrated by Kimberly-Clark, the manufacturer of Huggies disposable diapers. The company took its existing product line, made the diapers more waterproof, and began marketing them as disposable swim pants call Little Swimmers. Sara Lee Hosiery boosted its market by expanding its offerings to appeal to more customers and more customer needs. For example, Sara Lee Hosiery introduced Sheer Energy pantyhose for support, Just My Size pantyhose aimed at larger sizes, and recently introduced Silken Mist pantyhose aimed at African American women in shades better suited for darker skin tones.

These big investments go a long way toward determining the future of the company, but they don't always work as planned. Just look at Burger King's development of its new french fries.

It looked like a slam dunk great idea. Burger King took an uncooked french fry and coated it with a layer of starch that made it crunchier and kept it hot longer. Spending over $70 million on the new fries, the company even gave away 15 million orders on a "Free Fryday." Unfortunately, they didn't go down with consumers and Burger King was left to eat the loss. Given the size of the investment we're talking about, you can see why such a decision is so important.

CONCEPT CHECK

1. Why is it so difficult to find an exceptionally profitable project?
2. Why is the search for new profitable projects so important?

CAPITAL-BUDGETING DECISION CRITERIA

Objective **2**

In deciding whether to accept a new project, we focus on cash flows. Cash flows represent the benefits generated from accepting a capital-budgeting proposal. In this chapter we assume a given cash flow is generated by a project and work on determining whether that project should be accepted.

We consider four commonly used criteria for determining acceptability of investment proposals. The first one is the least sophisticated, in that it does not incorporate the time value of money into its calculations; the other three do take it into account. For the time being, the problem of incorporating risk into the capital-budgeting decision is ignored. This issue is examined in Chapter 10. In addition, we assume that the appropriate discount rate, required rate of return, or cost of capital is given. The determination of the cost of capital is the topic of Chapter 11.

PAYBACK PERIOD

The **payback period** is the *number of years needed to recover the initial cash outlay*. Because this criterion measures how quickly the project will return its original investment, it deals with free cash flows, which measure the true timing of the benefits, rather than accounting profits. Unfortunately, it also ignores the time value of money and does not discount these free cash flows back to the present. The accept/reject criterion centers on whether the project's payback period is less than or equal to the firm's maximum desired payback period. For example, if a firm's maximum desired payback period is 3 years and an investment proposal requires an initial cash outlay of $10,000 and yields the following set of annual cash flows, what is its payback period? Should the project be accepted?

payback period

YEAR	FREE CASH FLOW
1	$2,000
2	4,000
3	3,000
4	3,000
5	1,000

In this case, after 3 years the firm will have recaptured $9,000 on an initial investment of $10,000, leaving $1,000 of the initial investment to be recouped. During the fourth year a total of $3,000 will be returned from this investment, and, assuming it will flow into the firm at a constant rate over the year, it will take one-third of the year ($1,000/$3,000) to recapture the remaining $1,000. Thus, the payback period on this project is $3\frac{1}{3}$ years, which is more than the desired payback period. Using the payback period criterion, the firm would reject this project without even considering the $1,000 cash flow in year 5.

Although the payback period is used frequently, it does have some rather obvious drawbacks that are best demonstrated through the use of an example. Consider two investment

TABLE 9-1	Payback Period Example		
		PROJECTS	
		A	**B**
Initial cash outlay		−$10,000	−$10,000
Annual free cash inflows			
Year 1		$ 6,000	$ 5,000
2		4,000	5,000
3		3,000	0
4		2,000	0
5		1,000	0

projects, A and B, which involve an initial cash outlay of $10,000 each and produce the annual cash flows shown in Table 9-1. Both projects have a payback period of 2 years; therefore, in terms of the payback criterion both are equally acceptable. However, if we had our choice, it is clear we would select A over B, for at least two reasons. First, regardless of what happens after the payback period, project A returns our initial investment to us earlier within the payback period. Thus, because there is a time value of money, the cash flows occurring within the payback period should not be weighted equally, as they are. In addition, all cash flows that occur after the payback period are ignored. This violates the principle that investors desire more in the way of benefits rather than less—a principle that is difficult to deny, especially when we are talking about money.

Although these deficiencies limit the value of the payback period as a tool for investment evaluation, the payback period has several positive features. First, it deals with cash flows, as opposed to accounting profits, and therefore focuses on the true timing of the project's benefits and costs, even though it does not adjust the cash flows for the time value of money. Second, it is easy to visualize, quickly understood, and easy to calculate. Third, the payback period may make sense for the capital-constrained firm, that is, the firm that needs funds and is having problems raising additional investment funds. These firms need cash flows early on to allow them to continue in business and to take advantage of future investments. Finally, although the payback period has serious deficiencies, it is often used as a rough screening device to eliminate projects whose returns do not materialize until later years. This method emphasizes the earliest returns, which in all likelihood are less uncertain, and provides for the liquidity needs of the firm. Although its advantages are certainly significant, its disadvantages severely limit its value as a discriminating capital-budgeting criterion.

NET PRESENT VALUE

net present value (NPV)

The **net present value (NPV)** of an investment proposal is equal to the *present value of its annual free cash flows less the investment's initial outlay*. The net present value can be expressed as follows:

> ### BACK TO THE FOUNDATIONS
>
> The final three capital-budgeting criteria all incorporate **Principle 2: The Time Value of Money—A Dollar Received Today Is Worth More Than a Dollar Received in the Future** in their calculations. If we are at all to make rational business decisions, we must recognize that money has a time value. In examining the following three capital-budgeting techniques, you will notice that this principle is the driving force behind each of them.

$$NPV = \text{present value of all the future annual free cash flows} - \text{the initial cash outlay}$$
$$= FCF_1(PVIF_{k\%,\ 1\ yr}) + FCF_2(PVIF_{k\%,\ 2\ yr}) + \cdots + FCF_n(PVIF_{k\%,\ n\ yr}) - IO \qquad \textbf{(9-1)}$$

FINANCIAL MANAGEMENT
IN PRACTICE

FINDING PROFITABLE PROJECTS IN COMPETITIVE MARKETS—CREATING THEM BY DEVELOPING A COST ADVANTAGE

As we learned in **Principle 5: The Curse of Competitive Markets**, it is extremely difficult to find exceptionally profitable projects. We also noted that if you have the ability to produce at a cost below the competition, there is the opportunity for exceptionally large profits. Federal Express is one example of a company that has done exactly this.

Federal Express redefined the production-cost chain for rapid delivery of small parcels. Traditional firms such as Emery and Airborne Express operated by collecting freight packages of varying sizes, shipping them to their destination points via air freight and commercial airlines, and then delivering them to the addressee. Federal Express opted to focus only on the market for overnight delivery of small packages and documents. These were collected at local drop points during the late afternoon hours; flown on company-owned planes during early evening hours to a central hub in Memphis, Tennessee, where from 11 P.M. to 3 A.M. each night all parcels were sorted; and then reloaded on company planes and flown during the early morning hours to their destination points, from which they were delivered that morning by company personnel using company trucks. The cost structure thus achieved by Federal Express was low enough to permit guaranteed overnight delivery of a small parcel anywhere in the United States for a price as low as $11.

where FCF_t = the annual free cash flow in time period t (this can take on either positive or negative values)

k = the appropriate discount rate; that is, the required rate of return or cost of capital[1]

IO = the initial cash outlay

n = the project's expected life

$PVIF_{k\%, n\,\text{yr}}$ = the present value interest factor at $k\%$ and n years

The project's NPV gives a measurement of the net value of an investment proposal in terms of today's dollars. Because all cash flows are discounted back to the present, comparing the difference between the present value of the annual cash flows and the investment outlay does not violate the time value of money assumption. The difference between the present value of the annual cash flows and the initial outlay determines the net value of accepting the investment proposal in terms of today's dollars. Whenever the project's NPV is greater than or equal to zero, we will accept the project; whenever the NPV is negative, we will reject the project. If the project's NPV is zero, then it returns the required rate of return and should be accepted. This accept/reject criterion is illustrated here:

$NPV \geq 0.0$: accept

$NPV < 0.0$: reject

The following example illustrates the use of NPV as a capital-budgeting criterion.

TAKIN' IT TO THE NET

The same principles that guide us in capital-budgeting decisions also guide our decisions in personal finance. If you'd like to see an excellent selection of personal finance calculators, check out the Dinkytown Web site (www.dinkytown.net).

EXAMPLE

Ski-Doo is considering new machinery that would reduce manufacturing costs associated with its Mach Z snowmobile for which the free cash flows are shown in Table 9-2. If the firm has a 12 percent required rate of return, the present value of the free cash flow is $47,678, as calculated in Table 9-3. Subtracting the $40,000 initial outlay leaves an NPV of $7,678. Because this value is greater than zero, the NPV criterion indicates that the project should be accepted.

---

[1]The required rate of return or cost of capital is the rate of return necessary to justify raising funds to finance the project or, alternatively, the rate of return necessary to maintain the firm's current market price per share. These terms are defined in greater detail in Chapter 11.

TABLE 9-2   *NPV* Illustration of Ski-Doo's Investment in New Machinery

	FREE CASH FLOW
Initial outlay	−$40,000
Inflow year 1	15,000
Inflow year 2	14,000
Inflow year 3	13,000
Inflow year 4	12,000
Inflow year 5	11,000

CALCULATOR SOLUTION (USING A TEXAS INSTRUMENTS BA II PLUS):

Data and Key Input	Display
CF; −40,000; ENTER	CF0 = −40,000.
↓; 15,000; ENTER	C01 = 15,000.
↓; 1; ENTER	F01 = 1.00
↓; 14,000; ENTER	C02 = 14,000.
↓; 1; ENTER	F02 = 1.00
↓; 13,000; ENTER	C03 = 13,000.
↓; 1; ENTER	F03 = 1.00
↓; 12,000; ENTER	C04 = 12,000.
↓; 1; ENTER	F04 = 1.00
↓; 11,000; ENTER	C05 = 11,000.
↓; 1; ENTER	F05 = 1.00
NPV	I = 0.00
12; ENTER	I = 12.00
↓; CPT	NPV = 7,675.

TABLE 9-3   Calculation for *NPV* Illustration of Investment in New Machinery

	FREE CASH FLOW	PRESENT VALUE FACTOR AT 12 PERCENT	PRESENT VALUE
Inflow year 1	$15,000	.893	$13,395
Inflow year 2	14,000	.797	11,158
Inflow year 3	13,000	.712	9,256
Inflow year 4	12,000	.636	7,632
Inflow year 5	11,000	.567	6,237
Present value of free cash flows			$47,678
Initial outlay			−40,000
Net present value			$ 7,678

Note in the Ski-Doo example that the worth of the *NPV* calculation is a function of the accuracy of the cash flow predictions.

The *NPV* criterion is the capital-budgeting decision tool we find most favorable for several reasons. First of all, it deals with free cash flows rather than accounting profits. In this regard it is sensitive to the true timing of the benefits resulting from the project. Moreover, recognizing the time value of money allows comparison of the benefits and costs in a logical manner. Finally, because projects are accepted only if a positive *NPV* is associated with them, the acceptance of a project using this criterion will increase the value of the firm, which is consistent with the goal of maximizing the shareholders' wealth.

The disadvantage of the *NPV* method stems from the need for detailed, long-term forecasts of free cash flows accruing from the project's acceptance. Despite this drawback, the *NPV* is the most theoretically correct criterion that we will examine. The following example provides an additional illustration of its application.

EXAMPLE

A firm is considering the purchase of a new computer system, which will cost $30,000 initially, to aid in credit billing and inventory management. The free cash flows resulting from this project are provided in Table 9-4. The required rate of return demanded by the firm is 10 percent. To determine the system's *NPV*, the 3-year $15,000 cash flow annuity is first discounted back to the present at 10 percent. From Appendix E in the back of this book, we find that $PVIFA_{10\%,\ 3\ yr}$ is 2.487. Thus, the present value of this $15,000 annuity is $37,305.

Seeing that the cash inflows have been discounted back to the present, they can now be compared with the initial outlay because both of the flows are now stated in terms of today's dollars. Subtracting the initial outlay ($30,000) from the present value of the cash inflows ($37,305), we find that the system's *NPV* is $7,305. Because the *NPV* on this project is positive, the project should be accepted.

TABLE 9-4	*NPV* Example Problem of Computer System

	FREE CASH FLOW
Initial outlay	−$30,000
Inflow year 1	15,000
Inflow year 2	15,000
Inflow year 3	15,000

CALCULATOR SOLUTION

Data Input	Function Key
3	N
10	I/Y
15,000	PMT
0	FV

Function Key	Answer
CPT PV	−37,303

NPV = $37,303 − $30,000 = $7,303

SPREADSHEETS AND NET PRESENT VALUE

Although we can calculate the *NPV* by hand, it is more commonly done with the help of a spreadsheet. Just as with the keystroke calculations on a financial calculator, a spreadsheet can make easy work of *NPV* calculations. The only real glitch here is that Excel, along with most other spreadsheets, only calculates the present value of the future cash flows and ignores the initial outlay in its *NPV* calculations. Sounds strange? Well, it is. It is essentially just a carryforward of an error in one of the first spreadsheets. That means that the actual *NPV* is the Excel-calculated *NPV*, minus the initial outlay:

Actual *NPV* = Excel-calculated *NPV* − initial outlay

This can be input into a spreadsheet cell as:

= NPV (rate, inflow 1, inflow 2, ... inflow 29)-initial outlay

Looking back at the Ski-Doo example in Table 9-2, we can use a spreadsheet to calculate the net present value as long as we remember to subtract the initial outlay in order to get the correct number.

	A	B	C	D	E
2	Spreadsheets and NPV – the Ski-Doo Example				
3					
4	Looking at the example in Table 9.2, given a 12 percent				
5	discount rate and the following after-tax cash flows, the				
6	Net Present Value could be calculated as follows:				
7					
8			rate (i) =	12%	
9					
10			Year	Cash Flow	
11			Initial Outlay	($40.000)	
12			1	$15.000	
13			2	$14.000	
14			3	$13.000	
15			4	$12.000	
16			5	$11.000	
17					
18		NPV =	$7.674.63		
19					
20	Excel formula: =NPV(rate,inflow 1, inflow2, ...,inflow 29)				
21					
22	Again, from the Excel NPV calculation we must then				
23	subtract out the initial outlay in order to calculate the				
24	actual NPV.				
25					
26	Entered value in cell c26: =NPV(D16,D20:D24)−40000				
27					

Entered value in cell c15: =NPV(D8,D12:D16)−40000

PROFITABILITY INDEX (BENEFIT–COST RATIO)

The **profitability index (PI)**, or **benefit–cost ratio**, is the *ratio of the present value of the future free cash flows to the initial outlay*. Although the *NPV* investment criterion gives a measure of the absolute dollar desirability of a project, the profitability index provides a relative

profitability index (PI) or benefit–cost ratio

ACROSS THE HALL

MARKETING

When it comes to capital-budgeting decisions, marketing and finance have to work together to make good decisions. To do this, you, as a marketing major, have to know how your input is going to be used, how the capital-budgeting decision process works, and how the firm creates wealth. Capital budgeting doesn't just involve coming up with great ideas. It also involves taking those ideas and developing them into a product that consumers are going to embrace—a product that creates wealth for the firm. Whether that good idea makes it through the capital-budgeting process and becomes a new product depends on whether the present value of the expected benefits, measured by the free cash inflows, outweighs the present value of the costs. In a marketing position, you'll be working on pricing, promotional, and sales strategies that help sell lots of the product. But great sales numbers aren't the goal—the goal is to create wealth for the company. In effect, your pricing, promotional, design, and sales strategies will be evaluated in light of the net present value capital-budgeting technique we described earlier. Unfortunately, a mistake in any one of these areas can bring down an otherwise great product.

Marketing a new product is complicated enough without understanding how that new product will create wealth for the company. With a better understanding of how capital-budgeting decisions are made, you as a marketer will be better able to understand that great sales or excellent quality alone will not guarantee success. There is an almost unlimited list of examples of excellent new products that turned out to be flops and actually destroyed wealth for companies. For example, Gillette's "For Oily Hair Only" Shampoo failed not because it wasn't a good product but because its title reminded consumers of something they would rather not be reminded of—that they had oily hair. On the other hand, Ben-Gay Aspirin, Exxon Fruit Punch, Smucker's Ketchup, and Singles, Gerber's food for adults with flavors like blueberry delight, pureed sweet and sour pork, and chicken Madeira, failed because while they all might have been excellent products, consumers simply couldn't get by the brand name they were associated with and wouldn't buy them. Perhaps with a better understanding of how the firm creates wealth and how the capital-budgeting process actually works, marketers could have avoided these types of mistakes.

measure of an investment proposal's desirability—that is, the ratio of the present value of its future net benefits to its initial cost. The profitability index can be expressed as follows:

$$PI = \frac{\text{present value of all the future annual free cash flows}}{\text{initial cash outlay}} \tag{9-2}$$

$$= \frac{FCF_1(PVIF_{k\%,\,1\,\text{yr}}) + FCF_2(PVIF_{k\%,\,2\,\text{yr}}) + \cdots + FCF_n(PVIF_{k\%,\,n\,\text{yr}})}{IO}$$

where FCF_t = the annual free cash flow in time period t (this can take on either positive or negative values)

k = the appropriate discount rate; that is, the required rate of return or cost of capital

IO = the initial cash outlay

n = the project's expected life

$PVIF_{k\%,\,n\,\text{yr}}$ = the present value interest factor at $k\%$ and n years

The decision criterion is accept the project if the PI is greater than or equal to 1.00 and reject the project if the PI is less than 1.00.

$PI \geq 1.0$: accept

$PI < 1.0$: reject

Looking closely at this criterion, we see that it yields the same accept/reject decision as the NPV criterion. Whenever the present value of the project's free cash flows is greater than its initial cash outlay, the project's NPV will be positive, signaling a decision to accept. When this is true, then the project's PI will also be greater than 1 because the present value of the free cash flows (the PI's numerator) is greater than its initial outlay (the PI's denominator). Thus, these two decision criteria will always yield the same decision, although they will not necessarily rank acceptable projects in the same order. This problem of conflicting ranking is dealt with at a later point.

Because the *NPV* and *PI* criteria are essentially the same, they have the same advantages over the other criteria examined. Both employ free cash flows, recognize the timing of the cash flows, and are consistent with the goal of maximization of shareholders' wealth. The major disadvantage of the *PI* criterion, similar to the *NPV* criterion, is that it requires long, detailed free cash flow forecasts.

EXAMPLE

A firm with a 10 percent required rate of return is considering investing in a new machine with an expected life of 6 years. The free cash flows resulting from this investment are given in Table 9-5. Discounting the project's future net free cash flows back to the present yields a present value of $53,667; dividing this value by the initial outlay of $50,000 gives a profitability index of 1.0733, as shown in Table 9-6. This tells us that the present value of the future benefits accruing from this project is 1.0733 times the level of the initial outlay. Because the profitability index is greater than 1.0, the project should be accepted.

INTERNAL RATE OF RETURN

The **internal rate of return (IRR)** attempts to answer the question, what rate of return does this project earn? For computational purposes, the internal rate of return is defined as *the discount rate that equates the present value of the project's free cash flows with the project's initial*

internal rate of return (IRR)

TABLE 9-5	*PI* Illustration of Investment in New Machinery

	FREE CASH FLOW
Initial outlay	−$50,000
Inflow year 1	15,000
Inflow year 2	8,000
Inflow year 3	10,000
Inflow year 4	12,000
Inflow year 5	14,000
Inflow year 6	16,000

TABLE 9-6	Calculation for *PI* Illustration of Investment in New Machinery

	FREE CASH FLOW	PRESENT VALUE FACTOR AT 10 PERCENT	PRESENT VALUE
Initial outlay	−$50,000	1.000	−$50,000
Inflow year 1	15,000	0.909	13,635
Inflow year 2	8,000	0.826	6,608
Inflow year 3	10,000	0.751	7,510
Inflow year 4	12,000	0.683	8,196
Inflow year 5	14,000	0.621	8,694
Inflow year 6	16,000	0.564	9,024

$$PI = \frac{FCF_1(PVIF_{k\%,1\,yr}) + FCF_2(PVIF_{k\%,2\,yr}) + \cdots + FCF_n(PVIF_{k\%,n\,yr})}{IO}$$

$$= \frac{\$13,635 + \$6,608 + \$7,510 + \$8,196 + \$8,694 + \$9,024}{\$50,000}$$

$$= \frac{\$53,667}{\$50,000}$$

$$= 1.0733$$

cash outlay. Mathematically, the internal rate of return is defined as the value *IRR* in the following equation:

IRR = the rate of return that equates the present value of the project's free cash flows
with the initial outlay

$$IO = FCF_1(PVIF_{IRR\%,\, 1\, yr}) + FCF_2(PVIF_{IRR\%,\, 2\, yr}) + \cdots + FCF_n(PVIF_{IRR\%,\, n\, yr}) \qquad \textbf{(9-3)}$$

where *FCF*$_t$ = the annual free cash flow in time period *t* (this can take on either positive or negative values)

   IO = the initial cash outlay

   n = the project's expected life

   IRR = the project's internal rate of return

PVIF$_{k\%,\, n\, yr}$ = the present value interest factor at *k*% and *n* years

In effect, the *IRR* is analogous to the concept of the yield to maturity for bonds, which was examined in Chapter 6. In other words, a project's *IRR* is simply the rate of return that the project earns.

The decision criterion is to accept the project if the *IRR* is greater than or equal to the required rate of return. We reject the project if its *IRR* is less than the required rate of return. This accept/reject criterion can be stated as

IRR ≥ required rate of return: accept
IRR < required rate of return: reject

If the *IRR* on a project is equal to the shareholders' required rate of return, then the project should be accepted because the firm is earning the rate that its shareholders are requiring. However, the acceptance of a project with an *IRR* below the investors' required rate of return will decrease the firm's stock price.

If the *NPV* is positive, then the *IRR* must be greater than the required rate of return, *k*. Thus, all the discounted cash flow criteria are consistent and will give similar accept/reject decisions. One other disadvantage of the *IRR* relative to the *NPV* deals with the implied reinvestment rate assumptions made by these two methods. The *NPV* assumes that cash flows over the life of the project are reinvested back in projects that earn the required rate of return. That is, if we have a mining project with a 10-year expected life that produces a $100,000 cash flow at the end of the second year, the *NPV* technique assumes that this $100,000 is reinvested over years 3 though 10 at the required rate of return. The use of the *IRR*, however, implies that cash flows over the life of the project can be reinvested at the *IRR*. Thus, if the mining project we just looked at has a 40 percent *IRR*, the use of the *IRR* implies that the $100,000 cash flow that is received at the end of year 2 could be reinvested at 40 percent over the remaining life of the project. In effect, *the NPV method implicitly assumes that cash flows over the life of the project can be reinvested at the project's required rate of return, whereas the use of the IRR method implies that these cash flows could be reinvested at the IRR.* The better assumption is the one made by the *NPV*, that cash flows could be reinvested at the required rate of return, because cash flows could either be (1) returned in the form of dividends to shareholders who demand the required rate of return on their investments, or (2) reinvested in a new investment project. If these cash flows are invested in a new project, then they are simply substituting for external funding on which the required rate of return is demanded. Thus, the opportunity cost of these funds is the required rate of return. The bottom line to all this is that the *NPV* method makes the best reinvestment rate assumption, and, as such, is superior to the *IRR* method. Why should we care which method is used if both methods give similar accept/reject decisions? The answer, as we will see, is that although they may give the same accept/reject decision, they may rank projects differently in terms of desirability.

COMPUTING THE *IRR* WITH A FINANCIAL CALCULATOR

With today's calculators, the determination of an *IRR* is merely a matter of a few keystrokes. In Chapter 5, whenever we were solving time value of money problems for *i*, we were really solving for the *IRR*. For instance, in the example on page 142, when we solved for the rate at which $100 must be compounded annually for it to grow to $179.10 in 10 years, we were actually solving for that problem's *IRR*. Thus, with financial calculators we need only input the initial outlay, the cash flows, and their timing, and then input the function key "I/Y" or the "IRR" button to calculate the *IRR*. On some calculators it is necessary to press the compute key, CPT, before pressing the function key to be calculated.

SPREADSHEETS AND THE INTERNAL RATE OF RETURN

Calculating the *IRR* using a spreadsheet is extremely simple. Once the cash flows have been entered on the spreadsheet, all you need to do is input the Excel *IRR* formula into a spreadsheet cell and let the spreadsheet do the calculations for you. Of course, at least one of the cash flows must be positive and at least one must be negative. The *IRR* formula to be input into a spreadsheet cell is: **=IRR(values)**, where "values" is simply the range of cells in which the cash flows are stored.

	A	B	C	D	E
1					
2		**Spreadsheets and the IRR**			
3					
4	The three investment proposals just examined have the following				
5	cash flows:				
6					
7	Year	Project A	Project B	Project C	
8	Initial Outlay	($10.000)	($10.000)	($10.000)	
9	1	3.362	0	1.000	
10	2	3.362	0	3.000	
11	3	3.362	0	6.000	
12	4	3.362	13.605	7.000	
13					
14	IRR=	13.001%	8.000%	19.040%	
15					
16	Excel Formula: =IRR(values)				
17					
18	where:				
19	values =	the range of cells where the cash flows are stored.			
20		Note: There must be at least one positive and one			
21		negative cash flow.			
22					
23	Entered value in cell B14:=IRR(B8:B12)				
24	Entered value in cell C14:=IRR(C8:C12)				
25	Entered value in cell D14:=IRR(D8:D12)				
26					

Entered value in cell B14:=IRR(B8:B12)
Entered value in cell C14:=IRR(C8:C12)
Entered value in cell D14:=IRR(D8:D12)

COMPUTING THE *IRR* FOR EVEN CASH FLOWS USING THE TVM TABLES

In this section we are going to put our calculators aside and obtain a better understanding of the *IRR* by examining the mathematical process of calculating internal rates of return.

The calculation of a project's *IRR* can be either very simple or relatively complicated. As an example of a straightforward solution, assume that a firm with a required rate of return of 10 percent is considering a project that involves an initial outlay of $45,555. If the investment is taken, the free cash flows are expected to be $15,000 per annum over the project's 4-year life. In this case, the internal rate of return is equal to *IRR* in the following equation:

$$\$45,555 = \frac{\$15,000}{(1+IRR)^1} + \frac{\$15,000}{(1+IRR)^2} + \frac{\$15,000}{(1+IRR)^3} + \frac{\$15,000}{(1+IRR)^4}$$

From our discussion of the present value of an annuity in Chapter 5, we know that this equation can be reduced to

$$\$45,555 = \$15,000 \, (PVIFA_{i,\,4\,yr})$$

which can be solved using Appendix E which gives values for the $PVIFA_{i,\,n}$ for various combinations of *i* and *n*. Dividing both sides by $15,000, this becomes

$$3.037 = PVIFA_{i,\,4\,yr}$$

Hence, we are looking for $PVIFA_{i,\,4\,yr}$ of 3.037 in the 4-year row of Appendix E. This value occurs when *i* equals 12 percent, which means that 12 percent is the *IRR* for the investment. Therefore, because 12 percent is greater than the 10 percent required return, the project should be accepted.

CALCULATOR SOLUTION

Data Input	Function Key
4	N
−45,555	PV
15,000	PMT
0	FV

Function Key	Answer
CPT	
I/Y	12.01

COMPUTING THE *IRR* FOR UNEVEN CASH FLOWS

Unfortunately, although solving for the *IRR* is quite easy when using a financial calculator or spreadsheet, it can be solved directly in the tables only when the future free cash flows are in the form of an annuity or a single payment. With a calculator the process is simple: One need only key in the initial cash outlay, the cash flows, and their timing, and press the "IRR" button. Let's take a look at how you might solve a problem with uneven cash flows using a financial calculator. Every calculator works a bit differently, so you'll want to be familiar with how to input data into yours, but that being said, they all work essentially the same way. As you'd expect, you will enter all the cash flows, then solve for the project's *IRR*. With a Texas Instruments BA II Plus calculator, CFo indicates the initial outlay, which you'll want to give a negative value; C01 is the first free cash flow; and F01 is the number of years that the first free cash flow appears. Thus, if the free cash flows in years 1, 2, and 3 are all $1,000, then F01 = 3. C02 then becomes the second free cash flow, and F02 is the number of years that the second free cash flow appears. You'll notice that you move between the different cash flows using the down arrow ($\downarrow$) located on the top row of your calculator. Once you have inputted the initial outlay and all the free cash flows you then calculate the project's *IRR* by hitting the "IRR" button followed by "CPT," the compute button. Let's look at a quick example. Consider the following investment proposal:

Initial Outlay	−$5,000
FCF in year 1	2,000
FCF in year 2	2,000
FCF in year 3	3,000

**CALCULATOR SOLUTION
(USING A TEXAS INSTRUMENTS
BA II PLUS):**

Data and Key Input	Display
CF; −5,000; ENTER	CFo = −5,000.00
$\downarrow$; 2,000; ENTER	C01 = 2,000.00
$\downarrow$; 2; ENTER	F01 = 2.00
$\downarrow$; 3,000; ENTER	C02 = 3,000.00
$\downarrow$; 1; ENTER	F02 = 1.00
IRR; CPT	IRR = 17.50%

Thus, the IRR on this project is 17.50 percent. When a financial calculator is not available and these flows are in the form of an uneven series of flows, a trial-and-error approach is necessary. To do this, we first determine the present value of the future free cash flows using an arbitrary discount rate. If the present value of the future cash flows at this discount rate is larger than the initial outlay, the rate is increased; if it is smaller than the initial outlay, the discount rate is lowered and the process begins again. This search routine is continued until the present value of the future free cash flows is equal to the initial outlay. In effect, since the present value of the free cash inflows is equal to the initial outlay, the *NPV* must equal zero at this point. The interest rate that creates this situation is the *IRR*. This is the same basic process that a financial calculator uses to calculate an *IRR*.

EXAMPLE

Consider the following investment proposal:

Initial Outlay	−$10,010
FCF in year 1	1,000
FCF in year 2	3,000
FCF in year 3	6,000
FCF in year 4	7,000

CALCULATOR SOLUTION
(USING A TEXAS INSTRUMENTS
BA II PLUS)

Data and Key Input	Display
CF; –10,010; ENTER	CF0 = –10,010.00
↓; 1,000; ENTER	C01 = 1,000.00
↓; 1; ENTER	F01 = 1.00
↓; 3,000; ENTER	C02 = 3,000.00
↓; 1; ENTER	F02 = 1.00
↓; 6,000; ENTER	C03 = 6,000.00
↓; 1; ENTER	F03 = 1.00
↓; 7,000; ENTER	C04 = 7,000.00
↓; 1; ENTER	F04 = 1.00
IRR; CPT	IRR = 19.00%

TRIAL AND ERROR SOLUTION

Try different discount rates. The one that makes the present value of the free cash inflows equal to the initial outlay (i.e., makes the *NPV* equal to zero) is the *IRR*.

Discount Rate Guesses	NPV
15%	$1,075
20%	–$ 245
19%	$ 0

Thus, 19 percent is the project's *IRR*.

VIEWING THE *NPV–IRR* RELATIONSHIP: THE NET PRESENT VALUE PROFILE

Perhaps the easiest way to understand the relationship between the *IRR* and the *NPV* value is to view it graphically through the use of a **net present value profile**. A net present value profile is simply *a graph showing how a project's NPV changes as the discount rate changes*. To graph a project's net present value profile, you simply need to determine the project's *NPV*, first using a 0 percent discount rate, then slowly increasing the discount rate until a representative curve has been plotted. How does the *IRR* enter into the net present value profile? The *IRR* is the discount rate at which the *NPV* is zero.

net present value profile

Let's look at an example of a project that involves an after-tax initial outlay of $105,517 with free cash flows expected to be $30,000 per year over the project's 5-year life. Calculating the *NPV* of this project at several different discount rates results in the following:

Discount Rate	Project's NPV
0%	$44,483
5%	$24,367
10%	$ 8,207
13%	$ 0
15%	–$ 4,952
20%	–$15,798
25%	–$24,839

Plotting these values yields the net present value profile in Figure 9-1.

Where is the *IRR* in this figure? Recall that the *IRR* is the discount rate that equates the present value of the inflows with the present value of the outflows; thus, the *IRR* is the point at which the *NPV* is equal to zero—in this case, 13 percent. This is exactly the process that we use in computing the *IRR* for a series of uneven cash flows—we simply calculate the project's *NPV* using different discount rates and the discount rate that makes the *NPV* equal to zero is the project's *IRR*.

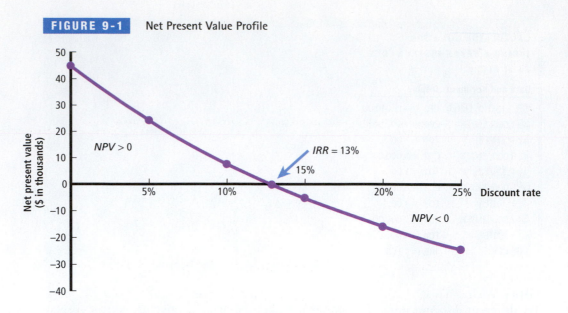

FIGURE 9-1   Net Present Value Profile

From the net present value profile you can easily see how a project's *NPV* varies inversely with the discount rate—as the discount rate is raised, the *NPV* drops. By analyzing a project's net present value profile, you can also see how sensitive the project is to your selection of the discount rate. The more sensitive the *NPV* is to the discount rate, the more important it is that you use the correct one in your calculations.

COMPLICATIONS WITH *IRR*: MULTIPLE RATES OF RETURN

Although any project can have only one *NPV* and one *PI*, a single project under certain circumstances can have more than one *IRR*. The reason for this can be traced to the calculations involved in determining the *IRR*. Equation (9-3) states that the *IRR* is the discount rate that equates the present value of the project's future net cash flows with the project's initial outlay:

$$IO = FCF_1(PVIF_{IRR\%,\ 1\ yr}) + FCF_2(PVIF_{IRR\%,\ 2\ yr}) + \cdots + FCF_n(PVIF_{IRR\%,\ n\ yr}) \qquad \textbf{(9-3)}$$

However, because equation (9-3) is a polynomial of a degree *n*, it has *n* solutions. Now if the initial outlay (*IO*) is the only negative cash flow and all the annual free cash flows (*FCF*) are positive, then all but one of these *n* solutions is either a negative or imaginary number and there is no problem. But problems occur when there are sign reversals in the cash flow stream; in fact, there can be as many solutions as there are sign reversals. A normal, or "conventional," pattern with a negative initial outlay and positive annual free cash flows after that (−, +, +, +, ... , +) has only one sign reversal, hence, only one positive *IRR*. However, an "unconventional" pattern with more than one sign reversal can have more than one *IRR*.[2]

	FREE CASH FLOW
Initial outlay	−$ 1,600
Year 1 Free cash flow	+$10,000
Year 2 Free cash flow	−$10,000

In this pattern of cash flows, there are two sign reversals from −$1,600 to +$10,000 and then from +$10,000 to −$10,000, so there can be as many as two positive *IRR*s that will make the present value of the free cash flows equal to the initial outlay. In fact, two internal rates of return solve this problem: 25 percent and 400 percent. Graphically, what we are

---

[2]This example is taken from James H. Lorie and Leonard J. Savage, "Three Problems in Rationing Capital," *Journal of Business* 28 (October 1955): 229–39.

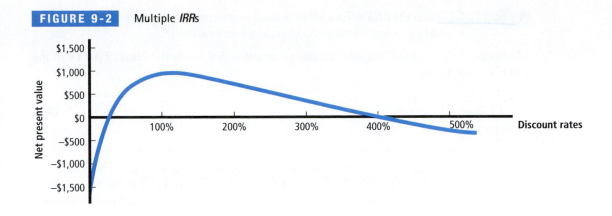

FIGURE 9-2   Multiple *IRR*s

solving for is the discount rate that makes the project's *NPV* equal to zero; as Figure 9-2 illustrates, this occurs twice.

Which solution is correct? The answer is that neither solution is valid. Although each fits the definition of *IRR*, neither provides any insight into the true project returns. In summary, when there is more than one sign reversal in the cash flow stream, the possibility of multiple *IRR*s exists, and the normal interpretation of the *IRR* loses its meaning. In this case, try the *NPV* criterion instead.

Modified Internal Rate of Return (MIRR)[3]

Problems with multiple rates of return and the reinvestment rate assumption make the *NPV* superior to the *IRR* as a capital-budgeting technique. However, because of the ease of interpretation, the *IRR* is preferred by many practitioners. Recently, a new technique, the modified internal rate of return (*MIRR*), has gained popularity as an alternative to the *IRR* method because it allows the decision maker to directly specify the appropriate reinvestment rate. As a result, the *MIRR* provides the decision maker with the intuitive appeal of the *IRR* coupled with an improved reinvestment rate assumption.

Is this really a problem? The answer is yes. One of the problems it creates is unrealistic expectations both for the corporation and for its shareholders. For example, the consulting firm McKinsey & Company examined one firm that approved 23 major projects over five years based on average *IRR*s of 77 percent.[4] However, when McKinsey adjusted the reinvestment rate on these projects to the firm's required rate of return, this return rate fell to 16 percent. The ranking of the projects also changed with the top-ranked project falling to the tenth most attractive project. Moreover, the returns on the highest-ranked projects with *IRR*s of 800, 150, and 130 percent dropped to 15, 23, and 22 percent, respectively, once the reinvestment rate was adjusted downward.

The driving force behind the *MIRR* is the assumption that all free cash flows over the life of the project are reinvested at the required rate of return until the termination of the project. Thus, to calculate the *MIRR*, we:

Step 1: Determine the present value of the project's free cash *out*flows. We do this by discounting all the free cash *out*flows back to the present at the required rate of return. If the initial outlay is the only free cash *out*flow, then the initial outlay is the present value of the free cash *out*flows.

Step 2: Determine the future value of the project's free cash *in*flows. Take all the annual free cash *in*flows and find their future value at the end of the project's life, compounded forward at the required rate of return. We will call this the project's *terminal value*, or *TV*.

[3]This section is relatively complex and can be omitted without loss of continuity.
[4]John C. Kellecher and Justin J. MacCormack, "Internal Rate of Return: A Cautionary Tale," *McKinsey Quarterly*, September 24, 2004, pp. 1–4.

Step 3: Calculate the *MIRR*. The *MIRR* is the discount rate that equates the present value of the free cash outflows with the project's terminal value.[5]

Mathematically, the modified internal rate of return is defined as the value of *MIRR* in the following equation:

$$PV_{\text{outflows}} = \frac{TV_{\text{inflows}}}{(1 + MIRR)^n} \qquad \text{(9-4)}$$

where PV_{outflows} = the present value of the project's free cash *out*flows
TV_{inflows} = the project's terminal value, calculated by taking all the annual free cash *in*flows and finding their future value at the end of the project's life, compounded forward at the required rate of return
n = the project's expected life
$MIRR$ = the project's modified internal rate of return

EXAMPLE: CALCULATING THE *MIRR*

Let's look at an example of a project with a 3-year life and a required rate of return of 10 percent assuming the following cash flows are associated with it:

	FREE CASH FLOWS		FREE CASH FLOWS
Initial outlay	−$6,000	Year 2	$3,000
Year 1	2,000	Year 3	4,000

The calculation of the *MIRR* can be viewed as a three-step process, which is also shown graphically in Figure 9-3.

Step 1: Determine the present value of the project's free cash *out*flows. In this case, the only *out*flow is the initial outlay of $6,000, which is already at the present; thus, it becomes the present value of the cash *out*flows.
Step 2: Determine the terminal value of the project's free cash *in*flows. To do this, we merely use the project's required rate of return to calculate the future value of the project's three cash *in*flows at the termination of the project. In this case, the *terminal value* becomes $9,720.
Step 3: Determine the discount rate that equates the present value of the *terminal value* and the present value of the project's cash *out*flows. Thus, the *MIRR* is calculated to be 17.446 percent.

For our example, the calculations are as follows:

$$\$6,000 = \frac{TV_{\text{inflows}}}{(1 + MIRR)^n}$$

$$\$6,000 = \frac{\$2,000\,(1+.10)^2 + \$3,000\,(1+.10)^1 + \$4,000\,(1+.10)^0}{(1+MIRR)^3}$$

$$\$6,000 = \frac{\$2,420 + \$3,300 + \$4,000}{(1+MIRR)^3}$$

$$\$6,000 = \frac{\$9,720}{(1+MIRR)^3}$$

$$MIRR = 17.446\%$$

[5]You will notice that we differentiate between annual cash inflows and annual cash outflows, compounding all the inflows to the end of the project and bringing all the outflows back to the present as part of the present value of the cost. Although there are alternative definitions of the *MIRR*, this is the most widely accepted definition. For an excellent discussion of the *MIRR*, see William R. McDaniel, Daniel E. McCarty, and Kenneth A. Jessell, "Discounted Cash Flow with Explicit Reinvestment Rates: Tutorial and Extension," *The Financial Review* (August 1988): 369–85.

FIGURE 9-3   Calculation of the *MIRR*

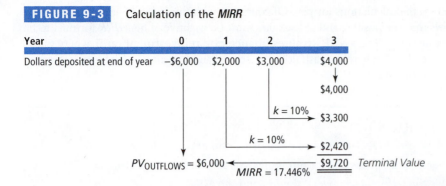

Thus, the *MIRR* for this project (17.446 percent) is less than its *IRR*, which comes out to 20.614 percent. In this case, it only makes sense that the *IRR* should be greater than the *MIRR*, because the *IRR* allows intermediate cash *in*flows to grow at the *IRR* rather than the required rate of return.

In terms of decision rules, if the project's *MIRR* is greater than or equal to the project's required rate of return, then the project should be accepted; if not, it should be rejected:

MIRR ≥ required rate of return: accept
MIRR < required rate of return: reject

Because of the frequent use of the *IRR* in the real world as a decision-making tool and its limiting reinvestment rate assumption, the *MIRR* has become increasingly popular as an alternative decision-making tool.

SPREADSHEETS AND THE MODIFIED INTERNAL RATE OF RETURN

As with other financial calculations using a spreadsheet, calculating the *MIRR* is extremely simple. The only difference between this calculation and that of the traditional *IRR* is that with a spreadsheet you also have the option of specifying both a *financing rate* and a *reinvestment rate*. The financing rate refers to the rate at which you borrow the money needed for the investment, whereas the reinvestment rate is the rate at which you reinvest the cash flows. Generally, it is assumed that these two values are one and the same. Thus, we enter the value of *k*, the appropriate discount rate, for both of these values. Once the cash flows have been entered on the spreadsheet, all you need to do is input the Excel *MIRR* formula into a spreadsheet cell and let

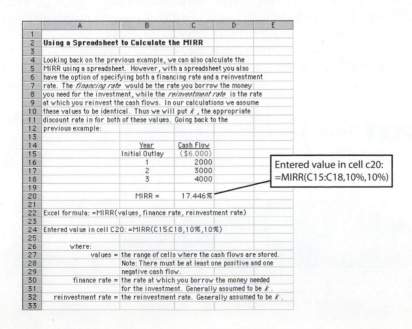

the spreadsheet do the calculations for you. Of course, as with the *IRR* calculation, at least one of the cash flows must be positive and at least one must be negative. The *MIRR* formula to be input into a spreadsheet cell is: =**MIRR(values,finance rate,reinvestment rate)**, where values is simply the range of cells where the cash flows are stored, and k is entered for both the finance rate and the reinvestment rate.

CONCEPT CHECK

1. Provide an intuitive definition of an internal rate of return for a project.
2. What does a net present value profile tell you and how is it constructed?
3. What is the difference between the *IRR* and the *MIRR*?
4. Why do the net present value and profitability index always give the same accept or reject decision for any project?

Objective **3**

CAPITAL RATIONING

capital rationing

The use of our capital-budgeting decision rules developed in this chapter implies that the size of the capital budget is determined by the availability of acceptable investment proposals. However, a firm may *place a limit on the dollar size of the capital budget*. This situation is called **capital rationing**. As we will see, an examination of capital rationing not only better enables us to deal with complexities of the real world but also serves to demonstrate the superiority of the *NPV* method over the *IRR* method for capital budgeting.

Using the *IRR* as the firm's decision rule, a firm accepts all projects with an *IRR* greater than the firm's required rate of return. This rule is illustrated in Figure 9-4, where projects A through E would be chosen. However, when capital rationing is imposed, the dollar size of the total investment is limited by the budget constraint. In Figure 9-4, the budget constraint of $X precludes the acceptance of an attractive investment, project E. This situation obviously contradicts prior decision rules. Moreover, the solution of choosing the projects with the highest *IRR* is complicated by the fact that some projects may be indivisible; for example, it is meaningless to recommend that half of project D be acquired.

PAUSE AND REFLECT

It is always somewhat uncomfortable to deal with problems associated with capital rationing because, under rationing, projects with positive net present values are rejected. This is a situation that violates the firm's goal of shareholder wealth maximization. However, in the real world, capital rationing does exist, and managers must deal with it. Often when firms impose capital constraints, they are recognizing that they do not have the ability to profitably handle more than a certain number of new and/or large projects.

FIGURE 9-4   Projects Ranked by *IRR*

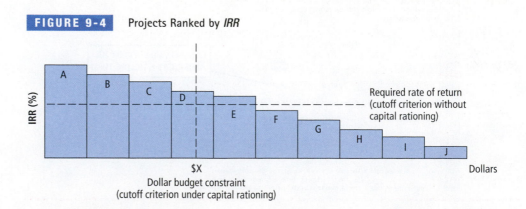

RATIONALE FOR CAPITAL RATIONING

We first ask why capital rationing exists and whether it is rational. In general, three principal reasons are given for imposing a capital-rationing constraint. First, management may think market conditions are temporarily adverse. In the period surrounding the downturn in the economy in the early 2000s, this reason was frequently given. At that time stock prices were depressed, which made the cost of funding projects high. Second, there may be a shortage of qualified managers to direct new projects; this can happen when projects are of a highly technical nature. Third, there may be intangible considerations. For example, management may simply fear debt, wishing to avoid interest payments at any cost. Or perhaps issuance of common stock may be limited to maintain a stable dividend policy.

Despite strong evidence that capital rationing exists in practice, the question remains as to its effect on the firm. In brief, the effect is negative, and to what degree depends on the severity of the rationing. If the rationing is minor and short-lived, the firm's share price will not suffer to any great extent. In this case, capital rationing can probably be excused, although it should be noted that any capital rationing that rejects projects with positive NPVs is contrary to the firm's goal of maximization of shareholders' wealth. If the capital rationing is a result of the firm's decision to limit dramatically the number of new projects or to limit total investment to internally generated funds, then this policy will eventually have a significantly negative effect on the firm's share price. For example, a lower share price will eventually result from lost competitive advantage if, because of a decision to arbitrarily limit its capital budget, a firm fails to upgrade its products and manufacturing processes.

CAPITAL RATIONING AND PROJECT SELECTION

If a firm decides to impose a capital constraint on investment projects, the appropriate decision criterion is to select the set of projects with the highest NPV subject to the capital constraint. In effect, we are selecting the projects that increase shareholders' wealth the most, because the NPV is the amount of wealth that is created when a project is accepted. This guideline may preclude merely taking the highest-ranked projects in terms of the PI or the IRR. If the projects shown in Figure 9-4 are divisible, the last project accepted may be only partially accepted. Although partial acceptance may be possible in some cases, the indivisibility of most capital investments prevents it. If a project is a sales outlet or a truck, it may be meaningless to purchase half a sales outlet or half a truck.

To illustrate this procedure, consider a firm with a budget constraint of $1 million and five indivisible projects available to it, as given in Table 9-7. If the highest-ranked projects were taken, projects A and B would be taken first. At that point there would not be enough funds available to take project C; hence, projects D and E would be taken. However, a higher total NPV is provided by the combination of projects A and C. Thus, projects A and C should be selected from the set of projects available. This illustrates our guideline: to select the set of projects that maximizes the firm's NPV.

PROJECT RANKING

In the past, we have proposed that all projects with a positive NPV, a PI greater than 1.0, or an IRR greater than the required rate of return be accepted, assuming there is no capital rationing. However, this acceptance is not always possible. In some cases, when two projects are judged acceptable by the discounted cash flow criteria, it may be necessary to select only one of them

TABLE 9-7 Capital-Rationing Example of Five Indivisible Projects

PROJECT	INITIAL OUTLAY	PROFITABILITY INDEX	NET PRESENT VALUE
A	$200,000	2.4	$280,000
B	200,000	2.3	260,000
C	800,000	1.7	560,000
D	300,000	1.3	90,000
E	300,000	1.2	60,000

mutually exclusive projects

because they are mutually exclusive. **Mutually exclusive projects** occur when a *set of investment proposals perform essentially the same task; acceptance of one will necessarily mean rejection of the others*. For example, a company considering the installation of a computer system may evaluate three or four systems, all of which may have positive *NPV*s; however, the acceptance of one system automatically means rejection of the others. In general, to deal with mutually exclusive projects, we simply rank them by means of the discounted cash flow criteria and select the project with the highest ranking. On occasion, however, problems of conflicting ranking may arise. As we will see, in general the *NPV* method is the preferred decision-making tool because it leads to the selection of the project that increases shareholder wealth the most.

> **CONCEPT CHECK**
> 1. What is capital rationing?
> 2. How might capital rationing conflict with the goal of maximization of shareholders' wealth?
> 3. What are mutually exclusive projects? How might they complicate the capital-budgeting process?

Objective **4**

PROBLEMS IN PROJECT RANKING: CAPITAL RATIONING, MUTUALLY EXCLUSIVE PROJECTS, AND PROBLEMS WITH THE *IRR*

There are three general types of ranking problems: the size disparity problem, the time disparity problem, and the unequal lives problem. Each involves the possibility of conflict in the ranks yielded by the various discounted cash flow capital-budgeting criteria. As noted previously, when one discounted cash flow criterion gives an accept signal, they will all give an accept signal, but they will not necessarily rank all projects in the same order. In most cases this disparity is not critical; however, for mutually exclusive projects the ranking order is important.

SIZE DISPARITY

The size disparity problem occurs when mutually exclusive projects of unequal size are examined. This problem is most easily clarified with an example.

EXAMPLE

Suppose a firm is considering two mutually exclusive projects, A and B; both have required rates of return of 10 percent. Project A involves a $200 initial outlay and a cash inflow of $300 at the end of 1 year, whereas project B involves an initial outlay of $1,500 and a cash inflow of $1,900 at the end of 1 year. The net present values, profitability indexes, and internal rates of return for these projects are given in Table 9-8.

In this case, if the *NPV* criterion is used, project B should be accepted; whereas if the *PI* or *IRR* criterion is used, project A should be chosen. The question now becomes, which project is better? The answer depends on whether capital rationing exists. Without capital rationing, project B is better because it provides the largest increase in shareholders' wealth; that is, it has a larger *NPV*. If there is a capital constraint, the problem then focuses on what can be done with the additional $1,300 that is freed if project A is chosen (costing $200, as opposed to $1,500). If the firm can earn more on project A plus the project financed with the additional $1,300 than it can on project B, then project A and the marginal project should be accepted. In effect, we are attempting to select the set of projects that maximizes the firm's *NPV*. Thus, if the marginal project has an *NPV* greater than $154.40 ($227.10 − $72.70), selecting it plus project A with an *NPV* of $72.70 will provide an *NPV* greater than $227.10, the *NPV* for project B.

TABLE 9-8	Size Disparity Ranking Problem

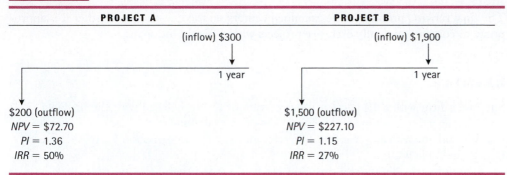

In summary, whenever the size disparity problem results in conflicting rankings between mutually exclusive projects, the project with the largest *NPV* will be selected, provided there is no capital rationing. When capital rationing exists, the firm should select the set of projects with the largest *NPV*.

TIME DISPARITY

The time disparity problem and the conflicting rankings that accompany it result from the differing reinvestment assumptions made by the net present value and internal rate of return decision criteria. The *NPV* criterion assumes that cash flows over the life of the project can be reinvested at the required rate of return or cost of capital, whereas the *IRR* criterion implicitly assumes that the cash flows over the life of the project can be reinvested at the *IRR*. Again, this problem may be illustrated through the use of an example.

EXAMPLE

Suppose a firm with a required rate of return or cost of capital of 10 percent and with no capital constraint is considering the two mutually exclusive projects illustrated in Table 9-9. The *NPV* and *PI* indicate that project A is the better of the two, whereas the *IRR* indicates that project B is the better. Project B receives its cash flows earlier than project A, and the different assumptions made about how these flows can be reinvested result in the difference in rankings. Which criterion would be followed depends on which reinvestment assumption is used. The *NPV* criterion is preferred in this case because it makes the most acceptable assumption for the wealth-maximizing firm. It is certainly the most conservative assumption that can be made, because the required rate of return is the lowest possible reinvestment rate. Moreover, as we have already noted, the *NPV* method maximizes the value of the firm and the shareholders' wealth.

TABLE 9-9	Time Disparity Ranking Problem

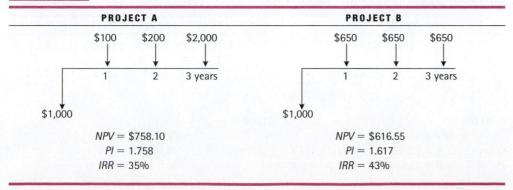

UNEQUAL LIVES

The final ranking problem to be examined centers on the question of whether it is appropriate to compare mutually exclusive projects with different life spans.

EXAMPLE

Suppose a firm with a 10 percent required rate of return is faced with the problem of replacing an aging machine and is considering two replacement machines, one with a 3-year life and one with a 6-year life. The relevant cash flow information for these projects is given in Table 9-10.

Examining the discounted cash flow criteria, we find that *NPV* and *PI* criteria indicate that project B is the better project, whereas the *IRR* criterion favors project A. This ranking inconsistency is caused by the different life spans of the projects being compared. In this case the decision is a difficult one because the projects are not comparable.

The problem of incomparability of projects with different lives arises because future, profitable investment proposals may be rejected without being included in the analysis. This can easily be seen in a replacement problem such as the present example, in which two mutually exclusive machines with different lives are being considered. In this case a comparison of the *NPV*s alone on each of these projects would be misleading. If the project with the shorter life were taken, at its termination the firm could replace the machine and receive additional benefits, whereas acceptance of the project with the longer life would exclude this possibility, a possibility that is not included in the analysis. The key question thus becomes, does today's investment decision include all future profitable investment proposals in its analysis? If not, the projects are not comparable. In this case, if project B is taken, then the project that could have been taken after 3 years when project A terminates is automatically rejected without being included in the analysis. Thus, acceptance of project B not only forces rejection of project A but also forces rejection of any replacement machine that might have been considered for years 4 through 6 without including this replacement machine in the analysis.

There are several methods to deal with this situation. The first option is to assume that the cash inflows from the shorter-lived investment will be reinvested at the required rate of return until the termination of the longer-lived asset. Although this approach is the simplest, merely calculating the *NPV*, it actually ignores the problem at hand—that of allowing for participation in another replacement opportunity with a positive *NPV*. The proper solution, thus, becomes the projection of reinvestment opportunities into the future—that is, making assumptions about possible future investment opportunities. Unfortunately, whereas the first method is too simplistic to be of any value, the second is extremely difficult, requiring extensive cash flow forecasts. The final technique for confronting the problem is to assume that reinvestment opportunities in the future will be similar to the current ones. The two most common ways of doing this are by creating a replacement chain to equalize life spans or by calculating the project's equivalent annual annuity. Using a replacement chain, the present example would call for the creation of a two-chain cycle for project A; that is, we assume that project A can be replaced with a similar investment at the end of 3 years.

TABLE 9-10   Unequal Lives Ranking Problem

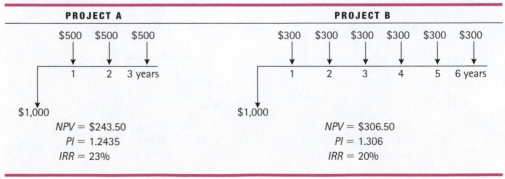

FIGURE 9-5 Replacement Chain Illustration: Two Project A's Back-to-Back

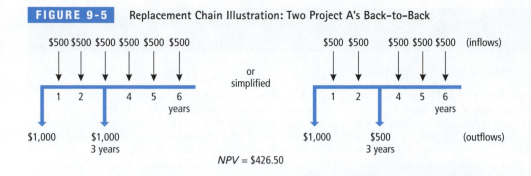

$NPV = \$426.50$

Thus, project A would be viewed as two project A's occurring back-to-back, as illustrated in Figure 9-5. The *NPV* on this replacement chain is $426.50, which is comparable with project B's *NPV*. Therefore, project A should be accepted because the *NPV* of its replacement chain is greater than the *NPV* of project B.

One problem with replacement chains is that, depending on the life of each project, it can be quite difficult to come up with equivalent lives. For example, if the two projects had 7- and 13-year lives, because the lowest common denominator is $7 \times 13 = 91$, a 91-year replacement chain would be needed to establish equivalent lives. In this case it is easier to determine the project's **equivalent annual annuity (EAA)**. A project's *EAA* is simply an *annuity cash flow that yields the same present value as the project's NPV*. To calculate a project's *EAA*, we need only calculate a project's *NPV* and then divide the number by the $PVIFA_{i, n}$ to determine the dollar value of an *n*-year annuity that would produce the same *NPV* as the project. This can be done in two steps as follows:

equivalent annual annuity (EAA)

Step 1: *Calculate the project's NPV.* In Table 9-10 we determined that project A had an *NPV* of $243.50, whereas project B had an *NPV* of $306.50.

Step 2: *Calculate the EAA.* The *EAA* is determined by dividing each project's *NPV* by the $PVIFA_{i, n}$ where *i* is the required rate of return and *n* is the project's life. This determines the level of an annuity cash flow that would produce the same *NPV* as the project. For project A the $PVIFA_{10\%, 3 \text{ yr}}$ is equal to 2.487, whereas the $PVIFA_{10\%, 6 \text{ yr}}$ for project B is equal to 4.355. Dividing each project's *NPV* by the appropriate $PVIFA_{i, n}$, we determine the *EAA* for each project:

$$EAA_A = NPV/PVIFA_{i, n}$$
$$= \$243.50/2.487$$
$$= \$97.91$$
$$EAA_B = \$306.50/4.355$$
$$= \$70.38$$

How do we interpret the *EAA*? For a project with an *n*-year life, it tells us the dollar value of an *n*-year annual annuity that would provide the same *NPV* as the project. Thus, for project A a 3-year annuity of $97.91, given a discount rate of 10 percent, would produce an *NPV* the same as project A's *NPV*, which is $243.50. We can now directly compare the equivalent annual annuities to determine which project is better. We can do this because we have found the level of annual annuity that produces an *NPV* equivalent to the project's *NPV*. Thus, because they are both annual annuities, they are comparable. To do this we need only calculate the present value of an infinite stream or perpetuity of equivalent annual annuities. This is done by using the present value of an infinite annuity formula—that is, simply dividing the *EAA* by the appropriate discount rate. In this case we find:

$$NPV_{\infty, A} = \$97.91/.10$$
$$= \$979.10$$
$$NPV_{\infty, B} = \$70.38/.10$$
$$= \$703.80$$

Here we have calculated the present value of an infinite-life replacement chain. Because the *EAA* method provides the same results as the infinite-life replacement chain, it really doesn't matter which method you prefer to use.

ETHICS IN FINANCIAL MANAGEMENT

THE FINANCIAL DOWNSIDE TO POOR ETHICAL BEHAVIOR

As we learned in **Principle 10: Ethical Behavior Is Doing the Right Thing, and Ethical Dilemmas Are Everywhere in Finance**. Knowing the inevitable outcome—for truth does percolate—why do bright and experienced people ignore it? For even if the truth is known only within the confines of the company, it will get out. Circumstances beyond even the best manager's control take over once the chance has passed to act on the moment of truth.

Johns Manville learned of the "crunching" lungs of asbestos workers in the 1930s, as reflected in the minutes of its board meetings. Instead of working on product development, warnings, or even safety equipment, the company forged onward with a strategy of trying to keep the scientific community from disclosing its findings and of limiting the increasing numbers of plaintiffs by settlements for silence.

Dow Corning didn't deserve its bankruptcy or the multibillion-dollar settlements for its silicone implants because the science didn't support the alleged damages. However, there was a moment of truth when those implants, placed on a blotter, left a stain. The company could have disclosed the possible leakage, researched the risk, and warned doctors and patients. Given the congressional testimony on the implants, many women would have chosen them despite the risk. Instead, they sued because they were not warned.

Beech-Nut's crisis was a chemical concoction instead of apple juice in its baby food products. Executives there ignored an in-house chemist who tried to tell them they were selling adulterated products. Kidder-Peabody fell despite warnings from employees about a glitch in its accounting system that was reporting bond swaps as sales and income.

These cases all have several things in common. First, their moments of truth came and went while the companies took no action. Second, employees who raised the issue were ignored, or, in some cases, fired. Third, there were lawyers along for the ride, as they have been with Ford and Firestone.

Never rely on a lawyer in these moments of truth. Lawyers give controlling legal authority but are not particularly good at controlling damage. Lawyers shouldn't make business decisions; moments of truth require managers. More importantly, moments of truth require managers with strong ethics who will do more than the law requires and less than the law allows.

As a now infamous memo reveals, Ford and Firestone did not feel obligated to reveal to the U.S. Transportation Department that certain tires were being recalled in overseas markets. The companies should have realized that it was not a question of whether the recall would be reported, but by whom.

Do businesses ever face the moment of truth wisely? One great example is James Burke, CEO of Johnson & Johnson at the time of the 1982 Tylenol capsule scare. The minute Tylenol was linked to the cyanide poisonings, Johnson & Johnson recalled and destroyed 31 million bottles of the product, at a cost of $100 million, and Mr. Burke bent over backwards to deal openly and forthrightly with the media and public. The result was one of the best crisis-management performances in history; the company won back nearly all its customers.

Source: *The Wall Street Journal*, "Manager's Journal: Ford-Firestone Lesson: Heed the Moment of Truth," September 11, 2000, page A44. Copyright © 2000, Dow Jones & Company, Inc. Reproduced with permission of DOW JONES & CO INC in the format Textbook via Copyright Clearance Center.

CONCEPT CHECK

1. What are the three general types of ranking problems?
2. In simple terms, what is an equivalent annual annuity (*EAA*)?

Objective **5**

ETHICS IN CAPITAL BUDGETING

Although it may not seem obvious, ethics has a role in capital budgeting. Firestone and Ford, Johns Manville, Dow Corning, and Beech-Nut provide examples of how these rules have been violated in the past and what the consequences can be. The Ethics in Financial Management article, "The Financial Downside to Poor Ethical Behavior," tells how important it is for firms to not only tell the truth but also make sure that consumers have all the facts they should have.

BACK TO THE FOUNDATIONS

*Ethics and ethical considerations continually crop up when capital-budgeting decisions are being made. This brings us back to **Principle 10: Ethical Behavior Is Doing the Right Thing, and Ethical Dilemmas Are Everywhere in Finance**. As the Ethics in Financial Management article points out, the most damaging event a business can experience is a loss of the public's confidence in the business's ethical standards. In making capital-budgeting decisions, we must be aware of this and that ethical behavior is doing the right thing and is the right thing to do.*

A GLANCE AT ACTUAL CAPITAL-BUDGETING PRACTICES

During the past 40 years, the popularity of each of the capital-budgeting methods has shifted rather dramatically. In the 1950s and 1960s, the payback period method dominated capital budgeting. Through the 1970s and 1980s, the *IRR* and the *NPV* techniques slowly gained in popularity until today, when they are used by the majority of major corporations in decision making.

Interestingly, a recent survey of 392 CFOs by John Graham and Campbell Harvey of Duke University found that 74.9 percent always or almost always use net present value and 75.7 percent always or almost always use the internal rate of return.[6] The payback period was also found to be very popular, with 56.7 percent indicating that they always or almost always use the payback period. The profitability index was found to be considerably less popular with only 11.9 percent of the CFOs surveyed indicating that they always or almost always use it. Moreover, the survey found that in firms headed by CEOs without an M.B.A. and headed also by older CEOs, the use of the payback period was more common.

This survey also found that large firms are significantly more likely to use *NPV* to evaluate capital-budgeting projects than are small firms. On the other hand, when it comes to capital budgeting, small firms use the payback period almost as frequently as they use *NPV* and *IRR*. One of the reasons commonly given for the use of the payback period approach is that it makes sense for the capital-constrained firm, that is, the firm that needs funds and is having problems raising additional investment funds. However, the survey didn't find any evidence of this being the case.

Without taking on new projects, a company simply wouldn't continue to exist. For example, Polaroid's inability to come up with a product to replace the instant camera that it produced resulted in that company going under in 2001. Finding new profitable projects and correctly evaluating them are central to a firm's continued existence—and that's what capital budgeting is all about. It may be your decision to buy a Burger King franchise and open a Burger King restaurant, or it may be to help in Burger King's decision to introduce the Big King, a new burger that looks an awful lot like the Big Mac. Regardless, when you're making an investment in fixed assets, it's a capital-budgeting decision. It may also involve taking your present technology and applying it in a different area. That's what Apple Computer did with the iPod, which is essentially a small, handheld computer with a hard drive that plays music.

Much of what is done within a business involves the capital-budgeting process. Many times it's referred to as strategic planning, but it generally involves capital-budgeting decisions. You may be involved in market research dealing with a proposed new product or its marketing plan, or in analyzing its costs—these are all part of the capital-budgeting process. Once all this information has been gathered, it is analyzed using the techniques and tools that we have presented in this chapter. Actually, almost any decision can be analyzed using the framework we presented here. That's because the *NPV* method "values" the project under consideration. That is, it looks at the present value of its benefits relative to the present value of its costs and, if the present value of the benefits outweighs the costs, the project is accepted. That's a pretty good decision rule, and it can be applied to any decision a business faces.

CONCEPT CHECK

1. What capital-budgeting criteria seem to be used most frequently in the real world? Why do you think this is so?

---

[6]John R. Graham and Campbell R. Harvey, "The Theory and Practice of Corporate Finance: Evidence from the Field," *Journal of Financial Economics* 60, 1–2 (May/June 2001), 187–243.

Objective **7**

FINANCE AND THE MULTINATIONAL FIRM: CAPITAL BUDGETING

Without question, the key to success in capital budgeting is to identify good projects, and for many companies these good projects are overseas. Just look at the success that Coca-Cola has had in the international markets, with more than 80 percent of its beverage profit coming from foreign markets and earning more in Japan than in the United States. This success abroad also holds true for Exxon Mobil, which earns over half its profits from abroad and is involved in gas and oil exploration projects in West Africa, the Caspian Sea, Russia, the Gulf of Mexico, and South America.

But how do you enter these markets initially? One approach that has been used successfully is through international joint ventures or strategic alliances. Under these arrangements two or more corporations merge their skills and resources on a specific project, trading things like technology and access to marketing channels. For example, GM and Suzuki Motors have a strategic alliance that provides Suzuki with access to Europe, North America, South America, and Africa, where GM has a strong presence, and provides GM with access to the Asia Pacific region, where Suzuki is well established. As John F. Smith, Jr., the GM chairman and CEO, said at the announcement of this joint venture, "Each company has specific competencies and market strengths, which can be better leveraged to the mutual benefit of both parties through this agreement."

An example of a successful market penetration using joint ventures is that of the U.S. oil giant Armco forming a joint venture with Mitsubishi to sell Armco's lightweight plastics in Japan. Similarly, Georgia-Pacific and Canfor Japan Corporation have a joint venture in which Georgia-Pacific gained access to Canfor's marketing expertise in Japan to sell pulp and paper products in Japan. Likewise, H. J. Heinz Co. announced a joint venture with an Indonesian firm to gain access to its Indonesian marketing channels. Joint ventures also provide a way to get around trade barriers. For example, India and Mexico require joint ventures for entry into their markets. As a result, U.S. firms like Apple Computer and Hewlett-Packard have been forced to enter into Mexican joint ventures in order to be allowed to ship their products into Mexico.

What is the alternative to not looking abroad for projects? It is losing out on potential revenues. Keep in mind that firms like Xerox, Hewlett-Packard, Dow Chemical, IBM, and Gillette all earn more than 50 percent of their profits from sales abroad. International boundaries no longer apply in finance.

CONCEPT CHECK

1. What methods do corporations use to enter the international markets?

SUMMARY

Objective **1**

Objective **2**

Objective **3**

Objective **4**

The process of capital budgeting involves decision making with respect to investment in fixed assets. Before a profitable project can be adopted, it must be identified or found. Unfortunately, coming up with ideas for new products, for ways to improve existing products, or for ways to make existing products more profitable is extremely difficult. In general, the best source of ideas for these new, potentially profitable products is from within the firm. We examine four commonly used criteria for determining the acceptance or rejection of capital-budgeting proposals. The first method, the payback period, does not incorporate the time value of money into its calculations. However, the net present value, profitability index, and internal rate of return do account for the time value of money. These methods are summarized in Table 9-11 on page 285.

This chapter introduces several complications into the capital-budgeting process. First, we examine capital rationing and the problems it can create by imposing a limit on the dollar size of the capital budget. Although capital rationing does not, in general, lead to the goal of maximization of shareholders' wealth, it does exist in practice. We also discuss problems associated with the evaluation

TABLE 9-11	Capital–Budgeting Criteria

1. Payback period = number of years required to recapture the initial investment

Accept if payback period ≤ maximum acceptable payback period
Reject if payback period > maximum acceptable payback period

Advantages:
- Uses free cash flows.
- Is easy to calculate and understand.
- Benefits the capital-constrained firm.
- May be used as rough screening device.

Disadvantages:
- Ignores the time value of money.
- Ignores cash flows occurring after the payback period.
- Selection of the maximum acceptable payback period is arbitrary.

2. Net present value = present value of the annual free cash flows less the investment's initial outlay

NPV = present value of all the future annual free cash flows − the initial cash outlay
$$= FCF_1(PVIF_{k\%, 1\ yr}) + FCF_2(PVIF_{k\%, 2\ yr}) + \cdots + FCF_n(PVIF_{k\%, n\ yr}) - IO$$

where FCF_t = the annual free cash flow in time period t (this can take on either positive or negative values)
$\quad k$ = the appropriate discount rate; that is, the required rate of return or the cost of capital
$\quad IO$ = the initial cash outlay
$\quad n$ = the project's expected life

Accept if $NPV \geq 0.0$
Reject if $NPV < 0.0$

Advantages:
- Uses free cash flows.
- Recognizes the time value of money.
- Is consistent with the firm's goal of shareholder wealth maximization.

Disadvantages:
- Requires detailed long-term forecasts of a project's cash flows.

3. Profitability index = the ratio of the present value of the future free cash flows to the initial outlay.

$$PI = \frac{\text{present value of all the future annual free cash flows}}{\text{initial cash outlay}}$$

$$= \frac{FCF_1(PVIF_{k\%, 1\ yr}) + FCF_2(PVIF_{k\%, 2\ yr}) + \cdots + FCF_n(PVIF_{k\%, n\ yr})}{IO}$$

Accept if $PI \geq 1.0$
Reject if $PI < 1.0$

Advantages:
- Uses free cash flows.
- Recognizes the time value of money.
- Is consistent with the firm's goal of shareholder wealth maximization.

Disadvantages:
- Requires detailed long-term forecasts of a project's cash flows.

4. Internal rate of return = the discount rate that equates the present value of the project's future free cash flows with the project's initial outlay.

IRR = the rate of return that equates the present value of the project's free cash flows with the initial outlay
$$IO = FCF_1(PVIF_{IRR\%, 1\ yr}) + FCF_2(PVIF_{IRR\%, 2\ yr}) + \cdots + FCF_n(PVIF_{IRR\%, n\ yr})$$

where IRR = the project's internal rate of return

Accept if $IRR \geq$ required rate of return
Reject if $IRR <$ required rate of return

Advantages:
- Uses free cash flows.
- Recognizes the time value of money.
- Is, in general, consistent with the firm's goal of shareholder wealth maximization.

Disadvantages:
- Requires detailed long-term forecasts of a project's cash flows.
- Possibility of multiple IRRs.
- Assumes cash flows over the life of the project can be reinvested at the IRR.

5. Modified internal rate of return = the rate of return that equates the present value of the cash outflows with the terminal value of the cash inflows.

$$PV_{outflows} = \frac{TV_{inflows}}{(1 + MIRR)^n}$$

where $PV_{outflows}$ = the present value of the project's free cash outflows

$TV_{inflows}$ = the project's terminal value, calculated by taking all the annual free cash *inflows* and finding their future value at the end of the project's life, compounded forward at the required rate of return

$MIRR$ = the project's modified internal rate of return

Accept if $MIRR \geq$ required rate of return

Reject if $MIRR <$ required rate of return

Advantages:
- Uses free cash flows.
- Recognizes the time value of money.
- Is consistent with the firm's goal of shareholder wealth maximization.
- Allows reinvestment rate to be directly specified.

Disadvantages:
- Requires detailed long-term cash flow forecasts.

Objective **5**

Objective **6**

Objective **7**

of mutually exclusive projects. Mutually exclusive projects occur when a set of investment proposals performs essentially the same task. In general, to deal with mutually exclusive projects, we rank them by means of the discounted cash flow criteria and select the project with the highest ranking. Conflicting rankings may arise because of the size disparity problem, the time disparity problem, and unequal lives. The problem of incomparability of projects with different life spans is not simply a result of the different life spans; rather, it arises because future profitable investment proposals may be rejected without being included in the analysis. Replacement chains and equivalent annual annuities are presented as possible solutions to this problem. Ethics and ethical decisions continuously crop up in capital budgeting. Just as with all other areas of finance, violating ethical considerations results in a loss of public confidence, which can have a significant negative effect on shareholder wealth. Over the past 40 years, the discounted capital-budgeting techniques have continued to gain in popularity and today dominate in the decision-making process.

The international markets provide another source for finding good capital-budgeting projects. In fact, many times a new project may simply involve taking an existing product and entering it in a foreign market. One approach that has been successfully used to enter foreign markets is international joint ventures or strategic alliances.

KEY TERMS

Benefit–cost ratio (see profitability index), 265

Capital budgeting, 260

Capital rationing, 276

Equivalent annual annuity (*EAA*), 281

Internal rate of return (*IRR*), 267

Mutually exclusive projects, 278

Net present value (*NPV*), 262

Net present value profile, 271

Payback period, 261

Profitability index (*PI*) or benefit–cost ratio, 265

STUDY QUESTIONS

9-1. Why is the capital-budgeting decision such an important process? Why are capital-budgeting errors so costly?

9-2. What are the criticisms of the use of the payback period as a capital-budgeting technique? What are its advantages? Why is it so frequently used?

9-3. In some countries, expropriation of foreign investments is a common practice. If you were considering an investment in one of those countries, would the use of the payback period criterion seem more reasonable than it otherwise might? Why?

9-4. Briefly compare and contrast the *NPV*, *PI*, and *IRR* criteria. What are the advantages and disadvantages of using each of these methods?

9-5. What are mutually exclusive projects? Why might the existence of mutually exclusive projects cause problems in the implementation of the discounted cash flow capital-budgeting criteria?

9-6. What are common reasons for capital rationing? Is capital rationing rational?

9-7. How should managers compare two mutually exclusive projects of unequal size? Would your approach change if capital rationing existed?

9-8. What causes the time disparity ranking problem? What reinvestment rate assumptions are associated with the *NPV* and *IRR* capital-budgeting criteria?

9-9. When might two mutually exclusive projects having unequal lives be incomparable? How should managers deal with this problem?

SELF-TEST PROBLEM

ST-1. You are considering a project that will require an initial outlay of $54,200. This project has an expected life of 5 years and will generate free cash flows to the company as a whole of $20,608 at the end of each year over its 5-year life. In addition to the $20,608 cash flow from operations during the fifth and final year, there will be an additional free cash inflow of $13,200 at the end of the fifth year associated with the salvage value of the machine, making the cash flow in year 5 equal to $33,808. Thus, the cash flows associated with this project look like this:

	CASH FLOW
Initial outlay	−$54,200
Inflow year 1	20,608
Inflow year 2	20,608
Inflow year 3	20,608
Inflow year 4	20,608
Inflow year 5	33,808

Given a required rate of return of 15 percent, calculate the following:

    a. Payback period   **b.** *NPV*   **c.** *PI*   **d.** *IRR*

Should this project be accepted?

STUDY PROBLEMS

9-1. (*IRR calculation*) Determine the *IRR* on the following projects:

    a. An initial outlay of $10,000 resulting in a single free cash flow of $17,182 after 8 years
    b. An initial outlay of $10,000 resulting in a single free cash flow of $48,077 after 10 years
    c. An initial outlay of $10,000 resulting in a single free cash flow of $114,943 after 20 years
    d. An initial outlay of $10,000 resulting in a single free cash flow of $13,680 after 3 years

9-2. (*IRR calculation*) Determine the *IRR* on the following projects:

    a. An initial outlay of $10,000 resulting in a free cash flow of $1,993 at the end of each year for the next 10 years
    b. An initial outlay of $10,000 resulting in a free cash flow of $2,054 at the end of each year for the next 20 years
    c. An initial outlay of $10,000 resulting in a free cash flow of $1,193 at the end of each year for the next 12 years
    d. An initial outlay of $10,000 resulting in a free cash flow of $2,843 at the end of each year for the next 5 years

9-3. (*IRR calculation*) Determine the *IRR* to the nearest percent on the following projects:

    a. An initial outlay of $10,000 resulting in a free cash flow of $2,000 at the end of year 1, $5,000 at the end of year 2, and $8,000 at the end of year 3
    b. An initial outlay of $10,000 resulting in a free cash flow of $8,000 at the end of year 1, $5,000 at the end of year 2, and $2,000 at the end of year 3
    c. An initial outlay of $10,000 resulting in a free cash flow of $2,000 at the end of years 1 through 5 and $5,000 at the end of year 6

9-4. (*NPV, PI, and IRR calculations*) Fijisawa, Inc., is considering a major expansion of its product line and has estimated the following cash flows associated with such an expansion. The initial outlay associated with the expansion would be $1,950,000, and the project would generate incremental free cash flows of $450,000 per year for 6 years. The appropriate required rate of return is 9 percent.

    a. Calculate the *NPV*.
    b. Calculate the *PI*.
    c. Calculate the *IRR*.
    d. Should this project be accepted?

9-5. (*Payback period, net present value, profitability index, and internal rate of return calculations*) You are considering a project with an initial cash outlay of $80,000 and expected free cash flows of $20,000 at the end of the year for 6 years. The required rate of return for this project is 10 percent.

    a. What is the project's payback period?
    b. What is the project's *NPV*?
    c. What is the project's *PI*?
    d. What is the project's *IRR*?

9-6. (*Net present value, profitability index, and internal rate of return calculations*) You are considering two independent projects, project A and project B. The initial cash outlay associated with project A is $50,000, and the initial cash outlay associated with project B is $70,000. The required rate of return on both projects is 12 percent. The expected annual free cash inflows from each project are as follows:

	PROJECT A	PROJECT B
Initial outlay	−$50,000	−$70,000
Inflow year 1	12,000	13,000
Inflow year 2	12,000	13,000
Inflow year 3	12,000	13,000
Inflow year 4	12,000	13,000
Inflow year 5	12,000	13,000
Inflow year 6	12,000	13,000

Calculate the *NPV*, *PI*, and *IRR* for each project and indicate if the project should be accepted.

9-7. (*Payback period calculations*) You are considering three independent projects, project A, project B, and project C. Given the following cash flow information, calculate the payback period for each.

	PROJECT A	PROJECT B	PROJECT C
Initial outlay	−$1,000	−$10,000	−$5,000
Inflow year 1	600	5,000	1,000
Inflow year 2	300	3,000	1,000
Inflow year 3	200	3,000	2,000
Inflow year 4	100	3,000	2,000
Inflow year 5	500	3,000	2,000

If you require a 3-year payback before an investment can be accepted, which project(s) would be accepted?

9-8. (*NPV with varying required rates of return*) Dowling Sportswear is considering building a new factory to produce aluminum baseball bats. This project would require an initial cash outlay of $5,000,000 and will generate annual free cash inflows of $1,000,000 per year for 8 years. Calculate the project's *NPV* given:

    a. A required rate of return of 9 percent
    b. A required rate of return of 11 percent
    c. A required rate of return of 13 percent
    d. A required rate of return of 15 percent

9-9. (*IRR calculations*) Given the following free cash flows, determine the *IRR* for the three independent projects A, B, and C.

	PROJECT A	PROJECT B	PROJECT C
Initial outlay	−$50,000	−$100,000	−$450,000
Cash inflows			
Year 1	$10,000	$ 25,000	$200,000
Year 2	15,000	25,000	200,000
Year 3	20,000	25,000	200,000
Year 4	25,000	25,000	—
Year 5	30,000	25,000	—

9-10. (*NPV with varying required rates of return*) Big Steve's, makers of swizzle sticks, is considering the purchase of a new plastic stamping machine. This investment requires an initial outlay of $100,000 and will generate free cash inflows of $18,000 per year for 10 years. For each of the listed required rates of return, determine the project's net present value.

    a. The required rate of return is 10 percent.
    b. The required rate of return is 15 percent.
    c. Would the project be accepted under part a or b?
    d. What is the project's *IRR*?

9-11. (*Internal rate of return with uneven cash flows*) The Boisjoly Corporation is considering introducing a new low-carb pasta product line. The required rate of return on this project is 12 percent. What is the *IRR* on this project if it is expected to produce the following cash flows?

Initial outlay	−$653,803
FCF in year 1	300,000
FCF in year 2	300,000
FCF in year 3	200,000
FCF in year 4	100,000

9-12. (*Internal rate of return with uneven cash flows*) The Tiffin Barker Corporation is considering introducing a new currency verifier that has the ability to identify counterfeit dollar bills. The required rate of return on this project is 12 percent. What is the *IRR* on this project if it is expected to produce the following cash flows?

Initial outlay	−$927,917
FCF in year 1	200,000
FCF in year 2	300,000
FCF in year 3	300,000
FCF in year 4	200,000
FCF in year 5	200,000
FCF in year 6	160,000

9-13. (*MIRR calculation*) Artie's Wrestling Stuff is considering building a new plant. This plant would require an initial cash outlay of $8 million and will generate annual free cash inflows of $2 million per year for eight years. Calculate the project's *MIRR* given:

    a. A required rate of return of 10 percent
    b. A required rate of return of 12 percent
    c. A required rate of return of 14 percent

9-14. (*Size disparity problem*) The D. Dorner Farms Corporation is considering purchasing one of two fertilizer-herbicides for the upcoming year. The more expensive of the two is better and will produce a higher yield. Assume these projects are mutually exclusive and that the required rate of return is 10 percent. Given the following free cash flows:

	PROJECT A	PROJECT B
Initial outlay	−$500	−$5,000
Inflow year 1	700	6,000

    a. Calculate the *NPV* of each project.
    b. Calculate the *PI* of each project.
    c. Calculate the *IRR* of each project.
    d. If there is no capital-rationing constraint, which project should be selected? If there is a capital-rationing constraint, how should the decision be made?

9-15. (*Time disparity problem*) The State Spartan Corporation is considering two mutually exclusive projects. The free cash flows associated with those projects are as follows:

	PROJECT A	PROJECT B
Initial outlay	−$50,000	−$50,000
Inflow year 1	15,625	0
Inflow year 2	15,625	0
Inflow year 3	15,625	0
Inflow year 4	15,625	0
Inflow year 5	15,625	100,000

The required rate of return on these projects is 10 percent.

    a. What is each project's payback period?
    b. What is each project's *NPV*?
    c. What is each project's *IRR*?
    d. What has caused the ranking conflict?
    e. Which project should be accepted? Why?

9-16. (*Unequal lives problem*) The B. T. Knight Corporation is considering two mutually exclusive pieces of machinery that perform the same task. The two alternatives available provide the following set of free cash flows:

	EQUIPMENT A	EQUIPMENT B
Initial outflow	−$20,000	−$20,000
Inflow year 1	12,590	6,625
Inflow year 2	12,590	6,625
Inflow year 3	12,590	6,625
Inflow year 4		6,625
Inflow year 5		6,625
Inflow year 6		6,625
Inflow year 7		6,625
Inflow year 8		6,625
Inflow year 9		6,625

Equipment A has an expected life of 3 years, whereas equipment B has an expected life of 9 years. Assume a required rate of return of 15 percent.

    a. Calculate each project's payback period.
    b. Calculate each project's *NPV*.
    c. Calculate each project's *IRR*.
    d. Are these projects comparable?
    e. Compare these projects using replacement chains and *EAA*. Which project should be selected? Support your recommendation.

9-17. (*Equivalent annual annuity*) The Andrzejewski Corporation is considering two mutually exclusive projects, one with a 3-year life and one with a 7-year life. The free cash flows from the two projects are as follows:

	PROJECT A	PROJECT B
Initial outlay	−$50,000	−$50,000
Inflow year 1	20,000	36,000
Inflow year 2	20,000	36,000
Inflow year 3	20,000	36,000
Inflow year 4	20,000	
Inflow year 5	20,000	
Inflow year 6	20,000	
Inflow year 7	20,000	

    a. Assuming a 10-percent required rate of return on both projects, calculate each project's *EAA*. Which project should be selected?
    b. Calculate the present value of an infinite-life replacement chain for each project.

9-18. (*Capital rationing*) The Cowboy Hat Company of Stillwater, Oklahoma, is considering seven capital investment proposals, for which the funds available are limited to a maximum of $12 million. The projects are independent and have the following costs and profitability indexes associated with them:

PROJECT	COST	PROFITABILITY INDEX
A	$4,000,000	1.18
B	3,000,000	1.08
C	5,000,000	1.33
D	6,000,000	1.31
E	4,000,000	1.19
F	6,000,000	1.20
G	4,000,000	1.18

    a. Under strict capital rationing, which projects should be selected?
    b. What problems are there with capital rationing?

WEB WORKS

9-WW. Since 2000, Harley Davidson has introduced several new products aimed directly at 18- to 34-year-old Generation X-ers in hopes of bringing a new generation of customers into motorcycling. One is the Buell Blast, a fun-to-ride, sporty motorcycle that is low cost and lightweight, and the other is a lower version of its 833 Sportster aimed at shorter riders. Harley was facing the problem that its customer base was rapidly aging. In fact, over the past 10 years the average age of a Harley rider has risen from 38 to 46. In addition, Harley wanted to add more women to its customer base. How did it go about doing this? Through its Buell motorcycle division that produces smaller, sportier, and less expensive motorcycles, which are more appropriate for less experienced motorcyclists. Harley hopes that once these new customers find the fun in motorcycling, they will eventually graduate to Harleys.

Take a look at the Harley Davidson website (**www.harley-davidson.com**). What type of customer do you think the Harley Davidson motorcycles appeal to? Now find the Buell Motorcycle Company website (**www.buell.com/en_us**). What type of customer do these motorcycles appeal to? What do you think of Harley's strategic plan?

COMPREHENSIVE PROBLEM

Your first assignment in your new position as assistant financial analyst at Caledonia Products is to evaluate two new capital-budgeting proposals. Because this is your first assignment, you have been asked not only to provide a recommendation but also to respond to a number of questions aimed at judging your understanding of the capital-budgeting process. This is a standard procedure for all new financial analysts at Caledonia, and it will serve to determine whether you are moved directly into the capital-budgeting analysis department or are provided with remedial training. The memorandum you received outlining your assignment follows.

To: The New Financial Analysts

From: Mr. V. Morrison, CEO, Caledonia Products

Re: Capital-Budgeting Analysis

Provide an evaluation of two proposed projects, both with 5-year expected lives and identical initial outlays of $110,000. Both of these projects involve additions to Caledonia's highly successful Avalon product line, and as a result, the required rate of return on both projects has been established at 12 percent. The expected free cash flows from each project are as follows:

	PROJECT A	PROJECT B
Initial outlay	−$110,000	−$110,000
Inflow year 1	20,000	40,000
Inflow year 2	30,000	40,000
Inflow year 3	40,000	40,000
Inflow year 4	50,000	40,000
Inflow year 5	70,000	40,000

In evaluating these projects, please respond to the following questions:

a. Why is the capital-budgeting process so important?
b. Why is it difficult to find exceptionally profitable projects?
c. What is the payback period on each project? If Caledonia imposes a 3-year maximum acceptable payback period, which of these projects should be accepted?
d. What are the criticisms of the payback period?
e. Determine the *NPV* for each of these projects. Should they be accepted?
f. Describe the logic behind the *NPV*.
g. Determine the *PI* for each of these projects. Should they be accepted?
h. Would you expect the *NPV* and *PI* methods to give consistent accept/reject decisions? Why or why not?
i. What would happen to the *NPV* and *PI* for each project if the required rate of return increased? If the required rate of return decreased?
j. Determine the *IRR* for each project. Should they be accepted?
k. How does a change in the required rate of return affect the project's internal rate of return?
l. What reinvestment rate assumptions are implicitly made by the *NPV* and *IRR* methods? Which one is better?

You have *also* been asked for your views on three unrelated sets of projects. Each set of projects involves two mutually exclusive projects. These projects follow.

m. Caledonia is considering two investments with 1-year lives. The more expensive of the two is the better and will produce more savings. Assume these projects are mutually exclusive and that the required rate of return is 10 percent. Given the following free cash flows:

	PROJECT A	PROJECT B
Initial outlay	−$195,000	−$1,200,000
Inflow year 1	240,000	1,650,000

1. Calculate the *NPV* for each project.
2. Calculate the *PI* for each project.
3. Calculate the *IRR* for each project.
4. If there is no capital-rationing constraint, which project should be selected? If there is a capital-rationing constraint, how should the decision be made?

n. Caledonia is considering two additional mutually exclusive projects. The free cash flows associated with these projects are as follows:

	PROJECT A	PROJECT B
Initial outlay	−$10,000	−$100,000
Inflow year 1	32,000	0
Inflow year 2	32,000	0
Inflow year 3	32,000	0
Inflow year 4	32,000	0
Inflow year 5	32,000	200,000

The required rate of return on these projects is 11 percent.
1. What is each project's payback period?
2. What is each project's *NPV*?
3. What is each project's *IRR*?
4. What has caused the ranking conflict?
5. Which project should be accepted? Why?

o. The final two mutually exclusive projects that Caledonia is considering involves mutually exclusive pieces of machinery that perform the same task. The two alternatives available provide the following set of free cash flows.

	EQUIPMENT A	EQUIPMENT B
Initial outlay	−$100,000	−$100,000
Inflow year 1	65,000	32,500
Inflow year 2	65,000	32,500
Inflow year 3	65,000	32,500
Inflow year 4		32,500
Inflow year 5		32,500
Inflow year 6		32,500
Inflow year 7		32,500
Inflow year 8		32,500
Inflow year 9		32,500

Equipment A has an expected life of 3 years, whereas equipment B has an expected life of 9 years. Assume a required rate of return of 14 percent.
1. Calculate each project's payback period.
2. Calculate each project's *NPV*.
3. Calculate each project's *IRR*.
4. Are these projects comparable?
5. Compare these projects using replacement chains and *EAA*s. Which project should be selected? Support your recommendation.

SELF-TEST SOLUTION

SS-1.

a. Payback period $= \dfrac{\$54,200}{\$20,608} = 2.630$ years

b. NPV = present value of all the future annual free cash flows – the initial cash outlay
$$= FCF_1(PVIF_{k\%,\,1\,yr}) + FCF_2(PVIF_{k\%,\,2\,yr}) + \cdots + FCF_n(PVIF_{k\%,\,n\,yr}) - IO$$
$$= \$20,608(2.855 + \$33,808(.497) - \$54,200$$
$$= \$58,836 + \$16,803 - \$54,200$$
$$= \$21,439$$

c.

$$PI = \dfrac{\text{present value of all the future annual free cash flows}}{\text{initial cash outlay}}$$

$$= \dfrac{FCF_1(PVIF_{k\%,\,1\,yr}) + FCF_2(PVIF_{k\%,\,2\,yr}) + \cdots + FCF_n(PVIF_{k\%,\,n\,yr})}{IO}$$

$$= \dfrac{\$75,639}{\$54,200}$$

$$= 1.396$$

d. IRR = the rate of return that equates the present value of the project's free cash flows with the initial outlay

$$IO = FCF_1(PVIF_{IRR\%,\,1\,yr}) + FCF_2(PVIF_{IRR\%,\,2\,yr}) + \cdots + FCF_n(PVIF_{IRR\%,\,n\,yr})$$

$$\$54,200 = \$20,608\,(PVIFA_{IRR\%,\,4\,yr}) + \$33,808\,(PVIF_{IRR\%,\,5\,yr})$$

Try 29 percent:

$$\$54,200 = \$20,608(2.203) + \$33,808(.280)$$
$$= \$45,399 + \$9,466$$
$$= \$54,865$$

Try 30 percent:

$$\$45,200 = \$20,608(2.166) + \$33,808(.269)$$
$$= \$44,637 + \$9,094$$
$$= \$53,731$$

Thus, the IRR is just below 30 percent and the project should be accepted because the NPV is positive, the PI is greater than 1.0, and the IRR is greater than the required rate of return of 15 percent.

⋘ LEARNING OBJECTIVES ⋙

After reading this chapter, you should be able to:

1. Identify guidelines by which we measure cash flows.

2. Explain how a project's benefits and costs—that is, its free cash flows—are calculated.

3. Explain the importance of options or flexibility in capital budgeting.

4. Explain what the appropriate measure of risk is for capital-budgeting purposes.

5. Determine the acceptability of a new project using the risk-adjusted discount method of adjusting for risk.

6. Explain the use of simulation for imitating the performance of a project under evaluation.

7. Explain why a multinational firm faces a more difficult time estimating cash flows along with increased risks.

Cash Flows and Other Topics in Capital Budgeting

In 2001 when Toyota introduced the first-generation model of its gas-electric hybrid car, the Prius, it seemed more like a little science experiment than real competition for the auto industry. But that's all changed. As gas prices climbed in 2004 and hovered around $2 a gallon, suddenly the gas-electric hybrid car seemed to be the way to go. About that time, Toyota introduced its second-generation Prius, and the future looked good. In fact, in late 2004 Toyota announced it would double the number of Prius cars that it sends to the U.S. market to 100,000 units annually in 2005, making it the Japanese automaker's third best-selling sedan.

How did Toyota gain leadership in the gas-electric hybrid car market? Its capital-budgeting decision to enter the gas-electric hybrid car market with the Prius vaulted Toyota into the lead, and that decision involved a very large investment in excess of $1 billion. This decision could leave Toyota in great shape to take on the future if strategic management consulting firm Booz Allen Hamilton is right in its forecast that cars equipped with hybrid engines could make up 20 percent of the overall car market by 2010 and 80 percent by 2015.

Still, according to many analysts, Toyota has yet to make a dime on the Prius. In fact, when the Prius first came out, Toyota had it priced so that it was losing about $3,000 on each car it sold. Although now Toyota claims to be finally making money on the Prius, many analysts feel that the automaker is really just breaking even.

Toyota's decision to introduce the Prius and enter the hybrid car market was a difficult one. Would it simply move Toyota customers from one Toyota car to another, or would it bring new customers to Toyota? Was this a chance to gain a foothold on the new technology of the future, or were hybrid cars simply a fad? It was indeed a difficult decision, especially when you consider the size of the investment. How did Toyota make the decision to go ahead with the Prius? It used the basic techniques described in the previous chapter, but before it could apply those techniques, Toyota had to come up with the cash flow forecasts and adjust for the risk associated with the project. That's what we'll be looking at in this chapter.

≪ WHAT'S AHEAD ≫

This chapter continues our discussion of decision-making rules for deciding when to invest in new projects. First, we examine what is a relevant cash flow and how to calculate the relevant cash flow. We then turn our attention to the problem of capital budgeting under uncertainty. In discussing capital-budgeting techniques in the preceding chapter, we implicitly assumed the level of risk associated with each investment proposal was the same. In this chapter we lift that assumption and examine various ways in which risk can be incorporated into the capital-budgeting decision.

In Chapter 9 we looked at decision criteria, assuming the cash flows were known with certainty. In this chapter, we see how difficult and complex estimating cash flows is. Not only will we develop an understanding of what a relevant cash flow is and how to measure it, but we will also try to understand the risks that Toyota or any other company faces in making capital-budgeting decisions, not knowing exactly what future competition it will face. We will also learn how Toyota or any other company can modify our capital-budgeting criterion to deal with risk.

GUIDELINES FOR CAPITAL BUDGETING

To evaluate investment proposals, we must first set guidelines by which we measure the value of each proposal. In effect, we are deciding what is and what isn't a relevant cash flow.

USE FREE CASH FLOWS RATHER THAN ACCOUNTING PROFITS

We use free cash flows, not accounting profits, as our measurement tool. The firm receives and is able to reinvest free cash flows, whereas accounting profits are shown when they are earned rather than when the money is actually in hand. Unfortunately, a firm's accounting profits and free cash flows may not be timed to occur together. For example, capital expenses, such as vehicles and plant and equipment, are depreciated over several years, with their annual depreciation subtracted from profits. Free cash flows correctly reflect the timing of benefits and costs— that is, when the money is received, when it can be reinvested, and when it must be paid out.

> **BACK TO THE FOUNDATIONS**
>
> *If we are to make intelligent capital-budgeting decisions, we must accurately measure the timing of the benefits and costs, that is, when we receive money and when it leaves our hands. **Principle 3: Cash—Not Profits—Is King** speaks directly to this. Remember, it is cash inflows that can be reinvested and cash outflows that involve paying out money.*

THINK INCREMENTALLY

Unfortunately, calculating free cash flows from a project may not be enough. Decision makers must ask, *What new free cash flows will the company as a whole receive if the company takes on a given project?* What if the company does not take on the project? Interestingly, we may find that not all cash flows a firm expects from an investment proposal are incremental in nature. In measuring free cash flows, however, the trick is to think incrementally. In doing so, we will see that only **incremental after-tax free cash flows** matter. As such, our guiding rule in deciding if a free cash flow is incremental is to look at the company with, versus without, the new product. As you will see in the upcoming sections, this may be easier said than done.

incremental after-tax free cash flows

> **BACK TO THE FOUNDATIONS**
>
> *In order to measure the true effects of our decisions, we analyze the benefits and costs of projects on an incremental basis, which relates directly to **Principle 4: Incremental Cash Flows—It's Only What Changes That Counts**. In effect, we ask ourselves what the cash flows will be if the project is taken on versus what they will be if the project is not taken on.*

BEWARE OF CASH FLOWS DIVERTED FROM EXISTING PRODUCTS

Assume for a moment that we are managers of a firm considering a new product line that might compete with one of our existing products and possibly reduce its sales. In determining the free cash flows associated with the proposed project, we should consider only the incremental sales brought to the company as a whole. New-product sales achieved at the cost of losing sales of other products in our line are not considered a benefit of adopting the new product. For example, when Quaker Oats introduced Cap'n Crunch's Cozmic Crunch, the product competed directly with the company's Cap'n Crunch and Crunch Berries cereals. (In fact it was almost identical to Crunch Berries, with the shapes changed to stars and moons, along with a packet of orange space dust that turns milk green.) Quaker meant to target the market niche held by Post Fruity Pebbles, but there was no question that sales recorded by Cozmic Crunch bit into—literally cannibalized—Quaker's existing product line.

Remember that we are only interested in the sales dollars to the firm if the project is accepted, as opposed to what the sales dollars would be if the project were rejected. Just moving sales from one product line to a new product line does not bring anything new into the company, but if sales are captured from competitors or if sales that would have been lost to new competing products are retained, then these are relevant incremental free cash flows. In each case these are the incremental free cash flows to the firm—looking at the firm as a whole, with the new product versus without the new product.

Look for Incidental or Synergistic Effects

Although in some cases a new project may take sales away from a firm's current projects, in other cases a new effort may actually bring new sales to the existing line.

For example, in 2002, GM's Pontiac division introduced the Vibe, an in-your-face-looking combination of a wagon and a sporty coupe. The idea was not only to sell lots of Vibes but also to help lure back young customers to Pontiac's other car lines. From 1994 until the introduction of the Vibe, the average age of Pontiac buyers had risen from 40 to 42. Thus, the hope was that the Vibe would bring younger customers into showrooms, who would in turn either buy a Vibe or lock on to another one of Pontiac's products. Thus, in evaluating the Vibe, if managers were to look only at the revenue from new Vibe sales, they would miss the incremental cash flow to Pontiac as a whole that results from new customers who would not have otherwise purchased a Pontiac automobile but did so only after being lured into a Pontiac showroom to see a Vibe. This is called a *synergistic* effect. The cash flow comes from any Pontiac sale that would not have occurred if a customer had not visited a Pontiac showroom to see a Vibe.

Work in Working-Capital Requirements

Many times a new project involves additional investment in working capital. This may take the form of new inventory to stock a sales outlet, additional investment in accounts receivable resulting from additional credit sales, or increased investment in free cash to operate cash registers, and more. Working-capital requirements are considered a free cash flow even though they do not leave the company. How can investment in inventory be considered a free cash outflow when the goods are still in the store? Because the firm does not have access to the inventory's cash value, the firm cannot use the money for other investments. Generally, working-capital requirements are tied up over the life of the project. When the project terminates, there is usually an offsetting cash inflow as the working capital is recovered, although this offset is not perfect because of the time value of money.

Consider Incremental Expenses

Just as cash inflows from a new project are measured on an incremental basis, expenses should also be measured on an incremental basis. For example, if introducing a new product line necessitates training the sales staff, the after-tax cash flow associated with the training program must be considered a cash outflow and charged against the project. If accepting a new project dictates that a production facility be reengineered, the cash flows associated with that capital investment should be charged against the project, and they will then be depreciated over the life of the project. Again, any incremental after-tax cash flow affecting the company as a whole is a relevant cash flow, whether it is flowing in or flowing out.

REMEMBER THAT SUNK COSTS ARE NOT INCREMENTAL CASH FLOWS

Only cash flows that are affected by the decision making at the moment are relevant in capital budgeting. The manager asks two questions: (1) Will this cash flow occur if the project is accepted? (2) Will this cash flow occur if the project is rejected? Yes to the first question and no to the second equals an incremental cash flow. For example, let's assume you are considering introducing a new taste treat called Puddin' in a Shoe. You would like to do some test-marketing before production. If you are considering the decision to test-market and have not yet done so, the costs associated with the test-marketing are relevant cash flows. Conversely, if you have already test-marketed, the cash flows involved in testing-marketing are no longer relevant in project evaluation. It's a matter of timing. Regardless of what you might decide about future production, the cash flows allocated to marketing have already occurred. Cash flows that have already taken place are often referred to as "sunk costs" because they have been sunk into the project and cannot be undone. As a rule, any cash flows that are not affected by the accept/reject criterion should not be included in capital-budgeting analysis.

ACCOUNT FOR OPPORTUNITY COSTS

Now we will focus on the cash flows that are lost because a given project consumes scarce resources that would have produced cash flows if that project had been rejected. This is the opportunity cost of doing business. For example, a product may use valuable floor space in a production facility. Although the cash flow is not obvious, the real question remains: What else could be done with this space? The space could have been rented out, or another product could have been stored there. The key point is that opportunity-cost cash flows should reflect net cash flows that would have been received if the project under consideration were rejected. Again, we are analyzing the cash flows to the company as a whole, with or without the project.

DECIDE IF OVERHEAD COSTS ARE TRULY INCREMENTAL CASH FLOWS

Although we certainly want to include any incremental cash flows resulting in changes from overhead expenses such as utilities and salaries, we also want to make sure that these are truly incremental cash flows. Many times, overhead expenses— heat, light, rent—would occur whether a given project were accepted or rejected. There is often not a single specific project to which these expenses can be allocated. Thus, the question is not whether the project benefits from overhead items but whether the overhead costs are incremental cash flows associated with the project and relevant to capital budgeting.

IGNORE INTEREST PAYMENTS AND FINANCING FLOWS

In evaluating new projects and determining cash flows, we must separate the investment decision from the financing decision. Interest payments and other financing cash flows that might result from raising funds to finance a project should not be considered incremental cash flows. If accepting a project means we have to raise new funds by issuing bonds, the interest charges associated with raising funds are not a relevant cash outflow. When we discount the incremental cash flows back to the present at the required rate of return, we are implicitly accounting for the cost of raising funds to finance the new project. In essence, the required rate of return reflects the cost of the funds needed to support the project. Managers first determine the desirability of the project and then determine how best to finance it.

CONCEPT CHECK

1. What is an incremental cash flow? What is a sunk cost? What are opportunity costs?
2. If Ford introduces a new auto line, might some of the cash flows from that new car line be diverted from existing product lines? How should you deal with this?

FINANCIAL MANAGEMENT
IN PRACTICE

UNIVERSAL STUDIOS

A major capital-budgeting decision led Universal Studios to build its Islands of Adventures theme park. The purpose of this $2.6 billion investment by Universal was to take direct aim at the first crack of the tourist's dollar in Orlando, Florida. Although this capital-budgeting decision may, on the surface, seem like a relatively simple decision, forecasting the expected cash flows associated with this theme park was, in fact, quite complicated.

To begin with, Universal was introducing a product that competes directly with itself. The original Universal Studios park features rides like "Back to the Future" and "Jaws." Are there enough tourist dollars to support both theme parks, or will the new Islands of Adventure park simply cannibalize ticket sales from the older Universal Studios park. In addition, what happens when Disney counters with a new park of its own? We will evaluate projects relative to their base case—that is, what will happen if the project is not carried out? In the case of Universal's Islands of Adventure, we could ask what would happen to attendance at the original Universal Studios park if the new park were not opened versus what the attendance

would be with the new park. Will tourist traffic through the Islands of Adventure lead to additional sales of the brands and businesses visibly promoted and available in the new park that fall under Universal's and Seagrams's corporate umbrella?

From Universal's point of view, the objective may be three-fold: to increase its share of the tourist market; to keep from losing market share as tourists look for the latest in technological rides and entertainment; and to promote Universal's, and its parent company Seagrams's, other brands and products. However, for companies in very competitive markets, the evolution and introduction of new products may serve more to preserve market share than to expand it. Certainly, that's the case in the computer market, where Dell, Compaq, and IBM introduce upgraded models that continually render current models obsolete. The bottom line here is that, with respect to estimating cash flows, things are many times more complicated than they first appear. As such, we have to dig deep to understand how a firm's free cash flows are affected by the decision at hand.

AN OVERVIEW OF THE CALCULATIONS OF A PROJECT'S FREE CASH FLOWS

Objective **2**

In measuring cash flows, we will be interested only in the incremental, or differential, after-tax cash flows that can be attributed to the proposal being evaluated. That is, we will focus our attention on the difference in the firm's after-tax cash flows *with* versus *without* the project—the project's *free cash flows*. The worth of our decision depends on the accuracy of our cash flow estimates. For this reason, we first examined the question of what cash flows are relevant. Now we will see that, in general, a project's free cash flows will fall into one of three categories: (1) the initial outlay, (2) the differential flows over the project's life, and (3) the terminal cash flow. Once we have taken a look at these categories, we will take on the task of measuring these free cash flows.

INITIAL OUTLAY

The **initial outlay** involves the immediate cash outflow necessary to purchase the asset and put it in operating order. This amount includes the cost of installing the asset (the asset's purchase price plus any expenses associated with shipping or installation) and any nonexpense cash outlays, such as increased working-capital requirements. If we are considering a new sales outlet, there might be additional cash flows associated with net investment in working capital in the form of increased inventory and cash necessary to operate the sales outlet. Although these cash flows are not included in the cost of the asset or even expensed on the books, they must be included in our analysis. The after-tax cost of expense items incurred as a result of new investment must also be included as cash outflows—for example, any training expenses that would not have been incurred otherwise.

Finally, if the investment decision is a replacement decision, the cash inflow associated with the selling price of the old asset, in addition to any tax effects resulting from its sale, must be included. It should be stressed that the incremental nature of the cash flow is of great importance. In many cases, if the project is not accepted, then status quo for the firm will simply not continue. In calculating incremental cash flows, we must be realistic in estimating what the cash flows to the company would be if the new project were not accepted.

initial outlay

TAX EFFECTS—SALE OF OLD MACHINE

Potentially, one of the most confusing initial outlay calculations is for a replacement project involving the incremental tax payment associated with the sale of an old machine. There are three possible tax situations dealing with the sale of an old asset:

1. The old asset is sold for a price above the depreciated value. Here the difference between the old machine's selling price and its depreciated value is considered a taxable gain and is taxed at the marginal corporate tax rate. If, for example, the old machine was originally purchased for $15,000, had a book value of $10,000, and was sold for $17,000, assuming the firm's marginal corporate tax rate is 34 percent, the taxes due from the gain would be ($17,000 − $10,000) × (.34), or $2,380.

2. The old asset is sold for its depreciated value. In this case, no taxes result, because there is neither a gain nor a loss in the asset's sale.

3. The old asset is sold for less than its depreciated value. In this case, the difference between the depreciated book value and the salvage value of the asset is a taxable loss and may be used to offset capital gains and thus results in tax savings. For example, if the depreciated book value of the asset is $10,000 and it is sold for $7,000, we have a $3,000 loss. Assuming the firm's marginal corporate tax rate is 34 percent, the cash inflow from tax savings is ($10,000 − $7,000) × (.34), or $1,020.

ANNUAL FREE CASH FLOWS OVER THE PROJECT'S LIFE

Annual free cash flows come from operating cash flows (that is, what you've made as a result of taking on the project), changes in working capital, and any capital spending that might take place. In our calculations we'll begin with our pro forma statements and work from there. We will have to make adjustments for interest, depreciation, and working capital, along with any capital expenditures that might occur.

Before we look at the calculations, let's look at the types of adjustments that we're going to have to make to go from operating cash flows to free cash flows. To do this we'll have to make adjustments for:

➤ **Depreciation and Taxes.** When accountants calculate a firm's net income, one of the expenses they subtract out is depreciation. However, depreciation is a non–cash flow expense. If you think about it, depreciation occurs because you bought a fixed asset (for example, you built a plant) in an earlier period, and now, through depreciation, you're expensing it over time—but depreciation does not involve a cash flow. That means net income understates cash flows by this amount. Therefore, we'll want to compensate for this by adding depreciation back in to our measure of accounting income when calculating cash flows.

In addition, although depreciation is not a cash flow item, it lowers profits, which in turn lowers taxes. For students developing a foundation in corporate finance, it is the concept of depreciation, not the calculation of it, that is important. The reason the calculation of depreciation is deemphasized is that it is extremely complicated, and its calculation changes every few years as Congress enacts new tax laws. Through all this, bear in mind that although depreciation is not a cash flow item, it does affect cash flows by lowering the level of profits on which taxes are calculated.

The Revenue Reconciliation Act of 1993 largely left intact the modified version of the Accelerated Cost Recovery System introduced in the Tax Reform Act of 1986. Although this was examined earlier, a review is appropriate here. This modified version of the old accelerated cost recovery system (ACRS) is used for most tangible depreciable property placed in service beginning in 1987. Under this method, the life of the asset is determined according to the asset's class life, which is assigned by the IRS; for example, most computer equipment has a 5-year asset life. It also allows for only a half-year's deduction in the first year and a half-year's deduction in the year after the recovery period. The asset is then depreciated using the 200 percent declining balance method or an optional straight-line method.

For our purposes, depreciation is calculated using a simplified straight-line method. This simplified process ignores the half-year convention that allows only a half-year's deduction in the year the project is placed in service and a half-year's deduction in the first year after the recovery period. By ignoring the half-year convention and assuming a zero salvage value, we are able to calculate annual depreciation by taking the project's initial depreciable value and dividing by its depreciable life as follows:

$$\text{Annual depreciation using the simplified straight-line method} = \frac{\text{initial depreciable value}}{\text{depreciable life}}$$

The initial depreciable value is equal to the cost of the asset plus any expenses necessary to get the new asset into operating order.

This is not how depreciation would actually be calculated. The reason we have simplified the calculation is to allow you to focus directly on what should and should not be included in the cash flow calculations. Moreover, because the tax laws change rather frequently, we are more interested in recognizing the tax implications of depreciation than in understanding the specific depreciation provisions of the current tax laws.

Our concern with depreciation is to highlight its importance in generating cash flow estimates and to indicate that the financial manager must be aware of the current tax provisions when evaluating capital-budgeting proposals.

➤ **Interest Expenses.** There's no question that if you take on a new project, you'll have to pay for it somehow—through either internal cash flow or selling new stocks or bonds. In other words, there's a cost to that money. We recognize this principle when we discount future cash flows back to the present at the required rate of return. Remember, the project's required rate of return is the rate of return that you must earn to justify taking on the project. It recognizes the risk of the project and the fact that there is an opportunity cost of money. If we discounted the future cash flows back to the present and also subtracted out interest expenses, then we'd be double counted for the cost of money—accounting for the cost of money once when we subtracted out interest expenses and once when we discounted the cash flows back to the present. Therefore, we want to make sure interest expenses aren't subtracted out. That means we'll want to make sure that financing flows are not included.

➤ **Changes in Working Capital.** Many projects require an increased investment in working capital. For example, some of the new sales may be credit sales resulting in an increased investment in accounts receivable. Also, in order to produce and sell the product, the firm may have to increase its investment in inventory. On the other hand, some of this increased working-capital investment may be financed by an increase in accounts payable. Since all these potential changes are changes in assets and liabilities, they don't affect accounting income. The bottom line here is that if this project brings with it a positive change in net working capital, then it means money is going to be tied up in increased working capital, and this would be a cash outflow. That means we'll have to make sure we account for any changes in working capital that might occur.

➤ **Changes in Capital Spending.** From an accounting perspective, the cash flow associated with the purchase of a fixed asset is not an expense. That means that when Marriott spends $50 million on building a new hotel resort, although there is a significant cash outflow, there is no accompanying expense. Instead, the $50 million cash outflow creates an annual depreciation expense over the life of the hotel. We'll want to make sure we include any changes in capital spending in our cash flow calculations.

TERMINAL CASH FLOW

The calculation of the terminal cash flow is in general quite a bit simpler than the preceding two calculations. Flows associated with the project's termination may include the salvage value of the project plus or minus any taxable gains or losses associated with its sale.

Under the current tax laws, in most cases there will be tax payments associated with the salvage value at termination. This is because the current laws allow all projects to be depreciated to zero, and if a project has a book value of zero at termination and a positive salvage value, then that salvage value will be taxed. The tax effects associated with the salvage value of the project at termination are determined exactly like the tax effects on the sale of the old machine associated with the initial outlay. The salvage value proceeds are compared with the depreciated value, in this case zero, to determine the tax.

In addition to the salvage value, there may be a cash outlay associated with the project termination. For example, at the close of a strip-mining operation, the mine must be refilled in an ecologically acceptable manner.

Now let's put this all together and measure the project's free cash flows.

MEASURING THE FREE CASH FLOWS

Free cash flow calculations can be broken down into three basic parts: cash flows from operations, cash flows associated with working-capital requirements, and capital-spending cash flows. Let's begin our discussion by looking at how to measure cash flows from operations and then move on to discuss measuring cash flows from working-capital requirements and capital spending.

Step 1: *Measure the project's change in operating cash flows.* An easy way to calculate operating cash flows is to take the information provided on a pro forma statement and simply convert the accounting information into cash flow information. To do this we take advantage of the fact that the difference between the change in sales and the change in costs should be equal to the change in earnings before interest and taxes (EBIT) plus depreciation.

Under this method, the calculation of a project's operating cash flow involves three steps. First, we determine the company's *earnings before interest and taxes (EBIT)* with and without this project. Second, we subtract out the change in taxes. Keep in mind that in calculating the change in taxes, we will ignore any interest expenses. Third, we adjust this value for the fact that depreciation, a non–cash flow item, has been subtracted out in the calculation of EBIT. We do this by adding back depreciation. Thus, operating cash flows are calculated as follows:

$$\text{Operating cash flows} = \text{change in earnings before interest and taxes} - \text{change in taxes} + \text{change in depreciation}$$

EXAMPLE

Let's look at an example to show the calculation of operating cash flows. Assume that a new project will annually generate revenues of $1,000,000 and cash expenses including both fixed and variable costs of $500,000, while increasing depreciation by $150,000 per year. In addition, let's assume that the firm's marginal tax rate is 34 percent. Given this, the firm's net profit after tax can be calculated as:

Revenue	$1,000,000
− Cash expenses	500,000
− Depreciation	150,000
= EBIT	$ 350,000
− Taxes (34%)	119,000
= Net income	$ 231,000

$$\text{Operating cash flows} = \text{change in earnings before interest and taxes} - \text{change in taxes} + \text{change in depreciation}$$
$$= \$350,000 - \$119,000 + \$150,000 = \$381,000$$

Step 2: *Calculate the cash flows from the change in net working capital.* As we mentioned earlier in this chapter, many times a new project will involve additional investment in working capital—perhaps new inventory to stock a new sales outlet or simply additional investment in accounts receivable. There also may be some spontaneous short-term financing—for example, increases in accounts payable—that result from the new project. Thus, the change in net working capital is the additional investment in current assets minus any additional short-term liabilities that were generated.

Step 3: *Determine the cash flows from the change in capital spending.* Although there is generally a large cash outflow associated with a project's initial outlay, there may also be additional capital-spending requirements over the life of the project. For example, you may know ahead of time that the plant will need some minor retooling in the second year of the project in order to keep the project abreast of new technological changes that are expected to take place. In effect, we will look at the company with and without the new project, and any changes in capital spending that occur are relevant.

Step 4: *Putting it together: calculating a project's free cash flows.* Thus, a project's free cash flows are:

Project's free cash flows = change in earnings before interest and taxes − change in taxes
+ change in depreciation − change in net working capital
− change in capital spending

To estimate the changes in EBIT, taxes, depreciation, net working capital, and capital spending we start with estimates of how many units we expect to sell, what the costs—both fixed and variable—will be, what the selling price will be, and what the required capital investment will be. From there we can put together a pro forma statement that should provide us with the data we need to estimate the project's free cash flows. However, you must keep in mind that our capital-budgeting decision will only be as good as our estimates of the costs and future demand. In fact, most capital-budgeting decisions that turn out to be bad decisions are not so because of using a bad decision rule but because the estimates of future demand and costs were inaccurate. Let's look at an example.

EXAMPLE

You are considering expanding your product line that currently consists of Lee's Press-on Nails to take advantage of the fitness craze. The new product you are considering introducing is "Press-on Abs" and you feel you can sell 100,000 of these per year for 4 years (after which time this project is expected to shut down because forecasters predict healthy looks will no longer be in vogue, being replaced with the couch potato look). The Press-on Abs would sell for $6.00 each, with variable costs of $3.00 for each one produced, while annual fixed costs associated with production would be $90,000. In addition, there would be a $200,000 initial expenditure associated with the purchase of new production equipment. It is assumed that this initial expenditure will be depreciated using the simplified straight-line method down to zero over 4 years. This project will also require a one-time initial investment of $30,000 in net working capital associated with inventory. Finally, assume that the firm's marginal tax rate is 34 percent.

INITIAL OUTLAY

Let's begin by estimating the initial outlay. In this example, the initial outlay will be the $200,000 initial expenditure plus the investment of $30,000 in net working capital for a total of $230,000.

ANNUAL FREE CASH FLOWS

Next, Table 10-1 calculates the annual change in earnings before interest and taxes. This calculation begins with the change in sales (Δ Sales) and subtracts the change in fixed and variable costs, in addition to the change in depreciation, to calculate the change in earnings before interest and taxes (EBIT). Depreciation was calculated using the simplified straight-line method, which is simply the depreciable value of the asset ($200,000 divided by the asset's expected life of 4 years). Taxes are then calculated assuming a 34 percent marginal tax rate. Once we have calculated EBIT and taxes we don't need to go any further, since these are the only two values from the pro forma income statement that we need. In addition, in this example there is not any annual

TABLE 10-1   Calculation of the Annual Change in Earnings Before Interest and Taxes for the Press-on Abs Project

Δ Sales (100,000 units at $6.00/unit)	$ 600,000
Less: Δ Variable Costs (variable cost $3.00/unit)	$ 300,000
Less: Δ Fixed Costs	$ 90,000
Equals: EBDIT	$ 210,000
Less: Δ Depreciation ($200,000/4 years)	$ 50,000
Equals: Δ EBIT	**$160,000**
Less: Δ Taxes: (taxed at 34%)	$ 54,400
Equals: Δ Net Income	$ 105,600

increase in working capital associated with the project under consideration. Also notice that we have ignored any interest payments and financing flows that might have occurred. As mentioned earlier, when we discount the free cash flows back to the present at the required rate of return, we are implicitly accounting for the cost of the funds needed to support the project.

The project's annual *change in operating cash flow* is calculated in Table 10-2.

TABLE 10-2   Annual Change in Operating Cash Flow, Press-on Abs Project

Δ Earnings Before Interest and Taxes (EBIT)	$160,000
Minus: Δ Taxes	−$ 54,400
Plus: Δ Depreciation	+$ 50,000
Equals: Δ Operating Cash Flow	**$155,600**

Remember: **The project's annual *free cash flow* is simply the *change in operating cash flow* less any *change in net working capital* and less any *change in capital spending***. In this example there are no changes in net working capital and capital spending over the life of the project. This is not the case for all projects that you will consider. For example, on a project where sales increase annually, it is likely that working capital will also increase each year to support a larger inventory and a higher level of accounts receivable. Similarly, on some projects the capital expenditures may be spread out over several years. The point here is that what we are trying to do is look at the firm with this project and without this project and measure the change in cash flows other than any interest payments and financing flows that might occur.

TERMINAL CASH FLOW

For this project, the terminal cash flow is quite simple. The only unusual cash flow at the project's termination is the recapture of the net working capital associated with the project. In effect, the investment in inventory of $30,000 is liquidated when the project is shut down in 4 years. Keep in mind that in calculating free cash flow we subtract out the change in net working capital, but since the change in net working capital is negative (we are reducing our investment in inventory), we are subtracting a negative number, which has the effect of adding it back in. Thus, working capital was a negative cash flow when the project began and we invested in inventory, and at termination it becomes a positive offsetting cash flow when the inventory is liquidated. The calculation of the terminal free cash flow is illustrated in Table 10-3.

TABLE 10-3   Terminal Free Cash Flow, Press-on Abs Project

Δ Earnings Before Interest and Taxes (EBIT)	$160,000
Minus: Δ Taxes	−$ 54,400
Plus: Δ Depreciation	+$ 50,000
Minus: Change in Net Working Capital	−($ 30,000)
Equals: Δ Free Cash Flow	$185,600

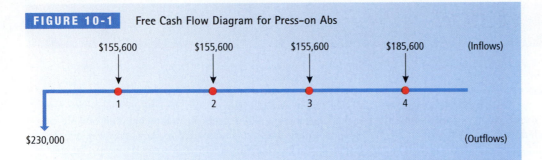

FIGURE 10-1   Free Cash Flow Diagram for Press-on Abs

If we were to construct a free cash flow diagram from this example (Figure 10-1), it would have an initial outlay of $230,000, the free cash flows during years 1 through 3 would be $155,600, and the free cash flow in the terminal year would be $185,600. Free cash flow diagrams similar to Figure 10-1 will be used throughout the remainder of this chapter with arrows above the time line indicating cash inflows and arrows below the time line denoting outflows.

A COMPREHENSIVE EXAMPLE: CALCULATING FREE CASH FLOWS

Now let's put what we know about capital budgeting together and look at a capital-budgeting decision for a firm in the 34 percent marginal tax bracket with a 15 percent required rate of return or cost of capital. The project we are considering involves the introduction of a new electric scooter line by Raymobile. Our first task is that of estimating cash flows. This project is expected to last 5 years and then, because this is somewhat of a fad project, to be terminated. Thus, our first task becomes that of estimating the initial outlay, the annual free cash flows, and the terminal free cash flow. Given the information in Table 10-4, we want to determine the free cash flows associated with the project. Once we have that, we can easily calculate the project's net present value, the profitability index, and the internal rate of return, and apply the appropriate decision criteria.

TABLE 10-4   Raymobile Scooter Line Capital–Budgeting Example

Cost of new plant and equipment:	$9,700,000
Shipping and installation costs:	$ 300,000
Unit sales:	

YEAR	UNITS SOLD
1	50,000
2	100,000
3	100,000
4	70,000
5	50,000

Sales price per unit:	$150/unit in years 1 through 4, $130/unit in year 5
Variable cost per unit:	$80/unit
Annual fixed costs:	$500,000
Working-capital requirements:	There will be an initial working-capital requirement of $100,000 just to get production started. Then, for each year, the *total* investment in net working capital will be equal to 10 percent of the dollar value of sales for that year. Thus, the investment in working capital will increase during years 1 and 2, then decrease in year 4. Finally, all working capital is liquidated at the termination of the project at the end of year 5.
The depreciation method:	We use the simplified straight-line method over 5 years. It is assumed that the plant and equipment will have no salvage value after 5 years. Thus, annual depreciation is $2,000,000/year for 5 years.

ACROSS
THE HALL

... MARKETING

A capital-budgeting decision is only as good as its free cash flow forecasts. Coming up with those cash flow forecasts and analyzing them involves an intersection of finance and marketing—and for you, the marketing student, understanding how this information is used by the folks in finance will help you in doing your job. While finance prepares the analysis used by the firm's management to make the go/no go decision on new products, marketers generally supply the sales forecasts that, in turn, feed into the cash flow forecasts on which those decisions are based. It is impossible to overstate the importance of the marketing input. One way marketers can improve the quality of cash flow forecasts is to test-market the new product. With test marketing the firm can gain a better handle on how consumers will react to the product and thereby make more accurate cash flow forecasts. Test marketing results also allow the firm to make adjustments that might improve the new product's chances in the marketplace. However, not only is test marketing expensive, but it also

alerts the competition to what is on the way and allows them to develop their own alternative. Whether to go ahead with test marketing is generally a decision that is handled outside of finance—in the marketing area—and its impact on whether the eventual capital-budgeting decision is good or not can be considerable. Look, for example, at Nabisco, which tried to take its Teddy Grahams to the breakfast table in the form of a breakfast cereal. It initially introduced a chocolate, cinnamon, and honey version of the cereal, but consumers weren't thrilled with it. So Nabisco reworked the formula, improved the taste, and immediately put it out without test marketing it. Unfortunately, although it tasted better, it didn't do that well in milk, leaving a gooey paste on the bottom of the cereal bowl. Consumers rejected it, store managers refused to restock it, and Nabisco dropped the project. In effect, the decision not to test-market the reformulated Teddy Grahams Breakfast Cereal turned a potentially good capital-budgeting project into a failure.

To determine the differential annual free cash flows, we first need to determine the annual change in operating cash flow. To do this we will take the change in EBIT, subtract out the change in taxes, and then add in the change in depreciation. This is shown in Section II of Table 10-5. We first determine what the change in sales revenue will be by multiplying the units sold times the sale price. From the change in sales revenue, we subtract out variable costs, which are $80 per unit. Then, the change in fixed costs is subtracted out, and the result is earnings before depreciation, interest, and taxes (EBDIT). Subtracting the change in depreciation from EBDIT then leaves us with the change in earnings before interest and taxes (EBIT). From the change in EBIT, we can then calculate the change in taxes, which are assumed to be 34 percent of EBIT.

Using the calculations provided in Section I of Table 10-5, we then calculate the operating cash flow in Section II of Table 10-5. As you recall, the operating cash flow is simply EBIT minus taxes, plus depreciation.

To calculate the free cash flow from this project, we subtract the change in net working capital and the change in capital spending from operating cash flow. Thus, the first step becomes determining the change in net working capital, which is shown in Section III of Table 10-5. The change in net working capital generally includes both increases in inventory and increases in accounts receivable that naturally occur as sales increase from the introduction of the new product line. Some of the increase in accounts receivable may be offset by increases in accounts payable, but, in general, most new projects involve some type of increase in net working capital. In this example, there is an initial working capital requirement of $100,000. In addition, for each year the total investment in net working capital will be equal to 10 percent of sales for each year. Thus, the investment in working capital for year 1 is $750,000 (because sales are estimated to be $7,500,000). Working capital will already be at $100,000, so the change in net working capital will be $650,000. Net working capital will continue to increase during years 1 and 2, then decrease in year 4. Finally, all working capital is liquidated at the termination of the project at the end of year 5.

With the operating cash flow and the change in net working capital already calculated, the calculation of the project's free cash flow becomes easy. All that is missing is the change in capital spending, which in this example will simply be the $9,700,000 for plant and equipment plus the $300,000 for shipping and installation. Thus, the change in capital

TABLE 10-5 Calculation of Free Cash Flow for Raymobile Scooters

SECTION I. CALCULATE THE CHANGE IN EBIT, TAXES, AND DEPRECIATION (THIS BECOMES AN INPUT IN THE CALCULATION OF OPERATING CASH FLOW IN SECTION II)

YEAR	0	1	2	3	4	5
Units sold		50,000	100,000	100,000	70,000	50,000
Sales price		$150	$150	$150	$150	$130
Sales revenue		$7,500,000	$15,000,000	$15,000,000	$10,500,000	$6,500,000
Less: Variable costs		4,000,000	8,000,000	8,000,000	5,600,000	4,000,000
Less: Fixed costs		500,000	500,000	500,000	500,000	500,000
Equals: EBDIT		$3,000,000	$ 6,500,000	$ 6,500,000	$ 4,400,000	$2,000,000
Less: Depreciation		2,000,000	2,000,000	2,000,000	2,000,000	2,000,000
Equals: EBIT		$1,000,000	$ 4,500,000	$ 4,500,000	$ 2,400,000	0
Taxes (@34%)		340,000	1,530,000	1,530,000	816,000	0

SECTION II. CALCULATE OPERATING CASH FLOW (THIS BECOMES AN INPUT IN THE CALCULATION OF FREE CASH FLOW IN SECTION IV)

Operating cash flow:						
EBIT		$1,000,000	$4,500,000	$4,500,000	$2,400,000	$ 0
Minus: Taxes		340,000	1,530,000	1,530,000	816,000	0
Plus: Depreciation		2,000,000	2,000,000	2,000,000	2,000,000	2,000,000
Equals: Operating cash flows		$2,660,000	$4,970,000	$4,970,000	$3,584,000	$2,000,000

SECTION III. CALCULATE THE NET WORKING CAPITAL (THIS BECOMES AN INPUT IN THE CALCULATION OF FREE CASH FLOWS IN SECTION IV)

Change in net working capital:						
Revenue		$7,500,000	$15,000,000	$15,000,000	$10,500,000	$6,500,000
Initial working-capital requirement	$100,000					
Net working-capital needs		750,000	1,500,000	1,500,000	1,050,000	650,000
Liquidation of working capital						650,000
Change in working capital	100,000	650,000	750,000	0	(450,000)	(1,050,000)

SECTION IV. CALCULATE FREE CASH FLOW (USING INFORMATION CALCULATED IN SECTIONS II AND III, IN ADDITION TO THE CHANGE IN CAPITAL SPENDING)

Free cash flow:						
Operating cash flow		$ 2,660,000	$ 4,970,000	$ 4,970,000	$ 3,584,000	$ 2,000,000
Minus: Change in net working capital	$ 100,000	650,000	750,000	0	(450,000)	(1,050,000)
Minus: Change in capital spending	10,000,000	0	0	0	0	0
Free cash flow	$(10,100,000)	$2,010,000	$4,220,000	$4,970,000	$4,034,000	$3,050,000

spending becomes $10,000,000. We then need merely to take operating cash flow and subtract from it both the change in net working capital and the change in capital spending. This is done in Section IV of Table 10-5. A free cash flow diagram for this project is provided in Figure 10-2.

Using the information provided in Section IV of Table 10-5 and Figure 10-2, we easily calculate the *NPV*, *PI*, and *IRR* for this project.

FIGURE 10-2 Free Cash Flow Diagram for the Raymobile Scooter Line

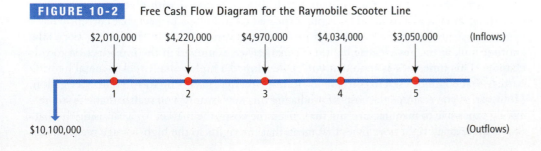

BACK TO THE FOUNDATIONS

In this chapter, it is easy to get caught up in the calculations and forget that before the calculations can be made, someone has to come up with the idea for the project. In some of the example problems, you may see projects that appear to be extremely profitable. Unfortunately, as we learned in **Principle 5: The Curse of Competitive Markets—Why It's Hard to Find Exceptionally Profitable Projects**, *it is unusual to find projects with dramatically high returns because of the very competitive nature of business. Thus, keep in mind that capital budgeting not only involves the estimation and evaluation of the project's cash flows, but it also includes the process of coming up with the idea for the project in the first place.*

Objective **3**   OPTIONS IN CAPITAL BUDGETING

The use of our discounted cash flow decision criteria, such as the *NPV* method, provides an excellent framework within which to evaluate projects. However, what happens if the project being analyzed has the potential to be modified after some future uncertainty has been resolved? For example, if a project that had an expected life of 10 years turns out to be better than anticipated, it may be expanded or continued past 10 years, perhaps going for 20 years. On the other hand, if its cash flows do not meet expectations, it may not last a full 10 years; it might be scaled back, abandoned, or sold. In addition, it might be delayed for a year or two. This flexibility is something that the *NPV* and our other decision criteria had a difficult time dealing with. In fact, the *NPV* may actually understate the value of the project because the future opportunities associated with the possibility of modifying the project may have a positive value. It is this value of flexibility that we will be examining using options.

Three of the most common option types that can add value to a capital-budgeting project are (1) the option to delay a project until the future cash flows are more favorable—this option is common when the firm has exclusive rights, perhaps a patent, to a product or technology; (2) the option to expand a project, perhaps in size or even to new products that would not have otherwise been feasible; and (3) the option to abandon a project if the future cash flows fall short of expectations.

THE OPTION TO DELAY A PROJECT

There is no question that the estimated cash flows associated with a project can change over time. In fact, as a result of changing expected cash flows, a project that currently has a negative net present value may have a positive net present value in the future. Let's take another look at the gas-electric hybrid car market we examined in the introduction to this chapter. This time, let's assume that you've developed a high-voltage nickel-metal hydride battery that could be used to increase the mileage on hybrid cars up to 150 miles per gallon. However, as you examine the costs of producing this new battery, you realize that it is still relatively expensive to manufacture and that, given the costs, the market for a car using this battery is quite small right now. Does that mean that the rights to the high-voltage nickel-metal hydride battery have no value? No, they have value because you may be able to improve on this technology in the future and make the battery even more efficient and less expensive. They also have value because oil prices may rise even further, which would lead to a bigger market for super fuel-efficient cars. In effect, the ability to delay this project with the hope that technological and market conditions will change, making this project profitable, lends value to this project.

Another example of the option to delay a project until the future cash flows are more favorable involves a firm that owns the oil rights to some oil-rich land and is considering an oil-drilling project. After all of the costs and the expected oil output are considered, this project may have a negative net present value. Does that mean the firm should give away its oil rights or that those oil rights have no value? Certainly not; there is a chance that in the future oil prices could rise to the point that this negative *NPV* project could become a positive *NPV* project. It is this ability to delay development that provides value. Thus, the value in this seemingly negative *NPV* project is provided by the option to delay the project until the future cash flows are more favorable.

THE OPTION TO EXPAND A PROJECT

Just as we saw with the option to delay a project, the estimated cash flows associated with a project can change over time, making it valuable to expand a project. Again, this flexibility to adjust production to demand has value. For example, a firm may build a production plant with excess capacity so that if the product has more than anticipated demand, it can simply increase production. Alternatively, taking on this project may provide the firm with a foothold in a new industry and lead to other products that would not have otherwise been feasible. This reasoning has led many firms to expand into e-businesses, hoping to gain know-how and expertise that will lead to other profitable projects down the line. It also provides some of the rationale for research and development expenditures in which the future project is not well defined.

Let's go back to our example of the gas-electric hybrid car and examine the option to expand that project. One of the reasons that most of the major automobile firms are introducing gas-electric hybrid cars is that they feel that if gas prices keep moving beyond the $2 per gallon price, these hybrids may be the future of the industry, and the only way to gain the know-how and expertise to produce a hybrid is to do it. As the cost of technology declines and the demands increase—perhaps pushed on by increases in gas prices—then they will be ready to expand into full-fledged production. This point becomes clear when you look at Honda, which first introduced the Insight in 2000, and Toyota, which introduced the Prius in 2001.

When they were first introduced, analysts estimated that Honda was losing about $8,000 on each Insight it sold, whereas Toyota was losing about $3,000 per car, with both expecting to break even in a few years. Still, these projects made sense because they allowed these automakers to gain the technological and production expertise to profitably produce a gas-electric hybrid car. And with Oak Ridge Labs estimating that there will be 1.2 million hybrids by 2008, it is a big market they're looking at. Moreover, the technology Honda and Toyota developed with the Insight and Prius may have profitable applications for other cars or in other areas. In effect, it is the option of expanding production in the future that brings value to this project.

THE OPTION TO ABANDON A PROJECT

The option to abandon a project as the estimated cash flows associated with a project can change over time also has value. Again, it is this flexibility to adjust to new information that provides the value. For example, a project's sales in the first year or two may not live up to expectations, with the project being barely profitable. The firm may then decide to liquidate the project and sell the plant and all of the equipment, and that liquidated value may be more than the value of keeping the project going.

Again, let's go back to our example of the gas-electric hybrid car and, this time, examine the option to abandon that project. If after a few years the cost of gas falls dramatically while the cost of technology remains high, the gas-electric hybrid car may not become profitable. At that point the manufacturer may decide to abandon the project and sell the technology, including all the patent rights it has developed. In effect, the original project, the gas-electric hybrid car, may not be of value, but the technology that has been developed may be. In effect, the value of abandoning the project and selling the technology may be more than the value of keeping the project running. Again, it is the value of flexibility associated with the possibility of modifying the project in the future—in this case abandoning the project—that can produce positive value.

OPTIONS IN CAPITAL BUDGETING: THE BOTTOM LINE

Because of the potential to be modified in the future after some future uncertainty has been resolved, we may find that a project with a negative net present value based upon its expected free cash flows is a "good" project and should be accepted—this demonstrates the value of options. In addition, we may find that a project with a positive net present value may be of more value if its acceptance is delayed. Options also explain the logic that drives firms to take on negative *NPV* projects that allow them to enter new markets. The option to abandon a project explains why firms hire employees on a temporary basis rather than permanently, why they may lease rather than buy equipment, and why they may enter into contracts with suppliers on an annual basis rather than long term.

CONCEPT CHECK

1. Give an example of an option to delay a project. Why might this be of value?
2. Give an example of an option to expand a project. Why might this be of value?
3. Give an example of an option to abandon a project. Why might this be of value?

Objective 4

RISK AND THE INVESTMENT DECISION

Up to this point we have ignored risk in capital budgeting; that is, we have discounted expected cash flows back to the present and ignored any uncertainty that there might be surrounding that estimate. In reality the future cash flows associated with the introduction of a new sales outlet or a new product are estimates of what is *expected* to happen in the future, not necessarily what will happen in the future. For example, when Coca-Cola decided to replace Classic Coke with its "New Coke," you can bet that the expected cash flows it based its decision on were nothing like the cash flows it realized. As a result, it didn't take Coca-Cola long to reintroduce Classic Coke. The cash flows we have discounted back to the present have only been our best estimate of the expected future cash flows. A cash flow diagram based on the possible outcomes of an investment proposal rather than the expected values of these outcomes appears in Figure 10-3.

FIGURE 10-3   Example Cash Flow Diagram Based on Possible Outcomes

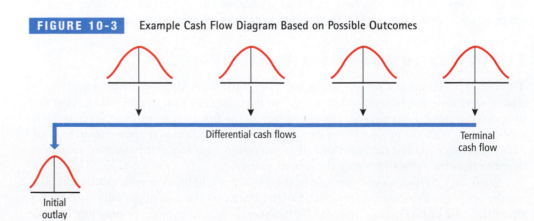

Differential cash flows

Terminal cash flow

Initial outlay

In this section, we assume that under conditions of risk we do not know beforehand what cash flows will actually result from a new project. However, we do have expectations concerning the possible outcomes and are able to assign probabilities to these outcomes. Stated another way, although we do not know what the cash flows resulting from the acceptance of a new project will be, we can formulate the probability distributions from which the flows will be drawn. As we learned in Chapter 8, risk occurs when there is some question about the future outcome of an event.

In the remainder of this chapter, we assume that although future cash flows are not known with certainty, the probability distribution from which they come can be estimated. Also, because we have illustrated that the dispersion of possible outcomes reflects risk, we are prepared to use a measure of dispersion or variability later in the chapter when we quantify risk.

In the pages that follow, remember that there are only two basic issues that we address: (1) What is risk in terms of capital-budgeting decisions, and how should it be measured? (2) How should risk be incorporated into capital-budgeting analysis?

WHAT MEASURE OF RISK IS RELEVANT IN CAPITAL BUDGETING?

Before we begin our discussion of how to adjust for risk, it is important to determine just what type of risk we are to adjust for. In capital budgeting, a project's risk can be looked at on three levels. First, there is the **project standing alone risk**, which is a *project's risk ignoring the fact that much of this risk will be diversified away as the project is combined with the firm's other projects and assets*. Second, we have the project's **contribution-to-firm risk**, which is the *amount of risk that the project contributes to the firm as a whole; this measure considers the fact that some of the project's risk will be diversified away as the project is combined with the firm's other projects and assets, but ignores the effects of diversification of the firm's shareholders*. Finally, there is **systematic risk**, which is the *risk of the project from the viewpoint of a well-diversified shareholder; this measure takes into account that some of a project's risk will be diversified away as the project is combined with the firm's other projects, and, in addition, some of the remaining risk will be diversified away by shareholders as they combine this stock with other stocks in their portfolios.* Graphically, this is shown in Figure 10-4.

project standing alone risk

contribution-to-firm risk

systematic risk

TAKIN' IT TO THE NET
Perhaps the best place to look to find information with respect to capital-budgeting projects currently being developed is Annual Reports.com, www.annualreports.com, which provides annual reports on over 1,000 companies.

FIGURE 10-4 Looking at Three Measures of a Project's Risk

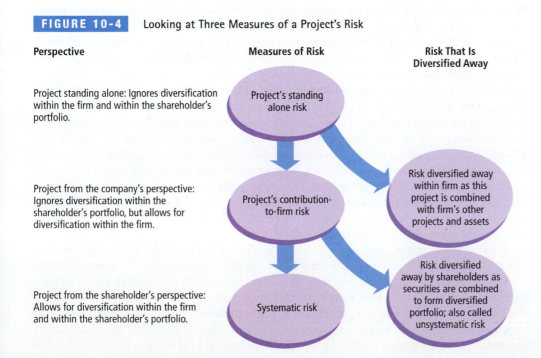

Perspective	Measures of Risk	Risk That Is Diversified Away
Project standing alone: Ignores diversification within the firm and within the shareholder's portfolio.	Project's standing alone risk	
Project from the company's perspective: Ignores diversification within the shareholder's portfolio, but allows for diversification within the firm.	Project's contribution-to-firm risk	Risk diversified away within firm as this project is combined with firm's other projects and assets
Project from the shareholder's perspective: Allows for diversification within the firm and within the shareholder's portfolio.	Systematic risk	Risk diversified away by shareholders as securities are combined to form diversified portfolio; also called unsystematic risk

Should we be interested in the project standing alone risk? The answer is no. Perhaps the easiest way to understand why not is to look at an example. Let's take the case of research and development projects at Johnson & Johnson. Each year Johnson & Johnson takes on hundreds of new R&D projects, knowing that they only have about a 10 percent probability of being successful. If they are successful, the profits can be enormous; if they fail, the investment is lost. If the company has only one project, and it is an R&D project, the company would have a 90 percent chance of failure. Thus, if we look at these R&D projects individually and measure their stand-alone risk, we would have to judge them to be enormously risky. However, if we consider the effect of the diversification that comes about from taking on several hundred independent R&D projects a year, all with a 10 percent chance of success, we can see that each R&D project does not add much risk to Johnson & Johnson. In short, because much of a project's risk is diversified away within the firm, the project standing alone risk is an inappropriate measure of the meaningful level of risk of a capital-budgeting project.

Should we be interested in the project's contribution-to-firm risk? Once again, at least in theory the answer is no, provided investors are well diversified and there is no chance of bankruptcy. From our earlier discussion of risk in Chapter 8, we saw that as shareholders, if we combined an individual security with other securities to form a diversified portfolio, much of the risk of the individual security would be diversified away. In short, all that affects the shareholders is the systematic risk of the project and, as such, is all that is theoretically relevant for capital budgeting.

MEASURING RISK FOR CAPITAL-BUDGETING PURPOSES WITH A DOSE OF REALITY—IS SYSTEMATIC RISK ALL THERE IS?

According to the capital asset pricing model (CAPM) we discussed in Chapter 6, systematic risk is the only relevant risk for capital-budgeting purposes; however, reality complicates this somewhat. In many instances a firm will have undiversified shareholders, including owners of small corporations. Because they are not diversified, for those shareholders the relevant measure of risk is the project's contribution-to-firm risk.

The possibility of bankruptcy also affects our view of what measure of risk is relevant. As you recall in developing the CAPM, we made the assumption that bankruptcy costs were zero. Because the project's contribution-to-firm risk can affect the possibility of bankruptcy, this may be an appropriate measure of risk if there are costs associated with bankruptcy. Quite obviously, in the real world there is a cost associated with bankruptcy. First, if a firm fails, its assets, in general, cannot be sold for their true economic value. Moreover, the amount of money actually available for distribution to stockholders is further reduced by liquidation and legal fees that must be paid. Finally, the opportunity cost associated with the delays related to the legal process further reduces the funds available to the shareholder. Therefore, because costs are associated with bankruptcy, reduction of the chance of bankruptcy has a very real value associated with it.

Indirect costs of bankruptcy also affect other areas of the firm, including production, sales, and the quality and efficiency of management. For example, firms with a higher probability of bankruptcy may have a more difficult time recruiting and retaining quality managers because jobs with that firm are viewed as being less secure. Suppliers also may be less willing to sell on credit. Finally, customers may lose confidence and fear that the firm may not be around to honor the warranty or to supply spare parts for the product in the future. As a result, as the probability of bankruptcy increases, the eventual bankruptcy may become self-fulfilling as potential customers and suppliers flee. The end result is that because the project's contribution-to-firm risk affects the probability of bankruptcy for the firm, it is a relevant risk measure for capital budgeting.

Finally, problems in measuring a project's systematic risk make its implementation extremely difficult. It is much easier talking about a project's systematic risk than measuring it.

Given all this, what do we use? The answer is that we will give consideration to both measures. We know in theory systematic risk is correct. We also know that bankruptcy costs and undiversified shareholders violate the assumptions of the theory, which brings us back to the concept of a project's contribution-to-firm risk. Still, the concept of systematic risk holds value for capital-budgeting decisions, because that is the risk that shareholders are compensated for assuming. Therefore, we will concern ourselves with both the project's contribution-to-firm risk and the project's systematic risk and not try to make any specific allocation of importance between the two for capital-budgeting purposes.

CONCEPT CHECK

1. In capital budgeting, a project's risk can be looked at on three levels. What are they and what are the measures of risk?
2. Is a project's standing alone risk the appropriate level of risk for capital budgeting? Why or why not?
3. What is systematic risk?
4. What problems are associated with using systematic risk as the measure for risk in capital budgeting?

INCORPORATING RISK INTO CAPITAL BUDGETING

Objective **5**

In Chapter 9 we ignored any risk differences between projects. This approach is simple but not valid; different investment projects do in fact contain different levels of risk. We now look at the risk-adjusted discount rate, which is based on the notion that investors require higher rates of return on more risky projects.

BACK TO THE FOUNDATIONS

All the methods used to compensate for risk in capital budgeting find their roots in **Principle 1: The Risk–Return Trade-Off—We Won't Take On Additional Risk Unless We Expect to Be Compensated with Additional Return.** *In fact, the risk-adjusted discount method puts this concept directly into play.*

RISK-ADJUSTED DISCOUNT RATES

The use of **risk-adjusted discount rates** is based on the concept that investors demand higher returns for more risky projects. This is the basic principle behind **Principle 1** and the CAPM, and this relationship between risk and return is illustrated graphically in Figure 10-5.

As we know from **Principle 1**, the expected rate of return on any investment should include compensation for delaying consumption equal to the risk-free rate of return, plus compensation for any risk taken on. Under the risk-adjusted discount rate approach, if the risk associated with the investment is greater than the risk involved in a typical endeavor, the discount rate is adjusted upward to compensate for this added risk. Once the firm determines the appropriate required rate of return for a project with a given level of risk, the cash

risk-adjusted discount rates

FIGURE 10-5 Risk–Return Relationship

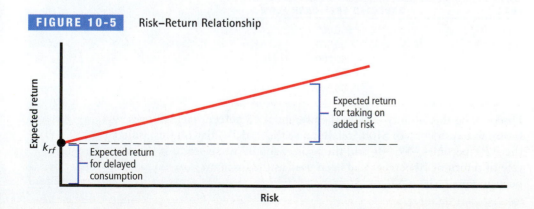

flows are discounted back to the present at the risk-adjusted discount rate. Then the normal capital-budgeting criteria are applied, except in the case of the *IRR*. For the *IRR*, the hurdle rate with which the project's *IRR* is compared now becomes the risk-adjusted discount rate. Expressed mathematically, the *NPV* using the risk-adjusted discount rate becomes

$$
\begin{aligned}
NPV = \;& \text{present value of all the} \\
& \text{future annual free cash} \\
& \text{flows discounted back} \qquad - \qquad \text{the initial cash outlay} \qquad \textbf{(10-1)}\\
& \text{to present at the risk-adjusted} \\
& \text{rate of return}
\end{aligned}
$$

$$
= FCF_1(PVIF_{k^*\%,\,1\text{ yr}}) + FCF_2(PVIF_{k^*\%,\,2\text{ yr}}) + \cdots + FCF_n(PVIF_{k^*\%,\,n\text{ yr}}) - IO
$$

where FCF_t = the annual free cash flow expected in time period t

IO = the initial cash outlay

k^* = the risk-adjusted discount rate

n = the project's expected life

$PVIF_{k\%,\,n\text{ yr}}$ = the present value interest factor for $k\%$ and n years

The logic behind the risk-adjusted discount rate stems from the idea that if the level of risk in a project is different from that of the typical firm project, then management must incorporate the shareholders' probable reaction to this new endeavor into the decision-making process. If the project has more risk than a typical project, then a higher required rate of return should apply. Otherwise, marginal projects will lower the firm's share price—that is, reduce shareholders' wealth. This will occur as the market raises its required rate of return on the firm to reflect the addition of a more risky project, whereas the incremental cash flows resulting from the acceptance of the new project are not large enough to offset this change fully. By the same logic, if the project has less than normal risk, a reduction in the required rate of return is appropriate. Thus, the risk-adjusted discount method attempts to apply more stringent standards—that is, require a higher rate of return—to projects that will increase the firm's risk level. This is because these projects will lead shareholders to demand a higher required rate of return to compensate them for the higher risk level of the firm. If this adjustment is not made, the marginal projects containing above-average risk could actually lower the firm's share price.

EXAMPLE

A toy manufacturer is considering the introduction of a line of fishing equipment with an expected life of 5 years. In the past, this firm has been quite conservative in its investment in new products, sticking primarily to standard toys. In this context, the introduction of a line of fishing equipment is considered an abnormally risky project. Management thinks that the normal required rate of return for the firm of 10 percent is not sufficient. Instead, the minimum acceptable rate of return on this project should be 15 percent. The initial outlay would be $110,000, and the expected cash flows from this project are given in the following table:

YEAR	EXPECTED FREE CASH FLOW
1	$30,000
2	30,000
3	30,000
4	30,000
5	30,000

Discounting this annuity back to the present at 15 percent yields a present value of the future free cash flows of $100,560. Because the initial outlay on this project is $110,000, the *NPV* becomes −$9,440, and the project should be rejected. If the normal required rate of return of 10 percent had been used as the discount rate, the project would have been accepted with a *NPV* of $3,730.

In practice, when the risk-adjusted discount rate is used, projects are generally grouped according to purpose, or risk class; then the discount rate preassigned to that purpose or risk class is used. For example, a firm with a required rate of return of 12 percent might use the following rate-of-return categorization:

PROJECT	REQUIRED RATE OF RETURN (%)
Replacement decision	12
Modification or expansion of existing product line	15
Project unrelated to current operations	18
Research and development operations	25

The purpose of this categorization of projects is to make their evaluation easier, but it also introduces a sense of arbitrariness into the calculations that makes the evaluation less meaningful. The trade-offs involved in the preceding classification are obvious; time and effort are minimized but only at the cost of precision.

RISK-ADJUSTED DISCOUNT RATE AND MEASUREMENT OF A PROJECT'S SYSTEMATIC RISK

When we initially talked about systematic risk or the beta, we were talking about measuring it for the entire firm. As you recall, although we could estimate a firm's beta using historical data, we did not have complete confidence in our results. As we will see, estimating the appropriate level of systematic risk for a single project is even more fraught with difficulties. To truly understand what it is we are trying to do and the difficulties we will encounter, let us step back a bit and examine systematic risk and the risk adjustment for a project.

What we are trying to do is use the CAPM to determine the level of risk and the appropriate risk–return trade-offs for a particular project. We then take the expected return on this project and compare it to the required return suggested by the CAPM to determine whether the project should be accepted. If the project appears to be a typical one for the firm, using the CAPM to determine the appropriate risk–return trade-offs and then judging the project against them may be a warranted approach. But if the project is not a typical project, what do we do? Historical data generally do not exist for a new project. In fact, for some capital investments— for example, a truck or a new building—historical data would not have much meaning. What we need to do is make the best of a bad situation. We either (1) fake it—that is, use historical accounting data, if available, to substitute for historical price data in estimating systematic risk— or (2) we attempt to find a substitute firm in the same industry as the capital-budgeting project and use the substitute firm's estimated systematic risk as a proxy for the project's systematic risk.

BETA ESTIMATION USING ACCOUNTING DATA

When we are dealing with a project that is identical to the firm's other projects, we need only estimate the level of systematic risk for the firm and use that estimate as a proxy for the project's risk. Unfortunately, when projects are not typical of the firm, this approach does not work. For example, when R. J. Reynolds introduces a new food through one of its food products divisions, this new product most likely carries with it a different level of systematic risk from what is typical for Reynolds as a whole.

To get a better approximation of the systematic risk level on this project, we estimate the level of systematic risk for the food division and use that as a proxy for the project's systematic risk. Unfortunately, historical stock price data are available only for the company as a whole, and as you recall, historical stock return data are generally used to estimate a firm's beta. Thus, we are forced to use accounting return data rather than historical stock return data for the division to estimate the division's systematic risk. To estimate a project's beta using accounting data we need only run a time-series regression of the division's return on assets (net income/total assets) on the market index (the S&P 500). The regression coefficient from this equation would be the project's accounting beta and would serve as an approximation for the project's true beta, or measure of systematic risk. Alternatively, a multiple regression model based on accounting data could be developed to explain betas. The results of this model could then be applied to firms that are not publicly traded to estimate their betas.

How good is the accounting beta technique? It certainly is not as good as a direct calculation of the beta. In fact, the correlation between the accounting beta and the beta calculated on historical stock return data is only about 0.6; however, better luck has been experienced with multiple regression models used to predict betas. Unfortunately, in many cases there may not be any realistic alternative to the calculation of the accounting beta. Owing to the importance of adjusting for a project's risk, the accounting beta method is much preferred to doing nothing.

THE PURE PLAY METHOD FOR ESTIMATING A PROJECT'S BETA

pure play method

Whereas the accounting beta method attempts to directly estimate a project or division's beta, the **pure play method** attempts to identify publicly traded firms that are engaged solely in the same business as the project or division. Once the proxy or pure play firm is identified, its systematic risk is determined and then used as a proxy for the project's or division's level of systematic risk. What we are doing is *looking for a publicly traded firm on the outside that looks like our project and using that firm's required rate of return to judge our project.* In doing so we are presuming that the systematic risk and the capital structure of the proxy firm are identical to those of the project.

In using the pure play method it should be noted that a firm's capital structure is reflected in its beta. When the capital structure of the proxy firm is different from that of the project's firm, some adjustment must be made for this difference. Although not a perfect approach, it does provide some insights about the level of systematic risk a project might have.

CONCEPT CHECK

1. What is the most commonly used method for incorporating risk into the capital-budgeting decision? How is this technique related to Principle 1?
2. Describe two methods for estimating a project's systematic risk.

Objective **6**

EXAMINING A PROJECT'S RISK THROUGH SIMULATION

SIMULATION: EXPLAINED AND ILLUSTRATED

simulation

Another method for evaluating risk in the investment decision is through the use of **simulation**. The risk-adjusted discount rate approach provided us with a single value for the risk-adjusted *NPV*, whereas a simulation approach gives us a probability distribution for the investment's *NPV* or *IRR*. Simulation *involves the process of imitating the performance of the project under evaluation. This is done by randomly selecting observations from each of the distributions that affect the outcome of the project, and continuing with this process until a representative record of the project's probable outcome is assembled.*

The easiest way to develop an understanding of the computer simulation process is to follow through an example simulation for an investment project evaluation. Suppose a chemical producer is considering an extension to its processing plant. The simulation process is portrayed in Figure 10-6. First, the probability distributions are determined for all the factors that affect the project's returns; in this case, let us assume there are nine such variables:

1. Market size
2. Selling price
3. Market growth rate
4. Share of market (which results in physical sales volume)
5. Investment required
6. Residual value of investment
7. Operating costs
8. Fixed costs
9. Useful life of facilities

FIGURE 10-6   Capital–Budgeting Simulation

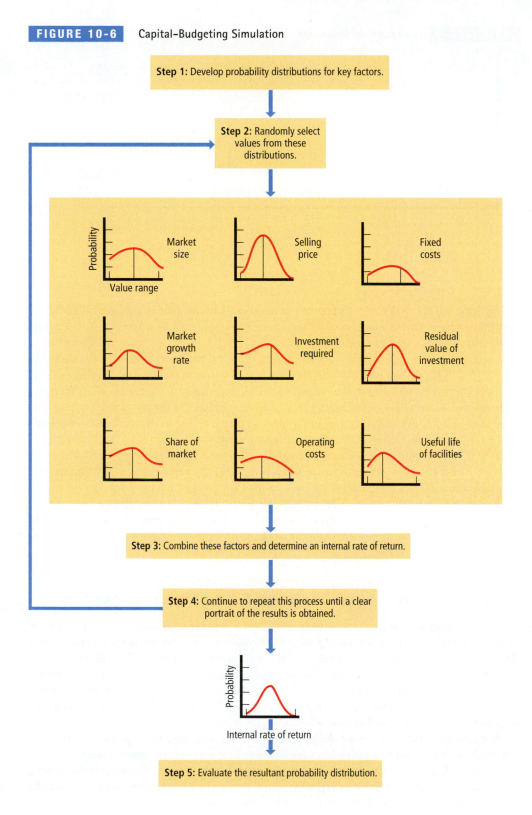

Then the computer randomly selects one observation from each of the probability distributions, according to its chance of actually occurring in the future. These nine observations are combined, and an *NPV* or *IRR* figure is calculated. This process is repeated as many times as desired, until a representative distribution of possible future outcomes is assembled. Thus, the inputs to a simulation include all the principal factors affecting the project's profitability, and the simulation output is a probability distribution of net present values or internal rates of return for the project. The decision maker bases

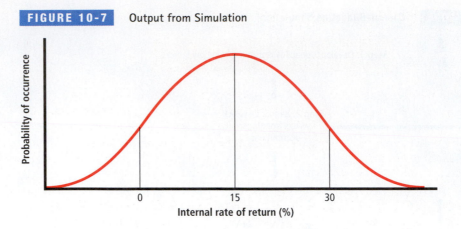

FIGURE 10-7 Output from Simulation

the decision on the full range of possible outcomes. The project is accepted if the decision maker feels that enough of the distribution lies above the normal cutoff criteria ($NPV \geq 0$, $IRR \geq$ required rate of return).

scenario analysis

Suppose the output from the simulation of a chemical producer's project is as shown in Figure 10-7. This output provides the decision maker with the probability of different outcomes occurring in addition to the range of possible outcomes. Sometimes called **scenario analysis**, this *examination identifies the range of possible outcomes under the worst, best, and most likely cases.* The firm's management examines the distribution to determine the project's level of risk and then makes the appropriate adjustment.

You'll notice that although the simulation approach helps us to determine the amount of total risk a project has, it does not differentiate between systematic and unsystematic risk. Because systematic risk cannot be diversified away for free, the simulation approach does not provide a complete method of risk assessment. However, it does provide important insights about the total risk level of a given investment project. Now we will look briefly at how the simulation approach can be used to perform sensitivity analysis.

SENSITIVITY ANALYSIS THROUGH SIMULATION APPROACH

sensitivity analysis

Sensitivity analysis involves *determining how the distribution of possible net present values or internal rates of return for a particular project is affected by a change in one particular input variable.* This is done by changing the value of one input variable while holding all other input variables constant. The distribution of possible net present values or internal rates of return that is generated is then compared with the distribution of possible returns generated before the change was made to determine the effect of the change. For this reason sensitivity analysis is commonly called *what-if analysis.*

For example, the chemical producer that is considering a possible expansion to its plant may wish to determine the effect of a more pessimistic forecast of the anticipated market growth rate. After the more pessimistic forecast replaces the original forecast in the model, the simulation is rerun. The two outputs are then compared to determine how sensitive the results are to the revised estimate of the market growth rate.

CONCEPT CHECK

1. Explain to yourself how simulations work.
2. What is scenario analysis? What is sensitivity analysis? When would you perform sensitivity analysis?

FINANCE AND THE MULTINATIONAL FIRM: CALCULATING CASH FLOWS AND THE INTERNATIONAL DIMENSION OF RISK

Objective **7**

The process of measuring the incremental after-tax cash flows to the company as a whole gets a bit more complicated when we are dealing with competition from abroad. One area in which this is certainly true is in calculating the right base case—that is, what the firm's incremental after-tax cash flows would be if the project is not taken on. In determining future cash flows we must always be aware of potential competition from abroad. We need only look to the auto industry to see that competition from abroad can be serious. During the 1970s, who would have thought that firms like Toyota, Honda, and Nissan could enter the U.S. markets and actually challenge the likes of Ford and GM? The end result of opening markets to international competition has led not only to increased opportunities but also to increased risks.

There are also other intangible benefits from investing in countries such as Germany and Japan, where cutting-edge technology is making its way into the marketplace. Here investment abroad provides a chance to observe the introduction of new innovations on a firsthand basis, allowing firms such as IBM, GE, and 3Com to react more quickly to any technological advances and product innovations that might come out of Germany or Japan.

Along with all the benefits from going multinational come the risks. One of the major risks involves currency fluctuations. For example, in 2002, Toyota finalized its plans for the introduction of the second-generation Prius, its gas-electric hybrid car, which it manufactures in Japan and imports to the United States. These plans included a pricing strategy to have the Prius sell below $30,000, at $29,990, because Toyota was worried that by crossing the $30,000 price threshold it might seriously lose sales. At that time, the Japanese yen was trading at around 134 yen per U.S. dollar. Unfortunately for Toyota, the yen to U.S. dollar exchange rate fell since then, to 103 Japanese yen per dollar at the beginning of 2005. What does this mean for Toyota? It means that Toyota receives only 77 percent as many yen on each Prius it sells in the United States. Since Toyota pays its workers in yen and its material costs are in yen, this placed a real strain on Toyota's profits.

CONCEPT CHECK

1. In what ways does the process of measuring the incremental after-tax cash flows to the company as a whole get a bit more complicated when we are dealing with competition from abroad?

2. What new risks does a firm face when it enters the international markets?

SUMMARY

In this chapter, we examine the measurement of incremental cash flows associated with a firm's investment proposals and methods that are used to evaluate those proposals. Relying on **Principle 3: Cash—Not Profits—Is King**, and **Principle 4: Incremental Cash Flows—It's Only What Changes That Counts**, we focus only on the incremental or differential after-tax cash flows attributed to the investment proposal. Care is taken to beware of cash flows diverted from existing products, look for incidental or synergistic effects, consider working-capital requirements, consider incremental expenses, ignore sunk costs, account for opportunity costs, examine overhead costs carefully, and ignore interest payments and financing flows.

Objective **1**

To measure a project's benefits, we use the project's free cash flows. These free cash flows include

Objective **2**

Project's free cash flows = project's change in operating cash flows
                − change in net working capital
                − change in capital spending

If we can rewrite this, inserting our calculation for project's change in operating cash flows, we get

Project's free cash flows = change in earnings before interest and taxes
− change in taxes
+ change in depreciation
− change in net working capital
− change in capital spending

Objective **3**

How do we deal with a project that has the potential to be modified in the future after some future uncertainty has been resolved? This flexibility to be modified is something that the *NPV* and our other decision criteria had a difficult time dealing with. It is this value of flexibility that we will be examining using options. Three of the most common types of options that can add value to a capital-budgeting project are (1) the option to delay a project until the future cash flows are more favorable (this option is common when the firm has exclusive right, perhaps a patent, to a product or technology); (2) the option to expand a project, perhaps in size or even to new products that would not have otherwise been feasible; and (3) the option to abandon a project if future cash flows fall short of expectations.

Objective **4**

We also cover the problem of incorporating risk into the capital-budgeting decision. First, we explore just what type of risk to adjust for: the project standing alone risk, the project's contribution-to-firm risk, or the project's systematic risk. In theory, systematic risk is the appropriate risk measure, but bankruptcy costs and the issue of undiversified shareholders also give weight to considering a project's contribution-to-firm risk as the appropriate risk measure. Both measures of risk are valid, and we avoid making any specific allocation of importance between the two in capital budgeting.

Objective **5**

Objective **6**

Two commonly used methods for incorporating risk into capital budgeting are (1) risk-adjusted discount rates and (2) simulation. The risk-adjusted discount rate involves an upward adjustment of the discount rate to compensate for risk. This method is based on the concept that investors demand higher returns for riskier projects. The simulation method is used to provide information about the location and shape of the distribution of possible outcomes. Decisions could be based directly on this method, or it could be used to determine input into the risk-adjusted discount rate method approach.

Objective **7**

The process of measuring the free cash flows to the company as a whole becomes more complicated when we are dealing with competition from abroad. One area in which this is certainly true is in calculating the right base case—that is, what the firm's free cash flows would be if the project is not taken on. Another complication involves the risks associated with currency fluctuations.

KEY TERMS

Contribution-to-firm risk, 311	**Project standing alone risk,** 311	**Scenario analysis,** 318
Incremental after-tax free cash flows, 296	**Pure play method,** 316	**Sensitivity analysis,** 318
Initial outlay, 299	**Risk-adjusted discount rate,** 313	**Simulation,** 316
		Systematic risk, 311

STUDY QUESTIONS

10-1. Why do we focus on cash flows rather than accounting profits in making our capital-budgeting decisions? Why are we interested only in incremental cash flows rather than total cash flows?

10-2. If depreciation is not a cash flow expense, does it affect the level of cash flows from a project in any way? Why?

10-3. If a project requires additional investment in working capital, how should this be treated in calculating cash flows?

10-4. How do sunk costs affect the determination of cash flows associated with an investment proposal?

10-5. In the preceding chapter we examined the payback period capital-budgeting criterion. Often this capital-budgeting criterion is used as a risk-screening device. Explain the rationale behind its use.

10-6. The use of the risk-adjusted discount rate assumes that risk increases over time. Justify this assumption.

10-7. Explain how simulation works. What is the value in using a simulation approach?

ST-1. The Easterwood Corporation, a firm in the 34 percent marginal tax bracket with a 15 percent required rate of return or cost of capital, is considering a new project. This project involves the introduction of a new product. This project is expected to last 5 years and then, because this is somewhat of a fad project, to be terminated. Given the following information, determine the free cash flows associated with the project, the project's net present value, the profitability index, and the internal rate of return. Apply the appropriate decision criteria.

Cost of new plant and equipment: $20,900,000
Shipping and installation costs: $ 300,000
Unit sales:

YEAR	UNITS SOLD
1	100,000
2	130,000
3	160,000
4	100,000
5	60,000

Sales price per unit: $500/unit in years 1 through 4, $380/unit in year 5
Variable cost per unit: $260/unit
Annual fixed costs: $300,000
Working–capital requirements: There will be an initial working-capital requirement of $500,000 just to get production started. For each year, the total investment in net working capital will be equal to 10 percent of the dollar value of sales for that year. Thus, the investment in working capital will increase during years 1 through 3, then decrease in year 4. Finally, all working capital is liquidated at the termination of the project at the end of year 5.
The depreciation method: Use the simplified straight-line method over 5 years. It is assumed that the plant and equipment will have no salvage value after 5 years.

10-1. (*Capital gains tax*) The J. Harris Corporation is considering selling one of its old assembly machines. The machine, purchased for $30,000 five years ago, had an expected life of 10 years and an expected salvage value of zero. Assume Harris uses simplified straight-line depreciation, creating depreciation of $3,000 per year, and could sell this old machine for $35,000. Also assume a 34 percent marginal tax rate.

   a. What would be the taxes associated with this sale?
   b. If the old machine were sold for $25,000, what would be the taxes associated with this sale?
   c. If the old machine were sold for $15,000, what would be the taxes associated with this sale?
   d. If the old machine were sold for $12,000, what would be the taxes associated with this sale?

10-2. (*Relevant cash flows*) Captins' Cereal is considering introducing a variation of its current breakfast cereal, Crunch Stuff. This new cereal will be similar to the old with the exception that it will contain sugarcoated marshmallows shaped in the form of stars. The new cereal will be called Crunch Stuff n' Stars. It is estimated that the sales for the new cereal will be $25 million; however, 20 percent of those sales will be former Crunch Stuff customers who have switched to Crunch Stuff n' Stars who would not have switched if the new product had not been introduced. What is the relevant sales level to consider when deciding whether to introduce Crunch n' Stars?

10-3. (*Calculating free cash flows*) Racin' Scooters is introducing a new product and has an expected change in EBIT of $475,000. Racin' Scooters has a 34 percent marginal tax rate. This project will also produce $100,000 of depreciation per year. In addition, this project will also cause the following changes:

	WITHOUT THE PROJECT	WITH THE PROJECT
Accounts receivable	$45,000	$63,000
Inventory	65,000	80,000
Accounts payable	70,000	94,000

What is the project's free cash flow?

10-4. (*Calculating free cash flows*) Visible Fences is introducing a new product and has an expected change in EBIT of $900,000. Visible Fences has a 34 percent marginal tax rate. This project will also produce $300,000 of depreciation per year. In addition, this project will also cause the following changes:

	WITHOUT THE PROJECT	WITH THE PROJECT
Accounts receivable	$55,000	$63,000
Inventory	55,000	70,000
Accounts payable	90,000	106,000

What is the project's free cash flow?

10-5. (*Calculating operating cash flows*) Assume that a new project will annually generate revenues of $2,000,000 and cash expenses including both fixed and variable costs of $800,000, while increasing depreciation by $200,000 per year. In addition, let's assume that the firm's marginal tax rate is 34 percent. Calculate the operating cash flows.

10-6. (*Calculating operating cash flows*) Assume that a new project will annually generate revenues of $3,000,000 and cash expenses including both fixed and variable costs of $900,000, while increasing depreciation by $400,000 per year. In addition, let's assume that the firm's marginal tax rate is 34 percent. Calculate the operating cash flows.

10-7. (*Calculating free cash flows*) You are considering expanding your product line that currently consists of skateboards to include gas-powered skateboards, and you feel you can sell 10,000 of these per year for 10 years (after which time this project is expected to shut down with solar-powered skateboards taking over). The gas skateboards would sell for $100 each with variable costs of $40 for each one produced, while annual fixed costs associated with production would be $160,000. In addition, there would be a $1,000,000 initial expenditure associated with the purchase of new production equipment. It is assumed that this initial expenditure will be depreciated using the simplified straight-line method down to zero over 10 years. This project will also require a one-time initial investment of $50,000 in net working capital associated with inventory and that working-capital investment will be recovered when the project is shut down. Finally, assume that the firm's marginal tax rate is 34 percent.

   a. What is the initial outlay associated with this project?
   b. What are the annual free cash flows associated with this project for years 1 through 9?
   c. What is the terminal cash flow in year 10 (that is, what is the free cash flow in year 10 plus any additional cash flows associated with termination of the project)?
   d. What is the project's *NPV* given a 10 percent required rate of return?

10-8. (*Calculating free cash flows*) You are considering new elliptical trainers and you feel you can sell 5,000 of these per year for 5 years (after which time this project is expected to shut down when it is learned that being fit is unhealthy). The elliptical trainers would sell for $1,000 each with variable costs of $500 for each one produced, while annual fixed costs associated with production would be $1,000,000. In addition, there would be a $5,000,000 initial expenditure associated with the purchase of new production equipment. It is assumed that this initial expenditure will be depreciated using the simplified straight-line method down to zero over 5 years. This project will also require a one-time initial investment of $1,000,000 in net working-capital associated with inventory and that working-capital investment will be recovered when the project is shut down. Finally, assume that the firm's marginal tax rate is 34 percent.

   a. What is the initial outlay associated with this project?
   b. What are the annual free cash flows associated with this project for years 1 through 4?
   c. What is the terminal cash flow in year 5 (that is, what is the free cash flow in year 5 plus any additional cash flows associated with termination of the project)?
   d. What is the project's *NPV* given a 10 percent required rate of return?

10-9. (*New project analysis*) The Chung Chemical Corporation is considering the purchase of a chemical analysis machine. Although the machine being considered will result in an increase in earnings before interest and taxes of $35,000 per year, it has a purchase price of $100,000, and it would cost an additional $5,000 to properly install this machine. In addition, to properly operate this machine, inventory must be increased by $5,000. This machine has an expected life of 10 years, after which it will have no salvage value. Also, assume simplified straight-line depreciation and that this machine is being depreciated down to zero, a 34 percent marginal tax rate, and a required rate of return of 15 percent.

   a. What is the initial outlay associated with this project?
   b. What are the annual after-tax cash flows associated with this project for years 1 through 9?
   c. What is the terminal cash flow in year 10 (what is the annual after-tax cash flow in year 10 plus any additional cash flows associated with termination of the project)?
   d. Should this machine be purchased?

10-10. (*New project analysis*) Raymobile Motors is considering the purchase of a new production machine for $500,000. The purchase of this machine will result in an increase in earnings before interest and taxes of $150,000 per year. To operate this machine properly, workers would have to go through a brief training session that would cost $25,000 after taxes. It would cost $5,000 to install this machine properly. Also, because this machine is extremely efficient, its purchase would necessitate an increase in inventory of $30,000. This machine has an expected life of 10 years, after which it will have no salvage value. Assume simplified straight-line depreciation and that this machine is being depreciated down to zero, a 34 percent marginal tax rate, and a required rate of return of 15 percent.

    a. What is the initial outlay associated with this project?
    b. What are the annual after-tax cash flows associated with this project for years 1 through 9?
    c. What is the terminal cash flow in year 10 (what is the annual after-tax cash flow in year 10 plus any additional cash flows associated with termination of the project)?
    d. Should this machine be purchased?

10-11. (*New project analysis*) Garcia's Truckin', Inc. is considering the purchase of a new production machine for $200,000. The purchase of this machine will result in an increase in earnings before interest and taxes of $50,000 per year. To operate this machine properly, workers would have to go through a brief training session that would cost $5,000 after taxes. It would cost $5,000 to install this machine properly. Also, because this machine is extremely efficient, its purchase would necessitate an increase in inventory of $20,000. This machine has an expected life of 10 years, after which it will have no salvage value. Finally, to purchase the new machine, it appears that the firm would have to borrow $100,000 at 8 percent interest from its local bank, resulting in additional interest payments of $8,000 per year. Assume simplified straight-line depreciation and that this machine is being depreciated down to zero, a 34 percent marginal tax rate, and a required rate of return of 10 percent.

    a. What is the initial outlay associated with this project?
    b. What are the annual after-tax cash flows associated with this project for years 1 through 9?
    c. What is the terminal cash flow in year 10 (what is the annual after-tax cash flow in year 10 plus any additional cash flows associated with termination of the project)?
    d. Should this machine be purchased?

10-12. (*Comprehensive problem*) Traid Winds Corporation, a firm in the 34 percent marginal tax bracket with a 15 percent required rate of return or cost of capital, is considering a new project. This project involves the introduction of a new product. This project is expected to last 5 years and then, because this is somewhat of a fad project, to be terminated. Given the following information, determine the free cash flows associated with the project, the project's net present value, the profitability index, and the internal rate of return. Apply the appropriate decision criteria.

Cost of new plant and equipment:	$14,800,000	
Shipping and installation costs:	$ 200,000	
Unit sales:		

	YEAR	UNITS SOLD
	1	70,000
	2	120,000
	3	120,000
	4	80,000
	5	70,000

Sales price per unit:	$300/unit in years 1 through 4, $250/unit in year 5
Variable cost per unit:	$140/unit
Annual fixed costs:	$700,000
Working-capital requirements:	There will be an initial working-capital requirement of $200,000 just to get production started. For each year, the total investment in net working capital will be equal to 10 percent of the dollar value of sales for that year. Thus, the investment in working capital will increase during years 1 and 2, then decrease in year 4. Finally, all working capital is liquidated at the termination of the project at the end of year 5.
The depreciation method:	Use the simplified straight-line method over 5 years. It is assumed that the plant and equipment will have no salvage value after 5 years.

10-13. (*Comprehensive problem*) The Shome Corporation, a firm in the 34 percent marginal tax bracket with a 15 percent required rate of return or cost of capital, is considering a new project. This project involves the introduction of a new product. This project is expected to last 5 years and then, because this is somewhat of a fad project, to be terminated. Given the following information, determine the free cash flows associated with the project, the project's net present value, the profitability index, and the internal rate of return. Apply the appropriate decision criteria.

Cost of new plant and equipment:	$6,900,000
Shipping and installation costs:	$ 100,000
Unit sales:	

YEAR	UNITS SOLD
1	80,000
2	100,000
3	120,000
4	70,000
5	70,000

Sales price per unit:	$250/unit in years 1 through 4, $200/unit in year 5
Variable cost per unit:	$130/unit
Annual fixed costs:	$300,000
Working–capital requirements:	There will be an initial working-capital requirement of $100,000 just to get production started. For each year, the total investment in net working capital will be equal to 10 percent of the dollar value of sales for that year. Thus, the investment in working capital will increase during years 1 through 3, then decrease in year 4. Finally, all working capital is liquidated at the termination of the project at the end of year 5.
The depreciation method:	Use the simplified straight-line method over 5 years. It is assumed that the plant and equipment will have no salvage value after 5 years.

10-14. (*Risk-adjusted NPV*) The Hokie Corporation is considering two mutually exclusive projects. Both require an initial outlay of $10,000 and will operate for 5 years. Project A will produce expected cash flows of $5,000 per year for years 1 through 5, whereas Project B will produce expected cash flows of $6,000 per year for years 1 through 5. Because project B is the riskier of the two projects, the management of Hokie Corporation has decided to apply a required rate of return of 15 percent to its evaluation but only a 12 percent required rate of return to project A. Determine each project's risk-adjusted net present value.

10-15. (*Risk-adjusted discount rates and risk classes*) The G. Wolfe Corporation is examining two capital-budgeting projects with 5-year lives. The first, project A, is a replacement project; the second, project B, is a project unrelated to current operations. The G. Wolfe Corporation uses the risk-adjusted discount rate method and groups projects according to purpose, and then uses a required rate of return or discount rate that has been preassigned to that purpose or risk class. The expected cash flows for these projects are given here:

	PROJECT A	PROJECT B
Initial investment	−$250,000	−$400,000
Cash inflows:		
Year 1	$ 30,000	$135,000
Year 2	40,000	135,000
Year 3	50,000	135,000
Year 4	90,000	135,000
Year 5	130,000	135,000

The purpose/risk classes and preassigned required rates of return are as follows:

PURPOSE	REQUIRED RATE OF RETURN
Replacement decision	12%
Modification or expansion of existing product line	15
Project unrelated to current operations	18
Research and development operations	20

Determine each project's risk-adjusted net present value.

10-WW. You've decided to use the pure play method for estimating a project's beta. Let's assume that your new product is in the pharmaceutical industry. The first thing you'll have to do is to calculate the beta on a drug company—let's pick Pfizer for this—that most closely matches your new product. To do this let's use the MoneyCentral site, which is a research site for the Microsoft network. If you have the company's ticker symbol, which is a unique one- to four-place alphabetical "nickname" for a company—for Pfizer the ticker symbol is pfe—you can go to a company report (**moneycentral.msn.com/investor/research/profile.asp?**). The report provides a one-page overview of the company, including its beta. Here you'll have to enter the symbol to get to the Pfizer page. The beta is listed as "Volatility (beta)."

You can also find the beta on Yahoo! Finance:

1. From the Yahoo home page (**www.yahoo.com**), choose "Yahoo! Finance" (first link in the top row, the same row in which the title "Yahoo!" appears).
2. Enter the ticker symbol in the first box and click on "Go"; choose "Key Statistics" from the left-hand column under "Company."
3. Go to the table under "Trading Information" and "Stock Price History" toward the bottom of the page on the right. Beta will be the first item in the first column.

Just as with MoneyCentral, in order to get the information for a given firm, you need to know its ticker symbol. The MoneyCentral site is a place to find the ticker symbol if you don't know it.

Let's look up four companies using both MoneyCentral and Yahoo! Finance:

- Pfizer (pfe)
- Amazon.com (amzn)
- Aetna (aet)
- Intel (intc)

What do you think the betas would be for these companies? Remember the beta of the market is 1.0. Less risky companies would be less than 1, and more risky companies would be more than 1.

Were you close? Are the betas on both sites the same? Why might there be differences in the betas?

It's been 2 months since you took a position as an assistant financial analyst at Caledonia Products. Although your boss has been pleased with your work, he is still a bit hesitant about unleashing you without supervision. Your next assignment involves both the calculation of the cash flows associated with a new investment under consideration and the evaluation of several mutually exclusive projects. Given your lack of tenure at Caledonia, you have been asked not only to provide a recommendation but also to respond to a number of questions aimed at judging your understanding of the capital-budgeting process. The memorandum you received outlining your assignment follows:

To: The Assistant Financial Analyst

From: Mr. V. Morrison, CEO, Caledonia Products

Re: Cash Flow Analysis and Capital Rationing

We are considering the introduction of a new product. Currently we are in the 34 percent marginal tax bracket with a 15 percent required rate of return or cost of capital. This project is expected to last 5 years and then, because this is somewhat of a fad project, to be terminated. The following information describes the new project:

Cost of new plant and equipment:	$7,900,000
Shipping and installation costs:	$ 100,000
Unit sales:	

YEAR	UNITS SOLD
1	70,000
2	120,000
3	140,000
4	80,000
5	60,000

Sales price per unit:	$300/unit in years 1 through 4, $260/unit in year 5
Variable cost per unit:	$180/unit
Annual fixed costs:	$200,000
Working–capital requirements:	There will be an initial working-capital requirement of $100,000 just to get production started. For each year, the total investment in net working capital will be equal to 10 percent of the dollar value of sales for that year. Thus, the investment in working capital will increase during years 1 through 3, then decrease in year 4. Finally, all working capital is liquidated at the termination of the project at the end of year 5.
The depreciation method:	Use the simplified straight-line method over 5 years. It is assumed that the plant and equipment will have no salvage value after 5 years.

a. Should Caledonia focus on cash flows or accounting profits in making our capital-budgeting decisions? Should we be interested in incremental cash flows, incremental profits, total free cash flows, or total profits?

b. How does depreciation affect free cash flows?

c. How do sunk costs affect the determination of cash flows?

d. What is the project's initial outlay?

e. What are the differential cash flows over the project's life?

f. What is the terminal cash flow?

g. Draw a cash flow diagram for this project.

h. What is its net present value?

i. What is its internal rate of return?

j. Should the project be accepted? Why or why not?

k. In capital budgeting, risk can be measured from three perspectives. What are those three measures of a project's risk?

l. According to the CAPM, which measurement of a project's risk is relevant? What complications does reality introduce into the CAPM view of risk, and what does that mean for our view of the relevant measure of a project's risk?

m. Explain how simulation works. What is the value in using a simulation approach?

n. What is sensitivity analysis and what is its purpose?

SELF-TEST SOLUTION

SS-1.

SECTION I. CALCULATE THE CHANGE IN EBIT, TAXES, AND DEPRECIATION
(THIS BECOMES AN INPUT IN THE CALCULATION OF OPERATING CASH FLOW IN SECTION II)

YEAR	0	1	2	3	4	5
Units sold		100,000	130,000	160,000	100,000	60,000
Sales price		$ 500	$ 500	$ 500	$ 500	$ 380
Sales revenue		$50,000,000	$65,000,000	$80,000,000	$50,000,000	$22,800,000
Less: Variable costs		26,000,000	33,800,000	41,600,000	26,000,000	15,600,000
Less: Fixed costs		$ 300,000	$ 300,000	$ 300,000	$ 300,000	$ 300,000
Equals: EBDIT		$23,700,000	$30,900,000	$38,100,000	$23,700,000	$ 6,900,000
Less: Depreciation		$ 4,240,000	$ 4,240,000	$ 4,240,000	$ 4,240,000	$ 4,240,000
Equals: EBIT		$19,460,000	$26,660,000	$33,860,000	$19,460,000	$ 2,660,000
Taxes (@ 34%)		$ 6,616,400	9,064,400	$ 11,512,400	$ 6,616,400	$ 904,400

SECTION II. CALCULATE OPERATING CASH FLOW
(THIS BECOMES AN INPUT IN THE CALCULATION OF FREE CASH FLOWS IN SECTION IV)

Operating cash flow:	0	1	2	3	4	5
EBIT		$ 19,460,000	$ 26,660,000	$ 33,860,000	$ 19,460,000	$ 2,660,000
Minus: Taxes		$ 6,616,400	$ 9,064,400	$ 11,512,400	$ 6,616,400	$ 904,400
Plus: Depreciation		$ 4,240,000	$ 4,240,000	$ 4,240,000	$ 4,240,000	$ 4,240,000
Equals: Operating cash flow		$ 17,083,600	$ 21,835,600	$ 26,587,600	$ 17,083,600	$ 5,995,600

SECTION III. CALCULATE THE NET WORKING CAPITAL
(THIS BECOMES AN INPUT IN THE CALCULATION OF FREE CASH FLOWS IN SECTION IV)

Change in net working capital:	0	1	2	3	4	5
Revenue		$ 50,000,000	$ 65,000,000	$ 80,000,000	$ 50,000,000	$22,800,000
Initial working-capital requirement	$ 500,000					
Net working-capital needs		$ 5,000,000	$ 6,500,000	$ 8,000,000	$ 5,000,000	2,280,000
Liquidation of working capital						$ 2,280,000
Change in working capital	$ 500,000	$ 4,500,000	$ 1,500,000	$ 1,500,000	($ 3,000,000)	($5,000,000)

SECTION IV. CALCULATE FREE CASH FLOW
(USING INFORMATION CALCULATED IN SECTIONS II AND III, IN ADDITION TO CHANGE IN CAPITAL SPENDING)

Free cash flow:	0	1	2	3	4	5
Operating cash flow		$ 17,083,600	$ 21,835,600	$ 26,587,600	$ 17,083,600	$ 5,995,600
Minus: Change in net working capital	$ 500,000	$ 4,500,000	$ 1,500,000	$ 1,500,000	($ 3,000,000)	($ 5,000,000)
Minus: Change in capital spending	$21,200,000	0	0	0	0	0
Free cash flow	($21,700,000)	$12,583,600	$20,335,600	$25,087,600	$20,083,600	$10,995,600

NPV	$38,064,020; Accept project; NPV is positive
PI	2.75; Accept project; PI is greater than 1.0
IRR	73.6%; Accept project; IRR is greater than the required rated return.

❦ LEARNING OBJECTIVES ❦

After reading this chapter, you should be able to:

1. Describe the concepts underlying the firm's cost of capital (technically, its weighted average cost of capital) and the purpose for its calculation.

2. Calculate the after-tax cost of debt, preferred stock, and common equity.

3. Calculate a firm's weighted average cost of capital.

4. Describe the procedure used by PepsiCo to estimate the cost of capital for a multidivisional firm.

5. Use the cost of capital to evaluate new investment opportunities.

6. Compute the economic profit earned by the firm and use this quantity to calculate incentive-based compensation.

7. Calculate equivalent interest rates for different countries.

Cost of Capital

THE COST OF CAPITAL: KEY DEFINITIONS AND CONCEPTS • DETERMINING INDIVIDUAL COSTS OF CAPITAL • THE WEIGHTED AVERAGE COST OF CAPITAL • CALCULATING DIVISIONAL COSTS OF CAPITAL: PEPSICO, INC. • USING A FIRM'S COST OF CAPITAL TO EVALUATE NEW CAPITAL INVESTMENTS • SHAREHOLDER VALUE–BASED MANAGEMENT • FINANCE AND THE MULTINATIONAL FIRM: WHY DO INTEREST RATES DIFFER BETWEEN COUNTRIES?

≪ WHAT'S AHEAD ≫

Having studied the connection between risk and rates of return for securities (Chapter 9) and the valuation of bonds and stocks (Chapters 7 and 8), we are prepared to consider the firm's cost of capital. A firm's cost of capital serves as the link between the firm's financing decisions and its investment decisions. The cost of capital becomes the hurdle rate that must be achieved by an investment before it will increase shareholder wealth. The term *cost of capital* is commonly used interchangeably with the firm's *required rate of return*, the *hurdle rate for new investments*, the *discount rate for evaluating a new investment*, and the firm's *opportunity costs of funds*. Regardless of the term used, the basic concept is the same. The cost of capital is the rate that must be earned on an investment project if the project is to increase the value of the common stockholders' investment.

The cost of capital is also the appropriate basis for evaluating the performance of a division or even an entire firm. In this case, the cost of capital becomes the key determinant of the capital cost associated with a firm's investments when we calculate a division's or firm's economic profit.

In this chapter, we discuss the fundamental determinants of a firm's cost of capital and the rationale for its calculation and use. This entails developing the logic for estimating the cost of debt capital, preferred stock, and common stock. Chapter 13 takes up consideration of the impact of the firm's financing mix on the cost of capital.

This chapter emphasizes Principles 1, 2, 3, 6, 7, 8, and 9: **Principle 1: The Risk–Return Trade-Off— We Won't Take On Additional Risk Unless We Expect to Be Compensated with Additional Return; Principle 2: The Time Value of Money—A Dollar Received Today Is Worth More Than a Dollar Received in the Future; Principle 3: Cash—Not Profits—Is King; Principle 6: Efficient Capital Markets—The Markets Are Quick and the Prices Are Right; Principle 7: The Agency Problem—Managers Won't Work for the Owners Unless It's in Their Best Interest; Principle 8: Taxes Bias Business Decisions; Principle 9: All Risk Is Not Equal— Some Risk Can Be Diversified Away and Some Cannot.**

Encore, Inc. and H&L Manufacturing are both faced with the need to assess financial performance. In one case, it is the anticipated performance of a new capital investment, and in the other, it is the performance of the firm as a whole. Consider the following scenarios:

- The Morristown division of Encore, Inc. is faced with an investment opportunity that requires the investment of $75 million to construct a new shipping and distribution facility. The new facility will free up existing factory space for additional productive capacity that the firm needs to meet growing demand.
- The management of H&L Manufacturing Company is trying to come to grips with the company's overall performance. Profits have grown by more than 20 percent per year over the past 5 years, but the firm's stock price has not kept pace with those of competitor firms.

In both the preceding scenarios the analyst needs a benchmark rate of return. Encore needs a benchmark return that can be used to evaluate whether the anticipated return from the new shipping and distribution investment is going to create or destroy shareholder wealth. H&L, on the other hand, needs a benchmark return to compare against the performance of the entire firm.

In this chapter, we learn that the benchmark return that is appropriate in both instances is the firm's cost of capital. We recognize Encore's problem as the capital-budgeting problem introduced earlier in Chapter 9, and H&L's problem is the focal point of shareholder value–based management (SVBM). Specifically, H&L wants to know whether it is creating value for its stockholders.

In July 1994, Boise Cascade adopted Economic Value Added (EVA®), a very popular method for implementing shareholder value–based management, as its key measure of financial performance. Its description of why it did so tells us a lot about the role of the cost of capital in managing a firm to create value for shareholders:[*]

> Economic value is created by earning a return greater than investors require and is destroyed by earning a return less than they require. The EVA measurement process encourages management to make business decisions that create economic value through improved operating efficiency, better asset utilization, and growth that generates returns which exceed the cost of capital.

But shareholder value–based management is about more than using the cost of capital as the standard for making financial choices. It is also about rewarding the firm's employees in ways that continually encourage them to seek out new ways to create shareholder value. Thus, the EVA system also involves rewarding employees for creating shareholder value as captured in the EVA performance metric. As we see in the following excerpt, Boise Cascade saw the need to connect EVA performance to compensation, following the old adage that what you measure and reward gets done:[**]

> We believe our emphasis on EVA will more closely align the interests of employees and shareholders. Therefore, we are also using EVA to determine incentive compensation for management. The compensation of plan participants, including corporate officers, will be tied directly to improvement in the EVA of their operations and the corporation as a whole. We believe this measurement, and the fact that incentive compensation is linked to it, will effectively encourage management decisions that maximize the market value of the capital contributed by investors.

Note: Stern Stewart & Co. has trademarked the term *Economic Value Added (EVA®)* to refer to its particular method for calculating a firm's economic profit using financial statement results.

[*]1994 Boise Cascade annual report.

[**]1994 Boise Cascade annual report.

Objective **1**

THE COST OF CAPITAL: KEY DEFINITIONS AND CONCEPTS

INVESTOR OPPORTUNITY COSTS, REQUIRED RATES OF RETURN, AND THE COST OF CAPITAL

In Chapter 9, we referred to the discount rate used in calculating net present value (*NPV*) simply as the appropriate discount rate. In this chapter, we define what we mean by this term. Specifically, the appropriate discount rate primarily reflects the **investor's required rate of return**, or the *minimum rate of return necessary to attract an investor to purchase or hold a security*. This rate of return considers the investor's opportunity cost of making the investment. This opportunity cost equals the return on the investor's next-best investment that is forgone should the project under consideration be accepted. This forgone return is the opportunity cost of undertaking the investment and, consequently, is the investor's required rate of return.

Is the investor's required rate of return the same thing as the cost of capital? Not exactly. Two basic considerations drive a wedge between the investor's required rate of return and the cost of capital to the firm. First, there are taxes. When a firm borrows money to finance the purchase of an asset, the interest expense is deductible for federal income tax calculations. Consider a firm that borrows at 9 percent and then deducts its

investor's required rate of return

interest expense from its revenues before paying taxes at a rate of 34 percent. For each dollar of interest it pays, the firm reduces its taxes by $.34. Consequently, the actual cost of borrowing to the firm is only 5.94% $[.09 - (.34 \times .09) = .09(1 - .34) = 0.0594,$ or 5.94%]. The second thing that causes the firm's cost of capital to differ from the investor's required rate of return is *any transaction costs incurred when a firm raises funds by issuing a particular type of security*, which are sometimes called **flotation costs**. For example, if a firm sells new shares for $25 per share but incurs transaction costs of $5 per share, then the cost of capital for the new common equity is increased. Assume that the investor's required rate of return is 15 percent for each $25 share; then $.15 \times \$25 = \$3.75$ must be earned each year to satisfy the investor's required return. However, the firm has only $20 to invest, so the cost of capital (k) is calculated as the rate of return that must be earned on the $20 net proceeds that will produce a dollar return of $3.75; that is,

flotation costs

$$\$20k = \$25 \times .15 = \$3.75$$

$$k = \frac{\$3.75}{\$20.00} = .1875, \text{ or } 18.75\%$$

We have more to say about both these considerations as we discuss the costs of the individual sources of capital to the firm.

FINANCIAL POLICY AND THE COST OF CAPITAL

A firm's **financial policy**—that is, *the policies regarding the sources of finances it plans to use and the particular mix (proportions) in which they will be used*—governs its use of debt and equity financing. The particular mixture of debt and equity that the firm utilizes can impact the firm's cost of capital. However, in this chapter, we assume that the firm maintains a fixed financial policy that is reflected in a fixed debt–equity ratio. Determination of the target mix of debt and equity financing is the subject of Chapter 12.

financial policy

The firm's overall cost of capital reflects the combined costs of all the sources of financing used by the firm. We refer to this overall cost of capital as the firm's **weighted average cost of capital**. The weighted average cost of capital is *the weighted average of the after-tax costs of each of the sources of capital used by a firm to finance a project, where the weights reflect the proportion of total financing raised from each source*. Consequently, the weighted average cost of capital is the rate of return that the firm must earn on its investments so that it can compensate both its creditors and stockholders with their individual required rates of return. Let's now turn to a discussion of how the costs of debt and equity can be estimated.

weighted average cost of capital

CONCEPT CHECK

1. How is an investor's required rate of return related to an opportunity cost?
2. How do flotation costs impact the firm's cost of capital?

DETERMINING INDIVIDUAL COSTS OF CAPITAL

Objective **2**

In order to attract new investors, companies have created a wide variety of financing instruments or securities. In this chapter, we stick to three basic types: debt, preferred stock, and common stock. In calculating the respective cost of financing from each of these types of financing instruments, we estimate the investor's required rate of return after properly adjusting for any transaction or flotation costs. In addition, because we will be discounting after-tax cash flows, we adjust our cost of capital for the effects of corporate taxes. In summary, the cost of a particular source of capital is equal to the investor's required rate of return after adjusting for the effects of both flotation costs and corporate taxes.

THE COST OF DEBT

The investor's required rate of return on debt is simply the return that creditors demand on new borrowing. We learned in Chapter 6 that we could calculate the value of a bond that has 3 years to maturity and pays interest annually plus the principal amount of the debt (M) at the end of 3 years as follows:

$$\text{Bond price } (P_d) = \frac{\text{interest for year 1 } (\$I_1)}{(1 + \text{bondholder's required rate of return } (R_d))}$$
$$+ \frac{\$I_2}{(1 + R_d)^2} + \frac{\$I_3 + \text{principal } (\$M)}{(1 + R_d)^3} \qquad \textbf{(11-1)}$$

Since firms must pay flotation costs when they issue new debt, the net proceeds from the bond issuance (NP_d) will be less than the bond price paid by the investor who buys it. The difference (i.e., the flotation costs) comprises the fees paid to an investment banker to prepare the documents needed to issue new bonds and for the sales commissions involved in selling them. Consequently, the cost of debt capital, k_d, will be higher than the investor's required rate of return, R_d. Specifically, we calculate the cost of capital for a firm's new debt as follows:

$$\text{Net proceeds } (NP_d) = \frac{\$I_1}{(1 + \text{cost of debt capital } (k_d))^1} + \frac{\$I_2}{(1 + k_d)^2} + \frac{\$I_3 + \$M}{(1 + k_d)^3} \qquad \textbf{(11-2a)}$$

Note that the adjustment for flotation costs simply involves replacing the market price of the bond with the net proceeds per bond (NP_d) received by the firm after paying these costs. The result of this adjustment is that the discount rate that solves equation (11-2a) is now the firm's cost of debt financing before adjusting for the effect of corporate taxes—that is, the before-tax cost of debt (k_d). The final adjustment we make is to account for the fact that interest is tax deductible. Thus, the after-tax cost of debt capital is simply $k_d(1 - T_c)$, where T_c is the corporate tax rate.

As we learned in Chapter 6, the interest payments on bonds are generally the same for each period. Under these conditions, equation (11-2a) can be restated using the interest factors in the present value tables found in the Appendixes at the back of the book, as follows:

$$NP_d = \$I_t(PVIFA_{k_d, n}) + \$M(PVIF_{k_d, n}) \qquad \textbf{(11-2b)}$$

BACK TO THE FOUNDATIONS

When we calculate the bondholder's required rate of return, we are discounting the interest and principal payments to the bondholder back to the present using a discount rate that makes this present value equal the current price of the firm's bonds. In essence, we are valuing the bond, which relies on two basic principles of finance: **Principle 1: The Risk–Return Trade-Off—We Won't Take On Additional Risk Unless We Expect to Be Compensated with Additional Return,** *and* **Principle 2: The Time Value of Money—A Dollar Received Today Is Worth More Than a Dollar Received in the Future.**

In addition, the calculation of the bondholder's required rate of return relies on the observed market price of the firm's bonds to be an accurate reflection of their worth. Buyers and sellers only stop trading when they are convinced that the price properly reflects all available information. **Principle 6: Efficient Capital Markets—The Markets Are Quick and the Prices Are Right.** *What we mean here, very simply, is that investors are ever vigilant and quickly act on information that affects the riskiness and, consequently, the price of a firm's bonds and other securities.*

EXAMPLE

Synopticom, Inc. plans a bond issue for the near future and wants to estimate its current cost of debt capital. After talking with the firm's investment banker, the firm's chief financial officer has determined that a 20-year maturity bond with a $1,000 face value and 8 percent coupon (paying $8\% \times \$1,000 = \$80$ per year in interest) can be sold to investors for $908.32. As we illustrated earlier in Chapter 7, equation (11-1) can be generalized to solve for the investor's required rate of return (R_d) for a 20-year bond. In this instance the bond pays 20 annual interest payments of $80 plus a $1,000 principal amount in the twentieth year; that is,

$$\$908.32 = \frac{\$80}{(1+R_d)^1} + \frac{\$80}{(1+R_d)^2} + \frac{\$80}{(1+R_d)^3} + \cdots + \frac{\$80}{(1+R_d)^{19}} + \frac{\$80 + \$1,000}{(1+R_d)^{20}}$$

In this case, Synopticom's creditors require a 9 percent rate of return. The cost of capital to the firm is higher than 9 percent, however, because the firm will have to pay flotation costs of $58.32 per bond when it issues the securities. The flotation costs reduce the net proceeds to Synopticom to $850. Substituting into equation (11-2), we find that the before-tax cost of capital for the bond issue (k_d) is 9.73 percent, that is,

$$\$850.00 = \frac{\$80}{(1+k_d)^1} + \frac{\$80}{(1+k_d)^2} + \frac{\$80}{(1+k_d)^3} + \cdots + \frac{\$80}{(1+k_d)^{19}} + \frac{\$80 + \$1,000}{(1+k_d)^{20}}$$

Once again, we can solve equation (11-2a) using a financial calculator, as we illustrate in the margin.

One final adjustment is necessary to obtain the firm's after-tax cost of debt capital. Assuming that Synopticom is in the 34 percent corporate income tax (T_c) bracket, we estimate the after-tax cost of debt capital as follows:

$$\text{After-tax cost of debt} = k_d(1 - T_c)$$
$$= 9.73\%(1 - .34) = 6.422\%$$

CALCULATOR SOLUTION

Data Input	Function Key
20	N
850	+/− PV
80	PMT
1000	FV

Function Key	Answer
CPT I/Y	9.73

BACK TO THE FOUNDATIONS

*The tax deductibility of interest expense makes debt financing less costly to the firm. This is an example of **Principle 8: Taxes Bias Business Decisions**. The tax deductibility of interest, other things remaining constant, serves to encourage firms to use more debt in their capital structure than they might otherwise use.*

THE COST OF PREFERRED STOCK

Determining the cost of preferred stock is very straightforward because of the simple nature of the cash flows paid to the holders of preferred shares. You will recall from Chapter 7 that the value of a preferred stock is simply

$$\frac{\text{Price of preferred}}{\text{stock } (P_{ps})} = \frac{\text{preferred stock dividend}}{\text{required rate of return for preferred stockholder}} \qquad \text{(11-3)}$$

where P_{ps} is the current market price of the preferred shares. Solving for the preferred stockholder's required rate of return, we get the following:

$$\frac{\text{required rate of return}}{\text{for preferred stockholder}} = \frac{\text{preferred stock dividend}}{\text{price of preferred stock}} \qquad \textbf{(11-4)}$$

Once again, where flotation costs are incurred when new preferred shares are sold, the investor's required rate of return is less than the cost of preferred capital to the firm. To calculate the cost of preferred stock, we must adjust the required rate of return to reflect these flotation costs. We replace the price of a preferred share in equation (11-4) with the net proceeds per share from the sale of new preferred shares (NP_{ps}). The resulting formula can be used to calculate the cost of preferred stock to the firm.

$$\text{cost of preferred stock } (k_{ps}) = \frac{\text{preferred stock dividend}}{\text{net proceeds per preferred share}} \qquad \textbf{(11-5)}$$

Note that the net proceeds per share are equal to the price per share of preferred stock minus flotation cost per share of newly issued preferred stock.

What about corporate taxes? In the case of preferred stock, no tax adjustment must be made because preferred dividends are not tax deductible.

EXAMPLE

El Paso Edison has an issue of preferred stock that pays an annual dividend of $4.25 per share. On November 23, 2004, the stock closed at $58.50. Assume that if the firm were to sell an issue of preferred stock with the same characteristics as its outstanding issue, it would incur flotation costs of $1.375 per share and the shares would sell for their November 23, 2004, closing price. What is El Paso Edison's cost of preferred stock?

Substituting into equation (11-5), we get the following cost of preferred stock for El Paso Edison:

$$k_{ps} = \frac{\$4.25}{(\$58.50 - \$1.375)} = .0744, \text{ or } 7.44\%$$

Note that there is no adjustment for taxes because preferred dividends are not tax deductible—that is, preferred dividends are paid after corporate taxes, unlike bond interest, which is paid with before-tax dollars.

THE COST OF COMMON EQUITY

Common equity is unique in two respects. First, the cost of common equity is more difficult to estimate than the cost of debt or preferred stock because the common stockholder's required rate of return is not observable. This results from the fact that common stockholders are the residual owners of the firm, which means that their return is equal to what is left of the firm's earnings after paying the firm's bondholders their contractually set interest and principal payments and the preferred stockholders their promised dividends. Second, common equity can be obtained either from the retention of firm earnings or through the sale of new shares. The costs associated with each of these sources are different from one another because the firm does not incur any flotation costs when it retains earnings but it does incur costs when it sells new common shares.

We discuss two methods for estimating the common stockholder's required rate of return, which is the foundation for our estimate of the firm's cost of equity capital. These methods are based on the dividend growth model and the capital asset pricing model, which were both discussed earlier in Chapter 7 when we discussed stock valuation.

THE DIVIDEND GROWTH MODEL

Recall from Chapter 7 that the value of a firm's common stock is equal to the present value of all future dividends. When dividends are expected to grow at a rate g forever and g is less than the investor's required rate of return, k_{cs}, then the value of a share of common stock, P_{cs}, can be written as

$$P_{cs} = \frac{D_1}{k_{cs} - g} \tag{11-6}$$

where D_1 is the dividend expected to be received by the firm's common shareholders 1 year hence. The expected dividend is simply the current dividend multiplied by 1 plus the annual rate of growth in dividends (i.e., $D_1 = D_0(1 + g)$). The investor's required rate of return then is found by solving equation (11-6) for k_{cs}.

$$k_{cs} = \frac{D_1}{P_{cs}} + g \tag{11-7}$$

Note that k_{cs} is the investor's required rate of return for investing in the firm's stock. It also serves as our estimate of the cost of equity capital, where new equity capital is obtained by retaining a part of the firm's current-period earnings. Recall that common equity financing can come from one of two sources: the retention of earnings (i.e., earnings not paid out in dividends to the common stockholders) or from the sale of new common shares. When the firm retains earnings, it doesn't incur any flotation costs; thus, the investor's required rate of return is the same as the firm's cost of new equity capital in this instance.

If the firm issues new shares to raise equity capital, then it incurs flotation costs. Once again we adjust the investor's required rate of return for flotation costs by substituting the net proceeds per share, NP_{cs}, for the stock price, P_{cs}, in equation (11-7) to estimate the cost of new common stock, k_{ncs}.

$$k_{ncs} = \frac{D_1}{NP_{cs}} + g \tag{11-8}$$

EXAMPLE

The Talbot Corporation's common shareholders anticipate receiving a $2.20 per share dividend next year, based on the fact that they received $2 last year and expect dividends to grow 10 percent next year. Furthermore, analysts predict that dividends will continue to grow at a rate of 10 percent into the foreseeable future. Given that the firm's stock is trading for $50 per share, we can calculate the investor's required rate of return (and the cost of retained earnings) as follows:

$$k_{cs} = \frac{D_1}{P_{cs}} + g = \frac{\$2.20}{\$50.00} + .10 = .144, \text{ or } 14.4\%$$

Should Talbot decide to issue new common stock, then it would incur a cost of $7.50 per share, or 15 percent of the current stock price. The resulting cost of new common equity capital would be

$$k_{ncs} = \frac{D_1}{NP_{cs}} + g = \frac{\$2.20}{\$50 - 7.50} + .10 = .1518, \text{ or } 15.18\%$$

Thus, Talbot faces two costs of capital with respect to common equity. If it retains earnings, then the cost of capital to the firm is 14.4 percent, and if it issues new common stock, the corresponding cost is 15.18 percent. This difference will prove to be important later when we calculate the overall or weighted average cost of capital for the firm.

> ### BACK TO THE FOUNDATIONS
>
> *The dividend growth model for common stock valuation relies on three of the fundamental principles of finance. First, stock value is equal to the present value of expected future dividends. This reflects **Principle 2: The Time Value of Money—A Dollar Received Today Is Worth More Than a Dollar Received in the Future**. Furthermore, dividends represent actual cash receipts to stockholders and are incorporated into the valuation model in a manner that reflects the timing of their receipt. This attribute of the dividend growth model reflects **Principle 3: Cash—Not Profits—Is King**. Finally, the rate used to discount the expected future dividends back to the present reflects the riskiness of the dividends. The higher the riskiness of the dividend payments, the higher the investor's required rate of return. This reflects **Principle 1: The Risk–Return Trade-Off—We Won't Take On Additional Risk Unless We Expect to Be Compensated with Additional Return**.*

ISSUES IN IMPLEMENTING THE DIVIDEND GROWTH MODEL

The principal advantage of the dividend growth model is its simplicity. To estimate an investor's required rate of return, the analyst needs only to observe the current dividend and stock price and to estimate the rate of growth in future dividends. The primary drawback relates to the applicability or appropriateness of the valuation model. That is, the dividend growth model is based on the fundamental assumption that dividends are expected to grow at a constant rate g forever. To avoid this assumption, analysts frequently utilize more complex valuation models in which dividends are expected to grow for, say, 5 years at one rate and then grow at a lower rate from year 6 forward. We do not consider these more complex models here.

Even if the constant growth rate assumption is acceptable, we must arrive at an estimate of that growth rate. We could estimate the rate of growth in historical dividends ourselves or go to published sources of growth rate expectations. Investment advisory services such as Value Line provide their own analysts' estimates of earnings growth rates (generally spanning up to 5 years), and the Institutional Brokers' Estimate System (I/B/E/S) collects and publishes earnings per share forecasts made by more than 1,000 analysts for a broad list of stocks. These estimates are helpful but still require the careful judgment of the analyst in their use because they relate to earnings (not dividends) and extend only 5 years into the future (not forever, as required by the dividend growth model). Nonetheless, these estimates provide a useful guide to making your initial dividend growth rate estimate.

THE CAPITAL ASSET PRICING MODEL

capital asset pricing model

Recall from Chapter 8 that the **capital asset pricing model (CAPM)** provides a basis for determining the investor's expected or required rate of return from investing in common stock. The model depends on three things:

1. the risk-free rate, k_{rf};
2. the systematic risk of the common stock's returns relative to the market as a whole, or the stock's beta coefficient, β; and
3. the market risk premium, which is equal to the difference in the expected rate of return for the market as a whole, that is, the expected rate of return for the "average security" minus the risk-free rate, or in symbols, $k_m - k_{rf}$.

Using the CAPM, the investor's required rate of return can be written as follows:

$$k_c = k_{rf} + \beta(k_m - k_{rf}) \tag{11-9}$$

EXAMPLE

Talbot Corporation's common stock has a beta coefficient of 1.40. Furthermore, the risk-free rate is currently 3.75 percent, and the expected rate of return on the market portfolio of all risky assets is 12 percent. Using the CAPM from equation (11-9), we can estimate Talbot's cost of capital as follows:

$$k_c = k_{rf} + \beta(k_m - k_{rf})$$
$$= .0375 + 1.4(.12 - .0375) = .153, \text{ or } 15.3\%$$

Note that the required rate of return we have estimated is the cost of internal common equity because no transaction costs are considered.

ISSUES IN IMPLEMENTING THE CAPM

The CAPM approach has two primary advantages. First, the model is simple and easy to understand and implement. The model variables are readily available from public sources, with the possible exception of beta coefficients for small and/or nonpublicly traded firms. Second, because the model does not rely on dividends or any assumption about the growth rate in dividends, it can be applied to companies that do not currently pay dividends or are not expected to experience a constant rate of growth in dividends.

Using the CAPM requires that we obtain estimates of each of the three model variables—k_{rf}, β, and $(k_m - k_{rf})$. Let's consider each in turn. First, the analyst has a wide range of U.S. government securities on which to base an estimate of the risk-free rate. Treasury securities with maturities from 30 days to 20 years are readily available, but the CAPM offers no guidance about the appropriate choice. In fact, the model itself assumes that there is but one risk-free rate, and it corresponds to a one-period return (the length of the period is not specified, however). Consequently, we are left to our own judgment about which maturity we should use to represent the risk-free rate. For applications of the cost of capital involving long-term capital expenditure decisions, it seems reasonable to select a risk-free rate of comparable maturity. So, if we are calculating the cost of capital to be used as the basis for evaluating investments that will provide returns over the next 20 years, it seems appropriate to use a risk-free rate corresponding to a U.S. Treasury bond of comparable maturity.

Second, estimates of security beta coefficients are available from a wide variety of investment advisory services, including Merrill Lynch and Value Line, among others. Alternatively, we could collect historical stock market returns for the company of interest as well as a general market index (such as the Standard and Poor's 500 Index) and estimate the stock's beta as the slope of the relationship between the two return series—as we did in Chapter 8. However, because beta estimates are widely available for a large majority of publicly traded firms, analysts frequently rely on published sources for betas.

Finally, estimation of the market risk premium can be accomplished by looking at the history of stock returns and the premium earned over (under) the risk-free rate of interest. In Chapter 8, we reported a summary of the historical returns earned on risk-free securities and common stocks in Figure 8-2. We saw that on average over the last 70 years, common stocks have earned a premium of roughly 7 percent over long-term government bonds. Thus, for our purposes, we will utilize this estimate of the market risk premium $(k_m - k_{rf})$ when estimating the investor's required rate of return on equity using the CAPM.

In addition to the historical average market risk premium, we can also utilize surveys of professional economists' opinions regarding future premiums.[1] For example, in a survey

TAKIN' IT TO THE NET
Ibbotson Associates maintains a historical database on rates of return earned on stocks and bonds, as well as the market risk premium. See its site www.ibbotson.com.

[1]The results reported here come from Ivo Welch, "Views of Financial Economists on the Equity Premium and on Professional Controversies," *The Journal of Business* 73–74 (October 2000): pp. 501–537; and Ivo Welch, "The Equity Premium Consensus Forecast Revisited," Cowles Foundation Discussion Paper No. 1325 (September 2001).

FINANCIAL MANAGEMENT
IN PRACTICE

IPOS: SHOULD A FIRM GO PUBLIC?

When a privately owned company decides to distribute its shares to the general public, it goes through a process known as an initial public offering (IPO). There are a number of advantages to having a firm's shares traded in the public equity market, including the following:

- **New capital is raised.** When the firm sells its shares to the public, it acquires new capital that can be invested in the firm.
- **The firm's owners gain liquidity of their share holdings.** Publicly traded shares are more easily bought and sold, so the owners can more easily liquidate all or part of their investment in the firm.
- **The firm gains future access to the public capital market.** Once a firm has raised capital in the public markets, it is easier to go back a second and third time.
- **Being a publicly traded firm may benefit the firm's business.** Public firms tend to enjoy a higher profile than their privately held counterparts. This may make it easier to make sales and attract vendors to supply goods and services to the firm.

However, all is not rosy as a publicly held firm. There are a number of potential disadvantages, including the following:

- **Reporting requirements can be onerous.** Publicly held firms are required to file periodic reports with the Securities and Exchange Commission (SEC). This is not only onerous in terms of the time and effort required, but also some business owners feel they must reveal information to their competitors that could be potentially damaging.

- **Private equity investors now must share any new wealth with the new public investors.** Now that the firm is a publicly held company, the new shareholders share on an equal footing with the company founders in the good (and bad) fortune of the firm.
- **The private investors lose a degree of control of the organization.** Outsiders gain voting control over the firm to the extent that they own its shares.
- **An IPO is expensive.** A typical firm may spend 15 to 25 percent of the money raised on expenses directly connected to the IPO. This cost is increased further if we consider the cost of lost management time and disruption of business associated with the IPO process.
- **Exit of company owners is usually limited.** The company founders may want to sell their shares through the IPO, but this is not allowed for an extended period of time. Therefore, the IPO is not usually a good mechanism for cashing out the company founders.
- **Everyone involved faces legal liability.** The IPO participants are jointly and severally liable for each others' actions. This means that they can be sued for any omissions from the IPO prospectus should the market valuation fall below the IPO offering price.

A careful weighing of the financial consequences of each of these advantages and disadvantages can provide a company's owners (and management) with some basis for answering the question of whether they want to become a public corporation.

Other Sources: Professor Ivo Welch's Web site: welch.som.yale.edu provides a wealth of information concerning IPOs.

conducted in 1998 by Yale economist Ivo Welch, the median 30-year market risk premium for all survey participants was 7 percent. When the survey was repeated in 2000, the corresponding market risk premium had fallen to 5 percent. These results suggest two things. First, the market risk premium is not fixed. It varies through time with the general business cycle. In addition, it appears that using a market risk premium somewhere between 5 percent and 7 percent is reasonable when estimating the cost of capital with the capital asset pricing model.

BACK TO THE FOUNDATIONS

*The capital asset pricing model, or CAPM, is a formal representation of **Principle 1: The Risk–Return Trade-Off—We Won't Take On Additional Risk Unless We Expect to Be Compensated with Additional Return**. By "formal" we mean that the specific method of calculating the additional returns needed to compensate for additional risk is specified in the form of an equation—the CAPM. The CAPM's recognition of systematic or nondiversifiable risk as the source of risk that is rewarded in the capital market is a reflection of **Principle 9: All Risk Is Not Equal— Some Risk Can Be Diversified Away and Some Cannot**.*

THE WEIGHTED AVERAGE COST OF CAPITAL

Objective **3**

Now that we have calculated the individual costs of capital for each of the sources of financing the firm might use, we turn to the combination of these capital costs into a single weighted average cost of capital. To estimate the weighted average cost of capital, we need to know the cost of each of the sources of capital used and the capital structure mix. We use the term **capital structure** to refer to *the proportions of each source of financing used by the firm.* Although a firm's capital structure can be quite complex, we focus our examples on the three basic sources of capital: bonds, preferred stock, and common equity.

capital structure

In words, we calculate the weighted average cost of capital for a firm that uses only debt and common equity using the following equation:

$$\begin{pmatrix} \text{weighted} \\ \text{average cost} \\ \text{of capital} \end{pmatrix} = \begin{pmatrix} \text{after-tax} \\ \text{cost of} \\ \text{debt} \end{pmatrix} \times \begin{pmatrix} \text{proportion} \\ \text{of debt} \\ \text{financing} \end{pmatrix} + \begin{pmatrix} \text{cost of} \\ \text{equity} \end{pmatrix} \times \begin{pmatrix} \text{proportion} \\ \text{of equity} \\ \text{financing} \end{pmatrix} \quad \textbf{(11-10)}$$

For example, if a firm borrows money at 6 percent after taxes, pays 10 percent for equity, and raises its capital in equal proportions from debt and equity, its weighted average cost of capital is 8 percent—that is,

Weighted
average cost $= [.06 \times .5] + [.10 \times .5] = .08$ or 8%
of capital

In practice, the calculation of the cost of capital is generally more complex than this example. For one thing, firms often have multiple debt issues with different required rates of return, and they also use preferred equity as well as common equity financing. Furthermore, when new common equity capital is raised, it is sometimes the result of retaining and reinvesting the firm's current period earnings and, at other times, it involves a new stock offering. In the case of retained earnings, the firm does not incur the costs associated with selling new common stock. This means that equity from retained earnings is less costly than a new stock offering. In the examples that follow, we address each of these complications.

CAPITAL STRUCTURE WEIGHTS

We opened this chapter with a description of an investment opportunity faced by the Morristown division of Encore, Inc. A critical element in the analysis of that investment was an estimate of the cost of capital—the discount rate—to be used to calculate the *NPV* for the project. The reason we calculate a cost of capital is that it enables us to evaluate one or more of the firm's investment opportunities. Remember that the cost of capital should reflect the riskiness of the project being evaluated, so a firm may calculate multiple costs of capital when it makes investments in multiple divisions or business units having different risk characteristics. Thus, for the calculated cost of capital to be meaningful, it must correspond directly to the riskiness of the particular project being analyzed. That is, in theory the cost of capital should reflect the particular way in which the funds are raised (the capital structure used) and the systemic risk characteristics of the project. Consequently, the correct way to calculate capital structure weights is to use the actual dollar amounts of the various sources of capital actually used by the firm.[2]

In practice, *the mixture of financing sources used by a firm will vary from year to year.* For this reason, many firms find it expedient to use target capital structure proportions in calculating the firm's weighted average cost of capital. For example, a firm might use its target mix of 40 percent debt and 60 percent equity to calculate its weighted average cost of capital even though, in that particular year, it raised the majority of its financing requirements by borrowing. Similarly, it would continue to use the target proportions in the subsequent year, when it might raise the majority of its financing needs by reinvesting earnings or through a new stock offering.

CALCULATING THE WEIGHTED AVERAGE COST OF CAPITAL

The weighted average cost of capital, k_{wacc}, is simply a weighted average of all the capital costs incurred by the firm. Table 11-1 illustrates the procedure used to estimate k_{wacc} for a firm that has debt, preferred stock, and common equity in its target capital structure mix. Two possible scenarios are described in the two panels. First, in Panel A the firm is able to finance all its target capital structure requirements for common equity through the retention of firm earnings. Second, in Panel B the firm must use a new equity offering to raise the equity capital it requires. For example, if the firm targets 75 percent equity financing and has current earnings of $750,000, then it can raise up to $750,000/.75 = $1,000,000 in new financing before it has to sell new equity. For $1,000,000 or less in capital spending, the firm's weighted average cost of capital would be calculated using the cost of equity from retained earnings (following Panel A of Table 11-1). For more than $1,000,000 in new capital, the cost of capital would rise to reflect the impact of the higher cost of using new common stock (following Panel B of Table 11-1).

TAKIN' IT TO THE NET

AFS Associates provides a cost of capital calculator at the Web site www.financeadvisor.com/coc.htm.

TABLE 11-1   Calculating the Weighted Average Cost of Capital

PANEL A: COMMON EQUITY RAISED BY RETAINED EARNINGS

SOURCE OF CAPITAL	CAPITAL STRUCTURE WEIGHTS	× COST OF CAPITAL	= PRODUCT
Bonds	w_d	$k_d(1 - T_c)$	$w_d \times k_d(1 - T_c)$
Preferred stock	w_{ps}	k_{ps}	$w_{ps} \times k_{ps}$
Common equity			
Retained earnings	w_{cs}	k_{cs}	$w_{cs} \times k_{cs}$
Sum =	100%	Sum =	k_{wacc}

PANEL B: COMMON EQUITY RAISED BY SELLING NEW COMMON STOCK

SOURCE OF CAPITAL	CAPITAL STRUCTURE WEIGHTS	× COST OF CAPITAL	= PRODUCT
Bonds	w_d	$k_d(1 - T_c)$	$w_d \times k_d(1 - T_c)$
Preferred stock	w_{ps}	k_{ps}	$w_{ps} \times k_{ps}$
Common equity			
Common stock	w_{ncs}	k_{ncs}	$w_{ncs} \times k_{ncs}$
Sum =	100%	Sum =	k_{wacc}

[2]There are instances when we will want to calculate the cost of capital for the firm as a whole. In this case, the appropriate weights to use are based on the market value of the various capital sources used by the firm. Market values rather than book values properly reflect the sources of financing used by a firm at any particular point in time. However, when a firm is privately owned, it is not possible to get market values of its securities, and book values are often used.

EXAMPLE

Ash, Inc.'s capital structure and estimated capital costs are found in Table 11-2. Note that the sum of the capital structure weights must sum to 100 percent if we have properly accounted for all sources of financing and in the correct amounts. For example, Ash plans to invest a total of $3 million in common equity into the $5 million investment. Because Ash has earnings equal to the $3,000,000 it needs in new equity financing, the entire amount of new equity will be raised by retaining earnings.

TABLE 11-2 Capital Structure and Capital Costs for Ash, Inc.

SOURCE OF CAPITAL	AMOUNT OF FUNDS RAISED ($)	PERCENTAGE OF TOTAL	AFTER-TAX COST OF CAPITAL
Bonds	1,750,000	35%	7%
Preferred stock	250,000	5%	13%
Common equity			
Retained earnings	3,000,000	60%	16%
	5,000,000	100%	

We calculate the weighted average cost of capital following the procedure described in Panel A of Table 11-1 and using the information found in Table 11-2. The resulting calculations are found in Panel A of Table 11-3, in which Ash, Inc.'s weighted average cost of capital for up to $5,000,000 in new financing is found to be 12.7 percent.

If Ash needs more than $5,000,000, it will not have any retained earnings to provide the additional equity capital. Thus, to maintain its desired 60 percent equity financing proportion, Ash will now have to issue new equity that costs 18 percent.

TABLE 11-3 Weighted Average Cost of Capital for Ash, Inc.

PANEL A: COST OF CAPITAL FOR $0 TO $5,000,000 IN NEW CAPITAL

SOURCE OF CAPITAL	CAPITAL STRUCTURE WEIGHTS	COST OF CAPITAL	PRODUCT
Bonds	35%	7%	2.45%
Preferred stock	5%	13%	0.65%
Common equity			
Retained earnings	60%	16%	9.60%
	100%	$k_{wacc} =$	12.70%

PANEL B: COST OF CAPITAL FOR MORE THAN $5,000,000

SOURCE OF CAPITAL	CAPITAL STRUCTURE WEIGHTS	COST OF CAPITAL	PRODUCT
Bonds	35%	7%	2.45%
Preferred stock	5%	13%	0.65%
Common equity			
Common stock	60%	18%	10.80%
	100%	$k_{wacc} =$	13.90%

Panel B of Table 11-3 contains the calculation of Ash's weighted average cost of capital for more than $5,000,000. The resulting cost is 13.9 percent.

In practice, many firms calculate only one cost of capital, using a cost of equity capital that ignores the transaction costs associated with raising new equity capital. In essence, they would use the capital cost calculated for Ash in Panel A of Table 11-3, regardless of the level of new financing for the year. Although this is technically incorrect, it is an understandable practice given the inexactness of the estimates of equity capital cost and the relatively small differences that result from the adjustment.[3]

---

[3]For a discussion of the imprecise nature of equity capital cost estimates, see Eugene F. Fama and Kenneth R. French, "Industry Costs of Equity," *Journal of Financial Economics 43* (1997), pp. 153–193.

Objective **4**

CALCULATING DIVISIONAL COSTS OF CAPITAL: PEPSICO, INC.

If a firm operates in multiple industries, each with its own particular risk characteristics, should it use different capital costs for each division? **Principle 1** suggests that the financial manager should recognize these risk differences in estimating the cost of capital to use in each division. This is exactly what PepsiCo did before February 1997, when it was operating in three basic industries.

PepsiCo went to great lengths to estimate the cost of capital for each of its three major operating divisions (restaurants, snack foods, and beverages).[4] We briefly summarize the basic elements of the calculations involved in these estimates, including the cost of debt financing, the cost of common equity, the target capital structure weights, and the weighted average cost of capital.

Table 11-4 contains the estimates of the after-tax cost of debt for each of PepsiCo's three divisions. Table 11-5 contains the estimates of the cost of equity capital for each of PepsiCo's three operating divisions using the CAPM. We will not explain the intricacies of their method for estimating divisional betas, except to say that they make use of beta estimates for a number of competitor firms from each of the operating divisions, which involves making appropriate adjustments for differences in the use of financial leverage across the competitor firms used in the analysis.[5]

The weighted average cost of capital for each of the divisions is estimated in Table 11-6 using the capital costs estimated in Tables 11-4 and 11-5 and using PepsiCo's target capital

TABLE 11-4   Estimating PepsiCo's Cost of Debt

	PRETAX COST OF DEBT	×	(1 – TAX RATE)	=	AFTER-TAX COST OF DEBT
Restaurants	8.93%	×	0.62	=	5.54%
Snack foods	8.43%	×	0.62	=	5.23%
Beverages	8.51%	×	0.62	=	5.28%

TABLE 11-5   Cost of Equity Capital for PepsiCo's Operating Divisions

	RISK-FREE RATE	+	BETA	×	(EXPECTED MARKET RETURN – RISK FREE RATE)	=	COST OF EQUITY
Restaurants	7.28%	+	1.17	×	(11.48% – 7.28%)	=	12.19%
Snack foods	7.28%	+	1.02	×	(11.48% – 7.28%)	=	11.56%
Beverages	7.28%	+	1.07	×	(11.48% – 7.28%)	=	11.77%

[4]PepsiCo spun off its restaurants division in February 1997. However, the example used here was based on the company before the spinoff.

[5]This method of using betas from comparable firms is sometimes referred to as the pure play method, because the analyst seeks independent beta estimates for firms engaged in only one business (i.e., restaurants or beverages). The betas for these pure play companies are then used to estimate the beta for a business or division.

FINANCIAL MANAGEMENT
IN PRACTICE

THE PILLSBURY COMPANY ADOPTS EVA® WITH A GRASSROOTS EDUCATION PROGRAM

A key determinant of the success of any incentive-based program is employee understanding. If employees simply view a new performance measurement and reward system as "just another" reporting requirement, the program will have minimum impact on employee behavior and, consequently, little effect on operating performance. In addition, if a firm's employees do not understand the measurement system, it is very likely that it will be distrusted and may even have counterproductive effects on firm performance.

So how do you instill in your employees the notion that your performance measurement and reward system does indeed lead to the desired result? Pillsbury took a unique approach to the problem by using a simulation exercise in which the value of applying the principles of Economic Value Added (EVA®) could be learned by simulating the operations of a hypothetical factory. Employees used the simulation to trace through the value-creation process from revenue to net operating profit after taxes to the weighted average cost of capital. The company trained 250 of its senior managers to coach the rest of their employees, rather than relying on the more traditional lecture format. The results were gratifying. One Pillsbury manager noted, "you saw the lights go on in people's eyes" as employees realized, "Oh, this really does impact my work environment."

Briggs and Stratton used a similar training program to instill the basic principles of EVA in its employees. Its business-simulation example was even more basic than the Pillsbury factory. Briggs and Stratton used a convenience store's operations to teach line workers the importance of controlling waste, utilizing assets fully, and managing profit margins. Recently, Stern Stewart Company, which coined the term *EVA*, has developed a training tool, the EVA Training Tutor.™ The EVA Training Tutor addresses four basic issues using CD-ROM technology:

- Why is creating shareholder wealth an important corporate and investor goal?
- What is the best way to measure wealth and business success?
- Which business strategies have created wealth, and which have failed?
- What can you do to create wealth and increase the stock price of your company?

In a more general sense, the education programs described briefly here are examples of the recognition by major corporations of the need to improve financial literacy if they are to be able to achieve the utmost from their human and capital resources.

Sources: Adapted from George Donnelly, "Grassroots EVA," CFO.com (May 1, 2000), www.cfo.com and The EVA Training Tutor™ (Stern Stewart and Company).

TABLE 11-6   PepsiCo's Weighted Average Cost of Capital for Each of Its Operating Divisions

	COST OF EQUITY TIMES THE TARGET EQUITY RATIO	+	AFTER-TAX COST OF DEBT TIMES THE TARGET DEBT RATIO	=	WEIGHTED AVERAGE COST OF CAPITAL
Restaurants	(12.19%)(0.70)	+	(5.54%)(0.30)	=	10.20%
Snack foods	(11.56%)(0.80)	+	(5.23%)(0.20)	=	10.29%
Beverages	(11.77%)(0.74)	+	(5.28%)(0.26)	=	10.08%

---

structure weights for each operating division. Note that the weighted average costs of capital for all three divisions fall within a very narrow range, between 10.08 percent and 10.29 percent.

CONCEPT CHECK

1. Why should firms that own and operate multiple businesses with very different risk characteristics use business-specific or divisional costs of capital?
2. Describe the process used to estimate the divisional costs of capital for PepsiCo.

Table 11-7 contains a summary of the formulas involved in estimating the weighted average cost of capital. If divisional costs of capital are to be estimated, then we must apply these formulas individually to each division where the opportunity costs of capital sources and the financing mix (proportions) used can differ, as we have just seen in the PepsiCo example.

TABLE 11-7   Summary of Cost of Capital Formulas

1. The After-Tax Cost of Debt, $k_d(1 - T_c)$
   a) Calculate the before-tax cost of debt, k_d, as follows:

$$NP_d = \sum_{t=1}^{n} \frac{\$I_t}{(1+k_d)^t} + \frac{\$M}{(1+k_d)^n} \tag{11-2a}$$

   where NP_d is the net proceeds received by the firm from the sale of each bond; $\$I_t$ is the dollar amount of interest paid to the investor in period t for each bond, $\$M$ is the maturity value of each bond paid in period n; k_d is the before-tax cost of debt to the firm; and n is the number of periods to maturity.
   b) Calculate the after-tax cost of debt as follows:

   after-tax cost of debt $= k_d(1 - T_c)$
   where T_c is the corporate tax rate.

2. The Cost of Preferred Stock, k_{ps}

$$k_{ps} = \frac{\text{preferred stock dividend}}{NP_{ps}} \tag{11-5}$$

   where NP_{ps} is the net proceeds per share of new preferred stock sold after flotation costs.

3. The Cost of Common Equity
   a) Method 1: dividend growth model
       Calculate the cost of internal common equity (retained earnings), k_{cs}, as follows:

$$k_{cs} = \frac{D_1}{P_{cs}} + g \tag{11-7}$$

   where D_1 is the expected dividend for the next year, P_{cs} is the current price of the firm's common stock, and g is the rate of growth in dividends per year. Calculate the cost of external common equity (new stock offering), k_{ncs}, as follows:

$$k_{ncs} = \frac{D_1}{NP_{cs}} + g \tag{11-8}$$

   where NP_{cs} is the net proceeds to the firm after flotation costs per share of stock sold.
   b) Method 2: capital asset pricing model, k_c

$$k_c = k_{rf} + \beta(k_m - k_{rf}) \tag{11-9}$$

   where the risk-free rate is k_{rf}; the systemic risk of the common stock's returns relative to the market as a whole, or the stock's beta coefficient, is β; and the market risk premium, which is equal to the difference in the expected rate of return for the market as a whole (i.e., the expected rate of return for the "average security") minus the risk-free rate, is $k_m - k_{rf}$.

4. The Weighted Average Cost of Capital

$$k_{wacc} = w_d k_d(1 - T_c) + w_{ps}k_{ps} + w_{cs}k_{cs} + w_{ncs}k_{ncs} \tag{11-10}$$

   where the w_i terms represent the market value weights associated with the firm's use of each of its sources of financing. Note that we are simply calculating a weighted average of the costs of each of the firm's sources of capital where the weights reflect the firm's relative use of each source.

Objective **5**

USING A FIRM'S COST OF CAPITAL TO EVALUATE NEW CAPITAL INVESTMENTS

If a firm has traditionally used a single cost of capital for all projects undertaken within each of several operating divisions (or companies) that have very different risk characteristics, then it will encounter resistance to the change from the high-risk divisions. Consider the case of the hypothetical firm Global Energy, whose divisional costs of capital are illustrated

FIGURE 11-1 Global Energy Divisional Costs of Capital

Using a company-wide cost of capital for a multidivisional firm results in systematic overinvestment in high-risk projects and underinvestment in low-risk projects.

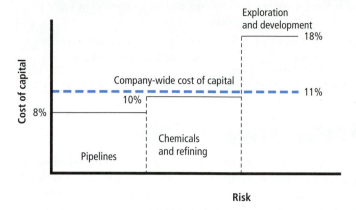

in Figure 11-1. Global Energy is an integrated oil company that engages in a wide range of hydrocarbon-related businesses, including exploration and development, pipelines, and refining. Each of these businesses has its unique set of risks. In Figure 11-1 we see that the overall, or enterprisewide, cost of capital for Global Energy is 11 percent, reflecting an average of the firm's divisional costs of capital, ranging from a low of 8 percent for pipelines up to 18 percent for exploration and development.

At present Global Energy is using 11 percent to evaluate new investment proposals from all three operating divisions. This means that exploration and development projects earning as little as 11 percent are being accepted even though the capital market dictates that projects of this risk should earn 18 percent. Thus, Global Energy overinvests in high-risk projects. Similarly, the company will underinvest in its two lower-risk divisions, where the companywide cost of capital is used.

Now consider the prospect of moving to division costs of capital and the implications this might have for the three divisions. Specifically, the exploration and development division is likely to see this as an adverse move for them because it will surely cut the level of new investment capital flowing into their operations. In contrast, the management of the remaining two divisions will see the change as good news because under the companywide cost of capital system they have been rejecting projects earning more than their market-based costs of capital (8 percent and 10 percent for pipelines and refining, respectively) but less than the company's 11 percent cost of capital.

BACK TO THE FOUNDATIONS

*The firm's weighted average cost of capital provides the appropriate discount rate for evaluating new projects only when the projects offer the same riskiness as the firm as a whole. This limitation of the usefulness of the firm's weighted average cost of capital is a direct extension of **Principle 1: The Risk–Return Trade-Off—We Won't Take On Additional Risk Unless We Expect to Be Compensated with Additional Return**. If project risk differs from that of the firm, then the firm's cost of capital (which reflects the risk of the firm's investment portfolio) is no longer the appropriate cost of capital for the project. For this reason, firms that invest in multiple divisions or business units that have different risk characteristics should calculate a different cost of capital for each division. In theory, each individual investment opportunity has its own unique risk attributes and, correspondingly, should have a unique cost of capital. However, given the impreciseness with which we estimate the cost of capital, we generally calculate the cost of capital for each operating division of the firm, not each project.*

Objective **6**

SHAREHOLDER VALUE–BASED MANAGEMENT

How do you know whether you are creating or destroying shareholder value? Asked somewhat differently, "how can you tell how much wealth a firm has created for its shareholders?" In recent years a whole host of systems have been developed that purport to answer these questions and in so doing provide guidance to a firm's management for use in making decisions that are expected to have the greatest positive impact on shareholder wealth. We refer to this cadre of methods as shareholder value–based management, or simply value–based management tools. We focus on one very popular method in our discussion that is based on the concept of economic profit.

HOW MUCH VALUE HAS A FIRM CREATED FOR ITS OWNERS?

market value added

In the introduction we described a firm, H&L Manufacturing, that was trying to come to grips with why its stock price was not growing as rapidly as its competitors'. In essence, H&L needs to know whether it is creating or destroying shareholder wealth. How can we tell? The answer is **market value added (MVA)**. *MVA* is a very simple concept. It represents *the difference in the current market value of the firm and the sum of all the funds that are invested in the firm*. If the market value of the firm exceeds the investment made in the firm, then the firm has created shareholder wealth. *MVA* is calculated as follows:

$$MVA = \text{total market value of the firm} - \text{invested capital} \qquad \textbf{(11-11a)}$$

The total market value of the firm is equal to the value of all the claims or securities the firm has issued; that is,

$$
\begin{matrix}
\text{Market value} & & \text{market value} & & \text{market value} & & \text{market value} \\
\text{of the} & = & \text{of the firm's} & + & \text{of the firm's} & + & \text{of the firm's} \\
\text{firm} & & \text{outstanding debt} & & \text{preferred stock} & & \text{common stock}
\end{matrix}
\qquad \textbf{(11-11b)}
$$

For firms whose debt and equity securities are traded in public markets we can calculate the market value of each type of security by simply multiplying the number of bonds or shares of stock by the most recent market price. It should be noted that most firms' debt is not publicly traded so it is common practice to approximate the market value of the firm's debt by using its book value. Invested capital is basically the sum total of the money invested in the firm to date. Invested capital is estimated by adjusting the firm's book value of total assets for things such as R&D expense and allowances for doubtful accounts receivable, which are not included in the total assets of the firm but, nonetheless, represent dollars that have been invested in the firm.[6]

In essence, *MVA* is the *NPV* of all the firm's investments.[7] A firm that is using its investments to produce what investors perceive to be positive *NPV*s will have a positive *MVA*.

---

[6]We will not go into the adjustments that are made to a firm's book assets to measure invested capital. The adjustments add equity equivalent reserves to capital and periodic changes in those reserves to after-tax operating profits. For example, equivalent reserves include such items as the deferred income tax reserve, LIFO reserve, cumulative amortization of goodwill, capitalized intangibles (including R&D), allowance for doubtful accounts, and warranty claim reserves.

[7]Technically, *MVA* overstates a firm's total wealth creation because it fails to incorporate an opportunity cost of the funds the firm invested in prior periods. As a consequence, our analogy to *NPV* is only truly accurate for the case of a start-up firm in which the firm's total invested capital is equal to total assets at the beginning of the period for which *MVA* is being measured. However, for our purposes *MVA* serves as a very useful and simple approximation to the wealth a firm has created for its investors.

TABLE 11-8			The Top and Bottom Five Firms in the 2004 Stern Stewart Performance 1,000					
2003 RANK	**2002 RANK**	**1999 RANK**	**COMPANY NAME**	**MVA**	**EVA**	**INVESTED CAPITAL**	**RETURN ON INVESTED CAPITAL**	**COST OF CAPITAL**
1	1	2	General Electric Co.	192,414	4,807	96,782	12.5%	7.3%
2	2	1	Microsoft Corp.	191,105	4,432	24,462	29.8%	11.8%
3	3	3	Wal-Mart Stores	184,890	4,350	82,470	11.6%	6.2%
4	23	10	Citigroup Inc.	133,567	6,367	133,048	13.0%	8.0%
5	5	17	Johnson & Johnson	121,222	4,861	53,566	17.6%	8.2%
996	999	18	Lucent Technologies Inc.	(43,785)	(8,398)	62,552	−3.5%	9.7%
997	110	999	SBC Communications Inc.	(51,464)	(8,859)	150,827	3.5%	9.3%
998	992	58	AT&T Corp.	(54,901)	(5,442)	88,332	2.3%	8.3%
999	1000	519	JDS Uniphase Corp.	(66,713)	(9,391)	69,699	−1.3%	12.2%
1000	993	9	Time Warner Inc.	(70,759)	(9,390)	161,329	2.2%	8.0%

Similarly, a firm that is using its invested capital in ways that investors feel destroy value will have a negative *MVA*. Note that because the market value of the firm's securities is based on expected future cash flows, *MVA* is a reflection of the expected *NPV*. Because *MVA* is not a measure of historical performance but instead reflects anticipated future performance, it can change dramatically as a firm's fortunes change. For example, in 1988, IBM's *MVA* was the largest of any U.S. company. By 1990, the fortunes of IBM had changed dramatically as the personal computer became the computer of the future. In 1991, IBM ranked thirty-first, and by 1993 its rank slipped to 1,000th. However, changes in the perceived fortunes of the company in 1997 resulted in a dramatic turnaround in investors' perceptions of IBM's future and raised its rank to sixteenth. Not every firm experiences this degree of volatility from year to year. The sources of the volatility in *MVA* are the market value of the firm's equity and adjustments the firm makes to its invested capital through acquisitions and sales of assets.

Table 11-8 contains the top and bottom five firms in terms of *MVA* for 2003. With the exception of Johnson&Johnson, all the top five wealth creators were ranked in the top 10 in 1999, which suggests that there is some stability among the top performers. Furthermore, of the bottom five performers were in the bottom 10 in 1999 (three Lucent Technologies, AT&T, and Time Warner).

DID THE FIRM CREATE SHAREHOLDER VALUE THIS YEAR?

MVA measures the wealth created by a firm at a particular point in time. However, the financial manager needs to evaluate the performance of the firm over a specific interval of time, say, 1 year. For this purpose, we calculate the firm's **economic profit**. Economic profit is defined as follows:

economic profit

$$\text{Economic profit} = \begin{pmatrix} \text{net operating} \\ \text{profit after tax} \\ (NOPAT) \end{pmatrix} - \begin{pmatrix} \text{invested} \\ \text{capital} \end{pmatrix} \times \begin{pmatrix} \text{cost of} \\ \text{capital} \end{pmatrix} \qquad \textbf{(11-12)}$$

Note that the distinction between economic and accounting profit (net operating profit) is the deduction of a return to the firm's invested capital. The product of the firm's invested capital (the total dollar investment made in the firm by its creditors and owners) and the cost of capital constitutes a capital charge. This capital charge is not a recognized accounting expense, but it is a very real expense from the perspective of the firm's bondholders and stockholders. The firm's accounting profits not only must be positive but also must cover the required rate of return on the firm's investment (the cost of capital) before shareholder value has been created. Thus, economic profit is simply accounting profit (net operating profit or income) less a charge for the use of capital.

FINANCIAL MANAGEMENT
IN PRACTICE

NEW USERS EXPLAIN THEIR GOALS AND OBJECTIVES IN ADOPTING EVA

The following excerpts taken from company annual reports and press releases document the rationale underlying the adoption of EVA as a system for implementing shareholder value–based management. The fundamental element throughout all the excerpts is the recognition of the need to place top priority on shareholder interests by considering the impact of all the firm's decisions on share value. In addition, we see the importance of tying compensation to EVA such that value creation is reinforced and rewarded.

OLIN CORPORATION (501 MERRITT 7, P.O. BOX 4500, NORWALK, CT 06856-4500)

The primary goal of any company is to manage its operations to create long-term value for shareholders and employees alike. Economic Value Added, or EVA, is a business management system that clearly shows how well a company is meeting that goal. EVA can help Olin to realize the sustained growth needed to meet the company's full potential.

We are using EVA to tie everything we do—investing in core businesses, financing activities, streamlining our business mix—to the goal of enhancing value for you, our shareholders. In fact, we are using EVA measures to tie compensation of our key managers to the achievement of tough multiyear goals. (Excerpts from "EVA: The Meaning of Our Success," and the *1995 Annual Report*. Olin Corp., used with permission.)

BOISE CASCADE CORPORATION (1111 WEST JEFFERSON STREET, P.O. BOX 50, BOISE, IDAHO 83728-0001)

In July 1994, Boise Cascade adopted EVA as its key financial measure. Economic value is created by earning a return greater than investors require and is destroyed by earning a return less than they require. The EVA measurement process encourages management to make business decisions that create economic value through improved operating efficiency, better asset utilization, and growth that generates returns which exceed the cost of capital.

We believe our emphasis on EVA will more closely align the interests of employees and shareholders. Therefore, we are also using EVA to determine incentive compensation for management. The compensation of plan participants, including corporate officers, will be tied directly to improvement in the EVA of their operations and the corporation as a whole. We believe this measurement, and the fact that incentive compensation is linked to it, will effectively encourage management decisions that maximize the market value of the capital contributed by investors. (Excerpt from *1994 Annual Report*, Boise Cascade, used with permission.)

EQUIFAX, INC. (1600 PEACHTREE STREET, NW, ATLANTA, GA 30309)

Our financial strategy is centered on creating shareholder value by maximizing Economic Value Added (EVA). The EVA framework helps us identify which "value drivers" will be the most effective in increasing the total return on capital employed in each of our operating units. These drivers fall within the general classifications of margin improvements, revenue growth and capital efficiency. (Excerpt from *1992 Annual Report*, Equifax, Inc., used with permission.)

JOHNSON WORLDWIDE ASSOCIATES, INC. (1326 WILLOW ROAD, STURTEVANT, WISCONSIN 53177)

Why was EVA chosen as a new financial measure at JWA?

We wanted a single concept to which all employees could relate. We reviewed many options and decided that EVA would provide the simplest, yet most comprehensive way to look at all aspects of managing our business, from inventory levels to sales programs and operating expenses.

So what? How does the use of economic profit help the financial manager? The answer is surprisingly simple. Most firms manage to earn positive profits. However, earning positive profits is no assurance that the firm is creating shareholder wealth because profits fail to incorporate any opportunity cost for the dollars that investors have tied up in the business. Economic profit, on the other hand, includes an explicit charge in the form of the capital charge, which recognizes the size of the investment made in the firm and the opportunity cost of that investment.

Consider the case of Kmart, which ranked 990th in the *MVA* rankings. Kmart's economic profit for 1999 can be calculated as follows:

$$\text{Economic profit} = NOPAT - (\text{invested capital} \times \text{cost of capital})$$
$$(\$568.979 \text{ M}) = \$950 \text{ M} - (\$19,727 \text{ M} \times .0770)$$

How can this be? Kmart earned a positive *NOPAT* of $950 million. The answer lies in the size of Kmart's *NOPAT* relative to its investment in assets. Compared with the firm's $19,727 million invested capital, its *NOPAT* represents a meager return of only 4.82 percent, which is less than the firm's 7.70 percent cost of capital. So long as Kmart continues to earn a return on its invested capital that is lower than its cost of capital, it will continue to destroy shareholder value no matter how large its profits. In fact, Kmart declared bankruptcy in January 2002.

How will the adoption of EVA change the financial environment of JWA?

We haven't managed the balance sheet as well as we should. EVA requires us to manage not only sales and profitability, but weighs these against what we invest in the business—its "capital." We will be focusing on earning an adequate return on that capital. That's what shareholders expect when they purchase our stock. If we don't earn the return investors expect, they will put their money elsewhere. As managers, we will be scrutinizing each of our business units to see that they are adding value.

What exactly do you mean by "adding value?"

Each business unit must cover the cost of operating—labor, materials, advertising and wear and tear on its equipment, for example. What remains after those costs are subtracted from sales revenue is the unit's operating profit. Each business unit will also deduct a charge for its cost of capital from its operating profit. The remainder is value created, or EVA. Over the long term, a business unit will not be successful unless its operating profits recover the cost of capital. Today, that is not always the case. Going forward, we want each unit to achieve net positive EVA, and to grow it every year. (Excerpt from *1996 Annual Report*, Johnson Worldwide Association, used with permission.)

SPX CORPORATION (700 TERRACE POINT DRIVE, MUSKEGON, MI 49443)

SPX adopted EVA because it:

- is easily understood and applied;
- fits into operational improvement efforts, because success requires continuous improvement in EVA;
- correlates closer to market value than any other operating performance measure;
- links directly to investor expectations through EVA improvement targets;

- focuses on long-term performance by using a bonus bank and predetermined improvement targets; and
- provides a common language for performance measurement, decision support, compensation and communication.

Today, people throughout SPX are making operating and strategic decisions using EVA decision support tools. We have trained our managers so they understand the link between daily operating decisions and shareholder value. Our recent restructuring of an operation in Germany was supported by EVA analysis. We chose the strategy that created the greatest EVA. (Excerpt from *1995 Annual Report*, SPX Corp., used with permission.)

BALL CORPORATION (345 SOUTH HIGH STREET, P.O. BOX 2407, MUNCIE, IN 47307-0407)

Ball joins a growing list of successful Fortune 500 companies which are focusing on EVA instead of exclusively monitoring more common measures such as earnings per share. Coca-Cola Co., a major customer of Ball, is among them.

A more in-depth explanation of the Economic Value Added concept begins with the understanding that investors require a minimum rate of return on their investment in the equity of a corporation to compensate them for the risk they assume. In turn, the corporation's management must earn at least this same rate of return to meet these investor expectations. When management earns a higher rate of return than the minimum required by investors, value has been created. The magnitude of that value depends on the amount of capital invested and the extent to which return on that capital exceeds investor expectations; this is economic value added. (Joan D. LaGuardia, "Adding Value: Ball Measures Up with a New Market Standard," *Ball Line Magazine*, No. 4, 1991, pp. 4–6.)

HOW CAN THE FIRM INCREASE ITS ECONOMIC PROFITS?

What can a firm do to improve its performance so it creates more shareholder value for its owners? The answer can be found by reviewing the variables that are found on the right-hand side of equation (11-12). These variables include the level of *NOPAT*, the cost of capital, and the amount of invested capital (often referred to as value drivers). One way to create additional value is by seeking ways to increase *NOPAT* without a corresponding increase in the firm's invested capital. This can be accomplished by increasing revenues and/or driving down expenses. There are a number of ways that a firm might reduce costs and increase profits without the need to spend additional capital. For example, the Domtar Corporation (a forest management company that deals in paper, pulp, and wood products) adopted an economic profit–based system and notes the following ways in which it can improve its economic profit by identifying operating efficiencies:

➤ cutting down on waste and damaged products
➤ operating machinery and equipment more efficiently
➤ improving product mix, devising methods to save on the purchase of raw materials
➤ improving health and safety performance, attracting and retaining customers
➤ making better use of time in the office and plant, implementing or improving preventative maintenance programs
➤ developing links with suppliers

A second way to improve economic profit is by growing the firm's investments in projects that earn returns in excess of the firm's cost of capital. For example, the firm might introduce new marketing plans that improve customer satisfaction and sales and profits, expand existing businesses that offer the potential to earn positive *NPV*s, or introduce new information systems to better trace customer buying habits and, correspondingly, increase firm sales.

The third and final approach to improving economic profits involves reducing the firm's capital charge (cost of capital × invested capital). This can be accomplished in either of two ways. If the firm is not using its minimum cost of capital financing mix, then restructuring its financing sources might lead to a lowering of the firm's cost of capital and a corresponding decrease in the firm's dollar cost of capital. Alternatively, the firm might consider withdrawing capital from its operations through the sale of underutilized assets (e.g., excess plant capacity, underperforming operating units, or real estate).

HOW CAN A FIRM LINK PAY FOR PERFORMANCE TO REINFORCE WEALTH CREATION?

Economic profit has become an important tool for aligning shareholder and manager interests in the running of the company. This is accomplished by basing management's incentive compensation on economic profit. A very simple version of such a compensation scheme is illustrated in equation (11-13).

$$\frac{\text{incentive}}{\text{compensation}} = \text{base pay} \times \frac{\text{percent}}{\text{incentive}} \times \frac{\text{actual economic profit}}{\text{target economic profit}} \quad \text{(11-13)}$$

TAKIN' IT TO THE NET
There is a wide array of vendors for value-based management systems, including Alcar www.Alcar.com, Holt Valuation www.holtvalue.com, Marakon www.Marakon.com, and Stern Stewart www.SternStewart.com.

For example, consider the case of the assistant treasurer for NewCo Oil, Inc. The assistant treasurer's base pay is $80,000 a year, and 20 percent of the total compensation for this position is designated by the company to be incentive based. If in a particular year NewCo set a target economic profit of $1 million and earned $1.2 million, then the assistant treasurer's incentive compensation would be calculated as following using equation (11-13):

$$\frac{\text{Incentive}}{\text{compensation}} = \text{base pay} \times \frac{\text{percent}}{\text{incentive}} \times \frac{\text{actual economic profit}}{\text{target economic profit}}$$

$$= \$80{,}000 \times 0.20 \times (\$1.2 \text{ million} / \$1 \text{ million})$$

$$= \$19{,}200$$

In this case, the assistant treasurer's total annual compensation would be $99,200 ($80,000 + $19,200). If NewCo earned only $800,000 in economic profit, then the incentive compensation paid to the assistant treasurer would be $12,800 [$80,000 × .20 × ($800,000/$1,000,000)].

Clearly, with this type of incentive compensation plan, the firm's managers will be very careful to manage for increased net operating profits while holding down the firm's invested capital and maintaining the lowest possible cost of capital. If they do this, they will maximize the contribution to shareholder wealth and also maximize their own year-end bonuses.

CONCEPT CHECK

1. What is market value added (*MVA*)?
2. Define economic profit and its determinants.
3. How is economic profit related to *MVA*?

FINANCE AND THE MULTINATIONAL FIRM: WHY DO INTEREST RATES DIFFER BETWEEN COUNTRIES?[8]

If borrowers and lenders can freely obtain money in one country and invest it in another, why are interest rates not the same the world over? Stated somewhat differently, if capital markets are fully integrated and money flows to the highest rate of interest, it would seem that the forces of competition would make interest rates the same for a given risk borrower.

Let's consider a hypothetical example to see how this might work. Assume that a U.S. borrower can borrow 1,000 yen in Japan for 5 percent interest, paying back 1,050 yen in 1 year. Alternatively, the U.S. firm can borrow an equivalent amount in the United States and pay 15.5 percent interest. Why the big difference? Is capital 10.5 percent cheaper in Japan, and if so, why don't U.S. firms simply switch to the Japanese capital market for their funds? The answer, as we will now illustrate, lies in the differences in the anticipated rates of inflation for Japan versus the United States.

Although it was not obvious in the preceding example, we assumed a zero rate of inflation for the Japanese economy and a 10 percent rate of inflation for the U.S. economy. With a zero anticipated rate of inflation, the nominal rate of interest in Japan (the rate we see quoted in the financial press) is equal to the real rate of 5 percent.[9] Under these assumptions, the nominal rate in the United States can be calculated using the Fisher model as follows:

$$\text{U.S. nominal rate of interest} = (1 + \text{real rate, U.S.})(1 + \text{inflation rate, U.S.}) - 1$$
$$= (1 + .05)(1.10) - 1 = .155, \text{ or } 15.5\%$$

To understand the reason for the different interest rates in Japan and the United States, we must extend the Fisher model to its international counterpart.

THE INTERNATIONAL FISHER EFFECT

In an international context, we must recognize that there can be different rates of inflation among the different countries of the world. For example, the Fisher model for the nominal rate in the home or domestic country ($r_{n,h}$) is a function of the real interest rate in the home country ($r_{r,h}$) and the anticipated rate of inflation in the home country (i_h). For the domestic economy, the Fisher relationship can be described as follows:

$$r_{n,h} = [(1 + r_{r,h})(1 + i_h)] - 1 = r_{r,h} + (i_h)(r_{r,h}) + i_h \tag{11-14a}$$

Using "f" as a subscript to denote a foreign country, we can define a similar relationship for any foreign country (Japan in our previous example):

$$r_{n,f} = [(1 + r_{r,f})(1 + i_f)] - 1 = r_{r,f} + (i_f)(r_{r,f}) + i_f \tag{11-14b}$$

The international version of the Fisher model prescribes that real returns will be equalized across countries through arbitrage—that is,

$$r_{r,h} = r_{r,f} \tag{11-14c}$$

Solving for the real rates of interest in (11-14a) and (11-14b) and equating the results produces the international version of the Fisher model—that is,

$$r_{n,h} - (i_h)(r_{r,h}) - i_h = r_{n,f} - (i_f)(r_{r,f}) - i_f \tag{11-15}$$

For simplicity analysts frequently ignore the intermediate product terms on both sides of equation (11-15) such that it reduces to the following:

$$r_{n,h} - i_h = r_{n,f} - i_f \tag{11-16}$$

[8]This section is from W. Carl Kester and Timothy A. Luehrman, "What Makes You Think U.S. Capital Is So Expensive?" *Journal of Applied Corporate Finance* (Summer 1992): pp. 29–41. Reprinted with permission.
[9]The real rate of interest is simply the rate of interest that is earned where the expected rate of inflation is zero.

FINANCIAL MANAGEMENT
IN PRACTICE

TYING INCENTIVE COMPENSATION TO ECONOMIC VALUE ADDED

In the following excerpts from company press releases, annual reports, proxy statements, and publications, we see evidence of the age-old adage, "What you measure and reward gets done." Specifically, these companies explicitly tie company incentive compensation to the creation of shareholder value as measured by EVA. Note that because EVA is a single-period-of-performance metric, many firms do not pay out the full EVA bonus in a single payment, but rather pay it into a bonus bank that gets paid out over several years. This payment practice is designed to encourage long-term value creation (i.e., multiple-year positive improvements in EVA) and to discourage gaming by managers that would increase one year's EVA at the expense of future years' EVA.

MATTHEWS INTERNATIONAL CORPORATION (TWO NORTHSHORE CENTER, PITTSBURGH, PA 15212-5851)

Annual incentive payments paid to officers in 1998 were based upon the improvement in economic value added over the prior two years' base. Economic value added is defined for this purpose as operating profit less associated capital costs of operating assets.

The incentive pools are determined based upon a percentage of absolute economic value added plus a percentage of the incremental economic value added over a two-year base. The incentive pools are distributed to individuals based upon each participant's target incentive and performance relative to achievement of personal goals.

Earned incentive awards that exceed target levels are deferred and paid in the subsequent two fiscal years. In 1998, certain executive officers received a payout of fifty percent of incentive reward amounts earned and deferred from fiscal 1997. The remaining fifty percent is payable in 1999. In fiscal 1998, certain executive officers earned incentive awards in excess of target levels. Amounts in excess of target have been deferred and are payable contingent upon economic value added performance and continued employment during fiscal 1999 and fiscal 2000. (*1999 Matthews International Corporation Notice of Annual Meeting and Proxy Statement*, pp. 24–25)

SPX CORPORATION (700 TERRACE POINT DRIVE, MUSKEGON, MI 49443)

In an EVA incentive compensation plan, managers and shareholders face similar risks. With EVA, compensation is tied to meeting investor expectations, not to meeting plan or budget. By disconnecting incentive compensation from planning and budgeting, and connecting it to investor expectations, managers focus on creating value, and not on negotiating performance targets.

Our EVA incentive compensation plan rewards managers only for continuous permanent improvement in EVA; failure to do so inflicts a cost. Meeting the EVA improvement target equates to meeting investor expectations and results in a competitive bonus. Exceeding the EVA improvement target results in a higher than competitive bonus. And falling short of the EVA improvement target produces a bonus that is less than competitive and can even be negative. Two-thirds of all bonuses above target are set aside in a "bonus bank," which is carried forward, payable only upon achieving EVA targets in subsequent years. Managers must earn back any negative bonuses accumulated in the bank before any bonus payment can be made.

The EVA incentive system simulates long-term ownership by tying bonuses to improvements in EVA over time. EVA improvement targets have been set for the next four years to provide strong incentives for management to increase long-term investor value.

The strong correlation between changes in EVA and in market value also means that the EVA compensation system is effectively "self-financing." That is, managers win only when the shareholders are winning. (*1995 SPX Annual Report*, p. 5)

BALL CORPORATION (345 SOUTH HIGH STREET, P.O. BOX 2407, MUNCIE, IN 47307-0407)

Effective January 1, 1992, the Corporation has established a new incentive compensation plan, entitled the "Ball Corporation 1992 Economic Value Added Incentive Compensation Plan for Key Members of Management." Referred to as the EVA Plan, it applies to all officers and key employees. The EVA Plan establishes a direct link between incentive compensation and the return earned on capital relative to a minimum required rate of return and historical actual performance. The EVA Plan establishes a specific target incentive amount for each participant based on a percentage of salary. (Ball Corporation *Notice of Annual Meeting and Proxy Statement*, 1992)

Rearranging terms, we get the following relationship between nominal interest rates in the domestic and foreign country and the differences in anticipated inflation in the two countries:

$$r_{n,h} - r_{n,f} = i_h - i_f \qquad \text{(11-16)}$$

Thus, differences in observed nominal rates of interest should equal differences in the expected rates of inflation between the two countries. This means that when we compare the interest rates for similar loans in two countries and they are not the same, we should immediately suspect that the expected rates of inflation for the two economies differ by an amount roughly equal to the interest rate differential.

INTEREST RATES AND CURRENCY EXCHANGE RATES: INTEREST RATE PARITY

Economists have formalized the relationship between interest rates of different countries in the interest rate parity theorem. This theorem is as follows:

$$\frac{(1+r_{n,\,b})}{(1+r_{n,\,f})} = \frac{E_1}{E_0} \tag{11-17}$$

where $r_{n,\,b}$ is the domestic one-period rate of interest, $r_{n,\,f}$ is the corresponding rate of interest in a foreign country, E_0 and E_1 are the exchange rates corresponding to the current period (i.e., the spot exchange rate) and one period hence (i.e., the one-period forward exchange rate).

To illustrate, let's consider the previous example, in which the domestic one-period interest rate $(r_{n,\,b})$ is 15.5 percent, the Japanese rate of interest $(r_{n,\,f})$ is 5 percent, the spot exchange ratio (E_0) is \$1 to 1 yen, and the forward exchange rate (E_1) is \$1.10 to 1 yen. Substituting into equation (11-17) produces the following result:

$$\frac{(1+.155)}{(1+.05)} = \frac{1.1}{1} = 1.10$$

The key thing to note here is that nominal interest rates are tied to exchange rates, and, as we learned earlier, differences in nominal rates of interest are tied to expected rates of inflation.

Why would we expect the interest rate parity relationship to hold? The answer lies in the fact that there are investors who stand ready to engage in arbitrage (trading) to enforce this relationship (within the bounds of transaction costs). Formally, we rely on the fundamental dictum of an efficient market (the law of one price). Very simply, the exchange-adjusted prices of identical loans must be within transaction costs of equality or the opportunity exists for traders to buy the low-cost loan and sell the higher-priced loan for a profit.

SUMMARY

The cost of capital: definitions and concepts

We opened our discussion of this chapter by discussing the investment opportunity facing Encore, Inc. The investment required that the firm invest \$75 million to renovate a production facility that will provide after-tax savings to the firm of \$25 million per year over the next 5 years. In Chapter 9, we learned that the proper way to evaluate whether to undertake the investment involves calculating its net present value (NPV). To calculate NPV, we must estimate both project cash flows and an appropriate discount rate. In this chapter, we have learned that the proper discount rate is a weighted average of the after-tax costs of all the firm's sources of financing. In addition, we have learned that the cost of capital for any source of financing is estimated by first calculating the investor's required rate of return, then making appropriate adjustments for flotation costs and corporate taxes (when appropriate). If Encore's weighted average cost of capital is 10 percent, then the NPV of the plant renovation is \$19.8 million and the investment should be made. The reason is that the project is expected to increase the wealth of Encore's shareholders by \$19.8 million. Very simply, the project is expected to return a present value amount of \$19.8 million more than Encore's sources of capital require, and because the common stockholders get any residual value left after returning the promised return to each of the other sources of capital, they receive the NPV.

Objective **1**

Determining individual costs of capital

To calculate the after-tax cost of debt capital, we must first calculate the before-tax cost of debt capital using the following formula:

$$NP_d = \sum_{t=1}^{n} \frac{\$I_t}{(1+k_d)^t} + \frac{\$M}{(1+k_d)^n} \tag{11-2}$$

Objective **2**

where NP_d = the net proceeds received by the firm from the sale of each bond
$\$I_t$ = the dollar amount of interest paid to the investor in period t for each bond
$\$M$ = the maturity value of each bond paid in period n
k_d = the before-tax cost of debt to the firm
n = the number of periods to maturity

Next, we adjust for the effects of corporate taxes because the bond interest is deducted from the firm's taxable income.

After-tax cost of debt = $k_d(1 - \text{corporate tax rate})$

The cost of preferred stock is relatively easy to calculate. We calculate the dividend yield on the preferred issue using net proceeds from the sale of each new share as follows:

$$\text{Cost of preferred stock} = k_{ps} = \frac{\text{preferred stock dividend}}{\text{net proceeds per preferred share}} \tag{11-5}$$

Note that no adjustment is made for corporate taxes because preferred stock dividends, unlike bond interest, are paid with after-tax earnings (i.e., preferred dividends are not tax deductible).

Common equity can be obtained by the firm in one of two ways. First, the firm can retain a portion of its net income after paying common dividends. The retention of earnings constitutes a means of raising common-equity financing internally—that is, no capital market issuance of securities is involved. Second, the firm can also raise equity capital through the sale of a new issue of common stock.

We discussed two methods for estimating the cost of common equity. The first involved using the dividend growth model:

$$k_{cs} = \frac{D_1}{P_{cs}} + g \tag{11-7}$$

where g is the rate at which dividends are expected to grow forever, k_{cs} is the investor's required rate of return, and P_{cs} is the current price of a share of common stock. When a new issue of common shares is issued, the firm incurs flotation costs. These costs reduce the amount of funds the firm receives per share. Consequently, the cost of external common equity using the dividend growth model requires that we substitute the net proceeds per share, NP_{cs}, for share price:

$$k_{ncs} = \frac{D_1}{NP_{cs}} + g \tag{11-8}$$

The second method for estimating the cost of common equity involves the use of the capital asset pricing model (CAPM), which we first discussed in Chapter 9. There we learned that the CAPM provides a basis for evaluating investors' required rates of return on common equity, k_c, using three variables:

1. the risk-free rate, k_{rf};
2. the systematic risk of the common stock's returns relative to the market as a whole, or the stock's beta coefficient, β; and
3. the market risk premium, which is equal to the difference in the expected rate of return for the market as a whole—that is, the expected rate of return for the "average security" minus the risk-free rate, $k_m - k_{rf}$.

The CAPM is written as follows:

$$k_c = k_{rf} + \beta(k_m - k_{rf}) \tag{11-9}$$

We found that all of the variables on the right side of equation (11-9) could be obtained from public sources for larger, publicly traded firms. However, for nonpublicly traded firms, the CAPM is more difficult to apply in the estimation of investor-required rates of return.

Objective 3

The weighted average cost of capital

The firm's weighted average cost of capital, k_{wacc}, can be defined as follows:

$$k_{wacc} = w_d k_d (1 - T_c) + w_{ps} k_{ps} + w_{cs} k_{cs} + w_{ncs} k_{ncs} \tag{11-10}$$

where the w terms represent the market value weights associated with the firm's use of each of its sources of financing. Note that we are simply calculating a weighted average of the costs of each of the firm's sources of capital where the weights reflect the firm's relative use of each source.

The weights used to calculate k_{wacc} should theoretically reflect the market values of each capital source as a fraction of the total market value of all capital sources (i.e., the market value of the firm). However, the analyst frequently finds the use of market value weights is impractical, either because the firm's securities are not publicly traded or because all capital sources are not used in proportion to their makeup of the firm's target capital structure in every financing episode. In these instances, we found that the weights should be the firm's long-term target financial mix.

Calculating divisional costs of capital and using a firm's cost of capital to evaluate new investments

The firm's weighted average cost of capital will reflect the operating or business risk of the firm's present set of investments and the financial risk attendant upon the way in which those assets are financed. Therefore, this cost of capital estimate is useful only for evaluating new investment opportunities that have similar business and financial risks. Remember that the primary determinant of the cost of capital for a particular investment is the risk of the investment itself, not the source of the capital. Multidivisional firms such as PepsiCo resolve this problem by calculating a different cost of capital for each of their major operating divisions.

Objective **4**

Objective **5**

Shareholder value–based management

How can we tell whether a firm's management is creating or destroying wealth? We found that a very commonsense measure known as market value added, or *MVA*, can be used for this purpose. *MVA* is simply the difference in the market value of the firm's securities (debt and equity) and the sum total of the funds that have been invested in the firm since its creation. If the market value of the firm's investments exceeds the total capital invested in the firm, then shareholder wealth has been created to the extent of this difference. Likewise, when the difference is negative, shareholder wealth has been destroyed.

Objective **6**

MVA measures the total shareholder wealth created by the firm at a particular point in time. How do we know whether shareholder wealth was created last year or last month? The answer is found in calculating the firm's economic profit, which is defined as follows:

$$\text{Economic profit} = \left(\begin{array}{c}\text{net operating} \\ \text{profit after tax} \\ (NOPAT)\end{array}\right) - \left(\begin{array}{c}\text{invested} \\ \text{capital}\end{array} \times \begin{array}{c}\text{cost of} \\ \text{capital}\end{array}\right) \qquad \textbf{(11-12)}$$

Thus, a firm's management has successfully created shareholder wealth when its after-tax net operating profits are sufficient to cover the opportunity cost of its invested capital.

Firms are increasingly using the concept of economic profit to link employee compensation to shareholder interests. The following general model can be used for this purpose:

$$\begin{array}{c}\text{Incentive} \\ \text{compensation}\end{array} = \text{base pay} \times \begin{array}{c}\text{percent} \\ \text{incentive} \\ \text{compensation}\end{array} \times \frac{\text{actual economic profit}}{\text{target economic profit}} \qquad \textbf{(11-13)}$$

If the firm manages to earn higher economic profits than were targeted for the period, then employee incentive compensation rises. Similarly, higher economic profits lead to greater shareholder value being created.

Calculating equivalent interest rates between countries

If borrowers and lenders can freely choose where they borrow and lend money, why aren't interest rates the same all over the world? The answer lies in differences in the anticipated rates of inflation between countries. In fact, the international Fisher Effect states that the differences in the rates of interest charged for the same loan in two different countries is equal to the difference in the anticipated rates of inflation in the countries. So, rates of interest are equal around the world only after we account for differences in rates of inflation between countries. Of course, the international Fisher Effect does not hold exactly due to political and other risk considerations that can serve to restrict capital flow between countries. However, the Fisher Effect does provide a useful starting point for understanding why there are differences in interest rates throughout the world.

Objective **7**

KEY TERMS

Capital asset pricing
model, 336
Capital structure, 339
Economic profit, 347

Financial policy, 331
Flotation costs, 331
Investor's required rate of
return, 330

Market value added, 346
Weighted average cost of
capital, 331

STUDY QUESTIONS

11-1. Define the term *cost of capital*.

11-2. Why do we calculate a firm's weighted average cost of capital?

11-3. In computing the cost of capital, which sources of capital do we consider?

11-4. How does a firm's tax rate affect its cost of capital? What is the effect of the flotation costs associated with a new security issue?

11-5. a. Distinguish between internal common equity and new common stock.

   b. Why is a cost associated with internal common equity?

   c. Describe the two approaches that could be used in computing the cost of common equity.

11-6. What might we expect to see in practice in the relative costs of different sources of capital?

SELF-TEST PROBLEMS

ST-1. (*Individual or component costs of capital*) Compute the cost for the following sources of financing:

   a. A $1,000 par value bond with a market price of $970 and a coupon interest rate of 10 percent. Flotation costs for a new issue would be approximately 5 percent. The bonds mature in 10 years and the corporate tax rate is 34 percent.

   b. A preferred stock selling for $100 with an annual dividend payment of $8. If the company sells a new issue, the flotation cost will be $9 per share. The company's marginal tax rate is 30 percent.

   c. Internally generated common stock totaling $4.8 million. The price of the common stock is $75 per share, and the dividend per share was $9.80 last year. The dividend is not expected to change in the future.

   d. New common stock when the most recent dividend was $2.80. The company's dividends per share should continue to increase at an 8 percent growth rate into the indefinite future. The market price of the stock is currently $53; however, flotation costs of $6 per share are expected if the new stock is issued.

ST-2. (*Weighted average cost of capital*) The capital structure for the Carion Corporation is provided here. The company plans to maintain its debt structure in the future. If the firm has a 5.5 percent after-tax cost of debt, a 13.5 percent cost of preferred stock, and an 18 percent cost of common stock, what is the firm's weighted average cost of capital?

CAPITAL STRUCTURE ($000)	
Bonds	$1,083
Preferred Stock	268
Common Stock	3,681
	$5,032

ST-3. (*Calculating the weighted average cost of capital*) ABBC Inc. operates a very successful chain of yogurt and coffee shops spread across the southwestern part of the United States and needs to raise funds for its planned expansion into the Northwest. The firm's balance sheet at the close of 2004 appeared as follows:

Cash	$ 2,010,000		
Accounts Receivable	4,580,000		
Inventories	1,540,000	Long-Term Debt	$ 8,141,000
Net Property, Plant and Equipment	32,575,000	Common Equity	32,564,000
Total Assets	$40,705,000		$40,705,000

At present the firm's common stock is selling for a price equal to its book value and the firm's bonds are selling at par. The company's management estimates that the market requires an 18 percent return on its common stock, the firm's bonds command a yield to maturity of 7.5 percent and the firm faces a tax rate of 35 percent. At the end of the previous year ABBC's common stock was selling for a price of 2.5 times its book value and its bonds were trading near their par value.

   a. What does ABBC's market value capital structure look like?

   b. What is ABBC's weighted average cost of capital?

   c. If ABBC's stock price were to rise such that it sold at 3.5 times book value such that the cost of equity falls to 15 percent, what would the firm's cost of capital be (assuming the cost of debt and tax rate do not change)?

ST-4. (*Divisional costs of capital and investment decisions*) Belton Oil and Gas, Inc., is a Houston-based independent oil and gas firm. In the past Belton's management has used a single firmwide cost of capital of 13 percent to evaluate new investments. However, management has long recognized that its exploration and production division is significantly more risky than the pipeline and transportation division. In fact, comparable firms to Belton's E&P division have equity betas of about 1.7 whereas distribution companies typically have equity betas of only .8. Given the importance of getting the cost of capital estimate as close to correct as possible, the firm's chief financial officer has asked you to prepare cost of capital estimates for each of the two divisions. The requisite information needed to accomplish your task is contained here:

- Cost of debt financing is 7 percent before taxes of 35 percent. However, if the E&P division were to borrow based on its projects alone the cost of debt would probably be 9 percent and the pipeline division could borrow at 5.5 percent. You may assume these costs of debt are after any flotation costs the firm might incur.
- The risk-free rate of interest on long-term U.S. Treasury bonds is currently 4.8 percent and the market risk premium has averaged 7.3 percent over the last several years.
- The E&P division adheres to a target debt ratio of 10 percent while the pipeline division utilizes 40 percent borrowed funds.
- The firm has sufficient internally generated funds such that no new stock will have to be sold to raise equity financing.

   a. Estimate the divisional costs of capital for the E&P and pipeline divisions.

   b. What are the implications of using a companywide cost of capital to evaluate new investment proposals in light of the differences in the costs of capital you estimated previously?

STUDY PROBLEMS

11-1. (*Individual or component costs of capital*) Compute the cost of the following:

   a. A bond that has $1,000 par value (face value) and a contract or coupon interest rate of 11 percent. A new issue would have a flotation cost of 5 percent of the $1,125 market value. The bonds mature in 10 years. The firm's average tax rate is 30 percent and its marginal tax rate is 34 percent.

   b. A new common stock issue that paid a $1.80 dividend last year. The par value of the stock is $15, and earnings per share have grown at a rate of 7 percent per year. This growth rate is expected to continue into the foreseeable future. The company maintains a constant dividend–earnings ratio of 30 percent. The price of this stock is now $27.50, but 5 percent flotation costs are anticipated.

   c. Internal common equity when the current market price of the common stock is $43. The expected dividend this coming year should be $3.50, increasing thereafter at a 7 percent annual growth rate. The corporation's tax rate is 34 percent.

   d. A preferred stock paying a 9 percent dividend on a $150 par value. If a new issue is offered, flotation costs will be 12 percent of the current price of $175.

   e. A bond selling to yield 12 percent after flotation costs, but before adjusting for the marginal corporate tax rate of 34 percent. In other words, 12 percent is the rate that equates the net proceeds from the bond with the present value of the future cash flows (principal and interest).

11-2. (*Individual or component costs of capital*) Compute the cost of the following:

   a. A bond selling to yield 7 percent after flotation costs, but before adjusting for the marginal corporate tax rate of 34 percent. In other words, 7 percent is the rate that equates the net proceeds from the bond with the present value of the future cash flows (principal and interest).

b. A new common stock issue that paid a $1.05 dividend last year. The par value of the stock is $2, and the earnings per share have grown at a rate of 4 percent per year. This growth rate is expected to continue into the foreseeable future. The company maintains a constant dividend–earnings ratio of 40 percent. The price of this stock is now $30, but 9 percent flotation costs are anticipated.

c. A bond that has a $1,000 par value and a contract or coupon interest rate of 12 percent. A new issue would net the company 90 percent of the $1,150 market value. The bonds mature in 15 years, the firm's average tax rate is 30 percent, and its marginal tax rate is 34 percent.

d. A preferred stock paying a 6 percent dividend on a $100 par value. If a new issue is offered, the company can expect to net $85 per share.

e. Internal common equity when the current market price of the common stock is $35. The expected dividend this forthcoming year should be $4, increasing thereafter at a 4 percent annual growth rate. The corporation's tax rate is 34 percent.

11-3. (*Cost of equity*) Salte Corporation is issuing new common stock at a market price of $27. Dividends last year were $1.45 and are expected to grow at an annual rate of 6 percent forever. Flotation costs will be 6 percent of market price. What is Salte's cost of equity?

11-4. (*Cost of debt*) Belton is issuing a $1,000 par value bond that pays 7 percent annual interest and matures in 15 years. Investors are willing to pay $958 for the bond. Flotation costs will be 11 percent of market value. The company is in an 18 percent tax bracket. What will be the firm's after-tax cost of debt on the bond?

11-5. (*Cost of preferred stock*) The preferred stock of Julian Industries sells for $36 and pays $3.00 in dividends. The net price of the security after issuance costs is $32.50. What is the cost of capital for the preferred stock?

11-6. (*Cost of debt*) The Zephyr Corporation is contemplating a new investment to be financed 33 percent from debt. The firm could sell new $1,000 par value bonds at a net price of $945. The coupon interest rate is 12 percent, and the bonds would mature in 15 years. If the company is in a 34 percent tax bracket, what is the after-tax cost of capital to Zephyr for bonds?

11-7. (*Cost of preferred stock*) Your firm is planning to issue preferred stock. The stock sells for $115; however, if new stock is issued, the company would receive only $98. The par value of the stock is $100 and the dividend rate is 14 percent. What is the cost of capital for the stock to your firm?

11-8. (*Cost of internal equity*) Pathos Co.'s common stock is currently selling for $23.80. Dividends paid last year were $.70. Flotation costs on issuing stock will be 10 percent of market price. The dividends and earnings per share are projected to have an annual growth rate of 15 percent. What is the cost of internal common equity for Pathos?

11-9. (*Cost of equity*) The common stock for the Bestsold Corporation sells for $58. If a new issue is sold, the flotation costs are estimated to be 8 percent. The company pays 50 percent of its earnings in dividends, and a $4 dividend was recently paid. Earnings per share 5 years ago were $5. Earnings are expected to continue to grow at the same annual rate in the future as during the past 5 years. The firm's marginal tax rate is 34 percent. Calculate the cost of (a) internal common equity and (b) external common equity.

11-10. (*Cost of debt*) Sincere Stationery Corporation needs to raise $500,000 to improve its manufacturing plant. It has decided to issue a $1,000 par value bond with a 14 percent annual coupon rate and a 10-year maturity. The investors require a 9 percent rate of return.

   a. Compute the market value of the bonds.
   b. What will the net price be if flotation costs are 10.5 percent of the market price?
   c. How many bonds will the firm have to issue to receive the needed funds?
   d. What is the firm's after-tax cost of debt if its average tax rate is 25 percent and its marginal tax rate is 34 percent?

11-11. (*Cost of debt*)

   a. Rework problem 11-10 as follows: Assume an 8 percent coupon rate. What effect does changing the coupon rate have on the firm's after-tax cost of capital?
   b. Why is there a change?

11-12. (*Economic profit*) The following table contains the firm market value (sum of debt and equity), invested capital, cost of capital, and return on invested capital for three prominent firms measured at year-end 1999:

A	B TOTAL MARKET VALUE ($ MILLIONS)	C INVESTED CAPITAL ($ MILLIONS)	D NET OPERATING PROFIT AFTER TAX (*NOPAT*)	E COST OF CAPITAL (K_{WACC}) (%)
Wal-Mart Stores	336,668	54,013	7,729.26	10.99
Yahoo!	137,595	8,847	(235.33)	15.99
Motorola	100,431	29,890	2,196.92	11.65

a. Based on the data presented here, which of these firms created value for its stockholders during 1999, based on their economic profit?

b. What is the *MVA* for each of these firms, and what does it tell you about each firm's success or failure to create wealth for its stockholders?

11-13. (*Incentive compensation*) The Navasar Manufacturing Company is implementing a new incentive compensation program for its top four executives that puts a portion of each executive's compensation "at risk" as an incentive to improve performance on the job. The chief financial officer is now estimating the total compensation (base pay plus the incentive portion) for each of these executives in an effort to determine whether the total is reasonable given the historical compensation paid to them. The following table contains the necessary information for evaluating compensation under the proposed plan, as well as the total compensation paid to each executive during the last calendar year:

EMPLOYEE TITLE	LAST YEAR'S COMPENSATION	% INCENTIVE PAY	PROPOSED TARGET PERFORMANCE	BASE COMPENSATION
Chief Executive Officer	$750,000	90%	$5,000,000	$ 75,000
Chief Operating Officer	500,000	80%	5,000,000	100,000
Chief Financial Officer	425,000	50%	5,000,000	212,500
Controller	275,000	30%	5,000,000	192,500

a. Calculate incentive and total compensation that will be paid to each of these officers of the firm when actual firm performance is 80%, 100%, and 120% of targeted performance. To calculate incentive pay, use the following relationship:

$$\text{Incentive compensation} = \text{base pay} \times \left(\begin{array}{c} \text{percent} \\ \text{incentive} \\ \text{compensation} \end{array} \right) \times \left(\frac{\text{actual performance}}{\text{target performance}} \right)$$

b. The chief financial officer is also considering a recommendation that incentive compensation be capped based on the firm's performance. For example, incentive pay would only begin when the firm's actual performance reaches 60 percent of target performance, and no additional incentive compensation would be paid once actual performance passed 150 percent of target performance. Under this plan, what are the minimum and maximum compensations that would be paid to each of the officers?

11-14. (*Divisional costs of capital*) LPT, Inc., is an integrated oil company headquartered in Dallas, Texas. The company has three operating divisions: oil exploration and production (commonly referred to as E&P), pipelines, and refining. Historically, LPT did not spend a great deal of time thinking about the opportunity costs of capital for each of its divisions and used a companywide weighted average cost of capital of 14 percent for all new capital investment projects. Recent changes in its businesses have made it abundantly clear to LPT's management that this is not a reasonable approach. For example, investors demand a much higher expected rate of return for exploration and production ventures than for pipeline investment. Although LPT's management agrees, in principle at least, that different operating divisions should face an opportunity cost of capital that reflects their individual risk characteristics, they are not in agreement about whether a move toward divisional costs of capital is a good idea based on practical considerations.

a. Pete Jennings is the chief operating officer for the E&P division, and he is concerned that going to a system of divisional costs of capital may restrain his ability to undertake very promising exploration opportunities. He argues that the firm really should be concerned about finding those opportunities that offer the highest possible rate of return on invested capital. Pete contends that using the firm's scarce capital to take on the most promising projects would lead to the greatest increase in shareholder value. Do you agree with Pete? Why or why not?

b. The pipeline division manager, Donna Selma, has long argued that charging her division the companywide cost of capital of 14 percent severely penalizes her opportunities to increase shareholder value. Do you agree with Donna? Explain.

c. "There is also the matter of the firm's EVA-based incentive compensation system," remarks Bill Simon, the firm's CEO. "If we move to divisional opportunity costs of capital, it seems to me that we should also define the divisional EVAs using a different cost of capital for each operating division." This, Bill contends, might make it seem as if the managers in the less risky divisions (those that carry a lower cost of capital) would have an easier time earning EVA-based bonuses. Is Bill correct in his contention that the firm will have to move toward the use of multiple EVA formulas in which the cost of capital varies across divisions?

11-15. (*Weighted average cost of capital*) Crawford Enterprises is a publicly held company located in Arnold, Kansas. The firm began as a small tool and die shop but grew over its 35-year life to become a leading supplier of metal fabrication equipment used in the farm tractor industry. At the close of 2004 the firm's balance sheet appeared as follows:

Cash	$ 540,000		
Accounts Receivable	4,580,000		
Inventories	7,400,000	Long-Term Debt	$12,590,000
Net Property, Plant and Equipment	18,955,000	Common Equity	18,885,000
Total Assets	$31,475,000		$31,475,000

At present the firm's common stock is selling for a price equal to its book value and the firm's bonds are selling at par. Crawford's management estimates that the market requires a 15 percent return on its common stock, the firm's bonds command a yield to maturity of 8 percent, and the firm faces a tax rate of 34 percent.

a. What is Crawford's weighted average cost of capital?

b. If Crawford's stock price were to rise such that it sold at 1.5 times book value such that the cost of equity falls to 13 percent, what would the firm's cost of capital be (assuming the cost of debt and tax rate do not change)?

11-16. (*Divisional costs of capital and investment decisions*) In May of this year Newcastle Mfg. Company's capital investment review committee received two major investment proposals. One of the proposals was put forth by the firm's domestic manufacturing division and the other came from the firm's distribution company. Both proposals promise internal rates of return equal to approximately 12 percent. In the past Newcastle's management has used a single firmwide cost of capital to evaluate new investments. However, management has long recognized that the manufacturing division is significantly more risky than the distribution division. In fact, comparable firms in the manufacturing division have equity betas of about 1.6 whereas distribution companies typically have equity betas of only 1.1. Given the size of the two proposals, Newcastle's management feels it can only undertake one so it wants to be sure that it is taking on the more promising investment. Given the importance of getting the cost of capital estimate as close to correct as possible, the firm's chief financial officer has asked you to prepare cost of capital estimates for each of the two divisions. The requisite information needed to accomplish your task is contained here:

- Cost of debt financing is 8 percent before taxes of 35 percent. You may assume this cost of debt is after any flotation costs the firm might incur.
- The risk-free rate of interest on long-term U.S. Treasury bonds is currently 4.8 percent, and the market risk premium has averaged 7.3 percent over the last several years.
- Both divisions adhere to target debt ratios of 40 percent.
- The firm has sufficient internally generated funds such that no new stock will have to be sold to raise equity financing.

a. Estimate the divisional costs of capital for the manufacturing and distribution divisions.

b. Which of the two projects should the firm undertake (assuming it cannot do both due to labor and other nonfinancial restraints)? Discuss.

Barnes & Noble (B&N) is a leading retailer of new books combining the power of traditional bricks-and-mortar storefronts throughout the nation with a state-of-the-art Internet marketing program. Use your answers to the following exercises to think about what the firm's cost of capital should be.

11-WW1. (*Defining B&N's capital structure*) Your first exercise is to assess B&N's capital structure. Begin by going to **www.sec.gov** to obtain the firm's most recent annual report (i.e., the firm's 10K). You may assume that the firm's liabilities are trading for prices that are reflected in their book values. Remember, however, that the only liabilities you want to include in the capital structure are permanent or long-term indebtedness, the current portion of the firm's long-term debt, and any short-term, interest-bearing notes payable. For the equity component of the capital structure you will need to determine the market value of B&N shares. To do this, you can multiply the ratio of price to book value of common equity (which can be found at **www.yahoo.com**) by the current book value of the firm's equity. For example, if the price to book ratio were 1.5 times and the book value of the firm's equity was $10 million, then the market value of the firm's common equity would be 1.5 times $10 million or $15 million.

11-WW2. (*Cost of debt*) Assuming that B&N's credit rating is AA, what is the current yield required on new debt with this rating? (See the Treasury Management Web site for current yield information—**www.tmpages.com/tmp55.htm**.)

11-WW3. (*Cost of equity*) Use the capital asset pricing model to estimate the cost of equity capital for B&N. You can assume an equity market risk premium of 7 percent. Use **www.yahoo.com** to get an equity beta for B&N and use the current yield for 20-year Treasury bonds to estimate the risk-free rate of interest (see the Treasury Management Web site for current yield information—**www.tmpages.com/tmp55.htm**).

11-WW4. (*Weighted average cost of capital*) If B&N's marginal tax rate is 35 percent, what is its weighted average cost of capital based on your answers to the preceding questions?

The balance sheet that follows indicates the capital structure for Nealon, Inc. Flotation costs are (a) 15 percent of market value for a new bond issue, and (b) $2.01 per share for preferred stock. The dividends for common stock were $2.50 last year and are projected to have an annual growth rate of 6 percent. The firm is in a 34 percent tax bracket. What is the weighted average cost of capital if the firm's finances are in the following proportions?

TYPE OF FINANCING	PERCENTAGE OF FUTURE FINANCING
Bonds (8%, $1,000 par, 16-year maturity)	38%
Preferred stock (5,000 shares outstanding, $50 par, $1.50 dividend)	15%
Common equity	47%
Total	100%

a. Market prices are $1,035 for bonds, $19 for preferred stock, and $35 for common stock. There will be sufficient internal common equity funding (i.e., retained earnings) available such that the firm does not plan to issue new common stock.

b. In part **a** we assumed that Nealon would have sufficient retained earnings such that it would not need to sell additional common stock to finance its new investments. Consider the situation now, when Nealon's retained earnings anticipated for the coming year are expected to fall short of the equity requirement of 47 percent of new capital raised. Consequently, the firm foresees the possibility that new common shares will have to be issued. To facilitate the sale of shares, Nealon's investment banker has advised management that they should expect a price discount of approximately 7 percent, or $2.45 per share. Under these terms, the new shares should provide net proceeds of about $32.55. What is Nealon's cost of equity capital when new shares are sold, and what is the weighted average cost of the added funds involved in the issuance of new shares?

SELF-TEST SOLUTIONS

The following notations are used in this group of problems:

k_d = the before-tax cost of debt

k_{ps} = the cost of preferred stock

k_{cs} = the cost of internal common stock

k_{ncs} = the cost of new common stock

t = the marginal tax rate

D_t = the dollar dividend per share, where D_0 is the most recently paid dividend and D_1 is the forthcoming dividend

P_0 = the value (present value) of a security

NP_0 = the value of security less any flotation costs incurred in issuing the security

SS-1. **a.**

$$\$921.50 = \sum_{t=1}^{n} \frac{\$100}{(1+k_d)^t} + \frac{\$1,000}{(1+k_d)^{10}}$$

RATE	VALUE
11%	$940.90
k_d%	$921.50
12%	$887.00

$\$19.40$

$\$53.90$

$$k_d = 0.11 + \left(\frac{\$19.40}{\$53.90}\right) 0.01 = 0.1136 = 11.36\%$$

$$k_{d(1-t)} = 11.36\%(1-0.34) = 7.50\%$$

b.

$$k_{ps} = \frac{D}{NP_0}$$

$$k_{ps} = \frac{\$8}{\$100 - \$9} = 0.0879 = 8.79\%$$

c.

$$k_{cs} = \frac{D_1}{P_0} + g$$

$$k_{cs} = \frac{\$9.80}{\$75} + 0\% = 0.1307 = 13.07\%$$

d.

$$k_{ncs} = \frac{D_1}{NP_0} + g$$

$$k_{ncs} = \frac{\$2.80(1+0.08)}{\$53 - \$6} + 0.08 = 0.1443 = 14.43\%$$

SS-2. Carion Corporation—Weighted Cost of Capital

	CAPITAL STRUCTURE	WEIGHTS	INDIVIDUAL COSTS	WEIGHTED COSTS
Bonds	$1,083	0.2152	5.5%	1.18%
Preferred stock	268	0.0533	13.5%	0.72%
Common stock	3,681	0.7315	18.0%	13.17%
	$5,032	1.0000		15.07%

SS-3. Given:

Cash	$ 2,010,000		
Accounts Receivable	4,580,000		
Inventories	1,540,000	Long-Term Debt	$ 8,141,000
Net Property, Plant and Equipment	32,575,000	Common Equity	32,564,000
Total Assets	$40,705,000		$40,705,000
Cost of debt financing	7.5%		
Cost of equity	18%		
Tax rate	35%		
Market to book ratio	2.50		

a. *What does the firm's market value capital structure look like?* Note that since the market to book ratio (market value of equity to book value of equity) is 2.5 the market value of the firm's equity is = 2.5 × $32,564,000 or $81,410,000. The market value of debt is assumed to equal its book value. Thus,

COMPONENT	MARKET VALUE BALANCE SHEET	PROPORTION	AFTER-TAX COST	PRODUCT
Long-Term Debt	$ 8,141,000	9%	4.88%	0.44318%
Common Equity	81,410,000	91%	18.00%	16.36364%
	$89,551,000			16.80682%

b. *What is ABBC's weighted average cost of capital? Based on the above calculations the answer is 16.8%*

c. *If ABBC's stock price were to rise such that it sold at 3.5 times book value such that the cost of equity falls to 15 percent, what would the firm's cost of capital be (assuming the cost of debt and tax rate do not change)?*

Cost of debt financing	8%
Cost of equity	15%
Tax rate	35%
Market to book ratio	3.50

COMPONENT	MARKET VALUE BALANCE SHEET	PROPORTION	AFTER-TAX COST	PRODUCT
Long-Term Debt	$ 8,141,000	7%	5.20%	0.34667%
Common Equity	113,974,000	93%	15.00%	14.00000%
	$122,115,000			14.34667%

SS-4. Given:

	E&P DIVISION	PIPELINE DIVISION
Equity beta	1.7	0.8
Tax rate	35.0%	35.0%
Cost of debt	9.0%	5.5%
Debt ratio	10.0%	40.0%
Risk-free rate	4.8%	
Market risk premium	7.3%	

a.

EXPLORATION AND DEVELOPMENT DIVISION			
COMPONENT	PROPORTION	AFTER-TAX COST	PRODUCT
Debt	10.0%	5.9%	0.6%
Equity	90.0%	17.2%	15.5%
			16.1%

PIPELINE DIVISION			
COMPONENT	PROPORTION	AFTER-TAX COST	PRODUCT
Debt	40.0%	3.6%	1.4%
Equity	60.0%	10.6%	6.4%
			7.8%

b. The very dramatic differences in the two divisional cost of capital estimates underscore the importance of careful analysis of capital costs that correspond as closely as possible to the riskiness of the use for which the funds are being requested. For example, using a 13 percent cost of capital for the firm as a whole leads to accepting E&P projects that fall well below the true cost of raising funds for these types of investments (16.1 percent). Similarly, using the 13 percent companywide cost of capital will result in the rejection of value-enhancing investments that earn in excess of the 7.8 percent cost of capital that is appropriate to the pipeline division.

► G. Bennett Stewart III is a senior partner with Stern Stewart & Co. (NY). (See opener for Part One for more information on Stewart and this company.) We asked Bennett some questions on the significance of the firm's decisions regarding capital structure and dividend policy and this is what he said:

Can you make some general comments on the significance of capital structure and dividend policy decisions to a firm's success?

Let me begin by saying that decisions management makes regarding what assets to buy, and the businesses in which it plans to compete, are the primary drivers of value creation. However, the financial side of the business is critically important, too. From a financing perspective it is management's responsibility to make sure that the cost of raising capital is as cheap as possible and the choice of the mix of debt and equity is an important determinant of a firm's cost of capital.

However, there is more to the firm's financial strategy than determining the mix of securities to use when financing the firm's investments. Specifically, the firm's financial strategy also includes the selection of the firm's dividend policy (the firm's strategy for returning cash to investors), the firm's overall risk management policy, its pension planning policy, and the policy it follows with respect to the use of surplus cash. In total, these policies can be described as the corporate financial strategy of the firm.

I would also like to point out that the determination of each of these policies is inextricably linked to minimizing taxes and transaction costs. In addition, a firm's financing policies include decisions regarding opportunities for employees to own part of the equity in the firm as a managerial strategy for improving firm performance. Consequently, setting a firm's financial policies provide crucial decision opportunities for the executive who wants proactively to seek out value creation opportunities.

Good companies are proactive about their financing decisions. They don't tend to let the cash flow of the business passively dictate their capital structure. Instead they think about the mix of debt and equity that will balance the tax and incentive benefits of debt financing against the need to preserve financial flexibility. In addition, the proactive manager thoughtfully examines the best way the firm will provide a return to their stockholders via cash distributions through dividends and share repurchases.

Can you give an example of a firm that is really good at managing capital structure and make a comment or two as to why you believe that to be so?

I think a good example of a company that has approached this very thoughtfully over the years is

the Coca-Cola Company. In the 1970s Coca-Cola was very passively financed. They had a AAA rating on their debt, what little debt they had, and they were an aggressive payer of dividends. When Roberto Goizueta came in as CEO in the early 80s he decided to stir up a more potent business model that emphasized global growth and product-line extensions. At the same time, he was a great believer in using debt financing much more aggressively to minimize the cost of capital. So the Coca-Cola Company began to borrow money and use the proceeds to repurchase the firm's common shares. This changed the firm's mix of debt and equity such that the firm lost its AAA bond rating. However, by raising the firm's use of debt, the firm reduced the overall cost of its capital. I think this is a crystal clear example of a company shifting from a passive to a proactive financial strategy.

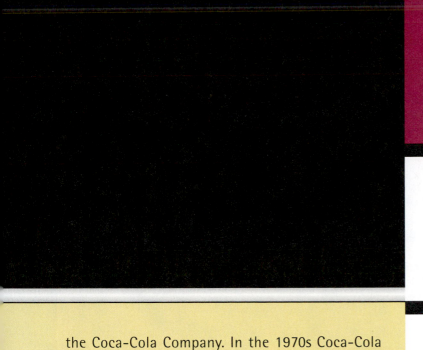

After reading this chapter, you should be able to:

1. Understand the difference between business risk and financial risk.

2. Use the technique of break-even analysis in a variety of analytical settings.

3. Distinguish among the financial concepts of operating leverage, financial leverage, and combined leverage.

4. Calculate the firm's degree of operating leverage, financial leverage, and combined leverage.

5. Understand the concept of an optimal capital structure.

6. Explain the main underpinnings of capital structure theory.

7. Understand and be able to graph the moderate position on capital structure importance.

8. Incorporate the concepts of agency costs and free cash flow into a discussion on capital structure management.

9. Use the basic tools of capital structure management.

10. Understand how business risk and global sales impact the multinational firm.

CHAPTER 12

Determining the Financing Mix

BUSINESS AND FINANCIAL RISK • BREAK-EVEN ANALYSIS • OPERATING LEVERAGE • FINANCIAL LEVERAGE • COMBINATION OF OPERATING AND FINANCIAL LEVERAGE • PLANNING THE FINANCING MIX • A QUICK LOOK AT CAPITAL STRUCTURE THEORY • BASIC TOOLS OF CAPITAL STRUCTURE MANAGEMENT • A GLANCE AT ACTUAL CAPITAL STRUCTURE MANAGEMENT • FINANCE AND THE MULTINATIONAL FIRM: BUSINESS RISK AND GLOBAL SALES

On July 12, 2000, Harley-Davidson Inc. issued a press release to the financial community and media that discussed its financial performance for the quarter ended June 25. Harley posted a fiscal second-quarter increase in net income of 32 percent over the 1999 second quarter. Harley noted that its sales revenue jumped by a pleasant 24 percent over the same period. Observe that Harley's increase in reported net income was 1.333 times the percentage hike in sales. Such disparate relationships between earnings increments and sales increments are commonly reported by numerous firms. Here are some other actual examples.

In fiscal 2004, Procter & Gamble (P&G) posted a sales increase of 18.5 percent over the level of reported sales for 2003. The firm's change in net income, however, rose by a larger 25.0 percent. Thus, the relative change in net income for P&G was 1.35 times the relative fluctuation in sales (i.e., 25.0 percent/18.5 percent).

We know that sales fluctuations are not always in the positive direction. International business conditions affected Coca-Cola's

⨳ WHAT'S AHEAD ⨳

Our work in earlier chapters allowed us to develop an understanding of how financial assets are valued in the marketplace. Drawing on the tenets of valuation theory, we presented various approaches to measuring the cost of funds to the business organization. This chapter presents concepts that relate to the valuation process and the cost of capital; it also discusses the crucial problem of planning the firm's financing mix.

The cost of capital provides a direct link between the formulation of the firm's asset structure and its financial structure. This is illustrated in Figure 12-1. Recall that the cost of capital is a basic input to the time-adjusted capital-budgeting models. Therefore, it affects the capital-budgeting, or asset-selection, process. The cost of capital is affected, in turn, by the composition of the right-hand side of the firm's balance sheet—that is, its financial structure.

This chapter examines tools that can be useful aids to the financial manager in determining the firm's proper financial structure. First, we review the technique of break-even analysis, which provides the foundation for the relationships to be highlighted in the remainder of the chapter. We then examine the concept of operating leverage, some consequences of the firm's use of financial leverage, and the impact on the firm's earnings stream when operating leverage and financial leverage are combined in various patterns. With this foundation to effectively analyze the variability in the firm's earnings streams, we move on to a discussion of capital structure theory and the basic tools of capital structure management. Actual capital structure practices are also placed in perspective. We close with a discussion involving the multinational firm and its relationship to both the business risk concept and global sales opportunities. Our immediate tasks are to distinguish two types of risk that confront the firm and to clarify some key terminology that is used throughout this chapter.

FIGURE 12-1 Cost of Capital as a Link Between a Firm's Asset Structure and Financial Structure

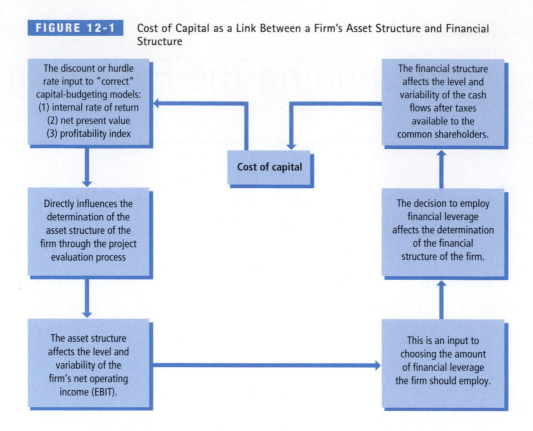

sales during 1998, and the company endured a 0.3 percent contraction in revenues. Importantly, Coke's net income contracted by a larger and more painful 14.4 percent.

The Boeing Company endured a similar result when financial results from 2002 were compared to 2001. Over this time period Boeing was confronted with a relative decline in revenues of 7.1 percent but saw net earnings decline by a magnified 17.9 percent.

What is it about the nature of business that causes changes in sales revenues to translate into larger variations in net income and, finally, the earnings available to the common shareholders? It would be a good planning tool for management to be able to decompose such fluctuations into those policies associated with the operating side of the business and those policies associated with the financing side of the business.

This chapter shows you how to do just that—and more. The United States was recession free from April 1991 until March 2001, when the tenth post–World War II recession officially commenced. This was the longest expansion, 120 months, in the history of credible business-cycle record keeping in the United States dating back to 1853. It took until July 17, 2003, for the National Bureau of Economic Research to announce that a "trough in business activity occurred in the U.S. economy in November 2001." A trough means a recession has ended. Note that this announcement happened a full 21 months after the recession was said to have ended. Business-cycle "dating" is an art subject to considerable debate among financial economists and executives. Even though this recession was officially over, the nation's labor markets continued to languish into July 2003, marked by very slow growth in payroll jobs. This postrecession adjustment period was a challenging one for many U.S. busi-

nesses that had loaded their balance sheets with debt over the "good times" of the 120-month expansion.

Financial executives had to delicately manage cash flows to service existing debt contracts or face bankruptcy. These same executives had to give considerable thought about how to finance the next (i.e., incremental) capital project.

Along these lines, Harley-Davidson, Inc., has taken a rather moderate exposure to financial risk in the management of its funds' sources. Harley has about 8,500 employees and, for reporting year 2001, ranked 466th among the *Fortune* 500 largest domestic corporations with sales revenues of $3.36 billion. Even though the overall economy was slow, Harley improved to a ranking of 392 for 2002 within this same set of 500 companies. For 2001, Harley generated $698.2 million in earnings before interest and taxes (i.e., *EBIT*) and incurred interest expense of $24.8 million. This put its times interest earned ratio at 28.2 times (i.e., $698.2/$24.8) for 2001. So in an adverse economic year, Harley's *EBIT* could slip to about one-twenty-eighth of its 2001 amount and the firm would still be able to pay its contractual debt obligations. This is a very safe interest coverage ratio. By the way, the times interest earned ratio is defined as earnings before interest and taxes divided by interest expense (refer to the Glossary at the back of this text).

If you understand the material and analytical processes in this chapter, you will be able to make positive contributions to company strategies that deal with the firm's financing mix. You will be able to formulate a defensible answer to the question, Should we finance the next capital project with a new issue of bonds or a new issue of common stock? You can also help a lot of firms avoid making serious financial errors, the consequences of which last for several years, because financing decisions typically impact the firm for several years.

BUSINESS AND FINANCIAL RISK

Objective **1**

risk

In studying capital-budgeting techniques, we referred to **risk** as the *likely variability associated with expected revenue or income streams*. Because our attention is now focused on the firm's financing decision rather than its investment decision, it is useful to separate the income stream variations attributable to (1) the company's exposure to business risk and (2) its decision to incur financial risk.

business risk

Business risk refers to the *relative dispersion (variability) in the firm's expected earnings before interest and taxes (EBIT)*.[1] Figure 12-2 shows a subjectively estimated probability distribution of next year's *EBIT* for Pierce Grain Company and the same type of projection for Pierce's larger competitor, Blackburn Seed Company. The expected value of *EBIT* for Pierce is $100,000, with an associated standard deviation of $20,000. If next year's *EBIT* for Pierce fell one standard deviation short of the expected $100,000, the actual *EBIT* would equal $80,000. Blackburn's expected *EBIT* is $200,000, and the size of the associated standard deviation is $20,000. The standard deviation for the expected level of *EBIT* is the same for both firms. We would say that Pierce's degree of business risk exceeds Blackburn's because of its larger coefficient of variation of expected *EBIT*, as follows:

$$\text{Pierce's coefficient of variation of expected } EBIT = \frac{\$20,000}{\$100,000} = .20$$

$$\text{Blackburn's coefficient of variation of expected } EBIT = \frac{\$20,000}{\$200,000} = .10$$

The relative dispersion in the firm's *EBIT* stream, measured here by its expected coefficient of variation, is the *residual* effect of several causal influences. Dispersion in operating income does not *cause* business risk; rather, this dispersion, which we call business risk, is the *result* of several influences. The company's cost structure, product demand characteristics, and intraindustry competitive position all affect its business risk exposure. Such business risk is a direct result of the firm's investment decision. It is the firm's asset structure, after all, that gives rise to both the level and variability of its operating profits.

financial risk

Financial risk, conversely, is a direct result of the firm's financing decision. In the context of selecting a proper financing mix, this risk applies to *(1) the additional variability in earnings available to the firm's common shareholders and (2) the additional chance of insolvency borne by the common shareholder caused by the use of financial leverage*.[2]

FIGURE 12-2   Subjective Probability Distribution of Next Year's *EBIT*

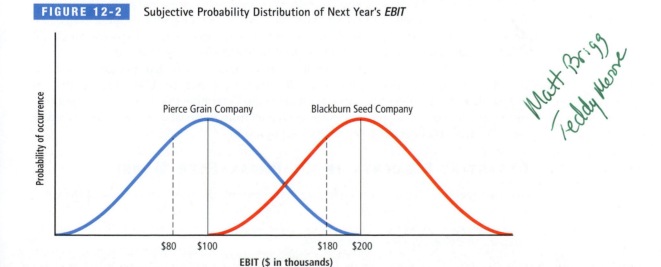

[1]If what accountants call "other income" and "other expenses" are equal to zero, then *EBIT* is equal to net operating income. These terms are used interchangeably.
[2]Note that the concept of financial risk used here differs from that used in our examination of cash and marketable securities management in Chapter 15.

financial leverage

Financial leverage means *financing a portion of the firm's assets with securities bearing a fixed (limited) rate of return* in hopes of increasing the ultimate return to the common stockholders. The decision to use debt or preferred stock in the financial structure of the corporation means that those who own the common shares of the firm are exposed to financial risk. Any given level of variability in *EBIT* is magnified by the firm's use of financial leverage, and such additional variability is embodied in the variability of earnings available to the common stockholder and earnings per share. If these magnifications are negative, the common stockholder has a higher chance of insolvency than would have existed had the use of fixed-charge securities (debt and preferred stock) been avoided.

operating leverage

In the rest of this chapter, we study techniques that permit a precise assessment of the earnings stream variability caused by (1) operating leverage and (2) financial leverage. **Operating leverage** refers to the *incurrence of fixed operating costs in the firm's income stream.* To understand the nature and importance of operating leverage, we need to draw on the basics of cost-volume-profit analysis, or *break-even analysis.*

CONCEPT CHECK

1. Explain the concept of business risk within the context of financial structure management.
2. Explain the concept of financial risk within the context of financial structure management.
3. Distinguish between financial leverage and operating leverage.

Objective **2**

BREAK-EVEN ANALYSIS

The technique of break-even analysis is familiar to legions of businesspeople. It is usefully applied in a wide array of business settings, including both small and large organizations. This tool is widely accepted by the business community for two reasons: It is based on straightforward assumptions, and companies have found that the information gained from the break-even model is beneficial in decision-making situations.

OBJECTIVE AND USES

The objective of break-even analysis is to determine the break-even quantity of output by studying the relationships among the firm's cost structure, volume of output, and profit. Alternatively, the firm ascertains the break-even level of sales dollars that corresponds to the break-even quantity of output. We develop the fundamental relationships by concentrating on units of output and then extend the procedure to permit direct calculation of the break-even sales level.

What is meant by the break-even quantity of output? It is that quantity of output, denominated in units, that results in an *EBIT* level equal to zero. Use of the break-even model, therefore, enables the financial officer (1) to determine the quantity of output that must be sold to cover all operating costs, as distinct from financial costs, and (2) to calculate the *EBIT* that will be achieved at various output levels.

ESSENTIAL ELEMENTS OF THE BREAK-EVEN MODEL

To implement the break-even model, we must separate the production costs of the company into two mutually exclusive categories: fixed costs and variable costs. You will recall from your study of basic economics that in the long run all costs are variable. Break-even analysis, therefore, is a short-run concept.

ASSUMED BEHAVIOR OF COSTS

FIXED COSTS

fixed costs

indirect costs

Fixed costs, also referred to as **indirect costs**, *do not vary in total amount as sales volume or the quantity of output changes* over some relevant range of output. Total fixed costs are independent

ACROSS THE HALL

ACCOUNTING—COST STRUCTURE, FORECASTING, AND INVESTMENT

Comments by Mr. Eric Gerstemeier

Mr. Eric Gerstemeier is a Senior Financial Analyst at Harcourt Education, a global education company providing print, assessment and development programs to students, teachers, and adults worldwide. Harcourt's corporate structure is composed of approximately a dozen primary divisions located across the United States and Canada, each division being responsible for its daily investment and operational decisions. Mr. Gerstemeier works for a 'shared services' division, a group providing a multitude of operational and financial services to each of the operating divisions. His responsibilities span a host of tasks ranging from budgeting and forecasting to process improvement, Sarbanes-Oxley compliance, and the valuation of acquisition prospects. Mr. Gerstemeier received his Bachelor's degree in finance and an M.B.A. from the University of Central Florida. He has worked in similar roles in both the technology and publishing industries.

A knowledge of cost structure, including fixed, variable, and semi-fixed costs is crucial to Mr. Gerstemeier's work. This base is also important to forecasting and capital investing decisions. His comments on these areas follow below.

Many decisions regarding the direction and funding of the ongoing business at Harcourt are made during the annual budget process and include the consideration of variables such as market conditions, risk assessments and the firm's operating cost structure. Similarly, the health of the company can be assessed and problem areas targeted through the analysis of such data. Indicative of the manufacturing industry, Harcourt's cost structure includes costs to produce the product (typically variable), costs to bring the product to market (variable and fixed) and infrastructure costs to support the business as a whole (generally fixed).

Furthermore, many cost drivers exhibit relationships with revenue, volumes shipped, or capital invested whereas others, typically those supporting the overall business, have fixed thresholds, i.e. a fixed number of IT professionals needed to support the general ledger system and its peripheral applications. Through quantification of these relationships, ratios and thresholds may be defined and Harcourt is able to create forward-looking income, cash flow, and balance sheet statements by which Harcourt manages the business (the budget). Some relationships (ratios) that Harcourt finds particularly valuable are as follows:

- Product investment needed to maintain or capture a given level of revenue (growth)
- Product investment and amortization
- Cost of goods sold and revenue (variable)
  - paper, print, and binding
  - freight
- Sales costs and revenue (fixed and variable)
  - Commissions (variable)
  - General labor costs (fixed/semi-fixed)
- General and administrative (fixed/semi-fixed)

Based on management's knowledge of these and other cost variables and coupled with an intimate knowledge of current and future market conditions, "pro-forma" statements of financial performance can be constructed. This provides the groundwork regarding where, when, and how much investment needs to take place in the near future. It also provides key metrics by which Harcourt can identify problem areas and justify the implementation of cost control and/or process improvement initiatives.

---

of the quantity of product produced and equal some constant dollar amount. As production volume increases, fixed cost per unit of product falls, as fixed costs are spread over larger and larger quantities of output. Figure 12-3 graphs the behavior of total fixed costs with respect to the company's relevant range of output. This total is shown to be unaffected by the quantity of product that is manufactured and sold. Over some other relevant output range, the amount of total fixed costs might be higher or lower for the same company.

In a manufacturing setting, some specific examples of fixed costs are

1. Administrative salaries
2. Depreciation
3. Insurance
4. Lump sums spent on intermittent advertising programs
5. Property taxes
6. Rent

VARIABLE COSTS

Variable costs are sometimes referred to as **direct costs**. Variable costs are *fixed per unit of output but vary in total as output changes*. Total variable costs are computed by taking the variable cost per unit and multiplying it by the quantity produced and sold. The break-even model

variable costs
direct costs

FIGURE 12-3   Fixed-Cost Behavior over Relevant Range of Output

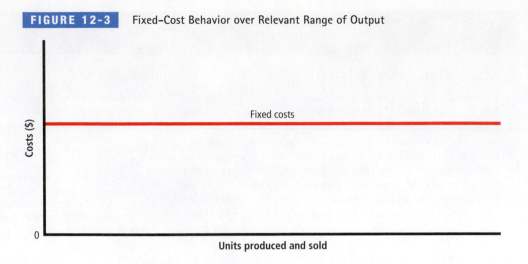

assumes proportionality between total variable costs and sales. Thus, if sales rise by 10 percent, it is assumed that variable costs will rise by 10 percent. Figure 12-4 graphs the behavior of total variable costs with respect to the company's relevant range of output. Total variable costs are seen to depend on the quantity of product that is manufactured and sold. Notice that if zero units of the product are manufactured, then variable costs are zero, but fixed costs are greater than zero. This implies that some contribution to the coverage of fixed costs occurs as long as the selling price per unit exceeds the variable costs per unit. This helps explain why some firms will operate a plant even when sales are temporarily depressed—that is, to provide some increment of revenue toward the coverage of fixed costs.

For a manufacturing operation, some examples of variable costs include

1. Direct labor
2. Direct materials
3. Energy costs (fuel, electricity, natural gas) associated with the production area
4. Freight costs for products leaving the plant
5. Packaging
6. Sales commissions

MORE ON BEHAVIOR OF COSTS

No one really believes that *all* costs behave as neatly as we have illustrated the fixed and variable costs in Figures 12-3 and 12-4. Nor does any law or accounting principle dictate that a certain element of the firm's total costs always will be classified as fixed or variable.

FIGURE 12-4   Variable-Cost Behavior over Relevant Range of Output

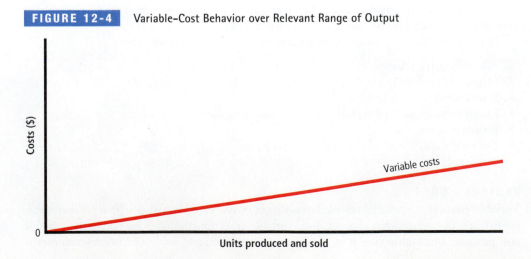

FIGURE 12-5   Semivariable-Cost Behavior over the Relevant Range of Output

This depends on each firm's specific circumstances. In one firm, energy costs may be predominantly fixed, whereas in another they may vary with output.[3]

Furthermore, some costs may be fixed for a while, then rise sharply to a higher level as a higher output is reached, remain fixed, and then rise again with further increases in production. Such costs may be termed either (1) *semivariable* or (2) *semifixed*. The label is your choice, because both are used in industrial practice. An example might be the salaries paid to production supervisors. Should output be cut back by 15 percent for a short period, the management of the organization is not likely to lay off 15 percent of the supervisors. Similarly, commissions paid to salespeople often follow a stepwise pattern over wide ranges of success. This sort of cost behavior is shown in Figure 12-5.

To implement the break-even model and deal with such a complex cost structure, the financial manager must (1) identify the most relevant output range for planning purposes and then (2) approximate the cost effect of semivariable items over this range by segregating a portion of them to fixed costs and a portion to variable costs. In the actual business setting this procedure is not fun. It is not unusual for the analyst who deals with the figures to spend considerably more time allocating costs to fixed and variable categories than in carrying out the actual break-even calculations.

TOTAL REVENUE AND VOLUME OF OUTPUT

Besides fixed and variable costs, the essential elements of the break-even model include total revenue from sales and volume of output. **Total revenue** means *total sales dollars* and is equal to the selling price per unit multiplied by the quantity sold. The **volume of output** refers to the *firm's level of operations* and may be *indicated either as a unit quantity or as sales dollars.*

total revenue
volume of output

FINDING THE BREAK-EVEN POINT

Finding the break-even point in terms of units of production can be accomplished in several ways. All approaches require the essential elements of the break-even model just described. The break-even model is a simple adaptation of the firm's income statement expressed in the following analytical format:

Sales – (total variable cost + total fixed cost) = profit   **(12-1)**

On a units-of-production basis, it is necessary to introduce (1) the price at which each unit is sold and (2) the variable cost per unit of output. Because the profit item studied in

---

[3]In a greenhouse operation, in which plants are grown (manufactured) under strictly controlled temperatures, heat costs will tend to be fixed whether the building is full or only half-full of seedlings. In a metal stamping operation, in which levers are being produced, there is no need to heat the plant to as high a temperature when the machines are stopped and the workers are not there. In this latter case, the heat costs will tend to be variable.

break-even analysis is *EBIT*, we use the acronym instead of the word *profit*. In terms of units, the income statement shown in equation (12-1) becomes the break-even model by setting *EBIT* equal to zero:

$$\left(\begin{array}{c}\text{Sales price}\\\text{per unit}\end{array}\right)\left(\begin{array}{c}\text{units}\\\text{sold}\end{array}\right)-\left[\left(\begin{array}{c}\text{variable cost}\\\text{per unit}\end{array}\right)\left(\begin{array}{c}\text{units}\\\text{sold}\end{array}\right)+\left(\begin{array}{c}\text{total fixed}\\\text{cost}\end{array}\right)\right]=EBIT=\$0 \quad \textbf{(12-2)}$$

Our task now becomes finding the number of units that must be produced and sold in order to satisfy equation (12-2)—that is, to arrive at *EBIT* = \$0. This can be done by (1) contribution margin analysis or (2) algebraic analysis. Each approach is illustrated using the same set of circumstances.

PROBLEM SITUATION

Even though Pierce Grain Company manufactures several different products, it has observed over a lengthy period that its product mix is rather constant. This allows management to conduct its financial planning by use of a "normal" sales price per unit and "normal" variable cost per unit. The "normal" sales price and variable cost per unit are calculated from the constant product mix. It is like assuming that the product mix is one big product. The selling price is \$10 and the variable cost is \$6. Total fixed costs for the firm are \$100,000 per year. What is the break-even point in units produced and sold for the company during the coming year?

CONTRIBUTION-MARGIN ANALYSIS

contribution margin

The contribution-margin technique permits direct computation of the break-even quantity of output. The **contribution margin** is the *difference between the unit selling price and unit variable costs*, as follows:

    unit sales price
   –unit variable cost
   =unit contribution margin

The use of the word *contribution* in the present context means contribution to the coverage of fixed operating costs. For Pierce Grain Company, the unit contribution margin is

unit sales price	\$10
unit variable cost	–6
unit contribution margin	\$ 4

If the annual fixed costs of \$100,000 are divided by the unit contribution margin of \$4, we find the break-even quantity of output for Pierce Grain is 25,000 units. Figure 12-6 portrays the contribution-margin technique for finding the break-even point.

FIGURE 12-6   Contribution–Margin Approach to Break-Even Analysis

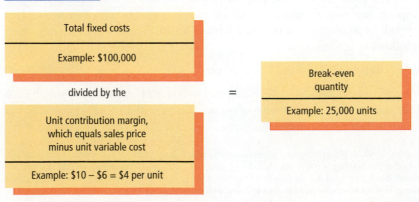

ALGEBRAIC ANALYSIS

To explain the algebraic method for finding the break-even output level, we need to adopt some notation.

Let

Q = the number of units sold
Q_B = the break-even level of Q
P = the unit sales price
F = total fixed costs anticipated over the planning period
V = the unit variable cost

Equation (12-2), the break-even model, is repeated on the following pages as equation (12-3), with the model symbols used in place of words. The break-even model is then solved for Q, the number of units that must be sold so that *EBIT* equals $0. We label the break-even point quantity Q_B.

$$(P \cdot Q) - [(V \cdot Q) + (F)] = EBIT = \$0 \qquad \textbf{(12-3)}$$
$$(P \cdot Q) - (V \cdot Q) - F = \$0$$
$$Q(P - V) = F$$

$$Q_B = \frac{F}{P - V} \qquad \textbf{(12-4)}$$

Observe that equation (12-4) says: Divide total fixed operating costs, F, by the unit contribution margin, $P - V$, and the break-even level of output, Q_B, will be obtained. The contribution margin analysis is nothing more than equation (12-4) in different garb.

Application of equation (12-4) permits direct calculation of Pierce Grain's break-even point, as follows:

$$Q_B = \frac{F}{P - V} = \frac{\$100,000}{\$10 - \$6} = 25,000 \text{ units}$$

BREAK-EVEN POINT IN SALES DOLLARS

In dealing with the multiproduct firm, it is convenient to compute the break-even point in terms of sales dollars rather than units of output. Sales, in effect, become a common denominator associated with a particular product mix. Furthermore, an outside analyst may not have access to internal unit cost data. He or she may, however, be able to obtain annual reports for the firm. If the analyst can separate the firm's total costs as identified from its annual reports into their fixed and variable components, he or she can calculate a general break-even point in sales dollars.

We illustrate this procedure using Pierce Grain Company's cost structure. Suppose that the reported financial information is arranged in the format shown in Table 12-1. We refer to this type of financial statement as an *analytical income statement*. This distinguishes it from audited income statements published, for example, in the annual reports of public corporations. If we are aware of the simple mathematical relationships on which cost-volume-profit analysis is based, we can use Table 12-1 to find the break-even point in sales dollars for Pierce Grain Company.

TABLE 12-1	Pierce Grain Company Analytical Income Statement
Sales	$300,000
Less: Total variable costs	180,000
Revenue before fixed costs	$120,000
Less: Total fixed costs	100,000
EBIT	$ 20,000

First, let us explore the logic of the process. Recall from equation (12-1) that

Sales − (total variable cost + total fixed cost) = *EBIT*

If we let total sales = *S*, total variable cost = *VC*, and total fixed cost = *F*, the preceding relationship becomes

$$S - (VC + F) = EBIT$$

Because variable cost per unit of output and selling price per unit are *assumed* constant over the relevant output range in break-even analysis, the ratio of total variable costs to sales, *VC/S*, is a constant for any level of sales. This permits us to rewrite the previous expression as

$$S - \left[\left(\frac{VC}{S} \right) S \right] - F = EBIT$$

and

$$S \left(1 - \frac{VC}{S} \right) - F = EBIT$$

At the break-even point, however, *EBIT* = 0, and the corresponding break-even level of sales can be represented as *S**. At the break-even level of sales, we have

$$S^* \left(1 - \frac{VC}{S} \right) - F = 0$$

or

$$S^* \left(1 - \frac{VC}{S} \right) = F$$

Therefore,

$$S^* = \frac{F}{1 - \dfrac{VC}{S}} \tag{12-5}$$

The application of equation (12-5) to Pierce Grain's analytical income statement in Table 12-1 permits the break-even sales level for the firm to be directly computed, as follows:

$$S^* = \frac{\$100,000}{1 - \dfrac{\$180,000}{\$300,000}}$$

$$= \frac{\$100,000}{1 - .60} = \$250,000$$

CONCEPT CHECK

1. Distinguish among fixed costs, variable costs, and semivariable costs.
2. Define the term *contribution margin*.
3. When is it useful or necessary to compute the break-even point in terms of sales dollars rather than units of output?

GENERAL MOTORS: PRICING STRATEGY IN A SLOW AGGREGATE ECONOMY

It was pointed out in Chapter 2 that the U.S. economy slipped into a formal recession during the initial quarter of 2001. As late as the summer of 2003, the economic recovery in the United States was muted at best. In fact, the highest-grade corporate bonds (those rated Aaa by Moody's) were yielding only 5.06 percent during the week of June 27, 2003, compared to a 22-year average (1981–2002) of 9.08 percent. Short-term interest rates were considerably lower. The target federal funds rate, for example, was set by Federal Reserve policymakers at a mere 1.00 percent. This put the commercial bank prime lending rate at 4.00 percent. The combination of (a) the slow overall economy and (b) extraordinarily low borrowing rates gave automobile manufacturers ample incentives to vigorously compete for sales via their pricing strategies.

The discussion just ended on break-even analysis demonstrated how firms and their financial analysts can use the contribution-margin metric to help formulate their pricing plans. Next, in an excerpt from a General Motors (GM) press release of July 2003, we see how that giant firm uses the break-even concept. Notice also the reference to GM's limited flexibility relative to managing fixed costs. This will directly relate to our subsequent discussion on operating leverage.

Over the past year and a half, GM has driven the U.S. auto industry into a price war of historic proportions as it battled the effects of a slowing economy. Last month GM's average per-vehicle incentive hit $3,934, a 51 percent increase over June 2002 and the highest average among large automakers.

With limited room to cut fixed costs, GM executives have defended their strategy as the best way to maximize profits and keep its factories running. GM's inventories were about 21 percent above normal at the end of June.

Source: Reuters at http://money.com/2003/07/08/pf/autos/gm_incentives.reut/index.htm.

OPERATING LEVERAGE

Objective **3**

If *fixed* operating costs are present in the firm's cost structure, so is operating leverage. Fixed operating costs do *not* include interest charges incurred from the firm's use of debt financing. Those costs will be incorporated into the analysis when financial leverage is discussed.

So operating leverage arises from the firm's use of fixed operating costs. But what is operating leverage? *Operating leverage* is the responsiveness of the firm's *EBIT* to fluctuations in sales. By continuing to draw on our data for Pierce Grain Company, we can illustrate the concept of operating leverage. Table 12-2 contains data for a study of a possible fluctuation in the firm's sales level. It is assumed that Pierce Grain is currently operating at an annual sales level of $300,000. This is referred to in the tabulation as the base sales level at *t* (time period zero). The question is, How will Pierce Grain's *EBIT* level respond to a positive 20 percent change in sales? A sales volume of $360,000, referred to as the forecast sales level at *t* + 1, reflects the 20 percent sales rise anticipated over the planning period. Assume that the planning period is 1 year.

Operating leverage relationships are derived within the mathematical assumptions of cost-volume-profit analysis. In the present example, this means that Pierce Grain's variable-cost-to-sales ratio of .6 will continue to hold during time period *t* + 1, and the fixed costs will hold steady at $100,000.

Given the forecasted sales level for Pierce Grain and its cost structure, we can measure the responsiveness of *EBIT* to the upswing in volume. Notice in Table 12-2 that *EBIT* is

TABLE 12-2 Concept of Operating Leverage: Increase in Pierce Grain Company Sales

ITEM	BASE SALES LEVEL, *t*	FORECAST SALES LEVEL, *t* + 1
Sales	$300,000	$360,000
Less: Total variable costs	180,000	216,000
Revenue before fixed costs	$120,000	$144,000
Less: Total fixed costs	100,000	100,000
EBIT	$ 20,000	$ 44,000

expected to be $44,000 at the end of the planning period. The percentage change in *EBIT* from t to $t+1$ can be measured as follows:

$$\text{Percentage change in } EBIT = \frac{\$44,000_{t+1} - \$20,000_t}{\$20,000_t}$$

$$= \frac{\$24,000}{\$20,000}$$

$$= 120\%$$

We know that the projected fluctuation in sales amounts to 20 percent of the base period, t, sales level. This is verified here:

$$\text{Percentage change in sales} = \frac{\$360,000_{t+1} - \$300,000_t}{\$300,000_t}$$

$$= \frac{\$60,000}{\$300,000}$$

$$= 20\%$$

By relating the percentage fluctuation in *EBIT* to the percentage fluctuation in sales, we can calculate a specific measure of operating leverage. Thus, we have

$$\begin{matrix} \text{Degree of operating} \\ \text{leverage} \\ \text{from the base sales level(s)} \end{matrix} = DOL_s = \frac{\text{percentage change in } EBIT}{\text{percentage change in sales}} \qquad \textbf{(12-6)}$$

Applying equation (12-6) to our Pierce Grain data gives

$$DOL_{\$300,000} = \frac{120\%}{20\%} = 6 \text{ times}$$

Unless we understand what the specific measures of operating leverage tell us, the fact that we may know it is equal to six times is nothing more than sterile information. For Pierce Grain, the inference is that for *any* percentage fluctuation in sales from the base level, the percentage fluctuation in *EBIT* will be six times as great. If Pierce Grain expected only a 5 percent rise in sales over the coming period, a 30 percent rise in *EBIT* would be anticipated as follows:

$$(\text{Percentage change in sales}) \times (DOL_s) = \text{percentage change in } EBIT$$
$$(5\%) \times (6) = 30\%$$

We will now return to the postulated 20 percent change in sales. What if the direction of the fluctuation is expected to be negative rather than positive? What is in store for Pierce Grain? Unfortunately for Pierce Grain, but fortunately for the analytical process, we will see that the operating leverage measure holds in the negative direction as well. This situation is displayed in Table 12-3.

TABLE 12-3	Concept of Operating Leverage: Decrease in Pierce Grain Company Sales	
ITEM	**BASE SALES LEVEL, t**	**FORECAST SALES LEVEL, $t+1$**
Sales	$300,000	$240,000
Less: Total variable costs	180,000	144,000
Revenue before fixed costs	$120,000	$ 96,000
Less: Total fixed costs	100,000	100,000
EBIT	$ 20,000	$ −4,000

At the $240,000 sales level, which represents the 20 percent decrease from the base period, Pierce Grain's *EBIT* is expected to be –$4,000. How sensitive is *EBIT* to this sales change? The magnitude of the *EBIT* fluctuation is calculated as

$$\text{Percentage change in } EBIT = \frac{-\$4,000_{t+1} - \$20,000_t}{\$20,000_t}$$

$$= \frac{-\$24,000}{\$20,000}$$

$$= -120\%$$

Making use of our knowledge that the sales change was equal to –20 percent permits us to compute the specific measure of operating leverage as

$$DOL_{\$300,000} = \frac{-120\%}{-20\%} = 6 \text{ times}$$

What we have seen, then, is that the degree of operating leverage measure works in the positive or negative direction. A negative change in production volume and sales can be magnified severalfold when the effect on *EBIT* is calculated.

To this point our calculations of the degree of operating leverage have required two analytical income statements: one for the base period and a second for the subsequent period that incorporates the possible sales alteration. This cumbersome process can be simplified. If unit cost data are available to the financial manager, the relationship can be expressed directly in the following manner:

$$DOL_s = \frac{Q(P - V)}{Q(P - V) - F} \qquad \textbf{(12-7)}$$

Observe in equation (12-7) that the variables were all previously defined in our algebraic analysis of the break-even model. Recall that Pierce sells its product at $10 per unit, the unit variable cost is $6, and total fixed costs over the planning horizon are $100,000. Still assuming that Pierce is operating at a $300,000 sales volume, which means output (Q) is 30,000 units, we can find the degree of operating leverage by application of equation (12-7):

$$DOL_{\$300,000} = \frac{30,000(\$10 - \$6)}{30,000(\$10 - \$6) - \$100,000} = \frac{\$120,000}{\$20,000} = 6 \text{ times}$$

Whereas equation (12-7) requires us to know unit cost data to carry out the computations, the next formulation we examine does not. If we have an analytical income statement for the base period, then equation (12-8) can be employed to find the firm's degree of operating leverage:

$$DOL_s = \frac{\text{revenue before fixed costs}}{EBIT} = \frac{S - VC}{S - VC - F} \qquad \textbf{(12-8)}$$

Using equation (12-8) in conjunction with the base period data for Pierce Grain shown in Table 12-3 gives

$$DOL_{\$300,000} = \frac{\$120,000}{\$20,000} = 6 \text{ times}$$

The three versions of the operating leverage measure all produce the same result. Data availability will sometimes dictate which formulation can be applied. The crucial consideration, though, is that you grasp what the measurement tells you. For Pierce Grain, a 1 percent change in sales will produce a 6 percent change in *EBIT*.

Before we complete this discussion of operating leverage and move on to the subject of financial leverage, ask yourself, "Which type of leverage is more under the control of management?" You will probably (and correctly) come to the conclusion that the firm's managers have less control over the operating cost structure and almost complete control over its financial structure. What the firm actually produces, for example, will determine to a significant degree the division between fixed and variable costs. There is more room for substitution among the various sources of financial capital than there is among the labor and real capital inputs that enable the firm to meet its production requirements. Thus, you can anticipate more arguments over the choice to use a given degree of financial leverage than the corresponding choice over operating leverage use.

IMPLICATIONS

As the firm's scale of operations moves in a favorable manner above the break-even point, the degree of operating leverage at each subsequent (higher) sales base will decline. In short, the greater the sales level, the lower the degree of operating leverage. As long as some fixed operating costs are present in the firm's cost structure, however, operating leverage exists, and the degree of operating leverage (DOL_s) will exceed 1.00. Operating leverage is present, then, whenever the firm faces the following situation:

$$\frac{\text{Percentage change in } EBIT}{\text{percentage change in sales}} > 1.00$$

The greater the firm's degree of operating leverage, the more its profits will vary with a given percentage change in sales. Thus, operating leverage is definitely an attribute of the business risk that confronts the company. We know that the degree of operating leverage falls as sales increase past the firm's break-even point. The sheer size and operating profitability of the firm, therefore, affect and can lessen its business risk exposure.

The manager considering an alteration in the firm's cost structure will benefit from an understanding of the operating leverage concept. It might be possible to replace part of the labor force with capital equipment (machinery). A possible result is an increase in fixed costs associated with the new machinery and a reduction in variable costs attributable to a lower labor bill. This conceivably could raise the firm's degree of operating leverage at a specific sales base. If the prospects for future sales increases are high, then increasing the degree of operating leverage might be a prudent decision. The opposite conclusion will be reached if sales prospects are unattractive.

CONCEPT CHECK

1. If a firm's degree of operating leverage happens to be six times, what precisely does that mean?
2. What does the degree of operating leverage concept suggest when a negative shock in production volume and sales occurs?
3. When is operating leverage present in the firm's cost structure? What condition is necessary for operating leverage not to be present in the firm's cost structure?

Objective **3**

FINANCIAL LEVERAGE

We have defined *financial leverage* as the practice of financing a portion of the firm's assets with securities bearing a fixed rate of return in hopes of increasing the ultimate return to the common shareholders. In the present discussion we focus on the responsiveness of the company's earnings per share to changes in its *EBIT*. For the time being, then, the return to the common stockholder being concentrated on is earnings per share. We are *not* saying that earnings per share is the appropriate criterion for all financing decisions. In fact, the weakness of such a contention is examined later. Rather, the use of financial leverage produces a certain type of *effect*. This effect can be illustrated clearly by concentrating on an earnings-per-share criterion.

Let us assume that Pierce Grain Company is in the process of getting started as a going concern. The firm's potential owners have calculated that $200,000 is needed to purchase the

TABLE 12-4	Pierce Grain Company Possible Capital Structures

PLAN A: 0% DEBT

		Total debt	$ 0
		Common equity	200,000[a]
Total assets	$200,000	Total liabilities and equity	$200,000

PLAN B: 25% DEBT AT 8% INTEREST RATE

		Total debt	$ 50,000
		Common equity	150,000[b]
Total assets	$200,000	Total liabilities and equity	$200,000

PLAN C: 40% DEBT AT 8% INTEREST RATE

		Total debt	$ 80,000
		Common equity	120,000[c]
Total assets	$200,000	Total liabilities and equity	$200,000

[a] 2,000 common shares outstanding.   [b] 1,500 common shares outstanding.   [c] 1,200 common shares outstanding.

necessary assets to conduct the business. Three possible financing plans have been identified for raising the $200,000; they are presented in Table 12-4. In plan A no financial risk is assumed: The entire $200,000 is raised by selling 2,000 common shares, each with a $100 par value. In plan B a moderate amount of financial risk is assumed: 25 percent of the assets are financed with a debt issue that carries an 8 percent annual interest rate. Plan C would use the most financial leverage: 40 percent of the assets would be financed with a debt issue costing 8 percent.

Table 12-5 presents the impact of financial leverage on earnings per share associated with each fund-raising alternative. If *EBIT* should increase from $20,000 to $40,000, then earnings per share would rise by 100 percent under plan A. The same positive fluctuation in *EBIT* would occasion an earnings-per-share rise of 125 percent under plan B, and 147 percent

TABLE 12-5	Pierce Grain Company Analysis of Financial Leverage at Different *EBIT* Levels

(1)	(2)	(3) = (1) − (2)	(4) = (3) × .5	(5) = (3) − (4)	(6)
EBIT	INTEREST	*EBT*	TAXES	NET INCOME TO COMMON	EARNINGS PER SHARE
PLAN A: 0% DEBT; $200,000 COMMON EQUITY; 2,000 SHARES					
$ 0	$ 0	$ 0	$ 0	$ 0	$ 0
20,000	0	20,000	10,000	10,000	5.00 } 100%
40,000	0	40,000	20,000	20,000	10.00
60,000	0	60,000	30,000	30,000	15.00
80,000	0	80,000	40,000	40,000	20.00
PLAN B: 25% DEBT; 8% INTEREST RATE; $150,000 COMMON EQUITY; 1,500 SHARES					
$ 0	$4,000	$(4,000)	$(2,000)[a]	$(2,000)	$(1.33)
20,000	4,000	16,000	8,000	8,000	5.33 } 125%
40,000	4,000	36,000	18,000	18,000	12.00
60,000	4,000	56,000	28,000	28,000	18.67
80,000	4,000	76,000	38,000	38,000	25.33
PLAN C: 40% DEBT; 8% INTEREST RATE; $120,000 COMMON EQUITY; 1,200 SHARES					
$ 0	$6,400	$(6,400)	$(3,200)[a]	$(3,200)	$(2.67)
20,000	6,400	13,600	6,800	6,800	5.67 } 147%
40,000	6,400	33,600	16,800	16,800	14.00
60,000	6,400	53,600	26,800	26,800	22.33
80,000	6,400	73,600	36,800	36,800	30.67

[a] The negative tax bill recognizes the credit arising from the carryback and carryforward provision of the tax code.

under plan C. In plans B and C, the 100 percent increase in *EBIT* (from $20,000 to $40,000) is magnified to a greater than 100 percent increase in earnings per share. The firm is employing financial leverage and exposing its owners to financial risk when the following situation exists:

$$\frac{\text{Percentage change in earnings per share}}{\text{percentage change in } EBIT} > 1.00$$

By following the same general procedures that allowed us to analyze the firm's use of operating leverage, we can lay out a precise measure of financial leverage. Such a measure deals with the sensitivity of earnings per share to *EBIT* fluctuations. The relationship can be expressed as

$$\text{Degree of financial leverage } (DFL) \text{ from base } EBIT \text{ level} = DFL_{EBIT} = \frac{\text{percentage change in earnings per share}}{\text{percentage change in } EBIT} \tag{12-9}$$

Using equation (12-9) with each of the financing choices outlined for Pierce Grain yields the following. The base *EBIT* level is $20,000 in each case.

Plan A: $DFL_{\$20,000} = \dfrac{100\%}{100\%} = 1.00$ time

Plan B: $DFL_{\$20,000} = \dfrac{125\%}{100\%} = 1.25$ times

Plan C: $DFL_{\$20,000} = \dfrac{147\%}{100\%} = 1.47$ times

Like operating leverage, the *degree of financial leverage* concept performs in the negative direction as well as the positive. Should *EBIT* fall by 10 percent, Pierce Grain Company would suffer a 12.5 percent decline in earnings per share under plan B. If plan C were chosen to raise the necessary financial capital, the decline in earnings would be 14.7 percent. Observe that the greater the *DFL*, the greater the fluctuations (positive or negative) in earnings per share. The common shareholder is required to endure greater variations in returns when the firm's management chooses to use more financial leverage rather than less. The *DFL* measure allows the variation to be quantified.

Rather than take the time to compute percentage changes in *EBIT* and earnings per share, the *DFL* can be found directly, as follows:

$$DFL_{EBIT} = \frac{EBIT}{EBIT - I} \tag{12-10}$$

In equation (12-10) the variable *I* represents the total interest expense incurred on *all* the firm's contractual debt obligations. If six bonds are outstanding, *I* is the sum of the interest expense on all six bonds. If the firm has preferred stock in its financial structure, the dividend on such issues must be inflated to a before-tax basis and included in the computation of *I*.[4] In this latter instance, *I* is in reality the sum of all fixed financing costs.

Equation (12-10) has been applied to each of Pierce Grain's financing plans (Table 12-5) at a base *EBIT* level of $20,000. The results are as follows:

Plan A: $DFL_{\$20,000} = \dfrac{\$20,000}{\$20,000 - 0} = 1.00$ time

Plan B: $DFL_{\$20,000} = \dfrac{\$20,000}{\$20,000 - \$4,000} = 1.25$ times

Plan C: $DFL_{\$20,000} = \dfrac{\$20,000}{\$20,000 - \$6,400} = 1.47$ times

---

[4]Suppose (1) preferred dividends of $4,000 are paid annually by the firm and (2) it faces a 40 percent marginal tax rate. How much must the firm earn *before taxes* to make the $4,000 payment out of after-tax earnings? Because preferred dividends are not tax deductible to the paying company, we have $4,000/(1 − .40) = $6,666.67.

As you probably suspected, the measures of financial leverage shown previously are identical to those obtained by use of equation (12-10). This will always be the case.

COMBINATION OF OPERATING AND FINANCIAL LEVERAGE

Objective **4**

Changes in sales revenues cause greater changes in *EBIT*. Additionally, changes in *EBIT* translate into larger variations in both earnings per share (*EPS*) and total earnings available to the common shareholders (*EAC*), if the firm chooses to use financial leverage. It should be no surprise, then, to find out that combining operating and financial leverage causes rather large variations in earnings per share. This entire process is visually displayed in Figure 12-7.

Because the risk associated with possible earnings per share is affected by the use of combined or total leverage, it is useful to quantify the effect. To illustrate, we refer once more to Pierce Grain Company. The cost structure identified for Pierce Grain in our discussion of break-even analysis still holds. Furthermore, assume that plan B, which carried a 25 percent debt ratio, was chosen to finance the company's assets. Turn your attention to Table 12-6.

In Table 12-6 an increase in output for Pierce Grain from 30,000 to 36,000 units is analyzed. This increase represents a 20 percent rise in sales revenues. From our earlier discussion of operating leverage and the data in Table 12-6, we can see that this 20 percent increase in sales is magnified into a 120 percent rise in *EBIT*. From this base sales level of $300,000 the degree of operating leverage is 6 times.

The 120 percent rise in *EBIT* induces a change in earnings per share and earnings available to the common shareholders of 150 percent. The degree of financial leverage is therefore 1.25 times.

The upshot of the analysis is that the 20 percent rise in sales has been magnified to 150 percent, as reflected by the percentage change in earnings per share. The formal measure of combined leverage can be expressed as follows:

$$\begin{pmatrix} \text{Degree of combined} \\ \text{leverage from the} \\ \text{base sales level} \end{pmatrix} = DCL_s = \begin{pmatrix} \dfrac{\text{percentage change}}{\text{in earnings per share}} \\ \overline{\text{percentage change in sales}} \end{pmatrix} \qquad \textbf{(12-11)}$$

This equation was used in the bottom portion of Table 12-6 to determine that the degree of combined leverage from the base sales level of $300,000 is 7.50 times. Pierce

FIGURE 12-7 Leverage and Earnings Fluctuations

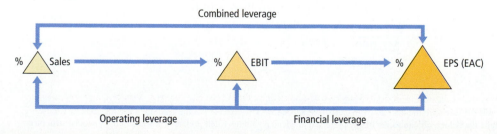

TABLE 12-6   Pierce Grain Company Combined Leverage Analysis

ITEM	BASE SALES LEVEL, t	FORECAST SALES LEVEL, $t+1$	SELECTED PERCENTAGE CHANGES
Sales	$300,000	$360,000	+ 20
Less: Total variable costs	180,000	216,000	
Revenue before fixed costs	$120,000	$144,000	
Less: Total fixed costs	100,000	100,000	
EBIT	$ 20,000	$ 44,000	+120
Less: Interest expense	4,000	4,000	
Earnings before taxes (EBT)	$ 16,000	$ 40,000	
Less: Taxes at 50%	8,000	20,000	
Net income	$ 8,000	$ 20,000	+150
Less: Preferred dividends	0	0	
Earnings available to common (EAC)	$ 8,000	$ 20,000	+150
Number of common shares	1,500	1,500	
Earnings per share (EPS)	$ 5.33	$ 13.33	+150

$$\text{Degree of operating leverage} = DOL_{\$300,000} = \frac{120\%}{20\%} = 6 \text{ times}$$

$$\text{Degree of financial leverage} = DFL_{\$20,000} = \frac{150\%}{120\%} = 1.25 \text{ times}$$

$$\text{Degree of combined leverage} = DCL_{\$300,000} = \frac{150\%}{20\%} = 7.50 \text{ times}$$

Grain's use of both operating and financial leverage will cause any percentage change in sales (from the specific base level) to be magnified by a factor of 7.50 when the effect on earnings per share is computed. A 1 percent change in sales, for example, will result in a 7.50 percent change in earnings per share.

Notice that the degree of combined leverage is actually the product (not the simple sum) of the two independent leverage measures. Thus, we have

$$(DOL_s) \times (DFL_{EBIT}) = DCL_s \qquad \text{(12-12)}$$

or

$$(6) \times (1.25) = 7.50 \text{ times}$$

It is possible to ascertain the degree of combined leverage in a direct fashion, without determining any percentage fluctuations or the separate leverage values. We need only substitute the appropriate values into equation (12-13):[5]

$$DCL_s = \frac{Q(P-V)}{Q(P-V) - F - I} \qquad \text{(12-13)}$$

The variable definitions in equation (12-13) are the same ones that have been employed throughout this chapter. Use of equation (12-13) with the information in Table 12-6 gives

$$
\begin{aligned}
DCL_{\$300,000} &= \frac{30,000(\$10 - \$6)}{30,000(\$10 - \$6) - \$100,000 - \$4,000} \\
&= \frac{\$120,000}{\$16,000} \\
&= 7.5 \text{ times}
\end{aligned}
$$

---

[5]As was the case with the degree-of-financial-leverage metric, the variable I in the combined leverage measure must include the before-tax equivalent of any preferred dividend payments when preferred stock is in the financial structure.

FINANCIAL MANAGEMENT
IN PRACTICE

COCA–COLA FINANCIAL POLICIES

Because financial leverage effects can be measured, management has the opportunity to formally shape corporate policy around the decision to use or avoid the use of leverage-inducing financial instruments (primarily debt issues). One company with very specific policies on the use of financial leverage is the Coca-Cola Company. The following discussion is from that firm's 1990 *Annual Report*.

Note how several of the key concepts and techniques presented throughout this book are mentioned in this excerpt. For example, mention is made of (1) the firm's primary objective, (2) its weighted average cost of capital, (3) investment risk characteristics, (4) the prudent use of debt capital, and (5) borrowing capacity.

Management's primary objective is to increase shareholder value over time. To accomplish this objective, the Coca-Cola Company and subsidiaries (the Company) have developed a comprehensive business strategy that emphasizes maximizing long-term cash flow by expanding its global business systems, increasing gallon sales, improving margins, investing in areas offering attractive returns and maintaining an appropriate capital structure.

Management seeks investments that strategically enhance existing operations and offer long-term cash returns that exceed the Company's weighted average cost of capital. For investments with risk characteristics similar to the soft drink industry and assuming a net-debt-to-capital ratio ceiling of 35 percent, that cost of capital is estimated by management to be approximately 12 percent after taxes.

The Company utilizes prudent amounts of debt to lower its overall cost of capital and increase its total return to shareholders. The Company has established a net-debt-to-net-capital ratio ceiling of 35 percent. Net debt is defined as total debt less excess cash, cash equivalents, and current marketable securities. Excluding the Company's finance subsidiary, net debt represented 22.8 percent of net capital at December 31, 1990.

Additional borrowing capacity within the 35 percent debt ceiling was approximately $940 million at December 31, 1990, excluding the Company's finance subsidiary. The Company anticipates using this additional borrowing capacity principally to fund investment opportunities that meet its strategic and financial objectives and, as a second priority, to fund the share repurchase program.

Source: Excerpt from *1990 Annual Report*, Coca-Cola Company, pp. 32–34. Used with permission.

IMPLICATIONS

The total risk exposure the firm assumes can be managed by combining operating and financial leverage in different degrees. Knowledge of the various leverage measures helps the financial officer determine the proper level of overall risk that should be accepted. If a high degree of business risk is inherent in the specific line of commercial activity, then a low posture regarding financial risk would minimize additional earnings fluctuations stemming from sales changes. Conversely, the firm that by its very nature incurs a low level of fixed operating costs might choose to use a high degree of financial leverage in the hope of increasing earnings per share and the rate of return on the common equity investment. Table 12-7 summarizes the salient concepts and calculation formats discussed thus far in this chapter.

CONCEPT CHECK

1. Explain the degree of combined leverage concept.
2. When would the degree of operating leverage and the degree of combined leverage be equal?

PLANNING THE FINANCING MIX

Objective **5**

Given our understanding of both operating and financial leverage, we now direct our attention to the determination of an appropriate financing mix for the firm. First, we must distinguish between financial structure and capital structure. **Financial structure** is the *mix of all items that appear on the right-hand side of the company's balance sheet*. **Capital structure** is the *mix of the long-term sources of funds used by the firm*. The relationship between financial and capital structures can be expressed in equation form:

financial structure
capital structure

(Financial structure) – (current liabilities) = capital structure   **(12-14)**

TABLE 12-7   Summary of Leverage Concepts and Calculations

TECHNIQUE	DESCRIPTION OR CONCEPT	CALCULATION	TEXT REFERENCE
BREAK-EVEN ANALYSIS			
1. Break-even point quantity	Total fixed costs divided by the unit contribution margin	$Q_B = \dfrac{F}{P-V}$	(12-4)
2. Break-even sales level	Total fixed costs divided by 1 minus the ratio of total variable costs to the associated level of sales	$S^* = \dfrac{F}{1 - \dfrac{VC}{S}}$	(12-5)
OPERATING LEVERAGE			
3. Degree of operating leverage	Percentage change in *EBIT* divided by the percentage change in sales; or revenue before fixed costs divided by revenue after fixed costs	$DOL_s = \dfrac{Q(P-V)}{Q(P-V)-F}$	(12-7)
FINANCIAL LEVERAGE			
4. Degree of financial leverage	Percentage change in earnings per share divided by the percentage change in *EBIT*; or *EBIT* divided by *EBT*[a]	$DFL_{EBIT} = \dfrac{EBIT}{EBIT-I}$	(12-10)
COMBINED LEVERAGE			
5. Degree of combined leverage	Percentage change in earnings per share divided by the percentage change in sales; or revenue before fixed costs divided by *EBT*[a]	$DCL_s = \dfrac{Q(P-V)}{Q(P-V)-F-I}$	(12-13)

[a] The use of *EBT* here presumes no preferred dividend payments. In the presence of preferred dividend payments, replace *EBT* with earnings available to common stock (*EAC*).

Prudent financial structure design requires answers to these two questions:

1. What should be the maturity composition of the firm's sources of funds; in other words, how should a firm best divide its total fund sources between short- and long-term components?
2. In what proportions relative to the total should the various forms of permanent financing be utilized?

The major influence on the maturity structure of the financing plans is the nature of the assets owned by the firm. A company heavily committed to real capital investment, represented primarily by fixed assets on its balance sheet, should finance those assets with permanent (long-term) types of financial capital. Furthermore, the permanent portion of the firm's investment in current assets should likewise be financed with permanent capital. Alternatively, assets held on a temporary basis are to be financed with temporary sources.

TABLE 12-8   Balance Sheet

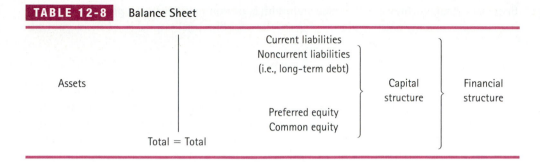

The present discussion assumes that the bulk of the company's current liabilities are comprised of temporary capital.

Accordingly, our focus in this chapter is on answering the second.of the two questions noted previously—this process is usually called *capital structure management*.

The objective of capital structure management is to mix the permanent sources of funds used by the firm in a manner that will maximize the company's common stock price. Alternatively, this objective may be viewed as a search for the *funds mix that will minimize the firm's composite cost of capital*. We can call this proper mix of funds sources the **optimal capital structure**.

optimal capital structure

Table 12-8 looks at equation (12-14) in terms of a simplified balance sheet format. It helps us visualize the overriding problem of capital structure management. The sources of funds that give rise to financing fixed costs (long-term debt and preferred equity) must be combined with common equity in the proportions most suitable to the investment marketplace. If that mix can be found, then holding all other factors constant, the firm's common stock price will be maximized.

Although equation (12-14) quite accurately indicates that the corporate capital structure may be viewed as an absolute dollar amount, the real capital structure problem is one of balancing the array of funds sources in a proper manner. Our use of the term *capital structure* emphasizes this latter problem of relative magnitude, or proportions.

It pays to understand the essential components of capital structure theory. The assumption of excessive financial risk can put the firm into bankruptcy proceedings. Some argue that the decision to use little financial leverage results in an undervaluation of the firm's shares in the marketplace. The effective financial manager must know how to find the area of optimum financial leverage use—this will enhance share value, all other considerations held constant. Thus, grasping the theory will make you better able to formulate a sound financial structure policy.

The rest of this chapter covers three main areas. First, we briefly discuss the theory of capital structure to provide a perspective. Second, we examine the basic tools of capital structure management. We conclude with a real-world look at actual capital structure management.

CONCEPT CHECK

1. What is the objective of capital structure management?
2. What is the main attribute of a firm's optimal capital structure?

A QUICK LOOK AT CAPITAL STRUCTURE THEORY

Objective **6**

An enduring controversy within financial theory concerns the effect of financial leverage on the overall cost of capital to the enterprise. The heart of the argument may be stated in the form of a question:

Can the firm affect its overall cost of funds, either favorably or unfavorably, by varying the mixture of financing sources used?

This controversy has taken many elegant forms in the finance literature. Most of these presentations appeal more to academics than financial management practitioners. To emphasize the ingredients of capital structure theory that have practical applications for business financial management, we will pursue an intuitive, or nonmathematical, approach to reach a better understanding of the underpinnings of this cost of capital–capital structure argument.

IMPORTANCE OF CAPITAL STRUCTURE

It makes economic sense for the firm to strive to minimize the cost of using financial capital. Both capital costs and other costs, such as manufacturing costs, share a common characteristic in that they potentially reduce the size of the cash dividend that could be paid to common stockholders.

We saw in Chapters 7 and 8 that the ultimate value of a share of common stock depends in part on the returns investors expect to receive from holding the stock. Cash dividends comprise all (in the case of an infinite holding period) or part (in the case of a holding period less than infinity) of these expected returns. Now, hold constant all factors that could affect share price except capital costs. If these capital costs could be kept at a minimum, the dividend stream flowing to the common stockholders would be maximized. This, in turn, would maximize the firm's common stock price.

If the firm's cost of capital can be affected by its capital structure, then capital structure management is clearly an important subset of business financial management.

ANALYTICAL SETTING

The essentials of the capital structure controversy are best highlighted within a framework that economists would call a "partial equilibrium analysis." In a partial equilibrium analysis, changes that do occur in several factors and have an impact on a certain key item are ignored to study the effect of changes in a main factor on that same item of interest. Here, two items are simultaneously of interest: (1) K_0, the firm's composite cost of capital, and (2) P_0, the market price of the firm's common stock. The firm's use of financial leverage is the main factor that is allowed to vary in the analysis. This means that important financial decisions, such as investing policy and dividend policy, are held constant throughout the discussion. We are only concerned with the effect of changes in the financing mix on share price and capital costs.

Consider a rarified economic world in which

1. corporate income is not subject to taxation;
2. capital structures consist only of stocks and bonds;
3. investors make homogeneous forecasts of net operating income (what we earlier called *EBIT*); and
4. securities are traded in perfect or efficient markets.

In this market setting, the direct answer to our question, "Can the firm affect its overall cost of funds, either favorably or unfavorably, by varying the mixture of financing sources used?" would be no. This view of capital structure importance was put into rather elegant form back in 1958 by two well-known financial economists, Franco Modigliani and Merton Miller, both of whom have been awarded the Nobel Prize in economics.

The Modigliani and Miller hypothesis, or the MM view, puts forth that within the perfect economic world previously described, the total market value of the firm's outstanding securities will be *unaffected* by the manner in which the right-hand side of the balance sheet is arranged. This means the sum of the market value of outstanding common stock plus outstanding debt will always be the same regardless of how much or little debt is actually used by the company. This MM view is sometimes called the *independence hypothesis*, as firm value is independent of capital structure design.[6]

---

[6]See Franco Modigliani and Merton H. Miller, "The Cost of Capital, Corporation Finance, and the Theory of Investment," *American Economic Review* 48 (June 1958), pp. 261–97; Modigliani and Miller, "Corporate Income Taxes and the Cost of Capital: A Correction," *American Economic Review* 53 (June 1963), pp. 433–43; and Merton H. Miller, "Debt and Taxes," *Journal of Finance* 32 (May 1977), pp. 261–75. The Modigliani–Miller capital structure theories and positions are put into a longer and broader perspective in Merton H. Miller, "The Modigliani–Miller Propositions after Thirty Years," in Joel Stern and Donald Chew, eds., *The Revolution in Corporate Finance*, 3rd ed. (Malden, MA: Blackwell Publishers Ltd., 1998), pp. 99–110. A most readable review of the Modigliani–Miller propositions is provided by D. Gifford, Jr., "After the Revolution," *CFO*, Vol. 14, No. 7 (July 1998), pp. 75–79. This source is widely followed by practicing financial professionals.

FIGURE 12-8 Firm Value and Capital Structure Design

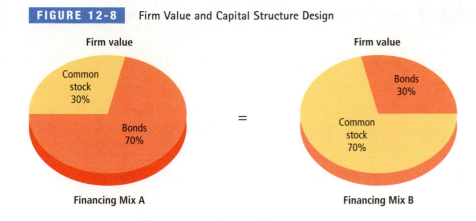

FIGURE 12-8 Firm Value and Capital Structure Design

The crux of this position on financing choice is illustrated in Figure 12-8. Here the firm's asset mix (i.e., the left-hand side of the balance sheet) is held constant. All that is different is the way the assets are financed. Under financing mix A, the firm funds 30 percent of its assets with common stock and the other 70 percent with bonds. Under financing mix B, the firm reverses this mix and funds 70 percent of the assets with common stock and only 30 percent with bonds. From our earlier discussions we know that financing mix A is the more heavily levered plan.

Notice, however, that the size of each "pie" in Figure 12-8 is exactly the same. The pie represents firm value—the total market value of the firm's outstanding securities. Thus, total firm value associated with financing mix A equals that associated with financing mix B. Firm value is *independent* of the actual financing mix that has been chosen.

This implication is taken further in Figures 12-9 and 12-10. They display how (1) the firm's cost of funds and (2) common stock price, P_0, relate to the firm's financing mix. In Figure 12-9 we see that the firm's overall cost of capital, K_0, is unaffected by an increased use of financial leverage. If more debt is used with a cost of K_d in the capital structure, the cost of common equity, k_c, will rise at the same rate additional earnings are generated. This will keep the composite cost of capital to the corporation unchanged. Figure 12-10 shows that because the overall cost of capital will not change with the leverage use, neither will the firm's common stock price.

The lesson of this view on financing choices is that debt financing is not as cheap as it first appears to be. This will keep the composite cost of funds constant over the full range of financial leverage use. The stark implication for financial officers is that one capital structure is just as good as any other.

Recall, though, the strict economic world in which this viewpoint was developed. We next turn to a market and legal environment that relaxes the extreme assumptions.

FIGURE 12-9 Capital Costs and Financial Leverage: No Taxes—Independence Hypothesis

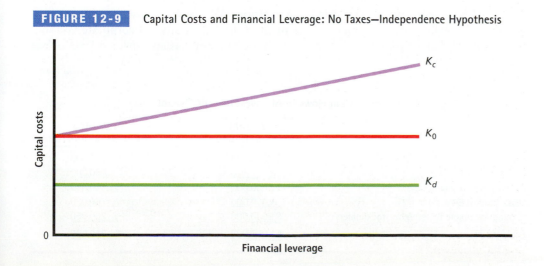

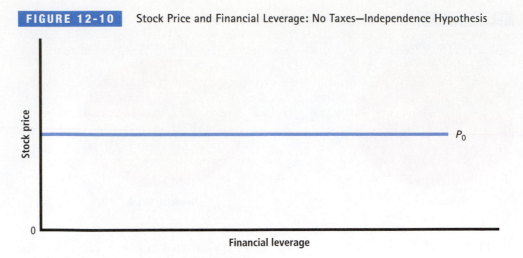

FIGURE 12-10   Stock Price and Financial Leverage: No Taxes—Independence Hypothesis

---

BACK TO THE FOUNDATIONS

*The suggestion from capital structure theory that one capital structure is just as good as any other within a perfect ("pure") market framework relies directly on **Principle 1: The Risk–Return Trade-Off—We Won't Take On Added Risk Unless We Expect to Be Compensated with Additional Return**. This means that using more debt in the capital structure will not be ignored by investors in the financial markets. These rational investors will require a higher return on common stock investments in the firm that uses more leverage (rather than less) to compensate for the increased uncertainty stemming from the addition of the debt securities in the capital structure.*

MODERATE POSITION: CORPORATE INCOME IS TAXED AND FIRMS MAY FAIL

We turn now to a description of the cost of capital–capital structure relationship that has rather wide appeal to both business practitioners and academics. This moderate view (1) admits to the fact that interest expense is tax deductible and (2) acknowledges that the probability of the firm's suffering bankruptcy costs is directly related to the company's use of financial leverage.

TAX DEDUCTIBILITY OF INTEREST EXPENSE

This portion of the analysis recognizes that corporate income is subject to taxation. Furthermore, we assume that interest expense is tax deductible for purposes of computing the firm's tax bill. In this environment, the use of debt financing should result in a higher total market value for the firm's outstanding securities. We see why subsequently.

Table 12-9 illustrates this important element of the U.S. system of corporate taxation. It is assumed that Skip's Camper Manufacturing Company has an expected level of net

---

TABLE 12-9   Skip's Camper Cash Flows to All Investors—The Case of Taxes

	UNLEVERED CAPITAL STRUCTURE	LEVERED CAPITAL STRUCTURE
Expected level of net operating income	$2,000,000	$2,000,000
Less: Interest expense	0	480,000
Earnings before taxes	$2,000,000	$1,520,000
Less: Taxes at 50%	1,000,000	760,000
Earnings available to common stockholders	$1,000,000	$ 760,000
Expected payments to *all* security holders	$1,000,000	$1,240,000

operating income (*EBIT*) of $2 million and faces a corporate tax rate (made simple for example purposes) of 50 percent. Two financing plans are analyzed. The first is an unlevered capital structure. The other assumes that Skip's Camper has $8 million of bonds outstanding that carry an interest rate of 6 percent per year.

Notice that if corporate income were *not* taxed, then earnings before taxes of $2 million per year could be paid to shareholders, in the form of cash dividends or to bond investors in the form of interest payments, or any combination of the two. This means that the *sum* of the cash flows that Skip's Camper could pay to its contributors of debt or equity is *not* affected by its financing mix.

When corporate income is taxed by the government, however, the sum of the cash flows made to all contributors of financial capital is *affected* by the firm's financing mix. Table 12-9 illustrates this point.

If Skip's Camper chooses the levered capital structure, the total payments to equity and debt holders will be $240,000 *greater* than under the all-common-equity capitalization. Where does this $240,000 come from? The government's take, through taxes collected, is lower by that amount. This *difference, which flows to the* Skip's Camper *security holders*, is called the **tax shield** on interest. In general, it may be calculated by equation (12-15), where r_d is the interest rate paid on the debt, M is the principal amount of the debt, and t is the firm's marginal tax rate:

tax shield

$$\text{Tax shield} = r_d(M)(t) \tag{12-15}$$

The moderate position on the importance of capital structure presumes that the tax shield must have value in the marketplace. Accordingly, this tax benefit will increase the total market value of the firm's outstanding securities relative to the all-equity capitalization. Financial leverage does affect firm value. Because the cost of capital is just the other side of the valuation coin, financial leverage also affects the firm's composite cost of capital. Can the firm increase firm value indefinitely and lower its cost of capital continuously by using more and more financial leverage? Common sense would tell us no! So would most financial managers and academicians. The acknowledgment of bankruptcy costs provides one possible rationale.

BACK TO THE FOUNDATIONS

The preceding section on the "Tax Deductibility of Interest Expense" is a compelling example of **Principle 8: Taxes Bias Business Decisions**. We have just seen that corporations have an important incentive provided by the tax code to finance projects with debt securities rather than new issues of common stock. The interest expense on the debt issue is tax deductible. The common stock dividends are not tax deductible. So firms can indeed increase their total after-tax cash flows available to all investors in their securities by using financial leverage. This element of the U.S. tax code should also remind you of **Principle 3: Cash—Not Profits—Is King**.

THE LIKELIHOOD OF FIRM FAILURE

The probability that the firm will be unable to meet the financial obligations identified in its debt contracts increases as more debt is employed. The highest costs would be incurred if the firm actually went into bankruptcy proceedings. Here, assets would be liquidated. If we admit that these assets might sell for something less than their perceived market values, both equity investors and debt holders could suffer losses. Other problems accompany bankruptcy proceedings. Lawyers and accountants have to be hired and paid. Managers must spend time preparing lengthy reports for those involved in the legal action.

Milder forms of financial distress also have their costs. As their firm's financial condition weakens, creditors may take action to restrict normal business activity. Suppliers may not deliver materials on credit. Profitable capital investments may have to be forgone, and dividend payments may even be interrupted. At some point the expected cost of default will be large enough to outweigh the tax shield advantage of debt financing. The firm will turn to other sources of financing, mainly common equity. At this point the real cost of debt is thought to be higher than the real cost of common equity.

FIGURE 12-11 Capital Costs and Financial Leverage: The Moderate View, Considering Taxes and Financial Distress

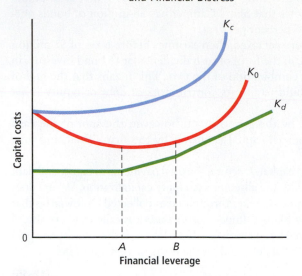

MODERATE VIEW: SAUCER-SHAPED COST OF CAPITAL CURVE

Objective **7**

This moderate view of the relationship between financing mix and the firm's cost of capital is depicted in Figure 12-11. The result is a saucer-shaped (or U-shaped) average cost of capital curve, K_0. The firm's average cost of equity, K_c, is seen to rise over all positive degrees of financial leverage use. For a while the firm can borrow funds at a relatively low after-tax cost of debt, K_d. Even though the cost of equity is rising, it does not rise at a fast enough rate to offset the use of the less-expensive debt financing. Thus, between points 0 and A on the financial-leverage axis, the average cost of capital declines and stock price rises.

Eventually, the threat of financial distress causes the cost of debt to rise. In Figure 12-11 this increase in the cost of debt shows up in the after-tax average cost of debt curve, K_d, at point A. Between points A and B, mixing debt and equity funds produces an average cost of capital that is (relatively) flat. The firm's **optimal range of financial leverage** lies between points A and B. *All capital structures between these two points are optimal because they produce the lowest composite cost of capital.* As we said earlier in this chapter, finding this optimal range of financing mixes is the objective of capital structure management.

optimal range of financial leverage

debt capacity

Point B signifies the firm's debt capacity. **Debt capacity** is the *maximum proportion of debt the firm can include in its capital structure and still maintain its lowest composite cost of capital.* Beyond point B, additional fixed-charge capital can be attracted only at very costly interest rates. At the same time, this excessive use of financial leverage would cause the firm's cost of equity to rise at a faster rate than previously. The composite cost of capital would then rise quite rapidly, and the firm's stock price would decline.

FIRM VALUE AND AGENCY COSTS

Objective **8**

In Chapter 1 we mentioned the agency problem. Recall that the agency problem gives rise to agency costs, which tend to occur in business organizations because ownership and management control are often separate. Thus, the firm's managers can properly be thought of as agents for the firm's stockholders.[7] To ensure that agent-managers act in the stockholders' best interests requires that (1) they have proper incentives to do so and (2) their deci-

[7]Economists have studied the problems associated with control of the corporation for decades. An early, classic work on this topic was A. A. Berle, Jr., and G. C. Means, *The Modern Corporation and Private Property* (New York: Macmillan, 1932). The recent emphasis in corporate finance and financial economics stems from the important contribution of Michael C. Jensen and William H. Meckling, "Theory of the Firm: Managerial Behavior, Agency Costs, and Ownership Structure," *Journal of Financial Economics* 3 (October 1976), pp. 305–60. Professors Jensen and Clifford Smith have analyzed the bondholder–stockholder conflict in a very clear style. See Michael C. Jensen and Clifford W. Smith, Jr., "Stockholder, Manager, and Creditor Interests: Applications of Agency Theory," in Edward I. Altman and Marti G. Subrahmanyam, eds., *Recent Advances in Corporate Finance* (Homewood, IL: Irwin, 1985), pp. 93–131.

sions are monitored. The incentives usually take the form of executive compensation plans and perquisites. The perquisites, though, might be a bloated support staff, country club memberships, luxurious corporate planes, or other amenities. Monitoring requires that certain costs be borne by the stockholders, such as (1) bonding the managers, (2) auditing financial statements, (3) structuring the organization in unique ways that limit useful managerial decisions, and (4) reviewing the costs and benefits of management perquisites. This list is indicative, not exhaustive. The main point is that monitoring costs are ultimately covered by the owners of the company—its common stockholders.

Capital structure management also gives rise to agency costs. Agency problems stem from conflicts of interest, and capital structure management encompasses a natural conflict between stockholders and bondholders. Acting in the stockholders' best interests might cause management to invest in extremely risky projects. Existing investors in the firm's bonds could logically take a dim view of such an investment policy. A change in the risk structure of the firm's assets would change the business risk exposure of the firm. This could lead to a downward revision of the bond rating the firm currently enjoys. A lowered bond rating in turn would lower the current market value of the firm's bonds. Clearly, bondholders would be unhappy with this result.

To reduce this conflict of interest, the creditors (bond investors) and stockholders may agree to include several protective covenants in the bond contract. These bond convenants are discussed in more detail in Chapter 7, but essentially they may be thought of as restrictions on managerial decision making. Typical covenants restrict payment of cash dividends on common stock, limit the acquisition or sale of assets, or limit further debt financing. To make sure management complies with the protective covenants means that monitoring costs are incurred. Like all monitoring costs, they are borne by common stockholders. Furthermore, like many costs, they involve the analysis of an important trade-off.

Figure 12-12 displays some of the trade-offs involved with the use of protective bond covenants. Note (in the left panel of Figure 12-12) that the firm might be able to sell bonds that carry no protective covenants only by incurring very high interest rates. With no protective covenants, there are no associated monitoring costs. Also, there are no lost operating efficiencies, such as being able to move quickly to acquire a particular company in the acquisitions market. Conversely, the willingness to submit to several covenants could reduce the explicit cost of the debt contract, but would involve incurring significant monitoring costs and losing some operating efficiencies (which also translates into higher costs). When the debt issue is first sold, then a trade-off will be arrived at among incurring monitoring costs, losing operating efficiencies, and enjoying a lower explicit interest cost.

Next, we have to consider the presence of monitoring costs at low and higher levels of leverage. When the firm operates at a low debt-to-equity ratio, there is little need for creditors to insist on a long list of bond covenants. The financial risk is just not there to require that type of activity. The firm will likewise benefit from low explicit interest rates when leverage is low. When the debt-to-equity ratio is high, however, it is logical for creditors to demand a great deal of monitoring. This increase in agency costs will raise the implicit cost (the true total cost) of debt financing. It seems logical, then, to suggest that monitoring costs will rise as the firm's use of financial leverage increases. Just as the likelihood of firm failure (financial distress) raises a company's overall cost of capital (K_0), so do agency costs. On the other side of the coin, this means that total firm value (the total market value of the

---

FIGURE 12-12   Agency Costs of Debt: Trade-Offs

No protective bond covenants	Many protective bond covenants
High interest rates	Low interest rates
Low monitoring costs	High monitoring costs
No lost operating efficiencies	Many lost operating efficiencies

FIGURE 12-13   Firm Value Considering Taxes, Agency Costs, and Financial Distress Costs

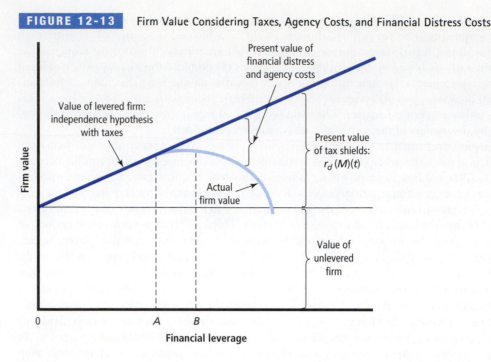

firm's securities) will be *lower* because of agency costs. Taken together, the agency costs and the costs associated with financial distress argue in favor of the concept of an *optimal* capital structure for the individual firm.

This discussion can be summarized by introducing equation (12-16) for the market value of the levered firm.

$$\begin{array}{c}\text{Market value of}\\\text{levered firm}\end{array} = \begin{array}{c}\text{market value of}\\\text{unlevered firm}\end{array} + \begin{array}{c}\text{present value}\\\text{of tax shields}\end{array} - \left(\begin{array}{cc}\text{present value} & \text{present value}\\\text{of financial} + \text{of agency}\\\text{distress costs} & \text{costs}\end{array}\right) \quad \textbf{(12-16)}$$

The relationship expressed in equation (12-16) is presented graphically in Figure 12-13. There we see that the tax shield effect is dominant until point *A* is reached. After point *A*, the rising costs of the likelihood of firm failure (financial distress) and agency costs cause the market value of the levered firm to decline. The objective for the financial manager here is to find point *B* by using all of his or her analytical skill; this must also include a good dose of seasoned judgment. At point *B* the actual market value of the levered firm is maximized, and its composite cost of capital (K_0) is at a minimum. The implementation problem is that the precise costs of financial distress and monitoring can only be estimated by subjective means; a definite mathematical solution is not available. Thus, planning the firm's financing mix always requires good decision making and management judgment.

AGENCY COSTS, FREE CASH FLOW, AND CAPITAL STRUCTURE

In 1986, Professor Michael C. Jensen further extended the concept of agency costs into the area of capital structure management. The contribution revolves around a concept that Jensen labels "free cash flow," which he defines as follows:

> Free cash flow is cash flow in excess of that required to fund all projects that have positive net present values when discounted at the relevant cost of capital.[8]

Jensen then proposes that substantial free cash flow can lead to misbehavior by managers and poor decisions that are not in the best interests of the firm's common stockholders.

---

[8]Michael C. Jensen, "Agency Costs of Free Cash Flow, Corporate Finance, and Takeovers," *American Economic Review* 76 (May 1986), pp. 323–29.

In other words, managers have an incentive to hold on to the free cash flow and have "fun" with it, rather than "disgorge" it, say, in the form of higher cash dividend payments.

But all is not lost. This leads to what Jensen calls his "control hypothesis" for debt creation. This means that by levering up, the firm's shareholders will enjoy increased control over their management team. For example, if the firm issues new debt and uses the proceeds to retire outstanding common stock, then management is obligated to pay out cash to service the debt—this simultaneously reduces the amount of free cash flow available to management to have fun with.

We can also refer to this motive for financial leverage use as the "threat hypothesis." Management works under the threat of financial failure; therefore, according to the "free cash flow theory of capital structure," it works more efficiently. This is supposed to reduce the agency costs of free cash flow, which will in turn be recognized by the marketplace in the form of greater returns on the common stock.

BACK TO THE FOUNDATIONS

*The discussions on agency costs, free cash flow, and the control hypothesis for debt creation return us to **Principle 7: The Agency Problem—Managers Won't Work for the Owners Unless It's in Their Best Interest**. The control hypothesis put forth by Jensen suggests that managers will work harder for shareholder interests when they have to "sweat it out" to meet contractual interest payments on debt securities. But we also learned that managers and bond investors can have a conflict that leads to agency costs associated with using debt capital. Thus, the theoretical benefits that flow from minimizing the agency costs of free cash flow by using more debt will cease when the rising agency costs of debt exactly offset those benefits. You can see how very difficult it is, then, for financial managers to identify precisely their true optimal capital structure.*

Note that the free cash flow theory of capital structure does not give a theoretical solution to the question of just how much financial leverage is enough. Nor does it suggest how much leverage is too much leverage. It is a way of thinking about why shareholders and their boards of directors might use more debt to control management behavior and decisions. The basic decision tools of capital structure management still have to be utilized. They are presented later in this chapter.

MANAGERIAL IMPLICATIONS

Where does our examination of capital structure theory leave us? The upshot is that the determination of the firm's financing mix is centrally important to the financial manager. The firm's stockholders are affected by capital structure decisions.

At the very least, and before bankruptcy costs and agency costs become detrimental, the tax shield effect will cause the shares of a levered firm to sell at a higher price than they would if the company had avoided debt financing. Because both the risk of failure and agency costs accompany the excessive use of leverage, the financial manager must exercise caution in the use of fixed-charge capital. This problem of searching for the optimal range of use of financial leverage is our next task.[9]

You have now developed a workable knowledge of capital structure theory. This makes you better equipped to search for your firm's optimal capital structure. Several tools are available to help you in this search process and simultaneously help you make prudent financing choices. These tools are decision oriented. They help us answer the question, The next time we need $20 million, should we issue common stock or sell long-term bonds?

---

[9] The relationship between capital structure and enterprise valuation by the marketplace continues to stimulate considerable research output. The complexity of the topic is reviewed in Stewart C. Myers, "The Capital Structure Puzzle," *Journal of Finance* 39 (July 1984), pp. 575–92. Ten useful papers are contained in Benjamin M. Friedman, ed., *Corporate Capital Structures in the United States* (Chicago: National Bureau of Economic Research and University of Chicago Press, 1985). A more recent treatment is Stewart C. Myers, "Still Searching for Optimal Capital Structure," in Joel Stern and Donald Chew, eds., *The Revolution in Corporate Finance*, 3rd ed. (Malden, MA: Blackwell Publishers Ltd., 1998), pp. 120–30.

FINANCIAL MANAGEMENT
IN PRACTICE

GEORGIA-PACIFIC ON CAPITAL STRUCTURE

The discussion that follows illustrates the care that Georgia-Pacific's key officers place on managing its financing mix.

As you read the discussion, notice that (1) Georgia-Pacific actually uses the weighted average cost of capital concept that you studied in Chapter 11; (2) the firm subscribes to what we called the "moderate view" of the relationship between financing mix and the company's average cost of capital [see Learning Objective 7]; and (3) the firm's management directly relates the stage of the aggregate business cycle to its capital structure planning process.

Georgia-Pacific tries to balance the mix of debt and equity in a way that will benefit our shareholders, by keeping our weighted average cost of capital low, while retaining the flexibility needed to finance attractive internal projects or acquisitions. Risk factors that contribute to the volatility of our cash flows include economic cycles, changes in industry capacity, environmental regulations and litigation.

On a market-value basis, our debt-to-capital ratio was 47 percent (year-end 1996). By employing this capital structure, we believe that our weighted average cost of capital is nearly optimized at approximately 10 percent. Although reducing debt significantly would somewhat reduce the marginal cost of debt, significant debt reduction would likely increase our weighted average cost of capital by raising the proportion of higher-cost equity.

Considering Georgia-Pacific's ability to generate strong cash flow—even at the bottom of the cycle—we believe the current debt structure is quite manageable. In fact, combining the lowest full-year cash flows from building products and pulp and paper operations over recent business cycles would still provide enough cash to pay taxes, cover interest on $5.5 billion of debt, pay dividends, and fund several hundred million dollars of reinvestment needed to maintain our facilities in competitive condition.

Source: Georgia-Pacific, *1996 Annual Report*, p. 15.

CONCEPT CHECK

1. What is the enduring controversy within the subject of capital structure theory?
2. Name the two financial economists, both of whom have won the Nobel Prize in economics, who back in 1958 challenged the importance of capital structure management.
3. Explain the independence hypothesis as it relates to capital structure management.
4. Explain the moderate view of the relationship between a firm's financing mix and its average cost of capital.
5. How do agency costs and free cash flow relate to capital structure management?

Objective **9**

BASIC TOOLS OF CAPITAL STRUCTURE MANAGEMENT

Recall from our earlier work that the use of financial leverage has two effects on the earnings stream flowing to the firm's common stockholders. For clarity, Tables 12-4 and 12-5 are repeated here as Tables 12-10 and 12-11. Three possible financing mixes for Pierce Grain Company are contained in Table 12-10, and an analysis for the corresponding financial-leverage effects is displayed in Table 12-11.

The first financial-leverage effect is the added variability in the earnings-per-share stream that accompanies the use of fixed-charge securities in the company's capital structure. By means of the degree-of-financial-leverage measure (DFL_{EBIT}), we explained how this variability can be quantified. The firm that uses more financial leverage (rather than less) will experience larger relative changes in its earnings per share (rather than smaller) after *EBIT* fluctuations. Assume that Pierce Grain elected financing plan C rather than plan A. Plan C is highly levered and plan A is unlevered. A 100 percent increase in *EBIT* from $20,000 to $40,000 would cause earnings per share to rise by 147 percent under plan C but only 100 percent under plan A. Unfortunately, the effect would operate in the negative direction as well. A given change in *EBIT* is *magnified* by the use of financial leverage. This magnification is reflected in the variability of the firm's earnings per share.

TABLE 12-10	Pierce Grain Company Possible Capital Structures

PLAN A: 0% DEBT

		Total debt	$ 0
		Common equity	200,000[a]
Total assets	$200,000	Total liabilities and equity	$200,000

PLAN B: 25% DEBT AT 8% INTEREST RATE

		Total debt	$ 50,000
		Common equity	150,000[b]
Total assets	$200,000	Total liabilities and equity	$200,000

PLAN C: 40% DEBT AT 8% INTEREST RATE

		Total debt	$ 80,000
		Common equity	120,000[c]
Total assets	$200,000	Total liabilities and equity	$200,000

[a] 2,000 common shares outstanding.   [b] 1,500 common shares outstanding.   [c] 1,200 common shares outstanding.

The second financial-leverage effect concerns the level of earnings per share at a given *EBIT* under a given capital structure. Refer to Table 12-11. At the *EBIT* level of $20,000, earnings per share would be $5, $5.33, and $5.67 under financing arrangements A, B, and C, respectively. Above a critical level of *EBIT*, the firm's earnings per share will be higher if greater degrees of financial leverage are employed. Conversely, below some critical level of *EBIT*, earnings per share will suffer at greater degrees of financial leverage. Whereas the first financial-leverage effect is quantified by the degree-of-financial leverage measure (DFL_{EBIT}), the second is quantified by what is generally referred to as *EBIT-EPS* analysis. (*EPS* refers, of course, to earnings per share.) The rationale underlying this sort of analysis is simple. Earnings is one of the key variables that influence the market value of the firm's common stock. The effect of a financing decision on *EPS*, then, should be understood because the decision will probably affect the value of the stockholder's investment.

TABLE 12-11	Pierce Grain Company Analysis of Financial Leverage at Different *EBIT* Levels

(1)	(2)	(3) = (1) − (2)	(4) = (3) × .5	(5) = (3) − (4)	(6)
EBIT	INTEREST	*EBT*	TAXES	NET INCOME TO COMMON	EARNINGS PER SHARE

PLAN A: 0% DEBT; $200,000 COMMON EQUITY; 2,000 SHARES

$ 0	$ 0	$ 0	$ 0	$ 0	$ 0
20,000	0	20,000	10,000	10,000	5.00
40,000	0	40,000	20,000	20,000	10.00
60,000	0	60,000	30,000	30,000	15.00
80,000	0	80,000	40,000	40,000	20.00

} 100%

PLAN B: 25% DEBT; 8% INTEREST RATE; $150,000 COMMON EQUITY; 1,500 SHARES

$ 0	$4,000	$(4,000)	$(2,000)[a]	$(2,000)	$ (1.33)
20,000	4,000	16,000	8,000	8,000	5.33
40,000	4,000	36,000	18,000	18,000	12.00
60,000	4,000	56,000	28,000	28,000	18.67
80,000	4,000	76,000	38,000	38,000	25.33

} 125%

PLAN C: 40% DEBT; 8% INTEREST RATE; $120,000 COMMON EQUITY; 1,200 SHARES

$ 0	$6,400	$(6,400)	$(3,200)[a]	$(3,200)	$(2.67)
20,000	6,400	13,600	6,800	6,800	5.67
40,000	6,400	33,600	16,800	16,800	14.00
60,000	6,400	53,600	26,800	26,800	22.33
80,000	6,400	73,600	36,800	36,800	30.67

} 147%

[a] The negative tax bill recognizes the credit arising from the carryback and carryforward provision of the tax code.

EBIT-EPS ANALYSIS

EXAMPLE

Assume that plan B in Table 12-11 is the existing capital structure for the Pierce Grain Company. Furthermore, the asset structure of the firm is such that EBIT is expected to be $20,000 per year for a very long time. A capital investment is available to Pierce Grain that will cost $50,000. Acquisition of this asset is expected to raise the projected EBIT level to $30,000, permanently. The firm can raise the needed cash by (1) selling 500 shares of common stock at $100 each or (2) selling new bonds that will net the firm $50,000 and carry an interest rate of 8.5 percent. These capital structures and corresponding EPS amounts are summarized in Table 12-12.

At the projected *EBIT* level of $30,000, the EPS for the common stock and debt alternatives are $6.50 and $7.25, respectively. Both are considerably above the $5.33 that would occur if the new project were rejected and the additional financial capital were not raised. Based on a criterion of selecting the financing plan that will provide the highest *EPS*, the bond alternative is favored. But what if the basic business risk to which the firm is exposed causes the *EBIT* level to vary over a considerable range? Can we be sure that the bond alternative will *always* have the higher *EPS* associated with it? The answer, of course, is no. When the *EBIT* level is subject to uncertainty, a graphic analysis of the proposed financing plans can provide useful information to the financial manager.

GRAPHIC ANALYSIS

The *EBIT-EPS* analysis chart allows the decision maker to visualize the impact of different financing plans on EPS over a range of *EBIT* levels. The relationship between EPS and *EBIT* is linear. All we need, therefore, to construct the chart is two points for each alternative. Part B of Table 12-12 already provides us with one of these points. The answer to the following question for each choice gives us the second point: At what *EBIT* level will the EPS for the plan be exactly zero? If the *EBIT* level *just covers* the plan's financing costs (on a

---

TABLE 12-12   Pierce Grain Company Analysis of Financing Choices

PART A: CAPITAL STRUCTURES

EXISTING CAPITAL STRUCTURE		WITH NEW COMMON STOCK FINANCING		WITH NEW DEBT FINANCING	
Long-term debt at 8%	$ 50,000	Long-term debt at 8%	$ 50,000	Long-term debt at 8%	$ 50,000
Common stock	150,000	Common stock	200,000	Long-term debt at 8.5%	50,000
				Common stock	150,000
Total liabilities and equity	$200,000	Total liabilities and equity	$250,000	Total liabilities and equity	$250,000
Common shares outstanding	1,500	Common shares outstanding	2,000	Common shares outstanding	1,500

PART B: PROJECTED *EPS* LEVELS

	EXISTING CAPITAL STRUCTURE	WITH NEW COMMON STOCK FINANCING	WITH NEW DEBT FINANCING
EBIT	$20,000	$30,000	$30,000
Less: Interest expense	4,000	4,000	8,250
Earnings before taxes (*EBT*)	$16,000	$26,000	$21,750
Less: Taxes at 50%	8,000	13,000	10,875
Net income	$ 8,000	$13,000	$10,875
Less: Preferred dividends	0	0	0
Earnings available to common	$ 8,000	$13,000	$10,875
EPS	$ 5.33	$ 6.50	$ 7.25

FIGURE 12-14   *EBIT-EPS* Analysis Chart

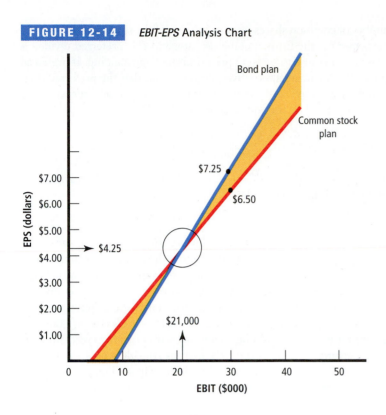

Handwritten annotations:
Buy all stock
or
All Bonds.
The Indifference Point
is the point
where it is finance
by all debt or all stock

before-tax basis), then *EPS* will be zero. For the stock plan, an *EPS* of zero is associated with an *EBIT* of $4,000. The $4,000 is the interest expense incurred under the existing capital structure. If the bond plan is elected, the interest costs will be the present $4,000 plus $4,250 per year arising from the new debt issue. An *EBIT* level of $8,250, then, is necessary to provide a zero *EPS* with the bond plan.

The *EBIT-EPS* analysis chart representing the financing choices available to the Pierce Grain Company is shown as Figure 12-14. *EBIT* is charted on the horizontal axis and *EPS* on the vertical axis. The intercepts on the horizontal axis represent the before-tax equivalent financing charges related to each plan. The straight lines for each plan tell us the *EPS* amounts that will occur at different *EBIT* amounts.

Notice that the bond-plan line has a *steeper slope* than the stock-plan line. This ensures that the lines for each financing choice will *intersect*. Above the intersection point, *EPS* for the plan with greater leverage will exceed that for the plan with lesser leverage. The intersection point, encircled in Figure 12-14, occurs at an *EBIT* level of $21,000 and produces *EPS* of $4.25 for each plan. When *EBIT* is $30,000, notice that the bond plan produces *EPS* of $7.25, and the stock plan, $6.50. Below the intersection point, *EPS* with the stock plan will *exceed* that with the more highly leveraged bond plan. The steeper slope of the bond-plan line indicates that with greater leverage, *EPS* is more sensitive to *EBIT* changes.

COMPUTING INDIFFERENCE POINTS

The point of intersection in Figure 12-14 is called the **EBIT-EPS indifference point**. It identifies the *EBIT level at which the EPS will be the same regardless of the financing plan chosen by the financial manager*. This indifference point, sometimes called the break-even point, has major implications for financial planning. At *EBIT* amounts in excess of the *EBIT* indifference level, the more heavily levered financing plan will generate a higher *EPS*. At *EBIT* amounts below the *EBIT* indifference level, the financing plan involving less leverage will generate a higher *EPS*. It is important, then, to know the *EBIT* indifference level.

We can find it graphically, as in Figure 12-14. At times it may be more efficient, though, to calculate the indifference point directly. This can be done by using the following equation:

EBIT-EPS indifference point

EPS: STOCK PLAN   *EPS*: BOND PLAN

$$\frac{(EBIT - I)(1-t) - P}{S_s} = \frac{(EBIT - I)(1-t) - P}{S_b} \qquad (12\text{-}17)$$

Handwritten annotation: *No Preferred Stock*

where S_s and S_b are the number of common shares outstanding under the stock and bond plans, respectively; I is interest expense; t is the firm's income tax rate; and P is preferred dividends paid. In the present case P is zero, because there is no preferred stock outstanding. If preferred stock is associated with one of the financing alternatives, keep in mind that the preferred dividends, P, are not tax deductible. Equation (12-17) does take this fact into consideration.

For the present example, we calculate the indifference level of *EBIT* as

$$\frac{(EBIT - \$4,000)(1 - 0.5) - 0}{2,000} = \frac{(EBIT - \$8,250)(1 - 0.5) - 0}{1,500}$$

When the expression above is solved for *EBIT*, we obtain $21,000. If *EBIT* turns out to be $21,000, then *EPS* will be $4.25 under both plans.

WORD OF CAUTION

Above the *EBIT-EPS* indifference point, a more heavily levered financial plan promises to deliver a larger *EPS*. Strict application of the criterion of selecting the financing plan that produces the highest *EPS* might have the firm issuing debt most of the time it raised external capital. Our discussion of capital structure theory taught us the dangers of that sort of action.

The primary weakness of *EBIT-EPS* analysis is that it disregards the implicit costs of debt financing. The effect of the specific financing decision on the firm's cost of common equity capital is totally ignored. Investors should be concerned with both the level and variability of the firm's expected earnings stream. *EBIT-EPS* analysis considers only the level of the earnings stream and ignores the variability (riskiness) inherent in it. Thus, this type of analysis must be used in conjunction with other basic tools in reaching the objective of capital structure management.

COMPARATIVE LEVERAGE RATIOS

In Chapter 4 we explored the overall usefulness of financial ratio analysis. Leverage ratios, one of the categories of financial ratios, are identified in that chapter. We emphasize here that the computation of leverage ratios is one of the basic tools of capital structure management.

Two types of leverage ratios must be computed when a financing decision faces the firm. We call these *balance-sheet leverage ratios* and *coverage ratios*. The firm's balance sheet supplies inputs for computing the balance-sheet leverage ratios. In various forms these balance-sheet metrics compare the firm's use of funds supplied by creditors with those supplied by owners.

Inputs to the coverage ratios generally come from the firm's income statement. At times the external analyst may have to consult balance-sheet information to construct some of these needed estimates. On a privately placed debt issue, for example, some fraction of the current portion of the firm's long-term debt might have to be used as an estimate of that issue's sinking fund. Coverage ratios provide estimates of the firm's ability to service its financing contracts. High coverage ratios, compared with a standard, imply unused debt capacity.

In reality we know that *EBIT* might be expected to vary over a considerable range of outcomes. For this reason the coverage ratios should be calculated several times, each at a different level of *EBIT*. If this is accomplished over all possible values of *EBIT*, a probability distribution for each coverage ratio can be constructed. This provides the financial manager with much more information than simply calculating the coverage ratios based on the expected value of *EBIT*.

INDUSTRY NORMS

The comparative leverage ratios calculated have additional utility to the decision maker if they can be compared with some standard. Generally, corporate financial analysts, investment bankers, commercial bank loan officers, and bond-rating agencies rely on industry classes from which to compute "normal" ratios. Although industry groupings may actually contain firms whose basic business-risk exposure differs widely, the practice is entrenched in American business behavior. At the very least, then, the financial officer must be interested in industry standards because almost everybody else is.

FINANCIAL MANAGEMENT
IN PRACTICE

THE WALT DISNEY COMPANY ON CAPITAL COSTS AND CAPITAL STRUCTURE

At the end of fiscal year 1998, the Walt Disney Company had a total market capitalization of $65 billion; this placed it among the 40 largest corporations in the United States, whereas its sales revenues of $23.0 billion placed it fifty-third on the 1999 *Fortune* 500 list. This multinational giant with 117,000 employees provides several real examples of the capital structure concepts presented in this chapter.

In the following discussion from Disney management, notice how the firm (1) relates capital costs to shareholder value; (2) believes in the "prudent degree of leverage" concept; (3) is concerned with its interest coverage ratio—measured as earnings before net interest, taxes, depreciation, and amortization, or *EBITDA*, divided by net interest expense; and (4) strives to maintain a minimum desired or target bond rating. Within the accompanying graph you see that Disney's coverage ratio for fiscal year 1998 of *EBITDA* to net interest expense is 8.1 times (i.e., $5,019 million/$622 million).

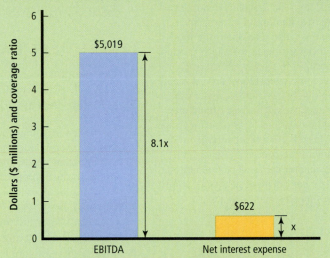

Disney's solid balance sheet allows the company to borrow at attractive rates, helping to reduce the overall cost of capital and thereby creating value for shareholders. As of year end, Disney maintained total borrowings of approximately $12 billion and a debt-to-total-capital ratio of 38%. The company believes that this level of debt represents a prudent degree of leverage, which provides for substantial financial flexibility to borrow should sound business opportunities present themselves. As measured by the ratio of earnings before net interest, taxes, depreciation and amortization (*EBITDA*) to net interest expense, the company covered its interest costs by a factor of more than eight times for the year ended September 30.

The company monitors its cash flow, interest coverage and its debt-to-total-capital ratio with the long-term goal of maintaining a strong single-A or better credit rating.

Source: The Walt Disney Company, *1998 Annual Report*, p. 12.

Several published studies indicate that capital structure ratios vary in a significant manner among industry classes.[10] For example, random samplings of the common equity ratios of large retail firms seem to differ statistically from those of major steel producers. The major steel producers use financial leverage to a lesser degree then do the large retail organizations. On the whole, firms operating in the *same* industry tend to exhibit capital structure ratios that cluster around a central value that we call a norm. Business risk varies from industry to industry. As a consequence, the capital structure norms vary from industry to industry.

This is not to say that all companies in the industry will maintain leverage ratios "close" to the norm. For instance, firms that are very profitable may display high coverage ratios and high balance-sheet leverage ratios. The moderately profitable firm, though, might find such a posture unduly risky. Here the usefulness of industry-normal leverage ratios is clear. If the firm chooses to deviate in a material manner from the accepted values for the key ratios, it must have a sound reason.

CONCEPT CHECK

1. Explain the meaning of the *EBIT-EPS* indifference point.
2. How are various leverage ratios and industry norms used in capital structure management?

---

[10]See, for example, Eli Schwartz and J. Richard Aronson, "Some Surrogate Evidence in Support of the Concept of Optimal Financial Structure," *Journal of Finance* 22 (March 1967), pp. 10–18; David F. Scott, Jr., "Evidence on the Importance of Financial Structure," *Financial Management* 1 (Summer 1972), pp. 45–50; and David F. Scott, Jr., and John D. Martin, "Industry Influence on Financial Structure," *Financial Management* 4 (Spring 1975), pp. 67–73.

Objective 9

A GLANCE AT ACTUAL CAPITAL STRUCTURE MANAGEMENT

We now examine some opinions and practices of financial executives that reinforce an emphasis on the importance of capital structure management.

TARGET DEBT RATIOS

Selected comments from financial executives point to the widespread use of target debt ratios. A vice president and treasurer of the American Telephone and Telegraph Company (AT&T) described his firm's debt-ratio policy in terms of a range:

> All of the foregoing considerations led us to conclude, and reaffirm for a period of many years, that the proper range of our debt was 30% to 40% of total capital. Reasonable success in meeting financial needs under the diverse market and economic conditions that we have faced attests to the appropriateness of this conclusion.[11]

A frequently mentioned influence on the level of target debt ratio is ability to meet financing charges. Other factors identified by executives as affecting the target are (1) maintaining a desired bond rating, (2) providing an adequate borrowing reserve, and (3) exploiting the advantages of financial leverage.

WHO SETS TARGET DEBT RATIOS?

We know that firms do use target debt ratios in arriving at financing decisions. But who sets or influences these target ratios? This and other questions concerning corporate financing policy were investigated in one study published in 1982.[12] This survey of the 1,000 largest industrial firms in the United States (as ranked by total sales dollars) involved responses from 212 financial executives.

In one portion of this study, the participants were asked to rank several possible influences on their target leverage (debt) ratios. Table 12-13 displays the percentage of responses ranked either number 1 or number 2 in importance. Ranks past the second are omitted in that they were not very significant. Notice that the most important influence is the firm's own management group and staff of analysts. This item accounted for 85 percent of the responses ranked number 1. Of the responses ranked number 2 in importance, investment bankers dominated the outcomes and accounted for 39 percent of such replies. Also notice that comparisons with ratios of industry competitors and commercial bankers have some impact on the determination of leverage targets.

TABLE 12-13   Setting Target Financial Structure Ratios

	RANK	
TYPE OF INFLUENCE	1	2
Internal management and staff analysts	85%	7%
Investment bankers	3	39
Commercial bankers	0	9
Trade creditors	1	0
Security analysts	1	4
Comparative industry ratios	3	23
Other	7	18
Total	100%	100%

Source: David F. Scott, Jr., "Financial Policies and Practices in Large Corporations." *Financial Management*, Vol. 11, No. 2 (Summer, 1982). Financial Management Association International, University of South Florida, Tampa, Florida 33620. Used with permission.

[11]John J. Scanlon, "Bell System Financial Policies," *Financial Management* 1 (Summer 1972), pp. 16–26.
[12]David F. Scott, Jr., and Dana J. Johnson, "Financing Policies and Practices in Large Corporations," *Financial Management* 11 (Summer 1982), pp. 51–59.

TABLE 12-14	Definitions of Debt Capacity in Practice	
STANDARD OR METHOD		**1,000 LARGEST CORPORATIONS (PERCENT USING)**
Target percent of total capitalization (long-term debt to total capitalization)		27%
Long-term debt to net worth ratio (or its inverse)		14
Long-term debt to total assets		2
Interest (or fixed charge) coverage ratio		6
Maintain bond ratings		14
Restrictive debt covenants		4
Most adverse cash flow		4
Industry standard		3
Other		10
No response		16
Total		100%

Source: David F. Scott, Jr., "Financial Policies and Practices in Large Corporations." *Financial Management*, Vol. 11, No. 2 (Summer 1982). Used with permission of Financial Management Association International, University of South Florida, Tampa, Florida 33620.

DEBT CAPACITY

Previously in this chapter we noted that the firm's debt capacity is the maximum proportion of debt that it can include in its capital structure and still maintain its lowest composite cost of capital. But how do financial executives make the concept of debt capacity operational? Table 12-14 is derived from the same 1982 survey, involving 212 executives, previously mentioned. These executives defined debt capacity in a wide variety of ways. The most popular approach was as a target percentage of total capitalization. Twenty-seven percent of the respondents thought of debt capacity in this manner. Forty-three percent of the participating executives remarked that debt capacity is defined in terms of some balance sheet–based financial ratio (see the first three items in Table 12-14). Maintaining a specific bond rating was also indicated to be a popular approach to implementing the debt-capacity concept.

BUSINESS RISK

The single most important factor that should affect the firm's financing mix is the underlying nature of the business in which it operates. In this chapter we defined business risk as the relative dispersion in the firm's expected stream of *EBIT*. If the nature of the firm's business is such that the variability inherent in its *EBIT* stream is high, then it would be unwise to impose a high degree of financial risk on top of this already uncertain earnings stream.

The AT&T financial officer referred to earlier has commented on the relationship between business risk and financial risk:

> In determining how much debt a firm can safely carry, it is necessary to consider the basic risks inherent in that business. This varies considerably among industries and is related essentially to the nature and demand for an industry's product, the operating characteristics of the industry, and its ability to earn an adequate return in an unknown future.[13]

CONCEPT CHECK

1. Identify several factors that influence target debt ratios in actual business practice.
2. Identify several methods used by executives to make the concept of debt capacity operational.

It appears clear that the firm's capital structure cannot be properly designed without a thorough understanding of its commercial strategy.

[13]Scanlon, "Bell System Financial Policies," p. 19.

Objective **10**

FINANCE AND THE MULTINATIONAL FIRM: BUSINESS RISK AND GLOBAL SALES

Early in this chapter we defined business risk as the relative dispersion (variability) in the firm's expected earnings before interest and taxes (*EBIT*). And when we discussed operating leverage and the degree-of-operating-leverage concept, we learned that changes or shocks to the firm's overall sales level will cause a greater percentage change in *EBIT* if fixed operating costs are present in the firm's cost structure. Thus, any event that induces a fluctuation in measured sales will impact a firm's business risk and its resulting *EBIT*.

Business risk is multidimensional and international. It is directly affected by several factors, including (1) the sensitivity of the firm's product demand to general economic conditions, (2) the degree of competition to which the firm is exposed, (3) product diversification, (4) growth prospects, and (5) global sales volume and production output. The latter factor is especially important to the multinational firm, and such firms are aware of it. Some seek to take advantage of it in an aggressive manner.

Consider the Coca-Cola Company. In his statement to shareholders published in 1998, Mr. M. Douglas Ivester, CEO and chairman of Coke's Board, commented on the firm's commercial strategy in both China and Russia.[14] He said, "In China, the world's largest market, our volume soared another 30 percent in 1997. But the average resident of China still drinks just six of our products a year—certainly a business in its infancy." Notice that although Coke's presence in China increases its total business risk exposure, Mr. Ivester views this exposure as a commercial opportunity for the firm.

In his discussion of the Russian market, Mr. Ivester offered, "In Russia, where we took the lead over our largest competitor in 1996, we widened that lead to 3-to-1 in 1997; we opened four more plants there on October 1, bringing our system's Russian investment to $650 million and pointing to strong future growth." Here we see that Coke is both cultivating the Russian consumer and simultaneously investing in plant and equipment there. Thus, Coke's broad commercial strategy, which impacts business risk, also encompasses the capital budgeting decision discussed earlier in this text.

CONCEPT CHECK

1. Identify several factors that directly affect a firm's business risk.
2. How might a firm's commercial strategy be influenced by its presence in foreign markets?

SUMMARY

Objective **1**

In this chapter we study the process of arriving at an appropriate financial structure for the firm and examine tools that can assist the financial manager in this task. We are concerned with assessing the variability in the firm's residual earnings stream (either earnings per share or earnings available to the common shareholders) induced by the use of operating and financial leverage. This assessment builds on the tenets of break-even analysis.

We then deal with the design of the firm's financing mix, particularly emphasizing management of the firm's permanent sources of funds—that is, its capital structure. The objective of capital structure management is to arrange the company's sources of funds so that its common stock price is maximized, all other factors held constant.

Objective **2**

Break-even analysis
Break-even analysis permits the financial manager to determine the quantity of output or the level of sales that will result in an *EBIT* level of zero. This means the firm has neither a profit nor a loss

---

[14] The Coca-Cola Company, *Annual Report*, 1997, pp. 5–6.

before any tax considerations. The effect of price changes, cost structure changes, or volume changes on profits (*EBIT*) can be studied. To make the technique operational, it is necessary that the firm's costs be classified as fixed or variable. Not all costs fit neatly into one of these two categories. Over short planning horizons, though, the preponderance of costs can be assigned to either the fixed or variable classification. Once the cost structure has been identified, the break-even point can be found by use of contribution margin analysis or algebraic analysis.

Operating leverage

Operating leverage is the responsiveness of the firm's *EBIT* to changes in sales revenues. It arises from the firm's use of fixed operating costs. When fixed operating costs are present in the company's cost structure, changes in sales are magnified into even greater changes in *EBIT*. The firm's degree of operating leverage from a base sales level is the percentage change in *EBIT* divided by the percentage change in sales. All types of leverage are two-edged swords. When sales decrease by some percentage, the negative impact on *EBIT* is even larger.

Objective **3**

Financial leverage

A firm employs financial leverage when it finances a portion of its assets with securities bearing a fixed rate of return. The presence of debt and/or preferred stock in the company's financial structure means that it is using financial leverage. When financial leverage is used, changes in *EBIT* translate into larger changes in earnings per share. The concept of the degree of financial leverage dwells on the sensitivity of earnings per share to changes in *EBIT*. The *DFL* from a base *EBIT* level is defined as the percentage change in earnings per share divided by the percentage change in *EBIT*. All other things equal, the more fixed-charge securities the firm employs in its financial structure, the greater its degree of financial leverage. Clearly, *EBIT* can rise or fall. If it falls, and financial leverage is used, the firm's shareholders endure negative changes in earnings per share that are larger than the relative decline in *EBIT*. Again, leverage is a two-edged sword.

Objective **4**

Combining operating and financial leverage

Firms use operating and financial leverage in various degrees. The joint use of operating and financial leverage can be measured by computing the degree of combined leverage, defined as the percentage change in earnings per share divided by the percentage change in sales. This measure allows the financial manager to ascertain the effect on total leverage caused by adding financial leverage on top of operating leverage. Effects can be dramatic because the degree of combined leverage is the product of the degrees of operating and financial leverage.

Capital structure theory

Can the firm affect its composite cost of capital by altering its financing mix? Attempts to answer this question have comprised a significant portion of capital structure theory for over three decades. Extreme positions show that the firm's stock price is either unaffected or continually affected as the firm increases its reliance on leverage-inducing funds. In the real world, an operating environment in which interest expense is tax deductible and market imperfections operate to restrict the amount of fixed-income obligations a firm can issue, most financial officers and financial academics subscribe to the concept of an optimal capital structure. The optimal capital structure minimizes the firm's composite cost of capital. Searching for a proper range of financial leverage, then, is an important financial management activity.

Objective **5**

Objective **6**

Objective **7**

Complicating the manager's search for an optimal capital structure are conflicts that lead to agency costs. A natural conflict exists between stockholders and bondholders (the agency costs of debt). To reduce excessive risk taking by management on behalf of stockholders, it may be necessary to include several protective covenants in bond contracts that serve to restrict managerial decision making.

Objective **8**

Another type of agency cost is related to "free cash flow." Managers, for example, have an incentive to hold on to free cash flow and enjoy it, rather than pay it out in the form of higher cash-dividend payments. This conflict between managers and stockholders leads to the concept of the *free cash flow theory of capital structure*. This same theory is also known as the *control hypothesis* and the *threat hypothesis*. The ultimate resolution of these agency costs affects the specific form of the firm's capital structure.

Tools of capital structure management

The decision to use senior securities in the firm's capitalization causes two types of financial-leverage effects. The first is the added variability in the earnings-per-share stream that accompanies the use of fixed-charge securities. We explain how this can be quantified by the use of the degree of financial-leverage metric. The second financial-leverage effect relates to the level of earnings per share (*EPS*) at a given *EBIT* under a specific capital structure. We rely on *EBIT-EPS* analysis to measure this second effect. Through *EBIT-EPS* analysis, the decision maker can inspect the impact of alternative financing plans on *EPS* over a full range of *EBIT* levels.

Objective **9**

A second tool of capital structure management is the calculation of comparative leverage ratios. Balance-sheet leverage ratios and coverage ratios can be computed according to the contractual stipulations of the proposed financing plans. Comparison of these ratios with industry standards enables the financial officer to determine if the firm's key ratios are materially out of line with accepted practice.

Capital structure practices

Surveys indicate that most financial officers in large firms believe in the concept of an optimal capital structure. The optimal capital structure is approximated by the identification of target debt ratios. The targets reflect the firm's ability to service fixed financing costs and also consider the business risk to which the firm is exposed.

Survey studies have provided information on who sets or influences the firm's target leverage ratios. The firm's own management group and staff of analysts are the major influence, followed in importance by investment bankers. Studies also show that executives put the concept of debt capacity in operation in many ways. The most popular approach is to define debt capacity in terms of a target long-term-debt-to-total-capitalization ratio. Maintaining a specific bond rating (such as Aa or A) is also a popular approach to implementing the debt capacity concept.

Objective **10**

The multinational firm: business risk and global sales

Business risk is both multidimensional and international. It is directly affected by several factors, including (1) the sensitivity of the firm's product demand to general economic conditions, (2) the degree of competition to which the firm is exposed, (3) product diversification, (4) growth prospects, and (5) global sales. On the last factor, we explored how the Coca-Cola Company related the firm's commercial strategy to include sales prospects in the huge markets of China and Russia.

KEY TERMS

Business risk, 369	Financial leverage, 370	Optimal range of financial leverage, 392
Capital structure, 385	Financial risk, 369	Risk, 369
Contribution margin, 374	Financial structure, 385	Tax shield, 391
Debt capacity, 392	Fixed costs, 370	Total revenue, 373
Direct costs (see variable costs), 371	Indirect costs (see fixed costs), 370	Variable costs, 371
EBIT-EPS indifference point, 399	Operating leverage, 370	Volume of output, 373
	Optimal capital structure, 387	

STUDY QUESTIONS

12-1. Distinguish between business risk and financial risk. What gives rise to, or causes, each type of risk?

12-2. Define the term *financial leverage*. Does the firm use financial leverage if preferred stock is present in the capital structure?

12-3. Define the term *operating leverage*. What type of effect occurs when the firm uses operating leverage?

12-4. A manager in your firm decides to employ break-even analysis. Of what shortcomings should this manager be aware?

12-5. If a firm has a degree of combined leverage of 3.0 times, what does a negative sales fluctuation of 15 percent portend for the earnings available to the firm's common stock investors?

12-6. Break-even analysis assumes linear revenue and cost functions. In reality, these linear functions over large output and sales levels are highly improbable. Why?

12-7. Define the following terms:

    a. *Financial structure*

    b. *Capital structure*

    c. *Optimal capital structure*

    d. *Debt capacity*

12-8. What is the primary weakness of *EBIT-EPS* analysis as a financing decision tool?

12-9. What is the objective of capital structure management?

12-10. Distinguish between (a) balance-sheet leverage ratios and (b) coverage ratios. Give two examples of each and indicate how they would be computed.

12-11. Why might firms whose sales levels change drastically over time choose to use debt only sparingly in their capital structures?

12-12. What condition would cause capital structure management to be a meaningless activity?

12-13. What does the term *independence hypothesis* mean as it applies to capital structure theory?

12-14. Who have been the foremost advocates of the independence hypothesis?

12-15. A financial manager might say that the firm's composite cost of capital is saucer-shaped or U-shaped. What does this mean?

12-16. Define the *EBIT-EPS* indifference point.

12-17. Explain how industry norms might be used by the financial manager in the design of the company's financing mix.

12-18. Define the term *free cash flow*.

12-19. What is meant by the *free cash flow theory of capital structure*?

12-20. In almost every instance, what funds source do managers use first in the financing of their capital budgets?

SELF-TEST PROBLEM

ST-1. (*Fixed costs and the break-even point*) Bonaventure Manufacturing expects to earn $210,000 next year after taxes. Sales will be $4 million. The firm's single plant is located on the outskirts of Olean, New York. The firm manufactures a combined bookshelf and desk unit used extensively in college dormitories. These units sell for $200 each and have a variable cost per unit of $150. Bonaventure experiences a 30 percent tax rate.

    a. What are the firm's fixed costs expected to be next year?
    b. Calculate the firm's break-even point in both units and dollars.

STUDY PROBLEMS

12-1. (*Leverage analysis*) You have developed the following analytical income statement for the Hugo Boss Corporation. It represents the most recent year's operations, which ended yesterday.

Sales	$ 50,439,375
Variable costs	(25,137,000)
Revenue before fixed costs	$ 25,302,375
Fixed costs	(10,143,000)
EBIT	$ 15,159,375
Interest expense	(1,488,375)
Earnings before taxes	$ 13,671,000
Taxes at 50%	(6,835,500)
Net income	$ 6,835,500

Your supervisor in the controller's office has just handed you a memorandum asking for written responses to the following questions:

    a. At this level of output, what is the degree of operating leverage?
    b. What is the degree of financial leverage?
    c. What is the degree of combined leverage?
    d. What is the firm's break-even point in sales dollars?
    e. If sales should increase by 30 percent, by what percent would earnings before taxes (and net income) increase?

12-2. (*EBIT-EPS analysis*) Two inventive entrepreneurs have interested a group of venture capitalists in backing a new business project. The proposed plan would consist of a series of international retail outlets to distribute and service a full line of ingenious home garden tools. The stores would be located in high-traffic cities in Latin America such as Panama City, Bogotá, São Paulo, and Buenos Aires. Two financing plans have been proposed by the entrepreneurs. Plan A is an all-common-equity structure. Five million dollars would be raised by selling 160,000 shares of common stock. Plan B would involve the use of long-term debt financing. Three million dollars would be raised by marketing bonds with an effective interest rate of 14 percent. Under the alternative, another $2 million would be raised by selling 64,000 shares of common stock. With both plans, $5 million is needed to launch the new firm's operations. The debt funds raised under plan B are considered to have no fixed maturity date, in that this portion of financial leverage is thought to be a permanent part of the company's capital structure. The two promising executives have decided to use a 35 percent tax rate in their analysis, and they have hired you on a consulting basis to do the following:

   a. Find the *EBIT* indifference level associated with the two financing proposals.
   b. Prepare an analytical income statement that proves *EPS* will be the same regardless of the plan chosen at the *EBIT* level found in part **a**.

12-3. (*Sales mix and break-even point*) CasaBlanca Appliances manufactures four lines of commercial kitchen equipment for hotels and restaurants. The lines produced are freezers (F), baking equipment (BE), commercial grilles (CG), and beverage dispensers (BD). The current sales mix for CasaBlanca and the contribution margin ratios (unit contribution margin divided by unit sales price) for these equipment lines are as follows:

PRODUCT LINE	PERCENT OF TOTAL SALES	CONTRIBUTION MARGIN RATIO
F	$11\frac{1}{4}$	60%
BE	$22\frac{1}{2}$	42
CG	$37\frac{3}{4}$	34
BD	$28\frac{1}{2}$	59

Total sales for next year are expected to be $800,000. Total fixed costs will be $220,000.

   a. Prepare a table showing (1) sales, (2) total variable costs, and (3) the total contribution margin associated with each product line.
   b. What is the aggregate contribution margin ratio indicative of this sales mix?
   c. At this sales mix, what is the break-even point in dollars?

12-4. (*EBIT-EPS analysis*) Four recent liberal arts graduates have interested a group of venture capitalists in backing a new business enterprise. The proposed operation would consist of a series of retail outlets to distribute and service a full line of vacuum cleaners and accessories. These stores would be located in Dallas, Houston, and San Antonio. Two financing plans have been proposed by the graduates. Plan A is an all-common-equity structure. Two million dollars would be raised by selling 100,000 shares of common stock. Plan B would involve the use of long-term debt financing. One million dollars would be raised by marketing bonds with an effective interest rate of 8 percent. Under this alternative, another $1 million would be raised by selling 50,000 shares of common stock. With both plans, then, $2 million is needed to launch the new firm's operations. The debt funds raised under plan B are considered to have no fixed maturity date, in that this portion of financial leverage is thought to be a permanent part of the company's capital structure. The fledgling executives have decided to use a 30 percent tax rate in their analysis, and they have hired you on a consulting basis to do the following:

   a. Find the *EBIT* indifference level associated with the two financing proposals.
   b. Prepare an analytical income statement that proves *EPS* will be the same regardless of the plan chosen at the *EBIT* level found in part **a** above.

12-5. (*Leverage analysis*) You have developed the following analytical income statement for your corporation. It represents the most recent year's operations, which ended yesterday.

Sales	$45,750,000
Variable costs	22,800,000
Revenue before fixed costs	$22,950,000
Fixed costs	9,200,000
EBIT	$13,750,000
Interest expense	1,350,000
Earnings before taxes	$12,400,000
Taxes at 50%	6,200,000
Net income	$ 6,200,000

Your supervisor in the controller's office has just handed you a memorandum asking for written responses to the following questions:

a. At this level of output, what is the degree of operating leverage?
b. What is the degree of financial leverage?
c. What is the degree of combined leverage?
d. What is the firm's break-even point in sales dollars?
e. If sales should increase by 25 percent, by what percent would earnings before taxes (and net income) increase?

12-6. (*Break-even point and operating leverage*) Footwear, Inc., manufactures a complete line of men's and women's dress shoes for independent merchants. The average selling price of its finished product is $85 per pair. The variable cost for this same pair of shoes is $58. Footwear, Inc., incurs fixed costs of $170,000 per year.

a. What is the break-even point in pairs of shoes for the company?
b. What is the dollar sales volume the firm must achieve to reach the break-even point?
c. What would be the firm's profit or loss at the following units of production sold: 7,000 pairs of shoes? 9,000 pairs of shoes? 15,000 pairs of shoes?
d. Find the degree of operating leverage for the production and sales levels given in part c above.

12-7. (*Break-even point and profit margin*) Mary Clark, a recent graduate of Clarion South University, is planning to open a new wholesaling operation. Her target operating profit margin is 26 percent. Her unit contribution margin will be 50 percent of sales. Average annual sales are forecast to be $3,250,000.

a. How large can fixed costs be for the wholesaling operation and still allow the 26 percent operating profit margin to be achieved?
b. What is the break-even point in dollars for the firm?

12-8. (*Leverage analysis*) You have developed the following analytical income statement for your corporation. It represents the most recent year's operations, which ended yesterday.

Sales	$30,000,000
Variable costs	13,500,000
Revenue before fixed costs	$16,500,000
Fixed costs	8,000,000
EBIT	$ 8,500,000
Interest expense	1,000,000
Earnings before taxes	$ 7,500,000
Taxes at 50%	3,750,000
Net income	$ 3,750,000

Your supervisor in the controller's office has just handed you a memorandum asking for written responses to the following questions:

a. At this level of output, what is the degree of operating leverage?
b. What is the degree of financial leverage?
c. What is the degree of combined leverage?
d. What is the firm's break-even point in sales dollars?
e. If sales should increase by 25 percent, by what percent would earnings before taxes (and net income) increase?

12-9. (*Break-even point and selling price*) Parks Castings, Inc., will manufacture and sell 200,000 units next year. Fixed costs will total $300,000, and variable costs will be 60 percent of sales.

  a. The firm wants to achieve a level of earnings before interest and taxes of $250,000. What selling price per unit is necessary to achieve this result?
  b. Set up an analytical income statement to verify your solution to part **a.**

12-10. (*Operating leverage*) Rocky Mount Metals Company manufactures an assortment of wood-burning stoves. The average selling price for the various units is $500. The associated variable cost is $350 per unit. Fixed costs for the firm average $180,000 annually.

  a. What is the break-even point in units for the company?
  b. What is the dollar sales volume the firm must achieve to reach the break-even point?
  c. What is the degree of operating leverage for a production and sales level of 5,000 units for the firm? (Calculate to three decimal places.)
  d. What will be the projected effect on earnings before interest and taxes if the firm's sales level should increase by 20 percent from the volume noted in part **c** above?

12-11. (*Sales mix and break-even point*) Toledo Components produces four lines of auto accessories for the major Detroit automobile manufacturers. The lines are known by the code letters A, B, C, and D. The current sales mix for Toledo and the contribution margin ratio (unit contribution margin divided by unit sales price) for these product lines are as follows:

PRODUCT LINE	PERCENT OF TOTAL SALES	CONTRIBUTION MARGIN RATIO
A	$33\frac{1}{3}$	40%
B	$41\frac{2}{3}$	32
C	$16\frac{2}{3}$	20
D	$8\frac{1}{3}$	60

Total sales for next year are forecast to be $120,000. Total fixed costs will be $29,400.

  a. Prepare a table showing (1) sales, (2) total variable costs, and (3) the total contribution margin associated with each product line.
  b. What is the aggregate contribution margin ratio indicative of this sales mix?
  c. At this sales mix, what is the break-even point in dollars?

12-12. (*Sales mix and break-even point*) Because of production constraints, Toledo Components (see problem 12-11) may have to adhere to a different sales mix for next year. The alternative plan is outlined here.

PRODUCT LINE	PERCENT OF TOTAL SALES
A	25
B	$36\frac{2}{3}$
C	$33\frac{1}{3}$
D	5

  a. Assuming all other facts in problem 12-11 remain the same, what effect will this different sales mix have on Toledo's break-even point in dollars?
  b. Which sales mix will Toledo's management prefer?

12-13. (*EBIT-EPS analysis*) A group of retired college professors has decided to form a small manufacturing corporation. The company will produce a full line of traditional office furniture. Two financing plans have been proposed by the investors. Plan A is an all-common-equity alternative. Under this agreement, 1 million common shares will be sold to net the firm $20 per share. Plan B involves the use of financial leverage. A debt issue with a 20-year maturity period will be privately placed. The debt issue will carry an interest rate of 10 percent, and the principal borrowed will amount to $6 million. The corporate tax rate is 50 percent.

  a. Find the *EBIT* indifference level associated with the two financing proposals.
  b. Prepare an analytical income statement that proves *EPS* will be the same regardless of the plan chosen at the *EBIT* level found in part **a.**
  c. Prepare an *EBIT-EPS* analysis chart for this situation.
  d. If a detailed financial analysis projects that long-term *EBIT* will always be close to $2.4 million annually, which plan will provide for the higher *EPS*?

12-14. (*EBIT-EPS analysis*) Four recent liberal arts graduates have interested a group of venture capitalists in backing a new business enterprise. The proposed operation would consist of a series of retail outlets to distribute and service a full line of vacuum cleaners and accessories. These stores would be located in Dallas, Houston, and San Antonio. Two financing plans have been proposed by the graduates. Plan A is an all-common-equity structure. Two million dollars would be raised by selling 80,000 shares of common stock. Plan B would involve the use of long-term debt financing. One million dollars would be raised by marketing bonds with an effective interest rate of 12 percent. Under the alternative, another $1 million would be raised by selling 40,000 shares of common stock. With both plans, then, $2 million is needed to launch the new firm's operations. The debt funds raised under plan B are considered to have no fixed maturity date, in that this portion of financial leverage is thought to be a permanent part of the company's capital structure. The fledgling executives have decided to use a 40 percent tax rate in their analysis, and they have hired you on a consulting basis to do the following:

    a. Find the *EBIT* indifference level associated with the two financing proposals.

    b. Prepare an analytical income statement that proves *EPS* will be the same regardless of the plan chosen at the *EBIT* level found in part **a**.

12-15. (*Assessing leverage use*) Some financial data for three corporations are displayed here.

MEASURE	FIRM A	FIRM B	FIRM C	INDUSTRY NORM
Debt ratio	20%	25%	40%	20%
Times interest covered	8 times	10 times	7 times	9 times
Price–earnings ratio	9 times	11 times	6 times	10 times

    a. Which firm appears to be excessively levered?

    b. Which firm appears to be employing financial leverage to the most appropriate degree?

    c. What explanation can you provide for the higher price–earnings ratio enjoyed by firm B as compared with firm A?

WEB WORKS

12-WW1. Please read the "Financial Management in Practice" box dealing with General Motors' pricing strategy found at the end of the break-even analysis discussion in this chapter (see p. 377). That will provide a useful background for this exercise. Pricing strategies and adjustments are more likely to occur when interest rates are low than when these rates are high. This is because the firm can borrow at lower rates in the financial marketplace to offset the total cost of any pricing incentives offered to potential customers.

The site **www.bankrate.com/ust/ratehm.asp** provides a listing of current major interest rates that are important to both corporate executives and investors. Here you can find (a) various lending rates, such as the prime lending rate and federal funds target rate, (b) rates on U.S. Treasury securities of differing maturities, and (c) other selected interest rates, such as on long-term corporate bonds.

Go to this site and inspect the current level of the prime interest rate and compare it to that rate one year earlier. Has the prime rate increased or decreased from a year ago? Given this information, would you recommend to your financial executive superior that the firm consider increasing or decreasing any pricing incentives aimed at your firm's customers? By the way, you work for a major automobile manufacturer.

12-WW2. The Coca-Cola Company consistently publishes an outstanding and useful annual report. It can be found at **www.coca-cola.com** or accessed through **www.reportgallery.com**. Coca-Cola is one of the few firms of which we are aware that actually includes a "glossary" in its annual report. For 2003 it is on the inside back cover and also can be accessed directly by clicking on "*Glossary of Terms*" at this site for the 2003 Summary Annual Report. Many of the entries in its glossary are of a financial nature. Check out (a) dividend payout ratio, (b) economic profit, (c) operating margin, and (d) return on common equity. Then see how its listings stack up against those noted in the glossary to this text. You will notice that the resulting definitions are very close in each case. **Key Points:** We don't make up this stuff and such concepts drive the decision-making processes of financial executives. Thus, you want to make such concepts a part of your everyday vocabulary.

12-WW3. This exercise focuses on capital structure management and its direct relationship to corporate capital costs. We will work with actual relationships from the Coca-Cola Company (ticker symbol KO). Find the 2003 10K report for Coke at **www.reportgallery.com**. Go to page 31 of this 10K report, which is filed annually with the SEC. There you will find that Coke's long-term debt was rated Baa by Moody's and BBB by Standard & Poor's as of December 28, 2003. One year earlier, by the way, Coke's debt by Moody's was actually higher at Aa. Next go to **www.federalreserve.com** to ascertain recent yield levels for Aaa-rated long-term bonds. Recall that you want to access the Fed's H.15 report on "Selected Interest Rates." Finally, go to **www.cnnfn.com** and click on "markets." The latter site will allow you to do some bond research of your own and find out what the current yield is on bonds rated Aa. **Then answer:** How many basis points (a basis point is one-hundredth of 1 percent) would Coke financial management gain if its bonds were rated Aaa rather than Aa? Then, using the sources noted previously, how many basis points would the firm give up if its long-term debt rating were lowered to Baa? **The Point:** You now understand the importance of bond ratings to corporate costs of capital.

12-WW4. The Federal Reserve Bank of St. Louis maintains an outstanding Web site at **www.stlouisfed.org**. It is a fertile source for financial and economic time series data. Go to the St. Louis Fed site and click on "Economic Research." Once you get there, click on "Economic-Data-FRED II." The latter acronym stands for "Federal Reserve economic data." Once you have pulled up FRED II, under "categories" click on the category labeled "Business/Fiscal." This will enable you to find the S&P 500 Composite Total Return (calculated by assuming monthly reinvestment of dividends). Inspect the direction of the index from August 2000 through December 2002. **The question:** Over the 2001–2002 time period, do you think nonfinancial corporate businesses raised more cash by issuing new corporate bonds or by issuing new corporate equities? **Hint:** You can verify your answer by going to any Federal Reserve Web site and searching for the statistical release Z.1, "Flow of Funds Accounts of the United States."

COMPREHENSIVE PROBLEMS

1. Imagine that you were hired recently as a financial analyst for a relatively new, highly leveraged ski manufacturer located in the foothills of Colorado's Rocky Mountains. Your firm manufactures only one product, a state-of-the-art snow ski. The company has been operating up to this point without much quantitative knowledge of the business and financial risks it faces.

Ski season just ended, however, so the president of the company has started to focus more on the financial aspects of managing the business. He has set up a meeting for next week with the CFO, Maria Sanchez, to discuss matters such as the business and financial risks faced by the company. Accordingly, Maria has asked you to prepare an analysis to assist her in her discussions with the president.

As a first step in your work, you compiled the following information regarding the cost structure of the company:

Output level	80,000 units
Operating assets	$4,000,000
Operating asset turnover	8 times
Return on operating assets	32%
Degree of operating leverage	6 times
Interest expense	$600,000
Tax rate	35%

As the next step, you need to determine the break-even point in units of output for the company. One of your strong points has been that you always prepare supporting work papers, which show how you arrive at your conclusions. You know Maria would like to see such work papers for this analysis to facilitate her review of your work.

Therefore, you will have the information you require to prepare an analytical income statement for the company. You are sure that Maria would like to see this statement; in addition, you know that you need it to be able to answer the following questions. You also know Maria expects you to prepare, in a format that is presentable to the president, answers to the following questions to serve as a basis for her discussions with the president.

- **a.** What is the degree of financial leverage?
- **b.** What is the degree of combined leverage?
- **c.** What is the firm's break-even point in sales dollars?
- **d.** If sales should increase by 30 percent (as the president expects), by what percentage would *EBT* (earnings before taxes) and net income increase?
- **e.** Prepare another analytical income statement, this time to verify the calculations from part **d.**

2. Camping USA, Inc. has only been operating for 2 years in the outskirts of Albuquerque, New Mexico, and is a new manufacturer of a top-of-the-line camping tent. You are starting an internship as assistant to the chief financial officer of the company, and the owner and CEO, Tom Charles, has decided that this is the right time to know more about the business and financial risks his company must deal with. For this, the CFO has asked you to prepare an analysis to support him in his next meeting with Tom Charles a week from today.

To make the required calculations, you have put together the following data regarding the cost structure of the company:

Output level	120,000 units
Operating assets	$6,000,000
Operating asset turnover	12 times
Return on operating assets	48%
Degree of operating leverage	10 times
Interest expense	$720,000
Tax rate	42%

The CFO has instructed you to first determine the break-even point in units of output for the company. He requires that you prepare supporting documents, which demonstrate how you arrived at your conclusion and can facilitate his review of your work. Accordingly, you are required to have the information needed to prepare an analytical income statement for the company to be presented to the CFO. In a format that is acceptable for a meeting discussion with the CEO, you also need to prepare answers to the following questions:

   a. What is the degree of financial leverage?
   b. What is the degree of combined leverage?
   c. What is the firm's break-even point in sales dollars?
   d. If sales should increase by 40 percent, by what percentage would *EBT* (earnings before taxes) and net income increase?
   e. Prepare another analytical income statement, this time to verify the calculations from part **d.**

SELF-TEST SOLUTION

SS-1.

a.
$$[(P \cdot Q) - [(V \cdot Q) + (F)]](1 - T) = \$210,000$$
$$[(\$4,000,000) - (\$3,000,000) - F](.7) = \$210,000$$
$$(\$1,000,000 - F)(.7) = \$210,000$$
$$\$700,000 - .7F = \$210,000$$
$$.7F = \$490,000$$
$$F = \underline{\$700,000}$$

Fixed costs next year, then, are expected to be $700,000.

b.
$$Q_B = \frac{F}{P - V} = \frac{\$700,000}{\$50} = \underline{14,000} \text{ units}$$

$$S^* = \frac{F}{1 - \dfrac{VC}{S}} = \frac{\$700,000}{1 - 0.75} = \frac{\$700,000}{0.25} = \underline{\$2,800,000}$$

The firm will break even (*EBIT* = 0) when it sells 14,000 units. With a selling price of $200 per unit, the break-even sales level is $2,800,000.

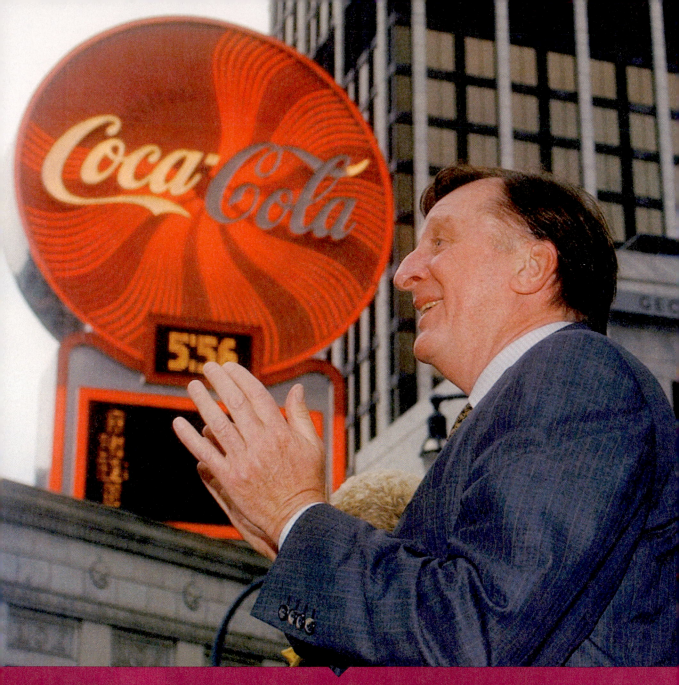

After reading this chapter, you should be able to:

1. Describe the trade-off between paying dividends and retaining the profits within the company.

2. Explain the relationship between a corporation's dividend policy and the market price of its common stock.

3. Describe practical considerations that may be important to the firm's dividend policy.

4. Distinguish among the types of dividend policies corporations frequently use.

5. Specify the procedures a company follows in administering the dividend payment.

6. Describe why and how a firm might pay noncash dividends (stock dividends and stock splits) instead of cash dividends.

7. Explain the purpose and procedures related to stock repurchases.

8. Understand the relationship between a policy of low-dividend payments and international capital budgeting opportunities that confront the multinational firm.

Dividend Policy and Internal Financing

The corporate choice to pay or not to pay a cash dividend to stockholders and the further choice to increase the dividend, reduce the dividend, or keep it at the same dollar amount represent some of the most challenging and perplexing areas of corporate financial policy. Because stockholder returns only come in two forms—stock price change and cash dividends received—it follows that the dividend decision directly impacts shareholder wealth.

We know that rational investors would rather be more wealthy than less wealthy. Accordingly, corporate boards of directors face a daunting decision every time the question of dividend policy and the possibility of changing the cash dividend is on the agenda.

In the simplest form, increasing the cash dividend simultaneously reduces the stock of internal financial capital (cash) available for capital expenditures. Thus, the firm's stockholders find themselves smack in the middle of **Principle 1: The Risk–Return Trade-Off—We Won't Take On Additional Risk Unless We Expect to Be**

Compensated with Additional Return. The cash dividend, after all, is in your hand to be spent today; the proposed capital expenditure is made based on the valuation of its expected, incremental net cash flows. Recall **Principle 4**.

The expected net present value (*NPV*) of the proposed capital project will be reflected in the firm's stock price. But, the arrival of new information over time about the success (or lack of success) of the capital project will be digested by the capital market and subsequently reflected in its stock price. So to be better off in a wealth context, the investor needs the firm to earn a higher rate of return on a dollar that is retained in the firm than that same investor could earn by investing that dollar elsewhere, given all economic considerations such as having to pay a personal tax on the dollar of cash dividends received. It is a perplexing corporate choice. But, indeed, financial executives and their firms come to grips with it. Consider the Coca-Cola Company. This firm said, "In 1996, our

❧ WHAT'S AHEAD ❧

The primary goal or objective of the firm should be to maximize the value, or price, of a firm's common stock. The success or failure of management's decisions can be evaluated only in light of their impact on the firm's common stock price. We observed that the company's investment (Chapters 9 and 10) and financing decisions (Chapter 12) can increase the value of the firm. As we look at the firm's policies regarding dividends and internal financing (how much of the company's financing comes from cash flows generated internally), we return to the same

basic question: Can management influence the price of the firm's stock, in this case through its dividend policies? After addressing this important question, we then look at the practical side of the question: What practices do managers commonly follow in making decisions about paying or not paying a dividend to the firm's stockholders? We conclude with a discussion of the multinational firm that chooses to follow a policy of low-dividend payments but is confronted, then, with the prospect of exploring international markets for high net present value projects.

dividend payout ratio was approximately 36 percent of our net income. To free up additional cash for reinvestment in our high-return beverages business, our Board of Directors intends to gradually reduce our dividend payout ratio to 30 percent over time."* This explicit statement describes Coca-Cola's dividend policy.

Starbucks Corporation, the retail coffee giant headquartered in Seattle, Washington, is just as adamant about clarity concerning its dividend policy. In this firm's 2001 annual report, management related, "The Company presently intends to retain earnings for use in its business and, therefore, does not anticipate paying a cash dividend in the near future."** You cannot get any closer to a straightforward statement concerning a zero dividend payout ratio than that.

The two preceding examples of actual dividend policy practice from Coca-Cola and Starbucks represent "north and south" pole stances on the choice to reinvest or pay out cash to shareholders. Coca-Cola feels it is prudent to pay out about 30 percent of after-tax earnings over time, whereas Starbucks' current policy is to retain earnings and put the cash to use in positive net present value projects. It is of no surprise that numerous other firms fall in between such staunch policies.

Harley-Davidson, Inc., provides a good example of a third position. Over the 7-year period 1997–2003, Harley's dividend payout ratio averaged 8.8 percent on a cash-weighted basis. Clearly, this payout ratio was more than zero but was not a large payout ratio by financial market standards. Still, Harley's absolute amount paid out in cash dividends increased each year from $0.07 per share in 1997 to $0.20 in 2003. During periods of strong internal corporate growth, firms tend to maintain modest dividend payout ratios. So, although not as severe a payout policy as that of Starbucks, Harley's policy was not as liberal as Coke's. You can see that firms have widely divergent views on appropriate dividend policies. Accordingly, dividend policy is the focus of this chapter. You will soon see that arguments and theories abound.

*The Coca-Cola Company, *Annual Report 1996*, p. 42.

**Starbucks Corporation, *Annual Report 2001*, p. 51.

KEY TERMS

Objective **1**

dividend payout ratio

Before taking up the particular issues relating to dividend policy, we must understand several key terms and interrelationships.

A firm's dividend policy includes two basic components. First, the **dividend payout ratio** indicates the *amount of dividends paid relative to the company's earnings*. For instance, if the dividend per share is $2 and the earnings per share are $4, the payout ratio is 50 percent ($2/$4). The second component is the stability of the dividends over time. As we observe later in the chapter, dividend stability may be almost as important to the investor as the amount of dividends received.

In formulating a dividend policy, the financial manager faces trade-offs. Assuming that management has already decided how much to invest and has chosen its debt–equity mix for financing these investments, the decision to pay a large dividend means simultaneously deciding to retain little, if any, profits; this in turn results in a greater reliance on external equity financing. Conversely, given the firm's investment and financing decisions, a small dividend payment corresponds to high profit retention, with less need for externally generated equity funds. These trade-offs, which are fundamental to our discussion, are illustrated in Figure 13-1.

FIGURE 13-1   Dividend Versus Retention/Financing Trade-Offs

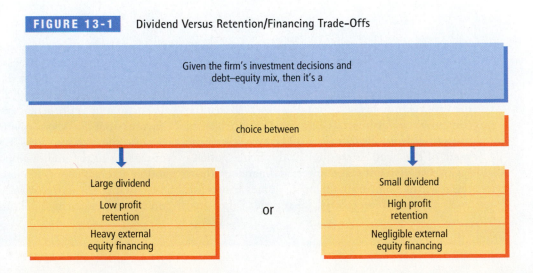

Given the firm's investment decisions and debt–equity mix, then it's a

choice between

Large dividend	or	Small dividend
Low profit retention		High profit retention
Heavy external equity financing		Negligible external equity financing

DOES DIVIDEND POLICY AFFECT STOCK PRICE?[1]

Objective **2**

The fundamental question to be resolved in our study of the firm's dividend policy may be stated simply as, What is a sound rationale or motivation for dividend payments? If we believe our objective should be to maximize the value of the common stock, we may restate the question as, Given the firm's capital-budgeting and borrowing decisions, what is the effect of the firm's dividend policies on the stock price? *Does a high dividend payment decrease stock value, increase it, or make no real difference?*

At first glance, we might reasonably conclude that a firm's dividend policy is important. We have already (Chapter 8) defined the value of a stock to be equal to the present value of future dividends. How can we now suggest that dividends are not important? Why do so many companies pay dividends, and why is a page in *The Wall Street Journal* devoted to dividend announcements? Based on intuition, we could quickly conclude that dividend policy is important. However, we might be surprised to learn that the dividend question has been a controversial issue for well more than three decades. Fischer Black, some 25 years ago, called it the "dividend puzzle." In his words:

> Why do corporations pay dividends? Why do investors pay attention to dividends? Perhaps the answers to these questions are obvious. Perhaps the answers are not so obvious. I claim the answers to these questions are not obvious at all. The harder we look at the dividend picture, the more it seems like a puzzle, with pieces that just don't fit together. What should the individual investor do about dividends in his portfolio? We don't know. What should the corporation do about dividend policy? We don't know.[2]

Twenty years later, in 1996, Peter Bernstein reexamined the "puzzle that fascinated Fischer Black."[3] He concluded the role of dividend policy in creating shareholder value is still very much a puzzle.

THREE BASIC VIEWS

Some would argue that the amount of dividend is irrelevant and any time spent on the decision is a waste of energy. Others contend that a high dividend results in a high stock price. Still others take the view that dividends actually hurt the stock value. Let us look at these three views in turn.

VIEW 1: DIVIDEND POLICY IS IRRELEVANT

Much of the controversy about the dividend issue is based in time-honored disagreements between the academic and professional communities. Experienced practitioners perceive stock price changes as resulting from dividend announcements and, therefore, see dividends as important. Professors who argue that dividends are irrelevant see a failure to carefully

[1]The concepts of this section draw heavily from Donald H. Chew, Jr., ed., "Do Dividends Matter? A Discussion of Corporate Dividend Policy," in *Six Roundtable Discussions of Corporate Finance with Joel Stern* (New York: Quorum Books, 1986), pp. 67–101; and a book of readings edited by Joel M. Stern and Donald H. Chew, Jr., *The Revolution in Corporate Finance* (New York: Basil Blackwell, 1986). A later discussion on the firm's dividend policy, but with the same conclusions as the other articles just listed, is Michael J. Barclay, Clifford W. Smith, and Ross L. Watts, "The Determinants of Corporate Leverage and Dividend Policies," *Journal of Applied Corporate Finance* 7, no. 4 (Winter 1995), pp. 4–19.
[2]Fischer Black, "The Dividend Puzzle," *Journal of Portfolio Management* 2 (Winter 1976), pp. 5–8.
[3]Peter L. Bernstein, "Dividends: The Puzzle," *Journal of Applied Corporate Finance* 9, no. 1 (Spring 1996), pp. 16–22.

define dividend policy and argue that the relationship between dividends and stock price may be an illusion.[4]

The position that dividends are not important rests on two preconditions. First, we assume that investment and borrowing decisions have already been made and that these decisions will not be altered by the amount of any dividend payments. Second, **perfect capital markets** are assumed to exist, which means that *(1) investors can buy and sell stocks without incurring any transaction costs, such as brokerage commissions; (2) companies can issue stocks without any cost of doing so; (3) there are no corporate or personal taxes; (4) complete information about the firm is readily available; (5) there are no conflicts of interest between management and stockholders; and (6) financial distress and bankruptcy costs are nonexistent.*

perfect capital markets

The first assumption—that we have already made the investment and financing decisions—simply keeps us from confusing the issues. We want to know the effect of dividend decisions on a stand-alone basis, without mixing in other decisions. The second assumption, that of perfect markets, also allows us to study the effect of dividend decisions in isolation, much as a physicist studies motion in a vacuum to avoid the influence of friction.

Given these assumptions, the effect of a dividend decision on share price may be stated unequivocally: *There is no relationship between dividend policy and stock value.* One dividend policy is as good as another. In the aggregate, investors are concerned only with *total* returns from investment decisions; they are indifferent whether these returns come from capital gains or dividend income. They also recognize that the dividend decision, given the investment policy, is really a choice of financing strategy. That is, to finance growth, the firm (a) may choose to issue stock, allowing internally generated funds (profits) to be used to pay dividends; or (b) it may use internally generated funds to finance its growth, while paying less in dividends but not having to issue stock. In the first case, shareholders receive dividend income; in the second case, the value of their stock should increase, providing capital gains. The nature of the return is the only difference; total returns should be about the same. Thus, to argue that paying dividends can make shareholders better off is to argue that paying out cash with one hand and taking it back with the other is a worthwhile activity for management.

The firm's dividend payout could affect stock price if the shareholder has no other way to receive income from the investment. However, assuming the capital markets are relatively efficient, a stockholder who needs current income could always sell shares. If the firm pays a dividend, the investor could eliminate any dividend received, in whole or in part, by using the dividend to purchase stock. The investor can, thus, personally create any desired dividend stream, no matter what dividend policy is in effect.

VIEW 2: HIGH DIVIDENDS INCREASE STOCK VALUE

The belief that a firm's dividend policy is unimportant implicitly assumes that an investor is indifferent about whether income comes through capital gains or through dividends. However, dividends are more predictable than capital gains; management can control dividends, but it cannot dictate the price of the stock. Investors are less certain of receiving income from capital gains than from dividends. The incremental risk associated with capital gains relative to dividend income implies a higher required rate for discounting a dollar of capital gains than for discounting a dollar of dividends. In other words, we would value a dollar of expected dividends more highly than a dollar of expected capital gains. We might, for example, require a 14 percent rate of return for a stock that pays its entire return from dividends, but a 20 percent return for a high-growth stock that pays no dividend. In so doing, we would give a higher value to the dividend income than we would to the capital gains. This view, which says *dividends are more certain than capital gains*, has been called the **bird-in-the-hand dividend theory**.

bird-in-the-hand dividend theory

The position that dividends are less risky than capital gains, and should, therefore, be valued differently, is not without its critics. If we hold to our basic decision not to let the

---

[4]For an excellent presentation of this issue, see Merton Miller, "Can Management Use Dividends to Influence the Value of the Firm?" in Stern and Chew, eds., *The Revolution in Corporate Finance* (New York: Basil Blackwell, 1986), pp. 299–305.

firm's dividend policy influence its investment and capital-mix decisions, the company's operating cash flows, in both expected amount and variability, are unaffected by its dividend policy. Because the dividend policy has no impact on the volatility of the company's overall cash flows, it has no impact on the riskiness of the firm.

Increasing a firm's dividend does not reduce the basic riskiness of the stock; rather, if a dividend payment requires management to issue new stock, it only transfers risk *and* ownership from the current owners to new owners. We would have to acknowledge that the current investors who receive the dividend trade an uncertain capital gain for a "safe" asset (the cash dividend). However, if risk reduction is the only goal, the investor could have kept the money in the bank and not bought the stock in the first place.

We might find fault with this bird-in-the-hand dividend theory, but there is still a strong perception among many investors and professional investment advisers that dividends are important. They frequently argue their case based on their own personal experience, as expressed by one investment adviser:

> In advising companies on dividend policy, we're absolutely sure on one side that the investors in companies like the utilities and the suburban banks want dividends. We're absolutely sure on the other side that … the high-technology companies should have no dividends. For the high earners—the ones that have a high rate of return like 20 percent or more than their cost of capital—we think they should have a low payout ratio. We think a typical industrial company which earns its cost of capital—just earns its cost of capital—probably should be in the average [dividend payout] range of 40 to 50 percent.[5]

BACK TO THE FOUNDATIONS

*The previous discussion specifying the "bird-in-the-hand" theory between the relationship of stock price and the firm's dividend policy relates directly to **Principle 2: The Time Value of Money—A Dollar Received Today Is Worth More Than a Dollar Received in the Future**. This theory suggests that because the dollar of dividends is received today it should be valued more highly than an uncertain capital gain that might be received in the future. The fundamental premise of this position is that the cash dividend in your hand (placed there today by the firm's payout policy) is more certain (less risky) than a possible capital gain. Many practitioners adhere to this theory; but many also adhere to the theory that is advanced in the next section. If nothing else, because it is controversial, dividend policy is important to the firm and its stockholders. And, in reality, many companies do pay cash dividends. Cash dividends are ubiquitous, so they are discussed in depth.*

VIEW 3: LOW DIVIDENDS INCREASE STOCK VALUE

The third view of how dividends affect stock price argues that dividends actually hurt the investors. This belief has largely been based on the difference in tax treatment for dividend income and capital gains. Contrary to the perfect-markets assumption of no taxes, most investors do pay income taxes. For these taxpayers, the objective is to maximize the *after-tax* return on investment relative to the risk assumed. This objective is realized by *minimizing* the effective tax rate on the income and, whenever possible, by *deferring* the payment of taxes.

Like most tax code complexities, Congress over the years has altered the outcome of whether capital gains are taxed at either (1) a lower or (2) similar rate as "earned income." Think of a water faucet being randomly turned on and then off. From 1987 through 1992, no federal tax advantage was provided for capital gains income relative to dividend income. A revision in the tax code that took effect beginning in 1993 did provide a preference for capital gains income. Then the Taxpayer Relief Act of 1997 made the difference (preference) even more favorable for capital gains as opposed to cash dividend income. For some

---

[5]From a discussion by John Childs, an investment adviser at Kidder Peabody, in Chew, ed., "Do Dividends Matter?" in *Six Roundtable Discussions of Corporate Finance with Joel Stern* (New York: Quorum Books, 1986), pp. 83–84.

taxpayers, if a minimum holding period had been reached, the tax rate applied to capital gains was reduced to 20 percent from the previous level of 28 percent. But wait, then came 2003 and Congress again felt the need to change the tax code as it pertained to both dividend income and capital gains income. On May 28, President Bush signed into law the Jobs and Growth Tax Relief Reconciliation Act of 2003. Recall that part of the impetus for this act was the recession that commenced in 2001 and the slow rate of payroll jobs creation that followed that recession.

In a nutshell this 2003 act lowered the top tax rate on dividend income to 15 percent from a previous top rate of 38.6 percent and also lowered the top rate paid on realized long-term capital gains to the same 15 percent from a previous 20 percent. Thus, you can see that the so-called investment playing field was (mostly) leveled for dividend income relative to qualifying capital gains. This rather dramatic change in the tax code will immediately remind you of **Principle 8: Taxes Bias Business Decisions**. In effect, a major portion of the previous bias against paying cash dividends to investors was mitigated. But, not all of it, as is pointed out next.

Actually a different benefit exists for capital gains returns relative to dividend income. Taxes on dividend income are paid when the dividend is received, whereas taxes on price appreciation (capital gains) are deferred until the stock is actually sold.

Thus, when it comes to tax considerations, many investors prefer the retention of a firm's earnings—in expectation of a later capital gain—as opposed to the near-term payment of cash dividends. Again, if earnings are retained within the firm, hopefully the stock price increases, but the increase is not taxed until the stock is sold.

Although the majority of investors are subject to taxes, certain investment companies, trusts, and pension plans are exempt on their dividend income. Also, for tax purposes, a corporation may generally exclude 70 percent of the dividend income received from another corporation. In these cases, and unlike the above situations, investors may prefer dividends over capital gains.

To summarize, when it comes to taxes, we want to maximize our *after*-tax return, as opposed to the *before*-tax return. Investors try to defer taxes whenever possible. Stocks that allow tax deferral (low dividends–high capital gains) will possibly sell at a premium relative to stocks that require current taxation (high dividends–low capital gains). In this way, the two stocks may provide comparable *after-tax* returns. This suggests that a policy of paying low dividends will result in a higher stock price. That is, high dividends hurt investors, whereas low dividends and high retention help investors. This is the logic of the advocates of the low-dividend policy. It does presume that the firm's management has a roster of positive net present value projects that will put the dollars retained to productive use. As pointed out, the 2003 act reduced the value of this logic and placed more emphasis on dividends paid to investors.

IMPROVING OUR THINKING

We have now looked at three views on dividend policy. Which is right? The argument that dividends are irrelevant is difficult to refute, given the perfect market assumptions. However, in the real world, it is not always easy to feel comfortable with such an argument. Conversely, the high-dividend philosophy, which measures risk by how we split the firm's cash flows between dividends and retention, is not particularly appealing when studied carefully. The third view, which is essentially a tax argument against high dividends, is persuasive. Even today, although the preferential tax rate for capital gains is limited, its "deferral advantage" is still alive and well. However, if low dividends are so advantageous and generous dividends are so hurtful, why do companies continue to pay dividends? It is difficult to believe that managers would forgo such an easy opportunity to benefit their stockholders. What are we missing?

The need to find the missing elements in our "dividend puzzle" has not been ignored. When we need to better understand an issue or phenomenon, we can either improve our thinking or gather more evidence about the topic. Scholars and practitioners have taken both approaches. Although no single definitive answer has yet been found that is acceptable to all, several plausible extensions have been developed. Some of the more popular additions include (1) the residual dividend theory, (2) the clientele effect, (3) the information effect, (4) agency costs, and (5) expectations theory.

THE RESIDUAL DIVIDEND THEORY

In perfect markets, we assume there is no cost to the firm when it issues new securities. However, in reality the process is quite expensive, and the flotation costs associated with a new offering may be as much as 20 percent of the dollar issue size. Thus, if management chooses to issue stock rather than retain profits to finance new investments, a larger amount of securities is required to receive the amount needed for the investment. For example, if $300,000 is needed to finance proposed investments, an amount exceeding the $300,000 will have to be issued to offset flotation costs incurred in the sale of the new stock issue. This means, very simply, that new equity capital raised through the sale of common stock will be more expensive than capital raised through the retention of earnings.

In effect, flotation costs eliminate our indifference between financing by internal capital and by new common stock. Given these costs, *dividends would be paid only if profits are not completely used for investment purposes;* that is, only when there are "residual earnings" after the financing of new investments. This policy is called the **residual dividend theory.**[6]

residual dividend theory

Given the existence of flotation costs, the firm's dividend policy should now be as follows:

1. Accept an investment if the *NPV* is positive; that is, if the expected rate of return exceeds the cost of capital.
2. Finance the equity portion of new investments *first* by internally generated funds. Only after this capital is fully utilized should the firm issue new common shares.
3. If any internally generated funds still remain after making all investments, pay dividends to the investors. However, if all internal capital is needed for financing the equity portion of proposed investments, pay no dividend.

Thus, dividend policy is influenced by (1) the company's investment opportunities and (2) the availability of internally generated capital, when dividends are paid *only* after all acceptable investments have been financed. According to this concept, dividend policy is totally passive in nature, having by itself no direct influence on the market price of the common stock.

Now, let us consider a dose of corporate reality. In the introduction to this chapter we talked briefly about the dividend policy of Starbucks Corporation. Recall that the company's management said, "The Company has never paid any dividends on its common stock. The Company presently intends to retain earnings for use in its business and, therefore, does not anticipate paying a cash dividend in the near future."[7]

Notice that management does not say, in absolute terms, that it will *never* pay a cash dividend. It just does not "anticipate" doing that for a while. Should Starbucks maintain its current policy of financing capital projects out of retentions, but then have cash left over and pay some of that out as dividends, the firm would be applying, in the pure sense, the residual dividend theory.

THE CLIENTELE EFFECT

What if the investors do not like the dividend policy chosen by management? In perfect markets, in which we have no costs in buying or selling stock, there is no problem. The investors may simply satisfy their personal income preferences by purchasing or selling

---

[6]The residual dividend theory is consistent with the "pecking order" theory of finance as described by Stewart Myers, "The Capital Structure Puzzle," *Journal of Finance* (July 1984), pp. 575–92.
[7]Starbucks Corporation, *Annual Report 2001*, p. 51.

securities when the dividends received do not satisfy their current needs for income. If an investor does not view the dividends received in any given year to be sufficient, he or she can simply sell a portion of stock, thereby "creating a dividend." In addition, if the dividend is larger than the investor desired, he or she will purchase stock with the "excess cash" created by the dividend. However, once we remove the assumption of perfect markets, we find that buying or selling stock is not cost free. Brokerage fees are incurred, ranging approximately from 1 percent to 10 percent. Even more costly is that the investor who buys the stock with cash received from a dividend will have to pay taxes before reinvesting the cash. And when a stock is bought or sold, it must first be reevaluated. Acquisition of the information for decision making also may be time-consuming and costly. Finally, aside from the cost of buying or selling part of the stock, some institutional investors, such as university endowment funds, are precluded from selling stock and "spending" the proceeds.

As a result of these considerations, investors may not be too inclined to buy stocks that require them to "create" a dividend stream more suitable to their purposes. Rather, if investors do in fact have a preference between dividends and capital gains, we could expect them to seek firms that have a dividend policy consistent with these preferences. They would, in essence, "sort themselves out" by buying stocks that satisfy their preferences for dividends and capital gains. Individuals and institutions that need current income would be drawn to companies that have high-dividend payouts. Other investors, such as wealthy individuals, would much prefer to avoid taxes by holding securities that offer no or small dividend income but large capital gains. In other words, there would be a **clientele effect**: *Firms draw a given clientele, given their stated dividend policy.*

clientele effect

The possibility that clienteles of investors exist might lead us to believe that the firm's dividend policy matters. However, unless there is a greater aggregate demand for a particular policy than the market can satisfy, dividend policy is still unimportant; one policy is as good as the other. The clientele effect only warns firms to avoid making capricious changes in their dividend policy. Given that the firm's investment decisions are already made, the level of the dividend is still unimportant. The change in the policy matters only when it requires clientele to shift to another company.

THE INFORMATION EFFECT

The investor in the world of perfect markets would argue with considerable persuasion that a firm's value is determined strictly by its investment and financing decisions and that the dividend policy has no impact on value. Yet we know from experience that a large, unexpected change in dividends can have a significant impact on the stock price. For instance, in November 1990, Occidental Petroleum cut its dividend from $2 to $1. In response, the firm's stock price went from about $32 to $17. How can we suggest that dividend policy matters little, when we can cite numerous such examples of a change in dividend affecting the stock price, especially when the change is negative?

Despite such "evidence," we are not looking at the real cause and effect. It may be that investors use a change in dividend policy as a *signal* about the firm's financial condition, especially its earning power. Thus, a dividend increase that is larger than expected might signal to investors that management expects significantly higher earnings in the future. Conversely, a dividend decrease, or even a less-than-expected increase, might signal that management is forecasting less-favorable future earnings.

Some would claim that management frequently has inside information about the firm that it cannot make available to investors. This *difference in accessibility to information between management and investors,* called **information asymmetry**, *may result in a lower stock price than would occur under conditions of certainty*. This reasoning says that, by regularly increasing dividends, management is making a commitment to continue these cash flows to the stockholders for the foreseeable future. So in a risky marketplace, dividends become a means to minimize any "drag" on the stock price that might come from differences in the level of information available to managers and investors.

information asymmetry

Dividends may, therefore, be important only as a communication tool; management may have no other credible way to inform investors about future earnings, or at least no convincing way that is less costly.

AGENCY COSTS

Up to this point, we have not allowed for separation between management and owners. However, with only a superficial look at the real world, we know that managers and investors are typically not the same people. Moreover, they do not have access to the same information about the firm; at times they do not even have the same incentives.

If the two groups are not the same, we must then assume that management is dedicated to the same goals as its owners. That is, we are making a presupposition that the behavior of companies with separate owners and managers will not differ from the behavior of owner-managed firms.

BACK TO THE FOUNDATIONS

*Principle 7 warned us there may be a conflict between management and owners, especially in large firms in which managers and owners have different incentives. That is, **Managers Won't Work for the Owners Unless It Is in Their Best Interest** to do so. As we shall see in this section, the dividend policy may be one way to reduce this problem.*

In reality, however, conflicts may still exist, and the stock price of a company owned by investors who are separate from management may be less than the stock value of a closely held firm. This potential difference in price is the *cost of the conflict to the owners*, which has come to be called **agency costs**.[8]

agency costs

Recognizing the possible problem, management, acting independently or at the insistence of the board of directors, frequently takes action to minimize the cost associated with the separation of ownership and management control. Such action, which in itself is costly, includes auditing by independent accountants, assigning supervisory functions to the company's board of directors, creating covenants in lending agreements that restrict management's powers, and providing incentive compensation plans for management that help "bond" management with the owners.

A firm's dividend policy may be perceived by owners as a tool to minimize agency costs. Assuming that the payment of a dividend requires management to issue stock to finance new investments, new investors may be attracted to the company only if management provides convincing information that the capital will be used profitably. Thus, the payment of dividends indirectly results in a closer monitoring of management's investment activities. In this case, dividends may make a meaningful contribution to the value of the firm.

EXPECTATIONS THEORY[9]

A common thread through much of our discussion of dividend policy, particularly as it relates to information effects, is the word *expected*. We should not overlook the significance of this word when we are making any financial decision within the firm. *No matter what the decision area, how the market price responds to management's actions is not determined entirely by the action itself; it is also affected by investors' expectations about the ultimate decision to be made by management.* This concept or idea is called the **expectations theory**.

expectations theory

---

[8]See M. C. Jensen and W. H. Meckling, "Theory of the Firm: Managerial Behavior, Agency Costs, and Ownership Structure," *Journal of Financial Economics* (October 1976), pp. 305–60.
[9]Much of the thinking in this section came from Miller, "Can Management Use Dividends to Influence the Value of the Firm?" in Stern and Chew, eds., *The Revolution in Corporate Finance* (New York: Basil Blackwell, 1986), pp. 299–303.

As the time approaches for management to announce the amount of the next dividend, investors form expectations about how much that dividend will be. These expectations are based on several factors internal to the firm, such as past dividend decisions, current and expected earnings, investment strategies, and financing decisions. They also consider such things as the condition of the general economy, the strength or weakness of the industry at the time, and possible changes in government policies.

When the actual dividend decision is announced, the investor compares the actual decision with the expected decision. If the amount of the dividend is as expected, even if it represents an increase from prior years, the market price of the stock will remain unchanged. However, if the dividend is higher or lower than expected, investors will reassess their perceptions of the firm. They will question the meaning of the *unexpected* change in the dividend. They may use the unexpected dividend decision as a clue about unexpected changes in earnings; that is, the unexpected dividend change has information content about the firm's earnings and other important factors. In short, management's actual decision about the firm's dividend policy may not be terribly significant, unless it departs from investors' expectations. If there is a difference between actual and expected dividends, we will more than likely see a movement in the stock price.

THE EMPIRICAL EVIDENCE

Our search for an answer to the question of dividend relevance has been less than successful. We have given it our best thinking, but still no single definitive position has emerged. Maybe we could gather evidence to show the relationship between dividend practices and security prices. We might also inquire into the perceptions of financial managers who make decisions about dividend policies, with the idea that their beliefs affect their decision making. Then we could truly know that dividend policy is important or that it does not matter.

To test the relationship between dividend payments and security prices, we could compare a firm's dividend yield (dividend/stock price) and the stock's total return. The question is, Do stocks that pay high dividends provide higher or lower returns to investors? Such tests have been conducted with the use of highly sophisticated statistical techniques. Despite the use of these extremely powerful analytical tools, which involve intricate and complicated procedures, the results have been mixed.[10] However, over long periods, the results have given a slight advantage to the low-dividend stocks; that is, stocks that pay lower dividends appear to have higher prices. More recently, researchers have found some modest relationships between a firm's dividend policy and share price, but still nothing convincing either way.[11] Thus, the findings are far from conclusive, however, owing to the relatively large standard errors of the estimates. (The apparent differences may be the result of random sampling error and not real differences.) We simply have been unable to disentangle the effect of dividend policy from other influences.

Several reasons may be given for our inability to arrive at conclusive results. First, to be accurate, we would need to know the amount of dividends investors *expected* to receive. Because these expectations cannot be observed, we can only use historical data, which may or may not relate to current expectations. Second, most empirical studies have assumed a linear relationship between dividend payments and stock prices. The actual relationship may be nonlinear, possibly even discontinuous. Whatever the reasons, the evidence to date is inconclusive and the jury is still out.

Because our statistical prowess does not provide any conclusive evidence, let's turn to our last hope. What do the financial managers of the world believe about the relevance of dividend policy? Although we may not conclude that a manager's opinion is necessarily the "final word on the matter," having these insights is helpful. If financial managers believe that dividends matter and act consistently in accordance with that conviction, they could

---

[10]See F. Black and M. Scholes, "The Effects of Dividend Yield and Dividend Policy on Common Stock Prices and Returns," *Journal of Financial Economics* 1 (May 1974), pp. 1–22; and M. H. Miller and M. Scholes, "Dividends and Taxes: Some Empirical Evidence," *Journal of Political Economy* 90 (1982), pp. 1118–41.
[11]Clifford Smith and Ross Watts, "The Investment Opportunity Set and Corporate Financing, Dividend, and Compensation Policies," *Journal of Financial Economics* 32 (1992), pp. 263–92.

influence the relationship between stock value and dividend policy. As stated by one group of researchers:

> In the matter of dividend policy, designing broad-based tests of actual corporate decision-making that would allow us to distinguish among these theories has proven to be quite difficult. The dearth of reliable empirical evidence on this topic has forced proponents of each theory to rely largely on anecdotes to buttress their arguments.[12]

To help us gain some understanding of management's perceptions, let's turn to a study by Baker, Farrelly, and Edelman that surveyed financial executives at 318 firms listed on the New York Stock Exchange.[13] The study favors the relevance of dividend policy, but not overwhelmingly so. For the most part, managers are divided between (a) believing that dividends are important or (b) having no opinion about the matter.

Regarding the question about the price–dividend relationship, Baker et al. asked the financial managers straight up, "Does the firm's dividend policy affect the price of the common stock?" Slightly more than 60 percent of the responses were affirmative, which is significant, but there were still almost 40 percent who had no opinion or disagreed. Thus, we could conclude that most managers think that dividends matter, but they have no mandate. Similarly, when asked if dividends provide informational content about the firm's future, the managers are basically split between no opinion and agreement. When asked about the trade-off between dividends and capital gains, almost two-thirds of the managers thought stockholders have a preference either for dividends or capital gains, with a lesser number (56 percent) believing that investors perceive the relative riskiness of capital gains and dividends to be different. Interestingly enough, though, almost half of the managers felt no clear responsibility to be responsive to stockholders' preferences.

WHAT ARE WE TO CONCLUDE?

We have now looked carefully at the importance of a firm's dividend policy as management seeks to increase the shareholders' wealth. We have gone to great lengths to gain insight and understanding from our best thinking. We have even drawn from the empirical evidence on hand to see what the findings suggest.

A reasonable person cannot reach a definitive conclusion; nevertheless, management is left with no choice. A firm must develop a dividend policy, based, it is hoped, on the best available knowledge. Although we can give advice with some reservation, the following conclusions would appear reasonable:

1. As a firm's investment opportunities increase, the dividend payout ratio should decrease. In other words, an inverse relationship should exist between the amount of investments with expected rates of return that exceed the cost of capital (positive *NPV*s) and the dividends remitted to investors. Because of flotation costs associated with raising external capital, the retention of internally generated equity financing is preferable to selling stock (in terms of the wealth of the current common shareholders).

2. The firm's dividend policy appears to be important; however, appearances may be deceptive. The real issue may be the firm's *expected* earning power and the riskiness of these earnings. Investors may be using the dividend payment as a source of information about the company's *expected* earnings. Management's actions regarding dividends may carry greater weight than a statement by management that earnings will be increasing.

3. If dividends influence stock price, this is probably based on the investor's desire to minimize and defer taxes and on the role of dividends in minimizing agency costs.

4. If the expectations theory has merit, which we believe it does, management should avoid surprising investors when it comes to the firm's dividend decision. The firm's dividend policy might effectively be treated as a *long-term residual*. Rather than project investment requirements for a single year, management could anticipate financing needs for several

[12]Barclay, Smith, and Watts, "The Determinants of Corporate Leverage and Dividend Policies," *Journal of Corporate Finance* 7, no. 4 (Winter 1995), p. 4.
[13]H. Kent Baker, Gail E. Farrelly, and Richard B. Edelman, "A Survey of Management Views on Dividend Policy," *Financial Management* 14 (Autumn 1985), pp. 78–84.

years. Based on the expected investment opportunities during the planning horizon, the firm's debt–equity mix, and the funds generated from operations, a *target* dividend payout ratio could be established. If internal funds remained after projection of the necessary equity financing, dividends would be paid. However, the planned dividend stream should distribute residual capital evenly to investors over the planning period. Conversely, if over the long term the entire amount of internally generated capital is needed for reinvestment in the company, then no dividend should be paid.

CONCEPT CHECK

1. Summarize the position that dividend policy may be irrelevant with regard to the firm's stock price.
2. What is meant by the bird-in-the-hand dividend theory?
3. Why are cash dividend payments thought to be more certain than prospective capital gains?
4. How might personal taxes affect both the firm's dividend policy and its share price?
5. Distinguish between the residual dividend theory and the clientele effect.

Objective **3**

THE DIVIDEND DECISION IN PRACTICE

In setting a firm's dividend policy, financial managers must work in the world of reality with the concepts we have set forth so far in this chapter. Again, although these concepts do not provide an equation that explains the key relationships, they certainly give us a more complete view of the finance world, which can only help us make better decisions. Other considerations of a more practical nature also appear as part of the firm's decision making about its dividend policy.

OTHER PRACTICAL CONSIDERATIONS

Many considerations may influence a firm's decision about its dividends, some of them unique to that company. Some of the more general considerations are given here.

LEGAL RESTRICTIONS

Certain legal restrictions may limit the amount of dividends a firm may pay. These legal constraints fall into two categories. First, *statutory restrictions* may prevent a company from paying dividends. Although specific limitations vary by state, generally a corporation may not pay a dividend (1) if the firm's liabilities exceed its assets, (2) if the amount of the dividend exceeds the accumulated profits (retained earnings), and (3) if the dividend is being paid from capital invested in the firm.

The second type of legal restriction is unique to each firm and results from restrictions in debt and preferred stock contracts. To minimize their risk, investors frequently impose restrictive provisions on management as a condition to their investment in the company. These constraints may include the provision that dividends may not be declared before the debt is repaid. Also, the corporation may be required to maintain a given amount of working capital. Preferred stockholders may stipulate that common dividends may not be paid when any preferred dividends are delinquent.

LIQUIDITY POSITION

Contrary to common opinion, the mere fact that a company shows a large amount of retained earnings in the balance sheet does not indicate that cash is available for the payment of dividends. The firm's current position in liquid assets, including cash, is basically independent of the retained earnings account. Historically, a company with sizable retained earnings has been successful in generating cash from operations. Yet these funds typically are either reinvested in the company within a short period or are used to pay maturing debt. Thus, a firm may be extremely profitable and still be *cash poor*. Because dividends are paid with cash, *and not with retained earnings*, the firm must have cash available for dividends to be paid. Hence, the firm's liquidity position has a direct bearing on its ability to pay dividends.

ABSENCE OR LACK OF OTHER SOURCES OF FINANCING

As already noted, a firm may (1) retain profits for reinvestment purposes or (2) pay dividends and issue new debt or equity securities to finance investments. For many small or new companies, this second option is not realistic. These firms do not have access to the capital markets, so they must rely more heavily on internally generated funds. As a consequence, the dividend payout ratio is generally much lower for a small or newly established firm than for a large, publicly owned corporation.

EARNINGS PREDICTABILITY

A company's dividend payout ratio depends to some extent on the predictability of a firm's profits over time. If earnings fluctuate significantly, management cannot rely on internally generated funds to meet future needs. When profits are realized, the firm may retain larger amounts to ensure that money is available when needed. Conversely, a firm with a stable earnings trend will typically pay out a larger portion of its earnings in dividends. This company has less concern about the availability of profits to meet future capital requirements.

OWNERSHIP CONTROL

For many large corporations, control through the ownership of common stock is not an issue. However, for many small and medium-sized companies, maintaining voting control takes a high priority. If the current common stockholders are unable to participate in a new offering, issuing new stock is unattractive, in that the control of the current stockholder is diluted. The owners might prefer that management finance new investments with debt and through profits rather than by issuing new common stock. This firm's growth is then constrained by the amount of debt capital available and by the company's ability to generate profits.

INFLATION

Before the late 1970s, inflationary pressures had not been a significant problem for either consumers or businesses. However, during much of the 1980s, the deterioration of the dollar's purchasing power had a direct impact on the replacement of fixed assets. In a period of inflation, as fixed assets become worn and obsolete, the funds generated from the depreciation tax shield ideally are used to finance the replacements. As the cost of equivalent equipment continues to increase, the depreciation funds become insufficient. This requires a greater retention of profits, which implies that dividends have to be adversely affected.

ALTERNATIVE DIVIDEND POLICIES

Objective **4**

Regardless of a firm's long-term dividend policy, most firms choose one of several year-to-year dividend payment patterns.

1. **Constant dividend payout ratio**. In this policy, the *percentage of earnings paid out in dividends is held constant*. Although the dividend-to-earnings ratio is stable, the dollar amount of the dividend naturally fluctuates from year to year as profits vary. *(constant dividend payout ratio)*

2. **Stable dollar dividend per share**. This policy *maintains a relatively stable dollar dividend over time*. An increase in the dollar dividend usually does not occur until management is convinced that the higher dividend level can be maintained in the future. Management also will not reduce the dollar dividend until the evidence clearly indicates that a continuation of the current dividend cannot be supported. *(stable dollar dividend per share)*

3. **Small, regular dividend plus a year-end extra**. A corporation following this policy *pays a small, regular dollar dividend plus a year-end extra dividend in prosperous years*. The extra dividend is declared toward the end of the fiscal year, when the company's profits for the period can be estimated. Management's objective is *to avoid the connotation of a permanent dividend*. However, this purpose may be defeated if *recurring* extra dividends come to be expected by investors. *(small, regular dividend plus a year-end extra)*

On July 20, 2004, technology giant Microsoft set a new financial market standard for the concept of an "extra or special dividend." Prior to the announcement, Microsoft had been paying a quarterly dividend of $0.04 per share or $0.16 annually. The special dividend was set at a comparatively whopping $3.00 per share. The company's common stock, which trades on the NASDAQ, at the time was selling for about $30.00 per share. Across all shareholders this extra dividend totaled approximately $32 billion. Simultaneously, Microsoft management stated that it would (1) double the regular common stock dividend amount to $0.32 per share annually, and (2) repurchase up to $30 billion of its common stock over the next 4 years. Microsoft valued the complex change in dividend policy at $75 billion over the ensuing 4 years. As a sidelight, Mr. William H. Gates III, the firm's chairman, was thought to personally receive $3.49 billion based on the number of common stock shares that he owned. It is fair to suggest that no prior action in corporate practice ever highlighted the importance of dividend policy to the extent of this shift in Microsoft's payout (retention) tendencies. The company had moved from a high-growth firm to a mature firm.[14]

increasing-stream hypothesis of dividend policy

Of the three dividend policies, the stable dollar dividend is by far the most common. In one study, corporate managers were found to be reluctant to change the dollar amount of the dividend in response to temporary fluctuations in earnings from year to year. This aversion was particularly evident when it came to decreasing the amount of the dividend from the previous level.[15] One explanation for the stable dividend is the **increasing-stream hypothesis of dividend policy**, which suggests that *dividend stability is essentially a smoothing of the dividend stream to minimize the effect of other types of company reversals.*[16] Thus, corporate managers make every effort to avoid a dividend cut, attempting instead to develop a gradually increasing dividend series over the long-term future. However, if a dividend reduction is absolutely necessary, the cut should be large enough to reduce the probability of future cuts.

EXAMPLE

We have discussed several alternative corporate-dividend policies. Here we have some actual data from Harley-Davidson that provide insight into that firm's payout policy. The table presents Harley's actual reported earnings and dividends per share, along with the calculated dividend payout ratio, which is shown in the right-hand column.

EARNINGS PER SHARE, DIVIDENDS PER SHARE, AND THE DIVIDEND PAYOUT RATIO: HARLEY-DAVIDSON, INC., 1997–2003

YEAR	EARNINGS PER SHARE	DIVIDENDS PER SHARE	PAYOUT RATIO %
1997	$0.57[a]	$0.07	12.3
1998	0.69	0.08	11.6
1999	0.86	0.09	10.5
2000	1.13	0.10	8.8
2001	1.43	0.12	8.4
2002	1.90	0.14	7.4
2003	2.50	0.20	8.0

[a]This series represents "diluted" earnings.

Source: Basic data from Harley-Davidson, Inc., *Annual Report 2003*, p. 8. Harley-Davidson maintains a fine Web site at www.HarleyDavidson.com. Go there, click on "site map" and then click on "investor relations" and you can review several annual reports.

[14]Owing to the enormity of the Microsoft extra or special dividend, major financial publications covered the decision extensively. See Gary Rivlin, "Microsoft to Pay Special Dividend to Stockholders," *The New York Times*, July 21, 2004, pp. A1 and C12; Robert A. Guth and Scott Thurm, "Microsoft to Dole Out Its Cash Hoard," *The Wall Street Journal*, July 21, 2004, pp. A1, 8; and Patrick Seitz, "Microsoft to Use Cash for a $30 Billion Buyback and One-Time Payout," *Investor's Business Daily*, July 21, 2004, pp. A1, 6.

[15]John Lintner, "Distribution of Income of Corporations among Dividends, Retained Earnings, and Taxes," *American Economic Review* 46 (May 1956), pp. 97–113.

[16]Keith V. Smith, "Increasing-Stream Hypothesis of Corporate Dividend Policy," *California Management Review* 15 (Fall 1971), pp. 56–64.

Now, which of the alternative dividend policies that we reviewed does the management of Harley seem to follow? Notice two important elements: (1) The payout ratio decreases on balance over the given 7-year time frame, and (2) the actual cash dividend paid over time increased each year. Also be aware that the alternative policies we have discussed are not always mutually exclusive. In other words, the actual data may not *precisely* fit any of the three popular policies. (*Hint:* Think about the results of the study reported by Dr. K. V. Smith and incorporate those into your analysis.)

DIVIDEND POLICY AND CORPORATE STRATEGY: THINGS WILL CHANGE—EVEN DIVIDEND POLICY

The recessions of 1990 to 1991 and 2001 induced a large number of American corporations to revisit their broadest corporate strategies that directly impact shareholder wealth. Today, the results of that "rethinking" are evident in many aspects of corporate behavior, including adjusted dividend policies.

One firm that altered its dividend policy in response to new strategies was W.R. Grace & Co., headquartered in Columbia, Maryland. The firm's core businesses include packaging, catalysts and silica products, and construction products. W.R. Grace & Co. ranked number 271 within the 1997 *Fortune* 500 list of the largest U.S. corporations with sales of $5.26 billion. The new corporate plans involved (1) divesting or discontinuing several product lines and (2) initiating a significant repurchase program of its own common stock. (Stock repurchase programs are discussed in depth later in this chapter.)

As a result, both the firm's payout ratio and actual cash dividend paid per share declined in significant fashion. The change in observed dividend policy is evident in Table 13-1. Notice that over the 1992 to 1994 period, W.R. Grace & Co. provided a good example of what we have called a "stable dividend policy." During this period the firm maintained a stable dollar dividend of $1.40 per share, whereas the payout ratio varied from 80.5 percent to 100.7 percent.

But when company policies changed dramatically, so did the associated dividend variables. The absolute dollar amount of the cash dividend per share was lowered to $0.50 in 1996, and the accompanying payout ratio fell to 20.7 percent. Importantly, the firm's total return to investors was a robust 30.9 percent during 1996, compared with its 10-year average of 16.4 percent. The market liked the change in dividend policy. So, although firms may be reluctant to change their dividend policies, it is possible with good planning and proper information dissemination to convince the financial markets that such a new direction might be good for investors.

TAKIN' IT TO THE NET

Go to www.homedepot.com and look up Home Depot's 1998 annual report. The firm's "Consolidated Statements of Cash Flows" reveals that cash dividends of $139 million, $110 million, and $90 million were paid over the 12-month periods ended February 1 of 1998, 1997, and 1996, respectively. Which of the alternative dividend policies that we have studied does Home Depot seem to follow?

TABLE 13-1 Earnings per Share, Dividends per Share, and the Dividend Payout Ratio: W.R. Grace & Company, 1992 to 1996

YEAR	EARNINGS PER SHARE[a]	DIVIDENDS PER SHARE	PAYOUT RATIO
1992	$1.70	$1.40	82.3%
1993	1.39	1.40	100.7
1994	1.74	1.40	80.5
1995	2.14	1.175	54.9
1996	2.41	0.50	20.7

[a]This series represents earnings from continuing operations but before special items.

Source: Basic data from W.R. Grace & Co., *Annual Report, 1996*, p. 55.

Objective **5**

DIVIDEND PAYMENT PROCEDURES

After the firm's dividend policy has been structured, several procedural details must be arranged. For instance, how frequently are dividend payments to be made? If a stockholder sells the shares during the year, who is entitled to the dividend? To answer these questions, we need to understand dividend payment procedures.

Generally, companies pay dividends on a quarterly basis. To illustrate, General Electric pays $6.72 per share in annual dividends. However, the firm actually issues a $1.68 quarterly dividend for a total yearly dividend of $6.72 ($1.68 × 4 quarters).

The final approval of a dividend payment comes from the board of directors. As an example, Emerson Electric on August 5, 1996, announced that holders of record as of August 16 would receive a $0.49 dividend. The dividend payment was to be made on September 10. August 5 is the **declaration date**—the *date when the dividend is formally declared by the board of directors*. The **date of record**, August 16, designates *when the stock transfer books are to be closed*. Investors shown to own the stock on this date receive the dividend. If a notification of a transfer is recorded subsequent to August 16, the new owner is not entitled to the dividend. However, a problem could develop if the stock were sold on August 15, one day prior to the record date. Time would not permit the sale to be reflected on the stockholder list by the August 16 date of record. To avoid this problem, *stock brokerage companies have uniformly decided to terminate the right of ownership to the dividend 2 working days before the date of record*. This prior date is the **ex-dividend date**. Therefore, any acquirer of Emerson Electric stock on August 14 or thereafter does not receive the dividend. Finally, the *company mails the dividend check to each investor* on September 10, the **payment date**. These events may be diagrammed as follows:

declaration date
date of record

ex-dividend date

payment date

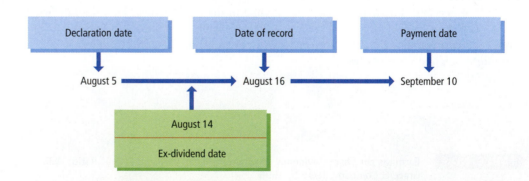

STOCK DIVIDENDS AND STOCK SPLITS

An integral part of dividend policy is the use of stock dividends and stock splits. Both involve issuing new shares of stock on a pro rata basis to the current shareholders, while the firm's assets, its earnings, the risk assumed, and the investors' percentage of ownership in the company remain unchanged. The only definite result from either a stock dividend or a stock split is the increase in the number of shares of stock outstanding.

To illustrate the effect of a stock dividend, assume that the Katie Corporation has 100,000 shares outstanding. The firm's after-tax profits are $500,000, or $5 in earnings per share. Currently, the company's stock is selling at a price–earnings multiple of 10, or $50 per share. Management is planning to issue a 20 percent stock dividend, so a stockholder owning 10 shares would receive two additional shares. We might immediately conclude that this investor is being given an asset (two shares of stock) worth $100; consequently, his or her personal worth should increase by $100. This conclusion is erroneous. The firm will be issuing 20,000 new shares (100,000 shares × 20 percent). Because the $500,000 in after-tax profits does not change, the new earnings per share will be $4.167 ($500,000/120,000 shares). If the price–earnings multiple remains at 10, the market price of the stock after the dividend should fall to $41.67 ($4.167 earnings per share × 10). The investor now owns 12 shares worth $41.67, which provides a $500 total value; thus, he or she is neither better nor worse off than before the stock dividend.

This example may make us wonder why a corporation would even bother with a stock dividend or stock split if no one benefits. However, before we study the rationale for such distributions, we should understand the differences between a stock split and a stock dividend.

STOCK DIVIDEND VERSUS SPLIT

The only difference between a stock dividend and a stock split relates to their respective accounting treatment. Stated differently, *there is absolutely no difference on an economic basis between a stock dividend and a stock split*. Both represent a proportionate distribution of additional shares to the current stockholders. However, *for accounting purposes* the **stock split** has been defined as a *stock dividend exceeding 25 percent*. Thus, a **stock dividend** is conventionally defined as a *distribution of shares up to 25 percent of the number of shares currently outstanding*.

stock split
stock dividend

The accounting treatment for a stock dividend requires the issuing firms to capitalize the "market value" of the dividend. In other words, the dollar amount of the dividend is transferred from retained earnings to the capital accounts (par and paid-in capital). This procedure may best be explained by an example. Assume that the L. Bernard Corporation is preparing to issue a 15 percent stock dividend. Table 13-2 presents the equity portion of the firm's balance sheet before the distribution. The market price for the stock has been $14. Thus, the 15 percent stock dividend increases the number of shares by 150,000 (1,000,000 shares × 15 percent). The "market value" of this increase is $2,100,000 (150,000 shares × $14 market price). To record this transaction, $2,100,000 would be transferred from retained earnings, resulting in a $300,000 increase in total par value (150,000 shares × $2 par value) and a $1,800,000 increment to paid-in capital. The $1,800,000 is the residual difference between $2,100,000 and $300,000. Table 13-3 shows the revised balance sheet.

What if the management of L. Bernard Corporation changed the plan and decided to split the stock two for one? In other words, a 100 percent increase in the number of shares

TABLE 13-2	L. Bernard Corporation Balance Sheet Before Stock Dividend
Common Stock	
Par value (1,000,000 shares outstanding; $2 par value)	$ 2,000,000
Paid-in capital	8,000,000
Retained earnings	15,000,000
Total equity	$25,000,000

TABLE 13-3   L. Bernard Corporation Balance Sheet After Stock Dividend

Common Stock	
Par value (1,150,000 shares outstanding; $2 par value)	$ 2,300,000
Paid-in capital	9,800,000
Retained earnings	12,900,000
Total equity	$25,000,000

would result. In accounting for the split, the changes to be recorded are (1) an increase in the number of shares and (2) a decrease in the per-share par value from $2 to $1. The dollar amounts of each account do not change. Table 13-4 reveals the new balance sheet.

Thus, for a stock dividend, an amount equal to the market value of the stock dividend is transferred from retained earnings to the capital stock accounts. When stock is split, only the number of shares changes, and the par value of each share is decreased proportionately. Despite this dissimilarity in accounting treatment, remember that no real economic difference exists between a split and a dividend.

RATIONALE FOR A STOCK DIVIDEND OR SPLIT

Although *stock* dividends and splits occur far less frequently than *cash* dividends, a significant number of companies choose to use these share distributions either with or in lieu of cash dividends. The extent of stock splits and stock dividends over the years can be made clear by a little price comparison. In 1926, a ticket to the movies cost 25¢—and even much less in the rural communities. At the same time, the average share price on the New York Stock Exchange was $35. Today, if we want to go to a new movie, we can pay $7 or more. However, the average share price is still about $35. The relatively constant share price is the result of the shares being split over and over again. We can only conclude that investors apparently like it that way. But why do they, if no economic benefit results to the investor from doing so?

Proponents of stock dividends and splits frequently maintain that stockholders receive a key benefit because the price of the stock will not fall precisely in proportion to the share increase. For a two-for-one split, the price of the stock might not decrease a full 50 percent, and the stockholder is left with a higher total value. There are two reasons for this disequilibrium. First, many financial executives believe that an optimal price range exists. Within this range, the total market value of the common stockholders is thought to be maximized. As the price exceeds this range, fewer investors can purchase the stock, thereby restraining the demand. Consequently, downward pressure is placed on its price. For instance, Hershey Foods Corporation in 1996 announced a two-for-one split on its shares, which were trading for $80. The reason given: The split would put it "in a more popular price range and should enhance trading liquidity." (*Liquidity* in this context means that more shares would be bought and sold by investors.)

The second explanation relates to the *informational content* of the dividend-split announcement. Stock dividends and splits have generally been associated with companies with growing earnings. The announcement of a stock dividend or split has therefore been perceived as favorable news. The empirical evidence, however, fails to verify these conclusions. Most studies indicate that investors are perceptive in identifying the true meaning of a share distribution. If the stock dividend or split is not accompanied by a positive trend in

TAKIN' IT TO THE NET

While a "plain vanilla" stock split merely represents a proportionate distribution of additional shares to current stockholders, more than a few investors believe that stock-split announcements contain useful information. Rightline Power Trading maintains a Web site at www.rightline.net. A proprietary model is used by the firm to identify stock-split candidates. The aim is to uncover "power trading" opportunities. The service is not free, but you can check it out.

TABLE 13-4   L. Bernard Corporation Balance Sheet After Stock Split

Common Stock	
Par value (2,000,000 shares outstanding; $1 par value)	$ 2,000,000
Paid-in capital	8,000,000
Retained earnings	15,000,000
Total equity	$25,000,000

earnings and increases in cash dividends, price increases surrounding the stock dividend or split are insignificant.[17] Therefore, we should be suspicious of the assertion that a stock dividend or split can help increase investors' net worth.

A second reason for stock dividends or splits is the conservation of corporate cash. If a company is encountering cash problems, it may substitute a stock dividend for a cash dividend. However, as before, investors will probably look beyond the dividend to ascertain the underlying reason for conserving cash. If the stock dividend is an effort to conserve cash for attractive investment opportunities, the shareholder may bid up the stock price. If the move to conserve cash relates to financial difficulties within the firm, the market price will most likely react adversely.

CONCEPT CHECK

1. From an economic standpoint, is there any meaningful difference between a stock split and a stock dividend?
2. What managerial logic might lie behind a stock split or a stock dividend?

STOCK REPURCHASES

Objective **7**

stock repurchase (stock buyback)

A **stock repurchase (stock buyback)** is when a *firm repurchases its own stock, resulting in a reduction in the number of shares outstanding*. For well over three decades, corporate managements have been active in repurchasing their own equity securities. For example, the Ford Motor Company on September 14, 2000, announced in a press release that it planned to buy back up to a full $5 billion of its stock. Immediately after the public announcement of this plan, shares of Ford common stock rose by 2.2 percent in the financial markets. Now, a key word in such announcements is the word *plan*. Companies give themselves room across time to execute these buybacks. And, Ford, at the time, was mired in a major-league tire-quality problem on some of its best-selling vehicles, so not all financial analysts and market watchers were sure when the actual repurchases would commence.

The Walt Disney Company provides another actual example of a firm seeking to increase shareholder total returns by using the stock repurchase mechanism. In its 2001 annual report, Disney management said, "In 2001, the company invested a total of $1.1 billion to purchase 63.9 million shares of Disney common stock at an average price of $16.62 per share. Since 1983, the company has repurchased nearly 549 million shares at a total cost of just under $4.4 billion. At the November 30 (2001) stock price, these shares represent a market value of more than $11 billion."[18] Clearly, Disney management is proud of its financial policy in this regard.

Also, if you were to look at the balance sheet of a firm such as the McDonald's Corporation, you would see that the firm's treasury stock—the amount paid for repurchasing its own stock—is severalfold the amount of the total amount originally invested by the stockholders. This situation is not unusual for many large companies. Several reasons have been given for *stock repurchases*. Examples of such benefits include

1. Means for providing an internal investment opportunity
2. Approach for modifying the firm's capital structure
3. Favorable impact on earnings per share
4. Elimination of a minority ownership group of stockholders
5. Minimization of the dilution in earnings per share associated with mergers
6. Reduction in the firm's costs associated with servicing small stockholders

Also, from the shareholders' perspective, a stock repurchase, as opposed to a cash dividend, has a potential tax advantage.

TAKIN' IT TO THE NET

Stock repurchase plans have become a rather common financial policy and activity within corporate America. IBM, for example, spent a robust $6.9 billion in 1998 and $7.1 billion in 1997 on the repurchase of its common stock. You can review management's discussion of the IBM repurchase plan at **www.IBM.com** by clicking on the "Stockholders' Equity Activity" section of the 1998 Annual Report.

---

[17]See James A. Millar and Bruce D. Fielitz, "Stock-Split and Stock-Dividend Decisions," *Financial Management* 2 (Winter 1973), pp. 35–45; and Eugene Fama, Lawrence Fisher, Michael Jensen, and Richard Roll, "The Adjustment of Stock Prices to New Information," *International Economic Review* (February 1969), pp. 1–21.

[18]The Walt Disney Company, *Annual Report* 2001, p. 12.

SHARE REPURCHASE AS A DIVIDEND DECISION

Clearly, the payment of a common stock dividend is the conventional method for distributing a firm's profits to its owners. However, it need not be the only way. Another approach is to repurchase the firm's stock. The concept may best be explained by an example.

EXAMPLE

Telink, Inc. is planning to pay $4 million ($4 per share) in dividends to its common stockholders. The following earnings and market price information is provided for Telink:

Net income	$7,500,000
Number of shares	1,000,000
Earnings per share	$7.50
Price–earnings ratio	8
Expected market price per share after dividend payment	$60

In a recent meeting, several board members, who are also major stockholders, question the need for a dividend payment. They maintain that they do not need the income, so why not allow the firm to retain the funds for future investments? In response, management contends that the available investments are not sufficiently profitable to justify retention of the income. That is, the investors' required rates of return exceed the expected rates of return that could be earned with the additional $4 million in investments.

Because management opposes the idea of retaining the profits for investment purposes, one of the firm's directors has suggested that the $4 million be used to repurchase the company's stock. In this way, the value of the stock should increase. This result may be demonstrated as follows:

1. Assume that shares are repurchased by the firm at the $60 market price (ex-dividend price) plus the contemplated $4 dividend per share, or for $64 per share.
2. Given a $64 price, 62,500 shares would be repurchased ($4 million ÷ $64 price).
3. If net income is not reduced but the number of shares declines as a result of the share repurchase, earnings per share would increase from $7.50 to $8, computed as follows:

$$\text{Earnings per share} = \text{net income/outstanding shares}$$
$$\text{(before repurchase)} = \$7,500,000/1,000,000$$
$$= \$7.50$$
$$\text{(after repurchase)} = \$7,500,000/(1,000,000 - 62,500)$$
$$= \$8$$

4. Assuming that the price–earnings ratio remains at 8, the new price after the repurchase would be $64, up from $60, where the increase exactly equals the amount of the forgone dividend.

In this example, Telink's stockholders are essentially provided the same value, whether a dividend is paid or stock is repurchased. If management pays a dividend, the investor will have a stock valued at $60 plus $4 received from the dividend. Conversely, if stock is repurchased in lieu of the dividend, the stock will be worth $64. These results were based on assuming (1) the stock is being repurchased at the exact $64 price, (2) the $7,500,000 net income is unaffected by the repurchase, and (3) the price–earnings ratio of 8 does not change after the repurchase. Given these assumptions, however, the stock repurchase serves as a perfect substitute for the dividend payment to the stockholders.

THE INVESTOR'S CHOICE

Given the choice between a stock repurchase and a dividend payment, which would an investor prefer? In perfect markets, in which there are no taxes, no commissions when buying and selling stock, and no informational content assigned to a dividend, the investor

FINANCIAL MANAGEMENT
IN PRACTICE

"MANY CONCERNS USE EXCESS CASH TO REPURCHASE THEIR SHARES"

Mattel, Inc. and General Dynamics are two firms, among many, that are repurchasing their own shares. These events, along with the rationale for the decision to repurchase their shares, are told in this *Wall Street Journal* article.

Stock buybacks are back. Faced with the prospect of only modest economic growth, many companies are using excess cash to buy their own shares rather than build new plants.

Consider the case of Mattel, Inc., the El Segundo, Calif., toy maker. It just announced plans to buy 10 million shares during the next four years, even though its stock, priced at $24, is selling at a healthy 16.6 times its past 12 month earnings. The reason: Plant capacity is sufficient to handle current sales growth of 10% to 12% yearly and excess cash is building up at the rate of $200 million a year.

"We don't need the cash to grow so we've decided to give it back," says James Eskridge, Mattel's chief financial officer. Actually, Mattel plans to use about half of the $200 million each year for buybacks and dividends and the rest for growth.

The effect [of a stock repurchase] on individual stocks can be significant, says Robert Giordano, director of economic research at Goldman Sachs & Co. A case in point is General Dynamics Corp., which last summer began selling some divisions and using the proceeds to buy its stock when shares were trading at about $65 each. After nearly $1 billion in buybacks, the stock has gained about 37%, closing yesterday at $89\frac{1}{2}$.

"The market reacts positively to purchases, and it appreciates a firm that does not squander excess cash," says Columbia Business School professor Gailen Hite.

Some of the buybacks have come from companies whose stock prices have been hurt. Drug makers, for example, have seen their stocks pummeled by fears that healthcare reform will sap profits. As a result, pharmaceutical companies have been big players in the buyback game.

But economists and analysts are much more intrigued by companies that are awash in cash, thanks to improving sales and several years of cost-cutting and debt reduction. At this stage of an economic recovery, many such companies would be investing heavily in plant and equipment. Not this time.

"Companies are throwing off more cash than they can ever hope to invest in plant, equipment or inventories," says Charles Clough, chief investment strategist for Merrill Lynch Capital Markets. Companies already have pared down debt, and now they're turning to equity, he says. His prediction: "He who shrinks his balance sheet the fastest wins in the '90s."

would be indifferent with regard to the choices. The investor could create a dividend stream by selling stock when income is needed.

If market imperfections exist, the investor may have a preference for one of the two methods of distributing the corporate income. First, the firm may have to pay too high a price for the repurchased stock, which is to the detriment of the remaining stockholders. If a relatively large number of shares are being bought, the price may be bid up too high, only to fall after the repurchase operation. Second, as a result of the repurchase, the market may perceive the riskiness of the corporation as increasing, which would lower the price–earnings ratio and the value of the stock.

FINANCING OR INVESTMENT DECISION

Repurchasing stock when the firm has excess cash may be regarded as a dividend decision. However, a stock repurchase may also be viewed as a financing decision. By issuing debt and then repurchasing stock, a firm can immediately alter its debt–equity mix toward a higher proportion of debt. Rather than choose how to distribute cash to the stockholders, management is using stock repurchase as a means to change the corporation's capital structure.

In addition to dividend and financing decisions, many managers consider stock repurchase as an investment decision. When equity prices are depressed in the marketplace, management may view the firm's own stock as being materially undervalued and representing a good investment opportunity. Although the firm's management may be wise to repurchase stock at unusually low prices, this decision cannot and should not be viewed in the context of an investment decision. Buying its own stock cannot provide expected returns as other investments do. No company can survive, much less prosper, by investing only in its own stock.

THE REPURCHASE PROCEDURE

If management intends to repurchase a block of the firm's outstanding shares, it should make this information public. All investors should be given the opportunity to work with complete information. They should be told the purpose of the repurchase, as well as the method to be used to acquire the stock.

Three methods for stock repurchase are available. First, the shares could be bought in the open market. Here the firm acquires the stock through a stockbroker at the going market price. This approach may place upward pressure on the stock price until the stock is acquired. Also, commissions must be paid to the stockbrokers as a fee for their services.

tender offer

The second method is to make a tender offer to the firm's shareholders. A **tender offer** is a *formal offer by the company to buy a specified number of shares at a predetermined and stated price. The tender price is set above the current market price in order to attract sellers.* A tender offer is best when a relatively large number of shares are to be bought because the company's intentions are clearly known and each shareholder has the opportunity to sell the stock at the tendered price.

The third and final method for repurchasing stock entails the purchase of the stock from one or more major stockholders. These purchases are made on a negotiated basis. Care should be taken to ensure a fair and equitable price. Otherwise, the remaining stockholders may be hurt as a result of the sale.

CONCEPT CHECK

1. Identify three reasons why a firm might buy back its own common stock shares.
2. What financial relationships must hold for a stock repurchase to be a perfect substitute for a cash dividend payment to stockholders?
3. Within the context of a stock repurchase, what is meant by a tender offer?

Objective **8**

FINANCE AND THE MULTINATIONAL FIRM: THE CASE OF LOW-DIVIDEND PAYMENTS; SO WHERE DO WE INVEST?

During late 2000 through March 2001, the U.S. economy continued an outstanding period of aggregate expansion that ultimately made it the longest in domestic business cycle history at 120 months. When such periods of relative prosperity occur, financially strong firms tend to focus their business strategies on growth; as a direct result, corporate dividend yields (i.e., cash dividends divided by common stock price) tend to decline. Firms retain more cash dollars for internal investment opportunities and disgorge less cash to investors. For growth-seeking companies, the capital-budgeting decision takes on greater importance, while the consequence of the dividend decision relative to both firm value and cash outflows shrinks. This might properly remind you of what we called the *residual dividend theory* earlier in this chapter.

During general economic prosperity, the multinational firm logically looks to international markets for prospectively high *NPV* projects. There are at least two solid reasons for such investing behavior: (1) to spread or dilute country-related economic risks by diversifying geographically and (2) to achieve a cost advantage over competitors. These two reasons for U.S. direct investment abroad should remind you of **Principle 9: All Risk Is Not Equal— Some Risk Can Be Diversified Away and Some Cannot**; and **Principle 5: The Curse of Competitive Markets—Why It's Hard to Find Exceptionally Profitable Projects**.

Table 13-5 identifies those countries, apart from the United States, that make up the so-called Group of Seven Industrialized Nations. Just think of them as the most advanced economies on the globe. They are referred to in the popular business press as the "G-7" countries. Government finance officials from the G-7 and sometimes their chief executive officers (such as the president of the United States) usually meet twice a year to discuss

TABLE 13-5 U.S. Direct Investment Abroad, 1998 Group of Seven Industrialized Nations

COUNTRY	AMOUNT ($ BILLIONS)	PERCENT OF TOTAL	PERCENT IN MANUFACTURING
Canada	$ 103.9	24.8%	44.7
France	39.2	9.4	48.4
Germany	42.9	10.3	51.9
Italy	14.6	3.5	58.5
Japan	38.2	9.2	37.2
United Kingdom	178.6	42.8	26.0
Total	$417.4	100.0%	

Source: *U.S. Net International Position at Year-End, 1998*. U.S. Department of Commerce (June 30, 1999), p. 10.

multinational economic policy. In Table 13-5 we can observe the historical dollar amounts U.S. multinational firms have invested internationally.

Notice that when corporate cash is available, U.S. multinational firms favor (1) the United Kingdom and (2) Canada as domiciles for direct investment. A full 67.6 percent of U.S. firms' investment in other G-7 countries is placed in those two countries. Also notice that the capital projects chosen by U.S. multinational firms tend to be concentrated in various manufacturing industries. For instance in Italy, a full 58.5 percent of the U.S. investment lies within the manufacturing sector. These relationships and the dominance of international manufacturing projects are displayed in Figure 13-2. A perceived cost advantage associated with overseas manufacturing, usually related to lower labor costs, explains the bias toward manufacturing-oriented projects by U.S. multinational firms. The competitive nature of a capitalist-based economy induces U.S. firms to seek low-cost labor inputs from their direct international investments.

CONCEPT CHECK

1. Identify two reasons why multinational firms might turn to international markets in search of high *NPV* projects.

2. Among the Group of Seven countries, which two are most favored with direct investment by U.S. companies?

FIGURE 13-2 U.S. Direct Investment Abroad, 1998 Group of Seven Industrialized Nations

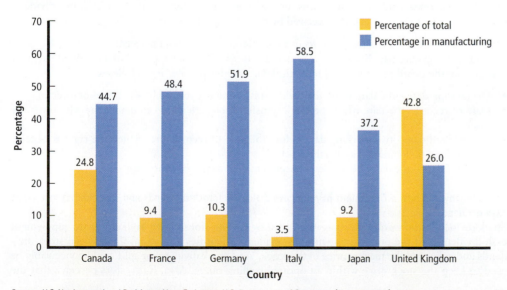

Source: *U.S. Net International Position at Year-End, 1998*. U.S. Department of Commerce (June 30, 1999), p. 10.

SUMMARY

Objective 1

Describe the trade-off between paying dividends and retaining the profits within the company

A company's dividend decision has an immediate impact on the firm's financial mix. If the dividend payment is increased, fewer funds are available internally for financing investments. Consequently, if additional equity capital is needed, the company has to issue new common stock.

Objective 2

Explain the relationship between a corporation's dividend policy and the market price of its common stock

In trying to understand the effect of the dividend policy on a firm's stock price, we must realize the following:

- In perfect markets, the choice between paying or not paying a dividend does not matter. However, when we realize in the real world that there are costs of issuing stock, we have a preference to use internal equity to finance our investment opportunities. Here the dividend decision is simply a residual factor, in which the dividend payment should equal the remaining internal capital after financing the equity portion of investments.
- Other market imperfections that may cause a company's dividend policy to affect the firm's stock price include (1) the deferred tax benefit of capital gains, (2) agency costs, (3) the clientele effect, and (4) the informational content of a given policy.

Objective 3

Describe practical considerations that may be important to the firm's dividend policy

Other practical considerations that may affect a firm's dividend payment decision include

- Legal restrictions
- The firm's liquidity position
- The company's accessibility to capital markets
- The stability of earnings
- The desire of investors to maintain control of the company
- Inflation rates

Objective 4

Distinguish among the types of dividend policies corporations frequently use

In practice, managers have generally followed one of three dividend policies:

- Constant dividend payout ratio, when the percentage of dividends to earnings is held constant
- Stable dollar dividend per share, when a relatively stable dollar dividend is maintained over time
- Small, regular dividend plus a year-end extra, when the firm pays a small, regular dollar dividend plus a year-end extra dividend in prosperous years

Of the three dividend policies, the stable dollar dividend is by far the most common. Please recall that the Jobs and Growth Tax Relief Reconciliation Act of 2003 reduced the top tax rate on dividend income to 15 percent and placed the top tax rate on realized long-term capital gains at this same 15 percent rate. This helped level the investment landscape for dividend income relative to qualifying capital gains. Taxes paid on capital gains, however, are still deferred until realized, but dividend income is taxed in the year that it is received by the investing taxpayer.

Objective 5

Specify the procedures a company follows in administering the dividend payment

Generally, companies pay dividends on a quarterly basis. The final approval of a dividend payment comes from the board of directors. The critical dates in this process are as follows:

- Declaration date—the date when the dividend is formally declared by the board of directors
- Date of record—the date when the stock transfer books are closed to determine who owns the stock
- Ex-dividend date—two working days before the date of record, after which the right to receive the dividend no longer goes with the stock
- Payment date—the date the dividend check is mailed to the stockholders

Objective 6

Describe why and how a firm might pay noncash dividends (stock dividends and stock splits) instead of cash dividends

Stock dividends and stock splits have been used by corporations either in lieu of or to supplement cash dividends. At the present, no empirical evidence identifies a relationship between stock dividends and splits and the market price of the stock. Yet a stock dividend or split could conceivably be used to keep the stock price within an optimal trading range. Also, if investors perceive that the stock dividend contains favorable information about the firm's operations, the price of the stock could increase.

Explain the purpose and procedures related to stock repurchases

As an alternative to paying a dividend, management can repurchase stock. In perfect markets, an investor would be indifferent between receiving a dividend or a share repurchase. The investor could simply create a dividend stream by selling stock when income is needed. If, however, market imperfections exist, the investor may have a preference for one of the two methods of distributing the corporate income. A stock repurchase may also be viewed as a financing decision. By issuing debt and then repurchasing stock, a firm can immediately alter its debt–equity mix toward a higher proportion of debt. Also, many managers consider a stock repurchase an investment decision—buying the stock when they believe it to be undervalued.

Objective **7**

The multinational firm: the case of low–dividend payments; so where do we invest?

During periods of general economic prosperity, financially strong firms tend to focus their business strategies on growth. As a result, dividend yield and cash dividend payments can decline. With internally generated cash to invest, the multinational firm will look to international markets for prospectively high *NPV* projects. This may allow the firm to (1) spread country-related economic risks by diversifying geographically and (2) achieve a cost advantage over competitors.

Objective **8**

KEY TERMS

Agency costs, 423

Bird-in-the-hand dividend theory, 418

Clientele effect, 422

Constant dividend payout ratio, 427

Date of record, 430

Declaration date, 430

Dividend payout ratio, 416

Ex-dividend date, 430

Expectations theory, 423

Increasing-stream hypothesis of dividend policy, 428

Information asymmetry, 422

Payment date, 430

Perfect capital markets, 418

Residual dividend theory, 421

Small, regular dividend plus a year-end extra, 427

Stable dollar dividend per share, 427

Stock dividend, 431

Stock repurchase (stock buyback), 433

Stock split, 431

Tender offer, 436

STUDY QUESTIONS

13-1. What is meant by the term *dividend payout ratio*?

13-2. Explain the trade-off between retaining internally generated funds and paying cash dividends.

13-3. a. What are the assumptions of a perfect market?

  b. What effect does dividend policy have on the share price in a perfect market?

13-4. What is the impact of flotation costs on the financing decision?

13-5. a. What is the *residual dividend theory*?

  b. Why is this theory operational only in the long term?

13-6. Why might investors prefer capital gains to the same amount of dividend income?

13-7. What legal restrictions may limit the amount of dividends to be paid?

13-8. How does a firm's liquidity position affect the payment of dividends?

13-9. How can ownership control constrain the growth of a firm?

13-10. a. Why is a stable dollar dividend policy popular from the viewpoint of the corporation?

  b. Is it also popular with investors? Why?

13-11. Explain declaration date, date of record, and ex-dividend date.

13-12. What are the advantages of a stock split or dividend over a cash dividend?

13-13. Why would a firm repurchase its own stock?

SELF-TEST PROBLEMS

ST-1. (*Dividend growth rate*) Schulz, Inc., maintains a constant dividend payout ratio of 35 percent. Earnings per share last year were $8.20 and are expected to grow indefinitely at a rate of 12 percent. What will be the dividend per share this year? In 5 years?

ST-2. (*Stock split*) The debt and equity section of the Robson Corporation balance sheet is shown here. The current market price of the common shares is $20. Reconstruct the financial statement assuming that (a) a 15 percent stock dividend is issued and (b) a two-for-one stock split is declared.

Debt	$1,800,000
Common	
Par ($2; 100,000 shares)	200,000
Paid-in capital	400,000
Retained earnings	900,000
	$3,300,000

STUDY PROBLEMS

13-1. (*Stock dividend*) STI Tech, located in the outskirts of Montevideo, Uruguay, designs and manufactures a wide variety of home security products. STI has 5,000,000 shares of common outstanding stock, a P/E ratio of 12, and net income of $2,500,000. The CEO of the company has planned a 25 percent stock dividend.

    a. After the stock dividend is paid, what will be the price of the stock?
    b. The son of the CEO, Claudio Pena, owns 500 shares. Will the total value of his 500 shares change as a result of the stock dividend?

13-2. (*Dividend policies*) Final earnings estimates for Chilean Health Spa & Fitness Center have been prepared for the CFO of the company and are shown in the following table. It has 7,500,000 shares of common outstanding stock. As assistant to the CFO, you are asked to determine the yearly dividend per share to be paid depending on the following possible policies:

    a. Stable dollar dividend targeted at 40 percent of the earnings over the 5-year period.
    b. Small, regular dividend of $0.60 per share plus a year-end extra when the profits in any year exceed $20,000,000. The year-end extra dividend will equal 50 percent of profits exceeding $20,000,000.
    c. Constant dividend payout ratio of 40 percent.

YEAR	PROFITS AFTER TAXES
1	$18,000,000
2	21,000,000
3	19,000,000
4	23,000,000
5	25,000,000

13-3. (*Flotation costs and issue size*) Your firm needs to raise $10 million. Assuming that flotation costs are expected to be $15 per share and that the market price of the stock is $120, how many shares would have to be issued? What is the dollar size of the issue?

13-4. (*Flotation costs and issue size*) If flotation costs for common stock issue are 18 percent, how large must the issue be so that the firm will net $5,800,000? If the stock sells for $85 per share, how many shares must be issued?

13-5. (*Stock dividend*) RCB has 2 million shares of common stock outstanding. Net income is $550,000, and the P/E ratio for the stock is 10. Management is planning a 20 percent stock dividend.

    a. What will be the price of the stock after the stock dividend?
    b. If an investor owns 100 shares before the stock dividend, does the total value of his or her shares change? Explain.

13-6. (*Stock split*) You own 5 percent of Trexco Corporation's common stock, which most recently sold for $98 before a planned two-for-one stock split announcement. Before the split there are 25,000 shares of common stock outstanding.

a. Relative to now, what will be your financial position after the stock split? (Assume the stock price falls proportionately.)

b. The executive vice president in charge of finance believes the price will only fall 40 percent after the split because she feels the price is above the optimal price range. If she is correct, what will be your net gain?

13-7. (*Dividend policies*) The earnings for Crystal Cargo, Inc. have been predicted for the next 5 years and are as follows. There are 1 million shares outstanding. Determine the yearly dividend per share to be paid if the following policies are enacted:

a. Constant dividend payout ratio of 50 percent.

b. Stable dollar dividend targeted at 50 percent of the earnings over the 5-year period.

c. Small, regular dividend of $.50 per share plus a year-end extra when the profits in any year exceed $1,500,000. The year-end extra dividend will equal 50 percent of profits exceeding $1,500,000.

YEAR	PROFITS AFTER TAXES
1	$1,400,000
2	2,000,000
3	1,860,000
4	900,000
5	2,800,000

13-8. (*Repurchase of stock*) The Dunn Corporation is planning to pay dividends of $500,000. There are 250,000 shares outstanding, with an earnings per share of $5. The stock should sell for $50 after the ex-dividend date. If instead of paying a dividend, management decides to repurchase stock

a. What should be the repurchase price?

b. How many shares should be repurchased?

c. What if the repurchase price is set below or above your suggested price in part **a**?

d. If you own 100 shares, would you prefer that the company pay the dividend or repurchase stock?

13-9. (*Flotation costs and issue size*) D. Butler, Inc. needs to raise $14 million. Assuming that the market price of the firm's stock is $95 and flotation costs are 10 percent of the market price, how many shares would have to be issued? What is the dollar size of the issue?

13-10. (*Stock split*) You own 20 percent of Rainy Corp., which recently sold for $86 before a planned two-for-one split announcement. Before the split there are 80,000 shares of common stock outstanding.

a. What is your financial position before the split, and what will it be after the stock split? (Assume the stock price falls proportionately.)

b. Your stockbroker believes the market will react positively to the split and that the price will fall only 45 percent after the split. If she is correct, what will be your net gain?

WEB WORKS

13-WW1. As mentioned in this chapter, the Jobs and Growth Tax Relief Reconciliation Act of 2003 included important changes in the tax code that relate to corporate dividend policy and the preference of investors for capital gains income relative to dividend income. Standard & Poor's provided a very concise, yet useful, three-page summary of these provisions found on the Franklin, Templeton Investments Web site. Visit that site at **www.franklintempleton.com/retail/jsp_cm/ corp/articles/common/ma_2003_taxact.jsp**. **The question**: What specific changes contained in the 2003 tax act might shift investors' preferences toward cash dividends, and what would you forecast the effect to be on dividend payout ratios?

13-WW2. Stock repurchase plans, as discussed in this chapter, have become a rather common financial policy activity in corporate America. IBM is one well-known firm that has had a long history of a vigorous repurchase program. You can review management's discussion of the IBM repurchase plan at **www.IBM.com** and find the firm's annual report for 2002. Page 55 of that report will give you details, for example, on how much IBM spent on common stock repurchases in the 2002 fourth quarter and how many fewer shares were left outstanding over the year due to the repurchase program.

13-WW3. Let us continue with a further look at IBM and its dividend policy. Visit the same Web site at **www.IBM.com** and this time look up the annual report for fiscal year 2003. On page 64 of that report you will find "management's discussion" of 2003 results and, specifically, how those results affected dividend policy and share repurchases. Notice that management said it returned $32.9 billion to investors in the form of dividends and share repurchases over the last 5 years (i.e., 1999–2003). **The exercise**: How much did IBM return to shareholders via dividend and share repurchases over each of the 5 years ended 2003? **Hint**: Go to page 65, and the sum of these five observations should add up to $32.9 billion.

COMPREHENSIVE PROBLEM

The following article appeared in the July 2, 1995, issue of the *Dallas Morning News*. Scott Burns, the author, argues the case for the importance of dividends.

Let us now praise the lowly dividend.

Insignificant to some. Small potatoes to others. An irksome sign of tax liability to many. However characterized, dividends are experiencing yet another round of defamation on Wall Street.

Why pay out dividends, the current argument goes, when a dollar of dividend can be retained as a dollar of book value that the market will value at two, three, or four dollars? With the average stock now selling at more than three times book value, investors should prefer companies that retain earnings rather than pay them out, even if they do nothing more with the money than repurchase shares.

The New Wisdom

Instead, the New Wisdom says, the investor should go for companies that retain earnings, reinvest them, and try to maximize shareholder value. Dividends should be avoided in the pursuit of long-term capital gains.

The only problem with this reasoning is that we've heard it before. And always at market tops.
- We heard it in the late 1960s as stock prices soared and dividend yields fell.
- We heard it again in the early '70s as investors fixated on the "Nifty Fifty" and analysts calmly projected that with growth companies yielding 1 percent or less, the most important part of the return was the certainty of 20 percent annual earnings growth.
- And we're hearing it now, with stock prices hitting new highs each day. The Standard & Poor's 500 Index, for instance, is up 19.7 percent since Dec. 31, the equivalent of more than seven years of dividends at the current yield of 2.6 percent.

Tilting the Yield

Significantly, we didn't hear that dividends were irrelevant in the late '70s, as stock valuations moved to new lows. At that time, portfolio managers talked about "yield tilt"—running a portfolio with a bias toward dividend return to offset some of the risk of continuing stock market decline. Indeed, many of the best performing funds in the late '70s were Equity-Income funds, the funds that seek above-average dividend income.

You can understand how much dividends contribute to long-term returns by taking a look at the performance of a major index, with and without dividend reinvestment. If you had invested $10,000 in the S&P's 500 Index in January 1982 and taken all dividends in cash, your original investment would have grown to $37,475 by the end of 1994.

It doesn't get much better than that.

The gain clocks a compound annual return of 10.7 percent, and total gain of $27,475. During the same period you would have collected an additional $14,244 in dividends.

Not a trivial sum, either.

In other words, during one of the biggest bull markets in history, unreinvested dividend income accounted for more than one-third of your total return.

If you had reinvested those dividends in additional stock, the final score would be even better: $60,303. The appreciation of your original investment would have been $27,475 while the growth from reinvested dividends would have been $22,828. Nearly half—45 percent—of your total return came from reinvested dividends. And this happened during a stellar period of rising stock prices.

Now consider the same investment during a period of misery. If you had invested $10,000 in the S&P's Index stocks in January 1968, your investment would have grown to only $14,073 over the next 13 years, a gain of only $4,073. During much of that time, the value of your original investment would have been less than $10,000. Dividends during the period would have totaled $7,088—substantially more than stock appreciation. Reinvested, the same dividends would have grown to $9,705, helping your original investment grow to $23,778.

In a period of major ups and downs that many investors don't like to remember, dividends accounted for 70 percent of total return (see accompanying table).

their ideas for improving the work processes and systems and where resources are made available for them to bring their ideas to fruition may be the most important part of the solution.

CHAPTER 14
SHORT-TERM
FINANCIAL PLANNING

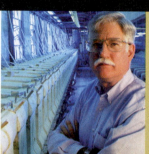

CHAPTER 15
WORKING-CAPITAL
MANAGEMENT

CHAPTER 16
CURRENT ASSET
MANAGEMENT

CHAPTER 17
INTERNATIONAL
BUSINESS FINANCE

➤ Milwaukee-based Harley-Davidson Corporation has a state of the art Parts and Accessories division, and the people that work there take tremendous pride of ownership for what happens in *their* part of the business. They simply feel they are the best. But it was not always this way.

In the early 1990's Harley-Davidson was experiencing tremendous growth in all segments of the business, including Parts and Accessories. Having come through a turnaround in the 1980's, the distribution and logistics functions in support of this business growth were strained and in need of change. In mid-1994 a team was formed to develop and implement a new strategy.

The issues at the time were significant. Their distribution center was a seven-level facility that was 84 years old and looked more like an old red brick school building than a modern warehouse. The facility was served by two freight elevators and limited technology support. In addition, the facility contained slightly over half the inventory, requiring off-site storage with daily shuttle runs to replenish stock.

Symptoms of Harley-Davidson's inventory problems included inventory turnover rates that were less than two turns per year; inventory accuracy levels in the 75 to 80% range; order cycle times from receipt of order to shipment in the 3- to 10-day range; lost inventory; inventory write-offs in the millions of dollars; and extremely low productivity.

The new strategy centered on designing a facility with appropriate storage, automation, and technology for each class of inventory. This would create optimum performance against a comprehensive set of metrics for cost, quality, and timing goals. In addition, a new relationship with employees called "partnering" was being instituted throughout the firm. The partnering program empowered employees and capitalized on their individual and collective knowledge and skills.

Brian Smith, general manager for Parts and Accessories with Harley-Davidson, describes the improvements as follows:

This project was implemented in 1997 and the results have been excellent. Inventory accuracy and fill rates have improved dramatically, and recovery time on stock-outs has been substantially improved. Turnover rates have more than doubled and are approaching world class. Slow moving and obsolete inventories have been reduced by over 60%. While order cycle times to customers have become top-notch. The majority of orders are shipped the same day as they are received, with very high levels of reliability.

Based on our experience, employees are typically the masters of the universe in which they work. They know more about the issues and possible solutions than anyone else. The creation of a culture where employees [are] encouraged to contribute

We could fiddle with these figures any number of ways. We could reduce the value of dividends by calculating income taxes. We could raise it by starting with the Dow Jones industrial average stocks, which tend to have higher dividends. But the point here is very simple: Whether you spend them or reinvest them, dividends are always an important part of the return on common stock.

Source: Scott Burns, "Those Lowly Dividends," *Dallas Morning News*, July 2, 1995, p. 1H. Reprinted with permission of the *Dallas Morning News*.

A Close Look at Dividends in Two Markets

ANATOMY OF THE BULL MARKET, 1982 TO 1994

Original investment		$10,000
Gain on original investment		$27,475
Total dividends	$14,244	
Gain on reinvested dividends	$ 8,584	
Total gain from dividends		$22,828
Total		$60,303
Compound annualized return equals 14.8%; 45% from dividends.		

ANATOMY OF A BEAR MARKET, 1968 TO 1980

Original investment		$10,000
Gain on original investment		$ 4,073
Total dividends	$ 7,088	
Gain on reinvested dividends	$ 2,617	
Total gain from dividends		$ 9,705
Total		$23,778
Compound annualized return equals 6.9%; 70% from dividends		

Source: Franklin/Templeton Group Hypothetical Illustration Program.

Based on your reading of this chapter, evaluate what Burns is saying. Do you agree or disagree with him? Why?

SELF-TEST SOLUTIONS

SS-1.

$$\text{Dividend per share} = 35\% \times \$8.20$$
$$= \$2.87$$

Dividends:

$$1 \text{ year} = \$2.87(1 + 0.12)$$
$$= \$3.21$$
$$5 \text{ years} = \$2.87(1 + 0.12)^5$$
$$= \$2.87(1.762)$$
$$= \$5.06$$

SS-2.

a. If a 15 percent stock dividend is issued, the financial statement would appear as follows:

Debt	$1,800,000
Common	
Par ($2 par; 115,000 shares)	230,000
Paid-in capital	670,000
Retained earnings	600,000
	$3,300,000

b. A two-for-one split would result in a 100 percent increase in the number of shares. Because the total par value remains at $200,000, the new par value per share is $1 ($200,000/200,000 shares). The new financial statement would be as follows:

Debt	$1,800,000
Common	
Par ($1 par; 200,000 shares)	200,000
Paid-in capital	400,000
Retained earnings	900,000
	$3,300,000

Short-Term Financial Planning

FINANCIAL FORECASTING • THE SUSTAINABLE RATE OF GROWTH • LIMITATIONS OF THE
PERCENT OF SALES FORECAST METHOD • CONSTRUCTING AND USING A CASH BUDGET

Forecasting is an integral part of the planning process, yet there are countless examples when our ability to predict the future is simply awful. Believing that the lower birthrates during the 1970s were permanent, school administrators began closing elementary schools. Then in the 1980s, birthrates and school enrollments increased again as a result of the fact that childless couples had simply deferred having children until later in life.

If forecasting the future is so difficult and plans are built on forecasts, why do firms engage in planning efforts? Obviously, they do, but why? The answer, oddly enough, does not lie in the accuracy of the firm's projections, for planning offers its greatest value when the future is the most uncertain. The value of planning is derived out of the process itself. That is, by thinking about what the future might be like the firm builds contingency plans that can improve its ability to respond to adverse events and take advantage of opportunities that may arise.

❧ WHAT'S AHEAD ❧

Chapter 14 has two primary objectives: First, it develops an appreciation for the role of forecasting in the firm's financial planning process. Basically, forecasts of future sales revenues and their associated expenses give the firm the information needed to project its future needs for financing. Also, this chapter provides an overview of the firm's budgetary system, including the cash budget, the pro forma (planned) income statement, and pro forma balance sheet. Pro forma financial statements give us a useful tool for analyzing the effects of the firm's forecasts and planned activities on its financial performance, as well as its needs for financing. In addition, pro forma statements can be used as a benchmark or standard to compare against actual operating results. Used in this way, pro forma statements are an instrument for controlling or monitoring the firm's progress throughout the planning period.

> **BACK TO THE FOUNDATIONS**
>
> *Financing decisions are made today in light of our expectations of an uncertain future. Financial forecasting involves making estimates of the future financing requirements of the firm.* **Principle 3: Cash—Not Profits—Is King** *speaks directly to this problem. Remember that effective financial management requires that consideration be given to cash flow and when it is received or disbursed.*

Objective 1

FINANCIAL FORECASTING

Financial forecasting is the process of attempting to estimate a firm's future financing requirements. The basic steps involved in predicting those financing needs are the following:

➤ Step 1: Project the firm's sales revenues and expenses over the planning period.
➤ Step 2: Estimate the levels of investment in current and fixed assets that are needed to support the projected sales.
➤ Step 3: Determine the firm's financing needs throughout the planning period.

SALES FORECAST

TAKIN' IT TO THE NET

To get economy-wide data on business, interest rates, and a wide range of economic time series, see **www.stls.frb. org/fred**. Often historical sales data for specific industries are available. For example, historical industry sales for semiconductors can be found at **www.e-insite.net/eb_mag**.

The key ingredient in the firm's planning process is the sales forecast. This projection is generally derived using information from a number of sources. At a minimum, the sales forecast for the coming year would reflect (1) any past trend in sales that is expected to carry through into the new year and (2) the influence of any anticipated events that might materially affect that trend.[1] An example of the latter is the initiation of a major advertising campaign or a change in the firm's pricing policy.

FORECASTING FINANCIAL VARIABLES

Traditional financial forecasting takes the sales forecast as a given and makes projections of its impact on the firm's various expenses, assets, and liabilities. The most commonly used method for making these projections is the percent of sales method.

PERCENT OF SALES METHOD OF FINANCIAL FORECASTING

percent of sales method

The **percent of sales method** involves *estimating the level of an expense, asset, or liability for a future period as a percentage of the sales forecast.* The percentage used can come from the most recent financial statement item as a percentage of current sales, from an average computed over several years, from the judgment of the analyst, or from some combination of these sources.

Table 14-1 presents a complete example that uses the percent of sales method of financial forecasting for Drew, Inc. In this example each item in the firm's balance sheet that varies with sales is converted to a percentage of 2005 sales of $10 million. The forecast of the new balance for each item is then calculated by multiplying this percentage times the $12 million in projected sales for the 2006 planning period. This method offers a relatively low-cost and easy-to-use way to estimate the firm's future financing needs.

Note that in the example in Table 14-1, both current and fixed assets are assumed to vary with the level of firm sales. This means that the firm does not have sufficient productive capacity to absorb a projected increase in sales. Thus, if sales were to rise by $1, fixed assets would rise by $0.40, or 40 percent of the projected increase in sales. If the fixed assets the firm currently owns are sufficient to support the projected level of sales, then fixed assets will not be converted to a percentage of sales and will be projected to remain unchanged for the period being forecast.

Also, note that accounts payable and accrued expenses are the only liabilities allowed to vary with sales. Both these liability accounts might reasonably be expected to rise and fall with the level of firm sales, hence, the use of the percent of sales forecast. Because these two

---

[1]A complete discussion of forecast methodologies is outside the scope of this book. The interested reader will find the following reference helpful: Paul Newbold and Theodore Bos, *Introductory Business Forecasting* 2nd ed. (Cincinnati: Southwestern, 1994).

TABLE 14-1   Using the Percent of Sales Method to Forecast Drew, Inc.'s Financing Requirements for 2006

	A	B	C	D	E	F	G	H	I	J
1	Drew, Inc.						Drew, Inc.			
2	**Income Statement for 2005**						**Pro forma Income Statement for 2006**			
3					% of 2005 Sales			Calculation		
4							Sales growth rate =	20%		
5	Sales		$ 10,000,000				Sales	$10 million x (1+.20) =	$ 12,000,000	
6	Net Income		$ 500,000	$500,000 / $10,000,000 =	5.0%		Net Income	$12 million x .05 =	$ 600,000	
7										
8										
9										
10	Drew, Inc.						Drew, Inc.			
11	**Balance Sheet for 2005**						**Pro forma Balance Sheet for 2006**			
12					% of 2005 Sales			Calculation		
13										
14	Current assets		$ 2,000,000	[$2m / $10m] =	20.0%		Current assets	.20 x$12m =	$ 2,400,000	
15	Net fixed assets		4,000,000	[$4m / $10m] =	40.0%		Net fixed assets	.40 x$12m =	$ 4,800,000	
16	Total		$ 6,000,000				Total		$ 7,200,000	
17										
18	Accounts payable		$ 1,000,000	[$1m / $10m] =	10.0%		Accounts payable	.10 x$12m =	$ 1,200,000	
19	Accrued expenses		1,000,000	[$1m / $10m] =	10.0%		Accrued expenses	.10 x$12m =	1,200,000	
20	Notes payable		500,000		NA*		Notes payable	No change	500,000	
21	Current Liabilities		$ 2,500,000				Current Liabilities		$ 2,900,000	
22	Long-term debt		2,000,000		NA*		Long-term debt	No change	$ 2,000,000	
23	Total Liabilities		$ 4,500,000				Total Liabilities		$ 4,900,000	
24	Common stock (par)		100,000		NA*		Common stock (par)	No change	100,000	
25	Paid-in-capital		200,000		NA*		Paid-in-capital	No change	200,000	
26	Retained earnings		1,200,000				Retained earnings	Calculation*	1,500,000	
27	Common Equity		$ 1,500,000				Common Equity		1,800,000	
28	Total		$ 6,000,000				Total Financing Provided		$ 6,700,000	
29							Discretionary Financing Needed (Plug)*		$ 500,000	
30							Total Financing Needed = Total Assets		$ 7,200,000	
31										
32	*Not applicable. These account balances do not vary with sales.									
33–34	*Projected retained earnings for 2006 equals $1,500,000 which is equal to the 2005 level of retained earnings of $1,200,000 plus net income of $600,000 less common dividends equal to 50% of projected net income or $300,000 .									
35–37	*Discretionary financing needed (DFN) for 2006 is a "plug figure" that equals the difference in the firm's projected total financing requirements or total assets equal to $7,200,000 and total financing provided which is $6,700,000. In this scenario DFN is $500,000.									
38										

categories of current liabilities normally vary directly with the level of sales, they are often referred to as sources of **spontaneous financing**, which include *the trade credit and other accounts payable that arise spontaneously in the firm's day-to-day operations*. Chapter 15, which discusses working-capital management, has more to say about these forms of financing. Notes payable, long-term debt, common stock, and paid-in capital are not assumed to vary directly with the level of firm sales. These sources of financing are termed **discretionary financing**, *which require an explicit decision on the part of the firm's management every time funds are raised. An example is a bank note that requires that negotiations be undertaken and an agreement signed setting forth the terms and conditions for the financing*. Finally, note that the level of retained earnings does vary with estimated sales. The predicted change in the level of retained earnings equals the estimated after-tax profits (projected net income) equal to 5 percent of sales, or $600,000, less the common stock dividends of $300,000.

In the Drew, Inc., example found in Table 14-1, we estimate that firm sales will increase from $10 million to $12 million, which will cause the firm's need for total assets to rise to $7.2 million. These assets will then be financed by $4.9 million in existing liabilities plus spontaneous liabilities; $1.8 million in owner funds, including an additional $300,000 in retained earnings from next year's sales; and finally, $500,000 in discretionary financing, which can be raised by issuing notes payable, selling bonds, offering an issue of stock, or some combination of these sources.

In summary, we can estimate the firm's discretionary financing needs (*DFN*), using the percent of sales method of financial forecasting, by following a four-step procedure:

Step 1: Convert each asset and liability account that varies directly with firm sales to a percentage of the current year's sales.

EXAMPLE: CURRENT ASSETS AS A PERCENTAGE OF SALES

$$\frac{\text{Current assets}}{\text{sales}} = \frac{\$2\text{M}}{\$10\text{M}} = .2 \text{ or } 20\%$$

Step 2: Project the level of each asset and liability account in the balance sheet using its percentage of sales multiplied by projected sales or by leaving the account balance unchanged when the account does not vary with the level of sales.

EXAMPLE: PREDICTING CURRENT ASSETS

$$\text{Projected current assets} = \text{projected sales} \times \frac{\text{current assets}}{\text{sales}} = \$12\text{M} \times .2 = \$2.4\text{M}$$

Step 3: Project the addition to retained earnings available to help finance the firm's operations. This equals projected net income for the period less planned common stock dividends.

EXAMPLE: PREDICTING ADDITIONAL RETAINED EARNINGS

$$\begin{array}{l}\text{Projected addition} \\ \text{to retained earnings}\end{array} = \text{projected sales} \times \frac{\text{net income}}{\text{sales}} \times \left(1 - \frac{\text{cash dividends}}{\text{net income}}\right) = \$12\text{M} \times .05 \times (1 - .5) = \$300,000$$

Step 4: Project the firm's *DFN* as the projected level of total assets less projected liabilities and owners' equity.

EXAMPLE: PREDICTING DISCRETIONARY FINANCING NEEDS

$$\begin{array}{l}\text{Discretionary financing needed} = \text{projected total assets} - \text{projected total liabilities} - \text{projected owner's equity} \\ = \$7.2\text{M} - 4.9\text{M} - \$1.8\text{M} = \$500,000\end{array}$$

ANALYZING THE EFFECTS OF PROFITABILITY AND DIVIDEND POLICY ON *DFN*

Projecting discretionary financing needed, we can quickly and easily evaluate the sensitivity of our projected financing requirements to changes in key variables. For example, using the information from the preceding example, we evaluate the effect of net profit margins (*NPMs*) equal to 1 percent, 5 percent, and 10 percent in combination with dividend payout ratios of 30 percent, 50 percent, and 70 percent, as follows:

Discretionary Financing Needed for Various Net Profit Margins and Dividend Payout Ratios

| NET PROFIT MARGIN | DIVIDEND PAYOUT RATIOS = DIVIDENDS ÷ NET INCOME | | |
	30%	50%	70%
1%	$716,000	$740,000	$764,000
5%	380,000	500,000	620,000
10%	(40,000)	200,000	440,000

If these *NPMs* are reasonable estimates of the possible ranges of values the firm might experience, and if the firm is considering dividend payouts ranging from 30 percent to 70 percent, then we estimate that the firm's financing requirements will range from ($40,000), which represents a surplus of $40,000, to a situation in which it would need to acquire $764,000. Lower *NPMs* mean higher funds requirements. Also, higher dividend payout percentages, other things remaining constant, lead to a need for more discretionary financing. This is a direct result of the fact that a high-dividend-paying firm retains less of its earnings.

ANALYZING THE EFFECTS OF SALES GROWTH ON A FIRM'S *DFN*

In Figure 14-1 we analyzed the *DFN* for Drew, Inc., whose sales were expected to grow from $10 million to $12 million during the coming year. Recall that the 20 percent expected increase in sales led to an increase in the firm's needs for financing in the amount of $500,000. We referred to this added financing requirement as the firm's *DFN* because all these funds must be raised from sources, such as bank borrowing or a new equity issue, that require that management exercise its discretion in selecting the source. In this section we want to investigate how a firm's *DFN* varies with different rates of anticipated growth in sales.

Table 14-2 contains an expansion of the financial forecast found in Table 14-1. Specifically, we use the same assumptions and prediction methods that underlie Table 14-1 but apply them to sales growth rates of 0 percent, 20 percent, and 40 percent. The *DFN* for these sales growth rates ranges from ($250,000) to $1,250,000. When *DFN* is negative, this means that the firm has more money than it needs to finance the assets used to generate the projected sales. Alternatively, when *DFN* is positive, this means that the firm must raise additional funds in this amount, by either borrowing or issuing stock. We can calculate *DFN* using the following relationship:

TAKIN' IT TO THE NET

An increasing variety of software products is becoming available to support a firm's efforts to build financing forecasts and model its financial requirements. For example, visit www.dataper.demon.co.uk/prophecy flash.htm.

$$DFN = \frac{\text{predicted change}}{\text{in total assets}} - \frac{\text{predicted change}}{\text{in spontaneous liabilities}} - \frac{\text{predicted change}}{\text{in retained earnings}} \quad \textbf{(14-1)}$$

Notice that in defining *DFN* we only consider changes in spontaneous liabilities, which you will recall are those liabilities that arise more or less automatically in the course of doing business (examples include accrued expenses and accounts payable). In Table 14-1 the only liabilities that are allowed to change with sales are spontaneous liabilities, so we can calculate the change in spontaneous liabilities simply by comparing total liabilities at the current sales level with total liabilities for the predicted sales level.

Equation (14-1) can be used to estimate the *DFN* numbers found in Table 14-2. For example, when sales are expected to grow at a rate of 10 percent (i.e., *g* equals 10 percent), *DFN* can be calculated as follows:

$$DFN(g = 10\%) = (\$6,600,000 - 6,000,000) - (\$4,700,000 - 4,500,000) - (\$1,475,000 - 1,200,000) = \$125,000$$

Sometimes analysts prefer to calculate a firm's **external financing needs** (*EFN*), which include *all the firm's needs for financing beyond the funds provided internally through the retention of earnings*. Thus,

external financing needs

$$EFN = \text{predicted change in total assets} - \text{change in retained earnings} \quad \textbf{(14-2)}$$

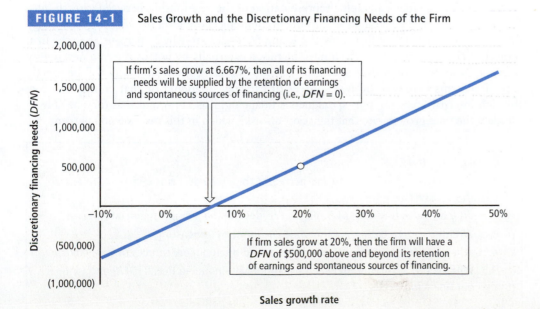

FIGURE 14-1   Sales Growth and the Discretionary Financing Needs of the Firm

If firm's sales grow at 6.667%, then all of its financing needs will be supplied by the retention of earnings and spontaneous sources of financing (i.e., *DFN* = 0).

If firm sales grow at 20%, then the firm will have a *DFN* of $500,000 above and beyond its retention of earnings and spontaneous sources of financing.

TABLE 14-2   Discretionary Financing Needs (*DFN*) and the Growth Rate in Sales

	A	B	C	D	E	F	G	H	I	J	K
1	Drew, Inc.						Drew, Inc.				
2	Income Statement for 2005						Pro forma Income Statement for 2006				
3					% of 2005 Sales						
4							Alternative Growth Rates in Sales		0%	20%	40%
5	Sales		$ 10,000,000				Sales		$ 10,000,000	$ 12,000,000	$ 14,000,000
6	Net Income		$ 500,000	$500,000 /$10,000,000 =	5.0%		Net Income		$ 500,000	$ 600,000	$ 700,000
7											
8											
9	Drew, Inc.						Drew, Inc.				
10	Balance Sheet for 2005						Pro forma Balance Sheet for 2006				
11					% of 2005 Sales			Calculation			
12											
13	Current assets		$ 2,000,000	$2m /$10m =	20.0%		Current assets	.20 x$12m =	$ 2,000,000	$ 2,400,000	$ 2,800,000
14	Net fixed assets		4,000,000	$4m /$10m =	40.0%		Net fixed assets	.40 x$12m =	4,000,000	$ 4,800,000	$ 5,600,000
15	Total		$ 6,000,000				Total		$ 6,000,000	$ 7,200,000	$ 8,400,000
16											
17	Accounts payable		$ 1,000,000	$1m /$10m =	10.0%		Accounts payable	.10 x$12m =	$ 1,000,000	$ 1,200,000	$ 1,400,000
18	Accrued expenses		1,000,000	$1m /$10m =	10.0%		Accrued expenses	.10 x$12m =	1,000,000	1,200,000	1,400,000
19	Notes payable		500,000		NAª		Notes payable	No change	500,000	500,000	500,000
20	Current Liabilities		$ 2,500,000				Current Liabilities		$ 2,500,000	$ 2,900,000	$ 3,300,000
21	Long-term debt		2,000,000		NAª		Long-term debt	No change	2,000,000	2,000,000	2,000,000
22	Total Liabilities		$ 4,500,000				Total Liabilities		$ 4,500,000	$ 4,900,000	$ 5,300,000
23	Common stock (par)		100,000		NAª		Common stock (par)	No change	100,000	$ 100,000	$ 100,000
24	Paid-in-capital		200,000		NAª		Paid-in-capital	No change	200,000	200,000	200,000
25	Retained earnings		1,200,000				Retained earnings	Calculationᵇ	1,450,000	1,500,000	1,550,000
26	Common Equity		$ 1,500,000				Common Equity		$ 1,750,000	$ 1,800,000	$ 1,850,000
27	Total		$ 6,000,000				Total Financing Provided		$ 6,250,000	$ 6,700,000	$ 7,150,000
28							Discretionary Financing Needed (Plug)ᶜ		$ (250,000)	$ 500,000	$ 1,250,000
29							Total Financing Needed = Total Assets		$ 6,000,000	$ 7,200,000	$ 8,400,000
30											
31											
32	ªNot applicable. These account balances do not vary with sales.										
33	ᵇProjected retained earnings for 2006 based on the 20% growth rate scenario is $1,500,000 and is calculated as follows: The 2005 retained earnings of $1,200,000 added to 2006 projected net income of $600,000 less common dividends of $300,000. Note that dividends are assumed to be 50% or net income so dividends vary across the three scenarios.										
34	ᶜDiscretionary financing needed (DFN) for 2006 and the 20% growth rate scenario is a "plug figure" that equals the difference in the firm's projected total financing requirements or total assets of $7,200,000 and total financing provided of $6,700,000. In this scenario DFN is $500,000.										
35											
36											
37											
38											

For an anticipated growth in sales of 10 percent, *EFN* equals $325,000. The difference between *EFN* and *DFN* equals the $200,000 in added spontaneous financing that the firm anticipates receiving when its sales rise from $10 million to $11 million. We prefer to use the *DFN* concept because it focuses the analyst's attention on the amount of funds that the firm must actively seek to meet the firm's financing requirements.

Figure 14-1 contains a graphic representation of the relationship between growth rates for sales and *DFN*. The straight line in the graph depicts the level of *DFN* for each of the different rates of growth in firm sales. For example, if sales grow by 20 percent, then the firm projects a *DFN* of $500,000, which must be raised externally by borrowing or a new equity offering. Note that when firm sales grow at 6.667 percent, the firm's *DFN* will be exactly zero. For firms that have limited sources of external financing or that choose to grow through internal financing plus spontaneous financing, it is important that they be able to estimate the sales growth rate that they can "afford," which in this case is 6.667 percent.

CONCEPT CHECK

1. If we cannot predict the future perfectly, then why do firms engage in financial forecasting?

2. Why are sales forecasts so important to developing a firm's financial forecast?

3. What is the percent of sales method of financial forecasting?

4. What are some examples of spontaneous and discretionary sources of financing?

5. What is the distinction between discretionary financing needs (*DFN*) and external financing needs (*EFN*)?

THE SUSTAINABLE RATE OF GROWTH

Objective **2**

The **sustainable rate of growth** (g^*) represents *the rate at which a firm's sales can grow if it wants to maintain its present financial ratios and does not want to resort to the sale of new equity shares*. A simple formula can be derived for g^* in which we assume that a firm's assets and liabilities all grow at the same rate as its sales, that is,

sustainable rate of growth

$$\text{Sustainable rate of growth } (g^*) = ROE\,(1-b) \qquad \textbf{(14-3)}$$

ROE is the firm's return on equity, which was defined in Chapter 3 as follows:

$$ROE = \frac{\text{net income}}{\text{common equity}}$$

and *b* is the firm's dividend payout ratio, that is, $\frac{\text{dividends}}{\text{net income}}$. The term $(1-b)$ is sometimes referred to as the **plowback ratio** because it indicates *the fraction of earnings that is reinvested or plowed back into the firm*. Equation (14-3) is deceptively simple. Recall that *ROE* can also be written as follows:

plowback ratio

$$ROE = \left(\frac{\text{net income}}{\text{sales}}\right) \times \left(\frac{\text{sales}}{\text{assets}}\right) \times \left(\frac{\text{total assets}}{\text{common equity}}\right)$$

Consequently, a firm's sustainable rate of growth is determined by its *ROE* (i.e., its anticipated *NPM*, asset turnover, and capital structure), as well as its dividend policy.

EXAMPLE: CALCULATING THE SUSTAINABLE RATE OF GROWTH

Consider the three firms found here:

FIRM	NET PROFIT MARGIN	ASSET TURNOVER	LEVERAGE (ASSETS ÷ EQUITY)	PLOWBACK RATIO	SUSTAINABLE GROWTH RATE (g^*)
A	15%	1.00	1.2	50%	9.0%
B	15%	1.00	1.2	100%	18.0%
C	15%	1.00	1.5	100%	22.5%

Comparing Firms A and B, we see that the only difference is that Firm A pays out half its earnings in common dividends (i.e., plows back half its earnings), whereas Firm B retains or plows back all of its earnings. The net result is that Firm B with its added source of internal equity financing can grow at twice the rate of Firm A (18 percent compared with only 9 percent). Similarly, comparing Firms B and C, we note that they differ only in that Firm B uses less debt financing than Firm C. The result is that Firm C's sustainable rate of growth is 22.5 percent, compared with only 18 percent for Firm B.

Before leaving our discussion of the sustainable rate of growth concept, it is important that we stress the underlying assumptions behind equation (14-3). For this equation to accurately depict a firm's sustainable rate of growth, the following assumptions must hold:

➤ First, the firm's assets must vary as a constant percentage of sales (i.e., even fixed assets expand and contract directly with the level of firm sales).
➤ Second, the firm's liabilities must all vary directly with firm sales. This means that the firm's management will expand its borrowing (both spontaneous and discretionary) in direct proportion with sales to maintain its present ratio of debt to assets.
➤ Third, the firm pays out a constant proportion of its earnings in common stock dividends regardless of the level of firm sales.

Because all three of these assumptions are only rough approximations to the way that firms actually behave, equation (14-3) provides a crude approximation of the firm's actual sustainable rate of growth. However, an estimate of g^* using equation (14-3) can be a very useful first step in the firm's financial planning process.

FINANCIAL MANAGEMENT
IN PRACTICE

SUSTAINABLE GROWTH—A BROADER PERSPECTIVE AT DUPONT*

The *financial* concept of a sustainable rate of growth is a very narrow one that pertains to the rate of growth in revenues that the firm can experience without being forced to change its key financial ratios and without having to resort to the sale of new shares of stock to finance the growth. The important thing to recognize here is that we *hold everything constant*. That is, we assume that the firm's profit margins and asset requirements do not change with growth in revenues. Although these conditions may hold as reasonable approximations, they almost certainly do not when we consider very-long-term growth. For example, some experts have extrapolated the resource requirements necessary to support the consumption level of the average American and estimate that it would take resources equal to approximately three times the world's known supplies. This is obviously not feasible, and it suggests a dim set of future prospects for earth's inhabitants.

Some business leaders, including DuPont Chairman and CEO Chad Holliday, who chairs the World Business Council for Sustainable Development (a coalition of 150 companies from 30 countries committed to environmental protection, social equity, and economic growth), have used these predictions as the basis for thinking about what level of growth is really sustainable. His approach at DuPont has been one of *undoing the assumptions* that underlie the predictions. For example, DuPont has set two goals for its use of the world's scarce resources for 2010: First, the company has targeted a reduction in greenhouse emissions by two-thirds while holding its energy use constant (flat). The company also plans to increase its use of renewable energy resources up to 10 percent of its global requirements.

*Adapted from Chad Holliday, "Sustainable Growth, the DuPont Way," *Harvard Business Review* (September 2001), pp. 129–34. Used by permission.

CONCEPT CHECK
1. What is a firm's sustainable rate of growth?
2. How is a firm's sustainable rate of growth related to the firm's profitability and dividend policy?

Objective **3**

LIMITATIONS OF THE PERCENT OF SALES FORECAST METHOD

The percent of sales method of financial forecasting provides reasonable estimates of a firm's financing requirements only when asset requirements and financing sources can be accurately forecast as a constant percent of sales. For example, predicting inventories using the percent of sales method involves the following predictive equation, where the subscript t refers to the period that is being forecast.

$$\text{Inventories}_t = \left[\frac{\text{inventories}_{t-1}}{\text{sales}_{t-1}}\right] \cdot \text{sales}_t$$

Figure 14-2a depicts this predictive relationship. Note that the percent of sales predictive model is simply a straight line that passes through the origin (i.e., has a zero intercept). There are some fairly common instances in which this type of relationship fails to describe the relationship between an asset category and sales. Two such examples involve assets for which there are scale economies and assets that must be purchased in discrete quantities ("lumpy assets").

Economies of scale are sometimes realized from investing in certain types of assets. For example, a new computer system may support a firm's operations over a wide range of firm sales. This means that these assets do not increase in direct proportion to sales. Figure 14-2b reflects one instance in which the firm realizes economies of scale from its investment in inventory. Note that inventories as a percentage of sales decline from 120 percent of sales, or $120 when sales are $100, to 30 percent of sales, or $300 when sales equal $1,000. This reflects the fact that there is a fixed component of inventories (in this

FIGURE 14-2a Percent of Sales Forecast

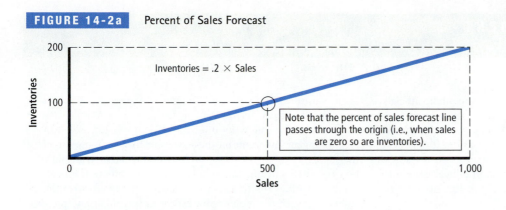

FIGURE 14-2b Economies of Scale

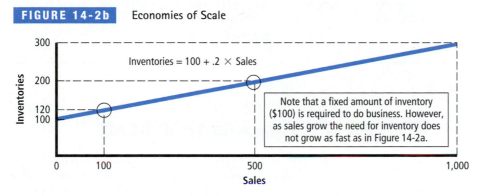

case $100) that the firm must have on hand regardless of the level of sales, plus a variable component (20 percent of sales). In this instance the predictive equation for inventories is as follows:

$$\text{Inventories}_t = a + b \text{ sales}_t$$

In this example, a is equal to 100 and b equals .20.[2]

Figure 14-2c is an example of *lumpy assets*, that is, assets that must be purchased in large, nondivisible components. For example, if the firm spends $500 on plant and equipment, it can produce up to $100 in sales per year. If it spends another $500 (for a total of $1,000), then it can support sales of $200 per year, and so forth. Note that when a block of assets is purchased, it creates excess capacity until sales grow to the point at which the capacity is fully used. The result is a step function like the one depicted in Figure 14-2c. Thus, if the firm does not expect sales to exceed the current capacity of its plant and equipment, there would be no projected need for added plant and equipment capacity.

FIGURE 14-2c Economies of Scale with Lumpy Investments

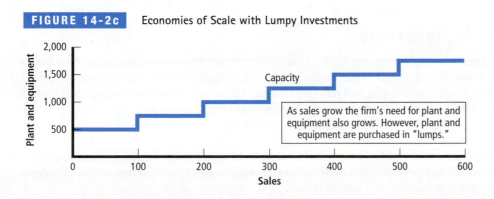

[2]Economies of scale are evidenced by the nonzero intercept value. However, scale economies can also result in nonlinear relationships between sales and a particular asset category. Later, when we discuss cash management, we will find that one popular cash management model predicts a nonlinear relationship between the optimal cash balance and the level of cash transactions.

FINANCIAL MANAGEMENT
IN PRACTICE

TO BRIBE OR NOT TO BRIBE

In many parts of the world, bribes and payoffs to public officials are considered the norm in business transactions. This raises a perplexing ethical question. If paying bribes is not considered unethical in a foreign country, should you consider it unethical to make these payments?

This situation provides an example of an ethical issue that gave rise to legislation. The Foreign Corrupt Practices Act of 1977 (as amended in the Omnibus Trade and Competitiveness Act of 1988) established criminal penalties for making payments to foreign officials, political parties, or candidates in order to obtain or retain business. Ethical problems are fre-

quently areas just outside the boundaries of current legislation and often lead to the passage of new legislation.

Consider the following question: If you were involved in negotiating an important business deal in a foreign country and the success or failure of the deal hinged on whether you paid a local government official to help you consummate the deal, would you authorize the payment? Assume that the form of the payment is such that you do not expect to be caught and punished; for example, your company agrees to purchase supplies from a family member of the government official at a price slightly above the competitive price.

CONSTRUCTING AND USING A CASH BUDGET

As we noted earlier, the principal virtue of the percent of sales method of financial forecasting is its simplicity. To obtain a more precise estimate of the amount and timing of the firm's future financing needs, we require a cash budget. The percent of sales method of financial forecasting provides a very useful, low-cost forerunner to the development of the more detailed cash budget, which the firm will ultimately use to estimate its financing needs.

BACK TO THE FOUNDATIONS

Budgets have many important uses; however, their use as a tool of managerial control is critically important and often overlooked in the study of financial management. **Principle 7: Agency Problems—Managers Won't Work for Owners Unless It's in Their Best Interest** *speaks to the root source of the problem, and budgets provide one tool for attempting to deal with it. Specifically, budgets provide management with a tool for evaluating performance and, consequently, maintaining a degree of control over employee actions.*

BUDGET FUNCTIONS

budget

A **budget** is simply *a forecast of future events*. For example, students preparing for final exams make use of time budgets to help them allocate their limited preparation time among their courses. Students also must budget their financial resources among competing uses, such as books, tuition, food, rent, clothes, and extracurricular activities.

Budgets perform three basic functions for a firm.

➤ First, they indicate the amount and timing of the firm's needs for future financing.
➤ Second, they provide the basis for taking corrective action in the event budgeted figures do not match actual or realized figures.
➤ Third, budgets provide the basis for performance evaluation and control. Plans are carried out by people, and budgets provide benchmarks that management can use to evaluate the performance of those responsible for carrying out those plans and, in turn, to control their actions.

CONCEPT CHECK

1. What, in words, is the fundamental relationship (equation) used in making percent of sales forecasts?
2. Under what circumstances does a firm violate the basic relationship underlying the percent of sales forecast method?

THE CASH BUDGET

Objective **4**

The **cash budget** represents a *detailed plan of future cash flows* and is composed of four elements: cash receipts, cash disbursements, net change in cash for the period, and new financing needed.

cash budget

EXAMPLE: CONSTRUCTING A CASH BUDGET

To demonstrate the construction and use of the cash budget, consider Salco Furniture Company, Inc., a regional distributor of household furniture. Management is in the process of preparing a monthly cash budget for the upcoming 6 months (January through June 2006). Salco's sales are highly seasonal, peaking in the months of March through May. Roughly 30 percent of Salco's sales are collected 1 month after the sale, 50 percent 2 months after the sale, and the remainder during the third month following the sale.

Salco attempts to pace its purchases with its forecast of future sales. Purchases generally equal 75 percent of sales and are made 2 months in advance of anticipated sales. Payments are made in the month following purchases. For example, June sales are estimated at $100,000; thus, April purchases are .75 × $100,000 = $75,000. Correspondingly, payments for purchases in May equal $75,000. Wages, salaries, rent, and other cash expenses are recorded in Table 14-3, which gives Salco's cash budget for the 6-month period ended in June 2006. Additional expenditures are recorded in the cash budget related to the purchase of equipment in the amount of $14,000 during February and the repayment of a $12,000 loan in May. In June, Salco will pay $7,500 interest on its $150,000 in long-term debt for the period of January to June 2006. Interest on the $12,000 short-term note repaid in May for the period January through May equals $600 and is paid in May.

TABLE 14-3 Salco Furniture Co., Inc. Cash Budget for the 6 Months Ended June 30, 2006

	A	B	C	D	E	F	G	H	I	J	K	L
1		October	November	December	January	February	March	April	May	June	July	August
2	Worksheet											
3	Sales (forecasted)	55,000	62,000	50,000	60,000	75,000	88,000	100,000	110,000	100,000	80,000	75,000
4	Purchases (75% of sales in 2 months)			56,250	66,000	75,000	82,500	75,000	60,000	56,250		
5												
6	Cash Receipts											
7	Collections:											
8	First Month after sale (30%)				15,000	18,000	22,500	26,400	30,000	33,000		
9	Second Month after sale (50%)				31,000	25,000	30,000	37,500	44,000	50,000		
10	Third Month after sale (20%)				11,000	12,400	10,000	12,000	15,000	17,600		
11	Total Cash Receipts				57,000	55,400	62,500	75,900	89,000	100,600		
12												
13	Cash Disbursements											
14	Payments (one-month lag of purchases from row 4)				56,250	66,000	75,000	82,500	75,000	60,000		
15	Wages and Salaries				3,000	10,000	7,000	8,000	6,000	4,000		
16	Rent				4,000	4,000	4,000	4,000	4,000	4,000		
17	Other Expenses				1,000	500	1,200	1,500	1,500	1,200		
18	Interest expense on existing debt[a]								600	7,500		
19	Taxes						4,460			5,200		
20	Purchase of Equipment					14,000						
21	Loan Repayment[b]								12,000			
22	Total Cash Disbursements				64,250	94,500	91,660	96,000	99,100	81,900		
23												
24	Net Change in Cash for the Period				(7,250)	(39,100)	(29,160)	(20,100)	(10,100)	18,700		
25	Plus: Beginning cash balance				20,000	12,750	10,000	10,000	10,000	10,000		
26	Less: Interest on short-term borrowing				0	0	(364)	(659)	(866)	(976)		
27	Equals: Ending cash balance before short-term borrowing				12,750	(26,350)	(19,524)	(10,759)	(966)	27,724		
28												
29	New Financing Needed[c]				0	36,350	29,524	20,759	10,966	(17,724)[d]		
30	Ending cash balance				12,750	10,000	10,000	10,000	10,000	10,000		
31	Cumulative borrowing				0	36,350	65,874	86,633	97,599	79,875		
32												
33												
34	[a]An interest payment of $600 on the $12,000 loan is due in May, and an interest payment of $7500 on the $150,000 long-term debt is due in June.											
35	[b]The principal amount of the $12,000 loan is also due in May.											
36	[c]The amount of financing that is required to raise the firm's ending cash balance up to its $10,000 desired cash balance.											
37	[d]Negative financing needed simply means the firm has excess cash that can be used to retire a part of its short-term borrowing from prior months.											
38												

FINANCIAL MANAGEMENT
IN PRACTICE

BEING HONEST ABOUT THE UNCERTAINTY OF THE FUTURE

Put yourself in the shoes of Ben Tolbert, who is the CFO of Bonajet Enterprises. Ben's CEO is scheduled to meet with a group of outside analysts tomorrow to discuss the firm's financial forecast for the last quarter of the year. Ben's analysis suggests that there is a very real prospect that the coming quarter's results could be very disappointing. How would you handle Ben's dilemma?

As Ben looks over a draft of the report he must submit to the company CEO, he becomes increasingly concerned. Although the forecast is below initial expectations, this is not what worries Ben. The problem is that some of the basic assumptions underlying his prediction might not come true. If this is the case, then the

company's performance for the last quarter of the year will be dramatically below its annual forecast. The result would be a potentially severe reaction in the investment community, causing a downward adjustment of unknown proportions in the firm's stock price.

Bonajet's CEO is a no-nonsense guy who really doesn't like to see his CFO hedge his predictions, so Ben is under pressure to decide whether to ignore the downside prospects or make them known to his CEO. Complicating matters is the fact that the worst-case scenario would probably give rise to a reorganization of Bonajet that would lead to substantial layoffs of its workforce. Here is Ben's dilemma: What should he tell the CEO in their meeting tomorrow morning?

Salco currently has a cash balance of $20,000 and wants to maintain a minimum balance of $10,000. Additional borrowing necessary to maintain that minimum balance is estimated in the final section of Table 14-3. Borrowing takes place at the beginning of the month in which the funds are needed. Interest on borrowed funds equals 12 percent per annum, or 1 percent per month, and is paid in the month following the one in which funds are borrowed. Thus, interest on funds borrowed in January will be paid in February equal to 1 percent of the loan amount outstanding during January.

The financing-needed line in Salco's cash budget determines that the firm's cumulative short-term borrowing will be $36,350 in February, $65,874 in March, $86,633 in April, and $97,599 in May. In June the firm will be able to reduce its borrowing to $79,875. Note that the cash budget indicates not only the amount of financing needed during the period but also when the funds will be needed.

CONCEPT CHECK

1. What is a cash budget?
2. How is a cash budget used in financial planning?

SUMMARY

Objective 1

This chapter develops the role of forecasting within the context of the firm's financial-planning activities. Forecasts of the firm's sales revenues and related expenses provide the basis for projecting future financing needs. The most popular method for forecasting financial variables is the percent of sales method.

Objective 2

A firm's sustainable rate of growth is the maximum rate at which its sales can grow if it is to maintain its present financial ratios and not have to resort to issuing new equity. We calculate the sustainable rate of growth as follows:

Sustainable rate of growth $(g^*) = ROE\,(1 - b)$

where ROE is the return on earned common equity and b is the dividend payout ratio (i.e., the ratio of dividends to earnings). Consequently, a firm's sustainable rate of growth increases with ROE and decreases with the fraction of its earnings paid out in dividends.

Objective 3

The percent of sales method presumes that the asset or liability being forecast is a constant percent of sales for all future levels of sales. There are instances when this assumption is not reasonable and, consequently, the percent of sales method does not provide reasonable predictions. One such instance arises when there are economies of scale in the use of the asset being forecast. For example, the firm may need at least $10 million in inventories to open its doors and operate even for sales as low as $100 million per year. If sales double to $200 million, inventories may only increase to $15 million. Thus, inventories do not increase with sales in a constant proportion. A second situation in which the percent of sales method fails to work properly is when asset purchases are lumpy. That is, if plant capacity must be purchased in $50 million increments, then plant and equipment will not remain a constant percentage of sales.

How serious are these possible problems and should we use the percent of sales method? Even in the face of these problems, the percent of sales method predicts reasonably well when predicted sales levels do not differ drastically from the level used to calculate the percentage of sales. For example, if the current sales level used in calculating percentage of sales for inventories is $40 million, then we can feel more comfortable forecasting the level of inventories corresponding to a new sales level of $42 million than when sales are predicted to rise to $60 million.

The cash budget is the primary tool of financial forecasting and planning. It contains a detailed plan of future cash flow estimates and is comprised of four elements or segments: cash receipts, cash disbursements, net change in cash for the period, and new financing needed. Once prepared, the cash budget also serves as a tool for monitoring and controlling the firm's operations. By comparing actual cash receipts and disbursements to those in the cash budget, the financial manager can gain an appreciation of how well the firm is performing. In addition, deviations from the plan serve as an early warning system to signal the onset of financial difficulties ahead.

Objective **4**

KEY TERMS

Budget, 456

Cash budget, 457

Discretionary financing, 449

External financing needs, 451

Percent of sales method, 448

Plowback ratio, 453

Spontaneous financing, 449

Sustainable rate of growth, 453

STUDY QUESTIONS

14-1. Discuss the shortcomings of the percent of sales method of financial forecasting.

14-2. What would be the probable effect on a firm's cash position of the following events?

    a. Rapidly rising sales

    b. A delay in the payment of payables

    c. A more liberal credit policy on sales (to the firm's customers)

    d. Holding larger inventories

14-3. A cash budget is usually thought of as a means of planning for future financing needs. Why would a cash budget also be important for a firm that has excess cash on hand?

14-4. Explain why a cash budget would be of particular importance to a firm that experiences seasonal fluctuations in its sales.

SELF-TEST PROBLEMS

ST-1. (*Financial forecasting*) Use the percent of sales method to prepare a pro forma income statement for Calico Sales Co., Inc. Projected sales for next year equal $4 million. Cost of goods sold equals 70 percent of sales, administrative expense equals $500,000, and depreciation expense is $300,000. Interest expense equals $50,000, and income is taxed at a rate of 40 percent. The firm plans to spend $200,000 during the period to renovate its office facility and will retire $150,000 in notes payable. Finally, selling expense equals 5 percent of sales.

ST-2. (*Cash budget*) Stauffer, Inc. has estimated sales and purchase requirements for the last half of the coming year. Past experience indicates that it will collect 20 percent of its sales in the month of the sale, 50 percent of the remainder 1 month after the sale, and the balance in the second month following the sale. Stauffer prefers to pay for half its purchases in the month of the purchase and the other half the following month. Labor expense for each month is expected to equal 5 percent of that month's sales, with cash payment being made in the month in which the expense is incurred.

Depreciation expense is $5,000 per month; miscellaneous cash expenses are $4,000 per month and are paid in the month incurred. General and administrative expenses of $50,000 are recognized and paid monthly. A $60,000 truck is to be purchased in August and is to be depreciated on a straight-line basis over 10 years with no expected salvage value. The company also plans to pay a $9,000 cash dividend to stockholders in July. The company feels that a minimum cash balance of $30,000 should be maintained. Any borrowing will cost 12 percent annually, with interest paid in the month following the month in which the funds are borrowed. Borrowing takes place at the beginning of the month in which the need for funds arises. For example, if during the month of July the firm should need to borrow $24,000 to maintain its $30,000 desired minimum balance, then $24,000 will be taken out on July 1 with interest owed for the entire month of July. Interest for the month of July would then be paid on August 1. Sales and purchase estimates are shown here. Prepare a cash budget for the months of July and August (cash on hand June 30 was $30,000, while sales for May and June were $100,000 and purchases were $60,000 for each of these months).

MONTH	SALES	PURCHASES
July	$120,000	$50,000
August	150,000	40,000
September	110,000	30,000

ST-3. (*Forecasting net income*) The chief financial officer of Clairmont Manufacturing, Inc., prepares a forecast of net income for the coming year as a starting point for developing financial plans. At the close of 2005, the firm's income statement appeared as follows (in $000):

Income Statement (000)

FOR THE YEAR ENDED 2005

Sales	$ 25,000
Cost of goods sold	(16,250)
Gross profit	8,750
Operating costs	(4,500)
Depreciation expense	(150)
Net operating profit	4,100
Interest expense	(1,580)
Earnings before taxes	2,520
Taxes	(882)
Net income	$ 1,638
Dividends	$ 1,500
Addition to retained earnings	$ 138

The CFO normally uses the most recent income statement to guide her estimate of what the future will bring. For example, she has made the following assumptions and estimates for 2006:

Sales growth rate	15%
COGS/sales	65%
Operating expenses/sales	18%
Depreciation expense (000)	$ 150
Interest expense (000)	$1,580
Tax Rate	35%
Dividends (000)	$1,500

Note that these estimates are derived from the 2005 income statement reflecting the fact that the CFO believes the only real change for the coming year is the level of sales, which she estimates to be 15 percent higher. Of course, cost of goods sold and operating expenses will rise in proportion to the increase in sales following the percent of sales noted earlier.

What do you estimate net income for the firm to be in 2006? If the firm retains its $1,500,000 dividend payment, how much do you estimate the firm will be able to retain in 2006?

STUDY PROBLEMS

14-1. (*Financial forecasting*) Zapatera Enterprises is evaluating its financing requirements for the coming year. The firm has only been in business for 1 year, but its CFO predicts that the firm's operating expenses, current assets, net fixed assets, and current liabilities will remain at their current proportion of sales.

Last year Zapatera had $12 million in sales, with net income of $1.2 million. The firm anticipates that next year's sales will reach $15 million, with net income rising to $2 million. Given its present high rate of growth, the firm retains all its earnings to help defray the cost of new investments.

The firm's balance sheet for the year just ended is found here:

Zapatera Enterprises, Inc.

BALANCE SHEET

	12/31/2006	% OF SALES
Current assets	$3,000,000	25%
Net fixed assets	6,000,000	50%
Total	$9,000,000	

LIABILITIES AND OWNERS' EQUITY

Accounts payable	$3,000,000	25%
Long-term debt	2,000,000	NA[a]
Total liabilities	$5,000,000	
Common stock	1,000,000	NA
Paid-in capital	1,800,000	NA
Retained earnings	1,200,000	
Common equity	4,000,000	
Total	$9,000,000	

[a] Not applicable. This figure does not vary directly with sales and is assumed to remain constant for purposes of making next year's forecast of financing requirements.

Estimate Zapatera's financing requirements (i.e., total assets) for 2006 and its discretionary financing needs (*DFN*).

14-2. (*Pro forma accounts receivable balance calculation*) On March 31, 2005, Mike's Bike Shop had outstanding accounts receivable of $17,500. Mike's sales are roughly evenly split between credit and cash sales, with the credit sales collected half in the month after the sale and the remainder 2 months after the sale. Historical and projected sales for the bike shop are given here:

MONTH	SALES	MONTH	SALES
January	$15,000	March	$25,000
February	20,000	April (projected)	30,000

    a. Under these circumstances, what should the balance in accounts receivable be at the end of April?

    b. How much cash did Mike's realize during April from sales and collections?

14-3. (*Financial forecasting*) Sambonoza Enterprises projects its sales next year to be $4 million and expects to earn 5 percent of that amount after taxes. The firm is currently in the process of projecting its financing needs and has made the following assumptions (projections):

1. Current assets will equal 20 percent of sales, while fixed assets will remain at their current level of $1 million.
2. Common equity is currently $0.8 million, and the firm pays out half its after-tax earnings in dividends.
3. The firm has short-term payables and trade credit that normally equal 10 percent of sales, and it has no long-term debt outstanding.

What are Sambonoza's financing needs for the coming year?

14-4. (*Financial forecasting—percent of sales*) Tulley Appliances, Inc., projects next year's sales to be $20 million. Current sales are at $15 million, based on current assets of $5 million and fixed assets of $5 million. The firm's net profit margin is 5 percent after taxes. Tulley forecasts that current assets will rise in direct proportion to the increase in sales, but fixed assets will increase by only $100,000. Currently, Tulley has $1.5 million in accounts payable (which vary directly with sales), $2 million in long-term debt (due in 10 years), and common equity (including $4 million in retained earnings) totaling $6.5 million. Tulley plans to pay $500,000 in common stock dividends next year.

    a. What are Tulley's total financing needs (i.e., total assets) for the coming year?

    b. Given the firm's projections and dividend payments plans, what are its discretionary financing needs?

    c. Based on your projections, and assuming that the $100,000 expansion in fixed assets will occur, what is the largest increase in sales the firm can support without having to resort to the use of discretionary sources of financing?

14-5. (*Pro forma balance sheet construction*) Use the following industry-average ratios to construct a pro forma balance sheet for Phoebe's Cat Foods, Inc.

Total asset turnover	1.5 times
Average collection period	
(assume 365-day year)	15 days
Fixed asset turnover	5 times
Inventory turnover	
(based on cost of goods sold)	3 times
Current ratio	2 times
Sales (all on credit)	$3.0 million
Cost of goods sold	75% of sales
Debt ratio	50%

		Current liabilities	
Cash		Long-term debt	
Accounts receivable	_____	Common stock plus	_____
Net fixed assets	$_____	Retained earnings	$_____

14-6. (*Cash budget*) The Sharpe Corporation's projected sales for the first 8 months of 2006 are as follows:

January	$ 90,000	May	$300,000
February	120,000	June	270,000
March	135,000	July	225,000
April	240,000	August	150,000

Of Sharpe's sales, 10 percent is for cash, another 60 percent is collected in the month following sales, and 30 percent is collected in the second month following sales. November and December sales for 2005 were $220,000 and $175,000, respectively.

Sharpe purchases its raw materials 2 months in advance of its sales equal to 60 percent of their final sales price. The supplier is paid 1 month after it makes delivery. For example, purchases for April sales are made in February, and payment is made in March.

In addition, Sharpe pays $10,000 per month for rent and $20,000 each month for other expenditures. Tax repayments of $22,500 are made each quarter, beginning in March.

The company's cash balance on December 31, 2005, was $22,000. This is the minimum balance the firm wants to maintain. Any borrowing that is needed to maintain this minimum is paid off in the subsequent month if there is sufficient cash. Interest on short-term loans (12 percent) is paid monthly. Borrowing to meet estimated monthly cash needs takes place at the beginning of the month. Thus, if in the month of April the firm expects to have a need for an additional $60,500, these funds would be borrowed at the beginning of April with interest of $605 (.12 × 1/12 × $60,500) owed for April and paid at the beginning of May.

    a. Prepare a cash budget for Sharpe covering the first 7 months of 2006.

    b. Sharpe has $200,000 in notes payable due in July that must be repaid or renegotiated for an extension. Will the firm have ample cash to repay the notes?

14-7. (*Percent of sales forecasting*) Which of the following accounts would most likely vary directly with the level of firm sales? Discuss each briefly.

	YES	NO		YES	NO
Cash	___	___	Notes payable	___	___
Marketable securities	___	___	Plant and equipment	___	___
Accounts payable	___	___	Inventories	___	___

14-8. (*Financial forecasting—percent of sales*) The balance sheet of the Boyd Trucking Company (BTC) follows:

Boyd Trucking Company Balance Sheet, December 31, 2005 ($ Millions)

Current assets	$10	Accounts payable	$ 5
Net fixed assets	15	Notes payable	0
Total	$25	Bonds payable	10
		Common equity	10
		Total	$25

BTC had sales for the year ended 12/31/2005 of $25 million. The firm follows a policy of paying all net earnings out to its common stockholders in cash dividends. Thus, BTC generates no funds from its earnings that can be used to expand its operations. (Assume that depreciation expense is just equal to the cost of replacing worn-out assets.)

    a. If BTC anticipates sales of $40 million during the coming year, develop a pro forma balance sheet for the firm on 12/31/06. Assume that current assets vary as a percent of sales, net fixed assets remain unchanged, and accounts payable vary as a percent of sales. Use notes payable as a balancing entry.

    b. How much "new" financing will BTC need next year?

    c. What limitations does the percent of sales forecast method suffer from? Discuss briefly.

14-9. (*Financial forecasting—discretionary financing needs*) The most recent balance sheet for the Armadillo Dog Biscuit Co., Inc. is shown in the following table. The company is about to embark on an advertising campaign, which is expected to raise sales from the current level of $5 million to $7 million by the end of next year. The firm is currently operating at full capacity and will have to increase its investment in both current and fixed assets to support the projected level of new sales. In fact, the firm estimates that both categories of assets will rise in direct proportion to the projected increase in sales.

Armadillo Dog Biscuit Co., Inc. ($ Millions)

	PRESENT LEVEL	PERCENT OF SALES	PROJECTED LEVEL
Current assets	$2.0		
Net fixed assets	3.0		
Total	$5.0		
Accounts payable	$0.5		
Accrued expense	0.5		
Notes payable	—		
Current liabilities	$1.0		
Long-term debt	$2.0		
Common stock	0.5		
Retained earnings	1.5		
Common equity	$2.0		
Total	$5.0		

The firm's net profits were 6 percent of the current year's sales but are expected to rise to 7 percent of next year's sales. To help support its anticipated growth in asset needs next year, the firm has suspended plans to pay cash dividends to its stockholders. In past years a $1.50-per-share dividend has been paid annually. Armadillo's accounts payable and accrued expenses are expected to vary directly with sales. In addition, notes payable will be used to supply the funds needed to finance next year's operations that are not forthcoming from other sources.

    a. Fill in the table and project the firm's needs for discretionary financing. Use notes payable as the balancing entry for future discretionary financing needs.

    b. Compare Armadillo's current ratio and debt ratio (total liabilities ÷ total assets) before the growth in sales and after. What was the effect of the expanded sales on these two dimensions of Armadillo's financial condition?

    c. What difference, if any, would have resulted if Armadillo's sales had risen to $6 million in 1 year and $7 million only after 2 years? Discuss only; no calculations are required.

14-10. (*Forecasting discretionary financing needs*) Fishing Charter, Inc., estimates that it invests $0.30 in assets for each dollar of new sales. However, $0.05 in profits are produced by each dollar of additional sales, of which $0.01 can be reinvested in the firm. If sales rise from their current level of $5 million by $500,000 next year, and the ratio of spontaneous liabilities to sales is 15 percent, what will be the firm's need for discretionary financing? (*Hint:* In this situation you do not know what the firm's existing level of assets is, nor do you know how those assets have been financed. Thus, you must estimate the change in financing needs and match this change with the expected changes in spontaneous liabilities, retained earnings, and other sources of discretionary financing.)

14-11. (*Preparation of a cash budget*) Lewis Printing has projected its sales for the first 8 months of 2006 as follows:

January	$100,000	April	$300,000	July	$200,000
February	120,000	May	275,000	August	180,000
March	150,000	June	200,000		

Lewis collects 20 percent of its sales in the month of the sale, 50 percent in the month following the sale, and the remaining 30 percent 2 months following the sale. During November and December of 2005, Lewis's sales were $220,000 and $175,000, respectively.

Lewis purchases raw materials 2 months in advance of its sales equal to 65 percent of its final sales. The supplier is paid 1 month after delivery. Thus, purchases for April sales are made in February and payment is made in March.

In addition, Lewis pays $10,000 per month for rent and $20,000 each month for other expenditures. Tax prepayments of $22,500 are made each quarter beginning in March. The company's cash balance as of December 31, 2005, was $28,000; a minimum balance of $25,000 must be maintained at all times to satisfy the firm's bank line of credit agreement. Lewis has arranged with its bank for short-term credit at an interest rate of 12 percent per annum (1 percent per month) to be paid monthly. Borrowing to meet estimated monthly cash needs takes place at the end of the month, and interest is not paid until the end of the following month. Consequently, if the firm needed to borrow $50,000 during April, then it would pay $500 (= .01 × $50,000) in interest during May. Finally, Lewis follows a policy of repaying its outstanding short-term debt in any month in which its cash balance exceeds the minimum desired balance of $25,000.

a. Lewis needs to know what its cash requirements will be for the next 6 months so that it can renegotiate the terms of its short-term credit agreement with its bank, if necessary. To evaluate this problem, the firm plans to evaluate the impact of a ±20 percent variation in its monthly sales efforts. Prepare a 6-month cash budget for Lewis and use it to evaluate the firm's cash needs.

b. Lewis has a $20,000 note due in June. Will the firm have sufficient cash to repay the loan?

14-12. (*Sustainable rate of growth*) ADP, Inc. is a manufacturer of specialty circuit boards in the personal computer industry. The firm has experienced phenomenal sales growth over its short 5-year life. Selected financial statement data are found in the following table:

	2005	2004	2003	2002	2001
Sales	$3,000	$2,200	$1,800	$1,400	$1,200
Net income	150	110	90	70	60
Assets	2,700	1,980	1,620	1,260	1,080
Dividends	60	44	36	28	24
Common equity	812	722	656	602	560
Liabilities	1,888	1,258	964	658	520
Liabilities and equity	2,700	1,980	1,620	1,260	1,080

a. Calculate ADP's sustainable rate of growth for each of the 5 years of its existence.

b. Compare the actual rates of growth in sales to the firm's sustainable rates calculated in part **a**. How has ADP been financing its growing asset needs?

14-13. (*Sustainable rate of growth*) The Carrera Game Company has experienced a 100 percent increase in sales over the last 5 years. The company president, Jack Carrera, has become increasingly alarmed by the firm's rising debt level even in the face of continued profitability.

	2005	2004	2003	2002	2001
Sales	$60,000	$56,000	$48,000	$36,000	$30,000
Net income	3,000	2,800	2,400	1,800	1,500
Assets	54,000	50,400	43,200	32,400	27,000
Dividends	1,200	1,120	960	720	600
Common equity	21,000	19,200	17,520	16,080	15,000
Liabilities	33,000	31,200	25,680	16,320	12,000
Liabilities and equity	54,000	50,400	43,200	32,400	27,000

a. Calculate the debt-to-assets ratio, return on common equity, actual rate of growth in firm sales, and retention ratio for each of the 5 years of data provided.

b. Calculate the sustainable rates of growth for Carrera for each of the last 5 years. Why has the firm's borrowing increased so dramatically?

14-14. (*Forecasting inventories*) Findlay Instruments produces a complete line of medical instruments used by plastic surgeons and has experienced rapid growth over the last 5 years. In an effort to make more accurate predictions of its financing requirements, Findlay is currently attempting to construct a financial-planning model based on the percent of sales forecasting method. However, the firm's chief financial analyst (Sarah Macias) is concerned that the projections for inventories will be seriously in error. She recognizes that the firm has begun to accrue substantial economies of scale in its inventory investment and has documented this fact in the following data and calculations:

YEAR	SALES (000)	INVENTORY (000)	% OF SALES
2001	$15,000	1,150	7.67%
2002	18,000	1,180	6.56%
2003	17,500	1,175	6.71%
2004	20,000	1,200	6.00%
2005	25,000	1,250	5.00%
			Average 6.39%

   a. Plot Findlay's sales and inventories for the last 5 years. What is the relationship between these two variables?
   b. Estimate firm inventories for 2006, when firm sales are projected to reach $30 million. Use the average percentage of sales for the last 5 years, the most recent percentage of sales, and your evaluation of the true relationship between the sales and inventories from part **a** to make three predictions.

14-15. (*Forecasting net income*) In November of each year the CFO of Barker Electronics begins the financial forecasting process to determine the firm's projected needs for new financing during the coming year. Barker is a small electronics manufacturing company located in Moline, Illinois, which is best known as the home of the John Deere Company. The CFO begins the process with the most recent year's income statement, projects sales growth for the coming year, and then estimates net income and finally the additional earnings he can expect to retain and reinvest in the firm. The firm's income statement for 2005 follows (in $000):

Income Statement (000)

YEAR ENDED DECEMBER 31, 2005	
Sales	$ 1,500
Cost of goods sold	(1,050)
Gross profit	$ 450
Operating costs	(225)
Depreciation expense	(50)
Net operating profit	$ 175
Interest expense	(10)
Earnings before taxes	$ 165
Taxes	(58)
Net income	$ 107
Dividends	$ 20
Addition to retained earnings	$ 87

The electronics business has been growing rapidly over the past 18 months as the economy recovers and the CFO estimates that sales will expand by 20 percent in the next year. In addition, he estimates the following relationships between each of the income statement expense items and sales:

COGS/sales	70%
Operating expenses/sales	15%
Depreciation expense (000)	$50
Interest expense (000)	$10
Tax rate	35%

Note that for the coming year both depreciation expense and interest expense are projected to remain the same as in 2005.

   a. Estimate Barker's net income for 2006 and its addition to retained earnings under the assumption that the firm leaves its dividends paid at the 2005 level.
   b. Reevaluate Barker's net income and addition to retained earnings where sales grow at 40 percent over the coming year. However, this scenario requires the addition of new plant and equipment in the amount of $100,000, which increases annual depreciation to $58,000 per year, and interest expense rises to $15,000.

WEB WORKS

14-WW1. Look up the most recent income statement and balance sheet for Starbucks (www.starbucks.com), Home Depot (www.homedepot.com), and Wal-Mart (www.walmart.com). For each firm calculate the ratio of current assets to sales for each of the last three years. If you projected that sales for each firm are anticipated to increase by 35 percent in the coming year, what would the percent of sales method of financial forecasting predict next year's current assets to be for each of the firms?

14-WW2. Assuming each of the firms analyzed in the preceding question retains its current dividend payout ratio and that the firm's net profit margin remains constant, how much should each firm expect to be able to reinvest out of next year's earnings?

COMPREHENSIVE PROBLEM

Phillips Petroleum is an integrated oil and gas company with headquarters in Bartlesville, Oklahoma, where it was founded in 1917. The company engages in petroleum exploration and production worldwide. In addition, it engages in natural gas gathering and processing, as well as petroleum refining and marketing primarily in the United States. The company has three operating groups: Exploration and Production, Gas and Gas Liquids, and Downstream Operations, which encompasses Petroleum Products and Chemicals.

In the mid-1980s, Phillips engaged in a major restructuring following two failed takeover attempts, one led by T. Boone Pickins and the other by Carl Ichan.[3] The restructuring resulted in a $4.5 billion plan to exchange a package of cash and debt securities for roughly half the company's shares and to sell $2 billion worth of assets. Phillips's long-term debt increased from $3.4 billion in late 1984 to a peak of $8.6 billion in April 1985.

During 1992, Phillips was able to strengthen its financial structure dramatically. Its subsidiary Phillips Gas Company completed an offering of $345 million of Series A 9.32% Cumulative Preferred Stock. As a result of this action and prior year's debt reductions, the company lowered its long-term debt-to-capital ratio over the last 5 years from 75 percent to 55 percent. In addition, the firm refinanced over a billion dollars of its debt at reduced rates. A company spokesman said, "Our debt-to-capital ratio is still on the high side, and we'll keep working to bring it down. But the cost of debt is manageable, and we're beyond the point where debt overshadows everything else we do."[4]

Summary Financial Information for Phillips Petroleum Corporation:
1986 to 1992 (in Millions of Dollars Except for per Share Figures)

	1986	**1987**	**1988**	**1989**	**1990**	**1991**	**1992**
Sales	$10,018.00	$10,917.00	$11,490.00	$12,492.00	$13,975.00	$13,259.00	$12,140.00
Net income	228.00	35.00	650.00	219.00	541.00	98.00	270.00
EPS	0.89	0.06	2.72	0.90	2.18	0.38	1.04
Current assets	2,802.00	2,855.00	3,062.00	2,876.00	3,322.00	2,459.00	2,349.00
Total assets	12,403.00	12,111.00	11,968.00	11,256.00	12,130.00	11,473.00	11,468.00
Current liabilities	2,234.00	2,402.00	2,468.00	2,706.00	2,910.00	2,503.00	2,517.00
Long-term debt	8,175.00	7,887.00	7,387.00	6,418.00	6,505.00	6,113.00	5,894.00
Total liabilities	10,409.00	10,289.00	9,855.00	9,124.00	9,411.00	8,716.00	8,411.00
Preferred stock	270.00	205.00	0.00	0.00	0.00	0.00	359.00
Common equity	1,724.00	1,617.00	2,113.00	2,132.00	2,719.00	2,757.00	2,698.00
Dividends per share	2.02	1.73	1.34	0.00	1.03	1.12	1.12

Source: Phillips annual reports for 1986 to 1992.

Highlights of Phillips's financial condition from 1986 to 1992 are found in the accompanying table. These data reflect the modern history of the company as a result of its financial restructuring following the downsizing and reorganization of Phillips's operations begun in the mid-1980s.

Phillips's management is currently developing its financial plans for the next 5 years and wants to develop a forecast of its financing requirements. As a first approximation, they have asked you to develop a model that can be used to make "ballpark" estimates of the firm's financing needs under the proviso that existing relationships found in the firm's financial statements remain the same over the period. Of particular interest is whether Phillips will be able to further reduce its reliance on debt financing. You may assume that Phillips's projected sales (in millions) for 1993 through 1997 are as follows: $13,000; $13,500; $14,000; $14,500; and $15,500.

    a. Project net income for 1993 to 1997 using the percent of sales method based on an average of this ratio for 1986 to 1992.

    b. Project total assets and current liabilities for 1993 to 1997 using the percent of sales method and your sales projections from part **a**.

    c. Assuming that common equity increases only as a result of the retention of earnings and holding long-term debt and preferred stock equal to its 1992 balances, project Phillips's discretionary financing needs for 1993 to 1997. (*Hint:* Assume that total assets and current liabilities vary as a percentage of sales as per your answers to part **b**. In addition, assume that Phillips plans to continue to pay its dividends of $1.12 per share in each of the next 5 years.)

---

[3]This discussion is based on a story in *The New York Times*, January 7, 1986.
[4]From *SEC Online*, 1992.

SELF-TEST SOLUTIONS

SS-1.

Calico Sales Co., Inc. Pro Forma Income Statement

Sales		$4,000,000
Cost of goods sold (70%)		(2,800,000)
Gross profit		1,200,000
Operating expense		
Selling expense (5%)	$200,000	
Administrative expense	500,000	
Depreciation expense	300,000	(1,000,000)
Net operating income		200,000
Interest expense		(50,000)
Earnings before taxes		150,000
Taxes (40%)		(60,000)
Net income		$ 90,000

Although the office-renovation expenditure and debt retirement are surely cash outflows, they do not enter the income statement directly. These expenditures affect expenses for the period's income statement only through their effect on depreciation and interest expense. A cash budget would indicate the full cash impact of the renovation and debt-retirement expenditures.

SS-2.

	MAY	JUNE	JULY	AUGUST
Sales	$100,000	$100,000	$ 120,000	$ 150,000
Purchases	60,000	60,000	50,000	40,000
Cash receipts:				
Collections from month of sale (20%)	20,000	20,000	24,000	30,000
1 month later (50% of uncollected amount)		40,000	40,000	48,000
2 months later (balance)			40,000	40,000
Total receipts			$ 104,000	$ 118,000
Cash disbursements:				
Payments for purchases—				
From 1 month earlier			$ 30,000	$ 25,000
From current month			$ 25,000	20,000
Total			$ 55,000	$ 45,000
Miscellaneous cash expenses			4,000	4,000
Labor expense (5% of sales)			6,000	7,500
General and administrative expense				
($50,000 per month)			50,000	50,000
Truck purchase			0	60,000
Cash dividends			9,000	—
Total disbursements			$(124,000)	$(166,500)
Net change in cash			(20,000)	(48,500)
Plus: Beginning cash balance			30,000	30,000
Less: Interest on short-term borrowing (1% prior month's borrowing)				(200)
Equals: Ending cash balance—without borrowing			10,000	(18,700)
Financing needed to reach target cash balance			20,000	48,700
Cumulative borrowing			$ 20,000	$ 68,700

SS-3. The projected net income for 2006 is found by first estimating firm sales. For 2006 the CFO anticipates 2005 sales of $25,000,000 will grow by 15 percent to $28,750,000. Deducting cost of goods sold and operating expenses as a proportion of sales, as well as taxes, and the fixed amounts we estimate for depreciation and interest expense, we estimate net income for 2006 to be $2,052,000. Details are provided in the pro forma income statement for 2006 that follows:

Income Statement (000)

	2005	2006		2005	2006
Sales	$ 25,000	$ 28,750	Interest expense	(1,580)	(1,580)
Cost of goods sold	(16,250)	(18,688)	Earnings before taxes	2,520	3,157
Gross profit	8,750	10,062	Taxes	(882)	(1,105)
Operating costs	(4,500)	(5,175)	Net income	$ 1,638	$ 2,052
Depreciation expense	(150)	(150)	Dividends	$ 1,500	$ 1,500
Net operating profit	4,100	4,737	Addition to retained earnings $	138	$ 552

Assuming that the firm's dividend payment remains constant at $1,500,000, we estimate that retained earnings will rise by $552,000 next year.

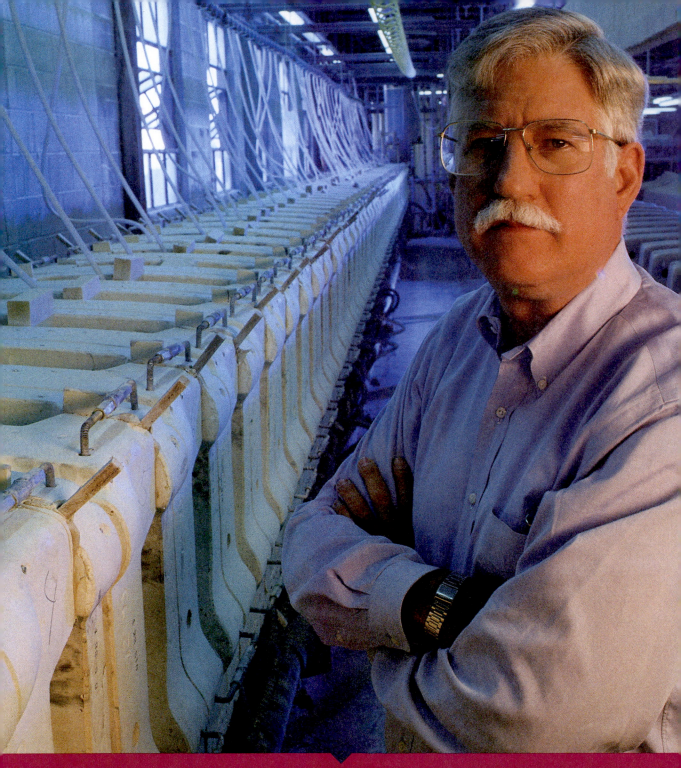

CHAPTER 15

Working-Capital Management

On average, U.S. companies invest more than $0.15 in working capital from each $1 of sales. In 1990, American Standard fit this mold very well, with more than $735 million invested in net working capital. By the mid-1990s, American Standard had revenues totaling $4.2 billion but had reduced its net working capital roughly by half.

In 1990, American Standard had three primary product lines: plumbing supplies, air conditioners, and brakes for trucks and buses. The firm faced static sales and huge interest payments (the result of a $3.1 billion junk bond issue used to stave off a hostile takeover

attempt by Black and Decker in 1989). To improve the firm's operating performance, its chairman, Emmanuel Kampouris, introduced a strategy aimed at reducing the firm's $735 million in net working capital to zero by 2000. This was feasible if the company could cut its inventories so low that they could be financed without borrowing. The idea was to deliver goods and bill customers more rapidly so that customer payments were sufficient to pay for minimal stocks of inventories. Kampouris sought to accomplish this ambitious goal through implementation of a lean manufacturing system known as

working capital

net working capital

⋙ WHAT'S AHEAD ⋘

Chapter 15 addresses two related topics: It introduces the principles involved in managing a firm's investment in working capital, and it presents a discussion of short-term financing. Traditionally, **working capital** is defined as the *firm's total investment in current assets.* **Net working capital**, on the other hand, is the *difference between the firm's current assets and its current liabilities.*

$$\text{Net working capital} = \text{current assets} - \text{current liabilities} \qquad \textbf{(15-1)}$$

Throughout this chapter, the term *working capital* refers to net working capital. In managing the firm's net working capital, we are concerned with *managing the firm's liquidity.* This entails managing two related aspects of the firm's operations: (1) its investment in current assets, and (2) its use of short-term or current liabilities.

Short-term sources of financing include all forms of financing that have maturities of 1 year or less—that is, current liabilities. There are two major issues involved in analyzing a firm's use of short-term financing: (1) How much short-term financing should the firm use? and (2) What specific sources of short-term financing should the firm select? We use the hedging principle of working-capital management to address the first of these questions. We then address the second issue by considering three basic factors: (1) the effective cost of credit, (2) the availability of credit in the amount needed and for the period that financing is required, and (3) the influence of the use of a particular credit source on the cost and availability of other sources of financing.

This chapter provides the basic principles underlying the analysis of all of these aspects.

demand flow technology. Under this system, plants manufacture products as customers order them. Suppliers deliver straight to the assembly line, thus reducing stocks of parts, and plants ship the products as soon as they are completed. The system dramatically reduces inventories of both parts and finished goods. To date,

American Standard has reduced its inventories by more than one-half, down to $326 million. Thus, American Standard invests only $0.05 out of each sales dollar in working capital, compared to the norm of $0.15. By saving interest payments on supplies, the company has increased its cash flow by $60 million a year.

Objective **1**

MANAGING CURRENT ASSETS AND LIABILITIES

A firm's current assets consist of cash and marketable securities, accounts receivable, inventories, and other assets that the firm's management expects to be converted to cash within a period of a year or less. Consequently, firms that choose to hold more current assets are, in general, more liquid than firms that do not.

THE RISK–RETURN TRADE-OFF

Actually firms that want to reduce their risk of illiquidity by holding more current assets do so by investing in larger cash and marketable securities balances. Holding larger cash and marketable securities balances has an unfortunate consequence, however. Because investments in cash and marketable securities earn relatively modest returns when compared with the firm's other investments, the firm that holds larger investments in these assets will reduce its overall rate of return. Thus, the increased liquidity (i.e., reduced risk of illiquidity) must be traded off against the firm's reduction in return on investment. Managing this trade-off is an important theme of working-capital management.

> ### BACK TO THE FOUNDATIONS
>
> *Many of the working-capital decisions made by financial managers involve risk–return trade-offs between liquidity and profitability. The principles that guide these decisions are the same ones set out in* **Principle 1: The Risk–Return Trade-Off—We Won't Take On Additional Risk Unless We Expect to Be Compensated with Additional Return***. The more current assets held and the more long-term financing used, the less the risk and the less the return.*

The firm's use of current versus long-term debt also involves a risk–return trade-off. *Other things remaining the same, the greater the firm's reliance on short-term debt or current liabilities in financing its assets, the greater the risk of illiquidity.* On the other hand, the use of current liabilities offers some very real advantages in that they can be less costly than long-term financing, and they provide the firm with a flexible means of financing its fluctuating needs for assets. However, if for some reason the firm has problems raising short-term funds or it should need funds for longer than expected, it can get into real trouble. Thus, a firm can reduce its risk of illiquidity through the use of long-term debt at the expense of a reduction in its return on invested funds. Once again we see that the risk–return trade-off involves an increased risk of illiquidity versus increased profitability.

ADVANTAGES OF CURRENT LIABILITIES: RETURN

FLEXIBILITY

Current liabilities offer the firm a flexible source of financing. They can be used to match the timing of a firm's needs for short-term financing. If, for example, a firm needs funds for a 3-month period during each year to finance a seasonal expansion in inventories, then a 3-month loan can provide substantial cost savings over a long-term loan (even if the interest rate on short-term financing should be higher). The use of long-term debt in this situation involves borrowing for the entire year rather than for the period when the funds are needed, which increases the amount of interest the firm must pay. This brings us to the second advantage generally associated with the use of short-term financing.

INTEREST COST

In general, interest rates on short-term debt are lower than on long-term debt for a given borrower. This relationship was introduced in Chapter 2 and is referred to as the term structure of interest rates. For a given firm, the term structure might appear as follows.

LOAN MATURITY	INTEREST RATE
3 months	4.00%
6 months	4.60
1 year	5.30
3 years	5.90
5 years	6.75
10 years	7.50
30 years	8.25

Note that this term structure reflects the rates of interest applicable to a given borrower at a particular time. It would not, for example, describe the rates of interest available to another borrower or even those applicable to the same borrower at a different time.

DISADVANTAGES OF CURRENT LIABILITIES: RISK

The use of current liabilities or short-term debt as opposed to long-term debt subjects the firm to a greater risk of illiquidity for two reasons. First, short-term debt, because of its very nature, must be repaid or rolled over more often, so it increases the possibility that the firm's financial condition might deteriorate to a point at which the needed funds might not be available.[1]

A second disadvantage of short-term debt is the uncertainty of interest costs from year to year. For example, a firm borrowing during a 6-month period each year to finance a seasonal expansion in current assets might incur a different rate of interest each year. This rate reflects the current rate of interest at the time of the loan, as well as the lender's perception of the firm's riskiness. If fixed-rate long-term debt were used, the interest cost would be known for the entire period of the loan agreement.

CONCEPT CHECK

1. How does investing more heavily in current assets while not increasing the firm's current liabilities decrease both the firm's risk and its expected return on its investment?
2. How does the use of current liabilities enhance firm profitability and also increase the firm's risk of default on its financial obligations?

APPROPRIATE LEVEL OF WORKING CAPITAL

Objective **2**

Managing the firm's net working capital (its liquidity) involves interrelated decisions regarding investments in current assets and use of current liabilities. Fortunately, a guiding principle exists that can be used as a benchmark for the firm's working-capital policies: the hedging principle, or principle of self-liquidating debt. This principle provides a guide to the maintenance of a level of liquidity sufficient for the firm to meet its maturing obligations on time.[2]

In Chapter 12 we discussed the firm's financing decision in terms of the choice between debt and equity sources of financing. There is, however, yet another critical dimension of

TAKIN' IT TO THE NET

Working-capital management is such a significant problem that specialized consulting firms have developed that devote significant parts of their practice to helping firms improve their working-capital management practices. See www.metapraxis.com.

---

[1]The dangers of such a policy are readily apparent in the experiences of firms that have been forced into bankruptcy. Penn Central, for example, went bankrupt when it had $80 million in short-term debt that it was unable to finance (roll over).
[2]A value-maximizing approach to the management of the firm's liquidity involves assessing the value of the benefits derived from increasing the firm's investment in liquid assets and weighing them against the added costs to the firm's owners resulting from investing in low-yield current assets. Unfortunately, the benefits derived from increased liquidity relate to the expected costs of bankruptcy to the firm's owners, and these costs are very difficult to measure. Thus, a "valuation" approach to liquidity management exists only in the theoretical realm.

the firm's financing decision. This relates to the maturity structure of the firm's debt. How should the decision be made about whether to use short-term (current debt) or longer-maturity debt? This is one of the fundamental questions addressed in this chapter and one that is critically important to the financial success of the firm.

HEDGING PRINCIPLE

hedging principle
principle of self-liquidating debt

Very simply, the **hedging principle**, or **principle of self-liquidating debt**, involves *matching the cash flow–generating characteristics of an asset with the maturity of the source of financing used to finance its acquisition*. For example, a seasonal expansion in inventories, according to the hedging principle, should be financed with a short-term loan or current liability. The rationale underlying the rule is straightforward. Funds are needed for a limited period, and when that time has passed, the cash needed to repay the loan will be generated by the sale of the extra inventory items. Obtaining the needed funds from a long-term source (longer than 1 year) would mean that the firm would still have the funds after the inventories they helped finance had been sold. In this case the firm would have "excess" liquidity, which it either holds in cash or invests in low-yield marketable securities until the seasonal increase in inventories occurs again and the funds are needed. The result of all this would be an overall lowering of firm profits.

Consider an example in which a firm purchases a new conveyor belt system, which is expected to produce cash savings to the firm by eliminating the need for two employees and, consequently, their salaries. This amounts to an annual savings of $24,000, whereas the conveyor belt costs $250,000 to install and will last 20 years. If the firm chooses to finance this asset with a 1-year note, then it will not be able to repay the loan from the $24,000 cash flow generated by the asset. In accordance with the hedging principle, the firm should finance the asset with a source of financing that more nearly matches the expected life and cash flow–generating characteristics of the asset. In this case, a 15- to 20-year loan would be more appropriate.

PERMANENT AND TEMPORARY ASSETS

permanent investments

The notion of maturity matching in the hedging principle can be most easily understood when we think in terms of the distinction between permanent and temporary investments in assets, as opposed to the more traditional fixed and current asset categories. **Permanent investments** in an asset are *investments that the firm expects to hold for a period longer than 1 year*. Note that we are referring to the period the firm plans to hold an investment, not the useful life of the asset. For example, permanent investments are made in the firm's minimum level of current assets, as well as in its fixed assets. **Temporary investments**, on the other hand, are composed of *current assets that will be liquidated and not replaced within the current year*. Thus, some part of the firm's current assets is permanent and the remainder is temporary. For example, a seasonal increase in level of inventories is a temporary investment: the buildup in inventories that will be eliminated when no longer needed. In contrast, the buildup in inventories to meet a long-term increasing sales trend is a permanent investment.

temporary investments

TEMPORARY, PERMANENT, AND SPONTANEOUS SOURCES OF FINANCING

Because total assets must always equal the sum of temporary, permanent, and spontaneous sources of financing, the hedging approach provides the financial manager with the basis for determining the sources of financing to use at any point.

Now, what constitutes a temporary, permanent, or spontaneous source of financing? Temporary sources of financing consist of current liabilities. Short-term notes payable constitute the most common example of a temporary source of financing. Examples of notes payable include unsecured bank loans, commercial paper, and loans secured by accounts receivable and inventories. Permanent sources of financing include intermediate-term loans, long-term debt, preferred stock, and common equity.

Spontaneous sources of financing consist of trade credit and other accounts payable that arise *spontaneously* in the firm's day-to-day operations. For example, as the firm acquires materials for its inventories, **trade credit** is often *made available spontaneously or on demand from the firm's suppliers when the firm orders its supplies or more inventory of products to sell*.

trade credit

TABLE 15-1   The Hedging Principle Applied to Working-Capital Management

Defined: A firm's asset needs that are not financed by spontaneous sources of financing should be financed in accordance with the following "matching rule"—permanent-asset investments are financed with permanent sources, and temporary-asset investments are financed with temporary sources of financing.

CLASSIFICATION OF A FIRM'S INVESTMENTS IN ASSETS	DEFINITIONS AND EXAMPLES	CLASSIFICATION OF A FIRM'S SOURCES OF FINANCING	DEFINITIONS AND EXAMPLES
Temporary investments	*Definition*: Current assets that will be liquidated and not replaced within the year. *Examples*: Seasonal expansions in inventories and accounts receivable.	Spontaneous financing	*Definition*: Financing that arises more or less automatically in response to the purchase of an asset. *Examples*: Trade credit that accompanies the purchase of inventories and other types of accounts payables created by the purchase of services (e.g., wages payable).
		Temporary financing	*Definition*: Current liabilities other than spontaneous sources of financing. *Examples*: Notes payable and revolving credit agreements that must be repaid in a period less than one year.
Permanent investments	*Definition*: Current and long-term asset investments that the firm expects to hold for a period longer than one year. *Examples*: Minimum levels of inventory and accounts receivable the firm maintains throughout the year as well as its investments in plant and equipment.	Permanent financing	*Definition*: Long-term liabilities not due and payable within the year and equity financing. *Examples*: Term loans, notes, and bonds as well as preferred and common equity.

Trade credit appears on the firm's balance sheet as accounts payable, and the size of the accounts-payable balance varies directly with the firm's purchases of inventory items. In turn, inventory purchases are related to anticipated sales. Thus, part of the financing needed by the firm is spontaneously provided in the form of trade credit.

In addition to trade credit, wages and salaries payable, accrued interest, and accrued taxes also provide valuable sources of spontaneous financing. These expenses accrue throughout the period until they are paid. For example, if a firm has a wage expense of $10,000 a week and pays its employees monthly, then its employees effectively provide financing equal to $10,000 by the end of the first week following a payday, $20,000 by the end of the second week, and so forth, until the workers are paid. Because these expenses generally arise in direct conjunction with the firm's ongoing operations, they, too, are referred to as spontaneous.

HEDGING PRINCIPLE: GRAPHIC ILLUSTRATION

The hedging principle can now be stated very succinctly: *Asset needs of the firm not financed by spontaneous sources should be financed in accordance with this rule: Permanent-asset investments are financed with permanent sources, and temporary investments are financed with temporary sources.*

The hedging principle is depicted in Figure 15-1. Total assets are broken down into temporary- and permanent-asset investment categories. The firm's permanent investment in assets is financed by the use of permanent sources of financing (intermediate- and long-term debt, preferred stock, and common equity) or spontaneous sources (trade credit and other accounts payable). For illustration purposes, spontaneous sources of financing are treated as if their amount were fixed. In practice, of course, spontaneous sources of financing fluctuate

FIGURE 15-1   Hedging Principle

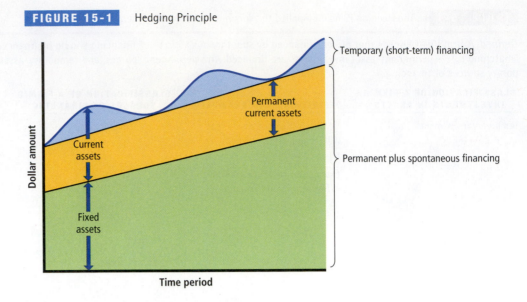

with the firm's purchases and its expenditures for wages, salaries, taxes, and other items that are paid on a delayed basis. Its temporary investment in assets is financed with temporary (short-term) debt.

CONCEPT CHECK

1. What is the hedging principle or principle of self-liquidating debt?
2. What are some examples of permanent and temporary investments in current assets?
3. Is trade credit a permanent, temporary, or spontaneous source of financing? Explain.

Objective | **3**   **ESTIMATION OF THE COST OF SHORT-TERM CREDIT**

APPROXIMATE COST-OF-CREDIT FORMULA

The procedure for estimating the cost of short-term credit is a very simple one and relies on the basic interest equation:

$$\text{Interest} = \text{principal} \times \text{rate} \times \text{time} \qquad \textbf{(15-2)}$$

where *interest* is the dollar amount of interest on a *principal* that is borrowed at some annual *rate* for a fraction of a year (represented by *time*). For example, a 6-month loan for $1,000 at 8 percent interest would require an interest payment of $40.

$$\text{Interest} = \$1,000 \times .08 \times \frac{1}{2} = \$40$$

We use this basic relationship to solve for the cost of a source of short-term financing or the annual percentage rate (*APR*) when the interest amount, the principal sum, and the time period for financing are known. Thus, solving the basic interest equation for *APR* produces[3]

$$APR = \frac{\text{interest}}{\text{principal} \times \text{time}} \qquad \textbf{(15-3)}$$

---

[3]For ease of computation, we assume a 30-day month and 360-day year in this chapter.

or

$$APR = \frac{interest}{principal} \times \frac{1}{time} \qquad (15\text{-}4)$$

This equation, called the *APR* calculation, is clarified by the following example.

EXAMPLE

The SKC Corporation plans to borrow $1,000 for a 90-day period. At maturity the firm will repay the $1,000 principal amount plus $30 interest. The effective annual rate of interest for the loan can be estimated using the *APR* equation, as follows:

$$APR = \frac{\$30}{\$1,000} \times \frac{1}{90/360}$$

$$= .03 \times \frac{360}{90} = .12 = 12\%$$

The effective annual cost of funds provided by the loan is, therefore, 12 percent.

ANNUAL PERCENTAGE YIELD FORMULA

The simple *APR* calculation does not consider compound interest. To account for the influence of compounding, we can use the following equation:

$$APY = \left(1 + \frac{i}{m}\right)^m - 1 \qquad (15\text{-}5)$$

where *APY* is the annual percentage yield, i is the nominal rate of interest per year (12 percent in the previous example), and m is the number of compounding periods within a year [$m = 1/time = 1/(90/360) = 4$ in the preceding example]. Thus, the effective rate of interest on the loan in the example problem, considering compounding, is

$$APY = \left(1 + \frac{.12}{4}\right)^4 - 1 = .126 = 12.6\%$$

Compounding effectively raises the cost of short-term credit. Because the differences between *APR* and *APY* are usually small, we use the simple interest values of *APR* to compute the cost of short-term credit.

> **CONCEPT CHECK**
> 1. What is the fundamental interest equation that underlies the calculation of the approximate cost-of-credit formula?
> 2. What is the annual percentage yield (*APY*) and why is it preferred to the annual percentage rate (*APR*)?

SOURCES OF SHORT-TERM CREDIT

Objective **4**

Short-term credit sources can be classified into two basic groups: unsecured and secured. **Unsecured loans** include all those *sources that have as their security only the lender's faith in the ability of the borrower to repay the funds when due*. Major sources of unsecured short-term credit include accrued wages and taxes, trade credit, unsecured bank loans, and commercial

unsecured loans

FINANCIAL MANAGEMENT IN PRACTICE

MANAGING WORKING CAPITAL BY TRIMMING RECEIVABLES

LaFarge Corporation is located in Reston, Virginia, and operates in the building materials industry. Last year LaFarge was able to dramatically improve its management of accounts receivable. This improvement is reflected in a decrease in the days of sales outstanding ratio (*DSO*); that is,

$$DSO = \frac{\text{accounts receivable}}{\text{sales}/365}$$

After reviewing this formula, you may recall that we referred to *DSO* in Chapter 4 as the average collection period. The company's success is due in large part to the fact that it ties incentive pay to the return on net assets (*RONA*) as defined here:

$$RONA = \frac{\text{earnings before interest and taxes}}{\text{net assets}}$$

Note that improvements in accounts receivable management that result in a decrease in *DSO* also lead to a reduction in the firm's net assets and a corresponding increase in *RONA*. Of course, this presumes that the reduction in *DSO* does not have an adverse impact on firm revenues and, consequently, earnings.

How Did They Do It?

Pete Sacripanti, vice president and controller of LaFarge's Calgary-based construction materials business, credits the firm's improved collections to 12 fundamental steps:[a]

1. **Focusing on customers and collections,** which involves all layers of management and is not just a finance responsibility.
2. **Building a base of preferred customers** that confers a competitive advantage.
3. **Delineating clear ownership of customer accounts** among the sales staff, which prevents passing the buck on delinquent accounts.
4. **Fixing clear guidelines** that govern LaFarge's commitments and responsibilities to customers.
5. **Articulating standard sales terms and conditions,** stipulating terms that are negotiable and those that are never negotiable.
6. **Establishing monthly collection targets by salesperson and division,** with collection targets based on the prior month's sales plus past-due accounts.

7. **Training salespeople on customer profitability,** with particular attention to (1) the link between past-due accounts and increased risk of bad debt write-offs, (2) the volume of business required to recover the cost of bad debts, and (3) higher borrowing costs for the company.
8. **Engaging in regular (weekly) credit and collection meetings** with the sales team, the credit manager, and the general manager.
9. **Encouraging constant "in-your-face" executive management,** featuring weekly status updates of collections by salespeople, including key account information.
10. **Facilitating collections through advance phone calls** to establish expected payment amount and availability and to provide a courier to pick up the payments.
11. **Developing collection skills,** including partial holdback releases; offsetting balances owed for services or equipment; use of construction liens, guarantees, letters of credit, and payment bonds; negotiation techniques for securing extras in lieu of write-offs; and better knowledge of the company's products, its industry, and its customers.
12. **Developing unique value** by building stronger relationships with customers, such as air-miles loyalty programs, engineered solutions, quality assurance, and new-product development.

The key thing to note in this list is that each item represents a managerial action aimed at improving the firm's success in collecting its receivables. The *DSO* metric captures the success of these actions, but it is these 12 steps that actually brought about the improvements.

Measuring Success

LaFarge engaged in a 3-year program aimed at reducing its investment in working capital. The success of the program is most clearly evident in the company's western Canadian construction-materials operation based in Calgary. This unit slashed its working capital by 38 percent to around $36 million while increasing sales by 10 percent to $425 million. The effect on *RONA* was dramatic because the firm simultaneously increased earnings (the numerator of the ratio) and decreased net assets (the denominator).

[a] From S. L. Mintz, "The 1999 Working Capital Survey: Dollars in the Details," *CFO Magazine* (July 1999), p. 58. Used by permission.

secured loans

paper. **Secured loans** involve the *pledge of specific assets as collateral in the event the borrower defaults in payment of principal or interest.* Commercial banks, finance companies, and factors are the primary suppliers of secured credit. The principal sources of collateral include accounts receivable and inventories.

UNSECURED SOURCES: ACCRUED WAGES AND TAXES

Because most businesses pay their employees only periodically (weekly, biweekly, or monthly), firms accrue a wages payable account that is, in essence, a loan from their employees. For example, if the wage expense for the Appleton Manufacturing Company is

$450,000 per week and it pays its employees monthly, then by the end of a 4-week month the firm will owe its employees $1.8 million in wages for services they have already performed during the month. Consequently, the employees finance their own efforts through waiting a full month for payment.

Similarly, firms generally make quarterly income tax payments for their estimated quarterly tax liability. This means that the firm has the use of the tax moneys it owes based on quarterly profits through the end of the quarter. In addition, the firm pays sales taxes and withholding (income) taxes for its employees on a deferred basis. The longer the period that the firm holds the tax payments, the greater the amount of financing they provide.

Note that these sources of financing *rise and fall spontaneously* with the level of firm sales. That is, as the firm's sales increase, so do its labor expenses, sales taxes collected, and income tax. Consequently, these accrued expense items provide the firm with automatic or spontaneous sources of financing.

UNSECURED SOURCES: TRADE CREDIT

Trade credit provides one of the most flexible sources of short-term financing available to the firm. We previously noted that trade credit is a primary source of spontaneous, or on-demand financing. That is, trade credit arises spontaneously with the firm's purchases. To arrange for credit, the firm need only place an order with one of its suppliers. The supplier checks the firm's credit and, if it is good, sends the merchandise. The purchasing firm then pays for the goods in accordance with the supplier's credit terms.

CREDIT TERMS AND CASH DISCOUNTS

Very often the credit terms offered with trade credit involve a cash discount for early payment. For example, a supplier might offer terms of 2/10, net 30, which means that a 2 percent discount is offered for payment within 10 days or the full amount is due in 30 days. Thus, a 2 percent penalty is involved for not paying within 10 days, or for delaying payment from the tenth to the thirtieth day (i.e., for 20 days). The effective annual cost of not taking the cash discount can be quite severe. Using a $1 invoice amount, the effective cost of passing up the discount period using the preceding credit terms and our *APR* equation can be estimated.

$$APR = \frac{\$.02}{\$.98} \times \frac{1}{20/360} = .3673 = 36.73\%$$

Note that the 2 percent cash discount is the *interest* cost of extending the payment period an *additional* 20 days. Note also that the principal amount of the credit is $0.98. This amount constitutes the full principal amount as of the tenth day of the credit period, after which time the cash discount is lost. The effective cost of passing up the 2 percent discount for 20 days is quite expensive: 36.73 percent. Furthermore, once the discount period has passed, there is no reason to pay before the final due date (the thirtieth day). Table 15-2 lists the effective annual cost of a number of alternative credit terms. Note that the cost of trade credit varies directly with the size of the cash discount and inversely with the length of time between the end of the discount period and the final due date.

STRETCHING OF TRADE CREDIT

Some firms that use trade credit engage in a practice called *stretching of trade accounts*. This practice involves delaying payments beyond the prescribed credit period. For example, a

TABLE 15-2	Effective Rates of Interest on Selected Trade Credit Terms
CREDIT TERMS	**EFFECTIVE RATES**
2/10, net 60	14.69%
2/10, net 90	9.18
3/20, net 60	27.84
6/10, net 90	28.72

firm might purchase materials under credit terms of 3/10, net 60; however, when faced with a shortage of cash, the firm might extend payment to the eightieth day. Continued violation of trade terms can eventually lead to a loss of credit. However, for short periods, and at infrequent intervals, stretching offers the firm an emergency source of short-term credit.

ADVANTAGES OF TRADE CREDIT

As a source of short-term financing, trade credit has a number of advantages. First, trade credit is conveniently obtained as a normal part of the firm's operations. Second, no formal agreements are generally involved in extending credit. Furthermore, the amount of credit extended expands and contracts with the needs of the firm; this is why it is classified as a spontaneous, or on-demand, source of financing.

UNSECURED SOURCES: BANK CREDIT

Commercial banks provide unsecured short-term credit in two basic forms: lines of credit and transaction loans (notes payable). Maturities of both types of loans are usually 1 year or less, with rates of interest depending on the creditworthiness of the borrower and the level of interest rates in the economy as a whole.

LINE OF CREDIT

line of credit

A **line of credit** is *generally an informal agreement or understanding between the borrower and the bank about the maximum amount of credit that the bank will provide the borrower at any one time.* Under this type of agreement there is *no legal commitment on the part of the bank to provide the stated credit.* In a **revolving credit agreement**, which is a variant of this form of financing, a *legal obligation is involved.* The line of credit agreement generally covers a period of 1 year corresponding to the borrower's *fiscal* year. Thus, if the borrower is on a July 31 fiscal year, its lines of credit are based on the same annual period.

revolving credit agreement

Credit Terms

Lines of credit generally do not involve fixed rates of interest; instead they state that credit will be extended at $\frac{1}{2}$ *percent over prime* or some other spread over the bank's prime rate.[4] Furthermore, the agreement usually does not spell out the specific use that will be made of the funds beyond a general statement, such as *for working-capital purposes.*

compensating balance

Lines of credit usually require that the borrower maintain a *minimum balance in the bank throughout the loan period,* called a **compensating balance**. This required balance (which can be stated as a percentage of the line of credit or the loan amount) increases the effective cost of the loan to the borrower, unless a deposit balance equal to or greater than this balance requirement is ordinarily maintained in the bank.

The effective cost of short-term bank credit can be estimated using the *APR* equation. Consider the following example.

EXAMPLE

M&M Beverage Company has a $300,000 line of credit that requires a compensating balance equal to 20 percent of the loan amount. The rate paid on the loan is 10 percent per annum, $200,000 is borrowed for a 6-month period, and the firm does not currently have a deposit with the lending bank. The dollar cost of the loan includes the interest expense and the opportunity cost of maintaining an idle cash balance equal to the 20 percent compensating balance. To accommodate the cost of the compensating-balance requirement, assume that the added funds will have to be borrowed and simply left idle in the firm's checking accounts. Thus, the amount actually borrowed (B) will be larger than the $200,000 needed. In fact, the needed $200,000 will constitute 80 percent of the total borrowed funds because of the 20 percent compensating-balance requirement; hence, $.80B = \$200,000$, such that $B = \$250,000$. Thus, interest is paid on a $250,000

---

[4]The *prime rate of interest* is the rate that a bank charges its most creditworthy borrowers.

loan ($250,000 \times .10 \times \frac{1}{2} = \$12,500.00$), of which only \$200,000 is available for use by the firm.[5] The effective annual cost of credit, therefore, is

$$APR = \frac{\$12,500.00}{\$200,000} \times \frac{1}{180/360} = .125 = 12.5\%$$

In the M&M Beverage Company example, the loan required the payment of principal (\$250,000) plus interest (\$12,500.00) at the end of the 6-month loan period. Frequently, bank loans will be made on a discount basis. That is, the loan interest will be deducted from the loan amount before the funds are transferred to the borrower. Extending the M&M Beverage Company example to consider discounted interest involves reducing the loan proceeds (\$200,000) in the previous example by the amount of interest for the full 6 months (\$12,500.00). The effective rate of interest on the loan is now

$$APR = \frac{\$12,500.00}{\$200,000 - \$12,500.00} \times \frac{1}{180/360}$$
$$= .1333 = 13.33\%$$

The effect of discounting interest was to raise the cost of the loan from 12.5 percent to 13.33 percent. This results from the fact that the firm pays interest on the same amount of funds as before (\$250,000); however, this time it gets the use of \$12,500.00 less, or \$200,000 − \$12,500.00 = \$187,500.00.[6]

TRANSACTION LOANS

Still another form of unsecured short-term bank credit can be obtained in the form of **transaction loans**. Here the loan is *made for a specific purpose*. This is the type of loan that most individuals associate with bank credit and is obtained by signing a promissory note.

    Unsecured transaction loans are very similar to a line of credit regarding cost, term to maturity, and compensating-balance requirements. In both instances commercial banks often require that the borrower *clean up* its short-term loans for a 30- to 45-day period during the year. This means, very simply, that the borrower must be free of any bank debt for the stated period. The purpose of such a requirement is to ensure that the borrower is not using short-term bank credit to finance a part of its permanent needs for funds.

transaction loans

---

[5]The same answer would have been obtained by assuming a total loan of \$200,000, of which only 80 percent, or \$160,000, was available for use by the firm; that is,

$$APR = \frac{\$10,000}{\$160,000} \times \frac{1}{180/360} = 12.5\%$$

Interest is now calculated on the \$200,000 loan amount ($\$-10,000 = \$200,000 \times .10 \times \frac{1}{2}$).

[6]If M&M needs the use of a full \$200,000, then it will have to borrow more than \$250,000 to cover both the compensating-balance requirement *and* the discounted interest. In fact, the firm will have to borrow some amount B such that

$$B - .2B - \left(.10 \times \frac{1}{2}\right)B = \$200,000$$
$$.75B = \$200,000$$
$$B = \frac{\$200,000}{.75} = \$266,666.67$$

The cost of credit remains the same at 13.33 percent, as we see here:

$$APR = \frac{\$13,333.33}{\$266,666.67 - \$53,333.33 - \$13,333.33} \times \frac{1}{180/360}$$
$$= .1333 = 13.33\%$$

UNSECURED SOURCES: COMMERCIAL PAPER

commercial paper

Only the largest and most creditworthy companies are able to use **commercial paper**, which is simply a *short-term promise to pay that is sold in the market for short-term debt securities.*

CREDIT TERMS

The maturity of the credit source is generally 6 months or less, although some issues carry 270-day maturities. The interest rate on commercial paper is generally slightly lower ($\frac{1}{2}$ to 1 percent) than the prime rate on commercial bank loans. Also, interest is usually discounted, although sometimes interest-bearing commercial paper is available.

New issues of commercial paper are either placed directly (sold by the issuing firm directly to the investing public) or dealer placed. Dealer placement involves the use of a commercial paper dealer, who sells the issue for the issuing firm. Many major finance companies, such as General Motors Acceptance Corporation, place their commercial paper directly. The volume of direct versus dealer placements is roughly 4 to 1 in favor of direct placements. Dealers are used primarily by industrial firms that either make only infrequent use of the commercial paper market or, owing to their small size, would have difficulty placing the issue without the help of a dealer.

COMMERCIAL PAPER AS A SOURCE OF SHORT-TERM CREDIT

Several advantages accrue to the user of commercial paper.

1. **Interest rate.** Commercial paper rates are generally lower than rates on bank loans and comparable sources of short-term financing.
2. **Compensating-balance requirement.** No minimum balance requirements are associated with commercial paper. However, issuing firms usually find it desirable to maintain line-of-credit agreements sufficient to back up their short-term financing needs in the event that a new issue of commercial paper cannot be sold or an outstanding issue cannot be repaid when due.
3. **Amount of credit.** Commercial paper offers the firm with very large credit needs a single source for all its short-term financing. Because of loan restrictions placed on the banks by the regulatory authorities, obtaining the necessary funds from a commercial bank might require dealing with a number of institutions.[7]
4. **Prestige.** Because it is widely recognized that only the most creditworthy borrowers have access to the commercial paper market, its use signifies a firm's credit status.

Using commercial paper for short-term financing, however, involves a very important risk. The commercial paper market is highly impersonal and denies even the most creditworthy borrower any flexibility in terms of repayment. When bank credit is used, the borrower has someone with whom he or she can work out any temporary difficulties that might be encountered in meeting a loan deadline. This flexibility simply does not exist for the user of commercial paper.

ESTIMATION OF THE COST OF COMMERCIAL PAPER

The cost of commercial paper can be estimated using the simple, effective cost-of-credit equation (*APR*). The key points to remember are that commercial paper interest is usually discounted and that if a dealer is used to place the issue, a fee is charged. Even if a dealer is not used, the issuing firm will incur costs associated with preparing and placing the issue, and these costs must be included in estimating the cost of credit.

EXAMPLE

The EPG Manufacturing Company uses commercial paper regularly to support its needs for short-term financing. The firm plans to sell $100 million in 270-day-maturity paper, on which it expects to pay discounted interest at a rate of 12 percent per annum ($9 million). In addition, EPG expects to incur a cost of approximately $100,000 in

---

[7]Member banks of the Federal Reserve System are limited to 10 percent of their total capital, surplus, and undivided profits when making loans to a single borrower. Thus, when a corporate borrower's needs for financing are very large, it may have to deal with a group of participating banks to raise the needed funds.

dealer placement fees and other expenses of issuing the paper. The effective cost of credit to EPG can be calculated as follows:

$$APR = \frac{\$9,000,000 + \$100,000}{\$100,000,000 - \$100,000 - \$9,000,000} \times \frac{1}{270/360}$$
$$= .1335 = 13.35\%$$

where the interest cost is calculated as $\$100,000,000 \times .12 \times (270/360) = \$9,000,000$ plus the $100,000 dealer placement fee. Thus, the effective cost of credit to EPG is 13.35 percent.

SECURED SOURCES: ACCOUNTS-RECEIVABLE LOANS

Secured sources of short-term credit have certain assets of the firm pledged as collateral to secure the loan. Upon default of the loan agreement, the lender has first claim to the pledged assets in addition to its claim as a general creditor of the firm. Hence, the secured credit agreement offers an added margin of safety to the lender.

Generally, a firm's receivables are among its most liquid assets. For this reason they are considered by many lenders to be prime collateral for a secured loan. Two basic procedures can be used in arranging for financing based on receivables: pledging and factoring.

PLEDGING ACCOUNTS RECEIVABLE

Under the **pledging accounts receivable** arrangement, the *borrower simply pledges accounts receivable as collateral for a loan obtained from either a commercial bank or a finance company.* The amount of the loan is stated as a percentage of the face value of the receivables pledged. If the firm provides the lender with a *general line* on its receivables, then all of the borrower's accounts are pledged as security for the loan. This method of pledging is simple and inexpensive. However, because the lender has no control over the quality of the receivables being pledged, it will set the maximum loan at a relatively low percentage of the total face value of the accounts, generally ranging downward from a maximum of around 75 percent.

Still another approach to pledging involves the borrower's presenting specific invoices to the lender as collateral for a loan. This method is somewhat more expensive because the lender must assess the creditworthiness of each individual account pledged; however, given this added knowledge the lender should be willing to increase the loan as a percentage of the face value of the invoices. In this case the loan might reach as high as 85 or 90 percent of the face value of the pledged receivables.

pledging accounts receivable

Credit Terms

Accounts receivable loans generally carry an interest rate 2 to 5 percent higher than the bank's prime lending rate. Finance companies charge an even higher rate. In addition, the lender usually charges a handling fee stated as a percentage of the face value of the receivables processed, which may be as much as 1 to 2 percent of the face value.

EXAMPLE

The A. B. Good Company sells electrical supplies to building contractors on terms of net 60. The firm's average monthly sales are $100,000; thus, given the firm's 2-month credit terms, its average receivables balance is $200,000. The firm pledges all its receivables to a local bank, which in turn advances up to 70 percent of the face value of the receivables at 3 percent over prime and with a 1 percent processing charge on *all* receivables pledged. A. B. Good follows a practice of borrowing the maximum amount possible, and the current prime rate is 10 percent.

The *APR* of using this source of financing for a full year is computed as follows:

$$APR = \frac{\$18,200 + \$12,000}{\$140,000} \times \frac{1}{360/360} = .2157 = 21.57\%$$

where the total dollar cost of the loan consists of both the annual interest expense (.13 × .70 × $200,000 = $18,200) and the annual processing fee (.01 × $100,000 × 12 months = $12,000). The amount of credit extended is .70 × $200,000 = $140,000. Note that the processing charge applies to *all* receivables pledged. Thus, the A. B. Good Company pledges $100,000 each month, or $1,200,000 during the year, on which a 1 percent fee must be paid, for a total annual charge of $12,000.

One more point: The lender, in addition to making advances or loans, may be providing certain credit services to the borrower. For example, the lender may provide billing and collection services. The value of these services should be considered in computing the cost of credit. In the preceding example, A. B. Good Company may *save* credit department expenses of $10,000 per year by pledging all its accounts and letting the lender provide those services. In this case, the cost of short-term credit is only

$$APR = \frac{\$18,200 + \$12,000 - \$10,000}{\$140,000} \times \frac{1}{360/360} = \$.1443 = 14.43\%$$

Advantages and Disadvantages of Pledging

The primary advantage of pledging as a source of short-term credit is the flexibility it provides the borrower. Financing is available on a continuous basis. The new accounts created through credit sales provide the collateral for the financing of new production. Furthermore, the lender may provide credit services that eliminate or at least reduce the need for similar services within the firm. The primary disadvantage associated with this method of financing is its cost, which can be relatively high compared with other sources of short-term credit, owing to the level of the interest rate charged on loans and the processing fee on pledged accounts.

FACTORING ACCOUNTS RECEIVABLE

factoring accounts receivable

factor

Factoring accounts receivable involves the *outright sale of a firm's accounts to a financial institution called a factor*. A **factor** is *a firm that acquires the receivables of other firms*. The factoring institution may be a commercial finance company that engages solely in the factoring of receivables (known as an *old-line factor*) or it may be a commercial bank. The factor, in turn, bears the risk of collection and, for a fee, services the accounts. The fee is stated as a percentage of the face value of all receivables factored (usually 1 to 3 percent).

The factor firm typically does *not* make payment for factored accounts until the accounts have been collected or the credit terms have been met. Should the firm wish to receive immediate payment for its factored accounts, it can borrow from the factor, using the factored accounts as collateral. The maximum loan the firm can obtain is equal to the face value of its factored accounts less the factor's fee (1 to 3 percent) less a reserve (6 to 10 percent) less the interest on the loan. For example, if $100,000 in receivables is factored, carrying 60-day credit terms, a 2 percent factor's fee, a 6 percent reserve, and interest at 1 percent per month on advances, then the maximum loan or advance the firm can receive is computed as follows:

Face amount of receivables factored	$100,000
Less: Fee (.02 × $100,000)	(2,000)
Reserve (.06 × $100,000)	(6,000)
Interest (.01 × $92,000 × 2 months)	(1,840)
Maximum advance	$90,160

Note that interest is discounted and calculated based on a maximum amount of funds available for advance ($92,000 = $100,000 − $2,000 − $6,000). Thus, the effective cost of credit can be calculated as follows:

$$APR = \frac{\$1,840 + \$2,000}{\$90,160} \times \frac{1}{60/360}$$

$$= .2555 = 25.55\%$$

SECURED SOURCES: INVENTORY LOANS

Inventory loans, or *loans secured by inventories*, provide a second source of security for short-term credit. The amount of the loan that can be obtained depends on both the marketability and perishability of the inventory. Some items, such as raw materials (grains, oil, lumber, and chemicals), are excellent sources of collateral, because they can easily be liquidated. Other items, such as work-in-process inventories, provide very poor collateral because of their lack of marketability.

inventory loans

There are several methods by which inventory can be used to secure short-term financing. These include a floating or blanket lien, chattel mortgage, field warehouse receipt, and terminal warehouse receipt.

Under a **floating lien agreement**, *the borrower gives the lender a lien against all its inventories*. This provides the simplest but least secure form of inventory collateral. The borrowing firm maintains full control of the inventories and continues to sell and replace them as it sees fit. Obviously, this lack of control over the collateral greatly dilutes the value of this type of security to the lender.

floating lien agreement

Under a **chattel mortgage agreement**, *the inventory is identified* (by serial number or otherwise) *in the security agreement and the borrower retains title to the inventory but cannot sell the items without the lender's consent.*

chattel mortgage agreement

Under a **field warehouse–financing agreement**, *inventories used as collateral are physically separated from the firm's other inventories and are placed under the control of a third-party field-warehousing firm.*

field warehouse–financing agreement

The **terminal warehouse agreement** differs from the field warehouse agreement in only one respect. Here *the inventories pledged as collateral are transported to a public warehouse that is physically removed from the borrower's premises.* The lender has an added degree of safety or security because the inventory is totally removed from the borrower's control. Once again the cost of this type of arrangement is increased because the warehouse firm must be paid by the borrower; in addition, the inventory must be transported to and, eventually, from the public warehouse.

terminal warehouse agreement

CONCEPT CHECK

1. What are some examples of unsecured and secured sources of short-term credit?
2. What is the difference between a line of credit and a revolving credit agreement?
3. What are the types of credit agreements a firm can get that are secured by its accounts receivable as collateral?
4. What are some examples of loans secured by a firm's inventories?

MULTINATIONAL WORKING-CAPITAL MANAGEMENT

Objective **5**

The basic principles of working-capital management are the same for multinational and domestic firms. However, because multinationals spend and receive money in different countries, the exchange rate between the firm's home country and each of the countries in which it does business poses an added source of concern when managing working capital.

Multinational firms, by definition, have assets that are denominated or valued in foreign currencies. This means that the multinational will lose value if that foreign currency declines in value vis-à-vis that of the home currency. Technically, the foreign assets of the firm are exposed to exchange-rate risk, the risk that tomorrow's exchange rate will differ from today's rate. However, the possibility of a decline in asset value may be offset by the decline in value of any liability that is also denominated or valued in terms of that foreign currency. Thus, a firm would normally be interested in its net exposed position (exposed assets – exposed liabilities) for each period and in each currency to which the firm has exposure.

If a firm is to manage its foreign-exchange risk exposure, it needs good measures. There are three popular measures of foreign exchange risk that can be used: translation exposure, transaction exposure, and economic exposure. Translation exposure arises because the foreign operations of multinational corporations have financial accounting statements denominated in the local currency of the country in which the operation is located. For U.S. multinational corporations, the reporting currency for their consolidated financial statements is the dollar, so the assets, liabilities, revenues, and expenses of the foreign operations must be translated into dollars. Furthermore, international transactions often require a payment to be made or received in a foreign currency in the future, so these transactions are exposed to exchange-rate risk. Economic exposure exists over the long term because the value of the future cash flows in the reporting currency (that is, the dollar) from foreign operations is exposed to exchange-rate risk. Indeed, the whole stream of future cash flows is exposed.

SUMMARY

Objective 1

Managing current assets and liabilities

Working-capital management involves managing the firm's liquidity, which in turn involves managing (1) the firm's investment in current assets and (2) its use of current liabilities. Each of these problems involves risk–return trade-offs. Investing in current assets reduces the firm's risk of illiquidity at the expense of lowering its overall rate of return on its investment in assets. Furthermore, the use of long-term sources of financing enhances the firm's liquidity while reducing its rate of return on assets.

Objective 2

Appropriate level of working capital

The hedging principle, or principle of self-liquidating debt, is a benchmark for working-capital decisions. Basically, this principle involves matching the cash flow–generating characteristics of an asset with the maturity of the source of financing used to acquire it.

Objective 3

Estimation of the cost of short-term credit

The key consideration in selecting a source of short-term financing is the effective cost of credit.

Objective 4

Sources of short-term credit

The various sources of short-term credit can be categorized into two groups: unsecured and secured. Unsecured credit offers no specific assets as security for the loan agreement. The primary sources include trade credit, lines of credit, unsecured transaction loans from commercial banks, and commercial paper. Secured credit is generally provided to business firms by commercial banks, finance companies, and factors. The most popular sources of security involve the use of accounts receivable and inventories. Loans secured by accounts receivable include pledging agreements, in which a firm pledges its receivables as security for a loan, and factoring agreements, in which the firm sells the receivables to a factor. In a pledging arrangement, the lender retains the right of recourse in the event of default, whereas in factoring, a lender is generally without recourse.

Loans secured by inventories can be made using one of several types of security arrangements. Among the most widely used are the floating lien, chattel mortgage, field warehouse financing, and terminal warehouse agreement. The form of agreement used depends on the type of inventories pledged as collateral and the degree of control the lender wishes to exercise over the loan collateral.

Objective 5

Multinational working-capital management

The problems of working-capital management are fundamentally the same for the multinational firm as for a domestic firm, with some complications. The primary source of complication comes from the fact that the multinational receives and makes payment with foreign currencies. This means that the multinational firm must be concerned not only with having sufficient liquidity but also with the value of its cash and marketable securities in terms of the value of the currencies of the countries in which it does business. Specifically, the multinational firm faces three types of currency exposure risk: translation exposure, transaction exposure, and economic exposure. All three types of currency risk must be managed by the multinational, in addition to the traditional risks of illiquidity.

KEY TERMS

Chattel mortgage agreement, 483

Commercial paper, 480

Compensating balance, 478

Factor, 482

Factoring accounts receivable, 482

Field warehouse–financing agreement, 483

Floating lien agreement, 483

Hedging principle, 472

Inventory loans, 483

Line of credit, 478

Net working capital, 469

Permanent investments, 472

Pledging accounts receivable, 481

Principle of self-liquidating debt (see hedging principle), 472

Revolving credit agreement, 478

Secured loans, 476

Temporary investments, 472

Terminal warehouse agreement, 483

Trade credit, 472

Transaction loans, 479

Unsecured loans, 475

Working capital, 469

STUDY QUESTIONS

15-1. Define and contrast the terms *working capital* and *net working capital*.

15-2. Discuss the risk–return relationship involved in the firm's asset-investment decisions as that relationship pertains to working-capital management.

15-3. What advantages and disadvantages are generally associated with the use of short-term debt? Discuss.

15-4. Explain what is meant by the statement "The use of current liabilities as opposed to long-term debt subjects the firm to a greater risk of illiquidity."

15-5. Define the hedging principle. How can this principle be used in the management of working capital?

15-6. Define the following terms:
  a. *Permanent asset investments*
  b. *Temporary asset investments*
  c. *Permanent sources of financing*
  d. *Temporary sources of financing*
  e. *Spontaneous sources of financing*

15-7. What distinguishes short-term, intermediate-term, and long-term debt?

15-8. What considerations should be used in selecting a source of short-term credit? Discuss each.

15-9. How can the formula "interest = principle × rate × time" be used to estimate the effective cost of short-term credit?

15-10. How can we accommodate the effects of compounding in our calculation of the effective cost of short-term credit?

15-11. There are three major sources of unsecured short-term credit other than accrued wages and taxes. List and discuss the distinguishing characteristics of each.

15-12. What is meant by the following trade credit terms: 2/10, net 30? 4/20, net 60? 3/15, net 45?

15-13. Define the following:
  a. Line of credit
  b. Commercial paper
  c. Compensating balance
  d. Prime rate

15-14. List and discuss four advantages of the use of commercial paper.

15-15. What risk is involved in the firm's use of commercial paper as a source of short-term credit? Discuss.

15-16. List and discuss the distinguishing features of the principal sources of secured credit based on accounts receivable.

SELF-TEST PROBLEMS

ST-1. (*Analyzing the cost of a commercial paper offering*) The Marilyn Sales Company is a wholesale machine tool broker that has gone through a recent expansion of its activities, resulting in doubling of its sales. The company has determined that it needs an additional $200 million in short-term funds to finance peak-season sales during roughly 6 months of the year. Marilyn's treasurer has recommended that the firm use a commercial paper offering to raise the needed funds. Specifically, he has determined that a $200 million offering would require 10 percent interest (paid in advance or discounted) plus a $125,000 placement fee. The paper would carry a 6-month (180-day) maturity. What is the effective cost of credit?

ST-2. (*Analyzing the cost of short-term credit*) The treasurer of the Lights-a-Lot Manufacturing Company is faced with three alternative bank loans. The firm wishes to select the one that minimizes its cost of credit on a $200,000 note that it plans to issue in the next 10 days. Relevant information for the three one-year loan configurations includes:

    a. An 18 percent rate of interest with interest paid at year-end and no compensating-balance requirement.

    b. A 16 percent rate of interest but carrying a 20 percent compensating-balance requirement. This loan also calls for interest to be paid at year-end.

    c. A 14 percent rate of interest that is discounted, plus a 20 percent compensating-balance requirement.

Analyze the cost of each of these alternatives. You may assume the firm would not normally maintain any bank balance that might be used to meet the 20 percent compensating-balance requirements of alternatives b and c.

ST-3. (*Analyzing the cost of a transaction loan*) The Ace Compost Company of Mart, Texas, has been in the business of converting feed lot manure into garden compost since 1984. The firm has approached the First State Bank of Mart about a short-term loan to help finance the firm's seasonal working-capital needs. Ace's management estimates that it will need a total of $100,000 for a period of 6 months during the coming year. The bank agreed to provide the financing under the following terms. Interest of 10 percent per annum will be paid along with the full principal amount of the loan at maturity. Furthermore, the bank has requested that Ace maintain a 15 percent compensating balance with the bank. Ace has kept an average account balance with the bank of $5,000 over the past year and plans to continue to do so. Consequently, Ace is $10,000 short of the mandatory compensating balance so it will have to borrow an additional $10,000 more than its $100,000 loan needed. What is the effective cost of credit for Ace if it accepts the bank's terms?

STUDY PROBLEMS

15-1. (*Estimating the cost of bank credit*) Paymaster Enterprises has arranged to finance its seasonal working-capital needs with a short-term bank loan. The loan will carry a rate of 12 percent per annum with interest paid in advance (discounted). In addition, Paymaster must maintain a minimum demand deposit with the bank of 10 percent of the loan balance throughout the term of the loan. If Paymaster plans to borrow $100,000 for a period of 3 months, what is the effective cost of the bank loan?

15-2. (*Estimating the cost of commercial paper*) On February 3, 2003, the Burlington Western Company plans a commercial paper issue of $20 million. The firm has never used commercial paper before but has been assured by the firm placing the issue that it will have no difficulty raising the funds. The commercial paper will carry a 270-day maturity and require interest based on a rate of 11 percent per annum. In addition, the firm will have to pay fees totaling $200,000 to bring the issue to market and place it. What is the effective cost of the commercial paper to Burlington Western?

15-3. (*Cost of trade credit*) Calculate the effective cost of the following trade credit terms, when payment is made on the net due date.

    a. 2/10, net 30

    b. 3/15, net 30

    c. 3/15, net 45

    d. 2/15, net 60

15-4. (*Annual percentage yield*) Compute the cost of the trade credit terms in problem 15-3 using the compounding formula, or annual percentage yield.

15-5. (*Cost of short-term financing*) The R. Morin Construction Company needs to borrow $100,000 to help finance the cost of a new $150,000 hydraulic crane used in the firm's commercial construction business. The crane will pay for itself in one year, and the firm is considering the following alternatives for financing its purchase:

Alternative A—The firm's bank has agreed to lend the $100,000 at a rate of 14 percent. Interest would be discounted, and a 15 percent compensating balance would be required. However, the compensating-balance requirement would not be binding on R. Morin because the firm normally maintains a minimum demand deposit (checking account) balance of $25,000 in the bank.

Alternative B—The equipment dealer has agreed to finance the equipment with a 1-year loan. The $100,000 loan would require payment of principal and interest totaling $116,300.

  a. Which alternative should R. Morin select?
  b. If the bank's compensating-balance requirement were to necessitate idle demand deposits equal to 15 percent of the loan, what effect would this have on the cost of the bank loan alternative?

15-6. (*Cost of short-term bank loan*) On July 1, 2003, the Southwest Forging Corporation arranged for a line of credit with the First National Bank of Dallas. The terms of the agreement call for $100,000 maximum loan with interest set at 1 percent over prime. In addition, the firm has to maintain a 20 percent compensating balance in its demand deposit account throughout the year. The prime rate is currently 12 percent.

  a. If Southwest normally maintains a $20,000 to $30,000 balance in its checking account with FNB of Dallas, what is the effective cost of credit through the line-of-credit agreement when the maximum loan amount is used for a full year?
  b. Recompute the effective cost of trade to Southwest if the firm borrows the compensating balance and it borrows the maximum possible under the loan agreement. Again, assume the full amount of the loan is outstanding for a whole year.

15-7. (*Cost of commercial paper*) Tri-State Enterprises plans to issue commercial paper for the first time in the firm's 35-year history. The firm plans to issue $500,000 in 180-day maturity notes. The paper will carry a $10\frac{1}{4}$ percent rate with discounted interest and will cost Tri-State $12,000 (paid in advance) to issue.

  a. What is the effective cost of credit to Tri-State?
  b. What other factors should the company consider in analyzing whether to issue the commercial paper?

15-8. (*Cost of accounts receivable*) Johnson Enterprises, Inc., is involved in the manufacture and sale of electronic components used in small AM/FM radios. The firm needs $300,000 to finance an anticipated expansion in receivables due to increased sales. Johnson's credit terms are net 60, and its average monthly credit sales are $200,000. In general, the firm's customers pay within the credit period; thus the firm's average accounts receivable balance is $400,000. Chuck Idol, Johnson's comptroller, approached the firm's bank with a request for a loan for the $300,000 using the firm's accounts receivable as collateral. The bank offered to make a loan at a rate of 2 percent over prime plus a 1 percent processing charge on all receivables pledged ($200,000 per month). Furthermore, the bank agreed to lend up to 75 percent of the face value of the receivables pledged.

  a. Estimate the cost of the receivables loan to Johnson when the firm borrows the $300,000. The prime rate is currently 11 percent.
  b. Idol also requested a line of credit for $300,000 from the bank. The bank agreed to grant the necessary line of credit at a rate of 3 percent over prime and required a 15 percent compensating balance. Johnson currently maintains an average demand deposit of $80,000. Estimate the cost of the line of credit to Johnson.
  c. Which source of credit should Johnson select? Why?

15-9. (*Cost of factoring*) MDM, Inc. is considering factoring its receivables. The firm has credit sales of $400,000 per month and has an average receivables balance of $800,000 with 60-day credit terms. The factor has offered to extend credit equal to 90 percent of the receivables factored less interest on the loan at a rate of $1\frac{1}{2}$ percent per month. The 10 percent difference in the advance and the face value of all receivables factored consists of a 1 percent factoring fee plus a 9 percent reserve, which the factor maintains. In addition, if MDM, Inc. decides to factor its receivables, it will sell them all, so that it can reduce its credit department costs by $1,500 a month.

  a. What is the cost of borrowing the maximum amount of credit available to MDM, Inc. through the factoring agreement?
  b. What considerations other than cost should be accounted for by MDM, Inc. in determining whether to enter the factoring agreement?

15-10. (*Cost of secured short-term credit*) The Sean-Janeow Import Co. needs $500,000 for the 3-month period ending September 30, 2003. The firm has explored two possible sources of credit.

1. S-J has arranged with its bank for a $500,000 loan secured by accounts receivable. The bank has agreed to advance S-J 80 percent of the value of its pledged receivables at a rate of 11 percent plus a 1 percent fee based on all receivables pledged. S-J's receivables average a total of $1 million year-round.

2. An insurance company has agreed to lend the $500,000 at a rate of 9 percent per annum, using a loan secured by S-J's inventory of salad oil. A field warehouse agreement would be used, which would cost S-J $2,000 a month. Which source of credit should S-J select? Explain.

15-11. (*Cost of short-term financing*) You plan to borrow $20,000 from the bank to pay for inventories for a gift shop you have just opened. The bank offers to lend you the money at 10 percent annual interest for the 6 months the funds will be needed.

   a. Calculate the effective rate of interest on the loan.
   b. In addition, the bank requires you to maintain a 15 percent compensating balance in the bank. Because you are just opening your business, you do not have a demand deposit account at the bank that can be used to meet the compensating-balance requirement. This means that you will have to put 15 percent of the loan amount from your own personal money (which you had planned to use to help finance the business) in a checking account. What is the cost of the loan now?
   c. In addition to the compensating-balance requirement in part **b**, you are told that interest will be discounted. What is the effective rate of interest on the loan now?

15-12. (*Cost of factoring*) A factor has agreed to lend the JVC Corporation working capital on the following terms. JVC's receivables average $100,000 per month and have a 90-day average collection period. (Note that JVC's credit terms call for payment in 90 days, and accounts receivable average $300,000 because of the 90-day average collection period.) The factor will charge 12 percent interest on any advance (1 percent per month paid in advance), will charge a 2 percent processing fee on all receivables factored, and will maintain a 20 percent reserve. If JVC undertakes the loan, it will reduce its own credit-department expenses by $2,000 per month. What is the annual effective rate of interest to JVC on the factoring arrangement? Assume that the maximum advance is taken.

15-13. (*Cost of a short-term bank loan*) Jimmy Hale is the owner and operator of the grain elevator in Brownfield, Texas, where he has lived for most of his 62 years. The rains during the spring have been the best in a decade and Mr. Hale is expecting a bumper wheat crop. This prompted Mr. Hale to rethink his current financing sources. He now believes he will need an additional $240,000 for the 3-month period ending with the close of the harvest season. After meeting with his banker, Mr. Hale is puzzling over what the additional financing will actually cost. The banker quoted him a rate of 1 percent over prime (which is currently 7 percent) and also requested that the firm increase its current bank balance of $4,000 up to 20 percent of the loan.

   a. If interest and principal are all repaid at the end of the 3-month loan term, what is the annual percentage rate on the loan offer made by Mr. Hale's bank?
   b. If the bank were to offer to lower the rate to prime if interest is discounted, should Mr. Hale accept this alternative?

WEB WORKS

15-WW1. Assume that you are the owner of an import business that specializes in the sale of floor tiles from around the world. Your business has grown dramatically over the two years since its founding and you are looking for a way to convert your accounts receivable to cash more quickly than the 90 days it presently takes to collect. Search the Internet for sources of factoring services. What types of information do factors typically ask for before initiating client services?

15-WW2. When Jaime Classwell arrived at work, he found a note on his cubicle asking him to come by his supervisor's office as soon as possible. When he arrived at her office, she asked him to look into inventory loans. She explained that the firm's rapid rate of growth was putting pressure on its ability to continue to finance its growth. Use the Internet to search out a list of sources of inventory loans. Prepare a brief report for Jaime's supervisor that describes the nature of the sources of financing that are available and any other information you feel should be included in such a preliminary analysis.

15-WW3. The Adirondack Furniture Company of Bentonville, Arkansas, makes and sells a line of lawn furniture throughout the United States. In May the company completed its annual planning process and came to the realization that the firm would have to increase its sources of financing if it was to be able to continue to expand its operations to meet rapidly growing demand for its products. After some deliberation, the firm decided that an increase in its line of bank credit was an important component of its financing plans. The problem the bank faced was that it had already reached the maximum loan it could obtain from the firm's long-time local bank. Thus, a broader search of credit sources and terms was needed. Assume that you have been asked to survey bank rates for a prime borrower. Use the Internet to establish current rates of interest being charged for short-term (less than one year) prime credit borrowers.

SELF-TEST SOLUTIONS

SS-1. The discounted interest cost of the commercial paper issue is calculated as follows:

Interest expense $= .10 \times \$200,000,000 \times 180/360 = \$10,000,000$

The effective cost of credit can now be calculated as follows:

$$APR = \frac{\$10,000,000 + \$125,000}{\$200,000,000 - \$125,000 - \$10,000,000} \times \frac{1}{180/360}$$
$$= .1066 = 10.66\%$$

SS-2.

a.
$$APR = \frac{.18 \times \$200,000}{\$200,000} \times \frac{1}{1}$$
$$= .18 = 18\%$$

b.
$$APR = \frac{.16 \times \$200,000}{\$200,000 - (.20 \times \$200,000)} \times \frac{1}{1}$$
$$= .20 = 20\%$$

c.
$$APR = \frac{.14 \times \$200,000}{\$200,000 - (.14 \times \$200,000) - (.2 \times \$200,000)} \times \frac{1}{1}$$
$$= .2121 = 21.21\%$$

Alternative a offers the lowest-cost service of financing, although it carries the highest stated rate of interest. The reason for this is that there is no compensating-balance requirement, nor is interest discounted for this alternative.

SS-3. Ace needs $100,000 to finance seasonal inventory needs for a period of 6 months during the coming year. However, the bank requires a minimum compensating balance of 15 percent of the loan or $15,000. This is $10,000 larger than Ace's average minimum balance over the past year so the firm will have to borrow $110,000 to get the funds it needs plus cover the minimum balance requirement. The *APR* for the loan can be calculated as follows:

$$APR = \frac{.10 \times (\$100,000 + \$10,000) \times .5}{\$100,000} \times \frac{1}{.5} = .11 \text{ or } 11\%$$

CHAPTER 16

Current Asset Management

WHY A COMPANY HOLDS CASH • CASH MANAGEMENT OBJECTIVES AND DECISIONS • COLLECTION AND DISBURSEMENT PROCEDURES • EVALUATION OF COSTS OF CASH MANAGEMENT SERVICES • COMPOSITION OF MARKETABLE-SECURITIES PORTFOLIO • ACCOUNTS–RECEIVABLE MANAGEMENT • INVENTORY MANAGEMENT

At the end of fiscal year 2003, the Walt Disney Company held 3.2 percent of its total assets of approximately $50.0 billion in the form of cash and short-term marketable securities. During 2003, Disney generated sales revenues of $27.061 billion. Based on a 365-day year, this means Disney "produced" $74,139,726 in sales revenues each day.

If Disney could have freed up only 1 day's worth of sales and invested it in 3-month U.S. Treasury bills yielding 2.21 percent, the

⊰ WHAT'S AHEAD ⊱

Chapter 15 provided an introduction and overview of the concept of working-capital management. In this chapter, we explore the management of the asset components of the working-capital equation. Accordingly, we focus on the alternatives available to managers for increasing shareholder wealth with respect to the most important types of current assets: (1) cash, (2) marketable securities, (3) accounts receivable, and (4) inventory. These are listed in order of declining liquidity.

Such alternatives include (1) techniques available to management for favorably influencing cash receipt and disbursement patterns, (2) investments that allow a firm to employ excess cash balances productively, (3) critical decision formulas for determining the appropriate amount of investment in accounts receivable, and (4) methods, such as those pertaining to order quantity and order point issues, for evaluating the most suitable levels of inventory.

These issues are important to the financial manager for several reasons. For example, judicious management of cash and near-cash assets allows the firm

to hold the minimum amount of cash necessary to meet the firm's obligations in a timely manner. As a result, the firm is able to take advantage of the opportunity to earn a return on its liquid assets and increase its profitability.

With such significance in mind, we begin the study of current asset management by exploring the various aspects of the management of cash and marketable securities. Afterward, we turn to an analysis of the important issues related to the management of accounts receivable and inventory.

Before proceeding to our discussion of cash management, it will be helpful to distinguish among several terms. **Cash** is the *currency and coin the firm has on hand in petty cash drawers, in cash registers, or in checking accounts (i.e., demand deposit accounts) at the various commercial banks.* **Marketable securities**, also called near cash or near-cash assets, are *security investments that the firm can quickly convert into cash balances.* Generally, firms hold marketable securities with very short maturity periods—less than 1 year. Together, cash and marketable securities constitute the most liquid assets of a firm.

firm's before-tax profits would have jumped by $1,638,488. That is a significant sum, and it demonstrates why firms like to have efficient treasury management departments in place. Shareholders enjoy the added profits that should, in turn, increase the market value of their common stock holdings.

Now, if Disney's management felt it could bear just a tad more risk, then the freed-up cash might be invested in bank certificates of deposit (CDs) of a similar maturity yielding 2.39 percent to investors. That difference of a mere 18 basis points (i.e., 2.39 – 2.21) may not seem like much, but when you put it to work on an investment of over $74 million, it produces a tidy income. Thus, by investing the excess cash in CDs rather than in Treasury bills, Disney's before-tax profits would be $133,451 greater (i.e., $1,771,939 – $1,638,488). This might be enough for the firm to hire a new business school graduate or two—just like you.

Managing the cash and the marketable-securities portfolio are important tasks for the financial executive. This chapter teaches you about sophisticated cash management systems and about prudent places to "park" the firm's excess cash balances so they earn a positive rate of return and are liquid at the same time. We also explore sound management techniques that relate to the other asset components of the firm's working capital—accounts receivable and inventory.

Objective

cash

marketable securities

WHY A COMPANY HOLDS CASH

A thorough understanding of why and how a firm holds cash requires an accurate conception of how cash flows into and through the enterprise. Figure 16-1 depicts the process of cash generation and disposition in a typical manufacturing setting. The arrows designate the direction of the flow—that is, whether the cash balance increases or decreases.

CASH FLOW PROCESS

The irregular increases in the firm's cash holdings can come from several external sources. Funds can be obtained in the financial markets from the sale of securities such as bonds, preferred stock, and common stock, or the firm can enter into nonmarketable-debt contracts with lenders such as commercial banks. These irregular cash inflows do not occur on a daily basis. The reason is that external financing contracts or arrangements usually involve huge sums of money stemming from a major need identified by the company's management, and these needs do not occur every day. For example, a new product might be in the launching process, or a plant expansion might be required to provide added productive capacity.

In most organizations the financial officer responsible for cash management also controls the transactions that affect the firm's investment in marketable securities. As excess cash becomes temporarily available, marketable securities are purchased. When cash is in short supply, a portion of the marketable-securities portfolio is liquidated.

Whereas the irregular cash inflows are from external sources, the other main sources of cash arise from internal operations and occur on a more regular basis. Over long periods, the largest receipts come from accounts-receivable collections and, to a lesser extent, from direct cash sales of finished goods. Many manufacturing concerns also generate cash on a regular basis through the liquidation of scrap or obsolete inventory. At various times fixed assets may also be sold, thereby generating some cash inflow.

FIGURE 16-1   The Cash Generation and Disposition Process

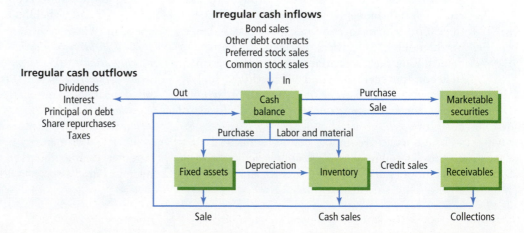

Apart from the investment of excess cash in near-cash assets, the cash balance experiences reductions for three key reasons. First, on an irregular basis, withdrawals are made to (1) pay cash dividends on preferred and common stock shares, (2) meet interest requirements on debt contracts, (3) repay the principal borrowed from creditors, (4) buy the firm's own shares in the financial markets for use in executive compensation plans or as an alternative to paying a cash dividend, and (5) pay tax bills. Again, by an *irregular basis* we mean items *not* occurring on a daily or frequent schedule. Second, the company's capital expenditure program designates that fixed assets be acquired at various intervals. Third, inventories are purchased on a regular basis to ensure a steady flow of finished goods off the production line. Note that the arrow linking the investment in fixed assets with the inventory account is labeled *depreciation*. This indicates that a portion of the cost of fixed assets is charged against the products coming off the assembly line. This cost is subsequently recovered through the sale of the finished-goods inventory. This is because the product's selling price will be set by management to cover all the costs of production, including depreciation.

MOTIVES FOR HOLDING CASH

The influences that affect the firm's cash balance can be classified in terms of the three motives put forth by John Maynard Keynes: (1) the transactions motive, (2) the precautionary motive, and (3) the speculative motive.[1]

TRANSACTIONS MOTIVE

Balances held for transaction purposes allow the firm to meet cash needs that arise in the ordinary course of doing business. In Figure 16-1, transaction balances would be used to meet the irregular outflows as well as the planned acquisition of fixed assets and inventories.

The relative amount of cash needed to satisfy transaction requirements is affected by a number of factors, including the industry in which the firm operates. It is well known that utilities can forecast cash receipts quite accurately, because of stable demand for their services. Computer software firms, however, have a more difficult time predicting their cash flows. New products are brought to market at a rapid pace, thereby making it difficult to project cash flows and balances precisely.

PRECAUTIONARY MOTIVE

Precautionary balances are a buffer stock of liquid assets. This motive for holding cash relates to the maintenance of balances to be used to satisfy possible, but as yet unknown, needs.

Cash flow predictability also has a material influence on the firm's demand for cash through this precautionary motive. The airline industry provides a typical illustration. Air passenger carriers are plagued with a high degree of cash flow uncertainty. The weather, rising fuel costs, and continual strikes by operating personnel make cash forecasting difficult for any airline. The upshot of this problem is that because of all the things that *might* happen, the minimum cash balances desired by the management of the air carriers tend to be large.

In actual business practice, the precautionary motive is met to a large extent by the holding of a portfolio of *liquid assets*, not just cash. Notice in Figure 16-1 the two-way flow of funds between the company's holdings of cash and marketable securities. In large corporate organizations, funds may flow either into or out of the marketable-securities portfolio on a daily basis.

SPECULATIVE MOTIVE

Cash is held for speculative purposes in order to take advantage of potential profit-making situations. Construction firms that build private dwellings will at times accumulate cash in anticipation of a significant drop in lumber costs. If the price of building supplies does drop, the companies that built up their cash balances stand to profit by purchasing materials in large quantities. This will reduce their cost of goods sold and increase their net profit

---

[1]John Maynard Keynes, *The General Theory of Employment, Interest, and Money* (New York: Harcourt Brace Jovanovich, 1936).

margin. Generally, the speculative motive is the least important component of a firm's preference for liquidity. The transactions and precautionary motives account for most of the reasons why a company holds cash balances.

CONCEPT CHECK

1. Describe the typical cash flow cycle for a firm.
2. What are the three motives for holding cash?

Objective **2**

CASH MANAGEMENT OBJECTIVES AND DECISIONS

RISK–RETURN TRADE-OFF

insolvency

A company wide cash management program must be concerned with minimizing the firm's risk of insolvency. In the context of cash management, the term **insolvency** describes the *situation in which the firm is unable to meet its maturing liabilities on time*. In such a case the company is *technically insolvent* in that it lacks the necessary liquidity to make prompt payment on its current debt obligations. A firm could avoid this problem by carrying large cash balances to pay the bills that come due.

The financial manager must strike an acceptable balance between holding too much cash and too little cash. This is the focal point of the risk–return trade-off. A large cash investment minimizes the chances of insolvency, but it penalizes company profitability. A small cash investment frees excess balances for investment in both marketable securities and longer-lived assets; this enhances company profitability and the value of the firm's common shares, but it increases the chances of running out of cash.

BACK TO THE FOUNDATIONS

*The dilemma faced by the financial manager is a clear application of **Principle 1: The Risk–Return Trade-Off—We Won't Take On Additional Risk Unless We Expect to Be Compensated with Additional Return**. To accept the risk of not having sufficient cash on hand, the firm must be compensated with a return on the cash that is invested. Moreover, the greater the risk of the investment in which the cash is placed, the greater the return the firm demands.*

OBJECTIVES

The risk–return trade-off can be reduced to two prime objectives for the firm's cash management system.

1. Enough cash must be on hand to meet the disbursal needs that arise in the course of doing business.
2. Investment in idle cash balances must be reduced to a minimum.

Evaluation of these operational objectives, and a conscious attempt on the part of management to meet them, gives rise to the need for some typical cash management decisions.

DECISIONS

Two conditions or ideals would allow the firm to operate for extended periods with cash balances near or at zero: (1) a completely accurate forecast of net cash flows over the planning horizon and (2) perfect synchronization of cash receipts and disbursements.

Cash flow forecasting is the initial step in any effective cash management program. Given that the firm will, as a matter of necessity, invest in some cash balances, certain types of decisions related to the size of those balances dominate the cash management process. These include decisions that answer the following questions:

1. What can be done to speed up cash collections and slow down or better control cash outflows?
2. What should be the composition of a marketable-securities portfolio?

CONCEPT CHECK

1. Describe the relationship between the firm's cash management program and the firm's risk of insolvency.
2. What are the fundamental decisions that the financial manager must make with respect to cash management?

COLLECTION AND DISBURSEMENT PROCEDURES

Objective **3**

The efficiency of the firm's cash management program can be enhanced by knowledge and use of various procedures aimed at (1) accelerating cash receipts and (2) improving the methods used to disburse cash. We will see that greater opportunity for corporate profit improvements lies with the cash receipts side of the funds flow process, although it would be unwise to ignore opportunities for favorably affecting cash disbursement practices.

MANAGING THE CASH INFLOW

The reduction of float lies at the center of the many approaches employed to speed up cash receipts. **Float** (or total float), which is *the length of time from when a check is written until the actual recipient can draw upon or use the "good funds,"* has the following four elements:

float

1. **Mail float** is caused by the time lapse from the moment a customer mails a remittance check until the firm begins to process it.
2. **Processing float** is caused by the time required for the firm to process remittance checks before they can be deposited in the bank.
3. **Transit float** is caused by the time necessary for a deposited check to clear through the commercial banking system and become usable funds to the company. Credit is deferred for a maximum of two business days on checks that are cleared through the Federal Reserve System.
4. **Disbursing float** derives from the fact that funds are available in the company's bank account until its payment check has cleared through the banking system.

We use the term *float* to refer to the total of its four elements just described. Float reduction can yield considerable benefits in terms of usable funds released for company use and returns produced on such freed-up balances.

REGULATION ALERT: "CHECK 21"

In October 2003, President Bush signed into law the Check Clearing for the 21st Century Act. The law took effect on October 28, 2004. This new law is now commonly referred to as "Check 21."[2] Prior to this new regulation, ordinary paper checks were physically transported

---

[2]See www.federalreserve.gov/check21 for a quick overview of the act and links to about 10 other sites dealing with it, including the full text of the law. Answers to frequently asked questions are also provided via a separate link.

A separate overview from the perspective of the financial institution affected by the act is provided by Robert W. Stasik, "Check 21 (the Check Clearing for the 21st Century Act) Potential Opportunities and Implications for Financial Institutions," Whitepaper Series (Mellon Financial Corporation, Pittsburgh, PA), 2004. This source is available at www.mellon.com/cashmanagement/enterprisecashmanagement/resourcecenter/pdf/check21wp.pdf.

A short piece on the argument over bank "hold" times is found in Richard Burnett, "Banks Have Check 21—What About Consumers?" *Orlando Sentinel* (January 16, 2005), pp. H1, 2.

by land carrier or air carrier from the depositing location to the financial institution that would eventually pay the check drawn against the firm's or individual's bank account.

Check 21 allows financial institutions the option of clearing a check image instead of the original check. Such digital substitutes can then be quickly processed within the banking clearing system in the same way that you use the Internet on your personal computer. These digital substitutes are being referred to as substitute checks or image replacement documents.

The impetus for this new law is threefold: (1) Bank regulators, like those at the Federal Reserve System, feel that Check 21 will accelerate check collection at the ultimate or payee bank, (2) it is forecast that out-of-pocket transportation costs to the banking system will be reduced, thereby increasing individual bank profitability, and (3) the high degree of physical risk exposure associated with carrier service can be minimized.

From the viewpoint of the firm's cash management system, "managing the float" will eventually be directly impacted. What has been called "disbursing float" could be dramatically reduced to a few hours instead of a day or two. But Check 21 does not require banks to alter their "hold" time on specific checks or substitute checks posted to the firm's account within the bank. (These are ultimately cash inflows that become "good" funds.)

So, although the check may clear within the bank clearing mechanism (i.e., from bank to bank), the firm may not have the use of "good" funds until banks are forced by a yet to be defined regulatory change to reduce their "hold" time on checks that have actually cleared. Thus, the effects of Check 21 on "transit float" (the third type of float mentioned previously) will occur gradually as pressure is put on individual financial institutions to reduce hold times and make the funds available for disbursement by the receiving firm.

The upshot for the firm and its cash management system is that the greatest profitability opportunities are still associated with reducing mail float and processing float. We move on now to an example of measuring such value.

EXAMPLE

The positive operating-profit effects that stem from the use of wise cash management techniques that result in float reduction can be dramatic when large total revenues are involved. Suppose that we want to estimate the value of a 1-day float reduction for Starbucks Corporation. Starbucks' 2004 sales revenues were reported at $5.294 billion. Let's assume that prudent investment in money-market securities will earn 4 percent annually. We ask, What is the estimated value of a 1-day float reduction to Starbucks? We can calculate this as follows:

$$\frac{\text{Annual revenues}}{\text{days in year}}$$

which for Starbucks in 2004 was

$$\frac{\$5.924 \text{ billion}}{365} = \$14,504,110$$

Thus, 1 day's freed-up balances for Starbucks will be $14,504,110. Then we find the annual (before-tax) value of the float reduction is

$$(\text{Sales per day}) \times (\text{assumed yield}) = \$14,504,110 \times .04 = \$580,164$$

Such prospective gains in operating profits make it worthwhile for the firm and its treasury management function to closely evaluate the cash management services offered by commercial banks—even when the bank fees can also be quite costly. We learn how to make decisions of this nature later in the chapter.

FIGURE 16-2 Ordinary Cash Collection System

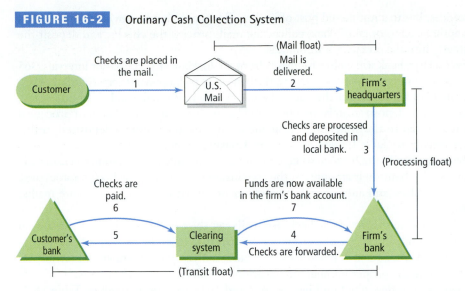

LOCKBOX ARRANGEMENT

The lockbox system is the most widely used commercial banking service for expediting cash gathering. Banks have offered this service since 1946. Such a system speeds up the conversion of receipts into usable funds by reducing both mail and processing float. In addition, it is possible to reduce transit float if lockboxes are located near Federal Reserve Banks and their branches. For large corporations that receive checks from all parts of the country, float reductions of 2 to 4 days are not unusual.

Figure 16-2 illustrates an elementary, but typical, cash collection system for a hypothetical firm. It also shows the origin of mail float, processing float, and transit float. The numbers represent the steps in this system. First, the customer places his or her remittance check in the U.S. mail, which is then delivered to the firm's headquarters. This causes the mail float. On the check's arrival at the firm's headquarters (or local collection center), general accounting personnel must go through the bookkeeping procedures needed to prepare them for local deposit. The checks are deposited. This causes the processing float. The checks are then forwarded for payment through the commercial bank clearing mechanism. The checks will be charged against the customer's own bank account. At this point the checks are said to be "paid" and become "good" funds available for use by the company that received them. This bank clearing procedure represents transit float and, as we said earlier, can amount to a delay of up to 2 business days.

The lockbox arrangement in Figure 16-3 is based on a simple procedure. The firm's customers are instructed to mail their remittance checks not to company headquarters or

TAKIN' IT TO THE NET

The Internet is revolutionizing the banking business as well as retail distribution. For an example of the type of firm offering banking services to e-commerce firms see www.magnetbanking.com.

FIGURE 16-3 Simple Lockbox System

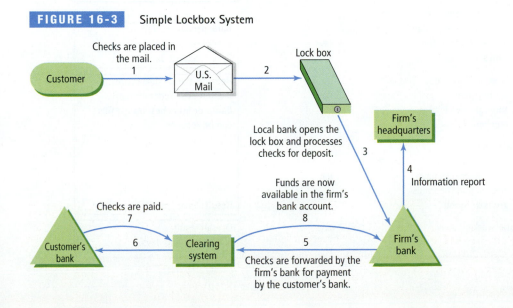

regional offices, but to a numbered post office box. The bank that is providing the lockbox service is authorized to open the box, collect the mail, process the checks, and deposit the checks directly into the company's account.

Typically a large bank will collect payments from the lockbox at 1- to 2-hour intervals, 365 days of the year. During peak business hours, the bank may pick up mail every 30 minutes.

Once the mail is received at the bank, the checks are examined, totaled, photocopied, and microfilmed. A deposit form is then prepared by the bank, and each batch of processed checks is forwarded to the collection department for clearance. Funds deposited in this manner are usually available for company use in 1 business day or less.

The bank can notify the firm via some type of telecommunications system the same day deposits are made about their amount. At the conclusion of each day, all check photocopies, invoices, deposit slips, and any other documents included with the remittances are mailed to the firm.

Note that the firm that receives checks from all over the country will have to use several lockboxes to take full advantage of a reduction in mail float. The firm's major bank should be able to offer as a service a detailed lockbox study, analyzing the company's receipt patterns to determine the proper number and location of lock-box receiving points.

The two systems described by Figures 16-2 and 16-3 are summarized in Table 16-1. There, the step numbers refer to those shown in Figure 16-2 (the ordinary system). Furthermore, Table 16-1 assumes that the customer and the firm's headquarters or its collection center are located in different cities. This causes the lag of 2 working days before the firm actually receives the remittance check. We notice at the bottom of Table 16-1 that the installation of the lockbox system can result in funds being credited to the firm's bank account a full *4 working days faster* than is possible under the ordinary collection system.

Previously in the introduction to this chapter we calculated the 2003 sales per day for Disney to be in excess of $74 million and assumed the firm could invest its excess cash in marketable securities to yield 2.21 percent annually. If Disney could speed up its cash collections by 4 days, as the hypothetical firm did in Table 16-1, the results would exceed $6.5

TABLE 16-1   Comparison of Ordinary Cash Collection System with Simple Lockbox System

STEPS	ORDINARY SYSTEM AND TIME		ADVANTAGE OF LOCKBOX
1	Customer writes check and places it in the mail.	1 day	
2	Mail is delivered to firm's headquarters.	2 days	Mail will not have to travel as far. Result: Save 1 day.
3	Accounting personnel process the checks and deposit them in the firm's local bank.	2 days	Bank personnel prepare checks for deposit. Result: Save 2 days.
4 and 5	Checks are forwarded for payment through the clearing mechanism.	1 day	Because the lockboxes are located near Federal Reserve Banks or branches, transit float can be reduced.
6 and 7	The firm receives notice from its bank that the checks have cleared and the funds are now "good."	1 day	Result: Save 1 day.
	Total working days	7 days	Overall result: Save 4 working days.

million to the firm's advantage. Specifically, the gross annual savings to Disney (apart from operating the lockbox system) would amount to $6.554 million as follows:

$$(\text{Sales per day}) \times (\text{days of float reduction}) \times (\text{assumed yield}) = \text{gross annual savings}$$
$$(\$74,139,726) \times (4) \times (.0221) = \$6,553,952$$

As you might guess, the prospects for generating revenues of this magnitude are important not only to the firms involved but also to commercial banks that offer lockbox services.

In summary, the benefits of a lockbox arrangement are

1. **Increased working cash.** The time required for converting receivables into available funds is reduced. This frees up cash for use elsewhere in the enterprise.
2. **Elimination of clerical functions.** The bank takes over the tasks of receiving, endorsing, totaling, and depositing checks. With less handling of receipts by employees, better audit control is achieved and the chance of documents becoming lost is reduced.
3. **Early knowledge of dishonored checks.** Should a customer's check be uncollectible because of lack of funds, it is returned, usually by special handling, to the firm.

These benefits are not free. Usually, the bank levies a charge for each check processed through the system. The benefits derived from the acceleration of receipts must exceed the incremental costs of the lockbox system or the firm would be better off without it. Later in this chapter, a straightforward method for assessing the desirability of a specific cash management service, such as the lockbox arrangement, is illustrated.

MANAGEMENT OF CASH OUTFLOW

The objective in managing cash outflows is to increase the company's float by slowing down the disbursement and collection process. This is exactly the opposite of our objective in managing cash collections. There we focused our attention on ways to shorten our customer's float, whereas now we wish to increase our own payment float. There are several tools at the disposal of the cash manager for accomplishing this end, and we describe three here. These are the use of (1) zero balance accounts, (2) payable-through drafts, and (3) remote disbursing. (See Table 16-2.)

ZERO BALANCE ACCOUNTS

Large corporations that operate multiple branches, divisions, or subsidiaries often maintain numerous bank accounts (in different banks) for the purpose of making timely operating disbursements. It does make good business sense for payments for purchased parts that go into, say, an automobile transmission to be made by the Transmission and Chassis Division of the auto manufacturer rather than its central office. The Transmission and Chassis Division originates such purchase orders, receives and inspects the shipment when it

---

TABLE 16-2   Features of Selected Cash Disbursal Techniques: A Summary

TECHNIQUE	OBJECTIVE	HOW ACCOMPLISHED
1. Zero balance accounts	(1) Achieve better control over cash payments, (2) reduce excess cash balances held in regional banks, and possibly (3) increase disbursing float.	Establish zero balance accounts for all of the firm's disbursing units. These accounts are all in the same concentration bank. Checks are drawn against these accounts, with the balance in each account never exceeding $0. Divisional disbursing authority is thereby maintained at the local level of management.
2. Payable-through drafts	Achieve effective central-office control over field-authorized payments.	Field office issues drafts rather than checks to settle up payables.
3. Remote disbursing	Extend disbursing float.	Write checks against demand deposit accounts held in distant banks.

arrives at the plant, authorizes payment, and writes the appropriate check. To have the central office involved in these matters would be a waste of company time.

What tends to happen, however, is that with several divisions utilizing their own disbursal accounts, excess cash balances build up in outlying banks and rob the firm of earning assets. Zero balance accounts are used to alleviate this problem. The objectives of a zero balance account system for the firm are (1) to achieve better control over its cash payments, (2) to reduce excess cash balances held in regional banks for disbursing purposes, and (3) to increase disbursing float.

zero balance accounts (ZBAs)

Zero balance accounts (ZBAs) *permit centralized control (at the headquarters level) over cash outflows while maintaining divisional disbursing authority.* Under this system the firm's authorized employees, representing their various divisions, continue to write checks on their individual accounts. Note that the numerous individual disbursing accounts are now *all* located in the same concentration bank. Actually these separate accounts contain no funds at all, thus their appropriate label, "zero balance." These accounts have all the characteristics of regular demand deposit accounts, including separate titles, numbers, and statements.

The firm's authorized agents write their payment checks as usual against their specific accounts. These checks clear through the banking system in the usual way. On a daily basis checks are presented to the firm's concentration bank (the drawee bank) for payment. As the checks are paid by the bank, negative (debit) balances build up in the proper disbursing accounts. At the end of each day the negative balances are restored to a zero level by means of credits to the ZBAs; a corresponding reduction of funds is made against the firm's concentration (master) demand deposit account. Each morning a report is electronically forwarded to corporate headquarters reflecting the balance in the master account as well as the previous day's activity in each ZBA. Using the report, the financial officer in charge of near-cash investments is ready to initiate appropriate transactions.

Managing the cash outflow through use of a ZBA system offers the following benefits to the firm with many operating units:

1. Centralized control over disbursements is achieved, even though payment and authority continue to rest with operating units.
2. Management time spent on superficial cash management activities is reduced. Exercises such as observing the balances held in numerous bank accounts, transferring funds to those accounts short of cash, and reconciling the accounts demand less attention.
3. Excess balances held in outlying accounts can be reduced.
4. The costs of cash management can be reduced, as wire transfers to build up funds in outlying disbursement accounts are eliminated.
5. Funds may be made available for company use through an increase in disbursement float. When local bank accounts are used to pay nearby suppliers, the checks clear rapidly. The same checks, if drawn on a ZBA located in a more distant concentration bank, will take more time to clear against the disbursing firm's account.

PAYABLE-THROUGH DRAFTS

payable-through drafts (PTDs)

Payable-through drafts (PTDs) are *legal instruments that have the physical appearance of ordinary checks but are not drawn on a bank. Instead, payable-through drafts are drawn on and payment is authorized by the issuing firm against its demand deposit account.*

Like checks, the drafts are cleared through the banking system and are presented to the issuing firm's bank. The bank serves as a collection point and passes the drafts on to the firm. The corporate issuer usually has to return by the following business day all drafts it does not wish to cover (pay). Those documents not returned to the bank are automatically paid. The firm inspects the drafts for validity by checking signatures, amounts, and dates. Stop-payment orders can be initiated by the company on any drafts considered inappropriate.

The main purpose of using a payable-through draft system is *to provide for effective control over field payments.* Central office control over payments begun by regional units is provided because the drafts are reviewed in advance of final payment. Payable-through drafts, for example, are used extensively in the insurance industry. The claims agent does not typically have check-signing authority against a corporate disbursement account. This agent can issue a draft, however, for quick settlement of a claim.

REMOTE DISBURSING

A few banks will provide the corporate customer with **remote disbursing**, a cash management service specifically designed to extend disbursing float. The firm's concentration bank may have a correspondent relationship with a smaller bank located in a distant city. In that remote city the Federal Reserve System is unable to maintain frequent clearings of checks drawn on local banks. For example, a firm that is located in Dallas and maintains its master account there may open an account with a bank situated in, say, Amarillo, Texas. The firm will write the bulk of its payment checks against the account in the Amarillo bank. The checks will probably take at least 1 business day longer to clear, so the firm can "play the float" to its advantage.

A firm must use this technique of remote disbursing with extreme care. If a key supplier of new materials located in Dallas has to wait the extra day for funds drawn on the Amarillo account, the possibility of incurring ill will might outweigh the apparent gain from an increase in the disbursing float. The impact on the firm's reputation of using remote disbursing should be explicitly evaluated. The practice of remote disbursing is discouraged by the Federal Reserve System.

remote disbursing

BACK TO THE FOUNDATIONS

*These collection and disbursement procedures are an illustration of **Principle 2: The Time Value of Money—A Dollar Received Today Is Worth More Than a Dollar Received in the Future**. The faster the firm can take possession of the money to which it is entitled, the sooner the firm can put the money to work generating a return. Similarly, the longer the firm can hold on to the liquid assets in its possession, the greater the return the firm can receive on such funds.*

CONCEPT CHECK

1. Define *float* and its origins in the cash management process (i.e., mail, processing, transit, and disbursing).
2. What is a lockbox arrangement and how does its use reduce float?
3. Describe the following methods for managing cash outflow: zero balance accounts and payable-through drafts.
4. What are the likely effects of Check 21 on the firm's cash management system?

EVALUATION OF COSTS OF CASH MANAGEMENT SERVICES

Objective **4**

A form of break-even analysis can help the financial officer decide whether a particular collection or disbursement service will provide an economic benefit to the firm. The evaluation process involves a very basic relationship in microeconomics:

$$\text{Added costs} = \text{added benefits} \qquad \textbf{(16-1)}$$

If equation (16-1) holds exactly, then the firm is no better or worse off for having adopted the given service. We will illustrate this procedure in terms of the desirability of installing an additional lockbox. Equation (16-1) can be restated on a per unit basis as follows:

$$P = (D)(S)(i) \qquad \textbf{(16-2)}$$

where P = increases in per check processing cost if the new system is adopted
D = days saved in the collection process (float reduction)
S = average check size in dollars
i = the daily, before-tax opportunity cost (rate of return) of carrying cash

Assume that check processing cost P will rise by $0.18 a check if the lockbox is used. The firm has determined that the average check size, S, that will be mailed to the lockbox location will be $900. If funds are freed by use of the lockbox, they will be invested in marketable securities to yield an *annual* before-tax return of 6 percent. With these data, it is possible to determine the reduction in check collection time D required to justify the use of the lockbox. That level of D is found to be

$$\$.18 = (D)(\$900)\left(\frac{.06}{365}\right)$$

$$1.217 \text{ days} = D$$

Thus, the lockbox is justified if the firm can speed up its collections by *more* than 1.217 days. This same style of analysis can be adapted to analyze the other tools of cash management.

CONCEPT CHECK

1. Describe the use of the break-even concept with respect to the management of cash.
2. How would you estimate the financial benefits of using a lockbox system?

Objective **5**

COMPOSITION OF MARKETABLE-SECURITIES PORTFOLIO

Once the design of the firm's cash receipts and payments system has been determined, the financial manager faces the task of selecting appropriate financial assets for inclusion in the firm's marketable-securities portfolio.

GENERAL SELECTION CRITERIA

Certain criteria can provide a financial manager with a useful framework for selecting a proper marketable-securities mix. These considerations include evaluation of the (1) financial risk, (2) interest rate risk, (3) liquidity, (4) taxability, and (5) yields among different financial assets. The following sections briefly delineate these criteria from the investor's viewpoint.

FINANCIAL RISK
Financial risk here refers to the uncertainty of expected returns from a security attributable to possible changes in the financial capacity of the security issuer to make future payments to the security owner. If the chance of default on the terms of the instrument is high (or low), then the financial risk is said to be high (or low).

In both financial practice and research, when estimates of risk-free returns are desired, the yields available on Treasury securities are consulted, and the safety of other financial instruments is weighed against them.

INTEREST RATE RISK
Interest rate risk refers to the uncertainty of expected returns from a financial instrument attributable to changes in interest rates. Of particular concern to the corporate treasurer is the price volatility associated with instruments that have long, as opposed to short, terms to maturity. An illustration can help clarify this point.

Suppose the financial officer is weighing the merits of investing temporarily available corporate cash in a new offering of U.S. Treasury obligations that will mature in either (1) 3 years or (2) 20 years from the date of issue. The purchase prices of the 3-year notes or 20-year bonds are at their par values of $1,000 per security. The maturity value of either class of security is equal to par, $1,000, and the coupon rate (stated interest rate) is set at 7 percent, compounded annually.

If after 1 year from the date of purchase prevailing interest rates rise to 9 percent, the market prices of these currently outstanding Treasury securities will fall to bring their yields to maturity in line with what investors could obtain by buying a new issue of a given instrument. The market prices of *both* the 3-year and 20-year obligations will decline. The price of the 20-year instrument will decline by a greater dollar amount, however, than that of the 3-year instrument.

One year from the date of issue, the price obtainable in the marketplace for the original 20-year instrument, which now has 19 years to go to maturity, can be found by computing *P* as follows:

$$P = \sum_{t=1}^{19} \frac{\$70}{(1+.09)^t} + \frac{\$1,000}{(1+.09)^{19}} = \$821.01$$

In the previous expression, (1) *t* is the year in which the particular return, either interest or principal amount, is received; (2) $70 is the annual interest payment; and (3) $1,000 is the contractual maturity value of the bond. The rise in interest rates has forced the market price of the bond down to $821.01.

What will happen to the price of the note that has 2 years remaining to maturity? In a similar manner, we can compute its price, *P*:

$$P = \sum_{t=1}^{2} \frac{\$70}{(1+.09)^t} + \frac{\$1,000}{(1+.09)^{2}} = \$964.84$$

The market price of the shorter-term note will decline to $964.84. Table 16-3 shows that the market value of the shorter-term security was penalized much less by the given rise in the general level of interest rates.

If we extended the illustration, we would see that, in terms of market price, a 1-year security would be affected less than a 2-year security, a 91-day security less than a 182-day security, and so on. Equity securities would exhibit the largest price changes because of their infinite maturity periods. To hedge against the price volatility caused by interest rate risk, the firm's marketable-securities portfolio will tend to be composed of instruments that mature over short periods.

LIQUIDITY

In the present context of managing the marketable-securities portfolio, *liquidity* refers to the ability to transform a security into cash. Should an unforeseen event require that a significant amount of cash be immediately available, then a sizable portion of the portfolio might have to be sold. The financial manager will want the cash quickly and will not want to accept a large price concession in order to convert the securities. Thus, in the formulation of preferences for the inclusion of particular instruments in the portfolio, the manager must consider (1) the period needed to sell the security and (2) the likelihood that the security can be sold at or near its prevailing market price.

TAXABILITY

The tax treatment of the income a firm receives from its security investments does not affect the ultimate mix of the marketable-securities portfolio as much as the criteria mentioned earlier. This is because the interest income from most instruments suitable for

TABLE 16-3 Market Price Effect of Rise in Interest Rates

ITEM	THREE-YEAR INSTRUMENT	TWENTY-YEAR INSTRUMENT
Original price	$1,000.00	$1,000.00
Price after one year	964.84	821.01
Decline in price	$ 35.16	$ 178.99

TABLE 16-4 Comparison of After-Tax Yields

	TAX-EXEMPT DEBT ISSUE (6% COUPON)	TAXABLE DEBT ISSUE (8% COUPON)
Interest income	$ 60.00	$ 80.00
Income tax (.34)	0.00	27.20
After-tax interest income	$ 60.00	$ 52.80
After-tax yield	$ 60.00 = 6%	$ 52.80 = 5.28%
	$1,000.00	$1,000.00

Derivation of equivalent before-tax yield on a taxable debt issue:

$$r = \frac{r^*}{1-T} = \frac{.06}{1-.34} = 9.091\%$$

where r = equivalent before-tax yield
r^* = after-tax yield on tax-exempt security
T = firm's marginal income tax rate

Proof: Interest income [$1,000 × .09091] $90.91
          Income tax (.34) $30.91
After-tax interest income $60.00

inclusion in the portfolio is taxable at the federal level. Still, some corporate treasurers seriously evaluate the taxability of interest income and capital gains.

The interest income from only one class of securities escapes the federal income tax. That class of securities is generally referred to as *municipal obligations*, or more simply as *municipals*. Because of the tax-exempt feature of interest income from state and local government securities, municipals sell at lower yields to maturity in the market than securities that pay taxable interest. The after-tax yield on a municipal obligation, however, could be higher than the yield from a non-tax-exempt security. This would depend mainly on the purchasing firm's tax situation.

Consider Table 16-4. A firm is assumed to be analyzing whether to invest in a 1-year tax-free debt issue yielding 6 percent on a $1,000 outlay or a 1-year taxable issue that yields 8 percent on a $1,000 outlay. The firm pays federal taxes at the rate of 34 percent. The yields quoted in the financial press and in the prospectuses that describe debt issues are *before-tax* returns. The actual *after-tax* return enjoyed by the investor depends on his or her tax bracket. Notice that the actual after-tax yield received by the firm is only 5.28 percent on the taxable issue versus 6 percent on the tax-exempt obligation. The lower portion of Table 16-4 shows that the fully taxed bond must yield 9.091 percent to make it comparable with the tax-exempt issue.

YIELDS

The final selection criterion that we mention is a significant one—the yields that are available on the different financial assets suitable for inclusion in the near-cash portfolio. By now it is probably obvious that the factors of (1) financial risk, (2) interest rate risk, (3) liquidity, and (4) taxability all influence the available yields on financial instruments. The yield criterion involves an evaluation of the risks and benefits inherent in all of these factors. If a given risk is assumed, such as lack of liquidity, a higher yield may be expected on the nonliquid instrument.

Figure 16-4 summarizes our framework for designing the firm's marketable-securities portfolio. The four basic considerations are shown to influence the yields available on securities. The financial manager must focus on the risk–return trade-offs identified through analysis. Coming to grips with these trade-offs will enable the financial manager to determine the proper marketable-securities mix for the company. Let us look now at the marketable securities prominent in firms' near-cash portfolios.

FIGURE 16-4   Designing the Marketable-Securities Portfolio

Considerations ⟶	Influence ⟶	Focus upon ⟶	Determine
Financial risk Interest rate risk Liquidity Taxability	Yields	Risk vs. return preferences	Marketable- securities mix

MARKETABLE-SECURITY ALTERNATIVES

Money-market securities generally have short-term maturity and are highly marketable, so the holder can quickly liquidate if the firm needs the cash. Table 16-5 summarizes the characteristics of the most widely used money market securities in terms of five key attributes: (1) the denominations in which securities are available; (2) the maturities that are offered; (3) the basis used (i.e., whether the security is sold at a discount or offers coupon interest payments); (4) the liquidity of the instrument, which relates principally to the availability of a secondary market for the security; and (5) taxability of the investment returns.

U.S. TREASURY BILLS

U.S. Treasury bills are the best known and most popular short-term investment outlet among firms. A Treasury bill is a direct obligation of the U.S. government sold on a regular basis by the U.S. Treasury. New Treasury bills are now issued in denominations as small as $1,000. Prior to recent years, the minimum purchase was a rather high amount of $10,000, which was blatantly difficult for small, individual investors. So now investors can participate in the Treasury bill market along with large corporations and increase their allocations in increments of $1,000 above the initial outlay of that same amount. At present, bills with maturities of 4 weeks, 13 weeks, and 26 weeks are issued every week (usually on Monday, unless it is a holiday) in an open market auction. Treasury bills are very popular among corporate treasurers who are responsible for managing the specific firm's cash position. You will see why later.

Of prime importance to the corporate treasurer is the fact that a very active secondary market exists for bills. After a bill has been acquired by the firm, should the need arise to turn it into cash, a group of securities dealers stands ready to purchase it. This highly developed secondary market for bills not only makes them extremely liquid, but also allows the firm to buy bills with maturities of a week or even less.

Because bills have the full financial backing of the U.S. government, they are, for all practical purposes, risk free. This negligible financial risk and high degree of liquidity makes the yields lower than those obtainable on other marketable securities. The income from Treasury bills is subject to federal income taxes, but *not* to state and local income taxes.

FEDERAL AGENCY SECURITIES

Federal agency securities are debt obligations of corporations and agencies that have been created to effect the various lending programs of the U.S. government. Five such government-sponsored corporations account for the majority of outstanding agency debt. The "big five" agencies are

1. The Federal National Mortgage Association (FNMA)
2. The Federal Home Loan Banks (FHLB)
3. The Federal Land Banks
4. The Federal Intermediate Credit Banks
5. The Banks for Cooperatives

It is not true that the "big five" federally sponsored agencies are owned by the U.S. government and that the securities they issue are fully guaranteed by the government. The "big five" agencies are now entirely owned by their member associations or the general public. In addition, the issuing agency, not the federal government, stands behind its promises to pay.

TAKIN' IT TO THE NET

The U.S. Department of the Treasury maintains a fine and useful Web site at www.treasurydirect.gov. There you can obtain detailed information on Treasury investment products, such as Treasury bills. It is clearly divided with separate information for (1) individual/personal investing, (2) corporate investing, and (3) government investing. In addition the Financial Management Service of the Treasury publishes on a quarterly basis its *Treasury Bulletin*. For Internet service subscribers this can be accessed at www.fms.treas.gov. The *Bulletin* contains a wide variety of data dealing with the fiscal operations of the U.S. government including recent market yields on Treasury bills, notes, and bonds that range in maturity from 1 month to 20 years.

TABLE 16-5   Features of Selected Money–Market Instruments

INSTRUMENTS	DENOMINATIONS	MATURITIES	BASIS	LIQUIDITY	TAXABILITY
U.S. Treasury bills—direct obligations of the U.S. government	$ 1,000 and increments of $ 1,000	91 days, 182 days, and 4 weeks	Discount	Excellent secondary market	Exempt from state and local income taxes
Federal agency securities—obligations of corporations and agencies created to effect the federal government's lending programs	Wide variation; from $1,000 to $1 million	5 days (Farm Credit consolidated discount notes) to more than 10 years	Discount or coupon; usually on coupon	Good for issues of "big five" agencies	Generally exempt at local level; FNMA issues are *not* exempt
Bankers' acceptance—drafts accepted for future payment by commercial banks	No set size; typically range from $25,000 to $1 million	Predominantly from 30 to 180 days	Discount	Good for acceptances of large "money-market" banks	Taxed at all levels of government
Negotiable certificates of deposit—marketable receipts for funds deposited in a bank for a fixed time period	$25,000 to $10 million	1 to 18 months	Accrued interest	Fair to good	Taxed at all levels of government
Commercial paper—short-term unsecured promissory notes	$5,000 to $5 million; $1,000 and $5,000 multiples above the initial offering size are sometimes available.	3 to 270 days	Discount	Poor; no active secondary market in usual sense	Taxed at all levels of government
Repurchase agreements—legal contracts between a borrower (security seller) and lender (security buyer). The borrower will repurchase at the contract price plus an interest charge.	Typical sizes are $500,000 or more.	According to terms of contract	Not applicable	Fixed by the agreement; that is, borrower will repurchase	Taxed at all levels of government
Money-market mutual funds—holders of diversified portfolios of short-term, high-grade debt instruments	Some require an initial investment as small as $1,000.	Shares can be sold at any time	Net asset value	Good; provided by the fund itself	Taxed at all levels of government

BANKERS' ACCEPTANCES

Bankers' acceptances are one of the least-understood instruments suitable for inclusion in the firm's marketable-securities portfolio. Their part in U.S. commerce today is largely concentrated in the financing of foreign transactions. Generally, an acceptance is a draft (order to pay) drawn on a specific bank by an exporter in order to obtain payment for goods shipped to a customer, who maintains an account with that specific bank.

NEGOTIABLE CERTIFICATES OF DEPOSIT

A *negotiable certificate of deposit (CD)* is a marketable receipt for funds that have been deposited in a bank for a fixed period. The deposited funds earn a fixed rate of interest. These are not to be confused with ordinary passbook savings accounts or non-marketable time deposits offered by all commercial banks. CDs are offered by major money-center banks. We are talking here about "corporate" CDs—not those offered to individuals.

COMMERCIAL PAPER

Commercial paper refers to short-term, unsecured promissory notes sold by large businesses to raise cash. These are sometimes described in the popular financial press as short-term corporate IOUs. Because they are unsecured, the issuing side of the market is dominated by large corporations, which typically maintain sound credit ratings. The issuing (borrowing) firm can sell the paper to a dealer, who will in turn sell it to the investing public; if the firm's reputation is solid, the paper can be sold directly to the ultimate investor.

REPURCHASE AGREEMENTS

Repurchase agreements (repos) are legal contracts that involve the actual sale of securities by a *borrower* to the *lender*, with a commitment on the part of the borrower to *repurchase* the securities at the contract price plus a stated interest charge. The securities sold to the lender are U.S. government issues or other instruments of the money market such as those described previously. The borrower is either a major financial institution—most often a commercial bank—or a dealer in U.S. government securities.

Why might the corporation with excess cash prefer to buy repurchase agreements rather than a given marketable security? There are two major reasons. First, the original maturities of the instruments being sold can, in effect, be adjusted to suit the particular needs of the investing corporation. Funds available for very short periods, such as 1 or 2 days, can be productively employed. The second reason is closely related to the first. The firm could, of course, buy a Treasury bill and then resell it in the market in a few days when cash is required. The drawback here would be the risk involved in liquidating the bill at a price equal to its earlier cost to the firm. The purchase of a repo removes this risk. The contract price of the securities that make up the arrangement is *fixed* for the duration of the transaction. The corporation that buys a repurchase agreement, then, is protected against market price fluctuations throughout the contract period. This makes it a sound alternative investment for funds that are freed up for only very short periods.

MONEY-MARKET MUTUAL FUNDS

The money-market mutual funds sell their shares to raise cash, and by pooling the funds of large numbers of small savers, they can build their liquid-asset portfolios. Many of these funds allow the investor to start an account with as little as $1,000. This small initial investment, coupled with the fact that some liquid-asset funds permit subsequent investments in amounts as small as $100, makes this type of outlet for excess cash suited to the small firm and even the individual. Furthermore, the management of a small enterprise may not be highly versed in the details of short-term investments. By purchasing shares in a liquid-asset fund, the investor is also buying managerial expertise.

Money-market mutual funds typically invest in a diversified portfolio of short-term, high-grade debt instruments such as those described previously. Some such funds, however, will accept more interest rate risk in their portfolios and acquire some corporate bonds and notes. Money-market mutual funds offer the investing firm a high degree of liquidity. By redeeming (selling) shares, the investor can obtain cash quickly. Procedures for liquidation vary among the funds, but shares can usually be redeemed by means of (1) special redemption checks supplied by the funds, (2) telephone instructions, (3) wire instructions, or (4) a letter. When liquidation is ordered by telephone or wire, the mutual fund can remit to the investor by the next business day.

THE YIELD STRUCTURE OF MARKETABLE SECURITIES

What type of return can the financial manager expect on a marketable-securities portfolio? This is a reasonable question. Some insight can be obtained by looking at the past, although we must realize that future returns are not guided by past experience. It is also useful to have some understanding of how the returns on one type of instrument stack up against another. The behavior of yields on short-term debt instruments over the 1980 to 2003 period is shown in Table 16-6.

TABLE 16-6   Annual Yields (Percent) on Selected Three–Month Marketable Securities

YEAR	T-BILLS	ACCEPTANCES	COMMERCIAL PAPER	CDS
1980	11.51	12.72	12.66	13.07
1985	7.48	7.92	7.95	8.05
1990	7.51	7.93	8.06	8.15
1995	5.51	5.81	5.93	5.92
1996	5.01	5.31	5.42	5.39
1997	5.06	5.54	5.60	5.62
1998	4.78	5.39	5.37	5.47
1999	4.64	5.24	5.22	5.33
2000	5.82	6.23	6.33	6.46
2001	3.40	—	3.65	3.71
2002	1.61	—	1.69	1.73
2003	1.01	—	1.11	1.15

Source: *Federal Reserve Statistical Release* G.13 (415), various issues, and *Statistical Supplement to the Federal Reserve Bulletin*, November 2004, p. 23.

CONCEPT CHECK

1. What are financial risk and interest rate risk?
2. Describe each of the following: Treasury bill, federal agency securities, bankers' acceptances, negotiable certificates of deposit, commercial paper, repurchase agreements, and money-market mutual funds.
3. What is meant by the yield structure of marketable securities?

Objective

ACCOUNTS-RECEIVABLE MANAGEMENT

We now turn from the most liquid of the firm's current assets (cash and marketable securities) to those that are less liquid—accounts receivable and inventories. All firms by their very nature are involved in selling either goods or services. Although some of these sales will be for cash, a large portion will involve credit. Whenever a sale is made on credit, it increases the firm's accounts receivable. Thus, the importance of how a firm manages its accounts receivable depends on the degree to which the firm sells on credit.

Accounts receivable typically comprise more than 25 percent of a firm's assets. In effect, when we discuss management of accounts receivable, we are discussing the management of one-quarter of the firm's assets. Moreover, because cash flows from a sale cannot be invested until the account is collected, control of receivables takes on added importance; efficient collection determines both profitability and liquidity of the firm.

SIZE OF INVESTMENT IN ACCOUNTS RECEIVABLE

The size of the investment in accounts receivable is determined by several factors. First, the percentage of credit sales to total sales affects the level of accounts receivable held. Although this factor certainly plays a major role in determining a firm's investment in accounts receivable, it generally is not within the control of the financial manager. The nature of the business tends to determine the blend between credit sales and cash sales. A large grocery store tends to sell exclusively on a cash basis, whereas most construction-lumber supply firms make their sales primarily with credit.

The level of sales is also a factor in determining the size of the investment in accounts receivable. Very simply, the more sales, the greater accounts receivable. It is not a decision variable for the financial manager, however.

The final determinants of the level of investment in accounts receivable are the credit and collection policies—more specifically, the terms of sale, the quality of customer, and the

FIGURE 16-5   Determinants of Investment in Accounts Receivable

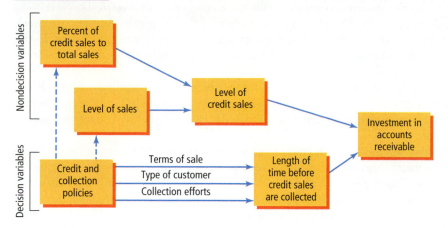

collection efforts. These policies *are* under the control of the financial manager. The terms of sale specify both the time period during which the customer must pay and the terms, such as penalties for late payments or discounts for early payments. The type of customer or credit policy also affects the level of investment in accounts receivable. For example, the acceptance of poorer credit risks and their subsequent delinquent payments may lead to an increase in accounts receivable. The strength and timing of the collection efforts can affect the period for which past-due accounts remain delinquent, which in turn affects the level of accounts receivable. Collection and credit policy decisions may further affect the level of investment in accounts receivable by causing changes in the sales level and the ratio of credit sales to total sales. The factors that determine the level of investment in accounts receivable are displayed in Figure 16-5.

TERMS OF SALE—DECISION VARIABLE

The **terms of sale** *identify the possible discount for early payment, the discount period, and the total credit period.* They are generally stated in the form *a/b* net *c*, indicating that the customer can deduct *a* percent if the account is paid within *b* days; otherwise, the account must be paid within *c* days. Thus, for example, trade credit terms of 2/10, net 30, indicate that a 2 percent discount can be taken if the account is paid within 10 days; otherwise it must be paid within 30 days. Failure to take the discount represents a cost to the customer. For instance, if the terms are 2/10, net 30, the annualized opportunity cost of passing up this 2 percent discount in order to withhold payment for an additional 20 days is 36.73 percent. This is determined as follows:

terms of sale

$$\text{Annualized opportunity cost of forgoing the discount} = \frac{a}{1-a} \times \frac{360}{c-b} \qquad \textbf{(16-3)}$$

Substituting the values from the example, we get

$$36.73\% = \frac{.02}{1-.02} \times \frac{360}{30-10}$$

In industry the typical discount ranges anywhere from 1/2 to 10 percent, whereas the discount period is generally 10 days and the total credit period varies from 30 to 90 days. Although the terms of credit vary radically from industry to industry, they tend to remain relatively uniform within any particular industry. Moreover, the terms tend to remain relatively constant over time, and they do not appear to be used frequently as a decision variable.

TYPE OF CUSTOMER—DECISION VARIABLE

A second decision variable involves determining the *type of customer* who qualifies for trade credit. Several costs always are associated with extending credit to less-creditworthy customers. First, as the probability of default increases, it becomes more important that the firm be able to identify which of the possible new customers is a poor risk. When more time is spent investigating the less-creditworthy customer, the costs of credit investigation increase.

Default costs also vary directly with the quality of the customer. As the customer's credit rating declines, the chance that the account will not be paid on time increases. In the extreme case, payment never occurs. Thus, taking on less-creditworthy customers results in increases in default costs.

Collection costs also increase as the quality of the customer declines. More delinquent accounts force the firm to spend more time and money collecting them. Overall, the decline in customer quality results in increased costs of credit investigation, collection, and default.

In determining whether to grant credit to an individual customer, we are primarily interested in the customer's short-run financial well-being. Thus, liquidity ratios, other obligations, and the overall profitability of the firm become the focal point in this analysis. Credit-rating services, such as Dun & Bradstreet, provide information on the financial status, operations, and payment history for most firms. Other possible sources of information would include credit bureaus, trade associations, chambers of commerce, competitors, bank references, public financial statements, and, of course, the firm's past relationship with the customer.

credit scoring

One way in which both individuals and firms are often evaluated as credit risks is through the use of credit scoring. **Credit scoring** involves the *numerical evaluation of each applicant*. An applicant receives a score based on his or her answers to a simple set of questions. This score is then evaluated according to a predetermined standard to determine whether credit should be extended. The major advantage of credit scoring is that it is inexpensive and easy to perform. For example, once the standards are set, a computer or clerical worker without any specialized training can easily evaluate any applicant.

The techniques used for constructing credit-scoring indexes range from the simple approach to adding up default rates associated with the answers given to each question, to sophisticated evaluations using multiple discriminate analysis (MDA). MDA is a statistical technique for calculating the appropriate importance to assign each question used in evaluating the applicant.

Edward Altman used multiple discriminant analysis to identify businesses that might go bankrupt. In his landmark study, Altman used financial ratios to develop the following index:

$$Z = 3.3\left(\frac{EBIT}{\text{total assets}}\right) + 1.0\left(\frac{\text{sales}}{\text{total assets}}\right) + .06\left(\frac{\text{market value of equity}}{\text{book value of debt}}\right) + 1.4\left(\frac{\text{retained earnings}}{\text{total assets}}\right) + 1.2\left(\frac{\text{working capital}}{\text{total assets}}\right) \quad \text{(16-4)}$$

Thus, to use the Altman Z-score model to predict a firm's likelihood of bankruptcy, we substitute the firm's values for each of the predictor variables on the right-hand side of equation (16-4). Altman found that firms that went bankrupt sometime during the next year tended to have a Z-score below 2.7, whereas firms that did not go bankrupt had Z-scores larger than 2.7.

EXAMPLE

To see how the credit-scoring model is used, let's consider the credit application of Jamison Electric Corporation. Column D contains the products of the credit-scoring model coefficients found in column B and Jamison's financial attributes found in column C. Adding up all the individual product terms produces a credit score of 2.00. Because this credit score is less than 2.7, we would anticipate that there is a high likelihood that Jamison will become bankrupt sometime during the coming year.[3]

---

[3]We should caution the user that the Z-score model was not a perfect predictor (although it was quite good). For example, of 100 firms that actually did go bankrupt over the period of one year, Altman found that the model correctly classified 94 firms. Similarly, of 100 firms that did not go bankrupt, the model correctly classified 97 as nonbankrupt.

	A	B	C	D
1	Variable	Coefficient	Firm Value	Product
2	EBIT/total assets	3.30	0.10	0.33
3	sales/total assets	1.00	0.85	0.85
4	market value of equity/book value of debt	0.06	4.00	0.24
5	retained earnings/total assets	1.40	0.20	0.28
6	Working capital/total assets	1.20	0.25	0.30
7			Z =	2.00
8				

COLLECTION EFFORTS—DECISION VARIABLE

The key to maintaining control over collection of accounts receivable is the fact that the probability of default increases with the age of the account. Thus, control of accounts receivable focuses on the control and elimination of past-due receivables. One common way of evaluating the current situation is *ratio analysis*. The financial manager can determine whether accounts receivables are under control by examining the average collection period, the ratio of receivables to assets, the ratio of credit sales to receivables (called the accounts-receivable turnover ratio), and the amount of bad debts relative to sales over time. In addition, the manager can perform what is called an aging of accounts receivable to provide a breakdown in both dollars and percentages of the proportion of receivables that are past due. Comparing the current aging of receivables with past data offers even more control.

Once the delinquent accounts have been identified, the firm's accounts-receivable group makes an effort to collect them. For example, a past-due letter, called a *dunning letter*, is sent if payment is not received on time, followed by an additional dunning letter in a more serious tone if the account becomes 3 weeks past due, followed after 6 weeks by a telephone call. Finally, if the account becomes 12 weeks past due, it might be turned over to a collection agency. Again, a direct trade-off exists between collection expenses and lost goodwill on one hand and noncollection of accounts on the other, and this trade-off is always part of making the decision.

INVENTORY MANAGEMENT

Objective **7**

inventory management

Inventory management involves the *control of the assets that are produced to be sold in the normal course of the firm's operations.* The general categories of inventory include raw-materials inventory, work-in-process inventory, and finished-goods inventory. The importance of the inventory management to the firm depends on the extent of the inventory investment. For an average firm, approximately 4.88 percent of all assets are in the form of inventory. However, the percentage varies widely from industry to industry. Thus, the importance of inventory management and control varies from industry to industry also. For example, it is much more important in the automotive dealer and service station trade, in which inventories make up 49.72 percent of total assets, than in the hotel business, in which the average investment in inventory is only 1.56 percent of total assets.

TYPES OF INVENTORY

The purpose of carrying inventories is to uncouple the operations of the firm—that is, to make each function of the business independent of each other function—so that delays or shutdowns in one area do not affect the production and sale of the final product. Because production shutdowns result in increased costs, and because delays in delivery can lose customers, the management and control of inventory are important duties of the financial manager.

Decision making in investment in inventory involves a basic trade-off between risk and return. The risk is that if the level of inventory is too low, the various functions of business do not operate independently, and delays in product and customer delivery can result. The

return results because reduced inventory investment saves money. As the size of inventory increases, storage and handling costs as well as the required return on capital invested in inventory rise. Therefore, as the inventory a firm holds is increased, the risk of running out of inventory is lessened, but inventory expenses rise.

RAW-MATERIALS INVENTORY

raw-materials inventory

Raw-materials inventory consists of *basic materials purchased from other firms to be used in the firm's production operations.* These goods may include steel, lumber, petroleum, or manufactured items such as wire, ball bearings, or tires that the firm does not produce itself. Regardless of the specific form of the raw-materials inventory, all manufacturing firms by definition maintain a raw-materials inventory. Its purpose is to uncouple the production function from the purchasing function—that is, to make these two functions independent of each other—so delays in shipment of raw materials do not cause production delays. In the event of a delay in shipment, the firm can satisfy its need for raw materials by liquidating its inventory.

WORK-IN-PROCESS INVENTORY

work-in-process inventory

Work-in-process inventory consists of *partially finished goods requiring additional work before they become finished goods.* The more complex and lengthy the production process, the larger the investment in work-in-process inventory. The purpose of work-in-process inventory is to uncouple the various operations in the production process so that machine failures and work stoppages in one operation will not affect the other operations. Assume, for example, there are 10 different production operations, each one involving the piece of work produced in the previous operation. If the machine performing the first production operation breaks down, a firm with no work-in-process inventory will have to shut down all 10 production operations. If a firm has such inventory, all remaining 9 operations can continue by drawing the input for the second operation from inventory.

FINISHED-GOODS INVENTORY

finished-goods inventory

Finished-goods inventory consists of *goods on which production has been completed but that are not yet sold.* The purpose of a finished-goods inventory is to uncouple the production and sales functions so that it is not necessary to produce the goods before a sale can occur—sales can be made directly out of inventory. In the auto industry, for example, people would not buy from a dealer who made them wait weeks or months when another dealer could fill the order immediately.

STOCK OF CASH

Although we have already discussed cash management at some length, it is worthwhile to mention cash again in the light of inventory management. This is because the *stock of cash* carried by a firm is simply a special type of inventory. In terms of uncoupling the various operations of the firm, the purpose of holding a stock of cash is to make the payment of bills independent of the collection of accounts due. When cash is kept on hand, bills can be paid without prior collection of accounts.

INVENTORY MANAGEMENT TECHNIQUES

The importance of effective inventory management is directly related to the size of the investment in inventory. Effective management of these assets is essential to the goal of maximizing shareholder wealth. To control the investment in inventory, management must solve two problems: the order quantity problem and the order point problem.

ORDER QUANTITY PROBLEM

order quantity problem

The **order quantity problem** involves *determining the optimal order size for an inventory item given its expected usage, carrying costs, and ordering costs.*

The economic order quantity (*EOQ*) model attempts to determine the order size that will minimize total inventory costs. It assumes that

$$\frac{\text{Total}}{\text{inventory costs}} = \frac{\text{total}}{\text{carrying costs}} + \frac{\text{total}}{\text{ordering costs}}$$

(16-5)

FIGURE 16-6 Inventory Level and the Replenishment Cycle

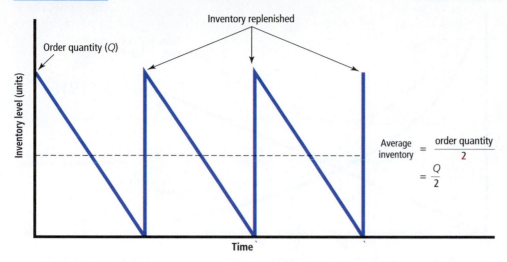

Assuming the inventory is allowed to fall to zero and then is immediately replenished (this assumption will be lifted when we discuss the order point problem), the average inventory becomes $Q/2$, where Q is inventory order size in units. This can be seen graphically in Figure 16-6.

If the average inventory is $Q/2$ and the carrying cost per unit is C, then carrying costs become

$$\frac{\text{Total}}{\text{carrying costs}} = \left(\frac{\text{average}}{\text{inventory}}\right)\left(\frac{\text{carrying cost}}{\text{per unit}}\right)$$

$$= \left(\frac{Q}{2}\right)C$$

(16-6)

where Q = the inventory order size in units
C = the carrying cost per unit

The carrying costs on inventory include the required rate of return on investment in inventory, in addition to warehouse or storage costs, wages for those who operate the warehouse, and costs associated with inventory shrinkage. Thus, carrying costs include both real cash flows and opportunity costs associated with having funds tied up in inventory.

The ordering costs incurred are equal to the ordering costs per order times the number of orders. If we assume total demand over the planning period is S, we order in lot sizes of Q, then S/Q represents the number of orders over the planning period. If the ordering cost per order is O, then

$$\frac{\text{Total}}{\text{ordering costs}} = \left(\frac{\text{number}}{\text{of orders}}\right)\left(\frac{\text{ordering cost}}{\text{per order}}\right)$$

(16-7)

$$= \left(\frac{S}{Q}\right)O$$

(16-7a)

where S = total demand in units over the planning period
O = ordering cost per order

Thus, total costs in equation (16-5) become

$$\text{Total costs} = \left(\frac{Q}{2}\right)C + \left(\frac{S}{Q}\right)O$$

(16-8)

Figure 16-7 illustrates this equation graphically.

TAKIN' IT TO THE NET

Inventory management is critical to many firms, and a whole host of software companies offers tools for managing all aspects of a firm's inventories. For an example of the breadth of areas in which software is available, check out www.accurateid.com and www.datastream.net.

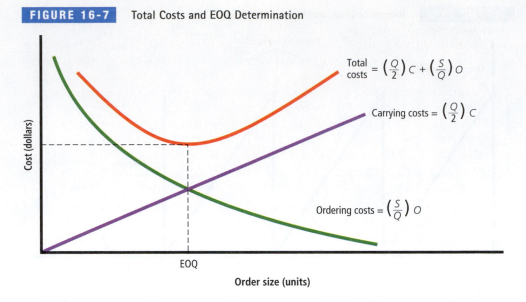

FIGURE 16-7 Total Costs and EOQ Determination

What we are looking for is the order size Q^* that provides the minimum total costs. By manipulating equation (16-8), we find that the optimal value of Q—that is, the economic order quantity (EOQ)—is

$$Q^* = \sqrt{\frac{2SO}{C}} \qquad\qquad (16\text{-}9)$$

The use of the EOQ model can best be illustrated through an example.

EXAMPLE

Suppose a firm expects total demand (S) for its product over the planning period to be 5,000 units, and the ordering cost per order (O) is \$200 and the carrying cost per unit (C) is \$2. Substituting these values into equation (16-9) yields

$$Q^* = \sqrt{\frac{2 \cdot 5,000 \cdot 200}{2}} = \sqrt{1,000,000} = 1,000 \text{ units}$$

Thus, if this firm orders in 1,000-unit lot sizes, it will minimize its total inventory costs.

EXAMINATION OF *EOQ* ASSUMPTIONS

Despite the fact that the EOQ model tends to yield quite good results, there are weaknesses associated with several of its assumptions. When its assumptions have been dramatically violated, the EOQ model can generally be modified to accommodate the situation. The model's assumptions are as follows:

1. **Constant or uniform demand.** Although the EOQ model assumes constant demand, demand may vary from day to day. If demand is stochastic—that is, not known in advance—the model must be modified through the inclusion of a safety stock.
2. **Constant unit price.** The inclusion of variable prices resulting from quantity discounts can be handled quite easily through a modification of the original EOQ model, redefining total costs and solving for the optimum order quantity.
3. **Constant carrying costs.** Unit carrying costs may vary substantially as the size of the inventory rises, perhaps decreasing because of economies of scale or storage efficiency or increasing as storage space runs out and new warehouses have to be rented. This sit-

uation can be handled through a modification in the original model similar to the one used for variable unit price.

4. **Constant ordering costs.** Although this assumption is generally valid, its violation can be accommodated by modifying the original *EOQ* model in a manner similar to the one used for variable unit price.

5. **Instantaneous delivery.** If delivery is not instantaneous, which is generally the case, the original EOQ model must be modified through the inclusion of a safety stock, that is, the inventory held to accommodate any unusually large and unexpected usage during the delivery time.

6. **Independent orders.** If multiple orders result in cost savings by reducing paperwork and transportation cost, the original *EOQ* model must be further modified. Although this modification is somewhat complicated, special *EOQ* models have been developed to deal with it.

These assumptions illustrate the limitations of the basic *EOQ* model and the ways in which it can be modified to compensate for them. An understanding of the limitations and assumptions of the *EOQ* model provides the financial manager with more of a base for making inventory decisions.

ORDER POINT PROBLEM

The two most limiting assumptions—those of constant or uniform demand and instantaneous delivery—are dealt with through the inclusion of **safety stock**, which is the *inventory held to accommodate any unusually large and unexpected usage during delivery time*. The *decision on how much safety stock to hold* is generally referred to as the **order point problem**; that is, how low should inventory be depleted before it is reordered?

Two factors that go into the determination of the appropriate order point: (1) the procurement or delivery-time stock and (2) the safety stock desired. Figure 16-8 graphs the process involved in order point determination. We observe that the order point problem can be decomposed into its two components, the **delivery-time stock**—that is, the *inventory needed between the order date and the receipt of the inventory ordered*—and the safety stock. Thus, the order point is reached when inventory falls to a level equal to the delivery-time stock plus the safety stock.

$$\begin{array}{l}\text{Inventory order point} \\ \text{[order new inventory} \\ \text{when the level of inventory} \\ \text{falls to this level]}\end{array} = \begin{array}{c}\text{delivery-time} \\ \text{stock}\end{array} + \begin{array}{c}\text{safety} \\ \text{stock}\end{array} \qquad \textbf{(16-10)}$$

safety stock

order point problem

delivery-time stock

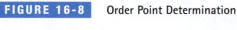

FIGURE 16-8   Order Point Determination

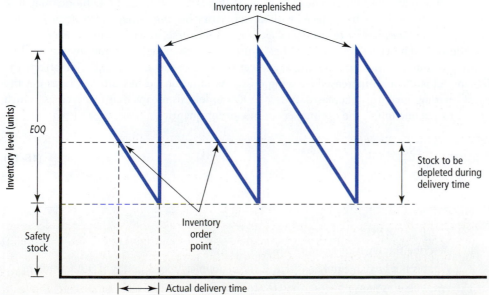

As a result of constantly carrying safety stock, the average level of inventory increases. Whereas before the inclusion of safety stock the average level of inventory was equal to $EOQ/2$, now it will be

$$\text{Average inventory} = \frac{EOQ}{2} + \text{safety stock} \qquad \text{(16-11)}$$

In general, several factors simultaneously determine how much delivery-time stock and safety stock should be held. First, the efficiency of the replenishment system affects how much delivery-time stock is needed. Because the delivery-time stock is the expected inventory usage between ordering and receiving inventory, efficient replenishment of inventory would reduce the need for delivery-time stock.

The uncertainty surrounding both the delivery time and the demand for the product affects the level of safety stock needed. The more certain the patterns of these inflows and outflows from the inventory, the less safety stock required. In effect, if these inflows and outflows are highly predictable, then there is little chance of any stock-out occurring. However, if they are unpredictable, it becomes necessary to carry additional safety stock to prevent unexpected stock-outs.

The safety margin desired also affects the level of safety stock held. If it is a costly experience to run out of inventory, the safety stock held will be larger than it would be otherwise. If running out of inventory and the subsequent delay in supplying customers result in strong customer dissatisfaction and the possibility of lost future sales, then additional safety stock is necessary. A final determinant is the cost of carrying additional inventory, in terms of both the handling and storage costs and the opportunity cost associated with the investment in additional inventory. Very simply, the greater the costs, the smaller the safety stock.

just-in-time inventory control system

Over the past decade or so, a different technique aimed at reducing the firm's investment in inventory has been adopted by numerous companies. It is known as the **just-in-time inventory control system**. The aim is to operate with the *lowest average level of inventory possible*. Within the *EOQ* model, the basics are to reduce (1) ordering costs and (2) safety stocks. This is achieved by attempting to receive an almost continuous flow of deliveries of component parts. The result is to actually have about 2 to 4 hours worth of inventory on hand. In effect, trucks, railroads, and airplanes become the firm's warehouses. This system has spawned a new emphasis on the dual relationship between the firm and its suppliers.

INFLATION AND *EOQ*

anticipatory buying

Inflation affects the *EOQ* model in two major ways. First, although the *EOQ* model can be modified to assume constant price increases, often major price increases occur only once or twice a year and are announced ahead of time. If this is the case, the *EOQ* model may lose its predictability and may be replaced with **anticipatory buying**—that is, *buying in anticipation of a price increase to secure the goods at a lower cost*. Of course, as with most decisions, there are trade-offs. The costs are the added carrying costs associated with the inventory. The benefits, of course, come from buying at a lower price. The second way inflation affects the *EOQ* model is through increased carrying costs. As inflation pushes interest rates up, the cost of carrying inventory increases. In our *EOQ* model this means that C increases, which results in a decline in Q^*, the optimal economic order quantity.

$$\downarrow Q^* = \sqrt{\frac{2SO}{C \uparrow}} \qquad \text{(16-12)}$$

CONCEPT CHECK

1. Describe the types of inventory that firms have.
2. What is the fundamental objective of the economic order quantity (*EOQ*) formula?
3. What assumptions underlie the *EOQ* formula?

SUMMARY

As you recall, several of the principles that form the foundations of financial management relate to the importance of cash and cash flows. In this chapter, we have developed many of the tools that a financial manager needs to manage the firm's cash and other current assets with the overall objective of ensuring that the firm has an appropriate level of liquidity or net working capital to carry out the goal of maximizing shareholder wealth.

Why a company holds cash

The firm experiences both regular and irregular cash flows. Once cash is obtained, the firm has three motives for holding cash rather than investing it: to satisfy transactions, precautionary, and speculative liquidity needs. To a certain extent, such needs can be satisfied by holding readily marketable securities rather than cash. A significant challenge of cash management, then, is dealing with the trade-off between the firm's need to have cash on hand to pay liabilities that arise in the course of doing business and the objective of maximizing wealth by minimizing idle cash balances that earn no return.

Objective **1**

Cash management objectives and decisions
Collection and disbursement procedures

Various procedures exist to improve the efficiency of a firm's cash management. Such procedures focus not only (although primarily) on accelerating the firm's cash receipts but also on improving the methods for disbursing cash. Generally, at the heart of attempts to accelerate cash receipts is a significant effort to reduce the mail, processing, and transit elements of the float.

Objective **2**

Objective **3**

On the cash disbursements side, firms try to prolong the time cash stays in their own accounts by increasing the disbursement float through the use of zero balance accounts; payable-through drafts; and, especially, remote disbursing. The first two methods also offer much better central-office control over disbursements. Before any collection or disbursement procedure is introduced, however, a careful analysis should be performed to ensure that expected benefits outweigh the expected costs of such procedures.

Evaluation of costs of cash management services
Composition of marketable-securities portfolio

Because idle cash earns no return, a financial manager looks for opportunities to invest such cash until it is required in the operations of the company. A variety of different readily marketable securities, described in the chapter, are available in the market today. The yields on such securities vary depending on four factors: the (1) financial risk, (2) interest rate risk, (3) liquidity, and (4) taxability of the security. By simultaneously taking into account these factors and the desired rate of return, the financial manager is able to determine the most suitable mix of cash and marketable securities for the firm.

Objective **4**

Objective **5**

Accounts-receivable management

When we consider that accounts receivable constitute approximately 25 percent of total assets for the typical firm, the importance of accounts-receivable management becomes even more apparent. The size of a firm's investment in accounts receivable depends on three factors: the percentage of credit sales to total sales, the level of sales, and the credit and collection policies of the firm. The financial manager, however, generally only has control over the terms of the sale, the quality of the customer, and the collection efforts.

Objective **6**

Inventory management

Although the level of investment in inventories by the typical firm is less than the investment in accounts receivable, inventory management and control remains an important function of the financial manager because inventories play a significant role in the operations of the firm. The purpose of holding inventory is to make each function of the business independent of the other functions. The primary issues related to inventory management are (1) How much inventory should be ordered? and (2) When should the order be placed? The *EOQ* model is used to answer the first of these questions. The order point model, which depends on the desired levels of delivery-time stock and safety stock, is applied to answer the second question. The relatively new just-in-time approach to inventory control is growing in popularity as an attempt to obtain additional cost savings by reducing the level of inventory a firm needs to have on hand. Instead of depending solely on its own inventories, the firm relies on its vendors to furnish supplies "just in time" to satisfy the firm's production requirements.

Objective **7**

KEY TERMS

Anticipatory buying, 516

Cash, 491

Credit scoring, 510

Delivery-time stock, 515

Finished-goods inventory, 512

Float, 495

Insolvency, 494

Inventory management, 511

Just-in-time inventory control system, 516

Marketable securities, 491

Order point problem, 515

Order quantity problem, 512

Payable-through drafts (PTDs), 500

Raw-materials inventory, 512

Remote disbursing, 501

Safety stock, 515

Terms of sale, 509

Work-in-process inventory, 512

Zero balance accounts (ZBAs), 500

STUDY QUESTIONS

16-1. What is meant by the cash flow process?

16-2. Identify the principal motives for holding cash and near-cash assets. Explain the purpose of each motive.

16-3. What is concentration banking and how may it be of value to the firm?

16-4. What are the two major objectives of the firm's cash management system?

16-5. What three decisions dominate the cash management process?

16-6. Within the context of cash management, what are the key elements of (total) float? Briefly define each element.

16-7. Distinguish between *financial risk* and *interest rate risk* as these terms are commonly used in discussions of cash management.

16-8. Your firm invests in only three different classes of marketable securities: commercial paper, Treasury bills, and federal agency securities. Recently, yields on these money-market instruments of 3 months' maturity were quoted at 6.10, 6.25, and 5.90 percent. Match the available yields with the types of instruments your firm purchases.

16-9. What factors determine the size of the investment a firm makes in accounts receivable? Which of these factors are under the control of the financial manager?

16-10. If a credit manager experienced no bad-debt losses over the past year, would this be an indication of proper credit management? Why or why not?

16-11. What are the risk–return trade-offs associated with adopting a more liberal trade credit policy?

16-12. What is the purpose of holding inventory? Name several types of inventory and describe their purpose.

16-13. Can cash be considered a special type of inventory? If so, what functions does it attempt to uncouple?

16-14. What are the major assumptions made by the *EOQ* model?

16-15. How might inflation affect the *EOQ* model?

SELF-TEST PROBLEMS

ST-1. (*Buying and selling marketable securities*) Mountaineer Outfitters has $2 million in excess cash that it might invest in marketable securities. To buy and sell the securities, however, the firm must pay a transaction fee of $45,000.

   a. Would you recommend purchasing the securities if they yield 12 percent annually and are held for

   1. One month?   4. Six months?

   2. Two months?   5. One year?

   3. Three months?

  b. What minimum required yield would the securities have to return for the firm to hold them for 3 months? (What is the break-even yield for a 3-month holding period?)

ST-2. (*EOQ calculations*) Consider the following inventory information and relationships for the F. Beamer Corporation:

1. Orders can be placed only in multiples of 100 units.
2. Annual unit usage is 300,000. (Assume a 50-week year in your calculations.)
3. The carrying cost is 30 percent of the purchase price of the goods.
4. The purchase price is $10 per unit.
5. The ordering cost is $50 per order.
6. The desired safety stock is 1,000 units. (This does not include delivery-time stock.)
7. Delivery time is 2 weeks.

Given this information

  a. What is the optimal *EOQ* level?
  b. How many orders will be placed annually?
  c. At what inventory level should a reorder be made?

STUDY PROBLEMS

16-1. (*Buying and selling marketable securities*) Pearl Islands Tour Operator, located in the Pacific Ocean near Panama City, has effectively collected $1,500,000 in excess cash that it plans to invest in marketable securities. The firm will have to pay total transaction costs of $30,000 to buy and sell the securities.

  a. Would you recommend purchasing the securities if they yield 8.25 percent annually and are held for
    1. One month?
    2. Two months?
    3. Three months?
    4. Six months?
    5. One year?
  b. What minimum required yield would the securities have to return for the firm to hold them for 3 months? (What is the break-even yield for a 3-month holding period?)

16-2. (*Cost of services*) As CFO of Portobello Scuba Diving, Inc. you are asked to look into the possibility of adopting a lockbox system to expedite cash receipts from clients. Portobello receives remittances totaling $24 million by check in a year. The firm records and processes 10,000 checks in the same period. The National Bank of Brazil has informed you that it could provide the service of expediting checks and associated documents through the lockbox system for a unit cost of $0.25 per check. After conducting an analysis, you project that cash freed up by the adoption of the system can be invested in a portfolio of near-cash assets that will yield an annual before-tax return of 8 percent. The company usually uses a 365-day year in its procedures.

  a. What reduction in check collection time is necessary for Portobello to be neither better nor worse off for having adopted the lockbox system?
  b. How would your solution to part **a** be affected if Portobello could invest the freed-up balances at an expected annual return of only 4 percent?
  c. What is the logical explanation for the differences in your answers to part **a** and part **b**?

16-3. (*Concentration banking*) Byron Sporting Goods operates in Miami, Florida. The firm produces and distributes a full line of athletic equipment on a nationwide basis. The firm currently uses a centralized billing system. Byron Sporting Goods has annual credit sales of $438 million. Austin National Bank has presented an offer to operate a concentration-banking system for the company. Byron already has an established line of credit with Austin. Austin says it will operate the system on a flat-fee basis of $200,000 per year. The analysis done by the bank's cash-management services division suggests that 3 days in mail float and 1 day in processing float can be eliminated.

Because Byron borrows almost continuously from Austin National, the value of the float reduction would be applied against the line of credit. The borrowing rate on the line of credit is set at an annual rate of 8 percent. Furthermore, because of the reduction in clerical help, the new system will save the firm $66,000 in processing costs. Byron uses a 365-day year in analyses of this sort. Should Byron accept the bank's offer to install the new system?

16-4. (*Concentration banking*) Treemont Shops operates in Naples, Florida. The firm distributes specialty gardening supplies nationwide. The firm currently uses a centralized billing system.

Treemont has annual credit sales of $362 million. Lasdon National Bank has presented an offer to operate a concentration-banking system for the company. Treemont already has an established line of credit with Lasdon. The bank says it will operate the system on a flat-fee basis of $175,000 per year. The analysis done by the bank's cash-management services division suggests that 3 days in mail float and 1 day in processing float can be eliminated. Because Treemont borrows almost continuously, the value of the float reduction would be applied against the line of credit. The borrowing rate on the line of credit is set at an annual rate of 7 percent. Furthermore, because of the reduction in clerical help, the new system will save the firm $57,500 in processing costs. Treemont uses a 365-day year in analyses of this sort. Should Treemont's management accept the bank's offer to install the new system?

16-5. (*Buying and selling marketable securities*) Miami Dice & Card Company has generated $800,000 in excess cash that it could invest in marketable securities. In order to buy and sell the securities, the firm will pay total transaction fees of $20,000.

    a. Would you recommend purchasing the securities if they yield 10.5 percent annually and are held for

        1. One month?
        2. Two months?
        3. Three months?
        4. Six months?
        5. One year?

    b. What minimum required yield would the securities have to return for the firm to hold them for 2 months? (What is the break-even yield for a 2-month holding period?)

16-6. (*Costs of services*) Mustang Ski-Wear, Inc., is investigating the possibility of adopting a lockbox system as a cash receipts acceleration device. In a typical year this firm receives remittances totaling $12 million by check. The firm will record and process 6,000 checks over this same period. The Colorado Springs Second National Bank has informed the management of Mustang that it will expedite checks and associated documents through the lockbox system for a unit cost of $0.20 per check. Mustang's financial manager has projected that cash freed up by adoption of the system can be invested in a portfolio of near-cash assets that will yield an annual before-tax return of 7 percent. Mustang financial analysts use a 365-day year in their procedures.

    a. What reduction in check collection time is necessary for Mustang to be neither better nor worse off for having adopted the proposed system?

    b. How would your solution to part **a** be affected if Mustang could invest the freed-up balances at an expected annual return of only 4.5 percent?

    c. What is the logical explanation for the difference in your answers to part **a** and part **b**?

16-7. (*Lockbox system*) Penn Steelworks is a distributor of cold-rolled steel products to the automobile industry. All its sales are on a credit basis, net 30 days. Sales are evenly distributed over its 10 sales regions throughout the United States. Delinquent accounts are no problem. The company has recently undertaken an analysis aimed at improving its cash management procedures. Penn determined that it takes an average of 3.2 days for customers' payments to reach the head office in Pittsburgh from the time they are mailed. It takes another full day in processing time prior to depositing the checks with a local bank. Annual sales average $4.8 million for each regional office. Reasonable investment opportunities can be found yielding 7 percent per year. To alleviate the float problem confronting the firm, the use of a lockbox system in each of the 10 regions is being considered. This would reduce mail float by 1.2 days. One day in processing float would also be eliminated, plus a full day in transit float. The lockbox arrangement would cost each region $250 per month.

    a. What is the opportunity cost to Penn Steelworks of the funds tied up in mailing and processing? Use a 365-day year.

    b. What would the net cost or savings be from use of the proposed cash acceleration technique? Should Penn adopt the system?

16-8. (*Cash receipts acceleration system*) Peggy Pierce Designs, Inc. is a vertically integrated, national manufacturer and retailer of women's clothing. Currently, the firm has no coordinated cash management system. A proposal, however, from the First Pennsylvania Bank aimed at speeding up cash collections is being examined by several of Pierce's corporate executives.

The firm currently uses a centralized billing procedure, which requires that all checks be mailed to the Philadelphia head office for processing and eventual deposit. Under this arrangement all the customers' remittance checks take an average of 5 business days to reach the head office. Once in Philadelphia, another 2 days are required to process the checks for ultimate deposit at the First Pennsylvania Bank.

The firm's daily remittances average $1 million. The average check size is $2,000. Pierce Designs currently earns 6 percent annually on its marketable-securities portfolio.

The cash acceleration plan proposed by officers of First Pennsylvania involves both a lockbox system and concentration banking. First Pennsylvania would be the firm's only concentration bank. Lockboxes would be established in (1) San Francisco, (2) Dallas, (3) Chicago, and (4) Philadelphia. This would reduce funds tied up by mail float to 3 days, and processing float will be eliminated. Funds would then be transferred twice each business day by means of automated depository transfer checks from local banks in San Francisco, Dallas, and Chicago to the First Pennsylvania Bank. Each DTC costs $15. These transfers will occur all 270 business days of the year. Each check processed through the lockbox system will cost $0.18.

    a. What amount of cash balances will be freed up if Peggy Pierce Designs, Inc., adopts the system suggested by First Pennsylvania?

    b. What is the opportunity cost of maintaining the current banking setup?

    c. What is the projected annual cost of operating the proposed system?

    d. Should Pierce adopt the new system? Compute the net annual gain or loss associated with adopting the system.

16-9. (*Marketable-securities portfolio*) The Alex Daniel Shoe Manufacturing Company currently pays its employees on a weekly basis. The weekly wage bill is $500,000. This means that on average the firm has accrued wages payable of ($500,000 + $0)/2 = $250,000.

Alex Daniel, Jr., works as the firm's senior financial analyst and reports directly to his father, who owns all of the firm's common stock. Alex Daniel, Jr., wants to move to a monthly wage-payment system. Employees would be paid at the end of every fourth week. The younger Daniel is fully aware that the labor union representing the company's workers will not permit the monthly payments system to take effect unless the workers are given some type of fringe benefit compensation. A plan has been worked out whereby the firm will make a contribution to the cost of life insurance coverage for each employee. This will cost the firm $35,000 annually. Alex Daniel, Jr., expects the firm to earn 7 percent annually on its marketable-securities portfolio.

    a. Based on the projected information, should Daniel Shoe Manufacturing move to the monthly wage-payment system?

    b. What annual rate of return on the marketable-securities portfolio would enable the firm to just break even on this proposal?

16-10. (*Valuing float reduction*) The Cowboy Bottling Company will generate $12 million in credit sales next year. Collection of these credit sales will occur evenly over this period. The firm's employees work 270 days a year. Currently, the firm's processing system ties up 4 days' worth of remittance checks. A recent report from a financial consultant indicated procedures that will enable Cowboy Bottling to reduce processing float by 2 full days. If Cowboy invests the released funds to earn 6 percent, what will be the annual savings?

16-11. (*Accounts payable policy and cash management*) Bradford Construction Supply Company is suffering from a prolonged decline in new construction in its sales area. In an attempt to improve its cash position, the firm is considering changes in its accounts-payable policy. After careful study, it has determined that the only alternative available is to slow disbursements. Purchases for the coming year are expected to be $37.5 million. Sales will be $65 million, which represents about a 20 percent drop from the current year. Currently, Bradford discounts approximately 25 percent of its payments at 3 percent, 10 days, net 30, and the balance of accounts is paid in 30 days. If Bradford adopts a policy of payment in 45 days or 60 days, how much can the firm gain if the annual opportunity cost of investment is 12 percent? What will be the result if this action causes Bradford Construction suppliers to increase their prices to the company by $\frac{1}{2}$ percent to compensate for the 60-day extended term of payment? In your calculations, use a 365-day year and ignore any compounding effects related to expected returns.

16-12. (*Interest rate risk*) Two years ago your corporate treasurer purchased for the firm a 20-year bond at its par value of $1,000. The coupon rate on this security is 8 percent. Interest payments are made to bondholders once a year. Currently, bonds of this particular risk class are yielding investors 9 percent. A cash shortage has forced you to instruct your treasurer to liquidate this bond.

    a. At what price will your bond be sold? Assume annual compounding.

    b. What will be the amount of your gain or loss over the original purchase price?

    c. What would be the amount of your gain or loss had the treasurer originally purchased a bond with a 4-year rather than a 20-year maturity? (Assume all characteristics of the bonds are identical except their maturity periods.)

    d. What do we call this type of risk assumed by your corporate treasurer?

16-13. (*Comparison of after-tax yields*) The corporate treasurer of Aggieland Fireworks is considering the purchase of a BBB-rated bond that carries a 9 percent coupon. The BBB-rated security is taxable, and the firm is in the 46 percent marginal tax bracket. The face value of this bond is $1,000.

A financial analyst who reports to the corporate treasurer has alerted him to the fact that a municipal obligation is coming to the market with a $5\frac{1}{2}$ percent coupon. The par value of this security is also $1,000.

    a. Which one of the two securities do you recommend the firm purchase? Why?

    b. What must the fully taxed bond yield before tax to make it comparable with the municipal offering?

16-14. (*Trade credit discounts*) Determine the effective annualized cost of forgoing the trade credit discount on the following terms:

    a. 1/10, net 20

    b. 2/10, net 30

    c. 3/10, net 30

    d. 3/10, net 60

    e. 3/10, net 90

    f. 5/10, net 60

16-15. (*Altman model*) The following ratios were supplied by six loan applicants. Given this information and the credit-scoring model developed by Altman (equation [16-4]), which loans have a high probability of defaulting next year?

	EBIT ÷ TOTAL ASSETS	SALES ÷ TOTAL ASSETS	MARKET VALUE OF EQUITY ÷ BOOK VALUE OF DEBT	RETAINED EARNINGS ÷ TOTAL ASSETS	WORKING CAPITAL ÷ TOTAL ASSETS
Applicant 1	.2	.2	1.2	.3	.5
Applicant 2	.2	.8	1.0	.3	.8
Applicant 3	.2	.7	.6	.3	.4
Applicant 4	.1	.4	1.2	.4	.4
Applicant 5	.3	.7	.5	.4	.7
Applicant 6	.2	.5	.5	.4	.4

16-16. (*Ratio analysis*) Assuming a 360-day year, calculate what the average investment in inventory would be for a firm, given the following information in each case.

    a. The firm has sales of $600,000, a gross profit margin of 10 percent, and an inventory turnover ratio of 6.

    b. The firm has a cost-of-goods sold figure of $480,000 and an average age of inventory of 40 days.

    c. The firm has a cost-of-goods-sold figure of $1.15 million and an inventory turnover rate of 5.

    d. The firm has a sales figure of $25 million, a gross profit margin of 14 percent, and an average age of inventory of 45 days.

16-17. (*EOQ calculations*) A downtown bookstore is trying to determine the optimal order quantity for a popular novel just printed in paperback. The store feels that the book will sell at four times its hardback figures. It would, therefore, sell approximately 3,000 copies in the next year at a price of $1.50. The store buys the book at a wholesale figure of $1. Costs for carrying the book are estimated at $0.10 a copy per year, and it costs $10 to order more books.

    a. Determine the *EOQ*.

    b. What would be the total costs for ordering the books 1, 4, 5, 10, and 15 times a year?

    c. What questionable assumptions are being made by the *EOQ* model?

16-18. (*Comprehensive EOQ calculations*) Knutson Products, Inc., is involved in the production of airplane parts and has the following inventory, carrying, and storage costs:

1. Orders must be placed in round lots of 100 units.
2. Annual unit usage is 250,000. (Assume a 50-week year in your calculations.)
3. The carrying cost is 10 percent of the purchase price.
4. The purchase price is $10 per unit.
5. The ordering cost is $100 per order.
6. The desired safety stock is 5,000 units. (This does not include delivery-time stock.)
7. The delivery time is 1 week.

Given the foregoing information:

- **a.** Determine the optimal *EOQ* level.
- **b.** How many orders will be placed annually?
- **c.** What is the inventory order point? (That is, at what level of inventory should a new order be placed?)
- **d.** What is the average inventory level?
- **e.** What would happen to the *EOQ* if annual unit sales doubled (all other unit costs and safety stocks remaining constant)? What is the elasticity of *EOQ* with respect to sales? (That is, what is the percentage change in *EOQ* divided by the percentage change in sales?)
- **f.** If carrying costs double, what will happen to the *EOQ* level? (Assume the original sales level of 250,000 units.) What is the elasticity of *EOQ* with respect to carrying costs?
- **g.** If the ordering costs double, what will happen to the level of *EOQ*? (Again assume original levels of sales and carrying costs.) What is the elasticity of *EOQ* with respect to ordering costs?
- **h.** If the selling price doubles, what will happen to *EOQ*? What is the elasticity of *EOQ* with respect to selling price?

WEB WORKS

16-WW1. Visit www.federalreserve.gov and click on "Research and Data." Find the H.15 (519) report on "Selected Interest Rates." This report is updated and published each week, with the last data entry being for Friday of that week. Here you can check both the available yields on different marketable securities that comprise the firm's short-term portfolio and the yield structure across different investment instruments within the portfolio. Interest rate data are available on commercial paper, certificates of deposit, and U.S. Treasury securities of varying maturities. It is a very useful weekly report.

16-WW2. The Procter & Gamble Company (P&G) is a major producer and distributor of a wide range of consumer goods. Familiar products include Tide, Bounty, Pringles, and Folgers. For fiscal year 2004, which ended June 30, P&G reached an annual sales volume of $51.41 billion, up from $43.38 billion in 2003. Find the firm's 2004 Annual Report at www.pg.com/investing or at www.reportgallery.com. Check out P&G's consolidated balance sheets for 2003 and 2004 on page 46. Now answer these questions dealing with current asset management: (1) What percentage of total current assets was represented by cash and cash equivalents in 2003 and 2004? (2) Was the amount invested in cash and cash equivalents more or less than the amount invested in accounts receivable? (3) Of the following three categories, cash and cash equivalents, accounts receivable, and inventories, which represented the largest investment for P&G each year?

16-WW3. Now call up the 2003 Annual Report for the Walt Disney Company at www.disney.com/investors and go to page 69. There you will find Disney's consolidated balance sheets for 2002 and 2003. We will focus on 2003. Notice that Disney had a total investment in current assets of $8.314 billion at the end of 2003. Now, of all the different current asset accounts, which single one dominated the others in terms of total dollars invested? Is it the same category that dominated P&G's current assets (from question 2)?

COMPREHENSIVE PROBLEM

New Wave Surfing Stuff, Inc. is a manufacturer of surfboards and related gear that sells to exclusive surf shops located in several Atlantic and Pacific mainland coastal towns as well as several Hawaiian locations. The company's headquarters are located in Carlsbad, California, a small southern California coastal town. True to form, the company's officers, all veteran surfers, have been somewhat laid back about various critical areas of financial management. With an economic downturn in California adversely affecting their business, however, the officers of the company have decided to focus intently on ways to improve New Wave's cash flows. The CFO, Willy Bonik, has been requested to forgo any more daytime surfing jaunts until he has wrapped up a plan to accelerate New Wave's cash flows.

In an effort to ensure his quick return to the surf, Willy has decided to focus on what he believes is one of the easiest methods of improving New Wave's cash collections, namely, adoption of a cash receipts acceleration system that includes a lockbox system and concentration banking. Willy is well aware that New Wave's current system leaves much room for improvement. The company's accounts receivable system currently requires that remittances from customers be mailed to the headquarters office for processing and then deposited in the local branch of the Bank of the U.S. Such an arrangement takes a considerable amount of time. The checks take an average of 5 days to reach the Carlsbad headquarters. Then, depending on the surf conditions, processing within the company takes anywhere from 2 to 4 days, with the average from the day of receipt by the company to the day of deposit at the bank being 3 days.

Willy feels pretty certain that such delays are costly. After all, New Wave's average daily collections are $150,000. The average remittance size is $750. If Willy could get these funds into his marketable-securities account more quickly, he could earn an annual rate of 5 percent on such funds. In addition, if he could arrange for someone else to do the processing, Willy could save $55,000 per year in costs related to clerical staffing.

New Wave's banker was pleased to provide Willy with a proposal for a combination of a lockbox system and a concentration-banking system. Bank of the U.S. would be New Wave's concentration bank. Lockboxes would be established in Honolulu, Newport Beach, and Daytona Beach. Each check processed through the lockbox system would cost New Wave $0.30. This arrangement, however, would reduce mail float by an average 2.5 days. The funds so collected would be transferred twice each day, 270 days a year, from each of the local lockbox banks to Bank of the U.S. Each transfer will cost $0.35. The combination of lockbox system and concentration banking would eliminate the time it takes the company to process cash collections, thereby making the funds available for short-term investment.

a. What would be the average amount of cash made available if New Wave were to adopt the system proposed by Bank of the U.S.?

b. What is the annual opportunity cost of maintaining the current cash collection and deposit system?

c. What is the expected annual cost of the complete system proposed by Bank of the U.S.?

d. What is the net gain or loss that is expected to result from the proposed new system? Should New Wave adopt the new system?

SELF-TEST SOLUTIONS

SS-1.

a. Here we must calculate the dollar value of the estimated return for each holding period and compare it with the transaction fee to determine if a gain can be made by investing in the securities. Those calculations and the resultant recommendations follow.

			RECOMMENDATION
1. $2,000,000 (.12) $\left(\frac{1}{12}\right)$	= $20,000	<$45,000	No
2. $2,000,000 (.12) $\left(\frac{2}{12}\right)$	= $40,000	<$45,000	No
3. $2,000,000 (.12) $\left(\frac{3}{12}\right)$	= $60,000	>$45,000	Yes
4. $2,000,000 (.12) $\left(\frac{6}{12}\right)$	= $120,000	>$45,000	Yes
5. $2,000,000 (.12) $\left(\frac{12}{12}\right)$	= $240,000	>$45,000	Yes

b. Let (%) be the required yield. With $2 million to invest for 3 months we have

$2,000,000(%)(3/12) = $45,000

$2,000,000(%)   = $180,000

= $180,000/2,000,000 = 9%

The break-even yield, therefore, is 9 percent.

SS-2.

    a. $EOQ = \sqrt{\dfrac{2SO}{C}}$

             $= \sqrt{\dfrac{2(300,000)(50)}{3}}$

          = 3,162 units, but because orders must be placed in 100-unit lots, the effective *EOQ* becomes 3,200 units

    b. $\dfrac{\text{total usage}}{EOQ} = \dfrac{300,000}{3,200} = 93.75$ orders per year

    c. Inventory order point = delivery time stock + safety stock

$$= \frac{2}{50} \times 300,000 + 1,000$$
$$= 12,000 + 1,000$$
$$= 13,000 \text{ units}$$

CHAPTER 17

International Business Finance

THE GLOBALIZATION OF PRODUCT AND FINANCIAL MARKETS • EXCHANGE RATES • INTEREST-RATE PARITY THEORY • PURCHASING-POWER PARITY THEORY • EXPOSURE TO EXCHANGE RATE RISK • MULTINATIONAL WORKING-CAPITAL MANAGEMENT • INTERNATIONAL FINANCING AND CAPITAL STRUCTURE DECISIONS • DIRECT FOREIGN INVESTMENT

Finding new projects doesn't necessarily mean coming up with a new product; it may mean taking an existing product and applying it to a new market. That's certainly been the direction that McDonald's has taken in recent years. Today, McDonald's operates in over 70 countries with more than 20,000 restaurants. One of the biggest is a 700-seat McDonald's in Moscow. Was this an expensive venture? It certainly was. In fact, the food plants that McDonald's built to supply burgers, fries, and everything else sold there cost more than $60 million.

In addition to the costs, there are a number of other factors that make opening an outlet outside of the United States both different and challenging. First, in order to keep the quality of what McDonald's sells identical with what is served at any McDonald's anywhere in the world, McDonald's spent 6 years putting together a supply chain that would provide the necessary raw materials at the quality level McDonald's demands. On top of that, there are risks associated with the Russian economy and its currency that are well beyond the scope of what is experienced in the United States.

These risks all materialized in 1998, when the Russian economy, along with its currency, the ruble, went in the tank. In an attempt to shore up the economy, the Russian government cut the exchange rate from 6,000 rubles for each U.S. dollar to a new rate of 6 rubles per U.S. dollar—in effect, they cut off three zeros. Unfortunately, that didn't solve the problems the Russian economy faced. In May 1998, the first Russian bank crashed and the value of the ruble started to drop. That summer, the Russian economy lost control, and in August the entire banking system failed.

When it was all over by the end of 1998, the exchange rate had fallen to 23 rubles per dollar, a change of more than 280 percent. Because McDonald's sells its burgers for rubles, when it came time to trade the rubles for U.S. dollars, McDonald's wasn't worth nearly as much as it was the year before. In spite of all this, the Moscow McDonald's has proven to be enormously successful since it opened. In fact, by 2004, McDonald's had 122 stores in 22 Russian cities, opening 20 new stores in 2004 alone, representing a total investment of about $300 million. It all goes to show that not all capital-budgeting projects have to be new products; they can be existing domestic products that are introduced into international markets.

≪ WHAT'S AHEAD ≫

This chapter highlights the complications that an international business faces when it deals in multiple currencies. Effective strategies for the reduction of foreign exchange risk are discussed. Working-capital management and capital structure decisions in the international context are also covered. For the international firm, direct foreign investment is a capital-budgeting decision—with some additional complexities.

Objective **1**

THE GLOBALIZATION OF PRODUCT AND FINANCIAL MARKETS

To say the least, the market for most products crosses many borders. In fact, some industries and states are highly dependent on the international economy. For example, the electronic consumer products and automobile industries are widely considered to be global industries. Ohio ranks fourth in terms of manufactured exports, and more than half of Ohio workers are employed by firms that depend to some extent on exports.

multinational corporation (MNC)

There has also been a rise in the global level of international portfolio and direct investment. Both direct and portfolio investments in the United States have been increasing faster than U.S. investment overseas. Direct investment occurs when the **multinational corporation (MNC)**, *a corporation with holdings and/or operations in more than one country*, has control over the investment, such as when it builds an offshore manufacturing facility. Portfolio investment involves financial assets with maturities greater than 1 year, such as the purchase of foreign stocks and bonds. Total foreign investment in the United States now exceeds such U.S. investment overseas.

A major reason for long-run overseas investments of U.S. companies is the high rates of return obtainable from these investments. The amount of U.S. *direct foreign investment (DFI)* abroad is large and growing. Significant amounts of the total assets, sales, and profits of American MNCs are attributable to foreign investments and foreign operations. Direct foreign investment is not limited to American firms. Many European and Japanese firms have operations abroad, too. During the last decade, these firms have been increasing their sales and setting up production facilities abroad, especially in the United States.

Capital flows between countries for international financial investment have also been increasing. Many firms, investment companies, and individuals invest in the capital markets in foreign countries. The motivation is twofold: to obtain returns higher than those obtainable in the domestic capital markets, and to reduce portfolio risk through international diversification. The increase in world trade and investment activity is reflected in the recent globalization of financial markets. The Eurodollar market is larger than any domestic financial market. U.S. companies are increasingly turning to this market for funds. Even companies and public entities that have no overseas presence are beginning to rely on this market for financing.

In addition, most national financial markets are becoming more integrated with global markets because of the rapid increase in the volume of interest rate and currency swaps. Because of the widespread availability of these swaps, the currency denomination and the source country of financing for many globally integrated companies are dictated by accessibility and relative-cost considerations, regardless of the currency ultimately needed by the firm. Even a *purely domestic firm* that buys all its inputs and sells all its output in its home country is not immune to foreign competition, nor can it totally ignore the workings of the international financial markets.

CONCEPT CHECK

1. Why do U.S. companies invest overseas?

Objective **2**

EXCHANGE RATES

FLOATING EXCHANGE RATES

floating-rate international currency system

Since 1973, a **floating-rate international currency system**, *a system in which exchange rates between different national currencies are allowed to fluctuate with supply and demand conditions*, has been operating. For most currencies, there are no parity rates and no bands within which the currencies fluctuate.[1] Most major currencies, including the U.S. dollar, fluctuate freely, depending on their values as perceived by the traders in foreign exchange markets. A

---

[1]The system of floating rates is referred to as the "floating-rate regime."

country's relative economic strengths, its level of exports and imports, the level of monetary activity, and the deficits or surpluses in its balance of payments (BOP) are all important factors in the determination of exchange rates.[2] Short-term, day-to-day fluctuations in exchange rates are caused by changing supply and demand conditions in the foreign exchange market.

THE EURO: THE NEW CURRENCY OF EUROPE

Since 2002, 11 countries in the European Union have used a new, single currency—the euro. These countries, often referred to as Euroland, are Germany, France, Italy, Spain, Portugal, Belgium, Netherlands, Luxembourg, Ireland, Finland, and Austria. Without question, Germany and France are the big players, accounting for over 50 percent of Euroland's output.

Why did the European Union go to a single currency? For several reasons: First, it makes it easier for goods, people, and services to travel across national borders. As a result, the economies of the European Union should flourish. A common currency eliminates the exchange costs that occur when you have to trade your German marks for French francs. It also eliminates the uncertainty associated with exchange rate fluctuations. It should also help eliminate cost differences for goods in different countries. For example, before the single European currency, "The Classics" Swatch watch was selling for an equivalent of 39.2 euros ($45.97) in Belgium and only 25.7 euros ($30.14) in Italy. With the introduction of the Euro, it made it easier to compare prices and reduce the discrepancies.

What does all this mean for the United States? First, it means the competition from abroad will be stronger. It also makes the exchange rate between the euro and the U.S. dollar a very important exchange rate. If the euro is strong, it should help U.S. exports by making them cheaper. On the other hand, if the euro is weak, U.S. exports may suffer. Fortunately, many U.S. multinational firms appear to be in good shape to cash in on any economic surge that may hit Euroland. For example, look at Wal-Mart, which has 21 stores in Germany. In Germany, Wal-Mart is doing just what it does here in the United States— it is wiping out the competition. For the Germans, this is their first sight of wide aisles— (bigger than some of the local streets)—and discount shopping. The euro will allow Wal-Mart both to offer even more bargains from all over Euroland and to provide a much more diverse selection of goods. That's because in Europe, with all the exchange rate uncertainties, most goods are regional in nature. That's the bottom line: The euro should introduce greater choice and greater competition—both good for the consumer.

THE FOREIGN EXCHANGE MARKET

The foreign exchange market provides a mechanism for the transfer of purchasing power from one currency to another. This market is not a physical entity like the New York Stock Exchange; it is a network of telephone and computer connections among banks, foreign exchange dealers, and brokers. The market operates simultaneously at three levels. At the first level, customers buy and sell foreign exchange (i.e., foreign currency) through their banks. At the second level, banks buy and sell foreign exchange from other banks in the same commercial center. At the last level, banks buy and sell foreign exchange from banks in commercial centers in other countries. Some important commercial centers for foreign exchange trading are New York, London, Zurich, Frankfurt, Hong Kong, Singapore, and Tokyo.

An example illustrates this multilevel trading. A trader in Texas may buy foreign exchange (pounds) from a bank in Houston for payment to a British supplier against some purchase made. The Houston bank, in turn, may purchase the foreign currency (pounds) from a New York bank. The New York bank may buy the pounds from another bank in New York or from a bank in London.

Because this market provides transactions in a continuous manner for a very large volume of sales and purchases, the currency markets are efficient: In other words, it is difficult to make a profit by shopping around from one bank to another. Minute differences in the

TAKIN' IT TO THE NET

Ohio State University provides an outstanding listing of Web sites dealing with international financial management fisher.osu.edu/fin/cern/world.htm. You'll find links to all kinds of excellent sites, all dealing with international finance.

---

[2]The balance of payments for the United States reflects the difference between the import and export of goods (the trade balance) and services. Capital inflows and outflows are tabulated in the capital account.

quotes from different banks are quickly eliminated. Because of the arbitrage mechanism, simultaneous quotes to different buyers in London and New York are likely to be the same.

Two major types of transactions are carried out in the foreign exchange markets: spot and forward transactions.

SPOT EXCHANGE RATES

exchange rate

A typical spot transaction involves an American firm buying foreign currency from its bank and paying for it in dollars. *The price of foreign currency in terms of the domestic currency* is the **exchange rate**. Another type of spot transaction is when an American firm receives foreign currency from abroad. The firm typically would sell the foreign currency to its bank for dollars. These are both **spot transactions** because *one currency is traded for another currency today*. The actual exchange rate quotes are expressed in several different ways, as discussed later. To allow time for the transfer of funds, the *value date* when the currencies are actually exchanged is two days after the spot transaction occurs. Four banks could easily be involved in the transactions: the local banks of the buyer and seller of the foreign exchange, and the money-center banks that handle the purchase and sale in the interbank market. Perhaps the buyer or seller will have to move the funds from one of its local banks to another, bringing even more banks into the transaction. A forward transaction entails an agreement today to deliver a specified number of units of a currency on a future date in return for a specified number of units of another currency.

spot transactions

direct quote

On the spot exchange market, contrasted with the over-the-counter market, the quoted exchange rate is typically called a direct quote. A **direct quote** *indicates the number of units of the home currency required to buy one unit of the foreign currency*. That is, in New York the typical exchange-rate quote indicates the number of dollars needed to buy one unit of a foreign currency: dollars per pound, dollars per euro, and so on. The spot rates in column 1 of Table 17-1 are the direct exchange quotes taken from *The Wall Street Journal*. Thus, according to Table 17-1, to buy 1 British pound (£1), $1.7888 was needed. To buy Swiss francs and euros, $.7923 and $1.2164 were needed, respectively.

indirect quote

An **indirect quote** *indicates the number of units of a foreign currency that can be bought for one unit of the home currency*. This reads as pounds per dollar, euros per dollar, and so forth. An indirect quote is the general method used in the over-the-counter market. Exceptions to this rule include British pounds, Irish punts, Australian dollars, and New Zealand dollars, which are quoted via direct quotes for historical reasons. Indirect quotes are given in the last column of Table 17-1.

In summary, a direct quote is the dollar/foreign currency rate ($/FC), and an indirect quote is the foreign currency/dollar (FC/$) rate. Therefore, an indirect quote is the reciprocal of a direct quote and vice versa. The following example illustrates the computation of an indirect quote from a given direct quote.

EXAMPLE

Suppose you want to compute the indirect quote from the direct quote of the spot rate for pounds given in column 1 of Table 17-1. The direct quote for the U.K. pound is $1.7888. The related indirect quote is calculated as the *reciprocal* of the direct quote as follows:

$$\text{Indirect quote} = \frac{1}{\text{direct quote}}$$

Thus,

$$\frac{1}{\$1.7888} = £.5590$$

Notice that the previous direct quote and indirect quote are identical to those shown in Table 17-1.

Direct and indirect quotes are useful in conducting international transactions, as the following examples show.

TABLE 17-1   Foreign Exchange Rates Reported September 2, 2004

KEY CURRENCY CROSS RATES

	DOLLAR	EURO	POUND	SFRANC	PESO	YEN	CDNDLR
Canada	1.2994	1.5806	2.3243	1.0295	.11284	.01187	...
Japan	109.49	133.19	195.86	86.751	9.508	...	84.266
Mexico	11.5154	14.0074	20.599	9.1237	...	.10517	8.8623
Switzerland	1.2621	1.5353	2.2577	...	.10960	.01153	.9713
U.K.	.55900	.6800	...	.4429	.04855	.00511	.43023
Euro	.82210	...	1.4706	.65135	.07139	.00751	.63269
U.S.	...	1.2164	1.7888	.79230	.08684	.00913	.76960

Source: Reuters

EXCHANGE RATES

The foreign exchange mid-range rates below apply to trading among banks in amounts of $1 million and more, as quoted at 4 p.m. Eastern time by Reuters and other sources. Retail transactions provide fewer units of foreign currency per dollar.

Country	U.S. $ EQUIVALENT	CURRENCY PER U.S. $	Country	U.S. $ EQUIVALENT	CURRENCY PER U.S. $
Argentina (Peso)-y	.3331	3.0021	New Zealand (Dollar)	.6494	1.5399
Australia (Dollar)	.6967	1.4353	Norway (Krone)	.1462	6.8399
Bahrain (Dinar)	2.6526	.3770	Pakistan (Rupee)	.01700	58.824
Brazil (Real)	.3403	2.9386	Peru (new Sol)	.2963	3.3750
Canada (Dollar)	.7696	1.2994	Philippines (Peso)	.01782	56.117
1-month forward	.7692	1.3001	Poland (Zloty)	.2749	3.6377
3-months forward	.7685	1.3012	Russia (Ruble)-a	.03420	29.240
6-months forward	.7674	1.3031	Saudi Arabia (Riyal)	.2667	3.7495
Chile (Peso)	.001600	625.00	Singapore (Dollar)	.5874	1.7024
China (Renminbi)	.1208	8.2781	Slovak Rep. (Koruna)	.03039	32.906
Colombia (Peso)	.0003904	2561.48	South Africa (Rand)	.1524	6.5617
Czech. Rep. (Koruna)			South Korea (Won)	.0008692	1150.48
Commercial rate	.03837	26.062	Sweden (Krona)	.1334	7.4963
Denmark (Krone)	.1636	6.1125	Switzerland (Franc)	.7923	1.2621
Ecuador (US Dollar)	1.0000	1.0000	1-month forward	.7931	1.2609
Egypt (Pound)-y	.1614	6.1950	3-months forward	.7947	1.2583
Hong Kong (Dollar)	.1283	7.7942	6-months forward	.7973	1.2542
Hungary (Forint)	.004908	203.75	Taiwan (Dollar)	.02959	33.795
India (Rupee)	.02162	46.254	Thailand (Baht)	.02408	41.528
Indonesia (Rupiah)	.0001077	9285	Turkey (Lira)	.00000066	1515152.
Israel (Shekel)	.2217	4.5106	U.K. (Pound)	1.7888	.5590
Japan (Yen)	.009133	109.49	1-month forward	1.7842	.5605
1-month forward	.009146	109.34	3-months forward	1.7752	.5633
3-months forward	.009174	109.00	6-months forward	1.7628	.5673
6-months forward	.009225	108.40	United Arab (Dirham)	.2723	3.6724
Jordan (Dinar)	1.4104	.7090	Uruguay (Peso)		
Kuwait (Dinar)	3.3927	.2948	Financial	.03500	28.571
Lebanon (Pound)	.0006604	1514.23	Venezuela (Bolivar)	.000521	1919.39
Malaysia (Ringgit)-b	.2632	3.7994			
Malta (Lira)	2.8462	.3513	SDR	1.4639	.6831
Mexico (Peso) Floating rate	.0868	11.5154	Euro	1.2164	.8221

Special Drawing Rights (SDR) are based on exchange rates for the U.S., British, and Japanese currencies. Source: International Monetary Fund.

a-Russian Central Bank rate. b-Government rate. y-Floating rate.

Source: *The Wall Street Journal*, September 3, 2004, p. C14.

EXAMPLE

An American business must pay 1,000 euros to a German firm on September 2, 2004. How many dollars will be required for this transaction?

$1.2164/€ × €1,000 = $1,216.40

EXAMPLE

An American business must pay $2,000 to a U.K. resident on September 2, 2004. How many pounds will the U.K. resident receive?

£.5590/$ × $2,000 = £1,118.00

EXCHANGE RATES AND ARBITRAGE

The foreign exchange quotes in two different countries must be in line with each other. If the exchange rate quotations between the London and New York spot exchange markets were *out of line*, then an *enterprising trader could make a profit by buying in the market where the currency was cheaper and selling it in the other*. Such a buy-and-sell strategy would involve a zero net investment of funds and no risk bearing, yet it would provide a sure profit. Such a person is called an **arbitrageur**, and the process of buying and selling in more than one market to make a riskless profit is called arbitrage. Spot exchange markets are efficient in the sense that arbitrage opportunities do not persist for any length of time. That is, the exchange rates between two different markets are quickly brought *in line*, aided by the arbitrage process. **Simple arbitrage** *eliminates exchange rate differentials across the markets for a single currency*, as in the preceding example for the New York and London quotes. **Triangular arbitrage** does the *same across the markets for all currencies*. **Covered-interest arbitrage** *eliminates differentials across currency and interest rate markets*.

Suppose that London quotes £.5700/$ instead of £.5590/$. If you simultaneously bought a pound in New York for £.5590/$ and sold a pound in London for £.5700/$, you would have (1) taken a zero net investment position because you bought £1 and sold £1, (2) locked in a sure profit of £.0110/$ *no matter which way* the pound subsequently moves, and (3) set in motion the forces that will eliminate the different quotes in New York and London. As others in the marketplace learn of your transaction, they will attempt to make the same transaction. The increased demand to buy pounds in New York will lead to a higher quote there, and the increased supply of pounds will lead to a lower quote in London. The workings of the market will produce a new spot rate that lies between £.5590/$ and £.5700/$ and is the same in New York and in London.

ASKED AND BID RATES

Two types of rates are quoted in the spot exchange market: the asked and the bid rates. The **asked rate** is the *rate the bank or the foreign exchange trader "asks" the customer to pay in home currency for foreign currency when the bank is selling and the customer is buying*. The asked rate is also known as the **selling rate** or the *offer rate*. The **bid rate** is *the rate at which the bank buys the foreign currency from the customer by paying in home currency*. The bid rate is also known as the **buying rate**. Note that Table 17-1 contains only the selling, offer, or asked rates, not the buying rate.

The banks sells a unit of foreign currency for more than it pays for it. Therefore, the direct asked quote ($/FC) is greater than the direct bid quote. *The difference between the asked quote and the bid quote* is known as the **bid-asked spread**. When there is a large volume of transactions and the trading is continuous, the spread is small and can be less than−1 percent (.01) for the major currencies. The spread is much higher for infrequently

Margin notes

arbitrageur

simple arbitrage

triangular arbitrage
covered-interest arbitrage

asked rate

selling rate
bid rate
buying rate

bid-asked spread

traded currencies. The spread exists to compensate the banks for holding the risky foreign currency and for providing the service of converting currencies.

CROSS RATES

A **cross rate** is *the computation of an exchange rate for a currency from the exchange rates of two other currencies*. These are given at the top of Table 17-1. The following example illustrates how this works.

cross rate

EXAMPLE

Taking the dollar/pound and the euro/dollar rates from column 1 and 2 of Table 17-1, determine the euro/pound and pound/euro exchange rates. We see that

$$(\$/\pounds) \times (€/\$) = (€/\pounds)$$

or

$$1.7888 \times .8221 = €1.4706/\pounds$$

Thus, the pound/euro exchange rate is

$$1/1.4706 = \pounds.6800/€$$

You'll notice that these rates are the same as those given in the top portion of Table 17-1 under Key Currency Cross Rates.

Cross-rate computations make it possible to use quotations in New York to compute the exchange rate between pounds, euros, and other currencies. Arbitrage conditions hold in cross rates, too. For example, the pound exchange rate in euros (the direct quote euros/pound) must be €1.4706/£. The euro exchange rate in London must be £.6800/€. If the rates were different from the computed cross rates, using quotes from New York, a trader could use three different currencies to lock in arbitrage profits through triangular arbitrage.

FORWARD EXCHANGE RATES

A **forward exchange contract** *requires delivery, at a specified future date, of one currency for a specified amount of another currency*. The exchange rate for the forward transaction is agreed on today; the actual payment of one currency and the receipt of another currency take place at the future date. For example, a 30-day contract on March 1 is for delivery on March 31. Note that the forward rate is not the same as the spot rate that will prevail in the future. The actual spot rate that will prevail is not known today; only the forward rate is known. The actual spot rate will depend on the market conditions at that time; it may be more or less than today's forward rate. **Exchange rate risk** is the *risk that tomorrow's exchange rate will differ from today's rate*.

forward exchange contract

exchange rate risk

As indicated earlier, it is extremely unlikely that the future spot rate will be exactly the same as the forward rate quoted today. Assume that you are going to receive a payment denominated in pounds from a British customer in 30 days. If you wait for 30 days and exchange the pounds at the spot rate, you will receive a dollar amount reflecting the exchange rate 30 days hence (i.e., the future spot rate). As of today, you have no way of knowing the exact dollar value of your future pound receipts. Consequently, you cannot make precise plans about the use of these dollars. If, conversely, you buy a futures contract, then you know the exact dollar value of your future receipts, and you can make precise plans concerning their use. The forward contract, therefore, can reduce your uncertainty about the future, and the major advantage of the forward market is that of risk reduction.

Forward contracts are usually quoted for periods of 30, 90, and 180 days. A contract for any intermediate date can be obtained, usually with the payment of a small premium. Forward contracts for periods longer than 180 days can be obtained by special negotiations with banks. Contracts for periods greater than 1 year can be costly.

Forward rates, like spot rates, are quoted in both direct and indirect form. The direct quotes for the 30-day, 90-day, and 180-day forward contracts on pounds, Swiss francs, Canadian dollars, and Japanese yen are given in column 1 of Table 17-1. The indirect quotes are indicated in column 2 of Table 17-1. The direct quotes are the dollar/foreign currency rate, and the indirect quotes are the foreign currency/dollar rate similar to the spot exchange quotes.

In Table 17-1 the 1-month forward quote for pounds is $1.7842 per pound. This means that the bank is contractually bound to deliver £1 at this price, and the buyer of the contract is legally obligated to buy it at this price in 30 days. Therefore, this is the price the customer must pay regardless of the actual spot rate prevailing in 30 days. If the spot price of the pound is less than $1.7842, then the customer pays *more* than the spot price. If the spot price is greater than $1.7842, then the customer pays *less* than the spot price.

The forward rate is often quoted at a premium or a discount from the existing spot rate. For example, the 30-day forward rate for the pound may be quoted as a .0046 discount (1.7842 forward rate −1.7888 spot rate). If the British pound is more expensive in the future than it is today, it is said to be selling at a premium relative to the dollar, and the dollar is said to be selling at a discount to the British pound. Notice in Table 17-1 that although the British pound is selling at a discount relative to the dollar, both the Swiss franc and Japanese yen are selling at a premium relative to the dollar. This premium or discount is also called the **forward-spot differential**.

forward-spot differential

Notationally, the relationship may be written

$$F - S = \text{premium } (F > S) \text{ or discount } (S > F) \qquad \textbf{(17-1)}$$

where F = the forward rate, direct quote
S = the spot rate, direct quote

The premium or discount can also be expressed as an annual percentage rate, computed as follows:

$$\frac{F-S}{S} \times \frac{12}{n} \times 100 = \text{annualized percentage}$$
$$\text{premium } (F > S) \text{ or discount } (S > F) \qquad \textbf{(17-2)}$$

where n = the number of months of the forward contract.

EXAMPLE

Compute the percent-per-annum premium on the 30-day pound.

Step 1: Identify F, S, and n.

$$F = 1.7842, S = 1.7888, n = 1 \text{ month}$$

Step 2: Because S is greater than F, we compute the annualized percentage discount:

$$D = \frac{1.7842 - 1.7888}{1.7888} \times \frac{12 \text{ months}}{1 \text{ month}} \times 100$$
$$= -3.086\%$$

The percent-per-annum discount on the 30-day pound is −3.086 percent.

EXAMPLES OF EXCHANGE RATE RISK

The concept of exchange rate risk applies to all types of international business. The measurement of these risks, and the type of risk, may differ among businesses. Let us see how exchange rate risk affects international trade contracts, international portfolio investments, and direct foreign investments.

EXCHANGE RATE RISK IN INTERNATIONAL TRADE CONTRACTS

The idea of exchange rate risk in trade contracts is illustrated in the following situations.

Case I

An American automobile distributor agrees to buy a car from the manufacturer in Detroit. The distributor agrees to pay $15,000 on delivery of the car, which is expected to be 30 days from today. The car is delivered on the thirtieth day and the distributor pays $15,000. Notice that from the day this contract was written until the day the car was delivered, the buyer knew the *exact dollar amount* of the liability. There was, in other words, *no uncertainty* about the value of the contract.

Case II

An American automobile distributor enters into a contract with a British supplier to buy a car from Britain for £10,600. The amount is payable on the delivery of the car, 30 days from today. Unfortunately, the exchange rate between British pounds and U.S. dollars may change in the next 30 days. In effect, the American firm is not certain what its future dollar outflow will be 30 days hence. That is, the *dollar value of the contract is uncertain*.

These two examples help illustrate the idea of foreign exchange risk in international trade contracts. In the domestic trade contract (Case I), the exact dollar amount of the future dollar payment is known today with certainty. In the case of the international trade contract (Case II), in which the *contract is written in the foreign currency*, the exact dollar amount of the contract is not known. The variability of the exchange rate induces variability in the future cash flow.

Exchange rate risk exists when the contract is written in terms of the foreign currency, or *denominated* in foreign currency. There is no direct exchange rate risk if the international trade contract is written in terms of the domestic currency. That is, in Case II, if the contract were written in dollars, the American importer would face *no* direct exchange rate risk. With the contract written in dollars, the British exporter would bear *all* the exchange rate risk because the British exporter's future pound receipts would be uncertain. That is, the British exporter would receive payment in dollars, which would have to be converted into pounds at an unknown (as of today) pound/dollar exchange rate. In international trade contracts of the type discussed here, at least one of the two parties to the contract *always* bears the exchange rate risk.

Certain types of international trade contracts are denominated in a third currency, different from either the importer's or the exporter's domestic currency. In Case II, the contract might have been denominated in, say, the Hong Kong dollar. With a Hong Kong dollar contract, both importer and exporter would be subject to exchange rate risk.

Exchange rate risk is not limited to the two-party trade contracts; it exists also in foreign portfolio investments and direct foreign investments.

EXCHANGE RATE RISK IN FOREIGN PORTFOLIO INVESTMENTS

Let us look at an example of exchange rate risk in the context of portfolio investments. An American investor buys a Hong Kong security. The exact return on the investment in the security is unknown. Thus, the security is a risky investment. The investment return in the holding period of, say, 3 months stated in HK$ could be anything from −2 to +8 percent. In addition, the U.S. dollar/HK$ exchange rate may depreciate by 4 percent or appreciate by 6 percent in the 3-month period during which the investment is held. The return to the American investor in U.S. dollars will, therefore, be in the range of −6 to +14 percent. Hence, the exchange rate fluctuations may increase the riskiness of the investments.

EXCHANGE RATE RISK IN DIRECT FOREIGN INVESTMENT

The exchange rate risk of a direct foreign investment (DFI) is more complicated. In a DFI, the parent company invests in assets denominated in a foreign currency. That is, the balance sheet and the income statement of the subsidiary are written in terms of the foreign currency. The parent company receives the repatriated profit stream in dollars. Thus, the exchange rate risk concept applies to fluctuations in the dollar value of the assets located abroad as well as to the fluctuations in the home currency–denominated profit stream. Exchange risk not only affects immediate profits, but it may affect the future profit stream as well.

ACROSS THE HALL

MARKETING

When reaching out to global markets, you not only need a good product, but you also need one that fits the culture of the market. As a result, although some products that are successful in the United States can be successfully introduced in global markets, others need to be adapted to the culture into which they are being introduced. For example, McDonald's has found great success globally, but it has done so by adapting its product line to fit the culture of the country it is entering. Understanding this is important because, whereas a new project will generally be evaluated using capital-budgeting techniques by the people in finance, determining how a product should be culturally adapted is the job of marketers. Their ability to modify and price the product so that it appeals abroad will go a long way toward determining whether or not a new capital-budgeting approach succeeds. For this reason, as a marketing student, you must understand exchange rates so you can price the new product in a way that creates wealth for the corporation. You also need to understand how the product must be culturally adapted for the new market. For example, while a Big Mac may taste pretty good to most people in the United States, that may not be the case around the world. As a result, McDonald's marketing staff many times offers alternative items that fit the cultural eating habits of different countries. For example, in Thailand McDonald's sells the McPork Burger with Thai Basil, while in Japan it offers the Tatsuta Burger, and in India it offers the Maharaja Mac, which has two all mutton patties, special sauce, lettuce, cheese, pickles, onions on a sesame seed bun—kinda sounds familiar, doesn't it? Similarly, when Gerber entered the baby food market in Japan, rather than strained peas and blueberry delight, it introduced sardines ground up in white radish sauce, cod roe spaghetti, and mugwort casserole. Moreover, a good product can fail abroad because of translation problems in its advertising campaign. A classic example is the Coors beer advertising slogan, "get loose with Coors," which translates in Spanish to "get the runs with Coors." The bottom line here is that in the international arena, marketing can take a good idea for a new product and help turn it into a success or a failure.

Although exchange rate risk can be a serious complication in international business activity, remember the principle of the risk–return trade-off: Traders and corporations find numerous reasons that the returns from international transactions outweigh the risks.

BACK TO THE FOUNDATIONS

*In international transactions, just as in domestic transactions, the key to value is the timing and amounts of cash flow spent and received. However, economic transactions across international borders add an element of risk because cash flows are denominated in the currency of the country in which business is being transacted. Consequently, the dollar value of the cash flows will depend on the exchange rate that exists at the time the cash changes hands. The fact remains, however, that it's cash spent and received that matters. This is the point of **Principle 3: Cash—Not Profits—Is King**.*

CONCEPT CHECK

1. What is a spot transaction? What is a direct quote? An indirect quote?
2. Who is an arbitrageur? How does an arbitrageur make money?
3. What is a forward exchange rate?
4. Describe exchange rate risk in direct foreign investment.

Objective **3**

INTEREST-RATE PARITY THEORY

Forward rates generally entail a premium or a discount relative to current spot rates. However, these forward premiums and discounts can differ between currencies and maturities. These differences depend solely on the difference in the level of interest rates between the two countries, called the *interest rate differential*. The value of the premium

FINANCIAL MANAGEMENT IN PRACTICE

"THE EURO HAS YET TO SPARK HOPED-FOR FINANCIAL REVOLUTION"

When the euro was launched in January 1999, it was hailed as a historic step that would alter the world's financial balance of power.

The new common currency, politicians and pundits predicted, would lure massive capital flows into Europe; challenge the dollar's hegemony; and accelerate European integration, forging its disparate member states into an economic and political superpower to rival the U.S.

That may happen one day.

"It was a real illusion to think the euro could do so much," says Serge Foucher, chief financial officer of Sony Europe GmbH, in Berlin. "The euro is a facilitator, but by itself it cannot resolve everything."

Some promised benefits from the euro, such as a cheaper and smoother cross-border payment system, haven't materialized. "We will be in a system for a long time where national payments will cost much less than cross-border payments," says Daniel Bouton, chairman of French bank Societe Generale SA.

Nor has the euro had any noticeable effect on equalizing consumer prices across the EU, as some economists predicted. Thanks to myriad national standards and rules, prices from country to country continue to vary widely. Swedish home-furnishing company Ikea, for example, says its production costs (and price tags) are higher in some countries because, among other things, rules oblige it to sew by hand the labels on items such as pillows and stuffed animals.

"We hope down the line we'll start moving in the direction of the U.S. market. It would make things a lot easier for a company like ours," says Lars Braberg, Ikea's director of EU affairs in Brussels.

In fact, differences in retail prices across Europe have widened for many products. An Opel Corsa costs 37% more, before taxes, in Germany than in Greece and other euro-zone states, more than twice as large as the gap a year ago, according to a July report by the European Commission.

Source: Excerpt from Christopher Rhoads and Geoff Winestock, "The Euro Has Yet to Spark Hoped-For Financial Revolution—Moves to Unify Markets, Lure Capital to Region Stall Without New Laws," *The Wall Street Journal* (September 10, 2001), Eastern Edition (staff-produced copy only). Copyright © 2001 by DOW JONES & COMPANY, INC. Reprinted with permission of DOW JONES & CO. INC. in the format Textbook via Copyright Clearance Center.

---

or discount can be theoretically computed from the **interest-rate parity (IRP) theory**. This theory states that *(except for the effects of small transaction costs) the forward premium or discount should be equal and opposite in size to the difference in the national interest rates for securities of the same maturity.*

Stated very simply, what does all this mean? It means that because of arbitrage, the interest rate differential between two countries must be equal to the difference between the forward and spot exchange rates. If this were not true, arbitrageurs would buy in the forward market and sell in the spot market (or vice versa) until prices were back in line and there were no profits left to be made. For example, if prices in the forward market were too low, arbitrageurs would enter the market, increase the demand for the forward foreign currency, and drive up the prices in the forward market until those prices obeyed the interest-rate parity theory.

interest-rate parity (IRP) theory

TAKIN' IT TO THE NET

When it comes to international business, the place to start is with the *Financial Times*, www.ft.com, which provides an excellent overview of what is happening in the world of business. The Markets page there offers in-depth coverage of global investing and the state of the euro.

CONCEPT CHECK

1. In simple terms, what does the interest-rate parity theory mean?

PURCHASING-POWER PARITY THEORY

Objective **4**

Long-run changes in exchange rates are influenced by international differences in inflation rates and the purchasing power of each nation's currency. Exchange rates of countries with high rates of inflation will tend to decline. According to the **purchasing-power parity (PPP) theory**, *in the long run, exchange rates adjust so that the purchasing power of each currency tends to be the same. Thus, exchange rate changes tend to reflect international differences in inflation rates. Countries with high rates of inflation tend to experience declines in the value of their currency.* Thus, if Britain experiences a 10 percent rate of inflation in a year that Japan experiences only a 6 percent rate, the U.K. currency (the pound) will be expected to decline in

purchasing-power parity (PPP) theory

value approximately by 3.77 percent [(1.10/1.06) − 1] against the Japanese currency (the yen). More accurately, according to the PPP theory,

Expected spot rate = current spot rate × expected difference in inflation rate

$$
\begin{array}{c}
\text{Expected spot rate} \\
\text{(domestic currency} \\
\text{per unit of foreign} \\
\text{currency)}
\end{array}
=
\begin{array}{c}
\text{current spot rate} \\
\text{(domestic currency} \\
\text{per unit of foreign} \\
\text{currency)}
\end{array}
\times
\frac{
\begin{array}{c}
\text{(1 + expected domestic} \\
\text{inflation rate)}
\end{array}
}{
\begin{array}{c}
\text{(1 + expected foreign} \\
\text{inflation rate)}
\end{array}
}
\tag{17-3}
$$

Thus, if the beginning value of the Japanese yen were £.00511, with a 6 percent inflation rate in Japan and a 10 percent inflation rate in Britain, according to the PPP, the expected value of the Japanese yen at the end of that year will be £.00511 × [1.10/1.06], or £.005303.

Stated very simply, what does this mean? It means that a dollar should have the same purchasing power anywhere in the world—well, at least on average. Obviously, this is not quite true. However, what the PPP theory tells us is that we should expect, on average, that differences in inflation rates between two countries should be reflected in changes in the exchange rates. In effect, the best forecast of the difference in inflation rates between two countries should also be the best forecast of the change in the spot rate of exchange.

THE LAW OF ONE PRICE

law of one price

Underlying the PPP relationship is the **law of one price**. This law is actually *a proposition that in competitive markets in which there are no transportation costs or barriers to trade, the same goods sold in different countries sell for the same price if all the different prices are expressed in terms of the same currency.* The idea is that the worth, in terms of marginal utility, of a good does not depend on where it is bought or sold. Because inflation will erode the purchasing power of any currency, its exchange rate must adhere to the PPP relationship if the law of one price is to hold over time.

There are enough obvious exceptions to the concept of purchasing-power parity that it may, at first glance, seem difficult to accept. For example, recently a Big Mac cost $2.36 in the United States, and given the then-existing exchange rates, it cost an equivalent of $2.02 in Mexico, $2.70 in Japan, and $3.22 in Germany. On the surface this might appear to violate the PPP theory and the law of one price; however, we must remember that this theory is based on the concept of arbitrage. In the case of a Big Mac, it's pretty hard to imagine buying Big Macs in Mexico for $2.02, shipping them to Germany, and reselling them for $3.22. But for commodities like gold and other items that are relatively inexpensive to ship and do not have to be consumed immediately, the law of one price holds much better.

INTERNATIONAL FISHER EFFECT

According to the domestic Fisher effect (FE), nominal interest rates reflect the expected inflation rate, a real rate of interest and the product of the real rate of interest and the inflation rate. In other words,

$$
\begin{array}{c}
\text{Nominal} \\
\text{interest rate}
\end{array}
=
\begin{array}{c}
\text{expected} \\
\text{inflation rate}
\end{array}
+
\begin{array}{c}
\text{real rate} \\
\text{of interest}
\end{array}
+
\left(
\begin{array}{c}
\text{expected} \\
\text{inflation rate}
\end{array}
+
\begin{array}{c}
\text{real rate} \\
\text{of interest}
\end{array}
\right)
\tag{17-4}
$$

Although there is mixed empirical support for the international Fisher effect (IFE), it is widely thought that, for the major industrial countries, the real rate of interest is about 3 percent when a long-term period is considered. In such a case, with the previous assumption regarding inflation rates, interest rates in Britain and Japan would be (.10 + .03 + .003) or 13.3 percent and (.06 + .03 + .0018) or 9.18 percent, respectively.

In effect, the IFE states that the real interest rate should be the same all over the world, with the difference in nominal or stated interest rates simply resulting from the differences in expected inflation rates. As we look at interest rates around the world, this tells us that we should not necessarily send our money to a bank account in the country with the highest interest rates. That course of action might only result in sending our money to a bank in the country with the highest expected level of inflation.

> **CONCEPT CHECK**
> 1. What does the law of one price say?
> 2. What is the international Fisher effect?

EXPOSURE TO EXCHANGE RATE RISK

Objective **5**

An asset denominated or valued in terms of foreign-currency cash flows will lose value if that foreign currency declines in value. It can be said that such an asset is exposed to exchange rate risk. However, this possible decline in asset value may be offset by the decline in value of any liability that is also denominated or valued in terms of that foreign currency. Thus, a firm would normally be interested in its net exposed position (exposed assets – exposed liabilities) for each period in each currency.

Although expected changes in exchange rates can often be included in the cost–benefit analysis relating to such transactions, in most cases there is an unexpected component in exchange rate changes, and often the cost–benefit analysis for such transactions does not fully capture even the expected change in the exchange rate. For example, price increases for the foreign operations of many MNCs often have to be less than those necessary to fully offset exchange rate changes, owing to the competitive pressures generated by local businesses.

Three measures of foreign exchange exposure are translation exposure, transaction exposure, and economic exposure. Translation exposure arises because the foreign operations of MNCs have financial statements denominated in the local currency of the country in which the operation is located. For U.S. MNCs, the *reporting currency* for its consolidated financial statements is the dollar, so the assets, liabilities, revenues, and expenses of the foreign operations must be translated into dollars. International transactions often require a payment to be made or received in a foreign currency in the future, so these transactions are exposed to exchange rate risk. Economic exposure exists over the long term because the value of future cash flows in the reporting currency (that is, the dollar) from foreign operations is exposed to exchange rate risk. Indeed, the whole stream of future cash flows is exposed. The Japanese automaker situation highlights the effect of economic exposure on an MNC's revenue stream. The three measures of exposure now are examined more closely.

TRANSLATION EXPOSURE

Foreign currency assets and liabilities are considered exposed if their foreign currency value for accounting purposes is to be translated into the domestic currency using the currency exchange rate—the exchange rate in effect on the balance sheet date. Other assets and liabilities and equity amounts that are translated at the historic exchange rate—the rate in effect when these items were first recognized in the company's accounts—are not considered to be exposed. The rate (current or historic) used to translate various accounts depends on the translation procedure used.

Whereas transaction exposure can result in exchange rate change–related losses and gains that are realized and have an impact on both reported and taxable income, translation exposure results in exchange rate losses and gains that are reflected in the company's accounting books but are unrealized and have little or no impact on taxable income. Thus, if financial markets are efficient and managerial goals are consistent with owner wealth maximization, a firm should not have to waste real resources hedging against possible paper losses caused by translation exposure. However, if there are significant agency or information costs or if markets are not efficient, a firm may indeed find it economical to hedge against translation losses or gains.

TRANSACTION EXPOSURE

Receivables, payables, and fixed-price sales or purchase contracts are examples of foreign currency transactions whose monetary value was fixed at a time different from the time

transaction exposure

when these transactions are actually completed. **Transaction exposure** is a term that *describes the net contracted foreign currency transactions for which the settlement amounts are subject to changing exchange rates.* A company normally must set up an additional reporting system to track transaction exposure, because several of these amounts are not recognized in the accounting books of the firm.

Exchange rate risk may be neutralized or hedged by a change in the asset and liability position in the foreign currency. An exposed asset position (such as an account receivable) can be hedged or covered by creating a liability of the same amount and maturity denominated in the foreign currency (such as a forward contract to sell the foreign currency). An exposed liability position (such as an account payable) can be covered by acquiring assets of the same amount and maturity in the foreign currency (such as a forward contract to buy the foreign currency). The objective is to have a zero net asset position in the foreign currency. This eliminates exchange rate risk because the loss (gain) in the liability (asset) is exactly offset by the gain (loss) in the value of the asset (liability) when the foreign currency appreciates (depreciates). Two popular forms of hedge are the money-market hedge and the exchange-market, or forward-market, hedge. In both types of hedge, the amount and the duration of the asset (liability) positions are matched. Note as you read the next two subsections how IRP theory ensures that each hedge provides the same cover.

MONEY-MARKET HEDGE

In a money-market hedge, the exposed position in a foreign currency is offset by borrowing or lending in the money market. Consider the case of the American firm with a net liability position (i.e., the amount it owes) of £3,000. The firm knows the exact amount of its pound liability in 30 days, but it does not know the liability in dollars. Assume that the 30-day money-market rates in both the United States and Britain are, respectively, 1 percent for lending and 1.5 percent for borrowing. The American business can take the following steps:

Step 1: Calculate the present value of the foreign currency liability (£3,000) that is due in 30 days. Use the money-market rate applicable for the foreign country (1 percent in the United Kingdom). The present value of £3,000 is £2,970.30, computed as follows: £3,000/(1 + .01).

Step 2: Exchange dollars on today's spot market to obtain the £2,970.30. The dollar amount needed today is $5,313.27 (£2,970.30 × 1.7888).

Step 3: Invest £2,970.30 in a United Kingdom 1-month money-market instrument. This investment will compound to exactly £3,000 in 1 month. The future liability of £3,000 is covered by the £2,970.30 investment.[3]

Note: If the American business does not own this amount today, it can borrow $5,313.27 from the U.S. money market at the going rate of 1.5 percent. In 30 days the American business will need to repay $5,392.97 [$5,313.27 × (1 + .015)].

Assuming that the American business borrows the money, its management may base its calculations on the knowledge that the British goods, on delivery in 30 days, will cost it $5,392.97. The British business will receive £3,000. The American business need not wait for the future spot exchange rate to be revealed. On today's date, the future dollar payment of the contract is known with certainty. This certainty helps the American business in making its pricing and financing decisions.

Many businesses hedge in the money market. The firm needs to borrow (creating a liability) in one market, lend or invest in the other money market, and use the spot exchange market on today's date. The mechanics of covering a net asset position in the foreign currency are the exact reverse of the mechanics of covering the liability position. With a net asset position in pounds: Borrow in the U.K. money market in pounds, convert to dollars on the spot exchange market, invest in the U.S. money market. When the net assets are converted into pounds (i.e., when the firm receives what it is owed), pay off the loan and the interest. The cost of hedging in the money market is the cost of doing business in three dif-

---

[3]Observe that £2,970.30 × (1 + .01) = £3,000.

ferent markets. Information about the three markets is needed, and analytical calculations of the type indicated here must be made.

Many small and infrequent traders find the cost of the money-market hedge prohibitive, especially because of the need for information about the market. These traders use the exchange-market, or forward-market, hedge, which has very similar hedging benefits.

THE FORWARD-MARKET HEDGE

The forward market provides a second possible hedging mechanism. It works as follows: A net asset (liability) position is covered by a liability (asset) in the forward market. Consider again the case of the American firm with a liability of £3,000 that must be paid in 30 days. The firm may take the following steps to cover its liability position:

Step 1: Buy a forward contract today to purchase £3,000 in 30 days. The 30-day forward rate is $1.7842/£.

Step 2: On the thirtieth day pay the banker $5,352.60 (£3,000 × $1.7842) and collect £3,000. Pay these pounds to the British supplier.

By the use of the forward contract the American business knows the exact worth of the future payment in dollars ($5,352.60). The exchange rate risk in pounds is totally eliminated by the net asset position in the forward pounds. In the case of a net asset exposure, the steps open to the American firm are the exact opposite: Sell the pounds forward and on the future day receive and deliver the pounds to collect the agreed-on dollar amount.

The use of the forward market as a hedge against exchange rate risk is simple and direct—that is, match the liability or asset position against an offsetting position in the forward market. The forward-market hedge is relatively easy to implement. The firm directs its banker that it needs to buy or sell a foreign currency on a future date, and the banker gives a forward quote.

The forward-market hedge and the money-market hedge give an identical future dollar payment (or receipt) if the forward contracts are priced according to the interest-rate parity theory. The alert student may have noticed that the dollar payments in the money-market hedge and the forward-market hedge examples were, respectively, $5,313.27 and $5,352.60. Recall from our previous discussions that in efficient markets, the forward contracts do indeed conform to IRP theory. However, the numbers in our example are not identical because the forward rate used in the forward-market hedge is not exactly equal to the interest rates in the money-market hedge.

CURRENCY-FUTURES CONTRACTS AND OPTIONS

The forward-market hedge is not adequate for some types of exposure. If the foreign currency asset or liability position occurs on a date for which forward quotes are not available, the forward-market hedge cannot be accomplished. In certain cases the forward-market hedge may cost more than the money-market hedge. In these cases, a corporation with a large amount of exposure may prefer the money-market hedge. In addition to forward-market and money-market hedges, a company can also hedge its exposure by buying (or selling) some relatively new instruments—foreign currency futures contracts and foreign currency options. Although futures contracts are similar to forward contracts in that they provide fixed prices for the required delivery of foreign currency at maturity, exchange-traded options permit fixed-price (strike price) foreign currency transactions anytime before maturity. Futures contracts and options differ from forward contracts in that, unlike forward contracts, which are customized regarding amount and maturity date, futures and options are traded in standard amounts with standard maturity dates. In addition, although forward contracts are written by banks, futures and options are traded on organized exchanges, and individual traders deal with the exchange-based clearing organization rather than with each other. The purchase of futures requires the fulfillment of margin requirements (about 5 to 10 percent of the face amount), whereas the purchase of forward contracts requires only good credit standing with a bank. The purchase of options requires an immediate outlay that reflects a premium above the strike price and an outlay equal to the strike price when and if the option is executed.

ECONOMIC EXPOSURE

The economic value of a company can vary in response to exchange rate changes. This change in value may be caused by a rate change–induced decline in the level of expected cash flows and/or by an increase in the riskiness of these cash flows. *Economic exposure* refers to the overall impact of exchange rate changes on the value of the firm and includes not only the strategic impact of changes in competitive relationships that arise from exchange rate changes but also the economic impact of transaction exposure, and if any, translation exposure.

Economic exposure to exchange rate changes depends on the competitive structure of the markets for a firm's inputs and outputs and how these markets are influenced by changes in exchange rates. This influence, in turn, depends on several economic factors, including price elasticities of the products, the degree of competition from foreign markets, and direct (through prices) and indirect (through incomes) impact of exchange rate changes on these markets. Assessing the economic exposure faced by a particular firm, thus, depends on the ability to understand and model the structure of the markets for its major inputs (purchases) and outputs (sales).

A company need not engage in any cross-border business activity to be exposed to exchange rate changes because product and financial markets in most countries are related and influenced to a large extent by the same global forces. The output of a company engaged in business activity only within one country may be competing with imported products, or it may be competing for its inputs with other domestic and foreign purchasers. For example, a Canadian chemical company that did no cross-border business nevertheless found that its profit margin depended directly on the U.S. dollar/ Japanese yen exchange rate. The company used coal as an input in its production process, and the Canadian price of coal was heavily influenced by the extent to which the Japanese bought U.S. coal, which in turn depended on the dollar/yen exchange rate.

Although translation exposure need not be managed, it might be useful for a firm to manage its transaction and economic exposures because they affect firm value directly. In most companies, transaction exposure is generally tracked and managed by the office of the corporate treasurer. Economic exposure is difficult to define in operating terms, and very few companies manage it actively. In most companies, economic exposure is generally considered part of the strategic planning process, rather than a treasurer's or finance function.

> **CONCEPT CHECK**
> 1. Give a simple explanation of translation exposure.
> 2. Give a simple explanation of transaction exposure.
> 3. Give a simple explanation of economic exposure.

Objective

MULTINATIONAL WORKING-CAPITAL MANAGEMENT

The basic principles of working-capital management for a multinational corporation are similar to those for a domestic firm. However, tax and exchange rate factors are additional considerations for the MNC. For the MNC with subsidiaries in many countries, the optimal decisions in the management of working capital are made by considering the market as a whole. The global or centralized financial decisions for the MNC are superior to the set of independent optimal decisions for the subsidiaries. This is the control problem of the MNC. If the individual subsidiaries make decisions that are best for them individually, the consolidation of such decisions may not be best for the MNC as a whole. To effect global management, sophisticated computerized models—incorporating many variables for each subsidiary— are solved to provide the best overall decision for the MNC.

Before considering the components of working-capital management, we examine two techniques that are useful in the management of a wide variety of working-capital components.

LEADING AND LAGGING

Two important risk-reduction techniques for many working-capital problems are called leading and lagging. Often forward-market and money-market hedges are not available to eliminate exchange risk. Under such circumstances, leading and lagging may be used to reduce exchange risk.

Recall that a net asset (long) position is not desirable in a weak or potentially depreciating currency. If a firm has a net asset position in such a currency, it should expedite the disposal of the asset. The firm should get rid of the asset earlier than it otherwise would have, or *lead*, and convert the funds into assets in a relatively stronger currency. By the same reasoning, the firm should *lag*, or delay the collection against a net asset position in a strong currency. If the firm has a net liability (short) position in the weak currency, then it should delay the payment against the liability, or lag, until the currency depreciates. In the case of an appreciating or strong foreign currency and a net liability position, the firm should lead the payments—that is, reduce the liabilities earlier than it would otherwise have.

These principles are useful in the management of working capital of an MNC. They cannot, however, eliminate the foreign exchange risk. When exchange rates change continuously, it is almost impossible to guess whether or when the currency will depreciate or appreciate. This is why the risk of exchange rate changes cannot be eliminated. Nevertheless, the reduction of risk, or the increased gain from exchange rate changes via the lead and lag, is useful for cash management, accounts-receivable management, and short-term liability management.

CASH MANAGEMENT AND POSITIONING OF FUNDS

Positioning of funds takes on an added importance in the international context. Funds may be transferred from a subsidiary of the MNC in country A to another subsidiary in country B such that the foreign exchange exposure and the tax liability of the MNC as a whole are minimized. It bears repeating that because of the global strategy of the MNC, the tax liability of the subsidiary in country A may be greater than it would otherwise have been, but the overall tax payment for all units of the MNC is minimized.

The transfer of funds among subsidiaries and the parent company is done by royalties, fees, and transfer pricing. A **transfer price** is the *price a subsidiary or a parent company charges other companies that are part of the MNC for its goods or services.* A parent that wishes to transfer funds from a subsidiary in a depreciating-currency country may charge a higher price on the goods and services sold to this subsidiary by the parent or by subsidiaries from strong-currency countries.

transfer price

> ### CONCEPT CHECK
> 1. Describe the risk-reduction techniques of leading and lagging.
> 2. How can a parent company use the concept of transfer pricing to move funds from a subsidiary in a depreciating-currency country to a strong-currency country?

INTERNATIONAL FINANCING AND CAPITAL STRUCTURE DECISIONS

Objective **7**

An MNC has access to many more financing sources than a domestic firm. It can tap not only the financing sources in its home country that are available to its domestic counterparts but also sources in the foreign countries in which it operates. Host countries often provide access to low-cost subsidized financing to attract foreign investment. In addition, the MNC may enjoy preferential credit standards because of its size and investor preference for its home currency. An MNC may be able to access third-country capital markets—countries in which it does not operate but which may have large, well-functioning capital markets. Finally, an MNC can also access external currency markets: Eurodollar, Eurocurrency, or Asian dollar markets. These external markets are unregulated, and because of their lower spread, can offer very attractive rates for financing *and* for investments. With the increasing availability of interest rate and currency swaps, a firm can raise funds in the lowest-cost maturities and currencies and swap them into funds with the maturity and currency denomination it requires. Because of its ability to tap a larger number of financial markets, the MNC may have a lower cost of capital; and because it may be better able to avoid the problems or limitations of any one financial market, it may have more continuous access to external financing compared with a domestic company.

Access to national financial markets is regulated by governments. For example, in the United States, access to capital markets is governed by SEC regulations. Access to Japanese capital markets is governed by regulations issued by the Ministry of Finance. Some countries have extensive regulations; other countries have relatively open markets. These regulations may differ depending on the legal residency terms of the company raising funds. A company that cannot use its local subsidiary to raise funds in a given market will be treated as foreign. In order to increase their visibility in a foreign capital market, a number of MNCs are now listing their equities on the stock exchanges of many of these countries.

The external currency markets are predominantly centered in Europe, and about 80 percent of their value is denominated in terms of the U.S. dollar. Thus, the most external currency markets can be characterized as Eurodollar markets. Such markets consist of an active short-term money market and an intermediate-term capital market with maturities ranging up to 15 years and averaging about 7 to 9 years. The intermediate-term market consists of the Eurobond and the Syndicated Eurocredit markets. Eurobonds are usually issued as unregistered bearer bonds and generally tend to have higher flotation costs but lower coupon rates compared with similar bonds issued in the United States. A Syndicated Eurocredit loan is simply a large-term loan that involves contributions by a number of lending banks.

In arriving at its capital structure decisions, an MNC has to consider a number of factors. First, the capital structure of its local affiliates is influenced by local norms regarding capital structure in that industry and in that country. Local norms for companies in the same industry can differ considerably from country to country. Second, the local-affiliate capital structure must also reflect corporate attitudes toward exchange-rate and political risks in that country, which would normally lead to higher levels of local debt and other local capital. Third, local-affiliate capital structure must reflect home-country requirements with regard to the company's consolidated capital structure. Finally, the optimal MNC capital structure should reflects its wider access to financial markets, its ability to diversify economic and political risks, and its other advantages over domestic companies.

BACK TO THE FOUNDATIONS

*Investment across international boundaries gives rise to special risks not encountered when investing domestically. Specifically, political risks and exchange rate risk are unique to international investing. Once again, **Principle 1: The Risk–Return Trade-Off—We Won't Take On Additional Risk Unless We Expect to Be Compensated with Additional Return** provides a rationale for evaluating these considerations. Where added risks are present, added rewards are necessary to induce investment.*

CONCEPT CHECK

1. What factors might an MNC consider in making a capital structure decision?

Objective **8**

DIRECT FOREIGN INVESTMENT

An MNC often makes direct foreign investments abroad in the form of plants and equipment. The decision process for this type of investment is very similar to the capital-budgeting decision in the domestic context—with some additional twists. Most real-world capital-budgeting decisions are made with uncertain future outcomes. Recall that a capital-budgeting decision has three major components: the estimation of the future cash flows (including the initial cost of the proposed investment), the estimation of the risk in these cash flows, and the choice of the proper discount rate. We will assume that the *NPV* criterion is appropriate as we examine (1) the risks associated with direct foreign investment and (2) factors to be considered in making the investment decision that may be unique to the international scene.

RISKS IN DIRECT FOREIGN INVESTMENT

Risks in domestic capital budgeting arise from two sources: business risk and financial risk. The international capital-budgeting problem incorporates these risks as well as political risk and exchange risk.

BUSINESS RISK AND FINANCIAL RISK

International business risk is due to the response of a business to economic conditions in the foreign country. Thus, the U.S. MNC needs to be aware of the business climate in both the United States and the foreign country. Additional business risk is due to competition from other MNCs, local businesses, and imported goods. Financial risk refers to the risks introduced in the profit stream by the firm's financial structure. The financial risks of foreign operations are not very different from those of domestic operations.

POLITICAL RISK

Political risk arises because the foreign subsidiary conducts its business in a political system different from that of the home country. Many foreign governments, especially those in the Third World, are less stable than the U.S. government. A change in a country's political setup frequently brings a change in policies with respect to businesses—and especially with respect to foreign businesses. An extreme change in policy might involve nationalization or even outright expropriation of certain businesses. These are the political risks of conducting business abroad. A business with no investment in plant and equipment is less susceptible to these risks. Some examples of political risk are listed here:

1. Expropriation of plant and equipment without compensation.
2. Expropriation with minimal compensation that is below actual market value.
3. Nonconvertibility of the subsidiary's foreign earnings into the parent's currency—the problem of *blocked funds*.
4. Substantial changes in the laws governing taxation.
5. Governmental controls in the foreign country regarding the sale price of the products, wages, and compensation to personnel, hiring of personnel, making of transfer payments to the parent, and local borrowing.
6. Some governments require certain amounts of local equity participation in the business. Some require that the majority of the equity participation belong to their country.

All these controls and governmental actions introduce risks in the cash flows of the investment to the parent company. These risks must be considered before making the foreign investment decision. The MNC may decide against investing in countries with risks of types 1 and 2. Other risks can be borne—provided that the returns from the foreign investments are high enough to compensate for them. Insurance against some types of political risks may be purchased from private insurance companies or from the U.S.-Government Overseas Private Investment Corporation. It should be noted that although an MNC cannot protect itself against all foreign political risks, political risks are also present in domestic business.

EXCHANGE RATE RISK

The exposure of the fixed assets is best measured by the effects of the exchange rate changes on the firm's future earnings stream: that being economic exposure rather than translation exposure. For instance, changes in the exchange rate may adversely affect sales by making competing imported goods cheaper. Changes in the cost of goods sold may result if some components are imported and their price in the foreign currency changes because of exchange rate fluctuations. The thrust of these examples is that the effect of exchange rate changes on income statement items should be properly measured to evaluate exchange rate risk. Finally, exchange rate risk affects the dollar-denominated profit stream of the parent company, whether or not it affects the foreign-operations profits.

TAKIN' IT TO THE NET

If you'd like information on Japan, try the Japan Information Network Web site web-japan.org/stat/index.html, which includes all Japanese direct investments abroad. This site also provides statistics on other aspects of Japan: major macroeconomics, financial and international transactions, including balance of payments, gold and foreign exchange reserves, trade in goods and services, and international investments.

CONCEPT CHECK

1. What are some of the risks associated with direct foreign investments?

SUMMARY

Objective **1**

Objective **2**

The growth of our global economy, the increasing number of multinational corporations, and the increase in foreign trade itself underscore the importance of the study of international finance.

Exchange rate mechanics are discussed in the context of the prevailing floating rates. Under this system, exchange rates between currencies vary in an apparently random fashion in accordance with the supply and demand conditions in the exchange market. Important economic factors affecting the level of exchange rates include the relative economic strengths of the countries involved, the balance-of-payments mechanism, and the countries' monetary policies. Several important exchange rate terms are introduced. These include the asked and the bid rates, which represent the selling and buying rates of currencies. The direct quote is the units of home currency per unit of foreign currency, and the indirect quote is the reciprocal of the direct quote. Cross-rate computations reflect the exchange rate between two foreign currencies.

Objective **3**

Objective **4**

The forward exchange market provides a valuable service by quoting rates for the delivery of foreign currencies in the future. The foreign currency is said to sell at a discount (premium) forward from the spot rate when the forward rate is less (discount) than the spot rate, in direct quotation. In addition, the influences of purchasing-power parity (PPP) and the international Fisher effect (IFE) in determining the exchange rate are discussed.

Objective **5**

Exchange rate risk exists because the exact spot rate that prevails on a future date is not known with certainty today. The concept of exchange rate risk is applicable to a wide variety of businesses, including export–import firms and firms involved in making direct foreign investments or international investments in securities. Foreign exchange exposure is a measure of exchange rate risk. There are different ways of measuring the foreign exposure, including the net asset (net liability) measurement. Different strategies are open to businesses to counter the exposure to this risk, including the money-market hedge, the forward-market hedge, futures contracts, and options. Each involves different costs.

Objective **6**

Objective **7**

In discussing working-capital management in an international environment, we find leading and lagging techniques useful in minimizing exchange rate risk and increasing profitability. In addition, funds positioning is a useful tool for reducing exchange rate risk exposure. The MNC may have a lower cost of capital because it has access to a larger set of financial markets than a domestic company. In addition to the home, host, and third-country financial markets, the MNC can tap the rapidly growing external currency markets. In making capital structure decisions, the MNC must consider political and exchange rate risks and host- and home-country capital structure norms.

Objective **8**

The complexities encountered in the direct foreign investment decision include the usual sources of risk—business and financial—and additional risks associated with fluctuating exchange rates and political factors. Political risk is due to differences in political climates, institutions, and processes between the home country and abroad. Under these conditions, the estimation of future cash flows and the choice of the proper discount rates are more complicated than for the domestic investment situation.

KEY TERMS

Arbitrageur, 532

Asked rate, 532

Bid rate, 532

Bid-asked spread, 532

Buying rate, 532

Covered-interest arbitrage, 532

Cross rate, 533

Direct quote, 530

Exchange rate, 530

Exchange rate risk, 533

Floating-rate international currency system, 528

Forward exchange contract, 533

Forward-spot differential, 534

Indirect quote, 530

Interest-rate parity (IRP) theory, 537

Law of one price, 538

Multinational corporation (MNC), 528

Purchasing-power parity (PPP) theory, 537

Selling rate, 532

Simple arbitrage, 532

Spot transactions, 530

Transaction exposure, 540

Transfer price, 543

Triangular arbitrage, 532

STUDY QUESTIONS

17-1. What additional factors are encountered in international as compared with domestic financial management? Discuss each briefly.

17-2. What different types of businesses operate in the international environment? Why are the techniques and strategies available to these firms different?

17-3. What is meant by arbitrage profits?

17-4. What are the markets and mechanics involved in generating (a) simple arbitrage profits and (b) triangular arbitrage profits?

17-5. How do purchasing power parity, interest rate parity, and the Fisher effect explain the relationships among the current spot rate, the future spot rate, and the forward rate?

17-6. What is meant by (a) exchange risk and (b) political risk?

17-7. How can exchange risk be measured?

17-8. What are the differences among transaction, translation, and economic exposures? Should all of them be ideally reduced to zero?

17-9. What steps can a firm take to reduce exchange risk? Indicate at least two different techniques.

17-10. How are the forward-market and the money-market hedges effected? What are the major differences between these two types of hedges?

17-11. In the New York exchange market, the forward rate for the Indian currency, the rupee, is not quoted. If you were exposed to exchange risk in rupees, how could you cover your position?

17-12. Compare and contrast the use of forward contracts, futures contracts, and options to reduce foreign exchange exposure. When is each instrument most appropriate?

17-13. Indicate two working-capital management techniques that are useful for international businesses to reduce exchange risk and potentially increase profits.

17-14. How do the financing sources available to an MNC differ from those available to a domestic firm? What do these differences mean for the company's cost of capital?

17-15. What risks are associated with direct foreign investment? How do these risks differ from those encountered in domestic investment?

17-16. How is the direct foreign investment decision made? What are the inputs to this decision process? Are the inputs more complicated than those to the domestic investment problem? If so, why?

17-17. A corporation desires to enter a particular foreign market. The DFI analysis indicates that a direct investment in the plant in the foreign country is not profitable. What other course of action can the company take to enter the foreign market? What are the important considerations?

SELF-TEST PROBLEM

The data for Self-Test Problem ST-1 are given in the following table:

COUNTRY	CONTRACT	$/FOREIGN CURRENCY
New Zealand—dollar	Spot	.3893
	30-day	.3910
	90-day	.3958

ST-1. You own $10,000. The U.S. dollar rate on the New Zealand dollar is 2.5823 NZ$/US$. The New Zealand dollar rate is given in the accompanying table. Are arbitrage profits possible? Set up an arbitrage scheme with your capital. What is the gain (loss) in dollars?

STUDY PROBLEMS

The data for Study Problems 17-1 through 17-6 are given in the following table:

COUNTRY	CONTRACT	$/FOREIGN CURRENCY
Canada—dollar	Spot	.8437
	30-day	.8417
	90-day	.8395
Japan—yen	Spot	.004684
	30-day	.004717
	90-day	.004781
Switzerland—franc	Spot	.5139
	30-day	.5169
	90-day	.5315

17-1. (*Spot exchange rates*) An American business needs to pay (a) 10,000 Canadian dollars, (b) 2 million yen, and (c) 50,000 Swiss francs to businesses abroad. What are the dollar payments to the respective countries?

17-2. (*Spot exchange rates*) An American business pays $10,000, $15,000, and $20,000 to suppliers in, respectively, Japan, Switzerland, and Canada. How much, in local currencies, do the suppliers receive?

17-3. (*Indirect quotes*) Compute the indirect quote for the spot and forward Canadian dollar, yen, and Swiss franc contracts.

17-4. (*Exchange rates*) The spreads on the contracts as a percentage of the asked rates are 2 percent for yen, 3 percent for Canadian dollars, and 5 percent for Swiss francs. Show, in a table similar to the preceding one, the bid rates for the different spot and forward rates.

17-5. (*Exchange rate arbitrage*) You own $10,000. The dollar rate in Tokyo is 216.6743. The yen rate in New York is given in the preceding table. Are arbitrage profits possible? Set up an arbitrage scheme with your capital. What is the gain (loss) in dollars?

17-6. (*Cross rates*) Compute the Canadian dollar/yen and the yen/Swiss franc spot rate from the data in the preceding table.

WEB WORKS

If you ever need to convert money from one currency to another, the Web is the place to go. There are a number of different currency converters available that are easy to use.

17-WW1. Take a look at the FX Converter (**www.oanda.com/convert/classic**). Use it to convert 100 Fiji dollars to U.S. dollars. How much are the 100 Fiji dollars worth in U.S. dollars?

17-WW2. Use the Bank of Canada currency converter (**www.bankofcanada.ca/en/exchform.htm**) to convert 100 Croatian kunas to U.S. dollars. How much are they worth?

17-WW3. Try the Yahoo! Finance currency calculator (**finance.yahoo.com/m3?u**) to convert 100 U.S. dollars into euros. How many euros would you get for $100?

17-WW4. Now use whatever currency calculator you'd like and move 100 U.S. dollars to euros. Convert those euros to Japanese yen and then convert those Japanese yen into U.S. dollars. How many U.S. dollars do you have?

COMPREHENSIVE PROBLEM

For your job as the business reporter for a local newspaper, you are given the assignment of putting together a series of articles on multinational finance and the international currency markets for your readers. Much recent local press coverage has been given to losses in the foreign exchange markets by JGAR, a local firm that is the subsidiary of Daedlufetarg, a large German manufacturing firm.

Your editor would like you to address several specific questions dealing with multinational finance. Prepare a response to the following memorandum from your editor:

To: Business Reporter
From: Perry White, Editor, *Daily Planet*
Re: Upcoming Series on Multinational Finance

In your upcoming series on multinational finance, I would like to make sure you cover several specific points. In addition, before you begin this assignment, I want to make sure we are all reading from the same script, because accuracy has always been the cornerstone of the *Daily Planet*. I'd like a response to the following questions before we proceed:

a. What new problems and factors are encountered in international, as opposed to domestic, financial management?
b. What does the term *arbitrage profits* mean?
c. What can a firm do to reduce exchange risk?
d. What are the differences among a forward contract, a futures contract, and options?

Use the following data in your responses to the remaining questions:

Selling Quotes for Foreign Currencies in New York

COUNTRY—CURRENCY	CONTRACT	$/FOREIGN
Canada—dollar	Spot	.8450
	30-day	.8415
	90-day	.8390
Japan—yen	Spot	.004700
	30-day	.004750
	90-day	.004820
Switzerland—franc	Spot	.5150
	30-day	.5182
	90-day	.5328

e. An American business needs to pay (a) 15,000 Canadian dollars, (b) 1.5 million yen, and (c) 55,000 Swiss francs to businesses abroad. What are the dollar payments to the respective countries?
f. An American business pays $20,000, $5,000, and $15,000 to suppliers in, respectively, Japan, Switzerland, and Canada. How much, in local currencies, do the suppliers receive?
g. Compute the indirect quote for the spot and forward Canadian dollar contract.
h. You own $10,000. The dollar rate in Tokyo is 216.6752. The yen rate in New York is given in the preceding table. Are arbitrage profits possible? Set up an arbitrage scheme with your capital. What is the gain (loss) in dollars?
i. Compute the Canadian dollar/yen spot rate from the data in the preceding table.

SELF-TEST SOLUTION

SS-1. The New Zealand rate is 2.5823 NZ$/$1, while the (indirect) New York rate is 1/.3893 = 2.5687 NZ$/US$.

Assuming no transaction costs, the rates between New Zealand and New York are out of line. Thus, arbitrage profits are possible.

Step 1: Because the New Zealand dollar is cheaper in New Zealand, buy $10,000 worth of New Zealand dollars in New Zealand. The number of New Zealand dollars purchased would be $10,000 × 2.5823 = 25,823 New Zealand dollars.

Step 2: Simultaneously, sell the New Zealand dollars in New York at the prevailing rate. The amount received upon the sale of the New Zealand dollars would be:

25,823 NZ$ × $.3893/NZ$ = $10,052.89

Net gain is $10,052.89 − $10,000 = $52.89.

APPENDIX A

USING A CALCULATOR

As you prepare for a career in business, the ability to use a financial calculator is essential, whether you are in the finance division or the marketing department. For most positions, it will be assumed that you can use a calculator in making computations that at one time were simply not possible without extensive time and effort. The following examples let us see what is possible, but they represent only the beginning of using the calculator in finance.

With just a little time and effort, you will be surprised at how much you can do with the calculator, such as calculating a stock's beta, or determining the value of a bond on a specific day given the exact date of maturity, or finding net present values and internal rates of return, or calculating the standard deviation. The list is almost endless.

In demonstrating how calculators may make our work easier, we must first decide which calculator to use. The options are numerous and largely depend on personal preference. We have chosen the Texas Instruments BA II Plus and the Hewlett-Packard 10bII.

We will limit our discussion to the following issues:

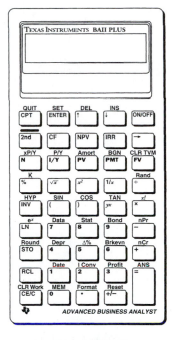

I. INTRODUCTORY COMMENTS

In the examples that follow, you are told (1) which keystrokes to use, (2) the resulting appearance of the calculator display, and (3) a supporting explanation.

The keystrokes column tells you which keys to press. The keystrokes shown in a white box tell you to use one of the calculator's dedicated or "hard" keys. For example, if +/− is shown in the keystrokes instruction column, press that key on the keyboard of the calculator. With the Texas Instruments BA II Plus, to use a function printed in a shaded box above a dedicated key, always press the shaded key 2nd first, then the function key. The HP 10bII has two shift keys, one purple (PRP) and one orange (ORG). To use the functions printed in purple (stats) on the keypad press the purple button first. To use the functions printed in orange (shift) on the keypad, press the orange button first.

II. AN IMPORTANT STARTING POINT - TEXAS INSTRUMENTS BA II PLUS

Example: You want to display four numbers to the right of the decimal.

Keystrokes	Display	Explanation
2nd		
FORMAT	DEC =	
4 ENTER	DEC = 4.0000	Sets display to show four numbers to the right of the decimal
CE/C CE/C	0.0000	Clears display

Example: You want to display two payments per year to be paid at the end of each period.

Keystrokes	Display	Explanation
2nd		
P/Y	P/Y =	
2 ENTER	P/Y = 2.0000	Sets number of payments per year at 2
2nd		
BGN	END	Sets timing of payment at the end of each period
CE/C CE/C	0.0000	Clears display

II. AN IMPORTANT STARTING POINT - HEWLETT-PACKARD 10BII

Example: You want to display four numbers to the right of the decimal. Note that ORG refers to the orange key, which is a "shifted" function used to access the functions printed in orange. There is also a purple shift key that gives you access to the statistical functions in purple.

Keystrokes	Display	Explanation
ORG, C ALL	0.00	Clears registers
ORG, Disp, 4	0.0000	Displays 4 decimal places

Example: You want to display two payments per year to be paid at the end of the period.

Keystrokes	Display	Explanation
ORG, C ALL	0.0000	Clears registers
2, ORG, P/YR	2.0000	Sets payments per year
ORG, BEG/END	2.0000	Sets END mode unless BEGIN enunciator on

III. CALCULATING TABLE VALUES - TEXAS INSTRUMENTS BA II PLUS

A. The compound sum of $1 (Appendix B)

Example: What is the table value for the compound sum of $1 for 5 years at a 12 percent annual interest rate?

Keystrokes	Display	Explanation
2nd		
P/Y	P/Y =	
1 ENTER	P/Y = 1.0000	Sets number of payments per year at 1
2nd		
BGN	END	Sets timing of payment at the end of each period
CE/C CE/C	0.0000	Clears display
2nd		
CLR TVM	0.0000	Clears TVM variables
1 +/−	PV = −1.0000	Stores initial $1 as a negative present value.
PV		Otherwise the answer will appear as negative.
5 N	N = 5.0000	Stores number of periods
12 I/Y	I/Y = 12.0000	Stores interest rate
CPT FV	FV = 1.7623	Table value

B. The present value of $1 (Appendix C)

Example: What is the table value for the present value of $1 for 8 years at a 10 percent annual interest rate?

Keystrokes	Display	Explanation
2nd		
P/Y	P/Y =	
1 ENTER	P/Y = 1.0000	Sets number of payments per year at 1
2nd		
BGN	END	Sets timing of payment at the end of each period
CE/C CE/C	0.0000	Clears display
2nd		
CLR TVM	0.0000	Clears TVM variables
1 +/−	FV = −1.0000	Stores future amount as negative value
FV		
8 N	N = 8.0000	Stores number of periods
10 I/Y	I/Y = 10.0000	Stores interest rate
CPT PV	PV = 0.4665	Table value

C. The sum of an annuity of $1 for *n* periods (Appendix D)

Example: What is the table value for the compound sum of an annuity of $1 for 6 years at a 14 percent annual interest rate?

Keystrokes	Display	Explanation
2nd		
P/Y	P/Y =	
1 ENTER	P/Y = 1.0000	Sets number of payments per year at 1
2nd		
BGN	END	Sets timing of payment at the end of each period
CE/C CE/C	0.0000	Clears display
2nd		
CLR TVM	0.0000	Clears TVM variables
1 +/−	PMT = −1.0000	Stores annual payment (annuity) as a negative number.
PMT		Otherwise the answer will appear as a negative.
6 N	N = 6.0000	Stores number of periods
14 I/Y	I/Y = 14.0000	Stores interest rate
CPT FV	FV = 8.5355	Table value

D. The present value of an annuity of $1 for *n* periods (Appendix E)

Example: What is the table value for the present value of an annuity of $1 for 12 years at a 9 percent annual interest rate?

Keystrokes	Display	Explanation
2nd		
P/Y	P/Y =	
1 ENTER	P/Y = 1.0000	Sets number of payments per year at 1
2nd		
BGN	END	Sets timing of payment at the end of each period
CE/C CE/C	0.0000	Clears display
2nd		
CLR TVM	0.0000	Clears TVM variables
1 +/−	PMT = −1.0000	Stores annual payment (annuity) as a negative number.
PMT		Otherwise the answer will appear as a negative.
12 N	N = 12.0000	Stores number of periods
9 I/Y	I/Y = 9.0000	Stores interest rate
CPT PV	PV = 7.1607	Table value

III. CALCULATING TABLE VALUES - HEWLETT-PACKARD 10BII

A. The compound sum of $1 (Appendix B)

Example: What is the table value for the compound sum of $1 for 5 years at 12 percent annual interest rate?

Keystrokes	Display	Explanation
ORG, C ALL	0.0000	Clears registers
1, ORG, P/YR	1.0000	Sets number of payments per year at 1
ORG, BEG/END	1.0000	Sets timing of payment at the end of each period
		(If BEGIN shows then press ORG, BEG/END again)
1, +/−, PV	−1.0000	Stores initial $1 as a negative present value.
		Otherwise the answer will appear as a negative.
5, N	5.0000	Stores number of periods
12, I/YR	12.0000	Stores interest rate
FV	1.7623	Table value

B. The Present Value of $1 (Appendix C)

Example: What is the table value for the present value of $1 for 8 years at a 10 percent annual interest rate?

Keystrokes	Display	Explanation
ORG, C ALL	0.0000	Clears registers
1, ORG, P/YR	1.0000	Sets number of payments per year at 1
ORG, BEG/END	1.0000	Sets timing of payment at the end of each period
		(If BEGIN shows press ORG, BEG/END again)
1, +/−, FV	−1.0000	Stores future amount as negative value
8, N	8.0000	Stores number of periods
10, I/YR	10.0000	Stores interest rate
PV	0.4665	Table value

C. The sum of an annuity of $1 for *n* periods (Appendix D)

Example: What is the table value for the compound sum of an annuity of $1 for 6 years at a 14 percent annual interest rate?

Keystrokes	Display	Explanation
ORG, C ALL	0.0000	Clears registers
1, ORG, P/YR	1.0000	Sets number of payments per year at 1
ORG, BEG/END	1.0000	Sets timing of payment at the end of each period
		(If BEGIN shows press ORG, BEG/END again)
1, +/−, PMT	−1.0000	Stores the annual payment (annuity) as a negative number. Otherwise the
		answer will appear as a negative.
6, N	6.0000	Stores the number of periods
14, I/YR	14.0000	Stores interest rate
FV	8.5355	Table value

D. The present value of an annuity of $1 for *n* periods (Appendix E)

Example: What is the table value for the present value of an annuity of $1 for 12 years at a 9 percent annual interest rate?

Keystrokes	Display	Explanation
ORG, C ALL	0.0000	Clears registers
1, ORG, P/YR	1.0000	Sets number of payments per year at 1
ORG, BEG/END	1.0000	Sets timing of payment at the end of each period
		(If BEGIN shows press ORG, BEG/END again)
1, +/−, PMT	−1.0000	Stores the annual payment (annuity) as a negative number.
		Otherwise the answer will appear as a negative.
12, N	12.0000	Stores number of periods
9, I/Y	9.0000	Stores interest rate
PV	7.1607	Table value

IV. CALCULATING PRESENT VALUES - TEXAS INSTRUMENTS BA II PLUS

Example: You are considering the purchase of a franchise of quick oil-change locations, which you believe will provide an annual cash flow of $50,000. At the end of 10 years, you believe that you will be able to sell the franchise for an estimated $900,000. Calculate the maximum amount you should pay for the franchise (present value) in order to realize at least an 18 percent annual yield.

Keystrokes	Display	Explanation
2nd		
BGN	END	Sets timing of payment at the end of each period
CE/C CE/C	0.0000	Clears display
2nd		
CLR TVM	0.0000	Clears TVM variables
10 N	N = 10.0000	Stores n, the holding period
18 I/Y	I/Y = 18.0000	Stores i, the required rate of return
50,000 PMT	PMT = 50,000.0000	Stores *PMT*, the annual cash flow to be received
900,000 FV	FV = 900,000.0000	Stores *FV*, the cash flow to be received at the end of the project
CPT PV	PV = −396,662.3350	The present value, given a required rate of return of 18 percent. (Note: The present value is displayed with a minus sign since it represents cash paid out.)

IV. CALCULATING PRESENT VALUES - HEWLETT-PACKARD 10BII

Example: You are considering the purchase of a franchise of quick oil-change locations, which you believe will provide an annual cash flow of $50,000. At the end of 10 years, you believe that you will be able to sell the franchise for an estimated $900,000. Calculate the maximum amount you should pay for the franchise (present value) in order to realize at least an 18 percent annual yield.

Keystrokes	Display	Explanation
ORG, C ALL	0.0000	Clears registers
ORG, BEG/END	0.0000	Sets timing of payment at the end of each period (If BEGIN shows press ORG, BEG/END again)
10, N	10.0000	Stores n, the holding period
18, I/Y	18.0000	Stores i, the required rate of return
50,000, PMT	50,000.0000	Stores PMT, the annual cash flow to be received
900,000, FV	900,000.0000	Stores FV, the cash flow to be received at the end of the project
PV	−396,662.3350	The present value, given a required rate of return of 18 percent. (Note: The present value is displayed with a minus sign since it represents cash paid out.)

V. CALCULATING FUTURE VALUES (COMPOUND SUM) - TEXAS INSTRUMENTS BA II PLUS

Example: If you deposit $300 a month (at the beginning of each month) into a new account that pays 6.25 percent annual interest compounded monthly, how much will you have in the account after 5 years?

Keystrokes	Display	Explanation
2nd		
BGN	END	Sets timing of payment at the end of each period
2nd		
SET	BGN	Sets timing of payments to beginning of each period
2nd		
P/Y	P/Y =	
12 ENTER	P/Y = 12.0000	Sets 12 payments per year
CE/C CE/C	0.0000	Clears display

(continues on next page)

Keystrokes	Display	Explanation
2nd		
CLR TVM	0.0000	Clears TVM variables
60 N	N = 60.0000	Stores *n*, the number of months for the investment
6.25 I/Y	I/Y = 6.2500	Stores *i*, the annual rate
300 +/− PMT	PMT = −300.0000	Stores *PMT*, the monthly amount invested (with a minus sign for cash paid out)
CPT FV	FV = 21,175.7613	The future value after 5 years

V. CALCULATING FUTURE VALUES (COMPOUND SUM) - HEWLETT-PACKARD 10BII

Example: If you deposit $300 a month (at the beginning of each month) into a new account that pays 6.25 percent annual interest compounded monthly, how much will you have in the account after 5 years?

Keystrokes	Display	Explanation
ORG, C ALL	0.0000	Clears registers
ORG, BEG/END	0.0000(BEGIN)	Sets timing of payments to beginning of each period
12, ORG, P/YR	12.0000	Sets 12 payments per year
60, N	60.0000	Stores *n*, the number of months for the investment
6.25, I/Y	6.2500	Stores *I*, the annual rate
300, +/−, PMT	−300.0000	Stores *PMT*, the monthly amount invested (with a minus sign for cash paid out)
FV	21,175.7613	The future value after 5 years

VI. CALCULATING THE NUMBER OF PAYMENTS OR RECEIPTS - TEXAS INSTRUMENTS BA II PLUS

Example: If you wish to retire with $500,000 saved, and can only afford payments of $500 at the beginning of each month, how long will you have to contribute toward your retirement if you can earn a 10 percent return on your contributions?

Keystrokes	Display	Explanation
2nd		
BGN	BGN	Verifies timing of payment at the beginning of each period
2nd		
P/Y	P/Y = 12.0000	
12 ENTER	P/Y = 12.0000	Sets 12 payments per year
CE/C CE/C	0.0000	Clears display
2nd		
CLR TVM	0.0000	Clears TVM variables
10 I/Y	I/Y = 10.0000	Stores *i*, the interest rate
500 +/− PMT	PMT = −500.0000	Stores *PMT*, the monthly amount invested (with a minus sign for cash paid out)
500,000 FV	FV = 500,000.0000	The value we want to achieve
CPT N	N = 268.2539	Number of months (since we considered monthly payments) required to achieve our goal

VI. CALCULATING THE NUMBER OF PAYMENTS OR RECEIPTS - HEWLETT-PACKARD 10BII

Example: If you wish to retire with $500,000 saved and can only afford payments of $500 at the beginning of each month, how long will you have to contribute toward your retirement if you can earn a 10 percent return on your contributions?

Keystrokes	Display	Explanation
ORG, C ALL	0.0000	Clears registers
ORG, BEG/END	0.0000(BEGIN)	Sets timing of payments to beginning of each period

12, ORG, P/YR	12.0000	Sets 12 payments per year
10, I/YR	10.0000	Stores I, the interest rate
500, +/–, PMT	500.0000	Stores PMT, the monthly amount invested (with a minus sign for cash paid out)
500,000, FV	500,000.0000	The value we want to achieve
N	268.2539	Number of months (since we considered monthly payments) required to achieve our goal

VII. CALCULATING THE PAYMENT AMOUNT - TEXAS INSTRUMENTS BA II PLUS

Example: Suppose your retirement needs were $750,000. If you are currently 25 years old and plan to retire at age 65, how much will you have to contribute at the beginning of each month for retirement if you can earn 12.5 percent on your savings?

Keystrokes	Display	Explanation
2nd		
BGN	BGN	Verifies timing of payment at the beginning of each period
2nd		
P/Y	P/Y = 12.0000	
12 ENTER	P/Y = 12.0000	Sets 12 payments per year
CE/C CE/C	0.0000	Clears display
2nd		
CLR TVM	0.0000	Clears TVM variables
12.5 I/Y	I/Y = 12.5000	Stores i, the interest rate
480 N	N = 480.0000	Stores n, the number of periods until we stop contributing (40 years × 12 months/year = 480 months)
750,000 FV	FV = 750,000.0000	The value we want to achieve
CPT PMT	PMT = −53.8347	Monthly contribution required to achieve our ultimate goal (shown as negative since it represents cash paid out)

VII. CALCULATING THE PAYMENT AMOUNT - HEWLETT-PACKARD 10BII

Example: Suppose your retirement needs are $750,000. If you are currently 25 years old and plan to retire at age 65, how much will you have to contribute at the beginning of each month for retirement if you can earn 12.5 percent on your savings?

Keystrokes	Display	Explanation
ORG, C ALL	0.0000	Clears registers
ORG, BEG/END	0.0000(BEGIN)	Sets timing of payments to the beginning of each period
12, ORG, P/YR	12.0000	Sets 12 payments per year
12.5, I/YR	12.5000	Stores I, the interest rate
480 N	N = 480.0000	Stores n, the number of periods until we stop contributing (40 years × 12 months/year = 480 months)
750,000, FV	750,000.0000	The value we want to achieve
PMT	−53.8347	Monthly contribution required to achieve our ultimate goal (shown as a negative since it represents cash paid out)

VIII. CALCULATING THE INTEREST RATE - TEXAS INSTRUMENTS BA II PLUS

Example: If you invest $300 at the end of each month for 6 years (72 months) for a promised $30,000 return at the end, what interest rate are you earning on your investment?

Keystrokes	Display	Explanation
2nd		
BGN	BGN	Sets timing of payments to beginning of each period

Keystrokes	Display	Explanation
2nd		
SET	END	Sets timing of payments to end of each period
2nd		
P/Y	P/Y = 12.0000	
12 ENTER	P/Y = 12.0000	Sets 12 payments per year
CE/C CE/C	0.0000	Clears display
2nd		
CLR TVM	0.0000	Clears TVM variables
72 N	N = 72.0000	Stores n, the number of deposits (investments)
300 +/−	PMT = −300.0000	Stores PMT, the monthly amount invested (with a minus sign for cash
PMT		paid out)
30,000 FV	FV = 30,000.0000	Stores the future value to be received in 6 years
CPT I/Y	I/Y = 10.5892	The annual interest rate earned on the investment

VIII. CALCULATING THE INTEREST RATE - HEWLETT-PACKARD 10BII

Example: If you invest $300 at the end of each month for 6 years (72 months) for a promised $30,000 return at the end, what interest rate are you earning on your investment?

Keystrokes	Display	Explanation
ORG, C ALL	0.0000	Clears registers
ORG, BEG/END	0.0000	Sets timing of payments to the end of each period
72, N	72.000	Stores n, the number of deposits (investments)
300, +/−, PMT	−300.0000	Stores PMT, the monthly amount invested (with a minus sign for cash
		paid out)
30,000, FV	30,000.0000	Stores the future value to be received in 6 years
I/YR	10.5892	The annual interest rate earned on the investment

IX. BOND VALUATION - TEXAS INSTRUMENTS BA II PLUS

A. Computing the value of a bond

Example: Assume the current date is January 1, 2006, and that you want to know the value of a bond that matures in 10 years and has a coupon rate of 9 percent (4.5 percent semiannually). Your required rate of return is 12 percent.

Keystrokes	Display	Explanation
2nd		
BGN	END	Verifies timing of payments to end of each period
2nd		
P/Y	P/Y = 12.0000	
2 ENTER	P/Y = 2.0000	Sets 2 payments per year; end mode (END) assumes cash flows are at
		the end of each 6-month period
CE/C CE/C	0.0000	Clears display
2nd		
CLR TVM	0.0000	Clears TVM variables
20 N	N = 20.0000	Stores the number of semiannual periods (10 years × 2)
12 I/Y	I/Y = 12.0000	Stores annual rate of return
45 PMT	PMT = 45.0000	Stores the semiannual interest payment
1,000 FV	FV = 1,000.0000	Stores the bond's maturity or par value
CPT PV	PV = −827.9512	Value of the bond, expressed as a negative number

SOLUTION Using the Bond Feature:

CE/C CE/C	0.0000	Clears display
2nd		
BOND	SDT = 1-01-1970	(This will be the last date entered)

2nd		
CLR WORK	SDT = 1-01-1970	Clears BOND variables
1.01.06 ENTER	SDT = 1-01-2006	Stores the current date (month, date, year)
↓	CPN = 0.0000	
9 ENTER	CPN = 9.0000	Stores the coupon interest rate
↓	RDT = 12-31-1990	(This will be the last date entered)
1.01.16 ENTER	RDT = 1-01-2016	Stores the maturity date in 10 years
↓	RV = 100.0000	Verifies bond maturity or par value
↓	ACT	
2nd		
SET	360	Sets calculations to be based on 360-day year
↓	2/Y	Verifies semiannual compounding rate
↓	YLD = 0.0000	
12 ENTER	YLD = 12.0000	Stores the investor's required rate of return
↓	PRI = 0.0000	
CPT	PRI = 82.7951	Value of bond as a percent of par value; i.e., value of bond is $827.95

B. Computing the yield to maturity of a bond

Example: Assume the current date is January 1, 2006, and that you want to know your yield to maturity on a bond that matures in 8 years and has a coupon rate of 12 percent (6 percent semiannually). The bond is selling for $1,100.

Keystrokes	Display	Explanation
2nd		
BGN	END	Verifies timing of payments to end of each period
2nd		
P/Y	P/Y = 12.0000	
2 ENTER	P/Y = 2.0000	Sets 2 payments per year; end mode (END) assumes cash flows are at the end of each 6-month period
CE/C CE/C	0.0000	Clears display
2nd		
CLR TVM	0.0000	Clears TVM variables
16 N	N = 16.0000	Stores the number of semiannual periods (8 years × 2)
1100 +/−	PV = −1,100.0000	Value of the bond, expressed as a negative number
PV		
60 PMT	PMT = 60.0000	Stores the semiannual interest payments
1,000 FV	FV = 1,000.0000	Stores the bond's maturity or par value
CPT I/Y	I/Y = 10.1451	The yield to maturity, expressed on an annual basis

SOLUTION Using the Bond Feature:

CE/C CE/C	0.0000	Clears display
2nd		
Bond	SDT = 1-01-1993	(This will be the last date entered)
2nd		
CLR WORK	SDT = 1-01-1993	Clears BOND variables
1.01.06 ENTER	SDT = 1-01-2006	Stores the current date (month, date, year)
↓	CPN = 0.0000	
12 ENTER	CPN = 12.0000	Stores the coupon interest rate
↓	RDT = 1-01-2003	(This will be the last date entered)
1.01.14 ENTER	RDT = 1-01-2014	Stores the maturity date in 8 years
↓	RV = 100.0000	Verifies bond's maturity or par value
↓	360	
2nd		

(continues on next page)

Keystrokes	Display	Explanation
SET	ACT	Sets calculations to be based on 360-day year
		Verifies semiannual compounding rate
↓	2/Y	
↓	YLD = 0.0000	
↓	PRI = 0.0000	
110 ENTER	PRI = 110.0000	Stores the bond value as a percentage of par value
↑	YLD = 0.0000	
CPT	YLD = 10.1451	Bond's yield to maturity

IX. BOND VALUATION - HEWLETT-PACKARD 10BII

A. Computing the value of a bond

Example: Assume the current date is January 1, 2006, and that you want to know the value of a bond that matures in 10 years and has a coupon rate of 9 percent (4.5 percent semiannually). Your required rate of return is 12 percent.

Keystrokes	Display	Explanation
ORG, C ALL	0.0000	Clears registers
2, ORG, P/YR	2.0000	Sets payments at 2 per year END mode
20, N	20.0000	Stores the number of semiannual periods
12, I/YR	12.0000	Stores annual rate of return
45, PMT	45.0000	Stores the semiannual interest payments
1000, FV	1,000.0000	Stores the bond's maturity or par value
PV	−827.9512	Value of the bond, expressed as a negative number

B. Computing the yield to maturity of a bond

Example: Assume the current date is January 1, 2006, and that you want to know your yield to maturity on a bond that matures in 8 years and has a coupon rate of 12 percent (6 percent semiannually). The bond is selling for $1,100.

Keystrokes	Display	Explanation
ORG, C ALL	0.0000	Clears registers
2, ORG, P/YR	2.0000	Sets payments at 2 per year END mode
16, N	16.0000	Stores the number of semiannual periods (8 years × 2)
1100, +/−, PV	−1,100.0000	Value of the bond expressed as a negative number
60, PMT	60.0000	Stores the semiannual interest payments
1000, FV	1,000.0000	Stores the bond's maturity or par value
I/YR	10.1451	The yield to maturity expressed on an annual basis

X. COMPUTING THE NET PRESENT VALUE AND INTERNAL RATE OF RETURN - TEXAS INSTRUMENTS BA II PLUS

A. Where future cash flows are equal amounts in each period (annuity)

Example: The firm is considering a capital project that would cost $80,000. The firm's cost of capital is 12 percent. The project life is 10 years, during which time the firm expects to receive $15,000 per year. Calculate the *NPV* and *IRR*.

Keystrokes	Display	Explanation
2nd		
BGN	END	Verifies timing of payments to end of each period
2nd		
P/Y	P/Y = 12.0000	
1 ENTER	P/Y = 1.0000	Sets 1 payment per year; end mode (END) assumes cash flows are at the end of each year
CE/C CE/C	0.0000	Clears display

	2nd		
CLR TVM	0.0000		Clears TVM variables
15,000 PMT	PMT = 15.0000		Stores the annual cash flows of $15,000
10 N	N = 10.0000		Stores the life of the project
12 I/Y	I/Y = 12.0000		Stores the cost of capital
CPT PV	PV = −84,753.3454		Calculates present value
+/−	84,753.3454		Changes *PV* to positive
−80,000 =	4,753.3454		Calculates net present value by subtracting the cost of the project
80,000 +/−	−80,000.0000		
PV	PV = −80,000.0000		
CPT I/Y	I/Y = 13.4344		Calculates the *IRR*

B. Where future cash flows are unequal amounts in each period

Example: The firm is considering a capital project that would cost $110,000. The firm's cost of capital is 15 percent. The project life is 5 years, with the following expected cash flows: $−25,000, $50,000, $60,000, $60,000 and $70,000. In addition, you expect to receive $30,000 in the last year from the salvage value of the equipment. Calculate the NPV and IRR.

Keystrokes	Display	Explanation
CE/C CE/C	0.0000	Clears display
CF	$CF_0 = 0.0000$	
2nd		
CLR WORK	$CF_0 = 0.0000$	Clears cash flow variables
110,000 +/−	$CF_0 = −110,000.0000$	Stores CF_0, the initial investment (with a minus sign for a negative cash flow)
ENTER		
↓	CO1 = 0.0000	Stores CF_1, the first year's cash flow (with a minus sign for a negative
25,000 +/−	CO1 = −25,000.0000	cash flow)
ENTER		
↓	FO1 = 1.0000	Stores the number of years CF_1 is repeated (in this case, 1 year only)
ENTER		
↓	CO2 = 0.0000	
50,000	CO2 = 50,000.0000	Stores CF_2
ENTER		
↓	FO2 = 1.0000	
ENTER	FO2 = 1.0000	Stores the number of years CF_2 is repeated
↓	CO3 = 0.0000	
60,000	CO3 = 60,000.0000	Stores CF_3
ENTER		
↓	FO3 = 2.0000	Stores the number of years CF_3 is repeated
2 ENTER		(here, 2 years, so our response is 2 to the FO_3 prompt)
↓	CO4 = 0.0000	
100,000	CO4 = 100,000.0000	Stores CF_4, $70,000 plus expected $30,000
ENTER		
↓	FO4 = 1.0000	Stores the number CF_4
ENTER		
2nd		
QUIT	0.0000	Ends storage of individual cash flows
NPV	I = 0.0000	
15 ENTER	I = 15.0000	Stores interest rate

(continues on next page)

Keystrokes	Display		Explanation
↓	NPV =	0.0000	
CPT	NPV = 29,541.8951		Calculates the project's *NPV* at the stated interest rate
IRR	IRR = 0.0000		
CPT	IRR = 22.0633		Calculates the project's *IRR*

X. COMPUTING THE NET PRESENT VALUE AND INTERNAL RATE OF RETURN - HEWLETT-PACKARD 10BII

A. Where future cash flows are equal amounts in each period (annuity)

Example: The firm is considering a capital project that would cost $80,000. The firm's cost of capital is 12 percent. The project life is 10 years, during which time the firm expects to receive $15,000 per year. Calculate the *NPV* and *IRR*.

Keystrokes	Display	Explanation
ORG, C ALL	0.0000	Clears registers
ORG, BEG/END	0.0000	Verifies timing of payments to end of each period
1, ORG, P/YR	1.0000	Sets 1 payment per year; end mode (END); assumes cash flows are at the end of each year
15,000, PMT	15,000.0000	Stores annual cash flows of $15,000
10, N	10.0000	Stores the life of the project
12, I/YR	12.0000	Stores the cost of capital
PV	−84,753.3454	Calculates present value
+/−	84,753.3454	Changes *PV* to positive
−80,000, =	4753.3454	Calculates net present value by subtracting the cost of the project
80,000, +/−	−80,000.0000	
PV	−80,000.0000	
I/YR	13.4344	Calculates the *IRR*

B. Where future cash flows are unequal amounts in each period

Example: The firm is considering a capital project that would cost $110,000. The firm's cost of capital is 15 percent. The project life is 5 years, with the following expected cash flows: −$25,000, $50,000, $60,000, $60,000, and $70,000. In addition, you expect to receive $30,000 in the last year from the salvage value of the equipment. Calculate the *NPV* and *IRR*.

Keystrokes	Display	Explanation
ORG, C ALL	0.0000	Clears registers
1, ORG, P/YR	1.0000	Sets 1 payment per year END mode
110,000, +/−, CFj	−110,000.0000	Stores CF0, the initial investment (with a minus sign for negative cash flow)
25,000, +/−, CFJ	−25,000.0000	Stores CF1, the first year's cash flow (with a minus sign for negative cash flow)
50,000, CFj	50,000.0000	Stores CF2
60,000, CFj	60,000.0000	Stores CF3
2, ORG, Nj	2.0000	Stores the number of years CF3 is repeated
100,000, CFj	100,000.0000	Stores CF4, $70,000 plus expected $30,000
15, I/YR	15.0000	Stores interest rate
ORG, NPV	29,541.8951	Calculates the project's *NPV* at the stated interest rate
ORG, IRR/YR	22.0633	Calculates the project's *IRR*

APPENDIX B

COMPOUND SUM OF $1 – $FVIF_{i\%, n \text{ years}}$

n	1%	2%	3%	4%	5%	6%	7%	8%	9%	10%
1	1.010	1.020	1.030	1.040	1.050	1.060	1.070	1.080	1.090	1.100
2	1.020	1.040	1.061	1.082	1.102	1.124	1.145	1.166	1.188	1.210
3	1.030	1.061	1.093	1.125	1.158	1.191	1.225	1.260	1.295	1.331
4	1.041	1.082	1.126	1.170	1.216	1.262	1.311	1.360	1.412	1.464
5	1.051	1.104	1.159	1.217	1.276	1.338	1.403	1.469	1.539	1.611
6	1.062	1.126	1.194	1.265	1.340	1.419	1.501	1.587	1.677	1.772
7	1.072	1.149	1.230	1.316	1.407	1.504	1.606	1.714	1.828	1.949
8	1.083	1.172	1.267	1.369	1.477	1.594	1.718	1.851	1.993	2.144
9	1.094	1.195	1.305	1.423	1.551	1.689	1.838	1.999	2.172	2.358
10	1.105	1.219	1.344	1.480	1.629	1.791	1.967	2.159	2.367	2.594
11	1.116	1.243	1.384	1.539	1.710	1.898	2.105	2.332	2.580	2.853
12	1.127	1.268	1.426	1.601	1.796	2.012	2.252	2.518	2.813	3.138
13	1.138	1.294	1.469	1.665	1.886	2.133	2.410	2.720	3.066	3.452
14	1.149	1.319	1.513	1.732	1.980	2.261	2.579	2.937	3.342	3.797
15	1.161	1.346	1.558	1.801	2.079	2.397	2.759	3.172	3.642	4.177
16	1.173	1.373	1.605	1.873	2.183	2.540	2.952	3.426	3.970	4.595
17	1.184	1.400	1.653	1.948	2.292	2.693	3.159	3.700	4.328	5.054
18	1.196	1.428	1.702	2.026	2.407	2.854	3.380	3.996	4.717	5.560
19	1.208	1.457	1.753	2.107	2.527	3.026	3.616	4.316	5.142	6.116
20	1.220	1.486	1.806	2.191	2.653	3.207	3.870	4.661	5.604	6.727
21	1.232	1.516	1.860	2.279	2.786	3.399	4.140	5.034	6.109	7.400
22	1.245	1.546	1.916	2.370	2.925	3.603	4.430	5.436	6.658	8.140
23	1.257	1.577	1.974	2.465	3.071	3.820	4.740	5.871	7.258	8.954
24	1.270	1.608	2.033	2.563	3.225	4.049	5.072	6.341	7.911	9.850
25	1.282	1.641	2.094	2.666	3.386	4.292	5.427	6.848	8.623	10.834
30	1.348	1.811	2.427	3.243	4.322	5.743	7.612	10.062	13.267	17.449
40	1.489	2.208	3.262	4.801	7.040	10.285	14.974	21.724	31.408	45.258
50	1.645	2.691	4.384	7.106	11.467	18.419	29.456	46.900	74.354	117.386

n	11%	12%	13%	14%	15%	16%	17%	18%	19%	20%
1	1.110	1.120	1.130	1.140	1.150	1.160	1.170	1.180	1.190	1.200
2	1.232	1.254	1.277	1.300	1.322	1.346	1.369	1.392	1.416	1.440
3	1.368	1.405	1.443	1.482	1.521	1.561	1.602	1.643	1.685	1.728
4	1.518	1.574	1.630	1.689	1.749	1.811	1.874	1.939	2.005	2.074
5	1.685	1.762	1.842	1.925	2.011	2.100	2.192	2.288	2.386	2.488
6	1.870	1.974	2.082	2.195	2.313	2.436	2.565	2.700	2.840	2.986
7	2.076	2.211	2.353	2.502	2.660	2.826	3.001	3.185	3.379	3.583
8	2.305	2.476	2.658	2.853	3.059	3.278	3.511	3.759	4.021	4.300
9	2.558	2.773	3.004	3.252	3.518	3.803	4.108	4.435	4.785	5.160
10	2.839	3.106	3.395	3.707	4.046	4.411	4.807	5.234	5.695	6.192
11	3.152	3.479	3.836	4.226	4.652	5.117	5.624	6.176	6.777	7.430
12	3.498	3.896	4.334	4.818	5.350	5.936	6.580	7.288	8.064	8.916
13	3.883	4.363	4.898	5.492	6.153	6.886	7.699	8.599	9.596	10.699
14	4.310	4.887	5.535	6.261	7.076	7.987	9.007	10.147	11.420	12.839
15	4.785	5.474	6.254	7.138	8.137	9.265	10.539	11.974	13.589	15.407
16	5.311	6.130	7.067	8.137	9.358	10.748	12.330	14.129	16.171	18.488
17	5.895	6.866	7.986	9.276	10.761	12.468	14.426	16.672	19.244	22.186
18	6.543	7.690	9.024	10.575	12.375	14.462	16.879	19.673	22.900	26.623
19	7.263	8.613	10.197	12.055	14.232	16.776	19.748	23.214	27.251	31.948
20	8.062	9.646	11.523	13.743	16.366	19.461	23.105	27.393	32.429	38.337
21	8.949	10.804	13.021	15.667	18.821	22.574	27.033	32.323	38.591	46.005
22	9.933	12.100	14.713	17.861	21.644	26.186	31.629	38.141	45.923	55.205
23	11.026	13.552	16.626	20.361	24.891	30.376	37.005	45.007	54.648	66.247
24	12.239	15.178	18.788	23.212	28.625	35.236	43.296	53.108	65.031	79.496
25	13.585	17.000	21.230	26.461	32.918	40.874	50.656	62.667	77.387	95.395
30	22.892	29.960	39.115	50.949	66.210	85.849	111.061	143.367	184.672	237.373
40	64.999	93.049	132.776	188.876	267.856	378.715	533.846	750.353	1051.642	1469.740
50	184.559	288.996	450.711	700.197	1083.619	1670.669	2566.080	3927.189	5988.730	9100.191

n	21%	22%	23%	24%	25%	26%	27%	28%	29%	30%
1	1.210	1.220	1.230	1.240	1.250	1.260	1.270	1.280	1.290	1.300
2	1.464	1.488	1.513	1.538	1.562	1.588	1.613	1.638	1.664	1.690
3	1.772	1.816	1.861	1.907	1.953	2.000	2.048	2.097	2.147	2.197
4	2.144	2.215	2.289	2.364	2.441	2.520	2.601	2.684	2.769	2.856
5	2.594	2.703	2.815	2.932	3.052	3.176	3.304	3.436	3.572	3.713
6	3.138	3.297	3.463	3.635	3.815	4.001	4.196	4.398	4.608	4.827
7	3.797	4.023	4.259	4.508	4.768	5.042	5.329	5.629	5.945	6.275
8	4.595	4.908	5.239	5.589	5.960	6.353	6.767	7.206	7.669	8.157
9	5.560	5.987	6.444	6.931	7.451	8.004	8.595	9.223	9.893	10.604
10	6.727	7.305	7.926	8.594	9.313	10.086	10.915	11.806	12.761	13.786
11	8.140	8.912	9.749	10.657	11.642	12.708	13.862	15.112	16.462	17.921
12	9.850	10.872	11.991	13.215	14.552	16.012	17.605	19.343	21.236	23.298
13	11.918	13.264	14.749	16.386	18.190	20.175	22.359	24.759	27.395	30.287
14	14.421	16.182	18.141	20.319	22.737	25.420	28.395	31.691	35.339	39.373
15	17.449	19.742	22.314	25.195	28.422	32.030	36.062	40.565	45.587	51.185
16	21.113	24.085	27.446	31.242	35.527	40.357	45.799	51.923	58.808	66.541
17	25.547	29.384	33.758	38.740	44.409	50.850	58.165	66.461	75.862	86.503
18	30.912	35.848	41.523	48.038	55.511	64.071	73.869	85.070	97.862	112.454
19	37.404	43.735	51.073	59.567	69.389	80.730	93.813	108.890	126.242	146.190
20	45.258	53.357	62.820	73.863	86.736	101.720	119.143	139.379	162.852	190.047
21	54.762	65.095	77.268	91.591	108.420	128.167	151.312	178.405	210.079	247.061
22	66.262	79.416	95.040	113.572	135.525	161.490	192.165	228.358	271.002	321.178
23	80.178	96.887	116.899	140.829	169.407	203.477	244.050	292.298	349.592	417.531
24	97.015	118.203	143.786	174.628	211.758	256.381	309.943	374.141	450.974	542.791
25	117.388	144.207	176.857	216.539	264.698	323.040	393.628	478.901	581.756	705.627
30	304.471	389.748	497.904	634.810	807.793	1025.904	1300.477	1645.488	2078.208	2619.936
40	2048.309	2846.941	3946.340	5455.797	7523.156	10346.879	14195.051	19426.418	26520.723	36117.754
50	13779.844	20795.680	31278.301	46889.207	70064.812	104354.562	154942.687	229345.875	338440.000	497910.125

n	31%	32%	33%	34%	35%	36%	37%	38%	39%	40%
1	1.310	1.320	1.330	1.340	1.350	1.360	1.370	1.380	1.390	1.400
2	1.716	1.742	1.769	1.796	1.822	1.850	1.877	1.904	1.932	1.960
3	2.248	2.300	2.353	2.406	2.460	2.515	2.571	2.628	2.686	2.744
4	2.945	3.036	3.129	3.224	3.321	3.421	3.523	3.627	3.733	3.842
5	3.858	4.007	4.162	4.320	4.484	4.653	4.826	5.005	5.189	5.378
6	5.054	5.290	5.535	5.789	6.053	6.328	6.612	6.907	7.213	7.530
7	6.621	6.983	7.361	7.758	8.172	8.605	9.058	9.531	10.025	10.541
8	8.673	9.217	9.791	10.395	11.032	11.703	12.410	13.153	13.935	14.758
9	11.362	12.166	13.022	13.930	14.894	15.917	17.001	18.151	19.370	20.661
10	14.884	16.060	17.319	18.666	20.106	21.646	23.292	25.049	26.924	28.925
11	19.498	21.199	23.034	25.012	27.144	29.439	31.910	34.567	37.425	40.495
12	25.542	27.982	30.635	33.516	36.644	40.037	43.716	47.703	52.020	56.694
13	33.460	36.937	40.745	44.912	49.469	54.451	59.892	65.830	72.308	79.371
14	43.832	49.756	54.190	60.181	66.784	74.053	82.051	90.845	100.509	111.190
15	57.420	64.358	72.073	80.643	90.158	100.712	112.410	125.366	139.707	155.567
16	75.220	84.953	95.857	108.061	121.713	136.968	154.002	173.005	194.192	217.793
17	98.539	112.138	127.490	144.802	164.312	186.277	210.983	238.747	269.927	304.911
18	129.086	148.022	169.561	194.035	221.822	253.337	289.046	329.471	375.198	426.875
19	169.102	195.389	225.517	260.006	299.459	344.537	395.993	454.669	521.525	597.625
20	221.523	257.913	299.937	348.408	404.270	468.571	542.511	627.443	724.919	836.674
21	290.196	340.446	398.916	466.867	545.764	637.256	743.240	865.871	1007.637	1171.343
22	380.156	449.388	530.558	625.601	736.781	865.668	1018.238	1194.900	1400.615	1639.878
23	498.004	593.192	705.642	838.305	994.653	1178.668	1394.986	1648.961	1946.854	2295.829
24	652.385	783.013	938.504	1123.328	1342.781	1602.988	1911.129	2275.564	2706.125	3214.158
25	854.623	1033.577	1248.210	1505.258	1812.754	2180.063	2618.245	3140.275	3761.511	4499.816
30	3297.081	4142.008	5194.516	6503.285	8128.426	10142.914	12636.086	15716.703	19517.969	24201.043
40	49072.621	66519.313	89962.188	121388.437	163433.875	219558.625	294317.937	393684.687	525508.312	700022.688

APPENDIX C

PRESENT VALUE OF $1 — $PVIF_{i\%, n \text{ years}}$

n	1%	2%	3%	4%	5%	6%	7%	8%	9%	10%
1	.990	.980	.971	.962	.952	.943	.935	.926	.917	.909
2	.980	.961	.943	.925	.907	.890	.873	.857	.842	.826
3	.971	.942	.915	.889	.864	.840	.816	.794	.772	.751
4	.961	.924	.888	.855	.823	.792	.763	.735	.708	.683
5	.951	.906	.863	.822	.784	.747	.713	.681	.650	.621
6	.942	.888	.837	.790	.746	.705	.666	.630	.596	.564
7	.933	.871	.813	.760	.711	.665	.623	.583	.547	.513
8	.923	.853	.789	.731	.677	.627	.582	.540	.502	.467
9	.914	.837	.766	.703	.645	.592	.544	.500	.460	.424
10	.905	.820	.744	.676	.614	.558	.508	.463	.422	.386
11	.896	.804	.722	.650	.585	.527	.475	.429	.388	.350
12	.887	.789	.701	.625	.557	.497	.444	.397	.356	.319
13	.879	.773	.681	.601	.530	.469	.415	.368	.326	.290
14	.870	.758	.661	.577	.505	.442	.388	.340	.299	.263
15	.861	.743	.642	.555	.481	.417	.362	.315	.275	.239
16	.853	.728	.623	.534	.458	.394	.339	.292	.252	.218
17	.844	.714	.605	.513	.436	.371	.317	.270	.231	.198
18	.836	.700	.587	.494	.416	.350	.296	.250	.212	.180
19	.828	.686	.570	.475	.396	.331	.277	.232	.194	.164
20	.820	.673	.554	.456	.377	.312	.258	.215	.178	.149
21	.811	.660	.538	.439	.359	.294	.242	.199	.164	.135
22	.803	.647	.522	.422	.342	.278	.226	.184	.150	.123
23	.795	.634	.507	.406	.326	.262	.211	.170	.138	.112
24	.788	.622	.492	.390	.310	.247	.197	.158	.126	.102
25	.780	.610	.478	.375	.295	.233	.184	.146	.116	.092
30	.742	.552	.412	.308	.231	.174	.131	.099	.075	.057
40	.672	.453	.307	.208	.142	.097	.067	.046	.032	.022
50	.608	.372	.228	.141	.087	.054	.034	.021	.013	.009

n	11%	12%	13%	14%	15%	16%	17%	18%	19%	20%
1	.901	.893	.885	.877	.870	.862	.855	.847	.840	.833
2	.812	.797	.783	.769	.756	.743	.731	.718	.706	.694
3	.731	.712	.693	.675	.658	.641	.624	.609	.593	.579
4	.659	.636	.613	.592	.572	.552	.534	.516	.499	.482
5	.593	.567	.543	.519	.497	.476	.456	.437	.419	.402
6	.535	.507	.480	.456	.432	.410	.390	.370	.352	.335
7	.482	.452	.425	.400	.376	.354	.333	.314	.296	.279
8	.434	.404	.376	.351	.327	.305	.285	.266	.249	.233
9	.391	.361	.333	.308	.284	.263	.243	.225	.209	.194
10	.352	.322	.295	.270	.247	.227	.208	.191	.176	.162
11	.317	.287	.261	.237	.215	.195	.178	.162	.148	.135
12	.286	.257	.231	.208	.187	.168	.152	.137	.124	.112
13	.258	.229	.204	.182	.163	.145	.130	.116	.104	.093
14	.232	.205	.181	.160	.141	.125	.111	.099	.088	.078
15	.209	.183	.160	.140	.123	.108	.095	.084	.074	.065
16	.188	.163	.141	.123	.107	.093	.081	.071	.062	.054
17	.170	.146	.125	.108	.093	.080	.069	.060	.052	.045
18	.153	.130	.111	.095	.081	.069	.059	.051	.044	.038
19	.138	.116	.098	.083	.070	.060	.051	.043	.037	.031
20	.124	.104	.087	.073	.061	.051	.043	.037	.031	.026
21	.112	.093	.077	.064	.053	.044	.037	.031	.026	.022
22	.101	.083	.068	.056	.046	.038	.032	.026	.022	.018
23	.091	.074	.060	.049	.040	.033	.027	.022	.018	.015
24	.082	.066	.053	.043	.035	.028	.023	.019	.015	.013
25	.074	.059	.047	.038	.030	.024	.020	.016	.013	.010
30	.044	.033	.026	.020	.015	.012	.009	.007	.005	.004
40	.015	.011	.008	.005	.004	.003	.002	.001	.001	.001
50	.005	.003	.002	.001	.001	.001	.000	.000	.000	.000

n	21%	22%	23%	24%	25%	26%	27%	28%	29%	30%
1	.826	.820	.813	.806	.800	.794	.787	.781	.775	.769
2	.683	.672	.661	.650	.640	.630	.620	.610	.601	.592
3	.564	.551	.537	.524	.512	.500	.488	.477	.466	.455
4	.467	.451	.437	.423	.410	.397	.384	.373	.361	.350
5	.386	.370	.355	.341	.328	.315	.303	.291	.280	.269
6	.319	.303	.289	.275	.262	.250	.238	.227	.217	.207
7	.263	.249	.235	.222	.210	.198	.188	.178	.168	.159
8	.218	.204	.191	.179	.168	.157	.148	.139	.130	.123
9	.180	.167	.155	.144	.134	.125	.116	.108	.101	.094
10	.149	.137	.126	.116	.107	.099	.092	.085	.078	.073
11	.123	.112	.103	.094	.086	.079	.072	.066	.061	.056
12	.102	.092	.083	.076	.069	.062	.057	.052	.047	.043
13	.084	.075	.068	.061	.055	.050	.045	.040	.037	.033
14	.069	.062	.055	.049	.044	.039	.035	.032	.028	.025
15	.057	.051	.045	.040	.035	.031	.028	.025	.022	.020
16	.047	.042	.036	.032	.028	.025	.022	.019	.017	.015
17	.039	.034	.030	.026	.023	.020	.017	.015	.013	.012
18	.032	.028	.024	.021	.018	.016	.014	.012	.010	.009
19	.027	.023	.020	.017	.014	.012	.011	.009	.008	.007
20	.022	.019	.016	.014	.012	.010	.008	.007	.006	.005
21	.018	.015	.013	.011	.009	.008	.007	.006	.005	.004
22	.015	.013	.011	.009	.007	.006	.005	.004	.004	.003
23	.012	.010	.009	.007	.006	.005	.004	.003	.003	.002
24	.010	.008	.007	.006	.005	.004	.003	.003	.002	.002
25	.009	.007	.006	.005	.004	.003	.003	.002	.002	.001
30	.003	.003	.002	.002	.001	.001	.001	.001	.000	.000
40	.000	.000	.000	.000	.000	.000	.000	.000	.000	.000
50	.000	.000	.000	.000	.000	.000	.000	.000	.000	.000

n	31%	32%	33%	34%	35%	36%	37%	38%	39%	40%
1	.763	.758	.752	.746	.741	.735	.730	.725	.719	.714
2	.583	.574	.565	.557	.549	.541	.533	.525	.518	.510
3	.445	.435	.425	.416	.406	.398	.389	.381	.372	.364
4	.340	.329	.320	.310	.301	.292	.284	.276	.268	.260
5	.259	.250	.240	.231	.223	.215	.207	.200	.193	.186
6	.198	.189	.181	.173	.165	.158	.151	.145	.139	.133
7	.151	.143	.136	.129	.122	.116	.110	.105	.100	.095
8	.115	.108	.102	.096	.091	.085	.081	.076	.072	.068
9	.088	.082	.077	.072	.067	.063	.059	.055	.052	.048
10	.067	.062	.058	.054	.050	.046	.043	.040	.037	.035
11	.051	.047	.043	.040	.037	.034	.031	.029	.027	.025
12	.039	.036	.033	.030	.027	.025	.023	.021	.019	.018
13	.030	.027	.025	.022	.020	.018	.017	.015	.014	.013
14	.023	.021	.018	.017	.015	.014	.012	.011	.010	.009
15	.017	.016	.014	.012	.011	.010	.009	.008	.007	.006
16	.013	.012	.010	.009	.008	.007	.006	.006	.005	.005
17	.010	.009	.008	.007	.006	.005	.005	.004	.004	.003
18	.008	.007	.006	.005	.005	.004	.003	.003	.003	.002
19	.006	.005	.004	.004	.003	.003	.003	.002	.002	.002
20	.005	.004	.003	.003	.002	.002	.002	.002	.001	.001
21	.003	.003	.003	.002	.002	.002	.001	.001	.001	.001
22	.003	.002	.002	.002	.001	.001	.001	.001	.001	.001
23	.002	.002	.001	.001	.001	.001	.001	.001	.001	.000
24	.002	.001	.001	.001	.001	.001	.001	.000	.000	.000
25	.001	.001	.001	.001	.001	.000	.000	.000	.000	.000
30	.000	.000	.000	.000	.000	.000	.000	.000	.000	.000
40	.000	.000	.000	.000	.000	.000	.000	.000	.000	.000

APPENDIX D

SUM OF AN ANNUITY OF $1 FOR n PERIODS — FVIFA$_{i\%, n \text{ years}}$

n	1%	2%	3%	4%	5%	6%	7%	8%	9%	10%
1	1.000	1.000	1.000	1.000	1.000	1.000	1.000	1.000	1.000	1.000
2	2.010	2.020	2.030	2.040	2.050	2.060	2.070	2.080	2.090	2.100
3	3.030	3.060	3.091	3.122	3.152	3.184	3.215	3.246	3.278	3.310
4	4.060	4.122	4.184	4.246	4.310	4.375	4.440	4.506	4.573	4.641
5	5.101	5.204	5.309	5.416	5.526	5.637	5.751	5.867	5.985	6.105
6	6.152	6.308	6.468	6.633	6.802	6.975	7.153	7.336	7.523	7.716
7	7.214	7.434	7.662	7.898	8.142	8.394	8.654	8.923	9.200	9.487
8	8.286	8.583	8.892	9.214	9.549	9.897	10.260	10.637	11.028	11.436
9	9.368	9.755	10.159	10.583	11.027	11.491	11.978	12.488	13.021	13.579
10	10.462	10.950	11.464	12.006	12.578	13.181	13.816	14.487	15.193	15.937
11	11.567	12.169	12.808	13.486	14.207	14.972	15.784	16.645	17.560	18.531
12	12.682	13.412	14.192	15.026	15.917	16.870	17.888	18.977	20.141	21.384
13	13.809	14.680	15.618	16.627	17.713	18.882	20.141	21.495	22.953	24.523
14	14.947	15.974	17.086	18.292	19.598	21.015	22.550	24.215	26.019	27.975
15	16.097	17.293	18.599	20.023	21.578	23.276	25.129	27.152	29.361	31.772
16	17.258	18.639	20.157	21.824	23.657	25.672	27.888	30.324	33.003	35.949
17	18.430	20.012	21.761	23.697	25.840	28.213	30.840	33.750	36.973	40.544
18	19.614	21.412	23.414	25.645	28.132	30.905	33.999	37.450	41.301	45.599
19	20.811	22.840	25.117	27.671	30.539	33.760	37.379	41.446	46.018	51.158
20	22.019	24.297	26.870	29.778	33.066	36.785	40.995	45.762	51.159	57.274
21	23.239	25.783	28.676	31.969	35.719	39.992	44.865	50.422	56.764	64.002
22	24.471	27.299	30.536	34.248	38.505	43.392	49.005	55.456	62.872	71.402
23	25.716	28.845	32.452	36.618	41.430	46.995	53.435	60.893	69.531	79.542
24	26.973	30.421	34.426	39.082	44.501	50.815	58.176	66.764	76.789	88.496
25	28.243	32.030	36.459	41.645	47.726	54.864	63.248	73.105	84.699	98.346
30	34.784	40.567	47.575	56.084	66.438	79.057	94.459	113.282	136.305	164.491
40	48.885	60.401	75.400	95.024	120.797	154.758	199.630	295.052	337.872	442.580
50	64.461	84.577	112.794	152.664	209.341	290.325	406.516	573.756	815.051	1163.865

n	11%	12%	13%	14%	15%	16%	17%	18%	19%	20%
1	1.000	1.000	1.000	1.000	1.000	1.000	1.000	1.000	1.000	1.000
2	2.110	2.120	2.130	2.140	2.150	2.160	2.170	2.180	2.190	2.200
3	3.342	3.374	3.407	3.440	3.472	3.506	3.539	3.572	3.606	3.640
4	4.710	4.779	4.850	4.921	4.993	5.066	5.141	5.215	5.291	5.368
5	6.228	6.353	6.480	6.610	6.742	6.877	7.014	7.154	7.297	7.442
6	7.913	8.115	8.323	8.535	8.754	8.977	9.207	9.442	9.683	9.930
7	9.783	10.089	10.405	10.730	11.067	11.414	11.772	12.141	12.523	12.916
8	11.859	12.300	12.757	13.233	13.727	14.240	14.773	15.327	15.902	16.499
9	14.164	14.776	15.416	16.085	16.786	17.518	18.285	19.086	19.923	20.799
10	16.722	17.549	18.420	19.337	20.304	21.321	22.393	23.521	24.709	25.959
11	19.561	20.655	21.814	23.044	24.349	25.733	27.200	28.755	30.403	32.150
12	22.713	24.133	25.650	27.271	29.001	30.850	32.824	34.931	37.180	39.580
13	26.211	28.029	29.984	32.088	34.352	36.786	39.404	42.218	45.244	48.496
14	30.095	32.392	34.882	37.581	40.504	43.672	47.102	50.818	54.841	59.196
15	34.405	37.280	40.417	43.842	47.580	51.659	56.109	60.965	66.260	72.035
16	39.190	42.753	46.671	50.980	55.717	60.925	66.648	72.938	79.850	87.442
17	44.500	48.883	53.738	59.117	65.075	71.673	78.978	87.067	96.021	105.930
18	50.396	55.749	61.724	68.393	75.836	84.140	93.404	103.739	115.265	128.116
19	56.939	64.439	70.748	78.968	88.211	98.603	110.283	123.412	138.165	154.739
20	64.202	72.052	80.946	91.024	102.443	115.379	130.031	146.626	165.417	186.687
21	72.264	81.698	92.468	104.767	118.809	134.840	153.136	174.019	197.846	225.024
22	81.213	92.502	105.489	120.434	137.630	157.414	180.169	206.342	236.436	271.028
23	91.147	104.602	120.203	138.295	159.274	183.600	211.798	244.483	282.359	326.234
24	102.173	118.154	136.829	158.656	184.166	213.976	248.803	289.490	337.007	392.480
25	114.412	133.333	155.616	181.867	212.790	249.212	292.099	342.598	402.038	471.976
30	199.018	241.330	293.192	356.778	434.738	530.306	647.423	790.932	966.698	1181.865
40	581.812	767.080	1013.667	1341.979	1779.048	2360.724	3134.412	4163.094	5529.711	7343.715
50	1668.723	2399.975	3459.344	4994.301	7217.488	10435.449	15088.805	21812.273	31514.492	45496.094

n	21%	22%	23%	24%	25%	26%	27%	28%	29%	30%
1	1.000	1.000	1.000	1.000	1.000	1.000	1.000	1.000	1.000	1.000
2	2.210	2.220	2.230	2.240	2.250	2.260	2.270	2.280	2.290	2.300
3	3.674	3.708	3.743	3.778	3.813	3.848	3.883	3.918	3.954	3.990
4	5.446	5.524	5.604	5.684	5.766	5.848	5.931	6.016	6.101	6.187
5	7.589	7.740	7.893	8.048	8.207	8.368	8.533	8.700	8.870	9.043
6	10.183	10.442	10.708	10.980	11.259	11.544	11.837	12.136	12.442	12.756
7	13.321	13.740	14.171	14.615	15.073	15.546	16.032	16.534	17.051	17.583
8	17.119	17.762	18.430	19.123	19.842	20.588	21.361	22.163	22.995	23.858
9	21.714	22.670	23.669	24.712	25.802	26.940	28.129	29.369	30.664	32.015
10	27.274	28.657	30.113	31.643	33.253	34.945	36.723	38.592	40.556	42.619
11	34.001	35.962	38.039	40.238	42.566	45.030	47.639	50.398	53.318	56.405
12	42.141	44.873	47.787	50.895	54.208	57.738	61.501	65.510	69.780	74.326
13	51.991	55.745	59.778	64.109	68.760	73.750	79.106	84.853	91.016	97.624
14	63.909	69.009	74.528	80.496	86.949	93.925	101.465	109.611	118.411	127.912
15	78.330	85.191	92.669	100.815	109.687	119.346	129.860	141.302	153.750	167.285
16	95.779	104.933	114.983	126.010	138.109	151.375	165.922	181.867	199.337	218.470
17	116.892	129.019	142.428	157.252	173.636	191.733	211.721	233.790	258.145	285.011
18	142.439	158.403	176.187	195.993	218.045	242.583	269.885	300.250	334.006	371.514
19	173.351	194.251	217.710	244.031	273.556	306.654	343.754	385.321	431.868	483.968
20	210.755	237.986	268.783	303.598	342.945	387.384	437.568	494.210	558.110	630.157
21	256.013	291.343	331.603	377.461	429.681	489.104	556.710	633.589	720.962	820.204
22	310.775	356.438	408.871	469.052	538.101	617.270	708.022	811.993	931.040	1067.265
23	377.038	435.854	503.911	582.624	673.626	778.760	990.187	1040.351	1202.042	1388.443
24	457.215	532.741	620.810	723.453	843.032	982.237	1144.237	1332.649	1551.634	1805.975
25	554.230	650.944	764.596	898.082	1054.791	1238.617	1454.180	1706.790	2002.608	2348.765
30	1445.111	1767.044	2160.459	2640.881	3227.172	3941.953	4812.891	5873.172	7162.785	8729.805
40	9749.141	12936.141	17153.691	22728.367	30088.621	39791.957	52570.707	69376.562	91447.375	120389.375

n	31%	32%	33%	34%	35%	36%	37%	38%	39%	40%
1	1.000	1.000	1.000	1.000	1.000	1.000	1.000	1.000	1.000	1.000
2	2.310	2.320	2.330	2.340	2.350	2.360	2.370	2.380	2.390	2.400
3	4.026	4.062	4.099	4.136	4.172	4.210	4.247	4.284	4.322	4.360
4	6.274	6.362	6.452	6.542	6.633	6.725	6.818	6.912	7.008	7.104
5	9.219	9.398	9.581	9.766	9.954	10.146	10.341	10.539	10.741	10.946
6	13.077	13.406	13.742	14.086	14.438	14.799	15.167	15.544	15.930	16.324
7	18.131	18.696	19.277	19.876	20.492	21.126	21.779	22.451	23.142	23.853
8	24.752	25.678	26.638	27.633	28.664	29.732	30.837	31.982	33.167	34.395
9	33.425	34.895	36.429	38.028	39.696	41.435	43.247	45.135	47.103	49.152
10	44.786	47.062	49.451	51.958	54.590	57.351	60.248	63.287	66.473	69.813
11	59.670	63.121	66.769	70.624	74.696	78.998	83.540	88.335	93.397	98.739
12	79.167	84.320	89.803	95.636	101.840	108.437	115.450	122.903	130.822	139.234
13	104.709	112.302	120.438	129.152	138.484	148.474	159.166	170.606	182.842	195.928
14	138.169	149.239	161.183	174.063	187.953	202.925	219.058	236.435	255.151	275.299
15	182.001	197.996	215.373	234.245	254.737	276.978	301.109	327.281	355.659	386.418
16	239.421	262.354	287.446	314.888	344.895	377.690	413.520	452.647	495.366	541.985
17	314.642	347.307	383.303	422.949	466.608	514.658	567.521	625.652	689.558	759.778
18	413.180	459.445	510.792	567.751	630.920	700.935	778.504	864.399	959.485	1064.689
19	542.266	607.467	680.354	761.786	852.741	954.271	1067.551	1193.870	1334.683	1491.563
20	711.368	802.856	905.870	1021.792	1152.200	1298.809	1463.544	1648.539	1856.208	2089.188
21	932.891	1060.769	1205.807	1370.201	1556.470	1767.380	2006.055	2275.982	2581.128	2925.862
22	1223.087	1401.215	1604.724	1837.068	2102.234	2404.636	2749.294	3141.852	3588.765	4097.203
23	1603.243	1850.603	2135.282	2462.669	2839.014	3271.304	3767.532	4336.750	4989.379	5737.078
24	2101.247	2443.795	2840.924	3300.974	3833.667	4449.969	5162.516	5985.711	6936.230	8032.906
25	2753.631	3226.808	3779.428	4424.301	5176.445	6052.957	7073.645	8261.273	9642.352	11247.062
30	10632.543	12940.672	15737.945	19124.434	23221.258	28172.016	34148.906	41357.227	50043.625	60500.207

APPENDIX E

PRESENT VALUE OF AN ANNUITY OF $1 FOR *n* PERIODS — $PVIFA_{i\%, n\ years}$

n	1%	2%	3%	4%	5%	6%	7%	8%	9%	10%
1	.990	.980	.971	.962	.952	.943	.935	.926	.917	.909
2	1.970	1.942	1.913	1.886	1.859	1.833	1.808	1.3783	1.759	1.736
3	2.941	2.884	2.829	2.775	2.723	2.673	2.624	2.577	2.531	2.487
4	3.902	3.808	3.717	3.630	3.546	3.465	3.387	3.312	3.240	3.170
5	4.853	4.713	4.580	4.452	4.329	4.212	4.100	3.993	3.890	3.791
6	5.795	5.601	5.417	5.242	5.076	4.917	4.767	5.623	4.486	4.355
7	6.728	6.472	6.230	6.002	5.786	5.582	5.389	5.206	5.033	4.868
8	7.652	7.326	7.020	6.733	6.463	6.210	5.971	5.747	5.535	5.335
9	8.566	8.162	7.786	7.435	7.108	6.802	6.515	6.247	5.995	5.759
10	9.471	8.983	8.530	8.111	7.722	7.360	7.024	6.710	6.418	6.145
11	10.368	9.787	9.253	8.760	8.306	7.887	7.499	7.139	6.805	6.495
12	11.255	10.575	9.954	9.385	8.863	8.384	7.943	7.536	7.161	6.814
13	12.134	11.348	10.635	9.986	9.394	8.853	8.358	7.904	7.487	7.103
14	13.004	12.106	11.296	10.563	9.899	9.295	8.746	8.244	7.786	7.367
15	13.865	12.849	11.938	11.118	10.380	9.712	9.108	8.560	8.061	7.606
16	14.718	13.578	12.561	11.652	10.838	10.106	9.447	8.851	8.313	7.824
17	15.562	14.292	13.166	12.166	11.274	10.477	9.763	9.122	8.544	8.022
18	16.398	14.992	13.754	12.659	11.690	10.828	10.059	9.372	8.756	8.201
19	17.226	15.679	14.324	13.134	12.085	11.158	10.336	9.604	8.950	8.365
20	18.046	16.352	14.878	13.590	12.462	11.470	10.594	9.818	9.129	8.514
21	18.857	17.011	15.415	14.029	12.821	11.764	10.836	10.017	9.292	8.649
22	19.661	17.658	15.937	14.451	13.163	12.042	11.061	10.201	9.442	8.772
23	20.456	18.292	16.444	14.857	13.489	12.303	11.272	10.371	9.580	8.883
24	21.244	18.914	16.936	15.247	13.799	12.550	11.469	10.529	9.707	8.985
25	22.023	19.524	17.413	15.622	14.094	12.783	11.654	10.675	9.823	9.077
30	25.808	22.397	19.601	17.292	15.373	13.765	12.409	11.258	10.274	9.427
40	32.835	27.356	23.115	19.793	17.159	15.046	13.332	11.925	10.757	9.779
50	39.197	31.424	25.730	21.482	18.256	15.762	13.801	12.234	10.962	9.915

n	11%	12%	13%	14%	15%	16%	17%	18%	19%	20%
1	.901	.893	.885	.877	.870	.862	.855	.847	.840	.833
2	1.713	1.690	1.668	1.647	1.626	1.605	1.585	1.566	1.547	1.528
3	2.444	2.402	2.361	2.322	2.283	2.246	2.210	2.174	2.140	2.106
4	3.102	3.037	2.974	2.914	2.855	2.798	2.743	2.690	2.639	2.589
5	3.696	3.605	3.517	3.433	3.352	3.274	3.199	3.127	3.058	2.991
6	4.231	4.111	3.998	3.889	3.784	3.685	3.589	3.498	3.410	3.326
7	4.712	4.564	4.423	4.288	4.160	4.039	3.922	3.812	3.706	3.605
8	5.146	4.968	4.799	4.639	4.487	4.344	4.207	4.078	3.954	3.837
9	5.537	5.328	5.132	4.946	4.772	4.607	4.451	4.303	4.163	4.031
10	5.889	5.650	5.246	5.216	5.019	4.833	4.659	4.494	4.339	4.192
11	6.207	5.938	5.687	5.453	5.234	5.029	4.836	4.656	4.487	4.327
12	6.492	6.194	5.918	5.660	5.421	5.197	4.988	4.793	4.611	4.439
13	6.750	6.424	6.122	5.842	5.583	5.342	5.118	4.910	4.715	4.533
14	6.982	6.628	6.303	6.002	5.724	5.468	5.229	5.008	4.802	4.611
15	7.191	6.811	6.462	6.142	5.847	5.575	5.324	5.092	4.876	4.675
16	7.379	6.974	6.604	6.265	5.954	5.669	5.405	5.162	4.938	4.730
17	7.549	7.120	6.729	6.373	6.047	5.749	5.475	5.222	4.990	4.775
18	7.702	7.250	6.840	6.467	6.128	5.818	5.534	5.273	5.033	4.812
19	7.839	7.366	6.938	6.550	6.198	5.877	5.585	5.316	5.070	4.843
20	7.963	7.469	7.025	6.623	6.259	5.929	5.628	5.353	5.101	4.870
21	8.075	7.562	7.102	6.687	6.312	5.973	5.665	5.384	5.127	4.891
22	8.176	7.645	7.170	6.743	6.359	6.011	5.696	5.410	5.149	4.909
23	8.266	7.718	7.230	6.792	6.399	6.044	5.723	5.432	5.167	4.925
24	8.348	7.784	7.283	6.835	6.434	6.073	5.747	5.451	5.182	4.937
25	8.422	7.843	7.330	6.873	6.464	6.097	5.766	5.467	5.195	4.948
30	8.694	8.055	7.496	7.003	6.566	6.177	5.829	5.517	5.235	4.979
40	8.951	8.244	7.634	7.105	6.642	6.233	5.871	5.548	5.258	4.997
50	9.042	8.305	7.675	7.133	6.661	6.246	5.880	5.554	5.262	4.999

n	21%	22%	23%	24%	25%	26%	27%	28%	29%	30%
1	.826	.820	.813	.806	.800	.794	.787	.781	.775	.769
2	1.509	1.492	1.474	1.457	1.440	1.424	1.407	1.392	1.376	1.361
3	2.074	2.042	2.011	1.981	1.952	1.923	1.896	1.868	1.842	1.816
4	2.540	2.494	2.448	2.404	2.362	2.320	2.280	2.241	2.203	2.166
5	2.926	2.864	2.803	2.745	2.689	2.635	2.583	2.532	2.483	2.436
6	3.245	3.167	3.092	3.020	2.951	2.885	2.821	2.759	2.700	2.643
7	3.508	3.416	3.327	3.242	3.161	3.083	3.009	2.937	2.868	2.802
8	3.726	3.619	3.518	3.421	3.329	3.241	3.156	3.076	2.999	2.925
9	3.905	3.786	3.673	3.566	3.463	3.366	3.273	3.184	3.100	3.019
10	4.054	3.923	3.799	3.682	3.570	3.465	3.364	3.269	3.178	3.092
11	4.177	4.035	3.902	3.776	3.656	3.544	3.437	3.335	3.329	3.147
12	4.278	4.127	3.985	3.851	3.725	3.606	3.493	3.387	3.286	3.190
13	4.362	4.203	4.053	3.912	3.780	3.656	3.538	3.427	3.322	3.223
14	4.432	4.265	4.108	3.962	3.824	3.695	3.573	3.459	3.351	3.249
15	4.489	4.315	4.153	4.001	3.859	3.726	3.601	3.483	3.373	3.268
16	4.536	4.357	4.189	4.003	3.887	3.751	3.623	3.503	3.390	3.283
17	4.576	4.391	4.219	4.059	3.910	3.771	3.640	3.518	3.403	3.295
18	4.608	4.419	4.243	4.080	3.928	3.786	3.654	3.529	3.413	3.304
19	4.635	4.442	4.263	4.097	3.942	3.799	3.664	3.539	3.421	3.311
20	4.657	4.460	4.279	4.110	3.954	3.808	3.673	3.546	3.427	3.316
21	4.675	4.476	4.292	4.121	3.963	3.816	3.679	3.551	3.432	3.320
22	4.690	4.488	4.302	4.130	3.970	3.822	3.684	3.556	3.436	3.323
23	4.703	4.499	4.311	4.137	3.976	3.827	3.689	3.559	3.438	3.325
24	4.713	4.507	4.318	4.143	3.981	3.831	3.692	3.562	3.441	3.327
25	4.721	4.514	4.323	4.147	3.985	3.834	3.694	3.564	3.442	3.329
30	4.746	4.534	4.339	4.160	3.995	3.842	3.701	3.569	3.447	3.332
40	4.760	4.544	4.347	4.166	3.999	3.846	3.703	3.571	3.448	3.333
50	4.762	4.545	4.348	4.167	4.000	3.846	3.704	3.571	3.448	3.333

n	31%	32%	33%	34%	35%	36%	37%	38%	39%	40%
1	.763	.758	.752	.746	.741	.735	.730	.725	.719	.714
2	1.346	1.331	1.317	1.303	1.289	1.276	1.263	1.250	1.237	1.224
3	1.791	1.766	1.742	1.719	1.696	1.673	1.652	1.630	1.609	1.589
4	2.130	2.096	2.062	2.029	1.997	1.966	1.935	1.906	1.877	1.849
5	2.390	2.345	2.302	2.260	2.220	2.181	2.143	2.106	2.070	2.035
6	2.588	2.534	2.483	2.433	2.385	2.339	2.294	2.251	2.209	2.168
7	2.739	2.677	2.619	2.562	2.508	2.455	2.404	2.355	2.308	2.263
8	2.854	2.786	2.721	2.658	2.598	2.540	2.485	2.432	2.380	2.331
9	2.942	2.868	2.798	2.730	2.665	2.603	2.544	2.487	2.432	2.379
10	3.009	2.930	2.855	2.784	2.715	2.649	2.587	2.527	2.469	2.414
11	3.060	2.978	2.899	2.824	2.752	2.683	2.618	2.555	2.496	2.438
12	3.100	3.013	2.931	2.853	2.779	2.708	2.641	2.576	2.515	2.456
13	3.129	3.040	2.956	2.876	2.799	2.727	2.658	2.592	2.529	2.469
14	3.152	3.061	2.974	2.892	2.814	2.740	2.670	2.603	2.539	2.477
15	3.170	3.076	2.988	2.905	2.825	2.750	2.679	2.611	2.546	2.484
16	3.183	3.088	2.999	2.914	2.834	2.757	2.685	2.616	2.551	2.489
17	3.193	3.097	3.007	2.921	2.840	2.763	2.690	2.621	2.555	2.492
18	3.201	3.104	3.012	2.926	2.844	2.767	2.693	2.624	2.557	2.494
19	3.207	3.109	3.017	2.930	2.848	2.770	2.696	2.626	2.559	2.496
20	3.211	3.113	3.020	2.933	2.850	2.772	2.698	2.627	2.561	2.497
21	3.215	3.116	3.023	2.935	2.852	2.773	2.699	2.629	2.562	2.498
22	3.217	3.118	3.025	2.936	2.853	2.775	2.700	2.629	2.562	2.498
23	3.219	3.120	3.026	2.938	2.854	2.775	2.701	2.630	2.563	2.499
24	3.221	3.121	3.027	2.939	2.855	2.776	2.701	2.630	2.563	2.499
25	3.222	3.122	3.028	2.939	2.856	2.776	2.702	2.631	2.563	2.499
30	3.225	3.124	3.030	2.941	2.857	2.777	2.702	2.631	2.564	2.500
40	3.226	3.125	3.030	2.941	2.857	2.778	2.703	2.632	2.564	2.500
50	3.226	3.125	3.030	2.941	2.857	2.778	2.703	2.632	2.564	2.500

APPENDIX F

CHECK FIGURES FOR SELECTED END-OF-CHAPTER STUDY PROBLEMS

CHAPTER 1
1-1. Taxable income = $526,800
Tax liability = $179,112
1-3. Taxable income = $365,000
Tax liability = $124,100
1-5. Taxable income = ($38,000)
Tax liability = $0
1-7. Taxable income = $153,600
Tax liability = $43,154
1-9. Taxable income = $370,000
Tax liability = $125,800
1-11. Taxable income = $1,813,000
Tax liability = $616,420

CHAPTER 2
2-1. Inferred real rate on Treasury bills: 0.63%
Inferred real rate on Treasury bonds: 3.10%
2-3. 11.28%
2-5. 12.35%

CHAPTER 3
3-1.

Total current assets	$32,650
Net buildings and equipment	$88,000
Total assets	$120,650
Total current liabilities	$5,400
Total liabilities	$60,400
Total equity	$60,250
Gross profits	$7,050
Operating income (EBIT)	$5,700
Net income	$3,360

3-3.

Total current assets	$491,800
Net fixed assets	$632,000
Total assets	$1,123,800
Total current liabilities	$237,900
Total liabilities	$571,900
Total equity	$551,900
Total liabilities and equity	$1,123,800
Gross profits	$276,000
Operating income (EBIT)	$131,000
Net income	$75,750

3-5.

After-tax cash flows from operations	$190
Increase in net working capital	$87
Increase in fixed assets	$55
Free cash flows	$48

3-7.

After-tax cash flows from operations	$442
Decrease in net working capital	$100
Purchase of fixed assets	($400)
Free cash flows	$142
Interest expense	($64)
Common stock dividends	($78)
Free cash flows—financing perspective	($142)

3-9.

After-tax cash flows from operations	$82,900
Increase in current assets	$23,100
Less increase in current liabilities	($6,000)
Increase in net operating working capital	$17,100
Purchase of fixed assets	$14,000
Interest paid to investors	($10,000)
Decrease in long-term debt	($10,000)
Common stock dividends	($31,800)

CHAPTER 4
4-1. $429,000
4-3. a. Gross profit $288,000; operating income $158,000; net income $93,200
b. Gross profit margin 72.0%; operating profit margin 39.5%
c. Times interest earned 9.41
4-5. $500,000
4-7. a. Total asset turnover = 2
b. Sales = $17.5m
Percentage increase = 75%
c. For last year, OROA = 20%
Projected OROA = 35%
4-9.

Current ratio	4.0x
Acid-test (quick) ratio	1.92x
Average collection period	107 days
Inventory turnover	1.36x
Operating return on assets	13.8%
Operating profit margin	24.8%
Total asset turnover	0.56x
Inventory turnover	1.36x
Fixed asset turnover	1.04x
Debt ratio	34.6%
Times interest earned	5.63x
Return on common equity	10.5%

4-11. a. Current ratio = 1.84
b. Acid-test ratio = 0.72
c. Debt ratio = 0.55
d. Times interest earned = 8
e. Inventory turnover = 5.48
f. Fixed asset turnover = 2.22
g. Return on equity = 23.4%

CHAPTER 5
5-1. a. $12,970
c. $3,019.40
5-2. a. n = 15 years
5-3. b. 5%
c. 9%
5-4. b. PV = $235.20
5-5. a. $6,289
c. $302.89
5-6. c. $1,562.96
5-7. a. FV_1 = $10,600
FV_5 = $13,380
FV_{15} = $23,970
5-9. a. $6,690
b. Semiannual: $6,720   Bimonthly: $6,740
5-11. Year 1: 18,000 books
Year 2: 21,600 books
Year 3: 25,920 books
5-13. $6,108.11
5-15. 8%
5-17. $658,197.85
5-21. b. $8,333.33
5-24. $6,509
5-26. 22%
5-27. $6,934.81
5-30. a. $1,989.73
5-33. $15,912
5-42. $2,054.81
5-45. $485.65
5-48. $18,071.11
5-50. b. 11.6123%

CHAPTER 6

6-1. $\bar{k} = 9.85\%$; $\sigma^2 = 6.99\%$; $\sigma = 2.64\%$

6-3. A: $\bar{k} = 16.7\%$; $\sigma^2 = 102.6\%$; $\sigma = 10.13\%$
B: $\bar{k} = 9.2\%$; $\sigma^2 = 12.76\%$; $\sigma = 3.57\%$

6-5. The beta is approximately 0.5.

6-7. 10.94%

6-9. a. Jazmon: For time = 4, 30%; Solomon for time = 3, 14.29%

6-11. a. 15.8%
b. 0.95

CHAPTER 7

7-1. a. 8%
b. $744.59

7-3. a. $865.80
b. 22%

7-5. a. Series A: For 5%, $1,310.21; for 8%, $1,037.68; for 12%, $783.20
Series B: For 5%, $1,033.33; for 8%, $1,004.63; for 12%, $968.75

7-7. 4.45%

7-9. 5.28%

7-11. a. $863.78
b. Market value $707.63 when required rate of return is 15%
Market value $1,171.19 when required rate of return is 8%

7-13. $547

CHAPTER 8

8-1. Stock A: Expected return = 12.86%
Stock B: Expected return = 11.81%

8-3. a. 6.33%
b. 14.96%

8-5. $116.67

8-7. a. 8.5%
b. $42.50

8-9. a. 18.9%
b. $28.57

8-11. 7.2%

8-13. $39.96

8-15. a. 10.91%
b. $36

8-17. $50

8-19.

Years	1	2	3	4	5	6
Free Cash Flows	$52	$59	$110	$120	$131	$209
Shareholder Value	$1,949					

CHAPTER 9

9-1. a. $IRR = 7\%$
b. $IRR = 17\%$

9-3. a. IRR = approximately 19%

9-5. a. payback period = 4 years

9-7. a. Project A:
Payback period = 2.5 years

9-13. b. $MIRR = 15.0749\%$

9-14. a. $NPV_A = \$136.30$
$NPV_B = \$455$
b. $PI_A = 1.2726$
$PI_B = 1.09$
c. $IRR_A = 40\%$
$IRR_B = 20\%$

9-16. a. Payback A = 1.589 years
Payback B = 3.019 years
b. $NPV_A = \$8,743$
$NPV_B = \$11,615$
c. $IRR_A = 40\%$
$IRR_B = 30\%$

CHAPTER 10

10-1. a. $6,800
b. $3,400
c. No taxes
d. $1,020

10-3. Free Cash Flow = $404,500

10-6. Operating cash flows = $1,522,000

10-9. a. $110,000
b. Free Cash Flow = $33,600

10-11. d. $NPV = \$106,477$

CHAPTER 11

11-1. a. $k_d(1 - t) = 6.53\%$
b. $k_{nc} = 14.37\%$
c. $k_c = 15.14\%$
d. $k_p = 8.77\%$
e. $k_d(1 - t) = 7.92\%$

11-3. $k_{nc} = 12.06\%$

11-5. $k_p = 9.23\%$

11-7. $k_p = 14.29\%$

11-9. a. $k_c = 17.59\%$
b. $k_{nc} = 18.25\%$

11-11. $P_0 = \$935.82$
$NP_0 = \$837.56$
Number of bonds = 597
$k_d(1 - t) = 7.08\%$

11-13. a.

	Incentive Compensation		
	80%	100%	120%
CEO	$540,000	$675,000	$810,000

b.

	60%	150%
CEO	$405,000	$1,012,500

11-15. a. 11.11%
b. 10.62%

CHAPTER 12

12-1. a. 1.67 times
b. 1.11 times
c. 1.85 times

12-3. b. 45.85%
c. $479,825.52

12-7. a. $F = \$780,000$
b. $S_B = \$1,560,000$

12-9. a. $P = \$6.875$ (selling price per unit)

12-10. a. 1,200 units
b. $600,000
c. $1.316 times
d. 26.32%

12-13. a. $EBIT = \$2,000,000$
b. EPS will be $1.00 for each plan
d. Plan B

CHAPTER 13

13-1. a. $4.80 per share
b. Value before and after dividend: $3,000.00

13-3. 95,238 shares; $11,428,560

13-5. Value before and after dividend: $275

13-9. 163,743 shares; $15,555,556

CHAPTER 14

14-1. Total assets = $11.75 million

14-3. Total assets = $1.8 million
Fixed assets = $1 million

14-5.

Cash	$526,712
Accounts receivable	$123,288
Current liabilities	$700,000
Net fixed assets	$600,000
Total assets	$2,000,000

14-9.   a. Notes payable $1.11 million
        b. Current ratio (before) = 2 times
           Current ratio (after) = 1.12 times
14-11. Cumulative borrowing (March) = $59,000
        Ending cash balance (June) = $107,724
14-13. a.   2005
           Debt-to-assets   61.11%
           ROE   14.29%
           Dividend payout   40.00%
           Actual growth rate   7.14%
        b. Sustainable rate of growth
           2001   6.00%
           2005   8.57%
14-15. a. $117,000
        b. $133,000

CHAPTER 15
15-1.   Rate = 13.79%
15-3.   a. Rate = 36.73%
        b. Rate = 74.23%
15-7.   a. Rate = 16.27%
15-11. a. APR = 10%
        b. APR = 11.76%
        c. APR = 12.5%
15-13. a. 9.8%
        b. Yes

CHAPTER 16
16-1.   b. Break-even yield is 8.0%.
16-3.   Yes; the company will save $250,000 annually by switching to the
        new concentration-banking system.

16-6.   a. Need to speed up collections by more than 0.5214 day.
        b. Cash collections would have to be accelerated by more than
           0.8110 day.
16-8.   a. $4 million
        b. $240,000
        c. $48,600
        d. Yes, net annual gain = $191,400
16-12. a. $912.44
        b. The loss will be $87.56.
        c. The capital loss here would be only $17.59.
        d. Interest rate risk. Thus leads to the maturity premium
           discussed in Chapter 2.
16-14. a. 36.36%
        b. 36.73%
        c. 55.67%
16-16. a. Average inventory = $90,000
        b. $53,333
16-18. a. *EOQ* = 7,071 units, or rounded to 7,100
        b. 35.2 orders per year

CHAPTER 17
17-1.   a. $8,437
        b. $9,368
        c. $25,695
17-3.   Canada; 1.1853; 1.1881; 1.1912
        Japan: 213.4927; 211.9992; 209.1613
        Switzerland: 1.9459; 1.9346; 1.8815
17-5.   Net gain = $149.02

GLOSSARY

Accelerated Depreciation Techniques. Techniques that allow the owner of the asset to take greater amounts of depreciation during the early years of its life, thereby deferring some of the taxes until later years.

Accounts-Receivable Turnover Ratio. A ratio, credit sales divided by accounts receivable, that expresses how often accounts receivable are "rolled over" during a year.

Accrual Method. A method of accounting whereby income is recorded when earned, whether or not the money has been received at that time, and expenses are recorded when incurred, whether or not any money has actually been paid out.

Acid-Test Ratio. (Current assets – inventories) ÷ current liabilities. This ratio is a more stringent measure of liquidity than the current ratio in that it subtracts inventories (the least liquid current asset) from current assets.

Acquisition. A combination of two or more businesses into a single operational entity.

Agency Costs. The costs, such as a reduced stock price, associated with potential conflict between managers and investors when these two groups are not the same.

Agency Problem. Problems and conflicts resulting from the separation of the management and ownership of the firm.

Amortized Loans. Loans that are paid off in equal periodic payments.

Analytical Income Statement. A financial statement used by internal analysts that differs in composition from audited or published financial statements.

Annuity. A series of equal dollar payments for a specified number of years.

Annuity Due. An annuity in which the payments occur at the beginning of each period.

Anticipatory Buying. Buying in anticipation of a price increase to secure goods at a lower cost.

Arbitrage-Pricing Model. A theory that relates stock returns and risk. The theory maintains that security returns vary from their expected amounts when there are unanticipated changes in basic economic forces. Such forces would include unexpected changes in industrial production, inflation rates, term structure of interest rates, and the difference between interest rates of high- and low-risk bonds.

Arbitrageur. A person involved in the process of buying and selling in more than one market to make riskless profits.

Arrearage. An overdue payment, generally referring to omitted preferred stock dividends.

Asked Rate. The rate a bank or foreign exchange trader "asks" the customer to pay in home currency for foreign currency when the bank is selling and the customer is buying.

Asset Allocation. Identifying and selecting the asset classes appropriate for a specific investment portfolio and determining the proportions of those assets within the portfolio.

Automated Depository Transfer Check (DTC) System. A cash management tool that moves funds from local bank accounts to concentration bank accounts electronically. This eliminates the mail float from the local bank to the concentration bank.

Average Collection Period. Accounts receivable divided by (annual credit sales divided by 365). A ratio that expresses how rapidly the firm is collecting its credit accounts.

Balance Sheet. A basic accounting statement that represents the financial position of a firm on a given date.

Balance-Sheet Leverage Ratios. Financial ratios used to measure the extent of a firm's use of borrowed funds, calculated using information found in the firm's balance sheet.

Bankers' Acceptances. A draft (order to pay) drawn on a specific bank by a seller of goods in order to obtain payment for goods that have been shipped (sold) to a customer. The customer maintains an account with that specific bank.

Bank Wire. A private wire service used and supported by approximately 250 banks in the United States for transferring funds, exchanging credit information, or effecting securities transactions.

Benefit-Cost Ratio. See **Profitability Index**.

Beta. The relationship between an investment's returns and the market returns. This is a measure of the investment's non-diversifiable risk.

Bid-Ask Spread. The difference between the bid quote and ask quote.

Bird-in-the-Hand Dividend Theory. The view that dividends are more certain than capital gains.

Bond. A long-term (10-year or more) promissory note issued by the borrower, promising to pay the owner of the security a predetermined and fixed amount of interest each year.

Bond Par Value. The face value appearing on the bond, which is to be returned to the bondholder at maturity.

Book Value. (1) The value of an asset as shown on the firm's balance sheet. It represents the historical cost of the asset rather than its current market value or replacement cost. (2) The depreciated value of a company's assets (original cost less accumulated depreciation) less the outstanding liabilities.

Book-Value Weights. The percentage of financing provided by different capital sources as measured by their book values from the company's balance sheet.

Break-Even Analysis. An analytical technique used to determine the quantity of output or sales that results in a zero level of earnings before interest and taxes (EBIT). Relationships among the firm's cost structure, volume of output, and EBIT are studied.

Business Risk. The relative dispersion or variability in the firm's expected earnings before interest and taxes (EBIT). The nature of the firm's operations causes its business risk. This type of risk is affected by the firm's cost structure, product demand characteristics, and intra-industry competitive position. In capital structure theory, business risk is distinguished from financial risk. Compare **Financial Risk**.

Buying Rate. The bid rate in a currency transaction.

Call Option. The right to purchase a given number of shares of stock or some other asset at a specified price over a given time period.

Call Premium. The difference between the call price and the security's par value.

Call Provision. A provision that entitles the corporation to repurchase its preferred stock from their investors at stated prices over specified periods.

Capital Asset. All property used in conducting a business other than assets held primarily for sale in the ordinary course of business or depreciable and real property used in conducting a business.

Capital Asset Pricing Model (CAPM). An equation stating that the expected rate of return on a project is a function of (1) the risk-free rate, (2) the investment's systematic risk, and (3) the expected risk premium for the market portfolio of all risky securities.

Capital Budgeting. The decision-making process with respect to investment in fixed assets. Specifically, it involves measuring the incremental cash flows associated with investment proposals and evaluating those proposed investments.

Capital Gain or Loss. As defined by the revenue code, a gain or loss resulting from the sale or exchange of a capital asset.

Capital Market. All institutions and procedures that facilitate transactions in long-term financial instruments.

Capital Rationing. The placing of a limit by the firm on the dollar size of the capital budget.

Capital Structure. The mix of long-term sources of funds used by the firm. This is also called the firm's capitalization. The relative total (percentage) of each type of fund is emphasized.

Cash. Currency and coins plus demand deposit accounts.

Cash Break-Even Analysis. Another version of break-even analysis that includes only the cash costs of production within the cost components. This means noncash expenses, like depreciation, are omitted in the analysis.

Cash Budget. A detailed plan of future cash flows. This budget is composed of four elements: cash receipts, cash disbursements, net change in cash for the period, and new financing needed.

Cash Flow Process. The process of cash generation and disposition in a typical business setting.

Cash Flow Statement. An accounting statement that computes the firm's cash inflows and outflows for a given time period.

Cash Flows from Investment Activities. Cash flows that include the purchase of fixed assets and other assets.

Cash Flows from Financing Activities. Cash flows that include proceeds from long-term debt or issuing common stock and payments made for stock dividends.

Cash Flows from Operations. Cash flows that consist of (1) collections from customers; (2) payments to suppliers for the purchase of materials; (3) other operating cash flows such as marketing and administrative expenses and interest payments; and (4) cash tax payments.

Certainty Equivalents. The amount of cash a person would require with certainty to make him or her indifferent between this certain sum and a particular risky or uncertain sum.

Characteristic Line. The line of "best fit" through a series of returns for a firm's stock relative to the market returns. The slope of the line, frequently called beta, represents the average movement of the firm's stock returns in response to a movement in the market's returns.

Chattel Mortgage Agreement. A loan agreement in which the lender can increase his or her security interest by having specific items of inventory identified in the loan agreement. The borrower retains title to the inventory but cannot sell the items without the lender's consent.

Clientele Effect. The belief that individuals and institutions that need current income will invest in companies that have high dividend payouts. Other investors prefer to avoid taxes by holding securities that offer only small dividend income but large capital gains. Thus, we have a "clientele" of investors.

Commercial Paper. Short-term unsecured promissory notes sold by large businesses in order to raise cash. Unlike most other money-market instruments, commercial paper has no developed secondary market.

Common Stock. Shares that represent the ownership in a corporation.

Company-Unique Risk. See **Unsystematic Risk.**

Compensating Balance. A balance of a given amount that the firm maintains in its demand deposit account. It may be required by either a formal or informal agreement with the firm's commercial bank. Such balances are usually required by the bank (1) on the unused portion of a loan commitment, (2) on the unpaid portion of an outstanding loan, or (3) in exchange for certain services provided by the bank, such as check-clearing or credit information. These balances raise the effective rate of interest paid on borrowed funds.

Compound Annuity. Depositing an equal sum of money at the end of each year for a certain number of years and allowing it to grow.

Compound Interest. The situation in which interest paid on the investment during the first period is added to the principal and, during the second period, interest is earned on the original principal plus the interest earned during the first period.

Compounding. The process of determining the future value of a payment or series of payments when applying the concept of compound interest.

Concentration Bank. A bank where a firm maintains a major disbursing account.

Concentration Banking. The selection of a few major banks where the firm maintains significant disbursing accounts.

Constant Dividend Payout Ratio. A dividend payment policy in which the percentage of earnings paid out in dividends is held constant. The dollar amount fluctuates from year to year as profits vary.

Contractual Interest Rate. The interest rate to be paid on a bond expressed as a percent of par value.

Contribution Margin. The difference between a product's selling price and its unit variable costs. It is usually measured on a per unit basis.

Contribution-to-Firm Risk. The amount of risk that a project contributes to the firm as a whole. This measure considers the fact that some of the project's risk will be diversified away as the project is combined with the firm's other projects and assets but ignores the effects of diversification of the firm's shareholders.

Convertible Debt. A hybrid security that combines debt or preferred stock with an option on the firm's common stock.

Convertible Preferred Stock. Stock that allows the stockholder to convert the preferred stock into a predetermined number of shares of common stock, if he or she so chooses.

Convertible Security. Preferred stock or debentures that can be exchanged for a specified number of shares of common stock at the will of the owner.

Corporate Bylaws. Regulations that govern the internal affairs of the corporation, designating such items as the time and place of the shareholders' meetings, voting rights, the election process for selecting members of the board of directors, the procedures for issuing and transferring stock certificates, and the policies relating to the corporate records.

Corporation. An entity that *legally* functions separate and apart from its owners.

Cost of Capital. See **Weighted Cost of Capital.**

Cost of Common Stock. The rate of return a firm must earn in order for the common stockholders to receive their required rate of return. The rate is based on the opportunity cost of funds for the common stockholders in the capital markets.

Cost of Debt. The rate that has to be received from an investment in order to achieve the required rate of return for the creditors. The cost is based on the debtholders' opportunity cost of debt in the capital markets.

Cost of Preferred Stock. The rate of return that must be earned on the preferred stockholders' investment to satisfy their required rate of return. The cost is based on the preferred stockholders' opportunity cost of preferred stock in the capital markets.

Cost-Volume-Profit Analysis. Another way of referring to ordinary break-even analysis.

Coupon Interest Rate. The interest to be paid annually on a bond as a percent of par value, which is specified in the contractual agreement.

Coverage Ratios. A group of ratios that measure a firm's ability to meet its recurring fixed-charge obligations, such as interest on long-term debt, lease payments, and/or preferred stock dividends.

Covered Interest Arbitrage. Arbitrage designed to eliminate differentials across currency and interest rate markets.

Credit Scoring. The numerical evaluation of credit applicants where the score is evaluated relative to a predetermined standard.

Cross Rate. The computation of an exchange rate for a currency from the exchange rates of two other currencies.

Cumulative Feature. A requirement that all past unpaid preferred stock dividends be paid before any common stock dividends are declared.

Cumulative Voting. Voting in which each share of stock allows the shareholder a number of votes equal to the number of directors being elected. The shareholder can then cast all of his or her votes for a single candidate or split them among the various candidates.

Current Assets. Assets consisting primarily of cash, marketable securities, accounts receivable, inventories, and prepaid expenses.

Current Ratio. Current assets divided by current liabilities. A ratio that indicates a firm's degree of liquidity by comparing its current assets to its current liabilities.

Current Yield. The ratio of the annual interest payment to the bond's market price.

Date of Record. Date at which the stock transfer books are to be closed for determining the investor to receive the next dividend payment. See **Ex-Dividend Date.**

Debenture. Any unsecured long-term debt.

Debt. Liabilities consisting of such sources as credit extended by suppliers or a loan from a bank.

Debt Capacity. The maximum proportion of debt that the firm can include in its capital structure and still maintain its lowest composite cost of capital.

Debt Ratio. Total liabilities divided by total assets. A ratio that measures the extent to which a firm has been financed with debt.

Declaration Date. The date upon which a dividend is formally declared by the board of directors.

Default Risk. The uncertainty of expected returns from a security attributable to pos-

sible changes in the financial capacity of the security issuer to make future payments to the security owner. Treasury securities are considered default free. Default risk is also referred to as "financial risk" in the context of marketable-securities management.

Degree of Combined Leverage. The percentage change in earnings per share caused by a percentage change in sales. It is the product of the degree of operating leverage and the degree of financial leverage.

Delivery-Time Stock. The inventory needed between the order date and the receipt of the inventory ordered.

Depository Transfer Checks (DTCs). A means for moving funds from local bank accounts to concentration bank accounts. The depository transfer check itself is an unsigned, nonnegotiable instrument. It is payable only to the bank deposit for credit to the firm's specific account.

Depreciation. The means by which an asset's value is expensed over its useful life for federal income tax purposes.

Direct Costs. See **Variable Costs.**

Direct Method. A format used to measure cash flow from operations, by which the different cash outflows occurring in regular operations of a business are subtracted from the cash flow collected from customers.

Direct Placement. See **Private Placement.**

Direct Quote. The exchange rate that indicates the number of units of the home currency required to buy one unit of foreign currency.

Direct Sale. The sale of securities by the corporation to the investing public without the services of an investment-banking firm.

Direct Securities. The pure financial claims issued by economic units to savers. These can later be transformed into indirect securities.

Disbursing Float. Funds available in the company's bank account until its payment check has cleared through the banking system.

Discount Bond. A bond that sells at a discount below par value.

Discounting. The inverse of compounding. This process is used to determine the present value of a cash flow.

Discount Rate. The interest rate used in the discounting process.

Discretionary Financing. Sources of financing that require an explicit decision on the part of the firm's management every time funds are raised. An example is a bank note

that requires that negotiations be undertaken and an agreement signed setting forth the terms and conditions of the financing.

Diversifiable Risk. See **Unsystematic Risk.**

Dividend Payout Ratio. The amount of dividends relative to the company's net income or earnings per share.

Dividend Yield. The dividend per share divided by the price of the security.

Dunning Letters. Past-due letters sent out to delinquent accounts.

DuPont Analysis. A method used to evaluate a firm's profitability and return on equity.

Earnings Before Interest and Taxes (EBIT). Profits from sales minus total operating expenses. Also called **Operating Income.**

Earnings Before Taxes (EBT). Operating income minus interest expense.

EBIT-EPS Indifference Point. The level of earnings before interest and taxes (EBIT) that will equate earnings per share (EPS) between two different financing plans.

Economic Failure. Situation in which a company's costs exceed its revenues. Stated differently, the internal rates of return on investments are less than the firm's cost of capital.

Efficient Market. A market in which the values of securities at any instant in time fully reflect all available information, which results in the market value and the intrinsic value being the same.

EPS. Typical financial notation for earnings per (common) share.

Equity. Stockholder's investment in the firm and the cumulative profits retained in the business up to the date of the balance sheet.

Equivalent Annual Annuity (EAA). An annuity cash flow that yields the same present value as the project's *NPV*. It is calculated by dividing the project's *NPV* by the appropriate $PVIFA_{i, n}$.

Eurobond. A bond issued in a country different from the one in whose currency the bond is denominated; for example, a bond issued in Europe or Asia by an American company that pays interest and principal to the lender in U.S. dollars.

Eurodollar Market. A banking market in U.S. dollars outside the United States. Large sums of U.S. dollars can be borrowed or invested in this unregulated financial market. Similar external markets exist in Europe and Asia and for other major currencies.

Exchange Rate. The price of a foreign currency stated in terms of the domestic or home currency.

Exchange Rate Risk. The risk that tomorrow's exchange rate will differ from today's rate.

Ex-Dividend Date. The date upon which stock brokerage companies have uniformly decided to terminate the right of ownership to the dividend, which is two days prior to the date of record.

Expectations Theory. The concept that, no matter what the decision area, how the market price responds to management's actions is not determined entirely by the action itself; it is also affected by investors' expectations about the ultimate decision to be made by management.

Expected Rate of Return. (1) The discount rate that equates the present value of the future cash flows (interest and maturity value) with the current market price of a bond. It is the rate of return an investor will earn if the bond is held to maturity. (2) The rate of return the investor expects to receive on an investment by paying the existing market price of the security. (3) The arithmetic mean or average of all possible outcomes where those outcomes are weighted by the probability that each will occur.

Ex-Rights Date. The date on or after which the stock sells without rights.

External Common Equity. A new issue of common stock.

Factor. A firm that, in acquiring the receivables of other firms, bears the risk of collection and, for a fee, services the accounts.

Factoring Accounts Receivable. The outright sale of a firm's accounts receivable to another party (the factor) without recourse. The factor, in turn, bears the risk of collection.

Fair Value. The present value of an asset's expected future cash flows.

Federal Agency Securities. Debt obligations of corporations and agencies created to carry out the lending programs of the U.S. government.

Federal Reserve System. The U.S. central banking system.

Field Warehouse–Financing Agreement. A security agreement in which inventories pledged as collateral are physically separated from the firm's other inventories and placed under the control of a third-party field-warehousing firm.

Financial Analysis. The assessment of a firm's financial condition or well-being. Its objectives are to determine the firm's financial strengths and to identify its weaknesses. The primary tool of financial analysis is the financial ratio.

Financial Assets. Claims for future payment by one economic unit upon another.

Financial Intermediaries. Major financial institutions, such as commercial banks, savings and loan associations, credit unions, life insurance companies, and mutual funds, that assist the transfer of savings from economic units with excess savings to those with a shortage of savings.

Financial Leverage. The use of securities bearing a fixed (limited) rate of return to finance a portion of a firm's assets. Financial leverage can arise from the use of either debt or preferred stock financing. The use of financial leverage exposes the firm to financial risk.

Financial Markets. Institutions and procedures that facilitate transactions in all types of financial claims (securities).

Financial Policy. The firm's policies regarding the sources of financing it plans to use and the particular mix (proportions) in which they will be used.

Financial Ratios. Accounting data restated in relative terms to identify some of the financial strengths and weaknesses of a company.

Financial Risk. The added variability in earnings available to a firm's common shareholders and the added chance of insolvency caused by the use of securities bearing a limited rate of return in the firm's financial structure. The use of financial leverage gives rise to financial risk.

Financial Structure. The mix of all funds sources that appears on the right-hand side of the balance sheet.

Financial Structure Design. The activity of seeking the proper mixture of a firm's short-term, long-term, and permanent financing components to minimize the cost of raising a given amount of funds.

Financing Costs. Cost incurred by a company that often include interest expenses and preferred dividends.

Finished-Goods Inventory. Goods on which the production has been completed but that are not yet sold.

Fixed-Asset Turnover. Sales divided by fixed assets. A ratio indicating how effectively a firm is using its fixed assets to generate sales.

Fixed Costs. Costs that do not vary in total dollar amount as sales volume or quantity of output changes. Also called indirect costs.

Fixed or Long-Term Assets. Assets comprising equipment, buildings, and land.

Float. The length of time from when a check is written until the actual recipient can draw upon or use the "good funds."

Floating Lien Agreement. An agreement, generally associated with a loan, whereby the borrower gives the lender a lien against all its inventory.

Floating Rate International Currency System. An international currency system in which exchange rates between different national currencies are allowed to fluctuate with supply and demand conditions. This contrasts with a fixed rate system in which exchange rates are pegged for extended periods of time and adjusted infrequently.

Flotation Costs. The transaction cost incurred when a firm raises funds by issuing a particular type of security.

Foreign Direct Investment. Physical assets, such as plant and equipment, acquired outside a corporation's home country but operated and controlled by that corporation.

Formal Control. Control vested in the stockholders having the majority of the voting common shares.

Forward Exchange Contract. A contract that requires delivery on a specified future date of one currency in return for a specified amount of another currency.

Forward-Spot Differential. The premium or discount between forward and spot currency exchange rates.

Future-Value Interest Factor ($FVIF_{i,\,n}$). The value $(1 + i)^n$ used as a multiplier to calculate an amount's future value.

Future-Value Interest Factor for an Annuity ($FVIFA_{i,\,n}$). The value $\left[\sum_{t=0}^{n-1}(1+i)^t\right]$ used as a multiplier to calculate the future value of an annuity.

Futures Contract. A contract to buy or sell a stated commodity (such as soybeans or corn) or financial claim (such as U.S. Treasury bonds) at a specified price at a specified future time.

General Partnership. A partnership in which all partners are fully liable for the indebtedness incurred by the partnership.

Gross Income. A firm's dollar sales from its product or services less the cost of producing or acquiring the product or service.

Gross Profit Margin. Gross profit divided by net sales. A ratio denoting the gross profit of the firm as a percentage of net sales.

Hedge. A means to neutralize exchange rate risk on an exposed asset position, whereby a liability of the same amount and maturity is created in a foreign currency.

Hedging Principle. A working-capital management policy which states that the cash flow–generating characteristics of a firm's investments should be matched with the cash flow requirements of the firm's sources of financing. Very simply, short-lived assets should be financed with short-term sources of financing while long-lived assets should be financed with long-term sources of financing.

High-Yield Bond. See **Junk Bond.**

Holding-Period Return. The return an investor would receive from holding a security for a designated period of time. For example, a monthly holding-period return would be the return for holding a security for a month.

Hostile Takeover. A merger or acquisition in which management resists the group initiating the transaction.

Hurdle Rate. The required rate of return used in capital budgeting.

Income Statement. A basic accounting statement that measures the results of a firm's operations over a specified period, commonly one year. Also known as the profit and loss statement. The bottom line of the income statement shows the firm's profit or loss for the period.

Increasing-Stream Hypothesis of Dividend Policy. The hypothesis that dividend stability is essentially a smoothing of the dividend stream to minimize the effect of other types of company reversals. Thus, corporate managers make every effort to avoid a dividend cut, attempting instead to develop a gradually increasing dividend series over the long-term future.

Incremental Cash Flows. The cash flows that result from the acceptance of a capital-budgeting project.

Indenture. The legal agreement between a firm issuing bonds and the bond trustee who represents the bondholders, providing the specific terms of the long agreement.

Indirect Costs. See **Fixed Costs.**

Indirect Method. An approach used to measure cash flows from operations, by which all operating expenses that did not result in a cash outflow for the period are added to net income.

Indirect Quote. The exchange rate that expresses the number of units of foreign currency that can be bought for one unit of home currency.

Indirect Securities. The unique financial claims issued by financial intermediaries. Mutual fund shares are an example.

Information Asymmetry. The difference in accessibility to information between managers and investors, which may result in a lower stock price than would be true in conditions of certainty.

Initial Outlay. The immediate cash outflow necessary to purchase an asset and put it in operating order.

Insolvency. The inability to meet interest payments or to repay debt at maturity.

Interest-Rate Parity Theory. The forward premium or discount should be equal and opposite in size to the differences in the national interest rates for the same maturity.

Interest Rate Risk. (1) The variability in a bond's value (risk) caused by changing interest. (2) The uncertainty that envelops the expected returns from a security caused by changes in interest rates. Price changes induced by interest rate changes are greater for long-term than for short-term financial instruments.

Internal Common Equity. Profits retained within the business for investment purposes.

Internal Growth. A firm's growth rate in earnings resulting from reinvesting company profits rather than distributing the earnings in the form of dividends. The growth rate is a function of the amount retained and the return earned on the retained funds.

Internal Rate of Return (IRR). A capital-budgeting technique that reflects the rate of return a project earns. Mathematically, it is the discount rate that equates the present value of the inflows with the present value of the outflows.

Intrinsic or Economic Value. The present value of an asset's expected future cash flows. This value is the amount the investor considers to be fair value, given the amount, timing, and riskiness of future cash flows.

Inventory Loans. Loans secured by inventories. Examples include floating or blanket lien agreements, chattel mortgage agreements, field-warehouse receipt loans, and terminal-warehouse receipt loans.

Inventory Management. The control of assets used in the production process or produced to be sold in the normal course of the firm's operations.

Inventory Turnover Ratio. Cost of goods sold divided by inventory. A ratio that measures the number of times a firm's inventories are sold and replaced during the year. This ratio reflects the relative liquidity of inventories.

Investment Banker. A financial specialist who underwrites and distributes new securities and advises corporate clients about raising new funds.

Investor's Required Rate of Return. The minimum rate of return necessary to attract an investor to purchase or hold a security. It is also the discount rate that equates the present value of the cash flows with the value of the security.

Junk Bond. Any bond rated BB or below.

Just-in-Time Inventory Control System. A production and management system in which inventory is cut down to a minimum through adjustments to the time and physical distance between the various production operations. Under this system the firm keeps a minimum level of inventory on hand, relying upon suppliers to furnish parts "just in time" for them to be assembled.

Law of One Price. The proposition that in competitive markets the same goods should sell for the same price where prices are stated in terms of a single currency.

Lead and Lag Strategies. Techniques used to reduce exchange rate risk where the firm maximizes its asset position in the stronger currency and its liability position in the weaker currency.

Least-Square Regression. A procedure for "fitting" a line through a scatter of observed data points in a way that minimizes the sum of the squared deviations of the points from the fitted line.

Leveraged Buyout (LBO). A corporate restructuring where the existing shareholders sell their shares to a small group of investors. The purchasers of the stock use the firm's unused debt capacity to borrow the funds to pay for the stock.

Limited Liability. A protective provision whereby the investor is not liable for more than the amount invested in the firm.

Limited Partnership. A partnership in which one or more of the partners has limited liability, restricted to the amount of capital he or she invests in the partnership.

Line of Credit. Generally an informal agreement or understanding between a borrower and a bank as to the maximum amount of credit the bank will provide the borrower at any one time. Under this type of agreement there is no "legal" commitment on the part of the bank to provide the stated credit. Compare **Revolving Credit Agreement.**

Liquidation Value. The dollar sum that could be realized if an asset were sold independently of the going concern.

Liquidity. A firm's ability to pay its bills on time. Liquidity is related to the ease and quickness with which a firm can convert its noncash assets into cash, as well as the size of the firm's investment in noncash assets vis-à-vis its short-term liabilities.

Liquidity Preference Theory. The shape of the term structure of interest rates is determined by an investor's additional required interest rate in compensation of additional risks.

Liquidity Ratios. Financial ratios used to assess the ability of a firm to pay its bills on time. Examples of liquidity ratios include the current ratio and the acid-test ratio.

Loan Amortization Schedule. A breakdown of the interest and principal payments on an amortized loan.

Long-Term Residual Dividend Policy. A dividend plan by which the residual capital is distributed smoothly to the investors over the planning period.

Mail Float. Funds tied up during the time that elapses from the moment a customer mails his or her remittance check until the firm begins to process it.

Majority Voting. Voting in which each share of stock allows the shareholder one vote, and each position on the board of directors is voted on separately. As a result, a majority of shares has the power to elect the entire board of directors.

Marginal Cost of Capital. The cost of capital that represents the weighted cost of each additional dollar of financing from all sources, debt, preferred stock, and common stock.

Marginal Tax Rate. The tax rate that would be applied to the next dollar of income.

Market Equilibrium. The situation in which expected returns equal required returns.

Market Risk. See **Systematic Risk**.

Market Segmentation Theory. The shape of the term structure of interest rates implies that the rate of interest for a particular maturity is determined solely by demand and supply for a given maturity. This rate is independent of the demand and supply for securities having different maturities.

Market Value. The value observed in the marketplace, where buyers and sellers negotiate a mutually acceptable price for the asset.

Market-Value Weights. The percentage of financing provided by different capital sources, measured by the current market prices of the firm's bonds and preferred and common stock.

Marketable Securities. Security investments (financial assets) the firm can quickly convert to cash balances. Also known as near cash or near-cash assets.

Maturity. The length of time until the bond issuer returns the par value to the bondholder and terminates the bond.

Maturity Date. The date upon which a borrower is to repay a loan.

Merger. A combination of two or more businesses into a single operational entity.

Money Market. All institutions and procedures that facilitate transactions in short-term instruments issued by borrowers with very high credit ratings.

Money-Market Mutual Funds. Investment companies that purchase a diversified array of short-term, high-grade (money-market) debt instruments.

Monitoring Costs. A form of agency costs. Typically these costs arise when bond investors take steps to ensure that protective covenants in the bond indenture are adhered to by management.

Mortgage Bond. A bond secured by a lien on real property.

Multinational Corporation (MNC). A corporation with holdings and/or operations in more than one country.

Mutually Exclusive Projects. A set of projects that perform essentially the same task, so that acceptance of one will necessarily mean rejection of the others.

Negotiable Certificates of Deposit. Marketable receipts for funds deposited in a bank for a fixed period. The deposited funds earn a fixed rate of interest. More commonly called CDs.

Net Income. A figure representing a firm's profit or loss for the period. It also represents the earnings available to the firm's common *and* preferred stockholders.

Net Income Available to Common Equity (also **Net Common Stock Earnings**). Net income after interest, taxes, and preferred dividends.

Net Income Available to Common Stockholders (Net Income). A figure representing a firm's profit or loss for a period. It also represents the earnings available to the firm's common and preferred stockholders.

Net Operating Loss Carryback and Carryforward. A tax provision that permits the taxpayer first to apply the loss against the profits in the three prior years (carryback). If the loss has not been completely absorbed by the profits in these three years, it may be applied to taxable profits in each of the 15 following years (carryforward).

Net Present Value (NPV). A capital-budgeting concept defined as the present value of the project's annual net cash flows after tax less the project's initial outlay.

Net Profit Margin. Net income divided by sales. A ratio that measures the net income of the firm as a percent of sales.

Net Working Capital. The difference between the firm's current assets and its current liabilities.

Nondiversifiable Risk. See **Systematic Risk**.

Nominal Interest Rate. The interest rate paid on debt securities without an adjustment for any loss in purchasing power.

Normal Probability Distribution. A special class of bell-shaped distributions with symmetrically decreasing density, where the curve approaches but never reaches the *x*-axis.

Offer Rate. See **Asked Rate**.

Operating Income. See **Earnings Before Interest and Taxes (EBIT)**.

Operating Return on Assets. The ratio of net operating income divided by total assets.

Operating Leverage. The incurring of fixed operating costs in a firm's income stream.

Operating Profit Margin. Net operating income divided by sales. A firm's earnings before interest and taxes. This ratio serves as an overall measure of operating effectiveness.

Opportunity Cost of Funds. The next-best rate of return available to the investor for a given level of risk.

Optimal Capital Structure. The capital structure that minimizes the firm's composite cost of capital (maximizes the common stock price) for raising a given amount of funds.

Optimal Range of Financial Leverage. The range of various capital structure combinations that yield the lowest overall cost of capital for the firm.

Option Contract. The right to buy or sell a fixed number of shares at a specified price over a limited time period.

Order Point Problem. Determining how low inventory should be depleted before it is reordered.

Order Quantity Problem. Determining the optimal order size for an inventory item given its usage, carrying costs, and ordering costs.

Organized Security Exchanges. Formal organizations involved in the trading of securities. Such exchanges are tangible entities that conduct auction markets in listed securities.

Other Assets. Assets not otherwise included in current assets or fixed assets.

Over-the-Counter Markets. All security markets except the organized exchanges. The money market is an over-the-counter market. Most corporate bonds also are traded in this market.

Partnership. An association of two or more individuals joining together as co-owners to operate a business for profit.

Par Value. On the face of a bond, the stated amount that the firm is to repay upon the maturity date.

Payable-Through Draft (PTD). A legal instrument that has the physical appearance of an ordinary check but is not drawn on a bank. A payable-through draft is drawn on and paid by the issuing firm. The bank serves as a collection point and passes the draft on to the firm.

Payback Period. A capital-budgeting criterion defined as the number of years required to recover the initial cash investment.

Payment Date. The date on which the company mails a dividend check to each investor of record.

Percent of Sales Method. A method of financial forecasting that involves estimating the level of an expense, asset, or liability for a future period as a percent of the sales forecast.

Perfect Capital Market. An assumption that allows one to study the effect of dividend decisions in isolation. It assumes that (1) investors can buy and sell stocks without incurring any transaction costs, such as brokerage commissions; (2) companies can issue stocks without any cost of doing so; (3) there are no corporate or personal taxes; (4) complete information about the firm is readily available; (5) there are no conflicts of interest between management and stockholders; and (6) financial distress and bankruptcy costs are nonexistent.

Permanent Investment. An investment that the firm expects to hold longer than one year. The firm makes permanent investments in fixed and current assets. Compare **Temporary Investments.**

Perpetuity. An annuity with an infinite life.

Pledging Accounts Receivable. A loan the firm obtains from a commercial bank or a finance company using its accounts receivable as collateral.

Plowback Ratio. The fraction of earnings that are reinvested, or plowed back, into the firm.

Portfolio Beta. The relationship between a portfolio's returns and the market returns. It is a measure of the portfolio's nondiversifiable risk.

Portfolio Diversification Effect. The fact that variations of the returns from a portfolio or combination of assets may be less than the sum of the variation of the individual assets making up the portfolio.

Preauthorized Check (PAC). A check that resembles an ordinary check but does not contain or require the signature of the person on whose account it is being drawn. A PAC is created only with the individual's legal authorization. The PAC system is advantageous when the firm regularly receives a large volume of payments of a fixed amount from the same customer over a long period.

Preemptive Right. The right entitling the common shareholder to maintain his or her proportionate share of ownership in the firm.

Preferred Stock. A hybrid security with characteristics of both common stock and bonds. It is similar to common stock in that it has no fixed maturity date, the nonpayment of dividends does not bring on bankruptcy, and dividends are not deductible for tax purposes. It is similar to bonds in that dividends are limited in amount.

Premium Bond. A bond that is selling above its par value.

Present Value. The value in today's dollars of a future payment discounted back to present at the required rate of return.

Present-Value Interest Factor ($PVIF_{i,\ n}$). The value $[1/(1 + i)^n]$ used as a multiplier to calculate an amount's present value.

Present-Value Interest Factor for an Annuity

($PVIFA_{i,\ n}$). The value $\left[\sum\limits_{t=1}^{n} \dfrac{1}{(1+i)^t} \right]$ used as a multiplier to calculate the present value of an annuity.

Price-Earnings (P/E) Ratio. The price the market places on \$1 of a firm's earnings. For example, if a firm has an earnings per share of \$2, and a stock price of \$30, its price-earnings ratio is 15 (\$30 ÷ \$2).

Primary Markets. Transactions in securities offered for the first time to potential investors.

Principle of Self-Liquidating Debt. See **Hedging Principle.**

Private Placement. A security offering limited to a small number of potential investors.

Privileged Subscription. The process of marketing a new security issue to a select group of investors.

Processing Float. Funds tied up during the time required for the firm to process remittance checks before they can be deposited in the bank.

Profit Budget. A budget of forecasted profits based on information gleaned from the cost and sales budgets.

Profit Margins. Financial ratios (sometimes simply referred to as margins) that reflect the level of firm profits relative to sales. Examples include the gross profit margin (gross profit divided by sales), operating profit margin (operating earnings divided by sales), and the net profit margin (net profit divided by sales).

Profitability Index (PI). A capital-budgeting criterion defined as the ratio of the present value of the future net cash flows to the initial outlay. Also called **Benefit-Cost Ratio.**

Pro Forma Income Statement. A statement of planned profit or loss for a future period.

Prospectus. A condensed version of the full registration statement filed with the Securities and Exchange Commission that describes a new security issue.

Protective Provisions. Provisions for preferred stock included in terms of the issue to protect the investor's interest. For instance, provisions generally allow for voting in the event of nonpayment of dividends, or they restrict the payment of common stock dividends if sinking-fund payments are not met or if the firm is in financial difficulty.

Proxy. A means of voting in which a designated party is provided with the temporary power of attorney to vote for the signee at the corporation's annual meeting.

Proxy Fight. A battle between rival groups for proxy votes in order to control the decisions made in a stockholders' meeting.

Public Offering. A security offering where all investors have the opportunity to acquire a portion of the financial claims being sold.

Purchasing Power Parity Theory. In the long run, exchange rates adjust so that the purchasing power of each currency tends to be the same.

Pure Play Method. A method of estimating a project's beta that involves looking for a publicly traded firm on the outside that looks like the project and using that outside firm's required rate of return to judge the project.

Put Option. The right to sell a given number of shares of common stock or some other asset at a specified price over a given time period.

Quick Ratio. See **Acid-Test Ratio.**

Raw-Materials Inventory. The basic materials purchased from other firms to be used in the firm's production operations.

Real Assets. Tangible assets like houses, equipment, and inventories; real assets are distinguished from financial assets.

Real Interest Rate. The nominal rate of interest less any loss in purchasing power of the dollar during the time of the investment.

Remote Disbursing. A cash management service specifically designed to extend disbursing float.

Repurchase Agreements. Legal contracts that involve the sale of short-term securities by a borrower to a lender of funds. The borrower commits to repurchase the securities at a later date at the contract price plus a stated interest charge.

Required Rate of Return. See **Investor's Required Rate of Return.**

Residual Dividend Theory. A theory that a company's dividend payment should equal the cash left after financing all the investments that have positive net present values.

Restrictive Covenants. Provisions in the loan agreement that place restrictions on the borrower and make the loan immediately payable and due when violated. These restrictive covenants are designed to maintain the borrower's financial condition on a par with that which existed at the time the loan was made.

Retained Earnings. Cumulative profits retained in a business up to the date of the balance sheet.

Return on Common Equity. Net income available to the common stockholders divided by common equity. A ratio relating earned income to the common stockholder's investment.

Return on Total Assets. Net income divided by total assets. This ratio determines the yield on the firm's assets by relating net income to total assets.

Return-Risk Line. A specification of the appropriate required rates of return for investments having different amounts of risk.

Revolving Credit Agreement. An understanding between the borrower and the bank as to the amount of credit the bank will be legally obligated to provide the borrower. Compare **Line of Credit.**

Right. A certificate issued to common stockholders giving them an option to purchase a stated number of new shares at a specified price during a 2- to 10-week period.

Risk. Potential variability in future cash flows. The likely variability associated with revenue or income streams. This concept has been measured operationally as the standard deviation or beta.

Risk-Adjusted Discount Rate. A method for incorporating a project's level of risk into the capital-budgeting process, in which the discount rate is adjusted upward to compensate for higher-than-normal risk or downward to compensate for lower-than-normal risk.

Risk-Free Rate of Return. The rate of return on risk-free investments. The interest rates on short-term U.S. government securities are commonly used to measure this rate.

Risk Premium. The additional return expected for assuming risk.

Safety Stock. Inventory held to accommodate any unusually large and unexpected usage during delivery time.

Sales Forecast. Projection of future sales.

Salvage Value. The value of an asset or investment project at the end of its usable life.

Scenario Analysis. Simulation analysis that focuses on an examination of the range of possible outcomes.

Secondary Market. Transactions in currently outstanding securities. This is distinguished from the new issues or primary market.

Secured Loans. Sources of credit that require security in the form of pledged assets. In the event the borrower defaults in payment of principal or interest, the lender can seize the pledged assets and sell them to settle the debt.

Securities and Exchange Commission (SEC). The federal agency created by the Securities Exchange Act of 1934 to enforce federal securities laws.

Securities Exchange Act of 1933. A regulation that requires registration of certain new issues of public securities with the Securities and Exchange Commission (SEC). The registration statement should disclose all facts relevant to the new issue that will permit an investor to make an informed decision.

Securities Exchange Act of 1934. This act enables the SEC to enforce federal securities laws. The major aspects of the 1934 act include (1) major securities exchanges are required to register with the SEC; (2) insider trading is regulated; (3) stock price manipulation by investors is prohibited; (4) the SEC has control over proxy procedures; and (5) the Board of Governors of the Federal Reserve System is given the responsibility of setting margin requirements.

Security Market Line. The return line that reflects the attitudes of investors regarding the minimum acceptable return for a given level of systematic risk.

Selling Group. A collection of securities dealers that participates in the distribution of new issues to final investors. A selling-group agreement links these dealers to the underwriting syndicate.

Selling Rate. See **Asked Rate.**

Sell-Off. The sale of a subsidiary, division, or product line by one firm to another.

Semifixed Costs. See **Semivariable Costs.**

Semivariable Costs. Costs that exhibit the joint characteristics of both fixed and variable costs over different ranges of output. Also called **Semifixed Costs.**

Sensitivity Analysis. The process of determining how the distribution of possible net present values or internal rates of return for a particular project is affected by a change in one particular input variable.

Shelf Offering. See **Shelf Registration.**

Shelf Registration. A procedure for issuing new securities where the firm obtains a master registration statement approved by the SEC.

Simple Arbitrage. Trading to eliminate exchange rate differentials across the markets for a single currency, for example, for the New York and London markets.

Simulation. The process of imitating the performance of an investment project through repeated evaluations, usually using a computer. In the general case, experimentation upon a mathematical model that has been designed to capture the critical realities of the decision-making situation.

Sinking-Fund Provision. A protective provision that requires the firm periodically to set aside an amount of money for the retirement of its preferred stock. This money is then used to purchase the preferred stock in the open market or through the use of the call provision, whichever method is cheaper.

Small, Regular Dividend Plus a Year-End Extra. A corporate policy of paying a small regular dollar dividend plus a year-end extra dividend in prosperous years to avoid the connotation of a permanent dividend.

Sole Proprietorship. A business owned by a single individual.

Spin-Off. The separation of a subsidiary from its parent, with no change in the equity ownership. The management of the parent company gives up operating control over the subsidiary, but the shareholders maintain their same percentage ownership in both firms. New shares representing ownership in the averted company are issued to the original shareholders on a pro rata basis.

Spontaneous Financing. The trade credit and other accounts payable that arise "spontaneously" in the firm's day-to-day operations.

Spot Transaction. A transaction made immediately in the marketplace at the market price.

Stable Dollar Dividend per Share. A dividend policy that maintains a relatively stable dollar dividend per share over time.

Standard Deviation. A statistical measure of the spread of a probability distribution calculated by squaring the difference between each outcome and its expected value, weighting each value by its probability, summing over all possible outcomes, and taking the square root of this sum.

Stock Buyback. See **Stock Repurchase.**

Stock Dividend. A distribution of shares of up to 25 percent of the number of shares currently outstanding, issued on a pro rata basis to the current stockholders.

Stock Market Value. See **Market Value.**

Stock Repurchase. The repurchase of common stock by the issuing firm for any of a variety of reasons, resulting in reduction of shares outstanding. Also called **Stock Buyback.**

Stock Split. A stock dividend exceeding 25 percent of the number of shares currently outstanding.

Straight-Line Depreciation. A method for computing depreciation expenses in which the cost of the asset is divided by the asset's useful life.

Stretching on Trade Credit. Failing to pay within the prescribed credit period. For example, under credit terms of 2/10, net 30, a firm would be stretching its trade credit if it failed to pay by the thirtieth day and paid on the sixtieth day.

Subchapter S Corporation. A corporation that, because of specific qualifications, is taxed as though it were a partnership.

Subordinated Debenture. A debenture that is subordinated to other debentures in being paid in case of insolvency.

Subscription Price. The price for which the security may be purchased in a rights offering.

Sustainable Rate of Growth. The rate at which a firm's sales can grow if it wants to maintain its present financial ratios and does not want to resort to the sale of new equity shares.

Syndicate. A group of investment bankers who contractually assist in the buying and selling of a new security issue.

Systematic Risk. (1) The portion of variations in investment returns that cannot be eliminated through investor diversification. This variation results from factors that affect all stocks. Also called **Market Risk** or **Nondiversifiable Risk.** (2) The risk of a project from the viewpoint of a well-diversified shareholder. This measure takes into account that some of the project's risk will be diversified away as the project is combined with the firm's other projects, and, in addition, some of the remaining risk will be diversified away by shareholders as they combine this stock with other stocks in their portfolios.

Target Capital Structure Mix. The mix of financing sources that a firm plans to maintain through time.

Target Debt Ratio. A desired proportion of long-term debt in a firm's capital structure. Alternatively, it may be the desired proportion of total debt in the firm's financial structure.

Taxable Income. Gross income from all sources, except for allowable exclusions, less any tax-deductible expenses.

Tax Expenses. Tax liability determined by earnings before taxes.

Tax Liability. The amount owed the federal, state, or local taxing authorities.

Tax Shield. The element from the federal tax code that permits interest costs to be deductible when computing a firm's tax bill. The dollar difference (the shield) flows to the firm's security holders.

Temporary Financing. Financing (other than spontaneous sources) that will be repaid within a period of one year or less. Included among these sources of short-term debt are secured and unsecured bank loans, commercial paper, loans secured by accounts receivable, and loans secured by inventories.

Temporary Investments. A firm's investments in current assets that will be liquidated and not replaced within a period of one year or less. Examples include seasonal expansions in inventories and accounts receivable. Compare **Permanent Investments.**

Tender Offer. A formal offer by the company to buy a specified number of shares at a predetermined and stated price. The tender price is set above the current market price in order to attract sellers.

Terminal Warehouse Agreement. A security agreement in which the inventories pledged as collateral are transported to a public warehouse that is physically removed from the borrower's premises. This is the safest (though costly) form of financing secured by inventory.

Term Loans. Loans that have maturities of 1 to 10 years and are repaid in periodic installments over the life of the loan. Term loans are usually secured by a chattel mortgage on equipment or a mortgage on real property.

Terms of Sale. The credit terms identifying the possible discount for early payment.

Term Structure of Interest Rates. The relationship between interest rates and the term to maturity, where the risk of default is held constant.

Times Interest Earned Ratio. Earnings before interest and taxes (EBIT) divided by interest expense. A ratio that measures a firm's ability to meet its interest payments from its annual operating earnings.

Total Asset Turnover. Sales divided by total tangible assets. An overall measure of the relation between a firm's tangible assets and the sales they generate.

Total Project Risk. A project's risk ignoring the fact that much of the risk will be diversified away as the project is combined with the firm's other projects and assets.

Total Revenue. Total sales dollars.

Trade Credit. Credit made available by a firm's suppliers in conjunction with the acquisition of materials. Trade credit appears on the balance sheet as accounts payable.

Transaction Loan. A loan where the proceeds are designated for a specific purpose—for example, a bank loan used to finance the acquisition of a piece of equipment.

Transfer Price. The price a subsidiary or a parent company charges other companies that are part of the same MNC for its goods or services.

Transit Float. Funds tied up during the time necessary for a deposited check to clear through the commercial banking system and become usable funds to the company.

Treasury Bills. Direct debt obligations of the U.S. government sold on a regular basis by the U.S. Treasury.

Trend Analysis. An analysis of a firm's financial ratios over time.

Triangular Arbitrage. Arbitrage across the markets for all currencies.

Unbiased Expectations Theory. The shape of the term structure of interest rates is determined by an investor's expectations about future interest rates.

Underwriting. The purchase and subsequent resale of a new security issue. The risk of selling the new issue at a satisfactory (profitable) price is assumed (underwritten) by the investment banker.

Underwriting Syndicate. A temporary association of investment bankers formed to purchase a new security issue and quickly resell it at a profit. Formation of the syndicate spreads the risk of loss among several investment bankers, thereby minimizing the risk exposure of any single underwriter.

Undiversifiable Risk. The portion of the variation in investment returns that cannot be eliminated through investor diversification.

Unique Risk. See **Unsystematic Risk**.

Unsecured Loans. All sources of credit that have as their security only the lender's faith in the borrower's ability to repay the funds when due.

Unsystematic Risk. The portion of the variation in investment returns that can be eliminated through investor diversification. This diversifiable risk is the result of factors that are unique to the particular firm. Also called **Company-Unique Risk** or **Diversifiable Risk**.

Value of a Bond. The present value of the interest payments, I_1, in period t, plus the present value of the redemption or par value of the indebtedness, M, at the maturity date.

Value of a Security. The present value of all future cash inflows expected to be received by the investor owning the security.

Variable Costs. Costs that are fixed per unit of output but vary in total as output changes. Also called **Direct Costs**.

Volume of Output. A firm's level of operations expressed either in sales dollars or as units of output.

Weighted Cost of Capital. A composite of the individual costs of financing incurred by each capital source. A firm's weighted cost of capital is a function of (1) the individual costs of capital, (2) the capital structure mix, and (3) the level of financing necessary to make the investment.

Weighted Marginal Cost of Capital. The composite cost for each additional dollar of financing. The marginal cost of capital represents the appropriate criterion for making investment decisions.

Wire Transfers. A method of moving funds electronically between bank accounts in order to eliminate transit float. The wired funds are immediately usable at the receiving bank.

Working Capital. A concept traditionally defined as a firm's investment in current assets. Compare **Net Working Capital**.

Work-in-Process Inventory. Partially finished goods requiring additional work before they become finished goods.

Yield to Maturity. (1) See Term **Structure of Interest Rates**. (2) The rate of return a bondholder will receive if the bond is held to maturity. (Equivalent to the expected rate of return.)

Zero and Very Low Coupon Bond. A bond issued at a substantial discount from its $1,000 face value and that pays little or no interest.

Zero Balance Accounts (ZBA). A cash management tool that permits centralized control over cash outflow while maintaining divisional disbursing authority. Objectives are (1) to achieve better control over cash payments; (2) to reduce excess cash balances held in regional banks for disbursing purposes; and (3) to increase disbursing float.

SUBJECT

CORPORATE